# THE WORLD STORMRIDER SURF GUIDE

LOW PRESSURE

Skeleton Bay
Namibia
ALAN VAN GYSEN

Mozambique
ALAN VAN GYSEN

Pipeline
Oahu, Hawaii
RYAN CRAIG

Lawrencetown
Nova Scotia, Canada
ADAM CORNICK

Witches Rock
Guanacaste,
Costa Rica
JEREMIAH KLEIN

Sunshine Beach
Sunshine Coast,
Queensland
NIGEL ARNISTON

Flame Balls
Vezo Reefs,
Madagascar
DAN HAYLOCK

Anchor Point
Central Morocco
CALLUM MORSE

Sultans
North Malé, Maldives
MATHIEU PELIKAN

Padang Padang
Bali, Indonesia
FEDERICO VANNO

Shipstern Bluff
Tasmania, Australia
STUART GIBSON

Lighthouse Beach
Kerala, India
GREG EWING

East Oaxaca
Mexico
RYAN CRAIG

Batu Islands
Indonesia
ANDREW SHIELD

Lance's Right
Mentawai Islands,
Indonesia
CRAIG LEVERS

Greenbush
Mentawai Islands,
Indonesia
FEDERICO VANNO

Rivermouth Bridge
Hainan, China
LARS JACOBSEN

Lighthouse
Mentawai Islands,
Indonesia
RUSSELL ORD

Cacimba do Padre
Fernando do Noronha,
Brazil
HENRIQUE PENGUIM

Teahupoo
Tahiti,
French Polynesia
BEN THOUARD

Fort Point
San Francisco,
California
JEREMIAH KLEIN

Lagundri Bay
Nias, Indonesia
TIMO JARVINEN

Queens
Honolulu, Oahu, Hawaii
ANDREW SHIELD

Whareakeake
Otago, New Zealand
CORY SCOTT

Pavones
Golfo Dulce,
Costa Rica
UNA OLA

La Piste
Capbreton, France
DAMIEN POULLENOT

Scotland
AL MACKINNON

Sunset Reef
Cape Town,
South Africa
ALAN VAN GYSEN

Teahupoo
Tahiti,
French Polynesia
DAMIEN POULLENOT

Chicama
La Libertad, Peru
WILSON FLORES

Title Page – **Lagundri Bay, Nias, Indonesia**

The World Stormrider Surf Guide
First published in 2018
by Low Pressure Ltd©
www.stormriderguides.com

Copyrighted surf information compiled using Low Pressure's SRDB and YEP's Worldwide Surfspots 2.0 database. Statistics taken from MSW 10-30yr historical data and Visual Planner software.

Creation of all maps graphic arrangements, pictograms, text and Spot Index Low Pressure Ltd 2018©



The representation in this guide of a road is no proof of the existence of a right of way, likewise the frontiers shown do not imply any recognition or official acceptance on the part of the publishers. Surfing is a dangerous and addictive activity. The authors and publishers take no responsibility for accident or injury as a result of using information contained within this guide.

A catalogue reference for this book can be obtained from the British Library. ISBN Hardback: 978-1-908520-44-9
Printed by Hong Kong Graphics and Printing using 100% chlorine-free paper stock from managed forests.

# THE WORLD STORMRIDER SURF GUIDE

TIMO JARVINEN

# THE WORLD STORMRIDER SURF GUIDE

# FOUR WORD

This project to combine the three volumes of *The World Stormrider Guide* into one behemoth book has been a long time coming, considering it was 1989 when the plan for a World guide was first hatched. This overambitious idea for a first book eventually morphed into the 1992 release of *The Stormrider Guide Europe*, which could then provide a chapter for the World project. The following year our paths crossed with French surf explorer Antony "YEP" Colas, who had been travelling extensively since the mid '80s and become a correspondent for the roughly-mapped, yellow-pages bulletin called *The Surf Report*. We shared a common love of surf travel and a belief that helping people to broaden their horizons and search for surf between and beyond the main spots on our maps would be a positive contribution to the surf world. By 1999, we had published four more guides, built up our international network of contributors and Antony had travelled to enough major surf zones so that we could finally publish *World Volume One*, containing 80 of the most famous surf zones on the planet. *Volumes Two* and *Three* followed over the next decade, shining some light on those places on the world map where you ask yourself "I wonder if this place has good waves?". Fast-forward another decade and the original vision of one big book is ready to hit the rollers. It has taken over four years to realise – more than enough time to build a house or earn a degree. In this case, we were renovating and seemingly simple tasks like title, extent, size, binding and price proved really difficult, let alone what the inside might look like. We discarded many working titles including the original Planet Surf and The Complete Stormrider Surf Guide until common sense prevailed and we ended up with *The World Stormrider Surf Guide*, a subtle yet appreciable tweak that would avoid confusion with the old title and fit snugly in our existing range of books.

Although most of the waves listed in this book are breaking in pretty much the same place and in the same way as they have done for the last three decades, the world we inhabit has changed massively. Since we started making *Stormrider Surf Guides* in 1989, the population of us humans has risen by 2.1 billion (40%). By the time you dry off after a two hour surf there are about 20,000 new brothers and sisters to share this planet with! The Surf World has also changed beyond all recognition. The internet has brought us the magic of Google Earth, webcams, surf alerts and super-accurate forecasts. Alongside this we've seen the unimaginable growth of the surf camp, surf charter and surf school. Now you can find a helping hand in all parts of the world offering everything from basic guiding to being dropped out the back by a dingy launched from a five star luxury cruiser. Wave discovery and media exposure since 1989 has grown exponentially, especially in the digital age of social media. The internet has become a bottomless pit of user-generated surf information – sorting the wheat from the chaff is the hardest part. In virtually every corner of the world there is now a web cam, board cam or phone cam broadcasting literally billions of images, yet quality

STU GIBSON

surf shots are still hard to find. The first place we looked to fulfil our photographic needs was the global army of professional surf photographers who are still scratching an existence, despite the number of mainstream surf periodicals that have moved online or disappeared altogether. They have embraced modern tech by combining their incredible artistic visions with drone mounted micro cameras to capture breathtaking aerial imagery only previously possible at great expense from the seat of an aircraft (pioneered by the 1963 Stern and Cleary *Surfing Guide to California*). Of course the professionals don't always make it to the less consistent or less desirable surfing areas, so each of these regions require us to find and contact an individual local photographer. Instant photo access via apps like Pinterest, Instagram and Facebook make this research a little easier, but overload is common and innumerable emails, Skypes, posts, messages and calls to our far-flung, fact-checking contributors have been sent out into the ether. Previously, maps were the result of many days tracing various resources, from tourist board brochures to marine charts, with as much detail and consistency as possible. But the rapid growth of mankind - new roads and towns, entire coastlines altered - meant that every map in this edition needed to be redrawn from the ground up. Even though online mapping has come of age and we all zoom in and out from earth to street views getting directions on our phones, the power of digital mapping does not translate to our analogue printed format, which still involves endless hours of detailed cartography.

Thankfully though, some things have not changed and we are all still globe-trotting. Antony has clocked up 200+ surf trips to over 50 countries, often exorcising his penchant for bore-riding, discovering new rivers to ride and new islands to surf in the Maldives. Surf and travel remain a massive focus for tens of thousands of us and hitting the road remains as joyful as ever. Turning a corner and seeing perfect lines rolling in and scrambling to get in the water as fast as you can will never get old. The challenge for us all now, is how to fairly balance and distribute wave resources among those that found and call spots home, with the billions of new people/surfers who must also be given the same rights to freely access the ocean's waves, just like the pioneers did. "I was here first" is just not an acceptable argument in a fair world where nobody owns the oceans.

As always with Stormrider Surf Guides we leave plenty of places out and the road less-travelled still remains sparsely populated with those who refuse to simply follow the crowd. This book is a starting point to explore a whole World of wave possibilities, where the experience of meeting new people and cultures with an open mind, is just as precious as the stoke of finding and riding a new wave, that may have otherwise gone unridden.

Ollie Fitzjones – *Publishing Director*
Bruce Sutherland – *Editorial Director*
Dan Haylock – *Creative Director*
Antony Colas – *Senior Contributing Author*

Cloudbreak, Fiji

# CONTENTS

## INTRODUCTION



## EUROPE



## AFRICA



## INDIAN OCEAN



## AUSTRALIA



## EAST ASIA

surf shots are still hard to find. The first place we looked to fulfil our photographic needs was the global army of professional surf photographers who are still scratching an existence, despite the number of mainstream surf periodicals that have moved online or disappeared altogether. They have embraced modern tech by combining their incredible artistic visions with drone mounted micro cameras to capture breathtaking aerial imagery only previously possible at great expense from the seat of an aircraft (pioneered by the 1963 Stern and Cleary *Surfing Guide to California*). Of course the professionals don't always make it to the less consistent or less desirable surfing areas, so each of these regions require us to find and contact an individual local photographer. Instant photo access via apps like Pinterest, Instagram and Facebook make this research a little easier, but overload is common and innumerable emails, Skypes, posts, messages and calls to our far-flung, fact-checking contributors have been sent out into the ether. Previously, maps were the result of many days tracing various resources, from tourist board brochures to marine charts, with as much detail and consistency as possible. But the rapid growth of mankind - new roads and towns, entire coastlines altered - meant that every map in this edition needed to be redrawn from the ground up. Even though online mapping has come of age and we all zoom in and out from earth to street views getting directions on our phones, the power of digital mapping does not translate to our analogue printed format, which still involves endless hours of detailed cartography.

Thankfully though, some things have not changed and we are all still globe-trotting. Antony has clocked up 200+ surf trips to over 50 countries, often exercising his penchant for bore-riding, discovering new rivers to ride and new islands to surf in the Maldives. Surf and travel remain a massive focus for tens of thousands of us and hitting the road remains as joyful as ever. Turning a corner and seeing perfect lines rolling in and scrambling to get in the water as fast as you can will never get old. The challenge for us all now, is how to fairly balance and distribute wave resources among those that found and call spots home, with the billions of new people/surfers who must also be given the same rights to freely access the ocean's waves, just like the pioneers did. "I was here first" is just not an acceptable argument in a fair world where nobody owns the oceans.
As always with Stormrider Surf Guides we leave plenty of places out and the road less-travelled still remains sparsely populated with those who refuse to simply follow the crowd. This book is a starting point to explore a whole World of wave possibilities, where the experience of meeting new people and cultures with an open mind, is just as precious as the stoke of finding and riding a new wave, that may have otherwise gone unridden.

Ollie Fitzjones – *Publishing Director*
Bruce Sutherland – *Editorial Director*
Dan Haylock – *Creative Director*
Antony Colas – *Senior Contributing Author*

Cloudbreak, Fiji

STU GIBSON

# CONTRIBUTORS

Lance's Right, Mentawai Islands

**Publishing Directors**
Ollie Fitzjones Bruce Sutherland Dan Haylock

**Editor** Bruce Sutherland

**Design and Production** Dan Haylock

**Everything Else** Ollie Fitzjones

**Senior Contributing Author** Antony 'YEP' Colas

**Accounts** Andrea Fitzjones

**Senior Editorial Contributors**
Stuart Butler Tony Butt Alex Dick-Read Craig Jarvis Drew Kampion Mike Kew Bruno Morand Tim Nunn Olivier Servaire Roger Sharp

**Thanks**
Mary Alegoet Kore Antonson Latif Benhaddad Jérome Blanco John Callahan Fabrice Colas Joël de Rosnay Gibus de Soultrait Nicolas Dejean Alex Dick-Read Benoit Duthu Pete Feehan Ben Freeston Camilo Gallardo Hugues Gosselin Val Gwyther Marc Hare Tom Hautzel Steven Jenkins Drew Kampion Mireille Lahiholle Philippe Lauga Simon Mahomo Laurent Masurel Ryall Mills Arthur Moreno Geoffroy Moreno Tim Nunn Gareth Parkinson Jim Pesket Tim Rainger Julia Ratsimandresy Vik Sell Erwan Simon David Sims Neil Stewart Ed Temperley Hayder Tuaima Graham Waldron Tiki Yates Patagonia

**Special Thanks**
Jo Finn Sandy Finn Haylock Maisie Finn Haylock Sue and John Haylock Paul and Hilary Finn Andrea Fitzjones Dillon Fitzjones Ty Ryder Fitzjones Sheila Fitzjones Jake Fitzjones Shani Fitzjones Marla Fitzjones Louise Millais Aedan Millais Jamie Millais Ella Millais Anna Millais Mireille Balbi Edgar Colas Edwige Colas Alfred Colas Jean Colas Bernadette Plazanet

*Dedicated to the memory of two incredible women who stood beside us on life's journey. **Sheila Fitzjones**, an amazing matriarch and **Louise Millais**, a much-loved wife, mother and talented artist.*

**Photographic Contributors**
Toby Adamson Hugo Alvaraz Javier Amezaga Adrian Araya Nigel Arnison Jean Pierre Baillot Robin Bakker Gonzalo Barandarian Bob Barbour Klaus Baumgartner Dan Beilich Ian Bird Luis Blanco Clarrie Bouma Kian Bourke-Steer Richard Brady Jeremy Brasset Ricardo Bravo Stuart Butler John Callahan Gilles Calvet Tom Carey Pierre Carreau Patrick Castagnet Sylvain Cazenave Francis Chagos Aaron Checkwood Philippe Chevodian Jason Childs Bruce Chrisner Antony Colas Gary Conley Dave Conner Adam Cornick Chris Corona Rick Cowley Tom Cozad Ryan Craig Dean Dampney Sean Davey Damian Davila Pierre De Champs Alex Dick-Read Jeff Divine Keegan Downes Tom Dugan Easydrop.com Patrick Eichstaedt Grant Ellis Rambo Estrada Greg Ewing Jason Feast Juan Fernandez Javier Fernandez Ollie Fitzjones Steve Fitzpatrick Tony Fleury Wilson Flores Nicolas Fojtu Murray Fraser Gavin Gallagher Luke Gartside Gecko Thierry Gibaud Stuart Gibson Ronan Gladu Aaron Golding Memo Gomez Kage Gozun Andy Guinand Mick Gullan Alan Van Gysen Quinn Haber Fabien Haegele Andrew Halsall Peter Harding Roy Harley Warren Hawke Dan Haylock Bob Henson Tobias Hettiger Eric Hilliard Georg Hilmarsson Phil Holden Alexandra Horvath ST Images Sebastian Imizcoz Anders Inglesten Jenya Ivkov Lars Jacobson Timo Jarvinen Krzysztof Jedrzejak Jack Johns Joli Paul Kennedy Kenyu Michael Kew Jeremiah Klein Tom Korber Florian Lang Christopher Lantz Guilluame Larre Alex Laurel Nick Lavecchia Yannick Le Touquin Craig Levers Michael Legge-Wilkinson Ingrid Lindfors Ranulf Lucas Jody Macdonald Al Mackinnon Marcelo Maragni Baby Marmootte Brad Masters Laurent Masurel Emiliano Mazzoni Russell McCarthy Simon McComb Joe McGovern Kody McGregor Mark Mcinnis Dudu Melao Menswave William Mertz Max Mills Kevin Moncayo Stephan Montiel Moonwalker Bill Morris Callum Morse Billy Mystic Nasser Mickey Nattz Pat Nolan Nicolas Olivera Russell Ord Craig Parry Yohann Peche Shane Peel Chris Peel Mathieu Pelikan Kristen Pelou Jean Claude Pereira Clement Phillipon Photogerson Izak Photography Henrique Pinguim Manuel Poppe Andy Potts Damien Poullenot Daniel Pullen Luke Rasmussen Uri Richter Jason Richter Stephane Robin Basilio Ruy Steve Ryan Kenji Sahara Pedro Salinas Carlos Sanchez Epes Sargent Cory Scott Olivier Servaire Roger Sharp Andrew Shield Micky Smith Dave Sparkes Ryan Struck Surfotos.cl Bruce Sutherland Booze Tentacle Bernard Testemale William Thomas Ben Thouard Luc De Tienda Patrice Touhar Amaury Treguer Takahiro Tsuchiya Seth Tyler U-SKE Willy Uribe Federico Vanno Flavio Vidigal Juan Virues Paige Vuoto Scott Walls Simon Williams Ryan Williams Alex Williams Jeremy Wilmotte Jimmy Wilson Louis Wulff Beach Break Surf Camp BlueTrailz.com Chicamasurf.com Ineika kwepunha.com Kura Kura Surf Camp Manoa Surf Tours N'Gor Island Surf Camp Salina Surf Camp Skeleton Safaris Surfers Paradise Surf Camp Swop Surfboards UnaOla Uritours.com Waidroka.com Wavegarden.com

**Editorial Contributors**
Andrew Abel Teymour Adham Joel Agostino Pedro Almendra Amadeus Nuno Amado Jeff Aniort Mickey Arandia Antoine Arutahi Karl Azzopardi Vergara B Tony Bafana Daniel Ballian Gonzalo Barandiaran Jeff Barksdale Alan Barnes Bizuka Barros Sebastien Barth Rob Beishuizen Greg Bertish Tama Blackburn Lena Blain Nick Blanche Jérôme Blanco Sam Bleakley Jérôme Boggio-Pasqua Chris Bond Olivier Bonnefon Jean-Luc Bourroullec Paul Breen Kristian Breivik John Callahan Guillaume Capette Belko Caquero Jay Chapelle Kiki Commarieu Marcos Conde Bill Cooksey Chuck Corbett Costasurf Paul Couderc Dan Crockett Adolfo Cruz Marc D'Offay Artur Nunes Da Silva Dale Dagger Brett Davies Lee De Louche Philippe de Marsan Alexis Deforges Glen Duncan Joe Dunn Mike Durand Benoit Duthu Benoit Duthu Paul Edmiston Hicham El Ouarga Scott Ellison Joe Entrikin Greg Ewing Hussein Fayaz Jason Feast Kyle Ferreira Mark Flint Adam Frost Patrice Galand Eric Gamez Walid Gebahi Gian Marcio Gey John Gibbons Gil Dane Gillett Guillermo Gomez John Gregg Sean Griffin Ray Guin Jr Gustavo Quinn Haber Ian Haight Sam Hammer Hamid Hamza Vince Han Jude Harbott Tony Harbott Peter Harding John Harrison Warren Hawke Jack Heckerman Steve Heron Erik Hesse Tobias Hettiger Michael Hill Russell Hill Georg Hilmarsson Ian Hodge Daniel Hopkins Stuart Horstman Woody Howard Dustin Humphrey Tony Hussein Victor Ika Bryan Jackson Simon James Rodney Jamieson Erik Jansen Kevin Johns Tor Johnson Harley Jones Tim Jones Lima Junior Tilbur Kattelbach Shaun Keane Adrian Kirby Ron Kirwan Fraser Kirwan Vasily Kiselev Benjamin Kromayer Nicolas Labat Regis Lacouture Gastón Lagrange Denis Lartigau Serginho Laus Philippe Le Leannec Yolin Lee Pascal Lefebvre Peter Lewis Nicholai Lidow Matt Lindsay Alicia Lippincott Richard Lippincott Dan Lodge Mike Loomis Mark Lumsden Ian Lyon Jon Madhava Hebel Magnus Lisa Makiiti Allois Malfitani David Malherbe Eric Marmora Todd Mazur John McCarthy Bob McClay Gavin McGlurg Kody McGregor Shayne McIntyre Dudu Melao SF-J Mercer Max Mills Noriyuki Mochizuki Henry Morales Arthur Moreno Andy Morrell Lance Moss Jesper Mouritzen Mr Chaundry Mr Zen Ian Muller Christian Münz John Murphy Sean Murphy Magnus Murray Nahu Peter Neely Mochizuki Noriyuki Charles Norman Jeff Norman Richard Norris Glen Novey Nicolas Nowak Ricardo Nuñez Jamie Nye Chris O' Gallagher Ingó Olsen Tommy Olsen Pedro Pablo Vangie Palacios Yiorgos Papandreou Robert Parker Sylvia Pascoe Rémi Paya Leonel Perez Yznez Allard Pheifer Steve Pike Haroon Pirzada Pension Poetana Des Pollock Lloyd Pollock Richard PublicBeach Rémi Quique Paul Raicevic Fred Ralaimihoatra Fabrice Ratti Reddog Pieter Regeer John Rei Jude Rigby Benny Risanto Stéphane Robin David Robinson Garth Robinson Pete Robinson Blair Rogers Colin Ross Benoît Rozé Dave Ryan Eddie Salazar Bob Samin Alejandro Sanchez Dave Scard Cory Scott Lawrence Scrafield Ian Sermonia Karin Sierralta Francisco Silva Erwan Simon Ivan Sinel Brendan Smith Diego Sotomayor Wayne Spence Justin Starow Mike Steadman Stella Tertius Strydom Vincent Stuhlen Bruno Suarez Sro Surf Jérôme Teigné Fanny Terrer Steve Thompson Dan Thorn Michael TuboLoco Junji Uchida Wim Van Cleynenbreugel Robin Van de Linde Kurt Van Duke Alan Van Gysen Dave Vanimolodge Úrsula Vargas Etienne Venter Felip Vergez Yvon Vivi Sergio VM Graham Walker Kevin Warren Andy Watson AJ Whilar Fred White Michael Wilkinson Ishack Wilmot Jody Wood Tiki Yates Hiroshi Yonekawa Zairil Zainal Austin Zammit Nik Zanella Ziggy

# CONTENTS

## INTRODUCTION



## EUROPE



## AFRICA



## INDIAN OCEAN



## AUSTRALIA



## EAST ASIA

## PACIFIC OCEAN



## NORTH AMERICA



## CENTRAL AMERICA AND THE CARIBBEAN



## SOUTH AMERICA

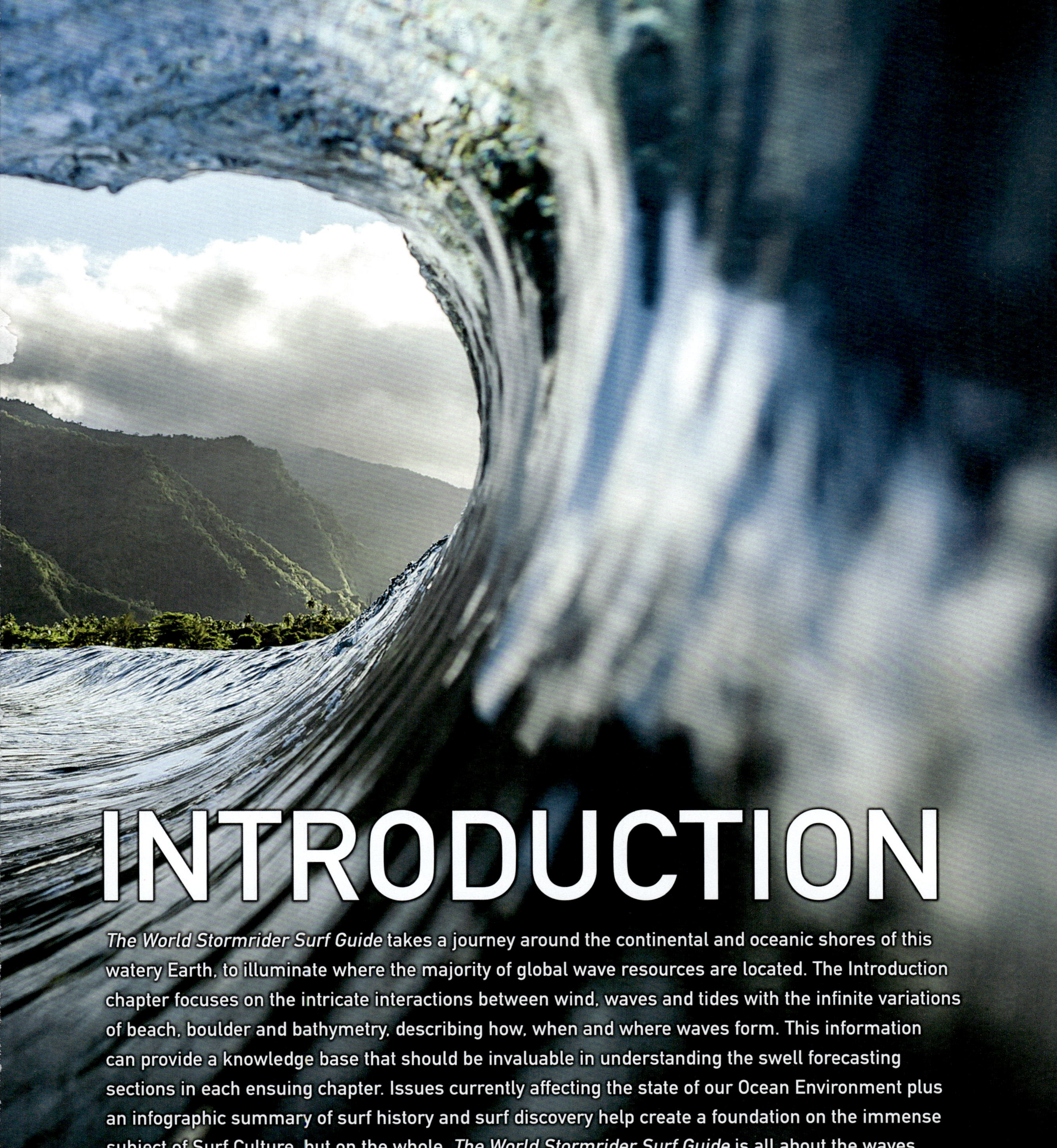

BEN THOUARD

# INTRODUCTION

*The World Stormrider Surf Guide* takes a journey around the continental and oceanic shores of this watery Earth, to illuminate where the majority of global wave resources are located. The Introduction chapter focuses on the intricate interactions between wind, waves and tides with the infinite variations of beach, boulder and bathymetry, describing how, when and where waves form. This information can provide a knowledge base that should be invaluable in understanding the swell forecasting sections in each ensuing chapter. Issues currently affecting the state of our Ocean Environment plus an infographic summary of surf history and surf discovery help create a foundation on the immense subject of Surf Culture, but on the whole, *The World Stormrider Surf Guide* is all about the waves.

Tahiti, French Polynesia

# The World's Oceans

Oceans and seas cover 71% of the Earth's surface, representing about 362,000,000km2. Surrounding this immense blanket of water is an estimated 400,000km of potentially surf-exposed coastlines. Of this extensive global coastline, about 20% is hardly ever exposed or too cold to surf and another 20% suffers from low consistency. This leaves 40% of the world's coastline providing waves on a weekly basis and a mere 20% considered highly consistent with surf more or less on a daily basis. These simplified statistics help shed some light on the geographical possibilities and limitations that face the global surf traveller in the unpredictable realm of surfing ocean waves. The southern hemisphere contains more of these highly consistent shores because it is dominated by water and hosts only two entire continents, Australasia and Antarctica.

**Atlantic Ocean 82,000,000 km²**

- The world's second largest ocean with 22% of the global sea area (increasing to 29% when the neigbouring seas are included).
- Bisected by the Equator, the greatest distance from east to west in the North Atlantic is 6,900km from Morocco to Florida and 6,500km from Cape Horn to Cape of Good Hope in the South Atlantic.
- Average depth is 3,660m and the deepest point is in the Puerto Rico Trench 8,648m.

The North Atlantic is the windiest and roughest ocean, with strong winter westerlies of over 55kmh, generating a band of seas greater than 15ft (5m) in the 30° to 60° zone, sending the biggest waves to the eastern shore of the basin. There is significant seasonal variation with much weaker winds and swells occurring in summer. The NE trade winds blowing from the sub-tropical highs around 30°N towards the Equator are sustained throughout the year, but weaker than those in the North Pacific. An extensive area of light winds or doldrums dominates the equatorial regions apart from a weak SW monsoon that is experienced in the Gulf of Guinea around July. The South Atlantic is the smallest ocean and is unusual because it has a complete lack of tropical storm activity. The barrier provided by the Andes produces a slight reduction of strength in the SE trade winds and a marked reduction of waves in the southwest throughout the year. Overall, the Atlantic trades are the weakest of all oceans.

**Indian Ocean 73,000,000km²**

- 20% of the global sea area, the Indian Ocean is quite similar in size to the Atlantic.
- Southern hemisphere location, with little area located north of the Equator. 6,400km wide at the equator.
- Average depth is 3,897m with the Java Trench bottoming out at 7,725m.

The low latitude of the westerly flow can clash with the icy polar easterlies, creating unpredictable and gusty winds. These winds have the greatest fetch of anywhere on the planet, leading to the term the 'Roaring Forties', which produce large ocean swells,

resulting in regular 'fully arisen seas'. Peak mean waves of over 15ft (5m) are observed in July/August and unlike the northern hemisphere, the seasonal change is minimal. The Asian/Australasian monsoon dominates the eastern half of the Indian Ocean throughout summer (Dec-March), when strong NW winds blow throughout Indonesia and northern Australia, while NE winds flow towards India. In the western half of the Indian Ocean there is a winter (July) SW monsoon, which reaches its greatest intensity around Somalia (Somalia Jet). The remainder of the sub-tropical to equatorial zone is mostly influenced by SE trades.

**Pacific Ocean – 165,000,000km²**

- 45% of the global ocean coverage. The largest body of water and single biggest feature on planet Earth.
- The widest point in an east-west direction is 19,300km extending almost halfway round the world. 15,500km from north to south.
- The deepest ocean with an average depth of 4,200m, plunging to the unequalled depth of 10,920m in the Mariana Trench.

In the winter, the northern half of the North Pacific is raked by high winds of over 55kmh, usually blowing from the west. These winds can generate sustained seas of over 5m to pound the western shores of North America and Hawai'i. The tropical band of the western North Pacific is under the influence of the Asian Monsoon. Strong E trades extend to the Equator in January and generate seas of up to 10ft. Generally light winds are experienced in the eastern Equatorial Pacific throughout the year and wave height is maintained by swell propagation from both the North and South Pacific westerlies. The South Pacific experiences strong westerlies flowing between the 35º to 60° mid-latitudes throughout the year. This broad corridor extending from New Zealand to Cape Horn, reaches maximum activity from June to September, when the S to SW swells primarily affect the central and eastern Pacific. In the tropics, the trade winds are less extensive and weaker than the North Pacific, so this area relies on long distance oscillations from the mid-latitude westerlies in either hemisphere.

# Wind and Currents

**The earth's weather is a complex system designed to redistribute the heat energy that the sun delivers. The sun's rays strike the equatorial regions with more concentration, causing the surrounding air to be heated. This lighter, hot air rises in updrafts, then travels towards the poles, high in the atmosphere. When it cools, the air sinks down to sea level and returns towards the equator, replacing the warm air and completing the heat exchange process. These parcels of air are measured by barometric pressure whereby falling air increases sea-level pressure resulting in a high pressure and rising air decreases the sea-level pressure so it is called a low pressure. The air in a high pressure is attracted to areas of low pressure and rushes towards it, creating winds. The rotation of the earth deflects the wind from taking a direct route between a high and a low pressure, a phenomenon known as the Coriolis force. In the northern hemisphere, this causes the air to spin clockwise around a high pressure and anti-clockwise around a low pressure. The winds spin in the opposite direction in the southern hemisphere and these rotations are mirrored by the ocean currents. The Coriolis effect is also responsible for bending any wind (or pressure system) in the northern hemisphere to the right of its direction of travel. This right turn will be regardless of which way it is flowing between the equator and the poles and will therefore be a left arc for winds south of the equator. This produces the NE and SE trade winds that blow towards the equator from each hemisphere and also angles the mid-latitude westerlies from the NW and SW respectively. Besides these two dominant bands of circulating winds, there are polar cells at the extremities of the planet and doldrums directly over the equator.**

▲
**The Earth's heat exchange system balances the difference in temperature between the equator and poles via the winds that form around pressure systems. Temperature differencials between land and sea drive offshore winds.**
▼

## WIND

A low pressure or depression will form when a small perturbation in pressure and temperature exists. The warm, lighter air slides over the top of the cold, denser air. If conditions are right this will lead to a self-perpetuating vortex. These mid-latitude systems become more energetic in the winter when the temperature difference between the equator and the poles increases. A primary influence on the west to east movements of these weather systems is the flow of air in the upper atmosphere called the jet stream. The jet stream moves at much higher speeds than the surface air and dictates the speed, intensity and trajectory of surface weather systems. A jet stream that takes a polar heading will create surface low pressures that deepen, while a jet leading towards the equator will cause the low to fill and fizzle out.

The most violent of all low pressures are formed over warm, tropical oceans when huge differences in temperature get a storm spinning extremely fast. Massive amounts of water vapour are drawn up into the vortex of these destructive tropical storms that are known by different names around the world. Hurricane is used in the Atlantic and north-eastern Pacific, typhoon is the word for the north-western Pacific and cyclone is favoured in the south-western Pacific and Indian Ocean.

Land and sea breezes are a small scale version of the global convection currents governed by heat. During the day, the land quickly heats up and hot air starts rising. This brings in cool air from the sea in the form of the afternoon onshore sea breeze. At night when the land cools, the flow is reversed and the offshores blow. These are the forces that drive the monsoon, which is basically a powerful land or sea breeze depending on the season.

## CURRENTS

These vast moving belts of water convey warm water from the equator and return cold water from the poles. Like a big heat exchanger, currents (and winds) keep the earth evenly distributed with warmth. Surface currents are mainly wind driven and can move extremely quickly (from 10km/h up to 220km per day) while deep ocean currents barely move (1m per

Sunset Reef, Cape Peninsula

day) and work on differences in ocean density and salinity. Open ocean, wind driven surface currents form large round circulation patterns known as gyres. As with the wind, they circulate in a clockwise direction in the northern hemisphere and anti-clockwise in the south. While the wind is the major motivating force, the currents do not follow the exact same path, because the Coriolis effect steps in to alter the current's course. Northern hemisphere currents will swing to the right (clockwise) of the dominant wind direction, while it's left and anti-clockwise south of the equator. Wherever there is a cold current heading back to the equator combined with trade winds blowing away from the land, the phenomenon of upwelling occurs. Warmer surface water is driven offshore and colder water rises up from depth to replace it. This colder water is usually rich in biological species, which is fortunate because these areas of upwelling are almost exclusively situated next to deserts.

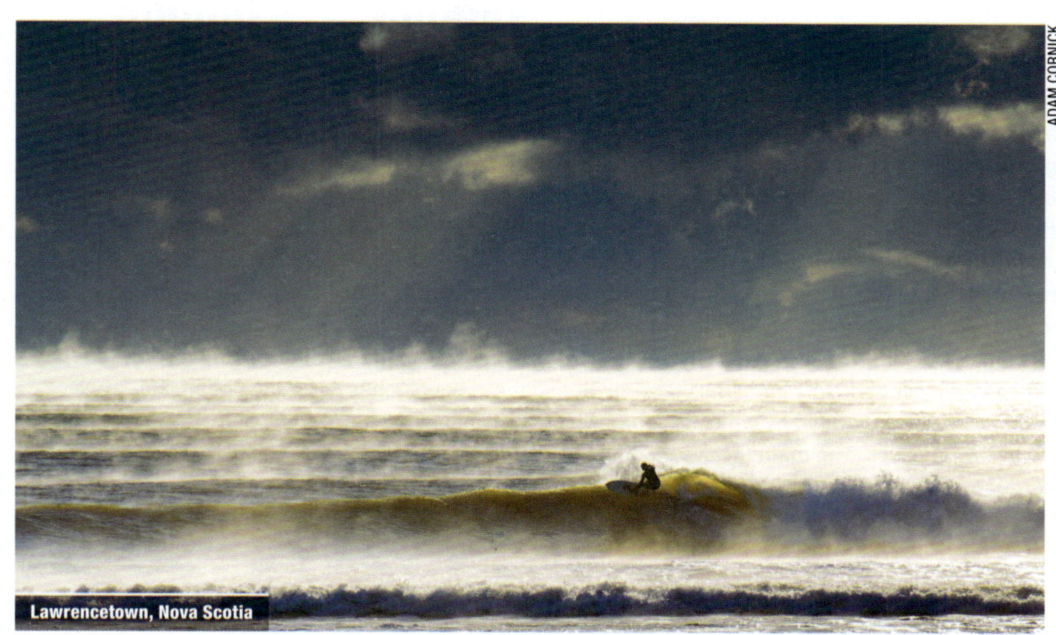

**Rare phenomena like sea smoke occur when cold air meets a warmer sea.**

**Lawrencetown, Nova Scotia**

ADAM CORNICK

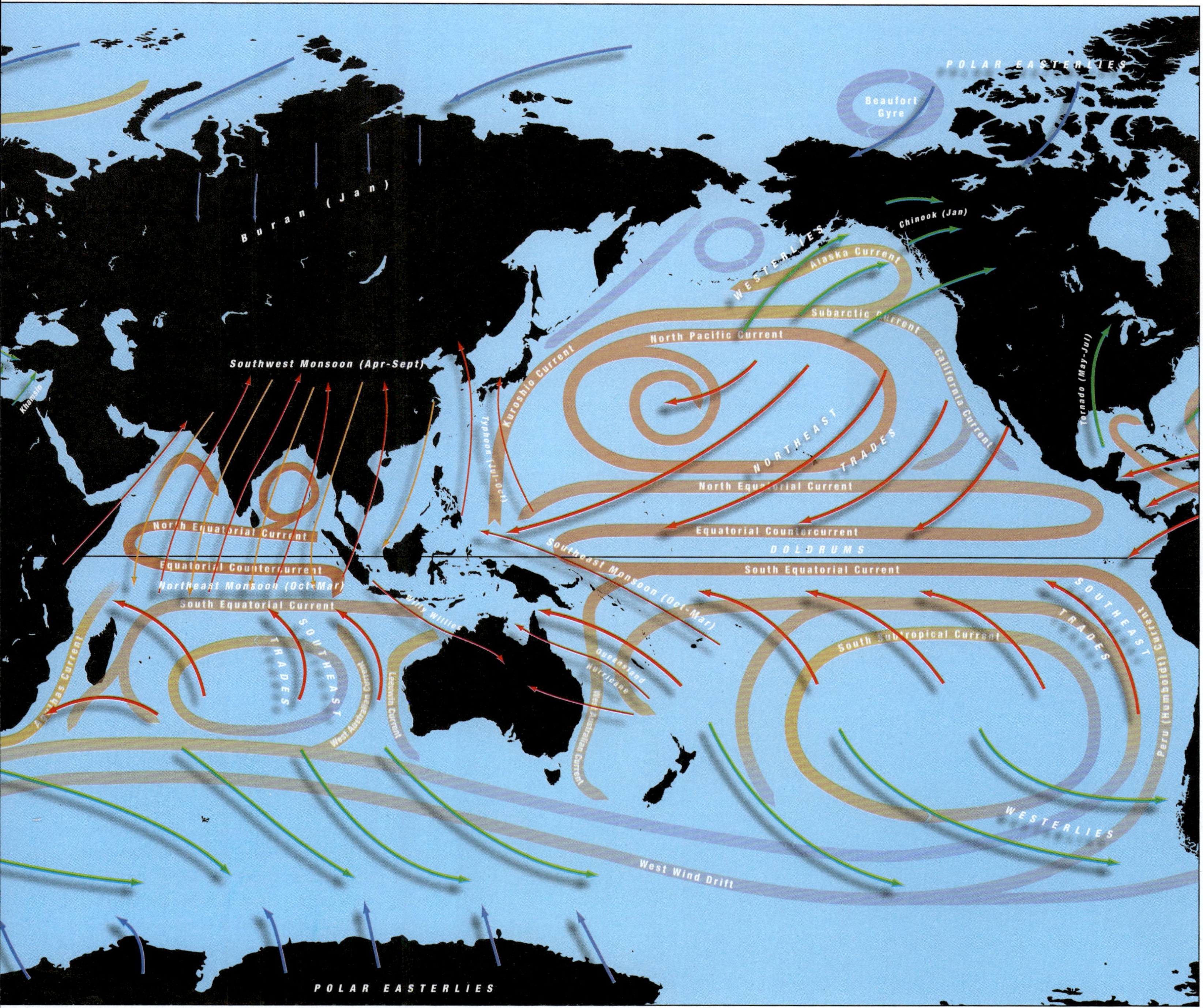

# Swell and Surf

**The main creator of rideable waves is wind blowing over the surface of the water. The wind comes in different strengths and goes by different names but essentially, it always has the same affect on wave creation. Wind blows across the surface of the globe from the four points of the compass and everything in between, but it also changes direction in the vertical plane, exerting a downward pressure on the surface of the sea. At first, this produces ripples on a calm surface, which are then easier for the wind to get a grip on and increase their size. This two-part process starts with the ripples or capillary waves, which are still small enough to be pulled back down by surface tension. As the ripples grow, small disturbances of rotating air form between the ripples adding more height to the waves, which in turn creates more uniform pockets of turbulence between the quickly growing waves. Surface tension is no longer strong enough to restore the rippling disturbance and gravity now attempts to push the waves back down. This self-perpetuating cycle increases wave height exponentially until gravity limits further growth and the wave reaches saturation point. The wave height can also be limited by white-capping, where storm force winds literally blow the tops off the cresting waves. The main factors that determine the size of the waves will be the strength and duration of the wind plus the fetch, meaning the distance over which the wind blows.**

## PROPAGATION, DISPERSION, GROUPING

Once the wind has done its job and the waves begin to travel or propagate away from the source, they organise themselves into lines of swell. As the swell fans out, the waves lose some height, which happens at a set rate. This is called circumferential dispersion, and the further a swell travels, the more this process will cause it to spread out. The width it spreads out is directly proportional to the distance it has travelled. For every doubling of the propagation distance, the height reduces by about one-third, which doesn't include other height reducing factors like white-capping and opposing winds in the propagation path.

Radial dispersion is the term used to describe how swell cleans itself up into the orderly lines that surfers love to see hitting their local beach. This revolves around wave speed,

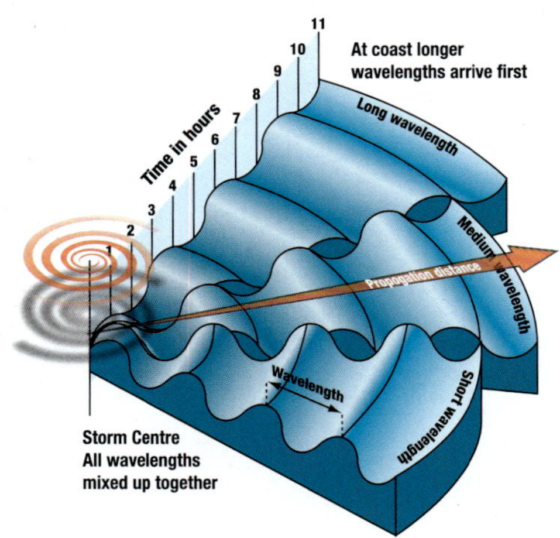


JENYA IVKOV

Convex refraction, Batu Karas, Java

which is governed by how far apart each wave is, known as wavelength. The longer the distance between two crests, the faster the waves will travel across the open ocean. When the swell is first created, many different wavelengths will be mixed in together, producing messy, disorganised waves. As the swell starts to propagate away, the faster waves with the longer wavelengths will progressively overtake the slower, shorter wavelength swells. Given enough time and distance, the faster swells will hit the coast first, bringing the clean, well-spaced corduroy lines that produce quality surf. The shorter wavelength swells will arrive later with less organisation and power, and some of the weaker, choppy waves won't even make it at all. Differences in wavelength are also responsible for the creation of sets. Technically referred to as wave grouping, sets are the result of two different swells travelling in the same direction and merging together. When the peaks of two different wave-trains coincide, a larger wave will result. However, when the peak of one wave-train coincides with the trough of another, a cancelling out effect occurs, resulting in the dreaded lulls at the beach. There are other complicated influencing factors and most non-surfing oceanographers are theoretically dismissive of wave grouping, indicating that further research is necessary to understand sets.

STU GIBSON

Concave refraction, Restaurants, Fiji

## SPEED, SHOALING AND REFRACTION

Wavelengths are also a major factor in determining the speed of waves. A straightforward equation is used for the velocity of deep water waves. Speed is equal to the wavelength divided by the period – the time it takes for two waves to pass a fixed point. This means that a well spaced, long period, big swell will travel at up to 40kmh (25mph).

As waves approach the coast and come in contact with the sea floor, they slow down, but only lose a little bit of energy to friction. The excess speed or velocity energy is channelled into making the waves higher, which happens when they start to feel the bottom at depths around one half of their wavelength. Unlike open ocean swell, the shallower the water, the slower a wave will travel, squashing together and forcing the wavelength to shorten, as the period must remain constant throughout the swell. Similar to traffic approaching a bottleneck, this slowing and bunching is termed shoaling, it increases wave height and the effect is more pronounced the steeper the shelf. If a section of one swell starts to feel the bottom while an adjacent section does not, then it will start to refract (bend) the swell. Depending on the swell direction, refraction will bend the swell one of two ways. If an obstacle (reef) is situated next to deep water, and a swell hits it straight on, then the part of the swell that hits the reef will slow down while the rest of the swell line will maintain speed. This faster travelling section will start to bend in towards the reef, resulting in concave refraction. The energy gets concentrated towards the peak, making the wave bigger, more sucky and bowly, but it often makes the wave shorter or far smaller on the inside. Convex refraction describes what happens at many classic pointbreaks, especially if they are at right angles to the prevailing swell direction. The swell lines squash together at one end as they slow down and break, whilst the other end keeps going faster resulting in a fanned-out appearance. Convex refraction spreads the wave energy over a wider area, so power and size will be less than in a concave set-up but the wave will be a long, walled-up type ride and sometimes even get bigger down the line.

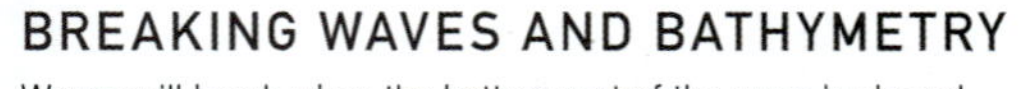

## BREAKING WAVES AND BATHYMETRY

Waves will break when the bottom part of the wave is slowed down so much that the top of the wave overtakes it and spills forward. A simple equation is used, stating that a wave will break in water at a depth of 1.3 times the wave height. This equation can be affected by other factors such as wind, swell type and beach slope. An offshore wind will hold up and delay the top of the wave from overtaking the bottom, resulting in the wave breaking in shallower water. Onshore winds have the opposite effect and can push the waves over before they reach the critical depth. Different types of swell may break in different depths of water. Fast, lined-up groundswell will get to

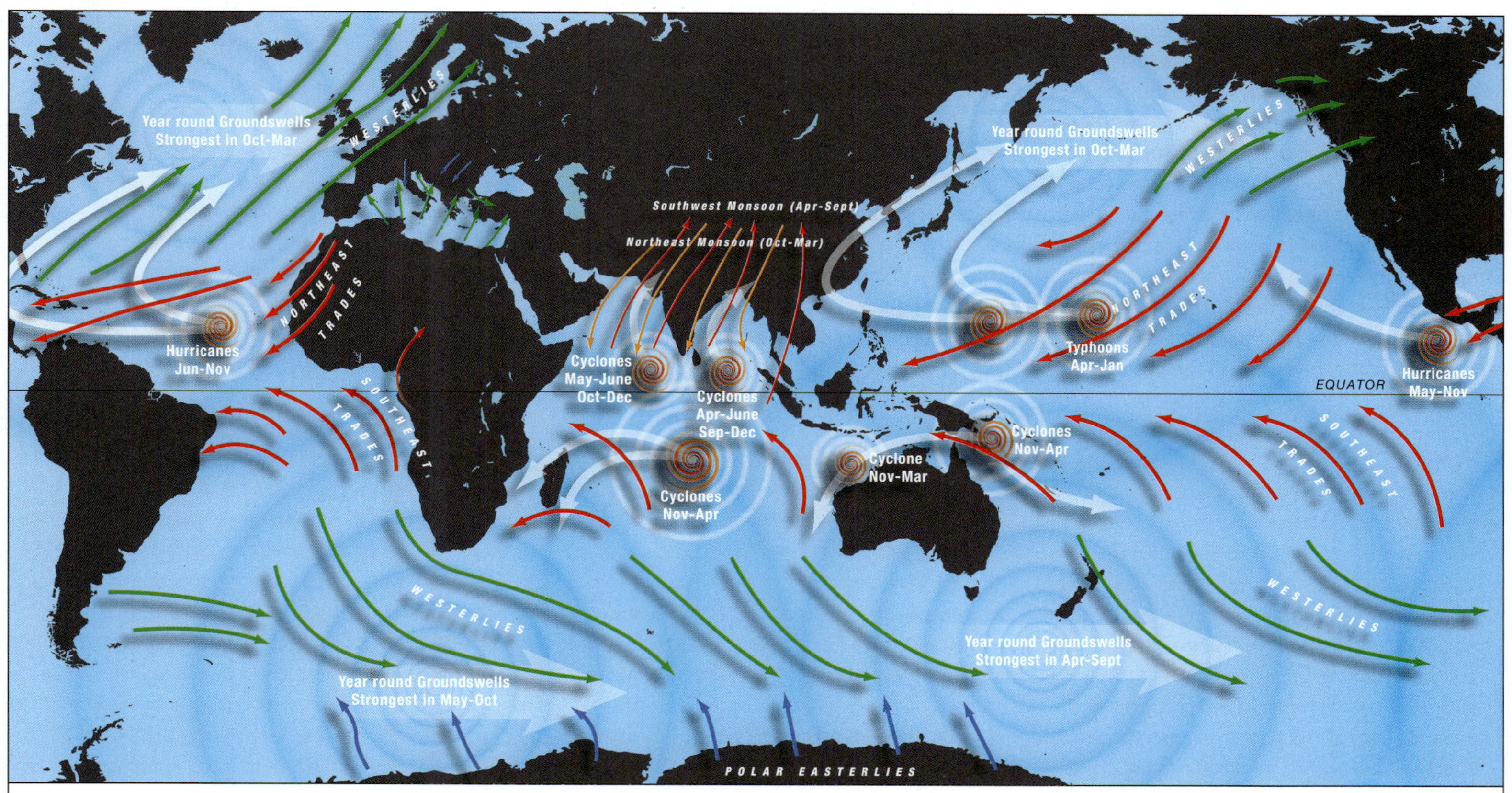


**Groundswell** – Defined as swell which has left the generating area and is propagating on its own, or "freewheeling". Produced by mid-latitude depressions between 30° and 60°. These low pressures travel from the west to the east so therefore send out more W swells than E. Waves are not affected by the Coriolis force, as they are just travelling energy, not material. Waves travel in great circular routes around the globe. Groundswells are the most consistent, powerful and sizeable of the ocean swells and are capable of travelling vast distances.

**Windswell** – Also called windsea, this type of swell still has the wind transferring energy from atmosphere to ocean, hopefully with enough fetch and duration to create rideable waves. Windswell is most prevalent where the east trades blow and its direction is totally governed by the wind. Most of the surf produced in the North Sea, Baltic and Mediterranean is courtesy of windswells, which are usually short lived, short period and disorganised, with little in the way of discernable swell lines.

**Tropical Storm Swell** – Hurricane, cyclone or typhoon swells are technically groundswells, born in sub-tropical latitudes (10° to 30°) by depressions often travelling from east to west. This produces more E swells than W but any swell direction is possible. Tropical storms only form at certain times of the year when the temperature contrasts between air and sea are at a maximum. These unpredictable, seasonal swells can produce a significant amount of sizeable waves as the storms can be slow moving. Hurricanes, cyclones and typhoons are given people's names from pre-determined alphabetical lists that alternate between male and female. Hurricanes are common off the east coast of North America, sending long-range swells to Europe.

shallower water before breaking while short wavelength, choppy windswell is more likely to crumble in deeper water. A gently sloping beach will cause waves to break prematurely while a steep slope makes them overshoot their normal breaking depth. Combining all these factors, a small, onshore, windswell wave, on a flat beach would break in very deep water, while a large groundswell in an offshore wind, on a steep reef would break in very shallow water.

Bathymetry refers to sea floor features like reefs and points (that are part of the refraction process). Two other important bathymetric features from a surfer's point of view are beaches and rivermouths. Beachbreaks need a certain shape of sandbar to provide a good forum for rideable waves. If the sand under the waves was totally flat and featureless, then when swell arrived it would almost certainly close-out. An ideal sandbar formation will be vaguely triangular with slightly deeper water on either side of the bar. This is formed when a wave breaks on a bar and starts pushing water towards the beach, picking up sand along the way. The water starts to get pushed sideways until it loses forward momentum and looks for a way back out to sea. This is where rips and currents form, aiding the circulation of water and sand. The rip gouges out a handy paddling channel and deposits more sand out towards the peak for more swell to focus upon. Rivermouths work on the same principle whereby sand is constantly deposited at the sandbar, and are far more reliable for well-shaped bathymetry.

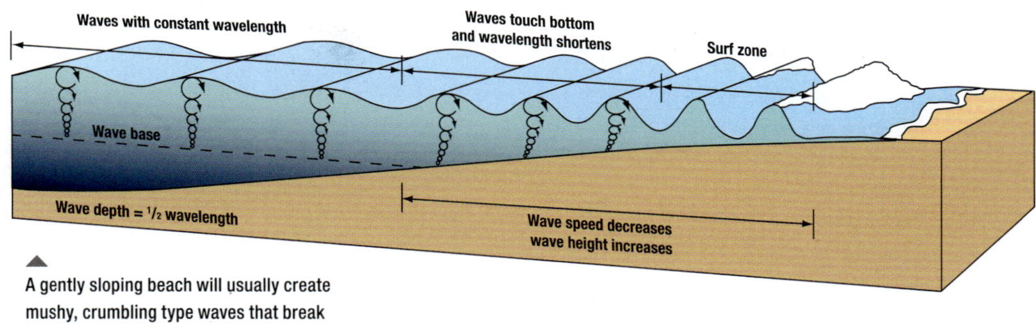


A gently sloping beach will usually create mushy, crumbling type waves that break in water deeper than the optimum depth of 1.3 x wave height.

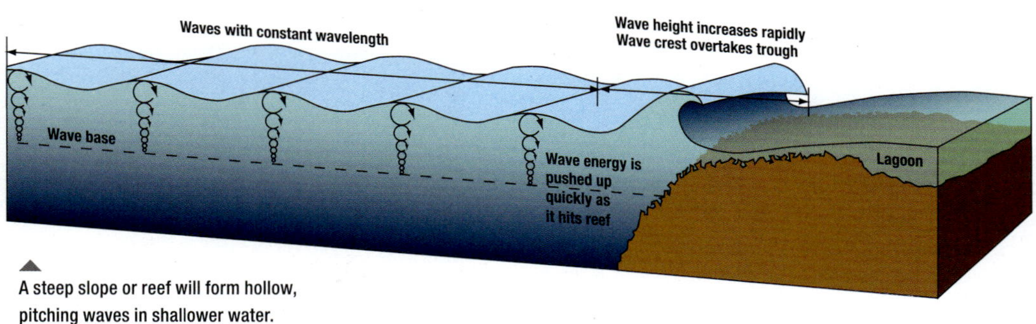


A steep slope or reef will form hollow, pitching waves in shallower water.

# Tropical Storms

**Cyclone, hurricane or typhoon are all geographically specific names for these strong tropical depressions, so choosing the correct name depends on where they form. Cyclone is the generic term used in the Indian Ocean and the Southwest Pacific Ocean (west of 160°E). Hurricane is the Atlantic word, plus it is used for any storm that appears in the Northeast Pacific (east of dateline or 160°E), while Typhoon and Super-Typhoon are reserved for the Northwest Pacific Ocean west of the dateline. There are also many different scales of measurement for tropical cyclones used by Regional Specialized Meteorological Centres and so the categories don't always match up and some measure winds at different heights, for different lengths of time, arriving at different averages. The Saffir–Simpson Hurricane Scale is used for hurricanes only and the winds must reach 119km/h (33 m/s, 64 kt, 74 mph) in order for the storm to be officially named as a Category 1 hurricane. However this is equal to Cat 3 on the Australian scale (see table). Tropical storm and tropical depression are further terms used at the lower end of the scale.**

## FORMATION

For all cyclones, hurricanes or typhoons to form, a handful of weather conditions must first combine.

- Surface water temps have to be above 26.5°C/80°F.
- Atmospheric instability – basically it is thunderstorm activity that allows the heat stored in the ocean waters to be liberated for the tropical cyclone development through fast cooling and moist convection.
- High humidity and relatively moist layers near the mid-troposphere 5km (3mi) up. Moisture is required for continuing development of widespread thunderstorm activity.
- Enough Coriolis force to get a low pressure centre spinning. That's why cyclones cannot form within 500km (300mi) of the equator.
- A pre-existing, near-surface disturbance with sizable spin and low-level inflow. Tropical cyclones cannot be generated spontaneously; they need some kind of spinning weather system to get started.
- Low vertical wind shear refers to the magnitude of wind change between the surface and the upper troposphere. Large values of vertical wind shear disrupt or destroy the tropical cyclone. Low values of less than about 37km/h (10m/s, 20kts, 23mph) of vertical wind shear are ideal.

## NAMING

Tropical cyclones have been given names since the practice was popularised by US Army Air Corp and Navy meteorologists, who were monitoring tropical cyclones over the Pacific during WWII. They chose girlfriends or wives' names, unlike the Australian forecaster that had dubbed them as political figures whom he disliked, years earlier. In 1945, the armed services publicly adopted a name list of typhoons of the western Pacific and in 1953 the US Weather Bureau switched to women's names until 1979 when men's names were included. Other regions followed this pattern until January 2000, whereby tropical cyclones in the Northwest Pacific basin are now given Asian names including flowers, animals, birds, trees, or even foods, etc, while some are simply descriptive adjectives. The Australian and South Pacific region started giving women's names to the storms in 1964 and both men's and women's names in 1974/1975. The Southwest Indian Ocean tropical cyclones were first named during the 1960/1961 season. The North Indian Ocean region tropical cyclones were slow on the name game and only started in 2006. Storm names are allocated alphabetically through any one season and traditionally provide surfers with a reference point, giving the storm a personality and allowing a deeper, more memorable interaction with the waves that are produced.

## TROPICAL STORM TRACKING

Forecasts for individual storms and their impacts are provided by NOAA's National Hurricane Center, which continuously monitors the tropics for storm development and tracking throughout the season using an array of tools including satellites, hurricane hunter aircraft, radars, buoys and advance computer modeling. Two of these hi-tech programs include the Hurricane Weather Research and Forecasting (HWRF) and the Geophysical Fluid Dynamics Laboratory (GFDL) models, boasting a vast improvement in forecasting a storm's track and intensity, which should save some lives. The Regional Specialized Meteorological Centres are strung across the seven major tropical cyclone basins, sited in Florida, Hawaii, Japan, India, Reunion, Australia and Fiji, plus a handful of regional offices, all working together as part of the World Weather Watch. From all these agencies, global trends and facts emerge like; annual average = 86 tropical cyclones (tropical storm intensity), 47 reach hurricane/typhoon strength and 20 become powerful tropical cyclones (Category 3+, severe, intense, super, major). The major surf forecasting websites often provide cyclone, hurricane and typhoon tracking tools that are specifically designed to help surfers with where, when and how big?

## TROPICAL STORM SURF CREATION

There are a few notable differences between the swell and waves produced by a cyclone, hurricane or typhoon and the surf produced by a normal (mid-latitude or extra-tropical) low pressure. They both create waves in exactly the same way by winds blowing across the surface of the ocean, but cyclones are usually much smaller in diameter with far less fetch than a sprawling winter, mid-latitude low that will produce greater wave height. These fetch-limited tropical storms can move extremely quickly and often change direction suddenly, which doesn't allow enough time for a good swell to spawn from a single direction. This can translate to really short swell events that decay rapidly over the open ocean, further limited by the small seasonal window that tropical storms are active in. Conversely, a storm that stalls or travels slowly in a straight line can make the surf pump for days on end and send out swell in many directions. Other factors to consider are how the bulk of the swell propagates out from the storm in the direction of travel, with the right side of the storm (regardless of hemisphere) always containing more energy, so the leading quadrant on the right should create more swell. Examples include strong SE swell for the US East Coast as a hurricane approaches on a direct E to W path towards the Caribbean and ideal NE swell for the East Coast of Australia as a cyclone heads south from New Guinea through the Coral Sea. Sailors dubbed the right half of the cyclone the dangerous semicircle since the heaviest rain, strongest winds and biggest seas were located in this half of the storm. Some storms can wind-up, make landfall, lose intensity and fizzle out or else head back out to sea and re-energize, even combining with the mid-latitude depressions and become an extra-tropical cyclone bringing swell to west-facing shores like Europe in the late summer. Knowing when a storm swell may arrive by calculating speed is fraught with variables, but if you know the swell period or the size of the storm then a few guess-timations can be made. Lower scale storms outputting swell periods of 10-12secs will travel about 650km (400mi) per 24hrs. Moderate scale with around 14secs period should cover 800km (500mi) while the big Cat 4 and 5 storms will see 16+sec period swells march over almost 1000kms (620mi) of open ocean if the storm track is heading your way. Anecdotal evidence suggests there is something about cyclone swells, which ramps up the power and also the number of waves in a set, as typhoon surfers often report sets of 12-15 waves compared to the average 4-6. No matter which ocean you are in, there is always a fine line between chasing down some tropical storm swell and getting caught in the storm itself, which brings strong winds, heavy rain and storm surges to low-lying areas. Storm surges are responsible for 90% of tropical storm deaths.

U-SKE

Typhoon generated surf, Japan

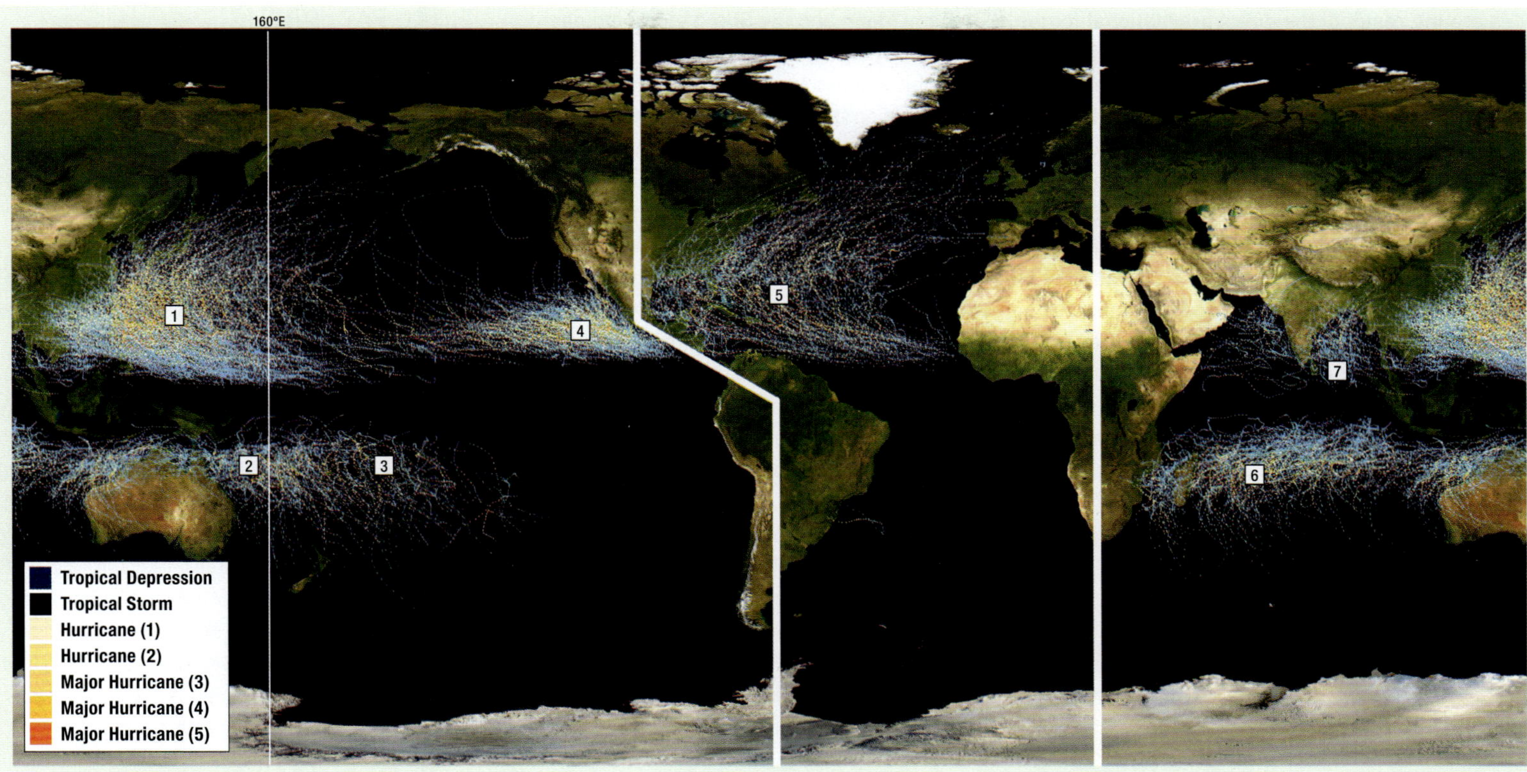


## THE MAGNIFICENT SEVEN

**1. Northwest Pacific (Apr – Jan)**
This region holds the record for tropical storms, spinning up the biggest, fastest and highest number of typhoons every year. Their tracks cover a vast area of ocean so a lot of countries are in the firing line. Micronesia, Philippines, Taiwan, China, Japan and then a second blast for those mid-Pacific islands if the storm throws a curve-ball and heads back east. June – Sept will be the heart of the typhoon season, which extends for 10 months, appreciably longer than any other region.

**2. Australia & 3. SW Pacific (Nov – Apr)**
These storms are harder to predict as historical data shows some fairly random tracks, with loops, stalls and sudden direction changes a common occurrence. Cyclones can also traverse the top of Australia, effectively linking the Pacific and Indian oceans. The Solomon's, New Hebrides, New Caledonia, Fiji, Tonga and Samoa can all take direct hits, but it is really Australia and even New Zealand that benefit the most from the west and south tracking storms while the South Pacific Islands further east are more likely to experience the lower category 1 and 2 storms. Whole seasons can pass without anything over category 3, so there's no banking on a cyclone swell in the temperamental SW Pacific.

**4. Northeast Pacific (May – Nov)**
These are the hurricanes that form off the coast of Mexico and Central America, then head in a west to north arc, bringing shorter, stronger swell events to these countries, plus longer distance waves to California and the West Coast USA, as well as the southeast exposed shores of Hawaii, thousands of miles away. Both coasts of North America experience their highest water temperatures in late August early September, so this usually coincides with prime hurricane time.

**TROPICAL CYCLONE CLASSIFICATIONS**

<table>
<tr><th colspan="3">10-MIN SUSTAINED WIND</th><th rowspan="2">BEAU-FORT</th><th rowspan="2">1 NORTHWEST PACIFIC (JAP)</th><th rowspan="2">1 NORTHWEST PACIFIC (US)</th><th rowspan="2">2 SW PACIFIC</th><th rowspan="2">3 AUSTRALIA</th><th rowspan="2">4 NORTHEAST PACIFIC</th><th rowspan="2">5 NORTH ATLANTIC</th><th rowspan="2">6 SOUTHWEST INDIAN OCEAN</th><th rowspan="2">7 NORTH INDIAN OCEAN</th></tr>
<tr><th>KNOTS</th><th>KMPH</th><th>MPH</th></tr>
<tr><td><28</td><td><52</td><td><32</td><td>0-6</td><td rowspan="3">Tropical Depression</td><td rowspan="3">Tropical Depression</td><td rowspan="3">Tropical Depression</td><td rowspan="3">Tropical Low</td><td rowspan="3">Tropical Depression</td><td rowspan="3">Tropical Depression</td><td>Tropical Disturbance</td><td>Depression</td></tr>
<tr><td>28-29</td><td>52-56</td><td>32-35</td><td rowspan="2">7</td><td rowspan="2">Tropical Depression</td><td rowspan="2">Deep Depression</td></tr>
<tr><td>30-33</td><td>56-63</td><td>35-39</td></tr>
<tr><td>34-47</td><td>63-89</td><td>39-55</td><td>8-9</td><td>Tropical Storm</td><td rowspan="3">Tropical Storm</td><td>Tropical Cyclone (1)</td><td>Tropical Cyclone (1)</td><td rowspan="3">Tropical Storm</td><td rowspan="3">Tropical Storm</td><td>Moderate Tropical Storm</td><td>Cyclonic Storm</td></tr>
<tr><td>48-55</td><td>89-104</td><td>55-64</td><td>10</td><td rowspan="2">Severe Tropical Storm</td><td rowspan="2">Tropical Cyclone (2)</td><td rowspan="2">Tropical Cyclone (2)</td><td rowspan="2">Severe Tropical Storm</td><td rowspan="2">Severe Cyclonic Storm</td></tr>
<tr><td>56-63</td><td>104-119</td><td>64-74</td><td>11</td></tr>
<tr><td>64-72</td><td>119-135</td><td>74-84</td><td>12</td><td rowspan="8">Typhoon</td><td rowspan="6">Typhoon</td><td rowspan="2">Severe Tropical Cyclone (3)</td><td rowspan="2">Severe Tropical Cyclone (3)</td><td>Hurricane (1)</td><td>Hurricane (1)</td><td rowspan="3">Tropical Cyclone</td><td rowspan="7">Very Severe Cyclonic Storm</td></tr>
<tr><td>73-85</td><td>135-159</td><td>84-99</td><td>13</td><td>Hurricane (2)</td><td>Hurricane (2)</td></tr>
<tr><td>86-89</td><td>159-167</td><td>99-104</td><td>14</td><td rowspan="3">Severe Tropical Cyclone (4)</td><td rowspan="3">Severe Tropical Cyclone (4)</td><td rowspan="2">Hurricane (3)</td><td rowspan="2">Hurricane (3)</td></tr>
<tr><td>90-99</td><td>167-185</td><td>104-115</td><td>15</td><td rowspan="3">Intense Tropical Cyclone</td></tr>
<tr><td>100-106</td><td>185-198</td><td>115-123</td><td>16</td><td rowspan="3">Major Hurricane (4)</td><td rowspan="3">Major Hurricane (4)</td></tr>
<tr><td>107-114</td><td>198-213</td><td>123-132</td><td rowspan="3">17</td><td rowspan="3">Severe Tropical Cyclone (5)</td><td rowspan="3">Severe Tropical Cyclone (5)</td></tr>
<tr><td>115-119</td><td>213-222</td><td>132-138</td><td rowspan="2">Super Typhoon</td><td rowspan="2">Very Intense Tropical Cyclone</td></tr>
<tr><td>>120</td><td>>222</td><td>>138</td><td>Major Hurricane (5)</td><td>Major Hurricane (5)</td><td>Super Cyclonic Storm</td></tr>
</table>

**5. North Atlantic Hurricanes (June – Nov)**
Forming around disturbances off the coast of West Africa, the storms have a fairly straight run down 'Hurricane Alley', a swathe of warm water that leads all the way to the east coast of Central America. That means there's a lot of good surfing real estate affected, either side of the alley including all the countries bordering the Caribbean, East Coast USA, the Gulf of Mexico coast and NE South America. Don't forget the chance of a hurricane re-energizing as it heads polewards and joining the procession of lows heading west to Europe. The South Atlantic isn't completely devoid of hurricanes (Catarina, Brazil, Cat2, 2004), but water temps and wind shear are usually against tropical storm formation.

**6. Southern Indian (Nov – Apr)**
Madagascar and the Mascarenes are in the favoured path of these cyclones that start off heading west before a short parabola to the south snuffs them out in the cooler waters. These inconsistent storms, which like the other Southern Hemisphere cyclones off both coasts of Australia, are generally less intense, shorter-lived and harder to track than their Northern Hemisphere cousins. Few of the bigger systems make landfall on Africa, while Madagascar bears the brunt and Western Australia is also prone to some cat 3 direct hits to the northwest coast.

**7. Northern Indian (Apr – Dec)**
The Bay of Bengal witnessed the most deadly cyclone ever, when Bhola surged ashore in Bangladesh, 1970. More recently, Nargis killed hundreds of thousands in Myanmar proving this basin may not be the most active, but it is certainly capable of occasionally producing powerful cyclones. Waves can result in India, Sri Lanka, Thailand, Andaman Islands and Sumatra, but high season is short from May-June. Across the Sub-Continent in the Arabian Sea is even less storm activity and little cyclone swell for established surf nations like the Maldives, which sit in the equatorial doldrums and experience too much decay in the swells from both the north and the south.

# Tides

**Tides are the result of the direct gravitational forces of both the Moon and the Sun creating bulges on the surface of the planet's oceans. Centrifugal forces create an equal bulge on the opposite side of the Earth, maintaining equilibrium for the planet during orbit.The two lunar bulges are the high tides and the areas in between are the low tides. The Earth spins on its axis and every point on the ocean's surface will experience at least one of these bulges every lunar day (24 hours and 50 minutes). Throughout the time it takes for the Moon to orbit the Earth (29.5 days or a lunar month), the Moon has four phases in relation to the Sun: opposition, quadrature, conjunction and quadrature (again). The Sun has 44% of the moon's gravitational pull on the oceans, which also produces bulges, every 24 hour solar day. So when the Sun and the Moon are lined up (in opposition or conjunction), their bulges are added together, making the tides bigger, known as spring tides. When the Sun is at an angle of 90° to the moon (quadrature), they create bulges at right angles to each other. The water is evened out over the Earth's oceans, producing neap tides. Maximum tide heights are achieved during perigean spring tides when both the sun and moon are closest to the Earth. Tides would be very predictable if the planet was covered only by water, but landmasses, the bathymetry of ocean basins, plus Earth's rotation and declination, all dynamically affect ocean tidal theory.**

## DECLINATION TIDES

When the Moon's orbit takes it 28.5 degrees north or south of the equator, the Earth's tidal bulges move with it. With only one bulge in either hemisphere, a point in the middle latitudes passes through only one crest and one trough during each tidal day, creating a diurnal or declination tide. The Sun adds gravitational pull to declination tides, particularly during the summer and winter solstice when it reaches 23.5 degrees north or south of the equator. Solar tides create higher tides in the Northern Hemisphere winter than in the summer. The Moon's orbit is inclined 5 degrees to the Earth and Sun orbits and takes 18.6 years to complete its cycle of maximum declination. Historical tidal records of at least 19 years are required to create fairly accurate tidal charts.

## TIDAL FACTORS

Over 150 factors can affect the tides and the greatest influences are the Coriolis effect, ocean depth and landforms. As with ocean currents and atmospheric systems, the Coriolis effect will bend trajectories to the right in the Northern Hemisphere and to the left in the south. Tides are considered an extreme example of a shallow-water wave (travelling in water depths less than 1/20th of its wavelength), because the extremely long wavelength of 20,000 kilometres travels in an average ocean depth of 4 kilometres. Theoretically, a tidal wave at the equator moves across Earth at 1,600 kilometres per hour, but friction with the ocean floor slows tides to a speed of about 700 kilometres per hour. Continents then get in the way and aided by the Coriolis effect, tidal waves break up into more than 12 major cells worldwide. In the middle of each cell is an amphidromic point, a tideless point in the ocean around which the tidal crests and troughs rotate through each tidal cycle. Owing to the shape of the ocean basins, the tidal crests and troughs cancel each other out at these 12 points. Co-tidal lines spoke out from each amphidromic point, joining places where high tide occurs simultaneously. The further away from the central point you travel, the higher the vertical difference between low and high tide (tidal range).

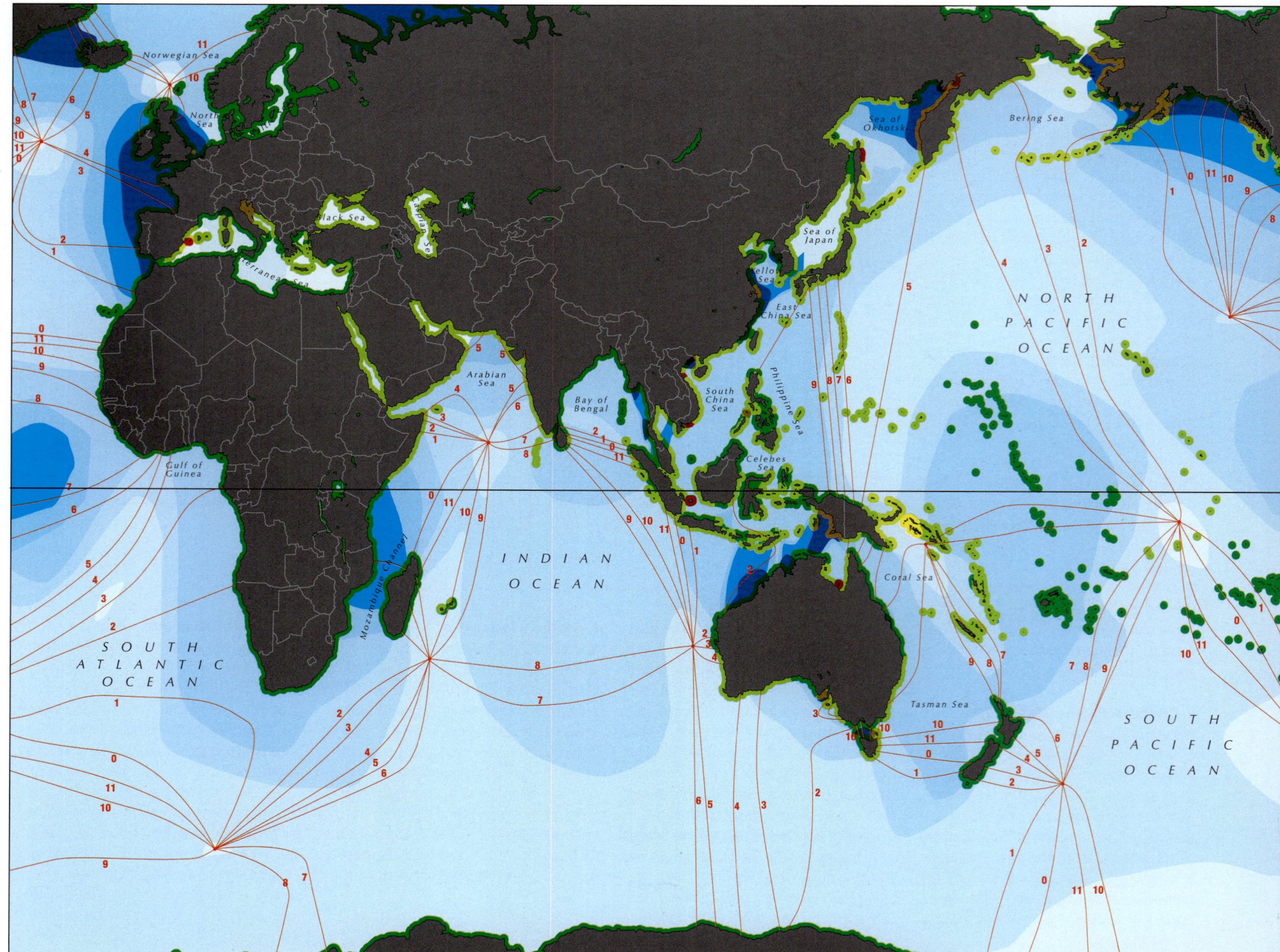

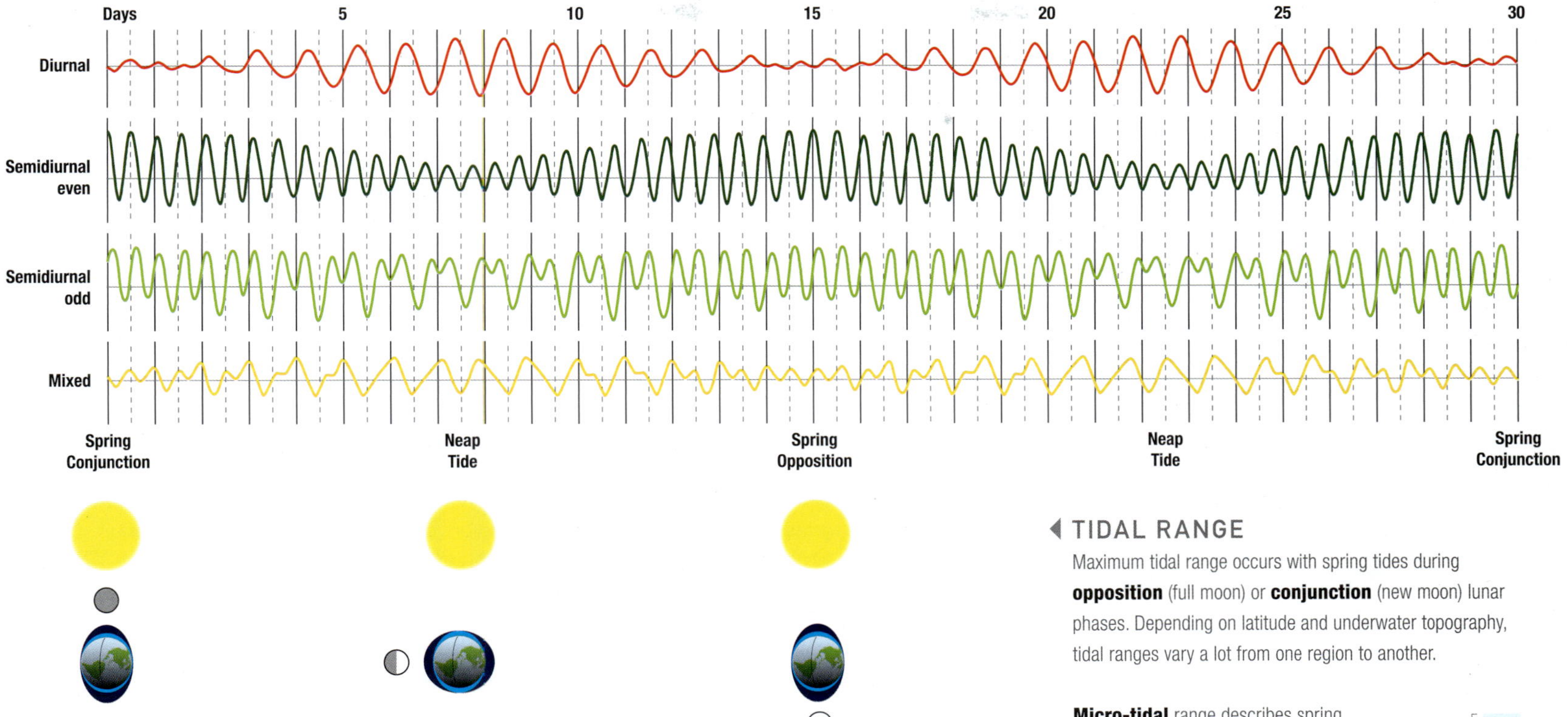

## TIDAL RANGE

Maximum tidal range occurs with spring tides during **opposition** (full moon) or **conjunction** (new moon) lunar phases. Depending on latitude and underwater topography, tidal ranges vary a lot from one region to another.

**Micro-tidal** range describes spring tide heights below 2m, a feature of many enclosed seas. Under 1m will be insignificant for most beaches but may affect shallow reefs, while up to 2m can mean some spots won't work on extreme tides.

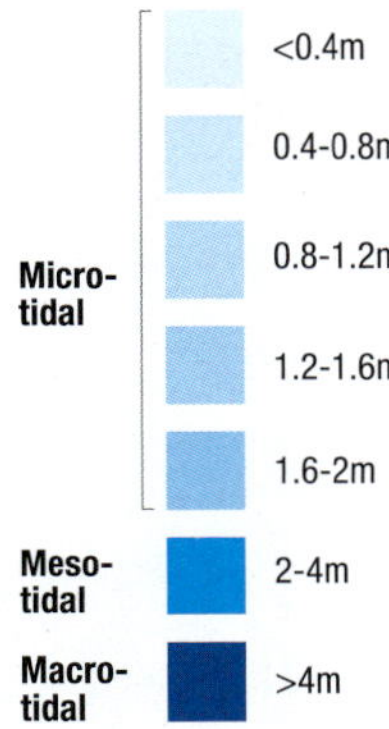


For **meso-tidal** range, spring tides will oscillate between 2m and 4m, meaning many tide sensitive spots will only work for about 1/3 of the tide (low, mid or high).

Regions like Atlantic Europe, North Brazil, Panama or Alaska that experience **macro-tidal** ranges over 4m for spring tides, will have extremely unstable surf conditions and tide will be the major factor when choosing a location to surf. Some tide charts use tidal coefficients to describe the tidal range amplitude, with larger numbers denoting a higher range and negative numbers also indicating a higher range as the tide drops below the zero **datum line**.

## TIDAL TYPES

Because of the Earth's rotation, different latitudes and uneven underwater topography, there are four types of tides.

**Diurnal** describes the coastal areas that experience a regular pattern of one high tide and one low tide each lunar day (24 hours, 50 minutes). This pattern is common in shallow or enclosed seas, such the Gulf of Mexico, the Alaskan Aleutians and the South China Sea, but is also found on the open ocean coast around Perth in Western Australia.

**Semidiurnal (even) tides** will manage to hit two high tides and two low tides of relatively equal range in a lunar day. This tidal type is most common throughout the Atlantic basin, Pacific Islands and eastern Australia.

**Semidiurnal (odd)** is a tidal pattern that experiences two high and two low tides per day, but the heights of both highs and both lows are different. This difference in tidal range is effected by the diurnal factor, but the semidiurnal factor remains dominant. Widely distributed along many Pacific coasts, Indonesia, the Arabian Sea and the Caribbean.

**Mixed tides** display characteristics of both semidiurnal and diurnal tides throughout the lunar month so one or two tides are possible per day. Mixed tides commonly have a tidal period of 12 hours, 25 minutes, but may also exhibit diurnal periods. These last two tidal types are usually combined into one type called Mixed Semidiurnal

**Amphidromic Points** indicate where the tidal range is almost zero.

11 **Co-tidal lines** join places where high tide occurs simultaneously. Numbers denote co-tidal hours from Greenwich Mean Time.

## TIDAL CYCLE

A tide cycle is made up of an incoming tide (flow) and an outgoing tide (ebb). The average length of a single semidiurnal tide cycle from low to high and back to low is 12 hours and 25 minutes, varying slightly on the relative locations of the Moon and the Sun. The tide moves at different speeds throughout the cycle, best depicted by the 'Rule of Twelfths'. By dividing the tidal range into 12 equal segments, it will show 50% of the tide flows or ebbs during the third and fourth hours, which only represents 33% of the time. Tidal movement is the least in the first and sixth hours, just after slack tide, when no perceptible ebb or flow can be measured at the top or bottom of the semidiurnal tide cycle.

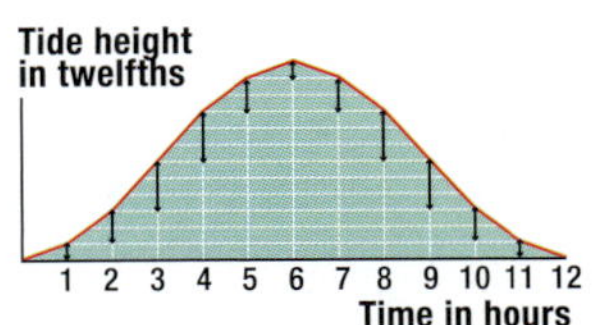

# The Ocean Environment

**An estimated 400,000km (250,000mi) of coastline separates the "Earth" from its defining feature – water. This thin frontier is where most human interaction takes place with the ocean environment and is the principle setting for the act of surfing. Many natural and human factors affect the ocean environment, altering conditions in the coastal zone and ultimately shaping the surfing experience. The central subjects that can crucially influence the ocean environment include pollution, erosion, access and hazards.**

RICARDO BRAVO

**Humans produce 300 million tons of plastic annually, then dump 8 million tons of it into our oceans every year. North Malé Atoll, Maldives.**

## POLLUTION

Pollution defines a wide range of harmful or poisonous substances introduced into an environment. Mankind dumps millions of gallons of effluent into the sea every day and yet expects the sea to continue to provide millions of tons of safe, edible food for harvest. Highly toxic industrial waste, heavy metals, radioactive material and thousands of tonnes of plastic are being deposited in the oceans daily, while at the same time, growing numbers of people are regularly entering the sea for recreation purposes. Cities concentrate and add pollution as vast areas of concrete are washed down by rain and returned to the sea with little or no treatment. Inland impurities are carried to the coast via aquatic arteries, which are choked and hardened on a centuries old diet of sewage and fertiliser. These pollution problems are all surmountable with modern treatment technologies and all that is required to effect change is money.

## EROSION

Paradoxically, large amounts of money have been spent in a vain attempt to halt the oceans' inexorable march inland, by construction of sea defences. Erosion is unavoidable, driven by the natural forces that have shaped the Earth over millenia, so the only intelligent response is to implement managed retreat. Resisting such powerful forces usually focuses the erosional process on adjacent coastlines and often increases damage whenever seawalls, jetties, breakwalls and harbours are constructed.

## ACCESS

These issues often take a back seat on the environmental front line, but are arguably the most crucial. Without access to the ocean environment, there is no interaction and no wave riding of any kind. Once again, financial gain is often at the heart of the matter as individuals, corporations and governments annexe coastal land resources and endeavour to restrict access or promote exclusivity.

## HAZARDS

Hazards come in many shapes and guises, encompassing a healthy number of natural examples that are elements of, or exist in the ocean environment. Supporting the emerging pattern, natural elements like dangerous sea creatures are not the biggest threat to surfers, but in fact, the man-made perils such as the humble surfboard are far more likely to inflict injury. Localism, or the territorial act of harassing visiting surfers has been around as long as surfing itself. Even the Hawaiian kings segregated the population and kept the best waves for themselves. Modern day surfers will be all too aware that localism sentiment exists at many a famous break, but in fact it is the quiet, semi-secret spots that often suffer the worst injustices, dealt out by "we were here first – not in my back yard" hypocrites and bullies, selfishly trying to preserve a natural resource for their exclusive enjoyment, yet perfectly happy to jet off to someone else's backyard and expect to be welcomed.

RICARDO BRAVO

**Coastal armouring against erosion is often ineffective and likely to cause further problems for adjacent coastlines, but jetties, groynes and harbour walls can also create some perfect surfing real estate. Figuera da Foz, Portugal.**

### RESPONSIBLE TRAVEL

Travelling responsibly means conserving natural resources, supporting local cultures, and minimizing our environmental impact as we travel.

### BEFORE TRAVELLING

- Research your destination as much as possible. Look into history, culture, natural environment, customs, legends, advisory notices and more. Avoid high season travel if possible.
- Learn a few words in the local language. People appreciate any effort to speak the local language and simple words like "Hello, Please" and "Thank you" can go a long way.
- Pack light and remove any new packaging items (cardboard, plastic, etc) that consume luggage space and create excess trash for foreign countries lacking recycling services. Take environmentally friendly clothing and travel gear made from recycled, reused, organic, and sustainable natural materials such as cotton, hemp, and bamboo. Use paperless ticketing, a reusable shopping bag and re-usable containers for toiletries that should be biodegradable.
- Pack rechargeable batteries, a battery charger and plug adapter. Single-use batteries are incredibly toxic and many countries do not have proper disposal facilities, so bring any used batteries back home.
- Take a reusable water bottle and use purification tablets, or decant from the largest bottles available locally to reduce waste from single-use plastic, disposable bottles.
- Book hotels that publish their environmental impact, employment and cultural policy. Newer hotels will be more energy efficient.
- Minimize transportation pollution and environmental impact by using alternative, fuel-efficient transport methods and offsetting your carbon emissions.
- Unplug your home and office appliances.

### WHILE TRAVELLING

- Engage in local culture. Eat local foods, shop in local markets and attend local festivals.
- Buy locally sourced products and services. Choose organic, ocean-friendly and sustainably sourced foods. Support locally owned businesses, community tour operators and artisans where your money will go directly to the local economy. Avoid buying products made from threatened natural resources and report poaching or other illegal activities to the local authorities.
- Refrain from over-aggressive bargaining and haggling over small change that could make a bigger difference to the vendor's life.
- Hire local guides who are knowledgeable about the destination.
- Tread lightly. Follow designated trails, respect signs, rules and caretakers and never remove archaeological/biological material from sites.
- Reduce, reuse, and recycle. Maintain normal environmental habits when traveling, including turning off lights and using less water. Turn off heating or air-con until you are in the room. Avoid excessive washing of sheets, towels and clothes in hotels. Opt for beverages in reusable glass bottles.
- Use the suggestion box to inform your hotel/hosts ideas on how to operate a more environmentally friendly business.

### AFTER TRAVELLING

- Share your responsible travel tips on how to positively impact the World, while still having an amazing journey. Share or donate your travel guides, brochures and literature to minimize waste.
- Give back. Traveling often opens your eyes and heart to something new. Donate to a local charity.

## SURF RELATED CHARITIES

**Surf AID** is a non-profit humanitarian organisation whose aim is to improve the health, wellbeing and self-reliance of people living in isolated regions connected to us through surfing. ***www.surfaidinternational.org***

**Surfrider Foundation**'s mission statement is all about the protection and enjoyment of oceans, waves and beaches through a powerful activist network. It's a grassroots organisation engaged with a wide range of environmental issues that affect coastlines. USA, Australia, Brazil, Canada, Europe, Japan ***www.surfrider.org***

**Waves 4 Water** has developed a DIY volunteer program called Clean Water Couriers. Surfers traveling to third-world countries add some water filters to their luggage and either deliver them to local non-profits or install the simple systems in remote villages. ***www.wavesforwater.org***

**Surfers Without Borders** is a humanitarian aid organization dedicated to creating projects that teach environmental awareness, reduce ocean pollution, promote sustainable development, and foster good relations between surfers and coastal communities around the world. ***www.surferswithoutborders.org***

**Surfers Against Sewage** (SAS) campaign for clean, safe recreational water, free from sewage effluents, toxic chemicals, nuclear waste and marine litter. ***www.sas.org.uk***

**Sustainable Surf** seeks to help transform the surf industry and community from its current unsustainable operating model to a global model of sustainability in action. ***www.sustainablesurf.org***

**Save The Waves Coalition** is a global nonprofit organisation dedicated to protecting and preserving the coastal environment, with an emphasis on the surf zone and educating the public about its value. Focused on fighting against coastal development that destroys surf spots, STW has established the World Surfing Reserves program that proactively identifies, designates and preserves outstanding waves, surf zones and their surrounding environments, around the world. ***www.savethewaves.org***

**Surfers for Cetaceans** calls on surfers everywhere to support the conservation and protection of whales, dolphins and other marine wildlife, while protesting against whaling, the killing of threatened or endangered species and the constant polluting and degradation of our marine environment. ***www.s4cglobal.org***

**Waves for Development** create life-enriching experiences in coastal communities through educational surf programs. Cultural exchange, environmental conservation, life skills, social entrepreneurship and sustainable tourism are values this surf NGO wants to promote. ***www.wavesfordevelopment.org***

**Surf Brands** have long been supporters of environmental causes and many have set up charitable or non-profit foundations to try and make a direct impact on issues that affect their customers. Quicksilver, O'Neill, Billabong, Hurley, Patagonia and even Kelly Slater (USA) have set up foundations or programs that give back to the surfing world.

## OTHER ORGANISATIONS

**Adventurers and Scientists for Conservation** is an organisation that uses adventure athletes to gather scientific data and knowledge of the natural environment, while on a trip to a remote area. Data collection can be expensive, time consuming, and physically challenging, so this partnership enables outdoor ambassadors to acquire the relevant skills before heading out into the more difficult to reach corners of the world. ASC has utilized the unique skills of climbers, mountaineers, divers, paddlers and other adventurers to acquire this data. ***www.adventureandscience.org***

**Greenpeace - Defending Our Oceans** is committed to defending the health of the world's oceans and the plants, animals and people that depend upon them. ***www.greenpeace.org/international/en/campaigns/oceans***

**Oceana** is the largest international group focused 100% on protecting and restoring the world's oceans. ***www.oceana.org***

**Reef Check** are an international non-profit organisation aimed at protecting and rehabilitating reefs worldwide, dedicated to conservation of two ecosystems: tropical coral reefs and California rocky reefs. ***www.reefcheck.org***

**WiLDCOAST** set out to protect some of the most beautiful and biologically significant coastal areas in California and Latin America. Today, WiLDCOAST operates 4 main programs – Wildlife Conservation, Marine Life Conservation, Coastal Conservation, and Climate Change. ***www.wildcoast.net***

**1% For the Planet** aims to build and support an alliance of businesses financially committed to creating a healthy planet. They offer a simple, tangible and proactive way for the business community to be a part of the solution. ***www.sustainablesurf.org***

## REGIONAL ORGANISATIONS

**UK:** 2 Minute Beach Clean; The Plastic Project
**USA:** Surfers' Enviro. Alliance; Sierra Club; Ocean Institute; LiVBLUE; Ocean Revolution
**Hawaii:** KAHEA – The Hawaiian-Environmental Alliance; North Shore Community Land Trust; Surfing Education Association
**Mexico:** LiVBLUE; Ocean Revolution; SurfEns
**Peru:** DGCostera
**New Zealand:** Surfbreak Protection Society
**Australia:** Nat'l Surfing Reserves
**Portugal:** Salvem o Surf

FEDERICO VANNO

Access to the surf is often made physically difficult or legally impossible, however boats open up many more possibilities. Banyak Islands, Indonesia

## ENVIRONMENTAL ACTIVISM

Human activity is inevitably altering the surrounding land and seascape, unbalancing natural ecosystems through pollution and over-exploitation of resources. Preventing the continued rape and pillage of the environment must centre on raising awareness, education and funding for research that will break the viscous circle of government sanctioned greed that permits mankind to desecrate the oceans. Mainstream organisations such as Greenpeace have the resources and membership to provide international monitoring and response to a wide range of global issues. Surfing orientated environmental activism is still in its infancy and has yet to develop a cohesive, worldwide organisation, relying instead on small localised groups, concentrating on local issues. The Surfrider Foundation represents the highest profile, largest membership environmental group focused on conservation, activism, research and education, providing an invaluable resource for surfers in North America, Australia, Europe, Japan and Brazil. Some of the challenges facing Surfrider and other groups include raising awareness at local, grassroots level, lobbying or advising governments, challenging inappropriate coastal developments, promoting low impact beach access, databasing coastal resources and monitoring pollution, not just for surfers, but all water users. Legislation on water quality has been introduced in most developed countries, although implementation and enforcement will prove to be both expensive and difficult unless full public support is forthcoming. Without a future plan for sustainable, environmentally sound, waste management, an erosion control policy, or adequate coastal access, surfers will continue to be denied the right to enjoy a clean, natural ocean environment.

Surfing is a hazardous sport, especially when considering riding powerful waves over shallow reefs, however it is often the actual surfboard that inflicts the most injuries. Table Top, Puerto Rico.

JIMMY WILSON

# Surf Culture

## HISTORY

The history of the Polynesian "Sport of Kings" was only preserved in song, so building an accurate time-line with exact dates is near impossible. It is thought that when the intrepid ocean travellers from Tahiti made landfall in Hawaii in the 4th Century AD, the paipo bellyboard was already part of the Polynesian culture. What isn't disputed is that Hawaii became the epicentre for *he'e nalu* or "wave sliding" while standing upright on a solid wood board and it was practised by the whole community from children to kings. In fact the royalty and chiefs (*Ali'i*) used surfing to maintain the status quo, reserving the best surf spots (*'ohu*) and longest boards (*olo*) for their own, exclusive use. Commoners used shorter, thinner and often wider boards (*alaia*) and there were many rituals, taboos and customs that revolved around all facets of surfing from choosing and harvesting the tree, to who was allowed to ride certain waves. One thing is for sure – Hawaiians loved surfing and it held pride of place in the community that downed tools when a good swell arrived, establishing a national identity, which survives to this day. While Peruvian fishermen may have been technically riding their totora reed horses for centuries or even millennia earlier, theirs seems to be a journey of necessity, adapting a fishing tool to slide effortlessly through the waves, as opposed to going surfing only for fun and recreation. In 1779, while Captain Cook's ships returned to England from the South Pacific, minus the Captain, his First Lieutenant completed the great explorer's journal, which contained the first detailed description of surfing. Polynesians riding "the greatest swell…with a most astonishing velocity" painted a picture for the rest of the world to marvel at. Some of Cook's sailors tried to surf in Hawaii, reporting that the boards were 'so finely tuned' that even their best swimmers couldn't stay on them for more than 30 seconds.

After Captain Cook's discovery of the Sandwich Isles, Christian missionaries spread throughout the Pacific region and generally frowned on the act of surfing, despite it's long cultural heritage and integral social role in Hawaii. By the late 19th century, when the USA finally annexed Hawaii and jailed Queen Lili'uokalani, the population had been decimated by *haole* diseases and only 40,000 survived from an estimated 400,000 a century earlier. In 1885, three young Hawaiian princes rode waves off the mouth of the San Lorenzo River in Santa Cruz using surfboards milled from local redwood. Surfing had almost disappeared except for isolated pockets of activity, one of which was based at Waikiki and had begun to pass on the ancient knowledge to a new type of visitor – the tourist.

Amongst these tourists was Alexander Hume Ford, who instantly identified with surf-riding, promoting the activity through notable author Jack London in 1907, then forming the Outrigger and Canoe Surf Club, before the Waikiki beachfront was swallowed by hotel developments. Three years later (1911), the predominately Hawaiian *Hui Nalu* club was co-founded

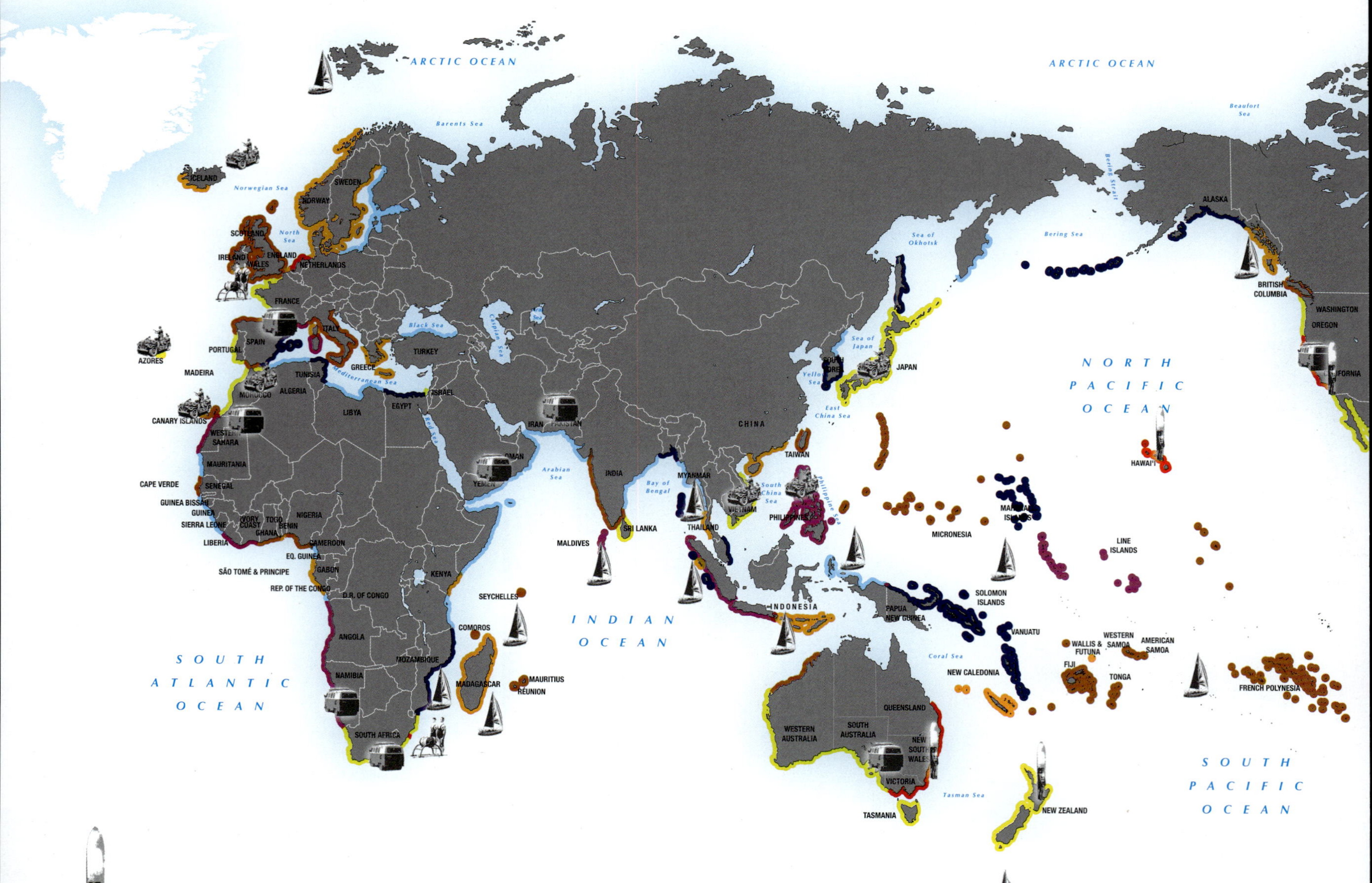

**Duke Kahanamoku** was surfing's ambassador and figurehead of the 20th Century, demonstrating the art of board-riding in California, New Jersey, Australia and New Zealand, attracting large crowds of onlookers and inspiring many to take up a board and contribute to global surf culture.

**US Servicemen** built a vital surfing link to the furthest flung countries and mid-ocean islands of strategic importance. The Canaries, Azores, Iceland, Morocco, Japan and all the Pacific islands where the US military are present, saw the first surfboards arrive with army, navy and marine personnel, who often left their boards behind for the locals to build their own scene.

**Lifeguards** spread the word through the seasonality of their work, living a truly endless summer. The Australian Surf Life Saving Association was instrumental in the propaS the world and the lifeguards would pass on their skills to a new and willing membership.

**Explorers** have added an important ingredient to the cultural melting pot, striking out into the unknown, searching for the perfect wave, which may be just around the next headland. Blake, Troy, Boyum, Rarick, Naughton and Peterson are just a few of the names who have pushed the frontiers and taken the road less travelled, but there are just as many unknown travellers that pioneered surfing in many countries and will remain incognito.

by a young local surfer and phenomenal swimmer, Duke Kahanamoku, who was honing his stroke to become the 1912 Olympic Champion in the 100m freestyle. Afterwards, he embarked on a worldwide swimming tour, which he unofficially used to introduce surfing to a waiting world. Surfing's foremost ambassador hit the waves in California and New Jersey (1912), Sydney (1914) and NZ (1915), sowing the seeds of today's global surf culture. Along with Duke, lifeguards like George Freeth patrolled the frontline, promoting many forms of surfing on various surfcraft and rescue equipment. They were exclusively Australian or American through the mid 20th century, and were joined by US servicemen, stationed to the outposts of the world. Meanwhile, a select cadre of global travellers with serious wanderlust struck out to the corners of the unknown surf world, pioneering some of the best waves on the planet, and converting the natives who took an interest.

*This map is a general representation of discovery periods and the first surfers may only have surfed a small portion of the country's coastline. There may still be coastline within a shaded region that remains undiscovered/unsurfed. Unshaded coastline is not covered in* The World Stormrider Surf Guide, *but may have some existing surf culture/history.*

**Some of the dates below represent when the country or spot was first exposed in the surf media. For more information refer to *The History of Surfing* and *The Encyclopedia of Surfing* – in book or online format by Matt Warshaw.**

### PRE-WAR

| | |
|---|---|
| 1907 | Redondo Beach – George Freeth, |
| 1909 | Manly – C.D. Paterson |
| 1922 | Miami – Tom Blake |
| 1923 | Jersey – Nigel Oxenden |
| 1925 | Malibu – Tom Blake, Sam Reid |
| 1928 | Durban – Charles MacAlister |
| 1929 | Cornwall – Lewis Rosenberg |
| 1930s | Brazil – Thomas Rittscher, Santos Osmar Gonçalves et al |
| 1930s | Kuta – Bob Koke |
| 1930s | Netherlands – Jan Nederveen |
| 1939 | Peru – Carlos Dogny |

### 1945 - 1959

| | |
|---|---|
| 1940s | Japan – US servicemen |
| 1940s | Baja – Unknown San Diego surfers |
| 1950s | Arpoador – Bruno Hermany, Jorge Paulo Lemann, Gilberto Laport, Arduino Colassanti, Irencyr Beltrao |
| 1950s | Tahiti – Unknown travellers |
| 1950s | Germany – Local lifeguards |
| 1953 | Portugal – António Jonet |
| 1954 | Morocco – US servicemen |
| 1956 | Israel – Dorian Paskowitz |
| 1956 | France – Peter Viertel, George Hennebutte, De Rosnay |
| 1956 | Elands Bay – John Whitmore |
| 1957 | Azores – US servicemen |
| 1960s | Puerto Rico – Jose Rodriguez, Guille Bermuda, et al |
| 1959 | Mexico – Bud Browne, Greg Noll |
| 1959 | Uruguay – Unknown |

### 1960 - 1969

| | |
|---|---|
| 1960s | Wales – Unknown |
| 1960s | Hong Kong – Derek Bailey |
| 1960s | Tonga – King Taufa'ahau Tupou IV |
| 1960s | Fiji – Unknown Australians |
| 1960s | Bahamas – Unknown Americans |
| 1960s | Jamaica – Cecil Ward, Pin Head, Apache, Ridgley |
| 1960s | Guatemala – Unknown Americans |
| 1960s | El Salvador – Unknown Americans |
| 1960s | Costa Rica – Unknown Americans |
| 1960s | Guam – Rick Value |
| 1960s | Federated States of Micronesia – local Pohnpeian |
| 1961 | Ireland – Ian Hill |
| 1962 | Spain – Jesús Fiocchi |
| 1962 | Panama – Unknown Americans |
| 1962 | Mauritius – Joel de Rosnay |
| 1963 | Italy – Peter Troy |
| 1963 | Argentina – Daniel Gil |
| 1963 | Ecuador – Snr Pousada |
| 1963 | Senegal – Endless Summer |
| 1963 | Ghana – Endless Summer |
| 1963 | Nigeria – Endless Summer |
| 1964 | Sri Lanka – Rusty Miller |
| 1964 | Canary Islands – Peter Troy |
| 1965 | Vancouver Island, Canada – Jim Sadler, Tofino locals |
| 1965 | Taiwan – Mao Guh, US Servicemen |
| 1965 | Barbados – Butch Linden, Jonny Fain |
| 1965 | Venezuela – Unknown |
| 1966 | Chicama – Carlos Barreda, Oscar Malpartida, Ivo Hunza |
| 1967 | Reunion – Unknown Aussies |
| 1967 | Seychelles – Ron Perrott, Geoff White |
| 1967 | Comoros – Ron Perrott, Geoff White |
| 1967 | Mavericks, California – Alex Matienzo, Jim Thompson, Dick Knottmeyer |
| 1968 | Scotland – Andy Bennetts, George Law |
| 1968 | Tamil Nadu – India – Claude Codgen |
| 1969 | Chile – Unknown |

### 1970 - 1979

| | |
|---|---|
| 1970s | Guadeloupe – Patrick Abadie, Francois De Corlieu |
| 1971 | Uluwatu – Albe Falzon, Steve Cooney, Rusty Miller |
| 1973 | Philippines – US servicemen |
| 1973 | Maldives – Tony Hinde, Mark Scanlon |
| 1974 | Grajagan – Bob Laverty, Bill Boyum |
| 1974 | Ivory Coast – Craig Naughton, Kevin Peterson |
| 1974 | Liberia – Craig Naughton, Kevin Peterson |
| 1974 | Angola – Randy Rarick |
| 1975 | Nias – Peter Troy, John Geisel, Kevin Lovett |
| 1979 | Kiribati – Chuck Corbett |

COURTESY THE SURFING MUSEUM

### 1980 - 1989

| | |
|---|---|
| 1980s | Iceland – US servicemen |
| 1980s | Sweden – Janne Ekstedt |
| 1980s | Denmark – Local windsurfers |
| 1980s | Nicobar Islands – Aussie dive instructors |
| 1980s | Wallis & Futuna – French expats |
| 1980s | Haiti – US Expatriates |
| 1980s | Madagascar – Unknown Sth Africans |
| 1980 | Mentawai – Wakefield, Goodnow, Fitzpatrick |
| 1980 | Phuket – Unknown Aussies |
| 1982 | Cloudbreak – Dave Clark |
| 1982 | Norway – Roar Berge, Per Ståle Grude |
| 1983 | Belgium – Kobbe |
| 1985 | Hainan, China – Peter Drouyn |
| 1986 | Cocos (Keeling) Islands – Jim Banks |
| 1986 | Teahupoo – Mike Stewart, Ben Severson |

### 1990 - 1999

| | |
|---|---|
| 1990s | PNG – Unknown Aussies |
| 1990 | Cherating – Unknown Aussies |
| 1991 | P-Pass – Alan Hamilton |
| 1992 | Cloud Nine – John Callahan, Taylor Knox, Evan Slater |
| 1992 | South Korea – John Callahan, Randy Rarick |
| 1993 | Cuba – Unknown Spanish & Quebec surfers |
| 1994 | New Ireland PNG – John Callahan, Chris Malloy, Ross Williams |
| 1995 | New Caledonia Sth – John Callahan, Chris Malloy, Donovan Frankenreiter |
| 1996 | Jurassic Point – Callahan, Chris Malloy et al |
| 1998 | Andaman Islands – Callahan, Chris Malloy, Jack Johnson, Sam George et al |
| 1999 | Antarctic Peninsula – Porter Turnbull |

### 2000 +

| | |
|---|---|
| 2000 | Myanmar – Callahan, Randy Rarick, Torsten Johnson |
| 2000 | Oman – Jeff Divine, Shayne and Shannon McIntyre, Surfer Magazine |
| 2000 | São Tomé and Principé – John Callahan, Randy Rarick, Sam George, Nuno Jonet, Thiago Olivera |
| 2001 | Pakistan – Stormrider, Oceansurf, Yep |
| 2003 | Yemen – Stuart Butler et al |
| 2003 | Andhra Pradesh, India – John Callahan, Yep, Randy Rarick, Shane McIntyre |
| 2004 | Central Maldives – Yep, Oxbow |
| 2005 | North Maldives – Yep, Callahan |
| 2005 | Chagos Islands – Ian & Mark Wilson |
| 2006 | Iran – Olivier Servaire |
| 2006 | Kamchatka – Rip Curl |
| 2007 | Namibia – Skeleton Bay – Local surfers |
| 2007 | Australia – The Right – Chad Jackson, Brad Hughes, Sean Virtue, Dean Harrington |
| 2007 | Libya – Yep |
| 2009 | East Algeria – Yep, Callahan |
| 2010 | Spain – Wavegarden Test Centre |
| 2011 | Gujarat, India – John Callahan, Sam Bleakley, Erwan Simon, Emi Cataldi, et al |
| 2015 | Wavegarden Surf Snowdonia – Wales |
| 2015 | KSWC Wave Ranch – Lemoore USA |
| 2017 | The Snake – Unknown – Rip Curl |
| 2018 | AWM BSR Surf Resort – Waco USA |

# Alternative Wave Resources

**With a rapidly growing world population, global wave resources are a seemingly finite resource. However, progress is being made with ever-improving technology in the wave pool genre, where increasingly impressive artificial waves are being manufactured for inland recreational purposes. While wave pools for swimmers have been around since 1927, the first board-surfable wave was built in Japan in 1966, until 1985 saw the first pro contest in a pool in Pennsylvania. Multiple attempts have been made the world over to create a ride that rivals the ocean, but all have fallen short. In the last decade, surf specific designs have raised the performance bar massively (see below). Tidal bores offer ultra long rides on traditional equipment and the inventory has increased in recent years to 64 rideable rivers around the world. Other surf creating ideas have fallen out of favour, including the near 100% failure rate of artificial reefs and the surf/snow/skate attitude of a thin layer of water creating a stationary wave over the fibreglass and rubber moulding of a FlowRider. Natural standing waves are increasingly popular, with the world's most famous example appearing in a small river in central Munich, Germany. Tow-in, tow-at and foilboarding have also opened up some new surfing real-estate.**

## WAVE POOLS

Early designs were based on the principle of building a very large swimming pool then quickly introducing a large volume of water to the pool displacing enough water to create a swell. Often using a giant cistern type system where tanks of water are literally flushed into the pool, wave height, direction and quality can be controlled, depending on the engineering. Recent developmental strides have been taken with two new designs which use a blade or foil pushing through the water to create a variety of wave shapes and heights that break over different bottom contours. A third design uses air chambers to create the requisite displacement. They all claim to be designed to cater for all surfing abilities, while trying to balance the quantity over quality quandary.

COURTESY WAVEGARDEN.COM

Wavegarden Cove

### WAVEGARDEN

Since commencing in 2005, Wavegarden has engineered two different wave-making systems. The first is Wavegarden's Lagoon technology, which is used at two public facilities: Surf Snowdonia in North Wales, and NLand Surf Park in Austin, Texas. Both surf parks make waves using a hydrodynamic wavefoil, which is pulled through the water by a cable. This is housed under a central pier, sending out a swell on both sides, which break differently depending on the engineered bathymetry of the eight various areas of the lagoon. The three wave types include a challenging Reef area for experts; point-style lefts and rights for intermediates through the Insides; and easy beginner-friendly rollers and white-water in the Bay areas at each end. Rides can go for up to 35 seconds and wave heights range from headhigh (2m) in The Reefs through to kneehigh (0.6m) in The Bays. When the foil has arrived at one end of the pier and a period of 1-2.5 minutes has elapsed to allow currents and backwash to subside, the bi-directional foil makes a pass in the opposite direction, minimising energy consumption and allowing for both offshore and onshore waves, depending on the local wind direction.

The second-generation technology is called the Wavegarden Cove. This technique uses a modular system that injects energy into the wave as it advances, recreating the same circular movement of water molecules as an ocean swell. Although the exact details are kept secret, the non-hydraulic, non-pneumatic technology is capable of making up to 1000 waves per hour, ranging from 0.6m-2.4m. There are approximately 30 different types of waves, suitable for all experience levels - from steep barrels for experienced surfers through to slow moving white-water for newcomers. A standard size facility can cater for up to 100 surfers at the same time (50 experts and 50 beginners). Experts and beginners surf in different areas and currents move in a circular fashion, returning surfers to the take-off zone. Wavegarden has developed a treatment system that keeps the water clean and crystal clear. There are currently 20 Coves in development around the globe, two of which are under construction (Melbourne, Australia; Bristol, England).
***www.wavegarden.com***

COURTESY WAVEGARDEN.COM

Surf Snowdonia

### THE WSL SURF RANCH

In 2015, The Kelly Slater Wave Company manufactured a wave pool in Lemoore California, designed to create a wave that would challenge the world's best surfers and ultimately serve as a forum for World Championship contests. The project has been shrouded in secrecy and technical details are vague, but it uses the same principle of a large blade or foil being drawn through the water beneath a 100 tonne, cable-driven vehicle running on twin tracks, much like a locomotive. Dubbed 'Groundswell Technology', the foil displaces a pulse that propagates out at an obtuse angle to the pier, forming a single left or a right, depending on which direction the foil is travelling down one side of the 600m pool. The resulting wave breaks back toward the fenced-off pier, conjuring rides up to 45 seconds with extremely long, hollow barrel sections, perfectly mimicking the best-shaped ocean waves found in the wild. The lips carry plenty of power and it's a high speed tube-ride that is sometimes difficult to read, with subtle differences possible on consecutive waves. The rights offer tube time up to 15 seconds on the first section, with a shorter but faster cover-up at the end of the wave. Lefts typically offer a ripable wall with more crumbling lip on the outside followed by a rapid tube on the inside. There is at least a 3 min turn-around to allow the pool to settle from the previous wave. While the prototype is firmly aimed at elite-level surfers, the wave technology is flexible and can also create variable waves for beginner and intermediate surfers.

In 2016, the WSL joined forces with KSWC to roll out the technology in order to promote the growth of high-performance surfing around the world and provide a valuable training facility offering a repeatable, controllable and scalable wave canvas. Pro competition started in September 2017 with the Future Classic and May 2018 with the team oriented Founders Cup, before the world tour scheduled stop in September 2018.
***www.kswaveco.com***

### AMERICAN WAVE MACHINES

Another pool for Texas has opened within the existing BSR water park, utilising AWM's Perfect Swell technology, generated by 7x3m wide air chambers, releasing the swell into a 75m pool. "Wave quality, size, duration, and frequency can be controlled at the touch of a button via an iPhone or iPad, with no wait time for waves." This flexibility allows for a greater number of different wave profiles including pointbreaks, beachbreak peaks, refraction wedges, or mush burgers. Firing all the chambers simultaneously would result in across the pool closeouts. Rides are as varied as the waves from barrels and ramps or walls and wedges. The machinery can produce up to 180 waves per hour, coming in sets of 3 after a short reload interval. Claimed wave face height ranges between 3ft and 8ft and rides last around 10-15 seconds. It costs $60/hr for a session. (See photo on page 299). ***www.bsrcablepark.com***

## TIDAL BORES

When the Earth was newly formed 5 billion years ago, there was a cosmic collision with the Mars-sized planet Theia, and the resulting debris coalesced to form the Moon. Back then the Earth spun a full rotation in 6 hours and tides reached 500m! The Moon helped slow the Earth's rotation and stabilised its orbit while slowly moving away from it. The Moon is 400 times smaller than the Sun, but it is 400 times closer, so they appear the same size in the sky. Between them, they exert a gravitational force on our planet that creates the tides (see Tides page 20). This force is measured at the equator as only being 60-90cm, so how do we get 18m tides in the Bay of Fundy? Other factors come into play like underwater topography, coastal morphology and resonance, barometric pressure and wind, just to name a few, but luckily for surfers, certain rivers that are open to an ocean with moderate to large tidal activity experience a wave phenomenon known as a tidal bore. Usually found in shallow, funnel-shaped estuaries between 50km and 100km long, the wave is created when river flow and ebbing tide runs in the opposite direction to a surging tide. This happens when the tide becomes asymmetrical: the tide floods into the river system in 3-4hr but takes 8-9hr to drain back out, meeting the new incoming tide back at the mouth of the estuary. A 4m tidal range at the mouth can reach a 6m maximum, 80km upstream. As the river narrows, the tide is condensed and shallower water causes the tidal wave to break, usually on each riverbank or away from the channels. Depth is crucial for a good bore wave, where most tropical and northern rivers are generally shallow while temperate latitudes are subject to strong rain causing higher water levels. Behind the larger leading wave can follow up to 15 lesser waves plus multiple corrugations, along with turbulent peaks, reflected off the banks and racing currents up to 8m/s (29km/h). With so many variables, the waves come in many patterns including chevrons, velour, antennae, spiders web and the chicken's foot, when viewed from the air. Due to the river's linear geography, bore waves offer the longest distance rides on the planet.

KENYU

The Baan, Hooghly River, Kolkata, India

All bore information taken from *Mascaret* by Antony "Yep" Colas – a detailed guide to how and where river bore waves form. French only.

YEP

Benak, Batang Lupar, Sri Anan, Malaysia

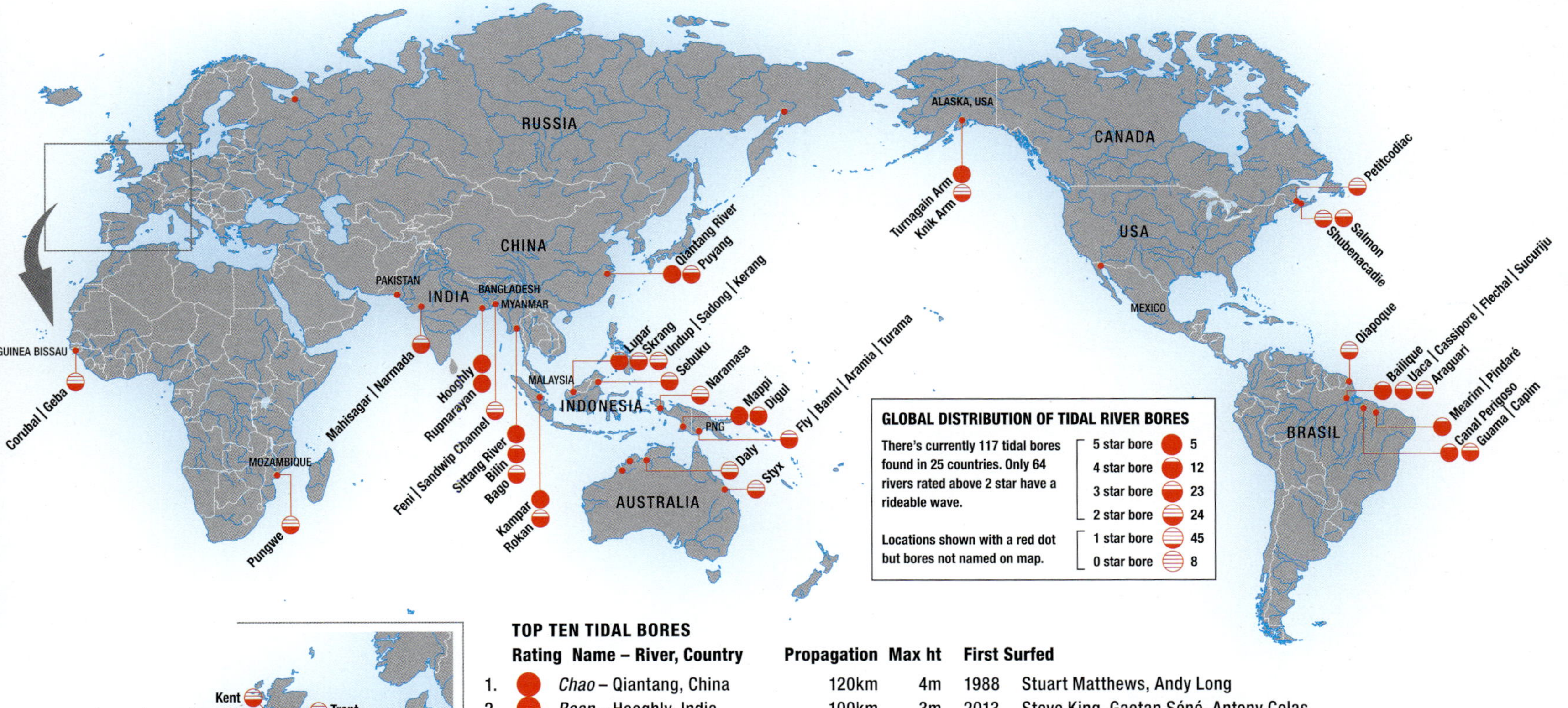


### TOP TEN TIDAL BORES

| | Rating | Name – River, Country | Propagation | Max ht | First Surfed | |
|---|---|---|---|---|---|---|
| 1. | ● | *Chao* – Qiantang, China | 120km | 4m | 1988 | Stuart Matthews, Andy Long |
| 2. | ● | *Baan* – Hooghly, India | 100km | 3m | 2013 | Steve King, Gaetan Séné, Antony Colas |
| 3. | ● | *Bono* – Kampar, Indo | 100km | 2.5m | 2011 | Patrick Audoy, Eduardo Bagé, Antony Colas, Fabrice Colas |
| 4. | ● | *Lhaine Lone* – Sittang, Myanmar | 60km | 2.5m | 2016 | Jérome Cordoba, Patrick Audoy, Gabriel Naveau, Antony Colas |
| 5. | ● | *Pororoca* – Canal Perigoso, Brasil | 70km | 2m | 1997 | Noélio Sobrinho, Gilvandro Junior, Silvio Santos, Jorge Junior |
| 6. | ● | *Kepala Arus* – Digul, Indonesia | 60km | 2m | 2015 | Eduardo Bagé, Kai Bates, Antony Colas |
| 7. | ● | *Benak* – Batang Lupar, Malaysia | 60km | 2m | 2009 | Antony Colas |
| 8. | ● | *Pororoca* – Mearim, Brasil | 50km | 2m | 2001 | Noélio Sobrinho, Geronimo Junior, Adrielson Grega, Vinicius Mirele |
| 9. | ● | *Bore* – Severn, England | 60km | 1.5m | 1955 | Jack Churchill |
| 10. | ● | *Mascaret* – Dordogne, France | 70km | 1.5m | 1982 | Roger Marcel |

LOCATION: IRELAND PHOTOGRAPHER: TIM NUNN

# EUROPE

Stretched along the eastern shore of the tempestuous North Atlantic Ocean, continental Europe presents a cornucopia of wave resources for the maturing surf cultures of the 'Old World'. This sublime continent has the ability to entertain the sweetest, small beachbreaks right alongside the meanest, mountainous reefbreaks, while new discoveries continue to raise Europe's profile and increase its inventory of world-class waves. Surf activists are looking to the next generation to carry on the fight to protect the ocean environment along this populated coastline. Meanwhile, surfer numbers are exploding from Iceland to Italy and beyond, as surfing comes of age on the European Continent.

LUKE GARTSIDE

Mundaka, País Vasco, Spain

# The Surf

## ICELAND

With 4970kms of coastline to explore, **Iceland** presents a rare opportunity to surf virgin territory, yet most Icelandic surfers only ride around the Reykjanes Peninsula, close to Reykjavik in the southwest. The Snaefellsness peninsula to the NW of Reykjavik also picks up plenty of swell from the S-W with more beachbreak than the Reykjanes but mainly 4WD access trails and few documented, bona fide surf spots. Westfjords has extensive beachbreaks facing S,W and N on its southern arm around Breiðavík. Straying off the Route 1 ring road is fraught in bad weather so checking towns like Blönduós in the north or the east coast from Breiðdalsvík where Route 1 hits the coast will be easiest. Invariably though it will be the tortuously twisting circuitous smaller roads that lead to an endless array of ash grey beachbreaks facing every conceivable direction that hold anything from fun longboard peelers to thumping peaks on empty lonely beaches in cold biting conditions. Vik is the southernmost point on the island and attracts any hint of swell down a submarine canyon onto quality black sandbanks. Challenging, hollow and powerful with strong rips and massive up to 5m tides, this is not a spot, or an island for the faint-hearted.

LAURENT MASUREL

Iceland

## THE BRITISH ISLES

**Ireland**'s sublime mix of reefs, points and beaches make the most of the near constant stream of Atlantic juice. Proximity to the storms can mean swells are disorganised and accompanied by strong winds but the contorted coastline usually means somewhere nearby is offshore. World-class waves can be found in many of the western counties while the east coast suffers from a lack quality and consistency, but once or twice a month, the Irish Sea can benefit from local wind generated waves and southerly groundswells. SE, S and huge SW swells enter St. George's Channel and bend around some of the east coast headlands. Well known east coast spots include White Rock & Killiney plus Bray in the Dublin area which generally work on N windswells. In **County Wicklow**, look for Magheramore, Brittas Bay and Greystones in all swell directions, while in **Wexford**, S swell bends off the pier and creates a nice wave in Courtown. **Southern Ireland** is predominantly onshore in the normal SW airstream, but there are some surprisingly good quality waves on occasion, mainly in winter. Plenty of surfers live close to the centres of Cork and Tramore, keenly awaiting the conversion of a big SW swell and N winds at breaks like Long Strand and Tramore. Stunning scenery surrounds the deep estuaries of The Ring of Kerry and provide much potential for discovery. Generally needs big SW swell to work, meaning cold, lonely waves are the norm. Autumn to sping in **County Kerry** and especially the Dingle Peninsula will see some great, but notoriously inconsistent waves. The highest concentration is around Brandon Bay on the north side, which requires exacting swell and wind directions. The other side of the peninsula, Inch Reef is a slumbering classic that rarely breaks, but is one of the longest waves in the country. There are some heavy water slabs just into County Clare, whose craggy W-facing coast receives ample swell but suffers from onshore winds most of the year. Summer can be prime, especially if a high pressure establishes in the vicinity but unstable weather patterns make Clare hard to call. **Galway** has a contorted craggy coastline of long-fingered promontories with lots of sheer cliffs and pocket beaches involving difficult access to the exposed parts. Between Clifden and Louisburgh is the area most likely to reward dedicated searchers. Achill island has some south-facing, beginner-friendly beachbreaks at Keel. In **County Mayo**, The Belmullet peninsula has a low-lying, west-facing coastline with squeaky clean beaches and a few reefs. Heavily exposed to the Atlantic breezes, it is often maxed-out or blown-out. Donegal Bay is the spiritual home of Irish surfing and an area blessed with several world-class waves that can fire at any time of the year. Counties **Sligo**, **Leitrim** and the spectacularly scenic, deeply indented coastline of **Donegal** hides many reefs, points and beaches, sprinkled around the countless headlands, bays and peninsulas. Bloody Foreland, Magheroaty, Dunfanaghy, Dooey and Loughros Beg are some of the spots that are readily surfable, year-round. The **Causeway Coast**, in Northern Ireland, is probably the most surfed area and the scene is centred on Portrush. It's only 26 miles from Ballycastle to Magilligan Head, home to north-facing, fast, French-style beachbreaks, plus the odd reef, that are offshore in the prevailing SW wind. Swells need to be from the NW or N although a massive W will wrap in, but this coast can pick up swell from the far flung lows spinning way up north in summer.

**Scotland** has an endless variety of waves and lies in one of the most consistent areas in Europe for surf. Boasting a 270-degree swell window, the west coast is peppered with islands, the north coast with beaches and there are slab reefs to the east. Being on the same latitude as Alaska means the winter months see a mere six hours of daylight, so getting the right tide at your favourite spot can be impossible. Conversely in the summer it's light for 20 hours or more a day, so a post-pub surf is possible. The **East Coast** is the least consistent area and only gets the dregs of big N/NE swells, but rare SE swells can bring a range of slumbering beaches and reefs to life. Dominant winds are cross-offshore from the SW. Edinburgh's Firth of Forth holds NE-facing beachbreak at Pease Bay or by the famous golf courses of St Andrews. Aberdeen's city beaches face more SE, keeping a large population of students and oil workers entertained, but it's not far to the **Moray Firth** coast and north-facing Fraserburgh, home to a brace of classy reefs. The Caithness zone introduces some great geology that is responsible for one of the finest waves in Europe at Thurso East. The wildly scenic North coast continues into the Highlands, swapping the flat slab reefbreaks and low-lying topography for the honey coloured rocks and sandy beaches of **Sutherland**. Empty and consistent, there are beautiful, peat-stained rivermouth sandbars at Melvich or Torrisdale and a pocket beach for most wind directions. Sandwood Bay on the west coast is the UK's most remote mainland beach. The Orkney and Shetland Islands lie to the NE and like most of Scotland's myriad islands are lightly surfed. The islands can get atrocious weather in the winter and it's possible to surf nearly right through the night around midsummer, which is a good time to go as is autumn. There are a lot of cliffs, but where the coast flattens out good reefbreaks and points abound. Skail Bay, Skara Brae and Marwick on Orkney are just some of the spots that lie in wait. The swell window is huge, catching swells from the W right round to SE. On Mainland in **Shetland**, the south has some beach and reefbreak at Boddam, Quendale and Sumburgh boat ramp near the airport, which all need S in the swell. Try Sandwick on the east coast and Sandness out west, where a boat would open up a world of opportunities on offshore islands like Papa Stour. To the west of the mainland lies the fractured archipelago of the **Hebrides**. The area has so many islands, islets and coastline, so the potential for empty waves is high. The Outer Hebrides receive the brunt of the Atlantic's force and have a helpful 180° swell window, but block and filter out much swell for the Inner Hebrides and mainland W coast, where the dominant winds are onshore. Tiree, Islay and the mainland surf beach of Machrihanish are the spots to check plus there are some sheltered gems that come to life in big W/NW swells, in the heart of Scotland's single-malt producing region. The Irish Sea is not a great place for a surfer unless you are on the south coast of the **Isle of Man** in a big winter SW storm. A handful of reefs can ridden just off Port St Mary and there are waves in Castletown.

JACK JOHNS

Rileys, Ireland

JASON FEAST

North Sea, England

**Wales** receives SW groundswell on most of its coastline, plus the north coast is rideable at Llandudno in W-NW gales. This region now boasts Surf Snowdonia, a wave pool utilising the Wavegarden technology. Anglesey is the least consistent area for waves due to its ultra narrow swell window. Quality surf only occurs when strong winter SW swells make it up St Georges Channel and hit a number of rocky beaches like Rhosneigr. The Lleyn Peninsula is a popular and versatile surf destination and has better exposure to the SW swell; the long beach at Hells Mouth is the most surfed area with a range of beachbreak and reef options. **Mid Wales** is home to a host of slumbering classic set-ups. From Harlech to Borth long stretches of beginner-friendly, west-facing beaches work in small swells. Aberystwyth is Cardigan Bay's surf centre and home to a brace of classy but inconsistent reefs. Along the Ceredigion coast lies a long stretch of boulder pointbreaks and secluded bays that come to life when huge winter swells are closing-out the open breaks to the south. **Pembrokeshire**'s coastal national park is a beautiful, unspoilt playground with three peninsulas offering a wealth of breaks facing all points on the compass. The main W-facing beaches receive SW/W swell, are offshore with wind in the E quadrant and are a consistent bet. Whitesands and Freshwater West are the name spots, popular with all kinds of surfcraft and both remain refreshingly undeveloped. The heartland of Welsh surfing has always been the **Gower Peninsula**. The majority of Welsh surf history and personalities are all interwoven with this wave-packed area. East from Swansea lies the industrialised landscape of **Glamorgan** then further south the wave rich town of Porthcawl, where inland surfers flock to Rest Bay, hoping the shallow, super-tidal Severn Estuary hasn't flattened the surf on a dropping tide. This region's reliable ride is the Severn Bore which breaks for miles through the **Gloucestershire** countryside on spring tides.

**England** has exposure to groundswell on most of its coastline, except for the Irish Sea coast in the NW of the country. SW to NW Atlantic swells and N swells coming down the North Sea are what surfers live for, but there are also a range of different windswell options around the less-fancied south and east coasts. SW winds predominate and as with most of the British Isles, September to November is prime time. **Cornwall**'s mild climate and consistent waves make it the most popular surfer and tourist destination in the whole country. South **Devon** is less consistent than its north coast and both hold quality beachbreaks like Croyde and Bantham, plus some moody point and reefbreaks. Easterly windswells coming down the English Channel can also provide waves for the desperate around Torquay. Summer can be painfully flat all along **Southern England**'s coast as the swell window narrows and the shallow English Channel saps the life out of swells. There are rideable waves and surf communities from Lyme Bay all the way past Brighton that make the most of their short-lived access to clean SW swells and generally make do with windswell. Kimmeridge and Bournemouth offer the best waves. The **Channel Islands** have some high quality breaks and good exposure to straight W Atlantic swells. Huge tides make local knowledge key at the most surfed beaches of Vazon Bay on Guernsey and St Ouen's Bay on Jersey. The islands large surf population ensure crowds at every session, year-round. Southeast England is inconsistent and polluted. The **Kent** coastline has got some surf spots but it's very rare for straight N groundswell to make it all the way down the North Sea. Joss Bay and the surrounding breaks generally work on short-range N/NE windswells. **Norfolk** never gets big waves but the flint-laden beaches of Cromer have good shape and offer sucky brown peaks in S-W winds. The **Yorkshire** coast is one of the best areas for surf in England, with favourable geology for slabby reefbreaks and a regular offshore SW airflow. Scarborough is surf central with breaks for all abilities. **The North East** is home to two contrasting surf experiences, the urban, polluted waves around Tyneside and Middlesbrough and the pristine, uncrowded wilds of Northumbria.

AL MACKINNON

Caithness, Scotland

## SCANDINAVIA & NORTHERN EUROPE

**Norway** has a staggering 83,000km of coastline punctured by fjords and dotted with islands that border four major seas including the Barents, Norwegian, North Sea and the Skagerrak. Low pressure systems usually track from the SW to NE bringing first SW and W swells then hopefully the more lined-up NW swells that get many of the best breaks firing, particularly Lofoten inside the Arctic Circle. North of Lofoten the swell window decreases with the water temperature and cliffs line the north coast. The Barents Sea receives regular, short-lived swells from the N and NE with plenty of quality boulder reef and beach setups yet to be ridden all the way round to the Russian border. **Svalbard** allegedly has some decent spots that have been surfed by Norwegian locals, but only in the summer when the treacherous waters become navigable and the sea is not frozen. Polar bear territory. Further south, Molde and the Stad-landet peninsula are frequented by Oslo surfers, looking for powerful peaks over both rock and sand in NW swells. Stavanger, in a lowland district called **Jæren**, is not the most consistent surf area, but the long sandy beaches and granite or boulder reefs provide numerous spots. The point at Sele and the consistent summer beachies at Bore are now regularly crowded. Breaks like Saltstein near Oslo are very unreliable, needing S in the swell. **Sweden** is very inconsistent with probably only 75 small, windy but rideable days a year between both coasts. SW swells roll into the Skagerrak, but the maze of rocky islands keep this coast's secrets for the locals. Check Nord-Koster, Öckerö and also the island of Rörö just off Göteborg in strong SW-NW winds. The shallow Kattegat, relies on very short fetch windswell from the SW to NW. Strong onshores are a necessary evil and if the wind swings offshore, the swell will drop rapidly. The scene is concentrated around Asa but it's the wind and kite surfers who will get the most water time. Malmö surfers can choose the Kattegat or the Skåne area of the Baltic around Vik in E swells. The islands of Gotland and Öland host many

ANDERS INGLESTEN

Faroe Islands

beaches and reefs that catch windswell from all directions. Toro attracts big crowds from Stockholm in SE-SW. North into the Gulf of Bothnia both Sweden (Sikhjalma, Smitingen, Härnösand, Salusand, Skeleftehamn) and **Finland** (Mäntyluoto, Yyteri, Tulliniementie) benefit from the 600km north-south fetch, during summer and autumn only as ice forms during winter/spring. The islands off Helsinki may get some SW slop on occasion, but the other end of the Gulf of Finland should be bigger in Sestroretsk, St Petersburg, **Russia**. More Russian surf can be found on the Baltic in the small exclave of **Kaliningrad** between Poland and Lithuania. Decent, year-round waves can be found at Malinovka, Pionersk, Donskoe, Baltiysk and the beach of choice for the Russian Surf Federation national competition at Zelenogradsk, where surf schools and crowds are materialising. Most of **Estonia** is blocked from the bigger SW-W swells by islands, but up near Tallinn, west-facing Vaana and Pakri will have waves in W gales. By far the best bet is on Hiiumaa Island at Ristna where a number of beach aspects help surfers and kiters deal with the strong winds. Wait for the wind to back off at **Latvia**'s straight beaches like Uzava or head to the breakwall sandbars of Pavilosta or Liepaja. **Lithuania** is fairly similar with rivermouth jetties at Šventoji and Molas and a long, straight W fetch. **Poland** represents the bulk of the southern Baltic's coastline. With dominant W winds blowing cross-shore, kitesurfing is ideal, especially on the Hel Peninsula where some waves can form between the multitude of wooden jetties at Chalupy and Wladyslawowo in bigger W swells. SW to W winds are offshore, but currents can be killer. From Karwia to Rowy, swell and wind exposed sands can have their day, particularly around the Leba rivermouth jetties. Unstabilised Dabki pulls in all swell directions onto some decent sandbars and works in SW winds. On the Baltic Sea coast of **Germany**, only a few spots face west like Hiddensee and Wustrow, so strong onshore winds from the NE-E are needed to get places like Pelzerharken, Hohwachter Bucht or Damp working. The key to good waves for all North Sea nations is strong onshore winds to build the swell then a brief period of cross or offshore winds before the short-fetch lines disappear in a matter of hours. Mid to high tides help the swell get over the offshore shoals that filter and reduce the potential power of the swell. Germany's west-facing coast receives swell from a decent swell window that ranges from the SW round to due N. NNW groundswells produce the best surf for the East Frisian Islands, while SW-W windswells bring the most waves to Sylt, the epicentre of German surfing and a big summer beach scene. This gently-curving, sandy, barrier island hosts 35kms of mostly unstabilised beachbreak, plus some small jetties and sand-covered boulders to help wave shape around Westerland. Further south, there are more shifting sandbars at St Peter Ording, another big resort town on the mainland but better waves can usually be found on the islands of Norderney and Borkum. **Denmark** is battered by fierce westerly winds all year-round and these winds can throw up some headhigh waves in half a day. The Jutland coastline of small bays and long, rock groynes help clean up the surf nicely, but expect messy onshores and all swells to come and go quickly. The best area is the stretch of beachbreaks from the mussel-covered reef in Klitmøller to Agger, with the popular Nr. Vorupør situated in the middle. Good windswell can be ridden in breezes from S to NE and the coast is well exposed to occasional groundswells from the SW to NW. It's less consistent and there's less protection from the wind heading south towards Hvide Sande, but E winds will bring semi-hollow, clean conditions. The Kattegat is the closest place to surf from Copenhagen but the waves are pretty pathetic. It takes at least 6 hours of 15m/s W or NW winds to kick up some autumn waves to ride between Gilleleje and Aalsgaarde on Zealand's north coast, while Hundested and Liseleje need N/NE. It's often during spring when strong E winds blow for at least 8 hours and the Baltic Sea can be surfed around Stevns Klint and in front of the harbour wall at Rødvig. Other areas with potential include Møn to the south, but the best Danish Baltic waves are on the island of Bornholm. Parts of the Danish administered **Faroe Islands** have been explored but the sheer sea cliffs and inhospitable nature of the environment mean most sessions take place in the north at Tjørnuvík where a barreling left and wedgy right grace each end of the deep sheltered cove. The Netherlands have long been wary of the North Sea, hiding behind the large dykes, seawalls and jetties that protect the below sea level countryside. Picking up both NW-N swells and SW windswell, it's the many jetties and seawalls that offer some protection and form to the waves. **Belgium** generally receives less swell than the Netherlands and the lack of depth offshore robs the swell of some power. A strong NW swell should see consistent jettybreaks like Blankenberge and Oostende get up to shoulder or even headhigh, but conditions are rarely clean as the onshores are a necessary evil. Summer is usually flat so aim for early winter before water temps drop to a chilly 5ºC (41ºF) in February and snowy sand is always a possibility.

## CONTINENTAL EUROPE

**France** sits at the heart of the European surf scene, occupying a geographically central position, which attracts all the tribes from the corners of the continent. Every conceivable wave type is represented along an extensive, swell-drenched coastline, from the cool Brittany pointbreaks, through the peerless beachbreak barrels of Biscay to the behemoth waves that unload on Basque bombies. Atlantic swells pour into the Bay of Biscay from a SW to NW direction, often without the accompanying strong winds. Hot summers see morning offshores and afternoon sea breezes that slowly relent through the best surfing months of autumn. While winter produces more NW winds and a maxed-out picture on Biscay's beaches,

KRZYSZTOF JEDRZEJAK

Gdansk Poland

Yerbabuena, Andalucia

JUAN VIRUES

the flanking reefs of Brittany and Cote Basque rumble into life, offering either protection or swell focusing power, under a range of wind directions. The macro-tides are a big issue hitting 9m in The Channel and diminishing to about 4.6m on a spring tide down south. The Channel coastline requires the biggest W swells or locally produced NW windswell to create any worthwhile rides. It lacks both power and consistency, but it's the closest surf to Paris and the chalk cliff scenery is a stunningly unique backdrop at spots like Etretat. The most consistent area is the northern part of the Cotentin Peninsula, which faces due W, while the coast of **Normandy** works mostly in winter SW storms. **Brittany** boasts a wide swell window and a rugged coastline, but large tides, swirling currents and offshore islands have a negative effect on the waves. The high cliffs and indented estuaries of the North Brittany coast hide many a fickle reef where local knowledge is indispensable. This jagged coast gives way to larger bays, low-lying land and longer stretches of beach in the **Finistere** area. Consistency quickly drops as the coast swings to face south along the **Morbihan** and **Loire Atlantique** coast. Such a contorted coastline means if there is swell, there will be waves somewhere, whatever the wind is doing, but allow plenty of time for navigating the slow roads and fast tides. Hotspots include Les Kaolins and La Côte Sauvage for hard-breathing beachbreak barrels. The Côte de Lumière region receives the highest sunshine hours on the French Atlantic coast. It's an intriguing mix of Brittany's broken up coastline and Aquitaine's long straight sand dunes, with a good selection of underrated waves. **Vendee** highlights include La Sauzaie, Sauveterre and the beachies of Les Conches/Bud Bud. Some interesting rocks and flat slab reefs can be found, particularly on the **Charente Maritime** islands of Île de Ré and Île de Oléron. Spring to autumn for the beachbreaks until the winter swells and winds divert the focus to the island reefbreaks. Aquitaine begins at the wide River **Gironde** that divides the rocky coastline of northern France from the endless sands of Europe's longest beach to the south. These 230 sandy kilometres represent the best beachbreak barrels in Europe, making **Landes** the place to be. On the downside, currents and longshore drift can be brutal, sandbars are constantly shifting, paddling-out channels are scarce at size, tidal ranges are large and wind protection is almost non-existent. The **Côte Basque** shares many characteristics with the north-facing Spanish coast and is blessed with some decent submarine geology, as slabs of reef dot the coast. From the summer beachies in Anglet to the winter reefs around Guéthary, there is always something to ride and there is always someone to ride it, regardless of the season.

**Spain** has a huge variety of surf, including some of the biggest, longest and most perfect waves on the planet. The wave climate tends to have a fairly large seasonal variation, with conditions quite a bit smaller in summer than in winter. Sea breezes, almost always from the NE, are a major factor in summer, which means either surfing before about midday or picking a west-facing beach. In the winter, it's either northerlies bringing heavy rain, low temperatures and bad surfing conditions, or southerlies delivering dry, sunny weather, warm temperatures and a constant stream of large, clean W-NW swells. The Basque Country region of **País Vasco** contains all types of reefs along with some world-class, big-wave spots and a world-class rivermouth called Mundaka. The coastal geology of **Cantabria** is slightly less abrupt than that of the Basque coast, so it has a multitude of good beachbreaks, plus a smaller number of good reefs. Therefore, big winter swells are not appreciated here quite as much and the best spots are those that work on small to medium summer swells. Cantabria also has a number of areas where one can find smaller, cleaner waves in huge storms or strong W to NW winds. There are one or two big-wave spots like the excellent righthander of Santa Marina. Star-rated spots include Liencres, a series of excellent and consistent beachbreaks, El Brusco, a hollow beachbreak and Santa Marina, which can be ridden up to around 15ft. In **Asturias**, the rugged, mountainous coastline is not particularly conducive for surfing, but there are some excellent west-facing beachbreaks and the regional classic Rodiles. Although the coastal rock formations of **Galicia** are not particularly good for surfing reefs, there are literally hundreds of beaches facing every different direction and some of these can produce excellent waves. Galicia has a wide swell window and one of the highest wave climates in Europe, even in summer. The surf in **Andalucia** is mainly centred on the coastline of "La Janda" in the province of Cadiz. Extensive, white sandy beaches face west out into the Atlantic, but Portugal's Cabo St Vincent creates

Liencres, Cantabria

JASON FEAST

# SWELL FORECASTING

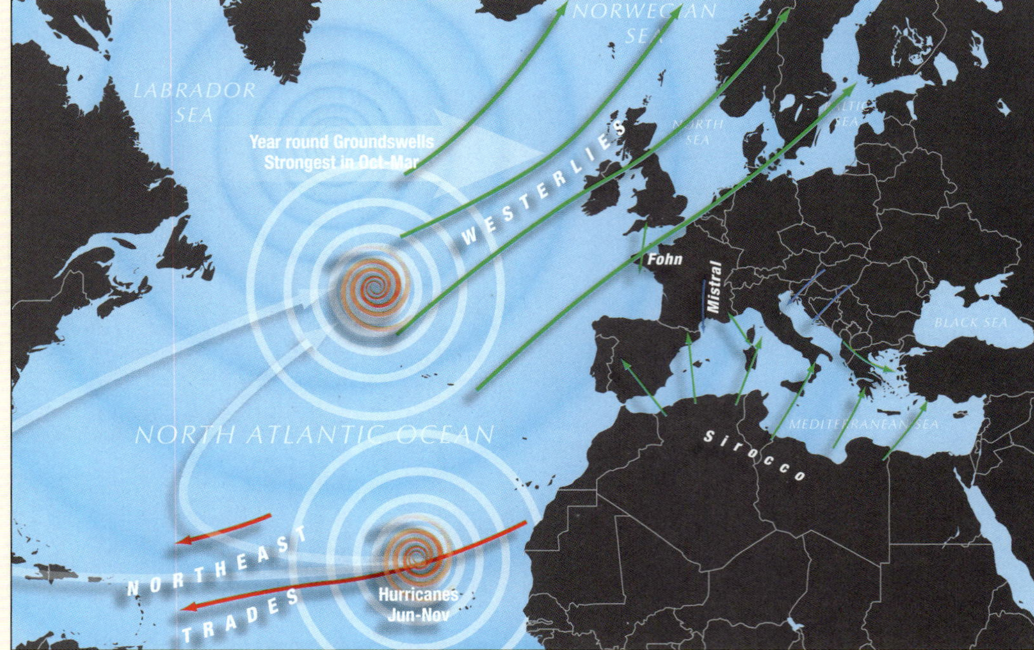


## THE ATLANTIC OCEAN

The surf in the eastern North Atlantic depends upon low pressure systems that form off the east coast of North America and track in a roughly easterly direction towards Europe. The westerly winds on the southern flanks of these lows generate swells that propagate towards Europe and North Africa. In winter, a fluid jet stream (winds at altitudes of 5-10km) produces a procession of deep, surface low pressure systems that can produce epic surf on many European coastlines. Clean, long period swells will march eastwards and southwards towards the Iberian Peninsula, Biscay and beyond to the Canaries and Morocco. Meanwhile in the British Isles and northern areas, out-of-control conditions on exposed coasts usually accompany the storm as it makes landfall. Winds can then swing to offshore for a brief period of good surf, depending on coastal orientation. A split jet stream occurs when a large high pressure (or blocking anticyclone) sits in the mid North Atlantic, hindering the formation of deep low pressures and reducing wave heights. In summer, the North Atlantic is noticeably less energetic than in winter, with small but consistent surf. Fully exposed areas such as western Ireland and Galicia probably offer the best options as the lows take a more northerly trajectory. In late summer and early autumn, surprisingly large swells can appear from ex-hurricanes that spin up just north of the Azores (a lot further south than normal). These rare swells can produce classic surf for the southwest-facing parts of the European coast.

## THE NORTH SEA

The North Sea has a narrow, long distance, groundswell window and instead relies on short fetch windswell for much of its wave action. These swells can appear from almost any direction, but are usually accompanied by the onshore winds that created them. When winter storms cross Britain, the SW winds continue into the North Sea to whip up swell for Denmark, Germany, The Netherlands and Belgium, while British North Sea surfers hope for the rare NE-SE winds to send a short swell. Summers are often flat, but autumn lows that track between Iceland and Scotland, first send westerly swells to Norway, then hopefully stall off the Scandinavian coast, pushing NW-N swells down to the North Sea Nations and the east coast of Britain. A blocking anticyclone will send more low pressure systems up north, so when the Atlantic is suffering from small swells, the North Sea is often pumping. The Baltic Sea nations hope these Atlantic lows continue their journey and blow long and hard enough for some short fetch windswell in the eastern Baltic.

## THE MEDITERANNEAN SEA

It is estimated that a minimum of 76 storms per year form in the Mediterranean Sea. 52 are spawned in the western Mediterranean, 14 arrive from northern Africa and only seven come from the northern Atlantic. These Mediterranean weather systems are notoriously difficult to forecast and even small depressions can produce strong local winds, generating decent swells from a variety of directions, mainly from the E-SE, SW-W and NW-NE. Depressions can form around the Balearics or in the Gulf of Lion and generally head towards Northern Italy or take a more southerly path to Sicily before weakening. Occasionally, a system will form over North Africa and kick into the sea off Tunisia. Far more reliable is the ever-present NW Mistral wind, which is the major wave producer in the western Mediterranean. Otherwise, windswells from all points of the compass bring waves to a diversity of shores from southern Spain to eastern Italy and beyond into the Ionian and Aegean. Wave heights rarely exceed 10ft and peak wave period typically ranges from 7 to 9 seconds.

## TIDES

The North Atlantic features the two largest tidal ranges in the world, and 15m ranges are experienced in the Bristol channel. Tides are absolutely crucial for many EU countries from Scotland to Portugal, while the micro-tidal ranges of the enclosed Baltic, Black and Mediterranean seas means anytime is a good time to surf.

RICARDO BRAVO

Figuera da Foz, Portugal

a swell shadow, so NW swells line up the best, but there is potential for Atlantic hurricane swells and S to W swells from more local systems. Andalucia is famous for windsurfing, thanks to the gusty, winter Levante from the east and the summer Poniente from the west. The coastline has some very useful bends and twists, giving rise to clean waves on most winds. The surfing epicentre really starts in El Palmar and extends all the way down to Tarifa, where both the winter swell and the wind are strongest. Highlights include the cluster of Canos de Meca, a long left reefbreak, Hierbabuena, a good right and Barbate's rivermouth lefts.

**Portugal** has always been steeped in seafaring traditions, yet the local surfing population has long been discovering new watery gold along the entire Portuguese coast. Its wealth lies in the variety, power and consistency of cool water waves that strike the gnarled, rocky reefs and explosive sandbanks over the narrow continental shelf. The main diet of W-NW swells pump in from autumn to spring, plus any summer windswells, making it a truly perennial destination. The northern provinces of **Minho and Douro** have a trove of super-consistent surf, grabbing the maximum from any swell direction. Rain, pollution and Porto's bleak industrial landscape combine to help deter visiting surfers. Late spring through to autumn will see lighter north winds that plague much of the country further south, and is also a good time for the featureless wind and swell exposed beachbreak of the Beira Littoral coast. The pin stripe candy town of Costa Nova and Figueria da Foz offer some protection, unlike Nazaré, the world's favourite new big wave spot for insane chargers, which has been added to the **Peniche** zone. Just down the coast, **Ericeira**, like Peniche, offers a truly staggering variety of waves, crammed into just a few kilometres of coast. The **Lisbon** surf zone has all the big city hassles of crowded waves, polluted waters, expensive living and traffic nightmares but it also has some classic waves, throughout the year. The Alentejo remains relatively undeveloped, and the northern half is an unexciting sandy strip of mediocre sandbars and shorepound on the Tróia Peninsula. A bit more swell hits around Praias Carvalhal, Pego and Lagoa do Melides. South of industrial Sines, the rocky coastline is a mix of pocket beaches like Porto Covo or long, consistent sands at Aivados or Malhão and though the NW swells may have lost some size, they tend to be orderly and break throughout the tide. Vila Nova de Milfontes is the main spot to check with a number of waves including the bowly left reef of Cogumelo, a few slab-style reefs and a long left that meanders up the rivermouth. The **Algarve** zone has become the busiest learn to surf destination in all

BRUCE SUTHERLAND

São Jorge, Azores

of Europe, thanks to the copious sunshine and flexible surfing inventory with the widest swell window in the country. The beautiful sandy beaches tucked up at the far eastern end of the Algarve do actually get a little windslop during the strong E/SE Levante winds of the summer, but wont win any quality awards.

## ATLANTIC ISLANDS

Rising from the abyssal plain to pierce the vastness of the North Atlantic, the nine major islands of the **Azores** are actually some of the tallest mountains on the planet. Spread over 600kms of ocean, some 1500kms from Lisbon, the Azores are perfectly situated to pick up swell from 360º. Low pressure systems often spin across the Atlantic somewhere to the north of the islands, deflected by the strongly established Azores High. This means winter swells usually arrive from the W-NW and slowly shift to N and then NE, before the next system moves through. Summer can see freak long-distance S swells all the way from the southern hemisphere or lined-up hurricane swell from the SW, along with localised windswells from just about any direction. Terceira simply means the third island, but some of its waves are first class. São Miguel is the biggest island and home to the most surfers. It's the only island in the chain with north-facing beachbreaks at Ribeira Grande and probably has the greatest variety of surf spots. **São Jorge** is long (56km), thin (8km at widest point) and extremely steep (1053m at the central peak). Short, rocky platforms called 'fajas' are the dominant coastal feature, formed by either lava flowing into the sea or piles of rocks that have fallen from the sheer cliffs. Of the 46 fajas, only three are ever surfed regularly by the locals. Faja dos Cubres has been touted as Portugal's longest wave yet it must be in close competition for the leg-burner crown with the Faja da Caldeira do Santo Cristo when it links up from the tip of Feiticeiras to the tail of Lago do Linho. These fajas work in all size swells and break with power over the boulders. S-SW winds can accelerate over the mid island ridge and W-NW winds can follow the cliffs cross-shore and basically behave in an erratic way. Faja dos Vimes is the only regular south coast option when SW swells and N winds combine. The rest of the island chain is even more lightly surfed; **Santa Maria** is the furthest island east and has an exposed right reefbreak on the NW coast at Anjos plus some rocky beachbreak on the south coast at Praia. Visible from all the other islands in the central group, **Pico** is Portugal's highest mountain and hides a few north coast breaks for those willing to walk some of the tracks or lucky enough to have access to a boat. Lajes do Pico has a SW-facing reef that picks up all the W and S swell action. Just to the west lies **Faial** and the rocky east coast breaks at Praia do Almoxarife that take big N and some S windswells. Praia do Norte is the main attraction open to all swells but best on W-NW to wrap down the left point. **Graciosa** is the most northern and smallest island in the Central Grupo and has a few east coast breaks between Praia and the port of Barra near Santa Cruz da Graciosa. The northwest coast has a couple of reefs to search out. **Corvo** is a logistical nightmare in bad weather for planes and boats and the cliffs prevent rideable surf along most of the coast – only the southern tip at Vila do Corvo has any waves. **Flores** has far more potential and the place to start exploring is the west coast and the rocky peaks around Faja Grande and Fajazinha.

Far to the SE, Madeira is another Portuguese island group that picks up lots of swell on a steep, cliff-lined coast. The smaller island of Porto Santo has a long stretch of SE-facing beachbreak which should shape up nearer the pier.

More Africa than Europe, the **Canary Islands** are blessed with warm water, volcanic reefs and a winter swell pattern that has earned them constant comparisons with Hawaii. The islands enjoy perfect bathymetry and abruptly focus the deep ocean swells onto the shallow lava reefs. The winter swell pattern extends from the W around to the N and summer sees constant N to NE trade-wind swells and onshore conditions for the north and east coasts. The 2m tidal range is enough for high or dry conditions on many of the volcanic slab reefs while the beachbreaks usually break through the tide. It's the power and magnificence of the autumn, winter and spring swells that really have given Lanzarote its "Hawaii of Europe" renown. The predominant NE trade winds can be a problem and grow in intensity in summer, when only a few spots remain rideable. **Fuerteventura** presents an arid, almost lunar landscape and is home to far more sandy beaches than the other islands. Strong winds are part of the deal, making this island a world-renowned kite/windsurfing spot, but there are plenty of waves to be found in the calmer winter months with it's North Coast being the epicentre. **Gran Canaria** may have the best weather in the world and it is also blessed with good surf. The most popular surfing area is Las Canteras with a variety of beach and reefbreaks, from El Confital to El Lloret. Countless spots can be seen along the north shore but many of them are dangerous and have difficult access like the slab reefs around Galdar. This coast is a swell magnet and can pick up small summer swells at beaches like Los Enanos, El Roque and Vagabundos. The west coast is a wall of sea cliffs so surf spots are almost non-existent. Tauro, Arguineguin and Maspalomas are the best spots in the south, working on large W swells, but this area is nowhere near as consistent as the north. The east coast breaks receive swell all year round and offers many good quality spots, including La Izquierda del Muelle, which works in the dominant NE winds. **Tenerife** is the biggest and most populated island in the chain, towered over by the snow-capped Pico de Teide (3718m) and countless coastal high-rise tourist developments. The two main surf zones couldn't be further apart: Bajamar in the northeast is home to some solid reefs in N swells and S winds plus the reliable beachbreak at Almáciga, while way down on the southern tip lie the waves of the overdeveloped Playa de las Americas resort. This area is crowded both on land and in the water and localism is rife at the famous La Izquierda reef. The NW swell window is narrow but the NE wind is almost dead offshore so clean conditions are commonplace. There are more spots to search for on the south-facing coast especially in summer SE-SW windswells. The east coast is largely poor to average beachbreak, but it gets a lot better way up north at Igueste de San Andres. **La Palma**, **Gomera** and **Hierro** are far less touristy and harder to get to and consequentially, have remained off the Canaries surf radar. La Palma's volcanoes are

PATRICE TOUHAR

Igueste de San Andres, Tenerife

still active and plunging sea cliffs are one obstacle to surfing on the north and west coast. The black sand beaches in the Porto Naos area like Los Guirres are worth a look for both beach and reef peaks in W–N swells. The coastal plain on the east coast is jagged and twisting, leaving few options for quality waves. On the NE-facing coast Nogales beach has some peaks that are difficult to get to but break all-year-round. Gomera is even more cliffy, so quality surf spots are few and far between. There are pocket beaches around the island that might have the odd wave but the main spot to check is the various peaks at Hermigua. The story is the same for Hierro with some rocky beaches on the northwest and east coasts that rarely offer quality, but west of Restinga in the south is a righthand reef at Tacoron worth searching out when the trades are blowing.

GECKO

La Couronne, French Med

## MEDITERRANEAN SEA & BLACK SEA

It could be called a big lake, an enclosed sea or a mini-ocean but the fact remains that the Mediterranean Sea holds its fair share of quality surf. The multi-directional windswells may not be huge, and are often all too short, but they sure can be sweet on the back of autumn and winter weather systems. The **Spanish Med** coast and Balearic Islands do get some semi-consistent waves from three main sources. The most common are the regular northerly Tramuntana winds, which after a few days blowing, can generate decent windswells breaking on northeast-facing breaks. The less consistent, warmer southerlies can blow with some force and generate surprisingly solid swells quite quickly. Lastly are the more potent Levantada gales from the east that are usually accompanied by wind and rain. Winter is surf time and autumn and spring can also produce the odd swell. Summer is famously flat for the Med surfer. Along the Eastern Spain mainland coast, there are thousands of kilometres of beachbreaks of below average quality. Hidden amongst all this dross are a few stand-out spots, which local riders are tuned into like a radar beacon. The **Costa del Sol** is the most unlikely of Med surfing coasts, but does occasionally break on the rarer E and S winter swells at Los Alamos and Playa de Carchuna. Pockets of locals surf the Cartagena and Benidorm areas and probably mission to some reefs near the Cabos de Palos and de la Nao. Murcia et Valenciana on the **Costa Blanca** can pick up NE swells, but the Balearics block and cut the fetch a lot. Jucar rivermouth is the name spot closer to Valencia, but it's basically just more, soft beachbreak. It's then empty miles up to the **Costa Brava** and the busy breaks around the metropolis of Barcelona. The quality of surf and quantity of surfers is surprising as winter NE/E swell brings waves right into the city at Barcelonetta and to a bunch of other breaks in the vicinity like Masnou. The **Balearic Islands** are usually associated with package tourists and nightclubs but there is some decent wave action for the patient surfer. Formentera is a small, quiet, exclusive island with one main, south-facing spot at Platja Migjorn. Ibiza has a small surf population who regularly ride the junky beachbreaks like Aguas Blancas in N/NE swells, but keep a close eye on the spots that work in a S swell. Mallorca is the biggest in terms of just about everything including surf spots and surfers. Check Peguera, Cala Major and Cero in the south or Calas Agulla and Mesquida up north. Menorca is definitely the most swell-exposed island and Platja de Cavalleria is the centre of the rugged north coast surf scene. There is more winter power and size to be found than the other islands, but luck is needed to get it good in spring or autumn.

GECKO

Alicante, Spanish Med

The **France Med** coast relies on windswell, often built by the ever-present Mistral breezes, which funnel down the mountain ranges from the N, then turn NW towards Italy. Tramontane is a N variation of the same phenomenon, while it's called Ponente when it blows from a straighter W direction. Other sources of windswell include the Grecale (NE), Levant (E), Sirocco (SE), Ostro (S) and Libeccio (SW). As soon as the wind drops, so does the swell and an offshore will flatten it very quickly. The extremely inconsistent **Golfe du Lion** stretches from Perpignan to Marseille, where the wind is usually offshore and swells from lows passing between Spain and Corsica are rare. Marseille starts to benefit from the westerly airflow and has a few quality reefs that work in SE to W winds and swells (La Couronne, Cassis and Cap Saint-Louis) however onshore conditions are the norm. The Six-Fours peninsula offers a wider swell and wind window. The **Côte d'Azur** resorts of St Tropez, Cannes and Nice all have rare SE-SW swell spots. Winter only and even then, it can be flat for weeks. Far better are the rocky shores of **Corsica**, facing directly into the Mistral and offering some good set-ups like Algajola in the north and Route des Sanguinaires in the west, where a number of long right points reside.

With 7600km of coastline and over 320 known surf spots, **Italy** has enough waves to keep legions of surfers entertained. Although the surf is often weak and windy, fun pointbreaks and hollow reefs can come to life in a surprising range of weather conditions. The Mistral is the driving force for surf in Northern Italy as the W-NW winds have enough fetch to build decent size swells for Sardinia or the reefs of **Liguria**. Varazze and Levanto hold some of the biggest waves on the mainland, but consistency is not too high with about 120 rideable days a year and most of them are small and onshore. Spring is often the best time, but a little wave can appear at any time of the year. There are classy spots along the **Tuscany** coast that attract surfers from far afield. Forte Dei Marmi, Viareggio, Livorno and Lillatro are all swell and people magnets. Offshore, Elba island presents an opportunity to ride some hollow, empty reefs in rare SE to SW swells. Lazio is the busiest surf zone being so close to Rome and it has a few hotspots around the crowded reefs of Santa Marinella. **Campagnia** spots are clustered around Naples. The swell window opens up to include SE swells driven in by the warm Scirocco winds, but once again consistency is low (50 days/yr) and long summer flat spells of weeks are not uncommon. Autumn to Spring is the best bet. Italy's East Coast on the shallow Adriatic, is the least consistent surf area yet it remains quite densely surfed. The few decent spots around Ravenna and Ancona attract surfers by the hundreds during the rare SE swells and frequent NE storms. This area can rely on 60-100 surfable days/year but this count includes also the many gutless NE windswell days. There are slow and easy righthand points in **Marche** and **Abruzzo** that continue to break in strong onshore winds. **Puglia** and **Molise** offers more challenging reefs in NE to SE swells with fewer people in the water. The Adriatic can have waves in summer when the descent of cold air currents from the former Soviet block triggers a gusty E to NE wind producing poor quality surf for many east coast spots. Otherwise it's those tricky SE and E windswells that can appear from autumn to spring but remember water temps can drop to 7ºC from the summer bath-like comfort of 30ºC. Way down south, **Calabria** and **Sicily** are perfectly exposed to African weather fronts and offer (to the very few locals) some of the sweetest left points in the Mediterranean. They rely on the less frequent, harder to forecast SE wind, which only hits this corner of the Med on about 50 days of the year. The north coast of Sicily does pick up NW swells and the biggest scene is around Palermo at Il Moletto. Malta is the most southerly member state in the EU, so good weather isn't a problem, just getting enough NW or E variation swell is.

The Balkans don't do too well for waves because winds and swells are usually NE or SE. **Croatia** is particularly bad with few spots working in the S or NW windslop. The rocky Kažela Beach is the place to go in a S swell and check the Golden Cape in a NW. Montenegro needs a proper S swell to get any waves and

Ulcinj is the sandy beginners beach for boards and kites in the steady afternoon onshores. Beside Bar harbour can be rideable in strong W-NW windswell. **Albania** has the longest fetch for summer's weak NW windswells and experiences the strongest winds and wave heights in the Adriatic, but S to NW swell is rarer than NE or SE. Durrës has sloppy peaks around the many piers.

**Greece** is not usually associated with surfing unless there is a sail or kite attached, despite being surrounded by six different seas. The northwest Epirus coastline faces the Ionian Sea and along with Crete, receives some of the longer fetch, larger waves from any W direction. Corfu sits at the entrance of the Adriatic but looks for swells coming from the S quadrant to hit Agios Giorgios or Glyfada. Athens and Peloponnisos have a number of marginal breaks with Vouliagmeni receiving the most traffic when a S swell arrives or Lagkouvardos and Kalo Nero in a W. On **Crete**, waist to shoulder-high windchop is the norm with a few dozen spots spread around the island. Head for Preveli in the south, Falasarna in the west and Mirabello Bay on the north coast. The Aegean islands are famous among sailors, so occasionally winds are heavy enough to kick up a bit of swell. In the south, Tinos pulls in N swells from the Meltemi winds and can even have a few waves in summer at Livada and Kolimpithra. Tourists islands like Mykonos, Naxos and surprisingly Kos and Rhodes all get swell on their north-facing coasts, plus Rhodes gets any E and S swells too, where Prasonisi will be biggest. Winter is the best time and if there is summer windslop, there can be clashes with lifeguards when red flags go up in tiny surf conditions at tourist beaches that are usually flat.

The Black Sea is another unlikely location to look for surf, yet there is some good geology and beaches catching winter storm surf. Eastern **Turkey**, **Georgia** and up into **Russia** towards Sochi and Anapa should be recipients of the most swell and wind seas combined. However, it's actually the N-NE-E swells of the Southwest Black Sea in Turkey that create the biggest waves. **Bulgaria** benefits with some solid waves from autumn to spring, close to the Turkish border at Silistar, Ahtopol, Varvara and up to Harmani. Heading north means less surf but Tyulenovo and Shabla are very exposed and jetties can provide

GARY CONLEY

Alanya, Turkish Med

some wind protection. Quality and quantity drop sharply as you head into **Romania**, so Vama Veche in the south is the best bet. Most swell is heading away from these northern shores, so forget Odessa and western Ukraine unless you are a long way east towards the entrance to the Sea of Azov in a S swell. The Mediterranean coast of **Turkey** misses out on the NW swell streaming out of the Aegean wind corridor and relies on scraps of SW-WSW swell arriving at a coast that has regular offshore winds, hindering the surf further. From Lara Beach, Antalya, through Side and Alanya and on to Anamur will be the biggest but expect weak, sloppy waves. **Cyprus** cuts out a lot of swell from eastern Turkey, catching it on the west and south coasts. Akdeniz Beach is a swell and wind magnet, shallow, sucky reefbreaks dot the Akamas peninsula, Potima has a sectiony right pointbreak, Helios Bay holds consistent peaks and Akrotiri reefs on the south coast regularly fire on any W swell. There is even waves on the east coast at Pernera Beach and Fig Tree. **Syria** is far too dangerous to surf while the civil war rages. **Lebanon** has a lot of seawalls, jetties and harbours, yet most of the surf spots break on open beaches and reefs north of Beirut. Try Batroun for reef peaks, Tam Tam and Nahr Ibrahim for beachbreaks or the jetty breaks called Mustafa's in front of Jiyeh Marina Resort. The Mediterranean chapter ends with the crowded beaches of Israel, beside the Gaza Strip, where the straight beach coastline has corners at jetties and harbours.

FEDERICO VANNO

Italy

# Reykjanes Peninsula ICELAND

With 4970kms of coastline to explore, Iceland presents a rare opportunity to surf virgin territory, yet most Icelandic surfers only ride around the Reykjanes peninsula, close to Reykjavik in the southwest. The Reykjanes peninsula is covered in old lava flows, so most of the waves break over volcanic reef or basalt rocks, sharp substances that take their toll on booties. The growing local surf population learn to surf at Sandvik, the only beachbreak in the area, which can hold waves as heavy as the reefs and points when it gets overhead.

+ PLENTY OF SWELL
+ LAVA RIGHTHAND POINTS
+ EMPTY LINE-UPS
+ DISCOVERY POTENTIAL

- INCONSISTENT SUMMERS
- LACK OF WINTER DAYLIGHT
- ARCTIC COLD
- EXPENSIVE DESTINATION

LAURENT MASUREL

Thorli

Beneath the lighthouse on the tip of the Reykjanes peninsula **Gardur** needs a considerable swell to swing around the corner and get the better north-facing, soft-shouldered A-frames working in SW winds and higher tides. **The Rock** sports a jacking take-off into a short, critical square barrel that occasionally sucks dry as tide increases and the break shifts closer to the beach. Super gnarly wave for pro's only. **Sandvik** is the Reykjanes main beachbreak that picks up a lot of swell and wind and it can get really heavy currents. Often has nice tapering peaks, but the paddle out can be punishing. **Grindavík** is an exposed, swell-magnet reefbreak with racy right walls at all sizes and some lefts. Friendly at 3ft, frightening at 8ft! Heavy water at size with crunching barrels over very shallow low tide reef that gets covered at high. Steep take-offs and bumpy faces unless due N winds. Very high consistency, even in summer, but always a lot of water moving over barely submerged rocks and urchins. **Rolling Stones** entices fat rights and lefts over a triangular boulder reef provided SW swell is over 10sec period on a full tide and any E wind. **Ollie's Shipwreck** is a long left reefbreak with easier shorter rights off the point in front of the lighthouse. Needs a bit of size, tide and some W in the swell for it to start working. **Thorli** is the most surfed place in Iceland, thanks to its deep paddling channel (no duckdiving!) and ability to handle all swells above chest high. Crumbly cutback corners when small turn into really long, workable walls at size. Rarely perfect, never closes out and a few inside sections wall up again and again. The long crescent of black sand at **Thorli Beach** has consistent peaks appearing on any swell with S in it. Can get big, hollow and heavy with swirling currents and lots of duck-diving.

Low pressure systems spawned in Baffin Bay, wind up south of Greenland, before sending W, SW, S and finally SE groundswells slamming into the Reykjanes peninsula, as they make their way along the transatlantic swell highway. These swells can be giant and very powerful, building suddenly and they are often accompanied by raw winds and stormy conditions. Winter is the most consistent swell season but it's difficult getting the right conditions to conspire in the very short span of daylight. Strong winds, chilling temperatures, snow storms and large tidal fluctuations are just some of the variables. September to November can be good months, with manageable air and water temperatures, and frequent low pressures. May-August sees plenty of summer flat spells in the southwest and could be a good time to explore the east and the north coasts for arctic windswells. Tides exceed 5m and few spots that can handle all tide heights.

GEORG HILMARSSON

The Rock

## TRAVEL INFORMATION

**Weather** – The warm Gulf Stream oceanic current brings very changeable weather throughout the year. The north of Iceland lies inside the Arctic Circle (66°) and freezing cold air occasionally affects the island in winter and spring. Summers are often cool and cloudy with short spells of sunny, pleasant weather. Much of the precipitation is actually snow during the wettest autumn and winter months. Winter water temps are surprisingly mild considering the latitude, bottoming out around 3-4°C (37-39°F) requiring seriously thick 6mm rubber and 7mm boots and gloves. Late summer water can hit 12°C (54°F) so a 4/3 and no gloves is doable, but remember the gusty windchill factor.

**Lodging and Food** – Accommodation is expensive - Northern Light Inn in Grindavik is $270/dble, Heimagisting Borg is $100/dble. Book a surf/snow/sup tour with Arctic Surfers. 68 campgrounds are open from June to mid-September and many campervan rentals are available (get a 4x4). Expect to pay $25 for a simple meal. Prices for beer at the pub have come down recently to $8-10. Arctic Surfers are a Surf/SUP/Snow tour operator with gear rental.

**Nature and Culture** – Natural hot springs and snowboard fields are flat day options for those with extra cash. Midnight sun and northern lights are part of the experience. Travel the 1339km long ring road around Iceland and gaze at glaciers, hot springs, geysers, active volcanoes and vast lava deserts.

**Hazards and Hassles** – Sharp volcanic rocks are unforgiving. Inclement weather can move in swiftly and bring thick fogs and sea mists. Lack of daylight and big tides can prevent sessions in winter and rip currents can be extra strong. Anywhere off the beaten track is a long way from help so solo missions are a bad idea. Take extra precautions.

**Handy Hints** – Equipment is hard to come by as there are no real surf shops selling hardware and if there were, prices would be very expensive. Take a gun and thicker board to float all the rubber. Two wetsuits can help!

| STATISTICS | | J F | M A | M J | J A | S O | N D |
|---|---|---|---|---|---|---|---|
| SWELL | Direction | | | | | | |
| | Size (ft) | 8 | 6-7 | 5 | 4 | 6 | 7 |
| WIND | Direction | | | | | | |
| | Force | F5-F6 | F5 | F4 | F3-F4 | F4-F5 | F5 |
| WATER | Wetsuit | | | | | | |
| | Temp/°C | 7 | 7 | 8 | 11 | 9 | 8 |
| WEATHER | Rainfall/mm | 76 | 59 | 42 | 53 | 80 | 78 |
| | days/mth | 18 | 18 | 15 | 15 | 20 | 19 |
| | Min temp/°C | -2 | 0 | 5 | 8 | 4 | -1 |
| | Max temp/°C | 3 | 5 | 11 | 14 | 11 | 3 |

# County Clare IRELAND

Despite the cold water, Ireland is often referred to as a surfer's paradise, thanks to its perfect positioning in the middle of the tracks of the Atlantic swell train. Every possible swell direction will hit the Emerald Isle somewhere and the twisted littoral outline offers protection from malevolent winds and waves. County Clare is exposed to any ripple from the west, focusing both ankle-snappers and tow-in giants onto a bunch of reefs, points and beaches, centred around the bustling seaside resort of Lahinch.

+ VERY CONSISTENT SWELLS
+ CHALLENGING WAVES
+ GOOD SUMMER SPOT
+ AWESOME LANDSCAPES

– OFTEN ONSHORE
– WINTER STORMS
– COLD WATER
– SUMMER CROWDS

The heavy, barrelling, righthand reef of **Crab Island** comes complete with vertical, jacking take-offs and thick-lipped slab sections to negotiate. It's a deceptively long paddle and judging the size from a distance is hard. Only for experts, who may have to swim back, against the current, with half a board. At its best, **Doolin Point** is a long, fast wall with barrelling sections, but unless the wind is perfectly offshore it'll be more peaky and sectiony. Difficult access in and out of the water and the uncompromising reef helps keep crowds low. At the base of the massive Cliffs of Moher is the scarily massive tow-in triangle, Aileens, for voyeurs only. Lahinch is a great little surf town with something for riders of all abilities. **Lahinch Beach** has good shape and is always busy; locals surf in front of the surf shop, beginners go for the gentler peaks to the north. Care is needed around high tide as the beach is covered. **Lahinch Left** is an extremely long, fun, left reef at the south end of the beach, popular with locals and intermediate surfers. Surfable on all tides when big, but better towards low when small. Further south, **Cornish Left** is a similar set-up but is a faster, hollower and shallower wave. Named after the brown river water flowing into the line-up, **Shit Creek** is a heavy, shallow left reef at low tide but mellows out and adds some rights at higher tides. **Cregg/Moy Beach** is a sheltered option when the swell is big. Fun little waves at this rocky cove. There are more waves further round the bay. **Green Point** is a rarely surfed, Mavericks-style peak that breaks close to the rocks, for experts and tow-freaks only. **Spanish Point** consists of Outside Point, a heavy, hazardous reef that hoovers up any size swell going, but the thick barrels are rarely surfed at any size. Middle Point has a long, fast wall and mid-tide tube sections. Inside Point only works when larger swells are running, creating short, funpark waves with a bit of wind protection. **Doughmore**'s rippy beachbreak peaks have full exposure to W swells, and a consistent right bank at the south end. Access hassles across private farmland and Trump's golf course, where permits to build 2 sea walls have been approved by local council. Sweet, hollow, lefthand reef in a sublime setting under the shadow of ruined **Doonbeg Castle**. Needs a macking, closing-out the rest of the coast, NW swell to get into the bay. Protected beachbreak peaks at **Killard** are offshore in prevailing SW winds, but need similar conditions to Doonbeg for anything to break.

## TRAVEL INFORMATION

**Weather** – County Clare has a mild but changeable climate all-year-round and is not noted for any extreme weather conditions. Winter temps occasionally drop below freezing but snow rarely lingers and annual average rainfall is equally distributed throughout the year. Clare is prone to the full force of Atlantic storms, bringing destructive winds and high rainfall. Use a 5/4 or 4/3mm fullsuit most of the year, discarding the boots/gloves/hood and dropping a millimetre from June to Sept.

**Lodging and Food** – Lahinch Hotel has double rooms and 8 bed dormitories from $22 per night, only 50m from beach with cooking facilities. Many B&B's, but price range is higher ($45-90). "Bord de Mer" is French run and faces Cregg Beach fr $68/dble. Camping is popular, free-camping still possible. Lots of great pubs, pay $15-20 for a meal or $7 for a meal in a glass – Guinness!

**Nature and Culture** – The Cliffs of Moher are amongst the tallest in Europe (203m). Burren is an ecological site with awesome lunar landscapes. Heaps of sacred sites (stone circles, dolmens, churches, castles). The county holds many traditional music festivals.

**Hazards and Hassles** – Huge waves over shallow reefs, brain-numbingly cold water, and long hold-downs are some of the dangers on offer. Aggressive localism is rare, especially if you act and surf respectfully. Best to surf with a friend in remote spots as coastal rescue is not too developed. Ask permission when break access is through private land.

**Handy Hints** – Lahinch surf school has boards for rent, lessons with ex Irish champ John McCarthy ($40/2h). Couple of surf shops in town (Lahinch, Green Room), but gear is expensive. Lahinch tends to become the Irish surfing capital during summer, when it gets very busy. Bring warm clothes for any season. Numerous campsites for campervans. Buses are cheap and take boards and useful for intercity travel.

GAVIN GALLAGHER

Crab Island

Lahinch gets battered by W swells in winter. Proximity to the storms can mean swells are disorganised and accompanied by strong onshore winds, August to October should maximise the likelihood of both good swell and the wind swinging to the elusive E direction. Prevailing winds blow from the SW almost year-round, but hopefully the contorted coastline can offer some shelter. The tidal range is crucial and can reach 4m, so most spots will be stable for 2hrs at low tide and high tide.

| STATISTICS | | J F | M A | M J | J A | S O | N D |
|---|---|---|---|---|---|---|---|
| SWELL | Direction | | | | | | |
| | Size (ft) | 6 | 5-6 | 3-4 | 2-3 | 4-5 | 5-6 |
| WIND | Direction | | | | | | |
| | Force | F5 | F4-F5 | F4 | F4 | F4-F5 | F5 |
| WATER | Wetsuit | | | | | | |
| | Temp/°C | 8 | 9 | 12 | 16 | 13 | 10 |
| WEATHER | Rainfall/mm | 85 | 63 | 61 | 70 | 87 | 97 |
| | days/mth | 17 | 13 | 12 | 16 | 17 | 18 |
| | Min temp/°C | 3 | 4 | 8 | 12 | 8 | 4 |
| | Max temp/°C | 8 | 12 | 17 | 19 | 16 | 10 |

GAVIN GALLAGHER

Lahinch Points

# Donegal Bay IRELAND

NW Ireland (Eire) is one of the most consistent surf destinations in Europe and Donegal Bay has become the epicentre of Irish surfing, since it is an area blessed with several world-class waves. The prevalent airflow from the SW and a mainly north-facing aspect, open to most Atlantic swells, means the low-lying coastline that passes through Counties Donegal, Leitrim, Sligo and Mayo is a true surfer's paradise. Perfect surf geology shapes triangulated reefs, rivermouth sandbars and assorted beachbreaks, evenly distributed around the bay. Bundoran is a regular international competition venue for both small and big waves. Further west, Easkey's consistent limestone reefbreaks are as popular as ever with travelling surfers.

+ UNCROWDED REEFBREAKS
+ POWERFUL SWELLS
+ PREDOMINANT OFFSHORES
+ COOL PEOPLE

- RAINY CLIMATE, COLD WATER
- WINDY CONDITIONS
- BIG TIDAL RANGES
- FAIRLY PRICEY

## TRAVEL INFORMATION

**Weather** – Ireland is known as the Emerald Isle for good reason – the land is very green, thanks to the amount of rain it receives. If the rain begins to get you down, then bear in mind the local saying "It doesn't rain in the pub". Despite the British Isles northerly latitude, it is not that cold because of the Gulf Stream's warming effects. It rarely snows in the winter and freezing temperatures occur only at night. However, winter is a hardcore time to surf in Ireland requiring a thick 5-4mm wetsuit, boots, hat and gloves. Summertime sees warm, sunny periods between showers and long daylight hours. A 3/2 steamer is ideal in summer and early autumn. Historical min/max of 8.1/16.1ºC (47/60ºF) measured in Bundoran for Mar/Aug.

**Lodging and Food** – Ireland is not a budget destination. B&B's will cost at least $50/dble. AirBnB can be better value. Bundoran Surf Co and TurfnSurf have lodges. There are campsites everywhere, but Ireland's wet climate can make this a miserable experience. Filling meals can be had for $20.

**Nature and Culture** – Western Ireland is a stunning patchwork of lonely valleys, lakes and low mountains, scattered with cottages and old castles. Irish culture centres around the pub, where drinking Guinness and listening to traditional music can be shared by all. Check out the Surfer's Bar in Rossnowlagh, Maddens Bridge Bar in Bundoran and the McGowan's in Easkey to name just a few.

**Hazards and Hassles** – You won't be leaving Ireland with a suntan, and if you don't like wind and rain, don't go. Many of the reefbreaks are treacherous. No lifeguards at most surf spots. Tidal ranges are large. Ireland is a very welcoming land, & hassles in the water are rare if you stick to the main spots. Travel in small groups, respect the locals by waiting your turn and smile.

**Handy Hints** – There are well-stocked surf shops/schools in Bundoran (Surfworld, Bundoran Surf Co), Rossnowlagh (Fin McCool) and Strandhill schools (iSurfIreland, Strandhill) or 7th Wave in Enniscrone.

AL MACKINNON

Pampa

LARS JACOBSEN

**Muckros** is the spot to go when NW'ers are destroying the rest of Donegal Bay. Beachbreak peaks in small bay are best at low incoming on a swell with W in it. Deepest into Donegal Bay, **Rossnowlagh** is always smaller and less powerful than surrounding breaks, with friendly rolling close-out walls and lines of whitewash perfect for the fleets of beginners that frequent the 3km strand. Occasionally has some nice peelers and is often the only option in big, onshore swells. The south end rip can hold up some lefts and rights and it's always better from mid to high. As famous for its place in Irish surf history as it is for its waves. Check out the memorabilia clad walls of the Surfers Bar or grab a Guinness at the Smugglers and meet some Irish legends. Lessons and hire available. **Tullan Strand** is a swell-magnet, ultra-consistent beachbreak, with a good low-tide wedge off the cliff at the southern end forming nice peaks for the local crowds. Big winter swells can scour out the sandbars and closeouts are prevalent up the beach so high tide is better. Rip along the bottom of the cliff is a handy conveyor belt out back. Lots of learners in the shorebreak. To the east of **The Peak** in Bundoran Bay is **3D's**, a spring

Tullahan Left

DAN HAYLOCK

high tide only reef. Spitting left and right barrels over a barely submerged slab for bodyboarders and tube freaks only. Heading west out of town, **Pampa** is the exposed headland at the end of Bundoran's bay. This is a serious wave for expert barrel riders as it sucks up heavily on the vert take-off and rifles off cylindrically over an unfriendly, incongruous reef. Easy enough to launch off the rocks but getting back in is tricky at size, which it handles with aplomb. The best locals have it dialled and don't take kindly to blow-ins who get out of their depth. **Black Spot** is the last break in Co Donegal on the next protruding point after Pampa. Pulls in the swell to an exposed peak that barrels hard on the quick low tide lefts, before pushing tide brings more manageable, longer rights, but still quite hollow. **Tullaghan Right** is a fairly fickle, high tide only, right reef/point. Can be dangerously shallow over the uneven, bouldery reef, especially when it's small. Safer depth when bigger but then the wave can be powerful and punishing. Quality **Tullaghan Left** rolls down the boulder point in big swells from the W-NW and is perfectly happy if the SW'ers are blowing. Even more sheltered is **Mullaghmore Strand**, the place to go on stormy big swells for variable size and quality beachbreaks. Perfect for longboarders and beginners in the lee of the headland and more push at the E end. Ireland's premier big-wave spot is **Mullaghmore** Head, where a savage, shallow, lefthand reefbreak produces massive tubes for those fearless or crazy enough to try and ride this most challenging of big waves. Handles any size swell, but needs to be well overhead to break clear of the exposed rocks and it's only surfable on higher tides. Handles a bit of SW wind so makes the most of big winter storms, but a bumpy face spells disaster. Has been paddled at size, but is usually a tow-in spot and jet-ski support is crucial for safety with the proximity of the rocks. **Streedagh Strand** is a banker for average beachbreak peaks when the SW'ers blow-out Bundoran. Doesn't handle too much size but will be bigger and more powerful at the E end on pushing tides. Other good waves in the area. **Strandhill**'s popular, reliable beachbreak sees a variety of options from hollow split peaks in the middle of the beach to Bluerock - a long righthand boulder point at the north end and more waves towards the southern end rivermouth. Uncrowded **Dunmoran Beach** is a good option for beginners/intermediates when the swell is up. Sheltered from big swells and SW winds. Consistent but rarely epic, **Easkey Right** can throw out some serious tubes but normally it's a long, whackable wall. W swell and low tide is best, attracting a decent crowd year-round. There are plenty of alternatives in the immediate vicinity. **Easkey Left** is even more popular since it works on all tides and any swell. Handles plenty of size, which ramps up the currents and SW winds are no problem. Nice drop to cover-up or coping and bends back over the shelf with a shreddable shoulder. **Pollacheeny Harbour** entertains a rarely seen righthand tube, breaking over boulders, with two sections breaking on either side of the harbour entrance channel. Long, fast, powerful and incredibly fickle. North of the pier at **Enniscrone**, a fast, hollow righthand pointbreak breaks over a sand-covered reef. High quality wave but needs a solid N swell to fire, as the swell window is limited and it is often blown out. Inishcrone has seaweed baths, a surf school and a beginner-friendly beach popular with kiters. **Kilcummin Harbour** deflects a powerful lefthander that breaks hollow and heavy at size and gets better the bigger it is. Can handle a W wind, but best on SW. Popular when other spots are maxing, so gets crowded. Respect the locals, the currents, the wave and avoid the unforgiving rocks on inside. **Lackan Bay** catches empty peaks along a scenic beach, with good shelter from W winds. **Bunatrahir Bay** provides deep shelter for a left reef north of the harbour on the west side of the bay. Needs the unlikely combo of a N swell with S winds to get going so low consistency spot that's rarely crowded.

Donegal Bay is so flexible it can fire at any time of the year, while September to November remains prime time. There are two standard weather scenarios, the most likely being that a low pressure system will travel E-NE across the Atlantic and hit Ireland, giving anything from 6-20ft predominantly W swells, producing sizeable surf on the north-facing beaches. Winds will start off as offshore from the S-SW before clocking around to the W, then NW and N, blowing out the bay. If a high pressure system establishes itself over the north Atlantic, (known as a blocking anticyclone), the storms are forced into higher latitudes, passing over Iceland towards Norway, yet the north-facing spots in Donegal Bay can still pick up the resultant NW-N swells. Dominant winds are SW-W year-round and are often in the F5 (30km/h+) strength band, although summer's frequently shifting breezes will be lighter. The tidal range can reach 4.8m and most spots will be stable for two hours at low tide and high tide. Never underestimate the tide factor.

**The Peak**

**LAT. 54.481310° LONG. -8.286972°**

Famous, flawless A-frame known as "The" Peak, since it offers a choice of a longer, high-performance, racy left wall or a shorter, slower, rip-bowl right. The cadence on the left is sweet with the odd pitching section until it gets beyond double-overhead and the sections come too thick and fast, making the deep channel paddle-out on the right far more attractive. Lower incoming tides are the go and any E wind round to S for the lefts, but it can be fun with onshore crumble offering hits and ramps. Always very crowded, unless it's big, so know your ability and surf with respect, among the locals who all know each other. Beginners and intermediates can surf the sandy bit of Main Beach and rippers can pull in at Inside Left over the low tide slab. Look out for rocks, urchins, rips and poor water quality after rains (always!).

| STATISTICS | | J F | M A | M J | J A | S O | N D |
|---|---|---|---|---|---|---|---|
| SWELL | Direction | | | | | | |
| | Size (ft) | 6 | 5-6 | 3-4 | 2-3 | 4-5 | 5-6 |
| WIND | Direction | | | | | | |
| | Force | F5 | F4-F5 | F4 | F4 | F4-F5 | F5 |
| WATER | Wetsuit | | | | | | |
| | Temp/°C | 8 | 9 | 12 | 16 | 13 | 10 |
| WEATHER | Rainfall/mm | 82 | 57 | 62 | 87 | 100 | 100 |
| | days/mth | 17 | 13 | 13 | 16 | 17 | 18 |
| | Min temp/°C | 3 | 4 | 8 | 12 | 9 | 5 |
| | Max temp/°C | 8 | 10 | 14 | 17 | 14 | 9 |

AL MACKINNON

Easkey Right

# Caithness SCOTLAND

All three of Scotland's coasts receive excellent waves, tempting more and more surfers to brave the cold and seek out Scotland's thick, heavy barrels, in uncrowded line-ups. The wildly scenic north coast has gained a reputation for flat slab reefbreaks in the county of Caithness that rival any in Europe and is home to the picture perfect rights of Thurso East. Good waves continue down the east coast, where short-lived swell from both North Atlantic and North Sea storms are groomed by a predominantly offshore wind.

+ QUALITY REEFS
+ THURSO EAST
+ HIGH LATITUDE SURFING
+ FANTASTIC SCENERY

- COLD WATER
- WET AND UNSTABLE WEATHER
- WINDY CONDITIONS
- HARD ACCESS

Ackergill

AL MACKINNON

Brimms Ness Bowl

JASON FEAST

Two incredibly inconsistent, short, sharp and heavy reefs that need low tide and some E in the swell to work, making **Ackergill** a very rare occurrence. Park near the jetty at Ackergillshore and paddle out through the harbour. The high quality beachbreak of **Sinclair's Bay** is visible from the A9, when a small to moderate NE swell is running. The rivermouth gives the banks good shape in middle of the beach and more shelter from SW wind can be found at the south end. The golf course means you will need to walk down or up from the few access points. **Keiss** is a long, left reef at the north end of Sinclair's Bay that also needs a big NE-E swell to break over fingers of reef. W wind is better than SW, which gets pretty strong around here. Low consistency and crowd factor. Sheltered **Freswick Bay** has low tide beachbreak peaks and a mid tide right off the rocks at south end of bay. Inconsistent as needs massive NE or SE swell to work. Park at the end of the northern access lane by the beach. **Skirza** is the most northerly spot on the east coast, enticing any E swell onto a scruffy, strata of reef. Classic, long lefthanders tour the reef, breaking up into different sections on a NE or walling up nicely with a straighter SE swell. Park considerately in the village, paddle out through the harbour. **Gills Bay** heavy, hollow, sectioning left point only fires on big NW swells, since N is blocked by the Orkneys. Best at mid tide when the long sections may link up. Experts only. Rarely crowded because it rarely works well. Fast, shallow lefts run down the reef at **Brunt Skerries** in NW swells or wall up in W swells. Sometimes a right breaks as well. Lower tides usually best. In front of the Castle of Mey. Inside Tang Head, a dishevelled platform of reef bends lined-up lefthanders in towards **Harrow Harbour**. NW swells align perfectly with the rocks, which need some tidal cover. Handles more size on the outside and more SW wind on the inside. Rocky

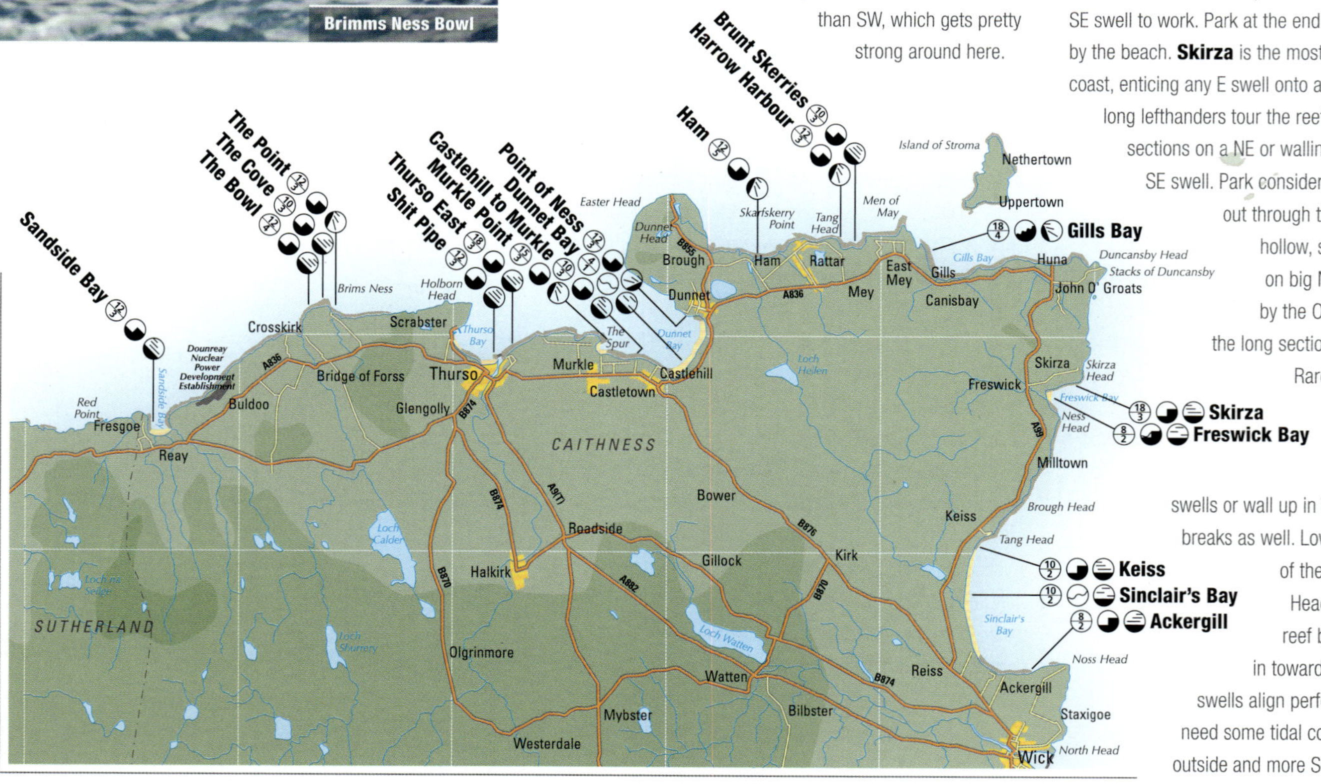

## TRAVEL INFORMATION

**Weather** – The weather is renowned for its extreme unpredictability, but it is not an arctic climate because the Gulf Stream warms things up a little. Snow is frequent in the winter with freezing temperatures occurring for four or five months of the year. The East Coast is drier with a more continental climate. The mountains get pretty foggy and are snowbound throughout the winter and spring. The coast is generally very windy and finding protection is a priority. Autumn is a good time to visit, with regular swells and reasonable water temperatures nearer the top of the 6-15ºC (43-59º) range. The coldest days may require a 6-5-4mm fullsuit, while hood, boots and gloves will be necessary until April/May.

**Lodging and Food** – Scotland is not a budget destination. B&Bs (Bed and Breakfasts) will cost at least $25-$100p/n or $80/dble for a hotel room. Rental caravans available from Easter to Oct or camping for the ultra-hardy. A filling, often deep-fried, meal shouldn't cost more than $15 – try authentic haggis, neeps and tatties. You will spend a lot of time and money at the pub.

**Nature and Culture** – Scotland is one of the least densely populated areas in Europe. Caithness is predominantly flat peat lands so head west into the Highlands to bag a Munro, meaning climb a peak over 3,000ft (914m). There are numerous castles (Sinclair, Old Keiss, Old Wick), stone rows and circles, burial cairns and a wide variety of rare wildlife.

**Hazards and Hassles** – If you can stand the rain, wind and ice-cream headaches, you'll have an unreal time. The reefbreaks are all heavy, spooky places to surf and only expert tube-jockeys should take on the semi-secret slabs like Baggies and The Dump. Strong rips and big tidal ranges greatly affect the surf. Thurso is a long way from anywhere - 2hrs drive to Inverness for city services. Be aware of the potential for radioactive particles around Sandside.

**Handy Hints** – Tempest Surf has a small range of essential equipment and a cafe. Take a more buoyant board to counteract the extra weight of all that neoprene. Near constant daylight in June-July is a magic experience - 6hrs in December is a real downer! Flat day fun is bowling or golf.

MARK MCINNIS

**Thurso East**

LAT. 58.602648° LONG. -3.509707°

Scotland's premier righthand reefbreak and a world-class barrel on its day. In NW swells at mid tide a relatively simple drop leads into one of the longest, hollowest rides in Europe. Even the biggest W swells won't get in without a touch of N; WNW swells are hollowest and the more N in the swell the mellower the wave as it tapers off to the shoulder. SW winds blow into the barrel and bump it up but it can still be fun in an onshore. Only moderate consistency and the smallish take-off zone quickly fills at the ideal mid tide. As crowds increase, locals are less tolerant of groups and those that don't wait their turn. Park responsibly in farmyard in front of the break, as there's not much room with the new barn. Alternatively, park by the harbour in town and paddle out in the peat-stained river that brings seriously cold water to the line-up in winter.

outcrops and currents. Scarfskerry Reefs face NW and are visible from the road. Check The Haven or the triangular Kirk O' Tang in smaller NW to N swells and any S wind. Empty and challenging, for experienced surfers only. Park considerately and don't block farmers' gates. **Ham** works in big NW swells and handles plenty of W wind, making it a stormy favourite. Powerful and shallow in places. Mid tides best. Gets big as the destroyed harbour can testify. Long, fun and bowly, **Point of Ness** hides in the lee of Dunnet Head. Easy paddle-outs and breaks through the tides up to high if big enough. Some shelter from N wind, but best on any E wind. Limited parking near the jetty. Below average beachbreak at **Dunnet Bay** is home to various beginner-friendly peaks in small swells. **Castlehill to Murkle** is a rarely surfed stretch of heavy reefs for the experienced and inquisitive. Formerly known as Nothing Left, this shallow, grunty left has been renamed Manson's after the death of long-time local Andrew Manson. Silos and The Pole are also thick, ledgy lefts found a little further west. Park at Castlehill, walk west and explore. Heavy, swell-exposed **Murkle Point** is a rarely surfed left breaking off a rocky outcrop known as The Spur. Good protection on the inside from SW to W gales. Watermen only. Access only from the lane south of the bay. The fun, split peak reef across the river from famous **Thurso East** is known as **Shit Pipe**, thanks to the peat coloured outflow. It's a little more offshore in SW winds that ruffle the longer right walls and the shorter, steeper left. W swell wont get in unless it is huge. Untaxing wave suitable for intermediates. Water quality is okay. Ample parking by harbour where the surf shop cafe is. **Brimms Ness Point** needs specific NW swell direction, low to mid tide and light S winds for the fickle, long, left point to work. Handles more size and is slightly more forgiving than the other 2 Brimms waves, but still requires a decent standard to make the drops. **Brimms Ness Cove** will be the shorter, peaky right between the Point and the Bowl. Can really lurch over the Caithness flagstone reef at low tide then relents to allow a few hacks before fizzling out in the channel. Mid tide safest and hopefully not too much W in the wind. The most western peak is **Brimms Ness Bowl**, a jacking, hollow, righthand tube for experts only. This corner of the reef is shallow and rocky, famous for rips and boils that can hold victims in the impact zone. The vikings named this point Brimms Ness, meaning Surf Point, so if it's flat here, then it's flat everywhere. Good place to watch if you don't have a late or air drop game and it hates extremes of tide and W winds. Highly consistent swell-wise, but the wind is often a problem on the exposed point, so when it is on, there is often a crowd. Parking either in the farmyard or out on the point depending on the state of the track and the goodwill of the landowner. Drive into and out of the area slowly as the residents are sick of speeding surfers. Quality left reef south of harbour in **Sandside Bay**. Dredging, thick, hollow first section and a long, whackable inside wall. Handles strong SW-W winds. Tens of thousands of radioactive particles from old reactors contaminated the shoreline and the seabed around the now defunct Dounreay Nuclear Reprocessing Plant. Experts regard the most radioactive of the grain-of-sand-sized particles are potentially lethal if ingested. Might explain why Sandside is rarely crowded!

JASON FEAST

Sandside

From September to April, North Atlantic low pressures frequently form around Greenland before traversing the Atlantic in an E-NE direction, producing major W-NW swells up to 20ft. The summer scenario often sees a high-pressure system covering the north Atlantic and the British Isles, pushing the lows into higher latitudes, therefore passing over Iceland and Norway and producing lined-up N swells. Many north-facing Caithness spots and the east coast will be offshore with the dominant, year-round SW-W winds, although summer sees much lighter, variable wind. Swells from the appreciably colder North Sea are usually N to NE but short fetch, short duration E to SE swell can be good for many spots. The tidal range can reach 5m; most spots will be stable for two hours at low and high tide, with the reefs generally being better at mid to high tide.

| STATISTICS | | J F | M A | M J | J A | S O | N D |
|---|---|---|---|---|---|---|---|
| SWELL | Direction | | | | | | |
| | Size (ft) | 7 | 6 | 4 | 3 | 5-6 | 6-7 |
| WIND | Direction | | | | | | |
| | Force | F5 | F4-F5 | F4 | F4 | F4 | F4-F5 |
| WATER | Wetsuit | | | | | | |
| | Temp/°C | 5 | 6 | 10 | 15 | 12 | 8 |
| WEATHER | Rainfall/mm | 48 | 40 | 50 | 80 | 60 | 57 |
| | days/mth | 11 | 10 | 11 | 11 | 12 | 12 |
| | Min temp/°C | 1 | 3 | 8 | 11 | 8 | 3 |
| | Max temp/°C | 6 | 9 | 15 | 18 | 14 | 8 |

# Outer Hebrides SCOTLAND

The Outer Hebrides, or Western Isles, sit a mere 28mi (45km) off the NW tip of Scotland and receive the brunt of the Atlantic's force through a helpful 180° swell window. The short continental shelf adds to the power of the waves and strong currents are the norm. A good range of beaches, points and reefs are surfed by the small, committed and knowledgable group of local surfers who get to surf until midnight on midsummer days.

+ POWERFUL AND CONSISTENT
+ BEACH AND POINTBREAKS
+ CLEAN WATER, NO CROWDS
+ LONG SUMMER DAYLIGHT

– HIGH LATITUDE WIND EXPOSURE
– COLD WATER
– LARGE TIDES
– CHANGEABLE, WET WEATHER

## TRAVEL INFORMATION

**Weather** – The Gulf Stream ocean current moderates the climate and despite the northerly latitude, winters are rarely cold on the coast and summers rarely warm. Despite being 800mi (1300km) north of London, the mean minimum temps are about the same. January is the windiest month, May is the driest and December the wettest. The famous Scottish "4 seasons in a day" weather is very changeable. In midsummer, there are barely 2 hours of darkness. August sea temps can top out at 14°C (58°F) and in March can dip below 7°C (45°F). Booties needed most of the time.

**Lodging and Food** – Fairhaven is Hebridean Surf's central Stornoway accommodation fr $30/p/n. Galson Farm Bunkhouse is $28/p/n or stay in the Guest House (fr $65/p/dbl). Cnip campsite is near Cliff or wild camp with permission away from homes. Outer Hebrides Campervan Hire in Stornoway. Expect to pay $25 for a good meal in a pub.

**Nature and Culture** – Watch whales, orcas and Risso dolphins, which are most sociable from Aug-Oct. Numerous lochs to fish salmon or trout. Great for diving, canoeing, sailing, mountain biking, climbing or coasteering. Don't miss the 5,000 yr old standing Stones of Calanais or The Broch at Carloway, a mere 2000 years old. Autumn Aurora Borealis can be seen.

**Hazards and Hassles** – Powerful waves, rips, winds, rocks and isolation can increase the fear factor. No dangerous animals. Stay warm and dry - bring appropriate clothing.

**Handy Hints** – Derek Macleod's Hebridean Surf shop at The Welcome In Filling Station in Lower Barvas sells and rents essential equipment with full surf school. Surf Lewis do lessons, board and SUP rental. Sunday is rest day, no transport. All place names and direction signs are in Gaelic.

AL MACKINNON

Barvas and Bus Stop

AL MACKINNON

Europie

East coast beachbreak **Tolsta** picks up any N swell and is directly offshore in the prevailing SW winds. Can be hollow and fast peeling, especially at low tides on this pristine stretch of sand. The **Port of Ness** is a protected pocket of sand facing the mainland that bends N swells onto sandbars and a scattering of rocks. Banks are always moving with the strong rips, although the southern end gets a right off the rocks. Quick check from **Europie** if wind is W. Consistent, fast, hollow beachbreaks at Europie shape up over transient bars and channels. In a N swell and SE wind the long right tubes are a sight to behold. Extremely rippy at size, which it can handle easily. The go to spot in most conditions, but beginners will struggle unless it is small. **Barvas** sports a very long, reeling, righthand boulder reef visible from the main road to the west coast. Can get big and heavy with any flavour N swell, E winds and higher tides. Across the bay, **Bus Stop** (also called Brue) attracts the goofies to a superb, ultra-long left point, breaking over boulders for up to 500m. There's an outside section that handles more swell, but less of the strong SW winds. Powerful and punishing. **Bragar** faces almost NE so has the ultimate aspect for taming the unruly SW-W gales. The pointbreak on the western flank of the bay is fast over the outside ledge then peels into the bay for a few hundred metres, working right through the tides if big enough. The beachbreak can also be fun and clean. **Dalbeg**'s protected cove promotes hollow, thumping waves over changeable sandbars and rocky fringes, sculpted by strong rips. Best in peaky, summer swells – out of control at double overhead. Popular **Dalmore** is a well-formed beachbreak that's fun when small, but serious and rippy at size. Walled-up peaks that speed over the changeable sandbars plus a grinding left in the corner at size. **Cliff** produces fast, hollow beachbreak, good tubes at low tide and long rides at other stages. Handles the most size of any UK beachbreak. Consistent and regularly surfed. Seriously heavy, rip torn and dangerous when big. Pack your gun and park on the grassy knoll above the beach. Small sandy beach at **Mangersta** is exposed to any W swell and wind. A couple of peaks best from low to mid tide providing the swell is no bigger than headhigh. On Harris, **Scarista**'s NW-facing crescent beach can handle some SW wind in the lee of the southern corner and can break with powerful lips and rips on bigger days. Head south to explore the islands of North Uist (Hosta), Benbeculla (Culla Bay), Barra and Vatersay for west-facing beachbreak.

The swell window extends from SSW around to NE swells arriving from the Norwegian Sea. When west-facing Lewis spots become out of control, the normally flat north or even east-facing spots start breaking and provide good shelter from the dominant and blustery SW-W winds. Spring into summer sees more E quadrant and slightly less W, but speeds remain F4 or higher. The "Hebs" are a year-round destination, but it can get real big and nasty in the winter. Large 5.5m tidal range affects the points and the beaches in smaller swells.

| STATISTICS | J F | M A | M J | J A | S O | N D |
|---|---|---|---|---|---|---|
| SWELL Direction | | | | | | |
| SWELL Size (ft) | 6-7 | 5-6 | 4-5 | 4 | 5-6 | 6-7 |
| WIND Direction | | | | | | |
| WIND Force | F5 | F4-F5 | F4 | F4 | F4-F5 | F5-F6 |
| WATER Wetsuit | | | | | | |
| WATER Temp/°C | 7 | 8 | 11 | 14 | 12 | 9 |
| WEATHER Rainfall/mm | 105 | 91 | 66 | 88 | 134 | 117 |
| WEATHER days/mth | 18 | 17 | 16 | 17 | 22 | 23 |
| WEATHER Min temp/°C | 1 | 2 | 7 | 10 | 7 | 2 |
| WEATHER Max temp/°C | 7 | 9 | 13 | 16 | 13 | 8 |

# Gower Peninsula WALES

Gower was the first area in the UK to be officially recognised an "area of outstanding natural beauty". This small peninsula projecting into the Bristol Channel has over 20 bays and sheltered coves along its rugged coastline. From long, expansive strands to tiny inlets, this stretch of coast provides a wide variety of breaks, combining multiple wind options with decent swell exposure.

+ DIVERSITY OF REEFS AND BEACHES
+ WIND FLEXIBILITY
+ MANY EASY WAVES
+ SCENIC AND CULTURALLY RICH AREA

- COLD WATER AND AIR
- TIGHT SWELL WINDOW
- MANY INCONSISTENT SPOTS
- WINDY AND CROWDED

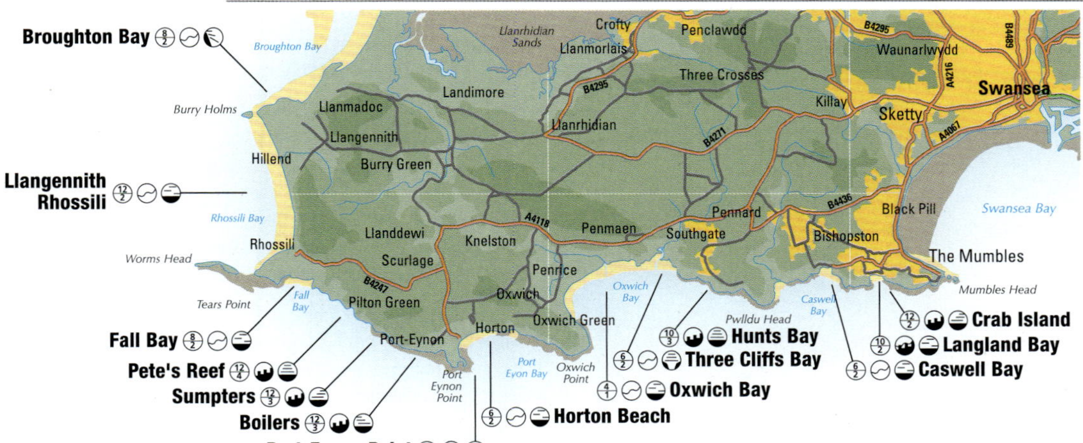


**Broughton Bay** features a long, gutless, longboard-friendly sand point. Needs a large SW swell to wrap in. Strong rip away from the line-up, so not suitable for beginners. **Llangennith**'s 3mi (5km) stretch of average yet consistent beachbreak, picks up all available swell and is popular with all abilities and types of wavecraft. Over head-height, the paddle-out is renowned for its difficulty. Three Peaks at the N end has more size and power, while Rhossili at the S end picks up less swell and has shelter from S quadrant winds. Remote cove at **Fall Bay** is home to a big swell, high tide wedge popular with bodyboarders. A hollow, low tide left reef separates it from Mewslade Bay, where the same conditions will bring scrappy, fast, dumpy, short beach peaks, but not many bother to make the long walk in. Swell magnet **Pete's Reef** peak works well on small summer swells. Very crowded and shallow reef, rocky entry and exit, strong rip on incoming tide and long walk in. **Sumpters** is a long walling right reef with some barrel sections. Deeper and an easier paddle-out so it's generally crowded with intermediates, despite the long walk in and lack of parking. Shallow left reefbreak at **Boilers** features a dredging take-off over barely-covered reef, running into a deeper gully. Rocky, rippy and sketchy leaving the water at high tide, so best at mid tide. Punchy **Port-Eynon Point** starts with a sucky take-off and first section before mellowing out into deeper water. In big wrapping swells Port Eynon beach can have small beginner-friendly waves. Good shorebreak when big swells wrap in to **Horton Beach**. Best at low, dumpy at high. Walk east to reach inconsistent Slade Bay, where right and left reefbreaks rely on solid swell and plenty of sand to fill in the gaps. Storm protected **Oxwich Bay** shapes hollow beachbreak, best at high. Needs massive winter swell to get going and is always crowded with mixed ability crew. Beautiful **Three Cliffs Bay** with sandbanks sculpted by a stream. Needs a big swell to get going. Very rippy and long walk in. **Hunts Bay** might have rights and lefts working in solid swell at mid to high tide. Rocks everywhere and it's easily blown-out in any W wind. Not a beginners spot. **Caswell Bay** doesn't handle much size before closing-out, is rarely clean, but is popular with tourists and surf schools. **Langland Bay** has something for everyone depending on the tide. At high tide there's The Shorey, until Rotherslade lefts and The Reef start working as the tide drops. At lower tides, Middle of the Bay, the Sandbar and Shit Pipe are all very busy all the time. The mythical, fast, hollow right reef at **Crab Island** only breaks well a few times a year. Tough current makes the drops harder and getting caught inside is punishing. Only the best will get waves off the devout local crew.

PHIL HOLDEN

Pete's Reef

## TRAVEL INFORMATION

**Weather** – The Gower has a real oceanic climate, allowing the peninsula to avoid experiencing the temperature extremes recorded in other parts of the UK, but freezing temperatures are still a regular occurrence in winter. The same moderation applies in summer and it rarely gets over 20°C (68°F), even in the warmest months of July and August. It rains every other day or more during the peak precipitation months between October and January, when water temperatures can dip below 8°C (46°F) or stay above 10°C (50°F) and never break 18°C (64°F) in July.

**Lodging and Food** – B&B's are the local flavour and there are many to choose from. Right behind the dunes of Llangennith, Hillend campsite is fine before it gets too cold. For maximum comfort try the Oxwich Bay Hotel ($100/n), the Worm's Head Hotel in Rhossili ($60/n) or the Carlton Hotel in Mumbles ($120/n). Try Welsh rarebit or laverbread, a seaweed dish.

**Nature and Culture** – There are medieval castles and churches, or megalithic burial tombs set among the beautiful natural landscape. Mumbles is widely reputed for partying, centred on the Mumbles Mile, an endless procession of pubs.

**Hazards and Hassles** – Water quality is improving despite neighbouring heavy industries. Breaks such as Llangennith suffer from strong rip-tide currents and flotillas of every type of surfcraft in summer.

**Handy Hints** – Good longboarding waves, check Guts Surfboards. Several surf shops including Gower Boardriders, Hotdog and legendary PJ's in Llangennith, who does hire and repairs. Many surf schools to choose from.

PHIL HOLDEN

Langland Bay

Ireland blocks all W to N swells and the Gower must rely on SW-W swells only. This means autumn and winter are most likely to produce groundswells from storms tracking on lower latitudes. Summers are usually quite lame, relying on the year-round onshore SW-W winds to kick up some low period windswell. These winds are consistently strong, only backing off and turning W during midsummer. The Gower handles NW winds, the bane of the West Cornwall coast. Late autumn, early winter is best. With 10.5m tides at Mumbles, tide tables are almost as important as thick rubber.

| STATISTICS | | J F | M A | M J | J A | S O | N D |
|---|---|---|---|---|---|---|---|
| SWELL | Direction | | | | | | |
| | Size (ft) | 6 | 5 | 3 | 1-2 | 4-5 | 5-6 |
| WIND | Direction | | | | | | |
| | Force | F5 | F4 | F3-F4 | F4 | F4-F5 | F5 |
| WATER | Wetsuit | | | | | | |
| | Temp/°C | 9 | 10 | 12 | 16 | 14 | 11 |
| WEATHER | Rainfall/mm | 100 | 70 | 75 | 100 | 115 | 135 |
| | days/mth | 16 | 13 | 13 | 15 | 16 | 18 |
| | Min temp/°C | 3 | 7 | 12 | 15 | 11 | 6 |
| | Max temp/°C | 6 | 9 | 15 | 18 | 14 | 11 |

# Cornwall ENGLAND

For travelling English speaking surfers, a European surfari will usually begin in England. No language barriers and the international transport links that London provides are the main reasons, but what many surfers fail to realise is England receives waves on all its lengthy coastline. The most consistent area is Cornwall, where year-round swells batter a mixture of small, rocky bays and long, sandy beaches on two very different coastlines.

- + VARIETY OF BEACH ASPECTS
- + BEAUTIFUL SCENERY
- + GOOD BEACH AND REEFBREAKS
- + YEAR-ROUND CONSISTENCY

- – COLD WATER
- – COOL AND WET CLIMATE
- – CROWDS
- – POLLUTION

JASON FEAST

Penhale, Perranporth

DAN AHYLOCK

Widemouth Bay

Bude's busy town beach **Crooklets** can entertain short, fast, sandbar rides plus at high tide Tower Rock has a short-lived, deceptive left on a swell. Rocks and backwash at high tide to contend with. Adjacent **Summerleaze** often holds the sand better and lines-up some bashable rights at Middle Beach. At mid to high tide on a solid swell, a right breaks off the sea-pool and meanders softly towards the rivermouth and harbour. Provides some wind and swell protection, so it's a surf school and beginners favourite, despite currents and crowds. Also check the speedy left wall to close-out off Barrel Rock at low tide. **Widemouth Bay**'s long stretch of average beachbreak and reef peaks includes Salthouse, Camel Rock and Black Rock. Each spot has its tidal nuance but there is always something to ride. It's consistent, crowded and home to more surf schools. **Crackington Haven** is a rocky beachbreak in a sheltered cove that filters the swell size and gives rare shelter from N winds. Lacks power and shape. Cambeak's huge outside bombora is awesome to watch, but never surfed. There's good beachbreak at **Trebarwith Strand** if the banks are cooperating, otherwise it is a hollow semi-close-out, popular with bodyboarders. The beach disappears at high tide and it's often crowded. Consistent, slow, intermediate-friendly walls, spread along **Polzeath** beach plus to the north, a reasonable right breaks off Pentire Point at size. Often crowded at this popular holiday spot. Around the headland, Lundy Bay is the low tide place for huge storm surf. North-facing **Harlyn** needs SW winds and a solid winter swell, offering friendly rolling walls for the crowds of longboarders and beginners who flock here during storm swells. Gets really fat and backwashy at high. Advanced surfers will check neighbouring Trevone for faster, steeper waves in similar conditions. Swell magnet, beachbreak **Constantine** has peaks in the middle of the bay, lefts off the reef at the south end, rights off the point at the north end (quality depends on sand flow from river) and Booby's to the north has a good but fickle low tide right reef. Can get very strong rips with an overhead swell and is not for beginners who should try Treyarnon. The fickle, exposed beachbreak at **Mawgan Porth** is best just after low, pushing up to mid tide. Left sandbar off the south end and right off the north side get a bit of extra push from a wedge coming off the cliffs. Normally messy and unrideable unless a perfectly clean, small swell is running. More of the same north at Bedruthan Steps. **Watergate Bay** stretches for 1.5mi (2.5km), entertaining fun peaks in all swells and through the tides. Popular with all standards including kitesurfers on W winds. Gets heavier and hollower at size, when the rips ramp up. Probably the best facilities of any beach in Britain: surf shop, school, bistro, bar, hotel and camping. Try the southern headland at Whipsiderry to escape the summer crowds. **Newquay Town Beaches** are a mixed bag from the confused, gutless straighthanders of Porth, through the low tide lumps of annual night-surf site Lusty Glaze to the ridiculously busy, punchy, high tide left at Tolcarne Wedge or the SW storm option of Towan to Great Western. Famous, fickle, big-wave

## TRAVEL INFORMATION

**Weather** – England's weather is notoriously famous for its mild rainy spells and unpredictability. Despite the northerly latitude it rarely snows in the winter and freezing temperatures only occur at night. During the autumn, air and water temperatures are still reasonable, swells consistent and the winds are often offshore. Cornwall is windy, requiring a 5/4mm wetsuit with boots, gloves and maybe a hat, as the water drops to 8°C (46°F). A 3-2 steamer is ideal in summer as the water touches 20°C (68°F).

**Lodging and Food** – B&B's are everywhere, from $45/n upwards. Fistral Beach Hotel is quality at a price. The Backpackers in Newquay or Fistral are good deals and surfer-friendly. A pub meal costs $20 and daytime "greasy spoon cafes" are cheaper.

**Nature and Culture** – North Cornwall is backed almost entirely by National Trust land, with little development marring its windswept beauty. There are many festivals in summer around Newquay. Cornwall and Devon are summer holiday hotspots in Britain. Resorts such as Newquay, Bude and Torquay become jam-packed and very lively.

**Hazards and Hassles** – Rocks, cold water, strong riptides, sewage and summer crowds. Cornwall suffers from intense traffic jams and over-subscribed beach parking on holiday weekends. The notoriously thin roads extend travelling times.

**Handy Hints** – There are a myriad of surf shops and board manufacturers like Ocean Magic. Boards: Nigel Semmens, Fluid Juice, Zuma Jay. A board costs $550.

JASON FEAST

## Fistral Beach

15/2

LAT. 50.418448° LONG. -5.099728°

The UK's most famous beach is home to a trio of quality breaks, a large local contingent and many of the country's top pros. Beneath the iconic Headland Hotel, Little Fistral is a high-performance, fast, hollow zipping left and right until the tide brings too many rocks into play. North Fistral draws in the most swell, hopefully with plenty of W, creating occasionally epic rights that get hollow at lower tides. Steep, with feathering lips and lots of opportunity to throw some big turns and airs, this is the contest site of choice for all high level competitions in the UK. South Fistral turns out lined-up lefts over sand and occasional rock bottom, with the headland providing good shelter from SW winds. Prefers higher tides, unlike North Fistral. The whole show is very consistent, hence the constant, year-round crowds. Surf centre and all facilities on the beach, plus Newquay is stacked with surf shops. Pathetic amount of pay parking for the most famous beach in the country.

spot Cribber rarely works as it needs to be perfectly clean and double overhead before it will break clear of the rocks. Rights are safer but the lefts can be good. Savage rips, nasty rocks and long hold-downs. Big-wave surfers only, but mere mortals can contest for waves at the UK's home of surf competitions, **Fistral Beach**. **Crantock** shapes a fast, hollow, right sandbar off rocks to the north and a rare left in the south corner on massive swells. The rivermouth sandbar is popular with longboarders, but quality is ever-changing and high tide does the beach no favours. Low crowd factor for Newquay, which continues at neighbouring Holywell Bay. From Penhale to **Perranporth** stretches a series of changeable peaks that can wall-up for long ripable rides beneath the towering sand dunes. To the north is Penhale Corner – a long, walling right peeling off Ligger Point at lower tides. The central Perran Sands beachbreaks are best at higher tides, but very open to swell and adverse winds. The main town beachbreaks are better at low tide with the highlight being a long left breaking underneath Droskyn Point if the river has shaped the sandbar. Rips are a problem, but it soaks up the big summer crowd from the huge campground. **St Agnes** attracts powerful, beachbreak peaks over a rocky beach. One of the few spots working in big SW swells and winds. Localised and crowded. **Porthtowan** produces proper powerful peaks with some good tube sections all the way up to the stream at Chapel Porth. Blows out easily unless you are in the southern corner and most of this stretch disappears at high. Consistent, often crowded, rippy and handles some swell, so not really for beginners. **Portreath** is best described as an average, all tides beachbreak, with good shelter from SW winds. There's nothing average about Portreath Wall, a dangerous, heavy granite reef righthander at the tip of the harbour wall. When it's on, it's thick, warping, hollow and mobbed with locals, many on bodyboards who also charge The V, a near dry shorey wedge on the inside. **Godrevy/Gwithian** is an extensive network of user-friendly sandbars offering better surfers more size and speed at the north end or beginners and improvers room to move. Works all tides and handles a fair bit of size. In big swells there might be a fast, hollow sandbar at Hayle Rivermouth or even more sheltered Carbis Bay. St Ives town beach **Porthmeor** faces NW, so only works in bigger swells. Good peak at the Boiler and a right off the island. **Gwenvor** is the most swell exposed beach in Cornwall, so no surf here means no surf anywhere. Solid beachbreak peaks and a fickle right point over sand/rock at the north end of the bay. Next door, **Sennen** is just as consistent, sucking in all swell directions for punchy peaks with barrels when offshore on a medium swell and tide. Rounding Lands End onto Cornwall's south coast passes protected bays like Porthcurno and Perranuthanoe that are irregular, big swell spots. **Praa Sands** is more consistent, attracting regular crowds to some well-shaped peaks that can get hollow in offshore N winds. Rips at low tide, shorepound at high and always busy when on. In large winter swells and cold N winds, picturesque **Porthleven** produces fast, hollow, perfect peaks over a ragged tongue of reef to the west of the harbour. Better known for short perfect righthand barrels, it also outputs some good lefts on certain swell directions. Cornwall's best reefbreak is always busy when on with a large local crew, pros and media. Dangerous at low tide and rippy at high – experts only. There's also another hollow left/right reef in front of the pier popular with lids.

Cornwall receives SW-WNW swells, but smaller NW groundswells are blocked out by Ireland, which explains summer flat spells. Autumn and winter are best, and the west coast is the most consistent with regular 2-12ft mainly W swells and SE to SW winds. The south coast is often onshore and the SW swell/NW wind combo for Porthleven works about 20-30 times a year. Prevailing winds are S-NW with more W in the summer time. The Newquay tide factor can reach 7.7m, totally dictating break choice.

JASON FEAST

Porthleven

| STATISTICS | | J F | M A | M J | J A | S O | N D |
|---|---|---|---|---|---|---|---|
| SWELL | Direction | | | | | | |
| | Size (ft) | 7 | 6 | 4 | 2 | 5-6 | 6-7 |
| WIND | Direction | | | | | | |
| | Force | F5 | F4-F5 | F4 | F4 | F4-F5 | F5 |
| WATER | Wetsuit | | | | | | |
| | Temp/°C | 9 | 10 | 12 | 16 | 14 | 11 |
| WEATHER | Rainfall/mm | 90 | 63 | 62 | 75 | 87 | 115 |
| | days/mth | 12 | 9 | 9 | 10 | 11 | 15 |
| | Min temp/°C | 4 | 5 | 9 | 13 | 11 | 6 |
| | Max temp/°C | 8 | 11 | 16 | 19 | 17 | 10 |

# Lofoten Islands NORWAY

The majority of Norway's surf scene is based around Stavanger, way down in the south, which has a handful of fun, reliable spots with decent exposure to the inconsistent swell patterns of the North Atlantic. However, way up north, above the Arctic Circle, Lofoten is now considered as Norway's primo surfing destination and has been highlighted in countless magazines and surf films. These mountainous islands 100km off the north Norwegian coastline, plunge steeply into the wild North Atlantic ocean, awaiting the arrival of autumn swells that are then transformed into some classy waves over boulders, reef and sand.

+ LONG EMPTY POINTBREAKS
+ MIDNIGHT SUN
+ UNRIVALLED ARCTIC SCENERY
+ FRIENDLY VIBE

- COLD SUMMER CONDITIONS
- SHORT SURFING SEASON
- DIFFICULT COASTAL ACCESS
- SUPER EXPENSIVE

Missing the flight or ferry from Bodø, means a 13h drive via Narvik's ski resorts to access Lofoten via bridges and the peninsula that joins to the mainland. The most northerly spot to check on Vestvågøy is **Kvalnes**, which is close to the coast road and faces north. It's rarely surfed, like the nearby break of Vinje which picks up most SW to N swells. Further down is **Eggum**'s beautiful pebble beach, which needs a big swell, S wind and is pretty sectiony. The boulders curve out to the west offering more exposed options. The breathtaking alpine scenery of Unstad's amphitheatre bay is home to three waves and has only recently become easily accessible as the tunnel leading to the village (pop 13) only opened in autumn 1995. **Unstad Right** is often considered a world-class pointbreak and possibly the best spot in Norway when it is on. Large open faces with a powerful pocket that hurtles down the line and serves up barrel sections in offshore easterlies, but the end section shuts down firmly. Needs a clean, longer period, W-NW swell to fire. Only experts can handle the speed, rocks and currents. Paddling from **Unstad Beach** is far safer than launching from the rocks, as it breaks over sand and some scattered boulders. Smaller, softer peaks provide the perfect place for beginners and the local surf school to get wet. **Unstad Left** churns out some awesome long lefthanders when a SW swell wraps onto the rocky shelf. Technically challenging with both crumbling sections and barrels mixed in. Winds can be funnelled offshore by the 800m mountain that looms over the break. Speed and nerve essential – experts only. Difficult entry and exit over the rocky shelf strewn with boulders. Exploring further south on Vestvågøy check the shining white sands of **Utakleiv** and Hauklands which are road accessible summer tourist beaches. On Flakstadøy, **Flakstad** faces NW so the wide beachbreak peaks have a little SW protection. Just north, Vikten is similar, but more wind exposed and flanked by boulder reefs. **Kvalvika**'s stunning bay (see the film *North of the Sun*) requires a solid hike to get to some average peelers that often close-out. Mostly uninspiring waves in a beautiful setting. Further down the island of Moskenesøy are two NW-facing sandy bays at Horseid and Bunes.

KIAN BOURKE-STEER/UNSTAD ARCTIC SURF

Unstad Left

KIAN BOURKE-STEER/UNSTAD ARCTIC SURF

Unstad Beach

Some North Atlantic depressions do get as far as Norway, but many of them die en-route so only autumn to winter brings regular, moderate period SW-W groundswells. Being so high in the Arctic Circle, it's mostly a venue for windswells from SW to N. Fairly strong, S quadrant winds dominate the year with a bit more N-NE in summer, when swell consistency stats are too low to plan a trip. Swells are short but powerful and can produce up to double overhead waves on the Unstad points. Unlike the Stavanger area where there are virtually no tides, most Lofoten islands are surrounded by strong tidal currents. The maelstrøm whirls are a direct consequence of major tidal action. Spring tidal range can reach 3m+ in Bodø.

## TRAVEL INFORMATION

**Weather** – Lofoten has a much milder climate than other parts of the world at the same latitude, such as Alaska and Greenland. The coastal climate makes winters comparatively mild and summers relatively cool. January and February are the coldest months, with an average temperature of –1°C. July and August are warmest with an average temperature of 12°C. The midnight sun is visible from 27 May - 17 July. Optimum timing is mid-September to mid-October, when water can be 7-12°C (45-54°F) so use a full 5/4 mm with 5mm+ booties, gloves and hood for the worst conditions.

**Lodging and Food** – The place to stay is Unstadt Arctic Surf which is a collection of cabins, a restaurant and surf school with rentals. Favour "rorbu" camping or self-catering units for cheaper stays, budget at least $50/d. If surviving on a budget (min $20/meal), cod and potatoes are cheap and shop in large supermarkets (Leknes or Svolvær).

**Nature and Culture** – "Skrei" (spawning cod) are caught during the winter, so boats could be available for chartering in autumn. Seals, killer whales and white-tailed eagles are often observed. Hiking, biking, downhill skateboarding, climbing, skiing and fishing. Northern lights from late autumn to early spring.

**Hazards and Hassles** – Rips and fin snapping boulders are the main dangers! Digging cars out of the snow and drying wetsuits can be major chores. Take plenty of cold water wax.

**Handy Hints** – Arctic Surf rent out a variety of boards and suits fr $40. Nearest shop is SrfSnoSk8 in Stavanger, 2000 km away! It takes 3 days to drive from Oslo to Unstad. Rental cars cost 800$/wk. Board and suit rental $100/d for both. Bring a pointbreak fast gunny board with extra float to carry the rubber. Alcohol is expensive.

| STATISTICS | | J F | M A | M J | J A | S O | N D |
|---|---|---|---|---|---|---|---|
| SWELL | Direction | | | | | | |
| | Size (ft) | 5-6 | 4-5 | 3-4 | 3 | 4-5 | 5-6 |
| WIND | Direction | | | | | | |
| | Force | F5 | F5 | F4 | F4 | F4-F5 | F5 |
| WATER | Wetsuit | | | | | | |
| | Temp/°C | 5 | 6 | 7 | 10 | 9 | 7 |
| WEATHER | Rainfall/mm | 61 | 51 | 41 | 59 | 101 | 89 |
| | days/mth | 15 | 16 | 17 | 18 | 20 | 16 |
| | Min temp/°C | -4 | -3 | 5 | 11 | 4 | -1 |
| | Max temp/°C | 2 | 4 | 12 | 15 | 9 | 3 |

# The Netherlands

Nearly a quarter of The Netherlands sits below sea level, so the population, who rely on dykes to defend the country from the worst North Sea swells, may not consider waves a blessing. Much of the seabed is shallow, continental shelf, so strong lows are needed to send NNW swells to endless flat beaches, where conditions improve in the vicinity of huge boulder jetties. There are 3 surfing regions: the Wadden Islands, Westkust and Zeeland to the south. Scheveningen is by far the most popular surf area as well as the major seaside resort.

+ MELLOW BEACHBREAKS
+ EXCELLENT BEACH FACILITIES
+ GOOD TRANSPORT LINKS
+ CLOSE TO AMSTERDAM

- LACK OF GROUNDSWELLS
- FLAT CROWDED SUMMERS
- FREEZING WINTERS
- EXPENSIVE

ROBIN BAKKER

Scheveningen Pier

**The Wadden Islands** are typical low-lying barrier islands with shifting sandbanks along open, unstabilised beaches. Big tides and big currents. Terscelling and Texel are the best bet. **Petten**'s lefthand jetty break gets hollow and fast on the inconsistent winter SW swells at mid incoming. Protection from S or SW winds. **Camperduin** is one of the most powerful jetty breaks in Holland and mid tide on the push is when the barrels happen for a couple of hours. Waves can even run from one jetty to the next in a good NW swell. Rip tides get fierce at high. Typical Dutch beachbreak at both **Bergen Aan Zee**, Egmond Aan Zee and down to Castricum dan Zee. Featureless, open beachbreak lacking shape and power. Hope for NW swells and slack winds to deter the kiteboarders. **Wijk Aan Zee/ Noordpier** is the premier spot closest to Amsterdam. Left and right walls in a NW swell and weaker disorganised corners in SW conditions, when the huge harbour jetty provides some wind protection. Onshore messy conditions are the norm and mid tides incoming are best. High tide there is too much water. **Zandvoort to Katwijk** sees open beaches with soft crumblers that can reform and break harder on the inside. Good for longboarding but beginners should note strong longshore currents. **Scheveningen Pier** holds some shape on the north side in SW swells and winds. Not as big, organised or crowded as **Scheveningen Nord**, a stretch of beach flanked by a huge harbour wall that gives SW wind protection and a paddling out channel. Often lacks in power and closes-out, therefore a lot of longboarders. Picks up all swell directions and breaks through the tide but best on a NW at high. **Scheveningen Zuid** also gets some quality peaks on the south side of the harbour jetty in big NW swells and remains ridable in gale force northerly winds. Hollow at times with defined lefts breaking into the paddling channel by the jetty and long rights wandering down the beach at high.

## TRAVEL INFORMATION

**Weather** – There is a moderate coastal climate with mild winters, drier springs and cool wetter summers.The SW-W wind can add a chill factor coming off the cold North Sea. Hardcore waveriders will have to handle 5°C (41°F) water or less and freezing air temps through autumn and winter. The heart of the winter requires 6/5/4 mm and all the other bits of rubber.

**Lodging and Food** – Expensive by European standards as it's a wealthy area. Scheveningen has the widest range of accommodation from deluxe Kurhaus Hotel sea view rooms to the campsite in the woods near Scheveningen. $20 should buy a decent meal.

**Nature and Culture** – Beach cafés and coffee shops are central to the vibe! There is a Flowrider at De Eemhof.

**Hazards and Hassles** – Summer brings surfing bans and lifeguards giving out tickets. Pollution is a problem from rivermouths and harbours. Expensive parking, wheel clamping and no overnight parking is enforced.

**Handy Hints** – Dutch, Belgian and German surfers mostly frequent this surf zone. Surfboards are available for rent ($10/h) at the Hart Beach Shop. Multiple surf schools fr $15/2hr lesson.

A good low tide option is **Kijkduin** that picks up all swells and gets hollow rights and lefts between short jettys in light winds. **Ter Heijde** holds more low tide jetty breaks that can shape up a few faster waves on a NW swell. The immense Europoort blocks SW swell from **Hoek Van Holland**, but on NW swells, it's a rounder and more powerful beachbreak, best around high tide with S winds. Undoubtedly suffers from harbour pollution. The huge Rotterdam port expansion buried some old spots (Slufter & Blokken) replacing them with the large recreational beach of **Maasvlakte 2**. The most northern surf break is Bel's (Parking 6), which generally has the biggest, most powerful waves coming out of deeper water in the shipping lane, but it is highly exposed to the wind. In Betweens (P5) faces WSW, needs more swell, but handles strong NW winds and becomes clean and hollow with N-NE winds. Both spots are shallow breaking waves with strong currents. Container's is a more forgiving wave, hosting multiple peaks between the yellow, blue and red access points with more than enough parking. South of here, Zeeland has a few breaks, but by far the most reliable are the pushier peaks between the wooden jetties of **Domburg**, or the rare, long, righthand walls of **Vlissingen**.

North Atlantic low pressure cells traverse the UK within 12 hours and resume their wave generation process in the North Sea. Most spots are best with NW swells and to a lesser degree W, N, and sometimes SW short period windswell. In the land of windmills, winds are pretty steady, though rarely very strong with SW dominance, tending S in winter and W in summer. There is a brief N-NE wind quadrant in May-June. Spring tidal range can reach 2.2m, and breaks usually favour low to mid-tide although some high tide spots can deliver shorebreak power.

| STATISTICS | | J F | M A | M J | J A | S O | N D |
|---|---|---|---|---|---|---|---|
| SWELL | Direction | | | | | | |
| | Size (ft) | 3 | 2-3 | 1-2 | 1 | 2-3 | 3 |
| WIND | Direction | | | | | | |
| | Force | F4 | F4 | F4 | F4 | F4 | F4 |
| WATER | Wetsuit | | | | | | |
| | Temp/°C | 6 | 7 | 13 | 17 | 17 | 11 |
| WEATHER | Rainfall/mm | 54 | 41 | 46 | 68 | 72 | 65 |
| | days/mth | 19 | 16 | 13 | 15 | 17 | 20 |
| | Min temp/°C | 1 | 4 | 11 | 14 | 11 | 4 |
| | Max temp/°C | 5 | 11 | 18 | 21 | 17 | 8 |

# South Finistère FRANCE

The large bays of Finistère and the attendant long peninsulas, offer a range of surfing real estate to cater in most swells and winds, despite regular fierce storms and a dramatic tidal range. Strict laws concerning coastal development, maintain long stretches of untouched coast and while most of the accessible spots will be crowded in small and clean conditions, there remains ample space for the growing surf population.

+ WIDE SWELL WINDOW
+ UNSPOILT CROZON PENINSULA
+ MULTI-ASPECT COASTLINE
+ RUGGED, SCENIC BEAUTY

– COLD, RAINY & WINDSWEPT
– LACK OF EPIC POINTBREAKS
– SUMMER CROWDS
– EXTREME TIDAL RANGES

With good westerly exposure, **Anse de Pen-hat** wears hollow peaks at both ends, shaped by strong rips and the waves will have some punch at the favoured tide of mid incoming. **Kerloch** has long rides with cutback walls that remains surfable with W winds in the north corner. Down the beach is Kersiguennou and the south end is Goulien where it will be bigger in W-NW swells. Scenic **Pointe de Dinan** is protected from N winds and holds some size as the long performance right walls rumble down the boulders. **La Palue**'s wide open, west-facing beachbreak picks up all available swells and is regularly crowded. Usually messy and weaker at low tide before lining-up on the push past mid. Long walls and the odd barrel section make it a fun intermediate spot. At low tide check Lostmarc'h, just to the north. **Cap de la Chèvre** has some big-wave options for experts only. **Pors-ar-Vag** has a good beachbreak for beginners isolated in Lestrevet. A long spinning wall cuts across the rocks of **Pointe Leydé** in a big SW swell and even handles W winds so attracts the hottest locals. The north coast of Cap Sizun conceals many little-known reefs and beaches like **Porz Théolen**. Impressive **Baie des Trépassés** picks up any small swell going, churning out some long low tide walls and also occasionally some hefty barrels off the high tide rock at the north end. There will be a crowd of all abilities on small swell weekends. **Saint Tugen** is the best beachbreak around in overhead conditions, delivering stand-up barrels at low tide. Faces straight into the SW swells, so any N wind will do and handles more size from more directions than most spots. **Pointe de Lervily** and Ile Aux Vaches are two shallow reef/pointbreaks that need decent size W or SW swell to break fast and ledgy. Inconsistent, crowded and rocky for experts only. When it's huge everywhere else, **La Gamelle** breaks on each side of a metallic beacon, the right being shorter and hollower. Gets an experienced crowd, despite 200m paddle offshore. The low to mid tide outer **Gwendrez** sandbars can hold some fine shapely peaks, with fast walled up sections and tube potential, plus there's a rare but feisty left off the rocks at the southern end. Big shoredump close-out for the bodyboarders. **La Torche** is the seminal Brittany surf spot with an ultra-consistent, walled-up peak breaking beside the rocky headland. Shorter but hollower rights break into the rip known as "the elevator" which flows straight to the peak. Lefts speed down the beach, but paddle back can be gruelling, so think about walking around to the rip. Many more breaks further north along beach at Tronoën, Plovan or Penhors. Ultra-crowded with all surf craft on weekends. **Pors Carn** beachbreak occasionally gets, hollow and wedgy and the curve of the beach means NE-SW winds are OK. There's a righthand reef at high tide and some offshore big-wave reefs for daredevils only. Usually quieter than La Torche, unless the swell is pumping or the N winds are howling. **Lesconil** requires a rare combination of S swell and N winds to provide anything else than windsurf conditions. When on, a reef close to the harbour offers hollow, powerful, low tide lefts and some lesser rights.

Swell averages hit 10-13ft in mid-winter but halve in summer when the dominant WSW groundswells are replaced by windswells that will have a bit more NW direction, in tandem with the wind. Predominant winds are from the SW-NW, with unfavourable W winds prevalent in summer after the morning easterlies. Apart from swell and wind combinations, tidal range is a significant factor. Crozon tides reach 6.4m so arrive well before optimum tide.

MENSWAVE

La Torche

KRISTEN PELOU

Pointe de Dinan

## TRAVEL INFORMATION

**Weather** – Brittany has a typical maritime climate with cool summers and mild, wet winters thanks to the Atlantic winds that keep the temperature above freezing in winter. Rain is frequent and quick, radical weather changes are a regular feature of Brittany's weather. Water temperature remains above 10°C (50°F) but summers wont exceed 18°C (64°F).

**Lodging and Food** – La Torche is lacking in facilities with no accommodation apart from a summertime campsite, 2 or 3 surf shops and a couple of crêperies. If you don't have a campervan, the guesthouses will cost ($60/dble) or budget hotels (fr $35/dble). Crêpes, seafood and apple dishes, often containing the famous Breton cidres. Pay $25 for a meal with cider.

**Nature and Culture** – Visit Oceanopolis in Brest, the biggest open-air aquarium in Europe. There are lots of festivals in the summer and locals party hard at the biggest one known as Fest-Noze.

**Hazards and Hassles** – Some spots have strong riptides but trying to get to the right spot before its optimum tidal phase is crucial. Some of the heavy slab reefs can be treacherous for the barrel-hunting bodyboard crew, who are mellow but numerous.

**Handy Hints** – Surf shops can be found at major spots and cities and the best shapers are in Quiberon, South Brittany. Motorways are toll-free in Brittany.

| STATISTICS | | J F | M A | M J | J A | S O | N D |
|---|---|---|---|---|---|---|---|
| SWELL | Direction | | | | | | |
| | Size (ft) | 7 | 6 | 4 | 2 | 5-6 | 6-7 |
| WIND | Direction | | | | | | |
| | Force | F5 | F4-F5 | F4 | F4 | F4 | F5 |
| WATER | Wetsuit | | | | | | |
| | Temp/°C | 10 | 10 | 13 | 16 | 15 | 12 |
| WEATHER | Rainfall/mm | 115 | 83 | 63 | 70 | 98 | 145 |
| | days/mth | 16 | 12 | 9 | 11 | 13 | 18 |
| | Min temp/°C | 4 | 6 | 9 | 13 | 10 | 6 |
| | Max temp/°C | 9 | 12 | 17 | 20 | 17 | 11 |

# Gironde FRANCE

The linear shores of Gironde can offer very attractive and challenging beachbreaks, particularly in the smaller swells of summer. Each coastal town has its own version of ever-changing, quality sandbanks, concentrating summer crowds at access points, but a 20min walk in either direction could be rewarded with empty waves.

- \+ EMPTY PEAKS TO FIND
- \+ UNCROWDED OFF-SEASON
- \+ MASCARET RIVER BORE
- \+ EXCELLENT WINES AND OYSTERS

- – BEACHBREAKS ONLY
- – SUMMER CROWDS
- – FREQUENT ONSHORES
- – COLD WATER IN WINTER

Lacanau

CLEMENT PHILLIPON

Inside the Gironde rivermouth, La Chambrette breaks hard and fast when the Atlantic coast is onshore and out of control, or **Le Verdon** will work in big swells and S winds. With the rivermouth creating offshore sandbanks, **Soulac** is always smaller but hollower than surrounding spots. At **L'Amelie**, occasionally fast and hollow waves form up by the blockhaus or the jetty. With a large swell and a bit of luck, long tubing lefts can appear at **Le Gurp**. Check the banks at La Négade to the north, or at Dépée next to the Euronat nudist camp. Nice peaks visible from the central **Montalivet** car park, but there's more for those that look around. One road bisects the 10km long Forêt du Flamand at **Le Pin Sec**. Endless choice of peaks along this quiet stretch that never gets crowded and has a good campsite nearby. More open beachbreak at **Hourtin** that can line-up nicely on its day. The soft reef helps to shape bowly waves, but high tide will kill it in small swells. **Le Crohot des Cavales** represents another large shadow zone west of the Hourtin lake accessible only by bicycle. May not be the hollowest and lined-up banks around but it is usually empty. Quieter than Lacanau, **Carcans** is often more walled-up than hollow, but still plenty of power. **Lacanau** is surf central for the Bordeaux area, with consistent surf, easily checked from the boardwalk at Plage Centrale. La Nord, La Sud or Super Sud are among 14km of beaches ideal with a medium size W-NW swell. Handles more size in summer when it is often bigger than Landes in the W windswells. Fast peeling low tide runners or mid to high tide shories tapering into the rips are sometimes separated by a deep trench, or spin all the way through. Like all Biscay beachies, it's fine for beginners when small and friendly, but a real challenge when overhead and bombing, not least because of the wicked rips. **Le Porge** can be a pretty picture when a morning offshore is ruffling some headhigh A-frames on the mid tide banks. Sucky and fast on the outside bank with a habit of closing-out at low. Consistent and often hollow peaks in small W swells at **La Jenny** are never too crowded thanks to the long walk in through the woods. **Le Grand Crohot** sports Lande-esque line-ups with plenty of bains and good shape on the outside bars in peaky summer swells. **Le Truc Vert**'s large camping overlooks the jetty influenced sandbanks that usually have good shape. **L'Horizon** is one of a dozen named semi-secret spots on the peninsula that can have great banks on any given day. Better with peaky, summer, W windswells, on smaller, lower tides. Beach markers are helpful to gauge the swift north to south currents. Beware of swift north to south currents, old bunkers and eroded jetties. Very large swells can wrap around Cap Ferret and break inside the Bassin d'Arcachon at **La Pointe**, throwing up tubey little rights. W winds are offshore, but the hellish currents can make for bumpy rides, so it is popular with bodyboarders. Great view of the massive Dune du Pyla in the background. There are lots more waves on the ocean side of Ferret, which will be smaller than those to the north, but plagued by strong currents.

Summer sees consistent WNW swells, which continue into winter adding the possibility of SW-W swell. Winds follow the same seasonal pattern plus there is a sizeable slice of N-NE year-round. Most spots won't handle more than 8ft, so shorter period, peaky swells are often the best. With high pressure over Biscay, morning offshores become a moderate sea breeze from around 11am. Tide ranges can exceed 5m, turning ugly mush into a perfect peak.

## TRAVEL INFORMATION

**Weather** – Gironde has a unique microclimate characterised by mild winters and relatively cool summers. Rain is frequent and gets stronger in autumn and winter. Summers are relatively hot with around 10 days per year above 30°C (86°F). Plan for water temps as low as 10°C (50°F) and as high as 23°C (74°F).

**Lodging and Food** – Always book in advance during summer, since Lacanau gets full. Wave Trotter's Guest House fr $21-31/n (ask at Mata Hari surf shop). Campgrounds are numerous. Try the excellent Arcachon oysters with a glass of Bordeaux white wine!

**Nature and Culture** – The Dune Du Pyla is the largest sand dune in Europe with excellent views over the Bassin d'Arcachon and the pine forest, plus it's the perfect training site for paragliding. Bordeaux vineyards are a tasty, flat-day idea. Topless and full nudity sunbathing is common along many stretches of the coast. Lively bars and nightclubs during peak season.

**Hazards and Hassles** – Big, stormy surf creates treacherous rips. Getting to the right spot before its optimum tide phase is crucial. In winter, beach trash builds up. Driving and parking are tricky from mid-July to mid-August.

**Handy Hints** – There are numerous surf shops, but only a few are open year-round (especially in small coastal towns). Try Mata Hari in Lacanau, or Surfers in Bordeaux. Be aware driving the forest trails is prohibited and the fine is expensive.

| STATISTICS | | J F | M A | M J | J A | S O | N D |
|---|---|---|---|---|---|---|---|
| SWELL | Direction | | | | | | |
| | Size (ft) | 7 | 5-6 | 4-5 | 2-3 | 4-5 | 6-7 |
| WIND | Direction | | | | | | |
| | Force | F5 | F4-F5 | F3-F4 | F3-F4 | F3-F4 | F5-F6 |
| WATER | Wetsuit | | | | | | |
| | Temp/°C | 12 | 13 | 15 | 20 | 18 | 14 |
| WEATHER | Rainfall/mm | 83 | 55 | 62 | 63 | 84 | 100 |
| | days/mth | 14 | 13 | 12 | 10 | 13 | 16 |
| | Min temp/°C | 2 | 5 | 11 | 14 | 10 | 4 |
| | Max temp/°C | 10 | 16 | 22 | 26 | 21 | 11 |

# Landes FRANCE

The 230km coastline called the Côte d'Argent is the longest uninterrupted stretch of sandy beach in Europe. Swells are focused then refracted on to the coast near Hossegor by a deep-water canyon, which helps shape sandbars that hold world-class beachbreaks. These exceptionally powerful, hollow, perfect peaks have attracted the world's best competitive surfers and the European surf industry to this corner of France. Big currents, large tidal ranges and extreme wind exposure do little to deter the ever-growing crowds of riders looking for some of the best beachbreaks on the planet.

+ TOP-QUALITY BEACHBREAKS
+ HOLLOW CONSISTENT WAVES
+ EMPTY PEAKS TO FIND
+ SUMMER PARTY SCENE

– STRONG RIPS
– NO SHELTERED SPOTS
– FREQUENT ONSHORES
– SUMMER CROWDS

North Landes

LAURENT MASUREL

**La Salie** has incredibly fast-shifting sandbars around the 800m long wharf, plus some good bodyboard shorebreak just to the north and more banks down at the blockhaus. Popular summer resort town **Biscarrosse-Plage** offers typical shifting bars, from high tide thumping shories to outer low tide bars that can be fast and hollow in sections. Seems to favour rights as the sand goes with the flow from N-S. Quiet **Mimizan-Plage** produces enough good waves on either side of the rivermouth that helps sculpt some organised sandbars, particularly from mid to high tide. The **Contis-Plage** lighthouse provides a birds eye view of the best sandbanks, especially those to the north, close to the bunker or rivermouth. **Cap de L'Homy** features more straight beachbreak that benefits from some swell angle or chopped up summer windswells. More performance oriented waves perfect for beginner/intermediates. With 12km of beachbreak to choose from, **St-Girons Plage** serves up something in between Hossegor barrels and average beachbreak walls. Favourite of foreign surfers and naturists with 2 massive camping sites and surf hire/schools for beginners. **Moliets Plage** soaks up the summer crowd on very shifty sandbanks that often shut down. High tide is usually no good. The Huchet River mouth from Leon Lake can shape some nice lower tide sandbars. Typical Landes plage, **Messanges** displays all moods of wave from onshore crumbly mess to morning A-frame barrels, depending on the luck of the sandbars. High tide will often kill it when small. North side of the lake entrance at **Vieux Boucau** has fast, hollow peaks on higher tides, but heavy longshore rips at headhigh plus. Port d'Albret on the south side leads into the Soustons stretch and has good shape for kilometers. Handles more size than the breaks to the north. **Casernes** campsite-fed beach access marks the northern limit of the Seignosse beaches. When the sand lines up, it can produce those speedy, lip smacking walls across a handful of mid tide sandbars. Despite the 500m walk from the car park and campground, it is often just as crowded as everywhere else.

**Le Penon** often holds some really good higher tide shorebreaks that entertain the mix of locals and travellers. Unmanageable rips and impossible paddle-outs at double overhead. Attracts huge summer crowds to the water park, fairground rides and tourist shops. **Les Bourdaines** is probably the most popular and consistent spot in Seignosse. Stable sandbanks have forged this reputation over the years and there always seems to be a defined left/right just south of the path and multiple peaks up towards Penon. Dead high tide will be a struggle when small and diagonal super rips can hold up the close-outs when the faces exceed 8ft. Top quality peaks appear when a good W-NW swell hits the sand at **Les Estagnots**. Handles a bit more size than Bourdaines and Penon, but expect severe long-shore drift when bigger. High tide inside banks can be hollow and fast. Always a crowd and the odd combative local. **Les Cul Nuls** is the link between the normal beachbreaks to the north and the heavy barreling shories of ✪**La Graviere**. Usually better at mid to high tides with a moderate swell, because of the steeper beach angle. Occasionally lines-up some long outside rights into rips, otherwise it's powerful action close to shore. **La Nord** is usually the only rideable beachbreak north of Capbreton when the swell heads towards 3m on the Biscay buoy. The shifting, outside bank holds triple overhead plus and favours rights into the rip torn paddling channel. Steep drops and fast walls

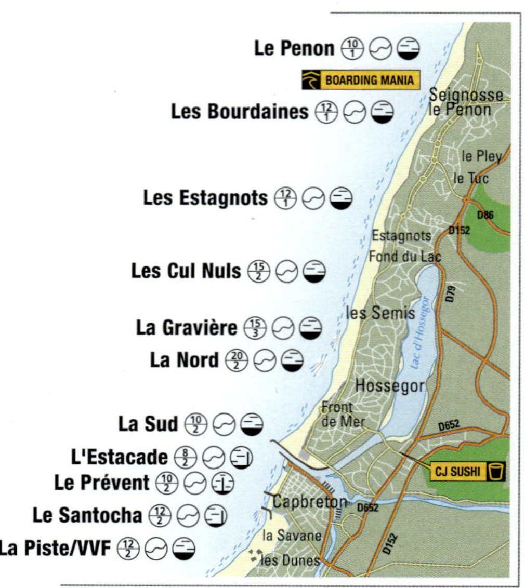


## TRAVEL INFORMATION

**Weather** – The Pyrenees mountains greatly influence the southern Landes weather bringing regular annual rainfall. Winters can be damp and cool, until stable weather arrives from March to October. March-April can have occasional warm spells, but spring is usually windy with squalls, rain and choppy swells. May and June are good months despite the cooler water. Summers can get some hot days before the sea breeze cuts in. Autumn weather can be perfect with cool mornings, warm daytime temps and comfortable water temps. Take a 4/3 fullsuit for winter, a 3/2 for mid-season, and a shorty or boardies for the warmer days that can reach 24°C (75°F).

**Lodging and Food** – Hossegor and Capbreton have multiple accommodation options for all budgets. There are dozens of summer surf camps/retreats/schools. Further up the coast, holiday rentals, VVF's and campgrounds are the go. Campervans will be fined for free-camping beach car parks during summer. Try cheaper Aire de Camping municipal sites. A typical restaurant bill is $20, not including wine. Seafood in Capbreton is big and foie gras along with duck dishes are regional favourites.

**Nature and Culture** – Golf, sailing, beach fishing, lake SUP, jet-skiing, water slides and skate parks plus crazy summer parties are some of the distractions. Rockfood is the most popular tourist bar right on the beach at Front de Mer, Hossegor. Winter is mellow as anything up to 75% of the region's coastal zone housing stock are second homes and often remain empty until the warmer months.

**Hazards and Hassles** – Getting to the right spot before the short window for optimum tide is crucial as spring and autumn equinox tides move fast. Beware of the extremely powerful rips; many visitors drown every year. In the winter, beaches get plenty of trash and driftwood from the ocean. Driving and parking are tricky from mid July to late August. Look out for thieves and vandals when parking in forest spots. Respect the large Hossegor surf community, who are amazingly tolerant, considering the huge increases in numbers every summer.

**Handy Hints** – There is a thriving surf industry at the Z.A. Pédebert in Soorts Hossegor, where you can get boards repaired, find a shaper and shop in one of the many factory outlets for all the big surf brands. You need a gun only for serious La Gravière or La Nord. Surf schools are everywhere. Boardingmania offer single lesson and week long training camps. Try to learn some French; it will be appreciated.

DAMIEN POULLENOT

## La Gravière

LAT. 43.666284° LONG. -1.443671°

Sited on an old gravel pit, this is the legendary Hossegor tube spot. Like all transient Landes sandbars, La Grav has its good years and bad years, but it's reliable enough to be the venue of choice for the annual pro-surfing competitions. Sometimes white-caps outside, rolls in and reforms, standing up over the shallow inside bars. Heavy, thick-lipped beasts, break perilously close to shore and often close-out, snapping more boards than just about anywhere. Tidal range radically affects the window for ideal conditions, as does swell period, which decides if it is messy and inconsistent or lined-up and bombing through. The rip speed usually rises in direct proportion with the swell height and on big days, only the tow crew will be able to get into the sets before being swept south in the current. Humbling for all, including the barrel experts and the pros. Spectator spot when big and usually rammed when smaller.

with barrel sections mean extra inches are a good idea. Can work at all tides but mid is the best bet. Heavy water when the rips are in full flow and La Nord is always crowded, often with the local SUP crew. Beside the rivermouth jetty, **La Sud** is always smaller and easier to handle than anywhere to the north. Far less current and a fuller wave profile gives beginner/improvers somewhere to surf away from the rippers. Plenty of straighthanders and turns into an unsurfable shorebreak on high tide. Tucked along the port's south jetty, **L'Estacade** is the ultimate shelter with laughable size compared to exposed beaches. Handles some N wind. Sometimes full and bloated, occasionally sucky and closing-out, but never perfect. Stronger winter swells concentrate surfers at **Le Prévent**, fighting for one of the steep, sucky, sand-churning slammers that might just hold up enough for a short, fast ride. There's often a left into the rips near the southern groyne and a stable right at the north end. Plenty of close-outs and terrible backwash on high tide. **Le Santocha** is the most regularly surfed wave in Capbreton, since it picks up swells that close-out the open beaches and forms up nice, fat peaks. Good drops followed by slopey walls and close-out inside section. A righthander tends to form along the groyne and it gets much hollower the further south you drift. **La Piste/VVF** is one of the most photographed beaches on the coast, thanks to perfect barrels being regularly on offer for those that can handle the air drops and some solid floggings amongst the packs of gifted locals and tube-hungry visitors. From low to mid tide is prime time, when the swell focuses on banks that seem to have a bit more punch and urgency than just about anywhere in Hossegor. **Capbreton Pointe** is actually just another stretch of the dead straight beach, but favourable sand formation can give the wave nice shape. Can be some bad vibes in the water and regular vehicle break-ins. With a moderate NW swell and offshores, heavy peaks, close to shore, provide tube time for the local **Labenne-Ocean** crew. **Tarnos Plage** is very similar to Labenne and Ondres, with weak low tide rides in small swell, before awakening in overhead to double-overhead W-NW swell and serving up chunky, powerful barrels. The extensive, curved jetty at **Boucau** helps shape the sandbanks and gives a little protection from S winds, but not from the pollution flowing out from the heavily industrialised Adour. Currents can be strong, but necessary to get out at size and only experienced surfers will handle the demanding, unfriendly line-up.

Consistent, high-latitude W-NW swells can reach up to 15ft, but the straight coastline has no protection from the dominant NW winds. As a cold front approaches, winds usually clock around from the SW to WNW, blowing-out the surf for several days with wet and windy conditions. When a high pressure system sits over the land, morning offshores are followed by a moderate NW sea breeze that blows from noon until dusk. The 4.5m tide factor is crucial and as the saying goes "If the waves look good, you've probably missed it".

DAMIEN POULLENOT

La Piste

STEPHAN MONTIEL

Boucau

| STATISTICS | | J F | M A | M J | J A | S O | N D |
|---|---|---|---|---|---|---|---|
| SWELL | Direction | | | | | | |
| | Size (ft) | 7-8 | 6-7 | 5 | 3 | 6 | 7 |
| WIND | Direction | | | | | | |
| | Force | F5 | F5 | F4 | F3 | F3 | F5 |
| WATER | Wetsuit | | | | | | |
| | Temp/°C | 12 | 13 | 17 | 21 | 18 | 15 |
| WEATHER | Rainfall/mm | 82 | 55 | 63 | 63 | 84 | 102 |
| | days/mth | 15 | 13 | 12 | 11 | 13 | 16 |
| | Min temp/°C | 2 | 5 | 11 | 14 | 10 | 4 |
| | Max temp/°C | 10 | 16 | 22 | 26 | 21 | 11 |

# Côte Basque FRANCE

The Côte Basque shares many characteristics with the north-facing Spanish coast and is blessed with some decent submarine geology. Slabs of reef dot the coast, focusing some of the most organised and unadulterated swell trains into scary, big-wave arenas, but there are also calm beginner coves, headlands, famous reefs and great jetty surf, offering a cornucopia of fun waves for all abilities and surfcraft.

- \+ VARIETY OF REEF AND BEACH
- \+ BEGINNER OR BIG-WAVE ZONE
- \+ SAME DAY SNOW AND SURF
- \+ RICH SURF CULTURE

- \- WET CLIMATE YEAR-ROUND
- \- POLLUTION/CROWDS IN SUMMER
- \- COLD WATER IN WINTER
- \- EXPENSIVE

Les Cavaliers

STEPHAN MONTIEL

Cotë des Basques

DAMIEN POULLENOT

The famous wave of **La Barre** has all but disappeared with the Adour river jetty extensions but peaks still form between the shorter jetties in heavy swells. Peak summer/autumn season often sees over 100 surfers in the water at **Les Cavaliers**, looking for tubes rivalling those of Hossegor or simply something to surf when everywhere else is flat. Handles stronger swells that unfurl over the outer banks at low tide, before edging inside and ending up as proper shore-dump for a couple of hours at high. Rips, pollution, surf schools and aggressive crowds bickering over the pretty A-frames. There's a lack of jetties and therefore less crowds sitting on the transient sandbars of Plage de l'Ocean, La Madrague through to Les Corsaires and Marinella, which can all be magic one day and junky the next, depending on the sand distribution and wind. Swell angle often dictates whether the longer **Sables d'Or** rights or hollower lefts will be better, with powerful tubes appearing on the good days. The jetty rips can help avoid a pounding when the swell jumps. Handles all tides and a bit more swell than the open spots just to the north. Crowds can be crazy with waterfront parking spots, surf shops and restaurants. **Le Club** often entertains a defined, bowly right off both the short and long jetty. When it works, good tubes are on offer, especially in the bodyboarder-friendly shorebreak at higher tides. **VVF**'s half-kilometre of sand pitches short sucky peaks or long, lined-up walls onto a variety of banks from the short jetty peak to the left in front of the crumbling cliffs below the lighthouse. All tides, all swell sizes up to 3m and it is nicely protected from all S winds. **Grande Plage** is the Basque coast's chic city beach that receives less swell than Anglet, but handles a very large variety of conditions. Rocks at the south end shape the banks and block S-SW winds. Sometimes the fat rolling peaks are fun and easy, other times they are sucky and close-out. **Côte des Basques** is popular with longboarders and surf schools enjoying mellow walls sheltered from northern winds. There's usually a peak close to the headland and another defined peak a bit further down the beach. High tide disappears the beach all the way down to Marbella and Milady. Better known for golfing and dining-out, **Ilbarritz** also hosts a couple of beaches that can produce good waves among the scattered reefs. It is often ill-defined and a mushy closeout, but lines up some shallow, bowly rights and a choice of peaks down the beach in front of the massive Camping Pavillion Royal. With mellow waves breaking over a mix of sand and rocks, **Erretegia** beach has long been popular with surf schools. Tucked beneath low cliffs, the beach all but disappears on big high tides so dropping tide is better on small to medium swell. **Bidart** has occasional memorable days with both fast walls outside and fun shorebreak hooks on the inside. Closes-out in bigger swells, is often crowded and there are some gnarly rocks to contend with. Next town of Guéthary is home to the rumbling rights of ✪**Parlementia**.

## TRAVEL INFORMATION

**Weather** – Due to the proximity of the Pyrenees mountains, it rains about 1500mm annually on the French Basque coast (1 day out of 2), which is less than the Spanish Basque country, but more than Hossegor. Summer stays light until 10pm and in the winter it's dark by 5.30pm. The weather is reasonably stable from March to October, although March/April will be much cooler than May/June or Sept/Oct, which are the prime months. Water temps bottom out at 11.3°C (53°F) in March then climb to 23.1°C (72°F) in August. Same wetsuit requirements as Hossegor.

**Lodging and Food** – Many hotels, from budget up to 4-star. On the N10, you can expect a double from $35, but the average in town is $50, especially in high season. Campsites are plentiful from May to September but beware of the wet climate. Typically, a restaurant bill is $20 not including wine. Hypermarkets have a huge selection of cheap food for self-caterers.

**Nature and Culture** – There is an aquarium in Biarritz and a Museum of Ocean and Surf (Cité de l'Océan et du Surf). The Longboard Surf Festival occurs in mid-July. If you are in the area in early August, then don't miss the Fete du Bayonne. Lots more festivals in October. Bars and nightclubs are very lively in peak season. The combination of sea and high mountains found in the Basque country make this area one of the most beautiful and enjoyable places in the world. Local sports that are well catered for include golf and mountain sports in the Pyrenees, whilst Pelote and Course du Vaches (jumping over charging cows in a bull ring) are interesting spectator sports.

**Hazards and Hassles** – Jetty rocks and shallow reefs can be threats. River runoff and tourist crowds equate to bad summer pollution, especially after storms. In the winter, beaches get covered in rubbish washed in by the big storms. Driving and parking are nightmarish during July and August.

**Handy Hints** – This is a developed area with everything you will need in the BAB (Biarritz, Anglet, Bayonne) city area. Some surf shops are open year-round and gear is expensive. You will need a gun to surf the reefs when they're big. The N10 major road can be annoyingly slow and the motorways are expensive, especially for vans. Apprenez du Français!

STEPHAN MONTIEL

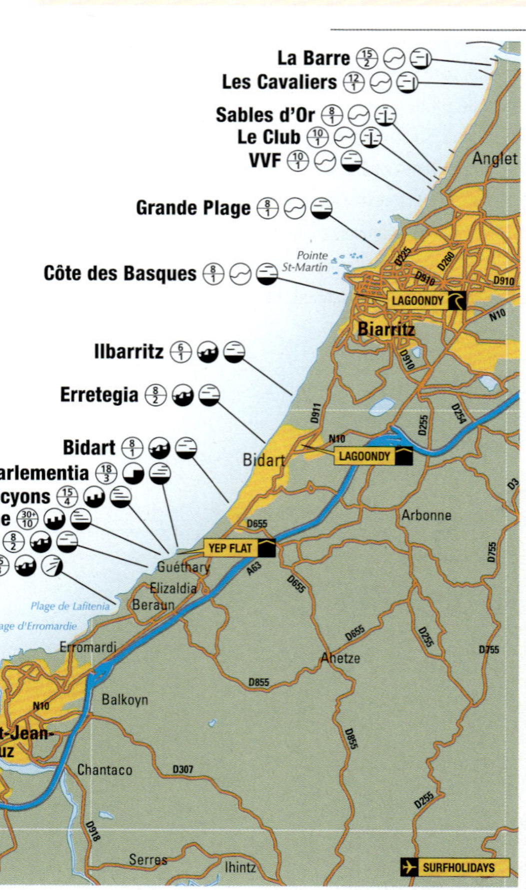

## Parlementia

LAT. 43.429882° LONG. -1.609024°

The Guéthary terrace gives the best view of this Sunset-like right with a shifting peak and short shoulder that holds up to 6m faces on a clean, NW swell. The outside bombora-style reef is quite deep, so the peak draws up a lot of water and only invites those on large, long, voluminous boards to get in early. There is also an attractive left off the peak, which rumbles back across the inner reef, sometimes walling up steeply or else sectioning and closing-out. On small to moderate days, faster rights break over this shallower reef shelf that entice the shortboarders, but eventually the sets off the west peak will punish with a circuit via the inside then the channel. Can be some fun, steeper, inside runners for the less gun happy and the wide playing field does give everybody a chance. Paddle out from the harbour to avoid the rock slalom at lower tides. Always deceptively bigger than it appears and it's always crowded with the longboard and pintail gun locals, who dominate the peak by knowing it backwards, plus a whole flotilla of others from groms and surf schools to granddads.

Across the bay, **Les Alcyons** short but powerful left reefbreak jacks on take-off and barrels across a shallow shelf. A heavy liquid and local current dominates the experts-only line-up. The outside reef of **Avalanche** is where a handful of experienced locals paddle into the biggest waves in the country and tow crews also frequent the line-up. Best on low tide, the long walls flex and flow with some high pockets and muscular shoulders. The rocky bay at **Cenitz** can tempt surfers to a few fun lefts and rights but needs a peaky swell and high tide to not close-out. Can be annoying with soft shoulders and not connecting up, but check on headhigh with more N in the swell. **Lafitenia** sculpts a beautiful righthand pointbreak, complete with steps in the steep take-off, that leads into a long fatter wall and occasionally hollow inside section. Frequented by multi ability surfers on various craft, it's a fairly friendly wave. Lower tides, any E wind and more W in the swell should get the wall lining up across the bay. The neighboring beaches of Mayarco and Erromardie usually lack quality. It's very rare for the enclosed, fashionable beach of St Jean de Luz to be worth riding, but a long right with a radical, sucky take-off wraps around the jetty on the north side of the bay at **Sainte-Barbe**. It then runs off through a series of wall to shoulder sections as it refracts around the reef for quite a distance to Inside Sainte-Barbe. Much closer to shore is Les Flots Bleus, a mini wave well-suited to kids and beginners. More N in the swell penetrates better, any NE to S wind will do and a dropping tide keeps it interesting. When it gets huge, spots work inside the bay near Ciboure or a soft peak breaks in the shadow of the Socoa Fort and it's offshore in a westerly. 2.5km offshore at **Belharra Perdun**, a 15m deep, seagrass covered shoal creates an A-frame peak on the two or three largest swells of the winter for the European tow-in crew. Has been a previous winner of the XXL contest with a wave estimated at 66ft. Only breaks on low tide unless it is psycho huge and can be watched from the coast road cliffs between Socoa and Hendaye. On the border with Spain, **Hendaye Plage** is the answer when everything else is closing-out. A long stretch of average beachbreaks offers a wide choice of peaks; usually better close to the casino or the south jetty. The place is perfect for beginners, which explains the amazing number of surf schools. Further out off the eastern headland is Vanthrax, an imaginatively named death peak that spews out massive left barrels a handful of times a year. Crazy bodyboarders and pros only.

LAURENT MASUREL

Sainte-Barbe

LAURENT MASUREL

Lafitenia

The coastline faces due west around to due north, catching the bulk of the very consistent North Atlantic swells. Unfortunately, it is not so well orientated for the dominant NW winds. When a low pressure approaches the coast, winds usually blow from the SW before turning WNW. Big storms are common and the surf can remain blown out for several days. Combine this with rain and cooler temperatures and it can get a little depressing! On the other hand, when a high pressure covers the country you will be blessed with sunny skies and in the mornings, light offshore breezes (about 1/3 of the time). In the afternoons it's usual for a light to moderate NW sea breeze to kick in. Tidal ranges can reach 4.50m on spring tides, at which time very few spots work properly, so timing the tides is crucial.

| STATISTICS | | J F | M A | M J | J A | S O | N D |
|---|---|---|---|---|---|---|---|
| SWELL | Direction | | | | | | |
| | Size (ft) | 7 | 6 | 4-5 | 2-3 | 5-6 | 6-7 |
| WIND | Direction | | | | | | |
| | Force | F5 | F5 | F4 | F3 | F3 | F5 |
| WATER | Wetsuit | | | | | | |
| | Temp/°C | 12 | 13 | 17 | 22 | 19 | 15 |
| WEATHER | Rainfall/mm | 132 | 126 | 105 | 84 | 130 | 161 |
| | days/mth | 14 | 13 | 12 | 12 | 14 | 16 |
| | Min temp/°C | 5 | 7 | 12 | 16 | 13 | 6 |
| | Max temp/°C | 12 | 15 | 20 | 24 | 22 | 14 |

# País Vasco SPAIN

The Basque Country is the most popular surfing area in Spain and it is not only because it is home to the world-class rivermouth called Mundaka. All types of reef can be found along this coast including mellow triangular peaks for longboarders or crazy, big-wave bombs for the chargers. There are also some good-quality beachbreaks, although these are not as prevalent as those in neighbouring France or Cantabria. The Basque Country or Pais Vasco in Spanish, picks up less swell than the rest of the north coast, particularly if it comes from the W, but in winter, there is rarely any lack of swell. There are also a host of spots surfable in stormy conditions and sheltered from strong W or SW winds. With its proximity to France and the highly populated coastal cities of San Sebastian and Bilbao, Pais Vasco has the highest level of surfing, the most crowds and the largest number of surf shops.

+ MAGICAL MUNDAKA!
+ HEAVY TUBING WAVES
+ FABULOUS SCENERY
+ EASY ACCESS

– CROWDED HOTSPOTS
– FEWER SUMMER SPOTS
– WINDY AND RAINY
– LARGE TIDAL RANGE

LAURENT MASUREL

Meñakoz to La Triangular

In downtown Donastia, **La Zurriola**'s crowded, consistent, medium-quality beachbreak can have good peaks on small swells; anything over about 5ft closes-out. Good luck parking in summer. Big city facilities including a surf school. Across the river, **Ondarreta** will start breaking when La Zurriola is overpowered, but dont expect much quality to the short, shorebreak straight-handers. Nicely tucked out of the strong SW or even W winds at the west end of the famous La Concha beach. Average beachbreak at **Orio** needs a large swell or stormy conditions to work. Sheltered from SW and OK on W winds. The higher the tide, the larger the swell needs to be before it breaks. **Zarautz** is very consistent, good quality and one of the most popular beachbreaks in Spain. Doesn't need much swell to work, although W swells struggle to get in here. A long beach with several peaks, mostly performance orientated. Competitive and always crowded in the water with a very high level of surfing. Dangerous and aptly named big-wave righthander **Roca Puta** starts perilously close to the uneven rocks with a critical first section into rapid tubular walls. Needs a large, clean, winter swell to work properly and clear the jumble of nasty rocks. Difficult entry and exit to a tight local line-up. There's a short, poor quality, semi-closeout beachbreak near the harbour wall of **Orrua**. Better at low tide, **Zumaia** is another consistent, small-wave beachbreak with good peaks when the banks are right. There are more big-wave spots and secrets along the snaky mountainous coast road to the picturesque fishing town of Lekeitio. **Carraspio**, a rivermouth beachbreak facing NE, provides some W wind shelter, but needs a fairly large swell to wrap in. Consistent **Laga** usually has good to excellent beachbreak, sometimes producing barrels. OK on most tides although the sandbars are very changeable. Sometimes crowded, especially at weekends. Picturesque spot in a pine forest with impressive cliffs, so it attracts summer beachgoers from nearby Gernika. **Laida** can be surfed as an uncrowded alternative to Mundaka or Laga on smaller days. Average beachbreak that's fairly consistent at low to mid tide. Easiest access is by paddling across the river from ✪**Mundaka**, a delightful fishing village and home to one of the world's best waves. The average to good lefthand pointbreak at **El Basurero** only works on the very biggest swells of the year when Mundaka closes-out. Sheltered from W and NW winds, it's better at low tide when some hazardous rocks appear. **Bakio** is a very consistent, popular beachbreak that can produce excellent waves with some barrel sections. People come here from Mundaka when the swell is small, adding to the already large local surfing population. Sandbar lefthander between a rivermouth and the pier, **Plentzia** breaks on large swells only, at low to mid tide. Sheltered from W and NW winds, it's moderately consistent in the winter and can be very crowded with longboarders at weekends. **Barrika** boasts consistent beachbreak with several shifting peaks. Works best on small swells at low to mid tide as the beach cuts off at high tide. Beware of uneven submerged rocks. Reasonably uncrowded with friendly locals and plenty of parking. Just to the west, **Meñakoz** is another world-class wave in the Basque zone. It's one of the most powerful, regularly-surfed waves in Europe and a highly dangerous big-wave spot. Starts breaking properly at about 12 foot. Hazards include

## TRAVEL INFORMATION

**Weather** – Bizkaia province is subject to a changeable climate with numerous storms produced by the high latitude lows travelling from W to E. The mountains rising up directly behind the coast produce plenty of orographic rainfall as moisture sweeps in from Biscay. On average one day out of two sees rainfall, mainly in the autumn and winter, which is prime surf season. October water temps can fluctuate between 16-21ºC (61-70ºF) before bottoming out in March around 11ºC (53ºF). A 4/3 with boots will usually suffice on all but the coldest days or rivermouth sessions.

**Lodging and Food** – A myriad of accommodation options in the cities and most towns will have some surfer-friendly hotel or pensión for a reasonable price. Mundaka Portuondo campsite is open year-round and has low season 3 bed bungalows from $98/n. Pensions or hotels in Mundaka/Bermeo, start from $76/dble in low season, but farm guest houses are a good option in this area. Tapas bars are a great Spanish institution.

**Nature and Culture** – With San Sebastian and Bilbao to choose from, entertainment is not hard to find. Visit the Guggenheim or head to the nearby city of Pamplona in July for Spain's biggest street party, the Fiesta San Fermin with the famous Running of the Bulls. Urdaibi Valley is a UN protected biosphere with caves and monasteries worth visiting.

**Hazards and Hassles** – You have to be fit to survive a Mundaka session, the clean up sets, impact zone, long paddles and the rips quickly tire you out. Some guys wear helmets when it's packed. Localism used to be very severe, now it's just a very competitive line-up. Avoid week-ends, noon and the best tide.

**Handy Hints** – This is the home of Pukas, Europe's largest board shaping factory, which burnt down in 2017, but reopened in 2018 and has surf shops in Zarautz and San Sebastian. Mundaka Surf Shop has the full spectrum of equipment for sale or rent. Early risers will get a bit more space in the line-up. Free-camping the car parks in your van will attract attention and tickets in the summer.

DAMIEN POULLENOT

**Mundaka**

LAT. 43.408915° LONG. -2.695038°

A dream lefthand barrel and possibly the best rivermouth wave in the world. A long triangular sandbank builds up over summer and catches the stronger winter NW swells, creating a long flawless tube with rides of up to 150-200 meters possible. From the peak, the wave sucks up hard, making for steep challenging take-offs straight into a sick barrel section. The ensuing long, fast wall, allows a few turns if you are going close to warp speed. The final two sections of the wave can vary in quality depending on the sandbar, but frequently they offer difficult to negotiate, hollow cylinders with less crowd pressure. Perfect conditions include strong S-SW winds, low incoming tide and the first long period NW swell of autumn. Always crowded, which adds to the danger. Be careful of the handy outgoing rip in the rivermouth on the drop. Parking can be difficult when the wave is on. Camping and surf shop nearby.

razor-sharp rocks, very strong rips, shifting peaks, two-wave hold-downs, broken boards and broken bones. The locals won't tolerate inexperienced surfers or tow-ins here either. Picturesque amphitheatre-like setting, ideal for watching the surf. Moderately consistent, medium-quality lefthand reefbreak at **El Sitio** only works at low tide on small, well-lined-up swells. Locals can be a little hostile and this spot is right near a sewage outlet. **Sopelana** is a very consistent beachbreak and one of the most crowded, highly competitive spots in Spain. There are several spots working on small to medium swells, including the ripable, semi-permanent, high-tide peak at the western end of the beach. Every facility available including surf school, surf shops and camping nearby. A short, bowly lefthander shows at **La Triangular** reef when a lined-up moderate W swell swings across the fingers of rock. Has a bad habit of protruding rocks appearing during the ideal surfing window of low tide. Small crowded take-off zone. La Derecha de la Triangular sits at the eastern end of La Salvaje beach modelling as an excellent long righthand reef/pointbreak. Rather slow on smaller swells, it doesn't get going until a medium W swells hits at mid-high tide. Nice predictable walls making half the thick crowd ride longboards. Hazards include a strong rip and some barely submerged rocks. La Salvaje itself has very consistent, good-quality beachbreak with two semi-permanent peaks, mostly lefthanders. Surfable on small to medium swells at all tides. Always crowded and highly competitive. Parking is OK in winter, but restricted and metered in summer. Good beach facilities plus surf shops and camping nearby. Big Wave Tour venue **La Galea** is a highly dangerous right point breaking into the Bilbao rivermouth. Needs big lined-up swell, so only works well a few times a year. OK on NE winds and always uncrowded. Difficult entry and exit over razor-sharp rocks and very polluted. Sheltered deeper inside the Bilbao rivermouth, Yeffrys is a long, sectiony right point that only works a few times a year on the biggest swells, along with average beachbreak at Ereaga, but both will be extremely polluted, with a bathing ban still in force.

In general, the winter is the best time to visit when the low pressure systems come through more southerly latitudes, pumping out big NW swells, which means offshore SW winds for the north-facing coast. This northerly aspect is not so good for the small W swells of summer, when heading further west to Cantabria is a good idea. Good conditions at Mundaka rarely last for more than two days, as the large swells required, drop off. Therefore, this classy wave is only rideable about 50 days a year. The Urdaibi Valley funnels SW winds into a more southerly direction, whilst when a high pressure covers the country, the wind will frequently turn N-NE in the afternoons, the worst wind direction. Tide heights top out at 4.5m at Bermeo, and greatly effect the wave quality.

JAVIER AMEZAGA

La Galea

| STATISTICS | | J F | M A | M J | J A | S O | N D |
|---|---|---|---|---|---|---|---|
| SWELL | Direction | | | | | | |
| | Size (ft) | 5-6 | 4-5 | 3-4 | 2 | 4-5 | 5-6 |
| WIND | Direction | | | | | | |
| | Force | F5 | F5 | F4 | F3 | F3 | F5 |
| WATER | Wetsuit | | | | | | |
| | Temp/°C | 12 | 13 | 15 | 19 | 17 | 14 |
| WEATHER | Rainfall/mm | 105 | 82 | 78 | 75 | 125 | 140 |
| | days/mth | 15 | 13 | 13 | 12 | 14 | 17 |
| | Min temp/°C | 7 | 9 | 12 | 16 | 13 | 9 |
| | Max temp/°C | 12 | 15 | 19 | 22 | 19 | 14 |

# Asturias SPAIN

In Asturias, the mountains run close to the coast, creating a rugged, difficult to access coastline of sheer cliffs and steep-sided valleys. Small offshore islets interfere with the swell and many rocky coves have poor waves, but there are some excellent west-facing beachbreaks that are offshore in the summer NE sea breezes. Regional classic rivermouth Rodiles works on larger autumn to winter swells so there is usually something to surf all-year-round.

+ EPIC LEFT RIVERMOUTH
+ CONSISTENT YEAR-ROUND SWELLS
+ MANY EXPOSED BEACHBREAKS
+ EMPTY REMOTE BEACHES

- WET AND WINDY
- COLD WINTER WATER
- STEEP, SLOW ACCESS
- CROWDED SUMMERS

WILLY URIBE

Rodiles

**Rodiles** is the best wave in Asturias, forming up a world-class rivermouth lefthander similar to Mundaka, but slightly shorter and handles less size. Needs a moderate winter NW swell, 2hrs either side of low to produce lengthy walls with inviting pull-in sections. Always crowded, heavy localism, strong rips, car crime and estuarine pollution. The small beach at **Playa España** can have one or two good peaks plus some higher tide shorebreaks. **Peñarrubia**'s medium-quality lefthand reefbreak is best at low to mid tide and needs a fair swell to get going. Flanked by the playas Cagonera and Cervigon, where a low tide left reef breaks. **El Mongol** is Gijon's best wave, a powerful righthand reefbreak that needs a big NW swell to work. Gets going at headhigh, closes-out at double that. Best at high tide. Average-quality, city centre beachbreak **San Lorenzo**, picks up a limited amount of swell, but is surfable during most tides and SW winds. Often crowded, with surf school, surf shops and bars at hand. **Luanco**'s east-facing beachbreak and ultra-hollow, outside righthand reef only work on the biggest of swells. **Verdicio** consistently picks up plenty of swell, but the low tide sandbars between the rocky outcrops are pretty average with slow corners or close-outs. West-facing **Xago** is an ultra-consistent beachbreak with good peaks at all tides and shelter from summer NE sea breezes. Stretching from Playa El Espartal to **Salinas**, this is one of the most popular surfing beaches in Asturias. Fast, barrelling, consistent beachbreak peaks, working during all tides and summer NE sea breezes. In the small holiday resort of **Santa Maria del Mar**, average beachbreaks plus a fickle lefthand reef will appear on moderate NW swells around mid tide. Long, dune-backed **Playón de Bayas** has plenty of shifting, all tide peaks. Extremely consistent and a swell magnet, E winds, lower tide and a summer NW swell should line up the banks. Standard beachbreak peaks at **Aguilar** are helped by some large rocky outcrops to shape the sandbars. Works during most stages of the tide, but W swells won't get in. **Cadavedo** is very sheltered, east-facing beachbreak and only an option on huge swells and stormy conditions. **Cueva**'s high quality, west-facing beachbreak matches rivermouth rights at the eastern end with rocky lefts at the other end. Very consistent. Best low to mid tide. **Otur** is a good option for small swells, works on most tides and gets hollower as it drops to low. Top quality, consistent beachbreak **Frejulfe** works on all tides – low for the eastern rivermouth and incoming to high for the rocky western end. Nearby Navia has a right reef at Moro and dirty lefts at the town beach.

## TRAVEL INFORMATION

**Weather** – The climate is humid, with mild, year-round temps, however weather patterns are unstable. Summer days are often cloudy and winters are very mild and rainy, even though the mountains may be cloaked in snow. A 4/3mm suit will cover all but the coldest winter days and spring thaws at the freezing rivermouths. During summer, a light steamer/springsuit combo will be needed as it gets colder further west.

**Lodging and Food** – Almost every Spanish beach has a campground with amenities: Rodiles has 3! They are cheap and very lively in summer. If you want to stay dry, look for pensions (P), hostels (Hs), or hotels (H) depending on budget. Beach hotels tend to be expensive. Meals cost $18. Local tapas are tasty, but they can leave an empty stomach and wallet!

**Nature and Culture** – Asturias offers 9th century "prerománica" architecture, in the old part of the Principado capital, Oviedo (with its Gothic cathedral) and Avilés. Check the high Picos de Europa (Covadonga), enjoy local music and apple cider fiestas in fall.

**Hazards and Hassles** – Hazards include polluted line-ups, summer jellyfish, rocks and jetties in rough seas, strong riptides and fishing lines. Localism can be heavy at urban spots and Rodiles.

**Handy Hints** – Avoid temporada alta (high season, summer), hotel prices double up and driving is crazy. In winter, you'll need a gun for serious spots (Mongol, Cabo Lastres). Tablas surf shop in Gijon sells all equipment and has a surf school plus webcam.

**Tapia** is a popular surfing beach and contest site that's often crowded thanks to a good-quality, consistent beachbreak with semi-permanent, hollow lefthander, fed by a stream. Best mid to low tide, outgoing, with some shelter from NE sea breezes in summer, but it is a year-round wave.

Swells arrive from the W and then shift to the NW and even due N while the low pressures track eastwards. Winds will start SW, sometimes at gale-force, before clocking W then NW as the front goes by. Summers suffer long flat spells and the light afternoon sea breeze is NW-NE. High pressure means constant S-SE in winter and morning offshores that can whistle down the valleys. Autumn is the best season but Dec-March can be a consistent period, with cool weather and potential for perfect surf. Tidal variation is huge (up to 4.15m), keeping surf session windows brief.

| STATISTICS | | J F | M A | M J | J A | S O | N D |
|---|---|---|---|---|---|---|---|
| SWELL | Direction | | | | | | |
| | Size (ft) | 5-6 | 4-5 | 3-4 | 2-3 | 4-5 | 5-6 |
| WIND | Direction | | | | | | |
| | Force | F4-F5 | F4-F5 | F4 | F3-F4 | F4 | F4-F5 |
| WATER | Wetsuit | | | | | | |
| | Temp/°C | 12 | 13 | 15 | 19 | 17 | 14 |
| WEATHER | Rainfall/mm | 105 | 83 | 78 | 75 | 125 | 143 |
| | days/mth | 15 | 14 | 14 | 12 | 14 | 17 |
| | Min temp/°C | 7 | 9 | 13 | 16 | 14 | 9 |
| | Max temp/°C | 12 | 15 | 19 | 22 | 20 | 14 |

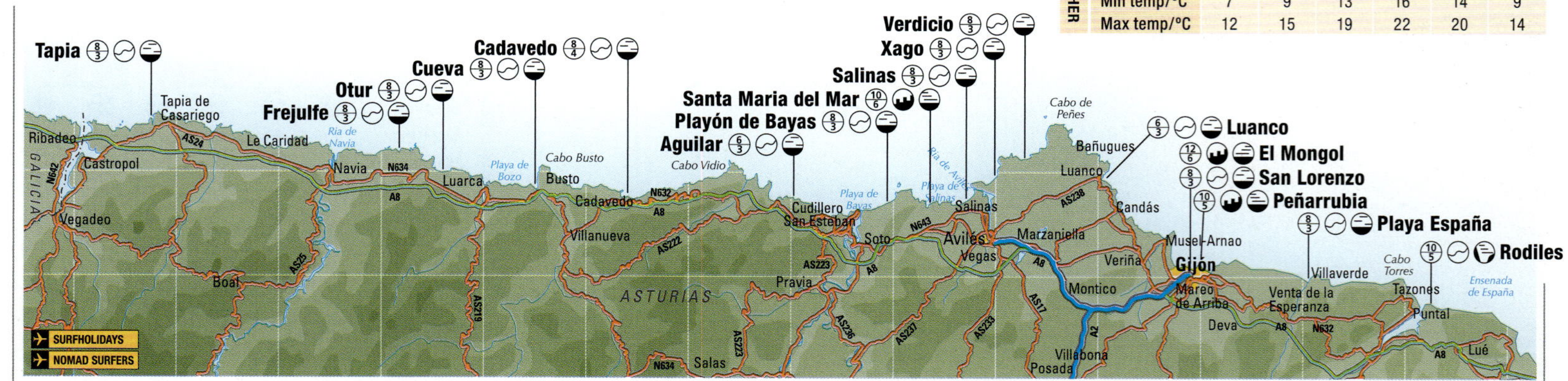

# Northwest Galicia SPAIN

Galicia's landscape of steep forested hills hidden behind clouds of misty drizzle earned it the "end of the world" nickname from the Romans. Since then, the Celtic inhabitants have been left alone in this un-Spanish corner of Iberia. Plunging valleys cut across the landscape, leading to large inlets and estuaries called rias. Similar to fjords, these flooded valleys deeply punctuate the coastline, and effectively filter the consistent North Atlantic swells. Galicia has mainland Europe's largest swell window and the jagged coastline means somewhere will always be offshore.

+ 180° SWELL WINDOW
+ MULTIPLE SWELL/WIND OPTIONS
+ BEAUTIFUL COUNTRYSIDE
+ CAMPERVAN FRIENDLY

- UNSTABLE CLIMATE
- YEAR-ROUND COOL WATER
- NO WORLD-CLASS BREAKS
- LONG DRIVES, HARD ACCESS

**Baleo** is a very consistent beachbreak with several decent peaks at lower tides that get crowd overspill from Pantín. Strong rips so beginners should try protected Villarube. **Rodo (Pantín)** is the most popular surf spot in Galicia and annual pro contest site. Ultra consistent, Pantin hoovers up W-NW swell into lined-up left and right peaks that barrels at low to mid but surfable on all tides. Strong rips with paddling channel at northern end. Similar conditions get **Valdoviño** going, with excellent quality peaks along the long arcing beach. There's a hollow right off a rocky island and a lagoon in the centre. **Campelo** offers challenging, walled-up beachbreak, with regular barrel sections, even on small swells, when low to mid tide is best. **Ponzos** holds another consistent, all tides beachbreak that makes the best of a NW swell at low tide and is OK on SW winds. Beautiful crescent of west-facing beachbreak at **San Xorxe** offers some S wind protection for the lefts in the southern corner and various other rippy peaks along length of beach. **Doniños** is the most popular wave in the area, thanks to superior quality and consistency along 2km's of swell sucking peaks that are hollowest at low to mid tide. Can be very crowded with surfers from Ferrol hence a degree of localism. A Coruña's crowded city beach **Riazor Orzán** needs some N in the swell and lower tide, but it is often a mushy close-out. Soft lefts and steeper rights at the north end channel. **Sabón** is a far more consistent, crowded and shapely low tide summer beachbreak, but the massive port construction has cut swell exposure and added to the river pollution. **Barrañan** receives lesser quality beachbreaks, but it's a reliable ride at mid to high tide. Check Valcobo for some rampy peaks. **Caion** is well-orientated to pick up tiny W-NW swells at this quality summer beachbreak. Usually best at mid tide, depending on sandbars. **Razo**'s big, open beachbreak is surfable when surrounding spots are too small. Excellent quality, fast, walled-up peelers, working on all tides. OK on SW winds, but destroyed by NW. Sheltered from W swells and winds, **Malpica** becomes a destination beachbreak when medium to large N swells turn on the punchy peaks. Lower tides can get crowded, sparking isolated cases of localism. If the beautiful, extensive, deserted beach at **Traba** is flat, then everywhere is. Highly changeable sandbars shaped by strong rips. Many similar west-facing beaches to the south (Nemiña, Larino/Louro, Rio Siera) or the crowded reef and beachbreaks of Patos near Vigo.

LAURENT MASUREL
Pantin

## TRAVEL INFORMATION

**Weather** – Galicia is the windiest, rainiest and cloudiest part of the country. Temperature variations are minimal throughout the year, with mild winters and gentle summers. Autumn and winter are the rainiest times but the good news is the rainfall never lasts long, as the weather can change many times during the day. The water is quite cold from the Canaries Current plus upwelling, dropping to 12°C (54°F) and maxing out at 20°C (68°F).

**Lodging and Food** – There are dozens of summer (May-Oct) campsites, ideal for campervans. There are pensions and Airbnb choices in Valdoviño and Doniños (±$30/n). Ferrol has some hotels from $38/n. Great seafood.

**Nature and Culture** – The region of Galicia to the south of Coruña is extremely picturesque. Ferrol has lots of bars and clubs for a large student population. The cultural highlight of a visit to Galicia is the famous pilgrimage town of Santiago de Compostela, which parties in late July. Spain's only surf museum, Océano Surf Museo, is in Valdoviño.

**Hazards and Hassles** – The strong rips in the rias, cold water and the unpredictable weather patterns are the main concerns. Beachbreaks near the main towns get busy in summer with parking problems. Some localism, particularly at Patos.

**Handy Hints** – Surf shops in Patos, Santiago and Vigo. A campervan is the best way to see and surf Galicia with plenty of freecamps, especially out of season.

DAN HAYLOCK
Razo

Jutting out into the Atlantic, Galicia gathers any swell from the SW to the NE. Straight W-NW swells average 4-15ft in winter and 2-10ft in the summer, when they tend to be from a more northerly direction. Many weather systems and up to 200 swells a year buffet this coast, but they are frequently disorganised and messy. The dominant wind is a strong W, more NW in summer and then SW in winter. The ideal surf conditions are a moderate W swell breaking into light east winds. Tidal ranges hit 4m in La Coruna, and play a big part in deciding where and when you will be surfing.

| STATISTICS | | J F | M A | M J | J A | S O | N D |
|---|---|---|---|---|---|---|---|
| SWELL | Direction | | | | | | |
| | Size (ft) | 6-7 | 5-6 | 4 | 2-3 | 5-6 | 6 |
| WIND | Direction | | | | | | |
| | Force | F4-F5 | F4-F5 | F4 | F3-F4 | F4 | F4-F5 |
| WATER | Wetsuit | | | | | | |
| | Temp/°C | 12 | 13 | 15 | 18 | 17 | 14 |
| WEATHER | Rainfall/mm | 99 | 80 | 50 | 38 | 75 | 130 |
| | days/mth | 13 | 14 | 12 | 10 | 14 | 16 |
| | Min temp/°C | 7 | 8 | 12 | 15 | 13 | 8 |
| | Max temp/°C | 13 | 16 | 19 | 23 | 21 | 14 |

# Minho and Douro PORTUGAL

Sitting on the western edge of Europe, Portugal has always been a little bit different. The northern provinces of Minho and Douro have largely skipped the attention of visiting surfers, despite having a super-consistent stretch of coast that grabs the maximum from any swell direction. There's a wide range of wave breaking surfaces from gentle beaches and rivermouths to sheer slab reefs.

+ HIGH SUMMER CONSISTENCY
+ LOTS OF OPEN BEACHBREAKS
+ LESS CROWDED THAN THE SOUTH
+ CULTURAL PORTO

- LACK OF EPIC POINTBREAKS
- COOL WATER IN SUMMER
- WETTEST REGION IN PORTUGAL
- POLLUTED AROUND PORTO

**Moledo do Minho** is a north Portugal hot spot with some reefs producing sectiony lefts at the southern end of the beach. The river that marks the border of Portugal and Spain forms a sandbar for hollow rights that can be epic when the currents, swells and tides all align. The huge beach at **Vila Praia de Âncora** produces fun, consistent sandbar peaks. The south end picks up more swell – NW is best. **Afife** has been likened to Supertubos, but without the crowds. Consistent and very fast, hollow peaks spit surfers out of barrels all over the place. SW swell and low to mid tide is best. With the power comes strong currents. **Viana do Castelo** is worth checking on a decent NW swell when the jetty can provide some hollow sheltered waves or head to the southern end of the beach for powerful peaks on smaller days. Very consistent west-facing beachbreaks stretch away to the north of **Esposende** and crowds are minimal in Portugal's coldest water. A series of jetties at **Fão** keep the sandbars stable and a decent, uncrowded peak can normally be found for beginners and improvers. **Aguçadoura** has a seemingly endless stretch of crowd-free beach that gathers any swell going, but is easily maxed-out. Different banks work at different stages of the tide and the water is super-clean. A large rock in the centre of **Póvoa do Varzim** beach can provide a high-class, short, sharp, shallow left. Outgoing tide and SW swell will attract many to this tight, tense take-off zone. A decent left breaks off a bunch of rocks on the **Vila do Conde** central beach. It's a short and hollow ride that gets busy. The consistent beach peaks of **Azuara** are nothing special unless the rivermouth bar lines up, but the high tide shorebreak is a hit with spongers. The first spot north of Porto with genuinely clean water. **Perafita** and neighbouring Praia do Aterro are backed by some serious factories, making the rocky low tide left off the point and the scrappy beachbreaks less appealing. There are similar concerns with water quality at **Leça**, where the harbour breakwall helps to shape up good sandbars and E offshores will hold the barrels open. If it's flat here then its flat everywhere. The north end of **Matosinhos** beach is sheltered by a large breakwater, which makes it a good option in massive NW swells. The south end peaks near the rocks are much more consistent and best at lower tides. High pollution risk, especially after rains, yet it is the most popular beach attracting all the surf schools. Semi sheltered sandbar waves at **Luz** prefer rights and can never be described as Portugal's best or cleanest wave. A rivermouth breakwall has killed the excellent Barra do Porto on the south side of the River Douro. **Miramar** island sitting just offshore has an occasional hollow, fast and high quality right barrelling off the shallow reef. A polluted stream flows straight into the line-up. **Espinho** is north Portugal's busiest and hassley jetty break. It runs through to the inside as a fast, walled up, sometimes tubey right that finally dies as a close-out over shallow rocks.

RICARDO BRAVO

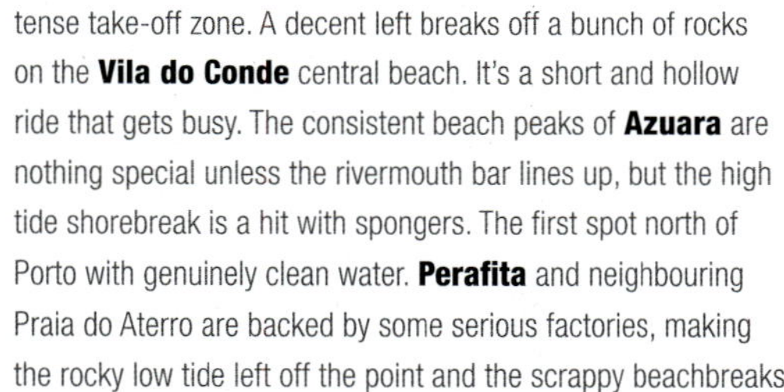
Aguçadoura

Portugal is hyper-consistent, year-round and often receives 8-10ft W-NW swells in winter and a solid 4-6ft W-NNW in summer. Dominant la Nortada winds are moderate NW-N, blowing from April to September. Summer sea breezes often mess up the waves and winter sees more SE-SW. Semi-diurnal tides reach up to 3.6m, shutting down many beachbreaks.

LAURENT MASUREL

Espinho

## TRAVEL INFORMATION

**Weather** – The typical maritime temperate climate means summers are sunny and gentle with occasional heat waves or oceanic fronts can bring rainy periods for a few days. Winter temps can occasionally drop below 0°C (32°F) at night and the weather is often rainy and windy for long stretches, although prolonged sunny periods do occur. Rain increases in frequency between September and late October. Water temp from 12°C in March to almost 20°C in autumn (54-68°F).

**Lodging and Food** – Surfivor Camp and school in Esmoriz has packages from $330/wk or dorm and breakfast from $18/n. Many pousadas, hotels, Airbnb and great camping in summer; Orbitür campsite in Viana do Castelo. Large variety of seafood, expect around $15 for a decent meal; try the caldo verde.

**Nature and Culture** – Visit Porto and its 1000yr old historic centre, classified by Unesco. Also taste the typical wine called Porto. The region is home to many wineries, try the Vinho Verde Route. Serra da Estrela mountains are 3h from Porto.

**Hazards and Hassles** – Pollution is a major problem around Porto where the Douro river flows large amounts of industrial and residential effluent into the bordering line-ups, forcing beach closures that ban swimming and surfing. Locals can be protective of some spots, but are much less defensive on the roads - beware. Watch your belongings, especially if you're camping.

**Handy Hints** – Main surf schools are Os Perafinas in Vila do Conde, Salty Wave, Flower Power and Onda Pura in Matosinhos. Surf supplies are available in the main surf hubs, try the Big Wave Surf Shop in Vila do Conde. Ear plugs can be useful to avoid diseases due to high pollution level.

| STATISTICS | | J F | M A | M J | J A | S O | N D |
|---|---|---|---|---|---|---|---|
| SWELL | Direction | | | | | | |
| | Size (ft) | 6-7 | 5-6 | 4 | 3 | 5 | 6 |
| WIND | Direction | | | | | | |
| | Force | F4-F5 | F4-F5 | F4 | F3-F4 | F4 | F4-F5 |
| WATER | Wetsuit | | | | | | |
| | Temp/°C | 12 | 13 | 15 | 18 | 17 | 14 |
| WEATHER | Rainfall/mm | 137 | 120 | 63 | 23 | 77 | 158 |
| | days/mth | 17 | 15 | 10 | 5 | 13 | 18 |
| | Min temp/°C | 5 | 8 | 12 | 14 | 13 | 7 |
| | Max temp/°C | 13 | 17 | 21 | 25 | 22 | 16 |

# Peniche PORTUGAL

The age-old seafaring traditions are strong in Peniche, which is home to one of Portugal's biggest fishing fleets. Peniche is on a small peninsula at right angles to the Portuguese coast creating wind and swell protection on either side. Just to the north, rising out of the submarine canyon, Nazaré detonates some of the biggest, scariest waves on the planet.

+ WIDE SWELL WINDOW
+ FLEXIBLE WIND/SWELL COMBOS
+ QUALITY BEACHES AND REEFS
+ CHEAP EURO DESTINATION

- SUMMER ONSHORES
- INCREASINGLY CROWDED
- COOL WATER YEAR-ROUND
- SARDINE FACTORY STINK!

RICARDO BRAVO

Supertubos

**Nazaré** has become a global big-wave phenomenon, thanks to a finger of deep water that points directly at the beach, beckoning some of the largest surfable waves on the planet to smash onto the sands of Praia Norte. Huge, heavy and sometimes hollow beach peaks for the insanely brave. Currents can be strong, and giant clean up sets are guaranteed when it's on, which isn't that often as it's fully wind-exposed. The main town beach offers a sheltered little wedge on big swells. The huge wind and swell exposed beach at **Foz do Arelho** is punctured by a couple of small rivermouths that form good banks with minimal crowds. It's basically the same beach 10km south at **Ferrel**, where the shifting peaks are super-consistent until the N winds shred it. The languid **Lagide** left is a long ride over a shallow, urchin-sprinkled reef. Low tide is sharp and shallow and high tide a little bouncy at this consistent crowded favourite. The long, curving, scalloped **Praia do Baleal** is offshore in any S winds. The centre of the beach gathers plenty of swell whilst the corners are good on big and windy days, attracting many surf schools. It takes a big SW swell and N winds to awaken **Molho Leste**'s wedging peak beside the harbour wall. The thick righthand barrels require expertise to manage the air drops and speed to beat the crunching lip. Rippy, localised spot. **Supertubos** has become a regular stop on the world pro tour and a perfect warm-up for Pipeline. Long, heavy, gas-filled tubes are guaranteed as well as a few shut-down close-outs, such is the speed of this wave. The lefts are usually better, but plenty of shorter rights peel off the main peak, especially in NW conditions. It's at its best with NE winds, a decent SW swell and mid-tide, but these conditions don't come around everyday. There can be a few lesser peaks further along the beach to help dilute the concentration of bodyboarders and local tube-seekers, but there's no escaping the mega crowds. A long, fat right that gets seriously big, breaks to the south of **Consolação** headland, while to the north is a much more fickle but hollow left. Both waves are very heavy and the right has good N wind shelter. Further south down towards the Ericeira zone are a series of long beaches and the occasional mediocre reef. Check from Areia Branca to Santa Cruz in small summer swells, plus Praia Azul for a quiet, consistent, high quality beachbreak with some wind shelter.

Portugal is the European yardstick for year-round consistency, and Peniche stylishly handles the regular NW swells. Average swell size is around 8-10ft in winter and summer is usually in the 4-6ft range. Storms are pretty frequent, but the peninsulas give flexibility during different wind and swell combinations. The Nortada is the dominant wind, blowing from the NW-N from April to September. Winter winds come from all directions but the standard pattern sees more NE-E winds and the occasional storms bringing S-SW winds. Max tidal range hits 3.6m and greatly affect where you surf.

## TRAVEL INFORMATION

**Weather** – The climate in Portugal is very pleasant year-round. Ericeira and Peniche are in the middle of the country, stuck between the dry Algarve and the damp regions north of Porto. The wettest season starts in November and lasts until March-April, and there is even snow in the Serra da Estrela (the snow resorts are only reliable in February). The best climate occurs during the change over seasons, even though mid-summer rarely gets too hot on the coast. The Nortada (north winds) always cool things down and conspire with the cold Canarian Current to prevent the water from ever reaching boardshorts temperature. A light 2/2 or 3/2 steamer will do except in mid-winter when a 4/3 and boots are necessary. August can see any temp between 17-22°C (63-72°F) and March can drop to 13°C (56°F).

**Lodging and Food** – Unless it's high season (June-Sept), finding quartos (rooms) or flats in Baleal/Peniche is easy, ask at the tourismo or try the pensaoes on Rua Jose Estevao in the old town. Baleal Surf Camp has 2 prime locations and a well-respected surf school. A meal costs around $12. Tasca do Joel is the restaurant frequented by the pros when the tour comes to town. Don't let the fish factory stench put you off the national dish of grilled sardines.

**Nature and Culture** – Don't miss Obidos, the fortified city to the east. Take a trip to the Berlenga islands, a bird-filled National Park, with nice beaches and snorkelling.

**Hazards and Hassles** – Portuguese bodyboarding is big, and it's the bodyboarders who control the line-ups, particularly at Molho Leste and Lagide. The atmosphere in the water is cool.

**Handy Hints** – There are a handful of surf shops in Peniche with good boards available; try Surfers Lab. Waves on the south side of the peninsula break harder than the more crumbly waves on the north side. There are lots of surf schools at Baia and Baleal Surf Camp do lessons and rentals.

LAURENT MASUREL

Nazaré

| STATISTICS | | J F | M A | M J | J A | S O | N D |
|---|---|---|---|---|---|---|---|
| SWELL | Direction | | | | | | |
| | Size (ft) | 5-6 | 5-6 | 4 | 3 | 4-5 | 5-6 |
| WIND | Direction | | | | | | |
| | Force | F2 | F2 | F2 | F2 | F3 | F3 |
| WATER | Wetsuit | | | | | | |
| | Temp/°C | 13 | 14 | 16 | 18 | 17 | 15 |
| WEATHER | Rainfall/mm | 90 | 80 | 30 | 4 | 31 | 100 |
| | days/mth | 10 | 8 | 4 | 1 | 6 | 10 |
| | Min temp/°C | 8 | 11 | 14 | 17 | 15 | 9 |
| | Max temp/°C | 15 | 19 | 23 | 28 | 25 | 16 |

# Ericeira PORTUGAL

As with Peniche, Ericeira has no shortage of Atlantic swell to play with. Numerous classic reef set-ups, rocky headlands and small rivermouth bays shape the swells into world-class waves such as Coxos. Ericeira can be considered the centre of Portuguese surfing with its concentration of classy breaks a mere 30km from Lisbon. It lacks much wind protection but for consistent, quality and challenging waves, Ericeira rules.

+ SUPER-CONSISTENT
+ CONCENTRATION OF SPOTS
+ WORLD-CLASS REEFS/POINTS
+ SKILLED SURFER PLAYGROUND

– FEW SHELTERED BREAKS
– LIMITED WIND OPTIONS
– COOL WATER YEAR-ROUND
– ALWAYS CROWDED

RICARDO BRAVO

Ribeira d'Ilhas

DAMIEN POULLENOT

Coxos

**São Lourenço**'s heavy right is one of Portugal's best-known big wave spots that can easily hold triple overhead, shifting, powerful and hollow surf. Big clean-up sets sweep in from the west, so organised NW swells are the best. Point/reefbreak gem **Coxos** peels down a series of rocky shelves and outcrops into a small bay. Coxos is long, fast and hollow when it hits the slabs just right, providing powerful and sometimes big waves if the longer interval NW swells are clean. Entry and exit is tricky, getting caught inside is harrowing, the rips are brutal and urchins love the place as do the large local crew. Across the bay, inconsistent **Crazy Left** is a suitably named, shallow, left reef that only works on SW swells at high tide. It's the hollowest left around and is full of hot bodyboarders. **Ribeira d'Ilhas** has become Europe's first World Surfing Reserve, since it is a very versatile set of reefs that normally have something worth getting wet for. Extremely long rights can start in front of the cliffs of Pontinha and finish on the rocky beach, but it's usually broken up into manageable sections. It can handle a bit of wind, most swell sizes if NW, and breaks throughout the tide. Swells come crashing out of deep water onto **Reef**, a barely submerged, urchin-infested rock shelf and produce the hollowest right in Ericeira. It's fickle and very short, needing gentle offshores and perfectly clean 3-6ft NW swell. **Backdoor** is normally a summer break, working best on N-NW swells. It holds some very hollow sections up to double-overhead and is sketchy on low tide. **Pedra Branca** is a short, sharp and very sweet left reef that can get hideously hollow and is suicidal at low tide. It's best on a SW swell with E winds and breaks up to double overhead. Inconsistent, crowded with rippers and carpeted in urchins. Ultra-reliable **Praia do Norte** accepts swells of almost any size and from any direction. Primarily a right reef at the north end, it's often sectiony, plus there can be a left further up and peaks down by the harbour wall. Sheltered **Praia do Peixe** inside the harbour is only worth a look on the biggest, stormiest days. Low tide is best for these shifty, uninspiring beach peaks. Another spot that won't win any awards for its quality but when the swell is too much for everywhere else, then **Furnas** will have some rights off the breakwall and shifty peaks. The cliffs shelter it from the worst of the strong N winds. Much of the time, the **Foz do Lizandro** rivermouth is deserted and a good place to go for lower quality, empty waves. Occasionally, the sandbars line-up properly and then this wave turns into a classy affair with long and hollow lefts. Best from mid-low tide on a small to moderate SW swell with light E winds. The water can be gross if there has been a lot of rain up river.

Ericeira's swell and wind synopsis is identical to Peniche, but the wind options are less flexible. All the breaks require E or even SE winds for due offshore so the summer Nortada is obviously bad news. Winter storms can mean some driving around to find places offering shelter from the wind and swell, which means Peniche or Lisbon. Autumn with its more easterly airflow is the best bet, but Ericeira can turn it on at any time of the year. Tides hit 3.5m and low tide can be suicidal on some reefs.

## TRAVEL INFORMATION

**Weather** – see Peniche

**Lodging and Food** – Apart from high season (June-Sept), finding quartos (rooms), pensãoes or hotels in Ericeira/Ribamar is easy starting at \$20-\$25/d. Surfholidays has multiple accommodation options for all budgets. A meal is ±\$12 if you can resist the more expensive seafood.

**Nature and Culture** – Ericeira is a typical fishing/tourist town with pastelerias, pretty streets and churches. It's lively year-round because of its proximity to Lisbon, but still fairly low key. A Saturday night out in Lisbon's Barrio Alto district can be interesting. Don't miss Sintra and the majestic castles of the old Royal City nearby.

**Hazards and Hassles** – The rocky ledges and reefs are more dangerous than the locals are but the area is getting increasingly overcrowded. Some of the remote car parks are tempting for thieves. Sitting out storm surf conditions is a regular occurrence.

**Handy Hints** – There are a few surf shops in Ericeira town (Boardculture). Semente Surfboards in Ribamar is Portugal's biggest board shaper. Na Onda Surf School is located in Praia do Lizandro. Bodyboarders outnumber stand-up surfers in most line-ups, except for Coxos and Ribeira d'Ilhas. Champion Surf Guides can customise intermediate/advanced surf trips along the coast from Lisbon to Nazaré.

| STATISTICS | | J F | M A | M J | J A | S O | N D |
|---|---|---|---|---|---|---|---|
| SWELL | Direction | | | | | | |
| | Size (ft) | 6-7 | 6 | 4-5 | 3 | 5 | 6 |
| WIND | Direction | | | | | | |
| | Force | F4 | F4 | F3-F4 | F3-F4 | F3-F4 | F4 |
| WATER | Wetsuit | | | | | | |
| | Temp/°C | 13 | 14 | 16 | 18 | 17 | 15 |
| WEATHER | Rainfall/mm | 90 | 80 | 30 | 4 | 31 | 100 |
| | days/mth | 10 | 8 | 4 | 1 | 6 | 10 |
| | Min temp/°C | 8 | 11 | 14 | 17 | 15 | 9 |
| | Max temp/°C | 15 | 19 | 23 | 28 | 25 | 16 |

# Lisbon PORTUGAL

**Lisbon interrupts the straight north-south geometry of Portugal's littoral line with a short stretch of mainly SW-facing coastline from Caiscais to Oeiras. When a big swell pounds the capital, coupled with the nation's dominant Nortada wind, perfect conditions arrive at several good set-ups along this rocky coast. Excellent powerful beachbreaks flank the city for summer fun, making Lisbon one of the best urban surfer playgrounds in the world.**

+ LARGE SWELL WINDOW
+ VERY CONSISTENT SWELLS
+ VARIETY OF BREAKS
+ EASY CITY ACCESS

- URBAN CROWDS
- NO EPIC POINTBREAKS
- COOL WATER YEAR-ROUND
- SOME LOCALISM/RIP-OFFS

**Praia das Maçãs** benefits from a bit of bounce off the cliffs that helps to boost up the wedgy lefts. Picks up any swell going as long as it isn't too big. **Praia Grande** is ultra-consistent and a very versatile beachbreak with long, but often slow waves at low tide and faster, shorter shorebreaks when the tide starts pushing up. Doesn't like a lot of wind and is busy whenever it's on. Better known for its kite/windsurfing conditions, **Praia Gunicho** is actually one of the better beachbreaks in the Lisbon area and certainly one of the most consistent. When it's good, wedgy, powerful rights break off the cliffs at the northern end. Mid-low tide on a NW swell is better, but it gets blown-out very easily. Sectiony and spacious, **Monte Estoril**'s righthander breaks off a jetty on both bigger and smaller days provided the wind isn't S to W. A high quality, fast and hollow, right reef at **Bolina** breaks with power over a shallow bottom. Busy, localised and not suitable for beginners. **Poça**'s popular mid-tide reef has a sucky, A-frame take-off, leading into a fast compression tube on the lefts. The rights have more wall and lip line than the lefts, which are always crowded with barrel-hunting bodyboarders. The sheltered and classy lefthander at **Azarujinja** is protected from W winds and is good to check in a big winter storm. There's a low tide right, but it's all about the powerful mid tide left that can get epic, but is often busy. São Pedro has two right pointbreaks, including **Bica**, a fat, but super-long right ideally suited to longboarders who crowd the place on a big NW swell, or better still SW. The same SW swell is ideal for neighbouring **Bafureira**, which handles less size but has more power than Bica. Inviting lefts and rights wall-up across the reef from mid to low tide, when rocks start popping up and rides shorten. **Parede** is an elusive right point that needs some S in the swell direction and only breaks a couple of hours either side of mid tide. When it's on, there can be some fast, firing rights, but as a visitor, don't expect too many waves. The original and still one of the best Portuguese surf spots, **Carcavelos** is a highly consistent and awesome beachbreak. Beside the fort at the eastern end, cylindrical lefts roll over shifting sandbars, attracting seemingly every surfer in the city and most of the foreign surfers on the Costa Estoril. Best on a SW swell, when power intensifies and the occasional right appears. **Santo Amaro** needs a huge swell to break, but when it does, it's a sick, muscular, righthand wall with fast tubular sections on a SW swell and incoming tide. Low consistency, always busy, rips, rocks, locals and the worst water quality in Portugal. **Costa Caparica** is the most consistent zone for Lisbon's surfers where a number of jetties provide variety and stability to the sandbars. Look for the low tide lefts at Covo do Vapor and Rio plus the 7 jetties referred to as CDS. Further south, check Praia da Rainha for average, open beachbreak. Set in beautiful countryside, **Largoa de Albuferia** is one of several beach access points that all provide quiet waves. A small rivermouth helps to form better than average sandbars on NW swell and outgoing tide. The fickle peak at **Bicas** has a faster walled left and a fatter right into the channel. Can hold a solid bit of W-NW swell, especially at the challenging left off the point. Check out **Sesimbra** harbour in SW swells and N winds for a left and sucky peaks.

Lisbon area soaks up the consistent year-round W-NW swells, but the rare SW swells can really light up the Estoril spots. Storms are frequent but Lisbon offers the perfect shelter to filter swells and get cross-offshore winds in summer NW or perfectly angled winter NE. Tides are 3.3m in Cascais - the vast majority of spots favour low tide. Water temps can be 0.5°C warmer than Peniche.

RICARDO BRAVO

Carcavelos

## TRAVEL INFORMATION

**Weather** - See Peniche

**Lodging and Food** – Caparica is a busy seaside resort with many cheap 'parques de campismo' to the south. Guincho is a good hub for the north side. A decent meal costs $12.

**Nature and Culture** – Great services, seaview restaurants (Europa Mar, Cafe do Mar) and bars in Caparica (Waikiki, Kontiki). Escape the city to the Arriba Fossil or the Albufeira lake area.

**Hazards and Hassles** – Avoid the summer tourist season from June-Sept. Thievery is common at Carcavelos and Praia Grande. The Tagus rivermouth spits out some shit and bordering beaches can be filthy. Traffic jams can be bad around Lisbon!

**Handy Hints** – Plenty of shapers: Matta, Lufi, Polen, with boards from $450+, expect some bargaining. Portugalsurfrentals.com (Carcavelos) offer high performance boards and airport collections fr $24/d. Try the Matta Surf Shop in Caparica. Only take a gun for winter west coast spots. Take surfing lessons with the Cascais or LX surf schools.

RICARDO BRAVO

Praia Guincho

| STATISTICS | | J F | M A | M J | J A | S O | N D |
|---|---|---|---|---|---|---|---|
| SWELL | Direction | | | | | | |
| | Size (ft) | 6-7 | 6 | 4-5 | 3 | 5 | 6 |
| WIND | Direction | | | | | | |
| | Force | F4 | F4 | F3-F4 | F3-F4 | F3-F4 | F4 |
| WATER | Wetsuit | | | | | | |
| | Temp/°C | 13 | 14 | 16 | 18 | 17 | 15 |
| WEATHER | Rainfall/mm | 93 | 83 | 31 | 4 | 32 | 100 |
| | days/mth | 10 | 9 | 5 | 1 | 6 | 10 |
| | Min temp/°C | 8 | 11 | 14 | 17 | 15 | 10 |
| | Max temp/°C | 15 | 19 | 23 | 28 | 25 | 16 |

# Algarve PORTUGAL

The Algarve is the southwestern corner of the Iberian Peninsula and is an intoxicating mix of Atlantic and Mediterranean influences. It was the last major European surf region to be explored and although it doesn't contain the classic reefs of central Portugal, the potential for good, uncrowded waves is high. The countryside is a gently undulating mesh of forests and small fields, leading down to an undeveloped coastline of high cliffs and long empty beaches scattered with rocks. The small, lively town of Sagres is well located to take advantage of the wide swell window of Cape St-Vincent, where the west and south coasts meet, creating a perfect corner for both beginners and experts to revel in the fun waves.

+ WIDE CHOICE OF BREAKS
+ REEFS AND BEACHES
+ SUPER-WIDE SWELL WINDOW
+ WARMEST EUROPEAN CLIMATE

- NO WORLD-CLASS SPOTS
- CROWDS & SURF SCHOOLS
- WEST COAST ONSHORES
- COOL WATER

DAN HAYLOCK

Praia do Amado

**Odeceixe** is the first spot in the Algarve region and while it consistently has waves, quality is hard to find as the river flow is constantly scouring out the sandbars and keeping the line-up in flux. The headland cliffs offer some N wind protection on the inside, but it is usually breaking on the fully wind-exposed outside because it only works at the lower stages of the tide. Often soft and perfect for beginners, it gets zooed in August and empty in winter. **Carriagem** is a long drive down a dirt road to isolated, exposed beachbreak. It's frustratingly fickle and usually best at mid tide, on a NW swell with slack or E winds. The drive in and the hike down a steep cliff face to get to the beach keeps it uncrowded. **Amoreira** is a rivermouth break, favouring rights at lower stages of the tide. The currents can be horrendous when it gets overhead and the wave itself is very fickle. Wind exposed, but gets lots of swell, preferably from the SW. Small summer swells best when it is sometimes crowded. The average stretch of rarely ridden beachbreak at **Monte Clérigo** is scattered with rocks and laced with rips. It breaks throughout the tide – high tide offers more shorey style waves, whilst low tide gives longer and mushier waves. The reefs to the south sometimes line-up, but it always seems to be windy here. No such problem for the regional hotspot ✪**Arrifana** which is sheltered by high cliffs from the N winds. **Praia da Bordeira** boasts to be one of the best, as well as one of the most beautiful, beaches in south Portugal. At low tide a long left winds off the Carrapateira cliffs below the car park and from mid-high tide the beach turns on the goods with often fast and hollow rights into the rivermouth. The left gets busy but the beach contains enough peaks to thin the crowds. Consistent but easily blown-out. Along a winding road to the south of Carrapateira village, **Praia do Amado** has more shelter than Praia da Bordeira and a right breaking off a large rock from mid-low tide. Average peaks break further down the beach. Popular with Algarve surf schools, despite the odd rip. **Praia da Cordama** looks out on more isolated beachbreak with a sprinkling of rocks below impressive cliffs. Small summer swells in glassy conditions will provide plenty of peaks between rips, but the N winds will destroy it. **Praia Castelejo** is a remote and beautiful beach with plenty of different options. It gathers maximum swell and is normally better in the autumn than spring as the sandbars tend to get destroyed over the course of the winter by big storms. Very wind exposed. Check the nearby coastline! As the best beach in the Sagres area, **Beliche** needs a hefty NW swell or a standard S to work and is offshore on N winds. When good it's a classy left wedge that handles up to double overhead. It's very hollow and fast and overrun with hot locals. **Tonel** is the most consistent of the Sagres beaches offering average peaks at lower tidal stages and a W swell. It doesn't pick up as much swell as the west coast so it is a popular place for beginner/intermediates and the many local bodyboarders. Highly consistent, often crowded, currents and localism, but the water is clean, and amenities include showers, lifeguard,

JASON FEAST

## TRAVEL INFORMATION

**Weather** – Despite its Atlantic position, the Algarve enjoys a Mediterranean climate with cool to mild winter temperatures, it never freezes and 20°C (68°F) at noon is common. Summers are hot, and less than 60mm winter rainfall per month, puts the Algarve at half the national average. Camping is still an option in winter. The water is warmer by 1-2°C (3-5°F) than central Portugal, with Sagres ranging from 14-22°C (58-72°F). Cold currents can hit the coast at any time so take a range of rubber.

**Lodging and Food** – Finding accommodation in Sagres or Lagos is easy. Many locals rent out rooms or whole houses at ± $15/room. There's a whole slew of surf camps in the Lagos area; The Surf Experience are the original outfit with week packages for all levels from $450. In Sagres try International Surfschool. A basic meal can be had for $12. The best fresh fish can be found at A Sagres Restaurante. Sagres has its own brand cheap beer.

**Nature and Culture** – Cape St-Vincent contains a fortress where Prince Henry the navigator, established his famous school of exploration. The nightlife in Sagres and even more so Lagos, is wild and raucous when summer brings the backpacking hordes. Beware the absinthe! Aljezur near Arrifana has some good ruins to visit.

**Hazards and Hassles** – Apart from rocks and some localism, there's little to worry about. The undeveloped west coast has few or no locals outside the towns and the Sagres surfers tend to stay at their home breaks. The area is slowly getting more and more crowded, but the vibe remains chilled-out as there are a lot of waves to choose from. Respect the sharp rocks at the pointbreaks and strong rips at certain breaks.

**Handy Hints** – There are surf shops in Lagos (Magic Board Center, Lagos Surf Center, Jah Shaka) and Surfers Lab in Sagres. The Algarve is a well-established tourist destination so English is widely spoken. Reckless driving is the national sport, and the N126 has an abnormally high death toll!

## Arrifana

**LAT. 37.294160° LONG. -8.872093°**

Beneath the white-washed village and massive cliffs is a busy and very ordinary beachbreak that works throughout the tide, picks up most swell and has decent N wind shelter. The real reason to visit Arrifana is the top-class, right pointbreak at the beach's northern end. Waves here are long, fast and very heavy with shallow boils and thick, hard to thread barrel sections. Works with plenty of W in the swell, but it needs to be at least 6ft to start breaking and holds up to triple overhead. Rocks can surface along the length of the ride and be careful of the two large rocks on the inside. It's always crowded with locals, travellers and legions of urchins. Beginners and intermediates should stick to the beachbreak which can get really good sometimes. Easy parking, showers, lifeguard (for the surf schools), a surf shop (in Aljezur) and camping nearby.

surf school, surf shops and camping in town. **Mareta**'s perfect but very rare wave needs a monster W-NW swell or a decent S. Also picks up a little wind slop on the summertime Levante winds. It's a hollow, bowly wave that gets very busy and is a little localised. **Zavial** is a fast, hollow and powerful right wedging up off the cliffs at the far end of the beach. It can be a mission getting a wave off the locals. Needs a moderate SW or big W-NW swell to break and mid tide to avoid closing-out. The most famous of the Algarve south coast spots and also the busiest with a local crew who are on it at the slightest sniff of a wave. If the scene here is too hectic then a drive around might reveal further goods. Medium consistency in slightly warmer water temps than the west coast. The curve of beach at **Praia da Luz** is flanked by a right and left pointbreak, which get good on any S or big W-NW swells. The left is particularly shallow and fast while the right known as Rocha Negra is a bit more manageable. The sandbanks benefit from a rivermouth that also brings stormwater to the line-up. On big S storms it's worth taking a look at Lagos town beach, **Praia Meia**, which can produce some fun and hollow little beach peaks. The eastern end of the beach picks up way more swell and a W wind is offshore. Best on a levante SE windswell. Great beginners zone. Tourist zoo in summer, with all facilities including a surf shop. A hollow and inconsistent left breaks off the jetty at **Praia da Rocha** in the heart of the major tourist resort of Portimão. Needs a big swell to work, it's renowned for its tubes and gets very busy. Pay to park.

Consistency is the best word to describe southern Portugal's surf. Average wintertime swells on the west coast are around 8-10ft, with 12-15ft maximums, whilst summer rarely goes flat and regularly gets to double overhead. The south coast works with either large filtered NW swells wrapping round the corner or much rarer winter SW-W swells banging straight in. The winds around Cape St Vincent are notoriously unpredictable and treated with suspicion by the local sailing fraternity, since strange swirling gusts and onshores when the weather map says offshore are known to happen. The Algarve area continues the national nortada trend with summer NW-N winds giving way to winter SW storm winds followed by NE to SE offshores. When the winter offshores do blow, they blow hard and make blind take-offs a regular occurrence. The S wind or levant as it is called in the Mediterranean disappears as quickly as it arrived – the SE-S swells produced by it are very fleeting, but light-up the beaches that are usually flat in summer. Maximum tidal range from Sines to Lagos is 3.4m and tends to swamp lots of breaks.

STUART BUTLER

Beliche

JASON FEAST

Zavial

| STATISTICS | | J F | M A | M J | J A | S O | N D |
|---|---|---|---|---|---|---|---|
| SWELL | Direction | | | | | | |
| | Size (ft) | 5 | 4-5 | 2-3 | 1-2 | 3-4 | 4-5 |
| WIND | Direction | | | | | | |
| | Force | F4 | F4 | F4 | F3 | F3 | F4 |
| WATER | Wetsuit | | | | | | |
| | Temp/°C | 15 | 16 | 18 | 21 | 19 | 17 |
| WEATHER | Rainfall/mm | 60 | 50 | 12 | 1 | 35 | 65 |
| | days/mth | 6 | 6 | 2 | 1 | 3 | 7 |
| | Min temp/°C | 9 | 12 | 16 | 20 | 17 | 11 |
| | Max temp/°C | 16 | 19 | 24 | 28 | 24 | 18 |

# Terceira AZORES

Only the very tallest undersea mountains manage to break the surface of the empty Atlantic Ocean. The 9 volcanic peaks of the Azores are all alone, almost equidistant from North America and Europe, with a full 360° swell window, right in the centre lane of the trans-Atlantic swell highway. Terceira simply means "3rd island", is fairly circular in shape and has the greatest concentration of east coast surf spots, including the sublime A-frame peak of Santa Catarina.

+ 360° SWELL WINDOW
+ EPIC SANTA CATARINA
+ EMPTY BIG WAVE SPOTS
+ BEAUTIFUL LANDSCAPES

– SHORT-LIVED, DISORGANISED SWELLS
– E-FACING SPOTS NEED BIG SWELLS
– RAPIDLY CHANGING CONDITIONS
– HEAVY WAVES, ROCKS AND BOULDERS

## TRAVEL INFORMATION

**Weather** – See São Miguel

**Lodging and Food** – Best is to stay in Praia. Good views from the 3star Hotel Varandas do Atlantico in Praia ($75/n). Pousadas normally $80-100 and any cheaper options have to be searched out. Azores has good dairy products, fish, wines and Europe's only tea plantation. A good restaurant meal will be $30-40.

**Nature and Culture** – Check the many natural swimming-pools like Biscoitos, set in volcanic rocks. May-October is Portuguese bullfighting season and whale watching time. Great views from Monte Brasil.

**Hazards and Hassles** – Volcanic eruptions, earthquakes and landslides are a threat. Locals surfers deserve maximum respect in the heavy waves. Basalt rocks can be ultra-sharp, some shark sightings at Quatro Ribeiras.

**Handy Hints** – Take a solid gun. If you break your board, there are two shapers in Porto Martins: Lucas makes SL surfboards and Tito does Titushapes. $600-750 for a new board. Spots like Santa Catarina might be destroyed by Tetrapods in new harbour projects. Visit neighbouring islands, especially Sao Jorge.

DAN HAYLOCK

Santa Catarina

Quatro Ribeiras
Vila Nova
Ponta do Queimado
Praia da Vitória
Santa Catarina
Ponta Negra
Pescadore
São Fernando
Contendas
Salga
Terreiro

**Vila Nova**'s banana-shaped bombora reef picks up and magnifies W-N swells into super-heavy rights and the odd left. Fast, thick barrels that wedge up and bend around this gnarly, offshore, boat access reef. Handles huge and is always bigger than it looks. Low tide is suicide and only experts with big everything should join the very few who have ridden this wave. North coast focal point **Quatro Ribeiras** has a choice of powerful, challenging set-ups. Lefts break off deepwater cliffs, wall-up and speed across bay before closing out on boulder beach. Righthander to the east is a bit mellower, but still very powerful. Needs to be overhead to start breaking. **Ponta do Queimado** is a sketchy spot with left at south end and more usable right at north end. Desperation check only - usually no waves at this end of the island. High performance righthander at **Terreiro** offers plenty of steep face to work with. Picks up all S swells but wraps in best on a W. Rocks can pop up in the face depending on the tide, making for a sectiony ride. Dangerous when big pointbreak **Salga** needs a SW-W swell to line-up properly. Changes with the tide from slopey shoulders to peeling walls and the inside section will stand up in front of the pool. **Contendas**' short, sucky peak goes dry on the rights, but the lefts can barrel on the peak. Works on a big SW, SE or E swell because it halves in size as it refracts and reforms into the bay. **São Fernando** works best on small N swells and is sheltered from NW winds. Easy, workable walls with a tendency to back off, especially as the tide pushes in from mid. Full-on sucky barrels at **Pescadore** break in seriously shallow water when a huge, long period, wrapping NW swell hits. Often crowded with the best local surfers and urchins blanket the nasty reef. Excellent, long, lefthander at **Ponta Negra** appears on big NW swells and winds from W-NE. Breaks hard and fast, bending over shallow sections of reef and throwing some big tubes. Often crowded and localised. Intermediates on smaller days, experts when it gets double overhead. **Santa Catarina** is the Azore's version of Pipeline, exploding on a shallow reef, just metres from shore. Jacking air drop take-offs into a cavernous pit that peels both ways for a short, but intense barrel ride. Perfect for bodyboarders and pro's, this wave is not for everyone. Needs a medium to big NW swell to wrap in and any W in the wind. Ultra polluted by three outfalls. Respect required. Assorted reef/beach waves at **Praia da Vitoria** include Dereitas and Esquerda do Chines that break off either side of an exposed rock. The left is a perfect hotdog wave in smaller N swells at high tide. Vietnam is the main left breaking wider than Chines with long, fun, ripable walls plus the odd cover-up section. Mid tide, big NW, N and NE swells and any W winds will be ideal. Busiest and easiest spot on the island where everyone learns.

DAN HAYLOCK

Praia da Vitoria

The Azores High is the major meteorological factor and if strongly established will hold off any storms from swinging straight over the top of the islands. This means 4-15ft winter swells usually arrive from the W-NW and slowly shift to N and then NE, before the next system moves through. Summer can see freak long-distance S swells all the way from the southern hemisphere or lined-up hurricane swell from the SW, along with localised windswells from just about any direction. Being so close to the systems means winds can be strong and variable, veering SW-W in winter and W-NW in summer. Swells are a bit raw and disorganised, jumping in size with little warning. Tides shift between 1.4m to 1.9m, but will affect many of the shallow reefs, while the beaches and points are generally unfazed.

| STATISTICS | | J F | M A | M J | J A | S O | N D |
|---|---|---|---|---|---|---|---|
| SWELL | Direction | | | | | | |
| | Size (ft) | 6 | 5-6 | 4-5 | 3 | 5 | 6 |
| WIND | Direction | | | | | | |
| | Force | F5 | F5 | F4 | F3 | F4 | F4 |
| WATER | Wetsuit | | | | | | |
| | Temp/°C | 16 | 17 | 18 | 22 | 22 | 19 |
| WEATHER | Rainfall/mm | 110 | 85 | 50 | 27 | 95 | 110 |
| | days/mth | 14 | 12 | 8 | 6 | 11 | 14 |
| | Min temp/°C | 11 | 11 | 14 | 17 | 16 | 13 |
| | Max temp/°C | 17 | 18 | 21 | 26 | 23 | 19 |

# São Miguel AZORES

Despite holding Portugal's highest peak, sailors referred to The Azores as 'The Disappearing Isles' because huge swells would obscure them from view. This kind of reputation is attracting the seasoned surf traveller to these wave-drenched shores. São Miguel is open to most swells and wind patterns, with the only N-facing beachbreaks in the chain, which have become a regular contest site for the world's pros.

+ VERY CONSISTENT SWELLS
+ UNCROWDED QUALITY WAVES
+ GOOD POINTBREAKS
+ EXPLORE NEARBY ISLANDS

- CHANGEABLE CONDITIONS
- SCARY REEFBREAKS
- COOL, WET CLIMATE
- HARD ACCESS TO MANY SPOTS

## TRAVEL INFORMATION

**Weather** – The Azores high is a bit of a misnomer, as the weather here is anything but settled and stable. It is more accurate to refer to a warm season and a cool season when almost every day sees some rain. Summer is mainly sunny and warm, winter is usually cool, windy and wet. Autumn, is the best time with ample swell and reasonable weather. Water temps stay above 14°C and below 25°C (58-77°F). Light fullsuit or a springsuit for June-Oct.

**Lodging and Food** – The Azores are not a budget destination; Ponta Delgada has plenty of hotels ranging from 4-star ($150/db) to 2-star ($46/db) or try Rabo de Peixe and Ribeira Grande (fr $32/n). Expect to pay about $20 for a meal.

**Nature and Culture** – Most tourists come to trek around the Sete Cidades Caldeira, (volcanic lake), bathe in the Furnas hot springs or watch whales. Ponta Delgada is a laid-back city - don't expect great nightlife.

**Hazards and Hassles** – Most reefs are sharp with uneven lava bottoms. Jellyfish can be a problem in summer on the south coast. Most of the local surfers are bodyboarders and don't bother getting up for the early.

**Handy Hints** – Bring at least two boards, including a semi-gun. Local surf shops sell little but wax and leashes. Be cool to the locals and they might share their secrets with you.

Serious big wave peak **Baixa de Viola** jacks up over a wind-exposed bombora reef, then rumbles along for a good distance. Big boards and experience needed. **Santa Iria**'s long, left pointbreak can be powerful with wrapping, bowly sections, but can also be easier performance walls suitable for beginner/improvers. Sectiony at low tide and at high tide access is blocked. Quality, black sand beachbreak at **Monte Verte** picks up a huge range of swells, but best on a NW. Can be powerful with various peaks and a semi-permanent right at the western end. Next door, **Santa Barbara**'s excellent beachbreaks are fast, hollow and bowly with wedging refracted peaks. Semi-pointbreak almost inside **Rabo de Peixe** harbour wall that destroyed a better wave outside the wall. Only breaks at lower tides and very close to the rocks. Vertical take-offs, powerful pockets and fast sections can change into easier drops and cutback shoulders depending on size, direction and tide. Fun, workable pointbreak **Mosteiros Right** is open to 180° of swell directions and lines-up best in W swell. Can be long, intermediate-friendly rides but dry rocks can pop up in the face below mid tide. **Mosteiros Left** is another rock strewn line-up holding average lefts that can be fast and hollow when the conditions come together. Cruisey righthander **Praia dos Mosteiros** starts with an easy take-off into steep performance walls with plenty of power in the pocket. A very big S, SW or W swell is needed to awaken **Santa Clara**, a heavy righthand reef with critical take-offs and high speed barrel sections for experts only. Extremely flexible city beachbreak **Populo** can be small and junky in the regular SW and W windswells with crumbly faces in the onshore breezes. Due S swells hit the rock-anchored sandbanks just right and line up powerful, hollow peaks in the long period swell. The most crowded spot in the Azores with both beginners and experts. **Santa Cruz/Lagoa** is a rocky left in the middle of town that needs a strong, clean S-SW swell for a short, fast and tubular ride over shallow reef. **Agua de Alto**'s south-facing beachbreak is the second option if Populo is too crowded. Has the same generous swell window, even picking up NE swells, with lots of peaks and plenty of room for beginners. The reef peak at **Vila Franca** is punchy and sucky at sub-mid tides, then fuller on the face and much more ripable at high. East of the town of **Ponta Garca** is a stretch of rocky beaches below cliffs. Usually mellow and unchallenging, it's a good place for learners who aren't afraid of a few rocks. Heavy **Ribeira Quente Left** peels down the side of a large jetty construction and ends in the beachbreak when it's big. Best on high tide and a S, SE or wrapping E-NE swell. Chunky, vertical walls at **Ribeira Quente Right** breaks down the seawall on the other side of town. Needs a strong swell to clear the boulders and strong S-W swell. **Faja do Araujo** is the only east coast wave and needs a huge NW swell of at least 15ft to start breaking at half that size as it refracts through 90°. Serious big water drops lead into cavernous barrels over tricky slabs of rock. When it is on, it's a world-class freight train for hundreds of metres and the best wave on the island. Extremely isolated requiring a half hour walk up the rocky shoreline, then difficult entry and exit to the water from the rocks 15 minutes paddle south of the point. Low tide, low consistency, high risk wave.

DAN HAYLOCK

Rabo de Peixe

RICARDO BRAVO

Santa Barbara

Swell Forecasting – see Terceira

# Lanzarote CANARY ISLANDS

The Canaries reputation for being the Hawaii of the Atlantic is well earned, as these volcanic islands have much in common with their Pacific cousins. NE trade winds fanning heavy reef waves, breaking close to shore in clear blue water, full of fierce locals, under a burning hot sun seems a fair description of both surf zones. The truth is there are many differences, like the climate and water temperature, but when it comes to the waves, the Canary Islands certainly has powerful, challenging surf. In terms of wave quality, Lanzarote is the island to head to where the heart of the surf scene is situated on the north shore between Famara and La Santa.

+ POWERFUL WAVES
+ LOTS OF SPOTS
+ DRY CLIMATE
+ DRAMATIC SCENERY

- SHARP, SHALLOW LAVA REEFS
- WINDY CONDITIONS
- FIERCE LOCALISM
- THEFTS AND CAR CRIME

## TRAVEL INFORMATION

**Weather** – Being so close to the Sahara desert, Lanzarote and Fuerteventura enjoy a semi-arid subtropical climate, that hardly ever sees rain. It gets very hot in the summer and also when E winds (Leste) blow in off the desert, which are partly responsible for depositing white sand on the east coast beaches. The worst phenomenon is 'La Calima', a strong E-S wind bringing downpours and a coating of yellowish-brown dust. The cold Canaries current means that winter water temps will be between 18-20°C (64-68°F), requiring a 3/2 fullsuit to battle the high wind-chill factor.

**Lodging and Food** – Most surfers stay in La Santa village guesthouses or Famara bungalows above the beach. Package holiday tourists end up in east coast resorts. Expect to pay around $300/w for accommodation and $15 for a basic meal.

**Nature and Culture** – Low-lying Lanzarote has a multitude of smooth volcanic cones and large dramatic black lava plains. Check the Timanfaya National Park or the lava tubes around Jameos del Agua. Hectic nightlife around Puerto del Carmen, as package holidaymakers pack out the bars and clubs.

**Hazards and Hassles** – There have been reports of some ugly rip-offs and violence towards travelling surfers. Hardcore locals usually control the big name line-ups, but if you avoid these spots then you shouldn't have much trouble. Avoid the impact zone, currents, urchins and hitting the reef.

**Handy Hints** – There are decent surf shops like El Cruce who also rent surf apartments and La Santa Surf Factory invite top international guest shapers to their shaping bay. Many surf schools and camps operate out of Famara.

La Santa Derecha

JUAN FERNANDEZ

La Santa Izquierda

JUAN FERNANDEZ

LAURENT MASUREL

The town of La Santa on the NW corner of the island is home to a concentration of quality reefs, including the world renowned tubing left of **El Quemao**. A mere 500m away, **La Santa Izquierda** creates a seriously thick left and right peak breaking over 'The Slab' with the left being the longer and the more fought over of the waves. Both waves produce classic powerful tubes, hold a lot of wind and swell directions but certainly not a crowd. The most ridden wave on the island but with a localism problem that makes it off limits to most. **La Santa Derecha** is better known as Morro Negro, a long righthand point with a couple of distinct sections that link up on the best days. This wave can be hollow on E winds and the best NW-N swell directions, but often provides large open faces. Handles size and even some N wind but W swells will section and bring nasty sneaker sets. Often crowded but the length of the wave can thin out the mix of tourists and locals. Slippery rocks, urchins, rips and beware of very shallow spots on smaller days. **The Complex** (aka Boca del Abajo) on La Isleta is a long, powerful wave with some very tubular sections and it holds considerable size. A W swell direction is vital here as is an offshore E-SE-S wind so consistency isn't high. Dramatic wave that is constantly breaking into shallow reef and boulders and is very size deceptive. **Caleta de Caballo Izquierda**'s very ordinary left breaks on the west side of the bay. Has an interesting rock that often pops up in the middle of the ride, which keeps things exciting. Often crowded with local crew when W winds blow out the La Santa breaks. Across the bay, **Caleta de Caballo Derecha** is a hollow right that only takes a few surfers to make a crowd, but numbers are often low due to the fierce nature of the wave. Powerful and fast breaking in very shallow water with a distinct take-off spot. Consistent **San Juan** is one of the most popular reefs on the island, because it's rideable on small swells, plus it can handle a light onshore wind. Starts as an A-frame peak running into a long lefthand wall while the right peters out immediately. The lower the tide the faster the wave and the more critical the drops. Shallow, urchin-infested reef and some localism. Dredgy, intense left over shallow reef at **Caleta de Famara** needs W swell to line-up. Inconsistent and when it is on the aggressive local crowd are not up for sharing. Dangerous below mid-tide. **Playa de Famara**'s 6kms of curving beach receives swell from W-N and handles wind from E-SW. Centre of the bay receives the most of the swell, but the sandbanks will close-out at around 8-10ft faces. North end can get fast and hollow at lower tide while south end is smaller and easier. Strong sideshore drift and currents. All the surf schools and kiteboarders congregate here, because it's super-consistent and relatively free of localism hassles. When sizeable swells hit the **Las Bajas** reef an enormous peak

Isla Graciosa
Playa de la Canteria
Jameos del Agua
Punta de Mujeres
Playa de la Garita
Playa Honda
Los Pocillos
Playa Blanca
West Coast
East Coast
SEE NORTH COAST MAP
SUDDEN RUSH
PERFECT WAVE
SURFHOLIDAYS
NOMAD SURFERS
EL CRUCE SURF
Arrecife
Teguise
Costa Teguise
Puerto del Carmen
Famara
La Santa
Tinajo
Yaiza
Playa Blanca
Órzola

### El Quemao

LAT. 29.11° LONG. -13.6673°

Known as Pipeline's Atlantic sister, because the longer lefts and shorter rights reel down a straight, shallow reef with intense power and ferocity. W swell makes the lefts more makeable than the rights, which resemble Backdoor by closing-out on the sharp lava reef shortly after take-off. When it's on, it's packed with the best of the island's stand-up surfers and bodyboarders and a Coliseum atmosphere pervades. One of the most photographed spots in the Canaries, but also one of the most localised. Does have its quieter moments on less epic days however the surfing level required to ride here is very high.

breaks top to bottom for tow-in crews and paddle-in hellmen only. A ferry plies the 2km wide El Rio straits to **Isla Graciosa** the smallest inhabited island of the archipelago and part of the Parque Nacional de los Islotes del Norte. Playa de las Conchas is the only long beach, a 1.5hr walk to the north-western shore, but it is more of a tourist beach and the surfing conditions are poor. There are several heavy reefs dotted around the island but this is a super-hard-core place where the reefs are really sharp, shallow and urchin-infested, making entry and exit a real hassle. Many of the waves are experts only and the locals from both the island and by the boatload from Lanzarote are not very gracious. Expect severe hassles and remember how isolated Graciosa is. There are no roads, only dirt or sand tracks so options include the 4X4 taxi service, hiking in or renting mountain bikes at the harbour in Caleta del Sebo, where there are basic facilities. **Playa de La Canteria** is nestled beneath cliffs where a mid to high tide peak breaks in the centre of the bay and a high tide righthander can peel down the rocks giving a fast and sometimes hollow ride. Swells over 6ft tend to close-out the bay. It's mainly a left point at **Jameos del Agua**, but on the biggest and cleanest of swells a solid right can also be found at the very end of the point. N swells wrap around the headland, lining-up sectiony walls and shoulders that lack a bit of power, however on classic days, it's definitely the longest wave on the island. Better at higher tides. Often surfable in strong N winds, so it can get very crowded. Perfect right and left peak at **Punta de Mujeres** that breaks on N swells and E windswells. Hollow both ways but very shallow with rocky fingers sticking up occasionally. Better at high tide. Extremely localised and always crowded. **Playa de La Garita** is mainly a slamming shoredump but the occasional wave will peel. Short, fast and hollow and a favourite for the local bodyboarders. Can produce waves on both N storm winds and SE Sirocco winds. The **East Coast** between Arrecife and Arrieta rarely works at all but strong N-E windswell can awaken a number of small wave spots. Most are rock scattered playas or the odd reef that work only on the rising tide and are all very fickle. **Playa Honda** parallels the airport runway offering small yet powerful beachbreak peaks and closeouts on howling N-E winds. The surf grows in size at the south end, but it is very exposed to the wind. **Los Piccolos** only works on the windiest days when swell is pushed down the east coast and into a long crescent of sandy beach. Lefts and rights with a half decent longboard wave at the north end. **Playa Blanca** is situated in Puerto del Carmen and not to be confused with the wave-less Playa Blanca resort to the south. This south-facing beach only really has waves during screaming onshore easterlies or the strongest of N-NE winds. The peaks in front of McDonalds are usually best. Low consistency and when there are waves, the lifeguards will red flag the beach – ask their permission before you surf. The **West Coast** beach/reefbreaks of El Golfo and Playa de Janubio are so exposed to swell and strong currents that they are usually unmakeable and too dangerous to surf – avoid.

GECKO

Jameos del Agua

Both Lanzarote and Fuerteventura consistently pull in the best of the NW-N swells that arrive throughout the major swell season from Oct to March. Deep North Atlantic lows send 4-15ft swells onto the exposed reefs, occasionally topped-up by long distance W swells created by hurricanes or weather systems off the Atlantic coast of America. Summer trades can produce surprisingly big east coast surf, but it is usually very disorganised, short period and wind-blown, hence the popularity of kitesurfing. Small, well-spaced, but rare S swells can also materialise through summer. Wind strength and direction will govern where you surf more than anything else does. The best conditions occur in late autumn/early winter (Nov-Jan), when the NE trades are at their lightest and have a more ENE aspect. Winds tend to get stronger and more NNE towards the end of winter then right through summer. The tidal range hits 2.9m in Arrecife affecting all shallow spots.

| STATISTICS | | J F | M A | M J | J A | S O | N D |
|---|---|---|---|---|---|---|---|
| SWELL | Direction | | | | | | |
| | Size (ft) | 5-6 | 5 | 4 | 2 | 4-5 | 5-6 |
| WIND | Direction | | | | | | |
| | Force | F4 | F4 | F4 | F4 | F3-F4 | F4 |
| WATER | Wetsuit | | | | | | |
| | Temp/°C | 18 | 18 | 19 | 22 | 22 | 20 |
| WEATHER | Rainfall/mm | 37 | 22 | 3 | 0 | 18 | 55 |
| | days/mth | 5 | 3 | 1 | 0 | 2 | 6 |
| | Min temp/°C | 14 | 15 | 18 | 21 | 20 | 16 |
| | Max temp/°C | 21 | 23 | 25 | 29 | 27 | 23 |

# Sardinia ITALY

Italy is hardly the most popular of European surf destinations, however the dominant NW Mistral wind blows with such regularity and power that Sardinia really does get consistent winter waves. It's the second largest island in the Med and there are waves all around it, but the west coast around Capo Mannu has a real concentration of reliable, quality spots.

+ FAIRLY CONSISTENT SURF
+ A VARIETY OF DIRECTIONS
+ MELLOW CROWDS
+ HISTORICAL & CULTURAL SITES

- WINDY CONDITIONS
- SHORT-LIVED SWELLS
- COLD WINTER CONDITIONS
- TOUGH ACCESS

## TRAVEL INFORMATION

**Weather** – Sardinia experiences a mixed Mediterranean and oceanic climate with low rainfall. Winters are cold and windy while spring and especially autumn bring plenty of sunshine and balmy temperatures. Avoid the summer heat, droughts, crowds and flat spells. 12-26°C (54-79°F) are the water temp extremes. Windchill factor is high. Take booties.

**Lodging and Food** – Stay in Oristano for the best hotel choices or Putzu Idu for apartments and villas. The Is Benas B&B Surf Camp and Resort, Capo Mannu (fr $295/3d). A good, basic meal is $20.

**Nature and Culture** – Italy has 50% of the World Heritage monuments. The west coast is beautifully untouched. In winter the only lively bars are in historic Oristano.

**Hazards and Hassles** – Weekends and holidays can get busy, but Italians are generally laid-back and good fun to be around. Beware of sharp rocks, urchins and plagues of jellyfish.

**Handy Hints** – Revolt Surf Shop carries a good range of equipment in the Capo Mannu area or try Wipeout in Cagliari. Kitesurfing is big all around the island.

DAN HAYLOCK

Sa Mesa Longa

On Sardinia's NW-facing coast, check Rena Majore, **Marinedda**, Badesi and La Ciaccia, hopefully when the wind backs off. More waves break deeper in the gulf on N and NE windchop or storms from the W-NW. **Silver Rock** is a powerful reef producing long ripable rights and fast hollow lefts over a rock bottom and is surfable in light onshore conditions. **Porto Ferro** is a very consistent spot that turns on in most swells. Several performance peaks with vertical walls over sand and rock. The left reef at the south end can line-up in big windy SW swells and stay clean. Strong currents, but very good water quality. Alghero has some south-facing, storm protected reefs plus an offshore island left at Maddalenedda. The top quality righthand pointbreak **La Speranza** produces powerful tubes in any W swell and handles the regular strong NW winds. Fast, hollow and shallow so intermediates or better. There are beachbreaks in front of the bar and more reefs to the south. Long line-up spreads the crowd. **S'Archittu** shapes up long righthanders over reef in solid SW storms and it holds up with strong onshores. On the best days the three sections connect and 700m rides are possible. The last section is the most powerful. Sharp rock bottom with sea urchins and strong currents on big windy days. Around the headland, **Islas Arenas** offers both reef peaks and beachbreaks along this swell and wind exposed stretch. North-facing reef and beach grace the next big bay at Su Crastu Biancu and Sa Boca Tunda respectively, but the real quality reefbreaks are found out on the Su Pallosu promontory. Outside the **Sa Mesa Longa** reef enclosing the lagoon, breaks a beautiful A-frame on a shallow rock bottom. Sa Mesa activates on any SW, W and especially sizeable NW swells but cannot be surfed with onshore wind. Use the channel on the left of the little island to get to the line-up. Often crowded with some attitude. Very famous among Mediterranean surfers, **Capo Mannu** area is a true swell and surfer magnet. The long right pointbreak peels down the south side of the Capo Mannu peninsula, one of the few spots sheltered from the NW gales. Easy take-off and hollow inside with 200m long rides possible. Highly consistent and often crowded, hazards include rips, sharp rocks on entry/exit plus it's seriously localised. Directly offshore in the NW Mistral, **Mini Capo** is one of the most consistent and technical waves in Italy. Mini Capo's reef peak offers several fast barrel sections and a steep inside, which makes for a long ride. The left is shorter but more intense. Always crowded with sharp locals, urchins and rocks. Easy access from little beach on left of carpark. La Punta is another nice right slide that needs W in the swell to wrap around the corner and into the bay to wake up protected Banzai and Lo Scivolo. Next beach is Putzu Idu, a curve of pretty average beachbreak that needs a big swell to have anything worth riding. A bit further south, **S'Arena Scoada** is better exposed with west-facing sandbars picking up some reasonably reliable peaks. Sardinia's surf continues down the rugged southwest coast and driving distances between spots increase markedly. Notable spots include the harbour jetty at Buggerru and the hard to find A-frame reef at Guroneddu. The islands of San Pietro and Sant'Antioco have surf in W swells but the half a dozen south coast spots around Chia also work on storms from the E and SE. A few waves will break around Cagliari and the marginal east coast in any NE-S pulses.

The consistent, forceful Mistral wind arrives from the WNW-NW bringing windswells that average 6-8ft with 8sec period, which can rise dramatically within hours. SW-facing spots are OK in the predominant NW winds. Winds can be variable with plentiful N and E winds. Cagliari tides never exceed 0.4m!

SHANE PEEL

S'Archittu

| STATISTICS | | J F | M A | M J | J A | S O | N D |
|---|---|---|---|---|---|---|---|
| SWELL | Direction | | | | | | |
| | Size (ft) | 3 | 2-3 | 2 | 1 | 2-3 | 3 |
| WIND | Direction | | | | | | |
| | Force | F4 | F4 | F4 | F4 | F4 | F4 |
| WATER | Wetsuit | | | | | | |
| | Temp/°C | 13 | 14 | 19 | 24 | 22 | 16 |
| WEATHER | Rainfall/mm | 50 | 37 | 19 | 5 | 42 | 67 |
| | days/mth | 8 | 6 | 2 | 1 | 5 | 9 |
| | Min temp/°C | 7 | 10 | 16 | 21 | 17 | 10 |
| | Max temp/°C | 14 | 18 | 25 | 30 | 25 | 18 |

# Lazio ITALY

Italy actually receives regular waves, sometimes as high as double overhead, despite most Italians saying there are no waves in the tranquil Mediterranean. It's true in summer when wave height is usually tiny and crowd size is huge, but winter brings low pressure systems from the Atlantic or western Med. Tuned-in surfers then track the storm, hoping for strong onshore winds to blow hard and long enough to bring swell to the Italian coastline. The Lazio coast receives these swells from a full 180° window, anytime from autumn through winter to spring, with the closest spots sitting a mere 30min from Rome.

+ STA. MARINELLA QUALITY REEFS
+ UNUSUAL SURF DESTINATION
+ MEDITERRANEAN CLIMATE
+ GREAT FOOD AND WINES

– MOSTLY INCONSISTENT SPOTS
– POTENTIAL CROWDS WHEN GOOD
– OFTEN ONSHORE OR VERY WINDY
– POLLUTION

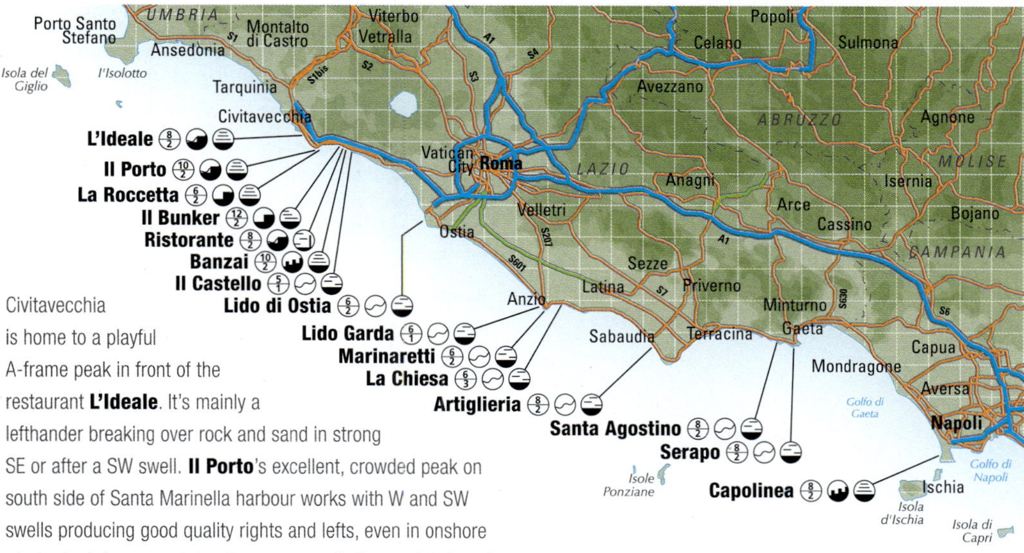


Civitavecchia is home to a playful A-frame peak in front of the restaurant **L'Ideale**. It's mainly a lefthander breaking over rock and sand in strong SE or after a SW swell. **Il Porto**'s excellent, crowded peak on south side of Santa Marinella harbour works with W and SW swells producing good quality rights and lefts, even in onshore winds. An A-frame peak breaks on a very shallow rock ledge at **La Roccetta**. The right is longer but slow, the left is shorter but intense and offers barrelling sections. Needs small windless SE, SW and also W swells. **Il Bunker** needs a big swell, preferably from the NW, to activate a powerful righthander breaking on a shallow reef in front of a WWII bunker. **Ristorante** is inconsistent but the short, fast rights off the jetty, just north of Banzai offer potentially good rides in less crowded conditions. Home to three generations of Italian surfers and the most crowded spot in Italy, the reef at **Banzai** miraculously breaks under SE, SW, W and NW swells. First place to check on any conditions and attracts big crowds from the capital. The reef holds righthanders with SW and W swells and lefthanders with SE. Gets shallow on the inside where sea-urchins lurk. Rome's longboarders often head to **Il Castello**, an average beachbreak just next to the castle in Santa Severa. Its peaks are best in SE windswell up to 5ft. The long sandy beach at **Lido di Ostia** (the closest to Rome) offers several average breaks in small, windless SW to NW swells. Surfable with moderate onshore and often a crowd of desperadoes. Mediocre beachbreak at **Lido Garda** needs W in the swell. More peaks beside local harbour. **Marinaretti** next to Anzio harbour might offer better quality waves and a little shelter from N winds, but it's really inconsistent. The beachbreak at **La Chiesa** offers short rides when Lido Garda & Marinaretti are too messy or overcrowded. **Artiglieria** in Sabaudia is a highly consistent beachbreak with plenty of fun peaks offering fast peeling waves with potential barrelling sections. Fast lefthanders on the south side of **Santa Agostino** beach when a SE swell hits a windless day. **Serapo**'s 2km of beachbreak in the heart of Gaeta offers several easy peaks under many conditions. The north side of the beach is surfable with big NW or small windless SW swells while the south side works in SE swells. The wide bay at **Capolinea** is conveniently exposed to SE, SW and NW swells. Rights and lefts break sheltered from the wind on rock bottom.

EMILIANO MAZZONI

Banzai

## TRAVEL INFORMATION

**Weather** – Rome offers a Mediterranean climate with hot summers and mild winters. In summer, temps rarely go under 28°C (82°F) but evenings are cooled by the Ponentino, a W wind from the Tyrrhenian Sea. The winter climate sees warm, sunny weather punctuated by frosts and occasional light snowfalls. Autumns feature heavy, persistent rain during the frequent SW and SE weather fronts. Spring or early autumn is the best weather with some waves. Use a 3/2mm fullsuit from December to April, a shorty or boardshorts for the rest of the year.

**Lodging and Food** – Accommodation is not cheap. Try Rifugio dei Cardinali in Santa Marinella (fr $70/n + apartments for rent). T-Village in Anzio (fr $400/w). Italy is renowned for excellent pastas, pizzas, wines and coffees. Expect $30 for a decent meal.

**Nature and Culture** – 28 centuries of history to visit; Roman ruins, archaeological sites, museums, churches or Renaissance art. Home of the Vatican, the world's smallest country!

**Hazards and Hassles** – Crowds are guaranteed every time it gets good. Watch out for rocks and urchins getting in/out of the water. Polluted breaks near the Tevere river. Shark attack on a surfer occurred in 1989 in Tuscany.

**Handy Hints** – A shortboard and a fish/fun/longboard for mushy days. Surf shops at the most popular breaks (Banzai Surf Shop in Santa Marinella) or in Rome (Waterworks, Salt Store). Booties are useful for sharp rocks and the dreaded sea urchins! There is no heavy localism in Lazio, but the crew at Banzai are famous for being straight and vocal if you show disrespect or waste waves.

FEDERICO VANNO

Lido di Ostia

Flexibility is the key as it is necessary to follow the swell and wind patterns, with SE-SW swell dominant. Only long periods of strong winds are able to generate sufficient windswells. The warm Sirocco wind originates over North Africa, where it can generate great SE swells but consistency is low (<50 days per year). A spell of Sirocco weather in autumn often ends with very heavy rain accompanied by thunder. Mistral (NW) is the main source of wind in summer, it will generate good waves if it blows strong enough. The Libeccio (SW to W) is the third wind option. Long summer flat spells of weeks are not uncommon. Lazio max tidal range is 45cm slightly influencing the shallow reefs of Santa Marinella.

| STATISTICS | | J F | M A | M J | J A | S O | N D |
|---|---|---|---|---|---|---|---|
| SWELL | Direction | | | | | | |
| | Size (ft) | 2 | 2 | 1-2 | 1 | 1-2 | 2-3 |
| WIND | Direction | | | | | | |
| | Force | F4 | F4 | F3-F4 | F3 | F4 | F4 |
| WATER | Wetsuit | | | | | | |
| | Temp/°C | 13 | 14 | 19 | 24 | 22 | 17 |
| WEATHER | Rainfall/mm | 67 | 54 | 42 | 18 | 81 | 111 |
| | days/mth | 9 | 7 | 5 | 2 | 7 | 11 |
| | Min temp/°C | 5 | 8 | 15 | 20 | 15 | 7 |
| | Max temp/°C | 12 | 17 | 25 | 30 | 24 | 15 |

# Malta and Gozo

The most southerly capital of the European Community sits in the middle of the Mediterranean Sea, where it has withstood a pounding from millennia of Mistral or Grecale wind-driven waves. Malta & Gozo have an incredible history, with megalithic evidence as old as 5000 BC and a constant trail of invasions up until independence in 1964. Surfers are yet to invade in numbers, since it's a winter-only destination, which leaves a handful of quality reefbreaks and fun beachbreaks to the small friendly crew of dedicated local surfers.

- \+ NW AND NE SWELLS
- \+ QUALITY REEFS & BEACHES
- \+ NO CROWDS
- \+ NO TIDES

- – WINTER ONLY
- – LACK OF CONSISTENT SPOTS
- – COASTLINE CLIFFS
- – JELLYFISH & SHALLOW ROCKS

## TRAVEL INFORMATION

**Weather** – Typically Mediterranean climate with hot, dry summers and short, cool winters. 75% of the total annual rainfall falls between October and March. Winds are strong and frequent; the most common are the cool NW (Majjistral), the dry NE (Grigal), and the hot humid SE (Xlokk). Water temps bottom out at 14°C (58°F) and top out at 28°C (82°F); take some neoprene for jellyfish in warmer months.

**Lodging and Food** – Package deal hotels are usually huge with lots of tourists. AirBnB, cheap guest-houses or small hotels from $30/n. In winter, stay in Mellieha, St-Paul's Bay or St-Julian's. Italian restaurants are good; $25 for a meal.

**Nature and Culture** – Scuba diving is big with countless diving centres around. There's an abundance of architecture (Mdina, Valletta) and ancient sites (Mnajdra Neolithic Temples) as well as lively pubs and discos in Paceville and Sliema.

**Hazards and Hassles** – The local scene is growing, creating super-friendly crowds at Ghajn Tuffieha, where sharing waves is normal. Beware with Pelagica Noctiluca jellyfish with SW winds and some reefs can be nasty. Traffic and driving can be mad with the planet's 2nd highest density of cars driving on the left.

**Handy Hints** – A fish and a longboard will do. Good kitesurfing. Surfing Malta run a mobile Mellieha surf hire service with boards, SUP's, windsurfers, wetsuits etc. Freeway sells/rents a few boards.

BRUCE SUTHERLAND

Riviera

On relaxed Gozo, the novelty wave on the **Inland Sea** occurs when NW or W storms penetrate the small tunnel through the cliffs, creating knee-high peaks over the rocky fingers of reef in the enclosed lagoon. A longboard and a large slice of swell and luck are needed. **Salt Pans** in Qbajjar is the best wave around, starting bigger on the outside of the point before cleaning up and offering a good wall for manoeuvres through the inside. Handles as big as it gets but needs NE direction to get into the bay. Scattered reefs to the east of **Marsalforn** harbour in NW-NE swells. Very difficult to negotiate in big swells. Sharp rocks. Gozo's main beach is **Ramla** where a decent NW swell will get lefts running down the beach or rights in NE swell. Can be some sucky take-offs and walls into the inside where strong currents and Roman sea defence ruins lurk. A steep concrete road leads to **San Blas** a secluded beachbreak with generally ugly waves in a beautiful setting on NW–NE swells. **Armier** faces the channel and surprisingly prefers big NE swells to create some shorebreak lefts over the sand and rock bottom. **Mellieha** is a popular kitesurf or SUP spot and will only have a weak wave in stormy NE swells. There's a backwashy wedge at the south end and more exposed beachbreak at Mgiebah. Spinning down the side of St Paul's Island and rarely surfed is **Apostle's Right**, a testing righthand reef during strong NE swells that is offshore in any S wind. Popular with windsurfers and surfers, **Ghallis Rock** is an exposed outer reef that throws up shallow fast lefts that can be challenging. Very exposed to any N wind, so it is often blown-out. Only experienced surfers should take on the rocky line-up and tricky access. **The Pole** has a gnarly inside death section and the lefts are suicide. Needs specific size and swell to be anywhere near good. **Marley's** at Palm Beach is a slab reef and the closest break to Valetta. Rights and lefts with shallow sections on a narrow beach, make it one of the more consistently rideable spots, despite missing out on NW swells. Need booties for the sharper rocks on the inside. On occasional SE swells, everyone heads to the ripable left at **St Thomas Bay**, which is good for all abilities. **Gnejna Bay** is sloppy, inconsistent and usually onshore in the NW wind, making it more of a kiteboarding spot. Malta's most consistent surf is found at **Riviera** in Ghajn Tuffieha Bay where a nice peak breaks next to the Riviera Bar and longer lefts wind into the inside with some great whackable and launchable sections. Jump off rock into channel beside the cliffs. Often crowded with the island's welcoming surf community. **Golden Bay** is worth a check in SW swells, which it usually picks up better than Riviera, producing some average longer lefts and rights along with strong currents.

With 500km of fetch in both the NW and NE direction, good-sized, longer period swells will build in the Ionian Sea and the Sicily Channel. The NW Mistral flux often regenerates in the Sicily Channel and produces the highest frequency of waves. The NE Grecale swells from the Ionian Sea are less frequent but can be good and chunky. Southern swells from Libya or due E swells are rare, short-lived and few south coast spots exist. Swells rarely hang around for more than 24 hours, 8ft is as big as it gets and only short and mid-term (3 days) forecasts can be reliable. 25cm tide in Malta.

YEP

Salt Pans

| STATISTICS | | J F | M A | M J | J A | S O | N D |
|---|---|---|---|---|---|---|---|
| SWELL | Direction | | | | | | |
| | Size (ft) | 2-3 | 2 | 1-2 | 2 | 1-2 | 2-3 |
| WIND | Direction | | | | | | |
| | Force | F5 | F5 | F4-F5 | F5 | F4 | F5 |
| WATER | Wetsuit | | | | | | |
| | Temp/°C | 15 | 16 | 20 | 25 | 23 | 18 |
| WEATHER | Rainfall/mm | 75 | 4 | 1 | 1 | 46 | 101 |
| | days/mth | 10 | 33 | 7 | 4 | 5 | 11 |
| | Min temp/°C | 10 | 12 | 17 | 22 | 20 | 14 |
| | Max temp/°C | 15 | 17 | 24 | 29 | 26 | 18 |

# Epirus GREECE

The Greeks have long had an affinity with the sea, which is now extending to surfing. With slightly more than 1000 islands, there is lots of choice from Crete, to the Aegean Sea islands like Chis, Kos, Naxos, Rhodos or Thinos or the Peloponnese peninsula, which is exposed on both sides. However, it's the coast of Epirus, right below Albania, that gets both S swells from the Ionian Sea as well as NW swells from the southern Adriatic Sea, which combined with the highest density of quality surf spots, make this region Greek surf central.

- \+ VARIOUS WINTER SWELLS
- \+ QUALITY WAVES FOR MED
- \+ BEST SPOT DENSITY IN GREECE
- \+ BEAUTIFUL MOUNTAINOUS REGION

- – INCONSISTENT
- – SHORT-LIVED SWELLS
- – WINTER CONDITIONS
- – LONG DRIVE FROM ATHENS

Kastro Point
Kattouristra
Krioneri/Panagis Is
Amoudia Right
Amoudia Left
Kerentza
Loutsa
Teris Point
Lygia
Little Bay
Lygia Reef
Kastrosika
Mytikas
Shark Reef

Parga's little beach town is packed with tourists and flat in summer, but SW storms produce one of the most scenic lefts in the Med, **Kastro**. Waves wrap around the cliffs and jack up a bit to give extra power and a hittable wall. It can get crowded but wave sharing and a really friendly vibe is the norm in Greece. Check the punchy rights at **Kattouristra** in the polluted port of Parga. **Krioneri Beach** has a rocky left and Panagis Island is a 200m paddle for softer lefts in the waist to chest high range. On the north side of a deep, scalloped bay, **Amoudia Right** breaks off the headland over sand, on SW swells and E winds. Nice peelers with workable faces. When short fetch, short duration NW swells hit, **Amoudia Left** is the place to check. A really long sandbank forms a fun pointbreak-style left off the rivermouth jetty and it works in onshore NW winds. **Kerentza** is well-protected from most winds and is usually uncrowded when a decent swell gets the rights working. Long and wide, **Loutsa Beach** is a sandy residential area and probably the most consistent beachbreak in Epirus. Picks up S-NW swells and it has easy parking and beach access in winter. **Teris Point** shelters some average beachbreaks that usually line-up into rights during S-W swells. **Lygia** main beach prefers S in the swell and N in the wind to clean up nice lefts and rights that occasionally throw up some hollow pockets. **Little Bay** hosts a rockier beach peak with good NW wind protection. A channel splits quality **Lygia Reef**, where fast, walled-up rights and lefts with hollow sections, spin over an urchin-infested reef during SW-W swells and an E wind. **Kastrosika** has average messy beachbreaks that appear during a SW storm and hopefully a NE wind to organise the peaks. A 200m paddle off **Mytikas**, a reliable left reefbreak lines-up best in summer W or NW swells. The same swells see good lefts unload on a flat, urchin-covered reef called **Sharks Reef** in Kalamitsi.

In Greece, generally speaking, SW swells happen in winter and N swells happen in summer. For the Greek islands, Meltemi N winds blow the strongest between June and September peaking July-August and creating excellent windsurf & kite conditions as well as 2-5ft onshore waves, although winter can also produce strong northern fetches. SW winds produce the longer period swells in winter, being able to wrap into sheltered spots like Kastro at around headhigh. Swells can last 2-3 days when the situation is perfect, but short-lived, 1 day swells are the norm. Epirus gets more offshore NE-SE winds than any other region, blowing down from the alpine mountains, especially in winter. That's when the beachbreaks like Loutsa or Amoudia or the reefs like Lygia or Mytikas get clean and totally rideable. Maximum 20cm tides in this zone!

YANNICK LE TOUQUIN
Kastro Point

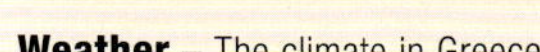

## TRAVEL INFORMATION

**Weather** – The climate in Greece is typically Mediterranean, but each area has its own unique micro-climate and weather forecast. The weather in Western Greece, particularly in the coastal regions of Epirus (Ipeiros) and the Ionian Islands is mild and characterised by relative humidity. Summers are hot, while winters are temperate and enjoyable. Rainfall in this area is frequent and among the highest in Greece. Due to its alpine nature, it gets colder away from the coast. The Mistro wind in summer is not as strong as Meltemi in the Aegean Sea, but is responsible for cooling down summer temps when the hopes of good surf is almost nil. In winter, the water can get down to 14°C (58°F) with the potential for high windchill factor.

**Lodging and Food** – During July/August, accommodation is tight but domatios can be found on the hill near Kastro, ranging from $50-65/n. Domatio owners usually meet the buses and offer their lodgings. In winter, it's cheaper and super easy. There are also three camp sites nearby. Expect $10-20 for a delicious meal in a small restaurant.

**Nature and Culture** – In Preveza, savour genuine local delicacies at the dozens of small tavernas that line the narrow streets. Ioanina is built on the shores of lake Pamvotida and is the largest and prettiest city in Epirus, with old buildings, narrow streets and natural charms. Check Perama's famous cave and the Mouzakei wax museum. Visit famous Greek temples. Drink some ouzo.

**Hazards and Hassles** – The beaches in summer are packed with thousands of sun-worshipping tourists. In winter, weather can be a bit chilly and wet with strong storms. Waves and locals are mellow, unlike the driving in Athens. Greek alphabet makes it hard to read the road signs when driving.

**Handy Hints** – There are two Frozen Wave surf shops; one in Athens near the airport and one in Glifada. Bring a longboard or a wider, thicker board to compensate for lack of power. Sell boards to the locals when leaving.

YANNICK LE TOUQUIN
Loutsa Beach

| STATISTICS | | J F | M A | M J | J A | S O | N D |
|---|---|---|---|---|---|---|---|
| SWELL | Direction | | | | | | |
| | Size (ft) | 2 | 1-2 | 0-1 | 0-1 | 1 | 2 |
| WIND | Direction | | | | | | |
| | Force | F4 | F4 | F3 | F3-F4 | F3-F4 | F4 |
| WATER | Wetsuit | | | | | | |
| | Temp/°C | 15 | 16 | 20 | 24 | 23 | 19 |
| WEATHER | Rainfall/mm | 133 | 81 | 24 | 15 | 114 | 179 |
| | days/mth | 12 | 8 | 4 | 3 | 9 | 14 |
| | Min temp/°C | 6 | 9 | 18 | 23 | 17 | 10 |
| | Max temp/°C | 14 | 18 | 28 | 33 | 27 | 17 |

# Southwest Black Sea TURKEY

The Black Sea is encircled by Bulgaria, Ukraine, Russia, Georgia and Turkey, with Istanbul straddling the narrow Bosphorus strait and therefore both the continents of Europe and Asia. There's a huge contrast between this bustling capital city and the rural Turkish coastline, where along the 'Kara Deniz' coastline, most families own just a tractor, and the roads are almost entirely clear. Turkey is one of the few surfing destinations where you actually surf in semi-fresh water, which greatly reduces buoyancy. Saltwater comes from the Mediterranean via the Bosphorus and the Sea of Marmara, whilst freshwater pours in from the bordering countries. Like bore-riders and lake surfers the world over, adjust your board accordingly. The winding coastal road from Erikli to Sinop reveals vast potential for untouched, empty waves.

- \+ TWO SWELL DIRECTIONS
- \+ NO TIDES
- \+ TOTALLY VIRGIN
- \+ SCENIC COASTAL ROAD

- – INCONSISTENT, SHORT-LIVED SWELLS
- – GUTLESS SMALL WAVES
- – COLD AND WET WINTER CLIMATE
- – LACK OF TOURIST INFRASTRUCTURE

YEP

Hardi

YEP

Zeus Temple

Near the town of Igneada, **Erikli** is one of the better waves in the Thrace region, a shallow rivermouth bar with short, thick rights and longer lefts. Both Port Kiyikoy and the long beach of **Kastro** are exposed to all swells with E in them and have rivermouths to sculpt some better sandbars. Across the Bosphorus are a few messy breaks round Sile and Cebeci, but consistency and size improve a long way east at **Bockoi Plaji**, a large beach with multiple set-ups. Located near an ancient **Zeus Temple** and the village of Kapisutu, this is a regional hotspot. A right point next to a longer rivermouth right sheltered by a grey granite cliff, plus a punchy beachbreak in the middle of the bay and good lefts on the west side of the cove. **Rivermouth Jetties** in Cide offer black sand beachbreak and NE wind protection.

**Yali Restaurant** in Cayyaka offers short dumpy beachbreak and potential for a right pointbreak. **Hardi** is a long lefthand pointbreak with several sections that needs a NNW swell to fire. A NE swell can see rights sweep past the rivermouth. A string of right points with rivermouths leads to **Hotel Touristik**, another righthand pointbreak with three distinctive sections. Big NNW swell should line up, while NE shoulders off. **Crane Beach** in Ayancik is an exposed cobblestone headland with a few rocks. Decent lefthander with 2 sections in W-NW swells. Excellent left pointbreak at **Oluza River** with 2-3 sections next to rivermouth. **Boat Shed** is a swell-puller that closes-out easily in a scenic cove with a single boat shed. A righthander breaks off a reef near the eastern headland. **Farmland**, a fast, ledgy right most suited to bodyboarding, is accessible via a dirt track. There's also a long beach with a quality peak in the corner sheltered from N winds. Inaccessible cliffs lead around to Sinop, where the left reefbreak at **Kalesi Plaji** was entombed by a harbour, but beach peaks break beside the wall to the west. New breakwalls have killed the lefts of **Kalesi Reef** but the easternmost reef is unaffected with scattered peaks on the outer reefs in bigger swells. Visible from main road 2km west of **Gerze**, a cobble reef off the headland holds decent rights and lefts depending on swell angle, with pebble beachbreak on either side.

## TRAVEL INFORMATION

**Weather** – Turkey gets extreme variations of temperature. The Black Sea coast receives the greatest amount of rainfall and is wetter in winter than summer and becomes more severe the further east you go. Because of a steep mountainous coastline, sun exposure can be very different from one spot to another. Temps get chilly in winter down to 5-15°C (41-59°F), whilst the weather can be pleasantly warm from 15-25°C (59-77°F) in summer. Transition months (Oct-Nov, April-May) are probably the best months to visit. There is snow on interior roads from Nov to April. Water gets down to 6-7°C (43-45°F), especially close to rivermouths. Take a 5mm fullsuit, boots, hood and gloves.

**Lodging and Food** – The best hotels in coastal towns won't cost more than $40, like Sinop Antik Otel. Staying in minor seaside resorts off-season will be a problem, with only cheap basic rooms to rent. Food is rich and varied, and everyone drinks tea. Expect to pay $10 for a meal. Beer is for sale in Tekel shops. Avoid Ramadan time.

**Nature and Culture** – Beautiful coastline between Amasra and Sinop. Go snowboarding in nearby Kartalkaya, Uludag or Ilgaz. Towns like Safranbolu or Amasra have a great feel to them, and Istanbul is a trip of its own. Try ferryboat rides in Yalova or Bandirma and visit the Prince's islands.

**Hazards and Hassles** – Driving can be sketchy on icy and snowy roads, and Istanbul traffic is mad. Beware of hypothermia if you surf on windy, cold days. Pollution problems in major coastal towns. Swells are short-lived and require a degree of forecasting skill.

**Handy Hints** – The Aegean and Mediterranean Sea both have coastal resorts with wind/kite surfing centres like Bodrum or Alacati, but no surfing equipment is available. Don't miss the big Bazar markets and the Mosque in Istanbul. You cannot access Bulgaria in a rental car.

Over its 1200km width, the Black Sea is hit by strong winter storms with a number of different fetches and a prevailing NW wind topped up by a good dose of NE days.. This stretch of coast receives 3-6ft swells during the storms, with 1-3ft clean surf in their aftermath. October through to March is the best season, but early winter has the mildest water temperatures. 2cm tides!

| STATISTICS | | J F | M A | M J | J A | S O | N D |
|---|---|---|---|---|---|---|---|
| SWELL | Direction | | | | | | |
| | Size (ft) | 3 | 2-3 | 2 | 1-2 | 2-3 | 3 |
| WIND | Direction | | | | | | |
| | Force | F4 | F4 | F4 | F4 | F4 | F4 |
| WATER | Wetsuit | | | | | | |
| | Temp/°C | 7 | 9 | 17 | 24 | 20 | 13 |
| WEATHER | Rainfall/mm | 70 | 65 | 42 | 35 | 71 | 87 |
| | days/mth | 10 | 10 | 7 | 4 | 7 | 9 |
| | Min temp/°C | 3 | 5 | 14 | 18 | 14 | 7 |
| | Max temp/°C | 10 | 14 | 21 | 26 | 23 | 15 |

Erikli
Kastro
Bockoi Plaji
Zeus Temple
Rivermouth Jetties
Yali Restaurant
Hardi
Hotel Touristik
Crane Beach
Oluza River
Boat Shed
Farmland
Kalesi Plaji
Kalesi Reef
Gerze

BLACK SEA
SEA OF MARMARA
Igneada
Kiliköy
Saray
Catala
Silivri
Kilyos
Istanbul
Sile
Pazarbaçi Burun
Cebeci
Kandira
Akçaova
Karasu
Akçakoca
Baba Burun
Eregli
Alapli
Devrek
Zonguldak
Caycuma
Amasra
Bartin
Kurucaçile
Cide
Kerempe Burun
Doganyurt
Inebolu
Abana
Turkeli
Ayancik
Ince Burun
Sinop Burun
Sinop
Gerze
Alacam
Bafra

# Tel Aviv ISRAEL

**Israel may seem an odd place to surf, having never been known for consistent or quality waves. It's not the place you'd go for a hard-core surf trip, but for learners and cruisers on all sorts of craft, there is enough winter windswell and some choppy summer waves to support a large community of keen riders. The long beaches are broken up by T-head groynes and jetties, which can bring some shape and permanence to the sandbars.**

+ GOOD JETTY SANDBANKS
+ UNUSUAL PLACE TO SURF
+ HISTORICAL SITES
+ TOP QUALITY HOTELS

- INCONSISTENT MUSHY WAVES
- CROWDED LINE-UPS
- PARKING HASSLES
- FAIRLY EXPENSIVE

In the northern city of Haifa, **Backdoor** is one of the best waves in the country as it is steep, occasionally hollow and breaks over a flat sandy reef between two jetties. Offshore in SW winds of winter but needs a bigger swell to break so it's inconsistent. Along Bat Galim beach past the **Casino**, good peaks will break a bit bigger, but mushier, offering something for longboarders and improvers, although the rocks make it unsuitable for learners. On the west-facing coast of Haifa, **The Peak** gets some SW wind protection from a parallel breakwall which collects sand into some wedgy peaks. Further north are some reef peaks for experienced surfers. To the south is a quieter jetty sandbar at Dado Beach. **Caesaria** has multiple options with beachbreaks at Shonit Beach and Sdot Yam, plus the quality, year-round peaks of Arubot Beach in front of the power station turbines. The fickle, shifting sands of **Netanya** are best surfed close to the groynes of Kontiki and Sironit beaches, but quality is rare. Might be more power down the beach at Argaman's Beach. **Herzliya**'s three breakwalls build up good sandbanks at tucked in Marina, Dabush and the open beachbreaks of Zvulun to the north, where wave heights will be higher. **Hazuk Beach** is a summer spot at the base of some cliffs, where there's plenty of space for anyone willing to ride sloppy little close-outs. The sandy reef at **Topsy**, will suit longboarders, where the fat, mushy sections are less crowded. In front of the **Hilton**, between the T-jetties, A-frames appear, with longer, hollower lefts, although there can be a powerful backwash. The inside sections are usually steeper and faster, but when it's big, it breaks outside of the jetties and the inside becomes mushy. The place gets very crowded, with lots of beginners despite the rocks making getting in and out tricky. **Dolphinairium** beach curves to face the NW, picking up the windswell better and will handle a SW wind, but it's nothing special. Easy parking - unusual for Tel Aviv! Surf beside the poles at **Hof Maravi** or there are more peaks in front of the short jetty and getting out can be hard when a bigger SW swell hits. In **Bat Yam**, have a look at Al Gal and Hagolshim for straight, exposed dune-backed beaches. On big swell days, a righthander will break down the southern side of the **Ashdod** harbour with power and hollow pockets. Down at the marina breakwall, nice peaks form in the protected corner, where there's a reliable, shapely left and a paddling channel for the big SW swells. Lots of occasionally hollow peaks between these two waves. Swell-sucking **Goote Beach** in Ashkelon cleans and softens NW swells around the jetties north of the marina or holds bigger, challenging peaks in winter W swells to the south.

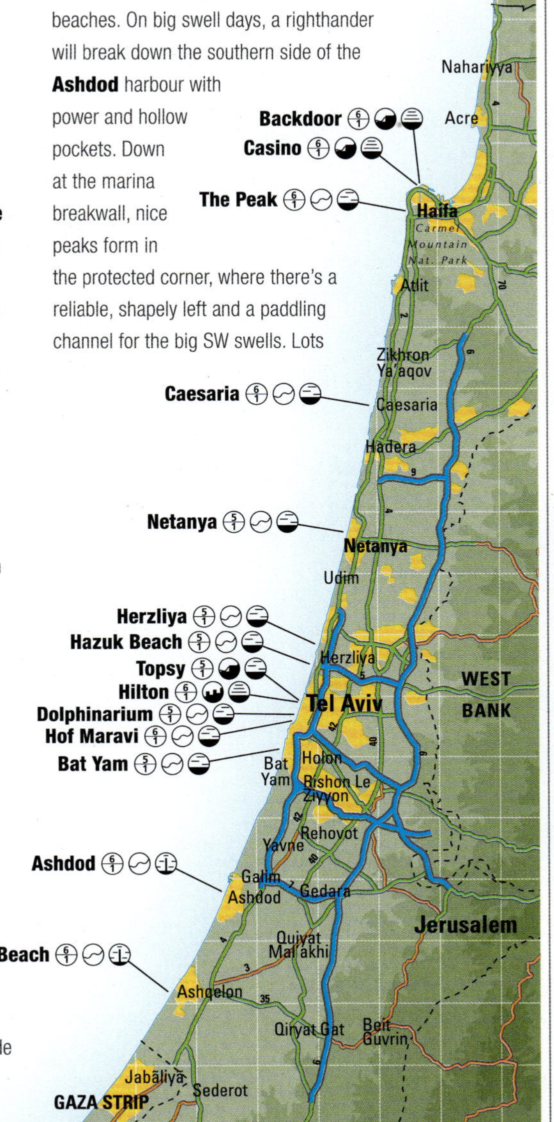

Herzliya

URI RICHTER

## TRAVEL INFORMATION

**Weather** – Winter (Nov-March) can get pretty cold, with temperatures as low as 5-10°C (41-50°F) in the morning. It can snow in Jerusalem. Winter rainfall can be quite heavy through Dec-Jan. Summers are hot and dry, especially when Sharav desert winds spread suffocating heat. For 2-3 months of the winter, you will need a fullsuit as the water drops to 18°C (64°F).

**Lodging and Food** – Tel Aviv is costly so if you can't afford the perfectly located Hilton ($380/d), then reckon on $90 for a guest house close to Hayarkon's Street (Gordon Inn). Eating falafel (chickpea sandwiches) will save you money on food.

**Nature and Culture** – Visit Jerusalem and the wonders of the old walled city. Plenty of flat days to float in the Dead Sea or drive five hours to Eilat and scuba dive in the Red Sea.

**Hazards and Hassles** – Most waveriders are kids on bodyboards, who crowd out the spots after 2 pm. Wake up early, especially if you need to park. Swarms of jellyfish in summer. Rain brings pollution to most line-ups. Terrorist attacks are random, but tend to be concentrated on the Gaza strip, the West Bank, Jerusalem and along the Lebanese border. Israeli stamps are a worry if you intend to visit Arab countries afterwards.

**Handy Hints** – Since the Paskotwitz/Kancepolsky dynasty launched surfing in the 50's, the surf industry has boomed. Board makers include Ultra-Wave (Herzliya), Inter Surf (Bat Yam) and Surf Club Israel, who do lessons and rentals.

Bat Yam

URI RICHTER

Mediterranean waves are almost exclusively generated by localised winds. Dominant winds are NW with a more N direction in summer and a SW-W theme in winter. Gusty summer winds will create 1-2ft chop while the best and more consistent swells are a result of winter SW-W winds with a longer fetch and period. Swells only last a day at a time and lack power and order. There are no sets to speak of, just typical short-spaced waves. Winter has some consistency with about 2 rideable days in a week in the 1-6ft range. Tides up to 45cm have little affect on the waves.

| STATISTICS | | J F | M A | M J | J A | S O | N D |
|---|---|---|---|---|---|---|---|
| SWELL | Direction | | | | | | |
| | Size (ft) | 2-3 | 2 | 0-1 | 1-2 | 0-1 | 2 |
| WIND | Direction | | | | | | |
| | Force | F4 | F3-F4 | F3 | F3 | F3 | F3 |
| WATER | Wetsuit | | | | | | |
| | Temp/°C | 18 | 19 | 23 | 27 | 25 | 21 |
| WEATHER | Rainfall/mm | 142 | 33 | 2 | 0 | 14 | 140 |
| | days/mth | 9 | 6 | 1 | 0 | 20 | 8 |
| | Min temp/°C | 9 | 12 | 18 | 24 | 21 | 14 |
| | Max temp/°C | 19 | 24 | 28 | 31 | 31 | 23 |

photo: m. lämmerhirt

# AFRICA

In terms of surf, Africa truly is the Dark Continent, representing the great unknown when it comes to vast tracts of swell-exposed coastline. The Atlantic dominates the continental mass, despite the best efforts of the Indian Ocean to pound the shorter eastern seaboard, while the Mediterranean marches out of the northern winter, bringing seasonal surf to the dusty, desert fringes. The two extremities of Morocco and South Africa are heavily surfed, mainstream destinations, but in-between them lays a whole continent of mysterious surf potential.

ALAN VAN GYSEN

J-Bay, St Francis Bay, South Africa

# The Surf

Wadi Naga, Libya

YEP

Casapeche, Algeria

JS CALLAHAN/SURF EXPLORE

## MEDITERRANEAN AFRICA

The enclosed nature of the Med limits the size and seasonality of the surf, as noted in Egypt and Tunisia so the same applies to **Libya**, where a legion of lefts march down the deserted desert coastline both east and west of Tripoli. Known spots include beachbreaks at Janzur just east of Tripoli, good reefbreaks around Misratah and the longest lefts in the Med at Wadi Naga on the NE coast. **Algeria** has less fetch in the western Mediterranean, but the most developed surf scene with a few regularly surfed beachbreaks around Algiers (Decaplage, Cherchell), but the best wave found so far is a left pointbreak out in the east at Ain Barbar, with a consistent, fun beachbreak nearby at Plage Mordjane. Swell size and frequency diminishes as the Med narrows toward the Straights of Gibraltar yet **Morocco** still manages to catch some rare NE windswell on both sides of the protruding promontory of Cap de Trois Fourches (La Bocana, Mina Rosita, Charrana) and even deeper west into the Alboran Sea at Playa de Targha, but by that time you are very close to Morocco's superior Atlantic coast.

## NORTHWEST AFRICA

Surfing in **Morocco** seems to be heavily concentrated around the two main hubs of Rabat to Casablanca and the surf-mad town of Taghazout in Central Morocco, but the rest of the coast is equally endowed. From El Jadida down to the hippy hang-out of Essaouira and on to Immesouane are any number of swell and wind exposed beachbreaks (Oualidia), plus quality right points (Sidi Bouzid, Cap Sim, Tafadna), including what is generally regarded as the best wave in the country at Safi. Down in the desert south beyond Tifnite are more exposed but often blown-out breaks, including Mirleft, Sidi Ifni and the legendary Boats Point, that hides itself well along this barren, stony coast. (See *Stormrider Surf Guide Europe* for more detail). **Western Sahara** may dispute its name and borders, but there is no argument about the quality of the waves, which would logically continue into **Mauritania**, but the empty, granular coastline lacks good set-ups and crumbly cliffs or open shapeless beaches dominate. Check the abandoned ghost town of Lagouira near Nouadhibou for several long, fast right points or the old wharf south of Nouakchott in deep winter. 600kms offshore, the **Cape Verde Islands** have some awesome setups throughout the archipelago with both N and S swell exposure if the angles are just right. While Sal is the go to island for surfers and kiters, Tarrafal on Santiago has a string of west-facing, boulder-strewn reefs. Many islands have steep craggy waveless coastlines for long stretches and inhospitable geology, blocking access to some waves on rocky beaches beneath the steep cliffs. (See *Stormrider Surf Guide Tropical Islands* for more info). **Senegal** has more to offer than just the epic concentration of waves on the Almadies Peninsula and limitless beachbreak stretches up to St Louis and down to **The Gambia** with a few rivermouths and points thrown in (Somone, Baobabs). This region suffers from an extensive continental shelf so the beaches near the Gambia rivermouth (Bakau, Fajara) tend to be bigger than the string of rocky outcrops to the south (Tanji, Sanyang, Gunjur). Cap Skirring in the Casamance region of Senegal is worth a look for a long right.

## WEST AFRICA

**Guinea Bissau** and **Guinea** are shielded by an extensive section of continental shelf, draining any swells of much power. **Sierra Leone** has slightly better prospects with regular fun lefts in S swells at Bureh Beach where a surf camp makes life easy. Check River Number Two's sand bars closer to Freetown and the Turtle Islands, where a long righthander chases the transient sands. The lefts in Northwest Liberia are touted amongst Africa's best, Ivory Coast has a wealth of well-documented beachbreak, while Ghana brings a mix of rocky and sandy points to the West Africa equation. Togo and Benin can occasionally shock with some powerful shorebreaks in the land of voodoo, but it is **Nigeria** that represents the longest coastline with dead-straight beachbreak as far as the eye can see, or dubious rivermouth shoals in the east. The main breaks are Lighthouse and Tarqua at the polluted mouth of the Lagos channel, or the Shipwreck, giving some shape to the waves. **Cameroon** is even less of a destination with poor exposure to swell, but in the wet season on a pushing tide check the Limbe beaches at Eseme, Mile 6 and 8. Way down south is some rock-strewn beachbreak at Kribi.

Nigeria

GREG EWING

## EQUATORIAL AFRICA

**Equatorial Guinea** is a surfing backwater and the NW-facing mainland coast is marginal. Bioko is far better placed to pick up SSW ground and windswells that resonate in the deepwater bowl beyond the continental shelf. There's a south coast left called Nacho or the east coast righthand point of Caracas, just north of Riaba. **São Tomé** will have some small, unpredictable waves in a crowdless zone where the surf season luckily coincides with the dry season. while Principe is a bit shadowed by São Tomé, but if there is a due S swell then south coast beaches like Praia Infante will hold some headhigh waves, albeit onshore. In **North Gabon** French expats and oil industry workers surf the beachbreaks around Port Gentil but the extensive littoral strip of jungle-clad beaches and lagoons in the Loango National Park remain untouched by all but the resident surfing hippos and elephants. Much further south, the large promontory of Mayumba organises long lines of lefthanders to hug the point for hundreds of metres. **Republic of Congo** has plenty of featureless beaches north of the main **Pointe-Noire** area while the confusingly named **Democratic Republic of Congo** has only 37kms of silted-up straight-handers apart

# SWELL FORECASTING

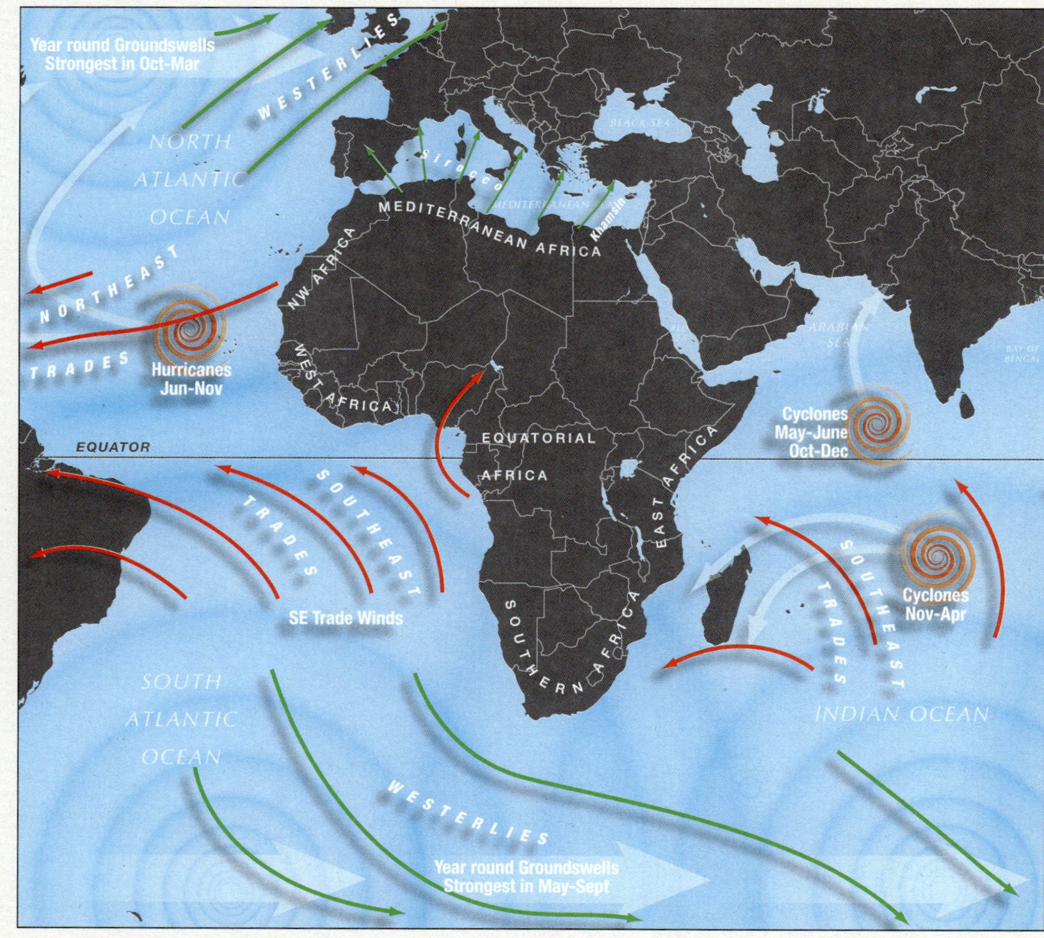


## MEDITERRANEAN AFRICA

This arid north-facing coastline relies on storms and cold fronts sweeping eastwards through the Mediterranean basin, driving windswell from the W, NW and N. The majority of these storms occur in December, January, February and March. The dominant wind in the northern Med, the Mistral, is the greatest swell producer, sending out NW pulses to Tunisia, Libya and sometimes as far as Egypt. Localised storms can bring windswell from all points of the compass and there is a name for most wind directions. The due N Tramontana brings N swell to Algeria, but the winter Poniente pattern will come from the SW-W, delivering swell to Europe. The Ionian sea can produce 24hr swells out of the SE for Tunisia when dust laden Sirocco winds blow out of the desert. All swells are usually short-lived, with a brief window of clean surf before the passing storm blows out exposed coasts, forcing a search for sheltered spots in a dropping swell scenario. There is an anti-cyclonic current running west to east across the north coast of Africa, but with micro-tides in the 0.37m range, when there is swell, waves are on tap all day.

## NORTHWEST AFRICA

The northwest African coast from Morocco to Senegal, receive exactly the same North Atlantic swells that provide Europe's surf. The best location for swell producing low pressures is between Nova Scotia and Iceland, especially if they drift south, closer to the Azores. North Africa has an ideal NW orientation, and Morocco in particular picks up plenty of winter swell from November-March. The harmattan NE trade winds blow parallel to the coast, favouring the abundant rights that pepper the coast in Morocco, the Canary Islands and all the way down to Senegal. May-November brings more N winds, which are bad for Morocco and the Canaries, but fine for the S-SW-facing breaks of Cape Verde and Senegal. These strong summer N-NE winds can whip up surprisingly large windswell for the east coasts of the islands, but are obviously accompanied by onshore winds, making them very popular with windsurfers. This part of Africa's coastline is scoured by the Canaries Current, a consistently cool offshoot from the main North Atlantic, clockwise circulating, surface current. This water started its Trans-Atlantic journey in the Gulf Stream off Florida, on the same latitude, but lost 8°C (14°F) on the way. This part of West Africa is the only true area of upwelling in the North Atlantic, fitting the global trend of being adjacent to a desert with strong offshore trade winds.

## WEST AFRICA

Most West African countries south of Senegal's Almadies peninsula rely on swell from the constantly raging storms that track between Cape Horn and the Cape of Good Hope, half a world away in the southern ocean. The strongest of these South Atlantic swells can make it as far as the Cape Verde islands, but swell decay is a big issue for all countries north of the equator. The west-facing coast of this region can receive remnants of storm activity off the SE coast of USA and some swell off the backend of hurricanes travelling west to the Caribbean, but it is wholly unreliable. When long range winter S swells do arrive, between April and September, they usually coincide with the SW monsoon bringing light onshores and an intense rainy season to the Gulf of Guinea. These swells are generally small, but very clean and organised, with long periods, providing fun peeling waves in Sierra Leone, Liberia, Ivory Coast and Ghana. Togo, Benin, Nigeria and Cameroon suffer from lower wave heights thanks to the draining influence of the continental shelf in the continent's "armpit". The same harmattan N winds blow straight offshore from Dec-April, shaping perfect, small beachbreaks, but it's often flat during these months. The water temperatures are no surprise, radiating warmth from the Guinea Current, which flows down to the Benguela Current off Angola.

## EQUATORIAL AFRICA

The South Atlantic is notable for its lack of tropical storm activity, because it doesn't have the contrast in sea and air temperatures to get a storm spinning enough to become a hurricane. This makes the south and west-facing shores of equatorial Africa a little unexciting compared to other areas near the equator. Sao Tome, Gabon and Congo are all dependant on S-SW swells marching up the Benguela Current corridor in the depths of winter, so June-August will be the best months to guarantee enough size. Angola has better exposure adding the shoulder seasons and extending the winter from April-Oct, coinciding with the southerly winds that often blow out the surf in this region by midday. SE winds blowing up from Namibia can create some windswell for S-facing spots when it glasses off.

ALAN VAN GYSEN

Hermanus, East Cape, South Africa

from the rivermouth and lighthouse at Muanda. The **Luanda and Bengo** zone only covers a fraction of **Angola**'s wave wealth but the northern coast is too straight until the rivermouth and points begin north of N'zeto. Ambriz and Catumbo have lefthand points, then south of Cabo Ledo is an array of lefthand pointbreaks down to Porto Amboim and beyond that, the arid south beckons to the adventurous.

## SOUTHERN AFRICA

This is the prime surfing real estate on the continent where the land meets the restless southern ocean and quality waves frequent all three sides of Cape Africa. **Namibia** has some of the longest, hollowest lefts on the planet, not only in the inhospitable wilderness of the **Skeleton Coast** but also around Swakopmund. There's no doubt that the incredible desert wilderness to the south through Luderitz and down to the border hides more gems that both the diamond mining companies and the harsh environment will conspire to maintain a restricted access policy. **South Africa**'s 2800kms of coast is utterly blessed with every type of wave from cold heavy water

### SOUTHERN AFRICA

The water temp drops severely because of the Benguela Current, but the surf gets bigger and more consistent in Namibia. Often shrouded in dense sea mist and sometimes plagued by SW onshores, Namibia nevertheless holds the promise of challenging waves in a challenging frontier. Once again, the cross/offshore SE winds and large coastal desert combine to provide the world's biggest area of upwelling. As the name suggests, you can't get closer to the Southern Ocean storms than South Africa. Consistent SW swells together with SW winds spray the coast from Cape Town to Durban then keep on giving by sending first S then SE swells all the way up the Mozambique Channel. Winters get cold and windy, but the long coastline conceals plenty of classic surf tucked away in bays, including the planet's best right pointbreak. As the lows march eastwards, the swell and wind directions change, but the SW winter and SE summer pattern is fairly reliable, as is the NE sea breeze that picks up strength from November to April. Cyclone swell is always a possibility for the eastern provinces of South Africa and Mozambique, during the tropical storm window from November to April. Benguela's icy grip is loosened across the southern coast of Africa as the warm Agulhas Current heralds the arrival of the Indian Ocean. Flowing out of the NE, the Agulhas Current is only 100km wide off the Transkei coast and is one of the fastest-flowing currents in the world at around 9km/h.

### EASTERN AFRICA

Since Mozambique and Madagascar cut off the supply of southern ocean swells to Tanzania, Kenya and Somalia, this East Africa coastline relies on high pressure systems settled over Mauritius, driving windswell in from the SE. The stronger SW monsoon typically sees SE winds blowing on the edge of the high create a regular 6-12ft windswell, mostly from June to September, which diminishes to 3-6ft by the time it reaches the coast. Most of that swell arrives with the strong SE onshores, so rights wrapping around reefs create the only options for side/offshore conditions. The weaker NE monsoon that blows from December to March does produce occasional windswells but exposure is far from ideal and countries like Kenya remain mostly flat during the high tourist season. This is also cyclone season when powerful E-SE swells may show up, despite the bulk of the swell usually following the storm's parabola and heading southwards. North of the equator, cyclones in the Arabian Sea form up in May-June and October-December which can affect the Horn of Africa and possibly a bit of action for northern Kenya. This zone is fed by the large South Equatorial gyre and the East African Coastal Current flows from south to north, getting warmer as it heads into the Arabian Sea.

Mozambique

ALAN VAN GYSEN

Ballito, North Kwazulu Natal

GREG EWING

to near tropical perfection. Here's a very brief summary of regions not featured in the Southern Africa zones. Namaqualand on the Northern Cape, continues the Namib theme of desert forbidden zone patrolled by De Beers diamond mining security, dense fogs and strong winds. Check around Port Nolloth, Kleinsee, Hondeklip Bay and Strandfontein before entering the **Western Cape** zone. There are plenty of beachbreaks through Yzerfontein, Melkbos and Blauuberg leading down to some of the best big city surfing in the world at **Cape Town**. From False Bay east, via Africa's southern tip at Cape Aghulas, the Overberg region offers some heavy stormy water and it's the shark cage-diving epicentre of the world. Highlights include secretive hollow slabs, big wave reefs and plenty of good sandbars outside the winter months in towns like Hermanus and Gansbaai. **The Garden Route** lures with the promise of empty righthanders, tucked in below the mountains that parallel the coast all the way to Tsitsikamma National Coastal Park. Every surfer has heard of J-Bay, the world's best righthand pointbreak, nestled in **St Francis Bay**, a zone that includes the city beaches of Port Elizabeth, which along with Port Alfred, could easily be a stand-alone destination. Check both the jetty waves at Port Alfred but don't expect to get it to yourself. Same goes for the most consistent surf in SA at **East London** which also has the dubious mantle of most shark attacks on surfers, particularly at the main spot, Nahoon. The beginning of the former Transkei or **Wild Coast** sees water temperatures start to rise and late summer or autumn should see the sand and rock symbiosis at its best, lighting up the numerous pointbreaks along this scenic coast and there's plenty of exploration potential by 4WD. Referred to as "The South coast" by Durbanites **Southern Kwazulu Natal** is a veritable wave feast of points, beaches and barrels galore, within easy strike distance of the city. The **Durban** surf scene is centred around the handful of piers and jetties in the Bay of Plenty that provide so many options for the city surfers in both summer and winter, plus there are the gaping tubes of Cave Rock just around the corner. The elephant in the room is the surf that stretches for at least 400kms into the Northern Kwazulu Natal up to the Mozambique border. Famous competition venues like Ballito are closer to Durban, but beyond lies a sub-tropical playground of summer lefts or winter rights depending on swell angle. Lots of shifting sandbars and further north sees coral reefs taking the wave energy a little offshore, where doubtless many secret spots reside. Access is difficult with lots of reserves and a ban on beach driving but since crowds are minimal, surfers gravitate to the hotspots like Alkantstrand in Richards Bay, where jetties provide wind protection, Cape Vidal's reefy peaks, or Sodwana Bay rights in big swells and A-frames over coral at Lighthouse.

## EASTERN AFRICA

**Mozambique** is more off the map than on it, with the **Inhambane** region representing around one sixth of the country's coastline. Access can be near on impossible for some stretches of coast and 4x4 driving is painfully slow. In the far south, Ponta do Ouro is one of the few known spots and sets the tone for Mozambique's plethora of righthand pointbreaks. Rock plus sand translates as fickle and the NE wind doesn't help, so choose early morning, lower tides and hope for a wrapping S swell. The sandy barrier islands are more wind/kitesurfing territory and heading north increases the swell shadow from Madagascar, but the Sofala, Zambezia and Nampula provinces have a south-facing aspect that should be offshore in N winds at the many rivermouths and long sandy beaches. **Tanzania** suffers from bad luck in the swell stakes, with major shadowing from Madagascar and the large offshore islands of Mafia, Zanzibar and Pemba. Dar es Salaam has good coral reef set-ups to the south and the main beachbreaks north of town are Coco Beach/Oyster Bay and Sea Cliff. People surf around the main tourist resorts on the northern tip of Zanzibar, but a boat is essential to access the real waves on offshore reefs like Mnemba where the dive boats operate. **Kenya** evokes images of safari rather than surfari but Mombasa, Malindi and Manda are all regularly ridden. Kidnappings, piracy and terrorist attacks have made the north of the country off limits for safe tourism and things only get scarier over the border in **Somalia**, where some waves have been ridden up in the north at Cape Hafun as well as in Mogadishu. A surf journalist was kidnapped in Galkayo and held for almost three years before a large ransom secured his release – forget about surfing here...

# Al Diffa EGYPT

Alexandria is the second largest city and the chief port of Egypt, located on the northwest fringe of the Nile Delta and stands on the frontier between the lush, irrigated lands and the outskirts of the Sahara. The evolution of surfing in and around the city has been slow, and there remains only a tiny population of local surfers compared with the much larger surfing population in neighbouring Israel, just over the Gaza Strip. There may only be 60 rideable days a year, but Alexandria boasts a coast ideally exposed to the NW, where small, empty waves hit numerous beaches and reefs.

+ GOOD JETTY SANDBANKS
+ HISTORICAL SITES
+ TOP QUALITY HOTELS
+ UNUSUAL PLACE TO SURF

- INCONSISTENT MUSHY WAVES
- POLITICAL UNREST
- PARKING HASSLES
- FAIRLY EXPENSIVE

YEP

Alexandria

Furthest west past Marsa Matruh is **Agiba Cove**, a perfect left that breaks over shallow and sharp reef in a fjord-like bay that needs a big swell to break up to shoulder high. **Agiba Beach** is a beautiful, turquoise-blue beachbreak that picks up all available swell and holds some of the biggest waves in the country. Nearby **Cleopatra Beach** can also offer up various rocky beachbreaks and a left point near the famous rock formation called Cleopatra's Bath. There are a variety of fast, sand and sandstone bottom breaks along the **Mersa Baghush** stretch of coast in NW swells, but there is no access to the exposed promontory of Ras El Hekma where there is a presidential residence. **Ghazala Bay** has deep water just offshore, so can pack some punch, but needs a large swell due to its easterly aspect. **Ras Gibeisa** is a real swell-puller, with a great left pointbreak possible and perfect longboard waves when small, however the coastguard can deny access. **Marakha** is another sand and sandstone break, with clean waves breaking opposite the Hilton. Between Marakha and **Sidi Krier**, over 30 access roads lead to large hotel complexes with Mediterranean blue beachbreaks, many of which are closeouts. Around **El Agamy** are a number of beach towns with unlimited beachbreak options; one good tip is the old WW2 jetty by the Bianky coastguard station. **Library**, so called because of its proximity to the oldest library in the world, is one of the best beachbreaks around Alexandria, consistent and capable of holding some of the largest surfable waves in Egypt. Watch out for a current that flows east; getting trapped on a rocky shoreline with no exit is the danger. Library is one of the only beaches where you are likely to encounter other surfers. Alexandria itself has a coastal road that provides good access to a number of different waves. The actual access to the beaches is harder to find, and some charge a small fee. **Stanley Bridge**, a tourist highlight, has a decent set up with both rights and lefts. However, concrete in the water and a police presence make actually surfing here unlikely. **Sidi Bishr** is the most reliable beach in Alex, with surprisingly consistent sets during a swell, just opposite the Ramada. Parking can be tricky. A second **Cleopatra Beach**, accessible from the Montazah Castle Resort, has a potential righthand point; this is dangerous when stormy so best in a clean NW swell. At the east end of the Maamoura resort town, **El Farasa** is a shifty beachbreak with vicious currents.

Over the winter, cold fronts sweep eastward and drive waves from the W or NW. These onshore winds have a potential fetch of 1500km from Sicily to Egypt so clean offshore swell can hit the coast 12-36hrs before the storms arrive and blow out all but the E-facing spots. During summer, the Greek Meltem blows a constant NNW wind over the Aegean Sea, which produces regular onshore 1-2ft conditions at the beachbreaks.

STUART BUTLER

Agiba Cove

## TRAVEL INFORMATION

**Weather** – Egypt receives fewer than 80mm of rain annually in most areas. Most rain falls along the coast, but even the wettest area around Alexandria does not exceed 200mm. Alexandria itself has relatively high humidity, but sea breezes help keep the moisture down to a comfortable level.

**Lodging and Food** – Adham Compound hotel has nice rooms with sports facilities. You could stay on the Corniche hotels, but it is expensive and getting out of Alex can be tricky. Food is cheap and varied, with seafood and Mediterranean cooking.

**Nature and Culture** – Don't miss the Great Sea of Sands at Siwa oasis, about 6h from Alex. Snowboard or buggy on the dunes! Visit the Library or Montazah castle in Alex or check out underwater temples scuba diving. The Giza pyramids near Cairo are only 3h away.

**Hazards and Hassles** – The sea in summer can be really polluted by the Nile, but the surf happens in winter and the water is cleaner. Some beach access can be private and coastguards in winter may try to arrest surfers.

**Handy Hints** – Take all gear with you and plan to leave things behind with the few friendly locals.

| STATISTICS | | J F | M A | M J | J A | S O | N D |
|---|---|---|---|---|---|---|---|
| SWELL | Direction | | | | | | |
| | Size (ft) | 1-2 | 1-2 | 0 | 1 | 1 | 1-2 |
| WIND | Direction | | | | | | |
| | Force | F4 | F3-F4 | F3 | F3-F4 | F3-F4 | F3-F4 |
| WATER | Wetsuit | | | | | | |
| | Temp/°C | 17 | 18 | 22 | 26 | 25 | 21 |
| WEATHER | Rainfall/mm | 35 | 65 | 0 | 0 | 3 | 44 |
| | days/mth | 6 | 2 | 0 | 0 | 1 | 5 |
| | Min temp/°C | 11 | 14 | 19 | 23 | 21 | 15 |
| | Max temp/°C | 19 | 22 | 27 | 30 | 29 | 23 |

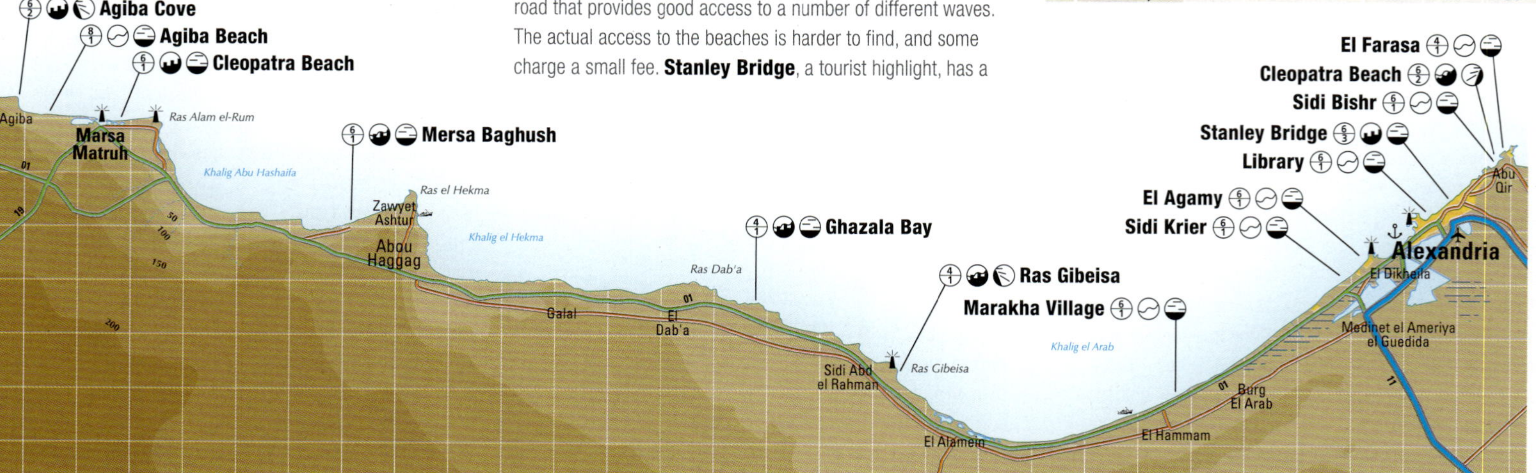

# Tunisia

When in need of a cheap escape from Europe, surfers traditionally go to Morocco or the Canaries, ignoring the Mediterranean Sea entirely. Tunisia, with cheap flights and 120 days of Mistral wind a year, offers a viable alternative destination with fairly consistent surf. Although Tunisia has been barely surfed for years, the wide swell exposure of the north coast and the potential for numerous lefts to break under the prevailing winter wind is attracting more French and Italian surfers.

- + HIGH MED CONSISTENCY
- + WIDE SWELL WINDOW
- + VIRGIN POINTBREAKS AND REEFS
- + CHEAP TOURIST DESTINATION

- – SHORT-LIVED SWELLS
- – CHILLY WINTER WEATHER
- – JELLYFISH PLAGUES
- – ROUGH NORTH COAST ROADS

Close to the Algerian border, **Cap Mérou** is a long, hollow, lefthand pointbreak offering one of the best rides in Tunisia. In the Tabarka area, the lefts at the **Amphithéâtre** de la Mer on the Cite Larmel side are a consistent option, particularly as they are side/offshore in a NW wind. **Fort Génois** is a right pointbreak needing size to clear the rocks and clean conditions to reveal its potential. Across the bay, near to Les Aiguilles, a short left also breaks in a solid swell. Along the **Route Touristique**, consistent beachbreak and coffee-rock reef options present themselves, between the hotels and golf course. Easy access to **Barboukech** leads to a beachbreak exposed to NW wind and swell. **Sidi Mechrig** is reached via a 45-minute detour off the main road and as well as ancient ruins, boasts exposed beach and reefbreaks. Driving west towards Bizerte, a 4WD helps access many of the coastal tracks leading to scenic bays. Between Cape Blanc and Cape Bizerte is **La Grotte**, with several lefthand reef options favouring clean conditions, but if a swell is running, head further east for the lefts of **La Corniche**. Driving from Bizerte to La Corniche with a good swell running reveals multiple sectiony lefthanders breaking right by the coastal road. Try the juicy left at Pointe du Daouli next to El Bistro restaurant. It is likely you will be surfing alone here, but unmarked gravel roads offer still more potential for seclusion. East of Bizerte and the canal crossing, a vast forest hides waves, including **Plage Remel** where three tankers have been shipwrecked. If the waves are clean they can be hollow. If the swell is too much for Corniche, drive eastwards towards Raf-Raf and be sure to check the **Metline Port**, very sheltered from NW winds but usually too small. **Raf Raf Plage** itself offers powerful rights and an attractive resort village, coastal range and island. Near the city of Tunis and the ancient ruins of Carthage, **Gammart** sometimes has mellow waves, but energy is sapped by the Gulf of Tunis. A straight N swell and NE wind can light-up the best right pointbreak in Tunisia, **Cap Méduse**, located near the Korbous ancient thermal station. Further up the cape lies **Sidi Daoud** and more wind exposed reefbreaks. Rounding the headland towards the Kelibia area, the impressive fortress at **El Mansourah** provides access to long, sandy beaches that pull plenty of swell. If an E-SE swell materialises, a drive down the east coast to Hammamet could be worthwhile, with long, sweeping lefts at Medina and more consistent peaks at Nhoza Beach. If in the area with time to spare, also check the reefs at Sousse and Monastir.

## TRAVEL INFORMATION

**Weather** – Whereas most of Tunisia experiences sub-Saharan climate, with dry warm temperatures year-round, North Tunisia has a Mediterranean climate with wet, mild winters and hot dry summers. During the winter surf season, expect a few rainy days requiring winter clothing because of wind chill.

**Lodging and Food** – In winter there is little choice of places to stay, few hotels are open and most guesthouses close. A 3-star hotel in Tabarka or Bizerte by the Corniche would be $30/dble. Food is good and cheap ($5/meal) but good restaurants on the road are rare and it's not easy to buy beer.

**Nature and Culture** – In Tabarka, there's golf or scuba diving for red coral, but in the off-season, options shrink to visiting the Genoese fortress. Bizerte is much bigger, including the double Kasbah near the old harbour.

**Hazards and Hassles** – Terror related attacks on tourists in 2015 have decimated the tourism industry. The surf is fairly safe unless you hit a rock or wreck. Little purple jellies called Pelagica Noctiluca are quite numerous in winter. Bring light gloves and booties to avoid stings. Apart from a handful of locals, there is never a crowd.

**Handy Hints** – Take a longboard for the smaller days and good walking boots for muddy fields. Internet facilities are rare and slow. Learn some French to get by at hotels and restaurants.

YEP

Cap Méduse

JS CALLAHAN SURFEXPLORE

Cap Mérou

| STATISTICS | | J F | M A | M J | J A | S O | N D |
|---|---|---|---|---|---|---|---|
| SWELL | Direction | | | | | | |
| | Size (ft) | 2-3 | 2 | 1 | 0-1 | 1-2 | 2-3 |
| WIND | Direction | | | | | | |
| | Force | F5 | F4 | F3-F4 | F3-F4 | F3-F4 | F4-F5 |
| WATER | Wetsuit | | | | | | |
| | Temp/°C | 14 | 15 | 19 | 24 | 23 | 17 |
| WEATHER | Rainfall/mm | 88 | 52 | 18 | 4 | 57 | 91 |
| | days/mth | 14 | 12 | 6 | 2 | 9 | 14 |
| | Min temp/°C | 7 | 9 | 15 | 19 | 16 | 9 |
| | Max temp/°C | 15 | 19 | 26 | 32 | 27 | 18 |

The majority of swell is provided by the NW Mistral and N Tramontana winds, when a day of clean surf arrives before the storm blows out exposed spots, then quickly fades. The Ionian Sea can create a short-lived SE windswell in the fetch from Libya, but doesn't carry enough power to wrap, so places that are offshore can often be flat. Tiny tides means waves all day.

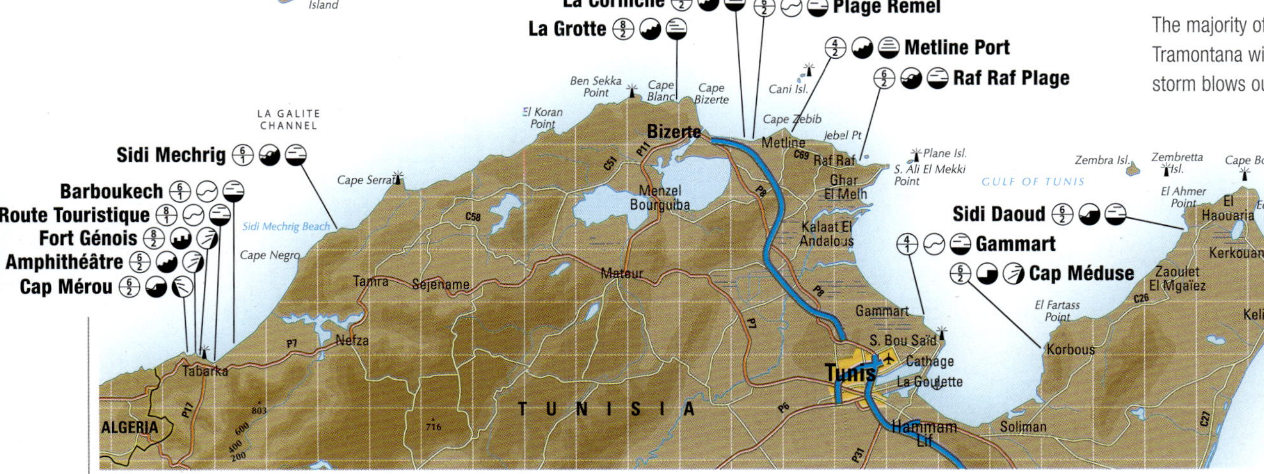

# Sal CAPE VERDE

**The Cape Verde islands are the southernmost group in the boomerang-shaped archipelago of Macaronesia. Made up of 10 major islands, Sal is the flattest island and the main tourist entry point. The island has become synonymous with wind and kitesurfing, since the year-round NE trades provide cross or offshore conditions on the west-facing lava reefs.**

- + GENERALLY UNCROWDED
- + SHAPELY REEF WAVES
- + EXPLORATION POSSIBILITIES
- + WIND/KITESURFING HEAVEN

- – INCONSISTENT, SEASONAL SWELLS
- – WINDY
- – FLAT DESERT LANDSCAPE
- – FAIRLY EXPENSIVE

Just south of the harbour at **Palmeira** sees a short, zippy left break into a clear channel on small to moderate swells and is worth the 35min drive if it is too small in Santa Maria. **Fontana** is a pretty place, located in a small bay that produces a mysto right when the swell is big. Needs E or SE winds so not very consistent. **Curral Joul** sits out on the tip of the exposed headland and will handle as big as it gets. The continuous line of rocks make the line-up difficult to read and it sections off badly in places, so experts only. Deeper in the bay and a much better bet is **Alibaba**, a superb walled-up righthander that motors down the rocky point, close to the cliffs, so it is less affected by the cross-shore NE'ers. **Monte Leão** can produce perfect, long rights and has the advantage of being quite sheltered from the wind by the Sleeping Lion mountain. It needs a big NW swell to wrap around the headland or a moderate WSW to sneak in between the other islands to begin breaking. The cluster of rocks at **Rife** is better suited to wave-sailing since the rights break lazily down towards the channel inside the protected bay. The best wave, 30 minutes walk from Santa Maria, is **Ponta Preta**, which has long rights peeling for up to 300m over sharp, black boulders. Barrel sections, speed walls and wind whipped copings are shared out between the surf and wind crews. This is a world-class wave so be sure your ability matches up. **Ponta do Sino** is a mixture of sand and reef that's usually bigger than Santa Maria, but often blown out. **Santa Maria** is an 8km (5mi) sandy beach on the southern tip of Sal that catches the all too rare SW swells and summer NE swells, along with big winter NW on the wrap. Mainly mellow, small beachbreaks, breaking around the wooden pier (Ponton) plus there are some lefts breaking on a reef close to the big hotel and old harbour. Nice, easy, beginner-friendly stretch at high tide over the sand and the left is used as an indicator to the west coast swell size. If you're lucky, and the persistent NE trade winds stop blowing, then the regulation 1-5ft (0.3-1.5m) NE windswell might clean up, meaning a check for rare long lefts, at the far end of **Fragata Beach** aka Kitebeach. There may be some good discoveries on the east coast in such conditions, but it's sharky. Don't forget about the other islands, with good waves to be found on Boa Vista, Santiago and Sao Vicente.

Only the biggest winter N and summer S groundswells will travel this far. Sal is blocked by Boa Vista island from the S-SE swells, and is only able to pick up NW swells, rare WSW and the omnipresent NE windswells. Strong NE winds are the standard, year-round trades with more favourable E in late autumn. Tidal ranges are less than 1m, but cause most waves to break too close to the rocks at high tide.

STUART BUTLER

Monte Leão

BERNARD TESTEMALE

Ponta Preta right

JODY MACDONALD

Alibaba

## TRAVEL INFORMATION

**Weather** – Sal is flat and extremely dry due to the strong NE trade winds. Much of the year is warm, but July to September is the so-called 'wet' season, when temps and humidity rise. The cold Canary Current requires a springsuit in the winter to counter the wind chill factor.

**Lodging and Food** – There's a wide variety of international hotels (RIU, Melia Tortuga, Morabeza fr $93/p/n/dble). Cheap 'pensãoes' (Hotel Santa Maria Beach fr $24/p/n/dble). The budget meal is cachupa, at $5, western food costs more like $25.

**Nature and Culture** – Sal is the place to learn to windsurf or kitesurf with one of the many schools. The diving is some of the best in the West Africa area, such as the Buracona hole.

**Hazards and Hassles** – Sharp lava rocks and urchins are a common danger. Most visiting surfers are actually windsurfers, while the locals tend to ride bodyboards. Minimal localism and only 1 shark fatality in 2001 on a diver.

**Handy Hints** – Bring everything including booties. There are a few surf shops (Surf 'n Soul, Tout'sab) and basic rental boards are available through the windsurf schools (Soultripping).

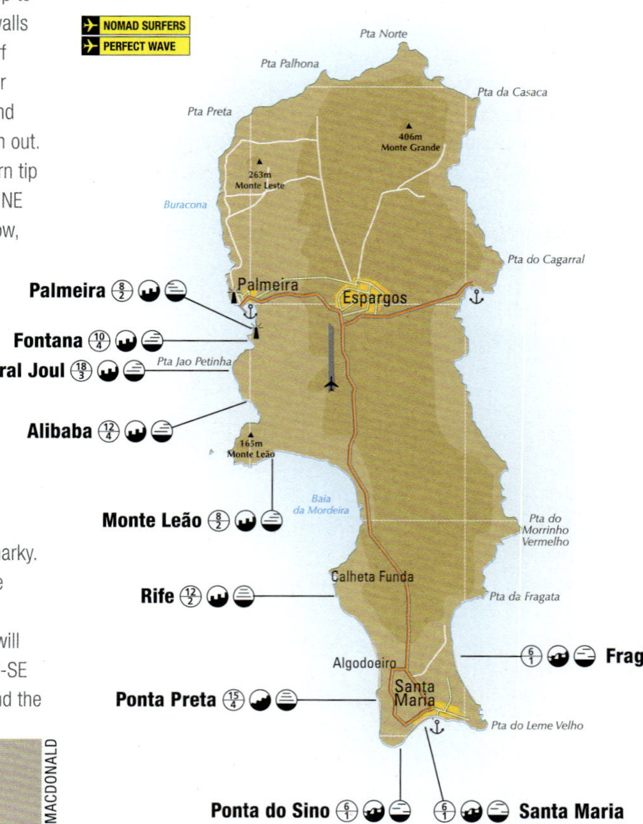


| STATISTICS | | J F | M A | M J | J A | S O | N D |
|---|---|---|---|---|---|---|---|
| SWELL | Direction | | | | | | |
| | Size (ft) | 4 | 3 | 2 | 0-1 | 2-3 | 4 |
| WIND | Direction | | | | | | |
| | Force | F4 | F4 | F4 | F4 | F4 | F4 |
| WATER | Wetsuit | | | | | | |
| | Temp/°C | 21 | 21 | 24 | 26 | 27 | 25 |
| WEATHER | Rainfall/mm | 3 | 0 | 0 | 10 | 30 | 16 |
| | days/mth | 2 | 0 | 0 | 2 | 3 | 2 |
| | Min temp/°C | 19 | 19 | 20 | 22 | 23 | 21 |
| | Max temp/°C | 23 | 24 | 25 | 27 | 26 | 25 |

# Rabat to Casablanca MOROCCO

Surfers arriving in Morocco in the winter surf season, usually head straight to the famous waves around Agadir. This is understandable when the weather in Northern Morocco is cold and the 1000kms of NW-facing beachbreaks are usually closed-out, cross-shore and uninviting. Despite being predominantly beach there are a few notable spots which offer wind and swell protection behind long, rivermouth jetties, plus a load of slabby reefbreaks and the rare opportunity to ride a left point, in a land of rights.

+ SWELL CONSISTENCY
+ PROTECTED JETTY BREAKS
+ EASY ACCESS
+ FASCINATING CULTURE

- NO WORLD-CLASS SPOTS
- COOL WINTER WATER
- URBAN HASSLES
- NO ALCOHOL

JEAN PIERRE BAILLOT

Medihya Plage

**Medihya Plage**, near the Kenitra army base, was first surfed in the late 1950s. The reliable, powerful Moone righthander breaks along the south jetty and is sheltered from northerlies. Chlihat, past the north jetty, or the town beachbreaks are a good summer bet, and when it's big enough, Charatane's left breaks deep inside the rivermouth. On the way to Salé is **Plage des Nations**, a wealthy resort with fast breaking, powerful beachbreaks and strong currents, so it is best in smaller swells. Rabat-Salé has a great combination of sensitive, small swell reefs, like **Kbeir**, a short, shallow and sucky left, and stormy condition spots inside the jetties, like **Doura** which had a Kirra-esque reputation before the rivermouth was dredged. There are eight spots around Rabat-Salé and the highest density of local surfers, serviced by the massive Oudayas Surf Club. There are several exits off the main highway south, leading to quality surf. Near Tamara, there's a fabled right called Smuggler's Point, but it's pretty fickle. **Skhirat** is a small swell left off a jetty, preferring low tides while the adjacent beachbreak provides overflow for the crowds. **Oued Cherrat** is the most consistent year-round spot because it is sheltered from westerlies. Regularly overrun by bodyboarders and there's a parking charge in summer. The neat fishing village at **Bouznika**, sits in a sheltered bay, hiding from the NW winds. At low tide there are chunky, long rights by the point; beware of the "table" rock section and urchins. Despite Mohammedia's many oil refineries, it is a good option. **Pont Blondin** pointbreak requires a combination of large swell and low tide, while the Oubaha reef is a good righthander that works on all tides. **Les Sablettes** beginners beachbreak is complimented by a well-defined right and a lefthander towards the rocks of La Piscine. The Marhaba Surf School attracts summer crowds. Casablanca, the financial capital, has plenty of beaches like **Zeneta** or Monica, an intense but short right, ideal for bodyboarders. Many prefer **No.23** beach in Aïn Diab for its consistency. Further south is **Dar Bouazza**, the best left pointbreak in Morocco. It's a long, wrapping, cutback wave with two main sections working fairly regularly.

| STATISTICS | | J F | M A | M J | J A | S O | N D |
|---|---|---|---|---|---|---|---|
| SWELL | Direction | | | | | | |
| | Size (ft) | 5-6 | 5 | 3-4 | 2 | 4 | 5-6 |
| WIND | Direction | | | | | | |
| | Force | F2-F3 | F2-F3 | F2-F3 | F2-F3 | F2-F3 | F2-F3 |
| WATER | Wetsuit | | | | | | |
| | Temp/°C | 16 | 18 | 20 | 22 | 21 | 18 |
| WEATHER | Rainfall/mm | 60 | 48 | 11 | 1 | 24 | 70 |
| | days/mth | 7 | 6 | 3 | 0 | 3 | 8 |
| | Min temp/°C | 9 | 12 | 16 | 20 | 17 | 11 |
| | Max temp/°C | 18 | 20 | 23 | 26 | 25 | 19 |

Avoid zillions of urchins and the rusty remains of the La Bobine wreck on shore. When it's too small, go to **Jack Beach**, a good, punchy beachbreak, and regular contest site. Further south you will see more bona-fide righthand points including the awesome freight-train barrels of Safi.

There is every chance a travelling surfer will pick up a few decent waves in winter, especially at the protected jetty breaks, but Northern Morocco is generally considered a spring to autumn destination although high summer will be windy. Many beaches max-out in winter NW swells, but that's when pointbreaks and sheltered spots come into their own. Tides vary from 0.6-2m.

## TRAVEL INFORMATION

**Weather** – The climate is warm but desert nights get chilly. In Rabat, winter rainfall peaks at 70mm per month. Summer gets extremely hot with virtually no rain. Water gets down to 16°C (61°F) which requires a 3/2mm fullsuit.

**Lodging and Food** – Budgeteers can pay from $5 for quite good quality hotel beds. Eating is cheap ($4 for a 3 course meal). Luxury is available at European prices. Tagines and couscous make for tasty local cuisine: no pork or alcohol.

**Nature and Culture** – Spectacular architecture includes the casbah's in Rabat and Salé and the world's tallest mosque (Hassan II Mosque) in Casablanca. Enjoy Sidi Bouknadel's exotic gardens, Rabat Surf club and open-air markets in medinas.

**Hazards and Hassles** – Avoid the sharp barnacles, urchins and rocks. Keep a close eye on personal possessions. Avoid carpet shops. Smoking hash is an illegal temptation; don't get caught with it! Beware of industrial and residential pollution at rivermouths (oued) after strong rains.

**Handy Hints** – Marhaba Surf School. Surf shops in Rabat (Ocean & Beaches) and many in Casa'. Avoid Ramadan month when everything slows down. Remember that small restaurants don't have toilet paper in the bathrooms. It's a muslim country (99% are Sunni), so dress respectfully.

JEAN CLAUDE PEREIRA

Dar Bouazza

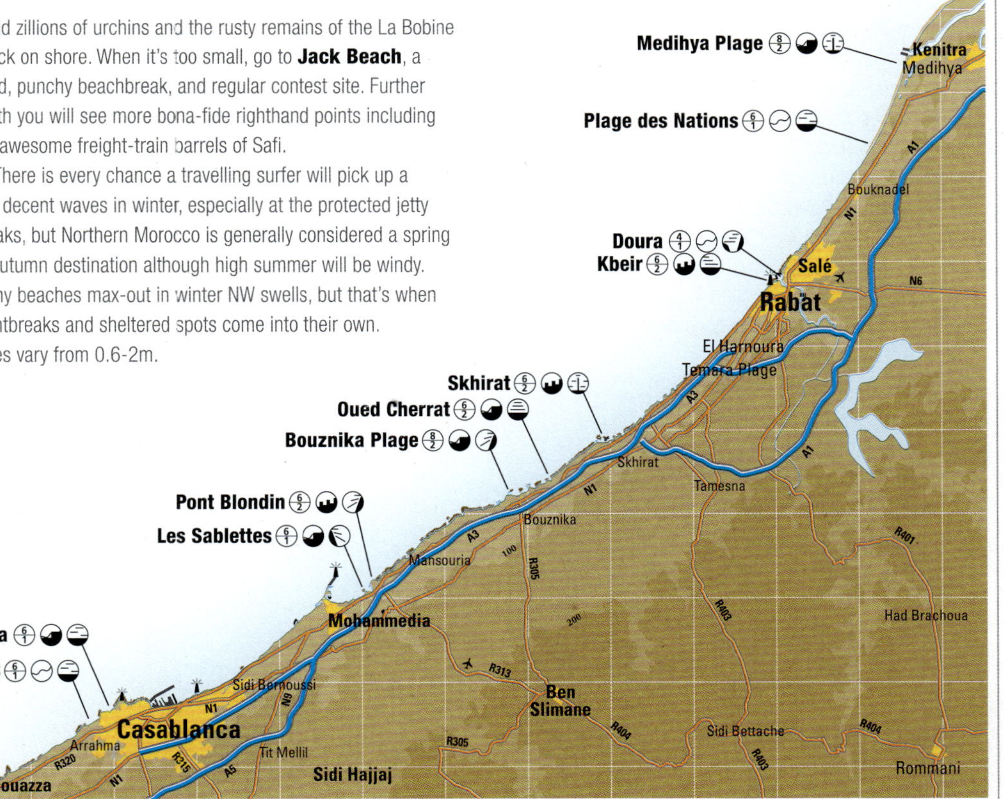

# Central Morocco

Despite its North African location, Morocco is very much a part of the European surf trail. Located between 20° and 35° latitude with a NW-facing coastline, Morocco has all the key elements for an outstanding surf destination. The Taghazout area in the south nestles behind a big cape, which funnels the predominant north winds into an offshore direction. The spots are all easily accessible by road with the waves generally breaking right over flat rock and sand. With balmy winter land temperatures, cheap living and a fascinating cultural diversity, Morocco is a must for the European surf traveller.

- + SWELL CONSISTENCY
- + LONG RIGHTHANDERS
- + BEGINNER-FRIENDLY AREA
- + GREAT WINTER WEATHER

- – FREQUENTLY MESSY LINE-UPS
- – STRONG NORTH WINDS
- – ANCHOR POINT CROWDS
- – POLLUTION AFTER RAIN

PATRICE TOUHAR

Immesouane

The scenic village turned modern fishing port of **Immesouane** sees long, mellow rights wrapping into the protected south-facing bay, while several defined peaks grace the more swell and wind exposed cathedral side. Highly consistent and often crowded mostly with longboarders. **Tamri** is a wind exposed rivermouth/beachbreak picking up plenty of swell on small days. On the southern tip of Cape Ghir is another small swell option called **Boilers**. This right sucks off a submerged ship boiler and rattles off fast, punchy, vertical walls, very close to the urchin infested rocks. The wind can be offshore on the wave as it whistles down from the mountains on the Cape, but onshore a few hundred meters out to sea! Check Draculas among the well-protected reefs and marginal beachbreaks on the drive south to **Killer Point**, named after the orcas sometimes seen here. Killers is the most consistent Taghazout pointbreak, sucking up all available N-W swells. It's always bigger than it looks and the paddle-out takes close to 15mins at high tide. In small swells, at low tide, the peak in front of the cliff has a short left (heading straight into some rocky caves) and a sectioning right. As the swell increases, the take-off area moves south and powerful, thicker walls rumble down the point. Occasional barrels and difficult to make sections for the crowds of competent surfers. **La Source** is a small swell A-frame that provides fun, performance walls and a venue for all abilities. Best on the push when the rights hold up towards the cliffs and the rarer lefts shoulder off towards the beach. **Mysteries** is a fickle, high tide righthander, but when the sand combines with the shallow reef it's a sucky, deceptively long wave with the odd barrel. Best on a clean, lined-up, medium-sized swell and after the exposed, low tide reef has been sufficiently covered. Next door is ✪ **Anchor Point**, a world famous right pointbreak, which holds massive swell and can break for up to 1km (0.6mi), all the way to the town of Taghazout. In Taghazout town, **Hash Point** is very protected from the swell and very dependant on how the sand lines up off the rocks. The name is a clue to the mellowness of this crumbly righthander that is good for starters and stoners. Could be some pollution from the town's sewers and when there is heavy rain. At the southern end of town is **Panoramas**, another right point that's often overlooked by Anchor's aficionados since it's fickle, fast and plagued by currents. Less crowds and good barrels are the trade-off when it does work. A long straight beach extends all the way down to Tamraght, offering easy, often mushy waves, more suited to beginners. Nestled south of a small rocky headland, a righthander can line-up off the **Devil's Rock** and peel towards the point at Banana Beach. Otherwise shorebreak lefts and rights offer fast punchy waves when the sand formation allows. Not as renowned as neighbouring spots but gets quite hollow. Good learner/improver spot with few crowds and mostly a sandy bottom. **Banana Beach** is tucked between the usually dry Aourir rivermouth and a cape offering some N wind protection. A surprisingly long, easy right can break from the point, otherwise it's a beginners beachbreak, which explains the surf schools in the village. Several spots are named after the number of kms they are from Agadir. The lefts of Km11 are fast and tubular on low tide, those of Km12 are softer but beware of boulders in the shorebreak. Both spots are crowded with local bodyboarders. Swell always struggles to get into the northern part of **Agadir**'s large bay

YOHANN PECHE

Devil's Rock

## TRAVEL INFORMATION

**Weather** – Morocco's central surf zone is a semi-tropical venue. The winter climate gives warm days, chilly nights and some rainfall. In Agadir, you may see 40mm of rain a month in mid-winter, making the rivermouth breaks very dirty. Summer gets extremely hot with virtually no rain. Minimum water temps get down to 16°C (60°F), but a 2mm short-sleeve fullsuit or a springy is ideal either side of winter.

**Lodging and Food** – Dozens of surf camps operate from Taghazout to Tamraght and offer everything from budget accommodation to all inclusive packages. Lessons and yoga are a big part of many camp deals. Surf Maroc has multiple locations around Taghazout with all inclusive packages fr $620. Zen Surf Morocco in Tamraght has packages fr $500 a week. Houses can be rented cheaply in Taghazout or basic cell-like rooms - ask around town for deals. Big resorts in Agadir. The food is excellent, like seafood and vegetable tagines. Alcohol is only available at tourist locations, but sweet mint tea is everywhere. A good meal shouldn't cost more than $8.

**Nature and Culture** – Morocco is a sensory feast full of amazing natural and cultural beauty. Unforgettable sights close to Agadir include the edge of the incomparable Sahara Desert, best seen around the small Oasis of Tata or to the east of Goulmine. Check the snow capped mountains of the High Atlas (ski resorts), or the Anti Atlas around Tafaroute. A trip around the ancient medina city of Marrakesh, with its colourful souks, is a must.

**Hazards and Hassles** – In the water the only dangers to worry about are urchins, rocks and crowds. On land, guard your possessions; there are a lot of thieves around. Smoking hash is illegal, and police regularly check tourist's luggage or cars for it and dish out heavy fines and stiff prison sentences. Huge black scorpions live under stones and bits of wood. Touts and scamming opportunists are everywhere; beware the carpet shop scam! On the whole Moroccan people are very friendly.

**Handy Hints** – Respect the Muslim culture, which is tolerant and far from Islamic fundamentalism. Women should avoid wearing skimpy clothing in the old medina cities and small traditional villages. The month long Ramadan festival can see a lot of shops closed and a reduced public transport service. Only use your right hand to eat. Surf gear is widely available from the dozens of surf schools, surf camps and surf shops in Taghazout, Tamraght and Agadir.

CALLUM MORSE

## Anchor Point

LAT. 30.544990° LONG. –9.725268°

A medium to large, long period NW swell is what's needed to light up this world-class right, first surfed by Aussies in the 1960's. From the steep take-off at the outside peak, a seemingly endless succession of speed walls and cutback hooks present themselves. Occasional emerald green rooms appear on the sandy sections down the point. It's easier to come in at one of the coves and walk back to jump off at the end between sets. Works on all but high tides, unless it's huge, which is when it may be possible to ride back to Taghazout. With all the recent growth in Taghazout, pollution is a real problem after heavy rain for the crowds of people escaping the northern winter.

GREG EWING

Boilers

DAMIEN POULLENOT

Draculas

and the beachbreak sucks anyway. The right at Anza gets quite good, but the proximity of the port, the refineries and untreated sewage outfall have terrible consequences on water quality. **Tifnite** holds several interesting set-ups around a fishing village settled on a rocky point. Reliable, small swell beachbreak with some sucky peaks, but N winds are not ideal. Look for other options north of town.

Morocco's coastline has the straightest swell exposure in the North Atlantic. The NW exposed beachbreaks can suffer from a swell excess in winter, but that's when the pointbreaks and sheltered spots are surfed. In winter, trade winds from the NE will make light to moderate cross-shores at most spots, whilst SW facing spots like Taghazout will be offshore. Mid-April sees the the NW-NE wind strengthen blowing out most exposed spots until mid-September. During this period, straight N winds blow for 40% of the time, with the relative lack of swell, this is the worst period to surf in Central Morocco. However, if you're into wind/kitesurfing, check out Essaouira. Tides vary from 0.6-2m.

| STATISTICS | | J F | M A | M J | J A | S O | N D |
|---|---|---|---|---|---|---|---|
| SWELL | Direction | | | | | | |
| | Size (ft) | 5 | 4-5 | 3-4 | 1-2 | 4 | 5 |
| WIND | Direction | | | | | | |
| | Force | F3 | F3 | F3 | F3 | F3 | F3 |
| WATER | Wetsuit | | | | | | |
| | Temp/°C | 16 | 17 | 19 | 22 | 21 | 18 |
| WEATHER | Rainfall/mm | 40 | 20 | 3 | 1 | 13 | 35 |
| | days/mth | 5 | 4 | 2 | 1 | 2 | 5 |
| | Min temp/°C | 9 | 11 | 15 | 18 | 16 | 10 |
| | Max temp/°C | 21 | 22 | 24 | 27 | 26 | 21 |

# Western Sahara

Western Sahara is the former Spanish Sahara, a large, lightly populated desert country south of Morocco. When Spain pulled out in 1976, the territory was occupied by troops from Morocco and Mauritania. The Mauritanians withdrew in 1979 and Morocco has occupied all of Western Sahara since then. It is slowly opening up to adventurous foreign tourists, most of whom are kiteboarders, revelling in the constant, strong desert driven winds howling down Dakhla's unique long bay.

+ CONSISTENT WINTER CONDITIONS
+ EPIC, EMPTY RIGHT POINTBREAKS
+ KITESURF AND FISHING HOTSPOT
+ DESERT BEAUTY AND WILDLIFE

- MOSTLY WINDY CONDITIONS
- REMOTE SURF SPOTS
- CHILLY DESERT CONDITIONS
- 4WD RENTAL NECESSARY

MOONWALKER

Foum Labouir

Tarfaya is the last major town in Morocco, where the beachbreak **Casamar** faces NW, right next to the fort. A sketchy desert track leads to **Yoyo**, an excellent right pointbreak at Km25, that's shallow and cylindrical, quite exposed to the winds, but it holds big swells. Over the frontier, 100km south is Laâyoune, the main city in the Sahara with 200,000 people. It's another 20km to reach the coast and the 11km long **La Corniche** of Foum El Oued, a kind of seaside resort with hotels. It's a long beachbreak, best with slack wind, high tide and small swells. Laayoune Beach is the main harbour at **Al Marsa** where two big jetties stick out up to 3km and provide some shelter from N winds. **Zbarat** is a small village, just off the main road with a really good right reefbreak. In **Tarf Noa**, there are reefs near the village and a good right set-up, 4km north towards Cap Cinq. **Boujdour** has a decent, sometimes hollow righthander out on the reef in front of the monuments at the cape. More reef peaks along the exposed beach extending north of town or at the port entrance. It will take a lot of effort to find **Skaymat**, and it only breaks in bigger swells, when quality 200m rides can be had, sometimes with protective expats who covet this wave. **Arish** rights can peel for almost 500m, under the wind shadow of the tall cliffs at N'Tirift. The first section is more exposed and an easy walk paddle between the rocks at low-mid. High tide breaks the wave up when small and makes the cruisey, slopey walls even fatter, but it is fun all the way for all surfcraft and abilities with multiple take-off spots down the sectiony line. The all male fishing village is heartbreakingly polluted by plastic. **Pointe de l'Or** is the closest spot for the many kiteboard camps to go wave-riding. The beachbreak can be anything from nice feathering peaks outside through to inside shorebreak speed-runs, but wind is the problem. The point has a sketchy right in big swells. Deep soft sand requires a 4WD to get there. **Foum Labouir** is the most popular spot in Dakhla, with reliable rights for most abilities. The wind-exposed first section can link through to the more popular take-off at the corner, which will wall up down a line of rock and sand for some nice open face carves and shoulder rebounds before ending up in the beachbreak. The end section is better protected from the howling winds by a low cliff. **La Sarga** sits at the tip of the promontory facing due S, so only bigger swells will wrap enough. Sand piles up into a perfect long bar, allowing rights to spin off with a bit more speed, power and occasional hollowness. It can be short steep sections or link up for longer rides and benefits from full NW wind protection. Military sometimes refuse access. Just over the Tropic of Cancer is **Lagtoua**, a killer set-up near a big fishing village where two long, right pointbreaks peel down dune-backed points. Sucks in plenty of swell, handles size and is consistently rideable for the few travellers who camp up their 4WD's on the beach here. 30km back up the coast is Porto Rico, a popular camp spot surrounded by reef and beachbreak options with good wind protection from the high cliffs.

The rule of thumb for surf trips to Morocco and Western Sahara is strong winds and small waves in summertime and the reverse in winter. Nov-Feb is the best window for swell with light winds but the N-NE wind can hit Force 7-8. Rips can be pretty intense despite low swell exposure and minor tidal phases up to 2.1m.

Casamar, Yoyo, La Corniche, Al Marsa, Zbarat, Tarf Noa, Msdoud, Skaymat, Arish, Pointe de l'Or, Foum Labouir, La Sarga, Lagtoua

MOROCCO, Cap Juby, Tarfaya, Hagounia, El-Aaiún Laayoune, N5, Smara, Cap Cinq, N1, N14, Boujdour, Bou Craa, WESTERN SAHARA, Guelta Zemmour, Oum Dreiga, N'Tireft, WEST POINT, OCEAN VAGABOND, Dakhla, N3, Argoub, Msyek, N1, Angra de Cintra, Aoussert, Zouerate

JS CALLAHAN/SURFEXPLORE

Arish

## TRAVEL INFORMATION

**Weather** – Hot, dry days and harsh, cold nights. Cold offshore air currents produce fog and heavy dew. Winter Atlantic lows bring rain fronts and S-SW winds. A light fullsuit for Jan - Apr.

**Lodging and Food** – Try Nagjir in Foum el Oued or Josephina in Al Marsa ($45-59/dble). In Dakhla, Sahara Regency is $120/n or Dakhla Hotel at $30/dble. Dakhla Attitude is a huge bayside bungalow village for all watersports (fr $260/w). Food is a bit pricey at $15 per meal. Fresh seafood at the Oyster farm restaurant.

**Nature and Culture** – Dramatic desert landscapes and not much else. Many camps offer surf-casting and lagoon fishing for bass and bone fish. Kiteboarders everywhere. Thermal spring at Asnaa.

**Hazards and Hassles** – Dust, sand, strong winds, personnel mines and some military activities. Cold morning wind chills. Currency is Moroccan dirham.

**Handy Hints** – The camps have surf shops but mainly for kite gear and some improving shortboard rental fleets. SUP, kayaking, wakeboarding and quad biking all available.

| STATISTICS | | J F | M A | M J | J A | S O | N D |
|---|---|---|---|---|---|---|---|
| SWELL | Direction | | | | | | |
| | Size (ft) | 4 | 3 | 2 | 1-2 | 2-3 | 4 |
| WIND | Direction | | | | | | |
| | Force | F4 | F4 | F4 | F4 | F4 | F4 |
| WATER | Wetsuit | | | | | | |
| | Temp/°C | 18 | 18 | 19 | 21 | 22 | 20 |
| WEATHER | Rainfall/mm | 32 | 20 | 3 | 0 | 115 | 44 |
| | days/mth | 6 | 3 | 2 | 0 | 4 | 7 |
| | Min temp/°C | 10 | 12 | 15 | 17 | 16 | 10 |
| | Max temp/°C | 20 | 21 | 23 | 25 | 25 | 23 |

# Almadies Peninsula SENEGAL

Most surfers who visit Senegal head straight to the prime surf area on the Almadies Peninsula, just outside Dakar. This westernmost tip of Africa juts out into the ocean and the peninsula has one of the largest swell windows in the world. Swells can appear from the SE all the way around to the NNE, which is about 260°! Another great thing about this zone is that most of the spots lie within easy walking distance of each other.

+ SPOT QUALITY & QUANTITY
+ EASY ACCESS
+ BUDGET TRIP
+ AFRICAN LIFESTYLE

– URCHINS
– ONSHORE WIND
– LOCAL HUSTLERS
– INCONSISTENT SW SIDE

## TRAVEL INFORMATION

**Weather** – It's dry most of the time, except from late July to early October. The water temp drops below 18°C (64°F) in the heart of the winter and combined with the wind chill, a 3/2mm is needed from Dec until May. Boardshorts from Aug-Oct.

**Lodging and Food** – N'gor Island surf Camp (from $300 p/w) offers surf tour packages and is quiet compared to mainland camps like Malika ($300 p/w) and Oumar ($350 p/w). All offer boat and van access. Food is cheap...lots of rice and fish!

**Nature and Culture** – Dakar is a big city with markets, shops and nightlife. Take the boat ride to the former slave island of Goré. Local surfers hang out at Secret Spot, below the Diarama hotel.

**Hazards and Hassles** – Sharks are rumoured to patrol the coastline, but fish are plentiful! Your main enemies are the sea urchins. Malaria and Yellow Fever are not major threats. Your biggest hassle will be street hustlers, eager to sell you things.

**Handy Hints** – Senegal is a very French destination. The Tribal Surf Shop at Le Virage has a good range of SAF boards and bodyboards. They also have a good board repair service. Locals use the south end of N'gor beach as a toilet.

N'GOR ISLAND SURF CAMP

Ouakam

If there's not enough swell to wrap around the Almadies Cape then **Yoff Beach**, to the North of N'gor, consistently picks up most swells and is a mellow, less challenging wave. **Yoff Island** holds a spoking left in bigger N swells, any S wind and medium tides. There's also a wind-exposed right 5 mins paddle west. **Le Virage** is a rocky bay where usually messy beachbreak finds a few corners as the tide pushes in. **N'gor Lefts** are consistent, long and wall-up for a lip smacking ride at a full range of sizes. On the other tip of the island, **N'gor Rights** featured in *The Endless Summer* and are always breaking, despite the regular onshores. There are different sections depending on the swell direction and size, but they are all powerful, well-shaped waves that mix speed and flow with cutback shoulders that can run for hundreds of metres. Avoid the two rocks (Mami and Papi) poking up mid wave and the carpet of urchins. Get a boat across the half-mile channel if not staying at a surf camp on the island. Across the deep channel, **Baie des Carpes** is a less crowded, punchy peak favouring lefts, while further out in front of the exclusive hotel and golf course are the fast lefts of **Gauche de Loic**. The SW-facing reefs are out of the wind, clean, and lined-up as the swells will have wrapped up to 180° around Almadies Point. **Club Med** hits a shallow curvy reef and concentrates a lot of power at the peak. Barrel sections and fast walls over a wide, shifting line-up. In bigger swells, **No Return** is a challenging down-the-line righthander with barrels aplenty. **Secret Spot** has lefts and rights in the bay with performance walls in S,SW,W and big NW swells for all abilities. **Vivier** is both a low tide righthander and a high tide left that sucks hard over boulders and reef. Both can be hollow and the left needs a good SW swell, which attracts keen bodyboarders. **Ouakam** stands out as Senegal's world-class spot. The right off the defined peak is usually longer and ruler-edged, while the left is fast, crisp and steep with plenty of barrel possibilities either way. The island of exposed rocks and the tight take-off zone dictate this is an experts only wave. Towards Dakar, there are consistent, but polluted reefs on the **Corniche Ouest**.

The winter NW swells can be powerful, reaching 8-10ft, and Senegal also receives consistent S/SW 3-6ft swells from May-October. Long distance southern hemi swells can sneak 1-4ft waves through a narrow window. The Harmattan (N-NE) trade winds blow from Nov to April becoming more NW from March to June. Sometimes the wind starts blowing before dawn and then calms down around noon. The short wet season typically has W-SW winds. Tidal range is never over 2m, but it can affect shallow spots.

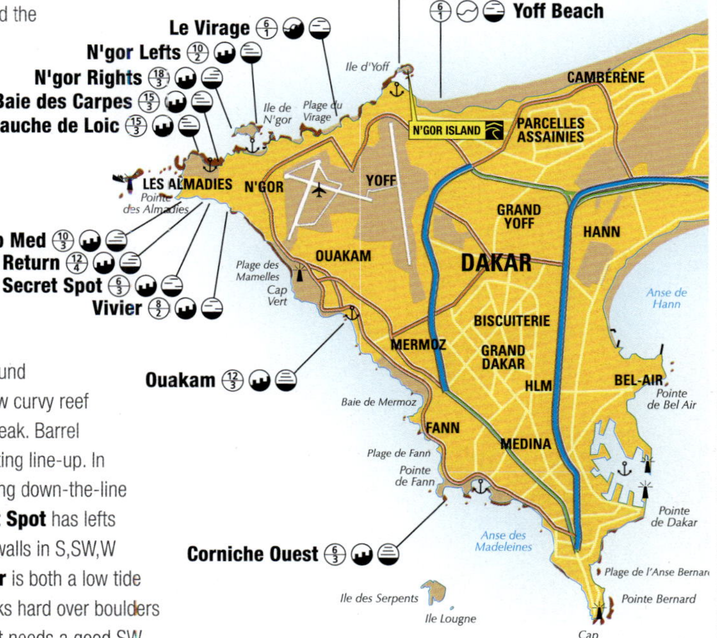

N'GOR ISLAND SURF CAMP

N'Gor Island

| STATISTICS | | J F | M A | M J | J A | S O | N D |
|---|---|---|---|---|---|---|---|
| SWELL | Direction | | | | | | |
| | Size (ft) | 4-5 | 4 | 3 | 2 | 3-4 | 4-5 |
| WIND | Direction | | | | | | |
| | Force | F3 | F3 | F3 | F3 | F3 | F3 |
| WATER | Wetsuit | | | | | | |
| | Temp/°C | 17 | 17 | 21 | 26 | 27 | 22 |
| WEATHER | Rainfall/mm | 1 | 0 | 5 | 135 | 105 | 2 |
| | days/mth | 1 | 0 | 1 | 10 | 7 | 1 |
| | Min temp/°C | 17 | 18 | 21 | 24 | 24 | 22 |
| | Max temp/°C | 25 | 24 | 28 | 30 | 30 | 26 |

GREG EWING

Club Med

# Northwest Liberia

The name Liberia comes from the word liberty and refers to the nation's origin as a colony of freed African American slaves returning to Africa from the United States in the early 19th century. Since 1989, two civil wars have plunged the country into chaos, led by violent military dictatorships, leading to the deaths of up to 200,000 people. Now peaceful, Liberia has the greatest concentration of quality lefthanders in just about all of Africa and combined with warm water, virgin line-ups and friendly locals, these empty barrels deserve more surfer's attention.

- + FAIRLY CONSISTENT SW SWELLS
- + UNCROWDED WAVES
- + BEST LEFT POINTS IN AFRICA
- + NOT TOO CHALLENGING

- – INCONSISTENT IN SUMMER
- – VERY WET DURING SURF SEASON
- – BUGS, MALARIA, YELLOW FEVER
- – RELATIVELY HIGH COSTS

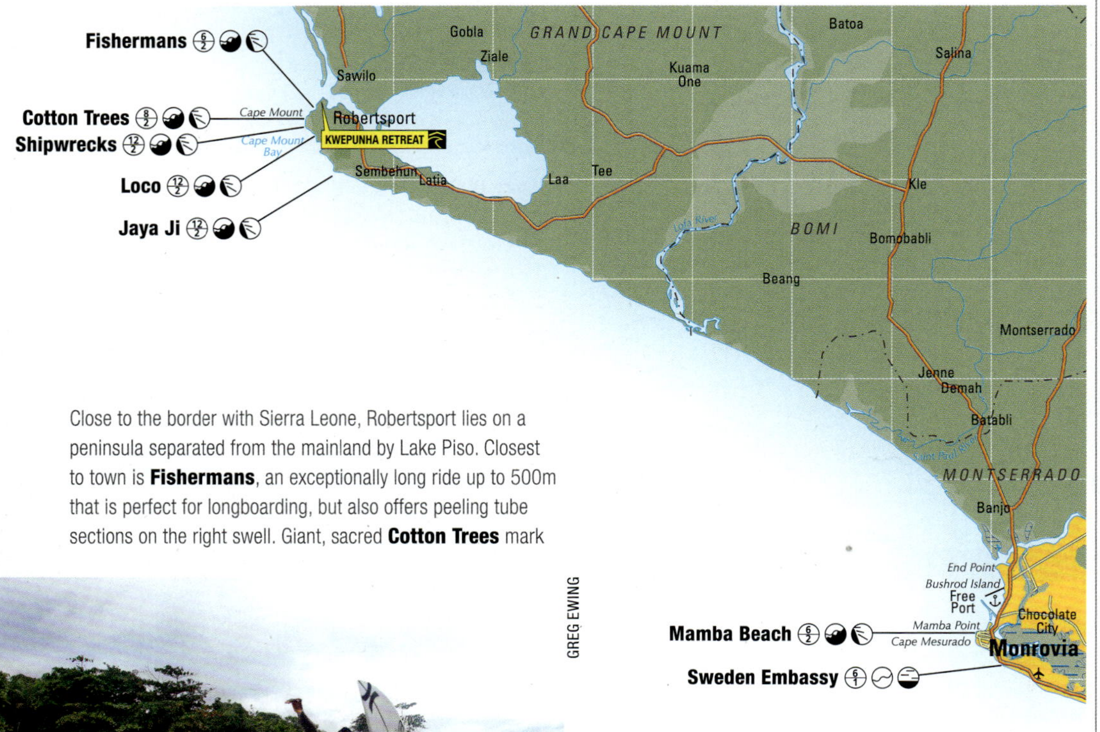


Close to the border with Sierra Leone, Robertsport lies on a peninsula separated from the mainland by Lake Piso. Closest to town is **Fishermans**, an exceptionally long ride up to 500m that is perfect for longboarding, but also offers peeling tube sections on the right swell. Giant, sacred **Cotton Trees** mark the take-off and end section of this wave that can connect into one long super-point, but it is often two waves. The end section can transform into a reverse Kirra, with dredging low tide barrels racing down the shallow sandbar. Exposed to the swell, **Shipwrecks** or Mid-Point will have fun waves when the other points are too small to ride and also handles up to double overhead. **Loco** faces due southwest and pulls in plenty of swell, but is a bit exposed to the wind and is a half hour hike from camp. Bigger, faster and gnarlier than the other points. Two hours hike south is **Jaya Ji**, where swells bounce off a rocky headland, creating a bowling, ripable wave that repeatedly doubles up as it rifles down the point, offering square tubes off the take-off and launch pads at the finish. A long, straight sandy coast with fewer kinks and a few rivermouths extends all the way to Liberia's capital city, Monrovia. South of the port the southern headland forms a very long, wind protected, lefthand pointbreak, known as **Dorothy's** after the elderly lady who runs the orphanage and school. The waves peel over a sandy rock bottom if there is enough SW swell wrapping in. It sections off and gets very close to the rocks if it is too small. There's some power close to the pocket and tapered shoulders for long, drawn-out cutbacks. Water quality is awful! On the other side of the protruding headland from Dorothy's, the SSW-facing city beaches host lots of random waves and it's probably easiest to surf **Mamba Beach** near the Mamba Point Hotel or out in front of the **Sweden Embassy**, where consistent beachbreaks cop onshores in the afternoon.

GREG EWING

Fishermans

Most swells are SSW swells from the South Atlantic, usually more frequent from April to September. The S-SW-facing coastline is mainly comprised of beachbreaks, generating waves from waist-high to double overhead. The beachbreaks are fun and can throw hard when it is on, while the pointbreaks are more fickle but offer perfect walls for intermediates. For guaranteed swells, choose July-August, but March-April will have better weather. Semi-diurnal tides 1.2m maximum tidal range.

Cotton Trees

KWEPUNHA.COM

## TRAVEL INFORMATION

**Weather** – Liberia has a year-round hot and extremely humid climate, but the heat is tempered by an almost constant breeze. Intense rainy season from May to October, (can back off in August) and the dry season really starts in December up to March. Surf in boardshorts all year.

**Lodging and Food** – In Robertsport, Kwepunha surf retreat has full board rooms fr $45/n, lessons ($30/h), rentals ($10/h) and guided tours ($25/d). In Monrovia, try Mamba Point Hotel on United Nations Drive at $150/d, Krystal Ocean View Hotel at $130/d or Tilda Guest House $110/d. Budget travellers can also get a room at St. Teresa's Convent, located a few blocks from Mamba Point Hotel ($25). Avoid dairy products.

**Nature and Culture** – Sapo National Park is popular for wildlife: elephants, viviparous toad, cross river gorilla, water buffalo, lions, zebra duiker, leopards, Diana monkey, iguanas, pigmy hippopotamus.

**Hazards and Hassles** – Chloroquine-resistant malaria is present year-round. Vaccination against yellow fever is mandatory, jabs for hepatitis A and typhoid is recommended. Ebola outbreaks from 2013-16 shut down Guinea, Liberia and Sierra Leone, but the current status is ebola-free. Local water is untreated; lots of bugs and mosquitoes because of the humidity that kills electronic gear.

**Handy Hints** – Take at least two boards and plan on leaving an old board behind! Only take folding US dollars. Check out the surf movie *Sliding Liberia*.

| STATISTICS | | J F | M A | M J | J A | S O | N D |
|---|---|---|---|---|---|---|---|
| SWELL | Direction | | | | | | |
| | Size (ft) | 2 | 2-3 | 3-4 | 4 | 3 | 2-3 |
| WIND | Direction | | | | | | |
| | Force | F2 | F2-F3 | F3 | F4 | F3 | F2 |
| WATER | Wetsuit | | | | | | |
| | Temp/°C | 27 | 27 | 28 | 26 | 27 | 28 |
| WEATHER | Rainfall/mm | 44 | 156 | 744 | 685 | 758 | 183 |
| | days/mth | 5 | 13 | 23 | 22 | 23 | 16 |
| | Min temp/°C | 21 | 22 | 22 | 23 | 22 | 21 |
| | Max temp/°C | 31 | 31 | 30 | 26 | 28 | 30 |

# Ivory Coast

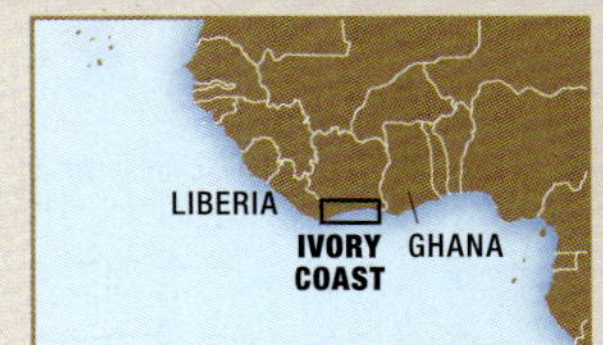




Located on the Gulf of Guinea, the Ivory Coast contains 515km (320mi) of exposed southerly facing shoreline. This equatorial country picks up the South Atlantic swells, which break on a variety of beaches and reefs, backed by swaying coconut trees and endless lagoons. Close to the Ghanaian border, Assinie is the most popular surf destination in the country with fast, hollow beachbreak conditions and a French run surf camp. When the swell picks up then there's reef and pointbreak action to the west and more mellow waves ideal for longboarders and beginners.

- \+ EMPTY LINE-UPS
- \+ LIGHT WIND PATTERNS
- \+ COOL BEACHES, EASY POINTS
- \+ JUNGLE SCENERY AND ANIMALS

- \- INCONSISTENT SWELL
- \- LACK OF BIG WAVES
- \- FAIRLY EXPENSIVE
- \- MALARIA & HYGIENE THREATS

MICHAEL KEW

Grand Drewin

From the Liberian border to San Pedro access to the remote coastline is difficult beyond the main towns of Tabou and Grand Bereby which both have some soft beachbreak. **San Pedro** has a black lava reefbreak, a number of beachbreaks to choose from and also a consistent low tide shorebreak. **Monogaga** is protected by a jutting headland so the righthand point needs a huge swell to work and will handle WSW winds. Rocky headlands like **Grand Drewin** hold a better righthander that breaks in a small sandy cove facing a fishing village. Faster walls and the suckier inside section keep the locals and visitors happy. **Sassandra** main beach is dirty, but the rights off the pink granite reef can produce rides of up to 100m. There are some other good right pointbreaks around that are worth searching for. There's also miles of average beachbreak nearby, but this area swarms with mosquitoes during the rainy months. **Dagbego**, in front of the 'Hotel Best of Africa', where there is a very nice beach with a right breaking from the tip of a rocky point. It needs a big swell to give long, workable walls, which won't be hollow. West of Abidjan is **Grand-Lahou**, a tourist zone with beachbreaks and a 'passe' where a sandbank holds a decent right and a left, best on an incoming tide. Either side of the capital Abidjan, a deep-water trench creates endless closeouts with horrendous rips and is locally known as 'La Barre'. The tourist beach town of **Grand Bassam** lacks quality banks, with either shoredump or messy chaos, but if the lagoons open to the sea between here and Assouinde, a quality passe may appear. Rips, rip offs and jellyfish can be a problem. **Assinie**, is the most popular surf destination in the country with bigger, more powerful beachbreak conditions, breaking fast and hollow and it always picks up any available swell. Handles overhead conditions before it closes out and is usually glassy in the morning and evening. Paddling out can be punishing when bigger. Winter conditions are often smaller and cleaner making it ideal for beginners. Peaks are named after the kilometre road signs. Currents and murky water up near the rivermouth.

Nov to April is the best time to catch the clean beachbreaks like Assinie, which only work on smaller swells anyway. The pointbreaks work on Southern Hemisphere wintertime groundswell, but it is also the rainy season when malaria is an issue. The Harmattan is a cool and dry N wind that blows offshore from December to May (10-20%), although around lunchtime a gentle onshore sea breeze picks up and ruins the waves. From June to September, the SW monsoon blows a mild onshore most of the time, but on the whole, wind strengths are fairly light. Tidal ranges are very low and only affect some shallow spots.

## TRAVEL INFORMATION

**Weather** – There is a short rainy season corresponding with the SW monsoon during Oct-Nov and again from mid-May to July. From Dec to mid-April and Aug to Sept, it's usually dry. Highest temps are around 35-37°C (95-99°F), occurring from March to June with 100% humidity. The coolest months are Aug, Sept and Jan. The water temp never drops below 23°C (73°F) and often hits 28°C (82°F). Take a rash vest for sun protection.

**Lodging and Food** – In Assinie you can rent a hut for cheap, but it's rough. Club Med hotel nearby but it's not cheap. Assinie surf camp bungalows cost $35/dble/full board. Local food is cheap - great selection of fruit.

**Nature and Culture** – This is a totally rural, African beach-life trip with little to do at night. When it's flat, Abidjan (2 hours away) is the best city trip to take. Jungle trips involve money and at least 2-3 days. Canoe trips around the lagoon, 10 minutes away from Assinie, will reveal crocodiles, birds and other exotic fauna.

**Hazards and Hassles** – Yellow fever injections and anti-malaria medication is a must. Avoid travel at night and don't leave possessions on the beach. Line-ups are always empty, except on weekends when expatriates from Abidjan hit the surf. Locals hardly ever surf as most West Africans have a healthy distrust for the ocean and can't swim. Jellyfish arrive with the onshores.

**Handy Hints** – There are two surf shops in Abidjan. The surf camp manager is a shaper who fixes and rents boards (±$14/d). The heat sometimes gets unbearable so it's best to get a room with A/C unless you're staying right on the beach.

LAURENT MASUREL

Assinie

| STATISTICS | | J F | M A | M J | J A | S O | N D |
|---|---|---|---|---|---|---|---|
| SWELL | Direction | | | | | | |
| | Size (ft) | 2 | 2-3 | 3-4 | 4 | 3 | 2-3 |
| WIND | Direction | | | | | | |
| | Force | F2 | F3 | F3 | F3 | F3 | F3 |
| WATER | Wetsuit | | | | | | |
| | Temp/°C | 27 | 28 | 27 | 25 | 24 | 26 |
| WEATHER | Rainfall/mm | 33 | 145 | 487 | 117 | 140 | 150 |
| | days/mth | 4 | 8 | 18 | 8 | 10 | 10 |
| | Min temp/°C | 23 | 24 | 24 | 23 | 23 | 23 |
| | Max temp/°C | 32 | 32 | 30 | 28 | 28 | 31 |

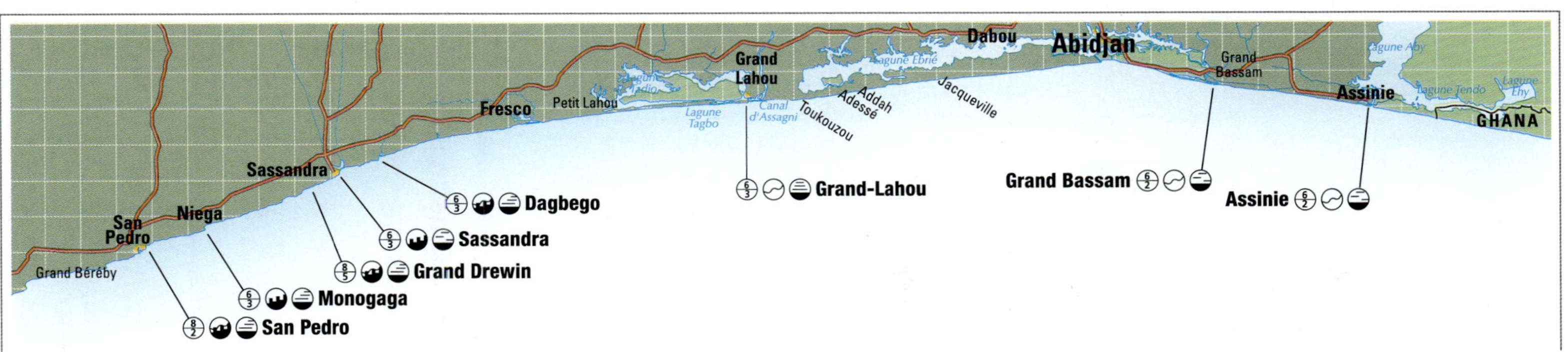

# Ghana

Most surfers would know little about surfing in Ghana, apart from the backwash waves that were surfed out to sea on *The Endless Summer*. Ghana claimed independence in 1957, avoided the region's wars and grew a democracy based on gold and cocoa. West of Accra, stretches 250km of golden sand and rocky patches, backed by flat, plains and numerous estuarine lagoons.

+ MELLOW RIGHT POINTBREAKS
+ CONSISTENTLY HEADHIGH
+ RELATIVELY CHEAP AND SAFE
+ VIRGIN, WARM WATER SURF

- LACK OF POWERFUL WAVES
- SMALL WAVES IN DRY SEASON
- BEACH POLLUTION
- HOT, HUMID AND MALARIAL

## TRAVEL INFORMATION

**Weather** – Temps vary between 21-32°C (70-90°F). Along the coast rainfall is light and the rainy season lasts from April until June with a short spell in October. No rubber necessary.

**Lodging and Food** – Busua has accommodation to suit all budgets. Mr Brights and Ahanta Waves organise accommodation, lessons and tours to spots where you'll be surfing all alone. Near Accra try Big Milly Backyard and Escape3points Lodge at Cape 3 Points is the best by far. Street food is dirt-cheap; expect $1 (3-5 cedis) for a meal. Soups, jollof rice, fufu and lobsters.

**Nature and Culture** – Besides palm-fringed beaches and slave forts, Ankasa national park is only 2h away. Fish markets are unavoidable! Laid-back atmosphere in Busua.

**Hazards and Hassles** – Yellow fever, malaria and other tropical diseases. Night walks along beaches invite muggings. Drink bottled water only. Locals use beach as toilet. Snakes and scorpions.

**Handy Hints** – Mr Brights and Ahanta Waves have the basics but bring your own gear if you're surfing beyond Busua.

JS CALLAHAN/SURFEXPLORE

Fete

**Mutrakni Point** is a well-regarded lefthand pointbreak over sand covered reef. There is also another left that shows itself in bigger swells out on the exposed isthmus plus a right on the east side beach corner. Further west lies Axim's hefty beachbreak by the beach resort with a fun reef nearby. **Cape Three Points** picks up maximum available swell, bending onto the main point for a mellow right slide that intermediates and longboarders will love. Out on the west side of the lighthouse is a left in sizeable swells, while the beachbreak stretching to the east is usually very fast, leading up to an inconsistent left point/reef. In Akwidaa **LP's** is a reliable and consistent, long right point that picks up most swell. Beachbreaks at Ketakor and Achenim add to the wave inventory. **Dixcove** is a well-known right reef below Fort Metal Cross, but the water by the rivermouth is murky and polluted. **Black Mamba's** breaks over round boulders full of urchins and is for more experienced surfers only. On its day it's easily the best wave in the area. Ghana's surfing centre is **Busua Beach** where the fun, mostly easy waves are ideal for the surf schools and locals to practice in. The rights at **Takoradi** can be ridden on the western side of the harbour. **Fort Sebastian** hosts another right point that is protected from westerly sea breezes. **Elmina**'s exotic beaches are fringed with palms, the obligatory fort and a slow breaking, right pointbreak. Cape Coast is the Central Region's capital, where below average close-out beachbreaks appear in front of the University and the castle. Further east at Winneba, **St Charles** is an outside righthand reef come pointbreak, which is nicely sheltered on the inside. It's possible to spend the night in the scenic **Fort Good Hope** in Senya Beraku, in order to ride the long, laid-back right pointbreak next to it. **Fete** needs clean morning conditions to shape up some long, shouldered walls between the tip of the point at Tills and the inside section at White Sands beach resort, which is sheltered by low cliffs from westerly sea breezes. Great fun when the sections all connect in due S swell at lower tides. It can be fat and suffer strong rips on bigger swells and like many other beaches is used for sanitary purposes by the local populace. Consistent, even when small, plus the beachbreak can hold some peaks. Just west is Tills beach, where quick-fire close-outs attract the kiteboarders of Accra. **Nyanyanu** is a small rivermouth right, best on low tide, that can connect up on bigger swells. The beachbreak at **Kokrobite** is best in small peaky 2-3ft surf with incoming tides to help reduce the amount of close-outs. The western point has some rocky, sectiony rights. A similar wave option, replete with expensive hotel for those who can afford it is **Labadi Beach** on the other side of Accra. It can be very polluted (tankers dump septic waste nearby) and there is a charge for beach access.

Long period organised S-SW groundswells arrive from April to Sept but will decay heavily and never exceed 8ft. Morning offshores become a gentle westerly sea breeze that destroys the beachbreaks. Nov to March is flat with due N winds. Tides are under 1m and only affect small beachbreaks at high.

GREG EWING

Busua Beach

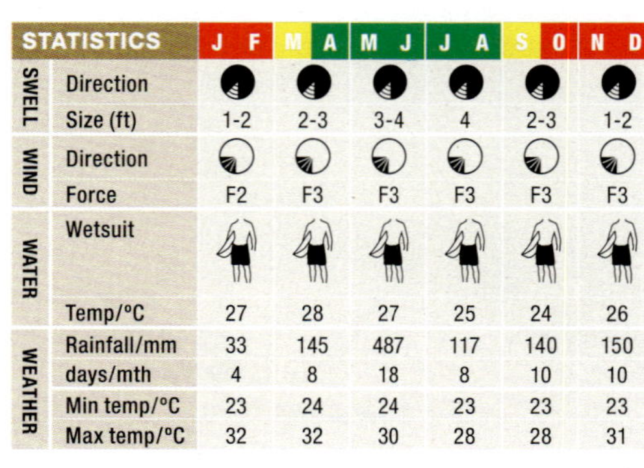

| STATISTICS | | J F | M A | M J | J A | S O | N D |
|---|---|---|---|---|---|---|---|
| SWELL | Direction | | | | | | |
| | Size (ft) | 1-2 | 2-3 | 3-4 | 4 | 2-3 | 1-2 |
| WIND | Direction | | | | | | |
| | Force | F2 | F3 | F3 | F3 | F3 | F3 |
| WATER | Wetsuit | | | | | | |
| | Temp/°C | 27 | 28 | 27 | 25 | 24 | 26 |
| WEATHER | Rainfall/mm | 33 | 145 | 487 | 117 | 140 | 150 |
| | days/mth | 4 | 8 | 18 | 8 | 10 | 10 |
| | Min temp/°C | 23 | 24 | 24 | 23 | 23 | 23 |
| | Max temp/°C | 32 | 32 | 30 | 28 | 28 | 31 |

# Togo and Benin

**Benin and Togo are largely off the map for both surfers and travellers. The two tiny nations, home to voodoo and friendly beachbreaks, offer a tropical climate and consistent, uncrowded surf potential. A combined trip to neighbouring Ghana will increase wave quantity and quality, yet Benin and Togo offer an escape into a unique and magical culture. The coast is made up of a series of steeply shelving beaches, almost entirely backed by lagoons and the best waves like Anécho appear where a natural or manmade feature creates sandbanks, breaking up the endless shore-pound.**

- \+ CONSISTENT, LONG-RANGE SWELL
- \+ NO CROWDS
- \+ EXPLORATION POSSIBILITIES
- \+ VOODOO CULTURE

- – NO EPIC SPOTS
- – LIGHT ONSHORES
- – RAIN IN SWELL SEASON
- – MALARIA

In the west of Togo, **Lomé-Rivage** is located a couple of kilometres to the east of Lomé centre and may be reached in a taxi. The spot itself usually has decent sandbars held in place by a large jetty, which has recently been extended. The massive harbour expansion project may have an effect on the surf, pollution and access, but it remains one of the most consistent spots. Visitors should be aware that this is also a private resort beach. Further east, it's straight beachbreak and the odd short jetty until you approach the border of Benin, where the beautiful German colonial town of **Anécho** (or Aného) hides one of the best waves in either country. A series of short rock jetties can hold some shape and the end jetty, which protects the rivermouth, will sculpt some longer and hollow rights down a triangulated sandbar. Slower shoulders or racy closeouts, but be warned, it is a little fickle, exposed to the wind and the lagoon/river outflow can bring muddy, polluted water. Crossing the border into Bénin, the first town is called Grand-Popo. The nearby beach, **Bouches de Roi**, offers low-quality closeout shorebreak, mostly unsurfable, with powerful and dangerous rips, especially at the lagoon opening to the east. At the fascinating town of **Ouidah**, a more attractive beach has marginally better potential, and becomes surfable at lower tides. The nearby snake temple is worth a visit if the waves aren't doing it. A track known as **Les Routes des Pêches** offers up more beachbreak surfing opportunities and the increased likelihood of encountering other surfers. Towards Cotonou, sandbars in front of the **Sheraton** and **Novotel** hotels will sometimes turn on, but pollution and beach crime can be an issue. The best waves in Bénin often break on a large sandbar in the **Cotonou Rivermouth**. Unfortunately, this spot is very polluted, and the top to bottom barrels usually go unsurfed due to the dubious water quality. There's a more popular right wedge in the corner of the beach next to the extensive harbour wall called La Meduse. Close to the Bénin-Nigeria border, **Kraké** receives more swell and can hold a good bank 50m (150yds) off the beach.

During the May-Sept wet season there are usually rideable waves from long-distance southern-hemisphere swells. Having travelled halfway around the world they are super-clean and orderly, with long lulls between sets, but wave faces rarely get above 6ft. The main problem with the wet season is that the wind is a light onshore S-SW almost all the time. Experienced West African surfers consider October or November to be the best months. Tides are small, but low tide can make a real difference to the quality of the beachbreaks.

Togo

STUART BUTLER

## TRAVEL INFORMATION

**Weather** – Togo and Benin are dominated by a strong SW monsoon between April and October with daily heavy rainfall. Even during the dry season, it still rains frequently near the coast. May-June and October are the rainiest months. March and April can be unbearably hot and humid. Dominant winds are SW and the water is warm enough for boardies year-round.

**Lodging and Food** – Every major coastal town has somewhere to stay and standards are, for West Africa, good. Budget at least $20/day for a double room with a/c and a shower. Food is renowned as the best in West Africa, with lots of spicy sauces and plenty of variety. Rat is the local delicacy of the coast. Basic meals don't cost more than $1.

**Nature and Culture** – Any trip is likely to leave the traveller with tales of encounters with the supernatural. The beautiful towns of Ouidah, Porto Novo and Anécho are all Voodoo centres, or check the fetish markets of Cotonou and Lomé.

**Hazards and Hassles** – Pollution around Cotonou and Lomé is a problem and there have been cases of robbery and worse on both city centre beaches. There is some political tension in Togo. Bénin is one of the safest countries in Africa. Malaria is a major problem in both countries.

**Handy Hints** – Take everything you need as there is no surf industry whatsoever. A standard day-to-day beachbreak board is perfect and don't forget sunscreen and plenty of wax.

| STATISTICS | | J F | M A | M J | J A | S O | N D |
|---|---|---|---|---|---|---|---|
| SWELL | Direction | | | | | | |
| | Size (ft) | 1-2 | 2-3 | 3-4 | 4 | 2-3 | 1-2 |
| WIND | Direction | | | | | | |
| | Force | F3 | F3 | F3 | F3 | F3 | F3 |
| WATER | Wetsuit | | | | | | |
| | Temp/°C | 27 | 28 | 27 | 24 | 25 | 27 |
| WEATHER | Rainfall/mm | 33 | 121 | 310 | 64 | 101 | 36 |
| | days/mth | 2 | 6 | 12 | 5 | 8 | 4 |
| | Min temp/°C | 24 | 26 | 23 | 23 | 23 | 24 |
| | Max temp/°C | 28 | 28 | 27 | 26 | 27 | 28 |

# São Tomé

São Tomé is the largest of 3 islands, followed by Príncipe which is 30min away by plane, and finally the tiny islet of Rolas (3km). São Tomé and Príncipe is a developing country where oil and tourism have taken over from an economy based on coffee and cocoa, hence the nickname of the "Chocolate Islands". Australian and American surfers visited as early as the '70s, but travelling surfers remain rare. There are many promising set-ups along the east coast plus the equator straddling Point Zero Left.

+ QUALITY, EMPTY POINTS
+ CONSISTENT SUMMER SWELLS
+ NO RAIN DURING SEASON
+ UNTOUCHED ISLAND

- MOSTLY SMALL WAVES
- NO ACCESS TO WEST COAST
- EXPENSIVE TRIP
- MALARIA

Santana

GREG EWING

The quickest check from the capitol is **Forte de São Tomé**, but the historical scenery is usually better than the short, dribbly, boulder rights that are often flat. **Lavaduro** could be a great right slab if it was not facing northeast, meaning the tubes are rarely big enough to clear the rocks. **Radiation Point** is fairly consistent, because even local SE windswell will wrap with enough size to ride, and the SW wind is cross-offshore on the biggest outside section. **Batismo** in Praia das Pombas is a great set up with long walls down the rocky point when a bigger S swell swings up the east coast. Lower tides and any W wind will do. The same conditions will see hollower waves at **Dique**, a shallow, urchin covered reef/point north of Santana village. Easily visible from the road, **Santana** throws down some pretty right walls over the reef hugging the point. Hollow pockets here and there on the low tide and it is still fun and bashable in light onshores. **Agua Izé** bay looks really nice and the right pointbreak set-up is obvious, but once again needs a strong pulse to fire. The cluster of rocks at the southern end of **Baia Coqueiro** hold the rivermouth sandbars nicely for some long, relaxing righthand shoulders into the bay. There's another good point/rivermouth named after the **Lo Grande** river which flows from the mountainous interior. This right picks up a bit more swell and the river flow decides how many holes are blown in the 300m line-up. Water can be murky and rippy. **Porto Alegre**, the African Nias, is the best wave on the island. It's a 200m long boulder/cobble right point that needs a big S swell and W quadrant winds to produce walls that are generally steeper and peel faster than the other pointbreaks on the island. Ilheu das Rolas is a small islet sitting on the equator off the southern tip of São Tome. It's an amazingly beautiful island and home to a very upscale dive resort. To reach the island catch the Cariouco boat from São João dos Angolares or Porto Alegre and cheaper accommodation is available at a Roça. **Praia Pestana**, or Fishermen's Bay, is a Waikiki-style reform, ideal to have fun on a longboard. The consistent **Point Zero Lefts** are bang-on the Equator, but suffer from sideshores and strong currents. There is now a decent new road providing access to Praia Jale **Ecolodge**, beach bungalows directly in front of a rocky lefthander that pulls in the swell, but it's often onshore. The west coast shows potential for long lefts, but the difficult access prevents many from exploring the multiple rivermouths and rocky coves. In the middle of the west coast is **Fim do Caminho** (end of the trail) near Santa Catarina. It's a long wrapping left pointbreak over a bunch of rocks, but it's a 2h drive from São Tomé.

It's usually flat from October to March until the Austral winter brings 2-8ft waves and the dominant SW winds get stronger. Rolas is the most exposed, but doesn't handle the stronger S swells that spots like Porto Alegre require to fire. 4ft max of tidal range affects Radiation Point at high.

## TRAVEL INFORMATION

**Weather** – São Tomé is fully equatorial and oceanic SW winds bring heavy rainfall and humidity, especially from February to May and again from October to November. When it rains, the sea becomes muddy. Despite the moisture it is often sunny, and the rains are mostly thunderstorms.

**Lodging and Food** – On Rolas, Pestana Equador Resort is a diving & fishing resort that costs $145/n/dbl: Jalé Beach Ecolodge bungalow for 2 from $45/day and the much newer Praia Inhame Ecolodge ($58/n/dbl/b&b). Allow $15 per meal. Roça are ex-plantation houses. Roça de São João dos Angolares: $55 for dble. Santomean cuisine is very rich! Eat Calulu, Blabla, Cachupa and Feijoada.

**Nature and Culture** – A paradise for bird watchers, hikers and biodiversity lovers. São Tomé Pico is a volcanic cone at 2024m. Don't miss Obo National Park. Visit coffee or cocoa plantations. Sea turtles can be seen at Mikolo Beach.

**Hazards and Hassles** – Protect against yellow fever and chloroquine-resistant malaria. Friendly locals on local wooden boards are becoming more common.

**Handy Hints** – Bring a longboard for the smaller days. Take USD$ and Euros - no cash machines. Dobras are used for local markets, taxis etc. Refuse to eat dishes made of sea turtles (meat or egg), or other protected species (shark, earth snails, forest pigeons etc).

Radiation Point

GREG EWING

| STATISTICS | | J F | M A | M J | J A | S O | N D |
|---|---|---|---|---|---|---|---|
| SWELL | Direction | | | | | | |
| | Size (ft) | 1-2 | 2-3 | 3-4 | 3-4 | 2-3 | 1-2 |
| WIND | Direction | | | | | | |
| | Force | F2-F3 | F3 | F3-F4 | F3-F4 | F3 | F3 |
| WATER | Wetsuit | | | | | | |
| | Temp/°C | 28 | 28 | 27 | 25 | 26 | 27 |
| WEATHER | Rainfall/mm | 94 | 140 | 81 | 0 | 66 | 103 |
| | days/mth | 7 | 9 | 5 | 0 | 6 | 8 |
| | Min temp/°C | 23 | 23 | 21 | 21 | 21 | 21 |
| | Max temp/°C | 30 | 30 | 28 | 28 | 29 | 29 |

# Northern Gabon

As a surf destination, Gabon remains a mystery to most and all of the known spots are located close to Port-Gentil or the capital, Libreville. Most surfers are French expatriates, but some foreign explorers have scoped the south and found bigger, longer, more powerful lefts over shifting sands in the jungle wilderness of Loango National Park.

- \+ MELLOW WAVES
- \+ NO CROWDS
- \+ SANDY LEFT POINTBREAKS
- \+ FISHING PARADISE

- – INCONSISTENT SWELLS
- – MALARIA AND DISEASES
- – SMALL, MUSHY WAVES
- – EXPENSIVE LOCAL PRICES

ALEXANDRA HORVATH

Palplanche

**Ferme aux Crocos** (Crocodile Farm) is a private beach resort reached by 4x4 with a wide beach and sloppy shorebreak waves. There is a rideable wave in Libreville at **Gueque** but it is very poor quality. On the west side of the Gabon Estuary are the ten neat beach bungalows, which make up Ekwata village. From here, it is a 15 minute walk up to **Ngombé** lighthouse where an occasional long, wrapping left breaks over the shiny black stones that line the coast. When it is on, it's a very long wave, so head for the beach and walk back to the peak under the shade of the trees. This estuarine area is a mere 40m deep, even at a full 20km out to sea, sucking the power from the swell. From Libreville, the Mandji Express catamaran ferry crosses the equator to Port-Gentil, Gabon's economic capital. Off the tip of the peninsula, Mandji Island rises out of deep water, unlike anywhere else in West Africa. This undoubtedly makes it the most consistent area to surf, plus it is home to a classy left, **Palplanche**, which breaks about 25-30 days a year. Opposite the rusty steel jetties of an old erosion prevention programme, the wave wraps around the NW of the island for up to 200m with some tube sections. **Cap Lopez** is the most reliable spot, on the other side of Village des Togolais. Open to all swells, these beachbreaks break predominately left, jack-up close to shore and produce hollow barrels with some shape. The water quality, like everywhere in this area, is a little murky but at least there is some power. **Ferme aux Cochons** (Pig Farm) probably gets some of the biggest surf, but the fast beachbreak cannot handle any wind. Closer to Port-Gentil are **PG2**, near the wharf where the transit ships for the oil platforms dock and **Plage du Dahu**, facing the Novotel. Heading southwards from here there is a vast 600km, SW-facing stretch of coastline down to Congo. Little is known but it's a fairly straight sandy shore with lagoons creating sandspits, which potentially could hold some insane lefts. **Olendé** is host to one of these with a 1km long, wrapping left, skirting the Barre des Portugais shore. It has only been surfed a handful of times. Unfortunately, the fishing camp at Olendé was closed in 2000 but there are two camps at Ozuri and Iguela, south of Omboué. Be warned that local surfcasters catch plenty of sharks and barracudas in this area. Either use a speed boat (very expensive) from Port-Gentil or fly to Omboué, the nearest main village. In December 2000 when the *National Geographic* Congotrek expedition hit the coast at **Petit Loango** they found hippos swimming in the waves, and wind-exposed beachbreaks stretching for miles.

Ferme aux Crocos
Gueque
Ngombé
Libreville
Owendo
Denis
Cap Santa Clara
Pte Pongara
Pte Kengere
Ile Conniquet
Ile Perroquet
EQUATOR
Kobékobe
Foulenzem
Batanga
Grand Bam-Bam 251m
Pte Tambinione
Baie de Nazaré
Pte Wézé
RESERVE DE WONGA WONGUE
Palplanche
Cap Lopez
Ferme aux Cochons
PG2
Plage du Dahu
Ile Mandji
Baie du Cap Lopez
Port-Gentil
Ntchengue
Gomo
Ozori
Olendé
Lagune Olendé
Barre des Portugais
Omboue
Lagune Nkomi
Mpanda
Petit Loango

April to September should see the biggest swells but the extended continental shelf and a predominately W-facing coast produce meagre wave heights of 2ft up to 5ft. Being right on the Equator and lacking straight exposure to S swells, the main surf spots lack consistency. Don't count on windswell or tidal range to help as 90% of all wind is less than Force 2, usually on a SE-SW quadrant and the biggest tide is a mere 2.1m. There is a constant south to north sideshore drift, getting stronger the further south you go.

## TRAVEL INFORMATION

**Weather** – Gabon is very hot and humid. Temps vary from 23-33°C (73-91°F) and during the 7-month-long rainy season, humidity wavers between 90-100%. The main rainy season is from mid-January to mid-May, with another smaller one from mid-October to mid-December. Only June-September is dry, luckily coinciding with the main swell season. Water temps rarely get below 25°C (77°F) but take a light neoprene rash-vest for wind protection.

**Lodging and Food** – Stay in the bungalows at Ekwata Village or Port-Gentil. Novotel is $50/d. L'Hirondelle is the cheapest at $35/dble. Ozuri or Iguela fishing camps from $1200/wk. $20 for a Western meal, $5 for a local one. Regab beer is $0.6.

**Nature and Culture** – There's plenty of African wildlife (chimps, birds, elephants). Port-Gentil has more restaurants, nightclubs and shops per capita than any other African city and also a casino. The fishing is excellent.

**Hazards and Hassles** – Yellow Fever immunisation is a must. Malaria is rife with lots of Nivaquine-resistant mosquitoes. Port-Gentil has a decent hospital. Water dangers include sharks, hippos and the strong equatorial sun.

**Handy Hints** – Bring all your gear with you as local surfers may buy it for a fair price. You won't need a gun as longboards/hybrids are ideal.

ALEX LAUREL

Olendé

| STATISTICS | | J F | M A | M J | J A | S O | N D |
|---|---|---|---|---|---|---|---|
| SWELL | Direction | | | | | | |
| | Size (ft) | 1 | 1-2 | 2-3 | 3 | 2 | 1 |
| WIND | Direction | | | | | | |
| | Force | F3 | F3 | F3 | F3 | F3 | F3 |
| WATER | Wetsuit | | | | | | |
| | Temp/°C | 27 | 28 | 25 | 23 | 24 | 26 |
| WEATHER | Rainfall/mm | 248 | 330 | 143 | 6 | 233 | 338 |
| | days/mth | 15 | 18 | 9 | 3 | 18 | 19 |
| | Min temp/°C | 24 | 23 | 24 | 22 | 23 | 24 |
| | Max temp/°C | 31 | 31 | 30 | 28 | 29 | 30 |

# Pointe Noire REPUBLIC OF CONGO

Only expats working in the oil industry are likely to be in a position to surf in Pointe-Noire, so knowing someone who works there or at the very least speaking some French are essential to find waves in the Republic of Congo. Despite all the difficulties to get there, Pointe-Noire is one of the safest coastal cities in Africa and truly an oasis in a turbulent region. The Republic of Congo coastline measures 170km, compared to the short 37km length of the often confused Democratic Republic of Congo's coast to the south. The Rep of Congo's shoreline is characterised by a succession of shaded bays and lagoons bordered by mangroves and only Pointe-Noire and Pointe Indienne stick out from the monotonous, straight beaches.

+ FAIRLY CONSISTENT SWELLS
+ TROPICAL & UNCROWDED
+ DRY DURING THE SURF SEASON
+ AMAZING WILDLIFE

– NO WORLD-CLASS SPOTS
– HIGH COSTS
– DIFFICULT TRAVELLING
– SOME HEALTH RISKS

STUART BUTLER
La Pyramide

## TRAVEL INFORMATION

**Weather** – Jan-Feb is the short dry season, March-May is the short wet season, June-Sept is the long dry season while Oct-Dec is the long wet season. Temps are relatively stable with less variation between the seasons than between day and night, which can be as high as 15°C (59°F). Annual average temps range between 20-27°C (68-80°F), although the cooling effect of the Benguela Current may produce lower temps 18°C (64°F). Use a shorty during July and August and boardshorts for the rest of the year.

**Lodging and Food** – Stay at the mid-priced Twiga hotel facing the beach; the owners surf! Best hotels are Novotel or Azur ($120-180) and other options are Palm Beach ($20-40) near Cote Sauvage or Migitel downtown ($40-80); Malonda lodge in Djeno costs $205 for a bungalow for two. No hotel at Pointe Indienne. Local food can be cheap ($5).

**Nature and Culture** – Sightseeing spots include the Wharf des Potasses, the harbour (old lighthouse), and Notre-Dame Cathedral. 5h north by 4WD is Conkouati Chimp Reserve and the Diosso canyon is nearby. Only 45min to Tchissanga Monkey World. Surf-casting and deep sea fishing, plus hang-gliding.

**Hazards and Hassles** – A yellow fever certificate and a really serious anti-malarial prophylactic, as some areas are chloroquine resistant. The heavy oil industry means you get occasional tar balls on the beach.

**Handy Hints** – One all-round board will be enough. Bagatelle surf shop may have changed its name, but it will still be expensive stuff! Don't get mixed up between Republic of Congo (Brazzaville) and the much larger Democratic Republic of Congo (Kinshasa) to the south and east. Check the nightclubs like Biblos, Colibri and Nels Club.

**Pointe Indienne** looks promising, but it's an ill-defined left point, where swells don't quite wrap in, because shallow outside sandbanks dissipate wave energy. Access from Plage de la Pointe Indienne is difficult and the line-up is fully exposed to the onshore wind with no action in the lee of the point. Bear in mind there are rumoured to be some quality lefts to the north towards Kouilou rivermouth on the way to Gabon. Piege à Sable no longer breaks as harbour and breakwall extensions have killed off one of the regions best waves. The best thing

STUART BUTLER
La Plage Sportive

about **La Plage Sportive** is that it's super-consistent and the beachbreak peaks hold good shape thanks to some reef formations holding the sand in place. It's also a good hangout since there are beach restaurants, showers, music, beachgoers and a general fun vibe. The waves turn from fun to serious when it exceeds headhigh, earning this stretch the Côte Sauvage name tag. **La Pyramide** is easy to find near an old derelict wharf that creates better banks, despite the frequent onshore winds, plus a few reefs add to the possibilities in this area that rarely sees a surfer. When Côte Sauvage gets out of control, especially in winter, it's an easy drive to **Djeno Point**, 30km south of Pointe Noire, where lefts wrap in on big swells, over a rock and sand bottom. Djeno is an oil terminal owned by ENI, producing 250,000 barrels/day so expect some tar balls. Further south is the fabled **M'Vassa**, where quality reefbreaks fire when a big SW swell meets clean, E wind conditions. The area is beautiful and pristine with turtles gracing the line-up, but getting there is quite difficult. Because of the large continental shelf, waves tend to spill rather than plunge, but this power decay actually helps the waves to peel off, rather than closing-out severely like a steep beachbreak.

If the S-SW onshore winds remain light and under 10 knots, the waves will be easy to ride up to 6ft. 2-3ft is the norm while 4-6ft swells happen several times a month during the winter season with 10ft days possible. June-August are the best months to surf the Congo, bringing lighter SE offshore winds. Semi-diurnal tides and a maximum tidal range of 2m.

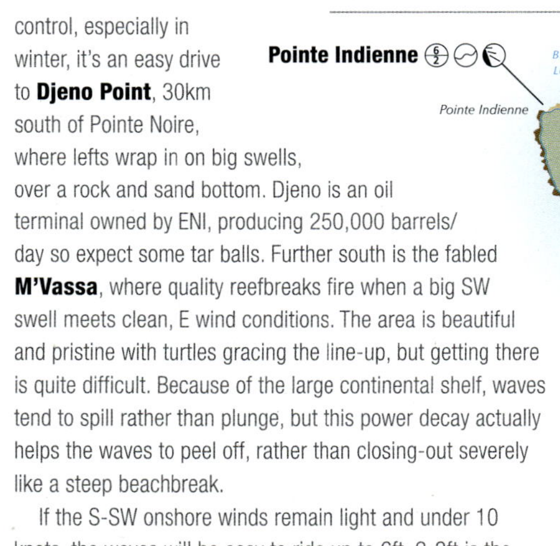

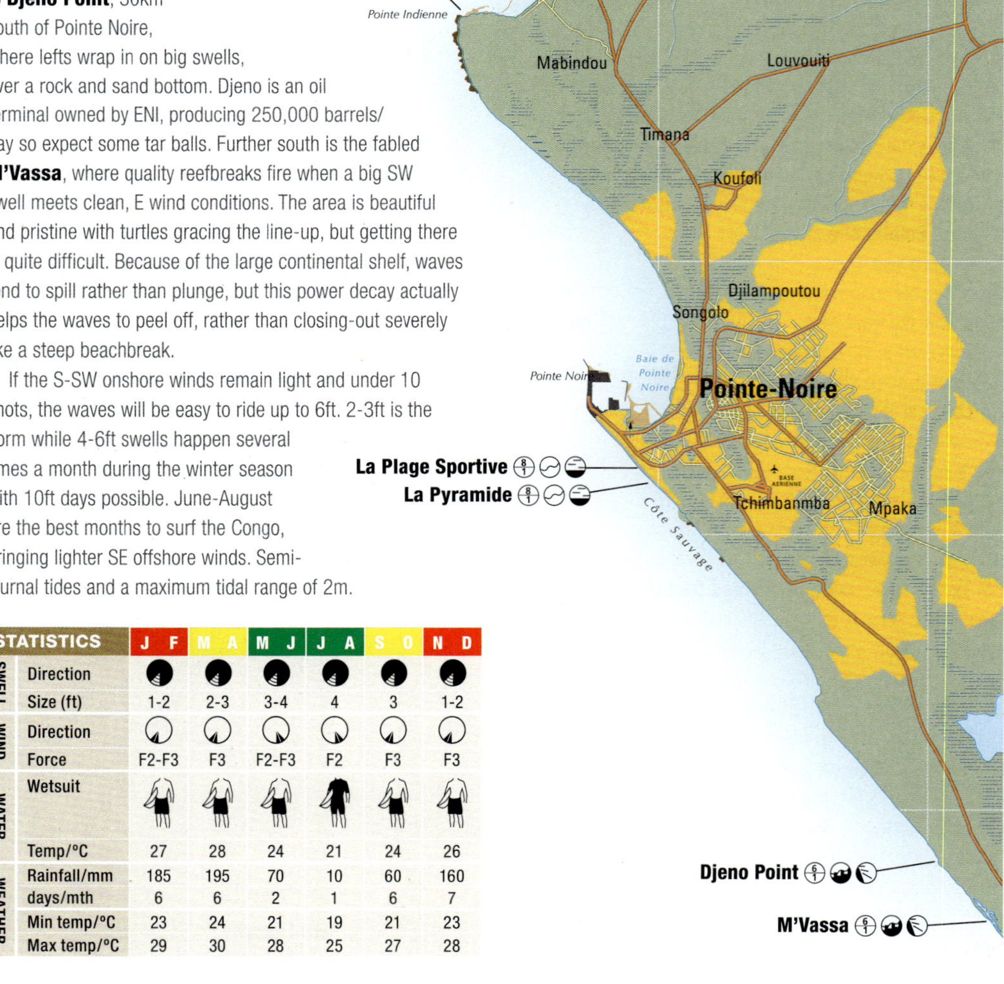


| STATISTICS | | J F | M A | M J | J A | S O | N D |
|---|---|---|---|---|---|---|---|
| SWELL | Direction | | | | | | |
| | Size (ft) | 1-2 | 2-3 | 3-4 | 4 | 3 | 1-2 |
| WIND | Direction | | | | | | |
| | Force | F2-F3 | F3 | F2-F3 | F2 | F3 | F3 |
| WATER | Wetsuit | | | | | | |
| | Temp/°C | 27 | 28 | 24 | 21 | 24 | 26 |
| WEATHER | Rainfall/mm | 185 | 195 | 70 | 10 | 60 | 160 |
| | days/mth | 6 | 6 | 2 | 1 | 6 | 7 |
| | Min temp/°C | 23 | 24 | 21 | 19 | 21 | 23 |
| | Max temp/°C | 29 | 30 | 28 | 25 | 27 | 28 |

# Luanda and Bengo ANGOLA

After 30 years of civil war, Angola is now seeing new economic prosperity from oil and mining, but only for a small selection of the population. The surfing areas in Luanda and Bengo are south of the capital and there's a long coastline of seemingly endless lefthanders that are often difficult to access beneath the impressive coastal cliffs. It's expensive to get around and 4x4 is crucial for exploration, but tourism infrastructure is growing with beach hotels at fishing towns like Cabo Ledo, where long lazy lefts provide quality rides for all surfing abilities.

+ EASY, LONG LEFT POINTS
+ CONSISTENT SWELLS
+ WARMISH WATER
+ UNDISCOVERED

- WINDY, EXPOSED SPOTS
- COSTLY FLIGHTS AND VISAS
- POST WAR REBUILDING
- SHARKS AND CROCS

The beaches closest to the capital city Luanda are not worth considering for foreign visitors with mushy beachbreaks at more suited to kitesurfing. **Buraco** is a gem, breaking close to shore down a sandy point with excellent shape and length. Long, leg-aching rides with some hollow sections over the ever-changing sands. Best at lower tides and S winds not a problem. Without a booming SW or moderate W swell it will be flat. Palmeirinhas hosts **Shipwreck** that picks up a lot of swell, but is also very exposed to the wind. This tubular spot needs to be hit early as it gets blown out by 10am. Drive to a more sheltered spot if the swell exceeds 6ft. The sunken freighter is now gone so finding it can be guesswork without a guide. **Onça** is a reliable beachbreak used by Angola Waves during small swells, not far from **Miradouro**, a short left pointbreak breaking in murky water with the major danger coming from falling cliffs. It needs a 4x4 at the best of times and is impassable with rain. South of the Cuanza river is **Barra da Cuanza** with several spots that are hardly ever ridden because of tough access. One of the three reefs is the only right in Angola, nestled under multi-coloured cliffs. Just remember not to paddle across the river because of sharks and crocs! **Sangano** is another long left, breaking in front of a large fishing village nestled below the escarpment. Usually has something fun for everyone on 2 sandy sections with scattered rocks. Much prefers low tide and offers good S wind protection on the inside beach section. More lefts to the north. Scalloped bay that's tucked away beneath the sea cliffs, **Queiroz** starts fast and hollow then offers high-speed walls and barrels for up to 400m. Definitely experts only and tricky to get to without a guide. **Doce Mar** beachbreaks offer easier rides for all abilities, a bit further south. **Cabo Ledo** has a NW-facing set-up that makes this a world-class pointbreak when measuring the fun factor. Really long lefthanders peel down the sandbank for up to 800m with predictable walls, tapered shoulders and it actually works best with a small swell making it ideal for less-experienced surfers. The first outside section facing the rocks has the most power and steepness, while the inside is usually glassy as the SW-W onshores are deflected by the headland. As the swell increases, the rips get pretty horrendous, but luckily, it is an easy walk back past the fish drying racks and out the point to jump in at the peak. Towards the Namibian border is a long stretch of coast with colder water but many more unsurfed, quality, left pointbreaks. Rio Seco is a W swell low tide beachbreak, while Porto Amboim, Kitoba and Sumbe are all lefthand pointbreaks in SW swells and higher tides.

Long range 4-8ft swell with long 15 second periods are most likely to hit from April to September, although at this latitude, some power has been lost along the way. The dominant S-SW winds start blowing from 10am so only the protected spots will break in the afternoon.. Some windswell waves can be observed whenever SE trades off Namibia blow with strength for a long period of time, but these swells will only reach the S-facing spots.and the tidal range never exceeds 5ft. As far as the semi-diurnal tides go, the range never exceeds 5ft max, with a slight diurnal inequality.

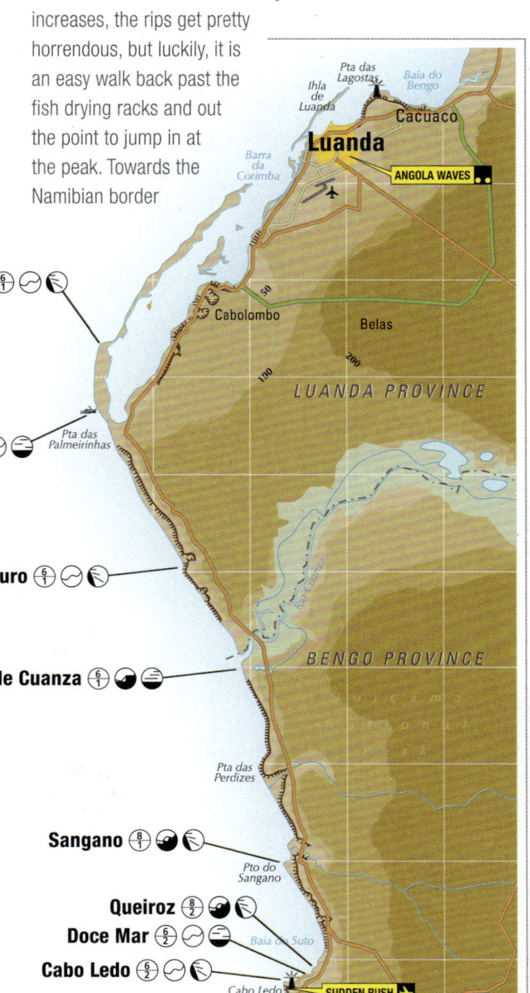


## TRAVEL INFORMATION

**Weather** – The Benguela current substantially reduces rain along the coast and in Luanda, the average annual rainfall is as low as 50cm. The rainy season is from November to March/April. The dry season (cacimbo) is often characterised by a heavy morning mist and holds the region to only 200 days of sunshine per year. The coolest months are July and August 18-25°C. Springsuits are probably only necessary on a windy day in June-September when water temps drop beneath 22°C.

**Lodging and Food** – Costs a fortune. International Hotel chains (Meridien, Continental) range from $250/n. Cheapest hotels would be $80/n. Angola Waves has 8 day, all-inclusive overland packages for $1050. Cabo Ledo is becoming a tourist hub with lots of hotel construction going on and investment in the local infrastructure.

**Nature and Culture** – Quissama National Park flanks the Atlantic for 120km, just south of the Cuanza River. Apart from world-class fishing with huge river tarpon there is a golf course and nightlife in town. Good place to buy diamonds.

**Hazards and Hassles** – Police checks can be hassley and expensive. A 4WD is needed to get anywhere and adds to the extremely high costs of travelling in Angola. There are regular shark sightings but no attacks on surfers. Except for rips, the sandy points are pretty harmless!

**Handy Hints** – Take everything. The left points are ideal for longboarding. Local currency is not exportable and dollars in cash are a must for the visitor.

MANUEL POPPE

Cabo Ledo Outside

JS CALLAHAN/SURFEXPLORE

Cabo Ledo Inside

| STATISTICS | | J F | M A | M J | J A | S O | N D |
|---|---|---|---|---|---|---|---|
| SWELL | Direction | | | | | | |
| | Size (ft) | 1-2 | 2-3 | 4 | 4-5 | 3-4 | 1-2 |
| WIND | Direction | | | | | | |
| | Force | F3 | F3 | F2-F3 | F2 | F2-F3 | F3 |
| WATER | Wetsuit | | | | | | |
| | Temp/°C | 26 | 26 | 24 | 21 | 23 | 25 |
| WEATHER | Rainfall/mm | 30 | 113 | 10 | 1 | 4 | 30 |
| | days/mth | 3 | 8 | 1 | 0 | 1 | 3 |
| | Min temp/°C | 24 | 24 | 22 | 18 | 21 | 23 |
| | Max temp/°C | 30 | 31 | 28 | 25 | 28 | 29 |

# Skeleton Coast NAMIBIA

**Namibia is one of the last frontiers of the surfing world. An isolated harsh environment, impossible access, heavy waves, strong currents, dense fog, very large sharks and the cold Benguela Current makes it a place suitable only for the most hardcore of riders. It receives consistent swell, but aside from one or two small patches of coastline close to the few towns, it remains almost completely unexplored.**

+ VIRGIN WAVES
+ CONSISTENT, POWERFUL SWELLS
+ UNCHARTERED COASTLINE
+ AMAZING SCENERY AND WILDLIFE

- HEAVY, SCARY CONDITIONS
- ONSHORE WINDS AND SEA FOG
- COLD WATER, DIFFICULT ACCESS
- SHARKS AND SEALS

In the Skeleton Coast National Park, coastal access becomes very difficult. This fragile ecosystem is characterised by flat gravel plains and patches of low dunes and though it might look uninhabited, wildlife flourishes here. This northern part of the Namib Desert can surprise the visitor with oryx, springbok, hyenas, jackals and even elephants and lions strolling down to the beach to check the surf – some indication of the true wildness of this region. There are definitely a few spots hidden away in coves and around headlands. However, visitors cannot just go off-road in a 4x4 to check the waves. The plant life, which forms the basis of the food chain, takes decades to grow and is easily destroyed by human interference. Under no circumstances are tourists allowed to leave the marked trails. In the middle of the reserve lies a long left pointbreak at **Ovahimba**. A wilderness camp 30kms inland provides access. This far north is expensive fly-in safari access only. Requires expert planning and surfing skills. **Terrace Bay** is about as far north as the average visitor will be permitted to go. There is an inconsistent left point here, and a more regular beachbreak, both of which are frequented by plenty of big sharks. Accommodation is available in basic blocks, which must be booked through the National Park office. Terrace is a popular fishing resort and offers the best beach shark fishing in the world. The left finishes up in front of the point where the fishermen gut their catches and throw all the entrails back into the sea! The next inhabited spot is **Torra Bay**, another average and often messy beachbreak. Small, glassy conditions offer the best chance of scoring waves. A highly fickle right point lines up at the southern end of the beach if the swell kicks in and the wind stays light. Camping is permitted here in Dec and Jan but must be booked in advance. There is also a mediocre but very consistent beachbreak located by the wreck of the **South West Sea**, a fishing vessel that ran aground here in the mid '70s. The Fur Seal Reserve at Cape Cross is home to two long left pointbreaks, which are offshore in the dominant S wind. **Main Break** is the most consistent wave, with long, fun lines, but the 100,000 seals lend a unique aroma to the surf! Further down the point is a slower section called **Graveyards**. **Factory Point**, in front of the Cape Cross Lodge, is not as good as the other two waves but is further from the seals.

At the north end of Swakopmund, is a reef/beachbreak known as **Fiji** (or Boulders), which is a good choice in smaller swells and light winds. **Vineta Point** breaks left (and sometimes right) in front of a rock groyne that works best at

Ovahimba
Terrace Bay
Torra Bay
South West Sea
Factory Point
Graveyards
Main Break

SEE MAP OPPOSITE

SKELETON SAFARIS

Skeleton Coast

## TRAVEL INFORMATION

**Weather** – Days are mostly warm to very hot 20-35°C (68-95°F), but the strong sea breezes can make the coast feel cold. It gets bitterly cold at night on the coast – down to 0°C (32°F). Morning fog occurs 340 days a year. Surfers need a 3/2 full suit from Dec-April and something thicker through the winter.

**Lodging and Food** – Excellent accommodation at the Cape Cross Lodge for $120 per night. Terrace Bay has a range of cheap $20 per night huts, and camping is allowed at Torra Bay. Free camping is neither permitted nor a sensible idea anywhere else. Skeleton Coast National Park is a protected area, and travellers will not be allowed in unless they have booked a place to stay at Terrace Bay. Skeleton Coast Wilderness Camp is close to Ovahimba ($450-670/n). Founded by the Germans in 1892, Swakopmund is a blend of colonial town and modern architecture with a variety of good hotels, pensions and coffee shops selling German cakes and pastries. Budget for between $40-$80 for daily living costs. Mile 4 Camping near Fiji.

**Nature and Culture** – The Skeleton coast is home to unique wildlife and plant life, including desert elephants and 'dead' plants that live for 2,000 years. Don't miss the Etosha National Park, a long drive inland and one of the best wildlife spectacles in Africa. Other highlights include the sand dunes of Sossusvlei and the remote Damaraland in the northwest. Although Swakopmund offers entertainment like a casino, aquarium and waterslides, you haven't come all this way to pretend you're at home.

**Hazards and Hassles** – There are lots of big sharks, not to mention jackals, hyenas and occasional lions on the beaches. The wildlife danger is over-hyped and a seal bite is far more likely than a shark bite. However, it's actually much safer than people believe. In reality you're more likely to be attacked by a seal during the breeding season (Oct-Nov), (there have been two reported bites by seals on surfers). A bigger danger is hitting shallow reefs. The cold water, currents and heavy surfing conditions are genuine risks. Sandstorms can make driving near impossible.

**Handy Hints** – Take all surfing equipment and a pair of binoculars for spotting the amazing flora and fauna. Namibia is a stunning pristine wilderness where human impact is minimal - an intimidating but rewarding destination. Namibia's best waves may be as yet unridden. Drive on the left.

ALAN VAN GYSEN

Factory Point

## Skeleton Bay

LAT. -22.933254° LONG. 14.423550°

It's a long drive around Walvisbaai and out onto the sand spit that leads to Pelican Point and the lighthouse. A curve in the beach creates the perfect angle for a freakishly insane, but fickle left to peel down parallel to the beach that is now famously known as Skeleton Bay. Requires exacting swell direction to line-up into a magical mile of peeling speed barrels that only the best pit jockeys will handle. Air drops into thick, freight train barrels that can keep you in the shade for the longest tubes of your life, if you can keep up. Heavy drift means walking back up the beach is a must, against the sandblasting wind. Seals everywhere and plagues of jellyfish at times.

ALAN VAN GYSEN

Skeleton Bay

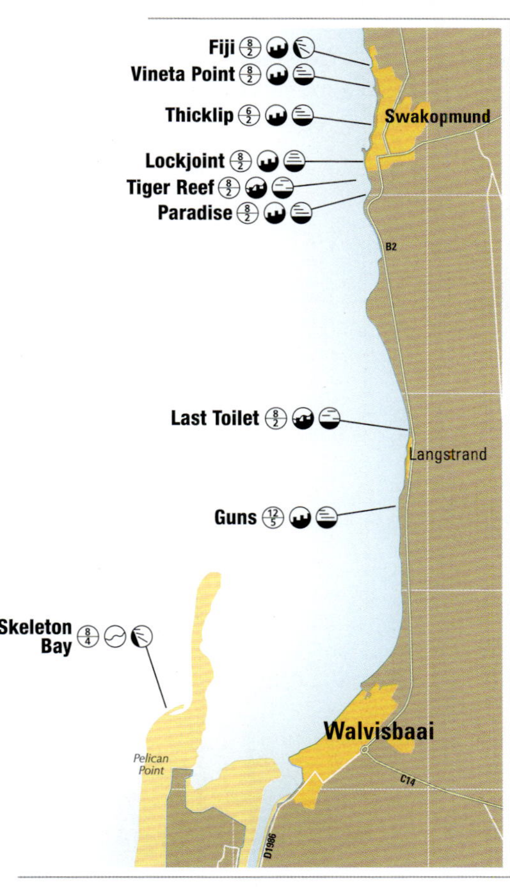


high tide. The shallow reef gives the wave a bowly take-off with barrels a possibility, so not for beginners. **Thicklip** is a bowly left reef, breaking near the rock groyne on Strand Street. It works best on a pushing tide with a moderate swell, but gets blown out easily. In town is the infamous **Lockjoint**, found halfway between the Pier and the Mole breakwater. It's a super-hollow, low tide reefbreak that unfortunately is very fickle. On the edge of town is **Tiger Reef**, a mess of peaks offshore that hold little quality. There's a sectiony left reef called **Paradise** that winds off a rocky point in a bay, a few kilometers south of Swakopmund. **Last Toilet** is found about 2km (1.25mi) beyond the railway restaurant on the Langstrand section. It's a small wave spot, working at low tide. Further south towards Walvisbaai is a powerful reefbreak called **Guns** the premier wave of the area. The left pointbreak produces classic long walls on a moderate W or a big SW swell. It's best from low to mid tide and can hold sizeable surf when everywhere else is maxed-out. Out on the sand spit that protects Walvisbaai is a freakishly insane, but fickle left with many names including Donkey Bay, Pelican Point or just ✪ **Skeleton Bay**.

The coast of Namibia picks up even the smallest of South Atlantic swells and receives waves on an almost daily basis, year-round. The best season is from May to Sept, with consistent 6-10ft SW swells. Most spots are difficult to find and fickle, hidden away behind miles of sand dunes. This is a windy stretch of coast and many breaks are highly sensitive to the wind. To score anywhere requires patience except for the Cape Cross points, which pick up lots of swell and are consistently offshore in the S winds. The dominant wind is from the S, varying very little from 45% in June to 62% in November, when it strengthens a little. While SE-S is the prevailing annual wind direction it usually veers a bit more S-SW at the coast. The tidal range can reach 2m and tide tables are available in Swakopmund.

| STATISTICS | | J F | M A | M J | J A | S O | N D |
|---|---|---|---|---|---|---|---|
| SWELL | Direction | | | | | | |
| | Size (ft) | 3 | 4 | 5 | 5 | 4 | 3 |
| WIND | Direction | | | | | | |
| | Force | F4 | F4 | F4 | F4 | F4 | F4 |
| WATER | Wetsuit | | | | | | |
| | Temp/°C | 20 | 18 | 15 | 13 | 14 | 16 |
| WEATHER | Rainfall/mm | 3 | 6 | 1 | 1 | 0 | 0 |
| | days/mth | 1 | 2 | 1 | 2 | 1 | 1 |
| | Min temp/°C | 15 | 14 | 10 | 8 | 10 | 13 |
| | Max temp/°C | 23 | 23 | 23 | 20 | 19 | 22 |

# Cape Peninsula SOUTH AFRICA

The coastline of South Africa is the oldest shoreline on earth, and aeons of erosion have created an underwater topography ideal for creating some of the best mid-latitude surf, anywhere in the world. The irregular shoreline of the Cape Peninsula, along with its 180° swell window, allows it to offer the best density of varied spots in the whole country, ranging from beginners beachbreak in False Bay to fearsome big-wave venues like Dungeons. Cape Town is a vibrant, cosmopolitan city, surrounded by natural beauty and overlooked by the iconic Table Mountain.

- \+ CONSISTENT, QUALITY WAVES
- \+ WIDE SWELL WINDOW
- \+ MOUNTAIN & SEASCAPES
- \+ CHEAP URBAN ENTERTAINMENT

- – COLD WATER YEAR-ROUND
- – UNSTABLE WINDY WEATHER
- – CITY INSECURITY
- – THICK KELP BEDS

Dunes

RYAN CRAIG

The west-facing stretch of average beachbreak at **Milnerton** can have some clean peelers in SE winds, but tends to closeout at low tide and when the swell gets much overhead. Peaks up and down the beach from the lighthouse spread the mellow crowd. Nestled in the southern corner of the long beach leading down to Cape Town Harbour and the container terminal, **The Wedge** benefits from the refraction of the swell around the numerous breakwalls, wedging into a sucky A-frame and short barrel over sandy reef. Local spongers love it and can be protective, while the pollution from the harbour and rivermouth should put off more surfers. **Thermopylae** is a long left reef that needs a sizeable swell to sweep around Mouille Point and set up a muscle-bound speed wall that grinds down the shelf to the first harbour breakwall. Halves the size of swell unless it is W-NW (rare) but makes up for it in the power stakes. High tide only and the wreck of the Thermopylae lurks right at the peak. Crowded, polluted and strong currents - only advanced surfers will handle the big days. There are a handful of tricky, localized reefs to the south including Off The Wall, Rocklands and Solly's at Sea Point. The rocks off **Glen Beach** hold some reliably good sandbars that can produce particularly hollow rights in smaller swells and low tides. Home turf for many rippers and popular with bodyboarders as it closes out a lot. To the north, Clifton is rarely any good and Camps Bay is usually a thumping shoredump at size. Popular summer spot **Llandudno** is well sheltered from SE gales, offering three spots, depending on how the sand is sticking to the rocks. The north end Gat section peaks up and throws out spitting right tubes, enlarged by the regular backwash. The middle peak and southern corner left are usually short sucky rides, with many a closeout. Always chilly when the SE wind blows offshore and it won't handle too much size, when a 20mins walk south to the nudist beach at Sandy Bay might reveal some more thumping barrels. ✪ **Dungeons** is Cape Town's big-wave pantheon. **The Hoek** is nestled under the cliffs below spectacular Chapman's Peak Drive and is considered a world-class, tubey A-frame when a small to medium SW-W swell is groomed by SE winds. The backwash off the rocks and eternally shifting sands decide which peak is providing the best air drop into short crystalline barrels, before closing out in the shallows. Stops working after mid tide. More consistent is **Noordhoek Beach**, which holds fun surf of variable quality along a 3.5km stretch of golden sands. The peaks can get classic on the right day and crowds thin out the further you walk from the car park, especially considering the high shark attack factor for this area. About two thirds of the way down Noordhoek Beach is **Dunes**, which can produce epic barrels, in moderate SW swells and summer SE'ers. Powerful and unpredictable with heavy paddle outs when it gets overhead. The 30min walk in doesn't deter the crowds these days as it can be so perfect. Worry more about the local fish than the local rippers. The outside bombora of Sunset is a hell of a drop for the local licensed tow crews and madmen. **Long Beach** faces N so any S wind will clean up the predominant lefts that bend around the outer reefs into a beautiful, triangular sandbar. Fast, hollow, high-performance walls into a slamming shorey that the bodyboarders love, especially further round the beach at Krans right. Holds some serious size and crowds since it is the only place to be in a SW'er, but it stops working at high tide. **Inner** and **Outer Kom** are open to plenty of swell and are consistent, yet rarely perfect or predictable. Inners has fun lefts which break over kelp beds, while Outers offers powerful shifting lefts that can easily catch you in the impact zone. Requires a late vertical drop and some barrel sense in the race to the channel. Rips increase once you are clear of the harbour and tend to head to the impact zone. **365's**, another kelp choked slab of reef down from The Kom will be barrel perfection in moderate W swells and NE Berg winds. Needs some tide to make life easier at this full-on experts only right and occasional

## TRAVEL INFORMATION

**Weather** – Winters (May-Sept) see many cold fronts and low pressures pass over, bringing wind, clouds and rain from the NW. As the cold front passes over, SE winds blow from False Bay to Table Bay, creating the famous misty tablecloth on Table Mountain.

**Lodging and Food** – Beachside BnB run by African Soul Surfer are the closest backpackers to the beach in Muizenberg. There are youth hostels in Camps Bay or in Kommetjie (Fendt Guesthouse or Tabankulu) for $20. Expect to spend $10 for a good meal. Local wine and lobster are both excellent and cheap.

**Nature and Culture** – There are plenty of cultural sites and some great bars and nightclubs. Take the classic cablecar ride up Table Mountain.

**Hazards and Hassles** – Since 1960 there have been 30 shark attacks in Cape Town, on average 1 every second year. The main worry is the thick kelp at some spots and the oceans' power. For such a big city, crowd pressure is low and it's ranked as South Africa's safest, but you still need to be careful.

**Handy Hints** – Stock up on cheap surf gear from the numerous well-supplied surf shops. Rental car from $150/w, gas is cheap ($0.90/l). Consider buying a car if you spend more than a couple of months travelling around the country. J-Bay is an 8-hour drive.

AL MACKINNON

## Dungeons

LAT. -34.061801° LONG. 18.324283°

Dungeons is one of the most challenging big waves in the world with double-up drops followed by long speed walls that can close-out. There's an inside Slab section that barrels on the smaller swells, a few outer peaks for rogue sets and the main Photo Bowl which is the end section of the wave. Light N winds, lower tides and long period bombing swell with W in it will get the guns dusted off. Access by boat or jet-ski from Hout Bay, where there is the occasional good day off the harbour wall. Home of Big Wave Africa comp and on the BWWT, this spooky, sharky outside reef is for hellmen only.

left that draws comparisons with Pipeline for both tube time and danger. **Crayfish Factory** is a ferocious right that needs a long period S-SW swell of large proportions to start breaking. It is one of Cape Town's best big wave spots, where extra length, experience and cojones are needed to make the heavy drop and then negotiate the refracting bowl sections further down the long line-up. Punishing hold downs for bailers and those stupid enough to get caught inside. Kelp, crowds, rips and sharks are lesser hazards than the wave itself. Down from the messy beachbreaks of Witsands is **Misty Cliffs**, where crowds might converge on small summer days when everywhere else is small and gutless. Mixture of shifty sandbars over rocky patches, which occasionally produce some hollow runners. Scarborough is a pointbreak setup that needs the rare conditions of overhead SW-W swell, E winds and incoming tide to fire. Luckily there are a couple of rights on the inside where the point meets the beachbreak and a righthand reef further north in front of the carpark. Small summer swells and SE winds will see some fun waves for most abilities. There are some good spots in the Cape Point Nature Reserve (entry fee= $10/p) like the rocky rights of **Olifantsbos Point** that rumble into life with a decent SW-W swell. Long, powerful and holds sizeable winter pulses if the wind blows SE. Rocky, some current and the odd crowd makes this an intermediates plus wave. Other waves to check down on the Cape are the fast kelpy lefts of Platboom and the super-sucky sponger pits of Dias Beach. Beware of the baboons and don't carry any food. **Buffels Bay** is an awesomely fast and furious righthand pointbreak that needs serious amounts of S swell to show. Offshore in stormy SW winds and swarmed with admirers on the too few classic days when the long walls appear. Fast down-the-line surfing plus patience is required to get one off the numerous dialled-in local crew, without getting caught inside. **Black Rocks** needs very similar conditions to Buffels, preferably with some huge SE swell and more W in the wind. It's a little more consistent and so it gets even more crowded, especially on the more fancied right. Needless to say, advanced surfers only. The coast road heading north around False Bay passes some fickle reefs like Glencairn and playful beachbreaks at Fish Hoek and Clovelly, before skirting the harbour to **Kalk Bay** Reef. This slab of reef regularly produces machine-like left pipes that are perfect for bodyboarders and pit pilots. Becomes a world-class wave when overhead SE swell meets understrength NW wind. Sucky, shallow and super-crowded! There's a similar ledge up the beach at Dangers or a less manic right at Baileys Cottage. **Muizenberg**'s long curve of sand invites fun rolling waves with enough peaks for everyone and is offshore in NW winds. The Corner and Cemetery are most popular, plus there are endless beginner-friendly options through Macassar and onto Strand, depending on the wind. All abilities and all surf craft at Cape Town's historical home of surfing.

Winter S-SW swells are consistent around 10ft at 12 seconds interval and can hit 30ft in August. March-April tend to be the cleanest, before the major winter cold fronts sweep across the Peninsula accompanied by NW winds and plenty of swell activity, meaning the S-facing spots are the go. Summers are usually warm and dry, as strong SE winds known as The Cape Doctor blow through in the afternoon. High pressure initiates warm, offshore Berg winds, meaning SW-exposed spots will have small, perfect conditions. Water temps hardly ever exceed 15°C (59ºF) and sometimes drop down to 9°C (48ºF) thanks to summer upwelling. Tidal range can reach 3m.

ALAN VAN GYSEN

Black Rocks

| STATISTICS | | J F | M A | M J | J A | S O | N D |
|---|---|---|---|---|---|---|---|
| SWELL | Direction | | | | | | |
| | Size (ft) | 3 | 5 | 6-7 | 7-8 | 5-6 | 3-4 |
| WIND | Direction | | | | | | |
| | Force | F4 | F4 | F4 | F4 | F4 | F4 |
| WATER | Wetsuit | | | | | | |
| | Temp/°C | 16 | 16 | 15 | 14 | 15 | 16 |
| WEATHER | Rainfall/mm | 10 | 30 | 82 | 77 | 37 | 14 |
| | days/mth | 2 | 4 | 9 | 10 | 11 | 2 |
| | Min temp/°C | 16 | 13 | 9 | 7 | 10 | 14 |
| | Max temp/°C | 26 | 24 | 19 | 18 | 20 | 24 |

# Western Cape SOUTH AFRICA

South Africa's Atlantic west coast north of Cape Town, shivers in the cold Benguela Current, which brings colder water temperatures in summer than winter, but also acts as a highway for swells to arrive at several kelp-covered, north-facing, left pointbreaks tucked behind headlands. Elands Bay has become a popular playground for Capetonian waveriders, whenever there is some significant swell action and there are plenty of other possibilities south of the mountainous Namaqualand area.

+ VARIETY OF LEFT POINTS
+ SOME EASY MELLOW WAVES
+ CHEAP AND UNCROWDED
+ SCENERY AND WILDLIFE

– FEW CONSISTENT SPOTS
– COLD WATER YEAR ROUND
– KELP AND MUSSELS
– LACKS TOURISM INFRASTRUCTURE

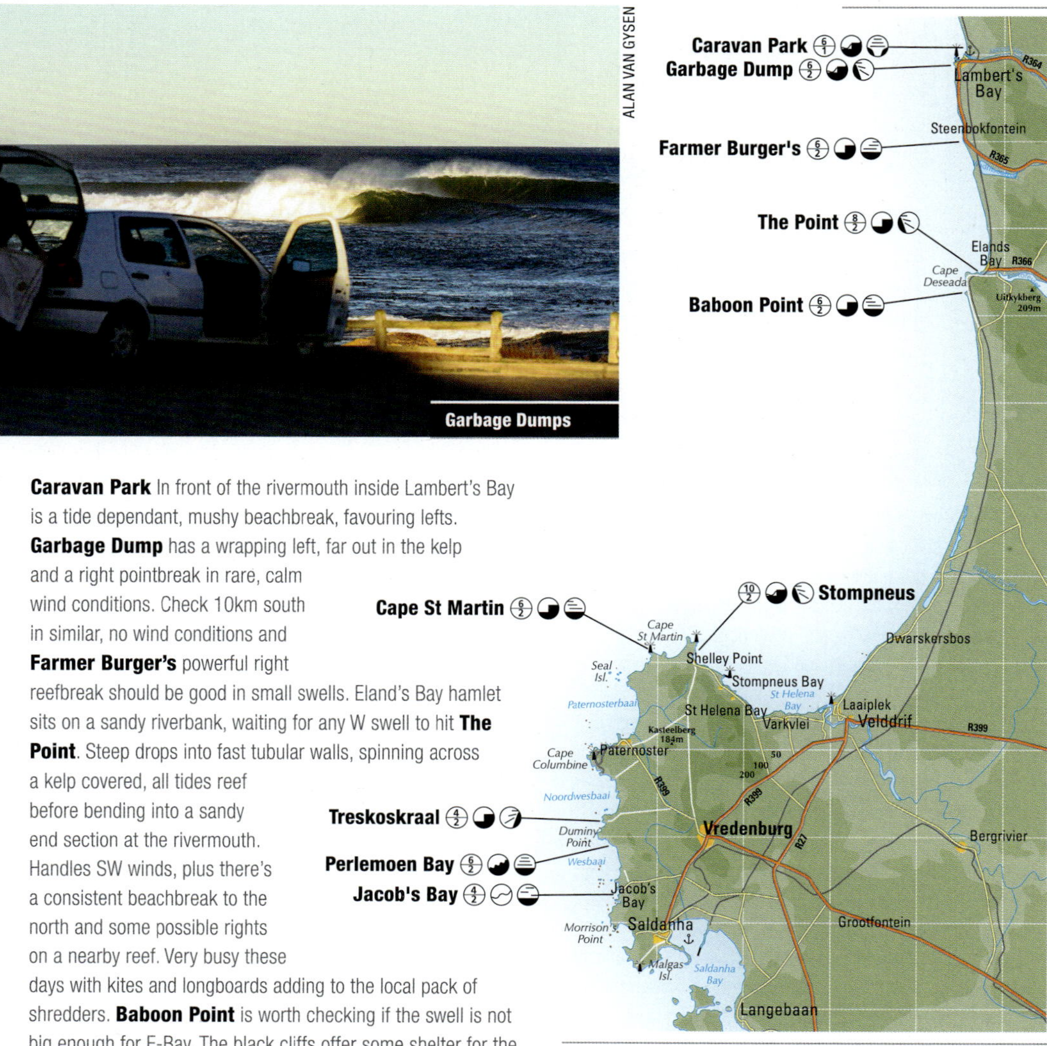


ALAN VAN GYSEN

Garbage Dumps

**Caravan Park** In front of the rivermouth inside Lambert's Bay is a tide dependant, mushy beachbreak, favouring lefts. **Garbage Dump** has a wrapping left, far out in the kelp and a right pointbreak in rare, calm wind conditions. Check 10km south in similar, no wind conditions and **Farmer Burger's** powerful right reefbreak should be good in small swells. Eland's Bay hamlet sits on a sandy riverbank, waiting for any W swell to hit **The Point**. Steep drops into fast tubular walls, spinning across a kelp covered, all tides reef before bending into a sandy end section at the rivermouth. Handles SW winds, plus there's a consistent beachbreak to the north and some possible rights on a nearby reef. Very busy these days with kites and longboards adding to the local pack of shredders. **Baboon Point** is worth checking if the swell is not big enough for E-Bay. The black cliffs offer some shelter for the lefts, but SW winds will blow out this spot. The long stretch of Santa Helena Bay would only suit beginners, lacking shape and shelter. **Stompneus** is the first break on the north side of the Vredenburg Peninsula. Not as epic as E-Bay and needs similar big swell conditions, but it combines an outside, low tide reef with an inside, high tide set-up that handles any swell size and even W winds. This area hides many other spots like Pastures, Heaven and Hell. Another fun left is to be found at **Cape St Martin** which works in similar conditions as Elands Bay but will be less crowded. **Trekoskraal** is an inconsistent right point in a deepwater bay that has some N wind protection. Sandy 4WD roads and great wild camping. **Perlemoen Bay** has a choice between a high tide righthand point in N winds or a fun, triangular lefthand reef over sand and boulders at lower tides. In the middle of **Jacob's Bay** a kelpy reef holds high tide peaks in overhead swells and light winds, otherwise pay a fee to check the small swell beachbreak at Swartriet Beach Resort.

N-exposed reefs like E-Bay definitely need strong winter SW swells to break. Common SW winds will be offshore and the day after a cold front passes is usually the classic day. Summer starts in October with strong SE winds (The Cape Doctor), bringing upwelling cold currents ashore and blown-out conditions after 10am. When a rare high pressure protects the West Coast, winds and swell diminish and warm NE Berg winds fan the SW-exposed spots, bringing small and perfect conditions. Tidal range can reach 3m, and most reefs and pointbreaks favour low tides, further reducing surf time.

## TRAVEL INFORMATION

**Weather** – Weather patterns are very unstable but rainfall is low. Winters (May-Sept) bring many cold fronts over the peninsula. Once the coastal low has passed, winds and clouds move in from the NW. Rain starts falling and the ocean gets rough. Summers are usually warm and dry but very windy in the afternoon. Because of the cold Benguela Current, water hardly ever gets over 15°C (59°F) and sometimes gets down to 9°C (48°F) on west-facing spots with summer upwelling. 4/3 fullsuit + booties required year-round.

**Lodging and Food** – E-Bay is tiny: stay in the beach caravan park ($3 per tent) Elands Bay Hotel from $25 p/n b&b. Eat as much red gold (crayfish) as you can. Seafood is cheap including anchovies, pilchards and long, thin, silvery snoek.

**Nature and Culture** – Plenty of birds like flamingos, pelicans and herons at E-Bay river or at the West Coast National Park. Don't expect city action, E-Bay has two pool tables and two cafes. Visit the Bobbejaanberg Cave in Baboon Point.

**Hazards and Hassles** – Most visitors are Capetonian weekenders so the crowd thins on weekdays. Have enough neoprene to protect your feet from the mussels. Frequent winds and a strong smell of fish can be a hassle as well as the thick kelp, which can hamper your board speed. Country towns are breeding grounds for the endemic racism that blights South Africa. On a positive note, sharks are not a problem in this area of SA.

**Handy Hints** – Use the designated town parking lot before walking out to the point. Living costs in SA are low.

| STATISTICS | | J F | M A | M J | J A | S O | N D |
|---|---|---|---|---|---|---|---|
| SWELL | Direction | | | | | | |
| | Size (ft) | 1-2 | 3-4 | 5 | 6 | 4 | 2 |
| WIND | Direction | | | | | | |
| | Force | F4 | F4 | F4 | F4 | F4 | F4 |
| WATER | Wetsuit | | | | | | |
| | Temp/°C | 16 | 15 | 14 | 13 | 14 | 16 |
| WEATHER | Rainfall/mm | 10 | 33 | 83 | 78 | 38 | 14 |
| | days/mth | 2 | 5 | 9 | 10 | 11 | 3 |
| | Min temp/°C | 16 | 13 | 9 | 8 | 10 | 14 |
| | Max temp/°C | 26 | 24 | 19 | 18 | 20 | 24 |

STUART GIBSON

The Point, Elands

# Garden Route SOUTH AFRICA

Half way between Cape Town and J-Bay are clusters of right pointbreaks, condensed in a popular area known as the Garden Route. This 250km stretch of coastal towns with exposed beachbreaks or sheltered bays, is also renowned for its unique flora and fauna, while the water teems with life as whales and dolphins frequent the wild ocean off South Africa's tip.

+ HIGH SWELL CONSISTENCY
+ VARIETY OF RIGHT POINTS
+ CHEAP AND UNCROWDED
+ GREAT NATURE ACTIVITIES

- COOL WATER YEAR-ROUND
- VIRTUALLY NO LEFTS
- NO MAJOR AIRPORT NEARBY
- PACKED TOURIST SEASON

**Jongensfontein** is a small, SE swell reefbreak that can be a long ride with some sucky hollow sections. High tides, SW swell and any strong winds don't agree with this place. **Still Bay** is an epic righthand pointbreak with powerful, ruler-edged walls and some tube time possible. Huge SW swells will halve in size by the time they have wrapped into the bay, before sectioning off between the tip and the harbour. Long rides, but rarely the full 1km link up, as rogue rocks and a gruelling rip pushes down the point. Low tide outside and high tide inside with W-SW winds, since NW can bump up the face, just like J-Bay. There are loads more spots in the immediate vicinity to escape the crowds. A solid SE or huge S-SW swell is needed for ultra-fickle **Vlees Bay** to get barreling through the three sections. Sharky, localised and tricky to find/access. Same deal at nearby Canon and Gourits Mouth. Mossel Bay holds a wealth of multi-peak, north-facing bays and **Outer Pool** is the pick, throwing up long, speedy walls with cavernous tubes at low tide, washed by a tiring drift down the point. Inner Pool prefers higher tides and is far slower and fatter. **Victoria Bay** is a popular right pointbreak zipping over the rocky headland beneath steep cliffs in a pocket bay. **Wilderness Beach** is a summer spot requiring small peaky S swells and any N winds, usually best at the west corner near Kaimansriver. On a NE wind, there's the novelty of a sucky left pointbreak at **Gerrickes**, but only in small summer conditions. **Goukamma**'s beautiful rivermouth peaks are totally sand dependant and the red alluvial soil in the outflow gives cover to the ever-present sharks. There are more breaks on the wild west side of Buffalo Bay Point, a consistent but messy right that only really fires up in SE swells. The most reliable spot is **Murphys** reef and sand peak, with punchy hollow lefts in most swells and even onshore winds. In touristy Plettenberg Bay, **The Wedge** is a bucking, rearing, beast of a wave when big SE-SW swells wrap into the huge bay. Bodyboard heaven as it doubles in size from the rock bounce, throws a huge cavern, then implodes on the beach. Air-drops, close-outs and sand slammers guaranteed, so stand-ups might want to check the Wreck on E swells. **Lookout Beach** is fairly ordinary beachbreak, with shifty sandbars, especially up by the rivermouth. Swell exposure and wave quality improves towards **Keurbooms**. It's an exposed beachbreak, getting epic on small, clean swell with no wind. Share the lefts and rights with a school of local dolphins in stunning scenery.

## TRAVEL INFORMATION

**Weather** – Rainfall is year-round but not torrential. Summers are usually warm and it's the only time the water feels bearable enough to wear springsuits. The rest of the year is not that cold although mid-winter, cloudy mornings are chilly while the SW winds require adequate clothing and fullsuits all the time (boots and even hoods), since the warm Agulhas Current heads offshore.

**Lodging and Food** – Avoid Dec-Feb when prices hit the roof. Robberg resort ($115/dble), Ohannas B&B ($45/dble) or Little Sanctuary self catering for 4 ($24p/n). Expect $10 for a meal.

**Nature and Culture** – Dive in cages to see white sharks. Whale and dolphin watching spots are plentiful. On either sides of the Route are two bungee jumping sites. Visit Tsitsikamma Park forests, Robberg in Plett has a reserve. Mossel Bay is scenic despite Mossgas' huge oil refinery.

**Hazards and Hassles** – The shark factor can be a problem, recent fatal attacks have occurred in Keurbooms, Buffel and Mossel Bay. Avoid sardine runs (well noticed by the media), sunset sessions and murky waters and all should be fine. Summer bluebottle flies can be much more of a hassle. Some localism at Mossel Bay.

**Handy Hints** - Loads of surf shops with cheap gear (board and wettie from $550). A semi-gun in winter might be necessary.

ALAN VAN GYSEN

Plettenberg Bay

JASON FEAST

Mossel Bay

Lows travel quickly from west to east, spinning clockwise, so the best coastal orientation is SE. Swells march against the W-flowing warm Agulhas current, building sandbanks in the SE-facing bays. Summer high pressures blow out most spots with the ENE winds. April to October sees morning NW Berg winds turning SW (sideshore) after noon. Any time a cold front passes, there will be E winds. Tides vary between 1-2m.

| STATISTICS | | J F | M A | M J | J A | S O | N D |
|---|---|---|---|---|---|---|---|
| SWELL | Direction | | | | | | |
| | Size (ft) | 2-3 | 4-5 | 5 | 5-6 | 4-5 | 3 |
| WIND | Direction | | | | | | |
| | Force | F4 | F4 | F4 | F4 | F4 | F4 |
| WATER | Wetsuit | | | | | | |
| | Temp/°C | 22 | 22 | 19 | 18 | 19 | 20 |
| WEATHER | Rainfall/mm | 53 | 60 | 64 | 65 | 70 | 58 |
| | days/mth | 5 | 6 | 6 | 6 | 8 | 6 |
| | Min temp/°C | 17 | 15 | 9 | 8 | 11 | 15 |
| | Max temp/°C | 25 | 24 | 21 | 20 | 21 | 23 |

# St Francis Bay SOUTH AFRICA

Halfway between Durban and Cape Town is South Africa's best and most consistent surf zone. The frequent winter SW swells turn on dozens of classic pointbreaks that are hidden away inside crescent shaped coves. Jeffreys Bay (J-Bay) is obviously the most renowned wave and is considered one of the best righthanders in the world. St Francis Bay is blessed with other quality waves, including the fickle Bruce's Beauties, which featured in the seminal '60s film, *Endless Summer*. Jeffreys Bay has quickly grown from laid-back hippie town into South Africa's major surf hub and a solid tourist destination in its own right.

+ J-BAY'S WORLD-CLASS RIGHTS
+ CONSISTENT SWELLS
+ FREQUENT OFFSHORE WINDS
+ SURF TOWN FACILITIES

- COOL WATER AND WIND CHILL
- MUSSEL COVERED ROCKS
- SHARKS
- PACKED J-BAY LINE-UP

## TRAVEL INFORMATION

**Weather** – The J-Bay area has an unstable climate but it's generally dry. The hot Berg winds can bring high temps and great weather off the mountains, followed a day later by a cold front coming off the sea, bringing a sudden drop in temperatures. Summers are warm and you could even surf in a shorty, but the remainder of the year requires a good 3/2 fullsuit.

**Lodging and Food** – During summer all accommodation may be full. In winter the crowds die down and prices drop and beds can be had in surfer's hostels for as little as $20/n or camping from $14. Better quality options include Jeffreys Bay Surftrips from ($40/n). Cape St-Francis Holiday Resort (fr $40/p/n), On the Beach Guesthouse (fr $50/p/n) and a multitude of others. A good meal costs $8. The fish is excellent.

**Nature and Culture** – There's very little to do here other than surf. The Drakensberg Mountains are a long but worthwhile trip. Port Elizabeth is known as the Friendly City, as well as the Windy City. Attractions include the Seaview Lion Park, Marine Rehab Centre, whale watching tours or the Shamwari Game Reserve.

**Hazards and Hassles** – Sharks are everyone's big fear, as Mick Fanning will testify, yet the first fatal J-Bay attack was in Oct 2013 on a swimmer. Avoid surfing during the sardine runs, heavy rain and at dawn or dusk. More realistic threats are the razor sharp mussels that line the rocks.

**Handy Hints** – Car rental, fuel and living costs are cheap. Surf gear bought from the J-Bay surf shops can be a very good deal.

ROY HARLEY

KODY MCGREGOR

Cape St Francis

SW-facing spots are exposed to plenty of Roaring Forties swell, but are often onshore in the best swell season. Oyster Bay, to the W of Seal Point, is one of these places, only really worth surfing during the predominant summer E winds. Out on the tip of the bay, sharky **Seal Point** is split into two sections by the annoying Full Stop rock. Bigger SE swells may link them up into a long, fast ride with barrel and carve sections. Plus there is the bonus of barreling **Cape St Francis Beach** is worth a look when the swell is small. All tides and S-NW winds should see somewhere working between The Corner, Lookouts and Ducks at the north end, where sandbars are held by reef patches and it will work in N winds. When a big S-E swell kicks **Bruce's Beauties** into life, the local chargers head to Cape St. Francis for some seriously heavy pits, that wrap dangerously close to the rocks on their grind down the long headland. Lower tides and SW winds produce a wave to rival Supertubes at J-Bay, but it is a fickle spot with low consistency. **Leftovers** is an underrated wave which can offer long rides when the swell comes up from the south. **Hullet's Reef** in the town of St. Francis Bay is the ideal place for beginners as it has mellow lefts on small swells. The town's beachbreak can get pretty epic in small clean swells and there are more options up the beach at the **Kromme Rivermouth**. The rare but quality left of **Clapton's Coils** near to Aston Bay works when an E swell meets a warm Berg wind. Fickle and fiercely protected by locals so look elsewhere. ✪ **J-Bay** is the benchmark by which all world-class righthand pointbreaks are measured. **Van Staden's Mouth**, on the way to Port Elizabeth, is situated inside the beautiful Van Stadens nature reserve, but the rivermouth beachbreak is usually completely blown out unless the winds are from the N. This coastline heading towards Cape Recife and Port Elizabeth (PE) is known as Wildside and made up of nature reserves and a largely undeveloped coastline. Many reef and sand options exist including Maitlands, Beachview, Laurie's Bay and a handful of semi-secret reefs that pick up tons of swell and clean up if the the wind swings any side of N. **Sardinia Bay** is quite reliable and powerful in small summer swells, with barrels to be had in the pristine environment. The sand has swallowed the road so park in the big lot and hope the thieves aren't on duty that day. Walking almost a km to the west will get you into **Doughnuts**, a bodyboarding favourite since there is always a hole in the middle. A good 300m offshore is the spooky lefthander on the Back Reef where fast spinning walls entice those skilled and brave enough to get some shack time without meeting the local wildlife. **Nordhoek Main Rights** is an easy access righthand reef thanks to the boat launching ramp and deeper channel that can make it a dry hair paddle out avoiding the the urchins and mussels that cover the rocks. Welcomes any S swell directions

KODY MCGREGOR

Bruce's Beauties

and can be a long, powerful ride with a few hollower sections. For proper barrels, paddle over the sharky channel to **Rocky's**, a slabby rock shelf that trips up SE-SW swells, but is less consistent and far less popular than the right, probably due to the heavy take-offs and thick lips. **Nordhoek Beach** faces due S and is usually overpowered and onshore, but can look good with small summer swells and NW winds that clean up the rights coming off the rocks in the western corner. There's also a decent right reef at the other end called **Non Kom** which will be dead offshore in NE winds. Rarely crowded with surfers unless Algoa Bay is flat, despite being the PE nudist beach. Out by the lighthouse, **The Beacon** (aka Boulders) is another small swell spot peeling right down the extended rock shelf. Usually better at high, eliminating the rock hop over the reef and keeping the cruisey walls breaking a bit more orderly. Improvers and longboarders will love it until it gets overhead, when the paddle-out and drift is too much. It's the same deal at **Pollock Beach** where The Pipe breaks in all small swells and is even rideable in light onshores from the E. The Clubhouse end will handle more size, but it is probably way better elsewhere. **Avalanche** may be the funnest wave in PE when the sand builds up just right on the reef. SW swells will bend into town, allowing this rocky outcrop to catch and focus the power as it zips down the line at varying speed with the odd hollow pocket. Pretty consistent and always crowded when it fires. South of the Shark Rock Pier and Hobie Beach is **Miller's Point**, another relatively mellow, messy sand-over-rock-shelf arrangement that needs some E in the swell to give it a bit of punch. However, on the dozen good days a year, it really fires at high tide with damn long rides and barrels that are missing when it's small. Gets crowded and a bit aggro on those days. Around the derelict pylons on **Humewood Beach** is a righthand sandbank that can deliver thick, throaty tubes for the hordes of bodyboarders and stand-ups good enough to make the vertical drop. Needs small to medium SE swell and SW winds to be primo, but SW wraps in if big enough. **The Fence** is found at the far end of Kings Beach where it meets the extensive harbour wall that provides the perfect reflection angle for wedging left peaks. Gets insanely hollow and working out which ones will get the perfect bounce takes time, but its allure guarantees weekend crowds. Higher tides and big SW or moderate NE-SE swells fanned by any W wind. Park at the waterslide and walk up Kings Beach, which can have some decent waves especially at lower tides when Fence isn't working.

KODY MCGREGOR

Port Elizabeth

## J-Bay

**LAT. -34.032934° LONG. 24.934619°**

The longest, most perfect righthand pointbreak on the planet, consists of no less than 10 different sections including Kitchen Windows, Magnatubes, Boneyards, Supertubes, Impossibles, Salad Bowls, Coins, Tubes, The Point and finally Albatross. Fingers of basalt hold the sand uniformly, creating the perfect bathymetry for 1km long rides between Boneyards and The Point when the swell is just the right size and perfectly lined up. Supertubes is the stellar section, where the pro competitions are held and the crew are most combative, while Point and Albatross are slower, more manageable walls for intermediates and longboarders. Maintaining high speed and a high line is critical for threading the multiple tube sections and cutting back is rarely a good idea. SW-W is offshore for most of the sections, while NW-NE Berg (or Devil) winds descend from the mountains, blowing into the barrels and creating a nasty chop that is hard to handle on a wave where speed is king. Currents can be unrelenting and sweep you down the point in a trice. Walking back up the point is de rigeur, but then you must find the keyhole through the sharp, mussel-coated boulders that are know locally as bricks. Booties and a strong board will help avoid damage and stave off the effects of upwelling fed cold water in the 15-19ºC (59-66ºF) bracket, further depressed by a lively windchill factor, despite being in a subtropical convergence zone where the warm Agulhas current meets the cold South Atlantic.

With a bit of luck, there will be weeks of back to back S-SW swells from March to Sept. Strong E winds or tropical cyclones occurring from Jan-March can provide short-lived NE-SE swells. Fast-paced depressions push strong SW winds and makes SE-facing spots like J-Bay a much better bet for good wind conditions. From Nov to March the wind changes direction and blows primarily from the E, not good for the majority of spots. From April to Oct light NW (berg) winds blow offshore in the morning, turning SW in the afternoon. Tidal range can be significant so get a tide table from the J-Bay surf shops.

| STATISTICS | | J F | M A | M J | J A | S O | N D |
|---|---|---|---|---|---|---|---|
| SWELL | Direction | | | | | | |
| | Size (ft) | 2-3 | 4-5 | 5 | 5-6 | 4-5 | 3 |
| WIND | Direction | | | | | | |
| | Force | F4 | F4 | F4 | F4 | F4 | F4 |
| WATER | Wetsuit | | | | | | |
| | Temp/°C | 21 | 19 | 17 | 15 | 16 | 19 |
| WEATHER | Rainfall/mm | 35 | 47 | 62 | 57 | 62 | 50 |
| | days/mth | 5 | 6 | 5 | 6 | 8 | 9 |
| | Min temp/°C | 16 | 14 | 9 | 7 | 11 | 14 |
| | Max temp/°C | 25 | 24 | 21 | 20 | 21 | 23 |

# East London SOUTH AFRICA

South Africa's only river port, is the gateway to the Sunshine Coast and the Wild Coast, and the swells that hit this Eastern Cape region are the most consistent for the whole South African coastline. Considering the warmer water and the number of legitimate right pointbreaks, East London is a world-class zone that sharks have managed to keep quiet. Many shark attacks have been recorded in and around the area so locals advise not to enter the water in the early morning or late afternoon, when birds and dolphins are seen feeding, and on no account to go out alone.

+ SWELLS YEAR-ROUND
+ UNCROWDED, OFTEN OFFSHORE
+ MANY LONG, RIGHT POINTS
+ WARMER WATER THAN J-BAY

– NOON SUMMER ENE WIND
– HIGH SHARK ATTACK STATS
– COOL, WINDY WINTERS
– SPOOKY, EMPTY LINE-UPS

LOUIS WULFF

Eastern Beach

**Kidd's Beach** is a popular holiday resort, offering a half-decent beachbreak best on small to mid S swells. **Igoda** is a better bet, facing south and sucking in plenty of swell at the eastern end rivermouth in front of the rocks forming really good tubes and beachbreak walls that are best on light NE or NW Berg winds. Nearby is **Naidoo Point**, producing nice tubular rights on small clean SW swells. In central East London, **Eastern Beach** delivers variable quality shifting sandbars, but on N winds and summer NE swells, it's the place to be. Countless contests are held at **Nahoon Reef**, the most popular right point in town. The outside section named Reef can handle very big swells, when huge drops and powerful bowl sections challenge the ever-present crowd. Corner, on the inside prefers E swells and any W wind and suffers less from the bad rips and bad shark attack record of Reef. Two rivermouths shape the sandbars to the north, but **Bonza's** is a below average spot needing Berg winds and small peaky E swells. **Gonubie Point** is a fine right point, requiring a medium E-SE swell to create angular pits over slabs of reef at lower tides. Crowded when on, there is also a consistent beachbreak, a tidal pool and plenty of accommodation. On the other side of the bay is **Gonubie Reef**, a consistent left pointbreak, which is a rarity in these parts. Really long, fun bashable walls on any swell direction or size.

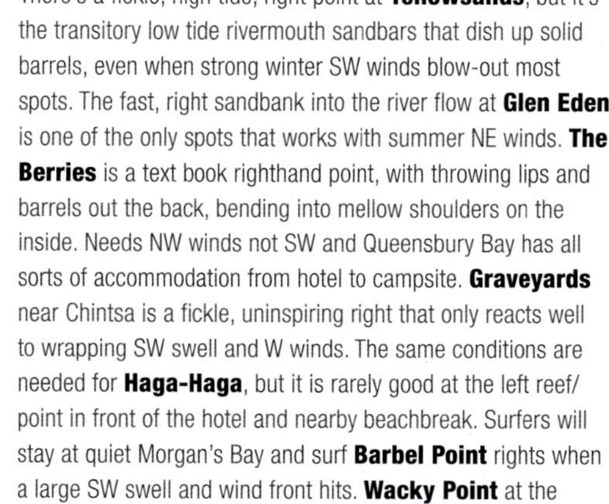

There's a fickle, high tide, right point at **Yellowsands**, but it's the transitory low tide rivermouth sandbars that dish up solid barrels, even when strong winter SW winds blow-out most spots. The fast, right sandbank into the river flow at **Glen Eden** is one of the only spots that works with summer NE winds. **The Berries** is a text book righthand point, with throwing lips and barrels out the back, bending into mellow shoulders on the inside. Needs NW winds not SW and Queensbury Bay has all sorts of accommodation from hotel to campsite. **Graveyards** near Chintsa is a fickle, uninspiring right that only reacts well to wrapping SW swell and W winds. The same conditions are needed for **Haga-Haga**, but it is rarely good at the left reef/point in front of the hotel and nearby beachbreak. Surfers will stay at quiet Morgan's Bay and surf **Barbel Point** rights when a large SW swell and wind front hits. **Wacky Point** at the Kei Mouth is somewhat fickle but an absolute gem when on. A couple of challenging, tubular sections unload over rocky shelves and it's rarely surfed by East London locals since it's a long drive along bad roads on the border of the Transkei.

The East London zone gets sheltered from the strong SW winds and cold rain squalls that affect most of the western part of the Eastern Cape Province. On clear winter days, it's offshore every morning, while in summer, it gets warm and humid as in Natal, but with less of the surf-destroying NE wind. Most of the right points work well with SW swells & winds. Tides can reach 2.1m, affecting rivermouth breaks.

## TRAVEL INFORMATION

**Weather** – East London enjoys a moderate subtropical climate, with few extremes. Winters are usually mild with temps between 10-23°C (50-74°F). From September to April, the climate is cool and wet with temps ranging from 12-25°C (54-77°F). Boardshorts, shorty, spring suit or light steamer will cover the seasons.

**Lodging and Food** – Stay at Dawn Patrol camp near Nahoon Reef or the Sugar Shack at Eastern Beach ($20 dble, surf hire/lessons). Expect $5 for a good meal. Wine and lobster are cheap.

**Nature and Culture** – Nahoon Fossil Prints, in Nahoon Bats Cave are the oldest homo sapiens footprints, 200,000 years old! Check the lion park where you can handle lion cubs.

**Hazards and Hassles** – Records show that shark attack is the main threat at most rivermouth spots. Buy a Shark Shield ($699) or Sharkbanz Shark leash ($180) to stop the Jaws theme playing in your head. Spots are fairly uncrowded and localism is rare. Wave power can be fierce in winter.

**Handy Hints** – Only drive during daytime. It takes 4-5h drive from J-Bay. Access to most of the spots is easy, just don't paddle across rivermouths when they run out to sea. Just Surfing and Boardriders have shops in East London.

| STATISTICS | | J F | M A | M J | J A | S O | N D |
|---|---|---|---|---|---|---|---|
| SWELL | Direction | | | | | | |
| | Size (ft) | 2-3 | 4-5 | 5 | 5-6 | 4-5 | 3 |
| WIND | Direction | | | | | | |
| | Force | F4 | F4-F5 | F5 | F5 | F5 | F4-F5 |
| WATER | Wetsuit | | | | | | |
| | Temp/°C | 22 | 21 | 19 | 18 | 19 | 21 |
| WEATHER | Rainfall/mm | 79 | 91 | 45 | 55 | 91 | 86 |
| | days/mth | 13 | 11 | 7 | 6 | 12 | 13 |
| | Min temp/°C | 18 | 16 | 11 | 10 | 13 | 16 |
| | Max temp/°C | 26 | 25 | 22 | 21 | 21 | 23 |

LOUIS WULFF

The Berries

# Wild Coast SOUTH AFRICA

The Wild Coast, once known as the Transkei homeland, is a 280km stretch of cliff faces, perfect beaches and rich tidal estuaries, running from Great Kei River (East London) to Mtamvuna River (Port Edward) on the border with KwaZulu Natal Province. Long distances between towns, the poor condition of the roads, a lack of facilities and some strenuous access to breaks; this region suits the more experienced searcher with some pioneering spirit. There is a balanced equilibrium between exposed, quality beachbreaks and protected right pointbreaks and many bays have both. A number of shark attacks on surfers have gone down at Nytlonyane and Port St Johns over the years, but stats show these encounters are becoming rarer. Coffee Bay is central enough to be used as a base for surfing missions and has some tourist facilities.

- + TOP-CLASS RIGHT POINTS
- + CROWD FREE
- + WARM WATER
- + CHEAP LIVING COSTS

- – SHARKS
- – POOR ROAD NETWORK
- – LACK OF FACILITIES
- – POVERTY & PETTY CRIME

Visit **Feldskoen Bay** for fun lefts and rights over a sand covered reef. Transkei's most consistent point, **Ntylonyane** (Breezy Point) has a J-Bay-like righthander that is super-consistent, but is more notorious for its ominous fatal shark attack record. **Sharpleys Point** needs S-SE swells to wrap in properly. **Hole-in-the-Wall** is a scenic sandstone arch that heavily filters big swell, allowing novelty lefts to reform down the boulders behind the island. **Coffee Bay Point** breaks right off the southern headland of the arcing Coffee Bay, needing smaller E swells or bigger S swells to reform over the rock shelf and sand bottom. On the other side of the headland is Mbomvu's rare, righthand rivermouth spot and White Clay, an average beachie that picks up most of the available swell. **Coffee Bay**'s main beach can produce classic waves when winds are light from the W and there is plenty of E in the swell. Multiple peaks but the gem waves are the high tide lefts running into the river flow in the southern corner. Both **Mdumbe** and **Lwandile** can be considered as epic righthand pointbreaks, especially when the rivermouth fed inside sandbanks link to the outside shelf creating some long, leg-burning rides. Beachbreak peaks can be found at **Presley's Bay**, but a better choice would be **Ebalow**. These rare but epic lefts are deep in 4WD country and peel into another sharky rivermouth. **Mpande Bay** can hold up in small swell, light offshore conditions but closes-out easily. Port St Johns is the main coastal town, exuding a strange melange of styles and cultures with several beaches close-by. On a very small swell, beachbreaks like **Mngazi** and **Second Beach** will hold some peaks, but not much quality. Further north, **Mzimpuni**'s large bay complete with big S-SE swell righthand pointbreak, is close to the small swell, beachbreak peaks of **Mbotyi**.

Most of the spinning lows send plenty of SE-SW swells to The Wild Coast, although occasionally one will parallel the coast bringing more E to the swells. E and SE swell can hit the righthand points too straight, bringing lots of big close-outs compared to the S-SW swells that refract around the headlands. NE summer winds bring some choppy headhigh windswell. Tides vary little but incoming or outgoing phases might create different current conditions at rivermouth spots.

GREG EWING

Lwandile

## TRAVEL INFORMATION

**Weather** – The climate along the Wild Coast is nearly always warm to hot, with humidity levels rising from Dec to March. Thunderstorms are frequent in summer. The Wild Coast lies in a summer-rainfall region, swelling many rivers that flow into the ocean. The drier, winter climate is most favourable during the months of May and June. Sea temperatures usually exceed 17°C (63°F) and can go as high as 23°C (74°F) when the warm Agulhas (or Mozambique) Current flows close to shore.

**Lodging and Food** – Tourist facilities are low but the coast is dotted with small lodges (from hotels to thatched rondavel huts). In Coffee Bay, Backpackers are fine like Bomvu or Coffee Shack ($12/day). Ocean View Hotel: from $69/b&b. Try Amapondo in PSJ or the Kraal in Mpande. A meal will cost $8.

**Nature and Culture** – Xhosa rural people live by tribal tradition and beliefs. Brightly coloured examples of the beadwork, together with traditional pottery and basketwork can be bought from roadside vendors and at some trading posts. Backpacker's activities: horse-riding, hiking, music, yoga and parties!

**Hazards and Hassles** – On remote beaches, beware of muggings and car break-ins. Reduce shark risks: don't surf too early or too late; don't surf near flooded rivermouth; don't piss in the sea (even if wearing a wetsuit) and avoid the sardine runs. Winter is less sharky as the rivers stop flowing out murky fresh water. Beware the strong weed.

**Handy Hints** – No shops or shapers in this zone. Old boards can be rented in Coffee Bay. An independent territory, Transkei reintegrated with the rest of South Africa in 1994 and boasts a predominantly Xhosa speaking population compared to Afrikaans (10%) and English (5%).

GREG EWING

Mdumbe

| STATISTICS | | J F | M A | M J | J A | S O | N D |
|---|---|---|---|---|---|---|---|
| SWELL | Direction | | | | | | |
| | Size (ft) | 2-3 | 4-5 | 5 | 5-6 | 4-5 | 3 |
| WIND | Direction | | | | | | |
| | Force | F4 | F4-F5 | F5 | F5 | F5 | F5 |
| WATER | Wetsuit | | | | | | |
| | Temp/°C | 22 | 21 | 19 | 18 | 19 | 21 |
| WEATHER | Rainfall/mm | 127 | 115 | 48 | 47 | 94 | 121 |
| | days/mth | 10 | 8 | 4 | 3 | 7 | 9 |
| | Min temp/°C | 20 | 18 | 15 | 13 | 16 | 18 |
| | Max temp/°C | 25 | 24 | 23 | 21 | 22 | 23 |

# Southern Kwazulu Natal SOUTH AFRICA

The huge province of Kwazulu Natal is split by Durban and the "South Coast" is well known as a sunny holiday playground, but also happens to be one of the world's most underrated surf zones. There are high quality, consistent waves everywhere, including hollow beachbreaks, heaps of righthand points and a few classic reefbreaks. The continental shelf drops away sharply, so catching the plentiful, year-round, open ocean swells is easier, attracting a variety of wave riders to this sub-tropical warm water zone.

+ VERY CONSISTENT SWELLS
+ MORNING OFFSHORES IN WINTER
+ HOLLOW PUNCHY RIGHT POINTS
+ UNCROWDED, WARM WATER

- BLOWN-OUT MOST AFTERNOONS
- SHARKS, UN-NETTED BEACHES
- ALMOST STRAIGHT COASTLINE
- SOME LOCALISM

Durban · Isipingo · Louis Botha Airport · Amanzimtoti · Kingsburgh · Umgababa · Danganya · Umkomaas · Palmcliffe · Vernon Crookes N.R. · Scottburgh · Park Rynie · Kelso · Pennington · Sezela · Ifafa Beach · Mtwalume · Mnamfu · Hibberdene · Umzumbe · Sunwich Port · Southport · Oribi Gorge Nature Reserve · Port Shepstone · Oslo Beach · Shelley Beach · St Michael's on Sea · Margate · Margate Airport · Ramsgate · Marina Beach · San Lameer · Trafalgar Marine Reserve · Glenmore · Port Edward

Amanzimtoti · Baggies · Toti Pipe · Green Point · Scottburgh · Happy Wanderers · Ifafa · The Spot · Umzumbe · Banana Beach · Sunwich Port · Shelley Beach · St Mike's · Lucien · Southbroom · T.O Strand

The Spot

ALAN VAN GYSEN

**T.O. Strand** just north of Port Edward needs a big SW groundswell and land breeze to produce heavy, rights over a rock shelf. **Southbroom** has very good mainly sand-bottomed rights that need strong S swells and a light SW-NW wind. The largest resort town is Margate, where **Lucien** is a steep, shorebreak wedge, perfect for bodyboarding in summer as the headland offers some NE protection. Don't overlook **St Mike's**, a popular consistent reef/point/beach-break, which can hold the biggest swells over a reef in front of the pool, leading into the screaming walls of the point, before detonating on the sand inside. **Shelley Beach** near Port Shepstone is only an average beachbreak, best in summer. A finger of reef holds the sand at **Sunwich Port**, which then sucks the sand back up into gaping barrels when a solid SW swell meets a W-NW wind. **Banana Beach** is a fast, peeling, shredable right that relies on sand from the rivermouth and the rocks off the southern point of this long beach. Very long rides are possible at **Umzumbe**, but the sandbanks vary a lot, affecting the rights off the point. Among the most famed south coast breaks is **The Spot**, with epic tubes and an inside bowl section, otherwise there's lots of close-outs. SW winds are OK, but there are no shark nets. Scottburg surfers visit **Ifafa** in small, clean swells for the high tide reefs and beachies including a crazy ledge called Heavy, which breaks to the south of the caravan park. Another caravan park at Kelso has private access to the fun, rolling walls of **Happy Wanderers**, otherwise pay a fee or walk around. The Point at **Scottburgh** is one of the most consistent waves around, breaking in front of the pool on a mussel infested reef, before winding into the highly changeable rivermouth sandbanks on the beach. Any S swell, any W wind and any tide, but remember your manners with the local crew. Next to Clansthal lighthouse is the legendary **Green Point**, which like many KZN righthanders, needs the right sands to build up. On medium S swells and light SW or land breeze, there should be a combination of hollow and slopey walls. Car break-in hot-spot. Beside the Warner Beach rock pool, **Baggies** is punchy and consistent on headhigh swells and any W winds. **Amanzimtoti** used to have the highest shark attack record in the world, before nets were deployed in 1962. Multiple fun beachbreaks from the swimming pool south to Inyoni Rocks and **Toti Pipe**, a fickle, serious shorebreak wedge, breaking over an old effluent pipe below the sand at high tide.

The winter months from May to August are consistent, when cold fronts sweep up the coast from the Cape, bringing solid 6-8ft SE-SW swells and winds, plus morning offshores. In summer, prevailing NE winds provide daily windswell, but a pesky onshore wind. Summer tropical cyclone swells forming off the east coast of Madagascar, often push in seriously big swell to the Kwazulu Natal coast. A lot of spots are at their best in these E swells although many of the points prefer SW. Tides are semi-diurnal, 2.4m max tidal range.

Scottburgh

GRANT ELLIS

| STATISTICS | | J F | M A | M J | J A | S O | N D |
|---|---|---|---|---|---|---|---|
| SWELL | Direction | | | | | | |
| | Size (ft) | 3 | 4 | 4-5 | 5-6 | 4-5 | 3 |
| WIND | Direction | | | | | | |
| | Force | F4 | F4 | F4 | F4 | F4-F5 | F4-F5 |
| WATER | Wetsuit | | | | | | |
| | Temp/°C | 26 | 25 | 23 | 21 | 22 | 24 |
| WEATHER | Rainfall/mm | 118 | 105 | 42 | 37 | 89 | 116 |
| | days/mth | 10 | 8 | 3 | 4 | 8 | 11 |
| | Min temp/°C | 21 | 18 | 12 | 11 | 15 | 18 |
| | Max temp/°C | 27 | 27 | 23 | 22 | 24 | 26 |

## TRAVEL INFORMATION

**Weather** – Summer months (September to April) are hot and humid with temps ranging from 23-33°C (74-92°F) and strong tropical thunderstorms occur almost daily in the afternoons from Dec-Feb. Winters are mild to warm and dry with temps between 13-25°C (56-77°F). Choose a really light fullsuit during winter and a shorty or boardshorts during summer.

**Lodging and Food** – Mantis & Moon in Umzumbe has dorms or treehouses ($25-48/dbl) or Southbroom Backpackers ($35-40/dbl) and Vulamenzi Lodge ($35-55). Expect $5 for a good meal. Good, cheap seafood.

**Nature and Culture** – Dive Aliwal Shoal, Protea Banks and do tiger shark diving to see the beasts! Check the wildlife at Hluhluwe 'Big-5' Game Park. Plenty of bars and nightclubs in high season.

**Hazards and Hassles** – Most of the beaches have shark nets but Natal Shark Board remove them during the June-August sardine runs. No attacks recorded for the last 15 years. Car thievery is a problem, crowds are fairly low outside high season, but tight-knit locals can be protective at some spots.

**Handy Hints** – No need for a gun, but take boards that can deal with barrelling point waves.

# Durban SOUTH AFRICA

Despite better waves elsewhere in South Africa, Durban has become the country's surf centre because of a high population density of surfers and a great year-round climate. South swells wrap around the Bluff Peninsula and focus on the long piers and groynes that trap the sand in perfect triangles. On the Bluff, powerful, hollow beachbreaks, plus the world-class tubes of Cave Rock are always bigger in S swells and cleaner in NE winds.

- + CONSISTENT
- + QUALITY BEACHBREAKS
- + URBAN ENTERTAINMENT
- + CHEAP

- – LOTS OF ONSHORE DAYS
- – CROWDS
- – STREET VIOLENCE
- – SHARKS AT UN-NETTED BEACHES

GREG EWING

Durban

**Brighton Beach** is an all-direction swell-magnet that has some hollow options like the left off the pool and the powerful shifting beachbreak, but it is easily blown out. When any S swell gets overhead, **Cave Rock** becomes a world-class, Hawaiian-style, righthand barrel that explodes across the dangerous shallow reef. The Pool section peels in front of the tidal sea pool while the gnarlier Rock rights are often faster and hollower at low to mid tides. Paddling out at either is a real mission so time the lulls carefully. **Anstey's** is only 800m up the beach (past the lefts of Inbetweens) where slightly less-critical peaks hit the sand on all small to medium swells. Gets crowded with average Joes escaping the town breaks, while the locals rule the other hollow spots on the Bluff. Next to the Natal Bay harbour entrance is **Vetch's Reef**, a rare right pointbreak over a semi-submerged old harbour jetty. Huge S wrap or cyclone NE-E swell will throw up hefty barrels from Pinnacle Rock or carvable walls on the inside Urchins reef section. **The Wedge** can be a quality, hollow left in E swells, giving goofies respite from the rights and thicker crowds on the other side of the New Pier. Beginners should drift south down to Addington and beyond. **New Pier** is Durban's most popular and impressive wave, bending any S swells into a speedy right with tube and turn sections up to double overhead. NE-E swells also work and at higher tides there are lefts running back towards the pier on the inside. Easy wave when small, but quickly transforms into a sucky, punishing experts-only wave. Gets hideously crowded at all times and sizes. **Dairy Beach** milks the swell into A-frame peaks and some good lefts in E swells, plus there's a bit of onshore wind protection at higher tides. **North Beach** is almost as good as New Pier, with the same firing right off the pier's end and a high tide left bowl on the inside. Gets packed with bodyboarders during the 9am-5pm surfing ban. **Bay of Plenty** used to be the best wave in town and main contest site but the sand has moved, making the right quite sectiony and less consistent than North or New piers. On its day, 200m rights will rifle over the triangular bank, allowing big rail work and short tube rides for a less zealous crowd. On average days there will be peaks up the beach and the usual inside left bowl at high tide. Between the shorter piers of **Snake Park** and Battery Beach, sand-dependant peaks will pick up more swell and wind, but less crowds than other town breaks. Tougher paddle-outs with fewer defined rips. **Country Club** is the new name for Africa Beach in front of the Golf Course and if the wind is calm, there can be a good shorebreaks from the casino to the Mgeni rivermouth. Always bigger in S swells but suffers in onshores and from longshore drift.

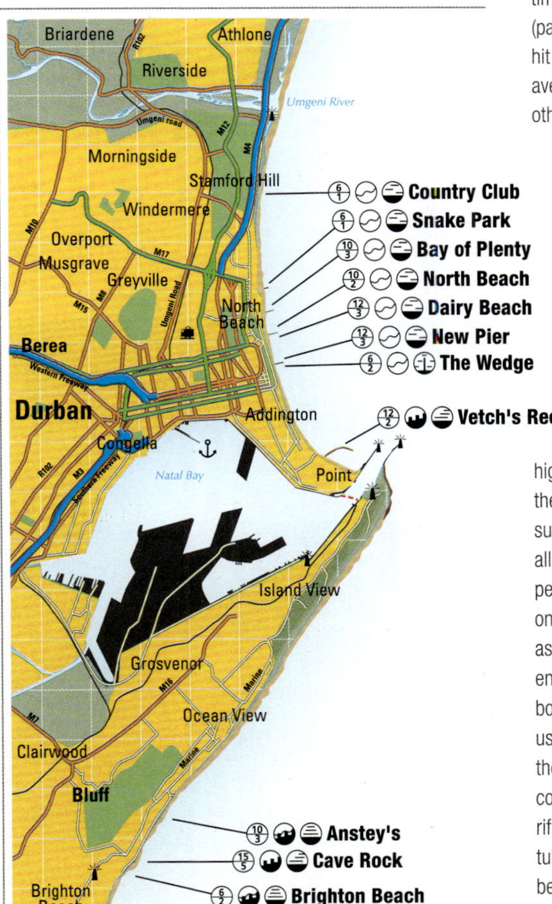

GREG EWING

Cave Rock

The lows have to travel pretty close to the coastline to provide 3-10ft S-SE swells on the Durban beaches. In summer (Nov-April) flat spells are common and long, although the pesky NE winds can produce headhigh, choppy, onshore waves. Occasionally, 4-8ft E swells come from tropical cyclones between Jan-March. Best conditions occur through the winter with plenty of S swells and offshore SW winds, before strong SE (onshore) winds blow out the surf by lunch time.

## TRAVEL INFORMATION

**Weather** – The Natal coast is subtropical and has 230 days of sunshine a year. Summers (Oct -Feb) range between 20°-30°C (68-86°F) with big afternoon thunderstorms. Winter temps never drop below 10°C (50°F) and often rise above 20°C (68°F). Cyclones occasionally hit the coast to the north of Durban. The Agulhas Current keeps water temps above 20°C (68°F). Wear a fullsuit only on the chilliest of mornings.

**Lodging and Food** – Downtown Durban offers the full range of accommodation options. Surfer friendly guesthouses starting at $15/d. More upmarket options include Blue Waters Hotel (fr $66/dbl/n). A good meal costs about $10.

**Nature and Culture** – Visit the Natal Sharks Board or the Timewarp Surfing Museum one onshore afternoon. Durban nightlife rocks. Go on safari in the Kruger and Kalahari Gemsbok national parks.

**Hazards and Hassles** – All town and Bluff beaches have shark nets - no surfer attacks since 1962. Beware of beach violence, theft and some localism at certain spots. Bluebottle jellyfish in summer.

**Handy Hints** – Surfboards are prohibited in the patrolled swimming zones from 9am-5pm. Avoid the barnacle encrusted pier pylons. Some of the cheapest surf gear in the world.

| STATISTICS | | J F | M A | M J | J A | S O | N D |
|---|---|---|---|---|---|---|---|
| SWELL | Direction | | | | | | |
| | Size (ft) | 2 | 4 | 4-5 | 5 | 4 | 2-3 |
| WIND | Direction | | | | | | |
| | Force | F4 | F4 | F4 | F4 | F4 | F4 |
| WATER | Wetsuit | | | | | | |
| | Temp/°C | 25 | 25 | 23 | 20 | 22 | 23 |
| WEATHER | Rainfall/mm | 125 | 102 | 47 | 32 | 75 | 122 |
| | days/mth | 10 | 8 | 4 | 3 | 8 | 11 |
| | Min temp/°C | 20 | 19 | 11 | 11 | 16 | 18 |
| | Max temp/°C | 28 | 27 | 23 | 22 | 23 | 26 |

# Inhambane Province MOZAMBIQUE

Surf explorers are finding plenty of waves along the 2,500km of Mozambique's coastline, most of which receives ample, seasonal swell and almost no crowds. Famous breaks like Ponta D'Ouro, a fabulous right point nestled up against the South African border, or Ilha de Inhaca, an island right near the capital, Maputo, both suffer from inconsistency and isolation. For the travelling surfer after quality and consistency, the best area to focus on is probably Inhambane province, a 6hr drive north from Maputo.

+ FAST, HOLLOW WAVES
+ WARM WATER
+ NO CROWDS
+ CHEAP & FRIENDLY

– FREQUENT ONSHORES
– LACK OF SPOT DENSITY
– INCONSISTENT
– MALARIA, TB AND AIDS

There is some potential exposed beachbreak around **Quissico**, but getting over the lagoon is tricky. **Praia de Závora** is a growing dive spot and has S-SW wind protection behind the jutting reef/point. Easy peaks over sand and outcrops of coral reef. Also check **Guinjata Bay** further north where there's a resort in front of a righthand point and protected peaks in the lee of the headland. Inhambane boasts a hospital, supermarkets and banks, but head to Tofo to stay on a long peninsula, sandwiched between the waves and a sheltered, mangrove hemmed lagoon with traditional wooden dhows ferrying people and goods to and from Inhambane's little port. On the swell-exposed side, there are a series of beaches and coves with plenty of consistent waves around Tofo. In the southern corner of Back Beach is **Backdoor**, a super-shallow, right tube that slams onto almost dry reef. **Back Beach** itself offers a reasonably hollow righthand beachbreak in S swells, but shuts down a lot over some nasty shallow patches of coral. In a NE-E swell, the left at the north end gathers up the most swell in the area. It's a short and hollow ride more suitable for bodyboarders with a freefall drop over a barely submerged razor sharp reef. The main attraction is **Tofinho** point, a high quality right that attracts plenty of swell. The take-off can be quite critical with a ledgy drop over a very shallow and sharp reef. After this initial section the wave peels quickly along the sandy edge of the reef and offers good tube sections. Further up the beach, **Dragons** conjures fun rights at the rocky outcrop and beach peaks stretch away to the north. **Praia Tofo** is generally a soft right point and weak inside beachbreak remaining small and fun, suitable for beginners or longboarders. **Dino's Left** needs an easterly swell combined with rare berg wind conditions to produce Indo-style lefts. The stunning **Barra Beach** is a long swathe of palm-backed white sand with good quality accommodation hidden behind the trees. The wave here is often little more than a closeout but sometimes it throws up a quality sandspit righthander at higher tides. It faces north so it is either nicely offshore or blown out trash in a NE sea breeze. There's a similar set-up but higher quality ride at Ponta Pomene, 100km north, or the more adventurous might travel 200km to check out the potential of the Bazaruto Archipelago.

GREG EWING

Praia Tofo

## TRAVEL INFORMATION

**Weather** – The rainy season coincides with the hot months between Nov and March. Winter lasts from July to September but the coast remains hot and sticky year-round and even on winter mornings, a shorty will suffice.

**Lodging and Food** – Ticket to Ride offer fully guided 4x4 adventures (fr $950/wk). Turtle Cove is owned by a surfer & has a yoga centre. Many surfers stay at Fatima's Nest (Tofo) and Fatima's Place (Maputo). Bamboozi Beach Lodge (fr $10) - the owner Des is an avid surfer. Seafood is the big thing all along the coast. General living costs are similar to South Africa. Expect $5-8 for a meal.

**Nature and Culture** – The diving around Tofo is superb - whale sharks, manta rays and dolphins are common year-round. The decaying old town of Inhambane is one of the highlights of Mozambique. Check out the markets and nightlife of Maputo.

**Hazards and Hassles** – Malaria is a very serious risk. The Aids rate is terrifyingly high. Droughts and floods occur with depressing regularity. The shark factor is overrated.

**Handy Hints** – Bring all equipment and spares. Rent a car in SA or just walk around Tofinho. Dhows can only explore calm bays. Summer sun protection is a must.

Mozambique's swell exposure is not ideal and it tends to be only the heart of the S-SE swell that makes it to shore. The best season is April to September when there are two or three solid swells a month, producing waves between 3-8ft. The rest of the year is likely to be flat on the points and small, mushy and onshore on the beaches. Cyclone generated heavy E-NE swells will produce either perfect lefts or widespread destruction. Tidal variations increase further up the Mozambique Channel and can have a big affect on the shallow reefs.

| STATISTICS | | J F | M A | M J | J A | S O | N D |
|---|---|---|---|---|---|---|---|
| SWELL | Direction | | | | | | |
| | Size (ft) | 1-2 | 2-3 | 3 | 3-4 | 2 | 1-2 |
| WIND | Direction | | | | | | |
| | Force | F3-F4 | F3-F4 | F4 | F4 | F4-F5 | F4 |
| WATER | Wetsuit | | | | | | |
| | Temp/°C | 25 | 25 | 23 | 21 | 22 | 24 |
| WEATHER | Rainfall/mm | 128 | 83 | 28 | 13 | 43 | 138 |
| | days/mth | 9 | 8 | 3 | 2 | 5 | 8 |
| | Min temp/°C | 22 | 20 | 15 | 15 | 17 | 21 |
| | Max temp/°C | 30 | 30 | 26 | 26 | 28 | 29 |

ALAN VAN GYSEN

Tofinho

# Kenya

Kenya and Tanzania have recently unveiled a few surfing secrets along their considerable Indian Ocean coastlines. A small expat surfing community has been tapping the surf here for decades, but Kenya is now starting to attract inquisitive surfers to the fringing reefs that break consistently during the southern hemisphere winter. Mombasa Island makes sense as a base for surf exploration, with waves right on its doorstep, plus easy access to the coastline north, featuring Arab and Portuguese forts, old towns and some of the finest beach hotels in Africa.

+ SEMI-CONSISTENT IN SUMMER
+ WARM WATER
+ VIRGIN REEFS & BEACHBREAKS
+ FASCINATING WILDLIFE

- LOTS OF ONSHORE MUSH
- MOMBASSA SHARKS
- REMOTE REEFS WITH TIDAL FLATS
- ROBBERIES AND MUGGINGS

MICHAEL KEW

Malindi

Visible from the Southside ferry, the **South Channel** outside reefs hold long, tapering, but sectiony rights and the SE trades blow cross-shore. It's a long paddle and shark sightings are frequent. **Baobabs** is where the local expats surf, over left reefs at the base of the cliffs, that suffer backwash at high tide and get really shallow at low. Nyali Beach provides access to the **North Channel** outside shallow reef, where the lefts are usually plagued by onshore SE trades, but it's a much shorter paddle and less sharky than the South Channel. 80km north, **Watamu** is a protected curve of aquamarine water with coral gardens and atolls, next to below average SE-facing reefs that are usually onshore and best at high tide. Malindi could be the surf capital of Kenya, thanks to a handful of expats promoting surf-tourism to take advantage of some semi-consistent waves. **Malindi Reefs** pick up any swell going and bend it around some quality righthand coral corners. The furthest of the four outside reefs sits 3km offshore, while it is only 1km from the long jetty to the most popular wave. From there, the large **Malindi Beach** extends north to a rivermouth, offering surprisingly consistent sandy peaks up to shoulder high, which are bigger at the north end and better at high tide. Driving to the island town of Lamu can be sketchy – ask around to find out if the road is safe. **Shela Beach** is lined with hotels and a virtually endless stretch of rolling sand dunes. It's one of the more consistent beachbreaks, bigger at the south end, but beware of currents and wildlife near the rivermouth. Because of its south-facing aspect, Shela is often onshore. Manda Island has wonderful beaches and even elephants have been known to swim across from the mainland to hang out. **Manda Lefts** can be long with racy sections over the live coral and it picks up and handles the most swell in Kenya, but is badly affected by the SE onshores. **Kiwayu** has some good set-ups with reefs and a decent beach, although outside reefs may filter the swell.

The NE monsoon blows hard from Dec-March and does produce occasional windswells but good days are rare during the high tourist season. The SW monsoon typically builds a strong high over Mauritius and the SE winds create a regular 6-12ft windswell, mostly from June to September, which diminishes to 3-6ft by the time it reaches the coast. Most of that swell arrives with very strong SE onshores, so rights wrapping around reefs create the only options for side/offshore conditions. Tides are semi-diurnal with diurnal inequality reaching 4m, making the beachbreaks better at high tide.

## TRAVEL INFORMATION

**Weather** – The climate is tropical dry tempered by the Indian Ocean. There are two main periods of rain from Mar to June and from Oct to Dec. Rain usually arrives in violent downpours that last for a few hours. The monsoon winds blow NE-SE onshore all year-round. Boardshorts only.

**Lodging and Food** – Cheap all-inclusive deals for Mombasa and Malindi. The Coconut Village in Malindi offers AC rooms for $70/pax in double rooms, Eden Roc is cheaper and only $8 for a basic backpacker room. Meals go from $4-15 with cheap Ugali or Githeri (maize & beans). Tusker beer is $2 up. Tamarind in Mombassa has the best seafood.

**Nature and Culture** – North of Mombassa has several world-class dive sites. Check Gede Ruins, Crocodile and Snake farms or day trip to Tsavo Game Park. Mombasa: Fort Jesus, Old Town, Yuls' Beach Bar, Pirates (Disco) or Mamba Village. Diani and Malindi attracts tourists with kite/windsurf, SUP, water-skiing, diving and deep-sea fishing.

**Hazards and Hassles** – Shallow live-coral reefs can be nasty and a shark encounter is likely, especially in the Mombasa Channel. Beware of weed patches in Malindi where thorns, logs, branches and crabs lurk. Nairobi is notorious for robberies and muggings, be vigilant in Mombasa.

**Handy Hints** – No surf stuff available. Bring a board and you might sell it. The areas bordering Somalia are all prone to banditry, kidnappings and terrorist attacks, making Lamu essential travel only.

JS CALLAHAN SURFEXPLORE

Manda Left

| STATISTICS | | J F | M A | M J | J A | S O | N D |
|---|---|---|---|---|---|---|---|
| SWELL | Direction | | | | | | |
| | Size (ft) | 1 | 1-2 | 3-4 | 4 | 3 | 1 |
| WIND | Direction | | | | | | |
| | Force | F4 | F3 | F4 | F4 | F3-F4 | F3-F4 |
| WATER | Wetsuit | | | | | | |
| | Temp/°C | 26 | 28 | 27 | 25 | 26 | 27 |
| WEATHER | Rainfall/mm | 27 | 118 | 191 | 72 | 81 | 85 |
| | days/mth | 3 | 7 | 15 | 12 | 9 | 5 |
| | Min temp/°C | 23 | 24 | 22 | 21 | 21 | 23 |
| | Max temp/°C | 31 | 31 | 29 | 27 | 29 | 30 |

# Come on a Surf Trip to the Banyak Islands onboard The Seriti!

# INDIAN OCEAN

Few surfers would disagree that the Indian Ocean is home to the best waves in the world, receiving copious, year-round swell from storms that circumnavigate the southern oceans, unimpeded by continental land masses. Indonesia and a sprinkling of Indian Ocean islands have proved themselves the most able catchers of this reliable swell, transforming it into a glut of world-class spots in balmy, tropical latitudes, fanned by trustworthy trades and monsoons. Surfers have been flocking to the region for the last four decades, as more and more incredible waves are discovered, spreading a feverish tide of exploration throughout the many islands, atolls and archipelagoes of this vast, warm water playground.

Padang Padang, Bali, Indonesia

# The Surf

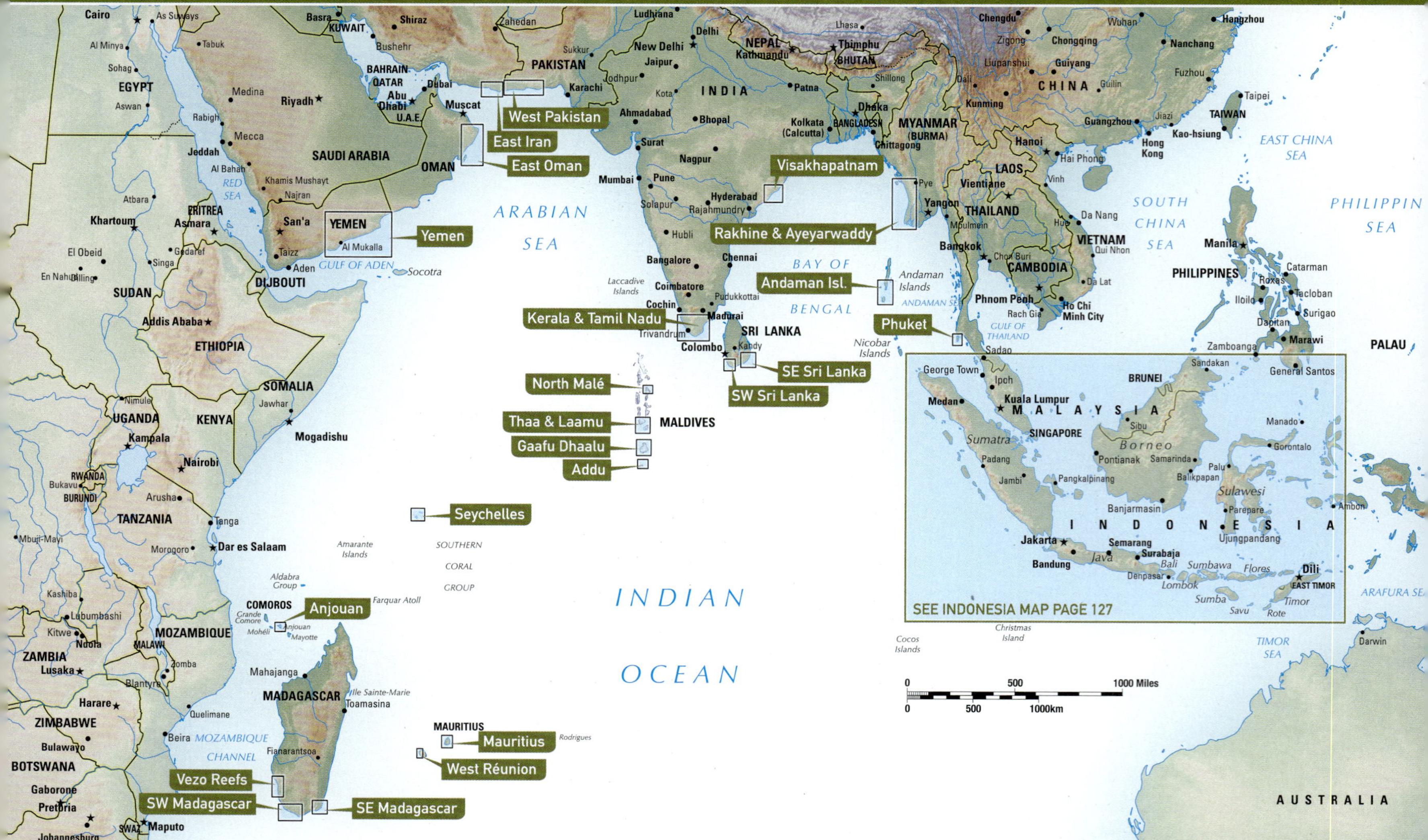
West Pakistan
East Iran
East Oman
Yemen
Visakhapatnam
Rakhine & Ayeyarwaddy
Andaman Isl.
Phuket
Kerala & Tamil Nadu
SE Sri Lanka
SW Sri Lanka
North Malé
Thaa & Laamu
Gaafu Dhaalu
Addu
MALDIVES
Seychelles
Anjouan
Mauritius
West Réunion
Vezo Reefs
SW Madagascar
SE Madagascar
ARABIAN SEA
BAY OF BENGAL
INDIAN OCEAN
SOUTH CHINA SEA
EAST CHINA SEA
PHILIPPINE SEA
MOZAMBIQUE CHANNEL
SEE INDONESIA MAP PAGE 127
AUSTRALIA

## MADAGASCAR

**Madagascar** is surprisingly under-explored, particularly in the north where swell is far less reliable. Even in the regularly surfed south, large gaps await the curious between **Vezo Reefs** and the beginning of the **SW Madagascar** zone, as well as the swell overloaded SE-facing coast from Cap Sainte Marie to the **SE Madagascar** region and the beginning of the east coast. The vast bulk of the east coast is featureless, windblown beachbreak, punctured by more rivermouths depositing murky, silt-laden water into unappealing, sharky line-ups. Up on the NE coast past Toamasina there is resort accommodation near the Foulpointe reefs and hazardous beachbreaks, where steep drop-offs, currents, and lots of rocks reside. Mahambo maintains a small local surf population and a few funky, shallow right and left reefbreaks in the vicinity. To the north are plenty of nooks and crannies to explore up to Diego Suarez, including Baie d'Antongil and the windblown barrier reef of Ile Sainte-Marie. The Mozambique Channel coastline is gouged by large estuarine rivermouths connected by straight sandy beaches and the migrating bars pile up some impressive looking left set-ups. The SW-facing coast around Maintirano and the Barren Islands hold some nice coral passes. The crazy sand deltas continue down the west coast past Morondava, Belo sur Mer and Morombe, until the fringing Vezo reefs of Toliara province reappear.

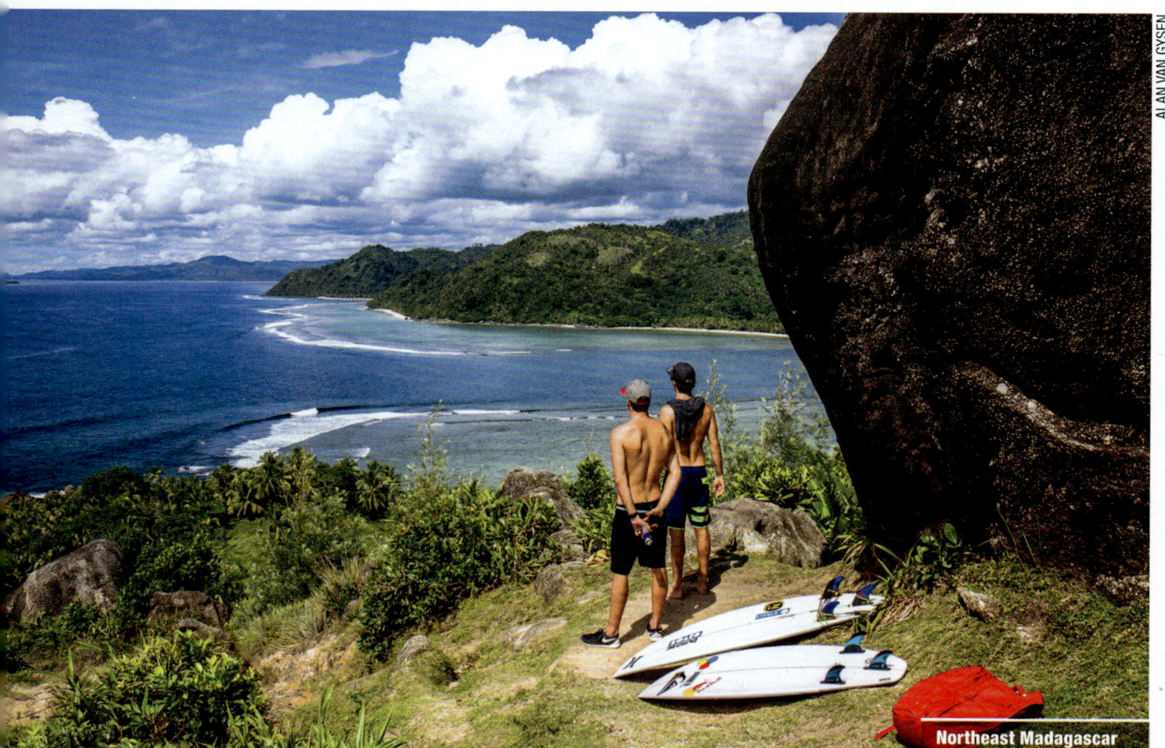

ALAN VAN GYSEN

Northeast Madagascar

## THE MASCARENES

**Réunion** is oft considered a one-wave island, rarely mentioned unless the boomerang bending lefts of St Leu are the topic of conversation. The rainy south and east coast is where the coral reefs give way to lava flows, basalt rocks and murky water at the many rivermouths, which are patrolled by the large Réunion shark population. The NE coast from Sainte-Rose to Saint-Denis offers very little opportunity, despite being

Barren Islands, Madagascar

JS CALLAHAN SURFEXPLORE

directly in the summer cyclone firing line and most locals will head to the NW coast for these rare swells. **Mauritius** shares a good few features with Réunion, being a bit more teardrop shaped, with a west side that is mainly NW-facing, which explains the consistency problems at Tamarin Bay. Consistency is never a problem on the swell-lashed S coast, but the SE winter trades are, so summer NE winds are the Christmas present for this coast. Unlike Réunion, the east coast has an extensive coral reef formation with multiple passes and cuts in the platform, but the pesky E trades exceed 32kmh for half the time in July and don't drop by too much through Jan. The relaxed outer-island of **Rodrigues**, is a windswept kite-surfing Mecca and has essentially one surf spot. Passe Jimmy is only surfable on small WSW swells and high tide, when the longer high-performance left and the abrupt hollow right break over very shallow, healthy live coral, often ruffled by hard offshores. The other Mauritian administered outer islands (Cargados Carajos Shoals, Agalega Islands and Tromelin) are all unsuitable places for a designated surf trip. **Anjouan** forms the bulk of the known surf in the **Comoros Islands**, plus there are some surf spots on Grande Comoros (Itzandra, Chomoni, Lac Sale), Moheli (Fomboni, Hoani) and even the reef-encircled French Territory of Mayotte, where one or two decent waves are accessible by boat, near the airport on slack wind days. The **Seychelles** look like they should be a surf paradise, but the five groups forming the Outer Islands are either a cluster of barely inhabited nature reserves and weather stations or exclusive resorts offering marginal surfing opportunities along straight barrier reefs.

## ARABIAN SEA

The recent political climate has left **Yemen** a no go zone and with little opportunity to expand the known surf spots beyond the eastern provinces. Socotra island presents the best potential and waves are ridden on the NW tip at the tourist hotspot Qalansiyah, by both surfers and wind/kitesurfers exploiting the strong windswell coming out of the Gulf of Aden from the W, NW or even NE. There are further mainly blown-out pointbreaks and beachbreaks all along both coasts. **Oman** has way more surfable coastline beyond Masirah Island and the Sharqiyah, but coastal angle is crucial to deciding whether too much wind or not enough swell will result. Furthest south there is some regular surf in the Gulf of Aden around Salalah. Either side of the Southwest monsoon should be best at the long city beaches in front of the tourist hotels. Heading south, check Mugsayl and Rakhyut or go north to Sadah for reef and beachbreak options. The Khuriya Muriya Islands have been surfed, but are very rugged and steep, while the adjacent coastline is similar in parts, interspersed with long straight beaches around Ash Shuwamiyah. The rocky beaches on the promontory at Ras Madrakah are worth investigating. The Gulf of Oman coast north of Muscat is marginal unless there is a cyclone off India. Spots have been surfed around Qurum Beach, Fujairah and Al Aqah, a right reef off Snoopy Island. Many surfers reside in Dubai, where four offshore constructions have left only two stretches of surfable beach open to the winter Persian Gulf windswell from the NW. This has caused crowding at Sunset Beach, which is under threat from marina expansion. Back in the open ocean beyond the **Iran** and **West Pakistan** zones of the Baluchistan desert, difficult access and bad bathymetry make Karachi the next place for some dumpy beachbreaks at Hawks Bay. The Indus river delta estuarine system extends down to the border and blocks land access to offshore sand shoals. In **India** the left point at Dwarka is the wave to check amongst the long, flat beaches of Gujarat State. Maharashtra has a myriad of river deltas surrounding Mumbai, where some long rivermouth waves can be found close to Alibag and Anjarle. Goa is party central around Christmas, yet mid-year will see regular chest-high days and a pick of the peaks at Baga, Calungute and Candolim. Gokarna is a popular hang out, with cheap accommodation and some powerful shoredump at high tides. Near the centre of Karnataka State, Murdeshwara offers clean beachbreaks in SW or NW onshores on either side of the peninsula, beneath the huge meditating statue of Shiva. Further south at Bhatkal, a series of cliff-lined coves offer multiple opportunities in a SW swell. Maravanthe is also dubbed 10,000 Peaks as the 6km stretch throws up an endless supply of corners and close-outs in equal measure. There's a short, speedy right off the lighthouse at Kapu Beach, followed by miles of average beachbreak in either direction. The Ashram Surf Retreat uses the Shambhavi River and a fast boat to access local breaks like Baba's Left, Tree Line, Swami's and Water Tank around Mulki, north of Mangalore. Crossing into Kerala sees consistency and size improve plus the appearance of more piers and jetties, which can provide stormy surf protection around Mahe from Thalassery to the big rivermouth at Talakkolattur. Between Mahe and Cherai is fairly straight and un-exciting except around the rivermouths and jetties. **Kerala and Tamil Nadu** are the most surfed regions in the country and are at centre stage of India's blossoming surf culture.

Gujarat State, India

JS CALLAHAN SURFEXPLORE

Qalansiyah, Socotra, Yemen

STUART BUTLER

## SWELL FORECASTING

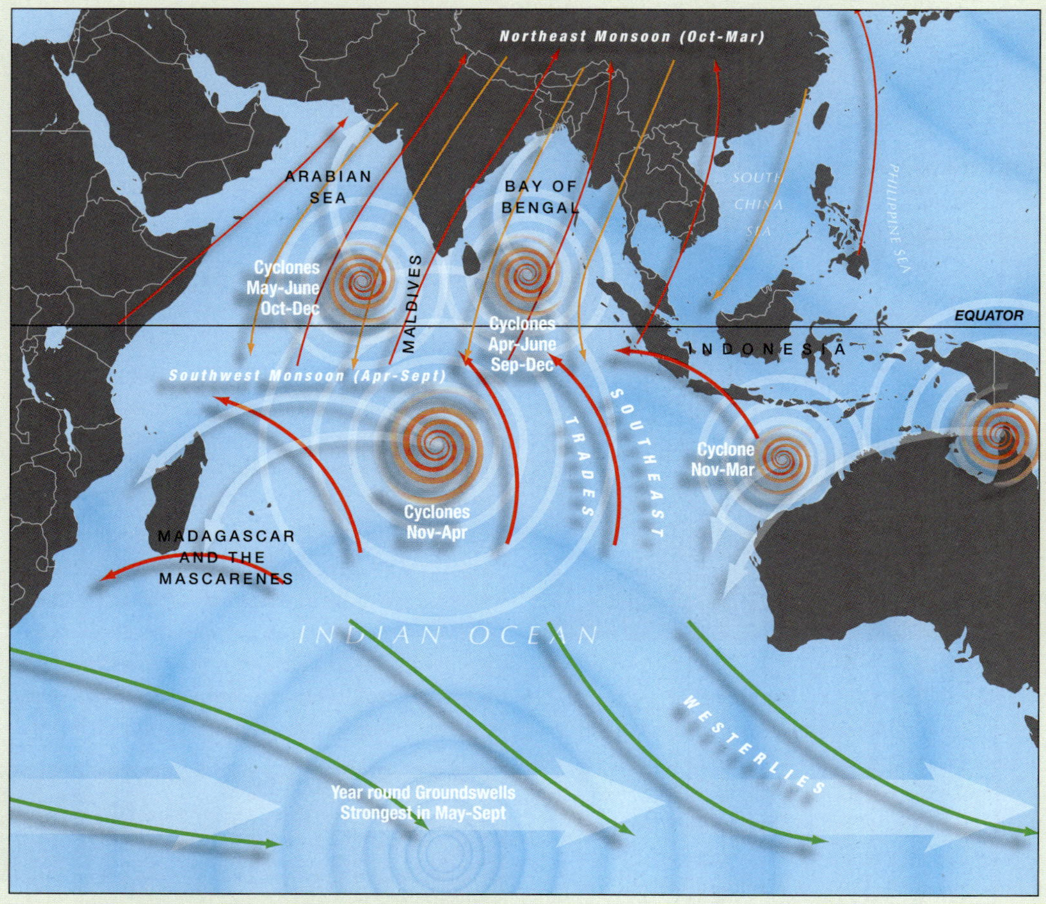


### MALDIVES

The Maldives are perfectly positioned to receive all the Southern Hemisphere groundswell with an unimpeded swell window for anything from the south. However, wave size usually deteriorates as the swells propagate northwards towards the Maldives and the swell often swings a bit to arrive from the SE. Locally generated windswell and occasional cyclone swells add to the inventory, but can't be relied on and the exposed western atolls are usually heavily blown out. While traditional monsoonal periods are stated as Dec-March for the NE and June-Oct for the SW, the actual wind conditions can be divided into three clear periods. The prevailing wind from April to August is SW-W, from September to November it swings SW-NW, changing again from December to March, when it predominately blows NW-NE. The currents switch with the seasons but have a negligible effect on water temperatures.

### BAY OF BENGAL

The Bay of Bengal fares better than the Arabian Sea when it comes to catching the long-range, southern hemisphere, SW swells that march across the equator in orderly lines. Sri Lanka is first in the firing line, but suffers from the SW onshores during the swell season and prefers a SE-S direction from the mix of wind and groundswells. The SW monsoon swells traverse the east coast of India losing plenty of height as they refract around headlands, before arriving in Myanmar and Thailand with the unavoidable onshore winds. The Andaman Islands suffer the same fate, which leaves a very short season of opportunity in spring when N winds greet early season swells that have not decayed too much over the long journey. Around 5 cyclones a year wind up in the Bay between April and June then again in September to December, taking a northwards trajectory toward Bangladesh, lighting up the east coast of India along the way. Winds are predictable providing the monsoon sticks to the schedule and drive the oceanic current reversal, but local coastal currents often run in the opposite direction with a series of complex gyres.

### MADAGASCAR AND THE MASCARENES

The Indian Ocean sits primarily in the southern Hemisphere, where most of the swells are generated between the Roaring Forties and the Great Southern Ocean located at 60° latitude. These low pressure systems make the journey from the Cape of Good Hope to the SW tip of Australia with year-round regularity, spraying out consistent, quality swell. Madagascar, Réunion, and Mauritius are much closer to the Roaring Forties lows and maintain some sizeable waves, but the SE to S trade winds can spoil the party in winter. Once the NE trades take over in November, it's time to watch out for cyclones forming in the 15°-25°S latitudes, which usually travel west towards the Mascarene Islands and Madagascar. These swell producers are a real plus, providing powerful swell for the east coasts of all the islands when the southern low pressures are at their weakest. Unfortunately, they are few and far between as well as being accompanied by the onshore NE winds. The SE trades reach maximum intensity from June to October. The anti clockwise rotation of the Agulhas Current (world's fastest at 9km/h) keeps Madagascar and the Mascarenes fed with warm water.

### ARABIAN SEA

Swell in this northern hemisphere basin is mainly controlled by the monsoon winds that blow NE from Dec to March before alternating to the SW from May/June to Sept/Oct. The SW monsoon brings the strongest winds to the tropical zone and constant, short period swell to the Arabian peninsula and the Indian subcontinent. Any Southern Ocean groundswell remnants will be too small to count on and the NE monsoon is not the greatest source for any organised, powerful swell. Major tropical storms also affect the Arabian Sea (May-June and Oct-Nov) meaning there are some waves going unridden in frontier surfing destinations such as Yemen, Oman, Pakistan, Lakshadweep and India. Currents are most notable in the North Indian Ocean because unlike the Pacific and Atlantic, a seasonal current reversal takes place. This coincides with the monsoon, flowing from the NE towards Africa in winter (Nov-Mar) and then in the opposite direction toward India in the summer months (June-Oct). Called the Somali Current, it follows the wind and can bring slight upwelling to the Horn of Africa region. The Arabian Sea also feeds the warmest sea (the Persian Gulf) and the saltiest sea (the Red Sea).

### INDONESIA

The SW-facing shores of Indonesia are at the end of the perfect propagation path for Roaring Forties swells. These weather systems serve up an almost constant supply of organised, long period swell that arrives at equatorial latitudes without too much decay and usually within 30° angle either side of due SW. The next piece of serendipity is the bulk of the archipelago is beyond the influence of the SW monsoon winds and the seasonal trade winds are reliably offshore. These SE winds groom the lefts on the western coasts from April to Oct, and the NW wet season winds leave south and east-facing coasts clean from Dec to March. The occasional Bay of Bengal cyclone swell can hit Sumatra and the even rarer Timor Sea storm, below Nusa Tenggara can bring SE swell in the wet season. A bit of vagueness during switchover and some non-committal directions in the northern equatorial regions barely detract from the glorious combinations of wind and swell that bless the Indonesian archipelago. Feeder currents from the South China Sea and the Timor Sea head west to mix into the Equatorial Counter Current and the South Equatorial Current, which flows westward back to Africa and the Agulhas.

## MALDIVES

The **Lakshadweep** is a Union Territory of India, (formerly known as the Laccadive Islands), but these atolls share far more in common with the Maldives than they do with the Subcontinent. Across the 12 atolls, the best place to look for surf is on the big ones like Androth, Amini, and Agatti, where the airport and main accommodation is. The reefs are often straight without any gaps so the tips of the islands will need investigation. Minicoy sits in isolation a long way south, putting it closer to the swell source and a more likely candidate for regular waves from June to September when a big SE or wrapping SW swell can bend onto the east coast, and be offshore in the W winds. The large concrete pier grooms these swells onto the reef, creating a flawless right barrel when the swell hits. The eight atolls north of Malé remain relatively untapped by foreign surfers for good reason. Long cruising distances in relatively rough seas with high monsoon wind factor, diminished swell exposure and a lack of quality set-ups (straight reefs or short shoulders) makes it a long shot for time restricted, travelling surfers. The main spots checked/surfed by the handful of exploration boat trips up to Haa Dhaalu atoll include the harbour channel rights and lefts at SW swell exposed Makunudhoo or small lefts across the channel at Kanditeem. The SE swell struggles to make it up to Haa Alifu, Haa Dhaalu, Shaviyani and Noonu, which all conceal some inconsistent passes. Lhaviyani Atoll does fire on a strong SE pulse at the sweet righthander Kakuni, plus five other passes with various swell/wind combos. Raa Atoll has a few set-ups on the SW side (Mushigiri, Kudathulhaadhoo), but the quality waves are SE-facing at Rasputins (Kinolhas) and Shipyard Rights (Iguraidhoo). Baa Atoll has been surfed around Fares, Eboodhoo, Hithaadhoo and Eydhafushi. While the Maldives surf scene revolves around the popular breaks of **North Malé**, there's also a number of breaks in the South Male Atoll area, including Quarters (Gulhi), Kate's (near Palm Tree Island Resort), Natives (Kandooma Resort, who claim exclusivity over the rights) and Riptides/Foxy's, a chunky mid channel right, facing a racy, shallow left. Vaavu misses out on east coast surf due to its extended south coast, but Meemu has a little cluster of waves accessed by the Medhufushi resort and occasional safari boats. Veyvah holds fun, zippy lefts with great length of ride. Tucked in a bit, Mulah needs more swell to serve up user-friendly rolling rights for improvers plus. Mulhi Inside is a full wrap right, that needs big swell but is SE wind protected, while the long walls of Outside work from tiny and are offshore in SW winds. The

Lakshadweep

ALAN VAN GYSEN

western atolls of Goidhoo, Alifu, Faafu and Dhaalu are wind exposed and cut off from the SE-S swell supply, but Maalhos and Kudahuvadhoo have lefts and rights respectively. **Thaa and Laamu** atolls are nicely placed at the bottom of the central chain to pick off the swell and **Gaafu Dhaalu** atoll is fast becoming popular with new charter and resort options. Crowds should never be a problem when travelling down to **Addu** atoll, where the waves get heavier and the remote islands give the feeling of real seclusion, almost 500kms from Male. The windswept **Chagos Archipelago** is surprisingly low on surf spots and Diego Garcia is home to a USA/UK Navy and Marines installation where it's actually illegal to surf, even for the troops who are stationed there. The archipelago is the world's largest nature reserve, where visitor permits and mooring fees are expensive and the waves are not worth it.

## BAY OF BENGAL

**Sri Lanka**'s surf scene has always centred on either Hikkaduwa or Arugam Bay, depending on the season. There is plenty more empty, soft beach and reefbreak along the west coast, both north and south of Colombo, but it's tiny during the NE monsoon. Wave size doubles by mid July, but the westerly winds usually put paid to any decent shape. Towns like Bentota and Wadduwa have shifting peaks in calm wind conditions, while other stretches of coast are armoured with breakwalls and jetties. That explains why the crowds are concentrated in **Southwest Sri Lanka**, leaving a lot of south-facing spots in seasonal limbo, some working in big swell and W-N winds, while others need the NE winds of winter. Much of the beachbreak is shoredump most of the time but there are a lot of rocky coves that can transform unruly swells into something worth searching for. Check out Dickwella, Nilwella, Tangalla and the extensive sands leading to Hambantota, before the main road heads inland to skirt the massive wilderness of the Yala National Park and onto the sandy right points of **Southeast Sri Lanka**. The NE, ravaged by civil war for decades, is basically one featureless and size deficient beachbreak.

Back on India's east coast just out of the Sri Lankan swell shadow is Pondicherry and Auroville, steep beach and jetty breaks that can get good in big monsoon or cyclone swells. Coastal armouring that protects the ancient Mahabalipuram Shore Temple has helped catch the sand and funnel some hollow righthanders down the point. Another good wave in this area is Big Rock, a proper left barrel over a rock shelf, just next to the reliable right point of Fisherman's Cove. The next state north is Andhra Pradesh where a lot of the good set-ups are found in the **Visag** area. Way up north in Orissa State, the dying swell hits straight beachbreaks at Puri; shorebreak when small or consistent lines of pounding whitewash when big. **Bangladesh** must be the most obscure Bay of Bengal country to cradle some surf and at Cox's Bazaar, one of the longest beaches anywhere, there is 120km of poor quality wave action from ankle-high mush to headhigh closeout barrels and everything in-between. Try Sept-Oct to avoid the rain. Silt from the Ganges Delta means the biggest waves are going to be found in the far SE at Teknaf, or on St Martins Island and Chera Deep.

Surfers have explored only a thin slice of **Myanmar**'s 2000kms of coastline in the state divisions of **Rakhine and Ayeyarwaddy**. Northern Myanmar's Baronga Islands offer the best potential. The Ayeyarwaddy Delta is a mess of silted, gently shelving estuaries and islets, cut off from the long distance Indian Ocean groundswell. Mon State holds so many estuaries and rivermouths that perfect sandbars must exist somewhere, but nobody is looking for them. Tanintharyi division starts off in a similar vein, until the 800 Mergui islands sieve out the meagre swell, leaving the many dive operators in the area to find the beach and reefbreaks that undoubtedly exist in this largely out of bounds area. The northwestern Thailand coastline has waves on Koh Phayam, which is open to SW swell. Far more consistent and conducive to year-round surfing is Cape Pakarang, where lefts run down the reef/point at easy, cruising speed. There are also rights to the south and the whole stretch down to the busy Khao Lak hotel area is quite consistent. The best spots to check are Nang Thong beach, Bang Niang rivermouth and Khuk Khak beach. A long, straight beachbreak ensues for 40km, through Thai Muang and down to **Phuket**, where most surf tourists congregate, hoping for some headhigh monsoonal swell without the onshore wind destroying it.

Cox's Bazaar, Bangladesh

STUART BUTLER

As outlined in **The Andaman Islands** zone, of the 550 islands, only a handful of them have been surfed and there is undoubtedly more spots to be discovered, especially in the north of the chain where swell regularity is much lower. Plenty of problems revolve around access, which is heavily restricted to most indigenous tribal regions and in fact a blanket ban exists for foreigners to travel to the Nicobar Islands, ostensibly for the protection of the indigenous tribal groups, unique flora and fauna. You do need a written permit from the Assistants Commissioner's office and the Forestry Department to access parts of the island inhabited by tribal groups, particularly around Indira Point, which is India's southernmost point. Recently, some Indian surfers explored this area and found some amazing world-class surf on the southwest coast of Great Nicobar, plus some tasty reefs and righthand pointbreaks along the SE coast up to the main area of habitation at Campbell Bay, where a fun peak hits the breakwall in a strong S swell. Car Nicobar, Teressa and Katchal Island all have ample swell exposure from the S-W, along with the promising reef bathymetry and Teressa and Katchal Island have been surfed by passing yachts (without permits).

Rasputins, North Maldves

ANDY GUINAND

SEBASTIAN IMIZCOZ

Sanding Island, Mentawai

## SUMATRA

The NW Indonesian province of **Aceh** is synonymous with the devastating 2004, ocean floor earthquake and subsequent massive tsunami. Reefs were thrust skyward, killing surf spots like fish out of water, but also new rides appeared along the devastated coast. The offshore islands shadow the coast SE of Ujong Karang from the staple diet of SW-W swells, unless it slips through the gaps for a rare day of waves. The coast is straight, sandy and rife with rivermouths bringing sediment and run-off from inland – hardly attractive when some of the best reefs in the world are a couple of hours sail away. **Simeulue and Banyak** still maintain a frontier status, avoiding the charter boat congestion of the Ments through a combination of lower consistency and spot density, treating smaller groups to some lively waves, including one of Indo's best rights. **Nias and the Hinako Islands** need no introduction, as Lagundri Bay is the original tropical paradise found. Once again, seismic activity has had a direct effect on the waves here, with the scorecard well in the black since Lagundri Bay has raised its reef and its game after the last 'quake. If you get stuck in the unlovely port of Sibolga, the offshore islands around Musala have some rare waves and are a beautiful place to hang out. Often referred to as the Telos, the 51 Batu Islands have dodged the bulk of the Nias and Mentawai crowds for much the same reason as the Banyaks. There are fewer big name spots and the best set-ups often require stronger swells, usually from the rarer W direction. However, consistent, year-round, headhigh surf can always be found with plenty of fun, easier line-ups that cater to most tastes and abilities. A few surf camps have opened, but for independent travellers, this place is a mission without a boat to get around and it has a reputation for malaria and other diseases. Most of the waves are found on the smaller islands to the NW, so check around and in between the larger islands of Telo, Sipika and the more exposed reefs of Pulau Sigata. On Tanahbala, there are some less-frequented breaks with longer travelling times between them especially if going all the way to Bojo. The camps all have their own names for the spots, so it depends on who you travel with, but there is no doubt this group holds some excellent waves and since the equator runs through here, winds are rarely a problem with plenty of glass and a spot for all wind/swell combos. The hulking mass of Siberut is the largest island in the Mentawai chain and has only been lightly surfed by long-range charter crews grabbing an opportunistic wave on the way to the Nias area. That means spots on the backside are more often seen from the northern tip at Tanjung Sigep, down to the impossibly sheltered Teluk Tabekat and out to the headland at Sikabaluan, but most will pass by like ships in the night. A good deal of the SW-facing coast is straight line reefs, exposed and messed up by wind and swell, but a few obvious jinks in the coast could produce a left or two at Tanjungs Sakaladat, Sataerataera and Simasuket. Many captains will have a few spots sussed for certain conditions and there are some mellow breaks in the Playgrounds area that get ridden like Taileleo, a fun mal slide facing south, Pearlers peak nestled behind Masokut and a righthander round the backside near the Muara harbour. It is important to recognise that while there are 40-60 named breaks in the **Mentawai Islands**, many more are out there, being surfed by experienced captains who know the deal. The Sumatran coastline behind the Mentawais should be a flat zone, yet it defies convention by regularly cobbling a wave together around the busy Padang coast. Swell filters through and hits a few beach/reef slots at Purus, Air Manis and often near the polluted rivermouths along Padang's main beach, but it is only for the desperate looking to tune up before heading out. It gets much worse down the grey sand coastline until the Mukomuko district of Bengkulu Province breaks free of the Mentawais shadow. Bengkulu City is regularly ridden at Pantai Panjang (Long Beach) and the long sheltered lefts of Tapak Padri. Just offshore is Pulau Tikus (Rat Island) where the barrier reef provides perfect snorkelling and more. Jalan Liwa skirts the coast past more promising headlands at Pantai Pasar and then Bintuhan where the coral reefs and bays start again, signalling the beginning of the great **Lampung** zone. Sitting way offshore in splendid isolation is Enggano with a rich assortment of coral reefs in fan formations and tiny atolls, slicing the S-W swells into some juicy bits, albeit plagued by slightly stronger winds.

## JAVA AND BALI

Once G-Land hit the surf press and the challenging reefs of **West Java** were mapped, people wondered what happened further along the coast in **Central Java** where unusual sand-sculpted rights were uncovered at Batu Karas. This still left a good 600kms of south-facing Javanese coast to search where the side to onshore wind exposure, plunging volcanic cliffs, islets and skerries, separated by long, current scoured, black sand beaches keeps the crowds away. Dangerous, thumping close-outs drum the sand in the swell season, but the potential for smaller, peaky, SE-SW swells to create piping beachbreaks in the shoulder and off season is always there. Luck plays a big part in identifying where rideable sandbars may be and finding other surfers to tackle lonely breaks is rare. Yogyakarta surfers are close to unruly Parangtritis Beach, but will head east to Pacitan where the deep protection of Teleng Ria Beach offers a sliding scale size of beachbreak plus a cultured left rivermouth that's protected from the trades. The crazed coastline of pocket bays and ragged rocky islets continues east, to Sudimoro, which has an E-wind-protected, left reef, but construction of a power plant and jetty has brought pollution. Round the corner the Banjar rivermouth and beachbreak has similar exposure and water quality problems. More scalloped bays of volcanic sand face into the SW swell and some have defined lefthanders in the eastern corners, nestling out of the sideshore winds.

CORY SCOTT

Watukarang, Java

Tambakrejo has rights and lefts over a dead coral shelf, but needs N quadrant winds. The limestone reef at Balekambang is fairly straight and exposed, but it's a popular tourist spot to see the island temple *a la* Tanah Lot. The islands of Sempu and Barung are way too cliffy and the big bay of beachbreaks between them can have some heavy barrels, but it's usually unappealing and windblown. This trend of cliff and close-out continues right through the mountainous Meru Betiri National Park and on to the serendipitous curve of **Grajagan Bay** out to the majestic lefts of G-Land. A short hop over the Bali Strait leads to what is fast becoming the wistful centre of the surfing universe, and all three coastlines of **Bali** are covered in detail.

Lombok

BRAD MASTERS

## NUSA TENGGARA

**Lombok** is a mere stone's throw from Bali and crossing the deeply cut channel leads to a different, drier world that is like an exploded version of the Bukit Peninsula on Bali, just without the 5 star hotels. The real touristy feel is reserved for the Gili's way up the north of the Lombok Channel, which feed off huge swells and NW winds, but there are further possibilities for surf along this east coast north of Sengigi and amongst the serene islands nestling behind Bangko Bangko. The south coast is cliffy and rocky, with lots of little islets and punctuated by a few really deep bays, which give **Lombok** way more flexibility in regards to swell size and beginners waves. The next surf zone of **West Sumbawa** has been surfed for decades, but due to lack of good transport links, it has remained a boat itinerary for most. Scar, Supersuck and Yo Yo's are firm favourites, but cruise around the corner and a wave wilderness opens up along the south coast for 180km. Once again the charters are in a hurry to get to the name breaks and safe anchorages so few spots are regularly surfed. The predominant coastal angle would favour NW wet season winds, but there are many deep bays backed by high coastal ranges that funnel winds down valleys to meet the sea at rivermouths and reef passes that are going to work during the dry season. Remoteness, rough seas and no roads are going to keep this coast off the maps for years to come. After the brief interruption of the surf ghetto at Lakey Peak in **Central Sumbawa**, normal service is resumed to the east of Wara Point out to Tanjung Langundu and the huge natural estuary that signals the end of the surf zone. What swell that does get through to Komodo and Flores is dashed against sea cliffs, proving this area is for divers and dragon hunters. **Sumba** is a large zone that is only lightly covered with dozens of scarily high quality waves interspersed between the major breaks on the map. Between Nihiwatu and Tarimbang a contorted playground of reefs, bays and rivermouths beckons the longer range boat charters, who are the only ones that are going to be able to access these waves that work in a range of different wind/swell combos, taking experienced captains quite a while to work out and extra diesel to keep commuting between safe anchorages and the empty line-ups. The same can be said of **Savu and Rote** a region that cops stronger wind than most places in Indonesia, which often brings cross-chop to line-ups that look like they should be offshore. Like Sumba, there are more breaks to be sniffed out, but wind direction and strength will be critical, as will the direction that the swell arrives through the narrow SSW to W window. West Timor's far southern coast is SW swell exposed at a couple of obvious reef set-ups, but it soon transforms into long sandy beaches and large rivermouths bringing sediment from the mountainous interior. Over the border into East Timor there's a few pockets of reef platform around Suai, Betano and Wedauberek, but wind strength, swell consistency and large saltwater crocs are the main worries. Timor translates as "east" and surfers should take note. To head further towards Irian Jaya is counter productive as Australia shuts the window, the continental shelf cuts the power and weather systems get funky. There is of course plenty of E windswell generated and in fact the north coasts of the islands strung between Flores and Pulau Wetar can get the odd sloppy wave, but what wind chop there is, usually heads straight to Sulawesi. Maluku is outlined in the Pacific chapter.

# Vezo Reefs MADAGASCAR

**Located in the middle of the Mozambique Channel the Tulear region has been likened to how Indonesia was 30 years ago. The 60km stretch of coastline between Ifaty and Anakao hosts more than 18 breaks, most of which are only accessible by boat from the well-protected harbour in Tulear. The harsh complexities of swell, wind, tide and access make for a difficult trip without the help of some local knowledge.**

+ QUALITY CORAL REEFS
+ YEAR-ROUND SWELLS
+ DESERTED SPOTS
+ CHEAP LOCAL COSTS

- STRONG ERRATIC TRADE WINDS
- LACK OF BEACHBREAKS
- UNDEVELOPED INFRASTRUCTURE
- EXPENSIVE FLIGHTS & TRANSFERS

22km north of Tulear, Ifaty lagoon boasts many tourist hotels at Mangily beach and a couple of reef passes lying 4-5kms offshore. The main north pass is poor quality while the rapid but inconsistent lefts of **South Pass** coupled with the shifty rights of **Laity Peak** can easily hold 10ft. To the south is the elusive **False Pass** and although there is an adjacent good right, it is known for the grinding world-class lefts which work best on a large groundswell. **The Right** is a perfect, fun, hot-dog wave on smaller swells. Tulear is a large, dusty harbour town sheltered by offshore reefs. **Googles** is the most consistent and powerful wave in the region – predominantly a left with a shorter right breaking over a sand/coral platform which extends from a headland. Can be surfed at all sizes, it's a board-breaker when big. **Pete's** is a sand bottom left located at the southern mouth of the Mangily river, ideally suited to beginner/intermediate surfers willing to make the 30min walk. At the northern extreme of the Tulear barrier reef is the classy left **Joeys**, which easily holds 15ft and peels left for 500m. Boating 1h/15km south from Tulear is **Jammies**, a reef pass with a left and barrelling right. At the southern extent of the Tulear reef is **Outers**, a solid right with a hollow inside section. The village of Sarodrano sits on a 3km-long sandspit, where a series of offshore waves are accessible by pirogue. On the north side of a submerged circular atoll is **TT's** (Tony's Tavarua, aka Nosy Manjaka), a 500m long, multi-barrel left that's perfect on moderate swells at higher tides. On the other side of the atoll breaks **Inners**, a rippable right with great speed sections. Across the pass is **Mussolini's**, a hollow left that needs more swell to break than Inners. It's possible to paddle out to **Three Rollers**, a beginners peak in front of Saradrano. Two hours from Tulear is Anakao, home to several low-key resorts. Off the northern tip of the island of Nosy Ve (marine and land sanctuary 5km offshore) is the technically demanding **Flameballs**, a fast, long spitting left with multiple barrelling sections over shallow fire coral. On the southern tip is **Pousse Pousse**, a hellman-fast, sectiony right with coral heads just below the surface that holds any size. Closer to Anakao beach, **Jelly Babies** is an ultra-consistent, fun peak, with crumbling walls, cutback shoulders and the occassional cover-up. Across the pass to the south is Indicators (aka Fafambé), another left breaking on medium/large swells.

ALAN VAN GYSEN

Flameballs

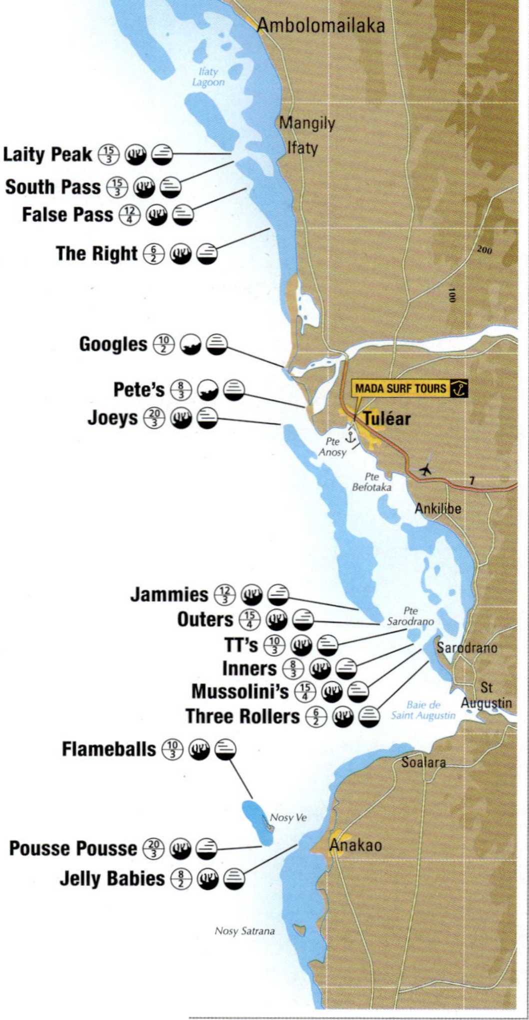


## TRAVEL INFORMATION

**Weather** – The driest region of Madagascar with Tulear sitting between the tropical west coast and the desert south. The dry season lasts nine months from March to Nov. During winter, air temps hover around 28°C (82°F), while the water temps rarely dip below 23°C (74°F), but take a shorty for windy days.

**Lodging and Food** – Mada Surf Tours provide mobile surf tour packages, hitting all the main spots (fr $55p/n). True Blue Travel also offer packages. Stay in Sunshine Resort in Anakao ($85/dbl, incl meals). Bamboo in Ifaty ($45/b'low), L'Escapade in Tulear ($22/n). Local food costs are ridiculously low and seafood is good.

**Nature and Culture** – Wild ringtail lemurs live near St Augustin Bay, where a visit to the Sarodrano Cave is a must. In Tulear check the 'Zaza Club' and dance the Minotsobe. Bird watching in Anakao and awesome forest hikes around Ifaty. Good diving facilities.

**Hazards and Hassles** – Shark threat is low, sunburn factor is high. Getting stuck in transit happens, take plenty of water and emergency kit. Regular swarms of jellyfish (hence Jelly Babies).

**Handy Hints** – Bring everything including a step-up for big days. Flame Balls is 30-40mins by local motor pirogue but can take an hour coming back into the windchop. Sailing pirogues are way slower and can't sail into the wind. Expect small crowds at Jelly Babies and Flame Balls.

From April to September, 4-12ft S-SW swells will shoot up the Mozambique Channel. The swell has to wrap around the NW-facing reefs so that the SE trades blow offshore, but they can get very strong. Early winter has the lightest winds. Tides in the Mozambique Channel can reach 1.8m, which is enough to bring live coral close to the surface. Most breaks prefer low tide, with the exception of TT's and Flame Balls.

| STATISTICS | | J F | M A | M J | J A | S O | N D |
|---|---|---|---|---|---|---|---|
| SWELL | Direction | | | | | | |
| | Size (ft) | 2 | 3-4 | 4-5 | 5-6 | 4 | 2-3 |
| WIND | Direction | | | | | | |
| | Force | F4 | F4 | F4 | F4 | F4 | F4 |
| WATER | Wetsuit | | | | | | |
| | Temp/°C | 27 | 27 | 25 | 23 | 24 | 26 |
| WEATHER | Rainfall/mm | 70 | 24 | 15 | 4 | 12 | 45 |
| | days/mth | 5 | 2 | 2 | 1 | 1 | 3 |
| | Min temp/°C | 23 | 21 | 16 | 15 | 17 | 21 |
| | Max temp/°C | 32 | 32 | 28 | 27 | 29 | 31 |

GREG EWING

TT's

# Southwest Madagascar

While the airport accessible Fort-Dauphin and Tulear have appeared in the surf press since the '80s, the stretch of coast in between has long remained a mystery due to the difficulty in getting there via dirt roads full of potholes. Hiring a tour guide with a 4WD from Fort Dauphin will almost certainly be necessary which makes it an expensive undertaking. Travel problems aside, there are undoubtedly some quality coral reefs and fun beachies to be savoured, along with a slow pace of life in this harsh, desert environment.

+ QUALITY LEFT REEFBREAKS
+ UNIQUE DESERT SURROUNDINGS
+ LONG, VIRGIN, MELLOW WAVES
+ 'BACK IN TIME' EXPERIENCE

- STRONG SE TRADES
- TRANSPORT NIGHTMARE
- EXTREMELY REMOTE
- LACK OF INFRASTRUCTURE

YEP

Lavanono Lefts

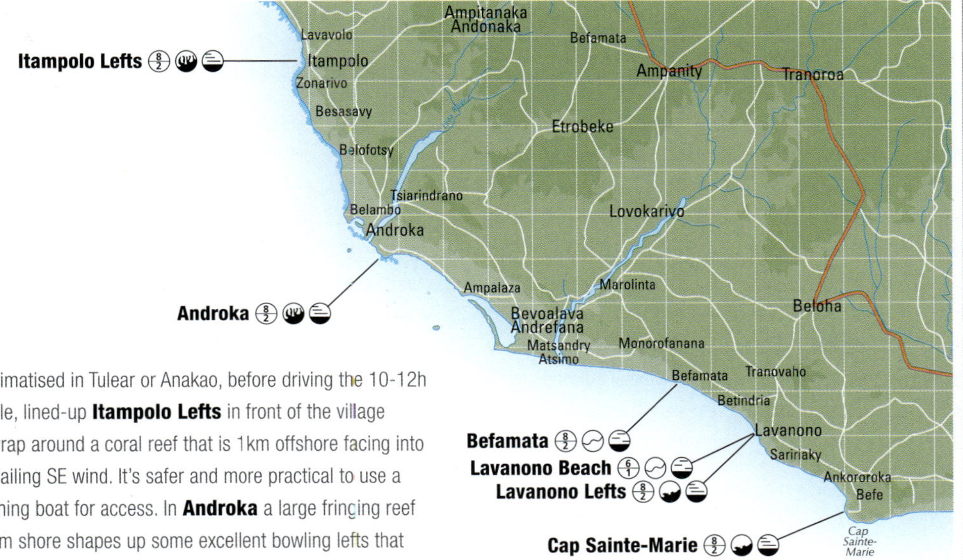


Get acclimatised in Tulear or Anakao, before driving the 10-12h to reliable, lined-up **Itampolo Lefts** in front of the village which wrap around a coral reef that is 1km offshore facing into the prevailing SE wind. It's safer and more practical to use a local fishing boat for access. In **Androka** a large fringing reef 3km from shore shapes up some excellent bowling lefts that bend into the main channel, while wind-exposed rights peel on the other side. Again a fisherman's help is essential and the whole process will takes heaps of time especially if you have to use the sail. Hardly anyone makes it to **Befamata**, an ultra-remote beachbreak with plenty of options but cross-shore in SE winds. Most surfers only go to Lavanono, the region's No1 spot, often travelling the long road from Fort-Dauphin and staying as long as they can at Sorona surf camp which has kick started many new initiatives. This tiny remote village epitomizes the Malagasy experience. **Lavanono Beach** produces crystal clear waves and an especially long mellow right, breaking further out and rolling all the way to the shore. **Lavanono Lefts** are reminiscent of St-Leu on Réunion Island, starting with long racing walls, usually ruffled by side-shores, before bending into a hollow, dead offshore, end bowl section, offering the odd barrel over flat, dead coral covered with kelp. On very low tides and small swell, the reef also holds longish rights, zipping inside the reef if the trades are low. Further inside where the village sits, a reform left breaks, where the village kids take turns on a couple of beat-up boards. Those who travel by 4WD from Fort-Dauphin, may get to stop at the barely accessible **Cap Sainte-Marie** near Ankororoka, where there can be extremely long lefts, sheltered from the blustery SE winds.

S-SW swells spin off the top edge of the east travelling Roaring Forties lows. From April to September, expect regular 4-12ft swells on the SW exposed shores, where most breaks average 3-8ft waves. Because the prevailing wind is E-SE, most setups experience cross-offshore conditions which are better angled for the lefts. The SE trades can be accelerated by the venturi effect of the coastal mountain range, and sometimes shift onshore as cold front cells approach the coast in winter. Early winter (April-May) is best for gentle winds. A varatraza onshore wind spell is a real bummer and usually happens from Sept-Oct, the windiest months. The tidal range is less than 0.6m in the far south, but it becomes significant 2m towards the Mozambique Channel, affecting navigation with local dug-outs to Androka or Itampolo reefs.

## TRAVEL INFORMATION

**Weather** – The climate of Madagascar is generally sub-tropical with two seasons: a hot, rainy one from November to April and a cooler, dry one from May to October. Neither the trade winds nor the monsoons reach the southern part of the island, which consequently receives little rain and is, in places, a semi-desert. The dryness is aggravated by a cold offshore current. Annual average rainfall is 390mm (16in). Thunderstorms are common during the rainy season and tropical cyclones are an important climatic feature; the island has already been significantly damaged by their impact. Temps vary between 14-28°C (58-82°F) in winter and range from 20-32°C (68-90°F) in summer. Use a springsuit or light fullsuit from May to December and boardies for the other months.

**Lodging and Food** – In Itampolo, stay at Chez Alain at $8-20/dble, they know about surfing. Lavanono Lodge has a camp with 10 bungalows facing the spot at $600p for all inclusive 5 night trip from Fort Dauphin. Local food is dirt cheap, expect $2-3 for a meal.

**Nature and Culture** – Expect a full-on desert, Antandroy means the land of thorns! It's bushy, spiny everywhere with zebu cows and goats eating the meagre vegetation. It's a world lost in time, very remote, very basic facilities. Meet the friendly lemurs on the Berenty Natural Reserve.

**Hazards and Hassles** – Sharks on this SW coast are rare. The reef in Lavanono is fairly flat but Androka and Itampolo are live coral. The SE wind can be a bother and it's coldish at night. Potential fleas in the beds! No mosquitoes but occasionally, small flies appear. Respect the local traditions.

**Handy Hints** – No need for a gun but kite-surf equipment would be useful. Take a beat-up board for the kids. There is no place on earth like Madagascar – be patient and open-minded and remember that all good things take time!

GILLES CALVET

Itampolo

| STATISTICS | | J F | M A | M J | J A | S O | N D |
|---|---|---|---|---|---|---|---|
| SWELL | Direction | | | | | | |
| | Size (ft) | 2 | 3-4 | 4-5 | 5-6 | 4 | 2-3 |
| WIND | Direction | | | | | | |
| | Force | F4 | F4 | F4 | F4 | F4 | F4 |
| WATER | Wetsuit | | | | | | |
| | Temp/°C | 25 | 25 | 22 | 21 | 21 | 23 |
| WEATHER | Rainfall/mm | 82 | 28 | 14 | 6 | 10 | 51 |
| | days/mth | 7 | 4 | 2 | 2 | 2 | 5 |
| | Min temp/°C | 22 | 18 | 16 | 14 | 16 | 20 |
| | Max temp/°C | 32 | 31 | 28 | 27 | 29 | 31 |

# Southeast Madagascar

Madagascar is one of the most uncrowded and potentially epic surf zones in the Indian Ocean, but it remains lightly surfed mainly because of a reputation for shark infested waters. While sharks are a bigger factor in the NE, they are far less numerous across the south coast between Fort Dauphin and Tulear. Fort Dauphin is the regional hub of the southeast, located on a peninsula with the sea on three sides and is home to a wide range of wave types.

+ UNCROWDED SPOTS
+ HOSPITABLE PEOPLE
+ CONSISTENT SWELLS
+ CHEAP LOCAL COSTS

- SHARK THREAT
- WINDY FROM SEPT TO NOV
- EXPENSIVE TRAVEL
- POOR ROADS

ALAN VAN GYSEN

Vinanibe

**Vinanibe** (a.k.a. Ambinanibe or Venom Bay) is the most powerful beachbreak of the region, where long, fast, hollow peelers break consistently all-year-round, groomed by the NE offshore winds. Currents and close-outs make it an experienced surfers spot. The 7km long **Baie des Singes** is peppered with peaks, ideal for all levels of surfing, windsurfing and kitesurfing. More super-fast waves offering perfect low tide barrels in the consistent N or NE wind. The town beach is a hang-out for local surfers with restaurants on hand for post surf parties. **Monseigneur Baie** is the classic regional reefbreak, offering 150m long, fun workable walls that go from nice and deep at the peak into shallow, flat rocks covered in live coral and urchins. Pumps from April to July when the S swells hit, but needs a S-SW wind making it inconsistent. Perfect for all but the complete novice. Wind and kitesurfers love the Fort Dauphin end of **Baie de Galion,** but cross-shore winds mean it rarely breaks properly for surfers amongst the many exposed and submerged shipwrecks. Only 15km along the beach, but a 2hr drive is the beautiful fishing village of **Evatra** which offers a SW-facing, left reef breaking into the rivermouth, well sheltered from the NE-E trades. Speedy bowls unload in SE-SW swells, often lining up perfectly, but it's best accessed by boat with a guide, as it can be a bit spooky due to 'big fish' and strong currents. **Lokaro** is a true gem of a beach just 40mins walk around the headland, offering perfect sheltered swimming or kitesurfing, but little surf thanks to offshore islets.

The best time to visit is April to July when regular S-SW swells reach 4-12ft. Most breaks in and around Fort Dauphin don't face directly into the SW swells, so average wave heights are reduced, but are still around 4-10ft in the winter. The eastern side of the island is the place to be from Nov-March (summer) when cyclone swells (without the bad weather) can reach 12-25ft on NE-E facing spots. However SE winds can dominate, strongest from Sept to Nov in Fort Dauphin. The tidal range is less than 0.5m.

ALAN VAN GYSEN

Monseigneur Bay

## TRAVEL INFORMATION

**Weather** – Moderate tropical climate with two seasons; Nov to March is the rainy season with stifling temperatures and thunderstorms. April to October is dry and warm with moderate cool spells, especially when the wind picks up in Sept - Nov. The 2,000m high peaks at the bottom of the eastern mountain range, create a microclimate with NE winds. Water averages 25ºC (77ºF) so take a shorty for windy days and cooler upwelling.

**Lodging and Food** – Various tour packages are available from TrueBlueTravel.co.za and Surfbornnaked.com. Kaleta Hotel ($25-65/r/n); Lavasoa (bungalows $50-85/n); Petit Bonheur overlooking Monseigneur Baie ($29-39/r/n); Gina Village (bungalows $25/n); Baie de Sainge Hotel (bungalows $20/n). Main courses for around $6-9; tasty rice & stew for less than $2; local beer = $1.

**Nature and Culture** – The Andohahela National Park, the Berenty & Nahampoana Private Reserves and Lac Anony are all well worth a visit. Whales migrate along the SE coast while dolphins and turtles often join surfers in the line-up. Local customs and belief in sorcery mix with religion, creating intriguing tombs with Zebu cattle skulls - ask permission before photographing. Poverty and malnutrition are rife – try to help.

**Hazards and Hassles** – There is malaria so take appropriate prophylaxis, spray and cover up in the evening. The sharks of Fort Dauphin appear to be uninterested in foraging inshore. A local guide can advise and always follow the rules of no surfing at dawn, dusk or in murky water or with an open wound.

**Handy Hints** – Malagasy currency is the Ariary (MGA); bring a mix of Euros or US dollars. Cash machines in major towns only and the max daily withdrawal is 400,000 Ariary ($196). Very few establishments outside of the capital can accept visa for payment. Speaking French is crucial or else book with Samson at www.surfbornnaked.com, the only British qualified surf instructor and lifeguard in Fort Dauphin. A group of 4 or 5 will fit into one 4WD making travel more cost effective. A tent will make it cheap and easy to visit remote breaks. Learn the regional 'fady' or taboos. For example, in Fort Dauphin it is considered extremely rude to touch another person's head.

| STATISTICS | | J F | M A | M J | J A | S O | N D |
|---|---|---|---|---|---|---|---|
| SWELL | Direction | | | | | | |
| | Size (ft) | 4 | 5 | 6 | 6-7 | 5-6 | 3 |
| WIND | Direction | | | | | | |
| | Force | F4 | F4 | F4 | F4 | F4-F5 | F4 |
| WATER | Wetsuit | | | | | | |
| | Temp/°C | 26 | 25 | 24 | 22 | 23 | 25 |
| WEATHER | Rainfall/mm | 242 | 130 | 10 | 10 | 30 | 200 |
| | days/mth | 16 | 9 | 2 | 2 | 7 | 15 |
| | Min temp/°C | 23 | 21 | 18 | 17 | 17 | 21 |
| | Max temp/°C | 30 | 29 | 24 | 25 | 27 | 30 |

# West Réunion

The beautiful volcanic island of Réunion is ideally placed to receive powerful and consistent Roaring Forties swells. Most of the 32 reported spots on the west coast break on fragmented barrier reefs, quite a distance from the beach. Rain from the mountainous interior brings murky water – good habitat for the sharks that have made Réunion's waters the most dangerous on the planet.

- + CONSISTENT
- + SPOT DIVERSITY
- + SCENERY
- + SUPERB ST LEU

- – SHARK ATTACKS
- – SURFING BANS
- – EXPENSIVE
- – CRAZY TRAFFIC

ALAN VAN GYSEN

St-Leu

St-Gilles is the area's main centre with bars, shops, hotels, good nightlife, and at least 17 breaks scattered around 12kms of coastline. **Cap Requin** swings left round a coral sweep in moderate swells, needing high tides for depth and SE winds for groomed, lip bashing walls. The name is a clue to its sharkiness, like La Cimetiere beachbreak just north, scene of two recent attacks. A 1200m shark net protects crowded **Boucan**, where a fun, reliable left reef breaks in swell up to 10ft, while the gnarly right only jacks up and barrels in solid size. **Aigrettes** is mainly a friendly left wall for improvers to hone their cutties. Netted **Roches Noires** has a string of rights that cover most abilities from the rare, N-swell-loving slabs of Cachera and L'Escalier down to Banc de Sable where even beginners can surf in big swells. The three sections of **La Digue** lefts occasionally link up into one extremely long left ride, offering intermediates a fast wall through the mid-section and shredders a tricky barrel on the inside. The fabulous natural lagoon reserve at **L'Hermitage Pass** offers surfers the choice between an epic tubing left and a short, intense barrelling right. A 5 knot current makes paddling out easy and coming in a nightmare. The three waves at **Trois-Bassins** are swell and crowd magnets, having waves when everywhere else is flat. La Barriere is the fast shallow right and odd left that works in any N or S swell. Most people ride The Peak closer to shore - a nice little A-frame with feathering lips and tapered shoulders over lava rocks, accessible to most surfers. South of the cut is a fairly fat left wall that occasionally connects up on a due S swell. **La Cafrine** is tucked in behind the St-Leu reef offering beginners a nursery right over a deep, urchin-covered, coral slab. The famous lefts of **St-Leu** provide a truly world-class wave when stronger SW swells hit. It starts with a quick drop and open face wall, ideal for carving big turns, before bending sharply round the reef into a couple of bowly, hollow sections that throw out a shallow tube. Needs to be overhead to start linking up for the full 300m ride, but will work in sections when it is smaller. **La Point-au-Sel** is a voyeurs dream as massive caverns hit a straight section of reef that looks perfect, but is unmakeable. **Etang-Salé** is the windsurfers equivalent of St-Leu, as the SE wind blows cross-shore, but if the winds are calm or NE, then barrels will appear out on the fringing reef. The south coast around St-Pierre is very consistent at **Pic du Diable** and **La Jetée** but the current shark factor is too high.

Saint-Denis
Pointe des Galets
La Possession
Le Port
Saint-Paul
Cap Requin
Boucan
Aigrettes
Roches-Noires
La Digue
Boucan Canot
Saint-Gilles-les-Bains
L'Hermitage-les-Bains
L'Hermitage
Passe de l'Hermitage
Trois-Bassins
Pointe des Trois-Bassins
Cirque de Mafate
Cirque de Salazie
Gros Morne
3070m Piton des Neiges
Grand Bénare
Cirque de Cilaos
La Caffrine
St-Leu
Saint-Leu
La Pointe-au-Sel
Pointe au Sel
Etang-Salé
L'Etang-salé les bains
Pointe de l'Etang-Salé
Saint-Louis
Saint-Pierre
Pic du Diable
Pic du Diable
La Jetée

SW swells varying in size from 3-15ft can occur year-round, while the summer season is characterised by occasional NE tropical storms (about 10 per season). SE trades blow constantly with a more E-NE direction during the summer (Dec-Mar) and more S-SE during winter (June-Sept). The wind can also produce 2-6ft onshore windswell on the windward coast, and side/offshore on the SW coast. Tides are significant at shallow spots.

## TRAVEL INFORMATION

**Weather** – The high mountains mean the windward coast is very wet, with record humidity levels, while the W coast is rather dry. The cyclone season lasts from Dec-March with major destructive cyclones hitting every three years or so. May-June and Sept-Oct are usually the best weather months. Springsuits help with windchill when water bottoms out at 24°C (75°F) around August.

**Lodging and Food** – St-Leu's 3-star Paladien Apolonia is plush but a double room starts at $175/night. Directly across the street from the wave is DodoSpot; a double room there starts at $32/night. The Campix campground is open March to November. Guesthouses ($40/$60) slightly out of town. Spicy Creole cuisine costs $15 or even less from bars.

**Nature and Culture** – Maïdo is a 2000m peak that has a breathtaking view over the W coast. Cirques like Mafate, Cilaos, and Salazie are great places for trekking and views. On the E side, Piton de la Fournaise is the second-most active volcano in the world.

**Hazards and Hassles** – In total 7 people have been killed in shark attacks in Reunion since January 2011. Don't surf in murky water, on your own, before dark, or after heavy rains. Fire coral, spiny urchins, and shallow reefs are also threats. Only 2 surf schools still operate, running SUP classes in protected lagoons.

**Handy Hints** – It's a French island with white "Zoreils" (the name of people from mainland France) raising the standard of living. Mixed-race locals speak Creole. The bars are lively and play local sega and maloya music. Surf gear is very expensive. Only surf the 2 protected beaches, despite a recent attack at Boucan due to a hole in the net.

ALAN VAN GYSEN

La Jetée

| STATISTICS | | J F | M A | M J | J A | S O | N D |
|---|---|---|---|---|---|---|---|
| SWELL | Direction | | | | | | |
| | Size (ft) | 4-5 | 5-6 | 6-7 | 7-8 | 6 | 3-4 |
| WIND | Direction | | | | | | |
| | Force | F4 | F4 | F4 | F5 | F4 | F3 |
| WATER | Wetsuit | | | | | | |
| | Temp/°C | 28 | 27 | 26 | 24 | 25 | 26 |
| WEATHER | Rainfall/mm | 240 | 225 | 77 | 60 | 45 | 247 |
| | days/mth | 12 | 11 | 11 | 11 | 7 | 10 |
| | Min temp/°C | 23 | 22 | 16 | 17 | 18 | 21 |
| | Max temp/°C | 30 | 29 | 27 | 25 | 26 | 28 |

# Mauritius

Mauritius has gained an exotic image in the heart of surfers thanks to the 1974 surf film, "Forgotten Island of Santosha". It focused on Tamarin Bay, a perfect, almond-eyed left that became a symbol of escapism. The epic 8-10ft swell featured in the film, captured the attention of the surfing world, but it turned out to be inconsistent, leaving many travelling surfers disappointed. Localism flared in the '90s, with incidents of violence from the now notorious *White Shorts* enforcers, but the aggression has thankfully calmed down. When it fires, Tamarin is a true slice of surfing paradise, plus there are a handful of quality reef passes on the exposed Morne Peninsula that are way more reliable and provide a great diversion on what is often referred to as the "Honeymoon Island".

+ TAMARIN'S FLAWLESS LEFT
+ QUALITY REEFBREAKS
+ EXOTIC CULTURE
+ BEAUTIFUL SCENERY

- CROWDS
- TAMARIN'S INCONSISTENCY
- LACK OF SHELTERED WAVES
- EXPENSIVE FLIGHTS

## TRAVEL INFORMATION

**Weather** – Mauritius differs from the classic monsoon pattern, and its year-round moderate rain generally falls at the end of the day. It's usually hotter and wetter, but with less cyclone risk during the summer (Dec-April). Winter begins in May, but temperatures remain warm enough for most visitors, and this period is considered the most pleasant time. The E coast is drier than the W coast. The water can get a little chilly in winter, requiring a springsuit as opposed to the usual boardies.

**Lodging and Food** – Surf Camp Mauritius offer accommodation and car packages fr $300/w, plus lessons and boat transport. At Chez Jacques, doubles start at $50/night. A double in Tamarin Hotel starts at $145/night half board. Le Morne has several luxury resorts facing the surf (Le Paradis, Dinarobin, Indian Resort, Les Pavillons); all expensive. Package deals are your best bet. Street food is good and spicy with Creole, French and Indian flavours on offer from local restaurants ($15/meal) or overpriced fusion food from the resorts.

**Nature and Culture** – Unlike Reunion, Mauritius is hilly rather than mountainous, and only the Trou aux Cerfs crater testifies to the ancient volcanic activity. The beaches are some of the most beautiful in the world. Port-Louis spice markets, Pamplemousse Gardens, and Moka Town are all worth a visit. Shellorama Museum next to Tamarin is interesting.

**Hazards and Hassles** – Tamarin locals can be surly, but other spots are cool and usually uncrowded. Coral heads are a worry at low tide Tamarin. Most coral reefs are dangerous and involve long paddles from shore. The island is generally safe for tourists and unprovoked shark attacks are not an issue, despite proximity to Rèunion. Bull sharks are around the passes and like the murky water at Mont Choisy.

**Handy Hints** – There are good shapers in Tamarin, and having a locally made board can make you feel safer in the Tamarin line-up! Mauritius is a peaceful blend of Catholics, Protestants, Hindus and Muslims. The Indian population is large. Go with an open mind and see what the melting pot of exotic culture is like. If the surf is flat, there are many ocean options like diving, snorkelling the lagoons, kitesurfing, SUP etc. Phoenix, the local beer, is the best in the Indian Ocean.

GREG EWING

Balaclava

GREG EWING

Black Rocks

GREG EWING

On the NE coast of Mauritius is the town of Grand Gaube; the barrier reef offshore has a couple of righthanders during the off-season, notably the right in front of **Ile Bernache**, fun and juicy when it breaks, which isn't very often. There is a kitesurfing/surf school nearby. Near **Grand Baie** is the island's second-best left, called "Tagore" by some, rivalling Tamarin when it's on, with localism and a nasty reef. Just south is the **Mont Choisy** beach area, where there are some shapely reefs offshore (two rights and two lefts), but require a long paddle or hiring a boat from shore. On the NW coast at Trou aux Biches there is a fairly gutless reef wave that is usually quite small, so good for novices. At **Balaclava** there is a pass in front of the Oberoi Hotel that has a fun left and a right when small and clean. At the south end of the bay (Baie de l'Arsenal) **Le Goulet** is a good but rare left that only breaks on the biggest of SW swells, having to wrap nearly 180°. At Baie de la Petite Rivière, there is a NW-facing pass in front of La Plantation d'Albion **Club Med** that has a left and a right, but both need a big winter swell or summer conditions to break. When the swell is small and clean, sometimes there are a few rideable spots on the barrier reef offshore of **Flic en Flac**. **Black Rocks** is a fast, powerful, folding wall that needs higher tides and more NE than SE wind to hold up the sections. It's situated across the deep channel from the famous reef at ✪**Tamarin Bay**, which will only start breaking when a moderate to big SW swell has enough power and period to wrap through 90° and hit the perfect curve of coral. Just down the coast, **La Preneuse** is a barrelling left along a corner of the barrier reef offshore of the Martello Tower museum. Yet another

Grand Baie
Ile Bernache
Mont Choisy
Balaclava
Le Goulet
Club Med
Flic en Flac
Black Rocks
Tamarin Bay
La Preneuse
Baie de la Petite Riviére Noire
Passe de l'Ambulante
One Eyes
Morne Rights
Macondé
Graveyards
Ilôt Sancho
Souillac
Ile des Deux Cocos
Port Louis
SURFCAMP MAURITIUS

## Tamarin Bay

LAT. -20.326852° LONG. 57.372085°

Hypnotic, cultured barrels tour the NW-facing reef when a moderate to large SW swell tacks in and long tube time is logged by the mix of locals and lucky holidaymakers. This long, perfectly-formed, barrelling left becomes ultra-shallow at low tide, so higher tides are safer. Tuck-ins and speed slashes are the order of the day so lesser surfers should stick to the inside reform or beachbreak. The blind aggression has gone, but behave and avoid eye-contact with the humourless crowds, foot-contact with the legion of urchins, face-contact with the coral crusted limestone and any contact with the ever-present sharks. Tamarin has been forgotten to an extent, since Indonesian consistency and price have deflected the hordes, but it is still a beauty to behold.

perfect, but inconsistent left exists at the entrance to **Baie de la Petite Riviére Noire** that requires a boat ride. Moving down to the consistent Le Morne Peninsula, there is **Passe de L'Ambulante**, a decent high tide left and right (the right is better) directly in front of Les Pavillons Hotel; it's almost 1km offshore so find a boat. The small pass opposite the southern tip of the Le Morne Peninsula and directly under the shadow of the towering granite Morne Brabant is called **One Eyes**. It's probably the most consistent and crowded wave on the island, especially on weekends, where shapely lefts spin down a straight reef that gets quite heavy and hollow when overhead. Low tide makes the line-up and the 20min lagoon paddle sketchy. When the swell is small and clean or the wind is NE, **Morne Rights** can be ridden out on the north side of Passe de la Prairie. Across the channel is the Manawa left and both are very consistent, long and hollow, but you need slack wind, incoming tide, and a boat to reach it. Horrendous out-going currents on the dropping tide. At Baie du Cap, **Macondé** is a short hollow left that can handle any size, but requires some N or E in the wind and a 10-minute paddle. All the spots further east only work in the morning or with summer NE winds. Facing the cemetery, **Graveyards** is another left that's rarely good, but usually rideable over the scary reef. Requires a long paddle-out, and needs N wind. One of the most consistent summer spots on the S coast is **Îlot Sancho**, which gets weird rights and lefts on the edge of the reef in the little cove. The right in **Souillac** breaks on a small swell and a N wind on the last bit of fringing reef before the coast gets cliffy. On huge south swells there is a psycho death righthand slab at Gris Gris—it would be a prime tow spot if jet skis were legal on Mauritius! Down at Blue Bay, there is a very good left behind **Île des Deux Cocos**, but it is always blown out during winter, hard to access and creates strong currents. The eastern reef of Mauritius has dozens of small passes and possible surf spots, but they are almost always flat and/or blown out.

GREG EWING

One Eyes

During the Southern Hemisphere winter (May-Oct) there are frequent SW swells varying in size from 2-20ft. Although these SW swells can appear year-round, the summer season is characterised by NE tropical storms, but with only about 10 depressions in six months, it's hardly consistent. Of these, 1-2 will be strong cyclones that can be dangerous and destructive. Winter SE-S trades blow constantly and with a greater strength and frequency from July-Sept. Summer winds veer more NE-E, which can also bring 2-6ft onshore windswell to the windward coast and side/offshore conditions on the surf-blessed SW corner. Tides are only significant at shallower spots.

| STATISTICS | | J F | M A | M J | J A | S O | N D |
|---|---|---|---|---|---|---|---|
| SWELL | Direction | | | | | | |
| | Size (ft) | 4 | 5 | 6 | 6-7 | 5-6 | 4 |
| WIND | Direction | | | | | | |
| | Force | F4 | F4 | F4 | F4 | F4 | F3-F4 |
| WATER | Wetsuit | | | | | | |
| | Temp/°C | 27 | 26 | 24 | 22 | 23 | 25 |
| WEATHER | Rainfall/mm | 205 | 174 | 81 | 61 | 38 | 82 |
| | days/mth | 11 | 10 | 7 | 6 | 4 | 6 |
| | Min temp/°C | 23 | 21 | 17 | 17 | 17 | 19 |
| | Max temp/°C | 30 | 29 | 26 | 24 | 26 | 29 |

# Anjouan COMOROS

Located in the north of the Mozambique Channel, between Africa and Madagascar, this volcanic archipelago is made up of four islands; Grande Comoros, Anjouan and Mohéli form the independent Comoros Union, while Mayotte remains a French territory. Tourism is undeveloped thanks to political instability (18 coups in 24yrs, often led by the well-known mercenary Bob Dénard) and a lack of infrastructure. With a mix of African, Malagasy, Arab and Persian origins, Comoros is one of the poorest countries in the world creating health problems like malaria and cholera. The Comoros have hidden their surf potential for a long time, until an expedition found waves on Anjouan, which has the best potential for regular surf at a variety of spots with good exposure to the different swells.

**+ EMPTY LINE-UPS**
**+ UNDISCOVERED WAVES**
**+ BEAUTIFUL LANDSCAPES**
**+ VARIETY OF SPOTS**

**- ONSHORE WINDS**
**- POLITICAL INSTABILITY**
**- DISEASES AND POVERTY**
**- INTER-ISLAND TRANSPORT**

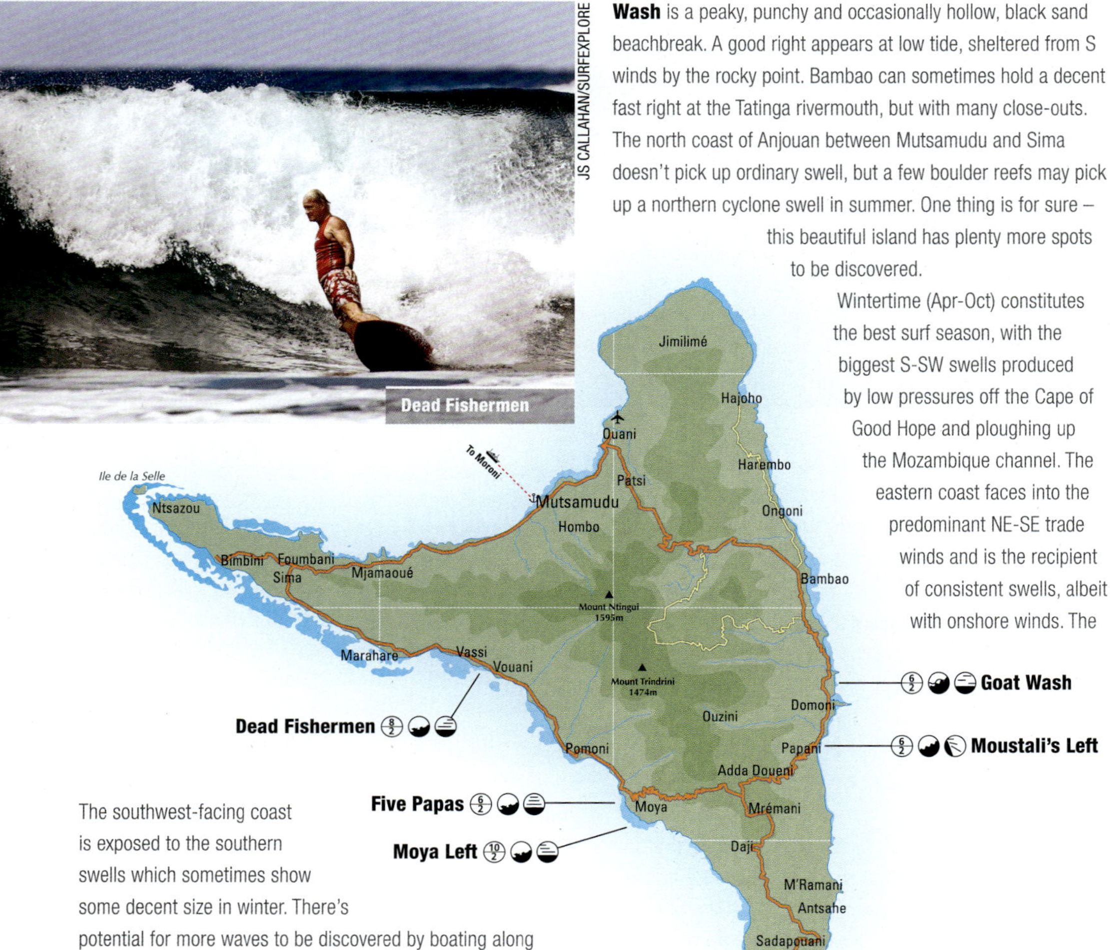


Dead Fishermen

Wintertime (Apr-Oct) constitutes the best surf season, with the biggest S-SW swells produced by low pressures off the Cape of Good Hope and ploughing up the Mozambique channel. The eastern coast faces into the predominant NE-SE trade winds and is the recipient of consistent swells, albeit with onshore winds. The Comoros is also in the road of the big summer cyclone swells, arriving from the N to NE, between December and March. The main winds blow from S-SE in winter, and from the N in summer. Tidal range can be very important and most of the beachbreaks are better at low tide.

The southwest-facing coast is exposed to the southern swells which sometimes show some decent size in winter. There's potential for more waves to be discovered by boating along the outer reefs between the northwestern tip of the island and Vouani. Just west of this village lies **Dead Fishermen**, a hollow, ledging right wall that sprints across the coral shelf in front of a big rock, offering proper barrels when it's clean. The wave packs a punch with heavy hold-downs. The little village of Moya is probably the best place to stay, with two spots breaking just in front of the hotel. **Five Papas**, a "V" shaped reef produces a longer walled left and short hollow right at mid-tide. **Moya Left** breaks on the outside coral reef, best at mid-high tide as the shallow reef drains down to dangerous levels at low and the strong current in the lagoon makes the paddle back to the beach tough. The long, black sand beach north of Moya offers nice peaks at low tide, with sandbanks stabilised close to the tunnel. Exposed to the NE windswell, the east coast can be regularly surfed in winter. **Moustali's Left** is the first spot accessible from the road south of Domoni, close to the filling station. The swell wraps around a bend in the coast covered in big black boulders and sometimes offers a nice wall. The place is exposed to the main onshore SE wind, so it needs to be glassy or NW to be any good. Just north of Domoni, **Goat Wash** is a peaky, punchy and occasionally hollow, black sand beachbreak. A good right appears at low tide, sheltered from S winds by the rocky point. Bambao can sometimes hold a decent fast right at the Tatinga rivermouth, but with many close-outs. The north coast of Anjouan between Mutsamudu and Sima doesn't pick up ordinary swell, but a few boulder reefs may pick up a northern cyclone swell in summer. One thing is for sure – this beautiful island has plenty more spots to be discovered.

## TRAVEL INFORMATION

**Weather** – The archipelago has a tropical, warm climate with lush vegetation, and a slight change between the 2 main seasons. East coast of Anjouan has a less humid climate than west coast (Moya) and the north coast (Mutsamudu). Water is boardshort warm year-round - take a rash or light wetsuit vest for when it's windy.

**Lodging and Food** – Moya Pension Bungalows is probably the best place to stay ($20/nt) just in front of the reefbreaks and close to the beachbreak. To stay in Domoni, check Loulou Motel ($40/nt) or Al Amal in Mutsamudu ($70/nt). Few restaurants in Mutsamudu and Domoni ($5-15), or find cheap food in the street shops.

**Nature and Culture** – Covered by tropical forests, hiking inland should uncover the endemic fauna (lemurs, giant fruit-bats) and flora. Hike Mount Trindrini from Domoni. Mosques and ancient monuments in Domoni show Arabic influences in the local architecture. Visit the old citadel of Mutsamudu at the top of the medina.

**Hazards and Hassles** – The Mozambique channel is known for its shark factor. Lack of hospitals, many diseases and health problems. Drink only sealed bottled water. Domestic flights are on the European black list. Be careful at all times – don't travel alone.

**Handy Hints** – With the lack of real hospital infrastructure, bring your own first aid kit, anti-malarials and pills to purify drinking water. No surf shop, so take usual boards, a semi-gun, a spare leash, wax, sunscreen and a ding repair kit.

| STATISTICS | | J F | M A | M J | J A | S O | N D |
|---|---|---|---|---|---|---|---|
| SWELL | Direction | | | | | | |
| | Size (ft) | 1-2 | 2 | 2-3 | 3 | 2-3 | 1-2 |
| WIND | Direction | | | | | | |
| | Force | F3-F4 | F3-F4 | F4 | F4 | F3 | F3 |
| WATER | Wetsuit | | | | | | |
| | Temp/°C | 29 | 28 | 27 | 26 | 25 | 27 |
| WEATHER | Rainfall/mm | 188 | 132 | 4 | 3 | 11 | 130 |
| | days/mth | 16 | 8 | 2 | 1 | 3 | 7 |
| | Min temp/°C | 23 | 23 | 19 | 18 | 21 | 23 |
| | Max temp/°C | 31 | 32 | 31 | 31 | 32 | 32 |

Moustali's Left

# Seychelles



In the Seychelles, small, clean, relatively uncrowded surf does exist, but Mahé suffers from a long, shallow shelf and sits too far W for the normal groundswell angles in the Indian Ocean. It's extremely inconsistent, relying on a major S swell to hit, or for consistent onshore winds to create surf on the few exposed beaches. However, it's an island of outstanding natural beauty, granite rock and lush mountains, with narrow coastal strips of gorgeous white-sand beaches.

+ USER-FRIENDLY WAVES
+ FEW CROWDS
+ WARM WATER
+ BEAUTIFUL SCENERY

- RARELY SURFABLE
- VERY EXPENSIVE
- WINDY
- LACK OF GOOD SPOTS

MICHAEL KEW

Anse aux Poules Bleues

## TRAVEL INFORMATION

**Weather** – From May to Oct, temps average 27°C (80°F) and 8 hrs sunshine per day. From Oct to Dec and Mar to May, there are light variable breezes, calm seas and higher temps/ humidity. From Dec to Mar, the period of fluctuating NW-NE winds brings frequent tropical rain, high humidity and average temps of 28°C (82°F).

**Lodging and Food** – Most hotels are in the surfless Beau Vallon area; try Coco d'Or Hotel ($165/dbl) or Augerine Guesthouse ($185/dbl). Victoria has several options. Numerous luxury resorts/hotels to choose from around the island. Camping is forbidden. Expect $20-30 for a basic meal; try some authentic Creole cuisine.

**Nature and Culture** – World-class sailing, diving, snorkelling, and fishing. Nightlife is limited to the entertainment at hotels and a few nightclubs. There are many species of flora and fauna unique to the island. The mountains offer some scenic hikes.

**Hazards and Hassles** – Most spots have shallow coral bottoms so there's a risk of hitting the reef. Never mind sharks or stonefish, but be very careful with the equatorial sun and possible theft, carried out by determined and possibly armed groups of 4 or 5 individuals. Watch your car.

**Handy Hints** – Because it is rarely good, crowds are increasing at the name breaks when they are on. Go with low expectations for surf. Seychelles is best viewed as a relaxing beach holiday, with any possible surf as just a bonus.

MICHAEL KEW

Barbarons

Most waves on Mahé are marginal coral reefbreaks. **Grande Anse** has a funky right reef at the north end of some poor beachbreak. Usually the biggest spot, but also blown-out. **Barbarons** is a shallow, ledgy left, accessed by walking through Le Meridien resort and south down the beach. Down the coast are a few decent but sheltered and extremely rare reefbreaks. **Anse aux Poules Bleues**, close to Anse à la Mouche, is a fun, shallow left that can be long; the SE trades blow offshore. Needs a huge SSW swell to break. This attracts an instant crowd on the three or so days it will break in a good year. With some SW groundswell, Baie Lazare has a few spots like **Anse Gaulette**, a fairly consistent reef and beachbreak. The reefs fronting the defunct Plantation Club hold headhigh walls, but it is very shallow so it needs a high spring tide of 1.8m and a proper offshore to truly work. **Anse Intendance** is fairly consistent beachbreak but rarely any good – usually closed-out or flat. On regular 1-2ft SE windswells, Anse Petite Police and the longer **Police Bay** are the island's most exposed beaches, but it's usually a rocky shore dump with strong currents and rarely worth a look. On the east coast, fringing reef keeps the surfline a good 200m offshore through Anse Forbans and further north at **Anse Bougainville** where racy righthand walls pitch down an angle in the otherwise straight reef. Best with summer NW winds, it can be surfed year-round, but getting good swell and winds is rare. A little further north, in a break in the reef before Anse Royale, **La Passe** occasionally shows when SE swell and NW winds combine. **Northeast Point** holds a short, very shallow right that's only approachable at high tides. It is shielded from swell by islets making it very inconsistent and requiring some E in the swell. On rare N summer swell, north-facing **Carana** Beach may produce some easy sand-bottom waves and it also throws up some wind slop in the SE trades. Praslin is encircled by shallow waters and usually flat, but there are some funky, mushy reefs at Anse Kerlan and Grande Anse on the east side. The tourist beach at Anse Lazio may have some shoredump close-outs. On neighbouring island La Digue **Grande Anse** may have a messy left at the north end if the SE'er isn't howling and is marginally better than neighbouring Petit Anse. On the northern tip, Anse Patate can have a right wedge off the rock.

The SE trades produce consistent 2-4ft (0.6-1.2m) wind chop on the east coast, but it is mostly unsurfable. Occasional SE to SSW groundswells hit the islands in winter and produce quality reefbreak surf if they wrap around to the west coast, where SE trades blow offshore at some spots. N windswell is a long shot and no cyclone has ever hit Mahé. Water is warm in summer, but winter trades can force temperatures to dip well below the average to 20°C (68°F). There are two different tides a day, with a max range of 1.5-2m.

| STATISTICS | | J F | M A | M J | J A | S O | N D |
|---|---|---|---|---|---|---|---|
| SWELL | Direction | | | | | | |
| | Size (ft) | 0-1 | 1-2 | 2 | 2-3 | 1-2 | 0-1 |
| WIND | Direction | | | | | | |
| | Force | F2-F3 | F2-F3 | F3 | F4 | F4 | F3 |
| WATER | Wetsuit | | | | | | |
| | Temp/°C | 28 | 28 | 27 | 25 | 26 | 27 |
| WEATHER | Rainfall/mm | 334 | 180 | 121 | 103 | 172 | 245 |
| | days/mth | 9 | 8 | 5 | 4 | 6 | 10 |
| | Min temp/°C | 25 | 28 | 28 | 26 | 26 | 25 |
| | Max temp/°C | 30 | 31 | 30 | 28 | 29 | 30 |

# Yemen

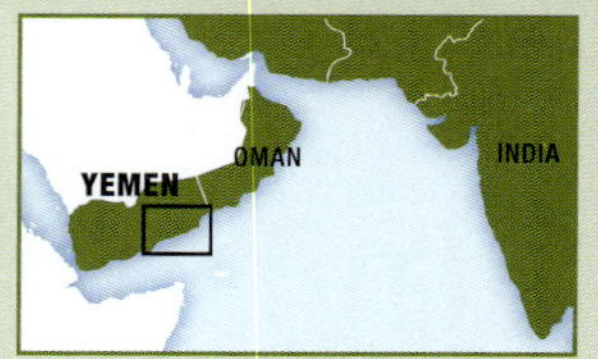


Yemen is a mountainous country, with rolling desert dunes, ancient caravan cities and a warm-hearted and friendly people for whom pride, hospitality and honour are the pillars of life. Several expeditions have ridden the waves breaking along Yemen's long south-facing Indian Ocean coastline and the remote island of Socotra. However governments are currently advising against all travel to Yemen which finds itself caught in the grips of widespread civil war complicated by foreign coalition interventions.

**+ RELIABLE MONSOON SWELL**
**+ POWERFUL, VIRGIN BEACHES**
**+ VERY WARM WATER**
**+ UNIQUE DESERT ENVIRONMENT**

**- WAR ZONE**
**- VERY UNSTABLE SECURITY**
**- MESSY WINDSWELL SURF**
**- VISAS, PERMITS, HIGH COSTS**

With the swells coming out of the SE and much of the Yemeni coast being blocked by Somalia the best bet for mainland surf will be east of Al Mukalla. This is not a trip to approach lightly. The desert provinces of Hadhramawt and Mahra are very remote areas and ample time, determination and money are required to explore this coast. Currently, the war makes travel to Yemen impossible as an independent surfer, so a recognised Yemeni tour agency will need to be appointed to provide all permits, drivers, 4WD jeeps, armed guards, tribal escorts and all day to day supplies such as food, water and camping equipment. None of this comes cheap and a two week trip here, (if/when the civil war ends) is going to cost plenty. Yemen is primarily beachbreaks with a couple of reefs and points. **Wadi** is the name given to a dry river bed and this one 20kms southwest of Mukalla leads to a bay with rights and lefts over volcanic rock. **Mukalla** has jetties with a small, polluted, right point breaking off one of them, but the old city has been surrounded by a wave-breaker since the late '80s, limiting the surf options. Check the rocky peninsula to the south of town. 15kms west of Ash Shihr, there is a village with huge circular oil storage tanks and three **Jetties**, which could provide sheltered surf when it's stormy and big but is completely out of bounds. **Sheba's Wedge** can be found on the long expanse of exposed beach that parallels the coast road. About 20kms west of Al Qumrah, a mini headland offers some shape. Imaginatively called **No Name** the rights are generally hollower and faster than the fat mushy lefts on the other side of the point, which are exposed to more SW wind. **Haswayn** does not look like a great set-up but the waves break with angle really close to shore. In **Al Ghaydah**, check the village by the coast, there is a sloppy SE-facing beachbreak. All the accessible spots in between are just waiting for someone to discover and name them!

From June to August, it's never flat in the Arabian Sea thanks to the SW monsoon, the world's most consistent weather system. By the time swells hits the Yemeni beaches, wave face height averages about 4ft (1.2m), rising to double this on big days and falling to 2-3ft on rare calm days, but always fast moving and powerful. The wind out at sea largely dies away by the time the swells make landfall and thanks to high coastal mountains the local winds are often funnelled offshore - at least for the mornings. Tidal range is average reaching 6ft max. Check Aden tide tables.

TOBY ADAMSON

Sheba's Wedge

TOBY ADAMSON

Sheba's Wedge

## TRAVEL INFORMATION

**Weather** – Summer surf season temperatures can average around 45ºC with highs nearer to 50ºC (113-122ºF), but the monsoon winds have a moderating influence on the coastal areas and the temperature in Al-Mukalla hovers around 30ºC (86ºF). Humidity is completely overwhelming. Afternoon winds can get strong and are very hot. Rainfall is unlikely but the eastern mountains catch a little cloud and mist from the monsoon. The water is in the high 20s to low 30s (85ºF).

**Lodging and Food** – Mukalla was the place to find a hotel from 10-50/dbl/n but war means all bets are off. Exploring the coast means camping out on the beaches. Food is cheap, but in the desert areas consists of little but fish and rice.

**Nature and Culture** – If the political situation ever calms down then Yemen will quite rightly become one of the biggest tourist destinations in the Islamic world. Highlights are the old town of Sana'a, the hundreds of fortified mountain villages, the ruins of ancient Kingdoms lost deep in the desert, the centuries old mud brick skyscraper cities of the Hadhramawt and simply mingling with the Yemenis and absorbing the culture and lifestyle of the worlds last remaining traditional Islamic society.

**Hazards and Hassles** – In the current situation it's not possible to visit Yemen, visas are not being issued and much of the surf area is in the hand of al-Qaeda. Terrorist attacks and kidnappings, lack of infrastructure, travel restrictions, high costs, sharks (on Socotra) and the heat make it a tough trip.

**Handy Hints** – There is no surf culture whatsoever, so bring everything. Respect the Islamic tradition and culture and keep an open mind. The tourist offices are of no real help. Lonely Planet's Oman, UAE and Arabia guide contains the best information on Yemen written by Stuart Butler, one of the few people to have surfed Yemen.

| STATISTICS | | J F | M A | M J | J A | S O | N D |
|---|---|---|---|---|---|---|---|
| SWELL | Direction | | | | | | |
| | Size (ft) | 1 | 0 | 4-5 | 5-6 | 3 | 1-2 |
| WIND | Direction | | | | | | |
| | Force | F3 | F2 | F3-F4 | F4 | F3 | F3 |
| WATER | Wetsuit | | | | | | |
| | Temp/°C | 25 | 27 | 29 | 25 | 26 | 26 |
| WEATHER | Rainfall/mm | 3 | 2 | 0 | 4 | 0 | 3 |
| | days/mth | 1 | 0 | 0 | 1 | 0 | 1 |
| | Min temp/°C | 22 | 24 | 28 | 28 | 26 | 23 |
| | Max temp/°C | 28 | 31 | 36 | 36 | 35 | 29 |

# East Oman

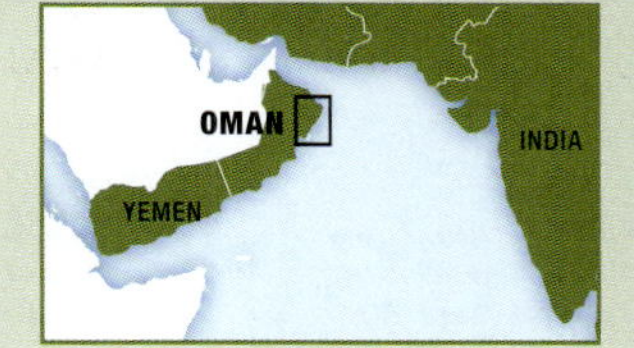




The Sultanate of Oman is 82% desert and the coastline extends from the Strait of Hormuz in the north, to Yemen in the south. It's possible to reach this coastline swept by summer monsoon swells in 7-8 hours drive from Dubai. Consequently ex pats had been riding some of these northerly spots for a decade before a Surfer Mag trip to the 'Empty Quarter' in 2000 exposed the area's potential.

+ CONSTANT SEASONAL WINDSWELL
+ FUN SIZE, VIRGIN WAVES
+ HOLLOW RIGHT POINTBREAKS
+ TROUBLE-FREE ENVIRONMENT

- MONSOON SEASON ONLY
- ONSHORE EXPOSED SPOTS
- NO FACILITIES, ENTERTAINMENT
- INLAND HEAT, GUSTY WINDS

Whale Rock

JS CALLAHAN/SURFEXPLORE

## TRAVEL INFORMATION

**Weather** – Masirah Island is hot and dry with short periods of very heavy rain in Oct-Dec and March-April. Temps peak at around 35°C (96°F) during May-June. June to August, sees the strong winds of the SW monsoon, known as the Khareef or Harif and humidity is high. Day and night temps vary a lot in the desert so bring a warm sleeping bag. Use a shorty for the high windchill factor.

**Lodging and Food** – A variety of accommodation can be found In Muscat, Al Ashkharah (hotels and Youth Hostel) and on Masirah ranging from $40-$80 p/r/p/n. Book early for the summer season! Camping is the only option to stay in front of Jazirah. Fish is cheap and plentiful - lots of dates and tea!

**Nature and Culture** – Gathering rare shells (like eloise), gazing at wild camels or huge green turtles in the water is about as fun as it gets. No beer or other addictive substances! Go fishing or wind/kitesurfing.

**Hazards and Hassles** – Despite the raw nature of the country, it's trouble free with regard to diseases, thefts or muggings. It is however, a desert with myriads of flies! Avoid sharp shells on rocks at pointbreaks. Plenty of stingray and jellyfish. Avoid Ramadan. Don't expect any locals, crowds, hustlers etc.

**Handy Hints** – Take everything, including a longboard/funboard and kitesurf for the numerous windy days. Don't forget books, music, games etc for killing time. This is an extremely peaceful set-up, relax and go slowly in the heat! Boats with 80hp outboards can be rented to explore the coastline.

In the Sharqiya region, **Sur** works in winter with a strong NE onshore wind, bringing some weak but rideable waves to the beaches along the corniche north of the harbour. **Ra's Al Hadd** should pick up more swell along a straight stretch of sand that's known as a green turtle nesting site. The east coast, aka the Pirate Coast gets S-SW monsoon swells in summer. A favourite with Dubai surfers and wind crew, Asilah has beachbreaks and, a sheltered right breaks off **Whale Rock** at the rivermouth, but the highlight is **Joe's Point**, a long, right pointbreak that needs bigger swells to wrap around the rocks. Gets really windy and strong rips parallel the beach heading north. In **Al Ashkharah** go to Shipwreck Beach, especially in decent sized, powerful surf. The reef extends out a fair way, so at low tide long, mellow righthanders break 100-200m off the beach. If it's small, there's a surfable shoredump at high tide and there are further righthand points to the south down to the protected low tide spot at **Bandar As Saqlah**. From Sana a ferry can be caught to Masirah, Oman's largest island. A quality righthander can allegedly be found close to the **BBC** telecom towers on a big swell but permission from the Jazirah military is needed to gain access. The closest spot to Hilf is **Ras Al Jazirah**, a sectiony, semi-long, righthand point breaking over rocks near a fishing camp. Getting in and out is fairly easy but bear in mind, there are usually strong cross-shore winds, rips and possibly some wind/kitesurfers. **Shi'inzi**'s powerful beach and reef combo closes out when it gets overhead. **Ras Al Ya**'s rights are tucked in behind the headland and handle the strong winds, but tend to be a bit fat and mushy. Masirah's SE-facing coast has at least eight potential righthand points and it's usually twice the size of the Jazirah area, but will be blown out from 10am onwards. **Haqal** hugs the rocks producing a juicy righthander that gets much better at high tide. **Ra's Kaydah** is the last headland before the coast turns too far into the wind. The outside tip of the reef has some sucky sections, providing the SW'er isn't blowing too hard. There is still much potential for discoveries on Masirah and the 500km of coast stretching south to the border of Yemen.

Masirah Island

JEFF DIVINE

The SW monsoon winds between June and September bring constant 8-12ft windswells from a SE-SW direction with a 6-12 sec period. Up north the swells don't have much power but the headhigh messy beachbreaks can be fun. The dominant monsoon winds are SW (Jun-Aug) and NE (Nov-Jan). 75% of cyclones that form in the Arabian Sea, end up on the Oman coast! Semidiurnal tides with diurnal inequality, reaching 5ft (1.6m) max; high tides are often the best time to surf.

| STATISTICS | | J F | M A | M J | J A | S O | N D |
|---|---|---|---|---|---|---|---|
| SWELL | Direction | | | | | | |
| | Size (ft) | 1 | 1-2 | 3-4 | 4-5 | 2-3 | 1 |
| WIND | Direction | | | | | | |
| | Force | F4 | F3-F4 | F3 | F3-F4 | F3-F4 | F3-F4 |
| WATER | Wetsuit | | | | | | |
| | Temp/°C | 22 | 23 | 25 | 24 | 23 | 23 |
| WEATHER | Rainfall/mm | 3 | 3 | 3 | 3 | 2 | 7 |
| | days/mth | 0 | 1 | 0 | 0 | 0 | 1 |
| | Min temp/°C | 24 | 26 | 29 | 30 | 28 | 25 |
| | Max temp/°C | 26 | 31 | 35 | 31 | 31 | 28 |

# East Iran

**Tucked between Iraq, Afghanistan and Pakistan, the political and geographical landscape of Iran isn't exactly perfect for a trouble-free surf trip. The southern province of Balochistan borders the Gulf of Oman, which connects with the Indian Ocean, providing real opportunities to discover new waves along a sparsely inhabited, desert seaboard among a string of small ports and even smaller fishing villages.**

+ WARM EMPTY WAVES
+ BREAK DIVERSITY
+ CONSISTENT IN MONSOON
+ EXOTIC CULTURE

- SHORT SWELL SEASON
- PAINFUL HEAT
- MILD ONSHORES
- LANGUAGE BARRIER

Boats abound in a village like **Tang**, but their operators rather stick to their routine than take curious surfers the 2km to the rights off the hammerhead peninsula. Access is an issue around Gurdin, requiring a good 4x4 to explore and also at **Pozm** where the lefts in front of the jetty break too close to the cliffs for comfort. The best waves are out the end of the Konarak peninsula but a naval base keeps the area shut down so head east on the reliable coastal road. Negotiate with employees of the **Aab** water desalination plant to surf the perfect beginner's beachbreak either side of the breakwalls. Chabahar is a fast growing city, thanks to being the biggest oceanic port in Iran and a free trade zone. The northern beaches are too sheltered from the swell, so head to Darya Bozorg (Big Sea) for a surf check, then head east to **Lakposht** where a good beachbreak can be surfed with only turtles for company. A stop at the **Maahi** fish cannery offers a great view of what may be the best pointbreak around. Unfortunately there's no way down the 60ft cliffs and only a boat ride from Ramin can reach the lefts that peel below. **Ramin** probably offers the best combo of surf and access. West of the port, a beachbreak offers mellow, crumbly waves, at least till the heavy shorebreak turns on. To the east lies a left pointbreak dubbed **Kabab** since it offers several sections instead of a straight ride. The waves start as a heavy peak facing the point before flattening out and then reforming into the bay to offer some of the best barrel opportunities around. There's a longer pointbreak setup towards the shrimp factory, **Meygou**, but the lefts don't line-up that well and cliffs complicate the access. The road then follows a string of consistent beachbreaks with plenty of potential under the shadow of the Mars Mountains. **Bod** has suffered from a harbour extension but there may be some sand build up on the E side jetty. Beachbreaks continue until reaching **Beris**, which features a large port and a couple of points. One of these offers a perfectly wrapping lefthander, but requires tons of swell to get going and only a boat or a very long paddle could get you to the bottom of the huge cliff. Neither Pusht or Pesabandar offer anything much different. There's a last treat towards **Gwatar** where water flowing from a man made irrigation canal forms a rivermouth righthander that peels for about 100m. Since the murky water is discharged by a nearby shrimp farm its quality is dubious at best.

In June, July and August, regular monsoonal SW winds create constant 3-12ft swells. Tropical storms can occasionally create even bigger waves. The monsoon produces onshore local winds from the southern quadrant which can temporarily blow out some spots, but mornings will be cleaner. Tides follow a semidiurnal tide pattern with diurnal inequality, reaching 3m on spring tides.

## TRAVEL INFORMATION

**Weather** – The place is called "Char-Bahar" which means four springs due to its mellow warm weather and cooling breeze from the Gulf of Oman. The zone is the warmest part of Iran in winter with average temps of 19°C (66°F) and the coolest part in summer with temps around 32°C (90°F). Boardies only for the summer surf season.

**Lodging and Food** – Chabahar's best hotel is the 4* Lipar located in the Free-Zone ($80 double). Sepideh, Daryayi and Keshtirani are much cheaper options in town. Remember that AC is a must. Kababs served with rice are the national dish. No beer, try doogh, a fizzy drink made from yoghurt, spices and aromatic herbs. Cheap food, usually $2-3 a meal.

**Nature and Culture** – The free zone provides shopping opportunities, but fishing villages don't. Check out the curiously eroded "Mars Mountains" or the Gelfeshan mud volcano.

**Hazards and Hassles** – Beachbreaks can hide some nasty rocks; remember you're a long way from medical attention. Heat is the main danger, don't go anywhere without water. Iran is an Islamic republic, don't stray from the laws. Getting to Iran might be discouraged by family, embassy and insurance.

**Handy Hints** – English is seldom spoken. Persian (Farsi) is the official language, although locals mainly speak "Baluchi" which is derived from Hindi languages. Even though it's 40°C, dress codes require long sleeves. T-shirts on land and boardshorts in the water seem tolerated… but only for men! Take plenty of wax and at least 2 boards.

OLIVIER SERVAIRE

Kabab

| STATISTICS | | J F | M A | M J | J A | S O | N D |
|---|---|---|---|---|---|---|---|
| SWELL | Direction | | | | | | |
| | Size (ft) | 0-1 | 1 | 3 | 4 | 2 | 0-1 |
| WIND | Direction | | | | | | |
| | Force | F3-F4 | F2-F3 | F4 | F3-F4 | F3 | F2-F3 |
| WATER | Wetsuit | | | | | | |
| | Temp/°C | 23 | 25 | 29 | 29 | 28 | 25 |
| WEATHER | Rainfall/mm | 18 | 9 | 5 | 55 | 8 | 7 |
| | days/mth | 2 | 1 | 1 | 2 | 1 | 1 |
| | Min temp/°C | 12 | 19 | 26 | 29 | 24 | 14 |
| | Max temp/°C | 25 | 31 | 36 | 35 | 33 | 29 |

Tang · Pozm · Aab · Lakposht · Maahi · Ramin · Kabab · Meygou · Bod · Beris · Gwatar

GULF OF OMAN

# West Pakistan

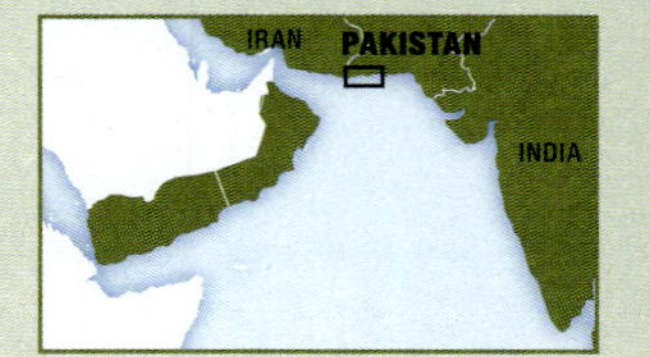


+ CONSTANT MONSOON SWELL
+ MELLOW RIGHT POINTBREAKS
+ DISCOVERY POTENTIAL
+ NO DISEASE OR BUGS

- SHORT SURF SEASON
- ONSHORE WINDS
- MILITARY RESTRICTIONS
- VERY HOT, WINDY AND DUSTY

Pakistan split from India in 1947 to form an independent nation for Muslims and has seen many changes in its short history. In June 2001 a crew of 12 people including four surfers explored the Makran Desert's coast looking for rideable surf in the Baluchistan province, its desert vistas containing formidable mountain ranges of amazing rock formations. However, they found that the deserted Arabian Sea coastline has shallow inshore sandbanks, especially around reefs and capes, which dissipate rather than focus the swell power. Subsequently the events of 9/11/2001 made any foreign travel in this region impossible and in more recent times huge infrastructure investment by China has resulted in a double edged sword. While the creation of the Makran Highway has cut travel times between the limited spots dramatically, dredging and harbour construction has changed or destroyed several potential setups.

DAN HAYLOCK

Mirages

The coastline features many exposed beaches such as **Ganz**, which could fire in the monsoon transition months when the SW winds aren't howling. Ras Pishukan should be better, but the line-up is shifty and unpredictable. Further inside the point, Pishukan had the potential for perfect headhigh rights, but a harbour development has now engulfed the line-up. Even deeper in the bay, **Pasao Kaur** is perfectly offshore, but won't get bigger than waisthigh peelers. On one side of the hammerhead peninsula is **Gwadar West**, a mushy, exposed beachbreak with boiling-hot water that has become trapped in the bay. To the east of Gwadar is **Surbandar**, an active fishing village and home to another new harbour development sheltered by a spectacular bluff. It is unclear whether the long 4-6ft mellow rights that were ridden in 2001 still work. Between Gwadar and Pasni, most of the coastal access points are very shallow, with **Ras Kappar** and **Shamal Bandar** providing the best possibilities. Pasni itself offers three types of breaks in a short stretch. **Jabal Zarain** is exposed and big and messy during the SW monsoon. The best bet for organised waves is **Ras Jaddi**, a rocky ledge filled with sand that throws up cross-shore lefts at high tide. Don't miss **Mirages**, 45mins drive away, a symmetrically perfect peeling right, which unfortunately rarely exceeds 3-4ft on the biggest swells.

The SW monsoon winds between June and August are the strongest winds on earth in the tropical zone producing constant 8-12ft windswell from a 240° direction with a 6-15 second period. These swells lack the power to refract around the capes and thus create 4-8ft onshore beachbreaks and 1-2ft clean right pointbreaks on the SE-E facing set-ups. The SW wind, although frequently strong later in the day, is often calm (never offshore) in the early morning. During the SW monsoon, ocean circulation and therefore currents and drift are clockwise (west to east), while during NE monsoon they are predominantly anticlockwise. Pakistan has semidiurnal tides with diurnal inequality, reaching 2.8m max and high tides are the best time to surf, since they help the swell get over the shallow shoals and into the beaches and points.

## TRAVEL INFORMATION

**Weather** – The Makran Coast lies outside the monsoon system of weather, therefore, the climate is extremely dry. The annual rainfall is less than 15cm, which combined with the natural geographical features makes it a daunting environment. Temps never drop below 30°C (86°F) and hover around 38°C (101°F) after noon. Airborne dust reduces visibility and gets into every nook and cranny. Sea surface temperature of the Arabian Sea varies between 24°C (75°F) and 30°C (86°F) from NE to SW monsoon.

**Lodging and Food** – Pearl Continental Hotel on the Gwadar Hammerhead provides A/C rooms ($130/dble w breakfast). A cheaper option is the basic Rest House, facing West Bay from $10/n. Dhal, nan, fish and dates (300 varieties) will be your food.

**Nature and Culture** – Gwadar is a huge chunk of rock 10km long, 2km wide and 200m high, linked by a narrow stretch of sand 20km long. The white clay cliffs are unreal. Check out the shipyards, the harbour, mud volcanoes and the lively Bazaar at night. It's incredibly cheap. Islamic beliefs are strong, but more liberal than neighbouring countries.

**Hazards and Hassles** – Apart from dozens of coastguard checks, the intense heat and dust, occasional sea and land snakes (garr) and rare sharks, it's pretty cool.

**Handy Hints** – Due to continuous upheaval in the region surf trips are still of an exploratory nature as tourist infrastructure is non-existent. Hire TRANSPAKISTAN services to organise transport, food, translation and guidance. Bring everything you need and let them take you to the surf spots.

| STATISTICS | | J F | M A | M J | J A | S O | N D |
|---|---|---|---|---|---|---|---|
| SWELL | Direction | | | | | | |
| | Size (ft) | 1 | 1-2 | 3-4 | 4-5 | 2-3 | 1 |
| WIND | Direction | | | | | | |
| | Force | F3-F4 | F2-F3 | F4 | F3-F4 | F3 | F2-F3 |
| WATER | Wetsuit | | | | | | |
| | Temp/°C | 24 | 26 | 29 | 29 | 28 | 25 |
| WEATHER | Rainfall/mm | 9 | 4 | 4 | 73 | 9 | 4 |
| | days/mth | 1 | 0 | 1 | 3 | 1 | 1 |
| | Min temp/°C | 16 | 23 | 29 | 29 | 26 | 18 |
| | Max temp/°C | 27 | 31 | 35 | 33 | 33 | 30 |

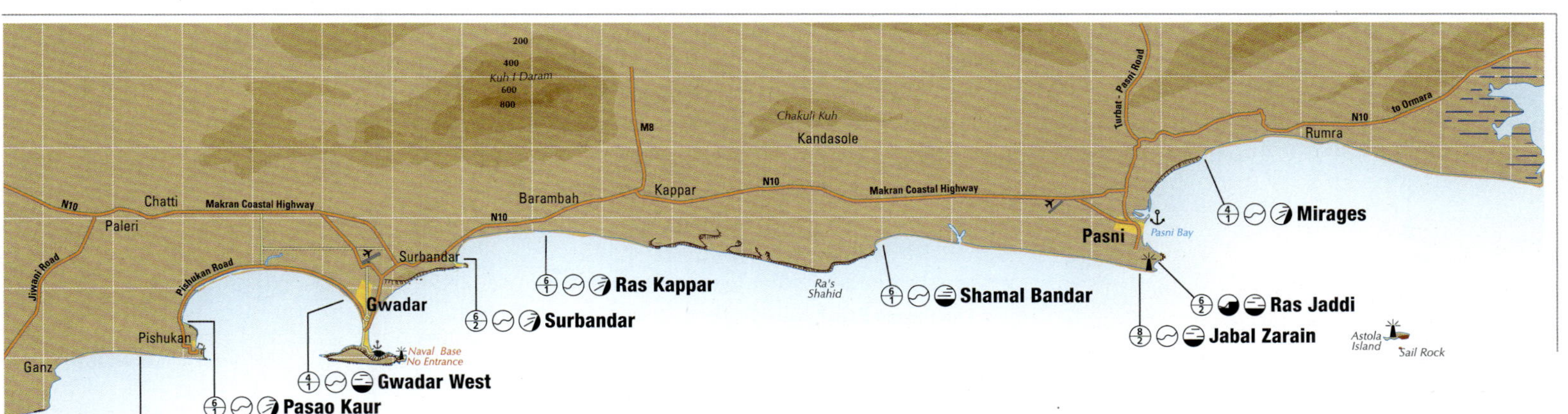

# Kerala and Tamil Nadu INDIA

On the southernmost tip of India, west-facing Kerala state is mainly all straight beachbreaks, punctuated by regular rivermouths and the occasional headland, which perfectly suits the small winter swells arriving between October and April. Rounding Cape Comorin southeast-facing Tamil Nadu has some playful pointbreaks that take advantage of larger S swells during the May to September period. This combination provides the flexibility to score fun, warm, uncrowded waves for most of the year, while experiencing the kaleidoscope of culture that defines India.

+ **CONSISTENT SWELLS**
+ **WARM, TROPICAL WATER**
+ **LAID BACK AND CHEAP**
+ **FASCINATING CULTURE**

- **ONSHORE, MUSHY CONDITIONS**
- **SMALL OR CLOSED-OUT BREAKS**
- **POLLUTED WATER & BEACHES**
- **LONG DISTANCES BETWEEN SPOTS**

## TRAVEL INFORMATION

**Weather** – Kerala is hot and humid but the Arabian Sea cools things down a bit compared to the interior. From June to September the SW monsoon's torrential rains feed a network of rivers and the backwaters. The temperature normally ranges from 28-32°C (82-90°F). Humidity is high and rises to 90%. From November to February, it's relatively dry and cool thanks to the NE monsoon (high tourist season). Highest temps occur April-May, the best time for surf. Expect boardshort-warm water year-round.

**Lodging and Food** – Travelling in India can suit any budget. Soul and Surf House near Varkala at $85 per night (soulandsurf.com) with surf guiding and rentals on offer. Vedanta Wake Up in Kovalam: A/C double room at $17 (low) and $28 (high). Most places serve a "thali" meal during the day.

**Nature and Culture** – Cruise in a traditional houseboat on the mesmerizing backwaters of Kumarakom or Aleppey. Enjoy Ayurvedic (oil) massages and treatments. Local surf numbers are growing thanks to Kovalam Surf Club (kovalamsurfclub.com).

**Hazards and Hassles** – Onshore surf can create intense rips, swimmers drown every year. Pollution can be extreme. Lots of reptiles: Cobra, viper, rat snake, flying snake.

**Handy Hints** – You can hire various surfboards and bodyboards on Kovalam beach and at Varkala from $6 a day. Plan to leave a board if possible with local surf organisations. Bring wax and leashes.

GREG EWING

Varkala

Heading south into Kerala the first real deviation from a straight coastline is the Sluice gate called **River Temple**. When the flow is slow an A-frame peak can be created, but beware of the outward rip and inside rocks. At **Ed's**, a short headland produces fast tubing lefts and creates a launching point for the local fishing boats. In **Varkala** the red cliffs and surrounding beaches can produce a few winter options including a good right over large rocks off the headland from April until the monsoon blows it out. Rips are often strong at the beachies and close-outs are the norm if it's onshore. Dawnies rule here. A series of boulder jetties at **Shirleys** creates some workable sandbars for small swell days. Climb over the large dune at **Jengos** to find two large jetties, which used to produce long point-style waves on the north side until they were extended in 2014. More recently, peaky rights have started to break on the south side all through the monsoon until the banks were washed away. Kovalam has cheap hotels, laid-back places to hang out and crowds of surfers. **Hawa Beach** faces directly into the SW swell, with disorganised lefts forming off the scattered rocks at the southern end. The right at the north end of **Lighthouse Beach** is excellent in the W swells that accompany the SW monsoon, but it needs clean conditions. To the south is a multi-purpose, artificial surf reef completed in 2010 by ASR. Commissioned by Kerala Tourism, the reef initially worked, producing a left barrel, but soon after the first monsoon became damaged and now rarely works. Kovalam locals use **Poovar** as a bolt-hole from their crowded home break so show a friendly attitude. It can hold fast barrels when the inland estuarine system breaches the sandbar, although the name may give a clue as to what is flowing out! On large S swells head to east-facing Tamil Nadu. Just past Kanyakumari, check Vattakottai Fort where the sandy shores of the west coast make way for some submerged reefs. On very big S swells, go 100km northeast to **Manapad Point**, one of the best surfing spots in India, where an ancient lava flow extends into the water forming a right point with 400m rides. To the north **Tiruchendur** has some good little waves breaking over a rock shelf just 200 metres south of the temple.

GREG EWING

Lighthouse Beach

Southern India is a year-round destination with constant S swells being generated from the roaring forties. During the SW monsoon (May to September) this mixes with W-NW monsoon swells that range from 4-12ft. Larger S swells with decent period (12-20secs) will produce wrapping conditions for spots on the east coast. During this time the west coast will often be an onshore, closed-out mess. West coast beachbreaks are better when there's no wind or NE monsoon winds (mornings from Nov-Apr), which coincides with smaller south swells, creating clean conditions for the beachbreaks. Tides are semi-diurnal with daily inequality. Maximum tidal range is only 1m, which has very little affect on most spots.

| STATISTICS | | J F | M A | M J | J A | S O | N D |
|---|---|---|---|---|---|---|---|
| SWELL | Direction | | | | | | |
| | Size (ft) | 2 | 2-3 | 4-5 | 5 | 3-4 | 2-3 |
| WIND | Direction | | | | | | |
| | Force | F3-F4 | F2-F3 | F4 | F4 | F4 | F3-F4 |
| WATER | Wetsuit | | | | | | |
| | Temp/°C | 27 | 29 | 28 | 27 | 27 | 27 |
| WEATHER | Rainfall/mm | 15 | 78 | 451 | 546 | 261 | 102 |
| | days/mth | 2 | 5 | 14 | 13 | 10 | 6 |
| | Min temp/°C | 22 | 25 | 23 | 23 | 23 | 23 |
| | Max temp/°C | 31 | 32 | 30 | 29 | 30 | 31 |

# Visakhapatnam INDIA

**Visakhapatnam is a large harbour city located on the Bay of Bengal coast of India. Very few tourists visit Visag meaning it is possibly India's most overlooked surf destination with a series of right pointbreaks and reefs located within an hours drive. A fledgling surf community has now started to develop since the early explorers arrived in 2004.**

**+ RIGHT POINTBREAKS**
**+ PERFECT LONGBOARD WAVES**
**+ SW MONSOON CONSISTENCY**
**+ FASCINATING CULTURE**

**- SMALL WAVES**
**- POOR HYGIENE**
**- INTENSE HEAT**
**- CRAZY TRAFFIC**

## TRAVEL INFORMATION

**Weather** – Andhra Pradesh climate is subtropical dry with heat-waves and droughts in April-May. Torrential rains in summer and winter with two-thirds falling during SW monsoon (June-Sept). The coastal region receives the highest rainfall. Occasional floods cause transport chaos.

**Lodging and Food** – 5 star Park Hotel in Visag has luxury facilities, sea views and direct access to the beach ($110 full board). Next door is Palm Beach; A/C double room is $20. For access to Mangamari use AP Tourism Hotel in Rushi Konda $25 double+b'fast. Avoid street food, ice and un-bottled water!

**Nature and Culture** – Visit temples including the 1098AD Simhachalam. Climb Kailash Giri Park for Lord Shiva Parvathi statue and Lawson's Bay view.

**Hazards and Hassles** – Hundreds of shitters on the beach may cause bad smell, diarrhoea and possibly transmit disease. Favour dropping tides! If you cut yourself, treat with care and avoid infections. The flat rocks on the points don't require booties. Drink lots of fluids to withstand the intense heat.

**Handy Hints** – There is a small, friendly expat and local surf community. A longboard/SUP will be useful for the smaller days. Take lots of wax and expect to surf long waves with no-one but your crew, so come in a group and surf early. May-June are the best months. Be ready to face poverty and infirmity. Learn to understand the local way of saying yes, nodding the head sideways.

Horrendous cross-town traffic means beaches south of Dolphins Nose, a huge rock promontory sheltering the harbour, are rarely worth visiting. The most popular beach along the Visag Beach Road is **Rama Krishna**, a rocky stretch that gets out of control in strong trades and large windswell but occasionally gets good surf when a sandspit develops off the northern reef. The assorted peaks opposite the **Park Hotel** need light NW conditions and a bit of size to clear the many rocks lurking in a line-up that favours lefts. Visag's best right is **Lawson's Bay**, with a 500m+ ride from take-off to the beach. The outside needs to be glassy to be rideable and the rock suck-outs can be intimidating, but give the wave some powerful sections. After a series of cutbacks, the wave reforms and there's some aerial action close to shore with the backwash! Despite improved sewage pipes, the beach itself is still used as a toilet. **Tenneti Park** holds the biggest waves wrapping in off Waltair Point, but it needs to be a clean, lined-up swell and SW-W winds. Hollow from take-off before filling into endless cutback shoulders. Effortless entry from the keyhole means dry hair paddle-outs. **Rushikonda** tourist beach has nice facilities and the recently established Lonely Surfers School teaches the locals. The shallow beachbreak surf set-up isn't great, but there are some fun rights in winter and lefts in summer. The standout right point is **Mangamari** (aka Malibupeta or M'peta), where a rocky shoreline straddles a golden sand beach and waves peel for up to 800m on big glassy days in summer monsoon only. When the lines start bending by Mangamari Peta point, there is still 90% of the swell size breaking on the first rock clusters. At high tide, despite some backwash, waves can unzip pretty fast with a real tubular wall, breaking in front of the rocks that cuts the wave in two at lower tides. Heavy refraction inside the bay means it is offshore all day in the SW monsoon and the fun sandbanks are perfectly suited to longboarding/SUP. Needless to say it's a long walk back, zigzagging between turds on the beach. The scenic rights of **Bhimuni** have a sucky take-off leading into long sectiony walls that work best at high tide on bigger wrapping S swells. Crazy art installations right on the beach. For the adventurous drive five hours north to Kalingapatnam, where small crumbly rights break on the outside of Sandy Point for such a distance that jelly-legs are guaranteed.

YEP
Rushikonda

The Bay of Bengal creates 3 types of swells. From May to August the SW monsoon produces 4-8ft wind-driven swells from Sri Lanka, but they decrease markedly in size when refracting inside the points. Exposed shores will be a messy 3-6ft, while north-facing bays break at 1-3ft with offshore conditions in S-SW winds. Mornings are often glassy, while moderate SE-SW seabreezes usually blow after 10am. Southern hemisphere, long period swells are not as frequent. Cyclones are rare (6 per year) pushing NE-E swells. The biggest tides reach 1.5-1.8m, affecting some rocky sections.

YEP
Mangamari

| STATISTICS | | J F | M A | M J | J A | S O | N D |
|---|---|---|---|---|---|---|---|
| SWELL | Direction | | | | | | |
| | Size (ft) | 1-2 | 2 | 3-4 | 3 | 2-3 | 2 |
| WIND | Direction | | | | | | |
| | Force | F3 | F3 | F4 | F4 | F3-F4 | F4 |
| WATER | Wetsuit | | | | | | |
| | Temp/°C | 26 | 28 | 29 | 28 | 28 | 27 |
| WEATHER | Rainfall/mm | 9 | 18 | 82 | 138 | 190 | 37 |
| | days/mth | 1 | 4 | 9 | 10 | 2 | 6 |
| | Min temp/°C | 19 | 25 | 28 | 26 | 25 | 23 |
| | Max temp/°C | 30 | 34 | 36 | 33 | 32 | 31 |

# Southwest Sri Lanka

The south coast of this extraordinarily beautiful country is open to plenty of long distance SW swells, but onshore monsoonal winds limit the surf season to the much quieter swell period of Dec-March. At this time of year, waist to headhigh waves are common and the glassy conditions are perfect. The centre of the south coast surf scene stretches from Hikkaduwa to Welligama with lots of options for all surf abilities.

+ QUALITY MELLOW WAVES
+ OFFSHORE NE MONSOON
+ BEAUTIFUL SCENERY
+ FRIENDLY LOCALS

– WIND & SWELL CONFLICT
– SMALL WAVES
– NO WORLD-CLASS SPOTS
– HIKKADUWA LOCALISM

ANDREW SHIELD

The Rock

On a big swell, **North Jetty** will catch some long lefts over a rugged reef bang in front of the harbour wall. The outside reef of **Benny's** offers a pretty radical and fairly long left that can hold big swells. The most consistent and crowded spot is **Main Reef**, which has fun, occasionally tubing, but generally slow lefts and rights on a flat coral reef facing the A-Frame Guest House. **Inside Reef** is another, left-leaning peak that deals out some power, without as many takers. The long stretch simply called **Beachbreak** varies from a fat beginners wave, to an occasionally fun, wedgy shorebreak, good for bodyboarders. If it ever gets big, the closed-up **Rivermouth** will have a rideable wave, although the water can be very dirty at this fishing beach. A rare right breaks in the old town of Gallé, but the often ignored **Dewata Beach** can have fun longboard waves and is one of the few spots that works off-season. Water quality is very suspect after heavy rains. The magnificent curl of beach at **Unawatuna** is largely sheltered from surf by fringing reefs, but a playful little right used to break off the western point. Sadly an new harbour wall has ruined it and only on the biggest days will it give a rolling, soft, inside right good for mals and surf schools. **Koggala** has a left reef with a bit more push or improvers can try the deep rolling reef peak at South Beach. **The Rock** is a super-consistent, focused peak, with fast-running lefts and shorter softer rights in all tides and NE winds. Always crowded from dawn but size certainly thins the crowd. **Kabalana Beach** can be a fun learner's wave with the occasional day of peeling waves. Just south of the Ahangama fishing poles, Rajith is the next reef with more longish walls both ways and it is a competition site so it's obviously consistent. The peak next to **Devil Island** holds user-friendly rights and lefts over sand and coral. SW swell is best and on bigger days you can get a 150m ride from the rock to the beach on the longer walling lefts up to headhigh. **Midigama Right** is a suckier little wave on the peak over the coral reef just a short easy paddle from shore. Fattens out into the channel that separates it from **Lazy Lefts**, where a short steep section then turns into a slow fat left that trundles along for 100m. Can get a bit of backwash at high so low tide is best. **Rams Right** is a short, powerful peak that breaks over a shallow reef and offers frequent tubes on the right and tapered left walls. A string of reef peaks to the east include Plantation, Coconuts, Ketature and Jungle Beach that can all have some quality on the odd day. Popular but polluted, **Weligama** beachbreak can be surfed even when small and is ideal for beginners. Beautiful **Mirissa** beach holds a very fickle right point at the western end of the bay plus a left. Madiha and **Sabine Reef** at Polhena have both fast lefts and righthanders that hold up to 6ft in a good SW swell. The eastern end of **Matara Beach** gathers in plenty of swell to a wide, open strand that is perfect for beginners and cruisers at low to mid tide.

CALLUM MORSE

Weligama

The consistent SW swell season (April-Oct) will be accompanied by frequent SW to WNW onshores. It's still possible to surf in the morning but expect rain, dirty water and strong winds. Shoulder season is best when NE winds are most likely to coincide with the bigger SW groundswells. During the dry season, waves are typically 2-6ft and clean, but the afternoons tend to go onshore. Tidal ranges are less than 1m, but affect the shallow reefs significantly.

## TRAVEL INFORMATION

**Weather** – Maha means NE monsoon (Nov-Mar) and is the driest and sunniest period. The transition periods have very hot temperatures (March-April), then the SW monsoon (Yala) lasts from April to Oct, bringing lots of strong onshores and rain. Water temperature averages 27°C (80°F) all year-round.

**Lodging and Food** – Sri Lanka has a myriad of accommodation from basic to luxury and dozens of surf camps/schools. Sion Surf Camp fr $555/wk inc yoga. The food in Sri Lanka is phenomenal - curries, plenty of seafood and fresh fruit from $5 for a meal.

**Nature and Culture** – Visit colonial Gallé, climb Adam's peak for the spectacular sunrise and see the Buddhist temples in Kandy. Wildlife (elephants and leopards) is plentiful in the national parks. Hikkaduwa has surprisingly good nightlife.

**Hazards and Hassles** – Localism in Hikkaduwa and increasingly Weligama - be mellow in the line-up. Sewage pollution and coral cuts mix badly.

**Handy Hints** – Many "surf shops"; try A-Frame and Cheeky Monkeys. Basic surf schools line the sands of the main beaches where battered boards can be rented for $3/h. Coaching quality is highly variable so stick to experienced outfits like Surf School Sri Lanka. Learn a few words of Sinhala and you'll be greeted with smiles.

North Jetty
Benny's
Main Reef
Inside Reef
Beachbreak
Rivermouth
Dewata Beach
Unawatuna
Kogalla
The Rock
Kabalana
Devil Island
Midigama Right
Lazy Lefts
Rams Right
Mirissa
Weligama
Matara Beach
Sabine Reef
PERFECT WAVE
SURF SCHOOL SRI LANKA
SION SURF CAMP
Ambalangoda
Akurala
Baddegama
Hikkaduwa
Dodanduwa
Galle
Talpe
Koggala
Weligama
Mirissa
Matara
Dondra
Gandara
Dikwella
Kirinda
Hakumana
Akuressa
Kananke

| STATISTICS | | J F | M A | M J | J A | S O | N D |
|---|---|---|---|---|---|---|---|
| SWELL | Direction | | | | | | |
| | Size (ft) | 3 | 3-4 | 5 | 6 | 4-5 | 3 |
| WIND | Direction | | | | | | |
| | Force | F3-F4 | F3 | F4 | F4 | F4 | F3 |
| WATER | Wetsuit | | | | | | |
| | Temp/°C | 27 | 28 | 28 | 28 | 27 | 27 |
| WEATHER | Rainfall/mm | 92 | 190 | 282 | 132 | 255 | 250 |
| | days/mth | 8 | 15 | 22 | 15 | 19 | 15 |
| | Min temp/°C | 22 | 23 | 25 | 25 | 24 | 22 |
| | Max temp/°C | 31 | 31 | 31 | 29 | 29 | 30 |

# Southeast Sri Lanka

First surfed in 1964, Arugam Bay is no surf secret. Despite the 2004 Boxing Day tsunami disaster, the waves are still breaking better than ever, with consistently small, perfect righthand peelers that make Arugam Bay an intermediates heaven. The civil war kept the village in its most basic form, but these days, there are new roads, bridges and more accommodation options for the growing stream of foreign surfers searching for the long, sheltered sand-bottom pointbreaks along this southeastern coast.

- + CONSISTENTLY CLEAN & RIDEABLE
- + LAID-BACK FRIENDLY VIBE
- + AMAZING SIGHTS AND WILDLIFE
- + CHEAP

- – CONSISTENTLY SMALL
- – CROWDED ARUGAM BAY
- – SLOW TRANSPORT
- – INTENSE HEAT AND INSECTS

Wave quality varies depending on sand build-up from point to point, which is heavily affected by river flows. **Sangakamanda** rivermouth is hardly ever surfed since access is difficult and wave quality not really worth it. **Komari** is a long walk from the end of the road, hard to find and gets blown out in the afternoon sea breezes. The best northern spot is **Pottuvil Point**, which can have 800m long rides from the tip to the beach, with a barrel in the middle in front of the huge granite rocks. **Pottuvil Beach** has a scalloped cove with point-style rights pushing wide and deep, making it a perfect beginners zone only 20mins tuk-tuk ride from Arugam Bay. The **Main Beach** is usually a close-out, but near the bridge, there can be a wedgy A-frame over the offshore rocks. The reform in front of **Mambo's** guesthouse can be a beginner's heaven, because it is always offshore, grooming tiny perfect walls, close to shore, making it simple to walk back up the beach. The southern point of **Arugam Bay** is a top-class wave breaking over an old coral reef, which can be dangerously shallow and sectiony at low tide. It's very consistent and often crowded with occasional barrels in front of the corner, but the afternoon SE sea breeze messes it up. South of the landmark **Crocodile Rock** is a sandy point with mushy rights, requiring a 20 min walk to get to. **Peanut Farm** is the best quality option within easy travel of Arugam, where sucky rights break close to the rocks, while the beachbreak is perfect for beginners. **Panama Rights** only works when the rivermouth is closed, offering rocky rights and a tiny reform by the boats. **Okanda**, is about 1h by tuk-tuk from A-Bay and picks up as much swell onto a sucky outside sandbar below a whale-shaped rock. The super-fun walls inside the cove are always offshore. Yala National Park offers a huge unexplored surf area that's consistent until the midday sea breeze sets in, but access should only be attempted by boat from Kumana. Ask the Rangers about surfing **Yala Rights**, but expect to pay entry fee and jeep hire. On the east side of Yala National Park, the most popular and expensive Block 1 entrance leads to **Palatupana** village, where there is a guest-house and a decent little right point off a rocky shore. **Kirinda** jetties hold some easy, small, but clean peeling waves.

The main swell producer is the SW monsoon pushing constant 4-10ft SW windswell from May-August. Long-distance S groundswells arrive between March and November. Swell direction matters and S-SE is obviously better than S-SW. Bengal Bay does produce some rare NE swells in the 2-4ft range, but it's mostly onshore. During the SW monsoon, light offshores blow up to 11am, before the low to moderate S-SE sea breeze starts messing up the outside sections. Tidal range is only 2ft max.

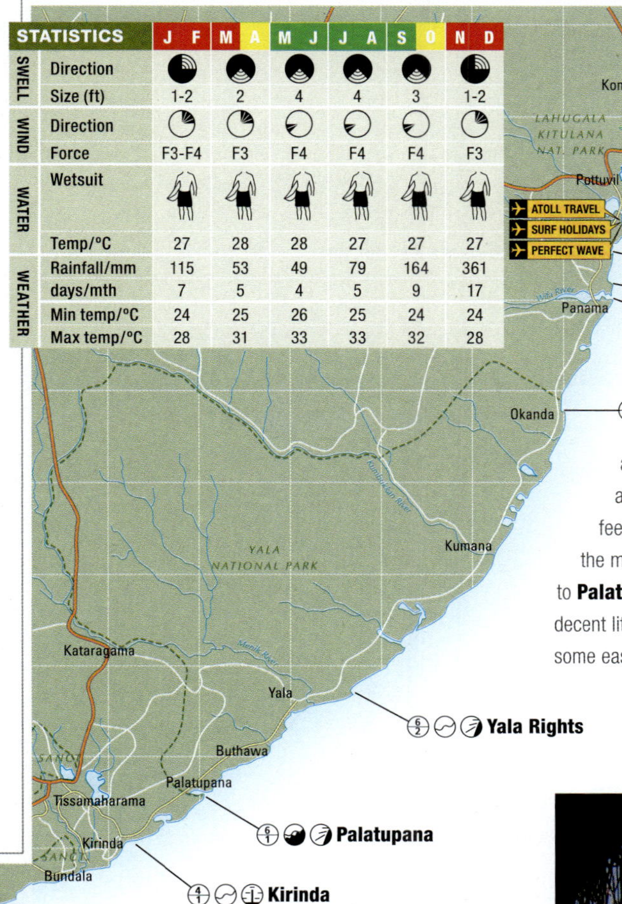

| STATISTICS | | J F | M A | M J | J A | S O | N D |
|---|---|---|---|---|---|---|---|
| SWELL | Direction | | | | | | |
| | Size (ft) | 1-2 | 2 | 4 | 4 | 3 | 1-2 |
| WIND | Direction | | | | | | |
| | Force | F3-F4 | F3 | F4 | F4 | F4 | F3 |
| WATER | Wetsuit | | | | | | |
| | Temp/°C | 27 | 28 | 28 | 27 | 27 | 27 |
| WEATHER | Rainfall/mm | 115 | 53 | 49 | 79 | 164 | 361 |
| | days/mth | 7 | 5 | 4 | 5 | 9 | 17 |
| | Min temp/°C | 24 | 25 | 26 | 25 | 24 | 24 |
| | Max temp/°C | 28 | 31 | 33 | 33 | 32 | 28 |



## TRAVEL INFORMATION

**Weather** – Arugam Bay area is ideally located to avoid the ravages of the two annual monsoons that hit the island from opposite directions - the SW (May-September) and NE (Nov-Feb). This southeastern corner is the driest part of the country and weather records show an average of 330 sunshine days/year! Boardshorts year-round.

**Lodging and Food** – Cheap beach guest-houses like Arugam Bay Surf Resort cost $20/d for room with fan. Medium priced Hideaway is $50/d/dbl and great food ($66B&B). A/C places include Siam Hotel ($45/n/tw), Tri-Star ($40-60). Book Stardust Hotel with Atoll Travel. Food is tasty, sometimes spicy, around $5 for a full meal.

**Nature and Culture** – Yala National Park is the main wildlife sanctuary; enter from Okanda (cheaper than Tissama), but you need to rent a car ($50-80/day). Check Kumana Bird Sanctuary, Hindu shrines like Katara-gama, Sigiriya citadel, Kandy Perahera Festiva. Ayurvedic massages. Full moon parties!

**Hazards and Hassles** – Crowding at A-Bay is heavy, especially July-Sept. Expect bad etiquette and drop-ins. The roads are slow, there's very little shade at most spots, so take enough water and make sure your tuk-tuk driver will pick you up after surfing.

**Handy Hints** – Bring cash, because the Bank of Ceylon in Pottuvil is a nightmare. You can rent NSP boards at Aloha and SurfNSun. Bring a fish type of board.

MICHAEL KEW

Crocodile Rock

JASON FEAST

Arugam Bay

# North Malé MALDIVES

The Maldives has gained a solid reputation for clean, almost beginner-friendly waves that break on the most exposed parts of the atoll reefs. Comprised of 26 atolls, surfing in the Maldives has remained focused on North Malé, which claims the best density of lefts and rights within a 2hr cruise. Combined with an appealing proximity to Hulhumalé international airport, it's an especially convenient, fun-wave playground for time-restricted, wealthy travellers. The Maldives surf has been one of the longest kept secrets, because Australian Tony Hinde managed to keep it quiet among his close friends between 1974 and 1988. These days, the four passes gathering the bulk of the swell are often crowded with all types and abilities of recreational surfers, from the resorts, guest-houses or charter boats, but the vibe is usually laid-back and friendly.

| | |
|---|---|
| + WORLD-CLASS WAVES | - CONSISTENTLY SMALL |
| + RARELY FLAT | - OFTEN CROWDED |
| + NO WIND BEFORE SW MONSOON | - BOAT ACCESS RESTRICTIONS |
| + UNIQUE BOATING LIFESTYLE | - TOP PRICES |

## TRAVEL INFORMATION

**Weather**– Typical, tropical, monsoon climate with plenty of rainfall. The NE monsoon (Iruvai) is the driest period with lighter winds from NE. During this period (Dec-Mar) temps soar and sunshine is plentiful. During May-Oct the monsoon comes from the SW (Hulhangu), bringing thunderstorms, gusty winds, overcast skies and occasional rainfall to the atolls. June-July is the worst. Most of the year averages around 27°C (80˚F), night and day, because there is no cooling land factor.

**Lodging and Food** – Stay in one of the few surf resorts, unless you can find/afford boat transport (speedboat $2000/d). North Malé atoll resorts are expensive, best prices (based on double occupancy) are Cinnamon Dhonveli at $431/n with surf transfers and Adaaran Select Hudhuranfushi around $500/n (+ $175 surf pass). Guest-house (Himmafushi, Huraa, Thulusdhoo) offer $80-130/d pricing + surf transfers on top, but don't serve any alcohol. Surf safari boat deals vary a lot depending on boat status, group size and the season (higher priced Oct-April): expect to pay between $120-350/d. Extras: beer ($5). Prices have increased rapidly as GST has increased from 3.5% in 2011 to 12% in 2014. Latest is the Green tax at $6/day.

**Nature and Culture** – Scuba-diving and snorkelling is among the world's top 10 because of huge species variety, quantity of fish (no nets allowed in the country) and perfect water temperatures (27-28ºC/80-82ºF). Coral gardens had recovered after the intense 1998 El Nino bleaching and again in 2010, while 2015 was another bad year with higher ocean temperatures. Hand-line fishing (spearguns prohibited), either trawling or at anchor is just intense: Spanish mackerel, yellow-fin tuna, barracuda, wahoo, rainbow fish, trevally, batfish, jobfish and triggerfish. Visiting villages will only take 1hr since most islands are tiny.

**Hazards and Hassles** – Despite loads of marine life it's safe. Although having a gentle slope and being quite smooth, pay attention to shallow reefs. Tidal rips and intense sunburn can be more of a threat. Crowds in North Malé are now a reality and boat wakes at some spots (Sultans) can be a hassle. Regimented group timetables may get on some people's nerves; talk with the captain/surf guide for optimum surf schedules.

**Handy Hints** – Bring 2 boards with spare fins, leash and at least 1 tropical wax bar for every 3 days. No need for a gun - take a fish instead. Boats don't necessarily have snorkelling and fishing stuff, bring your own. Also a surf hat and good sunblock. Don't bring alcohol or pork products.

ANDREW SHIELD

Pasta Point

LAURENT MASUREL

Chickens

Malé is the Maldivian capital and has one of the highest population densities in the world. It's mainly the 100 locals who surf **Raalhugandu**, the only reliable break in town, yet it is one of the most consistent and powerful waves in Maldives. Unfortunately development plans to build a bridge to the airport may kill off the fun peaks. On rare big SE swells, a few travellers manage to surf Rats treacherous lefts on the SW corner of Male, or across the channel on Vilingili where super-shallow rights spin across a bumpy reef. On nearby Furana, the Sheraton/**Full Moon** resort has started surfing programs for guests. The rights are fairly fickle, until a 2m+ SE swell hits with a 12 sec+ period, transforming it into one of the best rides in the country. **Half Moon** on Kanduoiygiri (Kadu for short) can also be good with similar big swell conditions, but will be smaller than everywhere else. Across the wide channel, Paradise Island tried to sell itself as a surf resort, but the lefts are little more than a closeout. The next reef pass north stands at the heart of the Maldivian surf scene, with no less than four epic breaks. First up is **Jailbreaks**, a right that becomes everyone's favourite for its length and soft-breaking sections, making it accessible to a wide range of skill levels. Honky's and **Sultan's** form the ultimate dream combination of rights and lefts breaking on both sides of Thamburudhoo island, which still belongs to the army and plans for a private luxury surf resort have been shelved. **Honky's** works in the typical NE winter winds enticing swell onto a nicely walled outside section that gets bigger and faster as it hits "Fred's Ledge" section on the inside. Offers short barrels and a bit more punch than most when the tide drains out, but beware of strong currents. **Pasta Point** is the classy lefthander reserved for the maximum thirty surfing guests booked into the exclusive Cinnamon Dhonveli Resort. It's consistent, handles NE-SE winds, starts and finishes fast with an edgy, lip-bashing wall in between. Thirty mins north by boat, in front of Club Med on

## Sultan's

LAT. 4.313543° LONG. 73.586281°

Impressive, righthand, point-style reefbreak that forms half of the Thamburudhoo Island double act, which also stars Honky's warping lefts during the NE monsoon. Some may argue that the shallower, faster waves to the north are better, but Sultans regularly delivers the biggest, longest waves in North Male, starting with a swift, steep drop into a carving wall that throws some hooks on the inside reef, a full 300m down the line. Currents and crowds can be big, but it's worth waiting for a tip to tail bomb.

Kanifinolhu, **Ninja's** rights appeal to improvers and cruisers on small, clean swells, as they tend to close-out over shoulder-high and lack shape. **Lohi's** keeps its old Lohifushi name, despite becoming Adaaran Select Hudhuranfushi resort. Being host to five WQS events (Deep Blue Open 2001-2005), Lohi's is a longer wave than Pasta, but not as perfect. The outside section holds the monsoon wind better, while the inside can be a dramatic freight train. Again, if you don't stay here, you don't surf here. Another 30mins sail north, the last pass is the safari boat favourite because it catches more S swell (and wind unfortunately!). **Coke's** (or Cola's, depending on your taste) has often been rated as the hardest breaking wave in North Male with a vert take-off, high barrel factor and nice shape over the shallow reef. Various new guesthouses and local crew add to the often crowded vibe and there are strong currents on the tide drop – experienced, fit surfers only. **Chicken's** left is home to long, playful lefts that can sometimes produce 10 second barrels, but not if the SW wind is up. Varies greatly in quality and crowds. On major SE swells and strong S winds, it might be worth checking the rights of Meerufenfushi Corner, but expect more than fast zipping lines!

Coke's

ANDY POTTS

The Indian Ocean is the most active ocean in the world with southern latitude swells remaining quite frequent, even during the austral summer. Lows tend to radiate a strong SW push of long 12-18sec period swell, that often arrives from a more S direction plus some shorter period (9-15) SE pulses. This groundswell is matched half of the time by windswells from various directions depending on the position of the high pressure systems. The full surfing season starts in March and ends in November, but generally speaking May-October is when the bulk of the swells arrive and most of the resorts and boats enter the high season. The SW monsoon tends to blow more W early and late season, with the dominant WSW averaging 10-20mph. December to February is the heart of the tourist season (NE monsoon) with countless honeymooners, cruisers, divers and small 2-3ft choppy windswells from the NE. March-April as well as November are transition months of weaker winds, sunny weather, less crowds but significantly less consistency with 3-5ft swells. Period is often more significant for wave size than wave height. Tides are unpredictable but create intense rips between islands, making it sketchy to paddle across channels. Depending on tide, you have either incoming or outgoing currents, so check with the dhoni/dingy captain. High tides are safer at most spots.

| STATISTICS | | J F | M A | M J | J A | S O | N D |
|---|---|---|---|---|---|---|---|
| SWELL | Direction | | | | | | |
| | Size (ft) | 2 | 3-4 | 4-5 | 5-6 | 4 | 2 |
| WIND | Direction | | | | | | |
| | Force | F3 | F2-F3 | F3 | F3 | F3 | F3 |
| WATER | Wetsuit | | | | | | |
| | Temp/°C | 27 | 28 | 27 | 26 | 27 | 27 |
| WEATHER | Rainfall/mm | 32 | 40 | 240 | 212 | 172 | 113 |
| | days/mth | 2 | 2 | 13 | 13 | 10 | 6 |
| | Min temp/°C | 23 | 25 | 25 | 24 | 24 | 25 |
| | Max temp/°C | 29 | 31 | 31 | 29 | 29 | 29 |

# Thaa and Laamu MALDIVES

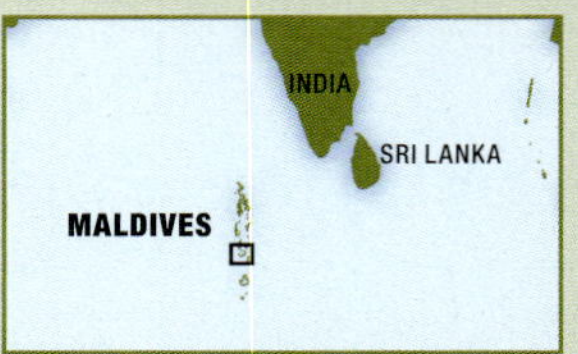


The Maldives are 26 flat coral atolls ringed with 1,200 islands, only a few of which are known for the quality of their surf. With an Indian Ocean swell window from direct E through S to W, Laamu atoll and Thaa atoll are fairly new central atoll surf zones with many high-quality reef pass setups. These two atolls alone present 150 islands and almost 650km of coastline to the frequent swell. The central atolls of the Maldives enjoy an abundance of medium-sized, perfect reefbreaks, the majority of which are righthanders. A settled and peaceful area of sparse population, access to the majority of these waves is by charter boat alone, despite planned resorts. Unlike other island chains, the expense and low number of boats in this area of the Maldives keeps crowds low. With waves such as Mikado and Yin Yang known for their pristine barrels, under the right conditions the central atolls are tropical perfection.

+ CONSISTENT IN SW MONSOON
+ LONG, WRAPPING REEF WAVES
+ WORLD-CLASS YINYANG, MIKADO
+ COMFORTABLE SAFARI BOATS

- LACK OF CONSISTENT LEFTS
- MORE CRUISING BETWEEN SPOTS
- HARDLY EVER BIG
- EXPENSIVE DOMESTIC FLIGHT

MICKEY NATTZ

Mikado

On the west coast of Thaa atoll, **Bowling Alley** is a scenic deep-water peak that closes out quickly onto a reef deep inside the atoll. When the wind blows from the SE, head to Hirilandhoo where a long, speedy, but inconsistent left called **Malik's** can offer high quality barrels. To the east lies **Adonis**, a sectiony right that favours N winds and breaks off the southeastern tip of Veymandhoo island. SE-SW swell first hits **Outside Mikado**, a fast right with a dodgy end section over uneven reef that needs higher tides to hold up. **Inside Mikado** is a perfect wraparound righthander that's inconsistent at low tide, but mid tide through high can deliver perfect peeling waves with short barrel sections. Inside Mikado is offshore in a SW wind, but a W or NW wind will spoil this flawless line-up. **Finnimas** is an exposed lefthander that needs NE, N or light NW winds to break well and across the next pass a right sometimes breaks.

Laamu atoll is more exposed and **Yin Yang** is the most consistent wave in the area, working best under strong SE swell when thick barrels and a powerful inside section can be punishing. The outside section breaks in deep water, and can be an option in NW winds that blow out the inside. In SW winds, the outside becomes choppy and the inside turns on. If the swell is big and the wind from the NW, it may be worth heading inside the pass to **Mada's**, a short and shallow left. On the east-facing coast of the atoll, **Bedhuge** is a remote, perfect right that breaks on big SE swells and any W wind. Across the pass **Refugee's Lefts** are short and shifty requiring specific SE swell direction to line up while **Refugee's Rights** are only for speed demons that can race the close-out sections. **Machine** is usually the best option; a winding, tubular right best on an incoming tide and is rideable even in small swells. On the northeast tip of the atoll is **Isdhoo Bank**, a rarely surfed righthander that comes alive in big S-SE swells with S-SW winds.

Late March through to mid May are generally clean and calm, ideal conditions for boat cruising. The wind doesn't get too strong, and even in the heart of the monsoon season clean days are common. Wind conditions can be divided into three clear periods. The prevailing wind from April to August is SW-W, from September to November it swings SW-NW, changing again from December to March, when it predominately blows NW-NE.

Kudahuvadhoo Kandu
Gaalee
Burunī
Kadufushi
Dhifushi
Olhugiri
Vilufushi
Kalhufahalafushi
Olhufushi
KOLHUMADULU
Madifushi
Dhiyamigili
Guraidhoo
Maalefushi
Kadoodhoo
Kakolhas
Vandhoo
Hirilandhoo
THAA
Thimarafushi
Gaadhiffushi
Kanimeedhoo
Fonadhoo
Veymandhoo
Kibidhoo
Omadhoo
Bowling Alley
Malik's
Finnimas
Inside Mikado
Outside Mikado
Adonis

BLUE K SAFARIS
MALDIVESURF
PERFECT WAVE
NOMAD SURFERS
WATERWAYS
ATOLL TRAVEL

LAAMU
Veymandoo Kandu
Isdhoo
Isdhoo Bank
Dhabidhoo
Machine
Fushi
Maabaidhoo
Mundoo
Refugee's Rights
Refugee's Lefts
Vadinalhu
Kalhaidhoo
Baresdhoo
Bedhuge
HADDHUNMATHI
Suaroge
Gan
Maavah
Huutimendhoo
Maamendhoo
Hithadhoo
Kunahandhoo
Gaadhoo
Fonadhoo
Kadhdhoo
Mada's
Yin Yang
Huvadhoo Kandu
ONE AND HALF DEGREE CHANNEL

MICKEY NATTZ

Yin Yang

## TRAVEL INFORMATION

**Weather** – The *Iruvai* is the NE monsoon (Dec-March), typified by dry weather and light N winds. The WSW monsoon, *Hulhangu* lasts from mid May through to mid November, and is likely to feature overcast weather and strong thunderstorms. 2704 hours of sunshine per year, help to keep water temperature between 28-30°C (82-86°F).

**Lodging and Food** – There is one high-end resort, Maalifushi by Como in Thaa atoll, and a Mikado guesthouse in Thimarafushi, but the majority of waves in this area are surfed using live aboard boats. Handful of boats operate on/off in this area: Horizon2 ($220/d), Hamathi ($230/d), Atoll Challenger (group only), Handhu and Handhufal. Cabins with air-conditioning are a luxury in the heat. Boats provide decent quality food and fresh fish is a certainty. Ask for Roshi Mashuni!

**Nature and Culture** – World class snorkelling and fishing sees tuna, Maori wrasse, swordfish, sailfish, marlin and even whale sharks visiting frequently. Expect friendly village culture.

**Hazards and Hassles** – Bring reef boots for shallow reefs. Sharks are usually small and benign, sea lice and urchins are rare. Avoid sunburn and sunstroke, take lycra and hats to minimise sunscreen use which harms the corals.

**Handy Hints** – There is very little surfing equipment available in Malé and it's expensive, so take everything. Also take entertainment for time off from the surf.

| STATISTICS | | J F | M A | M J | J A | S O | N D |
|---|---|---|---|---|---|---|---|
| SWELL | Direction | | | | | | |
| | Size (ft) | 2-3 | 4 | 5 | 6 | 4-5 | 2-3 |
| WIND | Direction | | | | | | |
| | Force | F3 | F2-F3 | F3 | F3 | F3-F4 | F3 |
| WATER | Wetsuit | | | | | | |
| | Temp/°C | 28 | 29 | 29 | 28 | 28 | 28 |
| WEATHER | Rainfall/mm | 32 | 40 | 240 | 212 | 172 | 113 |
| | days/mth | 2 | 2 | 13 | 13 | 10 | 6 |
| | Min temp/°C | 23 | 25 | 25 | 24 | 24 | 25 |
| | Max temp/°C | 29 | 31 | 31 | 29 | 29 | 29 |

# Gaafu Dhaalu MALDIVES

Gaafu Dhaalu (South Huvadhoo) has an exposed south-facing coast, boasting a dozen good passes, in a 2 hr cruising zone. Maldivian pioneer, Tony Hussein, discovered the areas potential in 1973, keeping it to himself until the first charters began in 1993. A short flight from crowded Malé drops surfers in this beautiful, undeveloped, secluded zone with a good choice of rights or lefts.

+ ATOLL PASS PERFECTION
+ FEWER CHARTER BOATS
+ CALM WATER CRUISING
+ GREAT FISHING/SCENERY

- STORMY WINTER SEAS
- GROWING SPRINGTIME CROWDS
- LONG TRANSFERS
- EXPENSIVE

YEP

Tiger Stripes

Fresh off the domestic flight, lucky punters will score good lefts at **Airport's** with a strong S-SW swell and NE wind, but the boat usually heads direct to Beacons, 2hrs away, at the first southern reef pass. Touted as the Maldives gutsiest wave, **Beacons**' powerful rights tube onto a shallow, unforgiving reef. SW swells will break down the reef, but a SE swell will create peaks slamming straight onto closeout sections of coral. Less intense is **Castaways**, exposed on an outside reef that is predictable, but shallow on the end section, especially at low tide. Anything N is offshore and the deserted island backdrop is idyllic. **Blue Bowls** is the most flexible right, tucked inside the pass and protected from SW-W winds. More of a point style wave, it has good length of ride and nice bowly sections for performance moves. All swells, all tides and all sizes. 30 minutes motoring east, **Five Islands** is another righthander that breaks hard and hollow on the shallow inside reef. The outside section encourages deep take-offs into racy walls and handles the biggest swells at all tides. **Two Ways** needs a big swell to hit its protected position, creating fun peeling, long walls with a bit of depth to the water making it a favourite with intermediates. Directly next-door are the reliable lefts of **Love Charms**, which can handle E winds and any size swell. Low tide is best when it is small, soft and broken into two distinct sections. Bigger swells morph it into a long, hollow wall, with powerful pockets. The next pass to the east is a narrow inlet between the islands of Gan and Gadhdhoo, where local surfers can be found. **Antiques** are the rights, which are always a couple of feet smaller and way more forgiving than the lefts. Named after the narrow gouges in the reef that give a striped effect, **Tiger Stripes** has some real growling lefts in a strong swell. Tricky take-offs into a long speed wall before committing to an inside tube section that wraps and peters out in the channel. Unimpressive when small, it always seems to be bigger than everywhere else. All tides, all variations of S swells and any N wind. **KH**'s is almost east coast and the two distinct take-off spots link together in bigger swell and tide conditions. There's scattered, quality surf like **Koodoo** and **Viligili**, located in Gaafu Alifu (North Huvadhoo Atoll), surfed by boats on their way to/from Male.

Huvadhu Kandu
ONE AND HALF DEGREE CHANNEL
Kolamaafushi
Viligili
Koodhoo
Maamendhoo
Viligili
Koodhoo
Nilandhoo
Dhaandhoo
GAAFU ALIFU
Dhevvadhoo
Funadhoo
Thinadhoo
Kaadedhdhoo
Madaveli
Hoadedhdhoo
HUVADHOO ATOLL
Kodey
Dhiyadhoo
Gemanafushi
Airports
Kaduhulhudhoo
Gadhoo
KH
GAAFU DHAALU
Nadallaa
Vashavarehaa
Boduhutaa
Gazeera
Gan
Tiger Stripes
Antiques
Vaadhoo
Love Charms
Fiyoari
Faruko
Two Ways
Five Islands
Beacons
Castaways
Blue Bowls
Addu Kandu
EQUATORIAL CHANNEL

BLUE K SAFARIS
MALDIVESURF
PERFECT WAVE
SUDDEN RUSH
SURFHOLIDAYS
NOMAD SURFERS
WATERWAYS
ATOLL TRAVEL

## TRAVEL INFORMATION

**Weather** – NE monsoon is the driest, sunniest period with lighter winds from NW to E and high humidity. Water temps remain around 28-30°C (82-86°F), meaning boardies, long sleeved lycra and sunhat!

**Lodging and Food** – All mod cons aboard a handful of safari boats including the original Horizon II and Anloran, booked through all the big agents (Atoll Travel, Maldivesurf, Perfect Wave, Waterways, etc). Ayada resort sits a mile from Two Ways but prices are around $800/d. One guesthouse in Blue Bowls around $90/d; speedboat transfers being an obvious extra at 500usd both ways. Food is varied as long as it is fish!

**Nature and Culture** – Typical boat trip culture of insane fishing, great snorkelling (no tanks available), surf vids and board games. Vaadhoo and Gadhdhoo offer telecom services and village scenery.

**Hazards and Hassles** – At 0° latitude, your worst enemy is the sun. Cover up and use waterproof sunscreen that protects you and the coral. Keep well hydrated and treat coral cuts carefully. Horrendous tidal currents rip through the passes. No alcohol, pornography, drugs, fishing rods or spear guns are allowed at customs.

**Handy Hints** – Bring two shortboards and reef equipment. Names are confusing - Gaafu Dhaalu is South Huvadhoo. Some boats have WIFI onboard now, buy a local card and 3G key at Malé airport for a reliable connection. GSM 99% coverage!

GREG EWING

Beacons

Due its size and location, Gaafu Dhaalu is the only atoll with total SW-SE exposure. May-Oct is the most consistent swell season, however, this coincides with the SW monsoon and the boats don't operate much during the stormy, windy conditions from May-August. Shoulder seasons either side of the NE monsoon are best for clean and sunny conditions during Feb to April (usually crowded) and Sept-Nov (very uncrowded). Winds will generally have a NW - NE direction but the monsoon can be early or late, bringing unwelcome SW winds to the transition periods. Any wind from the S to E quadrant kills off all the breaks, especially when it's small. Dec-Jan suffers flat spells, but exposure is better than Male Atolls.

| STATISTICS | | J F | M A | M J | J A | S O | N D |
|---|---|---|---|---|---|---|---|
| SWELL | Direction | | | | | | |
| | Size (ft) | 2-3 | 4 | 5 | 6 | 4 | 2-3 |
| WIND | Direction | | | | | | |
| | Force | F3 | F2-F3 | F3 | F3 | F3-F4 | F3 |
| WATER | Wetsuit | | | | | | |
| | Temp/°C | 28 | 29 | 29 | 28 | 28 | 28 |
| WEATHER | Rainfall/mm | 205 | 174 | 81 | 61 | 38 | 82 |
| | days/mth | 11 | 10 | 7 | 6 | 4 | 6 |
| | Min temp/°C | 25 | 25 | 25 | 25 | 24 | 25 |
| | Max temp/°C | 30 | 31 | 31 | 31 | 30 | 30 |

# Addu MALDIVES

Directly below the Equator is the southernmost Addu Atoll where Gan island was used as a British Royal Air Force base until 1976. The thriving population of 20,000, live in some of the biggest villages in the Maldives, connected by a system of roads and causeways. Best known for diving wrecks like *British Loyalty*, torpedoed by the Japanese in 1942, this part of the Maldives is slowly unveiling its potential for surfing. The reality is that Addu Atoll doesn't have Maldivian standard, perfectly shaped, soft-breaking waves. Beginner/improvers will struggle with the technical breaks that require speedy riding techniques and the super-fast shallow reefs can be intimidating.

**+ VIRGIN BREAKS**
**+ CONSISTENT, MORE SE WINDS**
**+ SOME OVERLAND ACCESS**
**+ INTERNATIONAL FLIGHTS**

**- LACK OF MELLOW WAVES**
**- EXPENSIVE DOMESTIC FLIGHT**
**- ONLY SW-EXPOSED PASS**
**- EXPENSIVE DHONI ACCESS**

## TRAVEL INFORMATION

**Weather** – Addu sees stronger, but less frequent showers than Malé and generally speaking, monsoons are less marked here with more SE winds in July-August. Thunderstorms can be really quick and strong. Water is bath warm, year-round.

**Lodging and Food** – Equator Village hotel does an all inclusive (with alcohol) price: $159/sgl, $226/dble and $303/triple. Buffet is usually generous with fish. Small local restaurants serve spicy food for around $12.

**Nature and Culture** – Visit Buddhist tombs dated before 1153. The 16km road can be a good biking trip and diving is world-class with plenty of sharks, big pelagics like barracuda and WWII relics.

**Hazards and Hassles** – Occasional small reef sharks at Gan and Viligili, but the main problem is the treacherous straight reef. Most spots are very shallow with deep water drop-offs. Beware when walking on garbage in Kottey. Shangri-la might ban free access to the Viligili breaks and cost $300-700/nt.

**Handy Hints** – As Addu Atoll is totally uncrowded, come with a group to share dhoni or van costs. Take a semi-gun as waves can get sizeable. Only dhoni to Viligili when it's clean. Take a van to Kottey for big stormy surf.

YEP

Madihera

**Kottey** fronts a garbage dump beside a muddy lagoon, but there's an interesting set of reefbreaks during the SW monsoon. The surf can get big and waves typically wedge up over the mainly dead coral reef, creating heavy, rippy, conditions and no

LAURENT MASUREL

Approach Lights

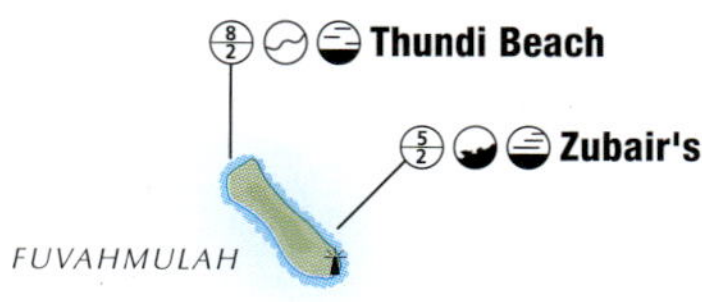


safe channel to paddle out. When the swell is small, drive to **Gaukendi Bridge** and surf the left on the south side or the peak in the middle, but avoid the north side close-outs. It's fairly safe on higher tides and not too shallow, although rides are short. The most obvious wave on Gan reels down a live coral reef right in front of the new runway and the **Approach Lights** usually mark the more rideable end section that's safer at higher tides. Outside sets can be 10ft+ and really throwing. It's possible to paddle across the wide lagoon, but it's safer to use a dhoni and jump straight into the line-up. Off the tip of **Madihera** islet is a quality left, wrapping round the reef pass like a pointbreak with two distinct sections. Outside can be sucky and barrelling but any S to NW wind will kill it, so glassy or NE conditions will be great and

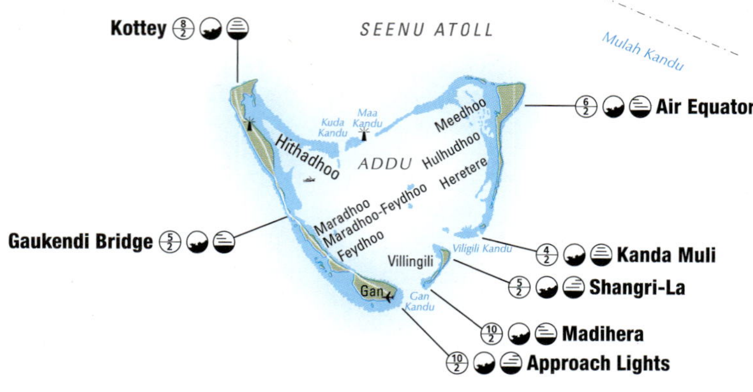


SE winds groom the speedy yet easy inside walls. Villingili is the site of the **Shangri-La** resort, which has access to some of the best waves in Addu and can sometimes ban surf access to outsiders. On small clean SE-SW swells, there is a nice right reefbreak wrapping along the east coast of the island that generally works best during the southern hemi summer. The eastern pass of Viligili hosts lots of peaks on the Milikédé side. **Kanda Muli** is a swell magnet reef that is far too straight, so it's important to avoid side winds, big swells and low tides. In case of a nice small swell and any N wind, there will be plenty of peaks favouring lefts. It takes 2h+ by dhoni to check the unridden Meedhoo lefts spotted by **Air Equator** airline pilot Andy Burr. It's offshore with NW winds and looks like a fast, full on barrel from the air. Remote Fuamullah does not have fully reliable breaks, but there's a good hotel, and the east side of **Thundi Beach** may be the only beachbreak (some reef too) in the Maldives. Wrapping rights and wedging peaks on a medium SE swell and SW winds, plus a pounding shorebreak for the kids. Near the harbour, local surfer **Zubair** surfs a fake reef pass where occasional rights are cleaned up by SW winds.

Swell exposure is obviously the best in the Maldives and unlike other atolls, it can be good in summer with small clean surf on the west side and Viligili. S to W winds are frequent during SW monsoon time (May-Sept) and the only surf will be in Kottey with side-offshore wedges. It's very unlikely to go flat, even during high tourist season from Dec-March. During spring tides, tide range is around a metre, while neap tides can be as little as a few centimetres. Avoid full/new moon weeks, because low tide on super shallow reefs will be very sketchy.

| | STATISTICS | J F | M A | M J | J A | S O | N D |
|---|---|---|---|---|---|---|---|
| SWELL | Direction | | | | | | |
| | Size (ft) | 2-3 | 4 | 5 | 6 | 4-5 | 2-3 |
| WIND | Direction | | | | | | |
| | Force | F3 | F3 | F3 | F3 | F3 | F3 |
| WATER | Wetsuit | | | | | | |
| | Temp/°C | 28 | 29 | 28 | 28 | 28 | 28 |
| WEATHER | Rainfall/mm | 45 | 52 | 250 | 221 | 178 | 114 |
| | days/mth | 2 | 2 | 12 | 11 | 10 | 7 |
| | Min temp/°C | 25 | 25 | 25 | 25 | 24 | 24 |
| | Max temp/°C | 30 | 31 | 31 | 31 | 30 | 30 |

# Rakhine & Ayeyarwaddy MYANMAR

**The secretive Buddhist nation of Burma has been re-christened Myanmar under the repressive military led dictatorship (SPDC). Tourism is in its infancy and the government controls almost all facets. Displacement, slave labour and illegal imprisonment are just some of the alleged human rights abuses, plus ethnic and religious tensions between armed militias and the army have been continuously flaring up in coastal regions. Most western governments advise their nationals not to visit or invest in Myanmar. The best waves are found in Rakhine state, which currently attracts a travel warning unless staying in the long-established, government-run Ngapali Beach resort, so until the country sees a more open regime, most of this beautiful country's surf will remain in the shadows.**

- \+ EXPLORATION POSSIBILITIES
- \+ NO CROWDS
- \+ CONSISTENT MONSOON SWELL
- \+ UNIQUE PEOPLE, COUNTRYSIDE

- – WET ONSHORE SWELL SEASON
- – REPRESSIVE DICTATORSHIP
- – ACCESS RESTRICTIONS
- – GOV. TOURISM FUNDS REGIME

The Myanmar coastline is 1900km long and can be divided into three parts: the Rakhine coastal area to the west, the Ayeyarwaddy delta in the middle and the Tanintharyi division with the Mergui Archipelago to the south. Weaving through the mass of government imposed restrictions and finding a suitable surfing beach is easier said than done as visitors have little choice as to where they can and cannot go. What this essentially boils down to is that only a handful of the thousands of swell exposed beaches along this coastline are open to foreigners. Every spot surfed so far, bar one, is within a kilometre or so of the handful of west coast beaches currently open to foreigners. Though nothing is likely to happen to any tourist who manages to visit and stay on a closed beach, the consequences for any Burmese perceived to have helped a foreign tourist can be severe. Nowadays, Burma does contain a small privately run tourist industry, including a few simple hotels, restaurants, tea houses and transport companies that should be favoured ahead of the government run establishments. It's normally fairly easy to tell them apart because the government places are always bigger, brighter and largely empty. **The Rock** is a little islet off the southern tip of Cheduba Island discovered in 2000 and shown in *The Surfers Journal* Vol 10 no.1. It's officially off-limits to foreigners. Ngapali Beach is the largest and oldest resort open to foreigners and is the easiest place for surfers to head to. The main beach gets poor quality waves but **Gottaung Beach**, 2kms to the north, can be wedgy and hollow, especially at low tide, but don't expect much above chest-high peelers. 30km south of Ngapali, **Peninsula Left** is clearly visible on Google Earth, but is hard to get to without a boat and has yet to be surfed. **Kanthaya**, a newly opened tourist beach 120km south of Ngapali, has a rivermouth to help create some sandbanks, but it's a slow, arduous road journey to get there. Just down the coast at **Gwa** an airfield makes it theoretically possible to fly from Yangon in 50mins (if there were flights!), but the curved beach is fairly protected at the southern end and is usually quite small. Another popular beach is **Chaungtha**, only 5hrs drive from the capital, attracting droves of middle-class holiday makers on the weekend to this northwest-facing beach with consistent waves, even in the regular onshores. **Ngwe Saung** is a recently developed area with 9km of consistent beachbreak and plenty of empty resort hotels (many with government connections) and not a surfer for miles.

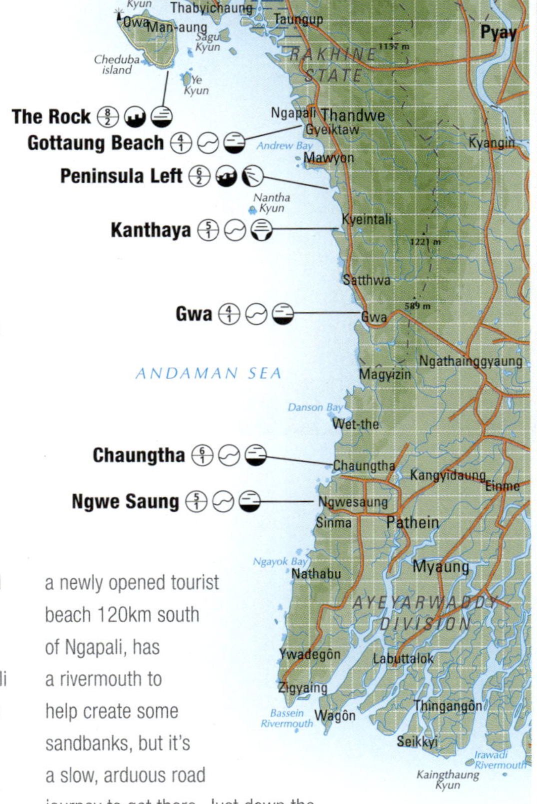


Antarctic swells are very clean with long lulls, but rarely get above 4-5ft. Between mid-May and late September, the Indian SW monsoon sweeps into the Bay of Bengal, blowing close to gale force on a daily basis and generating big, but messy, short period swells. Expect plenty of onshore wind and rain, so aim for the shoulder seasons. Tides are semi-diurnal and hit 7ft.

## TRAVEL INFORMATION

**Weather** – Coastal Burma has a typically hot and sticky tropical climate. Torrential afternoon rains begin around mid-May, peak in July and die away in early October. Temperatures are slightly lower, but humidity is intense. From late Oct to Feb, much of the country is dry and sunny. Water is boardies warm year-round. The devastating cyclone of 2008 killed over 100,000 people.

**Lodging and Food** – Avoid government run hotels and restaurants at all costs. There are now an increasing number of small, and often basic, locally run hotels where a room won't cost more than a few bucks. Every village has an abundance of basic restaurants serving very cheap and tasty Indian and Chinese influenced food.

**Nature and Culture** – Burma is stunningly beautiful and fairy tale exotic. Highlights are the Shwedagon Paya in Yangon and the temple ruins of Bagan, quite remote from the coast.

**Hazards and Hassles** – Very safe destination with crime against foreigners almost unheard of. Avoid all talk of politics and putting Burmese people into compromising situations. Beware of snakes!

**Handy Hints** – Take all surfing equipment with you as none is available anywhere in Burma. *Lonely Planet* is one of the few guidebooks available however the situation is constantly changing so take local advice. Package tours take busloads of elderly tourists to the major attractions around the country.

EMI MAZZONI

Gottaung Beach

JS CALLAHAN SURFEXPLORE

The Rock

| STATISTICS | | J F | M A | M J | J A | S O | N D |
|---|---|---|---|---|---|---|---|
| SWELL | Direction | | | | | | |
| | Size (ft) | 0-1 | 1-2 | 4-5 | 5-6 | 3 | 0-1 |
| WIND | Direction | | | | | | |
| | Force | F3 | F3 | F3-F4 | F4 | F3 | F3 |
| WATER | Wetsuit | | | | | | |
| | Temp/°C | 25 | 27 | 29 | 28 | 28 | 27 |
| WEATHER | Rainfall/mm | 4 | 30 | 394 | 555 | 287 | 40 |
| | days/mth | 0 | 1 | 18 | 25 | 15 | 2 |
| | Min temp/°C | 18 | 23 | 24 | 24 | 24 | 21 |
| | Max temp/°C | 33 | 36 | 32 | 29 | 31 | 31 |

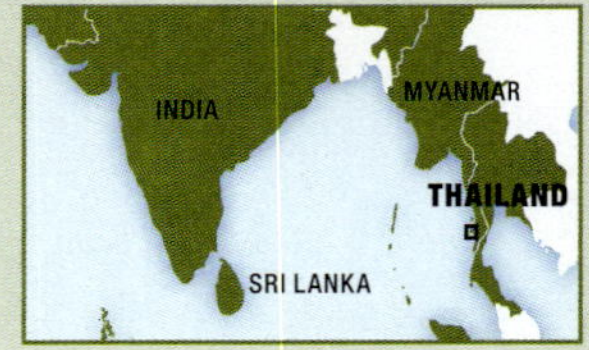


# Phuket THAILAND

Thailand's western shoreline has enough decent waves to attract surfers looking for cheap local costs and the famously warm Thai smile and hospitality. Regulars in the water are now a mixture of local Thais and foreigners from the sizeable expat community. Called "The Pearl of the South" by the tourist industry, Phuket is Thailand's largest island and is mostly mountainous with 70% forest cover. The western coast has 27 soft, white sand beaches, while the east coast beaches are muddy without waves.

+ UNCROWDED, MELLOW WAVES
+ OCCASIONAL POINTBREAKS
+ CHEAP, PARTY DESTINATION
+ EASY, SAFE TOURISM

- SHORT SWELL SEASON
- MUSHY AND ONSHORE
- INCONSISTENT AND RAINY
- MASS TOURISM

## TRAVEL INFORMATION

**Weather** – The dry season begins in December and lasts until March. The rainy season varies in the transition periods but generally runs from April - Nov and is the hottest time of year. The average rainfall in Phuket is about 2500mm (100in), with the vast majority of it falling within this period.

**Lodging and Food** – Endless accommodation options and during the monsoon, hotel rates are often half of the following high season rates. Dble room in a 4-star hotel is $150. A/C room in a guesthouse/bungalow fr$15. There's plenty of choice around Kamala and Kata. Check the Tube Surf Bar and Restaurant. Papaya salad, a popular Thai dish is $1.

**Nature and Culture** – Diving paradise although the Gulf of Thailand islands have the best visibility during SW monsoon. Don't miss Thai Boxing tournaments, Fantasea Show (trapeze artists, elephants, Vegas style), snake shows, Thalang Museum, Wat Chalong temples and Chalong Big Buddha. 1hr Thai massage is $10.

**Hazards and Hassles** – Waves are often mellow, but currents can be deceptively strong and tourists drown every year. There are some shallow rocks on a few of the points. A couple of spots are a bit localized, Muay Thai localism can put a downer on the rest of your trip. Beware of pickpockets and new friends who may slip a sleeping drug in your drink.

**Handy Hints** – You can rent boards, get lessons and find surf shops at many beaches. Try Saltwater Dreaming in Surin. Kata is the surf hub with many choices including the Rip Curl Surf house.

MOONWALKER
Kalim

MOONWALKER
Surin Beach

Flying into northern Phuket, check **Airport Reef**, a long curve of outer reef, 15mins paddle in shallow water, which can have fun drawn out rides. **Nai Thon** is an isolated bay with rocky headlands providing a bit of shape at either end, in front of a small bungalow complex. **Bang Tao** sports 8km of prime tourist sand that's popular with windsurfers, since the swell doesn't seem to make it in here very well. Much better is **Pansea Beach**, a small beach with nice sand banks at times and the northern headland near Chedi Resort offers a right pointbreak for experienced surfers. The wave tends to build in size and speed before closing out on bare reef. Take care! **Surin Beach** shelves steeply so can pack a punch. Best waves tend to be at each end…beware shallow rocks in the middle. The last rock at the northern end can create a great sandbank with fast rights. Visible from Khao Phanthurat pass, **Kamala Beach** sandbanks get stabilized by reefs and attract less crowds than Kata or Kalim. Waves get quite fat and slow when big and there is a small surfable, but inconsistent point/reef. When the surf is too big elsewhere, **Kalim** is one of the better breaks on Phuket, where a righthand reefbreak unfolds over shallow coral, plus there's an occasional left. The rides can be long and it gets very shallow at the end. It can get crowded - be respectful to the local crew. **Patong** is more famous for its shopping and nightlife and is often just a close-out. Obtaining day-pass access to **Relax Beach** gets expensive as it's private to Le Meridien Resort, but it can be excellent at the south end near the headland, where a S-SW-facing left can fire. The 3kms of sandbanks at **Karon Beach** constantly shift, but it does get ok on small swells with little or no wind and it's the favoured spot for the surf schools. SW-facing **Kata Beach** is the most popular spot because the waves are punchy, fast and often bigger, especially at the south end near Kata Beach Resort. Avoid after heavy rains, as it gets polluted. Surf shops, lessons and rentals available. Just south, near Kata Thani Resort is **Kata Noi Beach** with snappier waves at the northern end plus rights off the headland, where respect for the locals is required. Furthest south, **Nai Harn Beach** can hold bigger swells and gets very good. Near the lagoon outflow, nice sandbanks form even when it's small, producing speedy walls and longer rides favouring lefts.

Thailand's west coast, south of Ranong, boasts the best potential considering the WSW dominant swell direction and the shadowing effect of Sumatra. During the SW monsoon, 6ft seas are typical with many rain squalls. It's actually quite consistent during the monsoon, with 2-4ft almost every day from June to September.

| STATISTICS | | J F | M A | M J | J A | S O | N D |
|---|---|---|---|---|---|---|---|
| SWELL | Direction | None | | | | | None |
| | Size (ft) | 0 | 1 | 2 | 2-3 | 1-2 | 0 |
| WIND | Direction | | | | | | |
| | Force | F3 | F2-F3 | F3-F4 | F3-F4 | F3 | F3 |
| WATER | Wetsuit | | | | | | |
| | Temp/°C | 27 | 27 | 29 | 28 | 28 | 28 |
| WEATHER | Rainfall/mm | 31 | 89 | 306 | 283 | 360 | 121 |
| | days/mth | 4 | 7 | 18 | 19 | 20 | 11 |
| | Min temp/°C | 22 | 24 | 24 | 25 | 24 | 23 |
| | Max temp/°C | 31 | 32 | 30 | 30 | 29 | 29 |

# Andaman Islands INDIA

Dubbed "The land of the head-hunters" by Marco Polo, who was the first Western visitor to this chain of 572 islands, islets and rocks, now commonly referred to as the Andaman and Nicobar Islands. Geographic isolation, heavily restricted travel, mysterious Stone Age culture and totally uncharted waters characterise this zone. Whilst foreign tourists are permitted to visit the Andaman Islands, the Nicobars are only accessible to Indians and tribal areas are restricted. With only 36 of the 239 Andaman Islands inhabited, the dense tropical forests support an exotic, fragile ecosystem of unique flora and fauna, preserved and protected in 96 sanctuaries and nine national parks.

- \+ VIRGIN CORAL REEFBREAKS
- \+ KUMARI POINT
- \+ FEW BOATS, NO CROWDS
- \+ UNTOUCHED, WILD TRIBES

- \- ONSHORE IN SWELL SEASON
- \- SHORT IDEAL SEASON WINDOW
- \- EXPENSIVE BOAT OPTION ONLY
- \- OPPRESSIVE HUMIDITY

SOUTH ANDAMAN
Cape Barwell
Herbertabad
Palmer Point
Port Blair
Corbyn's Cove
North Sentinel Isl.
Tarmugli Isl.
Labyrinth Isl.
Manglutan
Boat Isl.
Chiriya Tapu
Macpherson Strait
Twins Isl.
Rutland Island
Portman Bay
Manners Strait
North Cinque Isl.
South Cinque Isl.
Passage Isl.
Sisters Isl.
Nancowry Strait
Neill Isl.
Hugh Rose Isl.
BAY OF BENGAL
Duncan Passage
South Sentinel Isl.
North Brother Isl.
South Brother Isl.
ANDAMAN SEA
Jackson Creek
Palalankwe
Tambeibui
Nachuge
LITTLE ANDAMAN
Butlers Bay
Jarawa Point
Hut Bay
South Point
Totem Reef
Sandy Point
Ignoitijala
Toibalewe
Muddy's
Kumari Point

Close to Port Blair is the main tourist beach of **Corbyn's Cove**, where the beachbreak is generally flat or a tiny closeout. There are no reliable breaks on the tiny Twin Islands off Rutland or the Cinque Islands. An exposed, wide reef pass on North Sentinel Island has been surfed, but these areas are off limits and the Sentinelese locals have a habit of attacking any strangers with spears and arrows! Little Andaman offers the best swell exposure from the S-W, as it isn't blocked by the Nicobars, sitting a little to the SE. **Jackson Creek** offers a safe anchorage inside a large shielding headland fringed by a wind and swell exposed reef. It is an excellent left, but needs E-S winds to be offshore and a decent swell to wrap so it's quite inconsistent. **Totem Reef** needs the same SE wind to be perfectly offshore, but can still be rideable during the NE monsoon. The SW tip of the island should show the most swell, especially at **Muddy's**, a solid, wedgy lefthander that works in NE winds and barrels hard in sections. Around Sandy Point is the main event, namely **Kumari Point**, which was the fastest and longest right pointbreak/reef in the country. Unfortunately, earthquakes have lifted this most photogenic of reefs out of the water and the line-up is now broken up into shorter peaky sections. It still shows some above average form when there's enough S-SW swell and winds from the N quadrant. The inside section has got even hollower as it spins down to the creek mouth channel in the reef. Most surfers concentrate on the reliable left reef up the east coast on the northern headland at Butler's Bay known as **Jarawa Point**, named after one of the indigenous tribes. Its positioning leaves W swells out of the equation, but anything S will hit a rocky, limestone shelf that curves into the bay, turning any N winds offshore. When it's on, a fast jetting left sucks up and peels from start to finish, with the chance of a few cover-ups at bigger sizes. Even when it's smaller, it still offers fun-park walls that tumble down the reef in sections, offering hits and shoulders. Most Andaman waves are fairly easy with good shape and fantastic colours on the reef below. Further south across the 10° Channel, the Nicobar Islands are off limits, protecting their undoubtedly high surf potential and their unique indigenous population from outside interference.

These islands receive a combination of long range groundswells and shorter fetch monsoon swells, which both arrive from the SW. Unfortunately, most of the breaks are directly onshore in the SW winds, so therefore, the season is a short spell from Mid-March to Mid-May when N winds prevail. Rough seas with constant 15-25 knot winds, make navigation difficult in the heart of the swell season. Semi-diurnal tidal phases are small, but affect some spots heavily.

## TRAVEL INFORMATION

**Weather** – During the SW monsoon from mid-May to October, heavy rains flush the islands, often bringing violent cyclones that leave the west coast beaches strewn with fallen trees. In November and December, less severe rains arrive with the NE monsoon. The driest period is between mid November and April, but humidity is high.

**Lodging and Food** – Butlers Bay has tourist huts available on the shore. Surfers have camped on the point, but prepare to be eaten alive by mosquitoes and sand flies. There's guesthouse and government accommodation in Hut Bay. The only boat charter is the family run, sailing yacht Scame (www.surf-sail.com) also bookable via soulandsurf.com (2500€ 10 day).

**Nature and Culture** – Home to stone-age tribes (Onge, Jarawa, Sentinelese) these reclusive aboriginal people live in impenetrable jungles, and still practise age old rituals. Little Andaman has elephant safaris through the rainforest. Trek to the White Surf and Whisper Wave waterfalls. World-class diving zone with large pelagics and amazing visibility. Great fishing.

**Hazards and Hassles** – Any emergency would take days to repatriate; take a well-stocked first aid kit. Beach sand flies are bloodthirsty and unavoidable. Avoid sea crocs and potentially hostile tribes.

**Handy Hints** – Take everything including reef boots and repair kit, plus snorkelling equipment for the many flat/windy days.

JS CALLAHAN SURF EXPLORE

Kumari Point

| STATISTICS | | J F | M A | M J | J A | S O | N D |
|---|---|---|---|---|---|---|---|
| SWELL | Direction | | | | | | |
| | Size (ft) | 2 | 3-4 | 4-5 | 5 | 4-5 | 1-2 |
| WIND | Direction | | | | | | |
| | Force | F3 | F2-F3 | F3-F4 | F4-F5 | F3-F4 | F3-F4 |
| WATER | Wetsuit | | | | | | |
| | Temp/°C | 27 | 28 | 29 | 28 | 27 | 27 |
| WEATHER | Rainfall/mm | 30 | 40 | 420 | 400 | 380 | 190 |
| | days/mth | 1 | 4 | 18 | 21 | 20 | 12 |
| | Min temp/°C | 23 | 25 | 26 | 25 | 25 | 25 |
| | Max temp/°C | 28 | 30 | 29 | 27 | 28 | 28 |

SWOP SURFBOARDS

Jarawa Point

# Aceh INDONESIA

Aceh, Indonesia's most western province, lost 100,000 people or 25% of its whole population in the 26th December 2004 tsunami, when 30-35ft waves left waterlines up to 60ft above sea level. Aceh boasts 1,500km of coastline on Sumatra, which is the sixth largest island in the world and the largest in Indonesia. The Aceh province has historically been independent and resistant to outside rule, sparking the 29 years of guerrilla warfare that finally ended post-tsunami. Aceh now has devolved governmental powers and is the only region in Indonesia to enforce Sharia law in the predominantly Muslim society. Plenty of pristine beaches and coral reefs with a variety of aspects are the drawcard to this lightly-surfed zone.

- + OFF-SEASON CONDITIONS
- + UNCROWDED WAVES
- + WILD SUMATRA
- + PULAU WEH DIVING

- – LACK OF CONSISTENT SWELLS
- – NOT INDO WORLD-CLASS
- – MALARIA
- – BASIC ACCOM & TRANSPORT

The surf around the capital of Banda Aceh on the northern tip has been documented by stoked adventurers since the 1980's. Pulau Weh, better known for diving (whale sharks and turtles) than its waves, has some mushy onshore beachbreaks around **Sabang** with some NE windswell. Surfers have even made their mark on Pulau Breueh at breaks like **Blangujung Rights** or the longer, more challenging right reef at **Lambaro**, which is easier to get to. Pulau Nasih is well worth the effort for long, hollow **Lam Tadoh Lefts** in a SSW-facing bay. Both islands are accessible by ferry from Banda Aceh and Weh has some of the most beautiful palm-fringed beaches in Sumatra with basic accommodation available. Aceh's west coast has a newly rebuilt road that flirts with the coastline all the way from Banda Aceh to Meulaboh. **Lampuuk** Beach is the place for easy beachbreak and is becoming the tourist hub for Banda, along with Lhok Nga where local surfers Taufik and Agus have become Aceh's first-ever lifeguards. Only 15km south of Banda, a beautiful little village holds a consistent, perfect **A-Frame** reefbreak out in front. South of A-frame is **Cement Factory**, producing great rights near Lafarge's huge cement extraction works and harbour jetty. **Pantai Camara** can have perfect, long rights off the rivermouth north of Leupung, but it needs swell. South of Mount Gurutee, where a new island has emerged with the uprising reef, fickle but good wet season rights peel at the rivermouth near **Lamno**, plus there's a quality right point. On the way to Lhok Kruet, near Keudeunga, look for the long **Left Point** in a deep bay facing WNW so it's offshore in SE winds. Further south is **Babah Nipah**, not easy to reach, but the rivermouth line-up promises long rides. Before **Calang**, have a look at the assorted reefbreaks facing west about 10km (6mi) north. After Calang, the shoreline becomes a straight sandy beach, dotted with various rivermouths and scattered rocks and reefs. On the **Kuala Bubon** cape, there are also some good lefts over rock and sand, facing WNW. Once in Meulaboh, it will probably be polluted by the headland and the **Ujong Karang** reef quality is questionable.

Unlike the rest of Indonesia, the surf season is Nov-March during the NE monsoon. During the Austral winter, constant WSW onshore winds shralp wave shape and quality won't be optimum, but smaller summer conditions will provide clean, fun, intermediate-style waves. There is 400km of fetch in the Andaman Sea, where the NE monsoon kicks up mushy 1-3ft windswells on the east coast. If the west coast goes flat, there's always a chance of rideable, unchartered waves in Banda Aceh or Lhokseumawe. With 2ft maximum tidal range, tides are rarely a problem, but winds really need to be right.

SIMON WILLIAMS

Blangujung Rights

SIMON WILLIAMS

Lam Tadoh Lefts

## TRAVEL INFORMATION

**Weather** – The weather is warm to hot with temps ranging from 23-30°C (73-86°F). Dry season runs from March through August and a rainy season from October to January. Northern Sumatra experiences heavy downpours and average annual rainfall is 1600mm. Boardshorts only.

**Lodging and Food** – Lhoknga Riverside resort do kiteboard/surf/SUP packages. Mami Diana's Losmen at Pantai Camara is a good base. Staying in Meulaboh is decent, although all village accommodation will be very basic losmen, but that will help the local population and it will be dirt cheap. Aceh coffee is amongst the most flavourful in the world.

**Nature and Culture** – Neat ancient architecture like The Great Baiturrahman Mosque, Museum Negeri, Kerkhof Churchyard, Syiah Kuala Grave. Takengon near Lake Laut Tawar in the central area of Aceh is cool 20°C (68°F) for a change with shoreline cliffs ideal for rock hiking and the lake is stocked with trout.

**Hazards and Hassles** – Serious travellers only as reliable medical help is far away and malaria is rampant.

**Handy Hints** – Oceanzone surfshop in Lhok Nga may have some stuff, but better plan to leave things behind than to buy. Remember to dress appropriately (Sharia Law), local women swim fully clothed.

| STATISTICS | | J F | M A | M J | J A | S O | N D |
|---|---|---|---|---|---|---|---|
| SWELL | Direction | | | | | | |
| | Size (ft) | 2-3 | 3 | 4 | 5 | 4 | 3 |
| WIND | Direction | | | | | | |
| | Force | F3 | F2-F3 | F3-F4 | F3-F4 | F3-F4 | F3 |
| WATER | Wetsuit | | | | | | |
| | Temp/°C | 28 | 29 | 29 | 29 | 28 | 28 |
| WEATHER | Rainfall/mm | 121 | 107 | 113 | 92 | 162 | 192 |
| | days/mth | 6 | 9 | 8 | 7 | 10 | 11 |
| | Min temp/°C | 23 | 23 | 23 | 23 | 23 | 23 |
| | Max temp/°C | 30 | 31 | 31 | 31 | 30 | 30 |

# Simeulue and Banyaks INDONESIA

Simeulue and Banyak still maintain a frontier status, avoiding the charter boat congestion of the Mentawais through a combination of lower consistency and spot density, treating smaller groups to some lively waves, including one of Indo's best rights. Not surprisingly, these "Many" islands have kept off the radar and some spots remain nameless, or have multiple names from the different boat operators that ply these waters. There's a wide choice of lefts and rights, ranging from shallow barrels to deeper, long, cruisey waves as well as some good off-season beachbreaks.

+ QUALITY REEF BREAKS
+ CONSISTENT HIGH SEASON SWELLS
+ LIGHT CROWDS
+ UNTOUCHED SCENERY

- NO BUDGET OPTIONS
- NO MEDICAL FACILITIES
- DANGEROUS NAVIGATION
- MALARIA

RYAN WILLIAMS

Lolok Point

**Tea Bags** is a challenging right that freight trains down a fringing reef when the swell is up. Other waves in the Busung village area include a sculpted right at the entrance to a deep bay, a fast left wall that hugs the corner of reef on the southern headland and an offshore bombie in the middle. Powerful beachbreaks hit the next bay south in small swells. There's also an easier left reefbreak on the SE tip of Simeulue called **Thailand** with a steep drop and plenty of shoulder for cutbacks, plus a heavy, shallow, fast right to the east. **Pulau Babi** is wide open to all swells, offering big drops into banking, full rail turns when it is pumping. Further inside peels a shorter, hollower right into the beach. The Banyak Islands spots are usually shallow and fast, especially when it is smaller and all are sensitive to swell direction, switching between carvable walls and gut wrenching barrels. **Turtles** is a fun, walling left and occasional slot beside the picturesque Pelanggaran Beach. At the southern end of the island is **Cobras**, a real swell magnet left that lines up a superlative long barrel on the right swell direction and is a go to spot when the swell is small. There's also a right named Warrens across the deep channel. The **Treasure Island** righthander is long and sweet, serving up multiple barrel sections with relatively easy take-offs in a pristine environment. It needs a medium S-SW swell to get going and NW winds and is one of the best waves in the region when it fires. The outside indicator reefs are for barrel-crazy experts only and further inside the bay is Minis, a playful right with a short barrel and workable face on large swells. The wide Bay of Plenty is very consistent and hosts several breaks. The left at **Lolok Point** is an excellent wave for those with sufficient tube-riding skills and lust for speed. Too shallow when small, a medium to heavy swell will produce majestic speed walls that head into shacking sections over the inside reef. Deeper into the bay, the intermediate-friendly lefts of **Dindos/Toy Town** peel predictably and playfully down the coral. Both work in E quadrant winds and higher tides. **Gunturs/Joystick** is a shorter good-natured right when small, but morphs into a seriously challenging, take-off barrel, linking into a hollow, shallow end section when overhead swells hit. Super-consistent, working on all swells and tides and clean when NW winds blow out the lefts.

Expect numerous 6-10ft SW swells (225º) per month between April and October, as well as occasional 3-6ft swells during off-season, with various 2-6ft cyclonic swells and some 1-2ft underlying windswell. The optimal season is June-August, yet it receives less swell than Nias, which can block some due S, so swells from 190º round to west (270º) are best. Due to the doldrums latitude, wind patterns are calm and variable, producing glassy to 8kmh wind conditions for 70% of the time. Tide ranges are only 0.6-1m, but matter plenty at shallow spots.

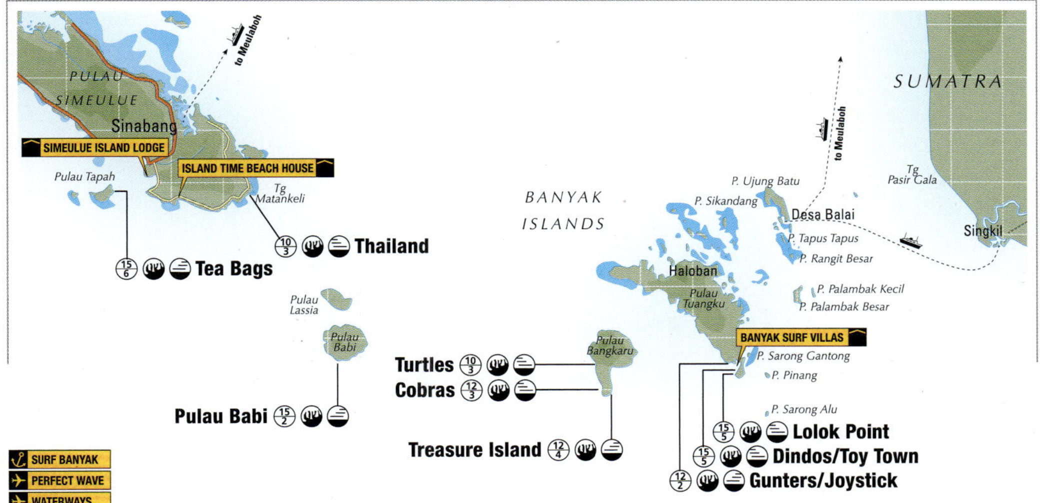


## TRAVEL INFORMATION

**Weather** – Typically equatorial with very high temperatures, dry season is May-Sept but expect late afternoon showers. During the October to April rainy season, it's rare to see more than half a day pass without any precipitation. Water is as warm as it gets.

**Lodging and Food** – SurfBanyak.com do an 11 night charter from $2895. Simeulue Island Lodge located in front of Dylans and Island Time Beach House in the village of Alus Alus have all inclusive packages from $350p/w. Banyak Surf Villas offers bungalows on the water in the Bay of Plenty at $1050p/w including boat transport to waves.

**Nature and Culture** – Trek and dive on Pulau Palambak or Pulau Balai. See the turtles laying eggs at night on Pulau Bangkaru. The untouched jungles offer unique flora and fauna and are best explored by boat.

**Hazards and Hassles** – Chloroquine-resistant malaria cases have been reported – use prophylaxis. Earthquakes and tsunamis are real threats. These shallow and treacherous reefs are far from medical attention; take a helmet, boots and serious medical equipment.

**Handy Hints** – Take everything, there are no exchange facilities and surfing equipment is unheard of. The Banyak Islands are getting increasingly popular with travellers and may not remain off the beaten path for long.

ALAN VAN GYSEN

Tea Bags

| STATISTICS | | J F | M A | M J | J A | S O | N D |
|---|---|---|---|---|---|---|---|
| SWELL | Direction | | | | | | |
| | Size (ft) | 3 | 4 | 4-5 | 5-6 | 5 | 3-4 |
| WIND | Direction | | | | | | |
| | Force | F2 | F2 | F2 | F2 | F3 | F3 |
| WATER | Wetsuit | | | | | | |
| | Temp/°C | 29 | 28 | 28 | 27 | 27 | 28 |
| WEATHER | Rainfall/mm | 120 | 110 | 130 | 130 | 200 | 220 |
| | days/mth | 6 | 8 | 7 | 7 | 10 | 10 |
| | Min temp/°C | 23 | 23 | 23 | 24 | 23 | 23 |
| | Max temp/°C | 30 | 31 | 31 | 31 | 30 | 29 |

# Nias and Hinako Islands INDONESIA

**The perfect righthander at Lagundri Bay on the island of Nias was the first world-class wave discovered in the Sumatra region. Nias was first surfed in 1975, by Aussie surf pioneers Peter Troy, Kevin Lovett and John Giesel. They put up with swarms of malarial mosquitoes and the most primitive of living conditions to ride absolute perfection in the jungle. These days, it's much easier to get to Nias Island and a slew of losmens fringe the deep bay, competing to accommodate the constant stream of surfers. The massive 2005 earthquake tipped the island, lifting reefs in the south with some waves improving and others disappearing. Just offshore in the Hinako Islands, the two super-consistent, crowd-spreading spots have also been affected; Bawa's bowly rights have suffered while Asu's lengthy lefts have got even hollower over the raised reefs.**

- \+ WORLD-CLASS RIGHTS
- \+ CALM WINDS
- \+ OFF THE BEATEN TRACK FEEL
- \+ INEXPENSIVE

- – LONG, HARD ACCESS
- – MALARIA
- – CROWDS
- – HEAT AND HEAVY RAINS

## TRAVEL INFORMATION

**Weather** – Nias has a typical equatorial climate with very high temperatures and humidity, which vary little year-round. Western Indo dry season is from May-Sept, but frequent 1-2 hour showers can still be expected, usually at night. The rainy season is from October-April. The water is some of the warmest in the surf world, getting close to 30°C (86°F) post Christmas.

**Lodging and Food** – The Sorake Beach Resort has closed so no 3 star options and intermittent electricity supply means a/c is often pointless and lamps/candles are the norm. There are at least 30 losmens (from 2-12 rm) built on stilts overlooking the point, which have cheap accommodation (from $5/n), plus you are expected to eat your meals in them. 3 camps at Asu (Asucamp fr $45/n, Puri Asu fr $130/n and Mama Silvi homestay cottages fr $21). Afulu now has 3 cottages at the wave from $40/n. Typical Indonesian meals based on fish and rice.

**Nature and Culture** – 1hr from Lagundri, Bawomataluo village has an impressive temple, shown on the 1000Rp note. Obstacle jumping and war dances are cultural showpieces.

**Hazards and Hassles** – Several surfers have contracted malaria in Lagundri but recent draining of swamps have greatly reduced the threat. It's more prevalent inland along with dengue fever. In the Hinako Islands chloroquine-resistant strains of malaria are present – take precautions! Lagundri is a deep-water spot, but most reefs around here are shallow so be prepared to hit the bottom. Lagundri attracts some petty criminals – keep your gear locked down. Theft has reduced, replaced by high pressure memento selling. Young local surfers make up a third of the crowd and are slim, fit, fast and have it wired, but are friendly and relaxed in the water although they take plenty of waves. Show respect as Nias people are proud and capable of getting angry.

**Handy Hints** – It's easy to buy, rent or repair boards. Bring boots, helmet and guns for the Hinakos. There is a small clinic and a police station in Lagundri. Best money exchange rate is back on the Sumatran mainland or in Gunungsitoli. There are ATM facilities and internet in Teluk Dalam.

PHILIPPE CHEVODIAN
Asu

PAUL KENNEDY
Afulu

The swell sucking Hinako Islands sit a mere 8km off Nias, but it's a good 65kms and 5hrs boat ride from Teluk Dalam in the south. Long, sweeping lefthand lines refract around the northern tip of tiny **Asu** island, stand up and pitch down the impressively long and shallow reef. Speed is essential to make some of the pinching sections and it gets heavy at size, which it handles with ease. Perfect barrels on its day but also easily blown out by shifty winds. Reef uplift (1-2m) has lowered wave quality, closing-out before the ridiculously shallow end "Nuclear Zone" reef that used to tempt the foolish into a terrifying barrel section among the skin-slashing coral heads. Unless you pay for a boat ride, getting in and out without injury is a real challenge as scrambling across the reef requires boots. It's possible to punch out from the tip of the point when it is smaller, otherwise take the longer but safer option of paddling from the jump off spots on the lava reef 300m beyond the Nuclear Zone. There's a camp in front of the wave and two others a short walk or boat ride away. If the wind swings onshore NW, then everyone will think about heading south to the remote and fickle right of **Bawa**, a growling beast that shifts around nastily as it unfolds over a gnarled slab reef. Consistently picks up more swell than anywhere and transforms a solid SW swell into round, cavernous pits through the sketchy inside bowl section. It's a challenging, powerful wave for chargers and tube junkies and a regular escape from the Lagundri circus. There are more lefts and rights to be sniffed out on the other tiny islands of Hamutala, Imana and Heruanga. Furthest north on Nias is **Afulu**, where pretty left lines swing down the reef that rose up to 2.5m in the '05 quake. It needs plenty of swell to break, light morning land-breezes and will be shallow over the uncompromising coral. Despite these prerequisites, it is fairly consistent and there are plenty more spots to search for in the area. It's a 15min walk from the nearest village, a short boat ride from the Hinako Islands, or long overland drive from Lagundri. Round the headland from Lagundri is **Shark Hole** (aka Secret or Hualohilho), an average left reef that is protected from any E wind and offers a barrel at take-off, a few racy sections and easier shoulders into deeper water. Improves with size and rarely crowded since it is a two hour walk from Sorake beach. The adjacent beachbreak peaks can get good right around the curve of Pantai Walohiu. Since the 2005 earthquake, all the waves in Lagundri Bay have been affected (uplift min 0.3m), including **Indicators**, a very shallow, hairy right with pinching barrels, where it's critical to wait for the right wave and then kick out before the disastrous end section. Only attracts a handful of locals and hellmen, on the few days a season it works. It's been called many things including Nias, Lagundri, Sorake and most often just ✪**The Point**, but whatever name is used, it always ends up in the world's top 10 waves. Here's why; the paddle out through the keyhole is dry hair

## The Point, Lagundri

LAT. 0.569781° LONG. 97.733914°

Legendary righthander with many names, but just one trick – to produce flawless, precision barrels. Answers to Nias, Lagundri, Sorake or simply The Point and is always high up all natural-footers dream-wave list. Recent earthquakes have improved length, hollowness and consistency, attracting ever-growing crowds to what was already a popular pilgrimage since the wave came to prominence in the '70s. It now works from tiny to tow-in, producing a more powerful, rounder barrel that can stay open for double digits, without feeling like the flat reef will gobble you up for falling. Easiest paddle-out in the world, helpful current, wind resilient and a postcard location with plenty of cheap accommodation just add to the positive vibe. Ride it at least once in your life, but you will never ride alone.

simplicity, the take-off is predictable, the barrel is a flawless almond shape that peels with precision at the perfect speed for up to 9 seconds, the reef is well-covered, even though the recent up-thrust has made it barrel harder from waist-high up to double overhead and beyond, plus the light seaward current from the channel deposits you nicely back at the peak, ironing out any shoulder bump on the way. It's all tides, all (light) winds, all year (with luck) and all too easy to stay encamped in one of the many losmens or hotels that line Sorake Beach. Negatives include the crowd, some localism, flying boards, sea-lice, the crowd… Losers in the new reef levels include Kiddieland, which has been replaced by a softer inside section of The Point and **The Machine**, an ultra hollow left barrel, deep in the bay, that now needs huge spring high tides and a macking swell. It has a new kink in it mid wave so making the channel is unlikely. There are also a variety of other lesser waves in the neighbourhood, within walking distance to the west (Sobatu) or back towards Teluk Dalam harbour (Rivermouth). **Hiliduha** aka Dipi, is a sheltered reef peak that turns on sucky, committed tubes when the swell is up. 10km north of Teluk Dalam harbour, in front of the village **Hilisataro** is a swift, sucky right at the south end of the bay that will be working when The Point is bigger, i.e. strong S-SW swell and light N-NW winds. Aka Rock Star, it attracts a few boats as it can be perfect, but challenging over the sharp, shallow reef.

Nias is only 60kms north of the equator, receiving plenty of organised swell from the Southern Ocean lows. Expect numerous 6-10ft SW swells from April-Oct and some occasional 3-6ft swells during the off-season along with various 2-6ft cyclone swells that can have lots of W in them as they head into the Bay of Bengal. Historical data shows a 100% swell consistency from April to September, averaging out at 7ft with a 14sec period and peaking at 12ft/21sec. The first half of the year shows mainly light NW for half the time plus oiled glass, zero winds for a whopping 20% of the time. Winds get a bit stronger through July to November with a more E-SE dominant direction, but it is still variable and early/late glass-offs are a given. October seems to be the windiest month with a combo of SE and NW at 16-32kmh. Tidal ranges are only 0.6-1m, but it has an effect on the super-shallow reefbreaks, especially since the earthquake, which saw some reefs rise by up to 2.5m while an island just 20km north subsided by 1.7m.

Hilidua

PAUL KENNEDY

| STATISTICS | | J F | M A | M J | J A | S O | N D |
|---|---|---|---|---|---|---|---|
| SWELL | Direction | | | | | | |
| | Size (ft) | 3-4 | 4-5 | 5 | 6 | 5-6 | 4 |
| WIND | Direction | | | | | | |
| | Force | F2 | F2 | F2 | F2 | F3 | F3 |
| WATER | Wetsuit | | | | | | |
| | Temp/°C | 29 | 28 | 28 | 27 | 27 | 28 |
| WEATHER | Rainfall/mm | 115 | 117 | 150 | 160 | 235 | 237 |
| | days/mth | 7 | 8 | 9 | 9 | 14 | 15 |
| | Min temp/°C | 22 | 22 | 23 | 23 | 22 | 22 |
| | Max temp/°C | 30 | 32 | 32 | 32 | 31 | 29 |

# Mentawai Islands INDONESIA

This wild and remote chain of islands are the undisputed home of many of "the best waves in the world". When a solid SW swell hits the Mentawais, the wave quality and quantity is unparalleled, thanks to the sheer concentration of truly world-class breaks and an unmatched flexibility when it comes to handling different swell and wind combinations. Unusual swell refraction creates unexpected waves on coral encrusted lava reefs round the back of islands and light, flukey winds provide a variety of directions unseen in other parts of Indonesia. Untouched rainforest houses the tribal inhabitants, many still clinging to a traditional subsistence lifestyle, while luxury yacht charters and an ever-increasing number of land camps cater to the growing procession of wave prospectors searching for surf gold.

+ VARIETY OF WORLD-CLASS SPOTS
+ YEAR-ROUND SWELL CONSISTENCY
+ LIGHT, VARIABLE WINDS
+ EXOTIC ISLANDS, UNIQUE CULTURE

- EXPENSIVE CHARTERS/CAMPS
- CROWDED LINE-UPS
- MALARIA
- LONG TRANSIT TIMES

SEBASTIAN IMIZCOZ

Ebay

## TRAVEL INFORMATION

**Weather** – Temperature variations are minimal year-round with a night/day range of 21-32°C (70-90°F). Equatorial Indo "dry" season is Jan-Aug, but frequent 1-2 hour showers can be expected, usually falling at night. Rainy season is Sept-Dec when it rains frequently. Water temp averages 27°C (80°F) and sometimes creeps up to 30°C (86°F)!

**Lodging and Food** – Most surfers will be aboard one of 50-60 charter boats or dozen or so land camps. Yacht charters offer unrivalled flexibility to be in the right place at the right time and carry up to 14, so factor in the instant crowd. Levels of luxury vary from pimped-up, gleaming white sports cruisers and catamarans to local sailing ketches. Land camps are now firmly established in the Playgrounds area (Ebay, Pitstop Hill, Wavepark, Kandui), Sipora (Aloita, Awera, Kingfisher, Katiet) and Nth Pagai (Macaronis). Trips are usually for 10-12 days and cost anything from $150-$400/d depending on the luxury of your boat/resort. Check out Atoll Travel, Freeline, Waterways, and Nomad Surfers for prices and options. Many boats/camps are booked out at least a year in advance, especially for peak season. Some villagers do put surfers up – be generous in return.

**Nature and Culture** – The virgin forest, rugged topography, rare flora and fauna and a unique tribal society make the Mentawai's an ideal spot for trekking tours. A local government tax of $77 per surfer, for up to a 15 day trip.

**Hazards and Hassles** – The surf is intense with strong rips and long hold-downs. Expect nasty reef cuts; take a well-stocked first aid kit. Staph infections are commonplace. Sea lice, heat exhaustion and sea sickness can strike anyone. Dangerous strains of malaria are a serious threat and many anchorages are close enough to shore for mozzies to attack.

**Handy Hints** – Bring lots of wax and leg-ropes. Bigger boards can help at spots like Thunders and Iceland. Try to charter with a group of surfers all at the same level of ability. Avoid paddling out en masse when other boat guests are already out. Try surfing the less crowded waves rather than hassling for bombs at Lance's and Maccas everyday.

CRAIG PARRY

## PLAYGROUNDS

**Promises** is a serious right tube that's rarely crowded because few can keep up with the flat-out speed barrel while ignoring the drought gripped polyp city just below their fin tips. Higher tides, W winds and an iron constitution. Conversely, **Burgerworld** is a relaxed intermediate wave that's perfect for snap and cutback combos or a little punt when the swell disappears. The friendly left reef at **Beng Bengs** works from tiny to fairly chunky with fast walls, a couple of hits and some pinchy cover-ups, before ending abruptly. **Ebay** is a lush, lefthand smoker with perfect form, especially when there's more W in the swell and E in the wind. Tight take-off zone, vert drop, quick turns then a race to the safety of the channel under the curtain, avoiding the two big rocks at high tide. **Pitstops** is a slurpy, fun-park right that wedges up and even barrels across a flatter coral shelf and a sandier inside. Prefers WSW swell and tides are not a problem. A fear-inducing righthander, **Bankvaults** bends and warps over the exposed, swell-sucking tip of Pulau Masokut. Deceptively fast, shifting sections look makeable from the channel, but only the real chargers will handle this complex line-up. Tucked into a corner close to shore, **Nipussi** gives lesser mortals a chance to work the consistent walls that are effectively the end of the Bank Vaults swell train. Longer drops can be had across a couple of sections of reef and the inside zippers can offer a short tube ride, before it goes dry at the sign-posted shut down. **Hideaways** produces a deceptively heavy left chamber that beckons chargers into a bendy bowl section, ending in a shouldered wall. Best in a decent period W swell and handles the S devil wind. Suicidally shallow at low tide –

SIBERUT
Muara
Gunung Paipai
Tandjung Sipaipal
Pulau Siloina
Tandjung Sidjagat
Pulau Djudjuat
Tandjung Maldai
Pulau Dodik
Beng Bengs
E-Bay
Pitstops
Burgerworld
Promises
Bankvaults
No-Kandui
PULAU MASOKUT
Tandjung Alogat
Hideaways
Pulau Simaimu
Tandjung Pulanggadjet
Pulau N'giau
Nipussi
Pulau Batiek
Karamba
Pulau Penanggalansabeu
A-Frames
4 Bobs
Rifles
PULAU KARANGMADJAT

PERFECT WAVE
ATOLL TRAVEL
SURFHOLIDAYS
NOMAD SURFERS
WATERWAYS

ANDREW SHIELD

No-Kandui

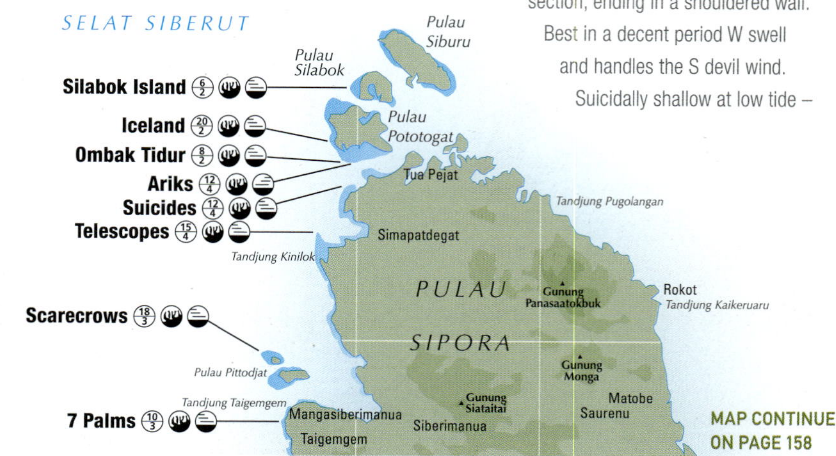


MAP CONTINUES ON PAGE 158

**Lance's Right**

LAT. -2.375301° LONG. 99.859299°

The pin-up centrefold for the Mentawai islands, bringing a new machine-like level to the word perfection. At the top of the coral platform, The Office section breathes in sharply, scooping up the next lucky expert who is hoping to be there when it exhales deeply, then launches through the Main Peak and into the inside where the shallowness of the Surgeons Table awaits. Size determines whether these 3 link and if any turns can be attempted. Perfection arrives with 6-8ft of S-SW swell, light W or no wind and at least 2hrs of tide. It's surprisingly consistent considering the swell refraction required and the afternoon land breezes can clean it up quickly. Dangers are coral heads appearing, trying to duck dive when caught inside and being pushed too deep by the entrenched crowd.

advanced surfers only. **No Kandui** is the perfect name for the most difficult and technically demanding left in the Mentawai. Cavernous barrels spin off down the 500m reef and only an air-drop to full tilt, in the barrel, speed pump will be good enough to get into the wave that rarely backs off enough to allow turns. Slap bang in the middle of Playgrounds anchorage, **Karamba** offers something for the longboard crew to check their speed and trim on predictable ruler-edged walls. Lefts offer surprisingly long rides around mid tide and it's usually uncrowded, as full refraction of S swell keeps size down. Across the channel **4 Bobs** is an enjoyable, warm-up right for the less intrepid. Take-off behind the peak for a whackable wall before a cutback section tapers off into deep water. Watch out for stunning, but shallow coral heads on the inside. **A-Frames**, aka Kandies Left, welcomes S swell onto a large, peaky, playing field. The wedges may offer a short right, but it's the left that attracts the boat crews sheltering in the safe anchorage. Drop, snap, tuck and fool around with this less daunting line-up that needs N quarter winds and a lower tide to spread the punters. **Rifles** riders have to maintain faster than a speeding bullet mentality to keep abreast of the constantly peeling sections and ahead of the foamball. It's not always perfect, often shutting down unmakeable sections, but when it aligns, it's one of the best waves on the planet. Slack or light NW wind, due S swell, not low tide and head to double over provide turbo-charged advanced surfers with a bona-fide dream wave.

## PULAU SIPORA

**Silabok Island** needs some W in the swell to be half the size of exposed breaks and is clean in the dreaded S winds. Manageable lefts hit the north coast at Muka Ikan (Fish Face) and Tikus (Rat) offering walls, shoulders and the occasional stress-free cover up for improvers and cruisers. **Iceland** is a brooding leviathan that ramps up swell size thanks to an abrupt transition from deep to reef. Powerful and moody, it's a cavernous barrel ride when a medium to large SW-W swell hits. **Ombak Tidur** translates as Sleeping Wave peeling down a long, straight, fatally-flawed reef south of Iceland. Likes more S in the swell to focus in on the reef, serving up racy walls and the odd heaving curtain call, hopefully groomed by the rare NE'er. **Ariks** needs a big SW-W swell to penetrate the channel and throw up a barrel on take-off before backing off and throwing again. Some days it's just a fun, smackable wall, but it's always littered with coral heads at low tide. **Suicides** shallow and square lefts spew down a coral shelf over the channel from Ariks in SW-W swells and SE winds. Yet another world-class left, **Telescopes** offers more flexibility than most waves in the area. The take-off is steep but not ridiculous and allows entry to a flawless, steady tube section then a whacking wall to a bend in the coral shelf where the next slot beckons. It's predictable and rarely pinches, is deeper than other reefs, can peel for 200m and handles the constant traffic of intermediates and experts alike. When it's big (up to triple overhead) the outer reef sets rumble in to the entry point with power and purpose – beware of the wide sets pinning you on the reef with its swirling currents. Prefers some W in the swell and mid tide will usually produce the epic sesh. Shifty, swell-sucking left reef, **Scarecrows** takes all swell directions, has plenty of water depth and is a crowd spreader on account of the wide clean-ups that roam towards the channel. Can be messy and very average at high, but always sneaks in a few good ones at some stage of the tide. Good for intermediates when small to medium size and experts will crack out the guns at size. Broken sections of reef at **7 Palms** hold small to medium swell lefts perfect for wall racing and cruising on a longboard. Consistent swell puller, but often sections and shuts down a bit. **Bintangs** equates to a surprisingly fun, frothing righthander that offers a great escape from the crowds at the left across the bay. Wont handle too much size, but when it's on, a slabby, take-off barrel section recedes into a bendy bashing wall that's always better with more water over it. **Lance's Left** works when the wind is in the E and there's a sniff of S swell, creating up to 3 defined sections, delivering anything from small lumpy walls to warp speed barrels at the top, centre and tail of the reef. Shifts mischievously in overhead swells and suckers the greedy into a corrugated, unmakeable end section. Super-consistent, better at mid tide and it will handle beyond double-overhead for the hellmen. **Lance's Right** is the ultimate hotspot (see map and statistics on page 158).

ANDREW SHIELD

Lance's Left

# Mentawai Islands continued

## THE PAGAI ISLANDS

Macaronis rights are usually ignored by the constant charter traffic that enters the beautiful deep-water anchorage of Teluk Pasangan. Flips between long carvable walls and some throwing tube sections. N-NE wind, a decent S swell and plenty of tide required to smooth out the juts in the reef. **Macaronis** is a machine-like, fun park left with all the rides. Barrel-riding, lip-smacking, air-popping and wall-gouging are religiously practiced by the hordes who come to ride the "world's funnest wave". The coral platform curves alluringly into the deep bay and the speed at which Macca's peels is fairly predictable, starting with a perfect pipe section and often ending with a ruler-edge quarter pipe wall. Jostling at the take-off is a given and it is easy to get pushed too deep when it's smaller. Looking further up the reef it sometimes looks doable and unlikely stories of pros making it right down the reef exist. The reef is sharp and shallow, but somehow less threatening than comparable depth spots. Getting caught inside will usually result in being flushed to the end if the sets are pouring through. Best at head and a half of SW swell, mid tide and E wind, it maxes out at double overhead, when the tubes go square. Remains surprisingly fun even if there is a direct onshore SW wind.

There's a land camp, viewing tower and anchorage for two pre-booked charters, to limit crowding. Extremely hollow uber-tube, **Greenbush** flourishes when the rare conditions of spring high tides and moderate S-SW swell meets a N quadrant wind. Vert drop, stall for the barrel then get on the gas as it coils and accelerates over ever shallower reef. May spit you out in the channel or slam the door, but it's safer in the barrel than straightening out. Finicky and fickle for tube-masters only. **Roxies** is forgiving without being soft due to a deeper, flat reef and easy paddling channel return to the peak. Fun from small to headhigh with whackable walls, turning into proper open barrels from take-off when overhead. **Rags Left** was one of the losers in the reef-rising earthquakes of recent times. It used to reel off perfectly down the front of the reef, but now it is prone to hideous boils and churning shallow fingers of coral. Up the top of the reef, perfection and ugly shut-downs happily co-exist and experts will need an air-drop, trusty pintail and a gung ho attitude to handle the big days. Toothy right with a bite to match its intimidating bark, **Rags Right** is close to the gnarliest wave in the Ments. Starts with a beyond vert, no mistakes, quick-as-you-can take-off followed by undulating, sometimes square barrels, vortexing down a featureless reef where eventually the coral heads are going to appear in the exit. **Thunders** rumbles in from deep water, serving up thick peaks that pop up in a range of spots, requiring a bigger board to negotiate the long drop leading to either shoulder hook or inside drainer barrel sections. Refracts heavily, focusing powerful whitewash on anyone caught inside, a situation guaranteed for most surfers. Works from tiny to huge and is the go-to spot when it's flat elsewhere. **Sibigau Rights** provide a N wind escape spot that rarely lines up needing more W in the swell to wrap in stop start walls along an ill-defined reef. Higher tides will be relaxed shoulders at half the size and regularity of Thunders around the corner, but offers an option for intermediates and crowd-free waves. **Solawi Lefts**, aka Turuns is another well-formed fringing reef around a tiny tropical idyll, offering up chunky left walls and tubes in SE winds and more westerly swells. There's a right off the south of the island if the wind switches N and there's also more waves to scope on Pagai Selatan. Scary left mincing machine that churns out lifetime best barrels and reef rash floggings in equal measure. **The Hole** needs very specific conditions to make it safe enough to surf. Swell needs to be very S just to get in and winds need to be NE-E or non-existent, while high tide moves the take-off to a shallower section up the reef. The inside bowl is the real danger and sets turn inside-out over this coral slab, entombing all but the best. Big wrap is required to hit **Lighthouse** and regularly does as S-SW swells coil around the island in pointbreak fashion. Down the line speed walls and the odd cover-up become heaving power pockets at 10ft+, but since it faces the same direction as Lances Right, a W quadrant wind is required.

During March-Nov, regular 6-12ft groundswells arrive from the S to SW and occasionally WSW to due W, translating to a maximum triple-overhead at the most exposed, big wave spots, but more likely averaging around headhigh to double overhead wave face heights. July and August offer the biggest days, longest periods and a very high percentage of forecasted 5-star rated days. This is also when SE winds dominate and pick up in speed. before returning to a NW wind regime that rarely exceeds 16kph and glassy conditions are frequent. There's also a chance of some 2-6ft cyclone swells coming from the west, plus locally generated SE windswells may provide some waves in flat spells. Tidal ranges are only 0.5-1m, but this will affect the many shallow spots where coral heads break the surface at low tide.

RYAN CRAIG

Macaronis

FEDERICO VANNO

Greenbush

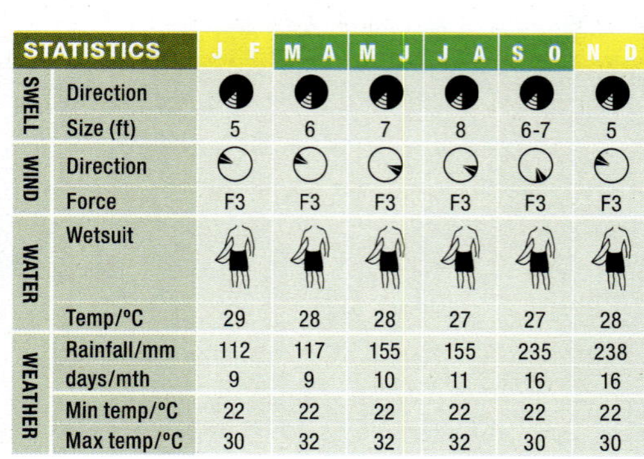

| STATISTICS | | J F | M A | M J | J A | S O | N D |
|---|---|---|---|---|---|---|---|
| SWELL | Direction | | | | | | |
| | Size (ft) | 5 | 6 | 7 | 8 | 6-7 | 5 |
| WIND | Direction | | | | | | |
| | Force | F3 | F3 | F3 | F3 | F3 | F3 |
| WATER | Wetsuit | | | | | | |
| | Temp/°C | 29 | 28 | 28 | 27 | 27 | 28 |
| WEATHER | Rainfall/mm | 112 | 117 | 155 | 155 | 235 | 238 |
| | days/mth | 9 | 9 | 10 | 11 | 16 | 16 |
| | Min temp/°C | 22 | 22 | 22 | 22 | 22 | 22 |
| | Max temp/°C | 30 | 32 | 32 | 32 | 30 | 30 |

# Lampung INDONESIA

Sumatra's mainland has an ideal orientation to Indian Ocean swell hitting the contoured coastline of the sixth biggest island in the world, yet it remains a quiet surfing backwater off the beaten Indonesian track. Lampung is scarcely populated, takes hours to get to and is rarely visited by tourists, but the fishing town of Krui has a growing reputation as the spot to hang out for the accessible lefts of Ujung Bocur and the heaving barrels of Way Jambu.

- \+ CONSISTENT, SIZABLE SURF
- \+ UNCROWDED FOR INDO
- \+ EXPLORATION POTENTIAL
- \+ CHEAP SURFCAMPS

- – CROSS-SHORE WINDS
- – FEW SERVICES, NO NIGHTLIFE
- – LONG OVERLAND ACCESS
- – MALARIA

FEDERICO VANNO
Ujung Bocur

## TRAVEL INFORMATION

**Weather** – May-Oct dry season is best with SE trades and mainly clear skies. The rainy season is a worry for travel, with morning drizzle and intense afternoon downpours. Strong equatorial sunshine, oppressive humidity and a zillion insects are a given. Boardies and booties.

**Lodging and Food** – Surfers spread between the surf camps that extend from Jimmy's to Way Jambu and provide all transportation and guiding services. Cheap losmens provide basic rooms and 3 meals a day from $20. Ombak Indah Losmen is the original Ujung Bocor camp, which organises all-inclusive tours through Freeline Indonesian Surf Adventures or World Surfaris (fr $90/n, ex Jakarta). Karang Nyimbor Hotel (fr $35/n); Paradise Surf Camp (fr $25/n) and Secret Sumatra (fr $120).

**Nature and Culture** – Explore the Bukit Barisan National Park maybe on an elephant's back. Fishing, snorkelling or tours to hot springs.

**Hazards and Hassles** – Close reef inspections are unavoidable, especially at low tides and at the treacherous Way Jambu. Check out the garbage thrown in Krui's river, explaining why rivermouths are off limits after the rain. Chloroquine-resistant malaria is a risk throughout Sumatra, so take appropriate prophylaxis.

**Handy Hints** – There's no bank to change money, very limited internet access and no surfshop. Wax & leashes at Ombak Indah. Water is warm, but a shorty provides protection against reef cuts and wind chill.

**Jimmy's Point** left is long with an intense barrel from take-off, while the right offers a hollow wall, but is plagued by a tricky shallow exit. Head south for the fun, chilled-out **Jenny's Rights**, perfect for wall cruising and the odd cover-up. **Pulau Pisang** has waves break along both sides of the island. The right is long, very fast and it favours the off-season W winds. The super-sucky lefts are usually flat out barrels requiring speed and skill at this crowd-free spot. The bustling town of Krui holds two reefs flanking a nice beach but pollution is an issue when the rivermouth opens. **Krui Right** is a zippy, peeling righthander that needs a bigger SW-W swell to break clear of the reef and is surfable through the tides. **Krui Left** is a hollow, quality sprint that compares to Bingin on Bali, but only the largest swells swing past the protruding southern point. **Ujung Walur** picks up far more swell, while still enjoying offshore winds. The ride is real short, but barrel technicians able to backdoor the hollow peak will be rewarded. Around the headland facing south is a tricky coral platform called **The Peak**, which is sensitive to wind, swell size and crowds. The thumping beachbreak barrels of **Mandiri** can get really good when the NE blows most mornings until 9am. The fine sand silts up the water, but it's the river flow that brings pollution in the wet season. Losmens line the point at **Ujung Bocur** the region's most consistent left that's sheltered from the SE trades. On smaller swells, it's a pretty mellow wave by Indo standards, flipping between long, drop and climb walls and a few half-face, hollow pockets, with rides up to 250m+. Gets a bit heavier and hollower as it reaches the double overhead mark, with barrels from the outset and thigh-burning walls through 3 to 4 take-off spots, so take a longer board. The set-up at **Way Jambu** is heavy and only experts will actually dare to tackle these hollow and powerful waves breaking dangerously close to sharp reef. Sectiony in the extreme, it varies greatly with tide and swell direction, but wide-open tubes are the constant theme at any size. An expedition south will pass by Bali Village, a clutch of rights and lefts facing a Balinese settlement. Despite being a promising set-up, **Siging** is a disorganised spot where the end of the reef is inside the point and well wind protected. **Benkunqut** is a proper pointbreak setup that faces due west so the SE winds blow offshore and Balimbing has the same aspect. Surfing Enggano requires a charter boat or local dugouts to explore the promising reefs that are often inside deep bays along the south shores of this remote island.

Plenty of 6-12ft swells hit from April-October and SSW is the perfect direction. Off-season is rarely flat with regular swells in the 2-6ft range. Cross-shore winds are the rule as the slowly increasing SE trades run from May-Oct, then NW winds dominate the rest of the year. Tides are mixed; Christmas Island (Aus) tidal charts are relatively accurate.

| STATISTICS | | J F | M A | M J | J A | S O | N D |
|---|---|---|---|---|---|---|---|
| SWELL | Direction | | | | | | |
| | Size (ft) | 5 | 6 | 7 | 8 | 6-7 | 5 |
| WIND | Direction | | | | | | |
| | Force | F3 | F3 | F2-F3 | F3-F4 | F3 | F3-F4 |
| WATER | Wetsuit | | | | | | |
| | Temp/°C | 28 | 28 | 28 | 27 | 28 | 28 |
| WEATHER | Rainfall/mm | 320 | 300 | 230 | 220 | 310 | 430 |
| | days/mth | 8 | 10 | 10 | 6 | 9 | 9 |
| | Min temp/°C | 23 | 23 | 23 | 23 | 23 | 23 |
| | Max temp/°C | 30 | 30 | 31 | 30 | 30 | 30 |

DAVE SPARKES
The Peak

# Panaitan and West Java INDONESIA

Close to the sprawling cities of Jakarta and Bandung, West Java is the most densely populated region in Indonesia with around 42m inhabitants. Despite the huge population, this SW tip of Java is a wild, unspoiled land in places, with large National Parks and World Heritage sites preserving the largest area of lowland rainforest in Java. One of Indonesia's most daunting yet rewarding barrels pinwheels down the coral crusted lava of Panaitan Island, nicely complemented by a mainland left that challenges for Indonesia's heavyweight, big wave crown. In between there are more reefs, beachbreaks and rivermouths with something to suit everyones style and ability.

+ HIGH CONSISTENCY
+ WORLD-CLASS PANAITAN ISLAND
+ VARIETY OF WAVES
+ CLOSE TO JAKARTA

- CROWDED CIMAJA
- SEA URCHINS, SHALLOW CORAL
- HARD ACCESS TO SOME SPOTS
- POLLUTION, DISEASE, MALARIA

Apocalypse

JASON CHILDS

Multi-peak, ripable rights break on the extensive outside reef of **Panaitan Bombie**, beyond the confines of the bay. Great when the swell is small and it is an easier wave than most on the island, despite the currents. Needs early/late glass or rare N winds to be good. Have no **Illusions**, it's rare to see perfect right peelers spin down the reef section tucked inside Sabini Point. Shallow and fast, Illusions needs more S in the swell to line up properly and will barrel nicely, but any SE wind will chop it up badly so early, late or off-season. **Apocalypse** – there's a clue in the name of this gnarly beast of a wave that sits deep in the bay and pretty well describes the end shutdown section. Air drops, a very square looking barrel and increasing speed to sudden close-out make this another experts wave, despite having better coral coverage than the left. Appeals to the experienced natural footers sick of getting out-run at One Palm. **Inside Rights** are where average surfers will revel in the lack of death-defying pits and have fun on a mix of lip-smacking walls and little hooks. A regular performer in off-season W winds and any SE-SW swell. Across the deep inner bay, **Inside Lefts** provide a reliable pressure valve and let-your-hair-down performance wall that intermediates will love and experts will shred. Long rides, low tides and good vibes prevail, as it usually has a wave when the banner waves don't thanks to its excellent wind protection. **Napalms** is a barrel machine further in the bay from One Palm and a little easier to master than its big brother. Lets you into a fast wall before sucking hard on the sharp inside coral heads. Low tide is risky and the SE winds give it a cross-shore chop you could do without. ✪**One Palm Point** is the main event and has been goading tube-junkies to pull in and hang on for the ride, or flogging of lifetime! There are more waves around the SE coast near the Rangers station.

On Java's SW tip, options are limited within the Ujung Kulon National Park until **Bayah Beach**, an empty, exposed, punchy beachbreak that requires small peaky swells to look at all tempting. Thumping close-outs and rips beyond headhigh. **Bayah Reef** is nestled behind the eastern headland, which provides a great vantage point to check this rarely ridden left. Nothing special other than some SE wind protection and the large rivermouth will bring filth after rains. A curve of decent beachbreaks is the backdrop for **Sawarna/Ciantir**, a long left shelf running down the eastern headland of the bay from Tanjung Layar. This wave has many moods and swells rear up from deep water, shifting around a bit, sometimes more hollow on take-off but generally a fast wall and always plenty of power. Should be more protected from the SE trades, but gets a nasty cross chop on it in the arvo, so get there early. Cheap accommodation in the village or take a boat from Cimaja. Just over the border from Banten Province into West Java Province sees more rocky reefs like **Batu Marob**, a nice righthand pointbreak with W wind protection. **Karang Haji** is a mellow longboard type right, breaking between the point and a rocky islet in smaller swells, with plenty of depth over the reef. There

## TRAVEL INFORMATION

**Weather** – Dry season (May-Oct) is the best time to visit. SE trades blow in from 11am and often die off around 4pm and the weather is reliably good, with only occasional evening thunderstorms. The rainy season, (Nov-April) can see morning drizzle, whereas afternoons have intense rains. Humidity levels are high in the rainy season and it brings out the insects. Water temperatures hover around 27-30ºC (80-86ºF), but some do wear wetsuits and booties at One Palm for reef protection.

**Lodging and Food** – Panaitan is a World Heritage site and the island remains uninhabited. Panaitan Island Ecosurf offer a choice of staying on small local craft, camping on Panaitan beach or staying at neighbouring Peucang Island Eco Lodge (fr$100/d). Yacht charters on Just Dreaming out of Anyer (fr $2000/9n) can be booked with Freeline. Various hotels/surf camps/losmens operate around Pelabuhan Ratu and Cimaja (Daun Daun Losmen, Pondok Kencana, fr $40/n). Down in Ujung Genteng, Mama's Losmen is rudimentary and cheap and Batu Besar (Big Rock) at Turtles can be part of a West Java tour. All these can be booked with the big agencies like Freeline, Surf Travel Company, and Surf the Earth.

**Nature and Culture** – Trek in the National Parks or book a boat trip out to witness the rapid rise of a new volcano Anak Krakatau (Child of Krakatoa), which has grown to over 300m since appearing in 1932 and is becoming increasingly active. There's rafting on the Citarik River or bathing in the Cisolok hot springs.

**Hazards and Hassles** – Both One Palm Point and Apocalypse are heavy duty waves and hitting the sharp reef is highly probable. Sharks are definitely present, but well fed. Cimaja is mellower than the Indo standard, but sea urchins and local crowds are not. Avoid rivermouths after rains, as hepatitis is common. Malaria is a much higher risk on Panaitan.

**Handy Hints** – A specialist board is needed for the heavier waves on Panaitan, where you must take everything you may need for survival. Be careful of local boat hire - stories of running out of fuel/food/water are rife and there is nothing/nobody out there to help. There are basic surf shops in Cimaja and some spares and board repair facilities at the main losmen in Ujung Genteng area. Many small local boats get into difficulty on the rough Sunda Strait, so the safer option is a proper surf yacht charter (Just Dreaming).

ANDREW SHIELD

Turtles

SEBASTIAN IMIZCOZ

## One Palm Point

LAT. -6.655053° LONG. 105.171153°

World-renowned left holding some of the longest barrels on earth in a pristine wilderness setting. It is super-shallow, very dangerous and hard to get to. Low tide equals suicide for all but the pros and mere journeymen have to wait for mid tide and/or smaller swells to make it from the air drop to deeper water in the channel. Requires a fairly high line to stay out of trouble, making it a real backhand challenge. Can be incredibly long when aligned on S-SW swells and any E wind. It's not always perfect by any stretch, but has rideable waves in the highly consistent bracket (7/10). Smart pig-doggers wear rubber!

Bayah Beach
Bayah Reef
Sawarna/Ciantir
Karang Haji
Indicators
Cimaja
Samudra
Loji
Ombak Tujuh
Turtles
Mama's
Ujung Genteng

Bayah
BANTEN PROVINCE
Karanghawu
Cimaja
Sawarna
Tg Layar
Pelabuhan Ratu
Cigaru
WEST JAVA PROVINCE
Cimarinjung
Ujung Genteng National Park
Ujung Genteng

is further soft, high tide beachbreaks at **Karang Hawu** and **Sunset**, perfect for beginners and stress-free sessions. The outside pointbreak of **Indicators** attracts experts on guns, who can paddle over from the main Cimaja line-up when the swell is really pumping. Jacking drops and slab sections across a reef littered with barnacle-encrusted boulders and urchins. Best on SW swells, higher tides and early mornings before the SE wind mashes it up. Tucked in a corner between rivermouths, the rocky shelf at **Cimaja** offers some outstanding right bowls when there is some W in the swell and either no or N wind. Attracts regular footers from as far as Jakarta so is often crowded with a bit of vibe, but the low tide barrels are worth a wait. Watch out for rocks and poor water quality after rain. Pelabuhan Ratu is a popular resort for Jakarta's well-off and breaking in front of the famous **Samudra** Hotel is a poor quality, small swell beachbreak that turns into a nasty close-out with strong rips at size. Just a short drive south of the Pelabuhan Ratu harbour is rare-bird **Loji**, a long, shapely pointbreak left that is not a challenging wave, is offshore all day, but needs a huge S-SW swell to break. There are more lefts up the beach at the dangerously polluted rivermouth if Loji is too small. **Ombak Tujuh** translates as Seven Waves and is definitely the big wave spot, capable of holding swells up to 20ft. The coral ledge protrudes into deep water, forcing the waves to jack up suddenly, making for elevator drops, right by the cliffs. Big wave experts only as the power and deepwater hold downs are serious, keeping crowds thin on big days. Needs a big swell to perform and longer pintails are a good idea. **Turtles** lurches abruptly onto the coral reef, making the take-off critical, then leading into some hooked walls and sucky barrel sections at lower tides. Gets classic and is a consistent option, despite SE winds ruffling it up. Remember to kick out before the sudden shutdown section past the rusty pipe pylons. **Mama's** losmen offers cheap accommodation and food, right in front of a moody high tide left. It's a fair way out over the reef platform/lagoon and swell direction will decide whether these speedy walls hold up nicely or close-out nastily on the sharp coralline shelf. Usually better in S swell conditions and the SE trades will keep it clean all day. On the SW tip of the Ujung Genteng National Park is the **Ujung Genteng Harbour**, where huge, intimidating lefts sweep around the reef and break along the entrance to the harbour channel. Sketchy in W swells, preferring S like Mama's to stop it sectioning off mercilessly. Higher skills at higher tides will get barrelled, but it's rarely good enough to make it worth risking a trip over the reef.

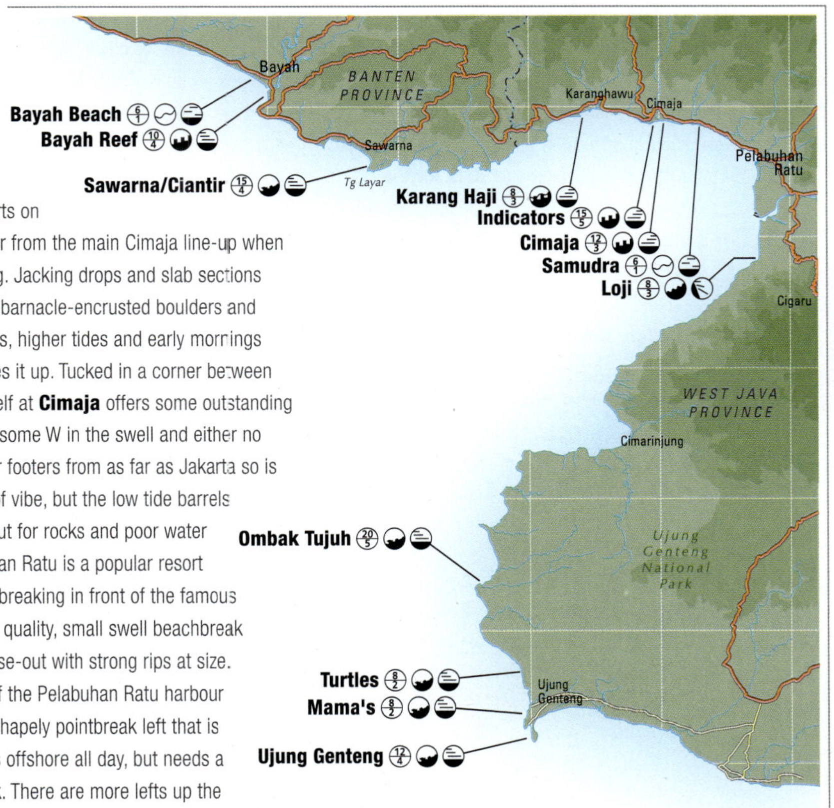

ANDREW SHILED

Ombak Tujuh

April-Oct swell consistency is really high and West Java usually averages 8ft at 14secs from June to September. The SSW direction is perfect for penetrating the prominent SW-facing bays on Panaitan Island. Off-season is rarely flat as constant swells in the 2-6ft range are aided by the Java Trench to focus wave energy on the coast. SE trade winds start in April blowing offshore for the lefts until Oct/Nov. Through the wet season (Dec-Mar), it shifts to W-NW with W first and then NW, grooming the rights on Panaitan. There's a big tide and a small tide every day that affects most breaks.

| STATISTICS | | J F | M A | M J | J A | S O | N D |
|---|---|---|---|---|---|---|---|
| SWELL | Direction | | | | | | |
| | Size (ft) | 4 | 5 | 6 | 7 | 6 | 4-5 |
| WIND | Direction | | | | | | |
| | Force | F3 | F3 | F4 | F4 | F4 | F3 |
| WATER | Wetsuit | | | | | | |
| | Temp/°C | 29 | 28 | 28 | 27 | 27 | 28 |
| WEATHER | Rainfall/mm | 229 | 117 | 105 | 55 | 77 | 172 |
| | days/mth | 18 | 13 | 8 | 5 | 7 | 13 |
| | Min temp/°C | 23 | 23 | 23 | 23 | 23 | 23 |
| | Max temp/°C | 29 | 31 | 31 | 31 | 30 | 30 |

# Central Java INDONESIA

With excellent surf at both ends of Java one could reasonably expect the remaining 1,000km of south-facing coastline to conceal more quality. A spine of volcanoes dominates the south of the island, creating many dangerous black sand beachbreaks that rely on shifty sandbanks and rare swell directions to produce quality waves. On the plus side, there are a few hidden gems – long sand point waves like Batu Karas provide great, low risk waves for all abilities.

- + FUN MELLOW WAVES
- + LOW CROWDS
- + WARM WATER
- + LAID-BACK ATMOSPHERE

- – LACK OF HIGH-CLASS WAVES
- – POOR BEACHBREAKS
- – REGULAR ONSHORE WINDS
- – LONG DRIVE FROM JAKARTA

**Bulak Benda** is highly exposed to swell, but needs a due S direction to get the fast, hollow right with serious barrels, reeling across the shallow reef ledge. Better at size, this open ocean, experts only spot needs offshore or glassy conditions. The fishing village of Batu Karas has a quiet, friendly vibe and is surfable all year, with more consistent and bigger swells during the dry season, but more favourable winds in the wet season. When S swells or larger SW swells wrap around **Batu Karas Point**, a long, fun right starts hollower on the take-off then shoulders into the wind-protected, sand-bottomed cove for rides up to 400 metres at low tide. **Batu Karas Reef** is more challenging, with an easy take-off and speedy workable walls across a lava rock reef. It prefers high tide, S swells and W winds making it mainly a wet season wave. Heading towards Pangandaran, the road passes a string of beachbreaks such as **Batu Hiu**. This area is plagued by really strong currents and the waves generally close-out too much, however the sandbanks tend to improve in the wet season. Popular with Javan holiday-makers, the long crescent of sand at **Pangandaran Beach** is home to seemingly endless beachbreaks that face S/SW, receive all available swell and are almost never flat. The set-up is remarkably similar to the Kuta/Legian beachbreaks in Bali, with wave quality depending on sandbank shape and swell size (close-outs are common with swells over 4'). During the dry season the sandbanks near the airstrip are best early mornings before the SE trades mess it up and the waves get progressively smaller and cleaner towards the nature reserve, making it a perfect learning curve. **Batu Mandi** is a short and punchy lefthand reefbreak that breaks hard and hollow on a sharp reef ledge. Best on small swells, it's extremely shallow at low tide, but even on high tide it's vital to exit the wave before the shut down end section. Further down the reef towards the 'White Sand Beach', a longish high tide left is surfable on huge SW swells. **Batu Layar** is on the E side of the peninsula and is an inconsistent right that needs headhigh S swell to show and a wet season W wind to be clean. Lower tides are faster as it gets fat at high. Nusa Kambangan Island is a nature reserve where the white sand beaches could conceal a few surfable breaks. Jailbreak is an average, often-sectiony right reef at the eastern tip of the island. For more challenging waves, head east to the Pacitan area.

June to Sept will be the best swell months but the E-SE winds will blow out the exposed waves. Shoulder season will have medium swells and some respite from the SE trades. Oct to Feb will be offshore W-NW all day but small to flat at spots like Batu Karas. The mixed tides reach 6ft and greatly affect many spots.

JENYA IVKOV

Batu Karas Reef

JENYA IVKOV

Batu Karas Point

## TRAVEL INFORMATION

**Weather** – The dry season, May-Oct is the best time to visit – the SE trades clear the skies everyday, producing rare thunderstorms in the evening. The rainy season can have morning drizzle then intense afternoon rain, or be mostly sunny, bringing intense humidity.

**Lodging and Food** – Backpacker to modest accommodation is available in Pangandaran. Bamboo House offers very basic rooms for $7/nt. Pantai Sari Hotel is close to Pangandaran beach and the best rooms have A/C ($14-30/nt). The stylish JavaCove Beach Hotel in Batu Karas has beachfront rooms starting at $40/nt for 2 people including their famous breakfast. Pick a fish for dinner and watch it being cooked in one of the many local warungs.

**Nature and Culture** – See wildlife such as deer, Javanese gibbons, echidnas and rare flora like the huge rafelesia flower in the Pangandaran National park. Cruise the 'Green Canyon' by boat along the Cijulang River. Citumang waterfall is a spectacular swimming hole.

**Hazards and Hassles** – The surf here is mellow by Indonesian standards, but the beachbreaks get heavy and strong rips are common. There are an increasing number of local surfers and travelling surfers, but crowds are not a problem.

**Handy Hints** – Pangandaran and Batu Karas have stocked surf shops and boards can be rented on the beach for $8/d. Avoid Indonesian holidays and weekends when prices rise.

| STATISTICS | | J F | M A | M J | J A | S O | N D |
|---|---|---|---|---|---|---|---|
| SWELL | Direction | | | | | | |
| | Size (ft) | 3-4 | 4 | 4-5 | 5-6 | 4-5 | 4 |
| WIND | Direction | | | | | | |
| | Force | F3 | F3 | F3-F4 | F4 | F4 | F3 |
| WATER | Wetsuit | | | | | | |
| | Temp/°C | 28 | 28 | 28 | 27 | 27 | 28 |
| WEATHER | Rainfall/mm | 340 | 260 | 100 | 30 | 60 | 280 |
| | days/mth | 12 | 10 | 5 | 2 | 4 | 12 |
| | Min temp/°C | 22 | 22 | 21 | 20 | 21 | 22 |
| | Max temp/°C | 28 | 30 | 30 | 30 | 31 | 30 |

# Grajagan Bay INDONESIA

Steeped in legend since it was first spotted from a plane back in the early '70s, Grajagan or G-Land has rightly become one of the planet's truly iconic waves. Peeling down the edge of a dense jungle that blankets the SE tip of Java, this perfect, magnificent, metric-mile reef, magically materialises some of the best lefts known to the surfing world. All the right ingredients are present to create what can only be described as a freak of nature and lifetime best tubes can be ridden by the hordes of surfers who invade this isolated wilderness every year.

+ WORLD-CLASS BENCHMARK SPOT
+ PERFECT LONG LEFT BARRELS
+ CONSISTENT SWELL & OFFSHORES
+ JUNGLE CAMP EXPERIENCE

- CROWDED LINE-UP
- ONE WAVE DESTINATION
- HEAVY WAVES, DANGEROUS REEF
- LONG OVERLAND TRANSIT

CORY SCOTT

G-Land

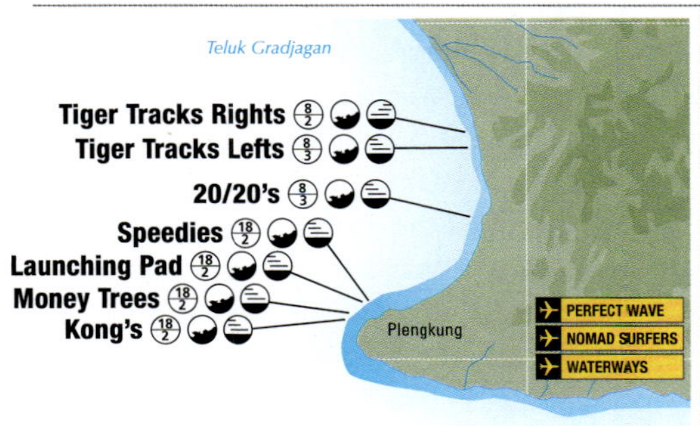


Furthest out on the perfectly angled G-Land reef is **Kong's**, often the shifty, messiest section of the reef, preferring W swell to barrel and works when small. **Money Trees**, attracts the bulk of the campers to what looks like perfect peeling barrels for 2-300m. The tubes can undulate from cavernous pits to tight, high envelopes and getting caught behind is guaranteed. **Launching Pad** only appears on moderate to heavy swells as wider rogue sets hit the patch of reef beyond the normal whitewash line and look like tapering into nothing, before jumping up and launching into the pedal-to-the-metal section – **Speedies**. Making the drop while drawing the right line and maintaining velocity are crucial as it doesn't let up or offer an easy escape for 200m of precision peeling. The reef whizzes by in clear menace, and is the sharpest, shallowest patch so surf it on the push from quarter tide. Chicken's is the very protected end of the reef for big day avoidance. A 20min walk north of camp arrives at **20/20's** where a break in the fringing reef allows some smaller, slower lefts to wrap into a sandy channel that also sports a swift, shallow right on the other side. A 1hr walk from camp, **Tiger Tracks Lefts** are assertive, walled-up and will occasionally tube down an ill-defined reef. On the other side of the sandy bay is **Tiger Tracks Rights**, a super-fun, forgiving righthander that invites hard turns and the odd barrel, mainly for frustrated regular footers from G-Land camp. All these spots need mid to high tide and are generally uncrowded. Tanjung Kucur is a long jungle hike through to the protected Bali Strait side, so it needs a real pumping S swell to break. Long rights are the lure, but the chances of scoring before the SE wind hits are slim.

The SE trade-season is usually April to Oct and the June-Sept high season slot shows incredibly high consistency (100%) for groundswell over 3ft (1m). Averages show a solid period of 14secs around the 8ft (2.5m) mark and bombing swells sometimes hit 13ft @ 20secs. Winds are reliably SE from April and can still have the odd offshore day as late as Dec, but transition months of March and Nov can have oscillating winds blowing mainly from the S before shifting W-NW for the wet-season. Tide charts are posted in the camps and on their websites. There is a big and a small tide each day with range reaching about 2.5m. G-Land veterans will always try to time their visits with a full or new moon.

## TRAVEL INFORMATION

**Weather** – The dry season from May-Oct is very warm, with gentle seabreezes and occasional overnight rains. Average air and water temps are 28°C (82°F) so not much relief getting wet. Camps are closed wet season depending on the winds and usually Dec and Jan are no go months, but tours start as early as late Feb, when rain and W wind is likely, but crowds are low.

**Lodging and Food** – There are 3 camps on land and some charters anchor in the bay. G-Land Bobby's Surf Camp (grajagan.com) is the original camp sited in front of Moneytrees, while G-Land Joyo's Surf Camp (g-land.com) is down closer to Speedies and G-Land Surf Camp (Raymond) is closest to Kongs. Prices start from $360 for 3 nights – see websites for details. You can pay extra for an upgraded menu, including extra beer.

**Nature and Culture** – There are snakes, the odd primate and all manner of bugs. The small black-tip reef sharks are well fed. Surf culture only!

**Hazards and Hassles** – Malarial mosquitoes are present at G-Land. The offshores start at 10 am so sunstroke, dehydration and heat exhaustion are real issues. Small sea snakes scurry around the channels, plus there are urchins in the crevices.

**Handy Hints** – Time your assaults with the crowd in mind. Early/late glassy sessions are often emptier. Paddle at high tide and walk carefully at low, preferably in booties. If possible, try to punch/fly/get out the back of shutdown sections rather than straighten out over the shallow reef. Time paddle outs between sets, pace yourself – G-land often rewards those who wait!

| STATISTICS | | J F | M A | M J | J A | S O | N D |
|---|---|---|---|---|---|---|---|
| SWELL | Direction | | | | | | |
| | Size (ft) | 4-5 | 5-6 | 6-7 | 7-8 | 6 | 4-5 |
| WIND | Direction | | | | | | |
| | Force | F3 | F2 | F3 | F3 | F3 | F3 |
| WATER | Wetsuit | | | | | | |
| | Temp/°C | 29 | 28 | 28 | 27 | 27 | 28 |
| WEATHER | Rainfall/mm | 300 | 177 | 105 | 55 | 77 | 172 |
| | days/mth | 18 | 13 | 8 | 5 | 7 | 13 |
| | Min temp/°C | 23 | 23 | 23 | 23 | 23 | 23 |
| | Max temp/°C | 29 | 31 | 31 | 31 | 30 | 30 |

JENYA IVKOV

G-Land

# Bali INDONESIA

Bali is "The island of 1000 temples" which the locals believe is blessed by the gods. The gods certainly have blessed the local surfers, because they live in a perfect, tropical surf paradise. Although 40 years of booming tourism development has drastically transformed the landscape and the line-ups, Bali remains an essential surfing experience. There is no denying the quality and quantity of its surf, when SW swells wrap consistent lines around the Bukit Peninsula into straight offshore winds, creating a list of world-class lefts, including Uluwatu, Padang Padang, Bingin and Kuta Reef. Add to these the quality beachbreaks of Kuta and Legian, plus the east side rights of Nusa Dua, Sanur and Keramas or Shipwrecks and Lacerations on Nusa Lembongan, then it becomes obvious that Bali has one of the highest concentration of quality waves on the planet.

+ MANY WORLD-CLASS SPOTS
+ WET & DRY SEASON WAVES
+ BEGINNER AND EXPERT SPOTS
+ UNIQUE BALINESE CULTURE
+ WILD NIGHT-LIFE

- VERY CROWDED WAVES
- TRAFFIC JAMS
- DANGEROUS DRIVING
- TOUTS AND HUSTLERS
- INCREASING POLLUTION

Medewi

JENYA IVKOV

## WEST COAST

**Medewi** is a slopey, light-lipped left that trundles down a smooth cobblestone and sand point, becoming the islands longest ride when it lines up on a S-SW swell. It's a typical, west coast, dawn patrol spot, so best bet is to stay at the losmens on the point. **Balian**'s rivermouth, rock-shelf peak is a reliable swell-magnet, focusing the bulk of its size and power on the long left. Can sometimes barrel on the smaller inside waves over the shallower part of the reef, but it is generally a wall to shoulder ride. The intermediate-friendly peaks at **Canggu** shift around a bit as the black sand moves around the reef, keeping the inevitable dawn crowd on their toes. The inside reef is tricky at low and high tide cuts off the beach in places so mid tide is often best, especially on the lefts. More peaks down the beach towards Pererenan. **Old Mans** forms the southern edge of the Canggu stretch and perennial favorite with the longboard and SUP crew as the long, lined-up rights skirt the lava reef. Generally fat and friendly up to headhigh, it can handle some sizable sets that will feather a long way out. It's mainly slop and shoredump between Canggu and **Brawa Beach,** where some rocky reefs anchor the sand and shape up some nice rights and a few lefts at mid to high tide. Good for improvers/intermediates and wont be as crowded as Canggu. In **Seminyak**, there's plenty of access roads leading to dozens of shifting sand bars that might be perfect A-framed peaks or surly, thumping close-outs as the swell gets overhead. Tides affect the quality and shape massively and often strong rips make it impossible to stay in position. Check Petitenget, Ku De Ta, and Double Six for the best banks. Famous, fine-grained **Kuta Beach** attracts surfers of all abilities to what can be super-fast tunnels or dribbly, knee-high corners. On any given day, there may be a dozen yellow rash vests, proning on their first ever waves alongside a Balinese local effortlessly punting a 360°. Usually better from mid to high, the trades are more offshore here, but water quality is very dubious after rain.

**Kuta Reef** sits a good 700m offshore, waiting for enough swell to swing around the projecting runway and hit a couple of sections of reef. The main reef is a fine left drop, stall, barrel, slash kind of wave and gets ledgy as it hits 8-10ft faces. Trades can really rip into the waves by the afternoon so the dawn patrol gets way overcrowded with boatloads paying to ride from the southern end of Kuta Beach, avoiding the 20min paddle. **Airport Reef** holds multi-peak ripable lefts that may not be perfect, but sure can be fun for the smaller crowd willing to go the extra mile. The two peaks sometimes link and open up, otherwise it's a performance wall that can give some long rides at higher tides. Book your boat ride back! One of Bali's premier waves, **Airport Rights** is fairly fickle, needing a chunky SW-W swell and higher tides to show its true colours. On its day, it can produce flawless deep pits, spinning the length of the reef triangle beside the airport runway. Seriously shallow and fast from headhigh up when it's an experts only wave and it's almost a 1km paddle, so get a boat from north Jimbaran Bay.

## EAST COAST

**Serangan** aka Turtle Island, is a wet-season, east-facing, crowd-pleaser that has something for everyone. Various lefts and rights peak up and pitch along a coral arc, ranging from softer shoulders to sucky shacks at all stages of the tide. It's strange to surf near a massive rock jetty in Bali, but it has little affect on the waves, which hit the nicely oriented SE reef. Picks up plenty of swell and breeze, drawing the crowds when the winds go W. Chilled out warung scene after clearing the security check to get on the island. In front of the upmarket hotel strip, **Hyatt Reef** is where tourists play in the calm waters of the lagoon on all sorts of craft and surfers make the long trek by boat out to the barrier reef for energetic righthanders that rumble off the furthest point. There's two sections separated by a big hole in the reef and the outside shares similarities with Nusa Dua, but the hap-hazard, rip torn peaks are even hollower. Further inside, rapid, walled rides guarantee tube-time as they suck over the shallower part of the reef. Nasty when big, it's an advanced break and a constant paddle against the current, until it backs off at dead high. **Tanjung Sari**, another hotel namesake line-up, where a big bend in the reef and a shallow channel provide both rights and lefts on either side. The rights can be picture perfect and peel for a good few hundred meters, providing the tide is lower and a good-sized S-SW swell has already awoken Sanur. Fast and sectiony is the vibe with scant coral cover, so each wave is a bit of a lottery. The lefts are easier, with a nice cover-up section before a short wall to the channel. **Sanur** is the east coast super-right that guillotines mercilessly over a sharp slab of coral and pinwheels at mach one for hundreds of meters, before closing out on the inside dry reef. Unfortunately, Sanur Reef needs a serious swell to even begin breaking and wont get classic until it is well overhead, meaning Nusa Dua will be twice as big. These huge swell conditions are rarer in the rainy season window when it's offshore all day, so consistency drops further. On smaller days at lower tides, it breaks up into funnelling walls and long shut-down sections, but with more swell and tide, barrel predictability and length of ride improves dramatically. The inside section is often unmakeable on all but the biggest tides and biggest days of the year and even then it will claim many victims. To say it is crowded is an understatement and some localism is likely. **Padang Galak** is a foot-burning black sand beachbreak that flips from low tide mushy shoulders to dredging shore-dump at high tide. Mid tide may conjure up something in-between and glassy mornings can be fun for the improvers trying to get some waves away from the crowds. Won't handle much above head high and needs some N in the wet season wind. The east coast reefs switch to a lava base at **Ketewel** and are every bit as intimidating as the coral. Spacious, angular pits unfold over an uneven base that demands high tide to be safe enough to challenge. Add in the southerly aspect and it means that morning glass and spring highs are the best option, so it's not too consistent. **Purnama** sits in a bucolic Bali backdrop of rice paddies and traditional houses, adding to the laid-back persona of this 2.5km strip of glinting lava particles. The sand will

Tanjung Sari

FEDERICO VANNO

**Keramas**

LAT. -8.598839° LONG. 115.339514°

Keramas is the jet-set plaything and latest pro contest hang-out as its reputation for barrels and high octane performance ramps grows. Picks up plenty of east coast swell and focuses it on a jagged lava reef that opens up straight from the drop then just asks to be bashed before the wave closes-out on the inside. Surprisingly consistent and increasingly crowded for the dawn glass sessions. Plenty of current when it gets bigger, always crowded and some bad vibes from over-zealous ex-pats and local surf guides.

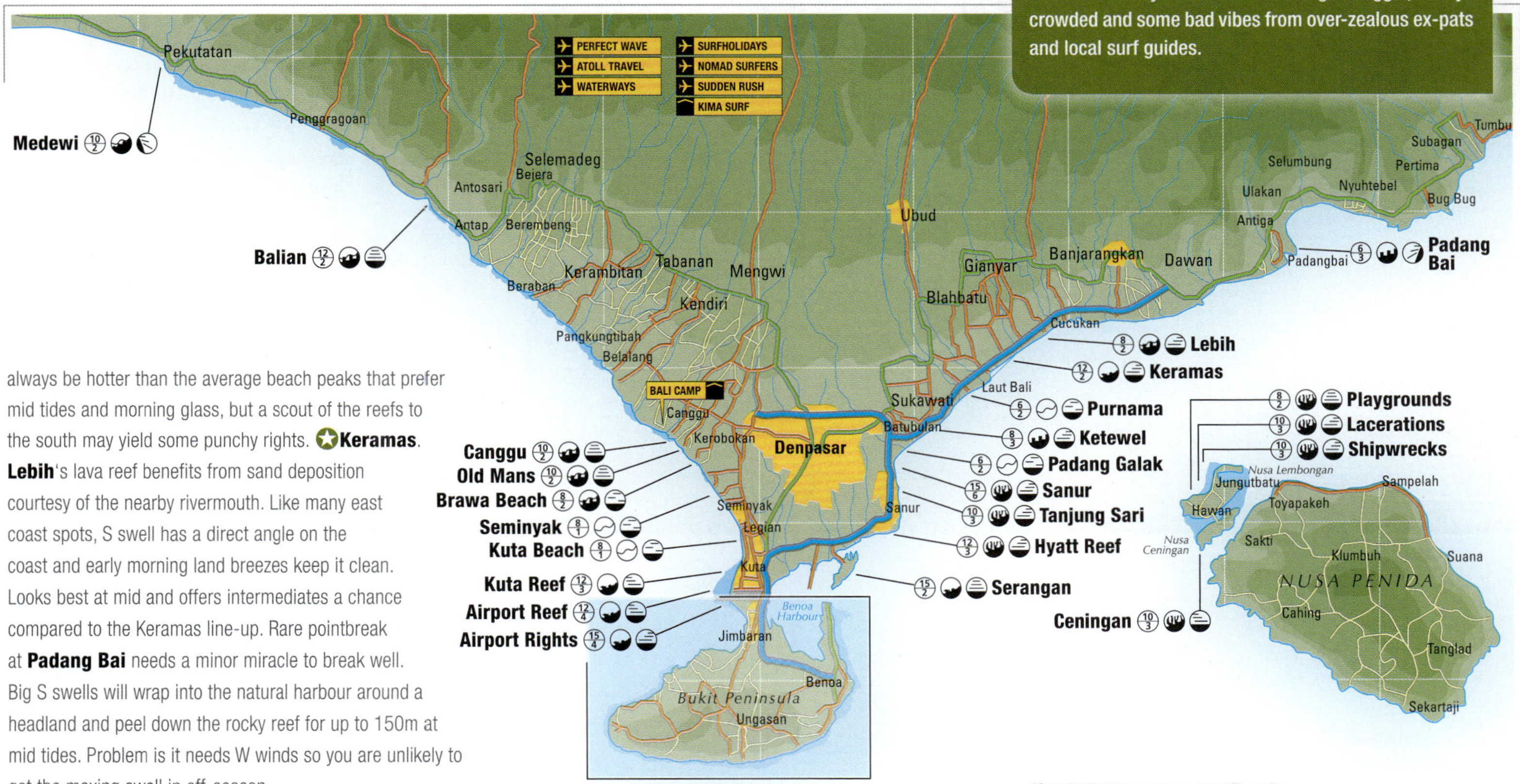

PERFECT WAVE
ATOLL TRAVEL
WATERWAYS
SURFHOLIDAYS
NOMAD SURFERS
SUDDEN RUSH
KIMA SURF
BALI CAMP

Medewi
Balian
Canggu
Old Mans
Brawa Beach
Seminyak
Kuta Beach
Kuta Reef
Airport Reef
Airport Rights
Padang Bai
Lebih
Keramas
Purnama
Ketewel
Padang Galak
Sanur
Tanjung Sari
Hyatt Reef
Serangan
Playgrounds
Lacerations
Shipwrecks
Ceningan

Pekutatan, Penggragoan, Selemadeg, Bejera, Antosari, Antap, Berembeng, Beraban, Kerambitan, Tabanan, Kendiri, Mengwi, Pangkungtibah, Belalang, Canggu, Kerobokan, Denpasar, Seminyak, Legian, Kuta, Jimbaran, Benoa Harbour, Benoa, Bukit Peninsula, Ungasan, Ubud, Gianyar, Blahbatu, Banjarangkan, Dawan, Cucukan, Laut Bali, Sukawati, Batubulan, Sanur, Selumbung, Ulakan, Antiga, Padangbai, Nyuhtebel, Subagan, Pertima, Bug Bug, Tumbu, Nusa Lembongan, Jungutbatu, Hawan, Nusa Ceningan, Toyapakeh, Sampelah, Sakti, Klumbuh, Suana, Nusa Penida, Caling, Tanglad, Sekartaji

BUKIT PENINSULA
SEE PAGE 166

always be hotter than the average beach peaks that prefer mid tides and morning glass, but a scout of the reefs to the south may yield some punchy rights. **Keramas**. **Lebih**'s lava reef benefits from sand deposition courtesy of the nearby rivermouth. Like many east coast spots, S swell has a direct angle on the coast and early morning land breezes keep it clean. Looks best at mid and offers intermediates a chance compared to the Keramas line-up. Rare pointbreak at **Padang Bai** needs a minor miracle to break well. Big S swells will wrap into the natural harbour around a headland and peel down the rocky reef for up to 150m at mid tides. Problem is it needs W winds so you are unlikely to get the maxing swell in off-season.

Over on Nusa Lembongan island, **Shipwrecks** is non-existent at low tide, but starts breaking on the push to mid and sets start rearing up out of the deep Lombok channel, peeling fast with a high, tight envelope and open shoulder. Gets packed with surfers of all standards so snagging one and avoiding the scratchers is part of the deal. Getting the tide just right is the trick - mid on springs, higher on neaps. **Lacerations** is a hard-core right with excellent, wide-open tube time on offer as the tide floods the sharp, shallow reef. It's a pitching, air-drop entry from the peak into a straight barrel section then a further sucky bowl as it approaches the channel marked by floating mooring lines that litter the bay. Not easy, not long and not empty. Nestled below cliffs, **Playgrounds** offers good SE trade protection and is the most user-friendly spot on Lembongan. It's an easier paddle, continues to break at lower tides, is a little bit deeper and offers more wall to work as opposed to the flat out barrels nearby. The lefts are better with a few lip-bashing opportunities along a tapered wall, while the rights may pitch slightly, but fade quickly. **Ceningan** Island is a lefthander that lines up rolling walls with a nice steep pocket and predictable sections. Some protection from the trades and it's a good small swell, low tide option when Lembongan isn't working.

JASON RICHTER

Lacerations

# Bali continued

BERNARD TESTEMALE

Bingin

## BUKIT PENINSULA

The mirage-like left spinner at **Balangan** is often a sectiony close-out, depending on swell direction and tide height. More south in the swell may make it a bit peaky and parallel the reef more, but the real deal starts at overhead to double on a SW-WSW and 0.4-1.4m tide co-efficient. Intermediates will deal with small swells, experts will charge the big days. **Dreamland's** once tranquil beach is now a tourist hotspot, with all mod cons and is well-suited to the masses, offering a decent left wall and short shouldering right off the peak, over a sandy reef platform that is good and deep. Best at low tides in small swell, otherwise becomes a fat, uninspiring shoredump. **Bingin** is best described as short, sharp and shallow. The tight take-off zone at the end of the shelf beneath the impressive Bukit cliffs is always packed with goofy's trying to nail the backdoor take-off and kick out before the dry reef shutdown a mere 50m later. **Impossibles** becomes possible when a moderate to large, long period S swell sweeps past Ulu's and Padang onto this long coral reef at low tide. There's usually three sections separated by straight bits of reef, so getting caught behind the curtain is a given. Looks picture perfect from the cliffs, but the reality is it's impossibly fast at some point in the wave. Same paddle-out as Padang, while getting in over the sharp low tide reef is best done in booties. ✪**Padang Padang** (see opposite). Ultra-consistent **Uluwatu** is the focal point of Balinese surfing thanks to its ability to handle any size swell from small to large and spread the biggest of crowds across a wide reef. Its sectioning, hollow walls always produce great waves, starting with faster, high tide, occasional tuck-ins up at Temples that lead down to the muscular, steep drops

JENYA IVKOV

Uluwatu

## TRAVEL INFORMATION

**Weather** – The two distinct seasons don't always run like clockwork and El Nino years in the Pacific usually extend the dry season to its limits of April-Nov when temps range from a night low of 23°C (74°F) to a day high of 33°C (92°F), tempered by sea breezes and the odd rain shower during the night. Conversely, La Nina patterns can bring unseasonal, torrential rains in mid dry season months. Nov-April is hotter, wetter, and more humid. Jan-Feb suffers from heavy afternoon rains and stifling humidity averaging at 85%. Water temps are usually a tepid 28°C (82°F), but can dip to 25°C (77°F). Surfing in a white T-shirt can aid cooling while a light vest may add a thin veneer of protection against the reef and cold mornings.

**Lodging and Food** – back-alley Kuta losmans (guest houses) that cost from $8-$25/night and finishing with the ridiculous exclusive resorts of Nusa Dua or Jimbaran for anything up to $8000 per night! There are many surf camps offering all inclusive packages (transfers, accom, board hire, lessons, transport, guiding, etc) for reasonable prices starting around $40/d (Balicamp, Kima) for room/bungalow to $70+ for self contained family houses. Classic Indonesian dishes like nasi goreng (fried rice) and sate ayam (chicken sate) are as cheap as $2-3. Great seafood available - try the Jimbaran fish restaurants.

**Nature and Culture** – Balinese practice an unusual form of Hinduism with a dash of Buddism and Animism, creating a fascinating religious culture centred on ritual ceremonies and offerings. Favourite tourist haunts include the artist village of Ubud, sunrise over Lake Batur and the lofty volcanic peak of Agung mountain, which dominates the landscape. There are also famous temples (Uluwatu, Tanah Lot, Besakih), myriad shopping opportunities and great restaurants. Kuta nightlife is a legendary, hedonistic melting pot of nightclubs and parties fuelled by cheap(ish) alcohol.

**Hazards and Hassles** – Mosquitos carry dengue fever, Japanese encephalitis and malaria (officially not present on Bali) - avoid bites. Considering the lack of sewage treatment and general sanitation levels, it's not surprising that cholera, typhoid, hepatitis, Bali-belly and TB are prevalent. Avoid rivermouths. Don't drink local water supply, ice or fruit/veg not freshly peeled/cooked. Dogs can carry rabies. Be careful of thieves, scammers and hustlers - drugs are a big no-no. Motorbike road-rash or shallow reef-rash are biggest threats. If injured seriously, many fly to Singapore or Darwin for hospital treatment as opposed to entering Denpasar Hospital. Private clinics and hospitals have improved treatment facilities but are expensive cash up front deals - get medical insurance!

**Handy Hints** – Kuta has the highest concentration of well-stocked surf shops in the world and prices may compare favourably when looking at high airline board charges. It is possible to sell your gear to local shops and giving kids your spare boards, boots, leg ropes is normal practice. Learn some basic Indonesian, which is easy to pick up. Be courteous to the local surfers.

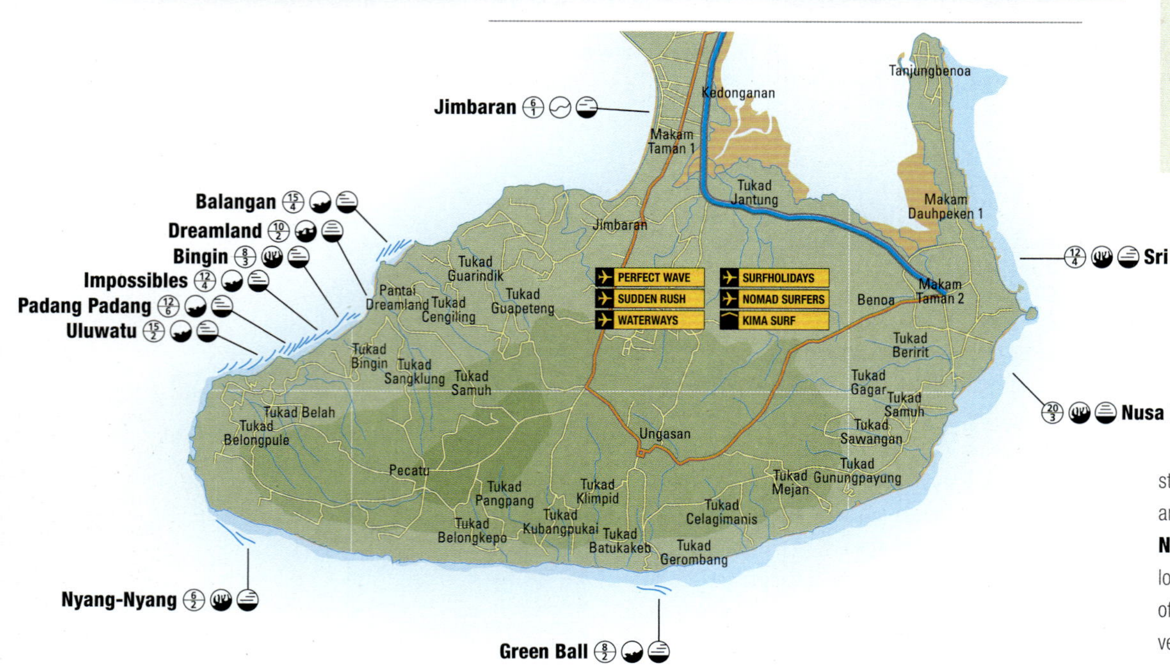


of The Peak where open face and hollow pockets unfold directly in front of the famous cave. It can sometimes jump the deadspot and barrel through to the start of the Racetrack, which twists and bends the wailing walls in an ever increasing race against the falling curtain. When swells exceed the 8-10ft mark, Outside Corner will rumble into life, with heavy, thick-lipped sections at low tide for experts on sturdy pintails. Main hazard is the crowd, followed by the reef and the constant, higher tide sweep to the north. **Nyang-Nyang** is Bali's "if it's flat here, it's flat everywhere" wave, located on the exposed south coast of the Bukit at the bottom of impressive cliffs. Blows out quickly and it also maxes out very quickly as the rights get overhead and the barrel sections become shut-down sections. The reef is ragged and always seems closer than it actually is, but higher tides will see more water in the channel and more chance of the lefts showing as well. Strong rips, sneaker sets and the hellish walk back up make this an advanced riders and fitness fanatics spot. **Green Ball** shares much with Nyang Nyang in that it is a swell-magnet right, horribly exposed to the trade winds and is at the bottom of a long, strenuous cliff path. If the wind isn't on it, then a fast, punchy right sucks and spins off the reef, then walls up nicely before pitting on the last bit of reef beside the channel. Home of the strongest current in Bali, which whips out to sea at various angles, making it hard to stay in position. Offshore **Nusa Dua** is a righthand supermarket with a confusing amount of aisles to go shopping in. All available swell is sucked into the entrance of the deep Lombok Strait and bent onto this 2km curve of coral reef. Unlike other Bukit set-ups, it focuses into a vast array of shifting peaks, hitting different lumps of the reef and drawing up into powerful, heavy-lipped bowls and long sections of speed carve walls. At size, the drops get serious and thick, while unpredictable sections add to the sense of roulette – eventually you will get one on the head. It rarely links up into a super-long ride, but the paddle back out always seems longer against the background drift north and if you try the zippy, open lefts on the far inside section, prepare to be punished paddling back out. Wet season, all-day-staple and dry season sneaky early. Conserve your strength and pay for a return boat ride out there. **Sri Lanka** is another quality wave that happens to be out the front of a Club Med. Off-season thrill a minute barrel when a big S-SW swell wraps enough to spin down the short, straight coral platform that faces out to the NE. Sucky and round from the take-off to the kick-out shut down section, but it has to to huge at Nusa Dua to be working well. It's only a medium consistency spot so when it finally breaks, the locals descend.

Bali benefits from an almost endless supply of Southern Ocean groundswell arriving form the S to WSW (180º-247º) but by far the most consistent direction is due SW (225º). These swells range from 3-12ft (1-4m), with averages around 5ft @ 11secs from Nov-March, then upping to 7-8ft @ 14secs in the middle of the April to Oct high season. Underlying windswell can mix in from the SE to the W, but has little bearing on the surf at most breaks. Sometimes, 6-10ft (2-3m) tropical cyclone swells can arrive from the western Indian Ocean or NW Australia through the southern hemisphere summer. Swells are focused onto the Bukit Peninsula because of the deep-water channels on either side of Bali, particularly the east side Lombok channel, which can draw in overhead waves to Nusa Dua when everywhere else seems too small. The ESE trade winds blow reliably from April to Oct, then shift SW-NW for the Dec to March wet-season. Wet season wind speeds are on the whole lower, usually staying below 10mph (16kph) compared to the dry season SE trades which regularly hit double that. Tide charts are posted in surf shop windows showing a big and a small tide each day, while full and new moons often see a jump in swell size as tidal range increases.

**Padang Padang**

**LAT. -8.809814° LONG. 115.099964°**

**Benchmark Bali barrel machine and all-round epic wave up there with the best lefts on the planet. Needs major swells to work as it is tucked into the peninsula below the cliffs where the SE trades blow dead offshore. The short 50m ride starts with a pitching lip take-off that sets up into a perfectly cylindrical wall, tempting experts to stand on the tail and see how deep they can push it. Barrel intensity increases as it draws more water off the shallow coral and forces a speed run to the exit before the wave runs out of water. Low is really sketchy, but there will still be someone out there risking their skin. Best described as a bear pit, attracting the biggest and the best grizzlies from the local, expat and tourist hordes. Respect.**

FEDERICO VANNO

Nusa Dua

| STATISTICS | | J F | M A | M J | J A | S O | N D |
|---|---|---|---|---|---|---|---|
| SWELL | Direction | | | | | | |
| | Size (ft) | 4-5 | 5-6 | 6-7 | 7-8 | 6 | 4-5 |
| WIND | Direction | | | | | | |
| | Force | F3 | F2 | F3 | F3 | F3 | F3 |
| WATER | Wetsuit | | | | | | |
| | Temp/°C | 29 | 28 | 28 | 27 | 27 | 28 |
| WEATHER | Rainfall/mm | 300 | 177 | 105 | 55 | 77 | 172 |
| | days/mth | 18 | 13 | 8 | 5 | 7 | 13 |
| | Min temp/°C | 23 | 23 | 23 | 23 | 23 | 23 |
| | Max temp/°C | 29 | 31 | 31 | 31 | 30 | 30 |

# Lombok INDONESIA

At its closest point, Lombok sits only 18km (11mi) east of Bali, yet major physical, cultural, linguistic and religious differences exist. The deep strait separating these islands links the Indian and Pacific oceans and is part of the "Wallace Line", an established physical division between Asia and Australia. Bali is green with lush, tropical vegetation, while Lombok is drier, more rugged, with completely different flora and fauna. When it comes to the waves, most Lombok surf breaks are generally regarded as being of lower quality and intensity than Bali's, with the notable exception of Desert Point, elected "Best Wave in the World" by *Tracks* magazine's readers.

+ VOTED WORLD'S BEST WAVE
+ YEAR-ROUND SURF
+ GREAT SCENERY
+ CHEAP LODGING AND FOOD

- OVERCROWDED DESERT POINT
- ONLY ONE OUTSTANDING BREAK
- HARD ACCESS TO EASTERN SPOTS
- LACK OF ACCOMMODATION

ALAN VAN GYSEN
Mawi

KURAKURA SURF CAMP
Tanjung A'an

KURAKURA SURF CAMP
Air Guling

RANULF LUCAS
Inside Ekas

Furthest west of the three small Gili islands (not shown on map), Gili Trawangan has a shallow fringing reef off the southern tip, serving up fast, hollow, but generally flawed right lines. Tricky wave to ride and plenty of current so experience required. Needs hefty S-SW swells to clear the coral that is usually frequented by snorkeling tourists. More a party, couples, chill out destination so don't expect many waves. Gili Air is over-protected from swell and dead onshore when the SE trades blow, meaning this is a very unlikely score. Huge SSW swell, big, dropping, spring high tide and light W-NW wind cook up some short, sharp barrels that peel perfectly down the SE tip. A surprising amount of locals do surf Sengigi, a circular reef that is mainly a left plus a sectiony right, which needs rare N winds. Plenty of SW swell and tide will clear the coral and fire off some cylindrical lefts, but it spends most days below the chest-high minimum required. ✪**Desert Point**. Decent lefts run at **Belongas** when the SSW swell hits this isolated reef just right and winds are E or even NE. Racy lip line with some tuck sections that will suit average surfers just fine at mid tide. **Mawi** is a quality, south coast, dry season break that works in all swell sizes, set in a beautiful west-facing bay. Consistent spot that attracts boats and land-based surfers from Kuta and Grupuk losmens when the SE blows strong. Small swells see a fun, peeling peak until the hollower right starts closing out at overhead size. The powerful left then rumbles on down the reef up to double overhead plus, offering a heavy drop/barrel section, hooking wall and final tube before shut down. Very strong currents in the channel and a nasty sharp reef mean intermediates need to be on their toes. Pointbreak style set-up on western fringe of pretty beach, **Mawun** causes SE-SW pulses to radiate round the reef for some long, high performance walls. Consistently has swell, but glassy or NW winds required, so it's a wet season spot. A short boat ride to the next bay west of Kuta unveils some low tide rights that trip into a fast inside barrel. **Air Guling** is exposed to swell and wind that needs to be more N than W, so it's rare to score after 9am. **Kuta** is the surfing hub of Lombok, another wet-season-centric spot as the righthander on the western headland is offshore in NW winds and likes a SE-S swell. Like Mawun and Air Guling, the left across the channel is lower quality and often messy, but both are fun, no consequence waves for all abilities and a lazy session instead of driving off in search of better waves. In front of the Novotel, **Segar** is a small swell, wind sensitive, fun righthander, plus occasional left. More peaks in either direction, but NE is offshore so early mornings or glassy, peaky off-season days will produce easy rides for the odd crowd. A straight shooting S swell will penetrate the bay and unload on **Tanjung A'an**, a nasty sharp reef with serious tubing intent. Guaranteed shade-time, this is heavy water, especially below mid tide and not a wave to be attempted by the meek. N winds or early glass make it less consistent than other spots nearby and due to its quality, has a few local "minders". Like the impressive twin peaks on the headland, **Outside Grupuk** is more rolling hill than impressive cliff. Orderly drop and plenty of shoulder real estate make it accessible to improvers when small and intermediates when big. Breaks consistently on any S swell at mid to high tides but is easily blown out and often crowded. **Don-Don** breaks in the middle of the bay, in front of the semi-submerged wooden fishing frames once the tide has moved in a few hours. Non-abrupt glide into predictable, easy walls that are a bit faster on the lefts. Like all the Grupuk spots, can get stupidly crowded with all skill levels in the water, so be wary and give the beginners room. **Inside Grupuk** is mainly rights, unless small and fairly similar to the other waves in the bay, namely rolling, simple drops and slopey walls ideal for improving turn combos and generally cruising. When there's a rare combination of S-SE swell and W wind, long bowling rights break at **Awang**, offering tubes over a shallow coral platform. **Inside Ekas** is a generously covered reef peak marooned in another deep bay/estuary that needs a moderate SW swell to wake up. Sucky and swift, the shorter rights feather up nicely and open up occasionally, as the SE trades blow into the barrel. Meanwhile, the longer lefts wall and roll predictably, inviting big hits in a playful, safe and therefore crowded environment. Low to mid tide for the rights, high for the lefts and any flavour E wind. The chaotic, powerful left at **Outside Ekas** shifts and jumps around the line-up below steep cliffs at the eastern headland. Consistently drags in far more swell than Inside Ekas, the high speed walls and odd tuck section can get really long at size, when it becomes an advanced surfers break.

## TRAVEL INFORMATION

**Weather** – Days are almost universally 12hrs long with sunrise at around 6.20 am and sunset at 6.30 pm. The daytime temperature averages 30°C (86°F) all-year-long, but take warm clothing if planning a trek of Mt. Rinjani. Lombok's tropical monsoon climate has two distinct seasons; dry (May to September) and wet (October to April). Monsoon refers to the wind – even in the wet monsoon the rain tends to be short lived and localised. May, June and July are considered the best, while Jan-Feb suffer heavy rains and stifling hot temps. Water remains around an ideal 28°C (82°F).

**Lodging and Food** – Basic rooms in Kuta cost under $5, for more comfort head to the Kuta Indah Hotel (fr $22) or the luxurious Novotel. Very basic hut accommodation is available at Bangko-Bangko (Deserts) and Laut Surga (Ekas), where there are also new, expensive, surf tourist options. Kura Kura Surf Camp in Kuta has all inclusive packages fr$420/5n. For surf charters check Freeline, Surf Travel Online and dozens more offering a range of vessels, duration and price. Lombok food revolves around poultry, meat and fish cooked with tropical veggies in spices and coconut milk sauce.

**Nature and Culture** – Trekking at least part of the way up Rinjani is the reason many tourists come to Lombok. Activities include kite surfing, diving, snorkelling, fishing, cycling, or even skateboard the bowl in Grupuk. Witness traditional culture in Relbitan and Sade, north of Kuta.

**Hazards and Hassles** – Desert Point is a super-gnarly wave; rips, shallow reef and crowds of frothing surfers all contribute to the danger; wear a helmet. Other spots break softer, but medical attention is more than an hour away in Mataram. Bring some reef boots. Theft stories are common. Tip someone to be a security guard for vehicles and belongings. Nearest bank is Praya (1hr), so take enough cash.

**Handy Hints** – Boards can be fixed or rented from Kuta Reef Surf Shop or Kimen Surf in Kuta. It's common practice to hire a local surfing guide. Bring a regular shortboard and a semi-gun, especially for Desert Point. Unlike in Hindu Bali, Islamic Sasaks make up 90% of Lombok's population.

**Desert Point** LAT. -8.726924° LONG. 115.837975°

When it is on, Desert Point is indeed one of the longest, makeable lefthand barrels on the planet with over 20secs tube time possible on one wave. The take-off area can shift around a little but generally rewards a deep attack. High speed is the key as it quickly winds up and starts peeling mercilessly across the shallow reef, cutting a trench in the coral where the mechanical lips have been slamming for centuries. The caverns get larger and faster as the inside section commits the tube rider to a lock-in that usually ends on dry reef. Only surfers good enough to deal with the tricky exit, the shallow reef, evil out-going currents and plenty of wave-starved rippers should apply. Desert's has a reputation for inconsistency, with only the biggest groundswells igniting it and high tides making it disappear as fast as it came. Surf charters keep flocking from Bali and dedicated hardcore surfers wait for weeks in basic beach shacks, forming a frenzied, barrel-hungry pack on those rare classic days.

Out on the exposed SE tip of Lombok, a series of reef cuts and passes offer small swell options, including the lip-smacking performance ramps of **Sereweh** up the eastern channel. If there's no sign of whitewash on these reefs, then Lombok is officially flat. Really a wet season option as a small SE swell and N winds are needed to make the long boat ride worth it. Hard to access by land, hard to scope by sea.

RUSSEL MCCARTHY

Outside Grupuk

Lombok receives the same swell that hits Bali and can also benefit from short-lived, wet season, tropical cyclone swell from a 180º window. Winds blow like clockwork: the mild E-SE trades start in April, blowing up until October. November is a transition month with oscillating winds around SE-SW. Then, it shifts to W-NW with W first and then NW until end of March. Get a tide table online or in Bali and pay attention to the range: there is a big and a small tide every day, with many spots working only at mid to high tide.

| STATISTICS | | J F | M A | M J | J A | S O | N D |
|---|---|---|---|---|---|---|---|
| SWELL | Direction | | | | | | |
| | Size (ft) | 4-5 | 5-6 | 6-7 | 7-8 | 6 | 4-5 |
| WIND | Direction | | | | | | |
| | Force | F3 | F2 | F3 | F3 | F3 | F3 |
| WATER | Wetsuit | | | | | | |
| | Temp/°C | 29 | 28 | 28 | 27 | 27 | 28 |
| WEATHER | Rainfall/mm | 310 | 150 | 70 | 35 | 65 | 220 |
| | days/mth | 19 | 15 | 8 | 3 | 7 | 16 |
| | Min temp/°C | 25 | 25 | 25 | 24 | 25 | 25 |
| | Max temp/°C | 30 | 30 | 29 | 28 | 29 | 30 |

# West Sumbawa INDONESIA

Heading east from Lombok, the climate remains dry, supporting a brown, parched landscape of scrub and bush, clinging to lowland hills and a smattering of volcanoes. Sumbawa's Mt Tambora ejected 4 times the magma of Krakatau, killing 72,000 and caused the "year of no summer" in 1816. These days the island remains sparsely populated, infrastructure is rudimentary with few good roads and the bustling tourist towns of Bali and beyond have yet to materialise here. Surfers have however, carved out a couple of epicentres alongside the two best west-facing surfing coasts. Across the Alas Strait from Lombok, a concentrated stretch of sharp, shallow reefs leave little to the imagination with names like Super Suck and Scar Reef, attracting thrill seekers who are usually on one of the many charters cruising between Bali and Rote.

**+ CONSISTENT SWELLS**
**+ WORLD-CLASS WAVES**
**+ SEMI-CROWDED**
**+ EXPLORATION POTENTIAL**

**– SE TRADES RESTRICT CHOICE**
**– SLOW OVERLAND ACCESS**
**– LACK OF ALTERNATE ACTIVITIES**
**– NO DIRECT FLIGHTS**

CORY SCOTT
Scar Reef

CORY SCOTT
Supersuck

**Northern Rights** is a treacherous angle of reef that needs the biggest, straightest SW swell, mid tides and a rare N wind to make the journey up the channel worth it. The harbour and rivermouth at Labuhan Lalar also needs a massive swell to refract onto the reefy beach at **Fly**, hitting a right triangle and a few easy peaks along its length. **Downtowns** becomes the default wave when Scar is too small or crowded and offers less critical peaks, including a nice right that sucks in swell and peels off the northern extremity of Jelenga Beach. **Scar Reef** is the main attraction in West Sumbawa, offering multiple barrel opportunities for advanced surfers willing to take a risk with possibly the sharpest reef in Indo. It starts off fast with a throwing take-off, then constant tongues of the lip flick out to swallow you as a series of backdoor sections demand high speed and clear positioning to thread the wave to the sketchy inside closeout. Its personality changes constantly as low tide madness becomes perfect mid-tide bowls, before giving way to fast sloping walls and envelopes at high. **Benete** is a major containership terminal and port, where the protected, deep bay needs a big bending swell to create another classic barrelling left over a shallow shelf beneath cliffs. Maluk Bay is the home of **Super Suck**, which will only show its world-class colours in a bigger SW-W swell. Take-offs are beyond critical and require an angled, straight into the barrel approach, which briefly lets up before increasing speed towards the inevitable straight reef shut-down. Crowded and intense. Sekongkang Bay is a swell magnet, with a couple of exposed slabs referred to as Yo-yo's thanks to the refraction off the cliffs. **The Wedge** does just that as smaller S-W swells bounce off the towering cliffs to form a steep but easy drop into a short punchy right that sucks up nicely before it ends abruptly. **The Hook** sits further down the reef where it curves into a proper channel and is more likely to hold up and spin off some makeable barrels. Neither spot handles SE trades nor major swells, so small, glassy mornings at mid tide are best. Around the headland the coast begins facing south around **Sejorong**, which is over-exposed to swell and wind, requiring off-season NW winds combined with smaller ground and windswells.

Sumbawa receives all the normal Indonesian swell trains and the 6-12ft swells from April-Oct are needed to penetrate the western bays. Due S direction and W swells are blocked, so only pulses that are 15° either side of SW will get in. The E-SE trades can be reliable (80% of the time) and very strong, averaging 25km/h in July. During the off-season the wind shifts to a W-NW direction. Download the diurnal tide chart so you know when the big tide is going to give the shallow reefs enough cover.

## TRAVEL INFORMATION

**Weather** – Warm to hot temperatures, regular sea breezes and some overnight rains temper the dry season from May-Oct. Nov-April is wetter, cloudier and hotter. Jan-Feb suffers from heavy rains and stifling hot temperatures. Water temps are a stable 28°C (82°F) year-round.

**Lodging and Food** – Many charter boats out of Bali go as far as Scar (fr $1000/7d). Cheap, land-based losmen accommodation is available at Jelinggah (Scar), Maluk (Super Suck) and Sekongkang (Yo-Yo's) from $5/n. Surfwestsumbawa.com has all inclusive packages from $400. Supersuck Hotel starts at $20/n.

**Nature and Culture** – Flat day options include good fishing, snorkelling and watching buffalo races in the rice paddies. Sumbawa is not as culturally rich as Bali.

**Hazards and Hassles** – Hitting the reef is going to be your major worry. Malaria is also a problem (take a net) and travelling overland will be slow and frustrating.

**Handy Hints** – Take everything you need (no surf shops) including an Indo gun for those frequent 8ft+ conditions. This trip is usually linked in with one to Lombok. Be very careful of cheap offers in Bali, scams happen!

| STATISTICS | | J F | M A | M J | J A | S O | N D |
|---|---|---|---|---|---|---|---|
| SWELL | Direction | | | | | | |
| | Size (ft) | 4 | 5 | 6 | 7 | 5-6 | 4 |
| WIND | Direction | | | | | | |
| | Force | F3 | F2 | F3 | F3 | F3 | F3 |
| WATER | Wetsuit | | | | | | |
| | Temp/°C | 29 | 28 | 28 | 27 | 27 | 28 |
| WEATHER | Rainfall/mm | 299 | 177 | 105 | 55 | 77 | 172 |
| | days/mth | 18 | 13 | 8 | 5 | 7 | 13 |
| | Min temp/°C | 23 | 23 | 23 | 23 | 23 | 23 |
| | Max temp/°C | 29 | 31 | 31 | 31 | 30 | 30 |

# Central Sumbawa INDONESIA

Just south of Hu'u, Lakey (Lakai) Beach, is a long, wide, palm-lined stretch of ivory sand, fronted by reef. Since its discovery by Australian surfers in the mid '80s, Hu'u has been known to offer a varied selection of waves for every ability and taste. This means it's a popular dry season destination, especially when early morning high tides are happening, producing the best waves in glassy conditions.

- \+ DENSITY OF WORLD-CLASS SPOTS
- \+ CONSISTENT CONDITIONS
- \+ LEFTS AND RIGHTS
- \+ DRY SURF SEASON

- − SOMETIMES VERY WINDY
- − LONG PADDLES
- − TRICKY LOW TIDES
- − CROWDS

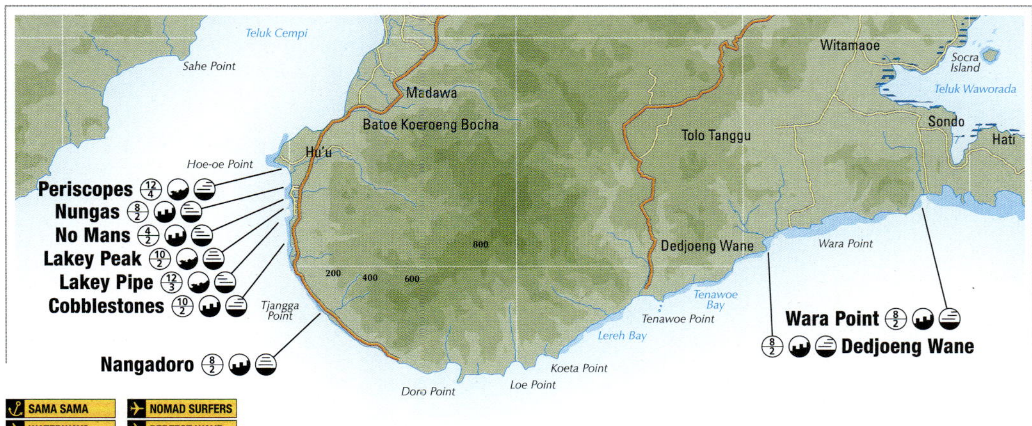


SAMA SAMA
WATERWAYS
NOMAD SURFERS
PERFECT WAVE

**Periscopes** is a 40 minute walk, but only a short 100m paddle-out. This wave requires a big swell with more S in it and can hold up to double overhead. Hit it early in the morning with a coinciding high tide, as this wave needs plenty of water over the reef to make it out of the barrel onto the shoulder. This is a natural footers tube riding paradise so expect crowds. **Nungas** can peel off like a mini version of G-land, grooming 200m long lefts with alternating shack and whack sections to play with. Many surfers get diverted on the long walk to Periscopes, opting for long ride, short walk. 300m right of Lakey Peak is a shut down section of reef called **No Mans** that may have a short shallow ride in small, lumpy swells. Perfect **Lakey Peak** peels off short lefts and rights into channels either side. The right will often throw up backdoor tube rides but gets too shallow at low tide, when the left is churning out predictable, ideal speed barrel rides. Mid tide lip-smacking sessions will appeal to intermediates and the flattish reef is user-friendly, except during full or new moon phases. Just 400 meters to the south is **Lakey Pipe**, a gnarly reef with a fairly sedate take-off, which then hits the shelf and throws out a solid backdoor barrel. Optimum at mid to high tide and double overhead. Walk 45mins (or rent a zodiac) to escape the Lakey crowds at a deep reef channel called **Cobblestones**. Nice walled-up rights on one side and lefts barrelling into the channel opposite, pick up more swell and handle some solid size at mid to high tides. Arrange a lift on a motorbike to get to **Nangadoro** that offers both a spinning left and two right reefs, which pick up more swell than any other spot. On small days with NW winds, venture to the south coast where great rights occasionally hit **Dedjoeng Wane**, or check the outside reefbreaks at **Wara Point**, 4km south of Sondo and a very long paddle.

RYAN CRAIG

Lakey Peak

## TRAVEL INFORMATION

**Weather** – The wet season generally occurs from Nov through Feb with heavy monsoon rainfall and clouds. The dry season, from May to Oct, can still experience rain but is generally fine, clear and hot. Temps are relatively warm, ranging from 23-32°C (74-90°F) all year-round. It can be breezy around Aug and Sept, but boardshorts and a rashie should do.

**Lodging and Food** – Growing number of places to stay in Lakey, 3km south of Hu'u. Aman Gati Hotel has 40 rooms (fr$52/p/dbl). Lakey Peak Surf Houses and bungalows (fr$35-$130/n). The original 22 room Mona Lisa Bungalows is well-maintained ($15/nt). Aircon can almost double room rate. Cheap food.

**Nature and Culture** – Visit Bima Sultan Palace on 99 old teak stilts, see Raba Dompu weaving village and Doro Bata relics in Dompu. Dompu is used by tourists as a stopover point to Mount Tambora. The trek takes 2 nights camping in a rain forest and 1 night to the 2,851m (9354ft) summit. Check Komodo island for its famous dragons.

**Hazards and Hassles** – The reef at Lakey Pipe can be nasty and long walks on low tide reef make booties almost compulsory. Surfing has 30 years of history, so there are now 2nd generation locals. It can be a bit aggro for the best conditions. Walk to the more remote spots – take good shoes and enough water. Low malaria risks.

**Handy Hints** – There are no surf shops around Lakey apart from wax at some of the hotels. A gun could be necessary for the 6-10ft (2-3m) days. There are rarely boat trips to Lakey area as boats go Bali - West Sumbawa or Sumba - Rote. The long overland trip from Bali is a real drag.

JIMMY WILSON

Periscopes

May-September is prime surf season, overloaded with 3-12ft swells, but plagued by sideshore afternoon trades. The SE trade winds start in April and the skies begin to dry. Mornings are often light offshores. The really windy season starts from the end of July until middle of November with 13-25 knots of cross-shore on the beach. November through February is not the best time of year for surf, but there is the chance of some cyclone swell and south coast spots will be offshore in the W-NW winds. The diurnal tide (one radical change per day) is a huge factor, so get a tide chart to plan your trip around AM highs.

| STATISTICS | | J F | M A | M J | J A | S O | N D |
|---|---|---|---|---|---|---|---|
| SWELL | Direction | | | | | | |
| | Size (ft) | 4 | 5 | 6 | 7 | 5-6 | 4 |
| WIND | Direction | | | | | | |
| | Force | F3 | F2 | F3 | F3 | F3 | F3 |
| WATER | Wetsuit | | | | | | |
| | Temp/°C | 29 | 28 | 28 | 27 | 27 | 28 |
| WEATHER | Rainfall/mm | 299 | 177 | 105 | 55 | 77 | 172 |
| | days/mth | 18 | 13 | 8 | 5 | 7 | 13 |
| | Min temp/°C | 23 | 23 | 23 | 23 | 23 | 23 |
| | Max temp/°C | 29 | 31 | 31 | 31 | 30 | 30 |

# Sumba INDONESIA

Deep offshore trenches and inter-island channels allow plenty of swell to hit the southwest-facing coast of Sumba, where waves of consequence get thrown onto the reefs of dead coral, volcanic rock and boulders. Sumba is not for everyone; the food and accommodation are basic and the mixed ethnic population speak three different languages. Huge megalithic tombs and thatched, peaked huts dot the landscape, while in the line-up, intrepid travellers are now sampling the oceanic power of this ancient island.

+ CONSISTENT GROUNDSWELLS
+ EMPTY TOP-CLASS SPOTS
+ BASIC OR LUXURY ROOMS
+ TRIBAL CULTURE

– WILD & WINDY SOMETIMES
– NO PUBLIC ACCESS TO NIHIWATU
– LACKS BEACH LODGING CHOICE
– EXPENSIVE TRANSPORT COSTS

KLAUS BAUMGARTNER

Millers Rights

**Pero Rights** are tricky and unforgiving with a sketchy cliff, dead-end section, requiring wet season NW-N winds. Across the rivermouth channel, **Pero Lefts** can be excellent as swell is refracted heavily into big bowl sections with ample tube-time. Highly consistent and holds as big as it gets. The fringing reef at **Wainjapu** consistently holds long makeable lefts, providing there's not too much W in the swell. Explore eastwards for a few quality, hard to find reefs. **Pantai Marosi** is actually a big, shifty, deepwater right with power and long hold-downs in chunky SW swells. The scenic bay is sensitive to wind plus there's an outside left and a small swell, hazard-free beachbreak. The often debated case of **Nihiwatu** is quite unique in Indonesia, since the deluxe resort claims exclusive use of "Occy's Lefts" for the happy-few who can afford it. The famous lefts work on any size, the bigger the better and get really fast and hollow at low tide. Fat righthanders break across the bay from Nihiwatu and there are Sunset style rights and lefts on the next point that can be accessed by boat or car in about one hour. The rivermouth at **Wainukaka** is better in the wet season and almost only rideable at high tide with quality rights and lefts over a constantly changing sandy bottom. Only 3hrs drive from Wainjapu, **Miller's Rights** in Tarimbang are Sumba's most ridden wave and the line-up is sometimes crowded from May to Sept. Fortunately, the wave is so long it soaks up a big crowd and fast, hollow sections split the pack into clusters between the softer shoulders that are quite accessible to improver/intermediates. Waves can be a bit funky with SE trades, but are usually clean early morning and during the wet season. Big wave chargers may look at the offshore location known as **Mangkudu Island**, where the challenging lefts can reach 15ft (5m) plus there is a mellower right on the other side, only offshore during the wet season. In Kallala, three fairly consistent lefts work on different swells and tides. **The Office** is an all-round wave, suited to most surfers, offering fun, lazy walls, the odd cover-up and a forgiving nature, plus there's empty beachbreak for beginners on the inside. **Racetrack** is more challenging with a steep drop into a barrel section and fast walls, best tackled at mid tide. **Five-O** hits a bend in the reef and throws some serious lips, attracting the skilled surfers willing to take a chance on the highest tides in exchange for some big shacks.

## TRAVEL INFORMATION

**Weather** – West Sumba is far wetter, turning green and fertile in the wet season, while East Sumba is more dry and mountainous. In many coastal areas not a drop of rain falls during most of the year. Boardshorts year-round.

**Lodging and Food** – Choose between cheap & basic homestays near the surf or hotels as far as 45mins away. East Sumba camps $60/d; Marthens (Tarimbang) $20/d inc. food; Ahong (Wainukaka) or Aloha Hotel are $10/d. Nihiwatu 5 days min. $5k+ (7n/dbl). Le Nautile (Marosi) $90/d. Story (Pero) $10/d. Cheap food at about $5 a meal. Most charters (Sama Sama, Sri Noa Noa) will sail out of Kupang, West Timor and take in Rote and Savu, before making the long crossing to Sumba.

**Nature and Culture** – Sumba is well known for its sandalwood, horses, impressive megalithic tombs and typical hand woven textile (ikat). The most spectacular ceremony is the Pasola, the ritual fight with spears featuring hundreds of horsemen.

**Hazards and Hassles** – Reef cuts and long hold-downs are guaranteed. Anticipation will be the key as spots work on specific conditions and hopping from one spot to another is slow and tedious by road. Take malaria pills. Be patient.

**Handy Hints** – Take a gun during dry season and as much supplies as you can carry. If you go feral, you need to speak Bahasa Indonesian.

Dry season (Mar-Oct) Indian Ocean swells can sometimes reach 12-15ft (4-5m) from a SSW- WSW direction. The main trend is the SE trades, which blow-out many exposed spots, especially from June-Sept. Thunderstorms can change wind patterns, so early and late glass-offs are common. The wet season (Nov -April) is also a good time to consider for friendlier conditions at the rights with NW winds being offshore. There's a big tide and small tide everyday, ranging up to 8ft.

| STATISTICS | | J F | M A | M J | J A | S O | N D |
|---|---|---|---|---|---|---|---|
| SWELL | Direction | | | | | | |
| | Size (ft) | 3 | 4 | 5 | 5-6 | 4-5 | 3 |
| WIND | Direction | | | | | | |
| | Force | F3-F4 | F2-F3 | F3-F4 | F3-F4 | F3 | F2-F3 |
| WATER | Wetsuit | | | | | | |
| | Temp/°C | 29 | 29 | 28 | 26 | 27 | 29 |
| WEATHER | Rainfall/mm | 340 | 140 | 20 | 5 | 10 | 150 |
| | days/mth | 8 | 5 | 1 | 0 | 1 | 13 |
| | Min temp/°C | 24 | 24 | 24 | 23 | 24 | 25 |
| | Max temp/°C | 28 | 30 | 31 | 30 | 32 | 31 |

GILLES CALVET

Pantai Marosi

# Savu and Rote INDONESIA

A hot, dry, arid landscape coupled with geographical isolation from the main Indonesian surf hubs, means the islands of Savu and Rote have remained a bit of a frontier. Tucked in above Australia, this region has a narrow swell window with only its SW corner facing the Indian Ocean swells, so can suffer flat spells when the rest of Indo is working on a due S. But in typical Indo fashion, minor islands can hide major surf breaks and Rote, Savu and the surrounding outcrops are no exception, roaring to life in a straight SW swell.

+ MELLOW, ACCESSIBLE WAVES
+ CHEAP LOSMEN OPTION
+ FEW CHARTER BOAT CROWDS
+ DRY SEASON WEATHER

- SMALL SWELL WINDOW
- STRONG TRADES AFTER 10AM
- LACK OF NIGHTLIFE
- ISOLATED, NO LAND ACCESS

DAMIEN POULLENOT

T-Land

More than a 160kms west of Rote lies tiny **Pulau Dana**, where its long, barrelling left pointbreak and attendant right pick up all available swell and the only locals are turtles. Left is offshore in the trades, the right isn't. **Raijua** has a set of classic lefts on the SW tip of this remote, desolate island, including a really long, smoking fast, lower tide left that can barrel top-to-bottom for long sections. There's also a wild, rippy outside bombie at high and an insane, cliff-hugging wedge. **Savu Lefts** hit a coral fringe near the main town Seba, lining up some heavy walls with hollow sections if the swell is strong enough and the trades are offshore. **Savu Rights** are extremely fickle, occasionally firing off perfect right drainers down a swell-sheltered reef that gets blown to bits by the trades. **Ndao**'s western reef tip has good exposure to swell and holds a left in any type of E wind plus there's a right further S in glass or N winds. Both feature fast, steep drops and racy walls. In the land of lefts, a long right like **Do'o** is welcomed, but facing almost north, it mainly works before or after the standard surf season in glassy or NW winds. Higher tides needed to cover the sharp coral reef. At tourist/surf town Nemberala Beach, **T-Land** is a consistent left with 3-4 sections that can connect for a 300m+ ride. It's an accessible wave, that peels at low tide and walls up at high tide if the swell is around the headhigh range. When a moderate to large SW pulse arrives, it transforms into a heavy barrel and speed wall combo at double to triple overhead. If the swell is breaking up, a 30min bike ride to the exposed outside reef of **Peanuts** will offer more intense barrels over a shallower, sharper reef. If there's enough push in the swell, **Boa** will wake up and hiss along an east-facing setup that's hollow, challenging and unlikely to be good unless its blowing W or light winds.

The swell window for the region is small and prefers plenty of W, which usually makes Sept more reliable than the biggest month June. The E-SE trade winds can be strong, kicking up an underlying SE windswell. The off-season is dominated by SW-NW winds, buffing the rare east-facing locations, but swells are inconsistent. Early/late season should be the best time for a boat trip, before the trades strengthen, making navigation and anchorage more difficult. There is a big tide and a small tide every day and some spots only work on certain stages.

| STATISTICS | | J F | M A | M J | J A | S O | N D |
|---|---|---|---|---|---|---|---|
| SWELL | Direction | | | | | | |
| | Size (ft) | 3 | 4 | 5 | 5-6 | 4-5 | 3 |
| WIND | Direction | | | | | | |
| | Force | F3-F4 | F3 | F3-F4 | F3-F4 | F3 | F2-F3 |
| WATER | Wetsuit | | | | | | |
| | Temp/°C | 29 | 29 | 27 | 26 | 27 | 29 |
| WEATHER | Rainfall/mm | 340 | 140 | 20 | 5 | 10 | 150 |
| | days/mth | 18 | 8 | 1 | 0 | 1 | 13 |
| | Min temp/°C | 24 | 24 | 24 | 23 | 24 | 25 |
| | Max temp/°C | 28 | 30 | 31 | 30 | 32 | 31 |

## TRAVEL INFORMATION

**Weather** – Central highlands and closeness to Australia make for irregular seasons in the area, but the long dry season (May-Oct) is rarely too hot, tempered by sea breezes and some overnight rains. Average air temp is 30°C (86°F) and the water around 28°C (82°F). Nov-April is rainier and cloudier, while Jan-Feb suffers heavy rains and is considered a time to avoid.

**Lodging and Food** – Cheap losmen accommodation close to T-Land usually includes food (Anugurah; Tirosa fr $10/n). Waterways and Atoll Travel all book the comfortable Nemberala Beach Resort (fr $190/p/n inc. surf boat transfers). Freeline book Malole Surf House (fr $1950/12n) plus the Sri Noa Noa (fr$2660/12n). The Sama Sama does early season charters (fr $2200/10n). Nightlife is quiet around Nemberala, with only a few little restaurants to try for a change of scene.

**Nature and Culture** – Nemberala's reef supports varied marine life for snorkelling. Check out the ikats (woven textiles), Rote's unique palm hats and dance to the sound of the sasando, the 20 stringed local guitars made of lontar palm that also supplies boat & housing material plus sweet, nutritious (sometimes alcoholic!) tuak. Animist rituals still take place on Savu.

**Hazards and Hassles** – T-Land gets crowded high season – a boat trip in this area guaranties empty waves. Chloroquine resistant malaria has been reported; take precautions.

**Handy Hints** – Pick up any surf accessories in Bali. Bring your shortboard and an Indo gun if you want to charge huge T-Land. Learning a little Indonesian will help you get around an area of many obscure dialects. Respect local beliefs in Savu, no matter how strange!

DAMIEN POULLENOT

Raijua

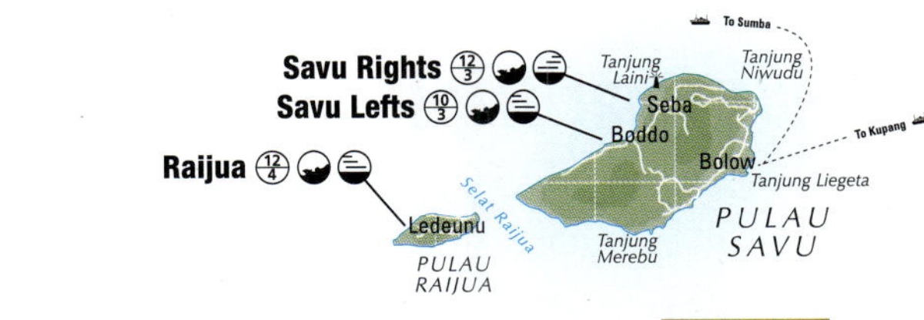


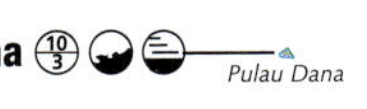

## THE BALICAMP & SAMA SAMA

### Customized Surf Guiding & Coaching and Trailblazing Boat Trips

This is about you. We can help you **follow your passion**, whether it be your first wave, or exploring uncrowded surf, pristine snorkelling and fishing, wild beaches, forests and culture.... or simply relaxing... in safety and comfort. We intimately know the seasons, weather conditions, locations and cultural sensitivities to guarantee an amazing surf, nature and cultural adventure.

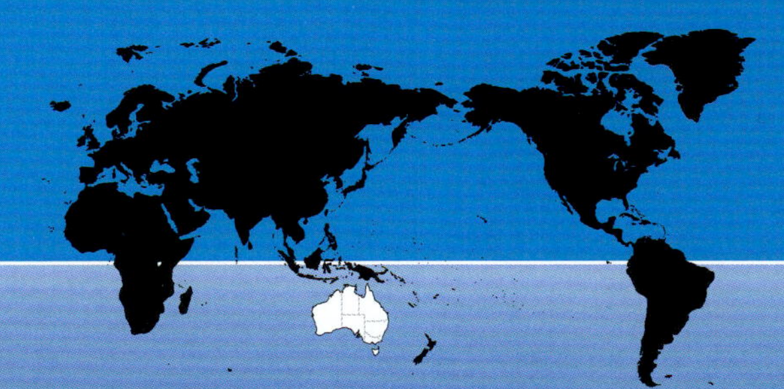

CRAIG PARRY

# AUSTRALIA

Australia is the only island continent on the planet, and within those two descriptive words are clues to this prolific surfing location. As an island it is surrounded by no less than three oceans, and four major seas, while as a continent it represents a surfable coastline of epic proportions. 90% of the population live in the narrow coastal zone and a high percentage consider themselves surfers, creating a nation where surf culture is mainstream. Australia offers an unrivalled diversity and quantity of waves, in a range of environments from tropical to trembling cold.

Byron Bay, New South Wales

# The Surf

## WESTERN AUSTRALIA

The Kimberley region of northern WA is an impressive wilderness and most of the surf comes courtesy of cyclones for a few months of the wet season. Apart from the multitude of offshore islands that must have some waves somewhere, the most popular spot is the 22km long Cable Beach in Broome. Plenty of locals surf here for the few weeks a year it works plus these days it is a popular tourist destination replete with big beach resorts. Down near Gantheaume Point and Riddels also work when it's big enough and you have to factor in the huge 10m tides, favouring mid to high. Some waves further north pick up big SW-W swell, but access is an issue with big fines for using washed out tracks and many vehicles are lost to the tides while beach driving. Next major mining centre is Karratha in the Pilbara, where offshore islands Angel and Gidley in the Dampier Archipelago spin up some righthanders, but are separated by 'clue in the name' Sharks Passage. More boat-access-only spots exist down to the Murion Islands and the beginning of the **Northwest WA** zone that includes the famous lefts of The Bluff. The 150km long Zuytdorp Cliffs link Shark Bay to the **Batavia Coast** at Kalbarri, extending down to Port Denison, where offshore reefs and skerries start to appear and hold some scary options for the brave in boats. Jurien Bay is the best place to launch from and Sandy Cape has land access beachies. A number of reefbreaks off Lancellin and Edward islands 500m to 2km offshore, work in moderate to large swells with light winds, plus there are some good peaks on the backbeach. When the Moore River opens to the sea, long barrels can form up for a short while. Check Two Rocks and the fun reef peaks at Derrs, that tend to be crowded. Yanchep

ANDREW SHIELD

Eyre Peninsula

PHOTOGERSON

Batavia Coast

has a handful of breaks including the areas best lefthander at The Spot, rights over the reef at Rafts and some sucky beachbreaks at Doggies for the bodyboarders. Clayton's is a full-on wedge growing from the bounce off the Mindarie Keys marina. Burns Beach benefits from a good reef peak, alongside average beachbreak options. For more of a challenge try Big Rock just down the coast before Trigg Beach and the start of the metropolitan **Perth** zone. A perimeter of fringing reefs suck the power and size from Perth's and Fremantle's surf so unless a heavy swell is running, waves are rarely overhead. Garden Island is off limits to all but navy personnel and boaters who remain in the channel and surf a few reefs in the south or across the channel at Point Peron to Penguin Island. Secret Harbour is one of the better Perth beachbreaks with something for all abilities throughout the year. More of the same at Golden Bay and Singleton, but Mandurah's 4th Groyne is a sucky barrel and guaranteed busy with bodyboarders. Between Falcon Bay and Avalon there are some reliable left reefs and the breakwall at the Dawesville channel has a rebound wedge, peaks at Pyramids and sandy reefs down at Melros. The straight sands of Yalgorup National Park leads down to Bunbury where a number of sand fed breaks get going in winter around the groynes and breakwalls of the harbour and back beach. Surf deteriorates as you go south into Geograph Bay and Busselton, since Cape Naturaliste cuts off the swell that makes **Southwest WA** so awesome and home to some of Australia's most consistent and challenging waves.

## SOUTHERN AUSTRALIA

Rounding the storm-battered lighthouse at Cape Leeuwin opens up the coastline to SE-S swell. Augusta Rivermouth is the first regular righthander, but is ultra-shark-friendly. Windy Harbour has beachbreaks either side, better in small swells. Mandalay and Conspicuous Beach holds more size for those fearless enough. Peaceful Bay has a serious left reef out of the W winds and an exposed big-wave right at the eastern end of the bay. A string of SE-facing beaches to the east include Parry, Lights, Lowlands and the most popular Ocean Beach where long rights can form off the rivermouth of Wilson Inlet. Mutton bird Beach gets hollow and powerful in S swell, N wind combo and like most of this coast, a 4WD makes life easier. The Bibbulmun Track winds for 1000km between Perth and Albany overlooking endless pounding surf that is always bigger than it looks from the towering granite cliffs. Albany's wave riches include Salmon Holes sucky reefs and protected Middleton Beach in town for all abilities. The coast turns to face the SE so winter becomes more consistent when breaks like Cheyne, Bremer and Hopetoun work with NW winds. Esperence is flanked by a number of quality waves from gentle, beginner friendly beachies to sucky reefs, points and is the jumping off point for Cyclops, one of the world's gnarliest big waves. The Cape Arid national park is bristling with quality waves, but signals the beginning of the longest line of sea cliffs in the world along the Great Australian Bight. Eucla is on the WA - SA border and has some ugly beachbreak by the jetty under the sand dunes, before the cliffs return up to Yalata's SW-facing 100km long beachbreak. Out of the desert pokes Point Sinclair and the concentrated quality of **Cactus**, SA's most famous and probably sharkiest surf. Offshore islands filter the swell until Streaky Bay where the excellent left at Granites resides. Check Scale Bay, Venus Beach and the heart-stopping lefts at Blackfellows in Elliston. Other Eyre Peninsula hotspots include Sheringa, Point Drummond, Greenly Beach, Coffin, Fishery and Sleaford Bays. **Adelaide** zone includes the Yorke Peninsula and Kangaroo Island, beyond which the 150km sands of the Coorong have few takers until Robe offers some civilisation and beach/reef options for all abilities. Head to Beachport east of the pier when the swell gets massive or try the fickle protected lefts at Southend. Engage 4WD to get to Cullens lefts in the Canunda National Park, showcasing the beauty of the Limestone Coast. Port MacDonnell is a popular crayfishing and surfing town with entry level beachbreaks at A-frames at Piccaninnie Beach and an assortment of heavy reefbreaks like Posties that handle the constant juice thrown at them by the Southern Ocean. Victoria's western coast continues the theme of a heaving ocean, howling winds and isolated reefs, toured by big sharks. Portland faces away from the SW swell which needs to be huge to get the insanely long rights of Blacknose to wheel down the point. Port Fairy accommodates three great reefbreaks out by the lighthouse and some fun beachbreak in town for large or SE swells. Warrnambool has mellow breakers at the west end of Lady Bay and more challenging peaks out at The Cutting and Japs. Monumental limestone ocean stacks dot the coast off Peterborough along with a couple of heavy barrelling righthanders made famous by Wayne Lynch, including the biggest, most powerful wave in VIC, Easter Reef. Port Campbell has a left reef at the entrance, breaking into the pier and beyond on macking swells. The 12 Apostles bring tourists flocking to this coast, but only experienced surfers should take on the powerful, rippy waves at the bottom of the cliff cut Gibson Steps, or the heavy peaks of Princetown. The **Great Ocean Road** surf needs little introduction and is immediately followed by the Mornington Peninsula and **Phillip Island** lowdown, all the way to Cape Paterson. Gippsland extends its isolated coast to the NSW border, shrouding some quality waves for searchers. West-facing Venus Bay is another of those long, lonely, windblown beaches, while Walkerville, Waratah Bay and Sandy Point is more protected and clean in N winds. The southern tip of the mainland at Wilsons Promontory is replete with adaptable beachbreaks at Derby, Squeaky and Oberon. Then starts the 90 Mile Beach closeout up to Lakes Entrance where sandbars improve and Red Bluff lefts work occasionally. Cape Conran lefts are out of the onshore E winds and more long, wilderness beaches lead out to Mallacoota and a good righthander at Bastion Point.

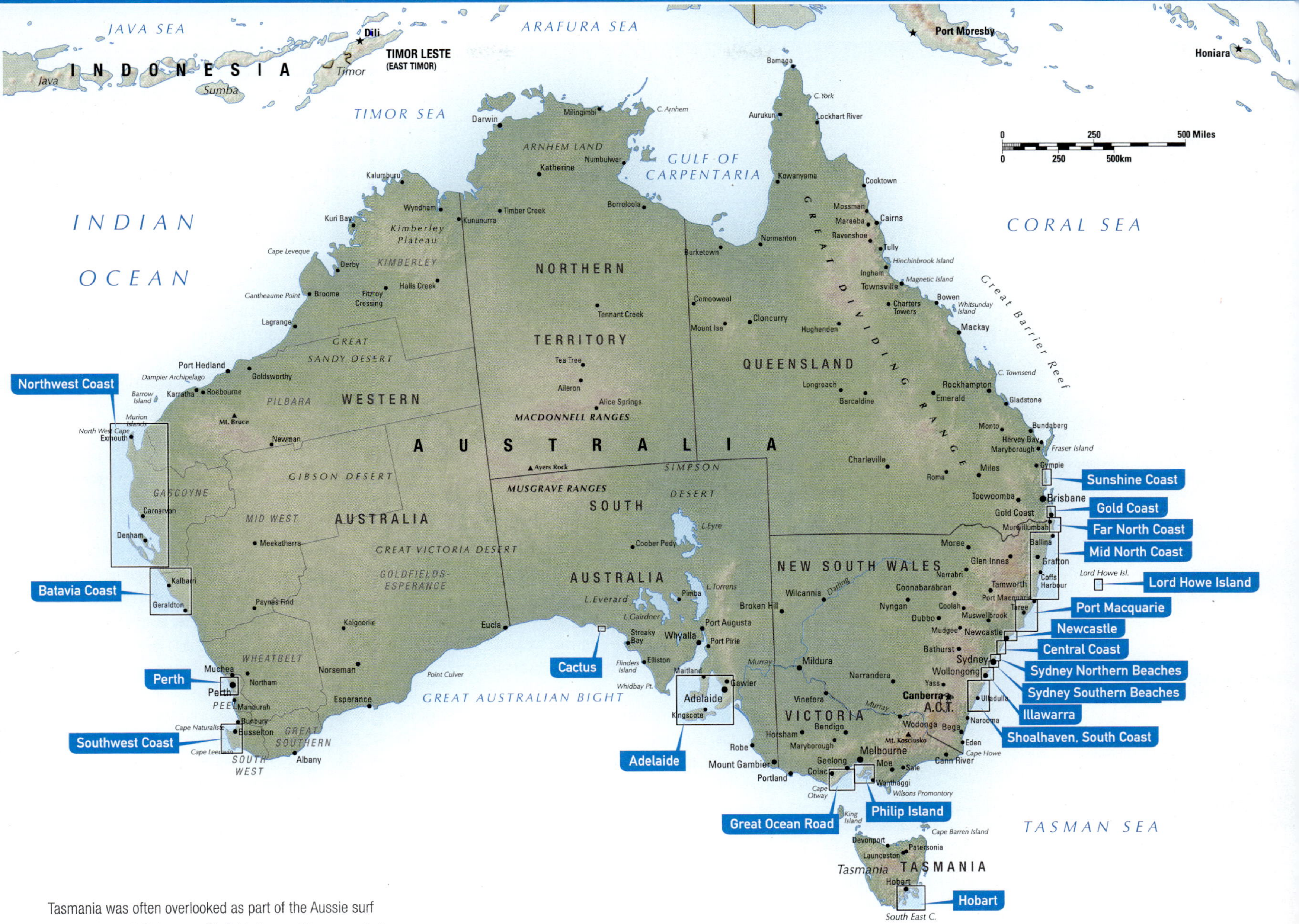

Northwest Coast
Batavia Coast
Perth
Southwest Coast
Cactus
Adelaide
Great Ocean Road
Philip Island
Hobart
Sunshine Coast
Gold Coast
Far North Coast
Mid North Coast
Lord Howe Island
Port Macquarie
Newcastle
Central Coast
Sydney Northern Beaches
Sydney Southern Beaches
Illawarra
Shoalhaven, South Coast

Tasmania was often overlooked as part of the Aussie surf experience until Shipsterns Bluff bludgeoned its way onto the scene and shone some light on the variety of waves around **Hobart**. The east coast of the Apple Isle is far less exposed to swell and is often small, but clean. North from Eaglehawk Neck requires some kind of E swell to get into the deep bays, where some fickle and locally sensitive spots work a few times a year. Little Swanport and Swansea's handful of right points awaken in big S-SE swells. North of the Freycinet Peninsula, stop in at Friendly Beach, Bicheno, 4 Mile, Scamander, Beer Barrel Beach, Binalong or any of the pristine beaches up through the Bay of Fires for some quality beach peaks. The north coast is inconsistent, relying on W-NW or NE swells which means summertime and lots of flat spells. Old Pier Beach in Bridport will be offshore in W winds and pick up NE swells, while the lusted over lefts of Tam O'Shanter need the much rarer NW pulses. Devonport Rivermouth is the most popular spot on the north coast, running long lefts when a W-NW hits. Wynyard has a number of reefs including Scuba Centre, Nurses and Golf Course, making them all easy to find. The best bet for west coast surf is to head to Marrawah where Anne Bay, Green Point

STU GIBSON
Tasmania

ANDREW SHIELD
King Island

Victorian Slab
STEVE RYAN

Merimbula Bar
DEAN DAMPNEY

and Lighthouse Beach receive consistent swell from the W, often accompanied by strong onshores. The wild west coast is a 4WD or hiking adventure with long, windswept beaches and some heavy, big wave reefbreaks at Trial Harbour or Granville Harbour, and beyond is the great wilderness of the Southwest National Park, where plenty of waves lurk for the real hardcore surfer.

## EASTERN AUSTRALIA

Australia's most populous and most surfed coastline is comprehensively covered in the zones of the **New South Wales (NSW)** and **Queensland (QLD)** coasts, with the only obvious gap being the Far South Coast of NSW. From the VIC border, cliffs dominate below the Nadgee moors and the Nature Reserve extends up to Wonboyne where Saltwater is a classical righthand point setup in a picturesque bay inside the Ben Boyd NP. Not very consistent, needing solid SE swell to extend the length of ride, which includes a vertical roll-in, thick wall, middle barrel section and open face before imploding in the beachbreak. Gets a crew on it when it pumps. Camping permits available. Dangers include some sharp rocks, sharp toothed fish and sharp tongued locals if you don't wait your turn. Asling is the main beach at Eden and provided there is some S in the swell it can throw up some decent hollow low tide peaks and is well protected from northerlies in Twofold Bay. The righthander at the Pambula Rivermouth is an east coast classic and high up the global wave charts, but works so rarely these days that legend may be more descriptive. The sandbar needs the river to be in flood conditions and more importantly, the rights require a huge NE swell to penetrate the bay and start spinning down the long sandbar. Speed is king as the barrel is fast and furious, leaving no time for turns. Low tide only adds to the fickleness and SW is offshore, more likely in winter S swell season. Fortunately, the beachbreaks just north of the rocky point get really good and are consistent, with good barrels on bigger swells. The rivermouth scores 1 for consistency and about 8 for crowds. It's also potentially sharky around the rivermouth. Another world-class rivermouth, Merimbula keeps the goofies happy at the north end of the bay from Pambula and is far more reliable as it works on SE swells, over a more stable sandbar. Usually switches between a ripable wall with tube sections popping up along the bar, which extends from 200m average to almost double that on a good day. Lower tides are usually better and watch out for the racing rip on dropping tides. Any N wind will be clean. Quality attracts the crowds and summer holidays can be packed. Long waves, long paddles and the rip help disperse the crowds, as do the regular visits from large sharks, feeding in the rivermouth. Boats punching in or out through the waves can be a real danger. Competent surfers only. Tahthra's beachbreak prefers NE-E swells so more a summer wave. Sometimes gets epic up at The Pole where it can be fast and hollow. All abilities including local pro Kai Otton. Summer holiday blues when the line-up fills up with lots of Victorians on holiday. Empty waves to the south at Wallagoot and Tura, plus options to the north in the Mimosa Rocks NP. Bunga Head creates a challenging righthand point that peaks up out the back and rumbles down the rocks, sometimes barreling, sometimes not. Not very consistent and gets a bit tense at the compact take-off. Advanced level surfers only. Bermagui has some beachies in town, but the best waves are found at Camel Rock, where if the sand aligns, long, sucky lefts will spin off in NE-SE swells. If it's blowing S, check out the Wallaga Lake entrance, over the headland. Narooma has a clutch of spots from the Breakwall outside rights, up through Bar Beach peaks and Kianga's righthand point. Something for everyone in most swells. Rips at the breakwall and of course sharks. Sand and reef peaks sit inside the lee of the headland that gives Dalmeny S wind protection. Fun, often easy walls that get mushy and fat at high tide. Right in front of the campground. More waves to the south of town at Yabbarra. Potato Point is really just beachbreaks benefitting from sand build up on either side of the headland. The rights on the north side are usually the best and a good paddling rip is often in place next to the rocks. Jemisons left gets sucky and holds a good double overhead swell with some N angle in it. There is a bonus righthander at Blackfellows, two headlands north which is also reliant on the sand to create some longer point-style waves. Chilled out area with low crowd factor and a density of spots. Something for most conditions and abilities. Congo attracts all swell directions onto some solid sandbars plus there's some serious barrels to be found out on the reef at The Suck. The entrance to the Moruya Rivermouth has a nicely groomed sandbar that fires off left with the odd right thrown in. Starts steep and round before walling up across the bay. Gets crowded with longboards and cruisers, so check the north side of the wall for suckier rights and lefts. Gets crowded in summer because it is more consistent than other south coast rivermouths. Batemans Bay area's most popular spot is probably South Broulee thanks to its consistency and the punchy peaks in the north corner that are clean in NE'ers. There are some heavy reef waves breaking off Broulee Island at Pink Rocks and Left Reef for experienced riders and more beachies up at North Broulee Beach. Something for all abilities but don't expect to be alone unless you walk down the beach. Mackenzie and Surf Beach to the north have pretty standard beach peaks closer to Batemans Bay.

Norfolk Island
ANDREW SHIELD

## SWELL FORECASTING

### WESTERN AUSTRALIA

Unlike any other continent, Australia has direct, unimpeded exposure to the Southern Ocean and its mountainous seas. The Roaring Forties storms that circulate around the 40°S latitude form a belt of efficient swell producers, spraying both the west-facing and south-facing coasts of Western Australia. Long period groundswell out of the S to WSW is guaranteed for most of the year, with only Dec-Feb dropping slightly in swell height and interval. The Northwest is fractionally less consistent than the Southwest corner around Margaret River, where winter regularly brings 20ft+ swells over 15secs for months on end, but the closer proximity to the storms means winds are stronger and often W-NW in this part of the state. In fact the Batavia coast may have the Goldilocks conditions between the two with 100% swell consistency from July to Sept, partnered with dominant E-SE winds. Perth suffers from swell shadowing by Rottnest and the Fremantle Doctor brings the summer sea breeze from Oct to March when sea and land temps vary the most. The vast south-facing coastline from Cape Leeuwin to the SA border in the Great Australian Bight is best described as rugged and windy. The S-SW swells overpower the bulk of the beaches, which require some kind of N wind and that is far more likely in the winter months. SE swells off the back of lows heading east are good for the Albany to Esperance stretch and the dominant W winds are offshore in some protected corners. The Southern Indian Ocean current becomes the West Australian Current as it turns northwards, bringing cold water out of the west, which is compounded by the blob of upwelling stationed off Southwest WA. The shallow, slow Leeuwin Current brings warm coastal eddies southwards and into the Great Australian Bight, making winter sea temperatures warmer than summer. Tides are huge in the far north of WA reaching 11.8m, but the surf zones are usually below 2m on a semi-diurnal or diurnal pattern.

### SOUTHERN AUSTRALIA

Once these Roaring Forties low pressure systems enter the Great Australian Bight, they lose little intensity and continue to bombard the southern coastline with SW swell. Cliffs ring the coastline of the Bight, which is largely inaccessible until the SW-facing shore of South Australia greets the swell head-on in one of the most inhospitable desert environments. Powerful 12 second period, 7-9ft swells, roll in year-round and SE winds are dominant from Nov-April, before swinging more SW-NW. The surf just keeps getting bigger into the state of Victoria and mountainous bomboras beckon the brave on the heavily exposed coast down to Cape Otway. The SE-facing coast of The Great Ocean Road is resplendent with righthand points and protection from the SW-NW gales that blow through summer and winter respectively. S swells are often the best and some spots need the rarer windswells out of the SE. Depending on their latitude, these spinning storms continue on their easterly course, blasting south or over the top of Tasmania, pounding the inaccessible western coast, then sending ultra-consistent 10-12ft @ 12secs SW swell wrapping around onto the eastern coast and hopefully swinging to a more due S or even SE swell for some of the sheltered spots that aren't lashed by the strong W-NW winds. The West Wind Drift or Antarctic Circumpolar Current directly affects the southern shores and Tasmania, despite the Leeuwin Current making it all the way to the Tasman Sea. Full rubber, year-round, is the southern surfer's lot, especially where seasonal upwelling occurs in SA south of Cactus, Yorkes and down to the border with Victoria. Tidal range hits 2.5m near Adelaide and the straits around Kangaroo Island, 3.2m off the Great Ocean Road and almost 4m for the Tasmanian north coast, but these are exceptions to what is usually a 1-2m range along the southern coast where both diurnal inequality and semi-diurnal tides can be found.

### EASTERN AUSTRALIA

As the southern ocean low pressure systems spin into the Tasman Sea, the fetch for due S swell then SE swell opens up along the entire East Coast all the way to southern QLD. Like all east-facing coasts, consistency drops markedly compared to the west and south, along with swell height, period and the ratio of solid groundswell to windswell. Proximity is key, illustrated by the average stats for mid winter in southern NSW as 8ft @ 9 secs, dropping to 6ft @ 9secs in Sydney. Further north consistency and size rises slightly as E windswell adds to the mix, but the real East Coast saviour is the summer cyclone swell. From November to early May, an average of 10 storms will form in Australian waters and around 6 will make landfall. Trying to predict a cyclone's path is near impossible, but generally speaking, a Coral Sea cyclone will wind-up in the warmer waters and either head towards Queensland, or parallel the coast and head south towards New Zealand. This means that cyclone swell is exclusively from the NE for most of the eastern seaboard and sometimes due E for Queensland and the Far North Coast of NSW. Summer is also characterised by NE sea breezes, which blow in as the land heats up, providing some small choppy windswells. In northern regions the winds tend more SE from the beginning of the year. During the winter months the winds can be a cold SW from the mountains of the Great Dividing Range, resulting in 6 months of S-SW for southern and central NSW, but further north it becomes increasingly S then turns SE for the Gold and Sunshine Coasts. The warm, southwards flowing, East Australia Current tempers the winter water temps in the southern half of the East Coast, while Queensland receives warmth directly from the South Equatorial Current.

### NORTHERN AUSTRALIA

The Great Barrier Reef remains an interesting surfing enigma, as there is definitely surf along its outer frontier. While PNG, the Solomons and New Hebrides can filter a bit of Pacific swell, there's enough open ocean at the end of the southern Pacific trade winds corridor. Most cyclones form up in this region so there are definitely seasonal opportunities. The northern coasts or top end of Australia is fairly devoid of surf apart from a handful of days in wet season Darwin when a low pressure stations off the coast to the NNW or a cyclone tracks west to east. Cyclone swells can also bring surf to the remote NW-facing coast of WA, but the extensive continental shelf, fringing reefs and massive tides make it a waste of time compared to the rest of the country. The top end of Australia experiences macro tidal ranges from 4 to 11.8m, and actually dictates if there will be any rideable surf or not. The South Equatorial Current brings year-round warmth to all Northern Australia waters.

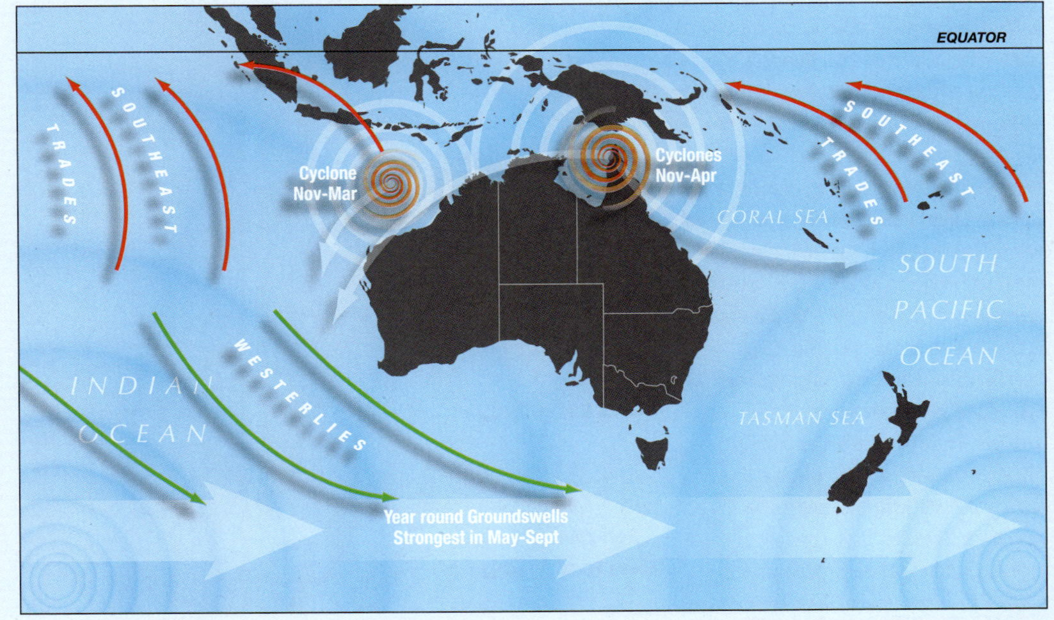


## NORTHERN AUSTRALIA

Above the Sunshine Coast zone there are more opportunities for regular waves before the Great Barrier Reef cuts off the swell supply. Fraser Island has some attractive righthanders over the shifting sandbars that build up in the lee of Indian Head and Waddy Point, but the shark threat is off the scale. Around Bundaberg a number of little towns with rocky beaches hold small waves. Check around Bargara then head up to Agnes Water for a righthand point and regulation beachbreaks. 1770 has a sandspit in Bustard Bay that is great for SUPing, but keep an eye out for Tony the (large) tiger shark. The Great Barrier Reef begins 85km due east of here and extends for 2300km northwestwards, and is the great unknown in surfing terms. Only locals with sturdy boats will ever be dropping anchor at one of the myriad passes that need summer tropical storms or strong windswell to work. The tourist frequented islands in the south have been surfed like Lady Musgrave and others nearby, but finding the right reef-line or a break in the reef, while there is swell and good winds, is unlikely without proper local knowledge. Back on the mainland, there are probably only a handful of good surf days and a few dozen marginal ones when storm events bring messy surf to coastal towns for the desperate, willing to risk box jellyfish, sharks and maybe even saltwater crocs in the far north. Cyclones bring rain and lots of it so surfing in brown, possibly polluted waters with howling, often onshore winds is the deal. Yeppoon and Mackay have regularly surfed waves during the Oct-March season in both SE windslop and NE-E cyclone swell. Whitsunday Island's famous Whitehaven Beach will occasionally catch NE swell. Townsville area has shifting sandbars offshore of Alva, while Florence Bay is the best of a few breaks on Magnetic Island, which picks up the most SE windswell and any N-NE groundswell. Mission Beach will have windslop at Bingil Bay and Cowley after 48hrs of continuous SE wind over 25km/h. Hinchinbrook and Great Palm islands have some opportunities for boaters. North of Cairns check Double Island and the small beaches below the cliffs en route to 4 Mile at Port Douglas. Those heading right up to Cape Tribulation may find a righthander in front of the camp site after heavy trade winds. Cooktown has dribble at Cherry Tree, Finch Bay and Archer Point, but north of here gets very marginal. In fact the next stop for any regularly surfed waves is Darwin, since the Gulf Of Carpentaria and Arnhem Land offer little chance of surf. A die-hard crew of city surfers await the month of rare, wet season cyclone swells to push into Darwin's gently shelving beaches at Nightcliff Beach, Rapid Creek or Dripstone Cliffs at Casuarina. It's only rideable for a very short tidal window in brown, turbid water which doesn't help with croc, shark and stinger paranoia.

# Northwest Coast WESTERN AUSTRALIA

**Western Australia is the largest state, but has the lowest population density in Australia. Travelling to the northwest-facing coast takes the word 'remote' to another level and accordingly most surf spots are uncrowded, with the exception of the world-class lefts at Gnaraloo. The natural habitat and unique wildlife is rich and diverse, especially along the 280km long Ningaloo Reef.**

- \+ WORLD-CLASS LEFTS
- \+ MOSTLY UNCROWDED
- \+ VERY HIGH CONSISTENCY
- \+ UNIQUE WILDLIFE & DIVING

- – CHALLENGING WAVES
- – STRONG WINDS
- – REMOTE, NO HOSPITAL
- – NATURAL DANGERS

Dunes

MICK GULLAN

An accessible option for quality offshore surfing can be found 10km NE of the tourist station of Exmouth. Plenty of boats head out to the dive site at Barrow Island where the consistent playful walls of **Murion Left** wrap around its northern tip. On North West Cape, chilled out **Dunes** is a series of reefs that can deliver long hollow lefts and more walled-up rights, but rips can be as worrying as the shark levels. When thick winter swells are running, chargers and hellmen boat out to the Exmouth **Lighthouse Bombie**, a monster left with awesome power breaks over a shallow, sandy reef ledge, creating a freefall take-off and gaping, do or die barrels. **Yardie Creek** is a famous gorge located 90km (56mi) from Exmouth in the Cape Range National Park. A boat is necessary to reach the excellent, long lefthander with a bowling, tubular inside section which needs a low to moderate swell and handles the sea breeze. Gnaraloo Station presents a high concentration of world-class wind/kite and surf spots. Facing Three Mile camp, **Tombstones** has a heavy paddle and a horrific take-off leading to thick, challenging barrel sections over shallow ledges. Experts only – razor sharp reef, rips, and sharks abound – it's a long way to hospital. 6km north of The Bluff is **Turtles**, where a quality barrelling left and fickle right, break over shallow, sharp reef. Most surfers come to this wilderness to ride **The Bluff**, an extremely fast left over a shallow, urchin infested limestone reef. Best at 5-6ft, the take-off is a vert drop into thick-lipped, express barrels! Helmet and booties strongly recommended. 60km north of Carnarvon, **Blow Holes** has easier waves for all abilities at a long sandy beach with some shelf action off an island at the northern end in NE winds. Dirk Hartog Island is a unique, remote eco-tourism destination with limited accommodation and access through Denham via car ferry (4WD only) or light plane. At the northern tip is **Turtle Bay**, where a long workable left is protected from S winds. Rips can be vicious and this is the entrance of the aptly named Shark Bay. At **Surf Point**, a shallow reef delivers long barrels at the island's south tip in a medium to big SW swell and NE-E winds. Very strong rips and an ultra-sharky channel make this break for hardcore surfers only. An adventurous 4WD track leads to **Steep Point**, the most westerly point of the mainland. It's a spooky spot that requires large SW-W swell to turn on, creating a serious left with powerful, long tubes, peeling over a shallow, sharp reef.

From April to September, it's rarely flat on the exposed spots, but wind will be the key factor. There are regular morning SE offshores, and occasional ENE winds. Winds tend to be stronger and more gusty from November to March and anything from the N-NW means heavy rain, which often causes all dirt roads in the area to become unpassable. Tidal range rarely exceeds 6ft in Exmouth and decreases heading south, but will heavily influence most of the reefs.

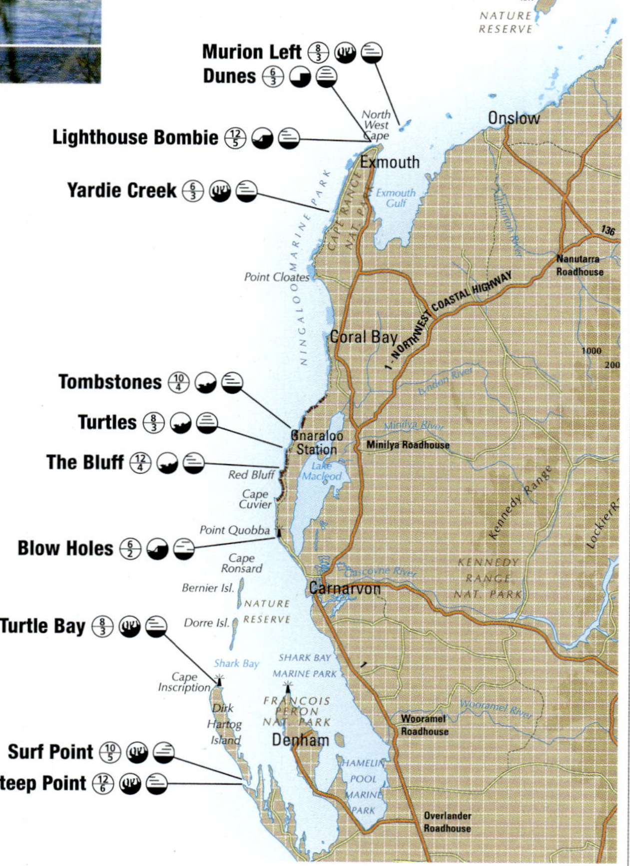

Red Bluff

MICK GULLAN

## TRAVEL INFORMATION

**Weather** – Temps range from 20-25°C (52-79°F) in winter and between 30-40°C (86-104°F) in summer. Most rain falls between May and August or from infrequent, decaying cyclones and tropical cloud bands between January and July. The dry season extends from early Sept through Dec. During the surfing season, a 2mm steamer offers sun, wind and reef protection, otherwise it is springsuit temperature.

**Lodging and Food** – Potshot resort in Exmouth has budget dorms from $33/night. Gnaraloo & Bluff camps (only basic accommodation options): 3 Mile Camp (10km from the Homestead) has a campground for $20/p/n. Also 4 bed cabins for $120/night. Excellent seafood and try the kangaroo meat.

**Nature and Culture** – Incredible sea life (fish, whales, dolphins, sharks, turtles, dugongs) and amazing corals. Bird watching, world-class fishing, quality snorkelling and diving sites. Shark Bay attracts many tourists.

**Hazards and Hassles** – Despite the high shark factor, attacks are rare, so reef cuts, strong currents and big, powerful waves are the real aquatic threats. Be fully prepared for desert survival, insects and snakes are plentiful. Population is low, but many are hardcore surfers, who can be as harsh as the environment to those who aren't humble.

**Handy Hints** – Bring a full quiver, repair kit, steamer for the cold winter mornings, booties, a first aid kit with magnaplasm for urchins. Also food, plenty of water, warm clothes, full camping gear. Internet at Gnaraloo station. Cape Hideaway Surf Shop in Exmouth. NW Surfboards in Carnarvon.

| STATISTICS | | J F | M A | M J | J A | S O | N D |
|---|---|---|---|---|---|---|---|
| SWELL | Direction | | | | | | |
| | Size (ft) | 4-5 | 5-6 | 6-7 | 7-8 | 6 | 4-5 |
| WIND | Direction | | | | | | |
| | Force | F5 | F4 | F4 | F4 | F4 | F4-F5 |
| WATER | Wetsuit | | | | | | |
| | Temp/°C | 26 | 26 | 24 | 22 | 22 | 23 |
| WEATHER | Rainfall/mm | 19 | 13 | 40 | 30 | 6 | 3 |
| | days/mth | 2 | 3 | 6 | 6 | 3 | 1 |
| | Min temp/°C | 22 | 20 | 14 | 12 | 15 | 20 |
| | Max temp/°C | 32 | 30 | 25 | 22 | 25 | 28 |

# Batavia Coast WESTERN AUSTRALIA

500km north of Perth The Gibson Desert and The Great Sandy Desert conspire with a rugged, dangerous coastline to remind surfers of their human frailties. Geraldton and Kalbarri form twin outposts of civilisation where a hardy crew of locals ride epic offshore reefs, which can be quite sensitive to the constant swell and strong winds. Knowing where and when is half the battle. Knowing your limitations is the other.

+ POWERFUL SWELLS
+ WORLD-CLASS SPOTS
+ BREAK VARIETY
+ UNCROWDED

- HOWLING SUMMER WINDS
- LONG PADDLES TO REEFS
- 4WD AND SUPPLIES REQUIRED
- DESERT DANGERS

DEAN DAMPNEY

Jake's

Kalbarri at the mouth of the Murchinson River has become a popular holiday resort. On smaller swells and the occasional NE winds, **Blue Holes** will produce nice rights and the odd left on a reef ledge just south of town. Peaky and sucky, this wave can pack a punch and the rocks are never far away, as it works at lower tides. The main event is **Jake's**, a kegging left point that breaks along a gnarly shelf for 200m+. Starts with an elevator drop as the wave goes sickeningly square over the barely covered reef causing corrugations in the face or double-ups at low tide right on the diminutive take-off spot. The barrel immediately starts grinding down the point, so down-the-line speed is imperative. Visitors will need to be very sure of their skills and very patient as they wait for scraps. **Bowes River** near Northampton is a great spot to camp for a few days. It's consistent and the mixed sand and reefbreaks are not too heavy. Further south and 5km off the North-West Coastal Highway, **Coronation** has fun reliable, beachbreak peaks, popular with windsurfers. A guided 4WD tour around here will undoubtedly uncover some other good spots, off the sealed road. A locals favourite are the hollow walls of **Drummonds**, better at high tide on big swells. **Sunset Beach**, next to the Suncity Tourist Park at the mouth of The Chapman River is rarely crowded despite quality lefts. Geraldton is known as the crayfish capital of the world. Many of the local fishermen are surfers who access the reefs sitting 20 minutes offshore. **Hell's Gate** is an all tides, powerful, shallow righthander, breaking 1km out from the Point Moore lighthouse. A sucky bodyboard wedge breaks left directly in front of the lighthouse. Whenever conditions don't suit the reefs the locals usually surf the stretch from Back Beach down to **Tarcoola**. South of Geraldton are Dongara's long lefts at Port Denison and the mixture of rock and sand peaks at Headbutts and Flat Rocks. The more adventurous can try and hire a crayfish boat to get to the dangerous waters of the Houtman Abrolhos Islands, some 40km off Geraldton, home of Supertubes and more virgin spots.

## TRAVEL INFORMATION

**Weather** – Being primarily in the short scrub desert, summer day and night temperature range can be as extreme as 30°C (86°F). Take warm clothing for dawn patrols and keep hydrated at midday. In winter, what little rainfall there is falls at night. Most days will be sunny and not too hot or windy. The water is very stable, varying a few degrees from 18°-21°C (65-70°F), requiring a light steamer (short sleeves or short legs are common) at most and boardies or a shorty on summer days.

**Lodging and Food** – Kalbarri is a popular resort and gets filled quickly during vacations. It offers anything from resorts ($55/dble), B&B (Seafront Villas: $35/dble), motel (Motor Hotel: $25) and dorms (Backpackers: $8). A basic meal is $10. The crayfish are fantastic and cheap.

**Nature and Culture** – In Kalbarri, Murchison River inland gorges and the Rainbow Jungle are good visits. To swim with dolphins, go to Monkey Mia, 4hr north. In Geraldton, check the museum (shipwreck stuff). Because of a mutiny aboard the Batavia in 1629, 2 sailors were dumped ashore, the first white men in Australia!

**Hazards and Hassles** – Despite abundant sea life (tiger, bronze whaler and mako sharks), reef cuts and powerful waves are the real threats. Be fully prepared for desert survival...the wrong decision could jeopardise your life! Insects and snakes are plentiful. Population is low but many are hardcore surfers, so remain humble. If the locals aren't surfing the main spots, then something is probably wrong.

**Handy Hints** – You need a gun for winter - Jake's holds real size. There are 3 surf shops in Geraldton and 1 in Kalbarri.

MICK GULLAN

Supertubes, Abrolhos

Well exposed to the Roaring Forties, so expect consistent 4-10ft SW swells. The best surfing season is the heart of winter when the biggest swells wrap into NW-facing coves and the SE-SW winds are cross/offshore. Southerly winds are dominant varying from 64% (Jan) to 14% (June). Summer (Oct-Mar) features gusty winds blowing endlessly for weeks. During winter, the wind compass pattern is wider and winds weaker with some perfect offshore E-NE winds. Tidal ranges are average, with spring tides never exceeding 2m but it gets more dramatic as you travel up north.

| STATISTICS | | J F | M A | M J | J A | S O | N D |
|---|---|---|---|---|---|---|---|
| SWELL | Direction | | | | | | |
| | Size (ft) | 4-5 | 5-6 | 6-7 | 7-8 | 6 | 4-5 |
| WIND | Direction | | | | | | |
| | Force | F5 | F4 | F4 | F4 | F4 | F4-F5 |
| WATER | Wetsuit | | | | | | |
| | Temp/°C | 21 | 21 | 20 | 19 | 18 | 19 |
| WEATHER | Rainfall/mm | 7 | 18 | 72 | 65 | 20 | 5 |
| | days/mth | 1 | 3 | 9 | 10 | 6 | 2 |
| | Min temp/°C | 20 | 17 | 12 | 10 | 11 | 16 |
| | Max temp/°C | 33 | 31 | 24 | 22 | 25 | 29 |

# Southwest Coast WESTERN AUSTRALIA

The Margaret River area of W.A. is perceived as Australia's most consistent and challenging big wave forum, where pretensions and pretenders are quickly washed away. Whilst the NW conceals Indo-like lefts, the area S of Cape Naturaliste is littered with rocky ledges and pointbreaks, that get battered by giant Roaring Forties swells. The scenic Caves Road skirts the coastline, meandering through forests, gentle hills and around vineyards that overlook the sea where a truly hardcore crew shreds dozens of world-class spots.

+ MASSIVE SWELL EXPOSURE
+ WORLD-CLASS REEFS
+ LOTS OF POWER
+ DRAMATIC COASTLINE

– COLD AND WET WINTERS
– ISOLATED, DANGEROUS REEFS
– WINDY
– 4WD ACCESS

## TRAVEL INFORMATION

**Weather** – The seasons are distinct with summer (Dec-Feb) enjoying hot temps and very little rain. Autumn is a great time but from May-Aug it gets pretty wet and cold with storms often hitting the coast accompanied by gusty SW-W winds. Sept marks the start of spring and some rainy days, but generally it's fine. A light steamer is the suit of choice year-round.

**Lodging and Food** – WA is full of campsites and caravan parks and the towns have plenty of cheap hotels. Recommended ones are in Gnarabup (Surf Point Lodge: $90/dble, 3 nights min stay), Margaret River (Innetown Backpackers: $20); Gracetown Chalets ($130/n – 5 people) and Yallingup (Chandlers Smiths Beach Villas: $720/w). A decent meal costs from $10.

**Nature and Culture** – The Margaret River area produces great wine, so a vineyard tour is a good way to kill a day on the unlikely chance of it ever going flat. The Mammoth Cave is a good visit. Take a boat to Flinders Island to see the bottlenose dolphins and the fur seal colonies.

**Hazards and Hassles** – The waves can be big and powerful, more suited to experienced surfers. Getting caught inside can be really heavy and many reefs are super shallow and urchined! The bush is full of spiders and snakes; watch out for the deadly Tiger snake. Locals are hardcore and don't like bad wave manners but the waves are plentiful, so there's rarely a problem.

**Handy Hints** – Take a gun or buy cheap, quality boards from many local surf shops in Dunsborough, Yallingup and Margaret River. Lots of opportunity to try wind/kiteboarding in afternoons.

Three Bears

MICK GULLAN

The Box

MICKEY SMITH

The protected reefs of Cape Naturaliste work when a huge SW-W swell is running, and the SW winds are blowing. The laid-back lefts at **Rocky Point** start with sloping walls from take-off, then hit a nice bit of reef further in, throwing out a bit more, but generally this wave is accessible to improvers up. There's more beginner-orientated beachbreaks and a few reefs further around at Bunkers Bay, with spots like The Farm, Boneyards and The Quarries working on similar conditions. The peak at **Windmills** works on small swells only and has tubey sections in an offshore E, as do other sandy reef peaks along this stretch, including a regular left up at the Other Side of the Moon nearer the Cape Naturaliste Lighthouse. A series of reef peaks affectionately called **Three Bears**, thanks to their ability to have something in the "just right" category in a wide range of swell sizes. The hierarchy is obvious with Papa's furthest out able to handle triple overhead plus. Mama's can be a perfect sucking barrel on those medium-sized SW swell days, with heavy drops and speedy walls, favouring the lefts at mid tides. Baby's isn't always the runt of the litter and can have nice spiralling lefts and a few decent rights off the peak in small to moderate SW-W swells. Makes the most of small swells and is prone to regular clean-up sets at any size. **Yallingup** is a major surf community, where steep, hollow waves, brush a scattering of hungry rocks along this curve of classic WA sand. Names like Mousetrap and Rabbit Hill refer to reliable clusters of rock and sand, but the whole stretch can fire all the way down to the learner-friendly peaks and occasionally thumping shorey facing the car park. **Supertubes** is aptly named and describes the wave right from the off. Vertical to air drops straight to double speedy tube section before kicking out or closing out. Critical, pitching rights are what most are looking for, but there are plenty of lefts as well, which can ledge and mutate over the shallow, angular reef. Smith's Beach is blessed with various beachbreak peaks, a rolling left off the point in big SW swells and a reef peak that draws in most swells and unfurls some beautiful, righthand barrels, plus some less challenging lefts that will handle more size than the right. **Pea Break** is another top-class righthand barrel searing over shallow reef in front of the car parks at Injidup. Typical, ledgy WA drop into full keg followed by Daytona wall for armco bashing and an inside exit ramp. The bendy bowl at the jostling, postage stamp peak offers a far more approachable left for intermediates. The point at **Injidup** needs a sizeable SW or moderate W swell before the lumbering lefts get going. Steep, open faces, interrupted by ill-tempered sections and it's tidally sensitive. Further south past the sucky lefts of Moses Point, are plenty of spooky waves with evocative names like Hangmans, Gallows and Guilotines found in the maze of heavy-duty 4WD tracks between Yallingup and Cowaramup. **North Point** is one of the most majestic and powerful righthand points in the country. It takes a fair amount of S to SW swell to swing onto the barnacle crusted reef where it rears up swiftly and roars straight into a throaty barrel section before slinging into the often hollower inside, where maintaining speed is crucial to survival. As size increases it is possible to multi-park under the thick, dredging lips along a length of ride that exceeds 300m. It's a massive paddle and really needs higher tides and an E wind to show its class. Non-experts will prefer **South Point**,

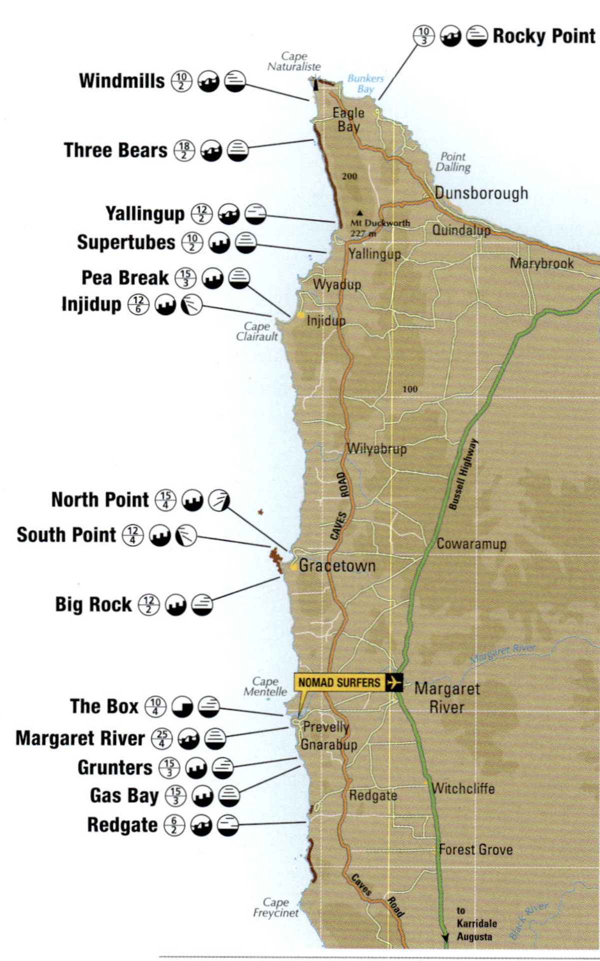

a functional, fun-lovin' left that runs a sloping wall down the jumbled rocks, standing up in places to work on those drawn-out roundhouses. Stays nice and smooth in SW wind, prefers higher tides and can get shallow over the urchin sprinkled reef. **Big Rock**, is another shallow, sucky right and along with Cobblestones, Noisies and Lefties, this area will always have a wave and a crowd when the swell and wind is down. **The Box** is a mutant righthand slab that earns its name from the square-shaped pits, just across the bay from Surfers Point. Make the air-drop then negotiate the dry sucks, boils or stepped faces to claim serious shack time. W swell helps make-ability as does more water over the sharp, sharky reef. Insane wave for the clinically insane or the pros when the comp is on. Next to ✪**Margaret River Surfers Point** triangular reef is Southside, another shelf of stone, facing into the SW swell and cultivating some tubular rights into the channel plus some seriously round, long lefts that close-out on the near-dry reef, leaving the rider particularly susceptible to clean-up sets. Beyond the big swell, lefthand reefs off Gnarabup Beach and down toward Gas Bay lies **Grunters**, an unpretentious wave that does what it says on the label. Seriously powerful righthanders wedge up a way offshore and explode with maximum force on the surprisingly shallow shelf. Often double sucks so be prepared to launch on what is already an air drop. S-SW swells and NE wind plus mid tides up. Inside **Gas Bay** is another grindy peak that will be smaller and more manageable, but still a challenge with heavy barrels and a covetous local crew. To the south, **Redgate** breaks mainly over sand creating hollow, punchy peaks in smaller swells. A-Frame shacks will also be found to the north along the Boodjidup stretch.

MICK GULLAN

North Point

### ✪ Margaret River

**LAT. -33.976355° LONG. 114.982214°**

**Sitting 10km west of the town of Margaret River, these famous lefts have been a proving ground and contest site for decades. It also holds some rights in swells up to 6ft but Margaret's is all about size and the lefts will handle plenty of that. Heart-stopping drops, lumpy bowls and cutback walls are all part of the waves' personality and it can handle a healthy dose of onshore wind, maintaining shape and some face smoothness for long, swooping turns. Watch out for speed bumps when cranking off the bottom and keep an eye on the horizon. Getting caught inside is no fun and positively dangerous if taking on the rights. Best conditions will be solid W swell, skimpy E wind and mid to high tide. The Rivermouth beachies nestled in the bay provide beginner/improver fun.**

The area from Cape Naturaliste to Cape Freycinet is fully exposed to the furious SW swells produced by the Roaring Forties. Waves can be large, although not necessarily clean and orderly, especially in winter, when there can be days of huge, onshore mush. Expect numerous 6-20ft swells in the winter, but usually only the sheltered spots will be rideable. Changeover seasons are the best bet as there are plenty of 4-12ft days at the most exposed spots. Even summertime is rarely flat, when regular 2-8ft swells can occur. WA is plagued by strong SW-W winds, while during the late summer/autumn there can be days with SE-S winds. When a high pressure sits over SW Australia, the mornings will typically be offshore, before an afternoon sea breeze (the Fremantle Doctor) blows out the surf. Tidal ranges are minimal and there is only one tide a day.

| STATISTICS | | J F | M A | M J | J A | S O | N D |
|---|---|---|---|---|---|---|---|
| SWELL | Direction | | | | | | |
| | Size (ft) | 5 | 6 | 7 | 8 | 6-7 | 5 |
| WIND | Direction | | | | | | |
| | Force | F4 | F4 | F4-F5 | F5 | F4-F5 | F4 |
| WATER | Wetsuit | | | | | | |
| | Temp/°C | 19 | 21 | 19 | 17 | 16 | 18 |
| WEATHER | Rainfall/mm | 21 | 52 | 200 | 195 | 95 | 32 |
| | days/mth | 3 | 8 | 18 | 21 | 14 | 7 |
| | Min temp/°C | 14 | 12 | 10 | 8 | 9 | 12 |
| | Max temp/°C | 24 | 23 | 18 | 16 | 18 | 22 |

# Perth WESTERN AUSTRALIA

Perth can't be taken seriously as a surf city as the shallow Five Fathom Bank (approx 10m/33ft) absorbs most of the swell. Surf is usually mushy and summers are mainly flat. Perth is an ideal place for learners to hone their skills before following their more experienced counterparts offshore to Rottnest Island, where some seriously heavy waves can be found only a 30min ferry ride from the city.

- \+ YEAR ROUND SOUTH SWELLS
- \+ ROTTNEST ISLAND SPOTS
- \+ GREAT CLIMATE
- \+ CABLE'S ARTIFICIAL REEF

- – PERTH'S INCONSISTENT SPOTS
- – INTENSE CROWDS
- – FREMANTLE DOCTOR'S ONSHORES
- – SHARKS

Strickland Bay

MICHAEL LEGGE-WILKINSON

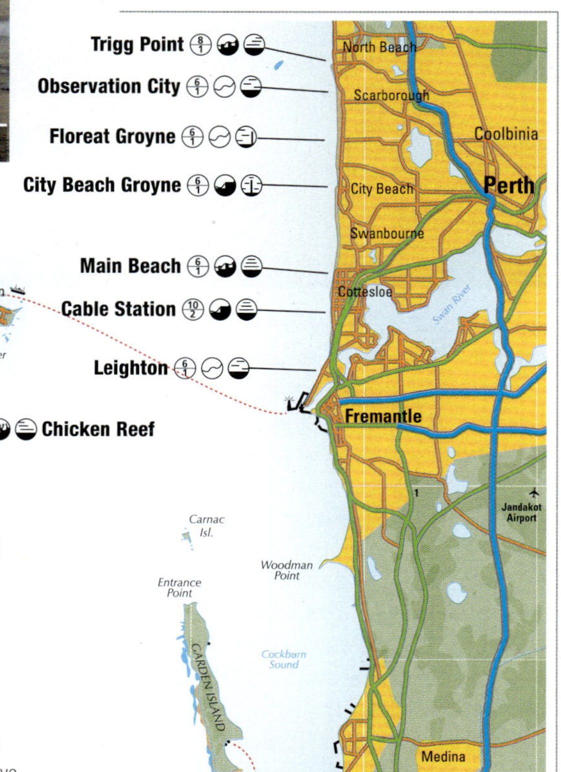


**Trigg Point** is Perth's most consistent and crowded wave, producing a longish, peeling righthander, over a sand-covered reef. The adjacent beachbreak can sometimes produce well-shaped peaks, spreading the inevitable crowds. The popular tourist beaches of Scarborough are just 2km south, but **Observation City** won't be any good unless there is a rare combo of huge swell, E winds and well-formed sandbanks. Check one of the webcams. **Floreat Groyne** offers wrapping lefts sheltered from dominant SW winds, but it rarely gets above headhigh. The **City Beach Groyne** is similar, with the option of night surfing, but beware of sharks. There are several spots in Cottesloe including **Main Beach** but there's a distinct lack of swell and a high density of surfers. In 2000 Cottesloe City Council voted to build "Artos" the first artificial surfing reef at **Cable Station**, 500m offshore of Mosman Beach Reserve where an underwater canyon funnels swell energy, but it is still a low frequency spot, needing a big NW swell to get going. When it's on, the peak can be good, but super-crowded. For fewer crowds, drive south and check **Leighton**, which will work on any major W swell. For experienced surfers a visit to the 11km long Rottnest Island (aka Rotto) is essential because it's often 2-3ft bigger than Perth's beaches. On the north side is **Stark Bay**, a growling, hollow, mid-high tide left in any sized SW-NW swell. A boat would help as it's remote and a board-snapper. Hellmen only. **Cathedral Rock** is just out of the brunt of the onshore SW'ers but the lefts are still hollow and punchy. **Radar Reef** is totally exposed to SW swells and winds and is a long paddle through strong currents to an isolated scary righthand bommie at higher tides. **Strickland Bay** is the most consistent break with superb lefts up to 12ft over a shallow reef ledge that has a lock-in end tube section. Decent rights on smaller swells. The reefs at **Salmon Point** are powerful and hollow on mid-sized SW swells and **Chicken Reef** is an insane tube over a sharp coral reef up to 10ft. Mid tides and N winds are best.

During Autumn and winter 6-12ft SW swells from the Roaring Forties make their way to Rottnest Island but 6ft is the minimum for Trigg Point or Artos reef to break. There can be plenty of N winds in autumn and winter, good for Rottnest's south coast. In summer S winds are predominant but wake up early as the SW "Fremantle Doctor" will ruin most of the spots by 11am. Rottnest Island is in the path of the warm Leeuwin Current, adding a couple of centigrade to the water temps. Tides are minimal (often less than 0.6m) and diurnal/semi-diurnal (once or twice a day), but manage to affect the very shallow reefs.

MICHAEL LEGGE-WILKINSON

Chicken Reef

## TRAVEL INFORMATION

**Weather** – The summer months (Dec-Mar) are hot with temps between 17-29°C (63-84°F). Summer afternoons are cooled by a strong SW sea breeze. Winter months (June to August) are mild and rainy, with average temps 9-18°C (48-64°F). Water is stable year-round at 18-20°C (64-68°F), a light steamer with short arms being ideal.

**Lodging and Food** – Favour Cottesloe to stay around Perth. Most of the 500,000 annual visitors to Rottnest come for the day. Rottnest Lodge is costly ($150/n), Villas/cottages are cheap (from $80/n for 4p). Camping pitch $25/up to 6p. At Thomson Bay, there's a store, bakery, bars and restaurants.

**Nature and Culture** – The Sorrento Quay and Hillary's Boat Harbour, 5km north of Trigg, house major attractions for tourists including Underwater World. Rottnest Island is a Reserve, has a record of 97 species of tropical fish and is popular for migrating humpback whales, bottlenose dolphins and sea lions.

**Hazards and Hassles** – On Perth town beaches, beware of robberies, crowds and sharks – Perth's city beaches have seen a spate of great white shark attacks, including a fatality. Rottnest surf conditions are often uncrowded but strong rips, razor-sharp reefs and sea urchins are prevalent. Use booties and designated pathways when accessing surf spots, to help protect fragile dune vegetation.

**Handy Hints** – Plenty of surf shops to get good gear. A couple of guns would be useful for a stay on Rottnest. Ask for the Rottnest Island Surf Map at the Tourist Information Centre. Buses and bicycles are the only form of transport on Rotto.

| STATISTICS | | J F | M A | M J | J A | S O | N D |
|---|---|---|---|---|---|---|---|
| SWELL | Direction | | | | | | |
| | Size (ft) | 3-4 | 4-5 | 5-6 | 6-7 | 5 | 3-4 |
| WIND | Direction | | | | | | |
| | Force | F4 | F4 | F4-F5 | F5 | F4 | F4 |
| WATER | Wetsuit | | | | | | |
| | Temp/°C | 20 | 20 | 19 | 18 | 16 | 19 |
| WEATHER | Rainfall/mm | 10 | 33 | 154 | 137 | 68 | 18 |
| | days/mth | 3 | 7 | 16 | 19 | 14 | 6 |
| | Min temp/°C | 19 | 15 | 11 | 9 | 11 | 15 |
| | Max temp/°C | 30 | 26 | 20 | 18 | 21 | 26 |

# Cactus SOUTH AUSTRALIA

Australia's interior consists mainly of desert while the coastline, which is more exposed to wet oceanic influences, is a lot greener. One exception is the Great Australian Bight coast of South Australia, where the treeless red dust of the Nullarbor Plain meets the ocean and the great waves of Cactus can be found. Despite the desolation, this is a real Mecca for the hardcore Australian surf traveller, since its discovery in the 1960s.

+ CONSISTENT SWELLS
+ QUALITY REEFBREAKS
+ POWERFUL LEFTS & RIGHTS
+ HARDCORE TRIP

- GREAT WHITE SHARKS
- COLD WATER
- DEADLY SNAKES
- FIERCE LOCALS

## TRAVEL INFORMATION

**Weather** – It's always hot in the afternoons, summers are suffocating and mornings are chilly, especially in the winter. Coastal upwelling and a cold offshore current means that the water temperature hardly ever gets above 14°C (57°F), which is a bizarre contrast when the summer land temps reach 40°C (105°F). The wind-chill factor can be pretty bad. Take a 4/3 steamer and booties, year-round.

**Lodging and Food** – Camping only. The land is private property (Foreshore Park) where you can camp for $13/d. There's no electricity and no luxuries other than the small shop selling basics. Take everything you need, including water.

**Nature and Culture** – There's very little around this area except dust, shimmering salt pans and flies, from whom there is no escape (except when surfing). It's a wild and untamed area which many people would consider hell.

**Hazards and Hassles** – The shark factor is very high and consequently the area remains uncrowded despite the good waves. On land, the flies can be mind numbingly annoying, but not as bad as the King Brown snakes, which have lethal bites.

**Handy Hints** – Cactus is not a place for the faint-hearted, so be prepared for a serious desert experience. Bring several boards (guns for the bigger days) and a winter suit. Gravelle is a good local shaper.

Cactus Waves

ANDREW HALSALL

Caves

BILL MORRIS

Supertubes
Crushers
Caves
Castles
Cactus
Cunns
Backdoor
Witzigs

From Penong, head another 21km south down a white lime, dirt road to Point Sinclair. The most southern spot is an outside break called **Witzig's**, which is a powerful left with dredging take-offs. Like just about all the breaks in Cactus, it's for confident, experienced surfers. **Backdoor** is a hectic right that barrels ferociously over a sharp, shallow reef near deep water below cliffs - get the picture? N-E winds and a wide swell-window but S-SW lines it up best. **Cunns** is a fairly inconsistent, mid tide left that's a good place to go if Cactus gets too crowded. It has S wind protection from the cliffs, walls can be a bit sectiony and it closes-out at the end. Strangely enough, **Cactus** itself is the least intimidating wave in the area as the lefts usually offer an easy entry with a nice little barrelling section. Once again, the locals will probably be surfing another break, unless it is having a good day on a headhigh swell at low to mid tides. Will close-out around 10ft and can be a longer ride than the other reefs. In the middle of the bay is **Castles**, where it's a case of inside zippery reforms on small days and outside grinding barrels on big days. Outside Castles is where most bites have occurred, including the attacks on a notorious, but now deceased local nicknamed 'Shark Bait', because he had been knocked off his board and mauled several times! The adjacent deep channel is the breeding ground for hundreds of Bronze Whalers and is easy access to the coast for great whites. Just on the other side of this spooky channel is **Caves**, a phenomenal right which is the locals favourite and regarded as the best spot in the Cactus area. With morning offshores and a decent swell, it can become a reeling, world-class, voluminous barrel breaking over a shallow ledge. Caves holds a good size, prefers lower tides and must be offshore NE. Guys have settled down here purely to surf this spot and they enforce strict laws about wave priority. On the other side of the small peninsula are two other board-breaking, shallow reefs, which are seldom ridden. **Crushers** is the left that needs a bit more W in the swell to get the barrels grinding across the regulation shallow reef. Seems to be the least crowded break on the Cactus stretch when there are lots of surfers about. **Supertubes** is the right, so fast, tubular tight envelopes are the go. It breaks a fair way out, only at low, which is strange considering how shallow it is. More W in the swell will take the edge off it.

Lows generally pass below South Australia, although in winter they will sometimes strike the coast in the east of the state. The winter swell exposure is massive with constant 6-12ft swells, but they are frequently messed up by onshore SW winds. Summers are still very consistent for swell, but the wind patterns aren't stable. Mornings are often offshore (NE), whilst afternoons suffer from strong onshore sea breezes. Early winter is a better bet for offshores than late winter. Tides vary a lot and affect the quality of the waves.

| STATISTICS | | J F | M A | M J | J A | S O | N D |
|---|---|---|---|---|---|---|---|
| SWELL | Direction | | | | | | |
| | Size (ft) | 4 | 4-5 | 5-6 | 6-7 | 5-6 | 4 |
| WIND | Direction | | | | | | |
| | Force | F3-F4 | F3 | F4-F5 | F4-F5 | F4-F5 | F4 |
| WATER | Wetsuit | | | | | | |
| | Temp/°C | 13 | 14 | 13 | 12 | 12 | 13 |
| WEATHER | Rainfall/mm | 11 | 17 | 48 | 40 | 21 | 13 |
| | days/mth | 3 | 4 | 10 | 10 | 7 | 3 |
| | Min temp/°C | 17 | 15 | 9 | 7 | 11 | 15 |
| | Max temp/°C | 25 | 23 | 19 | 18 | 21 | 24 |

# Adelaide SOUTH AUSTRALIA

Adelaide is South Australia's capital city of 1.25million people. It's a quick drive to the city spots but it's crowded and inconsistent because of a narrow swell window. Yorke Peninsula, 4h drive west of Adelaide has a concentration of quality waves on its tip in the Innes National Park suited to experienced fearless surfers. Kangaroo Island is 150km (96mi) long, and features many remote and spooky surf spots, exposed to the full force of the swell coming out of the Great Southern Ocean.

- + SOUTHERN OCEAN SWELLS
- + WIDE VARIETY OF SPOTS
- + CHOICE OF COASTLINES
- + LOW CROWD PRESSURES

- – COLD WATER, HOT AIR TEMPS
- – EXPERIENCED SURFER SPOTS
- – SOME LOCAL VIBES
- – SHARKS, SNAKES AND FLIES

## TRAVEL INFORMATION

**Weather** – Hot summers 16-27°C (61-81°F) with oppressive heatwaves of 35°C (97°F) flip to cool, mild winters 8-16°C (46-61°F) with harsh windchill factors and plenty of rain between May and August. Water temps are low – winter requires at least a 3/2 steamer and booties, summer will allow springsuits, but most surfers remain covered.

**Lodging and Food** – On Yorke, use cheap caravan parks. Marion Bay Seaside Apartments for groups: from $70/n. Around mid/south coasts, try backpackers for reasonable rates. Grosvenor Hotel in Victor Harbor from $20p/n. On Kangaroo, prepare to camp, or use Ozone Hotel in Kingscote.

**Nature and Culture** – Wild bush is the landscape. Main wildlife parks are Urimbirra Wildlife Park, Victor Harbor and Gorge Wildlife. Churches outnumbered by pubs and nightclubs. Don't miss Rodney Fox Shark Museum. Fishing is amazing. SA produces 50% of Australian wines. Kangaroos galore!

**Hazards and Hassles** – Bronze whalers and white pointers often patrol the area, be aware when to stay out of the water. Winds and tides cause strong rips. Avoid the brown snakes. Crowd pressure is much less than other parts of Australia.

**Handy Hints** – All kinds of waves so take a full quiver. Check out Cutloose or MidCoast Shop&Board in Lonsdale or Nasty Boards in Beverly. Victor Harbor has Surf Power, but no shops or shapers on Yorke.

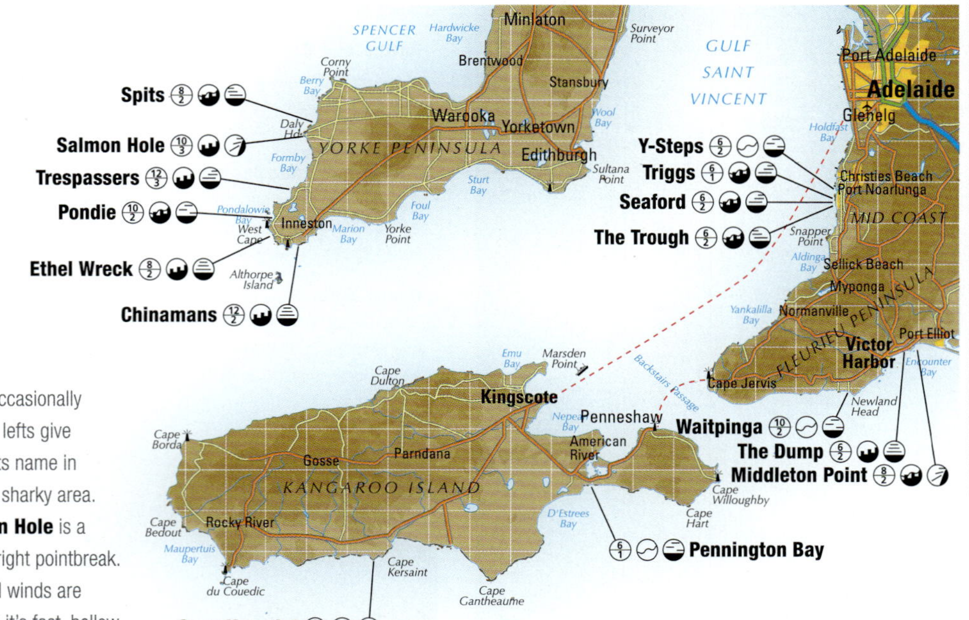


Long, occasionally spitting lefts give **Spits** its name in a rippy, sharky area. **Salmon Hole** is a scenic right pointbreak. When N winds are blowing it's fast, hollow and long, but avoid the suck rock in the middle. It's a long walk over private property to **Trespassers**, a right with a heavy take-off and workable walls at lower tides. Surf the sand covered reefs at **Pondie** in sizeable surf with strong S winds and low-mid tides, opposite a campsite. When everywhere is flat **Ethel Wreck** can produce

ANDREW SHIELD

Ethel Wreck

intense waves next to a shipwreck. Often rippy and disorganised but a crowd magnet when on. **Chinamans** is the classic South Australian spot for advanced surfers who dont mind the crowded small take-off zone and vertical drops over shallow, sharp reef. Getting in and out is tricky but the barrels are excellent. Baby Chinamans is a softer version, east of the main break. Lower tides and N winds. Over on the mid-coast in Adelaide if there is a major storm with gusty SW winds, try **Y-Steps** or the Hump at Christies Beach, where refraction can make A-frames with a bit of power. In large W-SW swell, **Seaford** rights offer the longest walls around, despite the sections and crowds. **Triggs** Beach has average rights and lefts working near the observation tower. The first section of **The Trough** delivers some punch before fattening out in the channel. The Fleurieu Peninsula is offshore in N winds so best surfed early before the summer S winds get up. Victor Harbor is SA's most popular holiday area, sometimes referred to as 'shark alley'! Expect brilliant sandbanks, mellow points and a few big waves. If the swell is tiny drive west to to **Waitpinga**, (windy place" in Aboriginal) which can be seriously hollow – beware of rips and white pointers. Check **The Dump** powerful reef rights, next to Granite Island. In Middleton a handful of surf spots can be checked in 10 minutes. For mal-riders/beginners, the rights at **Middleton Point** have room for everyone. The adventurous can take the ferry to Kangaroo Island, with countless turn-offs to rugged deserted spots. **Pennington Bay**'s shallow beachies can be fun on a medium swell with NE winds and, if swell and confidence get big, try **Cape Kersaint**'s left pointbreak, it's awesome!

Lashed by plenty of 3-20ft Southern Ocean swells but blocking islands and peninsulas have to be taken into account. Fleurieu Peninsula and Kangaroo Island work in small S summer swells. Yorke and the mid-coast needs strong SW-W winter swells. The wind is pretty much S-SW year round apart from winter when N-NE winds groom up the best surf conditions. Most of Yorke's spots work at low tide while the mid-coast is better on high, plan winter itineraries based on tide times. The narrow straights create significant tidal phases over 2.4m.

| STATISTICS | | J F | M A | M J | J A | S O | N D |
|---|---|---|---|---|---|---|---|
| SWELL | Direction | | | | | | |
| | Size (ft) | 2 | 3-4 | 5-6 | 6 | 5 | 2-3 |
| WIND | Direction | | | | | | |
| | Force | F3-F4 | F3 | F3-F4 | F3-F4 | F3-F4 | F4 |
| WATER | Wetsuit | | | | | | |
| | Temp/°C | 19 | 18 | 15 | 13 | 14 | 17 |
| WEATHER | Rainfall/mm | 20 | 35 | 70 | 65 | 50 | 25 |
| | days/mth | 5 | 8 | 14 | 16 | 12 | 7 |
| | Min temp/°C | 17 | 14 | 9 | 8 | 10 | 14 |
| | Max temp/°C | 30 | 25 | 18 | 16 | 21 | 27 |

ANDREW SHIELD

Chinamans

# Hobart TASMANIA

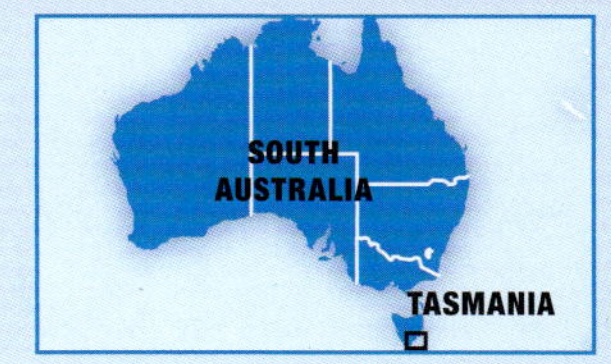




**Around 10,000 years ago, Australia's sixth state was joined to the mainland but it is now about 240km away across the shallow Bass Strait. Tasmania has become synonymous with the incredible right ledge on the Tasman Peninsula known as Shipstern Bluff, where the slightly insane take on triple lips, stepped faces and huge screaming barrels. The majority of surfers will be seeking less life-threatening spots and Hobart makes a good base to explore from.**

**+ ROARING FORTIES EXPOSURE**
**+ BEACHES AND POINTS**
**+ INDENTED COASTLINE**
**+ UNCROWDED, MOUNTAINOUS**

**– WINDY AND CHILLY WINTER SURF**
**– OCCASIONALLY FLAT SE COAST**
**– SLOW ACCESS**
**– EXPENSIVE**

Nine ferries a day make the 20min journey between Hobart and Bruny Island, home of some big waves that hold size better than most Tassie breaks. Furthest west is a rivermouth spot called **Lagoons**, where there is potential for long rights on a big swell, with the right sandbank, high tides and W-NW winds. On a medium swell, scenic **Cloudy Bay** can produce good beachbreaks, favouring rights breaking into the rip. Stop by **Coal Point** if the swell is big, because this is Bruny's best pointbreak. Hairy lefts unload over rock and kelp, the first section being fast with a challenging take-off. Other spots like **The Neck** are less consistent but it's a small island and waves are fairly easy to find. There are quite a few places to stay or camp. Betsey Island sits 1km off the South Arm's coastline, forcing large swells to wrap around it and reform into the sucky barrels of the occasionally crowded **Wedge**. Access is through private property. Another fun stretch of exposed beachie is **Goats** but **Clifton Beach** is Hobart's most popular spot, only 30min drive from the city centre. When the swell gets huge, other breaks on the east side get classic, small right points like **Cremorne**, Mays, Lauderdale or Seven Mile. Out on the Tasman Peninsula, the main town of Nubeena has access to **Roaring Beach**'s often surfed beachbreak and **Kelpies**, a long, hollow left pointbreak. **Shipstern Bluff** or Fluffys, an ironic tribute to its power, has become one of the world's iconic waves. Swells abruptly hit the granite ledge, only a few metres off a spectacular boulder-piled headland, creating a crazily difficult ride. Nowadays it is rarely ridden by paddle surfers and is the domain of a few crazy tow-in crews. Shipstern is a 2h/7km hike around the Tasman National Park. South of Port Arthur, **Remarkable Caves** is not only a tourist spot, but also has low tide peaks, and a scary paddle out past caves. A thin isthmus of land at Eaglehawk Neck attracts triangle sandbars along its extensive curve, plus a powerful, rare left point in NE swells. **Tessos**, a sucky, demanding, quality right over kelp-covered rock, is just next door. It needs huge SE swells to turn on but can handle any wind and works on high tide.

The west coast is usually big and onshore, the north coast needs major swells and the east coast is inconsistent. The south coast has the best winter surf, since most spots don't face the SW swell and filter wave height down to a manageable 4-6ft and the regular SW-N winds blow offshore. The extremely indented coastline is useful for offshores or sideshores and the 1.4m tides are a fraction of the north coast, but affect the reefs and points.

STU GIBSON

Mays Point

## TRAVEL INFORMATION

**Weather** – Temperate, maritime climate, meaning four seasons in one day! The west coast sees the highest average rainfall of Australia, but it's much lower in the east. Be prepared in winter with 5mm wetsuits, thick gloves, hoods and booties. A 3/2mm steamer may just be acceptable in summer.

**Lodging and Food** – Staying in Hobart is an option but driving times increase considerably. Favour Taranna (Masons cottages $77/dble), or Port Arthur (Sea Change Safety Cove, $127/dble). Enjoy a wide spectrum of berry fruits and apples, world-beating ales and wines or full flavoured cheeses.

**Nature and Culture** – 40% of Tassie is National Parks, making an outdoor playground free of pollution. Ski and surf in the same day (Ben Lomond resort). Climb Mt Wellington or visit Port Arthur's penal settlement. Keep eyes peeled for Tasmanian devils or the presumed extinct Tasmanian tigers!

**Hazards and Hassles** – Although crowds are rare, some spots are very sensitive, be very respectful with locals. Mind the nasty rips when close to rivermouths. Be ready to walk and get wet if camping.

**Handy Hints** – Plenty of well stocked surf shops in and around Hobart including RHS in town. Based at Clifton Beach tassiesurf.com/Coastrider Surf Academy offer a big range of surf lessons and equipment hire. Boards are AUS$30 a day and then $15 a day thereafter.

STU GIBSON

Shipstern Bluff

| STATISTICS | | J F | M A | M J | J A | S O | N D |
|---|---|---|---|---|---|---|---|
| SWELL | Direction | | | | | | |
| | Size (ft) | 2-3 | 4-5 | 5-6 | 6 | 5-6 | 3 |
| WIND | Direction | | | | | | |
| | Force | F3-F5 | F3-F5 | F3-F5 | F5 | F4-F5 | F4-F5 |
| WATER | Wetsuit | | | | | | |
| | Temp/°C | 15 | 13 | 11 | 11 | 11 | 13 |
| WEATHER | Rainfall/mm | 45 | 45 | 50 | 50 | 55 | 55 |
| | days/mth | 12 | 14 | 15 | 18 | 18 | 15 |
| | Min temp/°C | 12 | 10 | 6 | 5 | 7 | 10 |
| | Max temp/°C | 22 | 19 | 13 | 12 | 16 | 20 |

# Great Ocean Road VICTORIA

Victoria is the southern extent of the Australian mainland, hemmed in by the angry waters of Bass Strait and the Tasman Sea, but perfectly situated to receive the mountainous swells from the Southern Ocean. The Great Ocean Road twists torturously atop cliffs overlooking an eroded coast of limestone cliffs, sea stacks and caves, where a plethora of beach, reef and pointbreaks unload in a pristine and uncrowded environment. Since the early 60's, Torquay and Bells Beach have become a surfing epicentre, being home to leading surfwear manufacturers, Quiksilver and Rip Curl, plus the site of the longest running contest and the first Surfing Recreation Reserve on the planet. This 340km scenic drive west of Melbourne, is a surfer's dream as it passes the many right pointbreaks that line both sides of Cape Otway.

- \+ CONSISTENT SWELL
- \+ DOMINANT OFFSHORE WINDS
- \+ BIG-WAVE RIGHT POINTS
- \+ SPECTACULAR SCENERY

- – UNPREDICTABLE WEATHER
- – COOL WATER YEAR-ROUND
- – SUMMER FLAT SPELLS
- – CROWDED BREAKS

## TRAVEL INFORMATION

**Weather** – South Victoria has the coolest weather in mainland Australia, but not the wettest, with only 680mm. The weather is very changeable. Avoid June-Aug, if you're not into a cold trip. The changeover seasons can be pleasant, even though you still have to be prepared for cooler spells and gusty winds. Summers, (Dec to Feb), are fairly dry and warm, averaging 22°C (72°F). Summer water temps rarely get over 20°C (68°F) and winters dip down to 13°C (55°F). A 4/3 mm steamer for winter and a 3/2mm or springy for summer.

**Lodging and Food** – Plenty of cheap backpacker accommodation at around $25-50/p/n (Bells Beach and Anglesea Backpackers). Motels start from $75/p/n. Peppers The Sands resort in Torquay from 140/p/n. A good basic meal is $25.

**Nature and Culture** – Visit the Twelve Apostles and the Cape Otway National Park, plus the Australian National Surf Museum in Torquay. Go hiking around Point Addis. The Tower Hill Wildlife Sanctuary or Anglesea Golf Course are great for kangaroo spotting. The pub is a way of life in Oz, and Victoria is home to the country's favourite beers.

**Hazards and Hassles** – Aside from reef rubs, riptides and crowds, there is not much to worry about. The shark factor is low, but drownings are common in the big waves on the western side.

**Handy Hints** – Torquay is full of surf shops from the big Rip Curl boutique to core shop Strapper Surf. Every accessory under the sun and shortboards from $550.

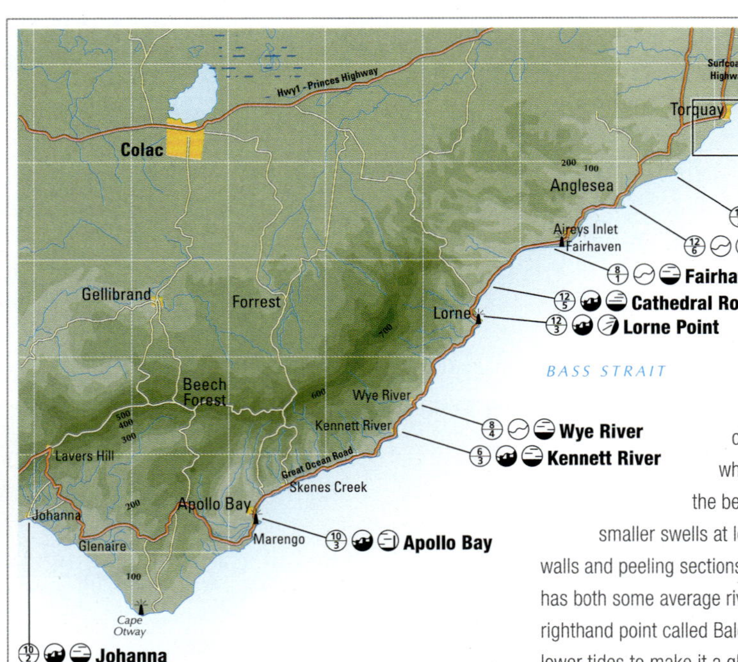

Johanna

The western side of Cape Otway picks up all the available swell so if it's small then the powerful beachbreaks of **Johanna** will be working. The sand is anchored by various bits of reef and there's a decent left at the eastern headland. Crowded in summer with the Torquay crew, it can be a punishing paddle-out and has a habit of dramatically increasing in size without warning. On the east side of Cape Otway is **Apollo Bay**, where there is a right off the harbour breakwall and outside jetty that can handle moderate size and will line up a bit better with some E in the swell at lower tides. There are also some nicely protected beachies perfect for beginners and escaping large, stormy conditions. Around the headland, Marengo offers a brace of more exposed reefs, a righthand point and some changeable, small swell beachbreak. **Kennett River** will have clean rivermouth peaks in S swells, which favour the rights running up the beach. Kennett Point is reliably fun in smaller swells at lower tides, offering a mixture of easy walls and peeling sections for most abilities. **Wye River** also has both some average rivermouth beachies and an option of a righthand point called Baldy, that relies on transient sand and lower tides to make it a glorious peeler for hundreds of meters. When the SW wind is howling and the swell is pumping, most surfers head for the protection of **Lorne Point** and hope they luck into one of the rare, magical days when the rights are hissing and barrelling for anything up to 500m all the way into the crumbly beachbreaks. Prefers a major SE swell, any W in the wind and low tide. **Cathedral Rock** needs a big SW or straight S swell to kick-start the sought after rights that speed down the knobbly reef. After the jacking take-off it stutters through barrel sections then fatter walls as it draws breath, before rifling off again along the reef. Experienced surfers only since getting caught inside is no fun and there's a local pecking order. Fairhaven offers due south-facing beachbreaks that scoop up the swell onto vastly varying sandbanks, that usually favour beginner-friendly, crumbling walls, but can occasionally throw up much better. Needs some angle in the swell to triangulate. Anglesea is a typical coastal town that has some decent beachbreaks at Main Beach for the hordes of groms

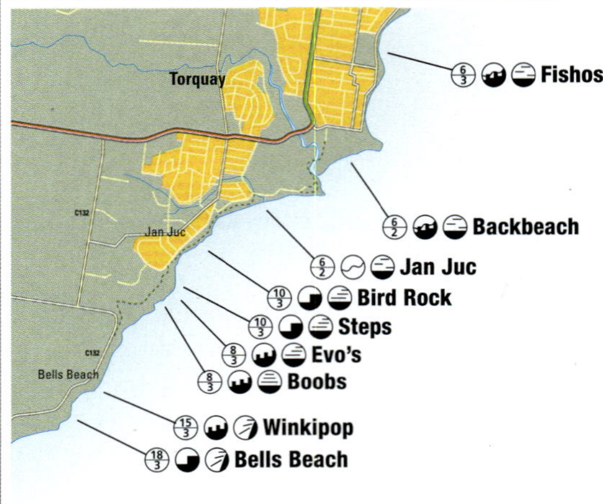

Winkipop

STEVE RYAN

Torquay Backbeach to Point Addis

ANDREW SHIELD

and fun rights at **Point Roadnight** for the mellow mal-riding dads. Needs a huge S-SE to be any good since it is nestled behind a long rocky finger, allowing the sand to build up on the lee side and providing protection from SW-W winds. Both right and lefthanders break off the scraggly reef at **Point Addis** with the lefthanders getting the nod if the SE swell is strong enough to produce some barrels. Otherwise it is a fairly tame affair offering lumbering walls and little else for the intermediates avoiding the gladiatorial line-ups up the road. **Bells Beach** is Victoria's most famous surf spot. Next door is **Winkipop**, a long, fast and hollow pointbreak that can handle solid swells over the shallow reef. Higher tides, 6-8ft and NW winds will create warp speed walls with impossibly long, makeable barrel sections that the locals hunt and slay with consummate ease. It breaks up into sections along the 400-odd-meters of rocky shelf and paddling against the constant sweep of the rip is a given. **Boobs** has a rare, tubey left off the peak if the wind isn't getting into it. It's a long walk round the cliffs from the car parks, keeping crowds down a bit. **Steps** has a few moods and once the rapid drop take-off is negotiated, it will wall and quite often stay overfed till the channel. This makes it a favourite with cruisers, while further out is the more challenging **Evo's**, which shifts across the shallow shelf at speed, squeezing off the odd barrel, or check the inside reef Sparrows, another potential barrel-ride in small to medium SW swells and N winds. All three breaks need mid to high tides to make them break and or safe. **Bird Rock** is a short, sucky, right reef, revered by the dedicated locals that dominate the tiny take-off zone. It jacks up quickly and rifles off fast so only the skilled will get a wave off the pack that is guaranteed when a clean, moderate SW swell hits. **Jan Juc**, a decent, but permanently crowded beachbreak, is best avoided at high tide. Packs coagulate around the car parks so walking can help, but it is the busiest spot on the coast. When the sand triangulates, it provides some tasty lips and ramps to launch from. Torquay is Victoria's surfing capital and **Backbeach** tames the SW swell and orders it into nice, easy rollin' rides for the hordes of beginners, longboarders and every other type of craft. S wind protection is afforded at **Fishos** during major swells or **Point Impossible** has further cruisey rights over flat reefs. **Bancoora**'s offshore reef occasionally sees quality rights on a humping SE swell and N wind combo. **13th Beach** stretches for over 6kms and faces into the SW swell stream. Furthest west is Turd Rock, a righthand point close to the sewage pumping station that most people think is shit. Next is Beacons which holds proper A-frames that hiss over the sandbars when it's on during a SW swell, N wind day. The peaks then stretch all the way up to Barwon Heads where **The Hole** is a rocky set of reefs and **Raffs** is a gentle beachbreak made for beginners, loggers, SUP'ers and those of a laid-back disposition. Point Lonsdale, an all-round beachbreak, completes the picture.

The southwest-facing coast can get huge, with S-W swells up to 15ft-20ft possible, which then wrap around Cape Otway to the SE-facing coastline, where the swells become much cleaner and orderly. While they lose some size, places like Bells will still regularly get triple overhead and bigger. Dominant SW-W winds will be cross/offshore on this side blowing into plenty of 2-15ft swells. Tasmania blocks Victoria from SE groundswells. Due S swells tend to be better for a lot of the SE-facing spots. Westerly winds dominate, tending more SW in summer and NW in winter. Tidal range is usually around 1.8m and the pushing tide can increase the wave size and quality.

### Bells Beach

**LAT. -38.371668° LONG. 144.283621°**

**A classic and consistent right point that breaks on almost any tide, any wind and any decent swell from SE-SW. It's usually broken into 3 sections, starting outside at Rincon, leading into Bells Bowl and finishing in the beachbreak. Power is always associated with this wave and few escape the flogging of an outside set on the head and gruelling paddle-outs as it grows beyond double overhead. When small it is playful and ripable, offering endless carve and cutback corners along a lengthy platform reef that is prone to some long, unmakeable sections. Best in wrapping SW swell and NW winds, but will still have takers in ugly onshore conditions. If the crazy crowd is too much, on the headland to the south there are less intimidating rights at Centreside plus some real decent lefts in SE swells and higher tides at Southside.**

| STATISTICS | | J F | M A | M J | J A | S O | N D |
|---|---|---|---|---|---|---|---|
| SWELL | Direction | | | | | | |
| | Size (ft) | 4 | 4-5 | 5-6 | 6-7 | 5-6 | 4 |
| WIND | Direction | | | | | | |
| | Force | F4 | F4 | F4 | F4-F5 | F4-F5 | F4 |
| WATER | Wetsuit | | | | | | |
| | Temp/°C | 18 | 19 | 16 | 13 | 14 | 16 |
| WEATHER | Rainfall/mm | 37 | 66 | 74 | 92 | 86 | 60 |
| | days/mth | 8 | 12 | 16 | 20 | 16 | 13 |
| | Min temp/°C | 14 | 13 | 9 | 8 | 9 | 12 |
| | Max temp/°C | 24 | 21 | 16 | 14 | 16 | 21 |

# Phillip Island VICTORIA

Surfers from Melbourne prefer to travel to the east-facing Great Ocean Road, because the dominant SW winds are offshore. However what the west-facing coast may lack in quality, it gains in consistency, rarely going flat. The indented coastline of headlands and islands also allows for a few offshore quality right corners when the SW'ers are blowing in stormy, winter conditions and plenty of quality beachbreaks in summer.

- \+ CONSISTENT SUMMER SWELL
- \+ RIGHT POINTBREAKS
- \+ EASY ACCESS
- \+ QUALITY, POWERFUL BEACHES

- – COOL/COLD WATER
- – COMPETITIVE CROWDS
- – RIPS AND ONSHORES
- – UNPREDICTABLE WEATHER

## TRAVEL INFORMATION

**Weather** – The coolest coastal weather on mainland Australia - winter gets quite cold. Spring and Autumn can be pleasant even though there will be cool spells with gusty winds. Summers from Dec to Feb are dry and warm, averaging 22°C (72°F). Summer water temps rarely reach 20°C (68°F) and in winter it dips down to 12°C (54°F). A 4/3mm steamer in winter and a 3/2 in summer.

**Lodging and Food** – On Mornington Peninsula, stay in Portsea (Clifton Lodge: from $53/dbl/n), cabins from $100/n/2 people. On Phillip Island, stay in Ventnor (Kil'n Time B&B: from $150/n) Expect $22 for a good meal.

**Nature and Culture** – Phillip Island switches gear for the 500cc Motorcycle Grand Prix in October. Don't miss the Seal Rocks Sea Life Centre, the Nobbies and the blowhole at Point Grant. Watch the Penguin Parade at sunset, when they cross Summerland Beach.

**Hazards and Hassles** – Apart from reef cuts and intense crowds, not much to fear. Shark factor is relatively low although great whites have been witnessed in the area. Big, gnarly waves on the SW coasts, and beware regular, strong rips.

**Handy Hints** – Famous Trigger Bros surfboards & shops in Sorrento: from $550 up to 6'6" to $900 for a longboard. Try Island surfboards and school in Cowes and Smiths Beach. East Coast Surf School at Pt Leo and Mornington Peninsula Surf School on St Andrews Beach both give lessons. Mornington is home of the Balin surf brand.

LUKE RASMUSSEN

Express Point

Out on Point Nepean, **Quarantines** is unusual, sometimes working when everywhere else is a mess. On a SE wind with a big swell, locals will boat in, otherwise it is a long trek to the unfriendly left line-up. The large expanse of Portsea's **Back Beach** has variable sandbanks. The most consistent spot on this SW exposed coast is powerful, fast and shapely **Gunnamatta**, home of many contests. Quality is dictated by the fast flowing rips. Takes a SW swell, NE winds and anything up to double overhead on the push. The lefts at **Cape Schanck** lighthouse hold some serious size, amidst stunning scenery. Flinders Beach is dotted with various reefbreaks, **Meanos** being the nastiest, tucked beneath the West Head cliffs. Even at high tide, the lefts can be intimidating, but the rights are easier, as is the inside reform. The main spot at Point Leo, **Suicides**, is a playful right point with long, workable walls, boosted by the incoming tide on bigger swells. If it's not big enough there are other breaks nearby. Philip Island is only 26km long and 9km wide, yet it is Victoria's leading tourist destination attracting 3.5 million visitors each year. The western tip, best known for its penguins, benefits from breaks on its north side like **Flynn's Reef**, an epic right that zips down the point and stays offshore in winds from NE to S. **Cat Bay** is the mellow beachie where all beginners should go, on decent swells and southerly winds. The south side has a number of good right points like **The Crack**, a section of the point at Summerland Bay. **Smith's Beach** is a rare, relaxed beachbreak with good low tide form and some wind protection, close to the experts-only **Express Point**, the most radical reef on the island. World-class, ledgy right tubes with elevator drops, mega crowds and a nasty reef. **Surfies Point** needs a bigger S to SE swell to make the big drops link through to the inside. The most reliable, powerful beachbreaks are at **Woolamai**, surf out front or walk east to Magic Lands to enjoy a bit more space. If Woolamai is flat, then **Kilcunda** may be on. This swell magnet is often too big and dangerous but power is the rule. Another spot to hold stormy conditions is **Eagle's Nest**, whose long slow rights can break in big S swells and W winds.

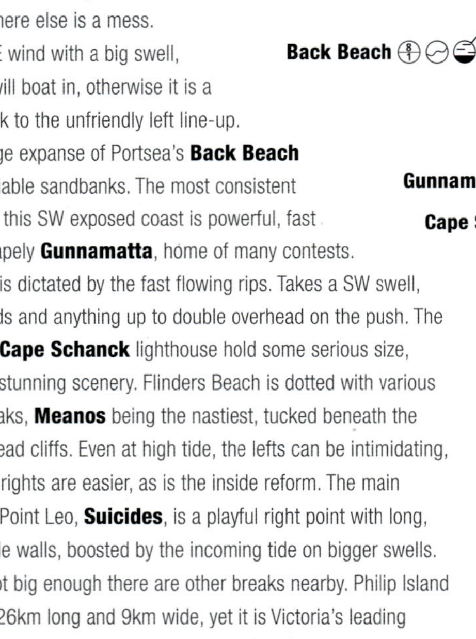
STEVE RYAN

Quarantines

Australia's SW-facing coast gets 15-20ft winter swells, but it is only on the more protected SE-facing headlands that they are groomed by the dominant NW-W winds. In summer, exposed SW-facing beaches enjoy plenty of messy onshore 2-6ft waves or smaller, cleaner waves on the sheltered right points. Tasmania can cause the low pressure systems to stall, sending S or even SE swells back to the coast. As cold storm fronts move in on the coast winds blow S, then E, then N on a cycle that can vary from a few hours to several days. Tide amplitude can reach 2.4m, so grab a Port Phillip Bay tide table and work out the variations for remote spots.

| STATISTICS | | J F | M A | M J | J A | S O | N D |
|---|---|---|---|---|---|---|---|
| SWELL | Direction | | | | | | |
| | Size (ft) | 4 | 4-5 | 5-6 | 6-7 | 5-6 | 4 |
| WIND | Direction | | | | | | |
| | Force | F4 | F4-F5 | F4-F5 | F4 | F4-F5 | F4-F5 |
| WATER | Wetsuit | | | | | | |
| | Temp/°C | 17 | 17 | 14 | 12 | 13 | 15 |
| WEATHER | Rainfall/mm | 50 | 55 | 55 | 50 | 65 | 60 |
| | days/mth | 9 | 11 | 15 | 17 | 15 | 12 |
| | Min temp/°C | 14 | 12 | 8 | 6 | 9 | 12 |
| | Max temp/°C | 26 | 22 | 16 | 14 | 18 | 21 |

# Shoalhaven, South Coast NSW

The South Coast generally refers to the coast south of Sydney down to the border with Victoria. Shoalhaven is the northernmost of three subregions, populated by retirees and visitors from Sydney and Canberra. The most popular tourist destination in New South Wales – a majestic stretch of coast with natural bays, white sand beaches, and a cloak of typical Aussie bush. Famed for its fish, dolphins and migrating whales, but also the unique reefs, points and beachbreak surf spots providing a great release valve for Sydney's weekend warriors.

+ VARIED QUALITY BREAKS
+ SWELL CONSISTENCY
+ LOW NSW CROWD LEVEL
+ SYDNEY ESCAPE

- COLDER THAN SYDNEY
- SHARKY WATERS
- WEEKEND CROWDS
- SOME LOCALISM

Booderee National Park is home to the all-time classic reefbreak **Black Rock** (aka Aussie Pipe, Wreck Bay or Summercloud Bay). One of the hollowest and most photogenic lefts in Australia, breaking intensely over a shallow cunjevoi and urchin-infested bottom. The local indigenous surfers can be protective. S swells, NE sea breezes and mid tide. **Coneeley's Reef** is a quality left and right reefbreak facing Swan Lake that needs a moderate SE to S swell and westerlies. Plenty of beachies nearby. All standards of surfer will find something at **Bendalong Beach**, where busy but highly consistent peaks can offer barrels on all swells and tides. It's a long walk and a longer paddle (over the Shark Pit) to the tip of **Green Island** where long, sectiony, bending, walled-up longboard lefts break in a moderate to big NE to S swell. Offshore in summer NE winds so often crowded. **Mollymook** has punchy beach peaks plus a zippy right off the reef at the south end. Ulladulla, a bustling fishing port and commercial centre is the hub of South Coast surfing. Locals show a real respect for **Golf Course Reef**, a left with long hollow walls peeling over shallow rocks in a big NE-SE. The bigger the better, but expect a heavy paddle-out. On a monster S swell, the locals head to the **Bommie**, a challenging, unpredictable and unforgiving open ocean right and occasional left. Rips and shallow bottom – watermen only. Neighbouring **Rennies Beach** offers great beach waves for intermediates and a right reef in the southern corner. On a medium NE to E swell, head to **Dolphin Point** where a gnarly left jacks-up hollow, barreling sections over a shallow ledge. Crampton Island is home to **Dum Dums**, a shallow reef that gets fast and hollow in a small NE to SE swell. **Guillotines** is a scary freefall drop into a growling barrel over a ledge, getting faster and shallower before shutting down. Further out on **Bawley Point**, is a short intense right barrel with a bottomless take-off in monster swells up to 15ft. It's really nasty getting in and out when over 6ft. Hellmen only. Explore the bush to find uncrowded spots like **Depot Beach** with S wind protection.

ANDREW SHIELD

Dum Dums

## TRAVEL INFORMATION

**Weather** – Winter temps range from 8-22°C (46-72°F) and summer temps are between 14-26°C (58-79°F). Winter days can be warm and dry or cool and wet with sudden downpours that are evenly distributed throughout the year. A 3/2 fullsuit and booties in winter. Springsuit the rest of the year. Boardshorts on the warmest days.

**Lodging and Food** – Large choice of motels, guest houses, cabins and tent sites. Book in advance for overnight camping in Booderee Nat Park ($25/night). South Coast Ulladulla Lodge ($25, $58/dbl) is the best backpacker option. Huskisson Beach Tourist Resort in Jervis Bay has 5pax cabins ($100/n) as does the legendary Don's at Green Island (from $50/dble). Caravan Parks everywhere including Sussex and Mollymook.

**Nature and Culture** – South Coast is a place to experience nature, with Jervis Bay, the Kangaroo Valley, Ettrema Wilderness, Budawang Ranges and Morton National Park being the main landmarks. The wild bush area that extends from Pretty Beach to Durras is well worth a visit.

**Hazards and Hassles** – Although crowds are usually not a major problem, some spots are very sensitive with tight take-off zones. Be very respectful with the locals. Many spots are for experts only, so do not overestimate your skills. Reef cuts, riptides and urchins are pretty common.

**Handy Hints** – Many surf shops in Ulladulla and Sussex Inlet. Surf schools in Ulladulla and Mollymook. Funnel-web spider bite is a life-threatening medical emergency – get to hospital with the spider (or definite id) quickly.

ANDREW SHIELD

Aussie Pipe

**North Durras** has a large reef in front of the lake entrance, where intermediates will enjoy excellent lefts and rights, but beware of the deep channel rips.

Consistent but rarely epic, most of the summer swell is generated by NE/SE wind. SE-S groundswells are more reliable and powerful from April to September. The surf is regularly 2-5ft, hitting 6-8ft a few times per month, with short flat periods in winter. SW winds are common in winter while summers are offshore in the morning before the NE sea breeze picks up. Most beachbreaks and reefbreaks work best on the incoming tide, even though tidal range is minimal.

| STATISTICS | | J F | M A | M J | J A | S O | N D |
|---|---|---|---|---|---|---|---|
| SWELL | Direction | | | | | | |
| | Size (ft) | 4-5 | 5-6 | 6 | 6 | 5 | 4-5 |
| WIND | Direction | | | | | | |
| | Force | F4 | F4-F5 | F4-F5 | F4-F5 | F4-F5 | F4 |
| WATER | Wetsuit | | | | | | |
| | Temp/°C | 20 | 20 | 17 | 15 | 16 | 17 |
| WEATHER | Rainfall/mm | 110 | 134 | 96 | 65 | 82 | 96 |
| | days/mth | 12 | 11 | 10 | 8 | 11 | 12 |
| | Min temp/°C | 16 | 14 | 9 | 7 | 10 | 14 |
| | Max temp/°C | 26 | 24 | 18 | 17 | 21 | 24 |

# Illawarra NEW SOUTH WALES

The Illawarra coastal region encompasses many landscapes from pristine bushland, lakes and rivers to the stark industrial views over Port Kembla steel-works. The towering escarpment of the Illawarra Range squeezes the narrow coastal strip into the sea, creating interesting geology and a high concentration of reefs and points, interspersed with long strands and shorter pocket beaches, offering waves in most conditions. Being an hours drive from Sydney doesn't help with crowd control, but there are some quiet spots between the banner waves.

- **+ GOOD REEF AND POINTBREAKS**
- **+ MULTIPLE BEACH OPTIONS**
- **+ NATIONAL PARK**
- **+ EASY COAST ROAD CHECKS**

- **– CITY CROWDS**
- **– LIMITED WIND PROTECTION**
- **– LOCALISED REEFS**
- **– POLLUTION ISSUES**

Bundeena
Waterfall
Helensburgh
Stanwell Park
Princes Highway
Coalcliff
Clifton
Scarborough
SUDDEN RUSH
Austinmer
Thirroul
Bulli
Woonona
B65
Fairy Meadow
Woollongong
Princes Motorway
Port Kembla
B65
Albion Park
Shellharbour
Shell Cove
Bombo
Kiama
400 200 600
SURFHOLIDAYS
Gerringong

Garie Beach
Stanwell Park
Coalcliff
Wombarra
Coledale
Sharkies
Headlands
Thirroul/Austinmer
Sandon Point
Bulli
Woonona
Towradgi
North Beach
South Beach
Port Kembla
Windang Island
Cowries
Redsands
The Farm
Mystics
Boneyards
Bombo
Kiama
Werri Beach

IAN BIRD

Mystics

**Werri Beach** sees solid beachbreaks in all swells plus a challenging right off the southern point in NE-E swells. Barrels hard over shallow rocks and is definitely an experienced surfers only spot. Nice A-frames at the northern end in NE swells and winds. **Kiama**'s main surfing beach holds punchy peaks in the middle and a left and right off the rocks at either end. This beach gets some raging rips so learners should head to Easts Beach for an easier ride. Experts will check The Pool, with rights around past the blowhole and lefts over the harbour entrance. It's easy to check **Bombo** from the road and if it's flat here, then forget it. Highly changeable banks at each end will break hard and hollow on the good days. Crowds, horrendous rips and a bad shark attack may just keep you driving. **Boneyards** is a heavy righthander over urchin-sprinkled rocks that has full S wind protection, even from SE sea breezes. Sucky at the drop zone, into a fast barrelling pocket and ripable wall. NE-E swells and a bit of water on the reef is best. Lefts appear on smaller swells over the inside reef. Experts only as the rips, sharks, urchins and locals are always lurking. Magical beachbreak peaks drum the sandbars at **Mystics** starting with the wedge at the north end that gets bounce off the cliffs all the way down to the Minnamurra end and the rivermouth. Insane barrels on many of the peaks that work in various swell directions. Powerful lips and rips so experienced surfers only. Inside the Killalea State Park, **The Farm** is a good option for improvers and longboarders as the waves are generally mellow, longer rides across the south-facing bay. Offshore even in summer NE'ers and more tide will help the corners hold up. An intimidating reef peak at **Redsands** squares up over the reef and turns inside out with heaving barrels on the right and shorter pinchier left. NE-E swell or big SE and more water never hurts, unlike not making the drop here. Loved by lids and chargers so expect a crowd. There are more reefs to check at Shallows and along the Shellharbour South Beach. **Cowries** hosts a grinding righthander over shallow shelf in moderate swells with some E. Awfully congested tiny take-off zone and the locals are on it in force when it works. On the next headland south, Pools rights and Shatters lefts provide some equally challenging options. To the north on Barrack Headland is **Mini Pipe**, lefts of intensity and hollowness in NE-E swells. Big wave chargers gravitate to **Windang Island** in heavy NE swells and N winds. It hugs the rocky cliffs and demands skill and confidence to master the drop, barrel to muscular wall. Lower tides keep it off the rocks that you don't want to get a close inspection of. A slew of reef and beachbreaks keep the local surfers happy around **Port Kembla** with the left reef at the northern end serving up solid lefts that are sheltered from the NE sea breezes. There are plenty of pitching peaks running down the beach southwards, spreading the regular crowds. Over Hill 60 are a number of heavy, localised waves along MM Beach including Bay and the fearsome Outer break, or Ollies sucky jetty rights in front of the steelworks. **South Beach** Wollongong comes into its own when a solid NE swell wraps around the headland and rifles off some hollow left bombs. Handles size and it's accessible via the rocks when too big to paddle. Most of the time it's average peaks and close-outs with good NE'er protection. **North Beach** Wollongong hates NE wind but likes a peaky NE-E swell or a S pulse. Busy city beach with all amenities. A lower tides reef by the **Towradgi** pool holds the sand and coaxes some rights and lefts to stand up and shoot through to the beachbreaks that extend south to Fairy Meadow or north to Corrimal and Bellambi. Super-reliable **Woonona** is the NE swell magnet in the region thanks to an outer reef bending the lines into the northern end of the beach. The lefts line up the best but there will be rights into the many channels also. Not ideal for beginners as the best surfers congregate here. More solid beachbreak at **Bulli** in peaky NE-SE swells. South end has a good right reef in the corner and the the northern headland

## TRAVEL INFORMATION

**Weather** – The steep escarpment of the Illawarra Range produces katabatic offshore flows, especially on cool winter mornings. The steepness aids convection forces driving summer sea breezes from 10am. The hottest months are Jan/Feb so expect onshores, continuing into March the wettest month.

**Lodging and Food** – Wollongong City Beach Hotel from $90. Camping and caravan parks are often good value for families and groups. Many holiday parks in Kiama and the council run Corrimal Beach and Bulli from $20/n/p.

**Nature and Culture** – The Royal National Park is prime Aussie bush – do the epic coast track 26km one way and stay at Era campground.

**Hazards and Hassles** – Shark worries are real and only Coledale, Austinmer, Thirroul, North and South Wollongong beaches are netted. Wollongong locals have an aggressive reputation at hotspots like Sandon. Water and air pollution blight the 'Gong. Summer NE winds bring stinging bluebottle jellyfish and urchins abound.

**Handy Hints** – Check legendary Byrne Surfboards in Thirroul.

CLARRIE BOUMA

Redsands

has a kamikaze left plus an extremely fickle rocky right called Peggies for experts only. The car park is packed when it's pumping at **Sandon Point**. **Thirroul** offers nice peaks up and down the beach in all swells and can have some hollow shories at higher tides. Consistent and enough space to spread the summer crowds. Both **Austinmer** and Little Austinmer to the north have variable beachbreaks that prefer NE swells. Prone to close-outs above headhigh, but the rights off the pool will hold up better and the left shelf at Little Austi can get fast and hollow. **Headlands** is a temperamental righthander that bends in all swell directions to cook up some sort of barrel over the crescent slab reef. An easier roll-in at higher tides leads to a sudden, sucking bowl section further inside that positively gapes in NE swells and often draws dry at low. S swells will wrap in a far more manageable fashion and may cut down on the numbers of bodyboarders looking for the hideous square pits on a NE. Often crowded because the epic days are few, but even a bad day at Headies will usually output some shade time. The peak at **Sharkies** is a reef sand combo that swell direction will dictate which side to ride with lefts in NE'ers and rights in SE/S swells. Good intermediates wave and low hassle factor. Check Thommo's fun left on the northern headland in NE swells. **Coledale** prefers some south in the swell and lower tides to get the sucky wedges in the south corner going, provided there's some sand in the bay. Look for the lefts called Shithouse in a solid NE pulse. **Wombarra** reef only works when the sand has filled in the holes in the reef and the rights can spin off for a good 200m in a E-S swell. Doesn't happen often, but when it does, the tubes are excellent. Various breaks can have their day at **Coalcliff**, but the peak in front of the carpark is the only reliable one. The Ledge by the pool can be sucky and intense on E swell and low tides and very occasionally the point can line up into it. The big Bommie left is fluky and the rest of the beachbreaks are average. **Stanwell Park** is a pretty beach under the shadow of the National Park and is the regions top S swell-magnet. Lefts can be long and hollow in NE swells and south end rights are more common in S swells. Shorey can be punchy, attracting plenty of lids. Good beginner beach on average days, but rips can be very strong and drownings have occurred. The main coastal access point for the Royal National Park (Nasho) is Garie Beach, a swell magnet and a beautiful place to surf. It catches NE swells the best, with lefts hitting the northern headland and the sand dependant banks all the way down to Little Garie. You have to walk everywhere from the main carpark and North Era beach will also have a left off the point, but less bodies in the water. Even further south is Burning Palms which is a shorter beach and easily overwhelmed by moderate swell. Peaky, small summer swells and light winds are the go, but beware the rips that get horrendous. Pay your day entrance fees or get an annual membership for all NSW National Parks.

**Sandon Point**
**LAT. -34.330505° LONG. 150.930933°**

**This stellar east coast righthand pointbreak is a testing, teasing ride that offers a high risk to reward ratio. The small swell fun walls are quickly replaced by muscled-up lines, throwing thick lips over the ledge, where take-offs become a leap into the unknown. Low tide and more E in the swell opens the barrels, while big S rumbles down the line with awesome power. Getting caught inside is not recommended (surfers have drowned here), but is almost guaranteed. Locals dominate and are intolerant to those who are out of their depth or out of order. The Jetty as it is sometimes called is high consistency and absolutely always crowded.**

CLARRIE BOUMA
Stanwell Park

The Illawarra and Coal Coasts generally receive the same swell patterns and weather as Sydney, but often can be a touch bigger in marginal summer windswells particularly from the SE-S. By far the most common swell direction is SE in the 5-6ft range, right through winter and tending more E for the high summer months. Winds are reliably SW winter and NE summer with onshores in between. Tidal range averages a metre affecting the slabs a lot.

CLARRIE BOUMA
Shithouse, Coledale

| STATISTICS | | J F | M A | M J | J A | S O | N D |
|---|---|---|---|---|---|---|---|
| SWELL | Direction | | | | | | |
| | Size (ft) | 4 | 4-5 | 5 | 5 | 4 | 4-5 |
| WIND | Direction | | | | | | |
| | Force | F4 | F3 | F3-F4 | F4 | F3-F4 | F4 |
| WATER | Wetsuit | | | | | | |
| | Temp/°C | 23 | 22 | 19 | 18 | 18 | 21 |
| WEATHER | Rainfall/mm | 143 | 145 | 109 | 73 | 84 | 105 |
| | days/mth | 10 | 9 | 7 | 6 | 7 | 9 |
| | Min temp/°C | 18 | 15 | 10 | 8 | 11 | 15 |
| | Max temp/°C | 25 | 23 | 19 | 18 | 21 | 24 |

# Sydney Southern Beaches NSW

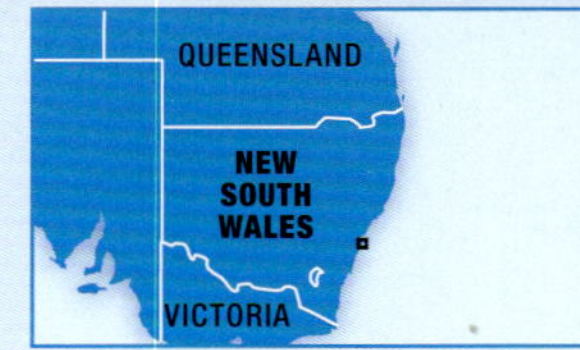


Sydney's indented, jagged coastline is broken and divided by four large riverine estuaries. Cronulla on the southerly outskirts, is sandwiched between the large Port Hacking estuary and the famous "discovery" anchorage of Botany Bay, which is still the location for most foreign arrivals at the international airport built into the bay. Sydney's city beaches extend from Maroubra to that most iconic symbol of Aussie life, Bondi Beach, sitting a mere 8km from the skyscrapers of the Central Business District of downtown Sydney. With easy modern transport links, Bondi has become a must see melting pot of beach culture for Sydney's myriad tourists and backpackers, plus plenty of city workers looking to cool down in some typical Aussie beachies or take on the challenge of some of the heavy reefs that stud this crowded urban coastline.

+ QUINTESSENTIAL AUSSIE BEACHES
+ BONDI BEACH SCENE
+ URBAN ENTERTAINMENT
+ GOOD TRANSPORT LINKS

- LIMITED OPTIONS
- THICK CITY CROWDS
- LOCALISED REEFS
- EXPENSIVE

## TRAVEL INFORMATION

**Weather** – Sydney has a subtropical climate, which makes the best time to visit the changeover seasons of autumn (Mar-Apr) and spring (Oct-Nov), when temperatures of around 24°C (75°F) are normal. Winters are never very cold, with afternoon temperatures frequently hitting 20°C (68°F). Mid summer is not a great time to be in Sydney as it's hotter, wetter, humid and less consistent surf. Use a 3/2 steamer for the May-September period, springsuit or boardies for the remainder of the year.

**Lodging and Food** – Cronulla YHA from $25/n. Bondi Backpackers and YHA from $20/n. Air BnB from $65/n. Manly Paradise Motel ($150-280/dble), Narrabeen Sands Hotel ($140/dble), Whale Beach B&B ($90). Food is cheap, especially from the take-aways and coffee shops. Meals from $16.

**Nature and Culture** – Sydney is a cosmopolitan city with plenty of nightlife. Climb the Harbour Bridge for stunning views. The Northern Beaches have large areas of parkland and natural Australian bushland.

**Hazards and Hassles** – Shark worries are minimal as the beaches are all netted. The locals are very competitive but aggressive localism is fairly rare. Parking can be difficult and expensive. All of Sydney's beaches can suffer from sewage pollution in onshores and stormwater after rain. Summer NE winds bring stinging bluebottle jellyfish.

**Handy Hints** – There are a multitude of surf shops where you can find cheap gear.

Bondi
Tamarama
Bronte
Coogee
Lurline Bay
Maroubra
Malabar
Voodoo
Wanda/Greenhills
The Wall/Elouera
The Alley
Cronulla Point
Shark Island

It's not the fish you should be worrying about when taking on the sinister square shacks of **Shark Island**. A solid S/SE swell and SW wind at **Cronulla Point** racks up some seriously powerful righthand walls that would fit into the world-class category. Long, thick and challenging, especially at size, which it handles with aplomb, as do the local chargers that rule this coveted line-up. Will break hollower in smaller NE/E swells but fragments a bit. The reef is cungey covered and always ready to catch out those sitting inside because the crowd is so thick. Experts only when it hits d-o-h. **The Alley** is a reliable reef near the pool that can be accommodating for intermediates at high tide, but gets dredgy and shallow at low tide. Bigger swells will roll in off the outside sandbars and the current can drag you a bit deep. Loved by bodyboarders who don't want to take on the Island. In front of **The Wall** is a stretch of above average beachbreaks that work in most swell directions and have a little more southerly protection than the breaks to the north as the beach curves around. Can be picture perfect on a SE swell NW wind combo at mid tide, when it gets crowded and maybe a bit aggro on the good days. **Elouera** continues the long beachbreak theme, offering something for everyone from summer slop in a SE'er to bombing A-frames in moderate peaky swells. Spreads the crowd over a number of banks and there's easy roadside parking. The ever-curving beach heads up to the **Wanda** and **Greenhills** section, providing more room to move between the main access points. There's a tendency for more closeouts as replenishing sand has been starved by mining and dune stabilisation. NE swells are filtered out by Kurnell Point, but winds from the N are increasingly offshore. SE swells and mid tides should keep anyone willing to walk rewarded. The further north you go into the Greenhills stretch usually results in lower wave heights, lower quality sandbanks, and lower crowds. Summer NE sea breezes are less of a problem also. Good stretch for beginners/improvers and alternative wavecraft. The lurching left at **Voodoo** is not for the weak of heart and mind. Sucks hard over the outside shelf, going angular at low and shoots down the line with power and pace. Difficult access, always crowded with protective locals and it's tricky to exit the water so only the most competent and confident of surfers should make the trek out through the National Park. There are a few other kelpy reefs in the vicinity like Suck Rock, but again the local crowd don't take too kindly to strangers and bodyboarders dominate the slab. The Potters Point sewage outfall adds further risk to surfing this area. More barely rideable slabs like Ours and the newly exposed big wave spot Cape Fear stud the Kurnell coast, but are heavily localised and only ridden by the most

DAN BEILICH
Cronulla Point

DAN BEILICH
Voodoo

## Shark Island

LAT. -34.059679° LONG. 151.160134°

**The original slab from hell has fascinated the surf press for decades, and while it may have lost some of its cachet to slightly scarier mutant barrels in other parts of the world, Shark Island is still one of the most fearsome pits on the planet. Air drop, hopefully ollying the staircase, into a way wider than higher tube before being spat out into the surge or driven onto the shelf. The rights are best on a SE swell while less deadly lefts appear in E/NE'ers. Bodyboarders love it, hellmen charge it and most everyday surfers should avoid it. Localism, attitude and crowds of disdainful bodyboarders add to the hazardous nature of this cunjevoi covered outcrop. Paddle from the point and don't think about the name.**

Bondi

MORNING BONDI

skilled or foolhardy. Cliquey reefbreaks continue on the other side of the entrance to Botany Bay before arriving at the city beaches. Long Bay is the other name for **Malabar** and the S/SE swell needs to be big to penetrate here. Sucky lefts at low tide fatten out through the push and it's protected from any N wind. Urchins lurk on the reef and water quality is dubious. Often crowded as everywhere else will be maxed out. The most consistent of the city beaches is **Maroubra**, which will have a wave in all swell directions from NE-S and the headlands provide a bit of protection from N or S winds. Lefts at the north end in a summer NE swell, peaks through the middle in any swell and rarer rights at the southern end reef. Poor water quality and manners regularly blight this line-up. **Lurline Bay** is the big wave spot when the beaches are closed out and a solid SE/S swell rumbles into town. Dangerous rocky spot for experts only. **Coogee** is probably the worst beachbreak in the Eastern Suburbs, suffering from deeper water, shadowing from Wedding Cake Island and a general lack of any consistent shape. Improves in bigger swells when the reef, bombie and even the island start to deliver. The shoredump makes Coogee less than ideal for beginners. **Bronte** is a small beach with a beachbreak and a reef nestled in behind the cliffs at the southern end, giving it decent S wind protection. The inconsistent reef gets hollow in moderate E swells but works in S as well. There's a rippy channel between the reef and the left beachbreak. **Tamarama** is a pocket beach that produces running lefts off the point in NE/E swells. Predominantly sand bottom but the rocks at the southern headland can appear all to quickly. Surfing banned in summer while lifeguards are on duty so only early or late sessions allowed. Gets packed with glamorous sunbathers, but can be rippy and dangerous in S swells and winds. McKenzies Bay is totally dependant on sand as to whether it will break. Only NE swells will get the wedge-effect off the cliffs and winter storms tend to scour out the bay. NE winds are fine so late summer is the best bet. **Bondi** is Australia's most famous beach, but it's a bit of a let down in the wave department. The south end is always bigger but starts to close out as the waves go overhead. The north end is perfect for beginners and there are literally thousands of them. SE-S swell goes straight in and any N wind is fine. High tide may hold up the shoulders a bit longer. A writhing mass of humanity throughout the year since Bondi is on every tourist and backpackers itinerary. Pollution, bluebottles and expensive parking are not on the brochures.

Sydney is pretty consistent but rarely epic, with SE to S groundswells the most reliable swell providers from April-September. NE to E windswells in summer may include the rare cyclone generated swells in Feb/March but there is still a lot of small SE windswells from the Tasman. The surf is usually waist to headhigh on the beachbreaks, although it can easily exceed double overhead on the best swells. Prevailing winds are SW in the winter, while summers are typically offshore NW in the mornings, before the NE sea breeze picks up. Tidal range reaches a max of 1.9m, which affects the fickle reefs and slabs.

| STATISTICS | | J F | M A | M J | J A | S O | N D |
|---|---|---|---|---|---|---|---|
| SWELL | Direction | | | | | | |
| | Size (ft) | 4-5 | 5 | 5 | 5 | 4 | 5 |
| WIND | Direction | | | | | | |
| | Force | F4 | F3-F4 | F4 | F4 | F4 | F4 |
| WATER | Wetsuit | | | | | | |
| | Temp/°C | 23 | 22 | 19 | 18 | 18 | 21 |
| WEATHER | Rainfall/mm | 103 | 125 | 129 | 92 | 75 | 84 |
| | days/mth | 11 | 12 | 11 | 10 | 10 | 10 |
| | Min temp/°C | 18 | 15 | 10 | 8 | 12 | 16 |
| | Max temp/°C | 26 | 23 | 19 | 18 | 22 | 25 |

# Sydney Northern Beaches NSW

In 1914, when Duke Kahanamoku arrived in Australia to show off his swimming prowess, he also gave a surfing demonstration at Freshwater Beach. It was a momentous occasion that was to change the image of Australia across the world - surfing had arrived! Since that time, surfing has grown intensely in popularity right around Australia's 25,260km coastline. Since the World Championships in 1964, Sydney has produced a string of talented surfers, unequalled by any other world surf location. This large city population takes pride in its beach culture, and has in many ways ruled the Aussie surf scene. Sydney Harbour (which has some breaks in huge swells) separates the city from The Northern Beaches, which can turn on great waves, especially in the rarer E-NE groundswells and most days have some sort of rideable waves. Protection from all wind directions except SE/E is possible, and the variety of spots caters to all surfing abilities.

- + WIDE SWELL WINDOW
- + BEACHES AND REEFS
- + URBAN ENTERTAINMENT
- + EASY ACCESS

- – RARELY CLASSIC
- – ALWAYS CROWDED
- – AGGRESSIVE LINE-UPS
- – EXPENSIVE

**TRAVEL INFORMATION**

See Sydney Southern Beaches

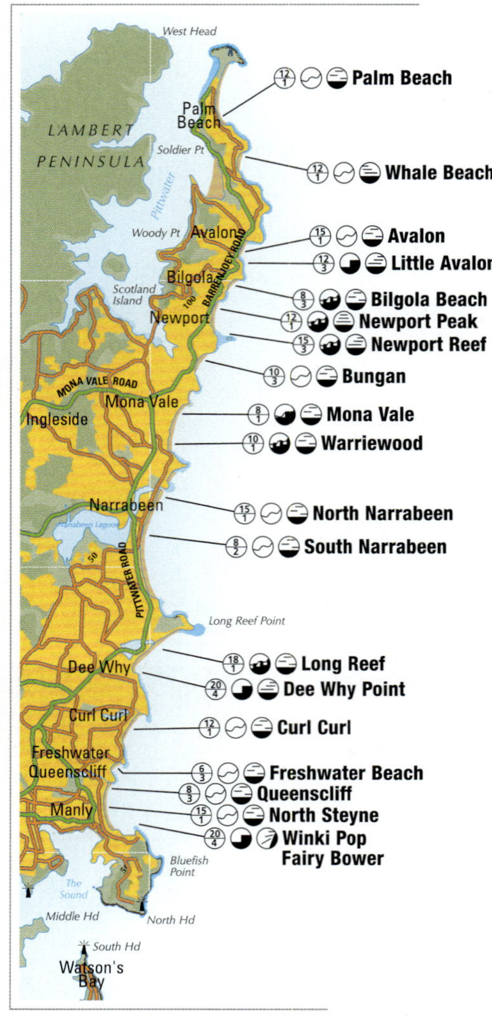

MURRAY FRASER

Winki Pop

Manly's southern headland is home to **Winki Pop** and **Fairy Bower**, consistent, quality righthanders that handle big swells from most directions. Winki's hits a shelf directly in front of the cliffs and sucks hard, making the drop and race to the corner an experts only pursuit. The Bower starts at the tip of the point and bends beautifully round the headland into the Racetrack section before petering out in deep water off Shelley Beach. South quadrant winds, some E in the swell, lower tides to avoid any bounce off the cliffs and enough height to break clear of the rocks. Rabid crowd always ready to spin and go if you fall, or even if you don't. Cliff-top carpark gets packed with peanut gallery when a big swell hits. The southern corner of Manly, is protected and always crowded with swimmers and tourists. South Steyne produces classic lefts on a NE swell, there's more peaks along the central Mid Steyne stretch, whilst **North Steyne** is a good beachbreak even on the usual S wind, S swell combination. At the north end, a rivermouth can groom some good banks for **Queenscliff**, but it is always crowded, with hot locals. Way outside, Queenscliff Bombie can test the mettle of any big wave rider with lurching peaks out of nowhere in 10ft plus swells. The Manly stretch is always a little smaller than exposed beaches like Curl Curl, but it seems to maintain better sandbanks and will have cleaner conditions during southerly busters. The flip side is mushy onshore conditions when summer NE'ers blow in. **Freshwater** or Harbord Beach is a small protected cove that can have a good righthander at the southern end but crowds out quickly with overprotective locals. This is where The Duke first demonstrated surfing to the Australian public. **Curl Curl** is an exposed beach, picking up the most swell on the northern beaches and works reasonably well in most conditions, although it's rarely perfect. Soaks up a big crowd along its length and often suffers from strong rips, which gouge out the sand to combat the Curly close-out. The challenge of **Dee Why Point** has been attracting surfers for years, and the ledgy, sucking right gets classic with the frequent winter S swell, S wind combo. It's a very technical wave ruled by the hardcore locals that patrol a small take-off zone in front of a swimming pool built on the rock ledge. Dee Why beach holds some great beachbreaks as well, handling

MURRAY FRASER

Queenscliff

IAN BIRD

Dee Why Point

## North Narrabeen

**LAT. -33.705382° LONG. 151.307893°**

**The Alley is basically a rivermouth set-up when they bulldoze the sand from the lake entrance and while the rights can be messier and rippy, they still pack plenty of punch. The majestic lefts are just waiting for a NE-E groundswell, NW-NE winds and lower tides to light up the line-up as barrels spin from tip to tail of the triangulated bank down towards the Carpark Rights section. Here the wave changes into a thick, heaving peak that demands skill to avoid the shut-downs and slams on the shallow sandbar. To say North Narra gets ultra crowded and competitive is an understatement, especially when you consider the crew that call it home. From old-timers Terry Fitzgerald, Mark Warren, Simon Anderson, Bruce Raymond and World Champ Damien Hardman, to the latest crop of pros like Hedgey, Davo and fly-boy Ozzie Wright. Then there is a whole strata of underground rippers who don't want to see you catch any of "their" waves if they can help it. Expect snaking, abuse and drop-ins, but don't try it on yourself! A walk south can turn up empty, lower quality options.**

Avalon

IAN BIRD

a bit more size when the No Mans stretch is closed-out, plus there's a kiddies corner behind the pool. At **Long Reef** there are dependable beachbreaks plus many different bombora reefs that handle swells up to as big as it gets. 'Longie Bombie' will focus S swell and be dead offshore in the common NE wind. Peaks up and occasionally barrels at low tide, the lip can have some power but the waves can often fatten up and meander, so it is often the realm of longboarders and SUP'ers. Long Reef headland hides some reefbreaks for experts before the shelter of Collaroy affords beginners a perfect training area in fat, rolling waves that give soft-toppers a chance to find their feet. The long crescent of **South Narrabeen** usually has uncrowded waves that are hollow and very fast. Perfect long lefts and shorter rights stalk the semi-permanent sandbank at **North Narrabeen**, creating one of Sydney's most iconic and reliable waves. **Warriewood** nestles below tall cliffs and is properly sheltered from strong S winds so when all the open beaches are blown to shreds, the righthanders off the point will still be rideable, but this means crowds can reach critical mass. Small to moderate E, SE and S swells will line up along the less-than-perfect rock line and any wind from SSE to NW should be clean enough. There's often a good left into the channel as well. **Mona Vale** entertains a bunch of decent peaks in front of the hospital and golf course. The protruding rocky shelf with sea pool has lefts running down the side in NE'ers and handles a bit of summer sea breeze. On the north side of the pool is The Basin, a deeper, rocky bay that is usually flat until a solid SE-S swell breaks outside, then reforms and wraps round the shelf, throwing up some pretty sick righthanders. Needs SW quadrant winds and it will be zooed when on. **Bungan** is a small beach and a long walk down the cliffs but has punchy waves in smaller swells. The north end rocks hold the sand, waiting for a moderate NE swell to transform it into a point-style left, but more often it's various beachbreak peaks in the centre. **Newport Reef** sits in front of the pool with an easier roll-in, long crumbly-section walls and lots of shoulder to work with. Works better at mid tides on E swells and less confident surfers will do better here as the take-off zone is spread out a bit and the waves more forgiving, although it will handle some sizeable swell. Experts may like the challenge of Crosswaves, further out off the island. **Newport Peak** is in plain view of Pittwater Rd, attracting a hefty crowd to one of Sydney's most competitive and crowded spots. Sand builds up around a platform reef and all swells will trip over it, with NE-E often being the best to bring the favoured lefts to life. Moves in and out with the tide, but always breaks with a bit of oomph, offering tubes, hooks and cutback walls in one short package. **Bilgola Beach** is a bit different, preferring to roll and crumble over the sandbars, producing mellow waves for beginners and improvers looking to escape the NE sea breezes and the rat races of Newport and Avalon. **Little Avalon** is a super-sucky, slab-hugging, righthand pit that peels off below the cliffs to the south of the main beach. Lurches onto the ledge so quickly that air-drops are inevitable and it has become the haunt of serious bodyboarders, looking to thread the cavernous barrels beneath thicker than normal lips. **Avalon** is a hotbed for talented surfers thanks to its shape and consistency. When a moderate NE swell hits, loping lefts start stomping down the north end and will look picture perfect in a hot NW breeze. Handles some big faces and gets intense at size, while down near the pool is another quality peak that works in all swell directions up to double overhead. Sharp drops at lower tides with plenty of hollow sections on the good days. **Whale Beach** would be just another selection of fun, unassuming beachbreak peaks if it didn't have the Wedge, tucked in below the northern headland. Only appearing in NE-E swells, a triangle of water pinballs off the rocks and wedges skywards, then landwards, resulting in short, sharp left shacks for the top of food chain. Luxury residential area **Palm Beach** sits beneath the lighthouse on Barrenjoey headland, where an occasionally grunty and walled-up left can spin down the rock and sand banks at the the north end. The bulk of "Palmy" is often a warbly mess of mush-burgers and close-outs, but the southern Kiddies Corner can hold a smaller wind-protected bank in summer NE'ers and S wraps.

Swell Forecasting see Sydney Southern Beaches.

# Central Coast NEW SOUTH WALES

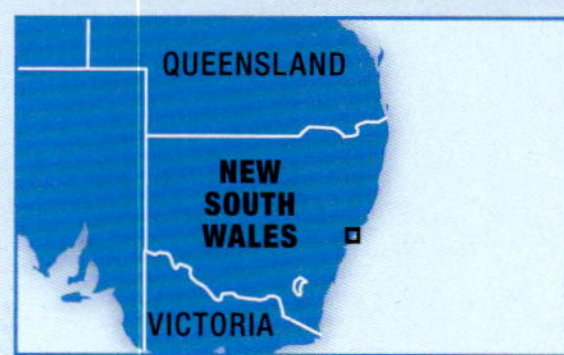


One hour from Sydney or Newcastle the Central Coast is home to some of the most beautiful, unspoiled beaches on the east coast, an attractive day-trip escape for many city dwellers and a big magnet for tourism and retirement. There's a real diversity of surf spots for surfers of all standards, from fun, pristine beachies to challenging, world-class, rock platform reefs and points.

+ CONCENTRATION OF SPOTS
+ SUITS ALL LEVELS
+ SYDNEY & NEWCASTLE NEARBY
+ BIG WAVE OPTIONS

- REGULAR SEA BREEZE
- GOOD SPOTS GET CROWDED
- SHARKY WATERS
- PRICEY ACCOMMODATION

## TRAVEL INFORMATION

**Weather** – In summer temps range between 13-27°C with occasional days over 30°C. June to Sept winter temps vary from 4-23°C. Hot days often tempered by cooling sea breezes and balmy evening temps. Annual average rainfall is 1300mm (52in), mostly falling between January and end of June. Use a 3/2mm fullsuit from May to Aug, a springsuit during spring and autumn, and a shorty or even boardshorts during summer.

**Lodging and Food** – Caravan parks like Dunleith at North Entrance have affordable tent sites from $30. Guest houses in Terrigal have double rooms from $100. If travelling with friends, a good option is The Palms (4pax villas $140-190/night) in Avoca Beach.

**Nature and Culture** – Visit Bouddi and Wyrrabalong National Parks, the Skillion Headland, Crackneck Lookout, The Australian Reptile Park and Gosford's Springtime Flora Festival in September. Also whale watching and good diving on an ex-military ship, sunk as an artificial reef at Terrigal.

**Hazards and Hassles** – Watch out for the guaranteed drop-ins, collisions and possible cuts on shallow reefs. Big wave spots require experience and humility. 13 shark incidents between Newcastle and Gosford but no fatalities.

**Handy Hints** – Any gear you want at bargain prices, shortboards from $450. Good shops are RMS near Shelly Beach, Wizstix in Long Jetty & Terrigal, Channel Surf Co and Oceanic Surf Co in The Entrance. Beginners can have a go with one of many surf schools.

**Box Head** is a rare, epic left point breaking up to 1500m along a sandbank at the mouth of the Hawkesbury River. Sucky barrels or slashable walls depending on the sand. Gruelling paddle-out. Long walk from Hawke Head Drive car park but plenty of surfers reach the peak by boat so it's often crowded. **MacMasters Point** has a critically vert take-off with a powerful bowl section over some large rocks when a big E to S winter swell wraps in. The sharp bottom and no nonsense locals means it is for experienced surfers only. Opposite is **Copacabana**, attracting a crew to the lefts on the northern point of the bay that suck over a shallow rock ledge before peeling through to the fun inside sandbars on higher tides and a S swell. Super-consistent **Avoca Beach** is a hotbed of talent, young and old. Excellent beachbreak peaks in many swell directions, the south end is well protected from southerlies and usually free of aggro. Not so at The Point, a hollow, crowded right that pumps on an E to SE swell and breaks very close to the rocks all the way along. Handy rip in the corner when big. In Terrigal, the smaller beginner peaks in the protected southern corner, often dump and close-out. Experienced surfers head to **Terrigal Haven** in solid E to SE winter swells when powerful, grinding, right-handers can peel and section for more than 200m. Mid tide with the odd dry rock surprise! **Wamberal** is a consistent beachbreak, so check Spoonies at the north end. Sensitive to sea breezes and crowds. One of the Central Coast's primo big-wave bombies is **Forresters** – hollow lefts and rights up to 15ft with a sizeable S swell. **Crackneck**, a secluded, fast-breaking, lefthand reef plus a short, suicidal right breaks over flat shelf strata. Best with NE-E swells from low to mid tide. **Shelly Beach** is a busy but consistent beachbreak ideal for learners. The north end can have awesome barrels, while the lefthand rock shelf holds up to 10ft. Reliable **Pelican Beach** often has plenty of epic peaks in small NE swells to spread a crowd. Neighbouring **Soldiers Beach** offers better protection from NE breezes, workable ledges that suit all levels, plus a fickle left point. If the swell is a big NE-E, **Norah Head** has a challenging reef known as Little Bombie and a shallow, ledgy right at Boat Ramp, which attracts a lot of bodyboarders. From Newcastle, the first place to check on a small to medium NE-SE swell is **Frazer Park**, a fun summer break with consistent peaky waves that tend to close out over 6ft.

Consistent, but epic conditions are rare. S to SE groundswells are more reliable from April-Sept, but some breaks need the summer NE windswell or longer period groundswell from cyclones up north. Prevailing SW winds are better in winter, while summers are typically NW offshore in the morning, before the NE sea breeze picks up. Most beachbreaks and reefbreaks work best on the incoming tide, even though tidal range is fairly small, but crucial for some points and Box Head. For Statistics see Newcastle opposite.

BRUCE SUTHERLAND

Terrigal Haven

ST IMAGES

Shelly Beach

# Newcastle NEW SOUTH WALES

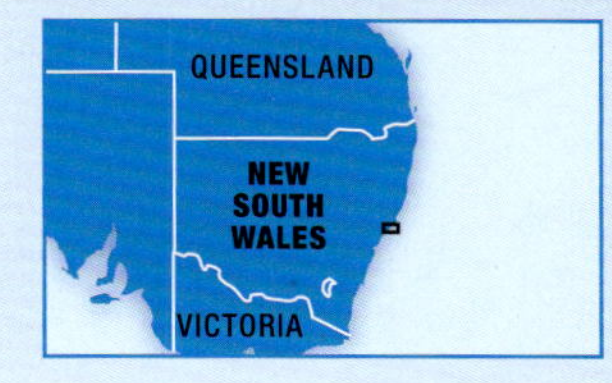




Newcastle and the surrounding Hunter region is fast developing with urban expansion attracting a whole lot of people priced out of Sydney, looking for the Aussie beachside lifestyle. This means more surfers hitting the waves at iconic beaches like Merewether where Mark Richards honed his inimitable style. However north of town, glorious countryside beckons the curious to open beaches and sheltered points around Hawks Nest.

+ EVERY TYPE OF BREAK
+ GOOD CITY BEACHBREAKS
+ LOWER CROWD FACTOR
+ CITY OR COUNTRY

- NEWCASTLE CROWDS
- INDUSTRIAL CITY LANDSCAPE
- SHARKY
- POLLUTION ISSUES

## TRAVEL INFORMATION

**Weather** – See Central Coast and Far North Coast.

**Lodging and Food** – Too many great campsites to list (fr $20/n). Backpackers Newcastle give free surfing lessons (fr $47/dbl/n). Noah's on the Beach (fr $130/n). Beach Hotel Merewether best dining view. Hunter Valley vineyards when the surf has got sour grapes.

**Nature and Culture** – Great fishing everywhere. Scuba dive Seal Rocks. Cruise Lake Macquarie. Newcastle nightclubs.

**Hazards and Hassles** – Record 8 day beach closure in Newcastle due to shark sightings. Many estuaries for nurseries and food. Locals can be brusque at the banner waves.

**Handy Hints** – M.R. has closed shop, Slimes stock his boards.

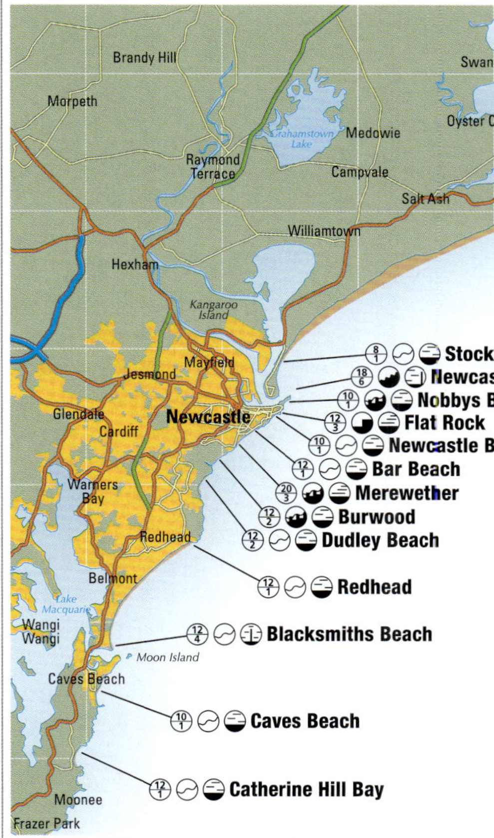


**Catherine Hill Bay** often has great shape and power, is super-consistent and often bigger than its neighbours, attracting surfers from both south and north. The southern end of **Caves Beach** prefers a bit of S in the swell, but NE is better for the Hams stretch up to the rocky sections of Frenchmans. The jetty protecting the entrance of Lake Macquarie at **Blacksmiths Beach** can occasionally have decent peaks on both sides, provided the NE-E swell is moderate and the tide is pushing. Often junky and weak, making it a great place to learn. **Redhead**, where the beach faces SE and picks up NE-E swells, offers good summer sea breeze protection. **Dudley Beach** is an oasis of green from the urban beaches and it can sometimes deliver equally picturesque lefts running down the banks in NE swells. More recreation area beachies at **Burwood** plus a righthand point called Leggies and some rocky lefts at the north end. **Merewether** is the home of Newcastle surfing and the southern reef known as Ladies can handle plenty of juice with triple overhead faces in a heavy E-SE swell. Roll in, barrel, hit lip and wait for inside section to unfold. **Bar Beach** regularly outputs some of the finest beachbreaks in Greater Newcastle, turning peaky small to moderate E swells into a barrel festival for the city slickers who dominate this break. **Newcastle Beach** is minutes from downtown and like Bondi, is popular with all kinds of beachgoers. It's also home for most pro contests, hoping to get the lefts off the point in good shape or some groomed peaks in the middle. **Flat Rock**, in front of the pools, is a sucking, dredging righthander that attracts bodyboarders and tube addicts. Tight take-off zone. **Nobbys Beach** invites chaotic, but often perfect peaks to bust over the patchy reef and sand bottom, churning out some impressive spinning lefts in NE swells. The shorie can be all time thick and thumping for the lids.

ASP

Merewether

The southern **Newcastle Harbour** jetty holds a freakish right when the biggest NE swells of the year penetrate the Hunter rivermouth. Thick, rumbling beast of a wave with barrel section, it's for hellmen only! Because **Stockton Beach** arcs for 32kms, there are plenty of swell and wind combos that might work between the sheltered corners. At **One Mile** the right off the point can get pretty good in E-SE swells and any S wind. Great longboarding and beginners wave when small. Walk around to NE protected Samurai beach for more powerful A-frames. The west-facing **Zenith Beach** at Shoal Bay can conjure some nice triangles, along with Box Beach where the waves get massive backwash off the cliffs and jack up insane wedging left pits. **Boulders** is a top shelf, lefthand point that breaks down the rocks inside the entrance to Port Stephens. Humping SE-S swell, any N wind and pushing tide might coalesce into the longest ride in NSW. Very sharky. Quality lefts are on the cards when **Hawks Nest** nets a small to moderate NE swell in light W winds. Hard-breaking and hollow peaks repeat for the 14kms up to Little Gibber which is offshore in N winds.

S to SE groundswells are more reliable from April-Sept, then the summer NE-E windswell or cyclone swell takes over. SW winds prevail through winter, while summers are typically NW offshore in the morning, before NE-SE sea breeze picks up. Tidal range is small, but the slab reefs and most points prefer mid tide.

IAN BIRD

Hawks Nest

| STATISTICS | | J F | M A | M J | J A | S O | N D |
|---|---|---|---|---|---|---|---|
| SWELL | Direction | | | | | | |
| | Size (ft) | 5 | 5-6 | 6 | 6 | 5 | 5-6 |
| WIND | Direction | | | | | | |
| | Force | F3-F4 | F4 | F4 | F4 | F4 | F4 |
| WATER | Wetsuit | | | | | | |
| | Temp/°C | 23 | 22 | 20 | 18 | 18 | 21 |
| WEATHER | Rainfall/mm | 129 | 148 | 120 | 78 | 76 | 100 |
| | days/mth | 12 | 13 | 11 | 9 | 11 | 12 |
| | Min temp/°C | 19 | 16 | 11 | 9 | 13 | 17 |
| | Max temp/°C | 26 | 24 | 19 | 17 | 19 | 21 |

# Port Macquarie NEW SOUTH WALES

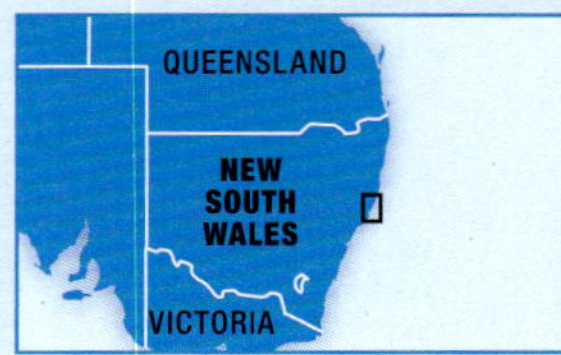


Technically the Mid North Coast starts in Seal Rocks and extends far beyond Coffs Harbour so this zone is just the beginning. It lacks the sheer number of righthand pointbreaks found further north, but makes up for it with some of the best and most reliable beachbreaks found on the entire NSW coastline. Both summer and winter swells are catered for and more people are realising that stopping in to this area is always worth the time and effort.

- \+ SUPER-CONSISTENT BEACHES
- \+ UNCROWDED LINE-UPS
- \+ SUMMER AND WINTER SPOTS
- \+ UNDEVELOPED COASTLINE

- – FEWER POINTBREAKS
- – SUMMER ONSHORES
- – LONG EXPOSED BEACHES
- – SHARKS

## TRAVEL INFORMATION

**Weather** – See Mid North Coast

**Lodging and Food** – Most towns are set up for tourists with campsites that often have cabins to rent (fr $20/n). Backpackers try Port Macquarie YHA who have boards and bikes (fr $19/n). Awesome fishing around all the rivermouths and estuaries. Hastings River Fish Co-op sell fish straight off the trawlers.

**Nature and Culture** – Great fishing everywhere. Scuba diving at Seal Rocks is famous for sighting grey nurse sharks year-round. Bush-walking in Myall Lakes National Park.

**Hazards and Hassles** – It's not just timid grey nurse sharks found in the gutters at Seal Rocks with bronze whalers and the odd bigger shark around.

**Handy Hints** – Stormriders Surf Shops in Port Mac, Kempsey and Forster (no relation). Saltwater Wine have 5 locations including a boardstore and espresso bar in PM.

Port Macquarie
North Haven
Old Bar
Saltwater Point
Tuncurry North Wall
One Mile Beach
Booti Booti Nat. Park
Boomerang Beach
Sandbar
Seal Rocks
Seal Rocks Lighthouse
Treachery

Treachery

Uber-consistent **Treachery** is powerful, offshore in summer NE'ers and usually a couple of feet bigger than anywhere else. Even small days will challenge beginners along with rips, locals, sharks and holiday crowds. **Seal Rocks Lighthouse Beach** just doesn't hold the same size, quality or allure of Treachery, but can have some fun, punchy peaks in each corner nestled out of the wind. In front of the popular campground is the soft righthand point at **Seal Rocks**, which needs serious NE-E swell to rumble and crumble down the fingers of rock. Great logging wave and fairly safe for improvers to try out a pointbreak. **Sandbar** sets a gold standard for beachbreaks with form and function on pretty much every swell direction and any N winds. Wedgie peaks in a SE or left runners in a NE, it's usually best just below Dangar Point. **Boomerang Beach** has a superb setup where the northern headland provides pesky NE wind protection, the middle peaks can triangulate perfectly in most swells and the southern pointbreak rolls into the beachbreak with powerful, ripable walls, that can handle a sizeable SE-S swell. Camping in the **Booti Booti National Park** right behind the beach at the southern corner will allow easy access to some solid peaks, which continue for miles up the beach. Just south, Elizabeth Beach can have some sucky wedges and dumpy close-outs in N-E swells. Popular with bodyboarders when big and surf schools when small. Consistent, sand-reliant, swell-catcher, **One Mile Beach** is happy in a W-NE breeze and prefers headhigh, peaky E swells. While Main Beach Forster offers some SE wind protection, it's all about the righthanders, Hayden Reef and Pebbly Beach, both needing serious NE juice. The **Tuncurry North Wall** attracts a crew when a beefy NE swell starts running down the breakwall at the mouth of Wallis Lake. Rights will gyrate down the sandbar and lefts can appear on the other side of the often defined paddling channel. Good S wind protection, but quality quickly deteriorates as you head north. **Saltwater Point** is a leg-burning righthand point that hugs the rocks in SE swell, creating open shreddable shoulders, while NE speeds it up, but often brings down the sections prematurely. **Old Bar** is a popular swell magnet beachbreak with shifting peaks over a big playing field. Up the beach is 2nd Corner which can be a bit bigger, while right up at Crowdy Head, there's good NE wind protection. **North Haven** is a typical rivermouth jetty break with protection from the southerlies and some good rights running down the wall when the sand builds up. **Port Macquarie** has various short rocky beaches in town like Flagstaff, Flynns and out by the Sea Acres Rainforest Centre which can all have their day in NE-SE swells and any W wind. The main event is the consistent north breakwall of the Hastings River, which handles big swells and fortunately, big crowds as the rights run down the triangular bar trapped by the wall. Peaks for as far as the eye can see to the north. There's a car ferry to get across the river and once you are on the other side there are no facilities. A 4WD will be handy to access the waves north of here.

The swell and wind scenario for this region differs little from Newcastle and shares a lot in common with Mid North Coast NSW. By far the most common swell direction is SE, which peaks in terms of consistency and size during April to May, and another spike during July. The established pattern of summer NW-NE winds from Dec-Mar and winter SE-SW winds from April-Nov starts to change as you move north where the NE winds may start as early as September. Maximum 1.7m tidal range at Port Macquarie does little to the beachies, but the slabs feel the low and the points feel the high tides, especially when wave height is small. For Statistics see Newcastle and Mid North Coast.

ANDREW SHIELD

Forster

IAN BIRD

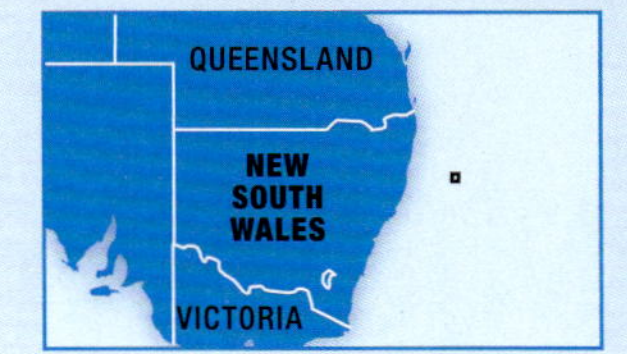




# Lord Howe Island NSW

Often described as Australia's most beautiful island, Lord Howe Is surrounded by the world's southernmost coral reef and is home to many rare and endemic plants and animals. With its protected marine park, no mobile phone reception, no jet skis, no big buildings, very few cars and only 400 visitor beds, the island is never crowded. Much of the island's coastline is exposed to waves that have unlimited fetch, hitting a great variety of breaks, creating fairly consistent surf all year. A barrier reef stretches for 6km along the west side of the island, enclosing a beautiful lagoon. It is sliced by several passages, most of them being home to quality surf breaks.

+ VARIETY OF BREAKS
+ ALWAYS OFFSHORE SOMEWHERE
+ LAID BACK, CROWD FREE
+ NATURE, BIRD & MARINE LIFE

– FICKLE CONDITIONS
– LONG PADDLE TO THE REEF
– EXPENSIVE FOOD & SUPPLIES
– NO CHEAP ACCOMMODATION

## TRAVEL INFORMATION

**Weather** – Lord Howe Island enjoys its own microclimate, best described as subtropical maritime, with very little annual variation in temperatures. Sea breezes prevent the summers from being too hot, while surrounding warm seas ensure pleasant winters. Mean annual rainfall in the lowlands is almost 1700mm, with a pronounced maximum in winter.

**Lodging and Food** – 17 properties to choose from (most are family operated, with capacity ranging from 4 to 85 beds). Camping is not permitted. For dining, be prepared to book and pay $25-45 for a meal. Coral Cafe and Bowling Club are cheaper alternatives to the Anchorage and Arajilla restaurants.

**Nature and Culture** – LHI is a protected marine park with quality snorkelling over pristine coral reefs. Excellent diving options (50 sites, 2 schools). Trekking up Mt Gower (8h) is a great experience. A trip to Ball's Pyramid costs $100/p.

**Hazards and Hassles** – Fishermen discovered in June 2001 the remains of a missing man, including a head, inside a 3m tiger shark caught off Lord Howe Island! No recorded attacks on surfers and only small reef sharks are seen at snorkelling locations. No snakes, no sand flies, no stingers but sea urchins! Doctor and small hospital on island. Most crew will use a dingy or paddle a kayak out to the reefs.

**Handy Hints** – Abemama is the new name of the only surf shop; board rentals ($20 half day, $30/d). ATM facilities at the Bowling Club or post office and credit cards widely accepted. Internet access at Visitor Centre.

IZAK PHOTOGRAPHY

West Coast Reefs

DAVE CONNOR

Blinky Beach

Paddling out from Dawson's Point or Old Settlement Beach is the best way to reach the North Passage and **La Meurthe**, a long, fast and hollow lefthander named after a nearby shipwreck. The other side of North Passage has a rideable right too, but the consistent lefts and rights at **Uli's** breaking near Rabbit Island have a wider swell window. Ideally take a boat, otherwise make the long paddle-out from Far Rocks, but be aware there is no channel, and set dodging is tricky. **Sunsets** is the only big wave spot, accessible through Erscott's Passage. The often disorganised setup can deliver a gnarly, shifting right hook with long walls. Experts or locals only! **Harry's** is the heaviest wave on LHI and outputs an extremely hollow, very fast and powerful righthander. Breaks over shallow coral so getting caught inside is a bad experience. **Little Reef** is a softer break closer to shore with good lefts for all levels. **Grinders** is a 30min paddle from Salmon Beach. Two main take-off spots launch into long lefthanders, with fast hollow sections and potential barrels. Depending on the tide stage, the channel can get very rippy so it is better to have a boat around. **Little Island**, a short but solid righthander breaking close to Salmon Beach offers wind protection from the surrounding cliffs when all other spots are blown out. The east coast receives less reliable swells, but close to the airport is **Blinky Beach**, the main beachbreak option on the island. The shifting sandbanks and few rocky patches are best on a E swell, W wind combo, and there is an interesting righthander at the south end. The southern end of **Middle Beach** features a great right over a coral shelf from mid to high tide with a rare SE swell. Under 3ft, it breaks over the inside platform; over 3ft, the righthander gains in quality with fast heavy bowls peeling over the outside shelf. **Ned's Beach** has various breaks the best one being the left point setup at the northern end known as Mexico, plus Surfers Hole, a fickle rocky peak best with a solid swell from the E. It's pretty inconsistent, due to the Admiralty Islands that block some swell.

LHI is unpredictable with good waves appearing anytime, summer being a safer bet. Clean swells arrive from the S, complimented by a few N cyclone swells. Summer winds can also generate occasional NE or SE swells, allowing the eastern spots to be ridden. In winter the swells are not as reliable and clean, but can occasionally provide excellent surf on the east coast. Summer tends to get more E to NE winds, while SW winds are more frequent in winter. Big tides up to 2m dangerously expose the west side reefs at low tide.

| STATISTICS | | J F | M A | M J | J A | S O | N D |
|---|---|---|---|---|---|---|---|
| SWELL | Direction | | | | | | |
| | Size (ft) | 2-3 | 2-3 | 3-4 | 4-5 | 3-4 | 2-3 |
| WIND | Direction | | | | | | |
| | Force | F2-F3 | F5 | F3 | F4-F5 | F4 | F3 |
| WATER | Wetsuit | | | | | | |
| | Temp/°C | 25 | 22 | 19 | 17 | 20 | 23 |
| WEATHER | Rainfall/mm | 99 | 117 | 158 | 148 | 114 | 112 |
| | days/mth | 12 | 17 | 22 | 22 | 16 | 13 |
| | Min temp/°C | 20 | 19 | 16 | 14 | 15 | 18 |
| | Max temp/°C | 25 | 22 | 19 | 17 | 20 | 23 |

# Mid North Coast NEW SOUTH WALES

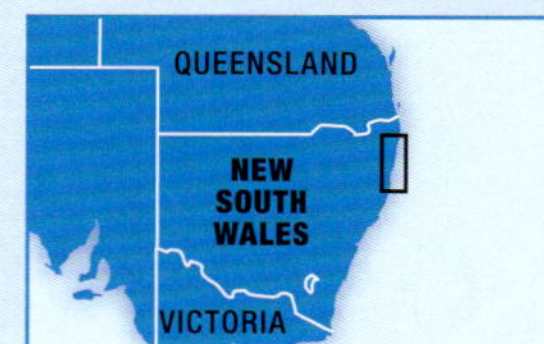

The Mid North Coast shimmers in warm sunshine most of the year and maintains a laid-back country feel, shunning the rampant development of other coastal regions. It is also where the classic Aussie righthand pointbreak begins to appear on many of the southern headlands, offering rides similar to the lifestyle this beautiful region encourages. The boulder and sand mix promotes cruisey walls and mellow shoulders, plus bonus sections of speed and hollowness.

+ PRISTINE POINTBREAKS
+ EMPTY BEACHBREAK OPTIONS
+ MILD WEATHER & WATER TEMPS
+ BEAUTIFUL BUCOLIC BACKDROP

– CROWDED POINTS
– SUMMER ONSHORES
– LONG DRIVES
– SHARK WORRIES

ST IMAGES
Park Beach

**Point Plomer** is not the most perfect or exciting right point on the coast, but it does offer entry level surfers a chance to get a taste of long pointbreak rights. Lower tides and a bit of size will increase the challenge. The beachbreak can be strong and dumpy, but if it blowing NE then Queens Head gets perfect in headhigh E swells. Pay National Park day ticket to park at the end of the vehicle testing dirt track, or stay in the campsite. **Crescent Head** has been a destination wave since its discovery in the '50s and longboarders especially like the spoking walls and shoulders that allow a full repertoire of manoeuvres. Short boarders can dial in a particular move using the paper-thin lips, between the copious amounts of cutbacks required to stay the 3-400m distance. Drops out in the rivermouth, across which can be some nice peaks. Crazy crowded during holiday season and weekends. Beginners should avoid as the rocks can pop up unexpectedly when it's small. Well sheltered from S winds and far less likely to be rammed, **Hat Head** gives intermediates up a chance to pick off a few peelers over the rocky shelf below the pointy headland. Any moderate E swell, any S wind and lower tides make the recipe for shorter rides than Crescent, but often with a bit more push. **South West Rocks** is protected from S swells so the Trial Bay crescent can be tiny and perfect for beginners. Horseshoe Bay is often rammed with swimmers in summer, but every now and then goes off with hollow righthanders off the point. Back Beach, like so many on this coast, can be good when the sand between the two rivermouths lines up on NE-E pulses. Likeable and lengthy, **Scotts Head** will bend SE swell around the rocky point, but mainly relies on the sand build up to allow it to rumble on for its full 300-400 metres. Handles plenty of size, when the sections get longer and much harder to make. Accessible for improvers when small, it gets pretty crowded with all abilities. The beachbreaks on both sides of the head are always worth a look. At **Nambucca Heads** rivermouth, the breakwall at Wellington Beach can trap the sand and line up some lefthanders, but the banks are constantly in flux and it rarely works any good. Most people go straight to **Valla** for solid, sucky beachbreaks with clout, forming up in front of the carpark on small, peaky NE-SE swells. A right can get good off the rocky platform in just the right SSE swell and the bodyboarders hit the peak at Humpies. Out on the south side of the **Sawtell** headland, the transitory sandbars at the rivermouth can line up great lefts in NE swells and the following sea breeze won't destroy it. Gets big and unruly, with bad rips, especially on dropping tides. The main surf beach to the north has easier waves and is patrolled. **Trapdoors** is a long pointbreak, breaking for a couple of hundred metres in the right SE swell, provided the sand has built up along the headland rocks. Sucky and fast at the take-off, it rifles off down toward the rivermouth, which can have some nice peaks when it is

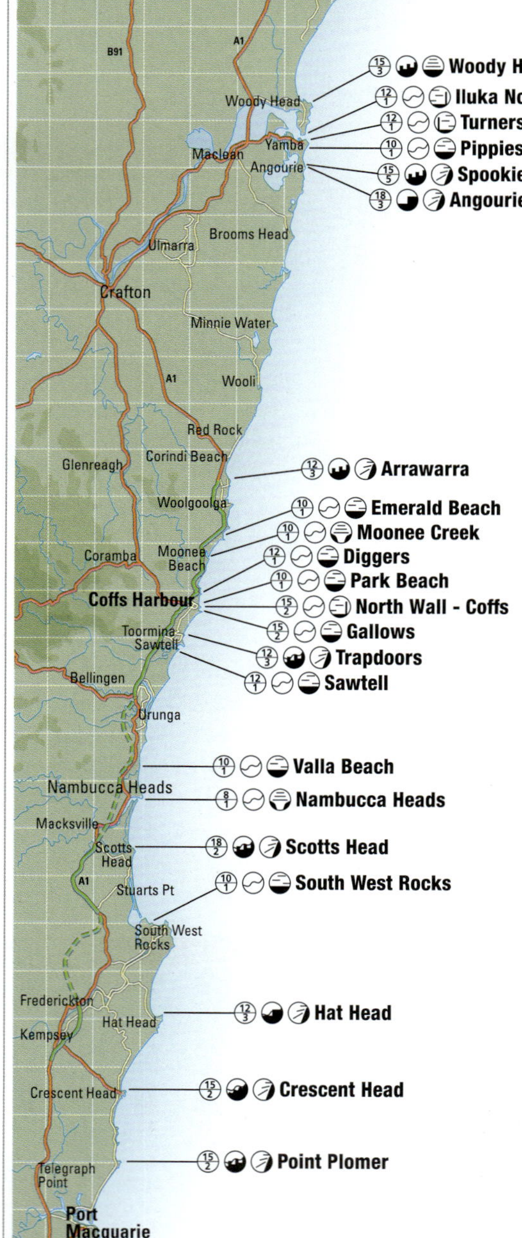


## TRAVEL INFORMATION

**Weather** – The sub-tropical climate improves the further north you travel. March is usually the wettest month and September the driest. The inland mountain ranges from Coffs Harbour receive more orographic rain than the coast, creating the awesome World Heritage listed rainforests of the Dorrigo National Park.

**Lodging and Food** – Coffs has all types of accommodation from Novotel (fr $120/dbl/n) to cheap Aussietel Backpackers with free board hire (fr $20/n). Typical coastal towns that are quiet in winter and bulging during school holidays with caravan parks and campgrounds. Holiday home rentals (Stayz fr $75/n). Many fancy and international restaurants in Coffs, but fresh seafood on the bbq is the real mid north coast vibe, along with bananas.

**Nature and Culture** – A string of National Parks, State Forests, Nature Reserves and Aboriginal Reserves stud this coastal region, containing an impressive range of biodiversity. Communing with nature is more the scene than nightclubbing in Coffs.

**Hazards and Hassles** – Many remote areas require 4WD especially after rain. The shark threat is ever-present on the Mid North Coast as great whites cruise between their nursery grounds around Hawks Nest to their seeming feeding grounds on the Far North Coast. Be very careful around rivermouths.

**Handy Hints** – Buy a season pass for the National Parks if you are going to camp for more than a week. Plenty of surf shops in all the big towns.

ANDREW SHIELD
Iluka North Wall

### Angourie

LAT. -29.482565° LONG. 153.367344°

**A perfect wave that never lets you relax. Elevates abruptly over a shelf, making for a tricky entry into multiple bending bowl sections and chunky walls that only experienced surfers will be able to deal with. NE-E ups the ante as it hits the reef square on, while big SE will rumble wider, but still with malicious power. Handles triple overhead and prefers lower tides unless it is bigger. Always crowded and with guys who have made this wave their life mission. Anga's Backbeach is awesome in any N wind and may even have a left off the point.**

smaller. Experts only and the local crew will be on it when it's good. **Gallows** wedges up and throws out hard and thick on most E swells, with rights barrelling back towards the rocks and lefts spinning down the beach. Guaranteed power, so it attracts the best stand-ups and bodyboarders. The **North Wall** of Coffs Harbour is a typical jetty break with a right spinning of it called the Wedge and a nice apex peak just next to it. Further out is Reef, a sucking slab off the rocks that goes square before shutting down, making it a favourite with bodyboarders. North of the polluted Coffs Creek rivermouth, **Park Beach** can serve up some sweet peaks in SE swells and the north end will be better in NE swells and winds. Consistent and not usually too crowded. **Diggers Beach** is nicely wind protected by high flanking headlands, yet seems to catch all available swell and it will handle a bit of size. Popular with longboarders when it's smaller, the reliable channel at the southern end gives some shape for both lefts and rights. More steep than hollow, but gets heavier as the swell shifts to overhead. Often crowded with all sorts of wave riders. The rip torn mouth of **Moonee Creek** helps sculpt some good sandbars and create a sucky barrel in the flow when the conditions are right. There is also a moderate swell right off the point and it is all sheltered from S winds. Lower tides and SE swell best. The rip makes this place unsuitable for beginners. **Emerald Beach** has some prime lefts worth diverting for when the creek has fed the sandbanks just right. Gets long hollow rides in all E swells. There's more possibilities to scope out up near Sandy Beach on both sides of the headland. Fun, but often fat righthander, **Arrawarra** is less daunting than most north coast points. From waisthigh to headhigh, the longboarders have the whip hand as any S swell refracts around the large headland, filtering out some size and power. Once it gets overhead, power increases and the inside runners close to the rocks will stand up in sections and offer faster ripable walls for shortboarders. Much better at lower tides, unless it is huge. With 400m easy rides on offer, it's no surprise the crowds can get crazy. If not working, check the handful of beaches back towards Woolgoolga including Mullaway, which has a much more powerful pointbreak and heavy beachbreak for advanced riders. Northwards the Pacific Hwy wanders inland and large tracts of bush separate small towns, usually at rivermouths that may organise some banks. Check Red Rock, the jetty at Wooli, Minnie Water and Broomes Head, but quality is rare. **Angourie** is the classic NSW righthand point that often resides in the world's Top 10 Waves list. Only experienced, confident surfers are good enough to handle the air drop to twisting barrel at **Spookies**, where the rocks are barely covered and mistakes are quickly punished. Needs some size to break clear of the rocks and lower tides help it break a bit earlier. Sometimes crowded with the best locals and blow-ins. **Pippies** is the local diet between swells, shelling out some cultured peaks in smaller swells, preferably from the NE-E, which gets the north end lefts going. Bigger swells shut it down along with the slabby righthander Razors, a bodyboard spot over the headland. The best peaks on the beach are often crowded when it is the only decent wave in town. Lefts off **Turners Wall** at the mouth of the Clarence River can be fast, hollow and punchy, with further peaks in the middle and a righthander at the south end. **Iluka North Wall** on the pther side of the Clarence River creates some real wedgy rights with the right E-SE swell and some bounce off the wall. More rights can rifle off down the beach and lefts appear in NE, but it's usually better back at Turners. Rippy, sharky and a long drive around the bridges from Yamba. Out in front of the **Woody Head** campground, a line of reef catches most swell and knocks out some nice sections which are mainly rights in a SE swell. Beautiful backwater that's empty most of the time.

Southwards there are more waves around Frasers Reef over rock and sand, while heading northwards into the Bundjalung National Park finds endless beachbreak that is never surfed except maybe at Black Rocks campsite or Jerusalem Creek.

SE swells are dominant throughout the year with a bit more E at the beginning of the year. NE cyclone swells give a big spike to the wave height and period averages but April, May, June are better bets as the summer onshores back off and a lot more SW-W-NW winds give clean conditions and rarely exceed 15-30kmh. Maximum 2.1m tidal range at Coffs affects most pointbreaks when swell, and more importantly period, is small.

ANDREW SHIELD

Pippies

| STATISTICS | | J F | M A | M J | J A | S O | N D |
|---|---|---|---|---|---|---|---|
| SWELL | Direction | | | | | | |
| | Size (ft) | 5 | 6 | 6 | 6 | 6 | 5 |
| WIND | Direction | | | | | | |
| | Force | F4 | F3 | F3 | F3 | F3 | F4 |
| WATER | Wetsuit | | | | | | |
| | Temp/°C | 25 | 24 | 22 | 20 | 20 | 23 |
| WEATHER | Rainfall/mm | 205 | 206 | 140 | 76 | 78 | 144 |
| | days/mth | 9 | 9 | 7 | 5 | 5 | 8 |
| | Min temp/°C | 19 | 17 | 10 | 8 | 12 | 17 |
| | Max temp/°C | 26 | 25 | 20 | 19 | 23 | 25 |

# Far North Coast NEW SOUTH WALES

Byron Bay is mainland Australia's easternmost tip, attracting surfers to a veritable array of long golden beaches and rocky headlands. From a sleepy coastal hippy town that encompassed the Far North Coast vibe, Byron has mutated into a virtual city, attracting movie stars, property developers and hordes of backpackers. While there are some epic set-ups, a lack of decent-sized swell dictates that conditions are fairly inconsistent, relying on summer cyclone swells or big winter S swells to create waves worth remembering. Typically, shoulder-high waves snap across the sandbanks in clean, small-size swells, while bigger days see the handful of quality pointbreaks rumble into life with locals descending from miles around.

- + BEAUTIFUL RIGHT POINTS
- + N-S SWELL WINDOW
- + BYRON BACKPACKER HEAVEN
- + WARM, CLEAR WATER & DOLPHINS

- – RARELY ANY BIG SWELLS
- – LACK OF REEFBREAKS
- – INTENSE CONSTANT CROWDS
- – VERY SHARKY

Broken Head

DAVID CONNOR

**Evans Head** breakwall at the rivermouth has its days with some rights protected from the S winds, but it doesn't break with the power or shape of the Ballina 'Walls'. The curious might find better shape over the backbeach called Chinamans and a rarity of a right point breaking off Snapper Rocks (NSW). The flags often take out the best peak closest to the wall leaving scattered groups on the peaks up the beach. Really sharky around here and over the back at Snapper Rocks/Chinamans where a large noah attacked a surfer in 2015. **Ballina South Wall** is a good call in summer NE'ers and small peaky swells for power pockets and A-frames down the beach. No facilities on this side and it's a bit of a diversion off the main roads, but it won't be empty on the good days. Quality, wedging peaks hit the **Ballina North Wall** groyne at the Richmond rivermouth. AKA Lighthouse Beach, there's great wind protection from S winds, but the talented local crew are always on it. Handles more size than the other town beaches to the north like Shelly and Angel, which also get good banks. **Flat Rock** is a symbiotic basalt reef/point that is nothing without a healthy covering of sand pushed in by summer NE'ers. Straight E-SE swells will wall up steady righthanders that appeal to intermediates who will struggle around the corner at ✪**Lennox Head**. Some decent beachies up towards Sharpes and maybe round the corner at Boulders in bigger S swells. **Broken Head** breaks on most NE-SE swells but needs the sand to line up with the rocky headland. There's lefts as well and the whole set-up is quite spread out. S to W winds and ideally a bit of N in the swell, making it more of a summer spot when the sand has been given a chance to build up. The beachbreaks are all abilities, but the point proper needs above average skill set. The sleepy streets of **Suffolk Park** occasionally lead to a good bank, with lefts often tubing down towards Taylors and Tea Tree Lake, on a mid tide, any E swell and any W in the wind. Get in before the wind does. **Tallows** is tucked out of the NE winds and is the place to be when the swell is small and from the S. Power is the key word, with thick-lipped triangles popping up randomly and peeling fast before usually closing-out or hitting one of the deeper channels and holes

## TRAVEL INFORMATION

**Weather** – The far north coast climate is much closer to Queensland's subtropical weather than Sydney. Summer temps average 21-28°C (70-82°F) and winter temps 15-21°C (59-70°F), giving Byron Bay an excellent year-round climate. The beaches around Byron offer clean, warm water, 26°C (79°F) in summer and 21°C (70°F) in winter, a springsuit should be enough for most sessions, the need for a light fullsuit only required on cold winter mornings or in cold SW'ers.

**Lodging and Food** – Byron real estate prices have sky-rocketed in recent years and boutique hotels, resorts and restaurants have sprung up. Backpacker dorms; Holiday Village $17 (free boards and bikes), YHA $20, Nomad & Aquarius $24. Air BnB from $57. The Byron at Byron Resort and Spa fr $225/dbl. Rae's on Watego's luxury fr $400/n. Expect $25 for a meal; there are lots of natural, organic food places, selling locally grown produce.

**Nature and Culture** – Hike the 3.7km Cape Byron walking track through rainforest, beach, grassland and clifftops to the lighthouse. Take binoculars to spy whales Feb-March and schools of dolphins May-October. Check the beautiful hinterland of National Parks and rainforest for bushwalking and waterfalls. Visit eclectic towns like Nimbin. Socialise with the huge international crew of visitors and locals in lively bars like the Beach Hotel, which displays big screen surf videos.

**Hazards and Hassles** – In 2015/16 alone, NSW recorded 21 unprovoked shark incidents, resulting in one fatality at Ballina. Attempts to net Lighthouse Beach and 7 Mile at Lennox failed. Bluebottles blow in on NE-SE winds. Crowds are bordering on insanity, especially when learners mix with the ultra-competitive local crew at breaks like The Pass.

**Handy Hints** – Shapers like McTavish and Maddog have showrooms both in town and the industrial estate. Expect $500+ for a shortboard and $1400 for a McTavish longboard. Beginners have a huge choice of surf schools in Byron Bay. Avoid Dec-Jan high season.

Byron Bay – Wategoes and The Pass

ANDREW SHIELD

## Lennox Head

**LAT. -28.805620° LONG. 153.604570°**

**Generally regarded as Australia's finest righthand point, surfers have flocked to the break, since the '60s. Few waves compare for speed, barrel sections, length of ride and an ability to handle the biggest NE-S swells. While a NE swell meeting a SW wind is considered primo, Lennox will also bend a S to its will, hitting a number of launch sites along the half kilometre headland. Expect full-throttle, ruler-edged walls to gusset multiple times and envelop those fast and canny enough to thread the right line. Holds proper size when the prospect of leaping off the rocks looks suicidal and the current running down the point is likely to challenge the strongest paddlers. So we know the current, difficult entry and exit over nasty boulders and the thick crowd of local rippers are hazards, so we won't mention the sharks.**

that scour the long beach. Because it is super-consistent and often perfect, Tallows can be very crowded, particularly at the northern peak of Cosy Corner. **Wategoes** sits astride the most eastern point of Australia and while the rock and sand try to coalesce into a defined righthand point, it's more often a bunch of mixed up, rolling peaks that shoulder and reform through the cove. This makes it ideal for any ability and any craft to get some action and it is still nicely offshore in the SE summer onshores. Absolutely always crowded with longboarders and soft-tops. Parking is damn near impossible on summer days. **The Pass** is the marquee break for Byron, welcoming all E swells into a balmy, pandanus-lined bay, transforming them into orderly righthanders that march in parallel lines to the sand. The outer take-off sucks strongly from the rocky outcrop and races through a fast vert section into the next entry point where crowds throng, waiting for a wider one or someone to fall. This starts an extremely long ride up to 500m as righthanders trundle down the sandy point towards Clarks Beach, perfect for longboarding or practising trim and cutbacks. Best on E-NE swells when the walls will be more extensive, but it can still break on big S-SE pulses with enough wrap, although the walls break up more and often fizzle-out. It is fairly protected from winds out of the ESE all the way round to SW and mid tide is the pick. Crowds are legion to the point of madness and all the locals descend on the quality days. The sweep down the point is shoulder-smashing and most people walk back to pick a moment to launch either behind or through the pass in the rocks. Drop-ins, hassling, shouting and general chaos are better left to the more adept. The Pass is also well-known for dolphin pods adding to the crowd and dropping in on anyone. **The Wreck** is right in town and usually noted for its rights, which wall up quick and throw in the odd spitting barrel. There are lefts as well which tend to be a bit slower and shouldery as the SE-E swells arrive at an angle in this deep bay. The rivermouth breakwalls at the mouth of the **Brunswick** River do a decent job of holding some sand together and the old adage of north wall in southerlies and south wall in northerlies holds true. North wall has some scattered rocks to help hold a right bank and when it gets real big there is a heavy right that unloads over the outside "Bar", deposited by the strong river flow. More peaky on the south side with rights and lefts in the summer northeasters. Long, lonely and usually blown-out linear beachbreak, with congregations at spots like Ocean Shores, Golden Beach and **Pottsville**, where variable sandbars will form along a deserted and sharky stretch of coast. Avoid high tide. Often chosen as a contest site for its consistency **Cabarita** has many moods. Stronger winter SE-S swells break outside with some lurching sections down towards the second outcrop that usually holds the barrel section if the sand is in place. Smaller days can see perfect peelers inside the first bay, out of the clutches of the SE sea-breezes. Check over the backside and all the way down to Hastings Point, to escape the crowds. **Kingscliff** has some good peaks shaped by the flow of the river, and the jetty protects from even SE winds, but too much S in the swell will see it sail straight past and the rip hardly ever lets up. The southern breakwall of the Tweed River next to the sand pumping jetty can have some peaky lefts in NE swells and offers some summer wind respite, followed by average but uncrowded beachies all the way south to **Fingal Head** where rolling walls and shoulders get hollow at headhigh before maxing out at about 10ft faces.

ANDREW SHIELD

**Cabarita**

April-September lows stationed in the Tasman Sea produce consistent E-S swells. In summer, December-April is the tropical cyclone season in the Coral Sea, but it is rare to get many long period NE swells and if the cyclone is too close, the surf will be choppy and erratic. E and SE swells are far more generous and help boost the annual mean wave height to 6-7ft. Wind is crucial, the best being SW, which often blows May to August. Summer sea breezes start off with N- NE dominance as early as Sept/Oct, before SE takes over by Feb/March. Occasional hot NW'ers will groom everything on the coast, but as temps rise, the NE'ers kick back in. As a general rule, beachies are better at high tides and pointbreaks on the low tides. Tide range can reach 1.9m.

| STATISTICS | | J F | M A | M J | J A | S O | N D |
|---|---|---|---|---|---|---|---|
| SWELL | Direction | | | | | | |
| | Size (ft) | 5 | 5-6 | 5-6 | 6 | 5 | 5 |
| WIND | Direction | | | | | | |
| | Force | F4 | F4 | F3 | F3 | F4 | F4 |
| WATER | Wetsuit | | | | | | |
| | Temp/°C | 26 | 25 | 22 | 21 | 21 | 24 |
| WEATHER | Rainfall/mm | 178 | 197 | 175 | 97 | 98 | 132 |
| | days/mth | 15 | 16 | 13 | 9 | 10 | 12 |
| | Min temp/°C | 21 | 18 | 13 | 12 | 15 | 19 |
| | Max temp/°C | 27 | 26 | 21 | 20 | 23 | 26 |

# Gold Coast QUEENSLAND

Queensland's Gold Coast is one of the most intense surf zones in the world, combining 40km of legendary spots with a huge, hungry surf population. It's the most visited stretch of coastline in Australia, but don't be misled by the name 'Surfer's Paradise', as the heart of this zone is dominated by skyscrapers, not palm trees and the hordes of tourists rule out anything approaching deserted. However, year-round warm temperatures, a raging nightlife and endlessly long, right pointbreaks tempt southerners and foreigners alike to try their luck in Australia's most competitive line-ups.

+ WORLD-CLASS RIGHT POINTS
+ SUBTROPICAL CLIMATE
+ FLAT DAY ENTERTAINMENT
+ INEXPENSIVE

- SUPER CROWDED SURF ARENA
- CONSTANT DROP-INS
- FEW LEFTS
- GENERALLY SMALL WAVES

## TRAVEL INFORMATION

**Weather** – November to April is the 'wet' season with some rainy days and warm temperatures. Cyclones usually only affect northern Queensland. It stays pleasant throughout the dry season (May-October) when nights can get a little bit chilly, so you may need a 2mm steamer in the early morning. Rest of the year it's boardshorts, or a shorty for the early mornings.

**Lodging and Food** – Coolangatta Sands Backpackers (fr $23). Komune is a high-rise hostel (fr $24). Rainbow Bay Resort from ($95/n/triple). Varied international menus from $15 for a meal.

**Nature and Culture** – Entertainment includes WhiteWater World, Sea World, Movie World, Dreamworld, Wet 'n' Wild, Cableski, Currumbin Sanctuary and Fleays Wildlife Pk. Also more than happy to separate you from your money is Jupiters Casino. There is some mega nightlife action on Orchid Avenue.

**Hazards and Hassles** – The most likely problems are drop-ins and collisions at zooed-out spots. You stand more chances being attacked by an aggro local, than a shark! NE winds bring in the nasty bluebottle jellyfish. The skin cancer rate is very high. Use more than just sunscreen.

**Handy Hints** – There are dozens of surf shops stocking all the gear at bargain prices. The Aussie beer culture leads to some serious nights out, but it's still crowded for the dawn patrol. Cheap food and drink at RSL Clubs. Queensland has a reputation as the 'Police State', with harsh drink driving penalties and draconian cannabis laws. Avoid where possible!

AL MACKINNON

Snapper Rocks and Greenmount

Even though **Duranbah** is technically in New South Wales, it has become one of the main surfing focal points of the "Goldie". The rivermouth jetties have helped form powerful wedging peaks that provide ample tube time at one of the world's finest beachbreaks. Crowds can be insane, mainly because when the points are sleeping, D-Bah will have thumping little A-frame wedges, somewhere along its length. Refraction off the breakwall helps to focus power on the peak and it will pick up any swell from NE around to S. Huge local crew dominate the line-up, so you might want to check some of the other beaches south of the river for less stressful sessions. **Snapper Rocks** has had a personality make-over ever since the Tweed Sand Bypassing Project started pumping sand northwards and is no longer second fiddle to Kirra when it comes to dredgy barrels. It starts from behind the rock, where just a few locals have dialled the launch into a square, thick-lipped pit before the backwash hits and twists the barrel just as it emerges out into the sandy expanses of what has been dubbed the Superbank. A frothing pack of rippers and longboarders then pounce on anything that moves, slashing and mainly burning any surfer perceived to be weak or undeserving. It then opens up to two parts wall one part barrel as it progresses 200m down towards the next rocks at Little Marley, before traversing Rainbow Bay for a further 400m of cruise and crack. E-SE provides the ideal swell direction, since too much S will by-pass the point, losing lots of size and shouldering off into deeper water, while NE will angle in and close-out whole sections of the sandbar and even blow holes in it. Handles S winds well and breaks through the tide, but the sweeping current is always there to drain your paddling power. The tree-lined **Greenmount** Point provides a curve of boulders for the sand to stick to, resulting in some long easy rights and a bit of protection from the dreaded SE winds. Since the advent of the Superbank, Greenmount and the adjacent Coolangatta Beach have been swallowed by sand and tacked onto the Snapper, Rainbow endless line-up. It still shows some of its longboarding heritage and can be less sucky than further up the line, but then again it can churn off relentlessly towards Big Groyne ✪**Kirra** if it's in the right mood. Handles more NE in the swell, which breaks up the sections and any S wind. **The Alley** at Currumbin has very long rights, well sheltered from the strongest SE winds. Rarely a barrel, it lazily peels for hundreds of metres, just asking to be ripped to pieces. It is such an accommodating wave that all types of surfcraft tackle it making the crowds of longboards, SUP and even kiteboarders a bit daunting. Best with a SE swell up to double-overhead, SW wind and lower, outgoing tides to hold up the walls across the rivermouth. The beaches south and north of the Alley through to Palm Beach hold plenty of less-crowded peaks. **Burleigh Heads** can be so awesome when the swell has S in it and the wind is SW offshore, shaping up thick, dredging barrels breaking over sand in front of a basalt boulder shoreline. After a long, leg-aching ride to the shorey shut-downs, it's a jog back up the point and over the slippery boulders before dashing for the outside against the rip that drags you back down the point. When the rest of the coast is closed-out, Burleigh will still be holding and barrel-hungry chargers will paddle out from the Tallebudgera rivermouth to the south, where there are more waves. Cyclone swells can blow holes in the set-up and it's rare for all four sections (Sharkies, The Cove, The Point and Rockbreak) to link-up. It's not as long as Kirra and not quite as crowded, but unfortunately it's more localised. The **Miami** stretch used to be a bit of a quiet spot away from the crowds, but these days nowhere is empty along the Goldie. Beat the wind by getting up early and avoid high tide when the waves go slack and the outside/inside channel cuts length of ride. **Broadbeach** is a continuation

South Stradbroke Island
Nerang Head
**The Spit**
Parkwood
Labrador
Main Beach
Southport
Molendinar
Ashmore
**Narrowneck**
Nerang
Surfers Paradise
**Surfers Paradise**
Gold Coast
Broadbeach
**Broadbeach**
Merrimac
Mermaid Waters
Miami
**Miami**
**Burleigh Heads**
Burleigh Heads
**Currumbin Alley**
QUEENSLAND
Palm Beach
Currumbin
Tugun
**Kirra**
**Greenmount**
**Snapper Rocks**
**Duranbah (D-Bah)**
Bilinga
Gold Coast Airport
Kirra
Coolangatta
Tweed
NSW

## Kirra

LAT. -28.164474° LONG. 153.535268°

**Kirra is Australia's and probably the world's best righthand point that breaks over sand. Air drops into various tube sections, which seem to suck-out below sea level, adding sand to the already ridiculously powerful and thick lips. Super long, slabby sections need breakneck speed to negotiate while praying the inevitable drop-in wont happen on the deepest tube of your life. It all depends on the constantly changing sand and breaks at about a third to a half the size of the prevailing swell. Big, solid SE groundswell is the preferred element, while E and even NE cyclone swells can also produce epic barrels if the sand is right. The sweep down the point is legendary, so many run back up the point after every ride.**

of the Surfers Paradise theme with plenty of fun beachbreaks to choose from, which range from straight-handers to long workable walls. Occasionally fires off some good barrels at lower tides and picks up NE swells better than SE, which shows better further north. This whole stretch will close-out when the wave faces exceed 6-8ft, which is when all the pointbreaks will be working. **Surfers Paradise** itself is more dedicated to swimmers, so don't surf between the flags as the lifeguards don't have a sense of humour. In-between the patrolled areas there are various peaks, sometimes slow and mushy, perfect for beginners and sometimes sucky and walled up with hollow bits, often in summer NE swells, when the crowds make it a real lucky dip as to whether you have a good session or not. All tides up to 6ft. Parking can be tricky and the backdrop of hi-rise hotels, casinos and swanky apartment buildings is a rare one for Australian waters. **Narrowneck** used to be off the surfer's radar until an artificial reef was built to create an erosion protection solution to prevent the beach being inundated during storm swells. While this part of the project is considered to have worked, the bonus surfing wave has been attracting plenty of takers since the sandbags trip up a decent right on SE swells and a left in NE'ers. 'Naz' is not the most exciting wave but can provide more shape on junky, onshore days than the long expanses of Surfers Paradise beaches stretching south. On its good days, there's pits to be found and a bit of extra power over the reef, plus a shorey section that bodyboarders like. Gets crowded as it is the first stop from Brisbane and is a regular local contest site. From *Sea World* you can take a look at **The Spit**, which isn't quite as developed as the rest of this coast, receives plenty of swell and has tons of empty peaks stretching as far as Main Beach. The main event is usually a left breaking between the Southport Seaway jetty and the Spit sand-pumping jetty, which provides plenty of raw materials for nice banks, both here and over the rivermouth at South Stradbroke Island. Its other fine quality is being able to tame the NE sea breezes better than any Goldy spot. The Spit is popular with tourists and beginners because there is less hassling and the waves are generally slopey and manageable when small. Can get hollow in a stronger, moderate swell, but it closes-out as it exceeds 6-8ft faces, plus the currents can ramp up quickly. The northern jetty is the most easily accessible of the South Straddie breaks and the trim peaks get insanely crowded as many dash across the channel that is famous for as much shark traffic as boat traffic.

ANDREW SHIELD

Burleigh Heads

December-March is tropical cyclone season in the Coral Sea, but most NE swells are usually small with short period. During this time E swells are far more common and SE to even S swells still arrive with greater height and period. Statistically speaking, March to July will have the biggest average size, more groundswell and mainly SE winds. The best SW winds often blow from May to August. September-December sees lots of N winds mess up the NE-facing coastline. As a general rule the pointbreaks crank from low-mid. Tidal range can reach 2m.

ANDREW SHIELD

Currumbin Alley

| STATISTICS | | J F | M A | M J | J A | S O | N D |
|---|---|---|---|---|---|---|---|
| SWELL | Direction | | | | | | |
| | Size (ft) | 4-5 | 4-5 | 2-3 | 2 | 2-3 | 3 |
| WIND | Direction | | | | | | |
| | Force | F4 | F4 | F4 | F4 | F4 | F4 |
| WATER | Wetsuit | | | | | | |
| | Temp/°C | 26 | 25 | 23 | 21 | 22 | 24 |
| WEATHER | Rainfall/mm | 185 | 170 | 114 | 66 | 72 | 118 |
| | days/mth | 13 | 13 | 9 | 7 | 8 | 10 |
| | Min temp/°C | 20 | 18 | 12 | 9 | 14 | 18 |
| | Max temp/°C | 28 | 27 | 22 | 21 | 24 | 28 |

# Sunshine Coast QUEENSLAND

A short drive from Brisbane lies a long coastal strip of pristine beaches, tropical landscapes, shimmering waterways and exciting towns. The Sunshine Coast is the northernmost stretch of reliable surf in Australia and home to the clutch of fabled right points at Noosa Heads. North of the waveless Brisbane zone are a string of modern tourist towns and miles of golden sand beachbreak, plus a few pointbreaks, while beyond Noosa the low tide beach becomes the 4WD highway to Double Island Point and the totally wild landscape of Fraser Island.

+ CYCLONE AND GROUNDSWELLS
+ LOTS OF RIGHT POINTBREAKS
+ EASY ACCESS BEACHBREAKS
+ BEGINNERS PARADISE IN NOOSA

– INTENSE CROWDS
– FICKLE POINTBREAKS
– LACK OF POWER AND SIZE
– FAIRLY EXPENSIVE

Caloundra has eight spots facing both north and south. **Kings Beach** often looks messy and crappy, but transforms to hollow, pitching peaks when NE'ers hit. The groyne at the southern end sits on a rock shelf and entertains thick, cylindrical lefts in most NE-SE swells and is protected from any N wind. A bit further south at Happy's, the sandbars that flank the Pumicestone Passage can output long, full lefts. **Moffats** is home of the mal and somewhere to tune-up on cutbacks between the long, crumbly sections, which are more makeable at higher tides. The Reef is 20mins paddle and should only be undertaken by accomplished surfers who can manage the drop and spitting keg. **Anne Street** Reef can get real good on moderate swells, when powerful lefts and rights appear, attracting a crowd. Dicky Beach and Neill St are hollow with a thumping shorey, so naturally a lot of bodyboarders. The surf becomes less crowded and more powerful towards Wurtulla and **Long Track** in the Currimundi Lake Conservation Park. When the lake flows out, the banks can get some sharp shape and assemble long, peeling walls in winter westerlies. **Kawana** has tons of access to consistent and hollow beachbreaks, sometimes stabilised on the rock bottom all the way up to The Corner, where NE wind is sideshore. **Point Cartwright** headland provides S wind shelter for a challenging right point, which shuts down on the eastern breakwall of the Mooloolaba Inlet. Thick walls arch and throw a barrel section on take-off, then it races down the line to the terminal shelf. All tides and winds from SE-W should be ok with any E swell up to 12ft, when it can start breaking past the rivermouth. Inside the usually flat bay on the other side of the river can see some awesome close-out barrels on a big NE swell S wind combo, otherwise it's a good learning area up to Mooloolaba Beach. In small swells, Alexandra Headland or **The Bluff** is a fat and forgiving righthand point that gets packed with longboarders in the water and tourists on the beach. Handles a bigger swell from the south, when rips increase and the walls have more power, but it is still a fairly benign wave. There's more rights on the inside at the Corner as it heads into the beachbreak lefts. The local longboard legends can be a bit greedy, but the vibe is fairly mellow. Maroochydore is the biggest centre on the Sunshine Coast, incorporating some walled-up beachbreaks and pockets of reef leading down to Alexandra Headland. Avoid the central beach masses by checking places like **Pin Cushion** behind the caravan park next to the Maroochy rivermouth. WSW winds, all tides and nice SE swell should see some hollow peaks. **Mudjimba Island** sees serious waves for experts off two sides of the island, with the longer, chunky lefts grinding down a barnacle encrusted reef, creating multi barrel opportunities in NW to NNE winds and a bit of S in the swell. The ledgy rights wrap around the top of the island so work in NE-SE swells and any S wind. Air drops and dry sucks are common, making this a favourite with the bodyboarders. Local vibe can be strong. Careful surfers will hire a boat, as the 30min paddle back is arduous and scary in the sharky waters. Always much bigger than the town beachbreaks, which are often nice and peaky as swell refracts around the island and hits at funny angles. The two tidally dependant, fickle NE-facing rocky beaches of Point Perry and Three Bays need a bit of size to get going, since they are sheltered from S swells and winds by Point Arkwright. At **Coolum Beach**, the peaks can get punchy and hollow on small to moderate

ANDREW SHIELD

Moffats

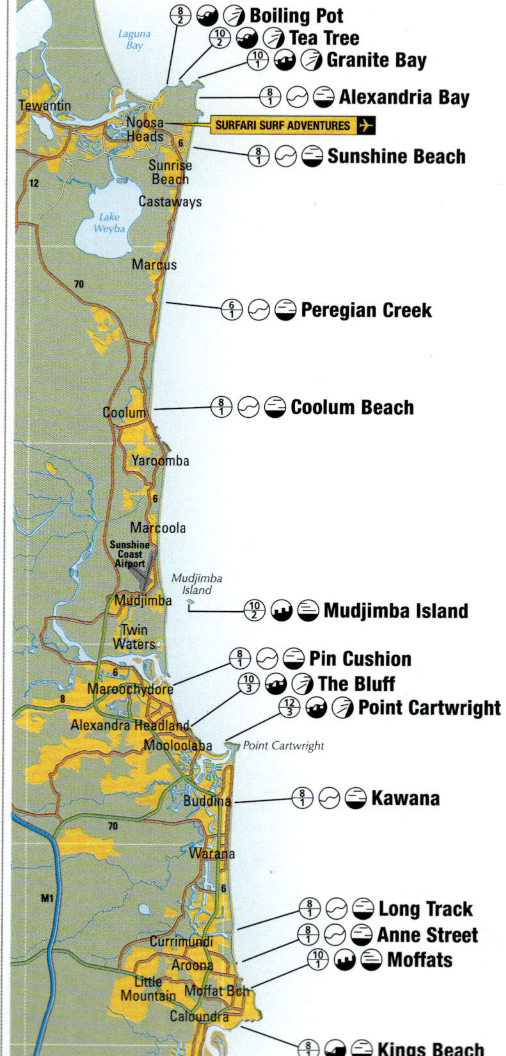

ANDREW SHIELD

Mudjimba Island

## TRAVEL INFORMATION

**Weather** – The Sunshine Coast enjoys a warm, subtropical climate with one of the highest sunshine readings in the world, averaging 7h a day. The variation between summer and winter is minimal and rainfall is concentrated in short wet seasons. Winter varies between 12-21°C (54-70°F) while summers average 17-28°C (63-82°F). Ocean temps get up to 26°C (79°F), so no wetsuits needed from Oct-April, while a springsuit or thin steamer is perfect from May-Sept.

**Lodging and Food** – Noosa YHA Halse Lodge offers free surf/bodyboards (fr $20/n), Nomads (fr $19), Noosa Backpackers Resort (fr $31), Sheraton (from $210/n). Other towns are easier to find deals. Expect $15 for a decent meal or cheaper for fast food.

**Nature and Culture** – Visit Underwater World in Mooloolaba, the Glasshouse Mountains, Australia Zoo with its amazing saltwater crocodile shows and Aussie World in Caloundra. Take a 4WD bus tour to Fraser Island for incredible natural beauty and wildlife on the world's largest sand island.

**Hazards and Hassles** – Australians suffer the highest skin cancer rates in the world – take precautions. Shark attacks, especially near islands, occur more frequently on cloudy, sultry summer days. Noosa hides many urchins in the eroded boulders but the constant, competitive crowd is the main hassle.

**Handy Hints** – Noosa longboards from $695-1350 or try Eternity Surf or Classic Malibu in Noosaville ($590 for a fish). Try long established Learn to Surf or Noosa Surf Lessons. Noosa Surf Festival happens in March.

**Noosa Heads**

**LAT. -26.376983 LONG. 153.107061°**

**Tea Tree is the locals favourite and a 20 minute walk into the Noosa National Park, which doesn't deter the crowds. Steeper and hollower than the other points, especially at low tide, when the first section sucks close to the rocks before sloping off over the inside sandbar. Holds a bit more swell and winds from E-S, but high tide is likely to bring you into conflict with the rocks, unless it is pumping. Hot doggin' locals rule the beautiful bay so take a good look over the left shoulder before going. The walk/jog/run through the bush is often a frenzied affair, stoked by glimpses of perfect lines, rattling the point. Stubbing toes on land and on the wade out is common. Boiling Pot is a bit more rocky and sucky on take-off with a speed section that will either fat out or transport you into the sandy National Park section in the bay in front of the car park. Walk through this sweet shoulder section and you might connect with Johnsons, which is effectively the lead in to First Point, where the swell loses some size and speed, making it mellow, smaller and perfect for beginners. Best waves will appear on headhigh to overhead NE-E swells, low to mid tide to keep off the rocks and any wind from SE to SW. The points which are closer to town suffer even bigger crowds as the novices and the lazy flock to the various take-off spots. Flying longboards, clueless tourists and wave-hog locals all need negotiating. Finding somewhere to park, both on land and in the sea can be tricky.**

E swells. Stumers Creek often has the goods and there are proper barrels on the good days. Parking quickly becomes a problem in summer. Coolum has many access routes leading to beachbreaks like **Peregian Beach** and Pitta Street, at the south end of town, where slabs of coffee rock hold the sand together when the surf hits a bit bigger from the SE. Ripable peaks and good shorey sections on high tides. **Sunshine Beach** is another swell magnet with powerful peaks in the lee of the northern headland. Nice holes and gutters help limit the close-outs and there are many access point all the way down through Sunrise and Castaways Beach. Holds it shape OK in the NE'ers. Relief from the masses requires a long walk through the National Park to **Alexandria Bay**, which is a consistent beachbreak that picks up any swell going. NE-SE windswell will be breaking here when everywhere else looks flat and the peaks can have some push around headhigh. Exposed to the sea-breezes, SW-N winds will be offshore and it's a classic Qld bush-backed beach that is worth making the effort to surf. Long slog from the National car park or else take the paths north from Sunshine Beach. The Noosa National Park is a natural wonder of the surfing world. Furthest out **Granite Bay** shows the most size, but relies on sand formations to join the rocks and rarely equals the other points for perfection, especially if there is more E in the wind. It is a bit gruntier, with more water moving and the first couple of sections can offer walled sections for shortboarders before it starts hitting deeper water and shoulders off. It's a long walk out to the low tide jump in spot at Picnic Cove and the rip can be strong in bigger swells. **Noosa Heads** is a wet dream for most surfers irrespective of their choice of surfcraft. Further north Double Island Point is a safe cyclone swell bet for extremely long rights by the lighthouse and occasional lefts on the beachbreak. Jelly legs and arms dictate walking back, decreasing the chance of meeting the abundant sharks. Reliable, local tour operators and surf schools can provide the necessary 4WD transport. There can be some attractive sandbars along the beach highway beside the Cooloola National Park, for those that don't mind feeling like bait. Sharks, rips and isolation make this an intermediates plus area. As for Fraser Island, there are some good waves up north around Indian Head, but only those with a chain mail shark suit would be able to safely take on the sheer volume and size of sharks that cruise this sandy coastline.

ONSAFARI.COM

Sunshine Beach

Winter produces consistent SE groundswells and coincides with the best winds (SE-SW) that often blow from May to August. February to April sees more E windswell bolstering the swell stats for cyclone season, when E-S winds dominate. Avoid the N winds of spring. The northerly drift of coastal sands is a local phenomenon. Summer and winter king tides can reach 2.1m and many beaches prefer more water.

ONSAFARI.COM

Three Bays, Coolum

| STATISTICS | | J F | M A | M J | J A | S O | N D |
|---|---|---|---|---|---|---|---|
| SWELL | Direction | | | | | | |
| | Size (ft) | 4 | 4 | 2-3 | 2 | 2-3 | 3 |
| WIND | Direction | | | | | | |
| | Force | F4 | F4 | F4 | F4 | F4 | F4 |
| WATER | Wetsuit | | | | | | |
| | Temp/°C | 26 | 25 | 23 | 21 | 22 | 24 |
| WEATHER | Rainfall/mm | 160 | 120 | 70 | 50 | 60 | 110 |
| | days/mth | 14 | 14 | 9 | 8 | 9 | 11 |
| | Min temp/°C | 21 | 18 | 12 | 10 | 15 | 19 |
| | Max temp/°C | 29 | 27 | 22 | 21 | 26 | 29 |

**YOUR OWN MALDIVES EXPERT OFFERS**

- **CHARTERED BOATS FOR GROUPS**
- **SCHEDULED BOATS FOR INDIVIDUALS**
- **GUESTHOUSES & SURF RESORTS**
- **BOARD AND SUP RENTALS**

THE ORIGINAL SURFMAP OF

# MALDIVES

The northern atolls are still being explored. There have been 10 waves discovered in the last 15 years – many of these made on Maldivesurf boat charters. There is a high chance of waves that still remain undiscovered, this is your chance to become a surf explorer.

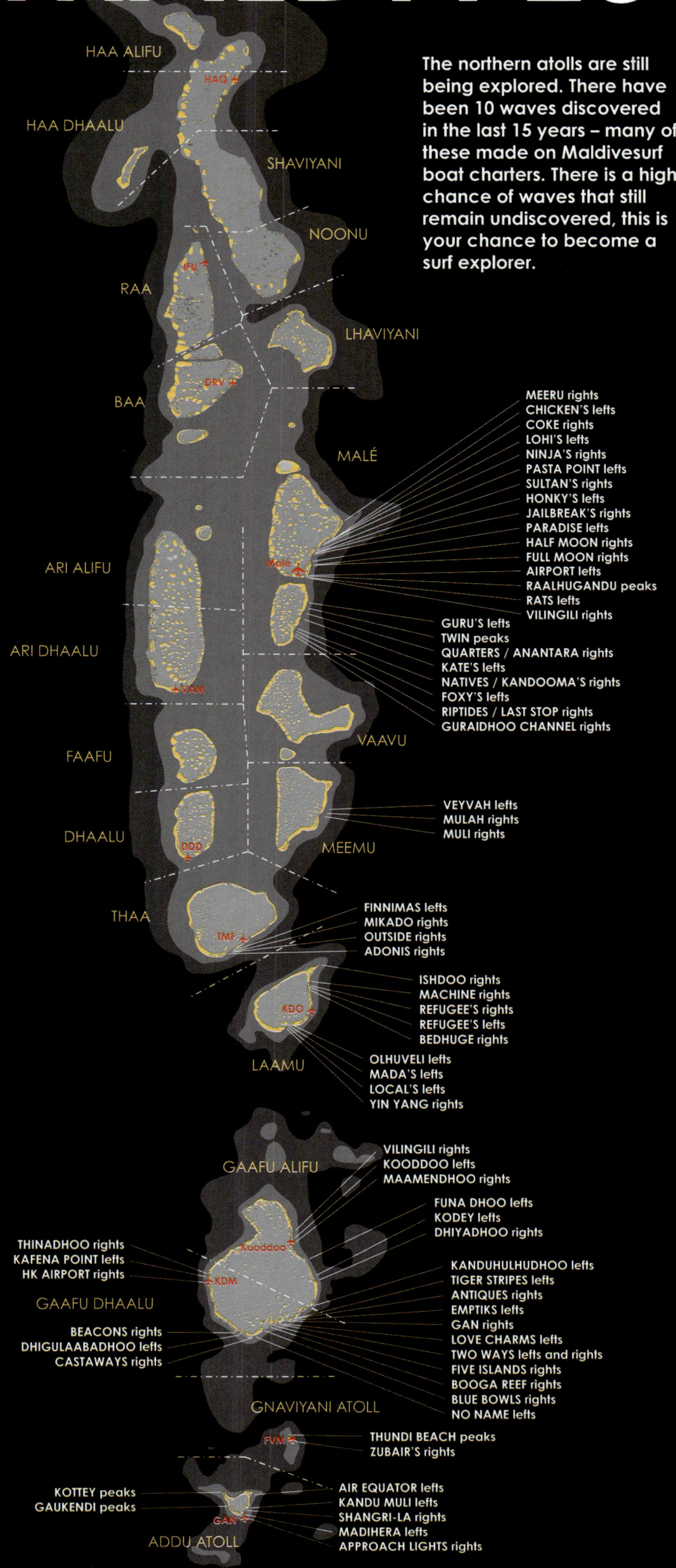

HAA ALIFU
HAQ
HAA DHAALU
SHAVIYANI
NOONU
RAA
IFU
LHAVIYANI
BAA
DRV
MALÉ

MEERU rights
CHICKEN'S lefts
COKE rights
LOHI'S lefts
NINJA'S rights
PASTA POINT lefts
SULTAN'S rights
HONKY'S lefts
JAILBREAK'S rights
PARADISE lefts
HALF MOON rights
FULL MOON rights
AIRPORT lefts
RAALHUGANDU peaks
RATS lefts
VILINGILI rights

Male

ARI ALIFU
ARI DHAALU
VAM

GURU'S lefts
TWIN peaks
QUARTERS / ANANTARA rights
KATE'S lefts
NATIVES / KANDOOMA'S rights
FOXY'S lefts
RIPTIDES / LAST STOP rights
GURAIDHOO CHANNEL rights

VAAVU
FAAFU
DHAALU
DDD
MEEMU

VEYVAH lefts
MULAH rights
MULI rights

THAA
TMF

FINNIMAS lefts
MIKADO rights
OUTSIDE rights
ADONIS rights

KDO

ISHDOO rights
MACHINE rights
REFUGEE'S rights
REFUGEE'S lefts
BEDHUGE rights

LAAMU

OLHUVELI lefts
MADA'S lefts
LOCAL'S lefts
YIN YANG rights

GAAFU ALIFU

VILINGILI rights
KOODDOO lefts
MAAMENDHOO rights

FUNA DHOO lefts
KODEY lefts
DHIYADHOO rights

Kooddoo

THINADHOO rights
KAFENA POINT lefts
HK AIRPORT rights

KDM
GAAFU DHAALU

KANDUHULHUDHOO lefts
TIGER STRIPES lefts
ANTIQUES rights
EMPTIKS lefts
GAN rights
LOVE CHARMS lefts
TWO WAYS lefts and rights
FIVE ISLANDS rights
BOOGA REEF rights
BLUE BOWLS rights
NO NAME lefts

BEACONS rights
DHIGULAABADHOO lefts
CASTAWAYS rights

GNAVIYANI ATOLL
FVM

THUNDI BEACH peaks
ZUBAIR'S rights

KOTTEY peaks
GAUKENDI peaks

GAN
ADDU ATOLL

AIR EQUATOR lefts
KANDU MULI lefts
SHANGRI-LA rights
MADIHERA lefts
APPROACH LIGHTS rights

OPERATED BY ANTONY "YEP" COLAS SINCE 2004

# EAST ASIA

The Asian corner of the Pacific may not have the same depth of surf culture that is apparent among the Polynesian nations to the east, nor does it benefit from both the booming northern and southern hemisphere swells, yet it is an enigmatic, challenging and ultimately rewarding surf destination when the conditions conspire. Follow the annual beat of the monsoon, or chase the biggest storms on earth as super-typhoons traverse the uber-deep water of the Mariana Trench and magic up swell events that awaken a host of waves throughout the Philippine and China Seas.

LAURENT MASUREL

Tuesday Rock, Siargao, Philippines

# The Surf

MICHAEL KEW

Vladivostock

## NORTHWEST PACIFIC BASIN

The Northwest Pacific surrounds **Russia**'s immense Kamchatka Peninsula, which has been surfed thanks to a handful of surf brands sending an expedition to take on the sub-polar climate and travel logistics that will keep this hardcore region a wilderness for a long time. The Kuril Trench exceeds 10km deep just offshore and volcanic sand beachbreaks abound from near the capital Petropavlovsk-Kamchatsky, north through Avacha Bay, while cliffs and reefs dominate the coast south to Cape Lopatka. In the summer surf season, the rivermouths sculpt the gravel and black sand, but are also a favourite feeding ground for the large bear population. The Kuril Islands trickle south to Hokkaido in splendid frozen isolation, with rocky beachbreak on both sides of Yuzhno-Kurilsk, the main settlement on Kunashir Island, however summer S swell exposure isn't great. Sakhalin represents an extensive coastline but you are only allowed in the sea around Yuzhno-Sakhalinsk and Okhotskoye, although other poor quality windslop appears on the south and even west coast around Yablochnoye. In the Sea of Japan, Vladivostok has the highest density of surf breaks in Eastern Russia with a dozen spots around the Primorsky Krai region. Typhoon season SE-SSW windswells will penetrate Ussuri Bay and hit some lined-up reefs and points within an hour of downtown, the pick being the rights at Patrokl or Zolotoy Bereg and the left at Emar. Tungus is another longer, lined-up left around the bay near Nakhodka, where solid beachbreak appears at Triozerye.

**Japan** appears to be ideally situated in the NW Pacific, ready to pick up wave energy anywhere along its 3000km length made up of almost 7000 islands. From the frozen north to the tropical south, there is far too much surfing real estate to cover every zone in detail and the seasonal variations are extreme. **Hokkaido** is more snowboarding than surfing with some bitter water and air temps in winter, however the hardy local contingent can be found picking off Sea of Japan waves on the west coast as far north as Wakkanai and Rashiri Island, or closer to Sapporo at the popular rivermouth breaks of Shioya, Fugoppe and Furubira. Summers can be very flat on the Sea of Japan but that is the time for SE swell and some typhoon action to roll into Uchiuwa Bay, which is ringed by volcanoes. Consistent peaks can be found at Hamaatsuma, Itankihama and in the city of Hakodate, but the island is heavily armed with tetrapods everywhere. There's a couple of surf shops and the town summer breaks will be far less crowded than Honshu, despite many holidaymakers from the south. **Tohoku** is the NE region of Honshu where incredible scenery is buried under some of the deepest snowfall figures in the world. Spring to autumn is usually the best surf season with more SE swell hitting every shape and size of sea defence known to man and creating some good beachbreaks right up north at Rokkasho, Veedol and Misawa harbour. The coastal mountains then lead down to Sendai where one of Japan's best beachbreaks will crank up in any size swell offering barrelling peaks for a large local contingent who surf Sendai-Shinko all-year-round. Fukushima used to be a great road trip for Tokyo surfers to escape for some quieter, cleaner waves up the northeast coast. Since the 2011 tsunami and nuclear power plant meltdown, this has become a no go zone thanks to high radiation levels and a forecast 40 year clean-up, which has yet to locate 600 tonnes of melted radioactive fuel and plans dumping millions of litres of tritium-laced water into the Pacific. Great beachbreaks like Toyoma and Kamioka are too close to the meltdown site in Futuba to be safe, but some locals take their chances. In **Kanto** Ibaraki is almost as close to Tokyo as Chiba but far less popular as it gets colder and windier and is only 100km from the reactor. The waves are generally high quality beachbreaks (Akamba, Kujigawa) and reefbreaks (Todai, Hitachi) among the sea defences and can be big and powerful with longer period E swells. Long beaches at Oarai and Onuki offer straight sandbars for the crowds of learners and cruisers between the jetties and are also home to some major tourist attractions. T-bar groynes litter the long beach southwards giving some shape to exposed beachies through Kashima all the way down to Chosi and the beginning of the most crowded zone in Japan, Chiba Prefecture. In Kanagawa Prefecture Shonan can easily push Chiba for highest crowd factor but a lack of consistency is the main problem for the closest beaches to downtown Tokyo. Nestled deep in Tokyo Bay with offshore islands filtering swell, it is either small windswell or pumping SE typhoon swell that gives the thousands of locals a chance to share a few waves. In the 10km stretch from the excellent walls and barrels of Osaki Reef in the east to the Shonan indicator beachbreaks of Kugenhama there are some quality storm reefs at Kabune, Tamaishi and Inamura, where a lack of quantity means competition for waves is intense. The Izu peninsula picks up more swell and E swell will start re-appearing at Shirahama, a consistent beachbreak used for comps and also at bays like Tattadohama, Iritahama and Ohama. Shizuoka Prefecture sees increases in water temps and decreasing crowds compared to Chiba, but is usually a summer/autumn destination working on SE-SW swells. Majestic Mt Fuji overlooks dozens of shifty beachbreaks plus a few reefs and rivermouths, so it pays to scout about. Highlights include the southeast-facing beaches around Shizunami, Katahama and Susuki, but the south-facing coast at Omaezaki boasts some serious barrels at Niinogawa Point, Sharks Point, and down to the nuclear plant at Hamaoka. Wind turbines are a bad omen here unless you have a sail or kite, particularly in winter, but when it's offshore, the whole south coast can fire through Toyohama, Hamamatsu, Kosai and Akabane. The **Kansai** region includes the coastal prefectures of Mie and Wakayama, providing plenty of waves for the surfers from the sprawling metropolis of Osaka and Kyoto. Ise has some good longboarding spots like Kounohama and check the rocky coast around the Toba Observatory. Pocket beaches with campgrounds like Atashika and Odomari need SE swells, while the long shingle beaches leading down to Shingu rivermouth pick up NE-SW, but have little quality. Wakayama is far more rocky with lots of hidden reefs like Nachi or Inami that require some decent swell from the southern quadrant. Gobo is really popular with city surfers since it's only a 2hr drive to the SW-facing beach, but if you want to see real crowds, try Isonoura on a summer swell and share with hundreds! Shikoku has some of Japan's finest rivermouth breaks and is a bigger region than our zone covers with plenty of exploration potential throughout Kochi Prefecture. From Cape Gamouda down to Kaifu is cliffy, boulder strewn bays and some steep protected beaches like Tainohama that may have some waves when the summer/autumn SE-SW swells arrive. Beyond the world-class cylinders of Nyodo Rivermouth, the coast goes vertical and contorted again, with some points and rocky bays to seek out, but much is inaccessible and too steep or rocky. Boulder strewn average beachbreaks at Ida, Tanoura, Futami and Hirano, pick up E-S swell or head a short way south for a long left point into a rivermouth and harbour in eastern Tosashimizu. Around the windswept and waveless Cape Ashizuri the rugged coast lacks opportunity except at rivermouths like Kainokawa. **Kyushu** fields two zones – Miyazaki on the east coast and Fukuoka found on the northwest coast facing the Japan Sea. The NE coast plunges into the sea apart from a few big bays that hit grey sand shingle beaches and usually close-out. The big rivermouths begin at Nobeoka then Hyuga and instantly the surf improves as long jetties hold sand and triangular bars are sculpted by the river flow. This theme runs through the Miyazaki zone, then continues around the tip of the island and onto the typhoon dependant peaks of Oniguchi, which sits under the shadow of the majestic volcanic cone Mt Kaimondake. This SW-facing coast suffers from a very small, typhoon dependant swell window, since Tanegashima and Okinawa block anything from the SE-S respectively. Those looking for adventure should try Amami Oshima, a large island between the two zones that holds at least a half dozen spots sprinkled about and few locals to share the rivermouths and reefs with.

The Sea of Japan coastline has enough surf potential to fill its own chapter. **Honshu** west coast breaks start in the far north in Aomori, Akita and Yamagata prefectures but its damn freezing. Ikarashi Cospo beach in Niigata is popular and the exposed Noto Peninsula of Ishikawa Prefecture should pick up maximum swell at rivermouth spots like Machino or Shibagaki and the jetties of Tokumitsu or Ataka near the city of Komatsu. Kyoto surfers make the drive to the west coast spots of the **Kansai** region when there's a storm to kick up the surf and gravitate towards Hamazume where sand builds up between the sea defences and there are "onsen" hot springs nearby to help thaw out. The **Chugoku** region represents the most westerly chance for Sea of Japan waves on the main island of Honshu. Tottori is a popular spot for tourists and surfers alike, where proper sandbars are fed by Japan's only mini-desert/sand dunes. Neighbouring Ishiwaki holds similar higher quality waves and this coastline receives anything from W around to NE swells, which often march in during winter. Scope out Kirara, Kokofu and the long north-facing beach at Odaohama comes complete with camping and a challenging right reef at Kohama. Even offshore islands like Tsunoshima have waves, leading down to the Kyu Shu zone of Fukuoka where shorter fetch and narrower swell window are offset by uncrowded quality and relatively warm water.

WWW.URITOURS.COM

North Korea

**North Korea** occupies the west coast of the Sea of Japan and despite the political situation in the world's most isolated country, a surf travel company has started guiding people around a few spots. Most surfing takes place around the Ma Jon Hotel beach and reefbreaks in the south central region with something in both small and big swells arriving from NE-SE directions. **South Korea** is far more accessible and picks up NE swells out of the Sea of Japan head-on, which suggests more waves in the cold winter, but typhoon season welcomes waves from SSE to SSW for the east and south-facing coasts. Best spot on the NE coast is right on the 38th Parallel which used to denote the North/South border before the war. Now it's a consistent, swell-pulling beachbreak with surf shop and some crowds on small summer weekends. Most of the east coast is empty through winter down to Busan, where a clutch of breaks around Haeundae help support the fast growing scene of surf schools, shops, shapers and a large local longboard contingent. The west coast in the Yellow Sea is pretty uninspiring windchop and on the rare occasions when swell comes up from the south the multitude of steep islets filter out swell. Try the Anmyeon-do resort beaches SW of Seoul if desperate. The south coast is also a maze of volcanic islands so just make the jump out to Jeju Do where there is plenty more surf.

U-SKE

Shonan Bay

Taiwan West Coast

## EAST AND SOUTH CHINA SEAS

Surfing is growing rapidly in **China** and it has been targeted as the next big market for the big surf brands to move into, as local governments inject cash into the tourism infrastructure. The islands of Taiwan and Hainan clearly represent the best bet for getting a wave in China, receiving the largest, most reliable surf and are both venues for top tier international contests.

Meanwhile, the extensive mainland coast receives swell from the Yellow Sea, East China Sea and South China Sea, where less than 500 surfers share around 10,000km of exposed beaches and reefs and amazingly, most of it is still unexplored. Winter NE swells in the 2-6ft range, are nearly constant from November to April, but summer flat spells can be long, tide range is huge (up to 7m) and the coast is often industrialised and polluted, with great amounts of plastic waste littering the shores. Getting around is also challenging with all communication in Mandarin only, as very few speak any English. Foreigners are not allowed to rent cars in China, unless they have a local license and boards are not accepted on most trains and buses. Without a Chinese friend or a professional driver managing hectic traffic, beach access and complicated weather forecasts, getting to the spots is near impossible. Northern water temperatures drop drastically in wintertime, bottoming out at 4ºC in Qingdao, the northern city of Shandong province. Qingdao's buildings and breweries exhibit its German colonial past and a group of about 30 locals enjoy the shifty sandbanks of Shilaoren Beach, a south-facing bay extracting the best from typhoon action and southerly windswells. Summer is hugely popular with swimmers and beach goers becoming a hazard, both here and down the coast at Golden Sands Beach, which picks up NE swell. The Zhejiang coast becomes shallow, marshy and muddy down to the 100km wide Hangzhou Bay, home to the mega-cities of Shanghai, Hangzhou and Ningbo. As the bay compresses the 8.93m tides, the world's biggest tidal bore appears on the Qiantang River, surging up to 4m high and producing rides up to 90mins. Known as the "Silver Dragon", it is the home of the yearly RedBull Shootout, but with many spectators lives lost every year, access is strictly forbidden with heavy fines imposed on those caught entering the water. Outside the bay, the Zhoushan archipelago offers a choice of low quality N and S-facing polluted beachbreak on the island of Shengsi or cleaner summer peaks on Zhujia Island. Heading south the unexplored coast is directly exposed to Pacific E swell, down to the consistent sand and rock setup of Airport Lefts, where there's some protection from the E and NE wind. Haitan or Pingtan Island is China's 5th biggest and marks the beginning of the South China Sea. NE-E swells hit a number of expert reefbreaks around Junshan village and the South Bay beside Pingtan's main sandy beach has high tide quality rides. Fujian Province is "terra incognita" boasting hundreds of kilometres of promising, untapped coast behind Taiwan. Wujiao Bay, on Dongshan Island also has good exposure to S and NE swell offering punchy beachbreak by the jetty and more windy, exposed beaches at Jinluan and Maluan where the kiters go. Another 200kms of SE-facing beachbreaks leads to the subtropical Hong Kong & Guangdong zone.

The epicenter of surfing in **Vietnam** is China Beach, a long, sandy beach that stretches 30 kilometres south from Da Nang. Further north the surf diminishes as Hainan blocks the predominant NE swell, but the central coast has lots of E-facing coast exposed to both monsoonal and typhoon swells. While typhoons can bring death and destruction to this region, they are also responsible for producing clean, four to five foot peaks, up and down the coast. Nah Trang gets it share of swell at the beginner-friendly beaches of Bai Dai where rentals and lessons are available. Nah Trang itself is usually just a shoredump, but just north of town at Hon Chong, there is a reefbreak that makes the most of stronger swells, despite losing wave height due to its sheltered position. Between Da Nang and Nah Trang, any number of unsurfed beaches would receive the same swell, but are off the usual backpacker trail and are rarely visited. Check Dung Quat's rocky peninsulas that may provide a sheltered left reef in big seas and other rock-based waves. Further south the beaches at Tuy Hoa and Tuy Hiep are proper swell magnets and guaranteed empty. The southern coast closest to the capital Ho Chi Minh City faces a little SE so doesn't receive the monsoon NE as readily as the central coast. The main surf spots to check out are Mui Ne, Ham Tien, Phan Thiet and closest to the city Vung Tau. Don't expect much in the way of shape or power unless a typhoon tracks from the SE.

Thanks to its protrusion into the NE swell chain, Eastern Peninsular **Malaysia** counts itself lucky to get four months rideable surf. Offshore islands filter the swell too much down south towards Singapore and in fact the Malaysian states on Borneo have a more favourable exposure, especially in the far north at beach and reefbreaks on the tip of Sabah at Tanjung Simpang Mengayau. More below-average waves at any number of beaches down the coast through Belud, and onto the Nexus resort sands around Kota Kinabalu.

Check the numerous T-groynes at Penanjong in **Brunei** which may hold the sand in storms, otherwise it's deadly straight sand all the way to Kuala Belait and the rivermouth jetty. Sarawak continues with minuscule mush on featureless beaches down to the many river deltas where the Benak river bore guarantees waves on 6m+ tides. West of Kuching picks up any N windswell at Pandan and Sematan.

## PHILIPPINE SEA

A glance at a map of the 7,107 islands of the **Philippines** could leave you feeling dizzy over the apparent possibilities this country offers to surfers. Drawing parallels to Indonesia, the quality of the reefs is similar, the climate much the same and the beaches as beautiful. It differs only in swell consistency, which is seasonally reliant on the monsoons and typhoons. **Luzon** is the birthplace of surfing in the Philippines, with US servicemen on the west coast, and actors dressed as servicemen at Baler on the east coast, where the famous surf scene from *Apocalypse Now* was shot. The film crew left their boards and the locals took to the water, creating a little surf scene and the first national champion. South of the Northwest Luzon zone, fringing reefs offer empty possibilities around Bolinao, before the coast angles back to Manilla Bay and requires rare SW-NW swell as opposed to the regular NE pattern. This is Zambales Province, which is fairly close to Manila on Luzon's west coast with sandy beachbreaks stretching for miles between major rivermouths at Botolah, San Felipe and Pundaquit, plus Capone Island has quality reef and beachbreaks, attracting city surfers in typhoon or SW-NW swells. There is more surf to sniff out in Illocos Norte, where the north coast of Luzon picks up NE swell head-on, but it is the reefbreaks around the resorts at Pagapud (Blue Lagoon) that occasionally go off in typhoon swell and SW winds. Winter onshores bring plenty of messed up swell which can wrap around the west coast at places like Saud beach. There's 90kms of grey sand beach fringing the northern part of Cagayan province. Check the jetty at Aparri and the reefs of Gonzaga. The NE coast of Cagayan and Isabela is a virtual wilderness, with the rough coastal road often washed out, but surf possibilities are high thanks to direct NE swell exposure,

Jelly Beans, Samar, Philippines

## SWELL FORECASTING

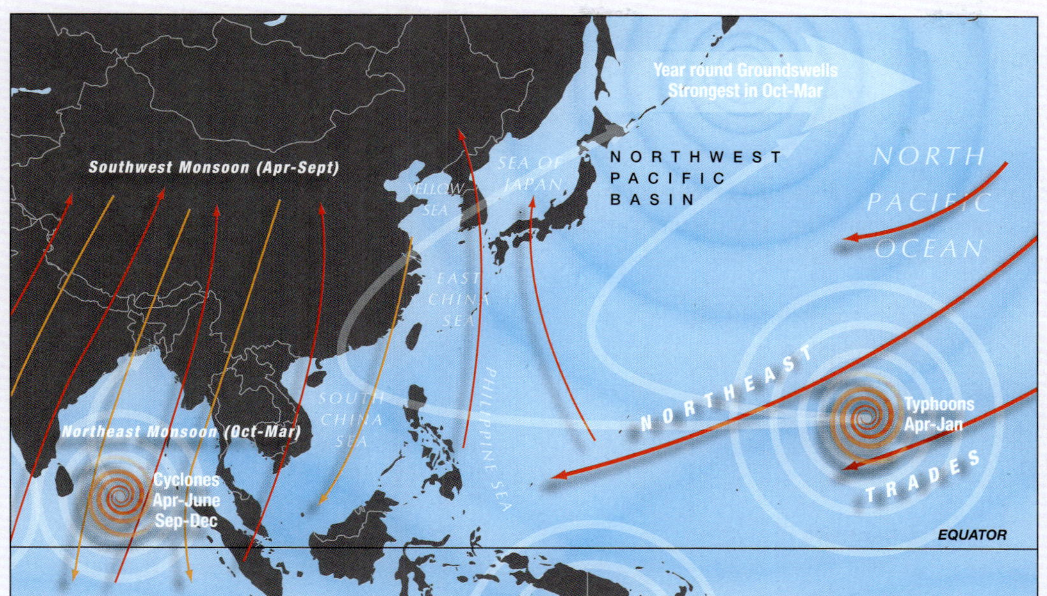


### EAST AND SOUTH CHINA SEAS

The NE monsoon plies the corridors of both the East China Sea and the South China Sea from November to March producing fairly reliable windswell and rideable waves in Taiwan, China, Vietnam, Malaysia and West Luzon. This is the primary surf season, bringing waist to headhigh windswell and occasional groundswell from NE-E slipping through the Luzon Strait. From May to mid-September the SW monsoon blows up and pretty much ends the surf season unless it's waisthigh onshore you are looking for. Typhoons on a rarer W-SW trajectory will bring in summer or autumn surf for Malaysia, Hainan and Hong Kong but are fleeting and difficult to predict. Taiwan, The Ryu Kyu islands, Jeju Do and the Chinese Mainland have better exposure from the typhoons that take the more common northwards arc. The surface currents follow the monsoon winds with a NE to SW flow and a anticlockwise gyre in winter switching to a SW to NE flowing current from April to Sept. Tidal range is 2m for the south but a massive 8m off the coast of China in the East.

### NORTHWEST PACIFIC BASIN

Asia's Pacific side experiences reliable, seasonal monsoon driven windswells and unpredictable, powerful typhoons. The NE monsoon blows hard and relentlessly through the winter months bringing constant swell and following wind for the bulk of the region. Short-lived NE groundswell is also sent down off the back of the big lows that spin across the North Pacific, mainly affecting Honshu in Japan and the more NE exposed parts of the Philippines. The monsoon wind reversal sees SW winds arrive in spring, often turning SE, bringing much rain in early summer to Japan. The warm North Equatorial Current hits the Philippines, then bends north into the Kuroshio Current, before the Kamchatka and Oyashio currents bring icy water down from the Aleutians and Bering Sea for northern Japan. The tidal range is minimal and mostly under 2m.

### THE SEA OF JAPAN

The vagaries of enclosed-sea swell production limit the amount of surfable days to a fraction of the year, usually in the depths of winter. Every now and then a summer or autumn storm will kick up fleeting windswell without the need for extreme full rubber, but you have to be lucky. SE-SW arrives off the back of summer typhoons, heading towards Russia, northern Japan, the Kuril Islands and finally Kamchatka, while rare W-N winds can produce for Southern Japan. NE swells dominate throughout winter, running parallel to Japan but hitting South Korea's east coast head-on, making for consistent surf from Nov-March. The warm Tsushima current flows northward up the west coast of Japan and on to thaw out Sakhalin in summer but the temps will hit zero degrees celsius in winter and the northern quarter freezes for 3-4 months. Micro-tidal range similar to the Mediterranean.

### PHILIPPINE SEA

The Philippine Sea holds the record for tropical storms, spinning up the biggest, fastest and highest number of typhoons every year. Their tracks cover a vast area of ocean so a lot of countries are in the firing line. Typhoons form in the open ocean over Melanesia and head due west towards the Philippines, then usually start on an arc northwards in the direction of Japan. It is this arc that produces N-E swell for the Philippines and Pacific Indonesia and SE-SW swells for Taiwan, China, Korea, Japan and beyond. June – Sept will be the heart of the typhoon season, which extends for 10 months (Apr – Jan), appreciably longer than any other region. The Philippine Sea is also fully affected by the NE monsoon and Northwest Pacific Basin NE groundswell during the winter months, plus picks up any residual and local swell in the water during the flatter summer months.

while hopefully finding protection from the following wind. **Baler Bay** is just a small slice of the exposed coast of Aurora Province where there are further waves at Diarabasin and Dingalan. The large islands off Quezon province filter much of the swell from the north and east, so by default should have some potential along the north-facing reefs. Camarines Norte is popular with Manilla weekend warriors who flock to Bagasbas Beach to learn while the Mercedes rivermouth near Daet provides a more challenging righthander over reef. Camarines Sur sees shallower offshore waters cut potential and it is shielded to the east by **Catanduanes**, where the regal rights of Majestics are awaited by patient barrel hunters.

**Eastern Samar** represents a real discovery zone with some surfers around Borongan and Calicoan Island, but there are plenty of other waves to search for. The Balicuatro Islands of Northern Samar are hard to get around without a boat and accommodation close to the waves is lacking, but amongst the unusual rock formations on Biri there are rights at Geron, Magasang and if you spot a perfect barrel, pinch yourself because you are not dreaming. On the north-facing coastline of Samar, Tamburusan Beach at Catarman is a palm fringed, sandy beach, surfable with southerly or westerly breezes wafting in from the San Bernardino Strait. Further east, Ojay Beach in Laoang is a similar inconsistent and soft beachbreak, but check the rights off Cahayagan Island. Relaxing beachbreaks can be found at Bato and somewhere south of Llorente and north of Calicoan is Jelly Beans, a long hollow left, breaking over a flat shelf of Philippine reef. For those looking to ride bigger, powerful waves, take a boat from Guiuan on a long journey out to Suluan Island and into the jaws of Jurassic Point.

Beyond the dreamy Cloud 9 peaks on **Siargao**, it's worth remembering the backside of the island accepts N-NE swells and offers E wind protection at remote reefs like Tangbo, Rizal, Dahican Island and the fringes of the Yohoho islands. The Bucas Grande islands have waves in stronger swells. Check Socorro and head south. A myriad of potential exists on small offshore islands and major landmasses alike, throughout Surigao Del Sur and Davao on Mindanao's southeastern coast. **Northern Mindanao** holds some serious peelers on rocky shelves and fringing reefs, plus the enigmatic Doot Poktoy, a rare rivermouth right that often attracts Mundaka comparisons. South of this zone is sand-bottom action for local surfers at Tandag, Tago and Dahican Beach. Finally, the long, thin flank of Palawan does get some small South China Sea N swell action with light offshore winds for 2-4 months (Nov-Feb) of the year. North is better so check around El Nido where spots like Mike's Point, Calaan, Nacpan and Duli are ridden by a few locals and visitors lucky enough to score a headhigh swell.

**North Maluku** and **West Papua** are the only regions of Indonesia that draw in Pacific juice and the islands of Morotai and Halmahera are stacked with waves. The N-E swell penetrates some of the deep bays like Kao and Buli, where some small islands bend lefts and rights around each reefy tip. Fast, throaty barrels can also be found on the east-facing coast around Dorosago and waves have been surfed on small islands all the way down to dive hot spot, Raja Ampat and Waigeo. The massive

JS CALLAHAN SURFEXPLORE

West Papua, Indonesia

Birds Head Peninsula is extremely tough access by road, so stay close to the cities of Sorong or Manokwari, where a left reef peels into Pantai Bakaro. Biak has a north coast road running from Wapur to Korem overlooking many possibilities along the coastal reef platform. Look for a left near the church at Warsa or find a boat out of Biak to the maze of reefs toward the east. Exploratory trips to Papua have gleaned huge potential but swell consistency is the problem and the short surf season coincides with the wet season. This means muddy rivermouths but the plethora of offshore islands offer reef curves with multiple aspects, so access to a decent boat is crucial. Kota Sarmi is a good base with waves around the harbour and Wakte Island has an attractive right reef set-up that's offshore in N winds. The regions capital Jayapura also has some mellow beachbreaks inside the bay at Pasir Hitam (Black Sand), Holtenkang and Skouw.

# Chiba, Honshu JAPAN

The east coast of Japan's main island Honshu is exposed to late summer typhoon swells, or short lived NE groundswells. Although the long tradition of fishing has had a negative influence on surfing, with harbours and tetrapods built in many of the areas that catch the best swells, surfing is now a well-established sport. The most popular surf zone for Tokyo-based surfers is the Chiba Peninsula, a mere 30 minute drive from the city.

+ THE FOUR M REEFBREAKS
+ WARM SUMMER CONDITIONS
+ TYPHOON SWELLS
+ UNIQUE CULTURE

- SUMMER FLAT SPELLS
- TOLL ROADS AND PARKING
- CROWDED WEEKENDS
- EXPENSIVE

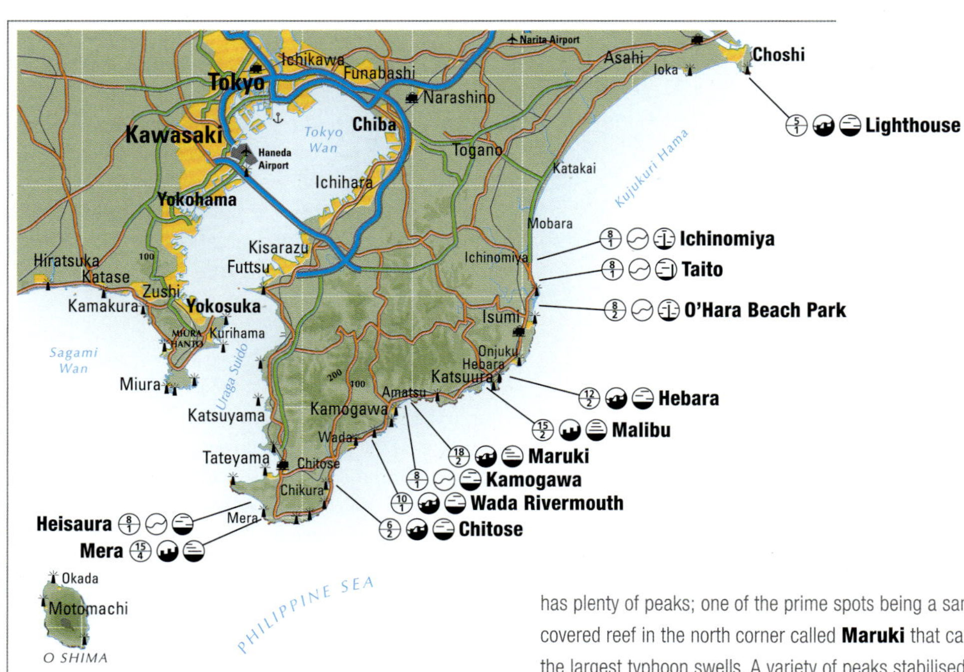

TAKAHIRO TSUCHIYA

Maruki

Near the Inubosaki **Lighthouse** at Choshi are a couple of wind and swell-exposed rock strewn bays with unremarkable waves. Below the south-facing cliffs are some more powerful, sand covered reefs that catch any S swells. From Iioka to Katakai, coastal defences and a lack of power makes it home to many surf schools. At **Ichinomiya**, T-shaped breakwaters create a diverse set of powerful beachbreaks that suck in E swell and hold some size. The same applies just south at Torami and 2020 Olympic venue **Shidashita**, which are at the heart of Japanese surf culture thanks to consistent waves at all sizes and reliable sandbars. **Taito** is a longboard-friendly right, peeling off the harbour breakwall. This whole stretch gets ultra-crowded, so expect drop-ins and poor water quality. From Izumi to **O'Hara Beach** Park there are less-crowded options in the gaps between the tetrapods. Crowded because they're consistent, Onjuku and **Hebara** hold some punchy, barrelling, reef/beach combos. **Malibu** is a Chiba typhoon classic; a right reefbreak that can hold triple overhead in a south-facing bay. A submarine canyon funnels the swell into **Kamogawa**, which has plenty of peaks; one of the prime spots being a sand-covered reef in the north corner called **Maruki** that can handle the largest typhoon swells. A variety of peaks stabilised by offshore tetrapods stertch southwards. Crowded **Wada** holds a clutch of consistent reefs that work well on various swell directions. More peaks at **Chitose** and Chikura – generally a longboard spot with mellow slides in waist to headhigh conditions. A rare bird, **Mera** is a serious left barrel with a small swell-window. Out on the end of the peninsula, 5km long **Heisaura** is a low tide beachbreak working in a S swell and N wind. To escape the crowds, take the ferry over to the quiet, mellow Izu islands and surf some powerful barreling waves on Nii-jima at Habushiura and Secrets.

The best swells originate from either typhoons to the S or lows to the NE. With an average of 15-30 swells per season (June-Nov), typhoons can send 2-20ft SE swells, which usually last two or three days, between the many flat spells of summer. Wintertime NE groundswells get good for hardy, experienced surfers. Winds blow from a NW direction in winter (cold and dry) whilst SE winds in high summer bring rain. In late summer the northerly kicks back in and typhoons continue to pump in swells. Tidal range doesn't exceed 2m but affects some spots.

## TRAVEL INFORMATION

**Weather** – Japan has sticky summers and bitterly cold winters as gusty NW winds come straight from Siberia adding to the wind-chill. Spring (April-May) is the best time with clear skies and pleasant temps. Summer is typhoon season, hot with heavy showers, but late summer is a good time for surf. The autumn gets cold very quickly. Despite freezing winter temps the water doesn't get that cold. Oct-May requires up to a 4/3 steamer and June-Sept a springsuit.

**Lodging and Food** – Splash Guest House on Hebara Beach (fr $50/n) are fully set up with surf & Sup rentals, school & guides. The Minshukus, (family run, basic lodging) around Katsuura are the cheapest places to stay – about ±$100/dble including breakfast. Local cuisine is tasty and healthy.

**Nature and Culture** – Tokyo is a city buzzing with life. Visit the central Ginza area for its shopping, Shinkuju for night-time entertainment or Akihabara for electronic goods. The perfect volcanic cone of Mt. Fuji is well worth a visit.

**Hazards and Hassles** – Locals are cool towards 'Gaijin' (foreigners). Avoid surfing on Sundays the beaches get engulfed by waveriders. Roads and traffic can be severe.

**Handy Hints** – In Tokyo, the Ochanomizu area has a whole street of shops dedicated to surf goods and culture. Murasaki Sports and Oshmans are nationwide chains that stock surf gear but at $900 a board, they are way overpriced. Crime rates are low, mutual respect is something that extends to all parts of daily life, including in the waves - there can be a hundred people on each peak, but no aggressive localism or jockeying for waves. Longboarding is becoming very popular.

| STATISTICS | | J F | M A | M J | J A | S O | N D |
|---|---|---|---|---|---|---|---|
| SWELL | Direction | | | | | | |
| | Size (ft) | 3-4 | 2-3 | 2 | 3-4 | 4 | 4 |
| WIND | Direction | | | | | | |
| | Force | F4-F5 | F4-F5 | F4 | F3-F4 | F4 | F4 |
| WATER | Wetsuit | | | | | | |
| | Temp/°C | 13 | 15 | 18 | 21 | 19 | 17 |
| WEATHER | Rainfall/mm | 67 | 117 | 155 | 145 | 215 | 80 |
| | days/mth | 7 | 11 | 12 | 11 | 13 | 6 |
| | Min temp/°C | -2 | 5 | 15 | 21 | 16 | 3 |
| | Max temp/°C | 9 | 15 | 23 | 29 | 24 | 14 |

TAKAHIRO TSUCHIYA

Taito and Shidashita

# Shikoku JAPAN

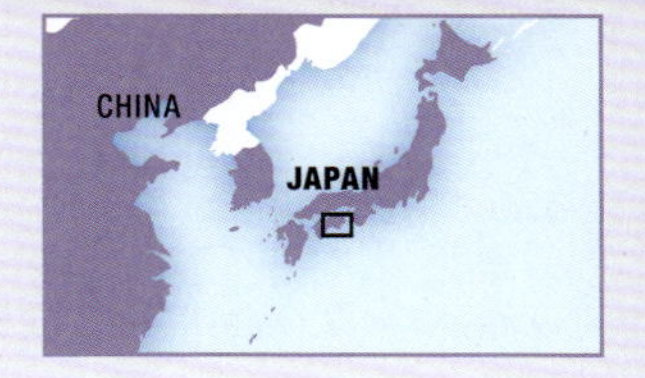


For those who have enough money and can handle the flat spells, Japan can be a rewarding surf destination. Amongst the best places in the country to head for is Shikoku, Japan's fourth largest island. The exposed SE-facing coastline has abundant rainfall that feeds numerous rivers. When these rivers spill into the sea, they help to form decent sandbanks for the typhoon generated swells to break on, resulting in some grinding righthand rivermouth breaks.

- \+ WORLD-CLASS RIVERMOUTH WAVES
- \+ WARM WATER IN THE SURF SEASON
- \+ LAID-BACK AMBIENCE
- \+ AMAZING CULTURAL EXPERIENCE

- – INCONSISTENT SWELLS
- – FLAT WINTERS
- – RELATIVELY WET CLIMATE
- – VERY HIGH LIVING COSTS

TAKAHIRO TSUCHIYA

Kaifu River

## TRAVEL INFORMATION

**Weather** – Shikoku winters are cold followed by hot, sticky summers, but it's not as extreme as the Chiba area further north. Spring and summer on the south coast are extremely wet; autumn sees a much drier weather pattern. Good news, as this is also the prime swell season. The water never gets very cold and during the autumn surf season it is at its warmest, never requiring more than a springsuit. Bear in mind that some typhoons hit the islands in the south of Japan.

**Lodging and Food** – Japan is ultra-expensive so avoid Osaka and the big cities. Hostels are about the cheapest accommodation (fr $25/n for a dorm bed!). Minshukus are family guesthouses, and are a much better option, although more expensive at ±$65/dble. The local food is delicious, sushi and rice will cost about $15 a meal.

**Nature and Culture** – There are spectacular views from the Seto-Ohashi Bridge outside of Osaka. There is a road in this area used by Buddhist pilgrims, along which are 88 temples. The Yosakoi Festival in Kochi in mid-Aug is unmissable.

**Hazards and Hassles** – Seismic activity is the highest in the world, but it's not really something to worry about. The largest typhoon swells can get a bit intimidating. Local surfers are supercool to foreigners (Gaijin) but despite this it's worth avoiding the popular spots and ridiculous crowds on Sundays.

**Handy Hints** – A growing surf industry is forming in this area and there are plenty of surf shops and shapers but gear is very expensive. Credit cards are accepted in major cities and larger outlets, but cash is the only option for many visitor attractions and small shops. Many ATMs in Japan do not accept cards issued outside of Japan (Post Offices and 7-Eleven stores do).

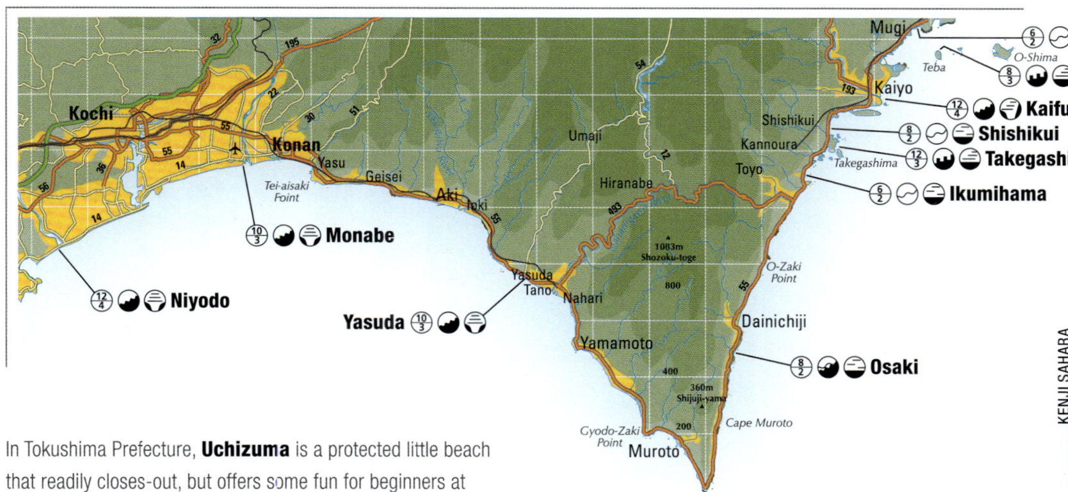


In Tokushima Prefecture, **Uchizuma** is a protected little beach that readily closes-out, but offers some fun for beginners at lower tides. A righthander skirts the rocks outside the harbour of **Teba** Shima island. Needs SE swell to wrap in properly and is rarely ridden, despite some quality. **Kaifu River** is one of the best quality rivermouth waves in Japan. It needs a moderate SE-S swell and any W wind to begin throwing up some seriously hollow rights for the big crowds that appear on the few days a season that it works. There's a short left off the peak and the neighbouring beach gets good too. Definitely for experienced surfers only as the rips are heavy, boulders are shallow and the tetrapods are close. **Shishikui** is a typical city beachbreak, with various peaks to choose from breaking outside the longshore seawalls. Sucks in any E-S swell and low tide is always better. **Takegashima** only breaks on higher tide when the nasty rocks are covered between the cliffs and the harbour wall. Sucks hard at take-off with boils and exposed rocks to avoid before the long walls to the harbour channel. **Ikumihama Beach** is very popular with surfers from Osaka, who use the overnight ferry from Nanko to surf the mellow waves. If a S swell hits, **Osaki** will have consistent peaky lines breaking over sand and boulders. Rounding Cape Muroto leads to a massive south-facing bay that is fed by many rivers from the mountainous interior. SW-facing towns like Nahari, **Yasuda**, Ioki and Aki all have rare rivermouth peaks that slumber until typhoons hit. The major one at **Monabe** gets epic a few times a year, provided the ever-shifting sandbar and boulders are in shape. Faces more due S and needs higher tides to be good. **Niyodo** is even better and on the rare good days, multiple barrel sections will implode over the cobble anchored sandbars. Rainfall often dictates the state of the sand and how many typhoons blow through the ESE-SSW window. It is a Japanese classic that gets heavily zooed on small days and weekends, when some localism is to be expected. On big days only the best surfers will handle the power and the rips.

The bulk of the swell comes from typhoons, bringing SE-SW swells between July-Nov. Expect many flat days and lots of 1-2ft wind chop. Cold, dry, offshore winds blow from the N in the winter, before shifting SE in the summer, bringing heavy rain. It rarely gets very windy, except when a passing low pressure system or a typhoon hits land. Tidal range doesn't exceed 2m but affects the rivermouth breaks a lot. Further south there are excellent beachbreaks around Shimanto where the mountainous coastal vistas and lower crowds make for a rewarding surf experience.

KENJI SAHARA

Niyodo

| STATISTICS | | J F | M A | M J | J A | S O | N D |
|---|---|---|---|---|---|---|---|
| SWELL | Direction | | | | | | |
| | Size (ft) | 1-2 | 1-2 | 2 | 3-4 | 4 | 4 |
| WIND | Direction | | | | | | |
| | Force | F4 | F4 | F3-F4 | F3 | F4 | F4 |
| WATER | Wetsuit | | | | | | |
| | Temp/°C | 17 | 16 | 22 | 27 | 25 | 20 |
| WEATHER | Rainfall/mm | 95 | 190 | 352 | 282 | 267 | 85 |
| | days/mth | 10 | 13 | 15 | 12 | 9 | 7 |
| | Min temp/°C | 3 | 8 | 16 | 23 | 18 | 6 |
| | Max temp/°C | 12 | 18 | 25 | 30 | 26 | 16 |

# Fukuoka, Kyushu JAPAN

**Fukuoka is situated on the northwest coast of Kyushu, Japan's westernmost island. Its coastline faces the Genkai Sea, a small body of water at the southwest tip of the Sea of Japan. Picking up northerly swells coming out of the Sea of Japan, this narrow swell window is offset by warm water and low crowds, compared to the surf zones further north and offers visitors a real taste of the Japanese surf experience.**

- + SOME QUALITY SPOTS
- + UNCROWDED SURF FOR JAPAN
- + PACIFIC COAST PROXIMITY
- + RELATIVELY WARM IN WINTER

- – NARROW SWELL WINDOW
- – COLD WINTER AIR TEMPS
- – INCONSISTENT GENKAI SEA
- – EXPENSIVE LOCAL COSTS

TAKAHIRO TSUCHIYA

Nishinoura

During winter when other nearby breaks are closing-out, **Waita** beachbreak can be a good, mellow option. Near the lighthouse at Tominohana is **Iwaya**, a fun contest site beachbreak with all facilities. **Same** (Sa-may) will be bigger and especially on NE swells, but is still suitable for beginners. Past Onga River is a shallow weak beachbreak at the **Shioirigawakakou** rivermouth, which breaks cleanly even on small swells from the W-NE. SW winds groom weak rights at **Hatsugyokou**, unless it is pumping, when the left offers a longer ride with backwash on full tide. One of Fukuoka's premier spots is **Kanezaki**, which offers tubing lefts and rights at each end of the beach. Consistent in winter and usually bigger than other breaks. **Tsurigawakakou** rivermouth is usually smaller, but has decent barrels when the sandbanks align. Next to Tougou Park and Kitakyushu Hospital, inconsistent **Tsuyazaki** right pointbreak is a quality wave, with a tube on take-off, then a playful wall up to 100m long. **Shingu** fishing port is a rivermouth where a long, fun lefthander breaks beside a seawall. Between the concrete tetra blocks, there's a shifting right and left peak. The left is usually smaller, but much faster than the longer rights. A thriving surf scene and many surf shops makes **Mitoma** beachbreak crowded. When it's bigger, there are long rides for those that make it out the back. The main attraction on the island of **Shikanoshima** is the rocky eastside reefbreak where slow lefts gradually build up speed to form long walls. West of the swell protected city of Fukuoka is **Nishinoura** a rocky, lefthander which tubes and peels for a long way. North of the tall torii shrine gate, is the highly consistent **Mitamigaura** beachbreak often used for contests. Slow and fat when small, but powerful when it gets overhead. A useful current runs out on the right side of the beach. When it's big **Oguchi** Bay has quality long reef-bottomed rights next to the rocks, if you can make the steep take-off. Hazardous on low tide. When it's smaller there's a fun beachbreak with some power. **Keya** is the main surfing break in western Fukuoka, which can handle some size. It's consistent, the waves are powerful and the curve of the beach means more wind directions (NE-SW) are possibly offshore.

The best seasons for Fukuoka are autumn and winter (September to March). There can also be surf in summer if a typhoon deviates northwest from the usual northeast path.

TAKAHIRO TSUCHIYA

Shikanoshima

## TRAVEL INFORMATION

**Weather** – Bordered on three sides by mountains, Fukuoka has rainy winters with occasional, brief snowfalls although temps rarely drop below 0°C/32°F, while spring is warm and sunny. Summers are humid and fairly hot (August hits 32°C/90°F) with a 6 week rainy season in June and July. Autumn is mild and dry – often considered as the best season for tourism. The typhoon season runs between August and September. Use a 3/2mm fullsuit from November to April and a springy or boardshorts for the rest of the year.

**Lodging and Food** – Anything from cheap 'capsules' ($40-60/n) to 5-star hotels. Centrally located Khaosan Int'l Hostel in Fukuoka suits the budget traveller. There's a peaceful campsite on Nokonoshima island or near Keya and Iwaya breaks. Try mentaiko cod-roe (spicy fish eggs) or hakata ramen (salty, oily pork noodle soup). Eat out at the night stalls known as yatai, in the Tenjin and Nakagawa districts.

**Nature and Culture** – Visit Dazaifu, Kyushu's old capital: the grand Tenmangu Shrine and the nearby Zen temple contrast differences between Shinto and Buddhist styles. For modern attractions, check out Robosquare near Fukuoka Tower. Don't miss Japan's largest basalt cave, Keya Oto and Uminonakamichi Marine Park. Most mountains are a bit over 1000m high.

**Hazards and Hassles** – Beware of stinging jellyfish in the water in late summer and early autumn. Fukuoka surfers have a reputation for friendliness, but they can become territorial when the surf gets good so always remember to be respectful and wait your turn in the line-up.

**Handy Hints** – Plenty of surf shops around, but gear is expensive. Better bring your own standard thruster and something for mellow waves. Most of the road signs are in English, but if you don't speak any Japanese, you might have trouble finding your way.

| STATISTICS | | J F | M A | M J | J A | S O | N D |
|---|---|---|---|---|---|---|---|
| SWELL | Direction | | | | | | |
| | Size (ft) | 2-3 | 1 | 0-1 | 1-2 | 2 | 3 |
| WIND | Direction | | | | | | |
| | Force | F4 | F4 | F3-F4 | F3-F4 | F4 | F4 |
| WATER | Wetsuit | | | | | | |
| | Temp/°C | 15 | 16 | 21 | 26 | 24 | 19 |
| WEATHER | Rainfall/mm | 54 | 78 | 52 | 280 | 80 | 53 |
| | days/mth | 9 | 11 | 10 | 10 | 9 | 8 |
| | Min temp/°C | 5 | 9 | 18 | 24 | 20 | 8 |
| | Max temp/°C | 12 | 17 | 26 | 31 | 28 | 15 |

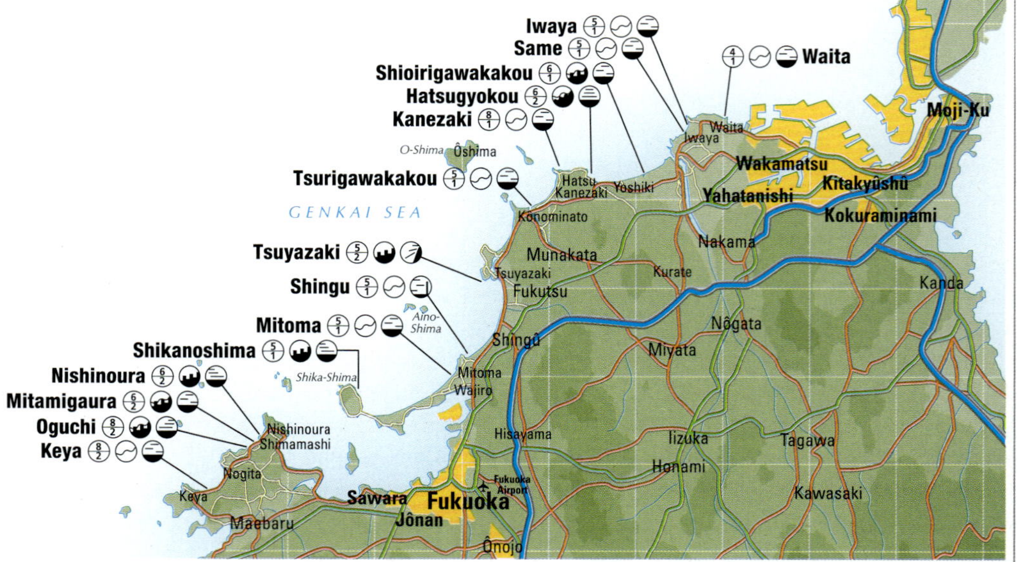

# Miyazaki, Kyushu JAPAN

**While not generally thought to be among Japan's top surfing destinations, Miyazaki's SE-facing shoreline is ideally located to catch typhoon swells. This coast is extensive and while the best waves do get crowded at times, there are lots of less accessible spots with good potential. Plenty of variety for surfers of all levels.**

+ WARM WATER TYPHOON SWELLS
+ LESS CROWDED POINTBREAKS
+ EXPLORATION POTENTIAL
+ JAPANESE CULTURE

– INCONSISTENT SWELLS
– COLD WINTER DAYS
– VERY EXPENSIVE
– COMMUNICATION HARD

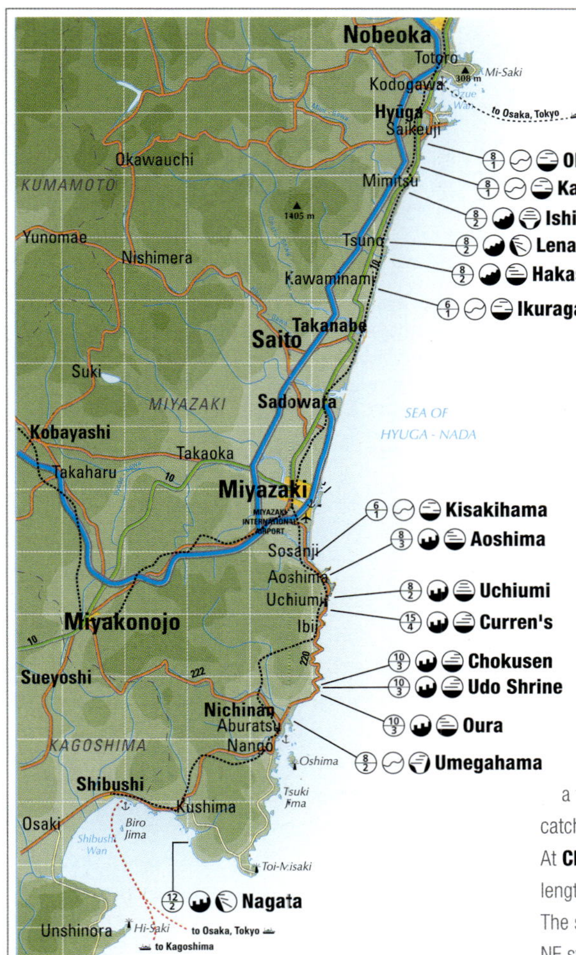


Much of this area's surfing is based around the reliable beachbreaks at **Okuragahama** or **Kanegahama**. Neither are particularly good but work on small swell with NW winds and have accommodation or camping to hand. On NE-E swells, **Ishinamigawa** (gawa means river) should have some hollow waves, spinning off the boulders around the rivermouth breakwall. **Lena** in Tsuno is a boulder pointbreak, breaking left for a long way near the rivermouth. Around the reef in front of the harbour past some other rideable peaks is **Hakashita**, another hollow left breaking over boulders when a solid E swell hits. On SE swells with NW wind check **Ikuragahama**'s fun but unchallenging beachbreak and many similar waves at rivermouths en route to Miyazaki. Miyazaki's main wave-riding area is Sosanji, where **Kisakihama** beach is plagued by intense crowds but localism is low, especially towards western surfers. **Aoshima** beachbreak is less consistent than Sosanji, but the lefthand reefbreak off the island that houses a beautiful Shinto temple can be long and workable when a solid E typhoon swell hits. It's a fairly predictable ride so gets crowded with longboarders looking to join the sections and ride a few hundred metres. **Uchiumi** is the start of the 50km long Nichinan coast, characterised by heavily striated reefs known as the Devils Washboard and many punchy waves. Uchiumi itself has rights and lefts depending on what the swell direction is. **Curren's**, named after Tom's epic ride on the long right reefbreak during 1991's classic conditions. It needs a typhoon to get the spot working, but paddling out and catching a wave requires plenty of experience and confidence. At **Chokusen**, the reef hugs a headland, giving it pointbreak length of ride with powerful walls and occasional cover-ups. The same goes for **Udo Shrine**, a nice-looking right peak on NE swells and S-W winds although crowded when it's classic. **Oura** is one those magic spots that can be perfect when everywhere else is messy, because the shallow lefts hold N winds. At **Umegahama** Rivermouth the high tide righthanders can be superb, pinwheeling over the groomed sandbars in SE swells. On the biggest SE typhoon swells, hit **Nagata** for a truly outstanding left pointbreak up to double-overhead.

Typhoons produce 4-6ft swells starting in July and climaxing in August-October. Occasional super-typhoons can deliver 12ft surf. They normally approach from the South China Sea before moving north usually accompanied by S winds. North Pacific lows as well as monsoonal NE winds produce some waves from November to February although good surf is rare despite dominant offshore winds. Winds often blow from the W-NE. Tidal range can reach 2.5m on spring tides and even more within deep bays, so get a tide table in a shop, and practice basic Japanese.

Chokusen

TAKAHIRO TSUCHIYA

## TRAVEL INFORMATION

**Weather** – Because of the warm Kuroshio Current, Kyushu experiences very different climate in winter and summer. Summers in Miyazaki are hot and humid with strong sunshine. Temps can exceed 30°C (86°F), even at night. May to August are really wet and prone to localised flooding. Autumn is warm and pleasant, the best time to visit unless a typhoon hits the coast (rare). Winter can be cold; but not often below freezing, snow is rare. Water feels tropical from July to October and doesn't drop much below 18°C (64°F) despite coldish winter days; take a light steamer and springsuit.

**Lodging and Food** – Most flats in the city are Japanese style: straw tatami mats on the floor, sliding shoji doors and a deep Ofuro (bathtub). A cheap Youth Hostel costs $50. A hotel like Kanko costs $90 (double). Seagaia Sheraton is $150 night (dble). Expect $20 for a meal at izakayas, udon, ramen and sushi shops.

**Nature and Culture** – Don't miss the Miyazaki shrine, Heiwadai Peace Park 37m tower built with stones collected from all over the world. Plenty of nightlife in Miyazaki. Seagaia Ocean Dome wave pool shut down in 2007.

**Hazards and Hassles** – Apart from getting lost due to communication problems, there is not much to fear. Crime is low to nil, locals will be very helpful with foreigners. Some spots are localised so show due respect. Typhoon swells can be intense and some shallow breaks can be dangerous.

**Handy Hints** – There are good supplies at the Blast surf shop in Huyga or PWS Surf Design but prices start from: longboard ($800), shortboard ($500), bodyboard ($230), springsuit ($200). Board rental is $25/ day. Most surf is in the 2-5ft range and shortboardable.

Uchiumi

ANDREW SHIELD

| STATISTICS | | J F | M A | M J | J A | S O | N D |
|---|---|---|---|---|---|---|---|
| SWELL | Direction | | | | | | |
| | Size (ft) | 2-3 | 2 | 1-2 | 2-3 | 3-4 | 3 |
| WIND | Direction | | | | | | |
| | Force | F4 | F4 | F3-F4 | F3 | F4 | F4 |
| WATER | Wetsuit | | | | | | |
| | Temp/°C | 18 | 17 | 22 | 27 | 25 | 21 |
| WEATHER | Rainfall/mm | 80 | 190 | 320 | 290 | 250 | 90 |
| | days/mth | 7 | 9 | 12 | 12 | 11 | 8 |
| | Min temp/°C | 3 | 10 | 18 | 23 | 18 | 7 |
| | Max temp/°C | 12 | 18 | 25 | 30 | 25 | 16 |

# Tanegashima JAPAN

Located 40km off the southern tip of Kyushu is one of the finest surf destinations in Japan. The island's long, narrow shape and good exposure to both Pacific and East China Sea swell, makes consistency high by Japanese standards. There's a variety of breaks to suit all levels and the water is warm all-year-round. Many surfers have moved to Tanegashima simply for the surf, which can get really good on both coasts, particularly when a typhoon roars past the region.

+ JAPAN'S MOST CONSISTENT SURF
+ WARM WATER YEAR-ROUND
+ QUALITY REEFS & RIVERMOUTHS
+ TWO SURFABLE COASTS

- RARELY WORLD-CLASS
- LIMITED ACCESS
- OFTEN ONSHORE
- SUPER-EXPENSIVE

## TRAVEL INFORMATION

**Weather** – Sub-tropical Tanegashima is relatively flat and dry, until summer brings considerable rainfall as tropical storms pass. The weather is hot and humid during summer but cold during winter and at night in autumn or spring. Boardshorts during summer, a shorty during spring and a 3/2mm fullsuit in the depths of winter.

**Lodging and Food** – Choose from western-style hotels or Japanese-style roll out futon mattresses in self-contained units to family-run minshuku guesthouses. Surf Villa Narai and Mauna Village cater specifically to surfers. Sushi, sashimi and sweet potatoes, are a prominent feature of the island's cuisine. Expect $15-20 for a meal.

**Nature and Culture** – Expect a relaxed island lifestyle offering a welcome escape from drab Japanese suburbia. Large limestone caves (Chikura and Matatenoiwaya) border the white sand beaches on the SE coast. Visit the Tanegashima Space Centre outside of launch times.

**Hazards and Hassles** – The best surf generally results from summer typhoon swells, however at such times access can be difficult with flights and ferries often cancelled. The line-up can get intense when the surf gets big and locals assert their priority, but you shouldn't have a problem if you are polite and friendly.

**Handy Hints** – It's possible to find some boards to rent but prices will be really high. There's a surprising array of ethnic cuisine, catering to the palates of well-travelled surfers. English knowledge is higher than the rest of Japan, but if you don't speak any Japanese, you might have a tough time communicating.

Injou

TAKAHIRO TSUCHIYA

Rock

TAKAHIRO TSUCHIYA

The furthest break north, **Chinbotsu**, breaks in front of a shipwreck and can hold some size on a NE-SE swell. Consistent and shallow, better when higher tides cover the boulders. **Kazamoto** rivermouth can be good when everywhere else is closed-out. Long rides over the boulder sand combo when it's overhead, incoming tide and offshore wind from the SW-W. **Azakou** rivermouth works on any E swell and can be uncrowded with fast take-offs and occasional tubes. Even when the surf is small beachbreaks like **Kanehama** are powerful enough to have fun waves with easy parking, showers and toilets. **Hungry** is a consistent, quality offshore reefbreak with great walls offering up to 200m long rides. It's usually a lefthander, but it also breaks right when it gets big. Best on a low tide and E swell. **Rock** is a right that breaks off Anjou Port, hollow when smaller, walling when bigger. The sheltered break of **Injou** is often glassy and handles wind from S round to NW. It's usually a long, righthand wall, but will break left too when it's big from the E. Beware of rocks on the shallow inside. **Nakayama** is a beautiful, long secluded beach with defined peaks, generally best on an incoming tide. **Toudaishita** is located next to the Space Centre and attracts a crowd to punchy low tide beach peaks and a soft left reef. Around the southernmost cape in front of the Iwasaki Hotel is **Hotel Mae**, a year-round beachbreak that gets crowded, because it is offshore in the regular NW-NE winds. A little further west is **Takezaki**, where A-frame peaks offer longer rides when the sandbanks are good and further reliable sandbars can be found next to the rivermouth groynes to the south. The west coast is less consistent and has fewer breaks than the east coast. **Yakutsu** is a fun beachbreak that will catch typhoon or winter SW-W swells as will **Nagahama**, where, at the northern end of the beach is a fickle, boulder and sand bottom rivermouth peak. The lefts in particular can offer long walls and even tubes. At **Sumiyoshi** port is a heavy righthand reefbreak, legendary for its large tubes and ability to handle the biggest W swells. Experts only as it's very shallow on the inside. **Yokino** is a picturesque stretch of white sand and reef just south of Nishinoomote, the main settlement of Tanegashima.

The Pacific east coast receives NE-SE swells all year-round, but the main surf season is from July to November when the summer typhoons can bring strong SE-SW swells. These swells can also hit the west coast of the island in the East China Sea in addition to winter low pressure systems bringing SW-W swells from December to February. Most of the surf is 2-6ft with occasional super-typhoon swells reaching 10-12ft. Tides are semi-diurnal with daily inequality, reaching 2.1m max on spring tides.

| STATISTICS | | J F | M A | M J | J A | S O | N D |
|---|---|---|---|---|---|---|---|
| SWELL | Direction | | | | | | |
| | Size (ft) | 2-3 | 2 | 1-2 | 2-3 | 3-4 | 3 |
| WIND | Direction | | | | | | |
| | Force | F4 | F4 | F3-F4 | F3-F4 | F4 | F4 |
| WATER | Wetsuit | | | | | | |
| | Temp/°C | 19 | 20 | 22 | 28 | 27 | 23 |
| WEATHER | Rainfall/mm | 124 | 158 | 173 | 392 | 60 | 83 |
| | days/mth | 10 | 12 | 13 | 11 | 11 | 9 |
| | Min temp/°C | 9 | 12 | 19 | 25 | 22 | 13 |
| | Max temp/°C | 15 | 19 | 25 | 30 | 26 | 20 |

# Okinawa JAPAN

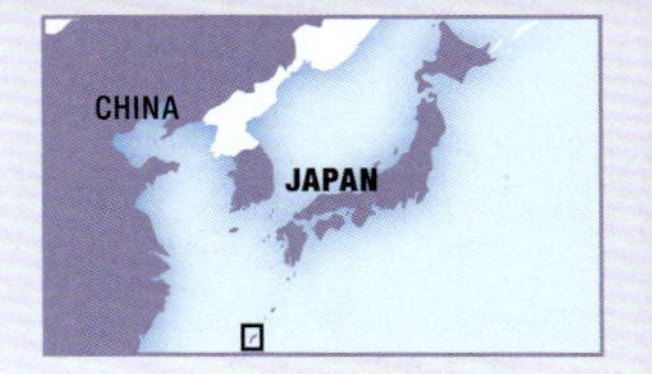


**Okinawa Prefecture consists of 161 islands, scattered over 1,000km, towards Taiwan. These Ryukyu Islands are now the most popular Japanese beach resort destination, thanks to its mild climate and fringing coral reefs. Sandwiched between the Pacific Ocean and the East China Sea, Okinawa picks up virtually any swell going. Most waves break at higher tides over very shallow shelves of reef and/or basaltic rock and crowds are heavy at the main spots, but most outer reefs and islands are still uncharted.**

+ EPIC TYPHOON SWELLS
+ SUBTROPICAL REEFBREAKS
+ SECRET SPOTS AND ISLANDS
+ ENGLISH SPEAKING JAPAN

- FLAT SPRING, MOSTLY WINDSWELL
- SHALLOW REEFS, NO BEACHES
- MAINLY HIGH TIDE SPOTS
- CROWDED PREMIERE SPOTS

The north side is less crowded at spots like **Ko-Chan**, aka Hedo Point, a summer right that is best with an E swell and S-SE winds. The take-off is steep, into a hollow barrel, followed by a 30m smooth, workable section. There are some easier peaks around the port of **Aha** that work on low tide but the lefts at Aha-yoko can be hollow and heavy. **Ikei** Island has some reefs facing the Big Time Hotel that enjoy a wide swell window and are fun at headhigh. If it gets bigger, the west side produces powerful rights. During rare E typhoon swells, nearby Tengan Pier will be firing and crowded. A 1h ferry trip from Baten Harbour is **Kudaka**, which has a very long left reefbreak with lots of sections but when they all link up, with the biggest NE swells, it's a beauty! **Suicide Cliffs** is the most consistent crowded summer spot with tricky cliff access when it's wet. Don't go if the swell is above 5ft and NW winds blow into the scattered, punchy peaks. Walk a lot further to **Castles**, which is just as consistent, much less crowded and offers a left point with two long sections. The west side winter breaks like **Aja** get crowded despite having to rely on the rare combination of N windswells and SE winds. Without doubt, **Sunabe Seawall** is the main surfing arena with half a dozen reefbreaks including Typhoon Breaks long lefts, Hotels sectiony rights, 5-Rocks short peaks, Californias, Hawaiians and **Bowls**. All prefer high tides to cover the reef - intermediates to pros depending on size. Further north, **Turtles** can produce massive lefts, among the biggest waves rideable on Okinawa but crazy currents have been known to drag unwary surfers to the seawall. Kamikaze bodyboarders head to scenic Cape Zanpa to ride one of the three breaks at **Mainside**. Consistent, tubey rights are common but the Outside reef is definitely the island's most radical wave! There's a left for the goofies as well. Check **Maeda** down the 300ft (100m) cliffs, for spinning lefts and rights plus good fishing and diving. Nago City's closest spot is **Buma**; two fun right and left reefbreaks of poor consistency.

Okinawa is usually flat in spring, before summer S swells are created by tropical disturbances and typhoons. August-October sees several monthly typhoons and occasional super-typhoons, which deliver up to 12ft surf on all corners of the island. The west coast gets three to four typhoons and the east about double that. The west coast gets choppy 3-8ft short period windswell from Nov-March, accompanied by NW winds that usually swing NE-E, which means clean surf, but size drops quickly. The east coast is reasonably consistent during the winter, but mostly onshore due to predominant NE winds. Tidal range can reach 7ft on spring tides: surf 2h before and after high tide for safety.

## TRAVEL INFORMATION

**Weather** – Okinawa enjoys Japan's only subtropical oceanic climate, with an annual mean temp of 22.5°C (73°F). N winds in winter and S winds in summer when temps exceed 30°C (86°F) but squalls can also occur. Okinawa is in 'Typhoon Alley' and has 7-8 per year. Winter temps rarely drop below 10°C (50°F). Water temps range from 20°C (68°F) to 30°C (86°F). In winter, the west side cools down so bring a springsuit. Then, warm water migrates north with the Kuroshio (the 'Black Current') bringing 6 months of boardshort surfing.

**Lodging and Food** – City hotels in Naha, Sunabe, Chatancho area on the west side and beach resorts in the central and northern parts are $50-60 a night. Island resorts like the Big AJ Resort on Ikei from $120. Facilities are very good. B&B costs from $45/n/dbl. Expect $15-20 for a meal, drink Awamori!

**Nature and Culture** – Beautiful white sand beaches, 40 golf courses, good diving or Togyu Bull fighting. See the Festival of Sun, Ocean & Joggers and Dragon boat races. It's the land of Karate and the Iriomote wildcat, a 'living fossil'.

**Hazards and Hassles** – Coral reefs are alive, sharp and shallow; avoid reef cuts and myriad urchins. Because of steep and hollow take-offs, many locals wear booties and helmets. There are shark sightings and shark attacks have occurred (Miyako 10/00). Very low crime so traffic and crowds will be the main problems.

**Handy Hints** – Expensive surf supplies at the Source Surf Shop or the Ryukyu Glass Factory; longboard ($800), shortboard ($500), bodyboard ($230), springsuit ($200). Rental is $25/day. 'Mensore' means welcome, most locals speak some English.

Sunabe

TAKAHIRO TSUCHIYA

Kudaka

JS CALLAHAN SURFEXPLORE

| STATISTICS | | J F | M A | M J | J A | S O | N D |
|---|---|---|---|---|---|---|---|
| SWELL | Direction | | | | | | |
| | Size (ft) | 3-4 | 2 | 1 | 2-3 | 3 | 3-4 |
| WIND | Direction | | | | | | |
| | Force | F4-F5 | F4 | F4 | F4 | F4 | F4-F5 |
| WATER | Wetsuit | | | | | | |
| | Temp/°C | 19 | 21 | 25 | 28 | 26 | 22 |
| WEATHER | Rainfall/mm | 130 | 165 | 290 | 240 | 160 | 130 |
| | days/mth | 4 | 5 | 6 | 9 | 7 | 5 |
| | Min temp/°C | 13 | 17 | 22 | 25 | 23 | 16 |
| | Max temp/°C | 18 | 22 | 27 | 30 | 28 | 22 |

# Taiwan

Surfing in Taiwan has a long history and surf arrives from a generous 225° swell window hitting all sides of the island. US soldiers were the first to ride the north coast beach of Jin Shan in 1965 and local pioneers like Mao Guh and his brothers ignored the government ban on access to the ocean, to take up surfing and open the first surf shop. With the lifting of Martial Law in 1987, surfing clubs popped up across the island and the R.O.C Surfing Association estimates that there could be 30,000 people riding waves across Taiwan. This is no surprise as the seasonal monsoons bring consistent waist to headhigh waves and a pair of boardshorts will do for all but the depths of winter, making Taiwan an increasingly alluring tropical destination.

+ SE TYPHOON & NE MONSOON
+ POWERFUL BEACHES & POINTS
+ CHEAP, EASY ACCESS FROM ASIA
+ BEAUTIFUL EAST COAST

- NO WORLD-CLASS BREAKS
- SUFFOCATING SUMMER HEAT
- DENSELY POPULATED TAIPEI
- DESTRUCTIVE TYPHOONS

ANDREW SHIELD

Cheng Gong

**Baishawan** is a north-facing, white sand beach with easy access from Taipei on the train/bus system. Often flat through summer, then cold and windy in winter it lacks power and shape, attracting kiteboarders, windsurfers and hang gliders. A much better bet is the high tide reefbreak called Wedding Plaza, a little further east. **Jin Shan** aka Green Bay or Golden Mountain is super popular in summer with huge crowds of clueless beginners hitting the various peaks between the north end left over boulders and the middle jetty. Also check Wan-Li. The eroding golden sands of **Fulong Beach** are split by the large Shuangshi rivermouth, which often floods the end of the access bridge. Weak, shifting peaks when small can transform into some decent walls at headhigh plus. Surfing closer to the harbour wall will cut the E wind. **Dashi**, aka Honeymoon Bay, benefits from clean water and some good, but unreliable sandbanks. Favours rights toward the southern end and is often the best option in the area. Gets crowded and a few rogue locals have been known to be aggressive to foreigners. Just north of Toucheng is **Wushi**, a decent black sand beach with south end jetties and some decent rights in winter NE'ers. Gets crowded because it has the best waves along the heavily armoured coast. Miles of sandy shoredump and rocky coast leads down to Hualien and 17km further south is **Gongs**, an inconsistent low to mid tide outside reef peak, that handles some size and N winds. Paddle from harbour jetty when big and plan exit away from shoreline tetrapods in front of peak. **Jici** is the sandiest beach in rocky Hualien, with average, often sloppy peaks in the southern corner. May pick up some power in a SE swell, but readily closes out. Serviced by Hualien Surf shop and there's a school for beginners. The coast road overlooks a stretch of rocky reefs down to and beyond **Fongbin**, a rivermouth beach that sucks in the swell and holds some good form, with powerful peaks hitting the ever-shifting black sandbars. Catching classic **Bashien Dong** lefts, at Eight Fairy Cave, will convince visitors of the power of Taiwanese surf. It's a long, boulder pointbreak that lines up great walling lefts on big NE swells, combined with NW winds. Usually soft shoulders outside and the odd short peeler on the rocky inside, before the heavy shorepound. The rivermouth can create intense rips and some rights to the north. South of Three Fairy Platform is **Cheng Gong** an epic left reef/point, breaking close to shore, but only on typhoon Category 4 or 5 from the E-SE or large NE. N or even NE winds are not a problem here. Sharp rocks and dead coral shelf,

ANDREW SHIELD

Donghe Rivermouth

## TRAVEL INFORMATION

**Weather** – Large differences in temperature and rainfall occur from north to south. Kenting has a warm tropical climate with rich and fertile vegetation. There is little change between seasons. Summer weather is cooled by the afternoon sea breeze and the cold wet winter NE winds that hit northern Taiwan are often blocked by the central mountains. A springsuit is enough for winter, even for the few weeks in Jan and Feb when air temps may dip to 10°C in morning offshores. Boardshorts from April to Nov and then some. Up north in winter may be as much as 6ºC cooler, requiring a steamer for a few months.

**Lodging and Food** – Dorm rooms for $10/night and $20-30 in hotels in off-season, but typhoon season is high summer season. Plenty of "Surf Houses" in Nanwan, backpacker style ($15). Motels and hotels price range is $45 to $120/p/n. surfingtaiwan.com do premium guided surf trips from Taitung county plus multi-activity and cultural tours (fr $750/p/dbl/6n). Similar deals from surftaiwan.com (fr $949/p/dbl/6n) with east and south coast options. Food is $3-10 per meal.

**Nature and Culture** – A steep central mountain range means the east coast is much less developed than the overcrowded west coast, which makes Taiwan second only to Bangladesh in population density. Lots of sightseeing near Taipei like museums, temples (Shihtoushan Buddhist) and waterfalls (Wulai). Tamsui Grass skiing resort near Baishawan. Many mountain peaks reach 3000m+, try hiking near Chushan or rafting on Hsiukuluan River (east coast). Kenting National Park protects some beautiful forests.

**Hazards and Hassles** – Waves hardly ever reach dangerous size except during typhoons when all beach activities are banned if a warning has been issued. Some volcanic reefs can be treacherous. Beware of concrete tetrapods! Crowds are increasing near Taipei and Nanwan, riding skills are improving and localism is an issue in places. Big cockroaches and aggressive mosquitoes.

**Handy Hints** – There's good gear among the dozens of surf shops. Expect $600 for a shortboard and $900 for a longboard. Rentals are $20/d. In Taipei (Johnny Rose, Tube Factory), Yilan (Blue Ocean, Cool), Kenting (Hotel California, Beach House) or Jialeshuei (Pintung), will help find lodgings, tours, school, rentals.

### Jialeshui

LAT. 21.985875° LONG. 120.847181°

Jialeshui or Jia le Shui is one of the main spots in south Taiwan, thanks to its bankability of having something to ride in most swells. Lefthanders skirt a rocky reef in the shadow of the extensive headland and can peel lazily for some distance attracting longboarders and improvers when NE-E swell wraps just right. In the middle of the beach a rivermouth peak examines the shifting sandbar, with long ripable rights and hollower shorter lefts leading into scattered beachbreak. Jialeshui holds consistent surf up to well overhead, before being overpowered on a major typhoon swell. Handles the regular onshores quite well, but beware the strong rips at the rivermouth and the often-present jellyfish/sea lice. Plenty of friendly locals, longboarders and many beginners. The town has quality board rentals, places to eat and drink and several accommodation options in the area from camping to boutique hotel. Further beach and reef possibilities down the coast to Fengchuisha.

plus rips and speedy lip line make this an experts only break. **Donghe Rivermouth** is extremely consistent and a swell-magnet, picking up all available seasonal swell onto shifting, river sculpted sandbars. There are two main peaks, either side of the rivermouth offering long walls with plenty of open face to dissect, plus some short barrel sections. It can hold a lot of swell and maintains good shape even on the bigger days. Wave quality is often the best on the island, so it's not the best place for beginners, especially as crowds are increasing, fed by a few new local surf shops nearby and visiting rippers looking to film and showcase Taiwan's surf. Further south the number of sandy beaches and reefbreaks increases, but the swell is less consistent. The wide beach at ✪ **Jialeshuei** may be Taiwan's most reliable spot. Facing SE, **Nanwan**, aka Binglang Beach, stands out as a shapely right reefbreak with nice curves and a sculpted face, but only on low-mid tide and S-SW swells. If the sand mix is just right, barrels are a given when it's bigger, which should help clear the water of weekend learner crowds. Summer typhoons should awaken a number of other reefs in the bay (Banana Bay, Windmills, Houbihu Harbour and Point) where the barrels and the coral reef are sharper. In Kaohsiung, go to **Sunyatsen Beach** facing the university for a short, bodyboard style shorebreak that's a low consistency break in the rare summer SW swells. It's easy to fly out to the 64 tiny Penghu Islands, but only go when a good S swell is running. **Sanshuei** is one of those picture-perfect beaches, ready to catch the occasional SE-SW summer swells, but a greater tidal range cuts surf time. Back on the heavily populated and usually flat NW coast of Taiwan, **Chu Nan**, needs a big winter N swell to create a slow, mushy, beginners beachbreak that's protected from NE winds by the harbour wall, just avoid lower tides.

ANDREW SHIELD

Nanwan

Taiwan sits smack dab in the middle of Typhoon Alley and the biggest swells of 8-12ft usually occur from July to October. Category 1-3 storms can appear in less than 24hrs, while super-typhoons Cat 4 and 5 usually take days to wind up, with potential for destruction, depending on the storm's track. Any violent storm activity in the western Pacific can create some waves, but consistency varies greatly, year to year. In the summer, knee to waist high is the average surf height pushed in by the SW monsoon winds without any typhoon activity. The most consistent surf is generated in winter from NE monsoon winds, which bring chest to headhigh waves almost everyday with potential 8-10ft peaks. North and east Taiwan has many spots that pick up even a sniff of swell (Yilan, Hualian) while the southern region has a myriad of breaks that need a bit of a look around to find (Taitung). Tides are semi-diurnal with diurnal inequality, but hardly reach more than 1m.

| STATISTICS | | J F | M A | M J | J A | S O | N D |
|---|---|---|---|---|---|---|---|
| SWELL | Direction | | | | | | |
| | Size (ft) | 4-5 | 2-3 | 1-2 | 3 | 3-4 | 4-5 |
| WIND | Direction | | | | | | |
| | Force | F5 | F4-F5 | F4 | F4 | F4-F5 | F4-F5 |
| WATER | Wetsuit | | | | | | |
| | Temp/°C | 23 | 24 | 27 | 29 | 28 | 25 |
| WEATHER | Rainfall/mm | 15 | 48 | 244 | 381 | 195 | 42 |
| | days/mth | 2 | 4 | 7 | 8 | 5 | 2 |
| | Min temp/°C | 13 | 17 | 22 | 23 | 21 | 15 |
| | Max temp/°C | 23 | 27 | 30 | 31 | 30 | 26 |

ANDREW SHIELD

Nanwan Point

# Jeju Do SOUTH KOREA

Lying off the southwest coast of the Republic of Korea, volcanic Jeju Island (Jejudo) is dominated by the lofty central peak of Halla mountain, which slopes steeply down to the north and south coasts, surrounded by 368 smaller volcanoes. The rocky coastline is short on sandy beaches so Jungmun in the south is the centre of surf culture on the island, where beach, reef and pointbreaks can be ridden. Koreans rarely swim in the sea, even when it's flat, so most lifeguards are over-cautious, particularly when there is typhoon swell, but a nucleus of local surfers are slowly altering these attitudes and loads more Koreans are learning to surf.

- + POWERFUL TYPHOON WAVES
- + BEACHES AND LAVA REEFS
- + WORLD HERITAGE ISLAND
- + GREAT TOURISM FACILITIES

- – INCONSISTENT SWELLS
- – SHORT SURF SEASON
- – UNPREDICTABLE TYPHOONS
- – OVER-PROTECTIVE LIFEGUARDS

Jungmun Beach

JS CALLAHAN/SURFEXPLORE

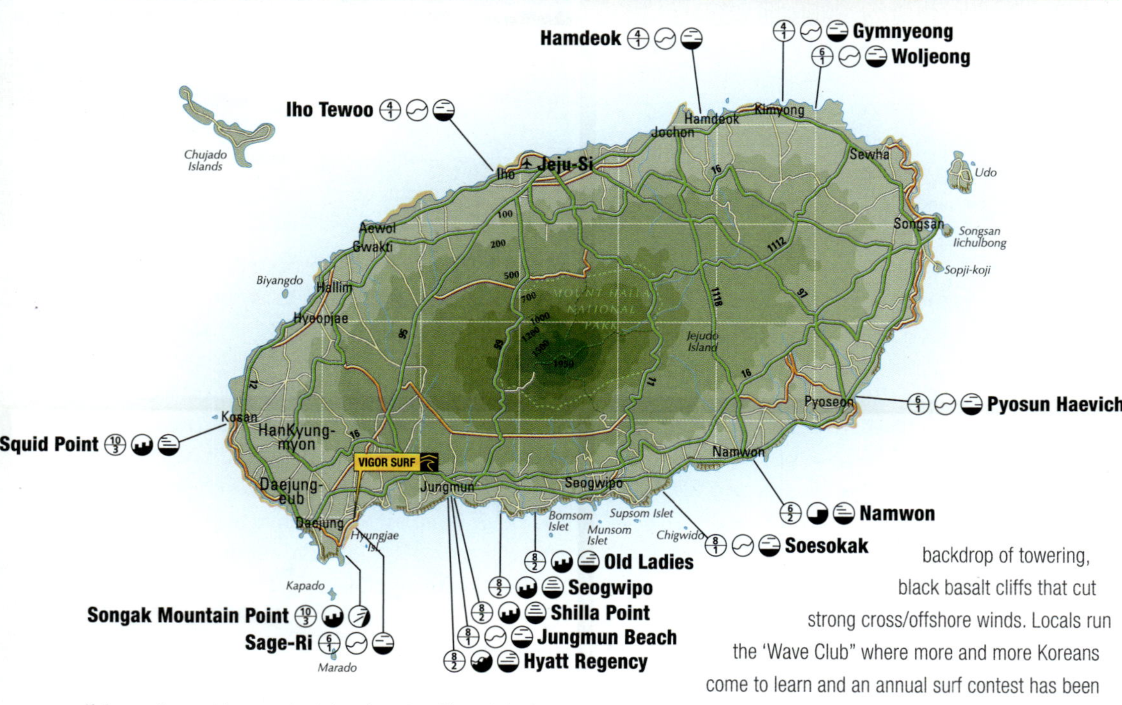


If the south coast is maxed out, head west to Chagwi-do harbour and **Squid Point**, a crumbly left that wraps onto the reef in front of the tetrapods. During rare typhoon swells, **Songak Mountain Point** can offer confident surfers both a long left point on the western side plus a righthander on the eastern side hugging the cliffs down towards the Mara Island ferry jetty. **Sage-ri** is a mellow beginners beach replete with surf school and lower crowd factor. Gets overpowered easily and beware the tongues of rock. In front of the **Hyatt Regency**, a boulder reef holds the sand and some decent low tide rights on any S swell variation, plus offers a bit of protection from W winds. **Jungmun Beach** has the highest concentration of different breaks on the island and a dramatic backdrop of towering, black basalt cliffs that cut strong cross/offshore winds. Locals run the 'Wave Club" where more and more Koreans come to learn and an annual surf contest has been held since 2005. The Centre Peak is the inside wave with lefts and rights, which can get very hollow and sucky when hitting the sandbar. The Outside is a mushier peak and shoulder that will roll through to connect with the inside and get hollow if the swell is bigger. Both are quite consistent and usually better at low tide. Beware of very strong currents on the left side of the beach and patches of reef underneath. On the eastern headland is **Shilla Point**, a reefbreak peak that's fast and hollow. The lefts peel nicely and can lead into the sucky sandbars on the beach. Beware of the big rock in the middle of the righthander that can only be seen at low tide. Experienced surfers can check the **Seogwipo** area for various rugged, rocky reef waves in bigger swells. **Old Ladies** is a quality right reefbreak, deep in a bay behind an island and affords good W wind protection. **Soesokak** needs a typhoon swell to get going but can have fun waves as the rivermouth sculpts some good sandbars. There is also rumoured to be a pointbreak nearby. Further east is a left slab at Namwon, which only turns on in special conditions of SE swell, NW wind. **Pyosan Haevich** is a super-popular tourist beach with gently shelving sands extending far out to sea at low tide. The outside waves can be ok and it picks up both NE and SE swells, making it more consistent than south-facing breaks. During winter, NE winds can kick up some short-period windswell on the north shore. **Woljeung** is probably the best north coast beach in terms of swell exposure, but it is usually flat outside the winter months so beginners will need fluky windslop in summer or thick rubber in winter. **Gymnyeong**, **Hamdeok** and **Iho Tewoo** are popular beginners spots with extensive shallow water.

Swell arrives from three sides, but lows in the Yellow Sea and NE windslop from the Sea of Japan is usually low quality. Typhoon swells winding up in the Philippine Sea need to track NW and send SSE-SSW swell between Taiwan and Japan so the best season is from June to October. Combine the skinny swell window with strong winds that often change direction many times during the day and you soon realise this is a fickle destination. Tides are semi-diurnal with diurnal inequality and spring tides rarely exceed 2m. Download a tide chart in English.

## TRAVEL INFORMATION

**Weather** – Jeju experiences both subtropical oceanic and temperate climates, so the winters are generally long, cold and dry, while summers are short, hot and humid. Spring and autumn are pleasant but short in duration. Temps range between 15°C-30°C (59-86°F) in summer and 3°C-16°C (37-61°F) during winter. Use a 4/3mm and boots mid winter, 3/2 from November to June and a springy or boardshorts from July through October.

**Lodging and Food** – Shilla Cheju Hotel super deluxe dbl room with ocean view is $470/night. In Seogwipo City, Daemyung Green Ville, New Kyongnam, Kal Seogwipo or Paradise Hotel are cheaper at $70-150/n. Jeju Guest-house, 25min N of Jungmun is $30/day. Meals are cheap: $7-12 for a full meal. Try kimchi, pickled fermented cabbage.

**Nature and Culture** – Visit the longest lava cave in the world. Women divers (Haenyeo) in ancient wetsuit and goggles, collect seaweed, shellfish and sea urchins, then sell them on the roadside. Sungsan's Sunrise Peak is the main tourist site. Many trails (Yongshil, Orimok) and waterfalls.

**Hazards and Hassles** – Lifeguards and police may stop you from entering the water during typhoon swells. Some lava reefs can be pretty nasty.

**Handy Hints** – Vigor Surf camp in Sage-ri has rentals and lessons. More shops on the mainland with expensive imported equipment at Busan and YangYang. North coast surf schools open in summer, but it's usually flat.

| STATISTICS | | J F | M A | M J | J A | S O | N D |
|---|---|---|---|---|---|---|---|
| SWELL | Direction | | | | | | |
| | Size (ft) | 2 | 1 | 1-2 | 2 | 2-3 | 2 |
| WIND | Direction | | | | | | |
| | Force | F4-F5 | F4 | F3-F4 | F3 | F4 | F4 |
| WATER | Wetsuit | | | | | | |
| | Temp/°C | 12 | 13 | 18 | 24 | 23 | 17 |
| WEATHER | Rainfall/mm | 60 | 82 | 130 | 227 | 119 | 66 |
| | days/mth | 4 | 5 | 7 | 12 | 7 | 5 |
| | Min temp/°C | 3 | 6 | 14 | 23 | 15 | 5 |
| | Max temp/°C | 8 | 16 | 24 | 29 | 25 | 15 |

# Hong Kong & Guangdong CHINA

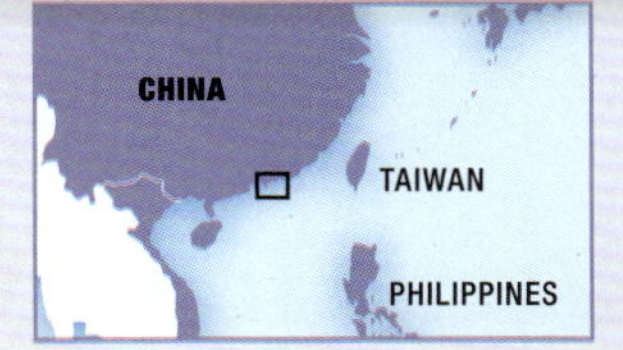


**Surfing in Hong Kong is far removed from the big city shopping, skyscrapers, crowded streets and junks jostling in the harbour. Set in a much more peaceful rural setting at least an hours drive away, the relatively consistent beachbreaks and fickle, secret reefbreaks can produce some quality waves, in seasonally specific conditions.**

+ CONSISTENT NE MONSOON
+ NEW SPOTS TO DISCOVER
+ OFFSHORE MORNINGS
+ CLOSE TO HONG KONG

- MOSTLY FLAT IN SPRING/SUMMER
- FEW SPOTS, MAINLY BEACHBREAK
- LANGUAGE BARRIER
- POLLUTION

Tai Long Wan is Cantonese for Big Wave Bay, but confusingly, there are three spots bearing this name. **Big Wave Bay LT** is on the rugged island of Lantau, which rises steeply up to 930m, but only gets waves on rare S and typhoon swells. There's lots of close-outs at **Cheung Sha**, attracting dozens of surfers on occasional 2-4ft days. It's a mini bus ride from the ferry, boasts one of Hong Kong's longest beaches and a small store that rents and sells boards. There's more mushy waves at **Pui O**, a short taxi ride from the Mui Wo ferry. The seven million residents of Hong Kong benefit from a modern, efficient road network, but it takes a while to get to the east-facing spots in quiet, bucolic areas. **Repulse Bay** is a popular tourist beach, surrounded by hi-rises, but it's rarely worth the trip because it faces southwest, is a shallow bay and offshore islands filter swell. **Shek O** can be a dumpy shorebreak in bigger winter swells, providing a bit more space and protection than neighbouring Big Wave Bay. **Big Wave Bay HK** is the centre of the surfing scene, attracting crowds of up to 100 surfers. Short shifting peaks will break in any swell from N to E, before it closes-out the bay over 6ft. Dangers include rocks at either end, strong rips, pollution and too many bodies in the water! The 3rd Big Wave Bay is **Tai Long Wan SK**, which has the biggest, most consistent and best shaped waves around. Consisting of four beaches facing NE to SE in a giant horseshoe bay, Fung Bay and Sai Wan are probably the best, catching any swell on offer, while Ham Tin offers a little protection from big swell and wind at the north end. Can get big, hollow and rippy, so not for beginners when a strong NE or typhoon swell hits.

## TRAVEL INFORMATION

**Weather** – Oct to Jan is the dry season, which is also the best time for swells. Jan and Feb is winter, with occasional cold fronts followed by dry northerly winds. June to September is the monsoon season with warm, sticky, sunny days, sudden rains and possible typhoons. A springsuit in winter for 2-3 months and a 3mm steamer on rare cold days.

**Lodging and Food** – HK hotels are relatively expensive; Stanford Hotel in Mongkok fr $75/n. China is cheaper; Zhelang has 3-star hotels for $30/night. Meals are cheap but not like a western Chinese take-away!

**Nature and Culture** – HK is the events capital of Asia for arts, sports, theatre, festivals and concerts. It's a vibrant city, but nature escapes are close by.

**Hazards and Hassles** – BWB HK, Shek O and Cheung Sha can have lots of local surfers and expats. Bad pollution everywhere – use ear plugs and keep your mouth shut. Traffic can be awful.

**Handy Hints** – Rent or buy boards at Eric's Shop on Big Wave Bay HK beach; rental boards $7/d and bodyboards $3/d, or store your own boards. 3 shops in HK sell boards ($390-780). In China, driving is illegal for gweela's (foreigners). Shenzhen is a Special Economic Zone (SEZ).

In winter, there is plenty of swell in the 2-4ft range over stable sandbars at mid to high tide. Most surfers camp overnight, since it is 2hrs from the city. On the mainland in Guangdong province, spots are few and far between as the sea has only recently receded, leaving a super indented coastline with flat rocks and myriads of granite islets. Eastwards, at **Xi-Chong and Dongchong**, good longboard waves peel lazily down some rivermouth sculpted sandbars, plus there is lots of rocky coast to explore. There's also good clean beach-hut accommodation and restaurants at Dongchong. **Pinghai Point** is a bit more accessible, holding some rights just near the Dongchong Hotel. Zhelang area or Hong Hoi Wan is the best bet with powerful, peaks near a series of jetties, but be aware this area sits next to a power plant and new industrial zone so pollution is a problem. The jetties have sculpted some excellent sand banks at **88**, sheltered from sideshore N-NE winds and it's usually offshore in the morning with a left breaking off the northern jetty and beautiful A-Frames inside. **Cherry Point** lefts only work on the bigger swells and are usually quite mushy.

Typhoon season is best from Aug-Oct, but it's very inconsistent, whereas the NE monsoon, from Nov to March registers 80% surf day consistency, mid-season. The best month is November with early NE swells and potential late season typhoons. The Taiwan Strait produces NE swells while the Luzon Strait gets direct E swells. Land breezes blow from the N, before shifting to light or moderate onshore NE-E later in the day. During SW season from May to September, waves are rare. Tides have unequal semi-diurnal cycles, reaching 2.4m and waves are often better at higher stages of tide.

YEP

Big Wave Bay HK

| STATISTICS | | J/F | M/A | M/J | J/A | S/O | N/D |
|---|---|---|---|---|---|---|---|
| SWELL | Direction | | | | | | |
| | Size (ft) | 3 | 1-2 | 0-1 | 1 | 2-3 | 3-4 |
| WIND | Direction | | | | | | |
| | Force | F4 | F4 | F3-F4 | F3 | F4 | F4 |
| WATER | Wetsuit | | | | | | |
| | Temp/°C | 19 | 21 | 27 | 28 | 27 | 22 |
| WEATHER | Rainfall/mm | 39 | 106 | 343 | 374 | 185 | 37 |
| | days/mth | 4 | 7 | 15 | 16 | 9 | 2 |
| | Min temp/°C | 13 | 17 | 24 | 26 | 24 | 16 |
| | Max temp/°C | 18 | 22 | 29 | 31 | 28 | 22 |

# Hainan CHINA

Hainan, the second largest of the Chinese islands after Taiwan, extends 1,500km of coastline into the South China Sea, with an eastern side exposed to consistent NE monsoon swells and seasonal typhoon swells. Hainan is advertised throughout China and Russia as a tropical holiday paradise, attracting around 10 million Chinese tourists every year, mainly to Sanya in the south of the island. The surf turns out to be quite consistent through winter, with hundreds of beaches and left points pulling in the NE-E swell and headlands provide size and wind protection on the big days. Visiting foreign surfers head straight for the lefthanders of Riyue Bay that have been deemed good enough to hold top level ISA and ASP events, but there's also a growing mix of Chinese surfers, keen to learn in the adjacent, beginner-friendly beachbreaks.

+ CHINA'S BEST SURF
+ QUALITY LEFT POINTBREAKS
+ CONSISTENT IN NE MONSOON
+ WARM WATER AND TROPICAL

- LACK OF POWER
- AVERAGE BEACHBREAKS
- RARE TYPHOON SWELLS
- DIFFICULT WITHOUT GUIDE

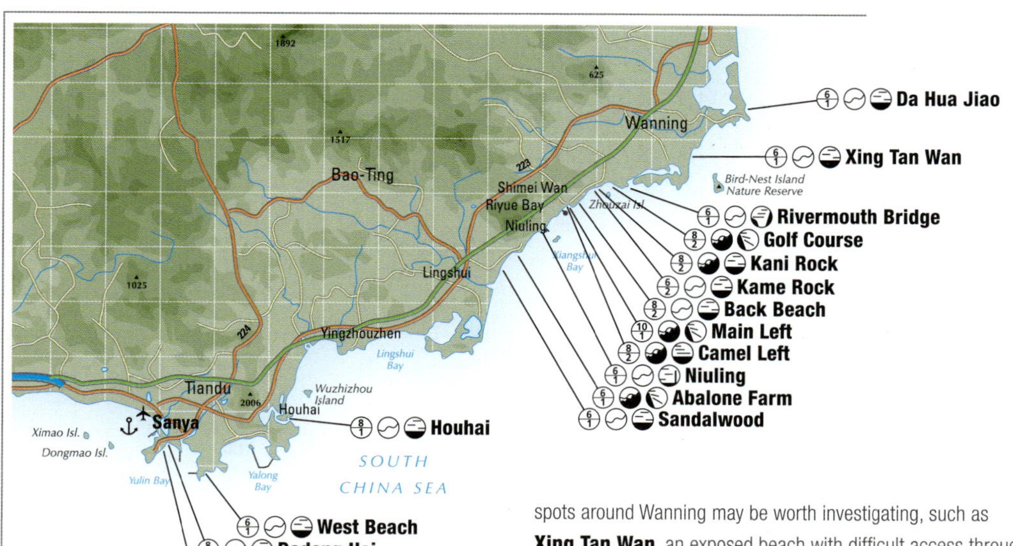

DAMIEN POULLENOT

Kame Rock

Between Haikou in the north and Sanya in the south, a 320km long expressway occasionally skirts the coastline. However, once off this major route the road network is poor, so exploring is time-consuming. The NE coast of Hainan around Wenchang is hard to access. Tongguling National Nature Reserve is more of a sightseeing area than a surfspot, but it overlooks the islet in the rivermouth at Moon Bay, which sometimes holds up between the close-outs or onshore mush. Getting to Buddha Beach is a mission, but the 16m statue lends a unique feel to the place. It's generally surfed on typhoon swells with SW winds, as the NE monsoon is onshore. Narrow rocky beach that picks up swell, but it's a poor set-up and there's often bad backwash. Da'ao Bay, needs the NE swell without the wind to create some soft corners, otherwise it will be flat or blownout. Long, lonely beaches extend south to Wanning, where **Da Hua Jaio** breaks near a military camp under similar small NE conditions. It's exposed to swell and wind so fairly consistent and messy. More spots around Wanning may be worth investigating, such as **Xing Tan Wan**, an exposed beach with difficult access through the muddy rice paddies. Small streams can cut a channel in the straight sandbars. South of here, the coast faces more SE and the likelihood of consistent, offshore surf soars. A huge curving jetty has been built at **Rivermouth Bridge** so sand has built up and it can pick up all swells with winds from SW-N keeping it groomed. The next three bays – Shimei Wan, Riyue Wan and Xiangshui Wan (wan means bay) hold major surf potential. **Golf Course**, in Shimei Wan, is a long left breaking down a sharp, rocky point by the Ocean Bay Golf Club. Best in bigger NE swells with N quadrant wins, it's a big paddle against sweeping currents to score the fast inside section. Small days are mellow, crumbling walls perfect for longboarding. There's another shorter left hugging the headland in the next bay east when the swell is bigger. At **Kani Rock**, powerful, low tide rights and lefts throw out close to shore over boulders and sand. **Kame Rock** is a hollow beachbreak with a good right next to the large rock. Some close-outs, but good barrels when the sandbars are right. **Back Beach** is just north of the headland in Riyue Wan and is a good option when the point is small. Powerful A-frames with great barrel potential are possible along this NE exposed stretch of sand on medium NE swells, low tide and offshore winds. Always bigger than everywhere else. Further south from ✪**Riyue Wan Main Left** the beachbreak leads down to a cluster of mussel encrusted rocks in front of the

## TRAVEL INFORMATION

**Weather** – Hainan is a tropical monsoon zone, with average temperatures between 22°C and 26°C (72-79°F). Annual rain is 1,639mm (66in), but much less in the leeward coasts around Niuling. Forest cover exceeds 50%. Surf without a wetsuit is possible in the early season because the water remains warm (25°C/77°F), but N winds can get chilly so take a springsuit in Nov-Dec and a light fullsuit in Jan-March. Because of the fairly shallow South China Sea, the water is coloured by sediment.

**Lodging and Food** – Lots of hotels have been built so the market is competitive. Compare Ocean Bay Golf with Le Meridien at top end, Sandalwood, WengQuan or Alila in Xiangshui Bay or overpriced 21 Century chain hotel in Riyue. Riyue Bay Surf Club offers spartan dormitory style accommodation ($9/n) or beachfront hotel basic room (fr $40/n/dbl). Chinese street food and restaurant cuisine is outstanding and very cheap. Try Wenchang Chicken, Jiaji Duck, Dongshan Mutton, Merry Crab. There is lots of fresh seafood available.

**Nature and Culture** – There is plenty to see and do: Nanwan Macaque island and a Buddhist statue 108m tall, Xinlong Botanical Garden with 1200 plant species, Hainan Marine Tropical World in Haikou, the Hot Spring region, Yalong bay near Sanya, Tinanya Haijiao rocks, and the Sanya Zoological Garden. There is buzzing nightlife in Sanya, and karaoke and massage are commonplace.

**Hazards and Hassles** – There are few local surfers, so localism is currently not an issue, but pay respect to the expat surfing community, local Hainan surfers and regulars from mainland China. There are some jellyfish, sea-lice and low tide rocks to be aware of. Hiring a cab can be difficult. Some beaches are off-limits and guards or the military may prohibit surfing in some areas.

**Handy Hints** – Very few people speak English or Japanese, only Mandarin. Internet facilities are very limited. The surf conditions cater for both short and longboards. During typhoon season, it's really hot. Bring all surf supplies, including wax.

JS CALLAHAN SURFEXPLORE

Golf Course

### Riyue Wan – Main Left

LAT. 18.630265° LONG. 110.222075°

The Main Left off the point of Riyue Bay can offer a low-mid tide 200m+ ride that starts about halfway out the headland. Nice and easy roll-ins lead onto a tapered wall or shoulder perfect for intermediates and longboarders to attack. Better surfers will make the paddle out to the Ghost Hotel on the tip which sucks up on sandbars and barrels for a short way before filling up and holding steep, ripable sections. into the bay. Even howling NE winds are not a problem, making it the most consistent winter wave in the area and an international contest site. The beachbreak can get some shape, especially in SE swells, keeping beginners off the point, but expect moderate crowds these days. Handles size during typhoon swells, when currents can be strong, but there is an easy paddling channel and it is user-friendly for improvers up.

tourist attraction called the Taiwanese Village. Sand builds up and creates **Camel Left**, a low tide racing wall with potential barrel sections when big NE swells wrap into the bay and winds blow more from the N. Intermediate to advanced surfers as the rocks are a bit nasty. **Niuling** has various peaks opposite the beach restaurants plus a punchy left off the harbour jetty, which has lost some quality since it was extended. Small swell at high tide will be ugly shoredump, but the north jetty may work in SW winds. If the wind is up from the NE, **Abalone Farm** offers long, shouldered lefts tucked into a sheltered cove with a massive new luxury hotel development. Another huge hotel hugs the sand at **Sandalwood** in Lingshui, where the open beachbreak is of good quality, has rivermouth jetties at the north end and is easily accessible from the highway. 45km NE of the tourist hub of Sanya, the small village of **Houhai** hosts a very consistent and powerful beachbreak, best on small to medium E and NE swells. Houhai is the winter hub for Sanya's booming surf scene with good wind and swell protection in the deep scalloped bay. Surfer friendly guesthouses and board rentals can be found here. Further south near Sanya and Yalong Bay, undeveloped **West Beach** needs SE swells but is often just a straighthander and not worth the effort. Access is via dirt tracks through the virgin forest. The main city break in Sanya is called **Dadong Hai** and is located in its busiest tourist district. This wide bay looks like a run down version of Waikiki without the consistent waves. Needs a summer typhoon swell to have anything bigger than the pleasure boat and jetski wakes. This spot favors low tide and can be crowded both with surfers and tourists jammed into their respective areas. In the next bay west, **Xiaodong Hai**, offers one of the best and rarest righthanders on the island. This long reef pass breaks on a sharp coral bottom and activates during SE typhoon swells producing high quality barrels, especially at high tide.

There are two main surfing seasons in Hainan. The typhoon season runs from August to October while the NE monsoon extends from November to March. November produces both early N swells and potential late season typhoons, while the mid to late season monsoon provides the most consistent waves in January and February. The Taiwan Strait also produces regular NE swells while the Luzon Strait gets direct but occasional E swells. The NNE wind becomes side/offshore on the ESE facing shorelines, mainly in Wanning, and can get strong at times. Winds shift a bit ENE in the afternoon but remain fairly offshore for the spots in the SE. During the SW season, from May to September, waves are rare and only found at south-facing spots. Typhoons can send awesome long period swells and sometimes the SW monsoon will produce 2-3ft of windswell on the south coast. Tide phases can get up to 1.5m, with very irregular changes between the two tides. A general rule of thumb is to favour the beachbreaks on high tide and the points on low tide.

LARS JACOBSEN

Rivermouth Bridge

| STATISTICS | | J F | M A | M J | J A | S O | N D |
|---|---|---|---|---|---|---|---|
| SWELL | Direction | | | | | | |
| | Size (ft) | 3-4 | 2 | 0-1 | 1-2 | 3 | 4 |
| WIND | Direction | | | | | | |
| | Force | F4-F5 | F4 | F4 | F4 | F4 | F4-F5 |
| WATER | Wetsuit | | | | | | |
| | Temp/°C | 24 | 26 | 29 | 29 | 29 | 25 |
| WEATHER | Rainfall/mm | 7 | 21 | 150 | 180 | 240 | 25 |
| | days/mth | 11 | 12 | 13 | 13 | 12 | 12 |
| | Min temp/°C | 19 | 21 | 24 | 25 | 24 | 20 |
| | Max temp/°C | 24 | 27 | 32 | 32 | 31 | 25 |

# Da Nang VIETNAM

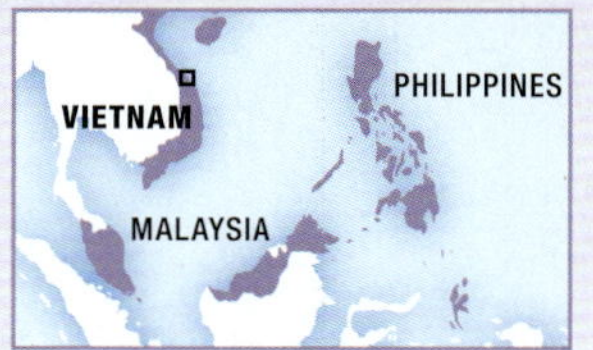


US servicemen first surfed China Beach back in the '60s and it is now Vietnam's most famous beach. Other areas with regular waves include Nha Trang and Phan Thiet along the exposed central coast and Vung Tau down south near Ho Chi Minh City. Most of Vietnam's surf is beachbreak with an outside sandbank, trough in the middle and a reform on the inside. The outside waves are the biggest, up to 8ft on the strongest NE wind push, which creates a choppy, disorganised line-up. The outside mushburgers quickly die in the trough before reforming into the shorey, which is where the power is. The best bet for a Vietnamese surf search is Da Nang because equipment is available to rent and unlike most surfing zones, crowds are never a nuisance.

+ RELIABLE SEASONAL WINDSWELL
+ SOFT, EMPTY BEACHBREAKS
+ DISCOVERY POTENTIAL
+ EXOTIC, WARM AND FRIENDLY

– SMALL DISORGANISED WAVES
– NO KNOWN REEFBREAKS
– SHORT SURF SEASON
– HEAVY RAIN AND HUMIDITY

## TRAVEL INFORMATION

**Weather** – Da Nang has a tropical climate that is characterised by strong monsoon influences with two distinct rainy and dry seasons. It's cooler during the swell season. Storms hit the area every year in September and October. Annual rainfall is even higher in the hills, especially those facing the sea. The N winds sometimes cool the water down to 23°C (74°F), but springsuits aren't really necessary.

**Lodging and Food** – The coast from My Khe to China beach has lots of options for all budgets - prices start at $8 for a basic room to $150 for a 5 star hotel option. Food is varied and very cheap ($3/meal). Best soups (pho) in the world.

**Nature and Culture** – Since Vietnam can't be a full-on surf trip, enjoy the scenery and the culture. Pay a visit to the Cham Museum, climb the Marble Mountains for awesome views of China Beach from Linh Ung Pagoda. Don't miss Hoi An and My Son. Vietnam's former capital city of Hue lies 4h north via scenic Hai Van pass.

**Hazards and Hassles** – During the surfing season excessive heat can be a problem. There is no malaria around Da Nang but it is still a problem in rural areas. Because of drugs and prostitution, AIDS is common. Motorbike rentals are cheap fun, but hazardous.

**Handy Hints** – In My Khe The Da Nang surf school has basic rental boards ($5-10/h) and lessons. Also check in at Tams Pub and surf shop for rentals, basic bits and food. Bring your everyday gear and maybe an old board to leave behind. The New Year Festival (late Jan, early Feb) can be fully booked. US dollars are still part of the economy.

JS CALLAHAN/SURFEXPLORE

China Beach

Furthest north, **Binh An** is usually small and lacks shape, but may have some crumblers for beginners staying in the beachfront resorts. Sandbars should be better closer to the Tu Hien rivermouth. Scenic **Lang Co** has better sandbars breaking both inside and outside and when the onshores shralp it, kitesurfers will appear. **Nam O Point** is probably the highest quality wave, but it won't break until the beaches are maxing out. Faster, steeper and shallower, the left is more wall than barrel. The beachbreak can be ok with some protection from NE winds behind the point and further peaks heading north past the rivermouth sandbars and up to the jetty. The rivermouth brings plenty of murky, polluted water to the line-up. **My Khe**, Non Nuoc, China Beach and Cua Dai are all part of the same stretch of below average beachbreak, that will break at low tide outside, before filling up in the central trough and reforming on the shorebreak sandbars. When a strong NE swell arrives on a glassy morning, **Non Nuoc** can have some nice tapered walls, but mostly its disorganised, choppy and lacking in power. **China Beach** is surf central for Da Nang and there are board rentals available for beginners and touring surfers. It's the most popular spot as it's usually the biggest and some kind of wave will be on offer for longboarding, SUP and occasionally shortboarders if the monsoon NE or typhoon NE/E swell arrives without the following winds. **Cue Dai Beach** has a steeper slope than China Beach and picks up more NE swell, but E is blocked by offshore islands. The large rivermouth grooms constantly changing sandbars but also brings some pretty polluted water to the less-developed beachfront. This 30km beach is backed by the verdant Marble Mountains, made up of five isolated limestone outcrops, each riddled with caves, grottoes, pagodas and shrines.

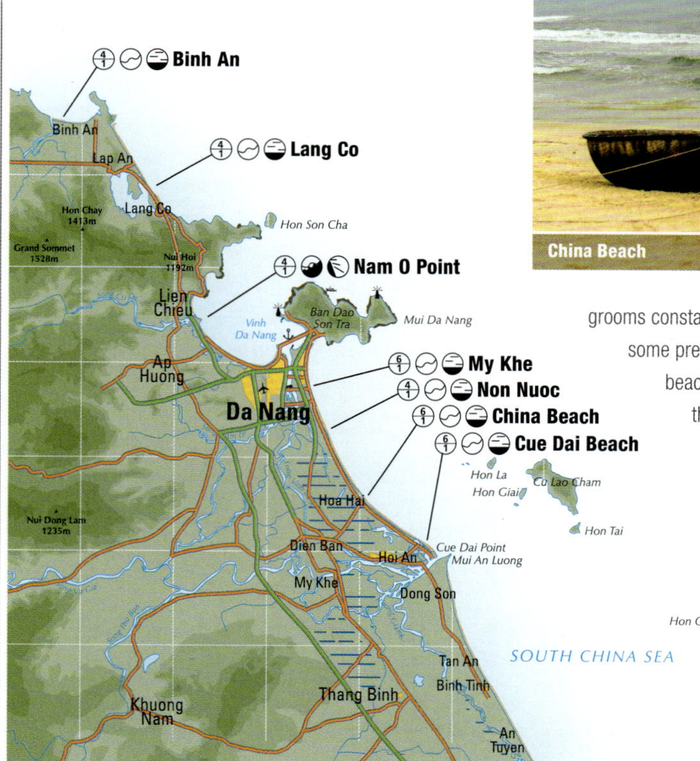

HUGO ALVARAZ

China Beach

The N-NE monsoon is a strong seasonal trend in the South China Sea starting in November until February-March. Expect messy 3-6ft on the most exposed beachbreaks and 1-2ft on the sheltered pointbreaks. During the June-October typhoon season, some major swell might hit with clean conditions but this is rare and short. During the SW monsoon, it's offshore everyday but mostly flat. Diurnal tides predominate in the South China Sea and won't exceed 1m.

| STATISTICS | | J F | M A | M J | J A | S O | N D |
|---|---|---|---|---|---|---|---|
| SWELL | Direction | | | | | | |
| | Size (ft) | 3-4 | 1 | 0 | 0-1 | 1-2 | 3-4 |
| WIND | Direction | | | | | | |
| | Force | F4 | F4 | F4 | F4 | F3-F4 | F4 |
| WATER | Wetsuit | | | | | | |
| | Temp/°C | 23 | 24 | 28 | 29 | 28 | 25 |
| WEATHER | Rainfall/mm | 65 | 15 | 45 | 110 | 490 | 215 |
| | days/mth | 11 | 4 | 8 | 12 | 19 | 21 |
| | Min temp/°C | 20 | 22 | 25 | 25 | 24 | 21 |
| | Max temp/°C | 25 | 29 | 34 | 34 | 30 | 26 |

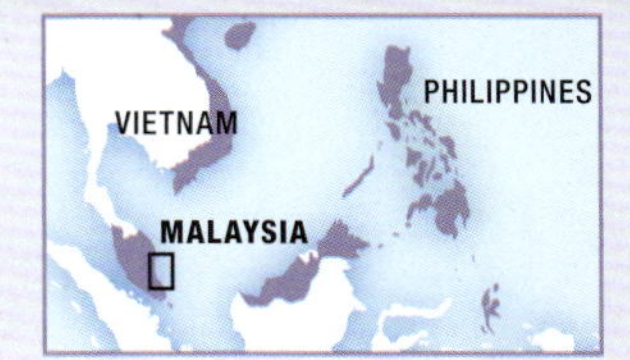


# Eastern Peninsular MALAYSIA

Malaysia is made up of Peninsular Malaysia and East Malaysia located on the northern part of Borneo island. The Peninsular's east coast comprises of mainly sandy beaches (91%) exposed to South China swells from the N and E. These exposed beachbreaks seemingly work best in the early monsoon season, when the sandbars have built up during flat summers. Some Malaysian locals have learned to surf at Sunway Lagoon in Petaling Jaya, between the airport and Kuala Lumpur, but surf time is very limited, no personal or fibreglass boards are allowed and entry plus rental is very expensive.

+ FREQUENT NE MONSOON SWELLS
+ MELLOW BEACHBREAKS
+ FRIENDLY LOCAL SURF POPULATION
+ CHEAP AND SAFE COUNTRY

– MAINLY MESSY WINDSWELL
– LACK OF REEFBREAKS
– MURKY MONSOON WATERS
– RAINY SWELL SEASON

The Terengganu surf community is growing fast and can be found surfing at the best spot **Batu Buruk** next to the long jetty that helps the sand formation. Straight exposed beaches stretch down the coast with average mushy peaks at spots like **Chendering** and **Pantai Kelulut**. The righthanders at **Marang** hug the curved wall of the harbour giving a pointbreak feel, but it's rarely surfed as a strong E swell is required for it to work. There's some beachbreak on either side of the harbour and the offshore resort islands like Perhentian, Redang, Gemia or Kapas may be worth investigation. In front of the resort nestled behind **Tanjong Jara** will see some protected peaks in big NE storms, but the point is a hoax and the north side beachies will be bigger. **Kerteh** beaches suffer from offshore banks killing the swell size and strength and it's rarely bigger than waist-high. The ivory sands of **Pantai Kemasik** hold small beginner or longboard waves south of the island. Further south is **Star Jetty Cruise**, a 500m long pier on stilts, which affords little or no wind protection. It needs a big swell and early season sandbars to be worth it. The most reliable beachbreak is **Kijal**, spreading the peaks along a 1km long coastal road and it's often best near the rocks at the south end. **Strawberry Resort** used to be the local's secret spot, boasting long walls and bowly sections down a sandy lefthand point, but access is often refused by the resort guards. It's best at low tide with no wind as it is fully exposed to the NE. **The Quarry** used to hold world-class lefts, but two rock jetties built in 2002 cut the spot in two. There's a short ride off the jetty's tip and then the wrapping pointbreak section on the inside. Still a good place to surf plus there are some rights to the south. On low tides and big swells **Chendor Beach** can hold weak wrapping lefts with many sections over migrating estuarine sandbars. It's a long walk and paddle to **Club Med**, visible from the Cherating line-up, sporting mellow, refracting lefts next to an island. There's always a pack on the sandspit lefts of **Tanjung Cherating**, Malaysia's best wave, which is 3-4h from KL. This long, protruding sandbank takes the NE breeze side-on and although it is not so powerful, Cherating can peel and section for up to 1km through the brown, rivermouth water. Take-off section can be hollow and it is always better at low tide. Intense rips require constant paddling to stay in position, so it's best to walk back up the beach after a wave. Surfers from KL usually hit **Teluk Cempedak** or **Baluk Beach** for sloppy, but beginner-friendly waves. 100km south and offshore Pulau Tioman holds a semi-right point and a protected deep bay beachbreak at Pantai Juara, popular with Singapore surfers sick of slow mushburgers at their nearest spot, Desaru.

During the NE monsoon from November to March, the winds blow from the NNE, bringing lots of stormy weather and swells down the South China Sea corridor. Between Nov and Jan, consistent 6-12ft swells produce waves in the 2-6ft range on exposed beachbreaks. From April to October it's basically flat apart from rare late summer typhoon swells. Tides have irregular semi-diurnal cycles and reach 2m on springs, which significantly affects the waves.

JS CALLAHAN/SURFEXPLORE

Tanjung Cherating

## TRAVEL INFORMATION

**Weather** –The tropical monsoon climate brings uniform annual temps, with January through April less humid and warm, while May to December are the wettest. Oct/Nov and end of Feb sees showers every 15 minutes and it is rare to have a full day with completely clear skies.

**Lodging and Food** – Matahari holiday huts is the base for Cherating Point surf school and has huts ($15 dble/n) and packages starting at $100 (2 lessons and 2 nts). Tanjung Inn is well located and has various options ($25 - $100/n). Decent variety of Malaysian or Chinese food.

**Nature and Culture** – In KL, check Petronas Towers, KLCC shopping mall, the Loft pub and nightclubs like Zouk, Passion or Beach Club. Visit the Cameron Highlands (jungle walks, waterfalls, tea plantations, gardens), Batu Caves towering limestone outcrop or Taman Negara jungle.

**Hazards and Hassles** – Malaysia is one of the most pleasant, hassle-free countries to visit in SE Asia. Frequent rains can be a bummer during swell season, but that keeps the numbers and prices down. Water is murky and tidal rips can be heavy, but it's fairly safe, sandy surf.

**Handy Hints** – Cherating Point surf school has rental boards and does surf packages. Ombok Cafe sells wax, 2nd hand boards and other basic surf accessories. Other popular surfer hangouts are the Cherating beach, Eco and Monkey bars. No ATM's in Cherating. Lots of potential for discovery.

| STATISTICS | | J F | M A | M J | J A | S O | N D |
|---|---|---|---|---|---|---|---|
| SWELL | Direction | | | | | | |
| | Size (ft) | 4 | 1-2 | 0-1 | 0-1 | 2 | 3-4 |
| WIND | Direction | | | | | | |
| | Force | F3 | F2-F3 | F2-F3 | F3 | F2-F3 | F3 |
| WATER | Wetsuit | | | | | | |
| | Temp/°C | 29 | 31 | 31 | 29 | 28 | 27 |
| WEATHER | Rainfall/mm | 203 | 150 | 172 | 206 | 246 | 548 |
| | days/mth | 9 | 12 | 16 | 15 | 19 | 20 |
| | Min temp/°C | 22 | 23 | 23 | 23 | 22 | 23 |
| | Max temp/°C | 29 | 32 | 33 | 33 | 32 | 30 |

# Northwest Luzon PHILIPPINES

North of the capital Manila is the west-facing South China Sea coast of Luzon that benefits from two distinct monsoonal surf seasons.

- \+ CONSISTENT NE MONSOON SWELL
- \+ OCCASIONAL SW TYPHOON SWELL
- \+ MANY UNCROWDED BREAKS
- \+ CHEAP LIVING COSTS

- \- SMALL SIZE WAVES
- \- CROWDED SAN JUAN SPOTS
- \- NATURAL/SOCIAL DISASTERS
- \- SEX TOURISM

The provinces of Ilocos Norte and Ilocos Sur contain an empty contorted coastline of shallow jagged reefs centred around the exclusive Badoc Island resort. Down south in La Union province the geology mellows and provides the perfect territory for beginner and intermediate surfers to hone their skills on a selection of rolling points and easy beaches within easy access of the crowded Philippine surfing mecca of San Juan.

QUINN HABER

Turtle Head

It's a 10min paddle across the bay to **Star Tubes** where fast, walling rights fold over a very shallow bottom covered by thick seaweed. Protected **Badoc Point**, close to shore in front of the Badoc Island Resort only breaks on a bigger typhoon swell – the beachbreak can also get good. Get the resort jetski out to **Badoc Island Lefts** a more consistent wave with nice pockets and walls. On the southern tip of Badoc Island is **Turtle Head**, marked by a spectacular rock that shelters this twisting, short right with its gaping tube section. Pinget Island is actually a peninsula with good potential for SW and NE swells. **Puro Pinget** is the best spot with a mix of beach and reefbreaks. In colonial Vigan, the small, friendly surfing community prefer the south-facing beach at **Manangat** that holds long rides during SW typhoon swell in summer. Lefts break off a huge seawall at **Parada Santa**, making the most of weak SW swells. **Nalvo**, near Santa Maria has reef and beachbreak with options for most surfers. **Darigayos** catches both SW and NE swells, so if it's flat there, it's flat everywhere. The province of La Union is the hub of the west coast winter surf scene with San Juan at its centre. About 15 mellow and easy reefs and beaches break on a 40km stretch down to San Fernando. **German Sunset Break** is located at the north end of a long beachbreak which work on most swells, opposite the German Sunset Beach resort. At the south end **Urbitzondo** holds long lefts over sand. NW Luzon's Malibu-esque right, **Mona Liza Point** faces the resort of the same name. The Point holds up to 10ft and will be busy when working but longboard rules are the go so be prepared to share. There is a beachbreak on the inside. When there is a large swell, the fabled spot is **Car-rille**, a 300m long right point, with some comparisons to Rincon. The Filipino navy runs a base at **Poro Point** so access to its inconsistent rights may be tricky. If venturing to **Bauang**, near the cemetery and an abandoned beach resort, there's some consistent beachbreak.

There are two windswell seasons plus an option for powerful typhoons. From October to March constant NE monsoon driven waves break in the 1-5ft range, with constant offshore winds favouring rights. Spring is mostly flat. From June to November the SW monsoon starts pushing occasional small swells favouring lefts. If the waves are generated in close proximity, the onshore winds are pretty weak courtesy of the Cordillera Mountains but stronger in Ilocos Norte than La Union. During this period tropical storms and typhoons hit Luzon resulting in 6-8ft+ conditions but also torrential rains and havoc if they hit the coast. As for tides, don't worry! Barometric tides will be more significant than astronomic ones.

KAGE GOZUN

Mona Lisa Point

## TRAVEL INFORMATION

**Weather** – Three pronounced seasons: November-February NE monsoon dry season; March to May spring hot/dry season; June-October SW monsoon extremely wet season. The Philippines are visited every year by 20 or so typhoons known as 'Baguiosi' during the SW monsoon season and Luzon is top of the hit list. Boardshorts only.

**Lodging and Food** – Stay (±$45/dble) in Urbitzondo: San Juan Surf Resort; Sebay Surf Resort. For better standards, go to San Fernando or book Badoc Resort: $65/day, exclusive access, 2 jetskis + outrigger, airport pick up. Contact Surf The Earth. Filipino cuisine has Chinese, Malay and Spanish influences.

**Nature and Culture** – Don't miss Vigan - oldest surviving Spanish colonial city, Hundred Islands National Park, the epic journey from Baguio to Banaue across Central Cordillera. Avoid Poro Point sex tourist traps. High Altitude in San Fernando is a cool disco. Many Karaoke bars!

**Hazards and Hassles** – It's a land of natural disasters! Typhoons pass periodically; nearly half of the Philippine's 25 major earthquake faults are in Luzon. Beware flash floods and transport failures. Coral reefs can be treacherous and there's some foul smelling kelp! Minimal localism.

**Handy Hints** – For beginners, it is possible to rent boards from San Juan resorts or get stuff in Yokohama Surf Shop in metro Manila. Yokohama is also a well-organised surf school in La Union. A gun won't be necessary but a wide board for slow waves in La Union will be. San Fernando population is 90,000. English is widely spoken.

| STATISTICS | | J F | M A | M J | J A | S O | N D |
|---|---|---|---|---|---|---|---|
| SWELL | Direction | | | | | | |
| | Size (ft) | 2-3 | 1 | 0-1 | 2-3 | 3-4 | 3 |
| WIND | Direction | | | | | | |
| | Force | F4-F5 | F4 | F3-F4 | F4 | F4-F5 | F4-F5 |
| WATER | Wetsuit | | | | | | |
| | Temp/°C | 24 | 26 | 26 | 27 | 26 | 25 |
| WEATHER | Rainfall/mm | 9 | 45 | 270 | 450 | 250 | 45 |
| | days/mth | 1 | 3 | 12 | 11 | 8 | 1 |
| | Min temp/°C | 22 | 24 | 26 | 25 | 25 | 23 |
| | Max temp/°C | 30 | 33 | 32 | 31 | 31 | 30 |

# Baler, Luzon PHILIPPINES

From Manila a nerve jangling 5-6 hour road trip over the rolling Sierra Madre mountain range ends in Baler, Aurora province where the surfing scene in *Apocalypse Now* was filmed at Charlie's Point. Since the film crew departed leaving their surfboards behind with the locals in a sleepy backwater a surf destination has grown complete with surf shops, camps and schools introducing surfing to an increasing number of foreign and local tourists.

- \+ FREQUENT NE MONSOON SWELLS
- \+ SCENIC SIERRA MOUNTAINS
- \+ CHEAP & ENTERTAINING
- \+ PINOY SURF CULTURE

- – NO WORLD-CLASS WAVES
- – ONSHORE BEACHBREAKS
- – TOUGH OVERLAND ACCESS
- – LANDSLIDES, RAINS, ROBBERY

JS CALLAHAN/SURFEXPLORE

Cemento

A bunch of quality spots lie north of Baler, but they are difficult to access if there has been heavy rainfall. These include Diarabasin, a snappy lefthand reefbreak, 45km to the north. Closer to Baler is **Dalugen Reef**, a fast and hollow left over a flat reef with adjacent beachbreaks for the less experienced. Only 15mins walk from Sabang is **Lindie's Point** where waves were created when government engineers opened up the mouth of the estuary to prevent floods during the rainy season. Left and right rivermouth sandbanks have formed, but the rips are strong. **Charlie's Point** is the *Apocalypse Now* spot where average quality rivermouth peaks break lazily over a sand/gravel bottom. Baler is located at the south end of a 10km stretch of grey sand beach, flanked by several resorts like Aliya Surf Camp, Bay's Inn Resort or MIA Surf and Sports. **Sabang Beach** is found right in front of Bay's Inn, where beginners brave the soft beachbreak with one of the many surf schools. Righthanders often form off the rivermouth sandbars, offering more speed and shape. The best spot around is undoubtedly **Cemento**, aka Cobra Reef, since the wave resembles the shape of a cobra about to strike. This is an excellent, exciting, heart-in-mouth righthander over a short, sharp coral reef, 40min walk, 20 min by tricycle or 10min by motor boat from Sabang. Better at lower tides with a good NE swell, Cemento is for experienced surfers and the local crew usually get the lion's share of the sets. It's a long winding drive or a punishing 45 minutes by boat through rough seas to ride **Dicasalarin Cove**, a secluded white sand beach facing east. Exposed beach peaks over dead coral and sand can get good. There is a maze of barely accessible bays, reefs and rivermouths heading south to the port town of Dingalan.

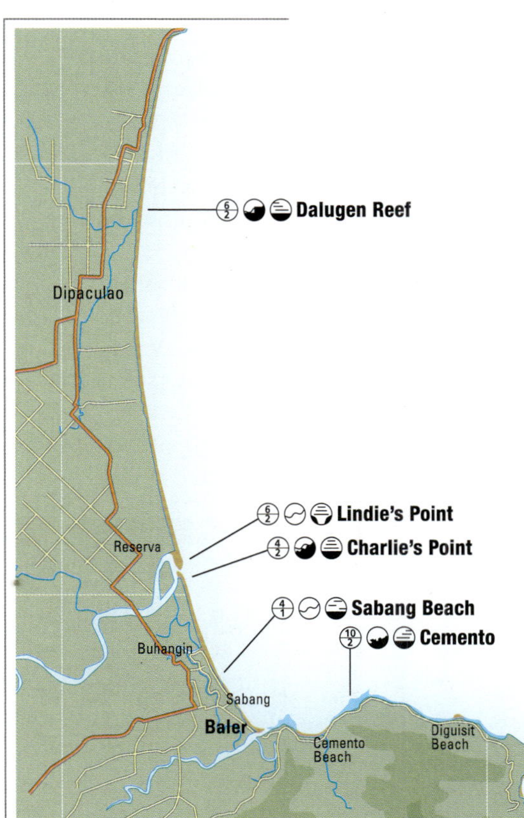


Aurora province is hit by typhoons at least 3 or 4 times a year, the season coinciding with the wet season from mid June to November and sometimes even December. The typhoons blow in from the Pacific during the SW monsoon, bringing good swells, but it can mean 3 or 4 days of high winds, heavy rains and tough travel. The best surf season runs from October to March, when the NE monsoon blows down from China, producing larger waves in the 3-8ft range. Winds will be onshore NE-E in the afternoon but mostly calm in the mornings. From March through June, the waves are relatively calm providing a good beachfront for swimmers. Tides are semi-diurnal with diurnal inequality, never exceeding 1m tidal range, even on spring tides.

## TRAVEL INFORMATION

**Weather** – Hot and humid with heavy rainfall throughout the year. Annual average rainfall is 3250mm (130in). Typhoons known as "bagyos" blow across the island about 20 times a year usually lasting 3 or 4 days. Two main wind currents – E-NE trade winds blow from November to April, then switches to a SW direction for the rest of the year. Average air temps 25°C (77°F) and water temps 26°C (79°F) vary little during the year.

**Lodging and Food** – Sabang Beach is action central. Bay's Inn Resort ($20 dble) basic rooms with fan, pool and restaurant. Aliya Surf Camp ($45 dble w b'fast) air con rooms, pool, billiards, surf school and restaurant. Lots of other accommodation. Cheap food – expect $5 for a really good meal.

**Nature and Culture** – Sierra mountains make for a beautiful tropical background. Check the small hot springs at Digisit near Cemento or Pimentel Falls near San Luis. Dilasag near Casiguran in the north is 8h away. Check the Banaue rice terraces in Isabela Province. Pinoys love partying plus karaoke and Philippine tourists come from Manila adding to the lively scene.

**Hazards and Hassles** – The Cobra section at Cemento can snap boards and smash bodies on the reef. Besides bugs and monsoon rains, watch out for thievery and pickpockets as there is much poverty. The journey from/to Manila can feel like a hassle, but is often an adventure! Typhoons can be pretty destructive over Aurora Province.

**Handy Hints** – Bay Inn and MIA Surf & Sports rent surfboards for $17-20 day. Plenty of surf schools and rental locations (Mahdox, MIA, Baler Surf School). Locations are named after barangays or local districts. Landslides, earthquakes, volcanic eruptions, floods, typhoons; the Philippines competes with Indo for catastrophes! Pinoys speak good English.

KAGE GOZUN

Sabang Beach

| STATISTICS | | J F | M A | M J | J A | S O | N D |
|---|---|---|---|---|---|---|---|
| SWELL | Direction | | | | | | |
| | Size (ft) | 4-5 | 3 | 1 | 1-2 | 2-3 | 5 |
| WIND | Direction | | | | | | |
| | Force | F4-F5 | F4 | F3-F4 | F4 | F4-F5 | F4-F5 |
| WATER | Wetsuit | | | | | | |
| | Temp/°C | 26 | 27 | 29 | 29 | 28 | 26 |
| WEATHER | Rainfall/mm | 182 | 221 | 256 | 228 | 342 | 370 |
| | days/mth | 13 | 10 | 10 | 10 | 15 | 17 |
| | Min temp/°C | 20 | 21 | 23 | 23 | 23 | 21 |
| | Max temp/°C | 29 | 31 | 33 | 33 | 32 | 30 |

# Catanduanes PHILIPPINES

Located just off the coast of South Luzon, Catanduanes island juts out into the Pacific as an ideal swell magnet for the NE typhoon swells. *Surfer* magazine published the story of a 1988 trip showing photos of a barreling righthander dubbed Majestics. However, the pictures were deceiving, not showing how quick, shallow or inconsistent the wave was. Many surfers end up spending weeks waiting for Majestics to do its thing, but those that do score it good, rate it as the Philippine's best barrel.

+ WORLD-CLASS RIGHTHANDER
+ EMPTY WAVES
+ EXOTIC, TROPICAL PARADISE
+ CHEAP AND MELLOW TRIP

- LONG FLAT SPELLS
- LACK OF SPOTS
- UNSUITABLE FOR BEGINNERS
- DIFFICULT ACCESS

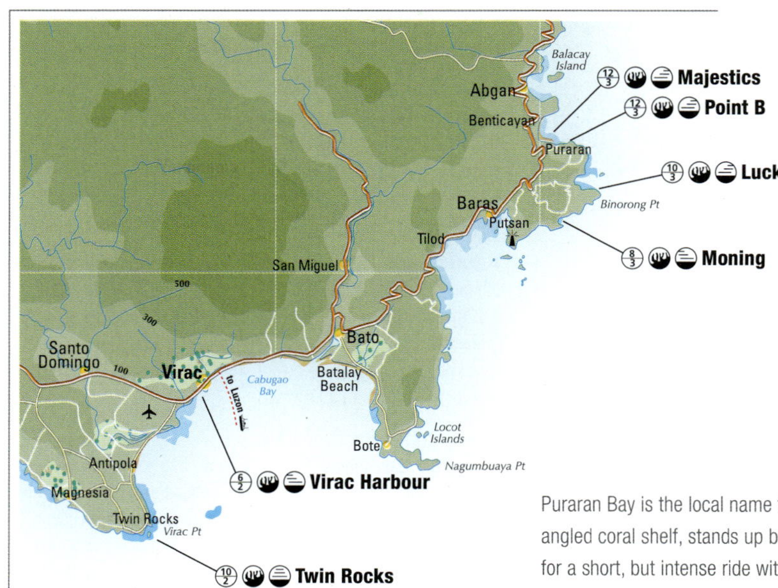

Point B

JS CALLAHAN/SURFEXPLORE

Puraran Bay is the local name for **Majestics**, which hits an angled coral shelf, stands up beyond straight and vortexes off for a short, but intense ride with an impressive power to size ratio. Needs at least a 2-3ft swell to clear the coral and it is best surfed from mid to high tide on the push. Having a light SW wind to hold up the lips is also a crucial factor, limiting the season to habagat months, which luckily coincide with the typhoons that bring the ideal E-NE swell direction. Intermediates might have fun on small days, but once it gets overhead, only tube-jockeys with an air-drop game will get into the heaving pits. Low tide can be ridden, but cuts are guaranteed to fallers and often result in infections and fevers, a long way from any hospital. Locals are usually cool and any hassles in the line-up may come from zealous regulars and transplants, irked by the wave's fickle nature. If conditions are too sketchy at Majestics, try **Point B** further to the S, but beware of the exposed rocks. It can be a brilliant wave but it's not suitable for beginners. By renting a boat you can reach **Lucky Point**, an exposed fringe of reef that needs E swell to line up properly. When Majestics and Point B are onshore go to **Moning**, a tidy right peeler that only works at high tide. Hire a boat in Baras to get out there. On big stormy days there can be a fun left inside **Virac Harbour**, which has plenty of opportunities to bust out some big moves. An hour south on the tip of the island, **Twin Rocks** has some fun lefts and rights and easy accommodation in a chilled-out atmosphere. None of the spots here ever get very busy, as there are only a handful of local and visiting foreign surfers. The island is big and certainly hides more spots. Hire a boat in Virac and go and explore.

Swell exposure is not great, coming only from typhoons travelling in a W-NW direction towards Japan. They can form at any time, but the majority occur between July and Nov, the peak months being Aug-Sept. There's an estimated 15-20 typhoons a year, each one providing 2-4 days of swell between 3-8ft, with peak swells hitting 12ft. From July to Oct the swells are cleaned up by the offshore SW wind. By Nov the wind is shifting round to an onshore, NE direction, although this transition period sees quite a lot of swell activity. The NE monsoon only brings small, onshore windswells. The May-June transition period will bring E-S winds, which fluctuate in strength and direction all the time, but generally it's quite calm and a good time for beginners. The tidal range is large and most of the shallow reefs are only rideable from mid to high tide.

Majestics

JS CALLAHAN/SURFEXPLORE

## TRAVEL INFORMATION

**Weather** – Hot and extremely humid year-round. The NE monsoon (amihan) lasts from Nov-April and not only brings onshores, but also huge amounts of rainfall. After the May-June transition period, the SW monsoon (habigat) starts blowing, bringing drier weather and offshore winds. Even though the swell comes from typhoons they rarely make landfall in the Philippines, although there is always the risk between July-Nov. If they do hit be prepared for devastation; super typhoon Loleng flattened every beach hut in Puraran in 1998.

**Lodging and Food** – Puraran Surf Beach Resort, Puting-Baybay Resort and Majestic Resort have beachfront local nipa huts on stilts fr $12/n and various rooms for less. Food is also cheap at $4-5 for a basic meal. Lots of seafood and rice.

**Nature and Culture** – Don't miss the 2500m Mayon volcano near Legaspi. The beaches here are some of the best in the world and the crystal clear water makes for excellent snorkelling and diving conditions. Climb up to the Puraran pass for some amazing views.

**Hazards and Hassles** – Reef cuts and malaria are your biggest enemies. Be prepared for flat days. Crowded line-ups are rare.

**Handy Hints** – Don't expect to find any surf gear available here. The local surfers, who are friendly and dedicated, always appreciate new gear. The annual Majestic Surfing Cup is usually held in October, contested by 48 surfers from around the country.

| STATISTICS | | J F | M A | M J | J A | S O | N D |
|---|---|---|---|---|---|---|---|
| SWELL | Direction | – | – | – | | | |
| | Size (ft) | 1 | 1 | 1-2 | 3 | 3-4 | 3-4 |
| WIND | Direction | | | | | | |
| | Force | F4 | F3 | F3 | F3-F4 | F3 | F3-F4 |
| WATER | Wetsuit | | | | | | |
| | Temp/°C | 24 | 24 | 25 | 26 | 25 | 24 |
| WEATHER | Rainfall/mm | 460 | 380 | 141 | 154 | 220 | 524 |
| | days/mth | 21 | 20 | 11 | 12 | 15 | 22 |
| | Min temp/°C | 23 | 23 | 24 | 24 | 24 | 23 |
| | Max temp/°C | 29 | 31 | 31 | 31 | 31 | 29 |

# Eastern Samar PHILIPPINES

Samar is the Philippines third largest volcanic island with rough, hilly terrain covered by lush tropical vegetation. Swell exposure is good with waves hitting both the north and east-facing coasts. Borongan, the provincial capital with 50,000 people is a good starting point to discover the 150km-long pristine coastline, which is largely unexplored, since travelling around Eastern Samar by road is challenging and slow, especially during the wet season. Samar was the natural choice for exploratory boat expeditions heading north from Siargao, resulting in discoveries like the secret spot Philippine Dream.

+ TYPHOONS AND WINDSWELLS
+ UNDISCOVERED QUALITY BREAKS
+ WARM AND TROPICAL
+ CHEAP AND LIVELY

- ERRATIC TYPHOON SWELLS
- MESSY WINDSWELLS
- HEAVY RAINS
- TIME CONSUMING TRAVEL

KAGE GOZUN

Sulingan Beach

A trike ride north of town, near the discos is an inconsistent beachbreak named **Boulevard**, which only works with a big swell due to the protection of the cove and offshore islets. There can be a fast right at the rivermouth on big NE swells. Fickle, challenging, short, hollow lefts, break over live coral at **Pirates Cove** in front of the so-called surf resort that offers a multitude of other activities as the waves are rarely any good. **Santa Monica** caters for fishermen, scuba divers and surfers if enough E swell is penetrating the bay. The reefs can hold some peaks and there is plenty of beachfront accommodation. The fine sand of **Lalawigan Beach** stretches south and the fringing reef holds low quality peaks all the way down to the Suribao rivermouth lefts and beachbreak at Omawas. Further south, 1h from Borongan, is **Llorente**, where beginners and improvers will appreciate some sand-bottomed peaks that seem to get plenty of swell and break through the tide. Once the biggest US Military base in the Philippines, Guiuan (pronounced Giwan) is 111km and 2 hours travel from Borongan and situated on a long, low, narrow coralline peninsula jutting out of Samar. Over the bridge on Calicoan Island, **Sulingan Beach** has a left and a right breaking on both sides of a narrow channel. Can have some power and gets shallow so pushing tides and wave faces up to 8ft before closing out. Beginners favour the centre part of the beach, sometimes referred to as ABC. The reef bottom of Sulingan has a gradual slope, devoid of the crevices of Siargao's Cloud 9, but the live coral is covered with sea urchins. Paddling out is fairly easy, though at low tide, expect a fair walk over coral in booties. The surf camp here was flattened by supertyphoon Yolanda in 2013.

Surfing in Samar presents a choice between the SW monsoon less rainy season (July-Sept) with dominant SW offshores and very erratic typhoon swells, or the NE monsoon very rainy season (Nov-Mar) with its dominant onshores but a consistent supply of windswell with occasional clean conditions. Usually, travellers aim for a lucky break between August-October hoping for the perfect ideal typhoon swell but many have been badly skunked, even on a month long trip. A better option may be to choose November, as the typhoon season switches to the NE monsoon windswell season. As far as tides go, they have a diurnal inequality so expect different tidal ranges during the day; they reach 1m on spring tides, which is significant enough on shallow reefs.

## TRAVEL INFORMATION

**Weather** – Humid and heavy rainfall year-round, with two distinct monsoon seasons: The more rainy NE monsoon from Nov-Mar. Occasional dry spells in May and June. Less rainy SW monsoon from July-Sept when westerly winds (Habagat) become dominant. Average yearly rainfall is 3000mm. 192 days of rain, average temp is 27°C (80°F). Frequent typhoons; the last one that hit land was in Dec '15. Water temps don't get super-warm, bring a light shorty and booties.

**Lodging and Food** – In Borongan, try Pension Alang-Alang, in front of Provincial Capital building ($4-8/d), or Domsowir Hotel in the same range. In Guiuan, try the Tanghay Lodge ($3-14/d), on the W-facing beach (flat). Expect to pay $3 for a decent meal.

**Nature and Culture** – Samar has the 2nd largest virgin forest in the Philippines. Close by are secluded waterfalls, caves and jungle treks. Try river tubing which involves lazily drifting downstream and enjoying the cool waters and tropical scenery. Local sailboats are called 'siling'. Borongan Fiesta in September. Cross Sohoton Natural Bridge!

**Hazards and Hassles** – Be ready to face buckets of rain especially in the NE monsoon season. Samar has now been decalred malaria free. A Yellow Fever certificate is required if arriving from infected areas. Coral reefbreaks can be very shallow.

**Handy Hints** – Take two all-round boards especially if staying for a while; the locals should be stoked to buy old gear upon departure. Rodel Aboy is the best local in Borongan. English is widely spoken.

JS CALLAHAN/SURFEXPLORE

Llorente

| STATISTICS | | J F | M A | M J | J A | S O | N D |
|---|---|---|---|---|---|---|---|
| SWELL | Direction | | | | | | |
| | Size (ft) | 3-4 | 2 | 0-1 | 1-2 | 3 | 4 |
| WIND | Direction | | | | | | |
| | Force | F4 | F4 | F3 | F3-F4 | F4 | F4 |
| WATER | Wetsuit | | | | | | |
| | Temp/°C | 23 | 23 | 24 | 25 | 24 | 23 |
| WEATHER | Rainfall/mm | 550 | 290 | 240 | 160 | 260 | 590 |
| | days/mth | 20 | 12 | 10 | 8 | 12 | 20 |
| | Min temp/°C | 22 | 23 | 23 | 23 | 23 | 22 |
| | Max temp/°C | 28 | 30 | 32 | 32 | 31 | 30 |

# Siargao PHILIPPINES

**Perfectly positioned as close to the plummeting depths of the Philippine Trench as possible, Siargao (pronounced Shar-gaw) represents the highest concentration of good surf to be found in the 7,107 islands of the archipelago. There are a number of world-class waves on the east-facing coastline, where many of the 32 documented spots are outside reefs and islets that can only be accessed by boat, while others break closer to the beach on a fringing reef. Cloud 9 is the most famous spot, located in General Luna, which is a good place to be based during the SW monsoon, while just up the coast, Pilar is a better bet during the NE trades.**

+ WORLD-CLASS REEFS
+ UNCROWDED SPOTS
+ TROPICAL CONDITIONS
+ CHEAP LIVING COSTS

- GENERALLY SMALL SURF
- LONG FLAT SPELLS
- LONG TRANSFER JOURNEY
- POLITICAL INSTABILITY

LAURENT MASUREL

Stimpy's

TOBIAS HETTIGER

Pacifico

Near San Isidro is **Pacifico**, a long, hollow and consistent left that likes N in the swell to stop closing-out. Long walk over the weedy reef lagoon best done in booties. Further north, Burgos and Alegria also have empty waves and pristine beaches. On SW winds with a good E-NE swell and full tide, **Caridad** reveals a perfect left with a low crowd factor. The place to be based during the NE trades is **Pilar**, only seven miles from General Luna, but a long boat or car ride. The Pilar area is generally not as crowded as the General Luna region and the deep bay holds a selection of good left reefs that can be surfed during NE storms. Get a boat to explore the coral reefs and rocky outcrops on the southern side of the bay like Salvation, Philippine Deep and Shifties. **Stimpy's** can be a ferocious, unpredictable left barrel that wraps around the coral heads and explodes with board-breaking power on overhead swells. Can also be mushy, fun walls and shoulders on smaller days when the regular NE blows, but there is usually something at this consistent, advanced spot. Take a longer board to make the drop and plenty of water and sun protection in the boat. These outer reefs get invaded by stinging jellyfish so a long sleeve rash vest can be a good idea. **Tuesday Rock**, Rock Island and Pancit Reef have all been used to describe this long, consistent, soft-peeling right that breaks in the shadow of a rocky islet, across the deep channel from Stimpy's. N-NE swells hit it perfectly and the SW monsoon is dead offshore, so it can hold double overhead waves and is best at lower tides when cutbacks can transform to cover-ups. Boat access only so crowds are variable. Improvers at high, intermediates up at low. **Jacking Horse** offers some relief from the crowds and an easier righthander, peaking up at the end of the reef as it turns a corner and faces NW. Can be a left out the back but it's short. NE swell and SW winds are ideal and lower tides link the sections better. Proper paddling channel and variable size makes it popular with intermediates while beginners surf the inside section called Little Pony. **Quicksilver** is Cloud 9's neighbouring reef peak and generally works at the same time. Short and fast peak, favouring rights and safer at higher tides. Good crowd relief valve and may offer more chances for those unable to get waves 150m down the reef. It takes about an hour to walk from General Luna to ✪**Cloud 9** but most of the established surf camps are located a lot

## TRAVEL INFORMATION

**Weather** – The Philippines is hot and extremely humid year-round. The Pacific side of the Philippines is subject to two monsoon patterns, the NE monsoon called amihan from Nov to April not only brings onshores and constant windswell, but also huge amounts of rainfall. In July the SW monsoon habagat starts blowing, this brings less rain and better weather patterns. Typhoons rarely make landfall this far S, but if they are going to then July-Dec is the risk period. The water is warm all year, so take boardshorts, a rash vest and booties for the reef walks.

**Lodging and Food** – There are 40 surf camps/resorts around Cloud Nine and General Luna from basic to full luxury; choose from Ocean 101 ($18-135 dbl), Sagana Resort (fr $80/p/n dble full board), Turtle ($36/n/dbl) or upmarket villas at Kawayan Resort (fr $120/n/dble). Closer to General Luna is Buddha's Surf Resort (fr $55/n/dbl) and Isla Cabana Resort (fr $100/n/4p) plus dozens more surf/guest houses. In Pilar try Lucod Beach Resort, Jafe Surf in Pacifico and White Sands in Burgos. Food ranges from cheap market stalls and street BBQ's to expensive resort restaurants; $5-10 a meal upwards.

**Nature and Culture** – The SUP, kite-boarding, kayaking, diving, snorkelling, fishing and jet-skiing are all excellent and many camps/hotels arrange hire and tours. Jump in a banca boat to the small outer islands. Explore the mangrove systems of Del Carmen or Pilar, natural hot springs near Lake Mainit, giant caves on Hikdop Island, Magpupungko rocks, Tak Tak waterfalls or whirlpools in the Surigao straits. For night-time entertainment go to General Luna and the videoke bars.

**Hazards and Hassles** – Siargao is hard to get to. There is a growing band of competitive local surfers and quite a lot of foreign surfers competing at Cloud Nine, but there are plenty of other spots that are empty. Rain, intense heat and malarial mosquitoes are present.

**Handy Hints** – Bring all your own surf gear, including a step-up for big days. Rentals for beginners and essential kit available from Hippie's Surf Shop and repairs are done in Catangnan.

### Cloud 9

**LAT. 9.813958° LONG. 126.167131°**

Cloud Nine is a perfect, top to bottom, barreling peak that's short but sweet when the conditions align. The more E in the swell the better as this will keep the door open to the safety of the channel, while N-NE tends to slam it. Higher tides also improve makeability as the coral lurks challengingly close to the open air. The rights are most coveted, while the lefts are shorter, yet just as hollow off the peak, before quickly shutting down. Sucks in the swell and can handle pretty large faces before maxing-out. Confident, nimble, experienced surfers will love it, while intermediates may struggle. The walk along the snaking, recently rebuilt pier gets you within 200m of the peak and avoids a lot of coral reef. The annual pro contest is a big event for Siargao, when it is a good time to visit for the party and pageantry, but not for getting shacked at Crowd 9! The tight take-off zone can be a hassle with locals and expats fighting for the bombs, but patience will be rewarded by the generally friendly local crew.

closer to this classy, world famous keg-fest. **Tuason Point** is a seriously heavy left that breaks hard and hollow down the fringe of exposed reef about 400m south of Cloud 9. On its day it is a fast throaty barrel for experienced surfers and low tide is sketchy. Despite its quality, Tuason is rarely crowded compared to its noisy neighbour. It's a 300m paddle out to **Horseshoe** (aka Hawaiian Jack), a wedgy, high tide right that shoulders off in deeper water and is best in headhigh swells. Multiple peaks and corners pop up all the way along a 2km fringing reef leading down to General Luna. It's difficult to assess size without making the 20min walk/paddle over the low tide reef, which many take from the cemetery, or pay for a 5 min boat ride from town. It's a bit more forgiving and rarely crowded, but blows out easily. General Luna itself is too sheltered, but is the best place to pick up a pump boat out to Daku Island, home to a long, fun right called **Barrio** (or Inside Dako) that breaks out in the channel. The reef's position cuts some swell size and the slower speed and deeper water make it a favourite with improvers. Dako Point has more challenging, sectiony rights on the islands northern fringe of reef that are also offshore in the SW monsoon, plus plenty of potential on the exposed eastern tip. Across the channel in front of Guyam Island there are a number of low to mid tide rides if there are too many boats at Barrio. **Pansukian** was one of the original waves ridden on Siargao, but these days is usually empty despite having some challenging peelers over the obligatory coral shelf in NE winds and E-SE swells. Daku blocks the NE swells. Short ride out via the bright white sands of Naked Island. It's a much longer boat mission to surf **Mabuntok**, which is close to the islands of East Bucas, Casulian, La Janosa, Mamon and Antokon. These waves aren't really suited to beginners but they're not especially critical. On the south side of Antokon there are various reefy peaks that are offshore in a NE'er.

LAURENT MASUREL

Tuesday Rock

Seasonally, the Philippines is fickle and difficult to predict, because the only real groundswell generator is from irregular typhoons travelling W-NW towards Japan. They may form at any time but July-Dec is the prime time, peaking through Sept-Oct. There is an estimated 15-20 swells in each season, that provide several days of E-NE swells between 3-8ft with occasional 12ft days. The best time for clean conditions is during the SW monsoon from July-Oct when the wind is predominantly offshore but both swell height and consistency is low. After this the wind switches around to the NE, bringing onshores and much bigger NE windswells that peak in Dec/Jan. Oct/Nov should bring the best chance of swell and some lighter winds. The calm May-June transition period sees low winds blowing from a E-SE direction, while swell is almost non-existent. The tidal range is minimal, but most shallow reefs are better surfed from mid-high tide.

| STATISTICS | | J F | M A | M J | J A | S O | N D |
|---|---|---|---|---|---|---|---|
| SWELL | Direction | | | | | | |
| | Size (ft) | 7-8 | 4-6 | 2-3 | 2 | 2-4 | 6-7 |
| WIND | Direction | | | | | | |
| | Force | F4 | F4 | F3 | F3-F4 | F3-F4 | F4 |
| WATER | Wetsuit | | | | | | |
| | Temp/°C | 24 | 24 | 24 | 25 | 24 | 24 |
| WEATHER | Rainfall/mm | 460 | 380 | 141 | 154 | 220 | 524 |
| | days/mth | 21 | 20 | 11 | 12 | 15 | 22 |
| | Min temp/°C | 23 | 23 | 24 | 24 | 24 | 23 |
| | Max temp/°C | 29 | 31 | 31 | 31 | 31 | 29 |

# Northern Mindanao PHILIPPINES

Mindanao, the second largest island of the Philippines, is an enchanting land of volcanic mountains cloaked in exotic tropical plants, leading down to squeaky white and pink sand beaches, where boldly-striped vintas ply the waters between houses perched precariously on stilts. Wave-rich Siargao island is close, so there is little wonder that intrepid travellers have searched around and discovered some perfect, typhoon swell gems like Lanuza's Doot Poktoy. An international longboard contest has been held there since Nov 2005, attracting some big Aussie names and exposure for this budding surf town, helped by the unusual "breaking of the board" opening ceremony.

+ WORLD-CLASS SAND POINT
+ MOSTLY UNCROWDED
+ CLOSE TO SIARGAO
+ VERY CHEAP, VIRGIN MINDANAO

– INCONSISTENT SWELLS
– SHORT SURF SEASON
– DIFFICULT ACCESS
– UN TRAVEL WARNINGS

Punta Left

JS CALLAHAN/SURFEXPLORE

A boat will be needed to surf the excellent **Auqui Lefts**, where a shallow coral reef set-up produces fast barreling waves even when small. Lanuza Bay is shallow, so from Cantilan to Lanuza there is an endless set of mushy beachbreaks and **Union** is the easiest village to get to near the mouth of the estuary. Legendary **Doot Poktoy** has incredible, fast rights barrelling over 300 meters of gravel sandbank at Lanuza's rivermouth. Low tide will be tubular, while high tide will be less intense but still a lot of fun. It has been compared to a reverse Mundaka in power and shape but is even more fickle. The surrounding town beachbreaks are perfect for learners. **Castor** is named after the land owner and holds gnarly lefts at high tide over a very sharp, shallow reef, so any S wind is imperative to clean up the faces. A 10min ride up the bumpy road is **Punta Left**, aka Big Star, another treacherous left reefbreak requiring booties which can handle any big N-NE swell. The most consistent wave around is probably **Moshi-Moshi**, a rivermouth peak with longer rights and shorter lefts. Large rocks mark the take-off spot and pop up along the line at low tide. A relatively recent discovery **Badjang**, aka Jelly's Point, has some high quality rights similar to Siargao reefs, working on any size NE swell and is fairly easy to get to, only 8km from Lanuza. On a clean, small swell, eyeball **Cauit Point**, which is a swell magnet left off the tip of the cape and only accessible by boat. When a typhoon swell maxes out Cauit, cruise down to **Glenda's** bowly lefts, which are a really long paddle from Cortes, so use a boat if possible. Before Tandag, there are heaps of unchartered east-facing reefs waiting for the curious who have time, a boat and the inclination to surf a new spot if the wind stays light.

Getting it good at Doot Poktoy is not easy, as it requires a powerful typhoon swell to push into the sheltered location, the sandbar to be in good condition and the tide as low as possible. Other less-sheltered spots require any NE swell to work. SW habagat monsoon wind is straight offshore (May to Oct). Typically, waves over boulders will be in the 2-6ft range, rivermouths will be more like 2-4ft and some reefbreaks might jump up to the 8-10ft range. Tides (reference is Davao) are semi-diurnal with daily inequality and tidal range can go over 1.8m, which is fairly significant for low tide rivermouths and high tide, shallow reefbreaks.

Doot Poktoy

TOBIAS HETTIGER

## TRAVEL INFORMATION

**Weather** – Monsoon winds blow from the SW from May to October and from the NE from November to February. Temperatures remain relatively constant during the year and seasons consist of periods of wet and dry. Wet months are from November to June with January as the wettest and September as the driest month. From June to December, typhoons often strike the archipelago and when accompanied by floods or high winds they may cause great damage. November through February constitutes the most agreeable season with cool air, invigorating at night and pleasant, sunny days. Temps usually range from 23-32°C (74-90°F). Boardies only.

**Lodging and Food** – Resorts and lodging houses are still very limited so look for home-stay program such as Mami's Surf Haus ($4pppn). Poktoy Palm Haven non-aircon rooms at $5 per guest per day while air-con room is $10. Lanuza Surf Camp is in front of Castor left with beds from $3.50/n.

**Nature and Culture** – Check Lanuza Marine Park and Sanctuary, Magkawas Falls, Green Paradise, Campamento Caves and Lanuza Wetland Park and Mangrove Forest. Ethnic tribes weave glorious tales of brave warriors and haughty princesses into colourful tapestries and fabrics.

**Hazards and Hassles** – It is advised against travel to SW Mindanao because of civil unrest. Northern Mindanao should be safer but check with the embassy. Some rocks can be dangerous, but waves are more beginner friendly than Siargao.

**Handy Hints** – Check with Lanuza Bay Surfing Company, their room rates are reasonable as well as their surfing rates at $4/hour for an instructor and $5/day surf board rental. They make surfboards from the local amakan tree, which costs $70/sq foot. Some of these Pinoy-made surfboards are exported to California.

| STATISTICS | | J F | M A | M J | J A | S O | N D |
|---|---|---|---|---|---|---|---|
| SWELL | Direction | | | | | | |
| | Size (ft) | 4 | 2-3 | 0-1 | 1 | 2 | 4-5 |
| WIND | Direction | | | | | | |
| | Force | F4 | F3 | F2-F3 | F3 | F4 | F3 |
| WATER | Wetsuit | | | | | | |
| | Temp/°C | 27 | 28 | 29 | 28 | 28 | 28 |
| WEATHER | Rainfall/mm | 313 | 250 | 136 | 127 | 136 | 342 |
| | days/mth | 21 | 20 | 11 | 12 | 15 | 22 |
| | Min temp/°C | 23 | 23 | 24 | 24 | 24 | 24 |
| | Max temp/°C | 28 | 29 | 31 | 31 | 31 | 29 |

# Northern Maluku INDONESIA

The original Spice Islands, the Malukus (Moluccas or Molluques) are the only Indonesian island chain in the Pacific. Despite waves as good as the Philippines, these islands remain largely ignored by travelling surfers. Occasional boat forays into the region have revealed an outstanding variety of breaks, most of which go unsurfed. A small number of feral surfers make the long trek through the jungles around Christmas time, to stay in remote villages and surf the better-known spots.

+ REGULAR N MONSOON SWELL
+ QUALITY, MID-SIZED WAVES
+ CALM WINDS, SMALL TIDES
+ NEWLY OPENED SURF AREA

- SHORT SURF SEASON
- LONG DISTANCES BETWEEN SPOTS
- FEW ORGANISED BOAT TRIPS
- VOLCANIC ACTIVITY AND QUAKES

DAN HAYLOCK

Serenade

Close to the bigger airport and optional boat charter departure point of Ternate, the reliable rights of **Sama Sama** break beneath the steep headland cliffs, peeling for about two or three turns. Changes constantly through the tide. Further north, Halmahera hides a bunch of great waves including the incredibly long, cruising walls of **Paniki Point** that bend through 130º bringing you almost back to the peak. Offshore on Loloda Utara islands the main attractions are on Salandageke Island. **Sidewalk** breaks down a natural rock spit, is ideally exposed to the NNE and can be an angry fast shut-down tube or a perfect, long, mellow righthander, ideal for longboarding when small. **Racing Lefts** across the channel are long and sectiony. **Coconut Swing** is a savage left break, but few waves are rideable. On the north coast of Halmahera **Double Dome** is ridden by local surfers on wooden planks. Lefts break down the angled reef into the town, offshore in westerlies. Pulau Rau has two setups dubbed **Nachos**, a fun high tide peak/left and **Tacos**, a super-fast left fringing reef over super-sharp coral. **Tanjung Padang** is a great set-up, with long, fast rights over the reef, flanked by a deep-water channel. Nearby **Short Ledge** is a thick high tide right barrel on the east side of a deep bay with further possibilities. Sopi, the northernmost bay on Morotai, is an obvious swell magnet. 40mins walk from the village where a few surfers hang out **Serenade** (named after one of the first boat trips to the area) is a stunning left. A ledgy take-off into an angular barrel section (which regularly slams shut) leads onto smooth, variable speed walls mixed with clean tapered shoulders. This easier wide section peaks up and runs off down the reef, leaving plenty of room for lip-tapping and roundhouses. Despite working on all tides, the two sections are distinctly separate on smaller swells and the fairly benign reef can get sketchy on the inside section close to the jungle shoreline. **Village Reform** is a rapid right that is shallow at low and fun, but sectiony at high. Outside **Indo Jiwa** is an epic right with fast outside sections and hollow walls, but needs plenty of size or N in the swell and higher tides. The east coasts of Morotai and Halmahera hide a multitude of breaks but do catch the E winds. **Pulau Kecil**, an island off the town of Berebere, has a long, wrapping righthander and a left. The **Tobelo Islands** pick up NE-E swell on a number of different reefs. Lefts off Kokara hit the same channel as the rights of Tagalaya while the reliable righthanders at Green Pools on Tupu Tupu, pick up the most swell at lower tides. Miti has the best left spinning over coral shelf and a short right further up the straight reef when small.

## TRAVEL INFORMATION

**Weather** – The climate is heavily influenced by the monsoon trends. Hot and humid is the rule with over 2500mm of rain a year. While SW monsoon (April-Oct) brings downpours the NE monsoon (Nov-March) surf season is somewhat clearer with small daytime temperature variation and frequent squalls and thunderstorms. Water is amongst the warmest on earth, at 29°C (84ºF).

**Food and Lodging** – There are cheap hotels ($5-10) in Ternate, Daruba or Tobelo. Ferals make the trek to Sopi for homestays. The most experienced/most regular charters are run by the BaliCamp/Sama Sama. Other irregular boat options include Bulan Baru; Raja Ampat; Lambo Cruises and The Anne Judith. Food is fresh and cheap - pay $3 for a meal in town.

**Nature and Culture** – There is not much in Maluku except thick jungle and rusted WW2 sunken ships and planes to dive on. There's superb snorkelling on untouched reefs. The waterfall shower at Paniki Point is a gem.

**Hazards and Hassles** – Virgin area with a low population. For land access malaria is present and humidity levels high. Travelling even short distances on motorbikes can take hours. Smoking volcanoes dominate the skyline and mini volcanic eruptions, with ash clouds, are a regular occurrence.

**Handy Hints** – Take at least 2 everyday boards - a longboard or groveller may come in handy when it is small. The water is extremely warm, so pack plenty of wax.

OLLIE FITZJONES

Sama Sama

Although the NW Pacific typhoon season (Sept-Oct) must have some epic days, it's safer to hit these islands at the heart of the winter NE monsoon season (Nov-March) for consistent 3-6ft wind-driven waves, with bigger days at exposed spots. Winds at this equatorial "doldrums" latitude are light and variable. Glassy days are the norm, but onshore ENE winds do occur, shifting NNW if the sun is shining. Tidal range varies up to 1m, and affects almost all the known spots. Tides are difficult to gauge and accurate information is hard to find – ask the local fishermen.

| STATISTICS | | J F | M A | M J | J A | S O | N D |
|---|---|---|---|---|---|---|---|
| SWELL | Direction | | | | | | |
| | Size (ft) | 4-5 | 2-3 | 0-1 | 1-2 | 2-3 | 4 |
| WIND | Direction | | | | | | |
| | Force | F3 | F3 | F2-F3 | F3 | F3 | F2-F3 |
| WATER | Wetsuit | | | | | | |
| | Temp/°C | 28 | 28 | 29 | 28 | 28 | 29 |
| WEATHER | Rainfall/mm | 123 | 207 | 577 | 501 | 198 | 123 |
| | days/mth | 13 | 17 | 23 | 21 | 14 | 12 |
| | Min temp/°C | 24 | 24 | 23 | 23 | 23 | 24 |
| | Max temp/°C | 31 | 30 | 28 | 27 | 28 | 31 |

# YOUR **SURF TRAVEL** SPECIALIS

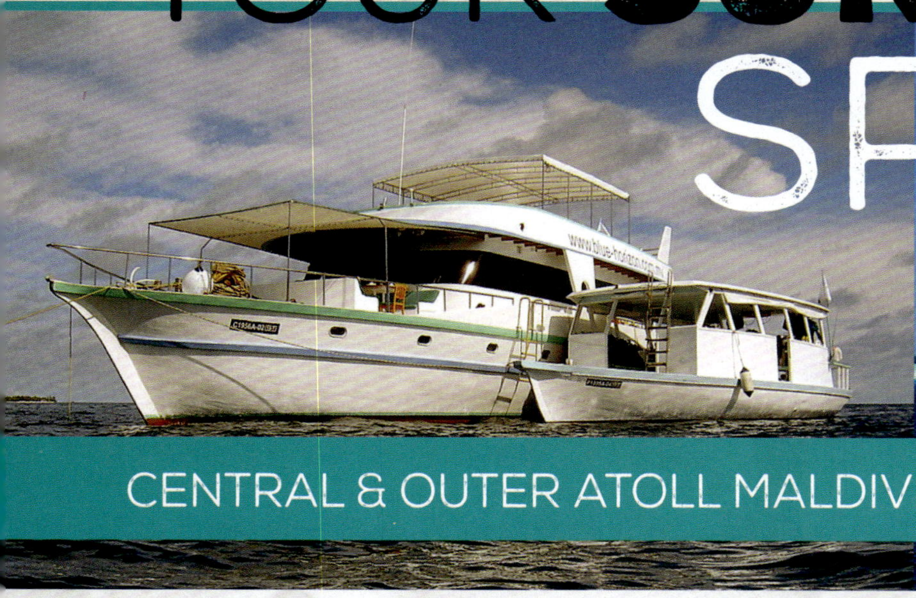
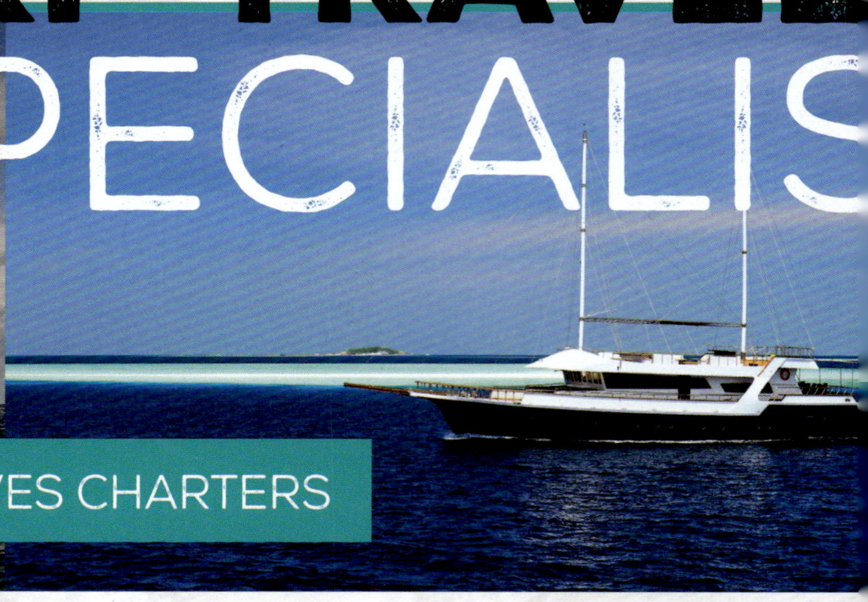

CENTRAL & OUTER ATOLL MALDIVES CHARTERS

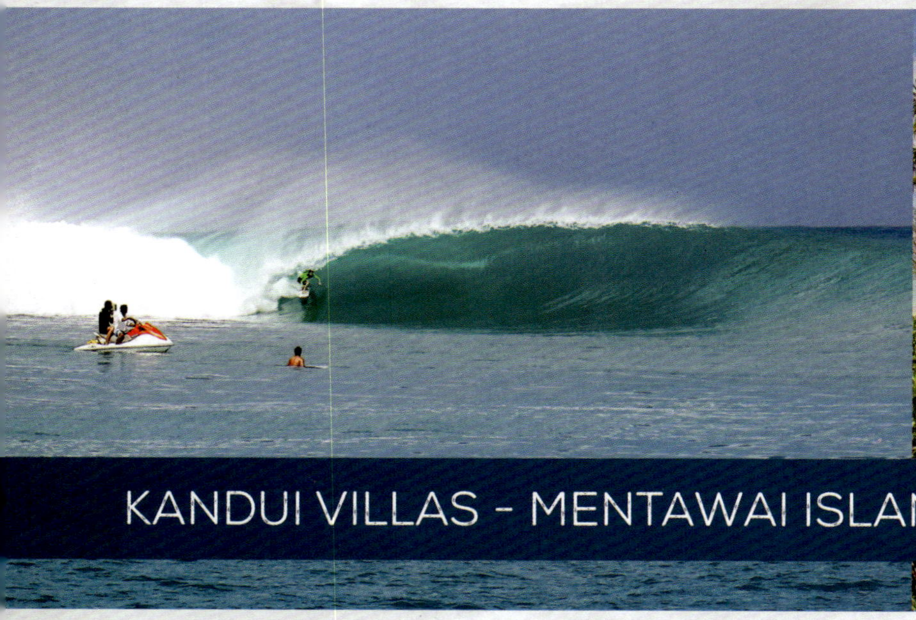
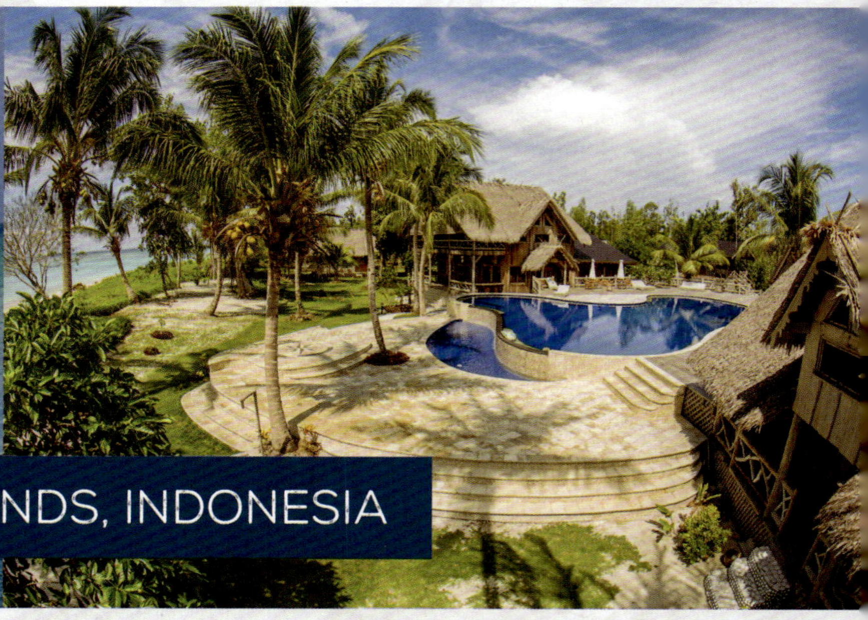

KANDUI VILLAS - MENTAWAI ISLANDS, INDONESIA

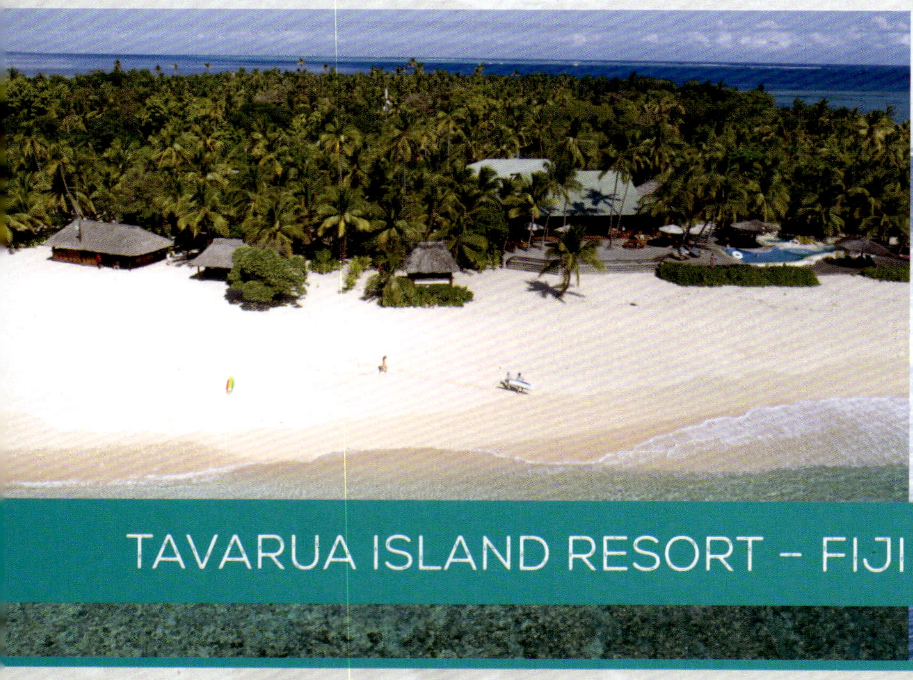
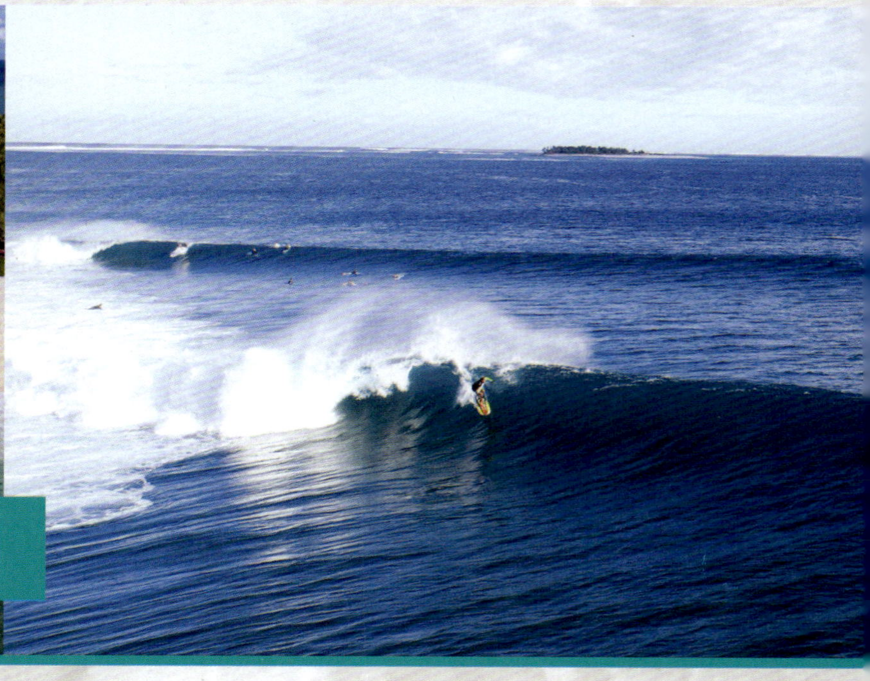

TAVARUA ISLAND RESORT – FIJI

FOR A FULL LIST OF THE WORLD'S PREMIER SURF PRODUCT, INFORMATION AND AVAILABILITY; **CONTACT THOSE WHO KNOW BEST!**

TS

Atoll Travel

WATERWAYS
SURF ADVENTURES

# PACIFIC OCEAN

Dwarfing the Atlantic with a surface area twice the size, the Pacific covers a third of the globe and is by far the Earth's biggest single feature. It is also the deepest ocean, holds the tallest mountains and the largest coral reef, but even more importantly, it is home to the planet's biggest surf! Booming winter Aleutian swells saturate the North Pacific, while southern hemisphere lines roar out of the forties latitudes almost year-round, peppering the South Pacific and beyond. Alongside these two main supply lines, there's always a chance of cyclones, hurricanes or typhoons, plus the ever-present east-flavoured trades can top up the islands with reliable windswell. The Pacific is encircled by 452 volcanoes and sitting majestically at the centre of this enormous lava-fed halo is Hawaii, which fittingly represents both the centre of The Ring of Fire and the centre of the surfing universe.

BEN THOUARD
Tahiti, French Polynesia

# The Surf

NORTH PACIFIC OCEAN

SOUTH PACIFIC OCEAN

Sandaun & East Sepik
Kavieng
New Georgia
Malaita & Makira
Pohnpei
Majuro
Kiritimati & Tabuaeran
Mamanucas
Efaté
Kadavu Passage
South Province
Tongatapu
Savai'i & Upolu
Tutuila
Rarotonga
Huahine & Raiatea
Tuamotu
Tahiti & Moorea
Northland and Auckland
Gisborne
Waikato
Taranaki
Mahia Peninsula
North Canterbury
Otago and Southland

SEE HAWAII MAP PAGE 251

## NEW ZEALAND

New Zealand sits at the bottom of the Ring of Fire, representing the 10th longest coastline in the world, offering 15,134km of Pacific wave-breaking rock and sand. After splitting off Australia, sinking then being thrust up by volcanic activity between the Earth's tectonic plates, New Zealand offers a unique surfing opportunity over a variety of points, reef, beaches and rivermouths in the temperate, stormy waters of the South Pacific.

**North Island** – The **Taranaki** zone and the world-class lefts of Raglan in the **Waikato** region are separated by the North Taranaki Bight which offers some winter swell protection and increasingly lonely waves beneath sheer cliffs on straight grey beaches and a bunch of lightly surfed spots at the harbours and rivermouths like Mokau and Awakino. The most populated region of NZ is described in the **Northland and Auckland** pages with the bulk of the city's inner beaches left for the kite crew while surfers hit the rare breaks on the North Shore or maybe even ferry across to Waiheke Island.

ANDREW SHIELD

Northland, New Zealand

The Coromandel Peninsula is a veritable feast of perfect mountain-backed bays and a heavy sprinkling of islands, all exposed to swell from NNW to SE. North-facing Fletcher Bay is shadowed by Great Barrier Island, but the beaches of Waikawau Bay or Matarangi, the reef at Kuaotunu and the shorie barrels of Otama are less compromised by the Mercury Islands. The east coast of the Coromandel shelves steeply and shapes barrels aplenty at Hot Water Beach, Tairua and popular summer surf town Whangamata, where the fickle rivermouth left gets epic. Bay of Plenty is well named with 200kms of broad golden sands from E-facing Waihi to NW oriented Cape Runaway Beach where peaks and rivermouth bars offer plenty of wind options. Highlights include restricted access Matakana

CORY SCOTT
Southland, New Zealand

Island, Mount Maunganui (despite the failed artificial reef), swell-sucking Newdicks, elusive Whakatane Heads rights and a dozen more shifty beachbreaks around to the Motu river delta in N flavour swells. **Gisborne** is the east coast Kiwi surfers town with ample swell window and a multi-aspect coastline, peppered with quality breaks. Exactly the same can be said for the **Mahia Peninsula** a mere 40km south and separated by a wild, mountainous coast that's hard to scope as the highway heads inland at Wharerata. Endless driftwood strewn, black sand beachbreak encircles Hawkes Bay and there are some fine rivermouth bars at Wairoa and Mohaka. Napier's best breaks are at Stingray Bay or Clive Rivermouth and the quality continues at Haumoana and Te Awanga mouths. Out of the bay and back in the full swell window, Ocean Beach gets big and unruly, Waimarama has more protection at the south end which is close to the challenging lefts of Cray Bay. Crowds dissolve into the rural hinterland and big arcing beaches like Porongahau, Herbertsville and Akitio, are punctured by rivers, providing empty surf in NW winds. Right reefs at Aramoana and Blackhead add to the inventory, before heading into the wilds of the Wairarapa region and some heavy waves on both the east and south coasts. The Gap at Castlepoint is encircled by cliffs, offering unrivalled protection from onshores. Heading toward Cape Palliser, the mountainous landscape hides some epic reefs at Tora where a number of sucky, powerful and long rights roll into the stream mouth beside surfer-filled free-camps. Around the cape, a concentration of west-facing reefs welcome competent surfers to try the muscular walls at Craps, Little Ning Nongs, Raspberries and Dee Dees. More lefts hug the rocky shore at Whatarangi on big days and into Palliser Bay there's a sucky shingle peak when the lake entrance is open and a sandy point in the western corner. Wainuiomata lefts get epic and are the first of a series that are biggest at Pencarrow Head then peel across shingle bars at various points all the way into Wellington Harbour at Eastbourne. The city beaches rely on SE-S swell squeaking through the narrow gap, hitting rocky spots like Breaker Bay, Propellers and Rat Island for the rippers and below average beachies for everyone at Wellington's surf central Lyall Bay or Houghton Bay. The NW-facing coast needs big NW to get around the top of the South Island and the W winds to back off, so it's very inconsistent. Top spot is Titahi Bay with lefts in the southern corner tucked out of the S winds, as are Wairaka and Pukerua, where high tide lefts appear in big NW seas. Small, mushy, empty beachbreak is the norm for Paekakariki, Waikane and then along an impressively long curve of ashen sand and dunes all the way up to the Taranaki zone. A shallow shelving profile and lack of swell exposure promotes this area as a longboard SUP playground. Head for the rivermouths at Hokio, Himatangi or Kotiata and increased W-SW swell exposure up towards Whanganui and its jetty breaks.

**South Island** – The east coast of the South Island is fairly well documented from the Kaikoura down to **North Canterbury** and into the chilly waters of **Otago and Southland**. The Canterbury Bight is featureless shorepound, except at rivermouths like Rakaia or the right points in Timaru. Check Oamaru or Kakanui has a right point bowling into rivermouth peaks. Between Otago and Southland lies The Catlins, a wild, scenic coastline with opportunities to ride both nuggety rocky points and endless golden sands, visited by fur seals and penguins. The South Coastal Track winds through fabulous Fiordland which signals the end of surfable coastline as the sea-flooded valleys and sounds meet the majestic Southern Alps. Go snowboarding instead. Beyond the many glaciers and frigid rivermouths of the West Coast region, Greymouth has waves on both sides of the river jetty and a sheltered right between them. Punakaiki River and Blowhole are regularly ridden amongst the pancake rocks. Westport Jetty has juicy peaks on either side and a sweet righthander deep inside the rivermouth on NW swells. Multiple rivermouths sculpt the bars up to Mokihinui and Little Wanganui with powerful lefts and rights that are often rip-torn. Karamea continues the theme with wide, estuary-fed sandbars. Head north into Tasman where the less-shifty lefts of Anatori Beach and its adjacent pretty peaks attract the campervan crew. Finally, Paturau River feeds more triangulated banks that are at their best in rarer NW swells.

## PAPUA NEW GUINEA

Half the biggest island in the Pacific means lots of surfing real estate, and Papua New Guinea represents an opportunity to search out new waves between the mainland bays of **Sandaun and East Sepik** and the island reefs off **Kavieng**. Tupira in Ulingan Bay is a consistent swell magnet close to five user-friendly, limestone bottomed breaks and has become a contest site for the world longboard championships. The north coast road of New Ireland works in any N swell and there's a surf camp located centrally at Rubio. Offshore islands like Simberi have been surfed and expats surf Rabaul, despite poor direct swell exposure. Bougainville and Manus islands present the biggest exploration possibilities within the swell window.

ANDREW SHIELD
Guam

## MICRONESIA

Festooned across the empty vastness of the Central Pacific and Mariana Basin, Micronesia incorporates the Marshall Islands, Gilbert Islands, Caroline Islands, Mariana Islands and a few outposts like the world's smallest republic Nauru and the US restricted zone of Wake Island. Within this region of Oceania, the **Federated States of Micronesia** contain the most documented spots, including the poster pin-up righthander of P-Pass on the volcanic island of **Pohnpei**. The **Marianas** include populous, localised **Guam**, which is inconsistent, but when it fires, it's hollow, fast and very, very shallow at breaks like Ricks, Boat Basin and Merizo. Saipan has a handful of breaks too and both islands prefer NW and W typhoon swells at west coast reefs. Kosrae has enough breaks in the coral fringe on all coasts to make it worthy of investigation. Further east the 34 atolls and islands of the **Marshall Islands** rely on US aid and missile base rent to fund the republic, while the few local surfers rely on scraps from both hemispheres on the crowded atoll of **Majuro**, where a glance at the map suggests great potential, but the reality is a dearth of top quality waves

RONAN GLADU

Solomon Islands

on the main island. Martin Daly (*Indies Trader*) has scoped all the Marshall's atolls and built a new resort on Ailinglaplap atoll, to access a handful of excellent reef passes on the north coast. ENE winds blow cross-offshore for the rights, making it a popular wind/kitesurfing spot. One deterrent is the Marshall's are the world's biggest shark sanctuary, covering nearly 2Mkm$^2$ of deep blue Pacific.

The **Solomon's** are the 3rd largest archipelago in the South Pacific, known for their unspoilt beauty and relaxed pace of life. They may not be in the ideal location to get the best Pacific swells, but there are some quality coral reefbreaks throughout the archipelago. The northern tip of Buka Island has a reefbreak and somewhere to stay at Hanpan. North Choiseul is wrapped in a fractured fringe of coral and some promising passes, again requiring a boat. A new resort built on Papatura Island off the NE-exposed coast of Santa Isabel claims access to a dozen breaks in a half hour cruising range with some flexibility when it comes to swell, wind and tide. Surprisingly, the majority of discoveries have turned up on the SW-facing coasts, when the Coral Sea cyclones kick in. The group's capital, Honiara, on Guadalcanal is the gateway to the Solomon's and under the right conditions, there's surf at Beaufort Bay and Yandina on Russel Island. The Western Provinces is where surfing has expanded, on the back of the diving resorts infrastructure, set up to explore the incredible lagoon – Marovo, which is blessed with 30m visibility and countless WWII underwater relics. Gizo is the capital of the Western Province and the starting point for riding some of the established waves on **New Georgia** like Skull Island, which is probably the longest righthander in the Solomons when a decent SE-SW pulse arrives from the Solomon Sea. Good waves have been ridden by a lucky few who have overcome the challenge of travelling to **Malaita and Makira**, which faces NE, picking up a variety of swell directions, but the main problem is access in this undeveloped region.

There is little doubt that if New Caledonia didn't block all the SW groundswell, **Vanuatu** would have some top notch surf. As it is, **Efate** has some nice set-ups that offer early morning, high tide barrels before the trades set in. The trade winds blow E in southern and central Vanuatu, but turn more S in the far north where there is a clear equatorial climatic influence. These scattering of small islands share more with the Solomons and are the frontier between Melanesia and Polynesia, suggesting N swell is a safer bet on the fringing reefs of the Torres Islands. The large mass of Espiritu Santo has some spots that a few locals ride, but it is extremely shadowed from E-SW and relies on W- NE swell for any action. There's some black sand beachbreak near Ipayato and Tasiriki in the southwest and rumours of a good reef on Sakau Island, but it takes huge effort to get there. Maewo and Pentecost Island have some windward coast potential, but will be blown out 90% of the time. Also inaccessible by land so only yachties willing to take the leap will surf these islands. The general consensus by those who have been is the surfing on Tanna is better than Efate as it picks up proper SW swell, sneaking round the tip of New Caledonia. In front of the wharf in Lenakel is one of a number waves in the area including friendly beachbreak and serious left reefbreaks that are offshore in the trades. Over the other side of the island, Port Resolution sees a massive expanse of reef, bend righthanders into the bay, plus small swell, wind exposed peaks nearby. Finally, Anelghowhat on Aneityum overlooks some very promising left reefbreaks including Mystery Island.

Triangulated with the Coral Sea and the Great Barrier Reef to the west and open to the Tasman Sea to the south, the elongated finger of **New Caledonia** is an unusual concoction of French chic and the Melanesian laid-back way of life. **South Province**'s outer reefs form part of an incredible 1500km barrier to the surf and encircle the world's largest lagoon, creating a spectacular playground for all types of water-sports lovers. Beyond the superb reef passes of Boulari, Dumbea, Tenia and Ouano lie dozens more to the south and all the way north beyond the land mass of Grande Terre. The coral defences continue on the east coast, but of course the trade winds and lack of any regular northern hemisphere swell kill off the chances of surf. Île des Pins off the SE corner of Grande Terre has a few land accessible waves around the main bays of Kuto and Rouleaux, where a boat would allow access to some more reef passes, but much of the island is a nature reserve so surfers and kiters are *interdite* (prohibited).

Comprising 844 islands and islets, **Fiji** covers 18,274 km$^2$ of solid land, but this doesn't include the staggeringly large 10,000 km$^2$ of reef. The Fiji Barrier Reef marine ecoregion supports at least 300 species of coral, over 475 species of molluscs, and 2,000 fish species, below the waves that arrive from all directions. The SW flank of the main island Viti Levu has held the surf world's gaze for decades and the perfect lefts of Cloudbreak in the **Mamanucas** have become one of the most iconic stops on professional surfing's "Dream Tour". Further south, land-accessible spots were found on the fringing reef before Frigates fantastic lefthander emphasised the wave potential of the **Kadavu Passage**. Exposure is the buzz word, but it also points out that the trade winds cause havoc for the swell drenched Eastern Division, so finding a pass or curve of reef that faces west is the challenge and only ocean-going yachties will get to explore the far-flung islands of Lau and Lomaiviti provinces where traditional life continues without resorts. Islands on the outer edges filter the SE-SW swell, but plenty still punches up through the wide channels, hitting the 4th largest island Taveuni at a large hammerhead reef at Lavena, or a protruding coral finger holding challenging rights at Nadillo (aka Purple Wall). Neighbouring Qamea has a surf camp set up at Maqai Beach in front of a handful of good waves including Maqai Wall, an all tide, all abilities, righthand barrel to carve-fest to inside rolling shoulders over a forgiving reef. Across the deep channel is Kavas, a gauntlet-throwing left sprint and Bula Bowls is an easier left on the other side of the Wall. There's even beginner-friendly inside reef waves and an artificial sandbag reef in front of the resort. The myriad of small islands sprinkled to the east probably all have surf at certain times of the year and are open to both S and N swells, mixed in with the constant underlying ESE windswell. Nanuku is one such speck where fast closeouts comb the outer reef until a

ANDREW SHIELD

Savai'i, Samoa

## SWELL FORECASTING

### NORTH PACIFIC

The North Pacific is constantly agitated by mid-latitude depressions that are more seasonal and more extreme than their southern counterparts. In winter, the ocean comes alive from October to March, as Aleutian low pressures usually start winding up in the Russian Kuril and blast across the North Pacific to Alaska. This will produce a swell train that favours centrally located islands like Hawaii, before losing some height as it propagates southwards and eastwards towards the north coasts of French Polynesia and the far flung eastern outposts of Rapa Nui and the Galapagos. Islands closer to Australia receive less of this swell, but long period, powerful NW-N pulses are more likely in the Dec-Feb window for Micronesia, Marshall Islands, Fiji, Tonga, Samoa and the Cook Islands. Typhoons mainly affect the shores outlined in the East Asia chapter, but can send some W-NW swell back towards Micronesian shores. Papua New Guinea and the Solomon Islands rely on windswell kicked up by the NW monsoon between Nov and April. Hurricanes forming off Central America are another source of unreliable, off-season swell, as they arc towards Hawaii bringing rare E-SE groundswell. The tropics belt is combed by dependable, often forceful easterly trade winds, quadrant opposed in each hemisphere by the Coriolis effect, which bends the winds towards the equator as the earth spins through its daily rotation. This is graphically illustrated by NE winds in the Northern Hemisphere islands of Hawaii and Micronesia to a decidedly SE dominance in all the South Pacific nations. Variations are rare, with a bit of wavering to the E, but it categorically means that west-facing spots are ideal for most Pacific islands while the windward east coasts get blown-out. The North Pacific gyre spins clockwise as the North Pacific Current flows eastwards across the top before bending south into the California Current then feeds into the North Equatorial Current, which races westwards before sweeping north into the fast flowing Kuroshio Current to complete the loop. There is an Alaskan and Aleutian offshoot plus a weird Equatorial Counter Current, which flows at odds to the other two Pacific Equatorial Currents. Tidal ranges across the Pacific are usually under 2m, but they matter on shallow reefbreaks, especially when the surf is smaller. The warmest ocean water on the planet is found in the western Pacific. The Indo-Pacific warm pool (IPWP) is the largest body of warm water in the world and has a major effect on global climate as it contracts and expands in size and varies in temperature over decades.

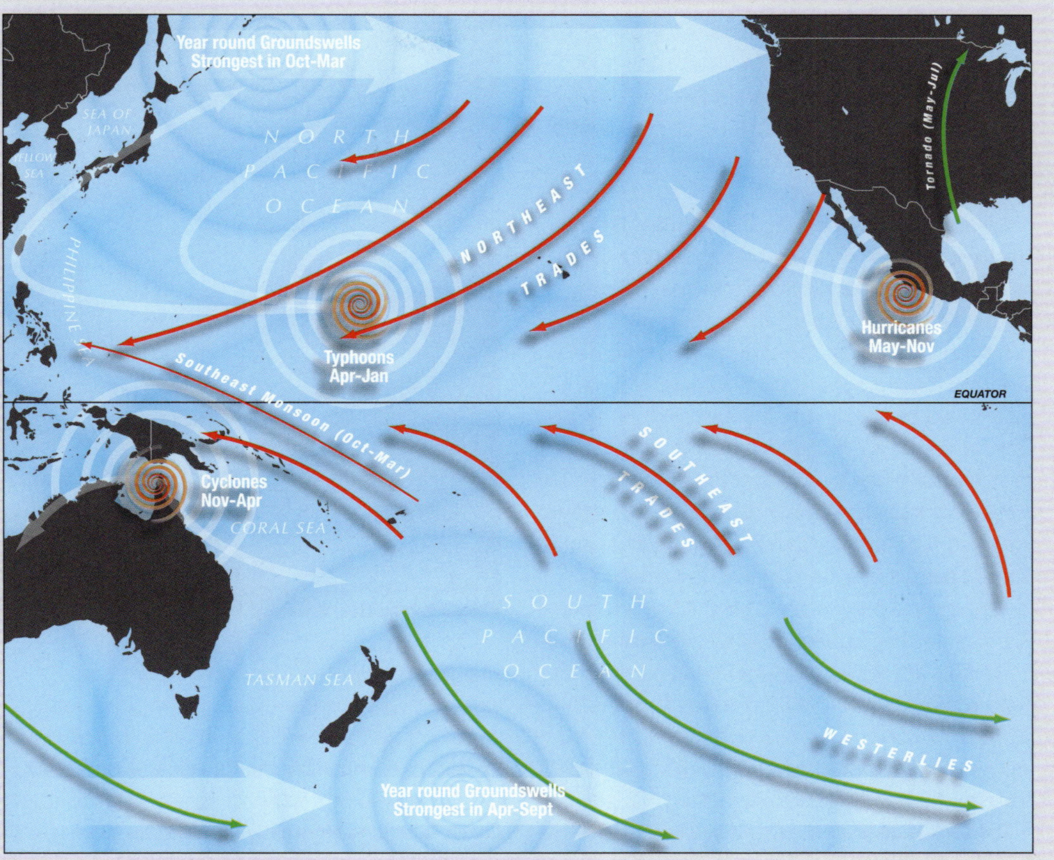

### SOUTH PACIFIC

Endlessly circling low pressures ply the landless waters of the great Southern Ocean, travelling from Australia towards South America, at latitudes between 35°and 60°S. These South Pacific lows are the source of most groundswells and statistics show a slightly less intense pattern than the Indian Ocean Roaring Forties or the North Pacific. Polynesia gets sprayed from April to September and the SW swells only fade slightly in the southern hemisphere summer. Many of the South Pacific islands suffer from the swell shadow cast by New Zealand, including New Caledonia, Fiji, Tonga and Samoa. This shadow doesn't stop all the SW swell and once the lows move further east, the S and SE swells will hit these Polynesian shores unhindered. Swell direction will often be an important factor at some reef passes, so waiting for the low pressures to enter the ideal window is crucial. The equator is no barrier and North Pacific nations will benefit from long period S quadrant swells during their summer, particularly further east in the Hawaiian chain.

Coral Sea tropical cyclone activity is the world's least predictable, usually forming just off the SE tip of New Guinea or Queensland and then heading south in an arc towards New Zealand, despatching solid NE-E groundswell. The dominant E-SE winds affect most of the South Pacific nations for the bulk of the year with exceptions in PNG and the Solomons, which are on the fringe of the monsoonal patterns in the northern hemisphere. The South Pacific sends cold water from the West Wind Drift into the Peru (or Humboldt) current, then up into the westwards flow of the South Equatorial Current. The powerful El Niño/Southern Oscillation (ENSO) occurs when the E equatorial trade winds slacken, which cause changes in circulation and sea surface temperatures (SST), allowing warmer than normal water (+ 2-4°C) to drift eastwards across the Pacific from the date line to Ecuador and Peru. This anomaly can affect world weather patterns and happens every 2-7 years, before reverting back to normal, cooler SST's known as the La Niña phase. Ocean surface temperatures in the Pacific fluctuate noticeably depending on the El Nino/La Nina cycle. Expect maximums around the Solomons to exceed 30°C (86°F) and minimums down to 8°C (46°F) in Dunedin NZ. The offshore islands of New Ireland, PNG see the biggest daily tidal change of up to 4m, otherwise it's micro-tidal ranges below 2m. Semi-diurnal even (two daily tides, same range) covers most of Polynesia and eastern Micronesia. Semi-diurnal odd (two daily tides, different range) describes the tides found across Hawaii, Melanesia, PNG and most of the Solomon's, which also experiences mixed tides, meaning sometimes one tide a day and sometimes two.

bigger swell wraps enough to create makeable lines on the western fringes at higher tides. Snaking along the frontier of the Northern Division and Vanua Levu, Cakaulevu Reef is about 200kms long and is the third longest continuous barrier reef in the world. While this Great Sea Reef is generally considered as diving territory, from November to March, NW-NE swells can arrive, helped along by the NE swing in the trade winds. Getting out to the reef takes plenty of time and money so few bother to explore during the N swell season. Labasa has direct access to the reef and there are enough curves and passes to expect to find some rideable waves, providing there is swell and the F4 winds haven't ripped it to pieces. Nukubati Resort boats out to Raviravi and Twin Passage, where lefts and better rights break with E wind protection in the shadow of Kia Island. Yasawa, Nacula and down to Naviti all face NW and are a little too far around the corner for any consistent S swell, making them another Nov-March N swell option, but far riskier than the Great Sea Reef. There are many fancy resorts, but none offer surfing, with flat water SUP, kite or wakeboarding more likely for the droves of honeymooners.

## POLYNESIA

The Kingdom of **Tonga** counts 174 islands spread over a 950km axis, yet we only describe waves on the NW corner of **Tongatapu**. This leaves literally hundreds of potential spots to be found on the other islands, starting with the main population centres in the Ha'apai, Vava'u and Niuas groups. High volcanic and low limestone islands characterise the Ha'apai, where the fringing, barrier and lagoon reefs catch the swell out of the Tonga Trench and there is enough variation in the reef architecture for good waves to appear. Same goes for Vava'u, where the west-facing reefs are always offshore, but reliant on more SW swell, making them fickle. Little exploring can be done without a boat, which explains why the short Ha'atafu stretch back on Tongatapu is so popular, with its easy 100m paddle to the reef. To surf the dredging peak at Ovaka takes a 1.5km paddle from private land and a sturdy, fast boat is essential to travel between the dozen known spots peeling off the circular reefs of uninhabited islands that dot the southern Vava'u seascape. The eastern reef gets way more swell and acts as a back-up for small NE or windswell days, but the SE trades

MICHAEL KEW

Tonga

usually frag it to hell. These winds and the exposed nature of the southern Vava'u islands make it hard for yachts to find safe anchorage. Tonga's summer (Dec-Mar) offers better hope as winds slacken and N swells arrive. The Niuas Group is closer to Samoa and outposts like Niuatoputapu, Tafahi and Niuafo'ou are volcanic and lack reef passes, so surf potential is minimal. On southern Eua Island there is a rare wave that breaks down the cliff side at Ufilei, plus a couple of high tide lefts and a right south of the harbour on moderate SW swells. Way up north, French-led Wallis island has a powerful, bowly, 200m left on the South Pass plus a handful of other fickle spots on the western outer reef. Futuna's rocky, ragged reef is much closer to shore, but set-ups are virtually non-existent.

**Samoa** is increasingly well-documented on **Savai'i and Upolu** although both island's northwestern coasts remain off the map, despite extensive fringing reef from Apia to the island of Manono. Apolima Island is far too steep with sheer cliffs dropping into the sea. Recent lava flows have engulfed large areas of land and reef around Mt Matavanu on the NE coast of Savai'i, wiping out some potentially prime surfing real estate by icing the reef in rugged igneous rock. Sitting 500km north, **Tokelau** is three low-lying atolls that should have great waves, if only there was a break or pass in the reef. This leaves a few sharp bends reliant on swell and wind direction to not close-out and east Atafu has an exposed, boat access only reef that should work in both N and S swells, wind permitting. Further west and the tiny undeveloped nation of **Tuvalu** suffers a similar fate with unbroken atoll rings like Vaitupu lacking any shape, or even a harbour for the ferry to dock. Funafuti is the capital where a total land area of 2.4km2 thinly encircles a lagoon area of 275km2 with many openings in the reef on the N and W sides. **Niue**'s rugged fringing reef sucks for surf.

**The Cook Islands** would appear to be an ideal destination, but the island's geology is less than ideal. **Rarotonga** has a few fun reefs around its circumference, enjoyed by low numbers of locals and tourists on round-the-world tickets. On Aitutaki, the ring of coral protecting the island is virtually unbroken, continuing the Cook Islands theme of shallow, sharp and prone to closing-out unless conditions are just right, plus the added hassle of needing a boat to access the waves. Many of the other islands are volcanic platforms with no appreciable surf. Classic atoll architecture returns on the northern outposts

MICHAEL KEW

Gilbert Islands

of the chain where the uninhabited Suwarrow atoll has a proper north-facing pass righthander and even further flung Penryhn has another couple of tidy set-ups at the Takuua and Tekasi passes, but only those lucky enough to have an ocean going yacht will ever see them.

**French Polynesia** is perfectly centred in the South Pacific, free from any swell shadowing and extremely welcoming to swells from either hemisphere. Once again, the numbers are staggering when simplified; 6 island chains made up of 130 islands spread over 2.5 million square kilometres of primo wave real estate, roughly equivalent to the size of Europe. Best known are the Society Islands and its Leeward Group of Huahine and Raiatea/Tahaa, Maupiti and Bora Bora which sit only 200km

BEN THOUARD

Tahiti, French Polynesia

west of Tahiti. Maupiti and Bora Bora only have one pass each – outriggers, canoes and SUP's rule the inshore waters. The the rest of the group is blessed with multiple openings in the fringing reef. **Huahine and Raiatea** have a reputation for fierce localism, while the islands of the Windward Group, namely **Tahiti and Moorea**, are world famous for fierce waves like Teahupoo and Temae. The north and west coasts are rich in reefbreaks, gyrating down the many deepwater passes, offering a range of lefts and rights with varying degrees of difficulty. There is also the occasional opportunity to ride fun reef, point and black sand beachbreak type waves on the windward coast at little bays like Tiarei and Faaone, while the offshore motus could be holding for those with a boat and the right angles of swell and wind. The 7 Austral Islands sink deep to the south, leaping the Tropic of Capricorn in a stormier, angry sea. Those seeking adventure will be relatively disappointed and only the twin passage on the south coast of Tubuai will tame the booming SE to SW swells into some manageable rides. Heading to the north of the Society Islands, the Tuamotu Archipelago barely breaks the surface with a procession of ringlet atolls that Darwin correctly guessed were the tips of old volcanoes. The western extremities have been shown to hold seriously good surf, so it makes sense that the impossibly remote central and eastern atolls and the far-flung Gambier Islands are similarly blessed. Of course avoid Mururoa and Fangataufa atolls, the site for the now infamous nuclear testing program run by the French Government in the SE corner of the **Tuamotu's**, but don't discount an atoll just because it is surrounded by others, because the swell seems to find a way in, as proven by the reef passes on the west side of Apataki. Mere mortals will never get this far in some of the most dangerous waters in the Pacific, where big sharks hunt in the passes and the rips take Herculean shoulders just to stay in position, in order to catch waves that will often test even the best riders. Further atolls flung like quoits lead to the cliff bound Pitcairn and Henderson islands, which aren't viable surf destinations. Skipping to the northeastern frontier of French Polynesia, the Marquesas couldn't be more different as monolithic basalt mountains rise from the submarine volcanic plateau and an arid, rocky landscape meets the South Equatorial Current. Plunging cliffs line deeply indented bays, where rocky beaches like Hanaiapa and Puamau are good starting points for exploration on the north coast of Hiva Oa and Atuona beach on the south. Ua Pou has a fun peak in Hakahau Bay, while kids bodysurf beside the wharf at Hakahetau and wind exposed Nuku Hiva picks up E swell at the pristine, white-sand beachbreak of Haatuatua. There is a small local surf population on all the islands who may choose to show visitors what the Marquesas have to offer to dedicated travellers willing to go to the ends of the earth.

The Republic of **Kiribati** is sprawled over an area of ocean way bigger than India, with a mere 3300km between the two main island groups of the Gilberts and the Line Islands. Most documented spots are on the planet's largest atoll, **Kiritimati and Tabuaeran**, which are closer to Hawaii than the Gilberts and where powerful, serious line-ups hold some epic waves for a small local crew. The Gilberts are less consistent, but the northern tip of the Tarawa atoll does hold a 500m long, walled-up, high tide right pointbreak at Naa, that relies on NE swell to fire and is a long way from help if you hit the reef. Other small islands like Abaiang are rumoured to have a wave in S swells at Ouba, Marakei has rights into a man-made channel, Abemama's NW passage and the offshore reefs of Tabiteuea have all been ridden by Chuck Corbett. He also surfed the arid, empty Phoenix Islands at Kanton passage, where large fish massively outnumber humans in the second biggest marine reserve in the world. The absence of deepwater passes limits the Gilberts severely and the man-made ones are always on the swell-starved SW coast. Find a conducive bend in the reef near the tips of islands that will wrap the winter NW swells or trade windswell and during El Nino, the wind reversal can mean rare E coast spots work.

## HAWAII

The Garden Island of **Kauai** is basically circular so all sorts of swells can wrap around the island bringing waves to unexpected coasts. The only stretch of the Garden Isle coastline that is not mentioned is the famed Na Pali coast, a primordial fringe of cliffs and jagged shoreline, facing the fury of the winter swells. The few valleys that allow access to the sea from the roller coaster Kalalau Trail are not blessed with great set-ups and notoriously dangerous, regularly taking swimmers, even in the calmer summer months. State Park permits required to camp on the 2 day hike or kayak in on one of the many organised tours.

DAMIEN POULLENOT

West Oahu

**Oahu** is Hawaii to the rest of the world – Waikiki, hula girls and beachboys, teaching the world the ancient Hawaiian art of *he'e nalu*, while the **North Shore** is where the modern heart of Hawaiian surfing resides. Pipe, Sunset, Waimea – a truly terrifying triumvirate of Pacific wave-power, ably supported by a glut of equally forceful and photogenic breaks, spooned onto the coastline like thick cream. West of Haleiwa, through Mokuleia, a few spots are ridden when the wind dies or goes some flavour of S, otherwise it is a bit of mess in NE-E trades. These cross-shore winds attract the wind/kite crew, but it is generally low crowds and hassle. Lefts and rights near the Pu'uiki Beach Park will run off way outside, depending on swell angle and kind winds. Mokuleia Beach Park is an easy check from the campground when N-NE pulses make the right hold up enough to connect between the rolling outside wall and the inside racetrack section over the coral. A mile west and there are more similar corners at Army Beach, which will conjure some lefts in NW swell under 8ft and hopefully S winds, otherwise the windy rigs will be flying all over the place. From here out to Kaena Point is hiking territory with trails into the Waianae Mountains and a taste of Hawaii au natural! The leeward West Side breaks are summarised (there are lots more) and the constant offshores meet both summer and winter swells, giving the tight-knit community plenty of opportunity to impart their wave-riding knowledge and traditions. The South Shore cityscape of Honolulu and Diamond Head provide the perfect backdrop for a gentle surf beyond the trampled sands of downtown Waikiki that has always been referred to as 'Town'. Incredibly, surfing on Oahu is not just about Town and there is a lot more Country than just the North Shore. The Windward Coast, or East Side is just waiting for kona winds to airbrush the constant E trade windswell into something sweet.

**Molokai**'s southern shore and particularly the western tip are littered with white sand beaches, including Hawaii's longest at Papohaku. The adjacent Kepuhi Bay is usually better, with a defined left and right at the northern end, but shorepound and rips can make it unsafe for swimmers. The north coast of the island is protected by some of the tallest sea cliffs on the planet, below which a leper colony was established at Kalaupapa in 1866. This flat tongue of land holds some good righthanders, but surfing is not encouraged. The spectacular north coast cliffs plunge straight into the ocean, and aside from trekking into Wailau Beach and checking the black sand and boulder set-ups near the rivermouth at Halawa Beach Park, there's no action until heading back into the Pailolo Channel opposite Maui. The twisting Kamehameha V road hugs the coast near Sandy Beach, in full view of some quality lefts where the local crew charge and visitors need a healthy dose of aloha to partake. In the main town of Kaunakakai a decent S or W swell can bring some surf to the outer reef and NE winds are offshore. Strong rips, spooky, sharky line-ups, nasty lava reef bottoms and some localism are all factors when surfing Molokai – tread slowly and carefully.

Out of all the Hawaiian Islands, **Maui** suffers the most swell shadowing from neighbouring islands and therefore some coastlines are not worth checking in certain swell patterns. Below the **Northwest Maui** zone, the busy Kihei stretch encompasses many of the tourist resorts and hotels on the island and is usually either flat or small, which is perfect for visiting non-surfers to hit the many surf schools and catch some perfect beginner waves. The Cove is the most popular spot, working best on W or S swells, with sandy peaks at the northern end of Kalama Park or a rocky left at the southern end. Makena State Park offers the occasional ride at Little Beach and Big Beach but it's rarely any good and better suited to bodyboard/bash. Super fast, bordering on the close-out and super shallow, bordering on the insane can be applied to both Dumps and La Perouse, lefts over nasty, coral-studded lava on the SW corner of the island. Picks up all S swell and is usually offshore all day, yet is pretty fickle and hard to read. Surf is at a premium from here all the way to Hana on the NE coast thanks to sheer cliffs, crazy volcanic rock formations and swell shadowing from the Big Island. Hana Bay is typical windward surf with some longer lefts sweeping towards the rivermouth with big N or E swell and kona winds. Round the corner back on the NE-facing coast are a couple of waves like Keanae, which gets some trade wind protection from the eastern headland and gives intermediates a chance to get some waves without much crowd pressure. Similar story at the deeply indented Honomanu Bay where there can be some good lefts on the exposed side in light or kona winds.

While Oahu and Kauai are known for their north/south shore divide, the **Big Island** is an east/west side story. The youngest island in the chain, Hawaii is known as the Big Island, due to its size, which is nearly double that of the others combined and being a live volcano, continues to grow. Lava flowing from Kilauea is continually shaping a new landscape on its way to the sea where it can both create future surf breaks or destroy existing ones. Whilst Oahu usually grabs the surf history limelight, Polynesian immigrants probably initiated surfing at Kealakekua Bay centuries ago, making the Big Island the birthplace of surfing and the aloha spirit. Crowds and localism do exist, but remote spots requiring long hikes or 4WD access will be empty and conditions will be less competitive than most Hawaiian line-ups.

LAURENT MASUREL

Molokai

# Taranaki NEW ZEALAND

Taranaki gets the most swell and has the greatest concentration of quality spots on New Zealand's North Island. The waves fan out around the base of Mt Taranaki (aka Mt Egmont) from Waitara in the north to Hawera in the south offering a range of swell and wind exposures. Streams and rivermouths cut the rural landscape, depositing boulders and eroding reefs into a plethora of quality and even world-class pointbreaks. The Surf highway provides limited access down the spoking side roads leaving plenty of scope for exploration.

**+ VARIETY OF CONDITIONS**
**+ CONSISTENT BIG SWELLS**
**+ QUALITY, UNCROWDED SPOTS**
**+ SNOWY, VOLCANIC SCENERY**

**- COLD AND WET CLIMATE**
**- WINDY CONDITIONS**
**- COLD WATER**
**- LACK OF PUBLIC TRANSPORT**

Fitzroy Beach

CORY SCOTT

**Ahu Ahu** is the last spot to give proper protection from any S wind with an outside left, an inside left and further peaks over the scattering of rocks buried in the sand. **Weld Road** is very similar with rolly, fun beginner peaks at high tide. It's a long walk in to **Kumera Patch**, a super-long, walling boulder left point with some hollower sections depending on tide and sand. Try the shorter, less popular left point at Komene Road 2km south. Puniho and Paora Roads lead to some classic waves like **Rocky Lefts & Rights** that straddle a boulder point and can get sucky and fast for more experienced surfers. Head north for more of the same at **Graveyards**. **Stent Road** is the finest right point in the country, working from tiny to thumping while holding a perfect line down the boulder strewn coastal protrusion. Very consistent and always crowded, bringing into play the lefts on either side. Coast Road heads south revealing many enticing setups including Crushers beach and Fin Fucker left point. When the winds turn to the N/NE in the spring/summer, head for the pocket beach of **Opunake** that hosts a fun, sheltered beachbreak. **Desperation Point** is a clutch of big wave peaks for more experienced surfers. At low tide, **Sky Williams** hugs the fringing reef and canters down the extensive line, occasionally galloping through the odd barrel, before trotting into the protected cove. On the same reef at mid to high tide **Mangahume** point has challenging hollow rights with a jacking take-off. Hidden 3km south, **Green Meadows** is a long right pointbreak broken into sections with barrels on the inside. An offshore shelf drains some power from southern Taranaki breaks, but summer swells bring good waves to the two groynes protecting the Patea Rivermouth and big winter swells will roll down the exceptionally long point at Fences, beside Waiinu Beach.

If the wind is calm (unusual), check **Waitara Bar** rivermouth on high tides and major swells when the reefs and sandbars can be hollow and firing. The hollow outside left reef at **Bell Block** requires a big swell and a long paddle. Beginners should stick to the beachbreak inside. In the town of New Plymouth, **Fitzroy Beach** provides wind and swell protection for the picture perfect beachbreak barrels to form all the way up to the groyne where the high tide classic Waiwhakaiho rivermouth thunders over the rocks at the north end along the coastal walkway. There are many good reefs in **New Plymouth** – Boulters Bay has a longboard left and right on either side, Bog Works is a big swell offshore peak with long walls for experts, while Belt Road is a lazy left point that occasionally goes off in big SW swells. The consistent, quality waves of **Back Beach** are where New Plymouth surfers head to get the most out of the swell and the north end banks are a regular contest site. **Oakura** is a popular, patrolled beachbreak with several streams cutting channels.

## TRAVEL INFORMATION

**Weather** – A moderate wet climate influenced by SW-W winds year-round. The weather changes quickly. Winter rainfall is quite heavy from May-Aug with cold temps and good ski conditions on Mt. Taranaki and bigger, consistent swells. Summers are mild. It's the same story in the water - a good 4/3mm fullsuit in winter and a 3/2mm fullsuit for summer.

**Lodging and Food** – There are plenty of backpackers, hostels and beach camps, all of which are cheap. The Wavehaven villa in Oakura from $20 for a dorm to $55/dble. The Opunake backpackers cost $22. New Plymouth is more upmarket. It shouldn't cost more than $15 for a basic meal.

**Nature and Culture** – Snow capped Mt. Taranaki dominates the skyline – the Manganui Ski Area has basic tow lifts and pistes for all levels. There is an 11km coastal walkway along the seafront of New Plymouth.

**Hazards and Hassles** – Be prepared for the cold, wind and rain. Most local surfers are cool and friendly to respectful visiting surfers. Shark attacks at Oakura (1966 fatal) and Opunake (2012).

**Handy Hints** – There are plenty of surf shops in New Plymouth. For cheap gear try Del Free 'n' Easy or Seasons Cheapskates. Always ask permission before crossing private property and close all farm gates.

Taranaki receives regular 4-12ft W-SW groundswells from the roaring forties year-round, with prime time between March and Aug. Rare NW swells or cyclones in summer (Dec-March) can fire up some normally dormant spots. The dominant wind comes from the SW-WNW, while any E winds occur through the summer months (Feb-Apr). The worst wind direction is NW-N, which occurs mostly in the spring. Tidal range is significant and effects most spots, especially rivermouths. Ask the fishermen.

Stent Road

CORY SCOTT

| STATISTICS | | J F | M A | M J | J A | S O | N D |
|---|---|---|---|---|---|---|---|
| SWELL | Direction | | | | | | |
| | Size (ft) | 5 | 5-6 | 7-8 | 6-7 | 6-7 | 6 |
| WIND | Direction | | | | | | |
| | Force | F4 | F4 | F4 | F4 | F4 | F4 |
| WATER | Wetsuit | | | | | | |
| | Temp/°C | 18 | 17 | 15 | 13 | 15 | 16 |
| WEATHER | Rainfall/mm | 80 | 87 | 225 | 125 | 97 | 97 |
| | days/mth | 7 | 9 | 11 | 13 | 9 | 8 |
| | Min temp/°C | 13 | 11 | 7 | 6 | 8 | 11 |
| | Max temp/°C | 21 | 18 | 14 | 12 | 15 | 18 |

# Waikato NEW ZEALAND

Incessant swells pummel the black sand beaches and rocky headlands of the Waikato region, home to New Zealand's most famous wave and surf town, situated a mere two hours drive from Auckland. Incredibly long and graceful lefthanders hug the headlands at a series of bays in Raglan, providing a world-class playground for a multitude of local, regional and international surfers.

+ CONSTANT SWELL SUPPLY
+ RAGLAN'S FAMOUS LEFTS
+ POINTS, RIVERMOUTHS & BEACHES
+ NZ'S FAVOURITE SURF TOWN

- HEAVY ONSHORES
- STRONG CURRENTS
- RAGLAN CROWDS
- SOME DIFFICULT ACCESS

Indicators to Manu Bay

RAMBO ESTRADA

At the south end of Sunset Beach, **Port Waikato**'s current scoured beach terminates at the headland cliffs where a throaty lefthand point breaks on the rocks below. Powerful walls and hollow sections when the sand joins the rocky fingers. Advanced to expert surfers only as the entry off the rocks is sketchy and locals intolerant. A gravel road leads to **Te Akau**, a powerful high tide beachbreak with scattered rocks north of Raglan. The rivermouth at Te Akau South helps break up the close-outs, on this wild stretch of coast. Both need small swells and any E wind. It's a long, arduous paddle across the current strafed Harbour entrance from Raglan to **Mussel Rock**. Sand commutes around the rocks with greatly varying results from slopey shoulders to fast tubes. Small days only. Same applies across the channel at **Raglan Bar,** where a changeable set of sandbanks will see some fast hollow peaks on calm wind days, which keeps the numerous kitesurfers on the beach. Tucked into the corner of Raglan Bay, **Ngarunui Beach** always serves up something to ride, catering for all abilities. The rip in the southern corner gives an armchair ride out the back where rolling walls stretch both ways for the regular crowds. It's the easiest check and surf in Raglan and where the surf schools ply their trade. More peaks down towards the harbour, but they will be messed up by the SW winds. **Manu Bay** is the innermost of the three Raglan points and starts with a hollow barrel section over the Ledge before bending into a walling section that can race for 300m or more past the boat ramp. Jumping from the rocks past the take-off spot requires good timing. Further west the Boneyards section may provide a relatively less crowded alternative. Despite having a reputation as being the lesser of Raglans three left points, **Whale Bay** can still pack a punch at smaller sizes when it breaks close to the rocks and sections on the headland to the east of the bay. On larger days the wall loses steepness and rolls along, unless the swell is more W-NW making it barrel over the boulders that have a tendency to pop up. Often slightly less crowded than the other two points with less locals, giving the intermediates a chance.

**Indicators** is the longest, fastest and most critical of Raglan's points. On smaller days Indicators splits into 2 or 3 sections. Outside Indicators has a heavy take-off into a throaty barrel and picks up the most size, but also the most wind. Indies has some hollow sections interspersed with performance and cutback walls. The final Valley section speeds up and hollows out again on lower tides. Larger days will occasionally break far enough out to link up with Whale Bay and maybe even Manu, but it's very unlikely to join the dots for the full 2km. All the points want SE offshores but handle a bit of SW, especially at Manu. **Ruapuke** is a summer alternative to the crowds found at the Raglan beaches – a powerful, swell-magnet spot. Usually blown out of control, the north end cleans up nicely in a NE wind and small swell. The Toreparu Stream can shape some bars down the south end at higher tides. Vicious rips when it gets overhead. The virtually inaccessible, locals only lefts of **Albatross Point** filter SW swells from Ocean Beach at Kawhia Harbour where you can dig a hot spring hole in the sand after surfing empty peaks. Located at the mouth of the Marokopa River, **Kiritehere** is a sectiony left point with powerful walls at higher tides.

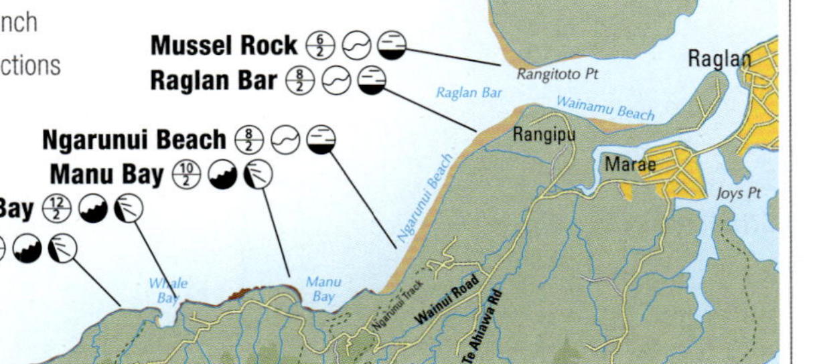


## TRAVEL INFORMATION

**Weather** – see *Taranaki*

**Lodging and Food** – Raglan is a full on surf town with every type of accommodation; basic (Raglan Backpackers, Karioi Lodge; fr $11/n), to the ideally located Whale Bay house rentals (fr $130 to $290/n) or eco options with Solscape and off-grid Indicators Beach House. Expect $12-25 for a meal from the varied Raglan eateries.

**Nature and Culture** – Kawhia hot springs can be dug out of the sand on Ocean Beach, 2hrs either side of low - take a shovel. Fishing is good in and outside the harbours.

**Hazards and Hassles** – Rips and mussel-coated rocks. A non-fatal shark attack took place in 2006 at Manu Bay.

**Handy Hints** – Raglan packs out in summer holidays. Many surf shops selling reasonably priced boards and accessories.

Raglan Bar

RAMBO ESTRADA

With 5 out of 6 days showing some SW-W swell arriving throughout the year, this is a very consistent coastline. A sprinkling of NW only reinforces the picture, with heights up to 24ft and 20 second period possible. The prevalent SW-W wind actually shares much of the winter months with E quadrant winds, before reasserting dominance in the summer months. N to E winds blow for about a quarter of the time annually. Semi-diurnal tides at Raglan with a 3.9m max tidal range.

| STATISTICS | | J F | M A | M J | J A | S O | N D |
|---|---|---|---|---|---|---|---|
| SWELL | Direction | | | | | | |
| | Size (ft) | 5-6 | 6-7 | 8 | 8 | 8 | 7 |
| WIND | Direction | | | | | | |
| | Force | F4 | F4 | F4 | F4 | F4 | F4 |
| WATER | Wetsuit | | | | | | |
| | Temp/°C | 18 | 17 | 15 | 13 | 15 | 16 |
| WEATHER | Rainfall/mm | 81 | 128 | 96 | 118 | 84 | 94 |
| | days/mth | 8 | 10 | 12 | 14 | 12 | 11 |
| | Min temp/°C | 16 | 12 | 8 | 7 | 9 | 12 |
| | Max temp/°C | 24 | 22 | 17 | 14 | 18 | 22 |

# Northland & Auckland NEW ZEALAND

Clear, warm sub-tropical waters wash both sides of a peninsula that benefits from a near 300° swell window. Any pulse from SSW all the way round to SE will hit countless uncrowded beaches, points and reefs. Northland is relatively narrow and at the widest point it's still less then 1 hours drive from east to west. The Twin Coast Discovery Highway leads to most of the surf locations so it's perfectly suited to campervan touring.

**+ SUPER-WIDE SWELL WINDOW**
**+ NZ'S WARMEST REGION**
**+ MOSTLY UNCROWDED**
**+ SHIPWRECK BAY LEFTS**

**– WEST COAST OFTEN ONSHORE**
**– 4WD ACCESS AT MANY SPOTS**
**– INCONSISTENT EAST COAST**
**– LONG HIKES TO SOME SPOTS**

## TRAVEL INFORMATION

**Weather** – Sub-tropical climate with warm, humid summers and mild, damp winters. Summer temps 14-23°C (58-74°F), rarely exceeding 27°C (80°F). Winter temps 8-17°C (46-63°F). SW winds prevail for much of the year and there's summer sea breezes. Tropical storms and cold fronts can cause occasional extreme conditions like hailstorms, but no snow. 3/2mm steamer or a springy for Dec-Feb.

**Lodging and Food** – Ahipara is a good base. Options include budget backpacker, homely B&B, spacious holiday park, family motel or luxury hotel from $15-150. Camping is a summer option. Good Vibrations run a surf camp/school/guiding from $55 day. Expect $12-25 for a meal. Try some of the seafood with fine Kiwi wines.

**Nature and Culture** – The Bay of Islands and The Poor Knights Islands marine reserve are well known. Don't miss Whangarei, the Scottish settlement at Waipu and the beautiful Whangaroa Harbour. Enjoy fine arts and crafts, fishing, diving and boating.

**Hazards and Hassles** – Main problem is the cold & wind and some rocks with razor-sharp mussels. Crowds are only a factor at Piha, Muriwai and North Auckland spots. Some shark attacks on both coasts over the years but mainly on swimmers and spear fisherman.

**Handy Hints** – Bookings are essential for the peak period of Dec-March. Various companies in Auckland offer shuttles to Orewa, Mangawhai, Piha, Muriwai or Shipwreck Bay. Good quality boards in Auckland and beach shops.

CRAIG LEVERS

Shipwreck Bay

✪**Piha** is New Zealand's most famous surf beach, 40km from the City of Sails. Endlessly long **Muriwai Beach** has lefts off the southern point but more surfers go round the corner to Maori Bay for hollow, better defined peaks in smaller swells and higher tides. Constantly moving sandbars shaped by strong rips for shape and some backwash in front of rocks. Crowds at Maori Beach when it's on, which is often. Big SW swells can create grinding rights off the inside sandbank at **Pouto** but it's rare. Being deep inside the mouth of the massive Kaipara Harbour means rips are strong. Around the corner on the ruler-edged beach up to Dargaville sees small swell, NE wind possibilities best accessed at Bayly's Beach. **Waipoua Reefs** are a 1h hike south from Waimamaku where isolated, gnarly, challenging waves greet small groups of experts. The beachbreak at Waimamaku breaks with size and power providing winds are from the E. West coast access is a real drag with 4WD forestry trails often gated and locked. West of Ahipara, **The Box** makes the most of smaller swells, ankle-tapping them into short, fairly cavernous tubes, hence the generic name. Needs water without wind to make the gut-wrenching drops doable. Ahipara is home to "Shippies" and 7 endless peeling lefts. Furthest west and more wind exposed, **Blue House** is a steep, fast and hollow beast, working well at higher tides. **Pines** serves up a mellower wall and shoulder with the odd cover-up section in smaller swells. Lower tides and lower crowds thanks to the long walk. **Supertubes** features a hell drop into a deep pit followed by a speed wall. Lower tides keep it peeling for the moderate crowd of advanced surfers, able to negotiate the drop, rip and shallow rocks. It's mainly sand under **Mukies 2**, which can make it a bit variable, but it works on all tides and is sometimes a hollow affair. Accommodates more intermediates and is an easier paddle out than other spots. The short sucky barrel section of **Mukies 1** is better at low tide and offers a bit more protection from westerlies. **Peaks** is a difficult paddle-out between the rocky outcrops and holds full-speed wailing walls, hollow pockets and tricky sections for experienced surfers to try and make it the full kilometre back to the beach. The take-off is a sucky launch into the barrel, so less-experienced surfers should ride the sweep down to the many other entry points. This would be NZ's most iconic wave if Raglan didn't exist. **Shipwreck Bay** ('Wreck Bay or Shippies) is perfectly angled to get SW swell on the wrap but not be ruffled by the following wind. Although it catches the least swell in the daisy chain of lefthand points and is a mellower ride over

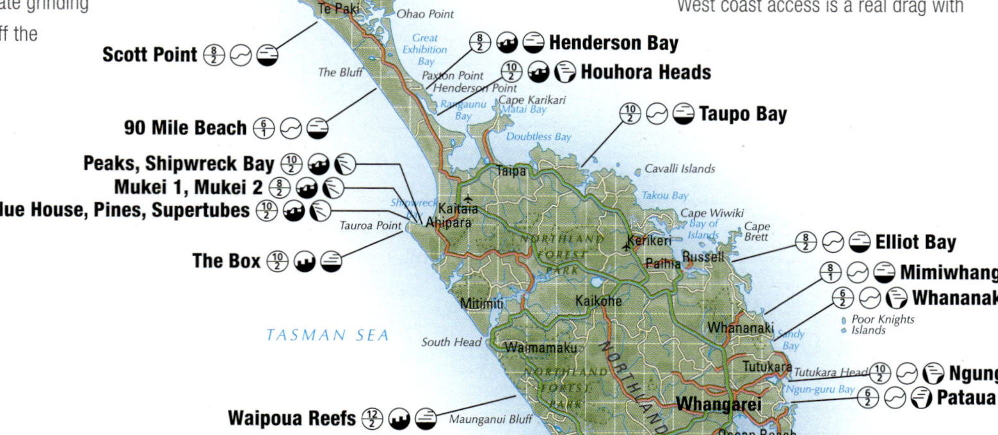

ANDREW SHIELD

Hendersons

sandbars, it still holds pristine peelers of real quality, attracting both rippers and improvers to a long, crowd-soaking line-up. All the points are offshore with any S wind variation and suffer from strong down the line drift. **90 Mile Beach** is one of the longest unspoilt beaches on earth, yet it is marked as National Highway at low tide! Beware of soft sand and incoming tides - a 4WD is crucial and many get stuck. Small peaky swells with NE winds will create good conditions, especially at The Bluff, the only headland about two-thirds of the way up. At the far end of 90 Mile. **Scott Point** is one of those swell magnets suited to adventurous and equipped surfers. There can be a fickle right in the lee of the headland, but mostly it is a wind and swell pounded mess. Small swell, light winds only. Between the northern wilds of Cape Reinga and the North Cape lurk some fine squeaky white strands that work on W and N swells at Te Werahi, Tapotupotu and Spirits Bay. **Henderson Bay** is a super-reliable beachbreak with scattered reefs forming sucky, tubular rides on all tides. Sucks in more swell than the white-as-snow sandbars to the north along Rarawa Beach and there's a rivermouth sandbar at **Houhora Heads**. N, NE or E swells should show somewhere on the Karikari Peninsula with Puheke and Tokerau good for wind and size options. Beautiful **Taupo Bay** cradles a series of sucky peaks barrelling up to almost double overhead, plus some thrusting rights breaking off the southern end in strong NE swells with all S winds covered. Gets a crowd plus there's a local surf school. Idyllic **Elliot Bay** will have clear water beachbreaks, often when the rest of the coast is flat. This means some crowds, despite the difficult access and walk over private land. **Mimiwhangata Bay** also requires payment to cross private farm land to access Okupe beach. Multiple peaks materialise in any E swell and preferably any W wind. Strong, organised fun for all abilities. A SE swell is the signal for **Whananaki North**, where rivermouth sandbars produce long peeling lefts with nice whackable sections, but close-out as it exceeds overhead. The Bar as it's known, is a pretty rare bird, so crowds flock when it's on. Another left over migrating sandbars at the **Ngunguru Bar** that rely on rare, sizeable SE swells, low incoming tide and any N winds to produce barrels. **Pataua Bar** has classic rivermouth rights, where the tricky take-offs and barrels rely on river flow and a NE swell. If the Bar isn't working, try Ocean Beach for larger, reliable, powerful peaks along a 6km stretch to the south. **Waipu Bar** is yet another transient rivermouth bank with lower tide rights being the usual fare on the north side of the flow. Sufficient peaks grace the long beach at higher tides down to Waipu Cove where rights can bank off the rocks and S winds aren't a problem. **Mangawhai Heads** is a wave and people magnet since the regulation rivermouth is aided and abetted by a spit of rocks to create some of the best lefthanders on this coast. Best in solid NE swells at lower tides, there's a bonus right back into the river and more small swell fun on the north side of the rocks. **Forestry** has something for everyone with its reliable beachbreaks and also a sweet left point in NE swells, which gets crowded on weekends. There's a right on the north side of Te Arai Point in E or SE swell squeaking past the Barrier Islands. Plenty of peaks stretching into the distance down Pakiri Beach. **Orewa Beach** with its rivermouth lefts and rights is great for learners, longboarders and SUPers with constant reforms. In the suburbs of **Auckland** are a series of reefs (Long Bay, Milford Reef, O'Neills, Takapuna) when big NE swells arrive, but they're always crowded with locals when on. Take the ferry to Great Barrier Island, home to many isolated beaches plus **Whangapoua**, a quality rivermouth right.

Over 300 days of SW-W swells from 2-15ft arrive on the west coast along with the onshore winds. November to March is cyclone season when solid groundswells may hit the NE coast, but as they move south, they turn into subtropical depressions, producing short-lived E-SE swells. During the summer period, high pressures dominate, blocking descending storms from the north and producing decent isobar fetch for the east coast with light onshores. When warm tropical air hits the Tasman Sea, sudden lows can form around Lord Howe producing unusual NW swells combined with E winds if a high is sitting over Northland. Semi-diurnal tides with 3m max tidal range. Piha tide is 3h later than Orewa Beach on the east coast.

**Piha**

**LAT. -36.9552° LONG. -9.725268°**

With rugged cliffs and the majestic Lion Rock standing guard over the beach, the scenery is dramatic and inspiring from the viewpoint on the drive down. South Piha has quality low tide lefts off the corner sandbar that roll in and reform in the shorey at high. The rip is fast and furious and there's a keyhole around the rocks. More currents flank Lion Rock, forming outside banks and helping with the paddle out that gets punishing at size, which Piha handles better than most beaches. When the swell is small, good peaks can often be found up the "Big Beach" at North Piha, usually at higher tides, sculpted by the streams and dangerous currents that claim many swimmers lives. When it's big, it's experts only and there's a few of them around. Beware the iron-sand gets mighty hot in the sun.

Mangawhai

CRAIG LEVERS

| STATISTICS | | J F | M A | M J | J A | S O | N D |
|---|---|---|---|---|---|---|---|
| SWELL | Direction | | | | | | |
| | Size (ft) | 3 | 3-4 | 5-6 | 6 | 5 | 4 |
| WIND | Direction | | | | | | |
| | Force | F4 | F4 | F4-F5 | F4-F5 | F4 | F4 |
| WATER | Wetsuit | | | | | | |
| | Temp/°C | 21 | 20 | 18 | 16 | 16 | 18 |
| WEATHER | Rainfall/mm | 81 | 88 | 123 | 126 | 97 | 83 |
| | days/mth | 9 | 11 | 17 | 17 | 14 | 12 |
| | Min temp/°C | 16 | 13 | 9 | 8 | 9 | 12 |
| | Max temp/°C | 23 | 22 | 17 | 14 | 17 | 21 |

# Gisborne NEW ZEALAND

Gisborne's grunty beachbreaks can get busy in summer, but further north on the East Cape, lies a high density of less-crowded quality points and reefs hidden amidst the sunniest and most untouched part of New Zealand. Although the surf is on average smaller than the west coast it is generally cleaner, as consistent and every bit as powerful.

- \+ MANY POINTBREAKS
- \+ CLEAN MID-SEASON SWELLS
- \+ HOLLOW, POWERFUL BEACHIES
- \+ UNTOUCHED COASTLINE

- – SMALL SUMMER SWELLS
- – SEMI-CROWDED MAIN SPOTS
- – CHILLY WINTER TEMPS
- – SOME DIFFICULT ACCESS

## TRAVEL INFORMATION

**Weather** – Gisborne and the East Cape enjoy a fairly dry, sunny climate with warm summers and mild winters. Sheltered by mountains to the west, strong, dry, Foehn winds descend from the NW. Sea breezes often occur on warm days. Sunniest months are February and October, followed by Nov-Dec-Jan. April is the wettest month when heavy rainfall comes in from the ESE, but westerly winds prevail. Min water temps are 13°C (55°F) requiring a 4/3mm fullsuit and max is 20°C (68°F) when a 3/2 fullsuit is recommended.

**Lodging and Food** – YHA Gisborne Backpackers has dorms for $22/dble for $45. Whales B&B, Wainui for $95/day or Chalet Surf Lodge with sea view rooms for $100/dble. A typical meal would be $15.

**Nature and Culture** – Try shark cage dives, horse trekking or winery visits. Maori culture runs deep on the East Cape. With 45,000 people, Gisborne is traditionally rural, with only a few happening places like Scotty's Bar & Grill.

**Hazards and Hassles** – No snakes or poisonous, dangerous creatures can be found in New Zealand. Localism can be felt at some spots or on classic days because of extra crowd pressure. Beware with rocks and rips. No shark attacks off the East Cape.

**Handy Hints** – Many surf shops to buy cheap quality gear: Blitz, Sequence or Exit Surf Shops; The Boardroom (Lost Surfboards), or the New Wave Surfboard factory sell custom boards. Rentals and lessons at the Chalet Surf Lodge. New Zealand Surfing Adventures offers 5-day all inclusive tours costing $1600.

CORY SCOTT

Waipaoa River

Hick's Bay cradles a long and beautiful beach, with easy rollers for beginners and longboarders. On a big E-NE swell, the adjacent **Horseshoe Bay** beachbreak might be maxed out but the righthand point may start working. Around the East Cape at the **Waiapu** rivermouth, the shingle beach picks up any S swell on shifty bars. **Waipiro Bay** is the place to be when moderate NE or strong SE swells awaken the clutch of right pointbreaks at the S end of this massive bay. Kitties is the inside section closer to the beach, while Frog Rock is shorter, faster and ends abruptly on the rocks. Outside is Creek, a fast hollow beast best left to experienced surfers. Expert surfers should check the fast barrelling right off the rocks at the north end of **Tokomaru Bay** and the adjacent average beachbreaks. **Three Points** is a right pointbreak with three sections that is rarely surfed because of access. Permission is needed and it's a long hike. It favours a medium E swell and there's decent beachbreaks. If the swell is big, check **Tolaga Bay**, a rivermouth right and beachbreak peaks with good S wind protection and a 600m pier. A steep 25 mins walk out onto the flanking **Cooks Point** is a low to mid tide righthander and further reefs off the Mitre Rocks. **Loisells** at Waihau Bay has exposed beachbreaks with the odd rocky patch which catches a lot of swell. **Whangara** has more surfers riding the beach in small conditions and the lefts off the island if the swell picks up. **Pouawa**'s beachbreaks are transient over the sandbars and scruffy reef outcrops, with a bit of NE wind protection up by the rivermouth. **North Makorori** is a long, soft left, great for longboarding. The long flat expanse of reef breaks in most swells at lower tides. It's a long paddle out to **Makorori Point**'s lengthy, meandering righthander, that is loved by longboarders and cruisers for its cutback walls and pedestrian pace in any SE-S swells. When the swell turns NE-E, shoulders become faster walls with hollower sections and more grunt. The beachbreaks spreading north are quality peaks with stable banks at Centres and Creeks. Some say **Wainui** is New Zealand's most consistent beachbreak/reef with many named sections like Whales, Chalet, Pines, School and the primo spot Stock Route. Can get very heavy and hollow and it handles sizeable swells. **Sponge Bay** is a reefy beach with easy rollers with a flanking left point and a right reef known as The Rock. Long hollow lefts break along the southern reef of **Tuamotu Island** when a medium E-S swell appears. Lower tides, NNE winds and a S swell should see epic waves, while more E or even huge NE swell will start the smaller intense rights at Inside Island, where NW is offshore. Requires a very long paddle (1.2km) from Sponge Bay for experts only. On large S swells **The Cliff** is an average left point located near the Gisborne yacht club. Waikanae and Midway Beach are ideal beginners waves, closer to the river, but **Gizzy Pipe** where the town sewer pipe heads 3km out to sea has built up top quality sandbars for some thumping tubes. On big swells check the **Waipaoa River Bar** (aka Big River), a deceptive, long, sandy pointbreak.

For Swell Forecasting see Mahia Peninsula.

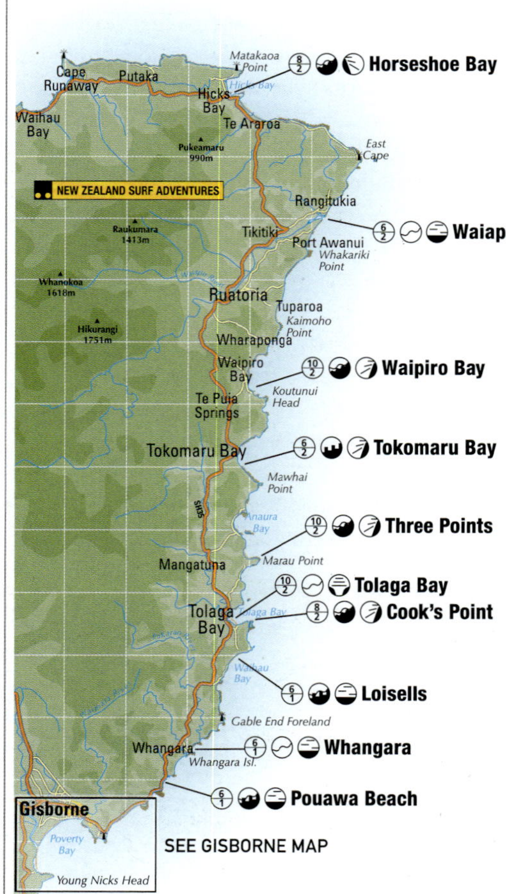


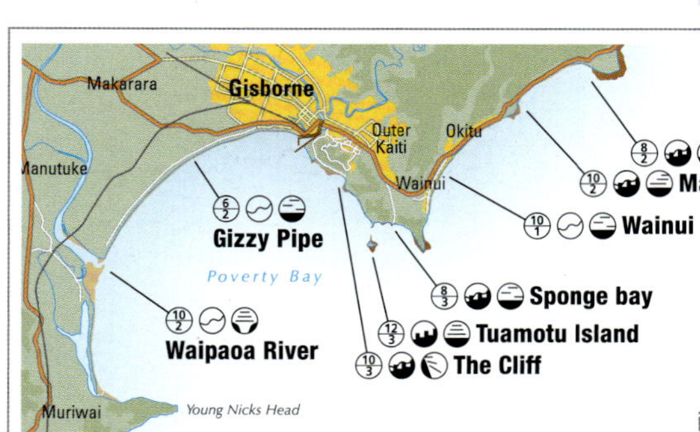

CORY SCOTT

Tuamotu island

# Mahia Peninsula NEW ZEALAND

The Mahia Peninsula is located on the east coast of the North Island, between the cities of Gisborne and Napier. The peninsula is a beautiful, hilly promontory, with isolated golden sand beaches and wonderfully clear water. It has a flexible array of reefs, points and beaches, which between them will catch any swell going from NE to SW. The predominant SW winds are perfect for many of the exposed eastern spots and somewhere will always be offshore, no matter what the wind direction. Everything remains truly wild but the laid-back, country feel is somewhat tempered by localism, so a low profile attitude is needed.

**+ VARIETY OF ASPECTS**
**+ DOMINANT OFFSHORE WINDS**
**+ CONSISTENT, QUALITY SPOTS**
**+ BEAUTIFUL, WILD AREA**

**– COLD AND WET CLIMATE**
**– WINDY**
**– COLD WATER**
**– SOME LOCALISM**

## TRAVEL INFORMATION

**Weather** – See Gisborne.

**Lodging and Food** – Mahia Beach Holiday Park in Opoutama has camping from $12pp (no power, off peak) or cabins $75 dble (off peak, shared kitchen) and motel rooms $125 dble (off peak). Self Catering at Mahanga Beach from $80-240 per night (6 people). For quality hotels you need to stay in Gisborne. Fish & chips are cheap at $8.

**Nature and Culture** – The peninsula is a wild area that is a paradise for divers, fishermen, kite & windsurfers, bird watchers and horse riders. It is a mellow place with no nightlife. Napier is an interesting Art Deco city and Gisborne is one of the surf cities of New Zealand.

**Hazards and Hassles** – Rolling boulders at Rolling Stones and other spots in large swells. Despite its peacefulness, there can be the occasional localism problem. Give the large local Maori population plenty of respect.

**Handy Hints** – Surf gear can be bought in Gisborne (see opposite) and Napier shops – Board Zone, Backdoor or Amazon.

CORY SCOTT
Annihilation Point

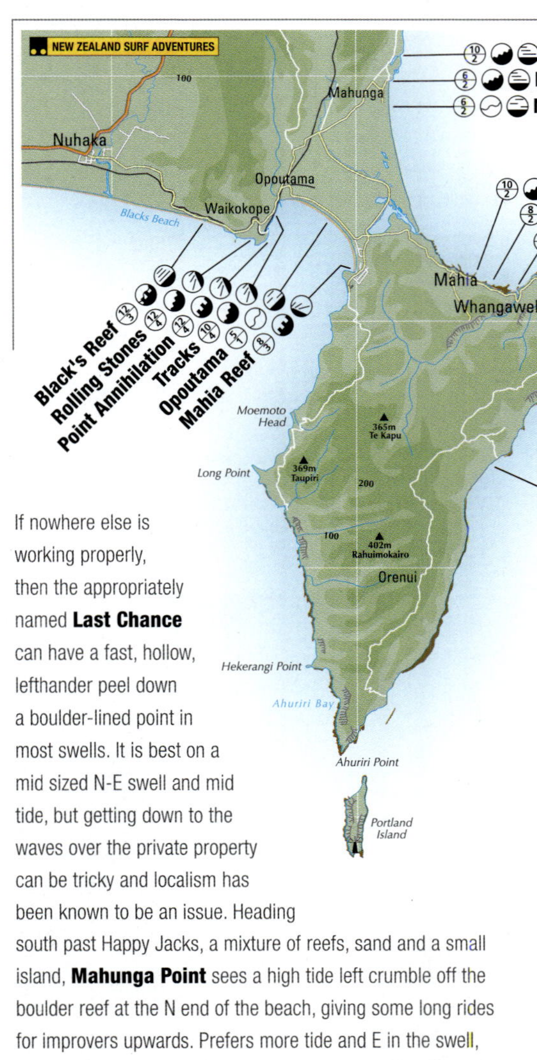


If nowhere else is working properly, then the appropriately named **Last Chance** can have a fast, hollow, lefthander peel down a boulder-lined point in most swells. It is best on a mid sized N-E swell and mid tide, but getting down to the waves over the private property can be tricky and localism has been known to be an issue. Heading south past Happy Jacks, a mixture of reefs, sand and a small island, **Mahunga Point** sees a high tide left crumble off the boulder reef at the N end of the beach, giving some long rides for improvers upwards. Prefers more tide and E in the swell, just like the adjacent 6km arc of fun, longboard-friendly peaks along **Mahunga Beach**. At its southern extent a rivermouth shapes the waves on Oraka Beach before the sands give way to a set of scattered cliff-lined sand and reef peaks called Old Mans, just north of Mahia town. **Mahia Spit** is a long, skinny finger of rock, beckoning NE swells to implode down the eastern side with a show of force and hollowness unequalled in this region. Square, super-shallow and fast, only experienced barrel-riders will emerge from the Spit's maw. The right off the tip and the inside is much easier, but it gets crowded at weekends. **Te Kapu** is a pair of quality reefbreaks called First and Second Reef, which are both fun rights with plenty of opportunities for high performance turns. The sketchy, barrelling righthander at **Boat Harbour** breaks very rarely, needing NE swell and S winds, but when it does, local Mahitians descend. Breaks super-shallow over the rock shelf and tests your ability to air drop into the square-floored barrel, making it a favourite with bodyboarders. Easier rights to the east at Aurora Pt and beyond. The remote beachbreak at **Diners Beach** is the last road accessible spot on the eastern peninsula and is fully exposed to swell and wind. Powerful triangular peaks are usually found at the north end and it's often empty. Over on the west side of the peninsula, **Mahia Reef** breaks around the base of the Mokotahi cliffs. Offers slopey lefts on major S swells that are good for improvers and longboarders as it shoulders quite predictably. The long, beautiful beach of **Opoutama** has more mellow easy rollers for beginners and loggers. Where the railway line meets the coast is **Tracks**, the most protected of three good quality righthand points. Requires a massive swell

CORY SCOTT
Rolling Stones

from the S, preferably with a bit of W in it. Consequentially, it's smaller and slower than the outer points, as the boulders shape up nice tapered walls and long shoulders. **Point Annihilation** has a clue in the name – make the powerful barrelling take-off to reach the dynamic walls. A small track leads down the cliff to **Rolling Stones**, where hollow, top-to-bottom, thick-lipped barrels grind down the boulder bank for expert surfers to take on the region's heaviest point. High tide makes the shorebreak too gnarly and pumps up the volume of the gnashing rocks. **Blacks Reef** is a quality, consistent reef peak, with a nice barrel section. The rights are hollower and longer, but lefts appear in more SE swells.

The East Cape gets SE-SSW longer period swells throughout the year, peaking between April and October. Mixed in are lots of short fetch windswells from the NE to SE. Summer cyclone swells are rare. Winds tend to be lighter than on the exposed west coast with a NW tendency in summer and SW in winter. Spring tides don't exceed 2m, yet it's enough range to affect some beachbreaks and most reefs.

| STATISTICS | | J F | M A | M J | J A | S O | N D |
|---|---|---|---|---|---|---|---|
| SWELL | Direction | | | | | | |
| | Size (ft) | 2-3 | 3-4 | 4-5 | 5 | 5 | 3 |
| WIND | Direction | | | | | | |
| | Force | F4 | F4 | F4 | F4 | F4 | F4 |
| WATER | Wetsuit | | | | | | |
| | Temp/°C | 18 | 16 | 13 | 12 | 12 | 15 |
| WEATHER | Rainfall/mm | 75 | 75 | 87 | 93 | 56 | 60 |
| | days/mth | 8 | 8 | 11 | 12 | 10 | 8 |
| | Min temp/°C | 14 | 11 | 6 | 5 | 8 | 12 |
| | Max temp/°C | 24 | 21 | 16 | 14 | 18 | 22 |

# North Canterbury NEW ZEALAND

The foothills of the snow-covered Kaikoura Range extend down to the Pacific coast leaving a narrow corridor for rail and road access. Surfing and snowboarding in one day are a real possibility. While much of the South Island relies on quality beachbreaks, this zone is sprinkled with pointbreaks and rivermouths, helping hardcore surfers avoid ice-cream headache paddle-outs.

+ CONSISTENT SWELLS
+ QUALITY RIGHT POINTBREAKS
+ UNCROWDED AND FRIENDLY
+ SURF/SNOWBOARD COMBO

- COLD WATER, STRONG WINDS
- POOR CHRISTCHURCH BEACHIES
- FREQUENT ONSHORES
- LONG FLIGHTS

WARREN HAWKE

Taylors Mistake

**Clarence** is home to a long-walled right pointbreak that is heavily dependent on swell angle, plus a sucky rivermouth right, both of which work on all tides in medium sized SE-S swells. **Blue Duck Stream** provides enough sand for the waves to keep breaking right through the high tide, but it will probably be a bit fat. **Mangamaunu** is a long, triple section right point that gets epic on NE-E swells, while the common SE-SW direction creates sections and rips. Cool, katabatic winds descend from the mountains creating offshores that blow every day in winter, despite prevailing NE winds. Hollow but not too powerful with long, cruisey rides for intermediates. It gets crowded, but there are other pointbreaks such as **Graveyards** out on the headland. Try the consistent, powerful peaks of **Meatworks** at lower tides on any S swell. Despite poor quality shingle beachbreaks in town, **Kaikoura** is one of the best places to stay. **Kahutara** could be Mangamaunu's twin, except it's heavier and less consistent. It hits the reef of gravel and boulders in front of the rivermouth, starting sucky and hollow, then a thick walling section before getting intense on the shorepound. Lots more breaks in the vicinity. **CC's** is a hollow beachbreak with good peaks at the rivermouth. **Gore Bay** is popular in summer and produces many peaks along its 5km stretch. High tide, SW winds and a big SE-S swell awakens the inconsistent point at **Port Robinson** accessed via a steep farm track. Softer peaks comb **Motunau Beach** at high tide, which is also necessary for boat access to the twin points that break down either side of Montunau Island. **Mid Shore** has a chunky E swell left point with difficult access through private farmland. The 50km sandy sweep of **Pegasus Bay** starts with a 4WD access left point called Fossils and extends south through multiple beachbreaks at Amberley, Leithfield, Waikuku and Pines, before the shifting Waimakariri Rivermouth bars attract surfers to the low tide lefts and rights and fishermen to the whitebait. Increasingly protected from S swells by the Banks Peninsula, making them smaller, weaker and messier are the **Christchurch** beaches of Spencerville, Waimairi and beach culture central New Brighton. Average beachbreaks on either side of the pier and also the only webcam. Very rarely, **Sumner Bar** sees fast hollow peaks line up in winter storms at the river estuary. Crowded **Taylor's Mistake** picks up E-NE swell and gets some chunky lefts and rights near the headlands at lower tides. Out on the Banks Peninsula, **Raupo Bay** has decent wedging sandbars, while **Hickory Bay** is the most consistent, with a 180º swell window. **Magnet Bay** lefts hug the low tide boulders, offering length of ride and some juicy walls at size.

SSE-SSW groundswells dominate for most of the year while summer sees short period NE-E windswells. SW-NW winds are typical in winter, then dominant NE winds give light onshores during summer. The Kaikoura Range will funnel local offshores. Semi-diurnal spring tides are 1.7m max.

WARREN HAWKE

Mangamaunu

## TRAVEL INFORMATION

**Weather** – The Southern Alps bring rapid weather changes so be prepared. Warm summers, especially when hot, dry, Foehn winds blow from the NW. Max air temps 18-26°C (64-79°F). Cold winters with frequent frost and air temps from 7-14°C (45-58°F). Cold water and intense windchill. Bring a 4/3mm, booties, gloves and hood in winter and a 3/2 fullsuit in summer.

**Lodging and Food** – Motels, motor inns, bed & breakfast, home-stays, holiday parks, farm-stays or backpacker hostels. Surfwatch Lodge at Mangamaunu is great: $140/dble. Topspot Backpacker in town. Expect $22/dble for a budget dorm room. Kaikoura means 'eat crayfish'. A typical meal would be $15.

**Nature and Culture** – Whale watching in Kaikoura; soak in the natural pools of Hanmer Springs; Canterbury's has 12 ski areas; alpine trekking in the Mt Cook region; "flightseeing" from Lake Tekapo or enjoy Christchurch, the garden city.

**Hazards and Hassles** – Shingle/boulder shorebreaks can be intimidating at high tides with some swell, be patient getting in and out. Seals are common in the water. Shark attack in Kaikoura 2007 and Christchurch a couple last century. Be ready for the cold. Crowds, if any, are mellow. Earthquakes are common and have recently affected some breaks and the road system.

**Handy Hints** – Get your gear at Kaikoura Surf Company. Custom boards from Surge Surfboards. Travel with NZ Surf Adventures, the all inclusive Searcher package covers both islands in a 12 day trip for $3000pp. Christchurch is only 4h from the west coast breaks between Westport and Greymouth.

| STATISTICS | | J F | M A | M J | J A | S O | N D |
|---|---|---|---|---|---|---|---|
| SWELL | Direction | | | | | | |
| | Size (ft) | 2-3 | 3-4 | 4-5 | 5 | 5 | 3 |
| WIND | Direction | | | | | | |
| | Force | F4 | F4 | F4-F5 | F4-F5 | F4 | F4-F5 |
| WATER | Wetsuit | | | | | | |
| | Temp/°C | 16 | 14 | 13 | 12 | 11 | 13 |
| WEATHER | Rainfall/mm | 65 | 70 | 90 | 90 | 70 | 70 |
| | days/mth | 9 | 11 | 15 | 15 | 12 | 11 |
| | Min temp/°C | 13 | 10 | 5 | 4 | 8 | 10 |
| | Max temp/°C | 21 | 18 | 13 | 11 | 16 | 19 |

# Otago and Southland NEW ZEALAND

Some of the most challenging and rewarding surf breaks to be found anywhere in New Zealand. Swells can get huge and it's no wonder that the Rex Von Huben memorial Big Wave contest is held here in October. North Otago spots are world-class but rare because of a lack of good NE swells. The Southern Scenic Route through the Catlins provides ample opportunity for exploration and is home to Papatowai, NZ's official tow-in break. A short hop west are the consistent Southland spots.

+ PLENTY OF SWELL ACTION
+ LOADS OF LONG POINTS
+ NZ'S BEST BEACHBREAKS
+ UNCROWDED NATURE

- COLD WATER, WINDY & WILD
- FARMLAND ACCESS, LONG HIKES
- RARELY CLASSIC ON POINTS
- LONG HAUL FLIGHTS

CORY SCOTT

Whareakeake

## TRAVEL INFORMATION

**Weather** – Cool winter temperatures ranging from 3-12°C (37-54°F). Some frosty nights but significant snowfall is uncommon. Spring can feature "four seasons in a day" weather. Mild, settled summers (Nov - Apr) with temps ranging from 7-19°C (45-66°F). Prevailing winds are either damp Southerlies or dry NW'ers. Use a 5/4mm fullsuit with boots and optional gloves and hood for winter, and a 4/3 for summer.

**Lodging and Food** – Plenty of accommodation to suit all budgets and tastes. Many backpackers from $40/n. Expect $20 for a meal. Great wines!

**Nature and Culture** – From June to Sept, 24 ski areas and 12 heli-ski operators offer some of the best alpine experiences in the world. Queenstown (Coronet Peak, Remarkable) or Wanaka (Treble Cone, Wardrona) or Mt Hutt in Canterbury are 4.5h from Dunedin. Go rock fishing or paua (abalone) diving.

**Hazards and Hassles** – Shark nets have been used in summer at St-Clair beach since 1970. Otago surfers are being driven out of the water by a growing population of sea lions. Harsh weather can close in quickly. Respect must be given to landowners if crossing private properties.

**Handy Hints** – Take a gun if visiting after April. Surf supplies abound in Dunedin city, Hydro Surf, Torpedo 7 and Amazon shops and Quarry Beach custom boards. Esplanade Surf School operates at St Clair. South Coast Boardriders, established in 1966, is one of the country's strongest surfing clubs.

Hollow **Karitane** rivermouth bar rights awaken on E swells while further outside, The Point is a sucky, challenging right, breaking close to the rocks from headhigh to scary big. **Potato Point** is well sheltered as the multi-section rights break beneath steep cliffs. The epic rights at **Whareakeake**, aka Murderers, need very rare NE swells, producing a fine mal wave when small, or a hollow racetrack at headhigh, with tube time when the sand is lined-up. **Aramoana** can throw square barrels when NE swells are greeted by S-SW winds, but this is rare. It's usually average peaks from the spit up to the rocky breaks at midway and gets bigger in front of the cliffs at the north end. The jetty provides easy entry for experts when big. Dunedin has some of the best beachbreaks in the country. Flat days are rare but strong rips and heavy storms are common. **Allans Beach** requires a long hike over sand hills down to a shapely beachie, often a bit bigger than town beaches. Not far is **Smails Beach** and neighbouring Tomohawk beach, suited to small S swells with an established left in the east corner and lots of rips. **St-Clair** is the hub of Dunedin surfing, with good quality beachbreak peaks and a long right point near the Salt Water hot pools when there's a big S swell. West of Blackhead's barreling beachbreak is **Brighton** where S swells bend around a large rock island. Easy workable walls after a hollow take-off, but positioning and paddle-out is tricky through the rocky channel at size. The Brighton beachbreak can get epic too with barrels on sandbanks anchored by patches of rock. On a medium S swell catch some ledgy lefts at **Long Point**. Take-offs can be hairy and walls are fast, but it's very ripable. Farmland access requires permission. At **Papatowai** tow-in teams and experienced paddlers try to ride the long barrelling right or lethal dredging left. Big boils and kelp add to the stress of this hellmen only wave. Hector's dolphins often play at **Porpoise Bay**, a rivermouth beachie with a selection of hollow and powerful peaks plus a bombie on big swells. The lack of roads on Stewart Island means taking a 1h boat ride from Half Moon Bay to get to **Mason Bay**, a very isolated west-facing beach. West of Invercargill, **Riverton Rocks** hold really long, cruisey rights if a big S swell wraps in at low tide. Check nearby **Colac Bay** beach and Nick's Point if it's not big enough. **Beatons** and **Porridge**, are a pair of grinding left pointbreaks with a mix of barrels and walls over rocky reef in S swells and NE winds. Farmers permission required. The last spot before Fjordland is **Frentzes Reef**, a left on large S swells.

This region is wide open to big Southern Ocean SE-SW swells all year. Cyclonic NE swells are very rare. The east coast normally remains off or sideshore unless high pressure brings E winds. Choose mid-seasons because summer might be a bit calm while winter will probably feel too icy and out-of-control. Semi-diurnal tides with 2.4m maximum tidal range. Dunedin (E) tide is 1.5h earlier than Porridge (S).

CORY SCOTT

Papatowai

| STATISTICS | | J F | M A | M J | J A | S O | N D |
|---|---|---|---|---|---|---|---|
| SWELL | Direction | | | | | | |
| | Size (ft) | 3 | 4 | 5 | 5-6 | 5 | 3-4 |
| WIND | Direction | | | | | | |
| | Force | F5 | F4-F5 | F4-F5 | F4-F5 | F4-F5 | F4-F5 |
| WATER | Wetsuit | | | | | | |
| | Temp/°C | 12 | 11 | 9 | 8 | 9 | 10 |
| WEATHER | Rainfall/mm | 73 | 70 | 75 | 68 | 65 | 69 |
| | days/mth | 11 | 12 | 12 | 11 | 12 | 12 |
| | Min temp/°C | 10 | 7 | 4 | 3 | 5 | 7 |
| | Max temp/°C | 19 | 17 | 12 | 11 | 15 | 18 |

# Sandaun and East Sepik PNG

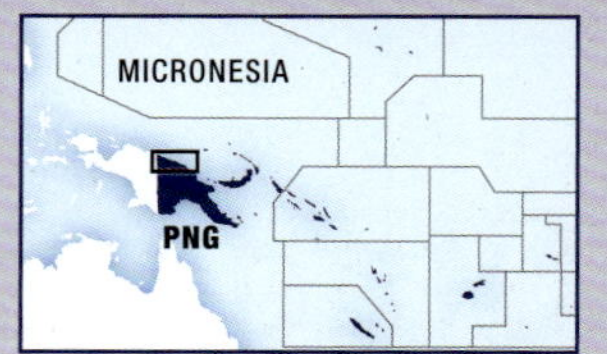


Papua New Guinea is known as 'the land of the unexpected' with its enormous diversity of cultures, peoples and landscapes. PNG is exposed to three seas of which the Bismarck Sea (backed by the Pacific Ocean) is the major swell producer. This NW-N monsoon swell affects Sandaun (the tok pisin word for sundown), an undeveloped region bordering Indonesia's Papua region, with 260km of mostly grey sand coastline where expats, based in Vanimo, working in the logging industry discovered good surf on this mountainous coast.

**+ CONSISTENT MONSOON SWELL**
**+ FUN-SIZED UNCROWDED WAVES**
**+ LOW TOURIST NUMBERS**
**+ CHEAP SURF CAMP OPTION**

**- NO OUTSTANDING BREAKS**
**- TRICKY ACCESS AND TRANSPORT**
**- HOT AND STICKY WEATHER**
**- STREET CRIME AND DISEASES**

MICHAEL KEW
Lido's Right

West of Vanimo lie the speedy, sucky left barrels of Yako and the longer walls of Waromo. Many surfers stay in the camp in Lido Village, a short walk from **Lido's Right** that peels down a long line of mainly limestone rubble reef and sand with a full variety of walls from easy crumbling lips to tuck and dash backdoor sections. **Lido's Left** can get really fast, hollow and is prone to a few sections as it bends through the inside. It's one of PNG's most consistent waves and can be surfed every afternoon even when the NW wind picks up. Different sections work depending on swell direction, but the reef lurks and it is not for beginners who should go to Town Beach for easy rides. In Vanimo, the province's only natural harbour, there is **Logs**, a freight train righthander of some consequence when the swell hits the big curve of reef out on the headland. The other end of the reef is **Jailbreak** a similarly fast, sectiony left. Further east is Narimo Island (aka Twin Rocks) where fun lefts and rights curl around the little paradise island. Endless beachbreaks lead down to **Sissano Lagoon**, where sandbanks form off the rivermouth. **Aitape** is Saudaun's largest settlement with 25,000 people and just off the point protecting the town's harbour, a superb left spins for 75m over a reef, working better on lower tides and any W wind. Aitape is connected by a rough coastal road to the large East Sepik Province. Offshore islands including **Tarawai**, Kairiru and Muschu have boat only surf spots along their coasts, like **Cape Barabar**. Back on land, follow the **Karawop** Plantation signs, which lead to fun wrapping lefts, breaking on boulders, protected from NW winds. **Wewak Point** is a reliable lefthand reefbreak, easy to check from town, tubular at low tide whilst at high tide, the harbour channel produces a soft left. **The Wharf**, aka Mission Point, is difficult to get to because the shallow outside reef peaks break 1km from shore. Travelling east, take Moem Barracks turn-off and check **Moem Point**, a mellow right reefbreak. If flat, drive further to **Forok Point**, a very consistent, all tides, right pointbreak with the occasional left, considered the best wave in East Sepik. Also called Dabiar Beach, the 7km of dirt access road is prone to flooding.

RYAN CRAIG
Wewak

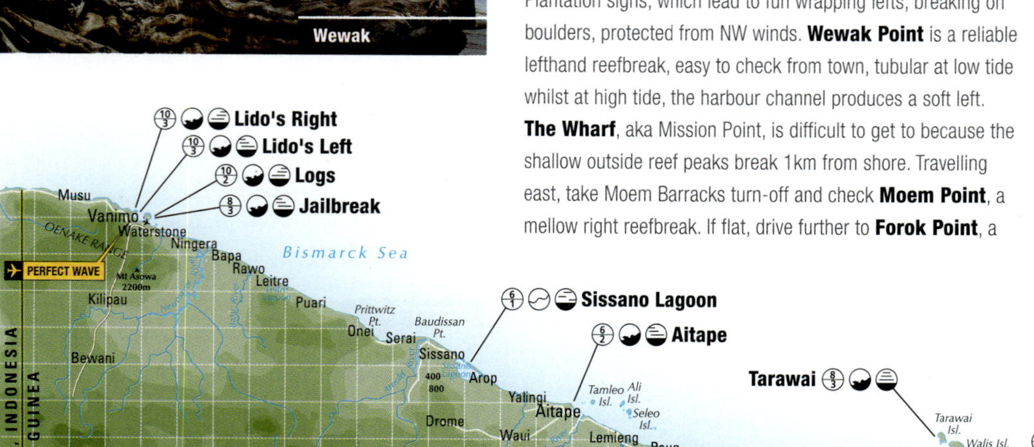


## TRAVEL INFORMATION

**Weather** – PNG has a hot wet climate all year. Vanimo, at the western end of the zone, is wettest during the surf season/wet season (Dec-Apr). Reduced visibility, 100% humidity, frenzied insects and washed-out roads. Wewak to the east of the zone is relatively dry during the surf season. Water remains super-warm year-round. Bring a rashie as the sun is fierce.

**Lodging and Food** – Lido Village has local homestays ($20/n). For A/C rooms, stay in Vanimo Beach Hotel ($130/n) or the Sandaun Surf Hotel ($120/n). Book basic Vanimo Surf Lodge ($100-149/n) through Perfect Wave. The Catholic churches run guesthouses ($50/n). Various hotels, guesthouses and backpackers available in Wewak including the Sepik Surf Site Lodge. An average meal is $10.

**Nature and Culture** – Vanimo is a pretty little seaside town with a free trade zone. Take a trip over the Indonesian border to the bustling city of Jayapura. Wewak is way busier, but don't expect nightlife or shopping. Visit the Japanese war memorial, WWII bomb craters, one of five markets to buy sacred masks and carvings or play golf.

**Hazards and Hassles** – Street crime stories are plentiful but PNG is big and Sepik is safe. Pack antibiotic cream for reef cuts. Transport and hygiene are hassley. This area is prone to earthquakes and tsunamis.

**Handy Hints** – There are surfboards for rent at Lido Village. Each surfer pays a one-off payment of AUD$50 plus AUD$12 per day as part of the Surf Management Plan run by the Surfing Association of PNG (SAPNG) to help with traditional rights, development, sustainable surf numbers and conservation.

The Sepik Provinces enjoy relatively consistent NW monsoon winds from November to April, producing regular 3-6ft waves with occasional 8-10ft, better suited to longboarders and lighter shortboarders. El Niño years are very inconsistent and worth avoiding, even though rainfall is lower. To the east offshore islands create some swell shadow, so Vanimo is the most consistent area. Exposed reefs need to be surfed in the morning when nearby mountains funnel offshores, before the W-NW sea breezes arrive. November is the least windy month while the dry season features SE winds and months of flatness. Maximum tidal range is 0.6m with unusual tide cycles combining diurnal and semi-diurnal phases.

| STATISTICS | | J F | M A | M J | J A | S O | N D |
|---|---|---|---|---|---|---|---|
| SWELL | Direction | | | | | | |
| | Size (ft) | 3-4 | 3 | 0-1 | 0-1 | 0-1 | 3 |
| WIND | Direction | | | | | | |
| | Force | F3-F4 | F3 | F2-F3 | F3 | F2-F3 | F3 |
| WATER | Wetsuit | | | | | | |
| | Temp/°C | 28 | 28 | 29 | 28 | 28 | 28 |
| WEATHER | Rainfall/mm | 268 | 253 | 169 | 142 | 185 | 220 |
| | days/mth | 18 | 19 | 15 | 14 | 15 | 17 |
| | Min temp/°C | 23 | 23 | 23 | 22 | 23 | 23 |
| | Max temp/°C | 29 | 30 | 30 | 30 | 30 | 30 |

# Kavieng, New Ireland PNG

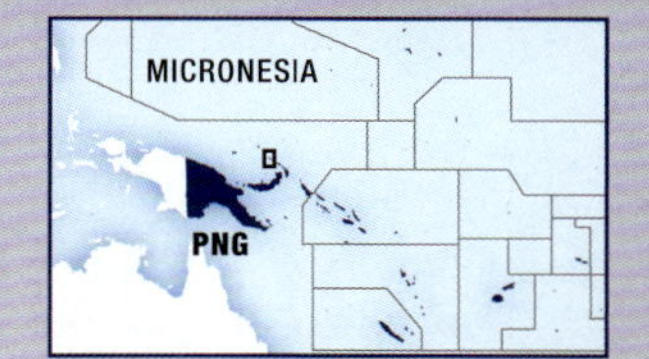


Some of PNG's best uncrowded waves break on tiny coral specks scattered through the Bismarck Archipelago.

**+ CONSISTENT, SEASONAL SWELLS**
**+ UNCROWDED, TROPICAL SURF**
**+ SHORT IDYLLIC BOAT RIDES**
**+ MELANESIAN/PAPUAN CULTURE**

**– OFTEN SMALL**
**– VERY RAINY SURF SEASON**
**– DIFFICULT, EXPENSIVE ACCESS**
**– HIGH MALARIA RISKS**

Melanesian in flavour, these islands bearing unlikely European names such as New Britain, New Ireland and New Hanover hold the best potential for maximizing the power of any WNW to ENE swells. Kavieng is the main town and jump off point for the islands that nestle not too far offshore.

CHRIS PEEL

Kavieng Lefts

Skirting around town and heading north is a shallow layer of reef known as **Pikinini**. Consistently rideable in shorter sections, it shows true class when a moderate WNW swell links up the speed runs into one, long racy barrel. All tides are doable, but high doesn't give any more tolerance over the live coral, so wear booties. Usually smaller close to Kavieng harbour, where kids paddle out on lumps of wood. **Nusa Lefts** hit the northern tip of the island where most surfers stay. This exposed spot jacks up out of deep water, then bowls out in places as the wall bends around the shelf. Fast and fluid with a nice coping, until the shallow inside section turns inside-out. Prefers more W than N in the swell with S quadrant winds and mid tide. A short boat ride away is **Long-Long**, named for its length of ride. It's rare since the swell has to be strong from the W-NW and winds from the N-E – an intermediate friendly deep water roll-in leads to a generous wall that invites tagging, spraying or some shade time. Across a short channel is **Nago**, a consistent peak more likely to work in N swells. The left usually makes the most of small swells with lip-bashing walls and an inside tuck section. The right is more fickle, needs more swell and can be a charging barrel. Prefers low to mid tides and the left even handles light onshores. **Edmago** is a top-drawer lefthander that needs W in the swell and SE winds to be any good. The adjacent right is more reliable, but far less impressive and neither spot likes the extremes of tide. When swell is in short supply, a longer trip to **Ral** is the call, since it sits in splendid isolation, open to all swells directions including NE and will have something to ride when all else is flat. Easy, fun and mushy when small, the rights on the western fringe of reef can be peaky or lined-up runners, depending on swell direction, which helps spread out the crowd on small days. The left is less reliable, both will become heavy over headhigh, but other spots will be better.

NW-NE windswells provide regular 3-6ft (1-2m) waves from Nov-April. While NW swell is ideal for many breaks, NNE-NE is more prevalent. Early offshores are prefered with onshores most afternoons. Nov has the lightest winds which turn increasingly E towards the end of the season. May-Oct sees offshore ESE winds, but is usually small or flat. Two daily tides with a different range (semi diurnal odd) with the biggest around 1m (3ft) between high and low. Most spots favour low to mid, high will be rideable, but mushier. It's not too hard to get a tide chart from Kavieng Harbour or the diving resorts.

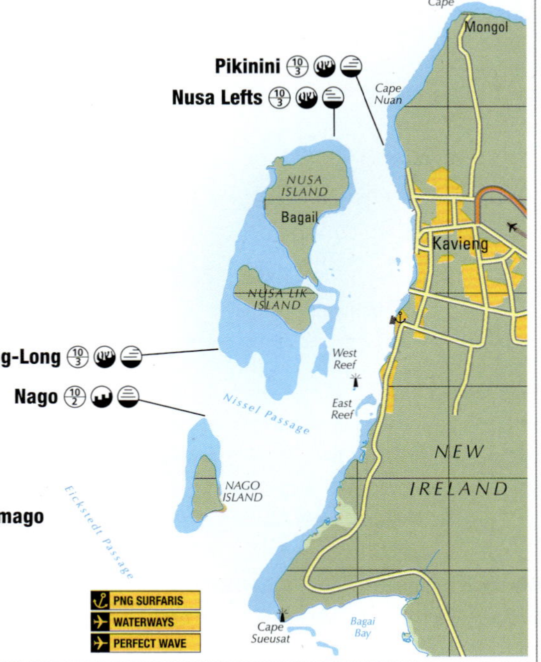


## TRAVEL INFORMATION

**Weather** – Dry season is a bit of a misnomer as it's very wet year round with a yearly average of 3.2m (10ft). The surf season corresponds with the rainy NW monsoon (Nov-Apr). It also gets very hot and is constantly sticky. Cyclones actually hitting this area are a rare occurrence.

**Lodging and Food** – There are a few hotels, B&B's and resorts in this area and they're all expensive. A basic hotel costs about $50/d, but most surfers stay at the Nusa Island Retreat on Nusa Lik, which will take no more than 12 people at a time and provide transport to the breaks ($250-299/n). Beach and waterfront bungalows, good restaurant and surf transfers are all part of the package. The fresh seafood is excellent.

**Nature and Culture** – World-class diving and fishing. On land you can play volleyball and snooker, visit the crocodile farm or WWII relics. Local people use coconut shell rattles and their voices to 'call the sharks'. Pidgin is a mix of local and English vocabulary which can be hard to interpret. The Surfing Association of Papua New Guinea promotes sustainable development by implementing the Kavieng Area Surf Management Plan that limits the total number of visiting surfers to 20 per day. Fees apply, regardless of where you stay and are distributed among the surfside communities. Book your place with the Kavieng Surf Club.

**Hazards and Hassles** – The Kavieng area is pretty safe and the locals are friendly and hospitable. Petty theft is quite rare, but remain vigilant. Reefs are super shallow and home to sharks, stonefish and sea snakes. A greater health risk is malaria and infection from reef cuts.

**Handy Hints** – Take lots of cash as credit cards either attract a surcharge or don't work. There is no surf gear available. Bring your standard shortboard, a fish for small mushy days and some reef boots. There is reasonable hospital care in Kavieng. Contact Perfect Wave for package trips to Nusa Lik or Waterways and Perfect Wave for PNG Explorer.

CHRIS PEEL

Kavieng Right

| STATISTICS | | J F | M A | M J | J A | S O | N D |
|---|---|---|---|---|---|---|---|
| SWELL | Direction | | | | | | |
| | Size (ft) | 4-5 | 3-4 | 1-2 | 0-1 | 1-2 | 3-4 |
| WIND | Direction | | | | | | |
| | Force | F3 | F2-F3 | F3 | F3 | F3 | F3 |
| WATER | Wetsuit | | | | | | |
| | Temp/°C | 28 | 28 | 28 | 27 | 27 | 27 |
| WEATHER | Rainfall/mm | 345 | 358 | 223 | 183 | 184 | 320 |
| | days/mth | 21 | 22 | 20 | 19 | 20 | 21 |
| | Min temp/°C | 24 | 23 | 23 | 22 | 23 | 24 |
| | Max temp/°C | 30 | 31 | 31 | 30 | 30 | 31 |

# Pohnpei MICRONESIA

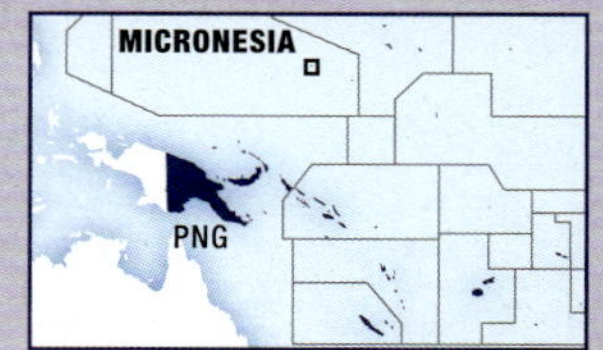


Pohnpei is one of eight island nations of the Federated States of Micronesia (FSM) and is the tip of a 5 million-year-old extinct shield volcano. The entire island is made up of black basalt rock, surrounded by a deep lagoon up to 8km wide, circled by many reefs. Secretly surfed by a lucky few until a *Surf Report* Issue in Feb 1998, P-Pass is now generally considered as the best wave in Micronesia.

**+ WARM, CRYSTAL CLEAR WATER**
**+ P-PASS PERFECTION**
**+ ISLAND SIGHTSEEING**
**+ SAFE, POLITICALLY STABLE**

**- INCONSISTENT N SWELLS**
**- OCCASIONAL CROWDS & RIPS**
**- EXTREMELY RAINY**
**- VERY EXPENSIVE TRIP**

ANDREW SHIELD

P-Pass

**P-Pass** has become the star of the Western Pacific by occasionally churning out impossibly perfect scary, double-overhead, super-sucky righthand pits, attracting pros and chargers to this remote island when the forecast looks right (2-5 times a year). Most of the time intermediates will enjoy the fun, consistent, headhigh, high tide sessions. It takes any swell from NW-NE, with straight N being the best direction. P-Pass works with no winds or with light NE-E trades, which blow dead offshore as the swell lines wrap around the reef. These rights can be surfed at any tide, but it does get very shallow on a full low tide. It's a 20min boat ride from Kolonia. It is only a 5min boat ride to **Sokehs Pass**, where small outside rights are rideable at high tide from 2-4ft, but there's nothing easy about the treacherous inside. **Lighthouse** breaks under the same conditions as P-Pass, but it is always bigger and has a super-shallow inside section. It's a challenging spot in big waves, with a west and a north take-off spot, a long wall and an incredible inside barrel section, inevitably drawing comparisons to Sunset Beach in Hawaii. Holds chunky swells and bigger is always better, because the reef can go dry at any tide on smaller days, when nearby Middle Pass may be working. The east side of Pohnpei has three different passes that work in totally different conditions in early season when the trade winds are low. **Mwahnd Lefts** holds big swell and can offer fun walls, good hooks and quick barrels. Across the channel, **Mwahnd Rights** handles any size swell from small to triple overhead. Reminiscent of Macaronis in Indo, **Aruh** has spinning lefts that require a huge N swell or an E swell without the E winds. Sharp bottom. **Nahpali** is a long sectiony right, which always has waves, but is usually blown out. It's rippy, sharky and a 40min boat ride. On the other side of the famous ruins of **Nan Madol**, more wind exposed rights peel and section off into the bay. **Nahlap** has a fun right reefbreak ideal for beginners. The waves pick up in SE swells from July until October, with 3-4ft faces and light or no winds.

Most of the swells that reach Pohnpei are generated by typhoons in the western Pacific or North Pacific winter storms from early October through to early May. During August and September, some breaks on the exposed windward side come alive with glassy or offshore conditions and E swells generated by local trade winds. SW swells can arrive with the strong monsoonal winds that blow in from western Micronesia and the Philippines. These waves hit the east to southwest sides of Pohnpei with less power and size. The NE trades blow strong from late December all the way to late May. Semi-diurnal tides with diurnal inequality, average 0.9m-1.8m max tidal range.

ANDREW SHIELD

Lighthouse

## TRAVEL INFORMATION

**Weather** – Pohnpei has a tropical, humid climate. One of the wettest places on earth with the largest part of the rainfall at night. Temps are constant, ranging from 23-30°C (74-86°F). Most of the year, there is a NE trade wind. A typical day in Pohnpei is cloudy with intermittent showers and the sun breaking through now and then. Major windstorms and destructive typhoons are rare. Boardshorts only in the "Pool", the warmest ocean temperatures in the world.

**Lodging and Food** – Pohnpei Surf Club costs between $199-225/night (peak season is Nov - Feb). 7 AC double rooms with all mod cons. P-Pass Surf Camp $170/d. Staying at the Village Hotel (fr $103) is possible, but finding a boat will be difficult and expensive. All-you-can-eat rotary Sushi for $8. Expect $15-20 for meals daily + stocking hotel rooms with supplies from the supermarket in Kolonia.

**Nature and Culture** – Waterfalls, ancient ruins of Nan Madol, world-class diving, deep-sea fishing, snorkelling, bird watching, canoeing. Hike Sokehs Ridge and WWII historical sites.

**Hazards and Hassles** – Boat access means no reef walking when you paddle in and out. Most surfers do not use booties, but they can be helpful at times.

**Handy Hints** – Small to mid-range boards (6'0"-7'0") work best in the barrels. PSC recommends bringing 4 boards and has a fleet of used hire boards for those who break all theirs. Bring everything with you including snacks.

| STATISTICS | | J F | M A | M J | J A | S O | N D |
|---|---|---|---|---|---|---|---|
| SWELL | Direction | | | | | | |
| | Size (ft) | 3-4 | 3 | 3-4 | 4-5 | 2-3 | 3-4 |
| WIND | Direction | | | | | | |
| | Force | F4 | F4 | F3-F4 | F3 | F3 | F3-F4 |
| WATER | Wetsuit | | | | | | |
| | Temp/°C | 28 | 28 | 29 | 29 | 29 | 29 |
| WEATHER | Rainfall/mm | 283 | 411 | 463 | 427 | 427 | 417 |
| | days/mth | 17 | 22 | 25 | 22 | 20 | 19 |
| | Min temp/°C | 24 | 24 | 23 | 23 | 23 | 23 |
| | Max temp/°C | 30 | 30 | 30 | 31 | 31 | 31 |

# Majuro MARSHALL ISLANDS

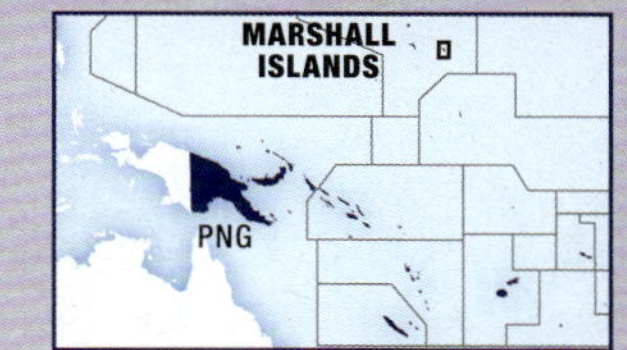


The Republic of the Marshall Islands are a Micronesian republic of 29 atolls plus five individual islands and all are open to swells from both hemispheres. Fickle at best, the Marshalls are not one of the world's great surfing destinations with few, if any world-class waves. Majuro has no honeymoon resorts, no extensive white sand beaches, and not much tourism infrastructure, yet it retains a peculiar charm in the smiles and ease of its people. Majuro atoll is the Marshalls nerve centre, home to the republic's primary government, most of its businesses, and about half of its entire population, making it one of the most densely populated atolls on Earth (31,000 people). International flights also go to Kwajalein Atoll, but it's strictly controlled by the US military, who have been testing ballistic missiles and nuclear detonations on surrounding islands, including the biggest ever explosion of a dry hydrogen bomb on Bikini Atoll in 1954.

**+ MELLOW ATOLL AMBIANCE**
**+ USER-FRIENDLY WAVES**
**+ CLEAN WATER**
**+ NO SURF CROWDS**

**– EXPENSIVE FLIGHTS**
**– LACK OF SURF SPOTS**
**– INCONSISTENT, SMALL WAVES**
**– POLLUTION AROUND D-U-D**

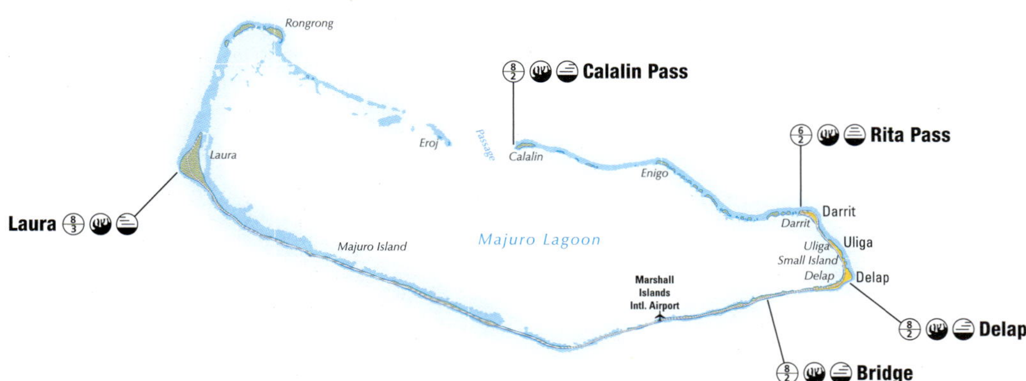


The majority of Majuro's surfing is done around the DUD Municipality, which is comprised of Darrit, Uliga, and Delap, crowded villages connected by a paved road, It's a dirty place, with lots of litter, dust, ramshackle buildings, and cars. Visiting surfers are rare. The handful living on Majuro are generally expat American teachers and Seventh Day Adventist church volunteers who frequent the sucky tubes at the **Bridge**, Majuro's marquee surf spot. Very shallow, hollow, and somewhat dangerous, the Bridge can provide quick, snappy rides if you're fast on your feet. The 4m high bridge was built to span a narrow channel the Japanese blasted through the reef in 1983, to spare small boats the long trip up to Calalin Channel, to gain access to the lagoon anchorages. On Majuro's southeast corner is **Delap**, in front of the hospital, which offers a fun, sectiony righthander during S swells. This is Majuro's most popular wave because it handles the prevailing NE trade wind. Darrit holds an occasionally fun left and right on either side of **Rita Pass**, but it's very sensitive to both NE trade wind and lower tide. At **Calalin Pass** there is an equally fickle righthander that suffers from lots of strong currents as it is the main passage into the lagoon. It's almost always onshore when it breaks in the N swell season, plus it's a 35km boat ride across the lagoon from the anchorage to access it. On the atoll's western tip, a rare S swell lefthander at **Laura** is dead offshore with the trades. It's possible to drive along the narrow road from D-U-D all the way west to Laura, which is considerably cleaner than DUD and more typical of natural Marshallese beauty. Just to the north is a quasi beachbreak (lots of coral heads) that can be fun and punchy during westerly windswells, but it is often blown-out or too small.

Most of Majuro's surf spots work on S swells, arriving from June-Sept. These swells have a long way to travel and can be shadowed and dissipated by the archipelagos to the south (Fiji, Kiribati, Tuvalu), resulting in often weak and inconsistent surf. The upside is that Majuro's surf is usually offshore on the atoll's south coast, and places like the Bridge and Laura are normally quite clean. In wintertime (Dec-Mar) northerly groundswells originate from the North Pacific and provide decent sized waves but unfortunately these coincide with the strong prevailing NE trade winds. Tides do exceed 1.5m and affect most waves.

MICHAEL KEW

Laura

## TRAVEL INFORMATION

**Weather** – Majuro's climate is pretty much the same all year: hot and humid, temps averaging 27°C (81°F). Rain is frequent. It can get very windy, especially during the winter. Ocean water temp is around 26°C (80°F). Boardshorts will do it plus a rashie for the wind and sun.

**Lodging and Food** – In DUD: Flame Tree, a cool hostel/restaurant with cheap rates ($25+/n). Hotel Robert Reimers, friendly and clean, with a good restaurant downstairs (Tide Table). Marshall Islands Resort ($80+/n), and its restaurant (Enra) offers great sea food. Long Island Hotel is $450/n. In Laura check out the Meyo Country Inn and Arno Beachcomber Lodge ($50dbl).

**Nature and Culture** – Beyond DUD, it's all coconut palms, coral rubble, turquoise lagoon, and blue Pacific. It's all very flat, and the atoll is so narrow in some places that it is only a stone's throw from the ocean to the lagoon. Culturally the Marshallese are some of the world's friendliest people, quick to share a smile and a meal.

**Hazards and Hassles** – The shallow coral reefs are your biggest concern, especially at the Bridge. Also beware of the searing tropical sun. Crime is not an issue.

**Handy Hints** – Bring plenty of sun cream and all surf gear, because there are no surf shops. If the surf is flat, take a lagoon tour or deep-sea fishing charter.

MICHAEL KEW

Bridge

| STATISTICS | | J F | M A | M J | J A | S O | N D |
|---|---|---|---|---|---|---|---|
| SWELL | Direction | | | | | | |
| | Size (ft) | 6-8 | 4-6 | 3-5 | 2-3 | 2-4 | 4-6 |
| WIND | Direction | | | | | | |
| | Force | F6 | F5 | F3 | F2 | F3-F4 | F5-F6 |
| WATER | Wetsuit | | | | | | |
| | Temp/°C | 26 | 26 | 26 | 26 | 26 | 26 |
| WEATHER | Rainfall/mm | 185 | 235 | 289 | 312 | 334 | 313 |
| | days/mth | 13 | 16 | 20 | 21 | 20 | 19 |
| | Min temp/°C | 25 | 25 | 25 | 25 | 25 | 25 |
| | Max temp/°C | 29 | 30 | 30 | 30 | 30 | 30 |

# New Georgia SOLOMON ISLANDS

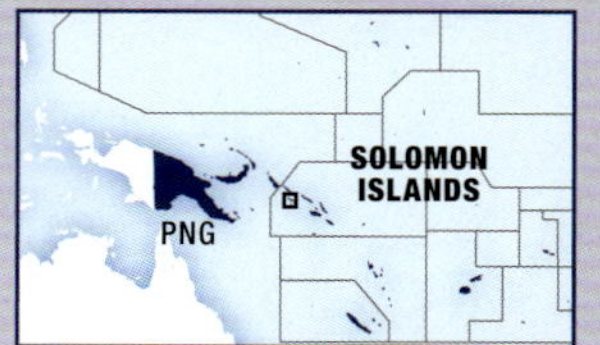


**With soaring mountain peaks, dense tropical rainforest, cascading waterfalls, palm-fringed beaches and traditional villages, the Melanesian Islands are known for their unspoilt beauty and relaxed pace of life. The Solomons may not be in the best location to get swells, but reports from divers and sailors have found that waves occur all over this area. The majority of discoveries have turned up on the SW-facing coasts, when the Coral Sea cyclone season kicks in and where surfing has expanded on the back of the diving resorts infrastructure.**

**+ CLEAN, GLASSY SWELLS**
**+ QUALITY REEFBREAKS**
**+ CRYSTAL CLEAR WATER**
**+ NO CROWDS**

**- ERRATIC SEASONAL SWELLS**
**- SHALLOW REEFS**
**- VERY HOT AND HUMID**
**- REMOTE ACCESS**

YEP

Titiana

Overlooked by majestic Kolombangra, the tallest volcano in the region, Gizo is the capital of the Western Province and Ghizo Island is the first accommodation option with surf in the locality. The main break is **Pailongge**, where long rights pick up any swell in front of the namesake village. On large swells, the two hollow sections will merge to become a long, perfect wave over the coral reef. Next to it is **Titiana**, a powerful left when it's on, usually during SE swells. These two are within walking and paddling distance from land. **Outside Naru** rights pick up SE swell straight on and it's only a short boat ride from Sanbis and Fatboys resorts on Mbabanga Island. 20mins boat ride from Gizo, another short, shallow left zips across the reef on **Makuti** Island but it needs S-SW swell since it is blocked by Green Reef. The second accommodation option is to stay on Lola Island at Zipolo Habu Resort, in order to shred **Skull Island** (2h boat trip from Gizo) when a mid to large swell hits. Possibly the longest rights in the Solomons, Skull is best at 3-6ft with NW-N wind. If the swell is too small, try **Despretes** further out; these peaky rights break close to shore with a great take-off that barrels down the line. Enter the beautiful lagoon through the reef pass. Not far eastward are two lefts and one right reef. **Mbirimbiri's** wrapping rights are super-shallow so avoid low tides and wait for N winds. Experts only since getting caught inside will be traumatic. **Lavata** works on rare W-NW swell, produced by windswell in the Solomon Sea, and **Kundu Kundu** is a deep water left, 150m offshore. It picks up all available swell, W being best, works all tides, especially at mid and holds up to 10ft, making it very long. There's a good chance of seeing fins but there has never been an attack. New discoveries are being made on Rendova, 45 minutes boat ride from Munda, where many exposed left reefbreaks go unridden. **Coves** is a real swell-magnet and breaks off a reef near a tiny beach. Best at 3-6ft, it's sheltered by high cliffs from any wind apart from W and the set-up is breathtaking.

The best time for swells is between December and April, when cyclones and lows build up to the east of northern Queensland, moving slowly south. They can last for more than a week at a time giving excellent, clean, good-sized swells. Also consistent smaller winter swells from May to August with lows travelling north from the Tasman Sea, hitting the east side of New Georgia Islands. The equatorial trough is an area of W-NW monsoonal winds, found close to, or south of the Solomons. NW windswells occur out of the Solomon Sea and E-NE are the most favourable winds, although winds often change and glassy days are not uncommon. Tides change from diurnal to semi-diurnal with diurnal inequality (different daily ranges), just remember they will not exceed 0.6m and full moon phases don't necessarily result in the biggest tides.

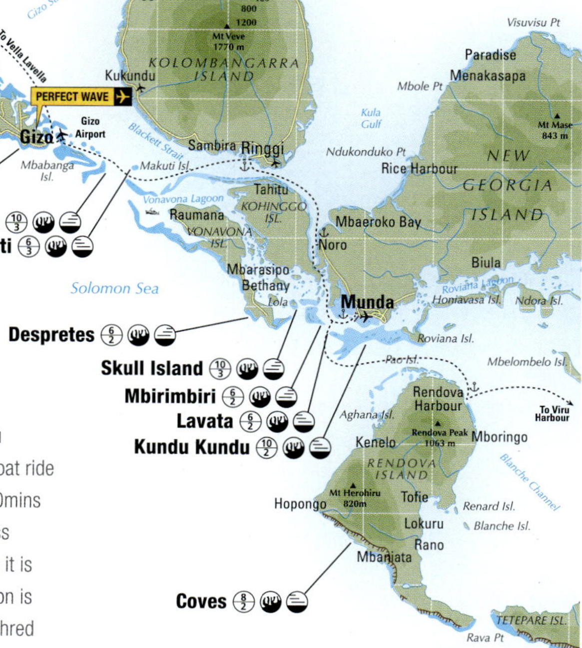

JEROME TEIGNE

Pailongge

## TRAVEL INFORMATION

**Weather** – Dec-April is the period of thunderstorms and the heaviest rainfall (average of 3600mm). Temps between 28°C (85°F) and 32°C (88°F), make it unbearably hot and sticky, so A/C is essential. Frequent thunderstorms build up over the mountainous interior on many afternoons and can drift towards coastal areas. Over the ocean, storms are likely to occur in the night or early morning. On average, cyclones hit the Solomons once or twice a year, although this decreases in the Western Province. Boardies are ideal; use a long sleeve rashie to protect against the fierce sun.

**Lodging and Food** – Flying to Munda (MUA) is easier, allowing bigger boards: Gizo Hotel has a/c, pool view rooms; Sanbis ECO Resort standard bungalow dbl from $200/n (+$125 + fuel p/d for boat and driver, up to 8 pax), some rentals available. Fatboys and Zipolo Habu Resort (Skull Island) can be booked through Surf The Earth. Full meal package includes BBQ tuna, chilli mud crab and lobster.

**Nature and Culture** – Dive Ghizo's WWII sunken military relics like the Tao Maru. Climb 1770m high Kolombangara Volcano. Visit the Megapode skull shrines and custom dances at Mbangopingo (Rendova).

**Hazards and Hassles** – Take anti-malarial medication, but the best defence is the prevention of mosquito bites. Drink bottled water. Be ready to face long boat rides in full sun exposure. Take reef boots.

**Handy Hints** – Take all gear including two boards, tropical wax and sunblock. Use the sea kayaks to access the surf to nearby breaks. Local costs are relatively inexpensive. 95% of the population are Christian.

| STATISTICS | | J F | M A | M J | J A | S O | N D |
|---|---|---|---|---|---|---|---|
| SWELL | Direction | | | | | | |
| | Size (ft) | 3-4 | 3 | 2 | 2-3 | 1-2 | 2-3 |
| WIND | Direction | | | | | | |
| | Force | F3 | F2-F3 | F2-F3 | F3 | F3-F4 | F2-F3 |
| WATER | Wetsuit | | | | | | |
| | Temp/°C | 29 | 29 | 29 | 28 | 28 | 29 |
| WEATHER | Rainfall/mm | 380 | 330 | 250 | 310 | 240 | 260 |
| | days/mth | 17 | 12 | 14 | 15 | 14 | 14 |
| | Min temp/°C | 24 | 23 | 23 | 23 | 23 | 23 |
| | Max temp/°C | 30 | 30 | 30 | 29 | 29 | 30 |

# Malaita & Makira SOLOMON ISLANDS

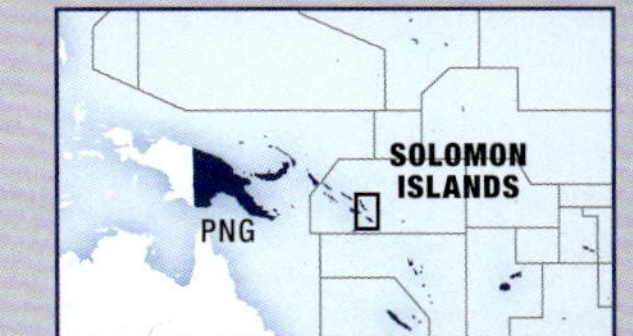


The Solomon Islands probably holds the largest, unexplored, quality surf territory in the South Pacific. The biggest island is Guadalcanal, next to Malaita and Makira, with other major islands being San Cristobal, Santa Isabel, Choiseul, Rennell, New Georgia and the Santa Cruz group. The topography varies from low-lying coral atolls to lofty volcanic peaks and the bulk of the population live within a subsistence economy, in one of the world's least developed countries. Very few have ventured along the northern sides of Malaita and Makira, but those that do are likely to ride some pristine set-ups catering for most abilities.

- **+ HUNDREDS OF SECRET SPOTS**
- **+ CLEAN TROPICAL PERFECTION**
- **+ NE & SE SWELLS**
- **+ DIVING PARADISE**

- **- SOME SWELL INCONSISTENCY**
- **- LACK OF TOURISM INFRASTRUCTURE**
- **- EXTREMELY REMOTE ACCESS**
- **- HIGH RAINFALL, MALARIA & DISEASE**

RONAN GLADU

Manu



On the northern tip of Malaita island, **Malu'u** Lodge provides a decent base for exploring the righthander bending round the reef on NE swells as well as the lagoon entrance. Heading SE, the Lau lagoon is home to Solwata Surf Camp, with access to a dozen reef passes, fringes and rivermouths nearby. The reef pass at **Manu** breaks right in two separate sections before shouldering into a deepwater channel cut by a river. **Fakanakafo Bay** has several spots nearby (Fouia & Atori), including a rivermouth peak and a long stretch of beachbreak that's quite a hike to reach. **Leli Island** is a scythe of reef, 20mins boat ride from the bay, where chunky, sectiony lefts will hug the curve of coral in big swells. Locals on strange home-made seko palm boards can sometimes be found at **Uruilangi**, a fun, small swell, easy access peak, a short boat ride from Atoifi. **Sinalangu** is an inconsistent, low tide right, next to the harbour entrance. Can be fast and shallow with long rides. Ulawa Island has a blanket of coral sand at **Su'ulausi Harbour**, one of the rare beachbreaks in the Solomons, with nice waves for all abilities. Down the coast at Su'ulofo village, a long, consistent left reef picks up any swell with E in it at **Su'uholo**, near Eresi Point. On Makira island, two thirds of the 40,500 Melanesian people live on the northern coast leaving the steep southern shore sparsely populated. Makira has more swamps than other islands making land transport tricky, especially to the good southern spots. Boat out to the north tip of **Malaupaina**, one of the Three Sisters Islands, which holds a pretty beefy right in light winds and large swells. The shallow reef is intimidating, as are the large saltwater crocodiles in the area! **Kirakira** is the main town to rent a boat, get supplies and maybe catch a few average black sand beachbreaks near the rivermouth. **Tawarogha** has been exposed to the surfing world, thanks to its long, hollow consistent rights, working with both SE and NE swells.

The N-NE swells from Dec to April are the most reliable. Typically, it will be a mellow 2-5ft, clean and often perfect with only occasional flat spells. The same time of year sees the most powerful waves arrive in the Coral Sea cyclone season, with 8ft SE swells possible on southern shores that are usually flat (no spots shown). Tasman lows send long-distance S swells in July-August, coinciding with ESE windswells, hitting east-facing

STEPHANE ROBIN

Tawarogha

shores like Ulawa island or Tawarogha. January to March sees a period of W- NW monsoonal winds. From May to October, the persistently strong SE trade winds blow, picking up plenty of moisture over the ocean and heavy rainfall is guaranteed, especially on the windward side. The transition months between the 2 seasons are marked by a greater frequency of calm winds. Most tides are small, but significant, with 1m max tidal range and diurnal cycles (1 tide a day).

## TRAVEL INFORMATION

**Weather** – Prepare for a wet tropical climate, featuring high, uniform humidity and temps (mean diurnal variation is 7°C/12°F), with abundant rainfall in all months. From December to March, NW equatorial winds bring hot weather and heavy rainfall that lessens during February when the equatorial trough is normally furthest south. From April to November, the islands are cooled by drier SE trade winds. Damaging, but rarely life-threatening, cyclones occasionally strike during the rainy season. Water temps are among the warmest on earth.

**Lodging and Food** – In Makira and Malaita, dirt cheap rest houses will be the norm with no A/C, maybe a fan & nets. Solwata Surf Camp will boat and drive you around the NE breaks; book through Surf the Earth. Basic fish & chips, sweet potatoes ($3-4 a meal). Auki, the province's capital, has a population of 4,000 and a variety of shops, hotels, and restaurants.

**Nature and Culture** – Islanders (Melanesians, Polynesians, Gilbertese) are unique and staunchly Christian. Towns are quiet, King Solomon Hotel operates Honiara's only nightclub. Makira: copra mill in Kira Kira, turtle beach and Natagera houses on Santa Ana Island. Malaita: Auki, relaxing provincial centre, shark calling, manufacture of shell money.

**Hazards and Hassles** – Medical facilities are limited; the nearest reliable hospitals are in Australia. High-risk area for chloroquine resistant malaria and dengue fever. Fresh and salt water crocodiles and sharks are common. Earthquake and tsunami prone area.

**Handy Hints** – Solomon's takes a lot of dedication and patience to score the best surf. Take everything you need, but not too much because of transport restrictions. Road system is light, take motorized canoes and boats (cheap). One strong all-round board, leash, wax and good snorkelling stuff.

| STATISTICS | | J F | M A | M J | J A | S O | N D |
|---|---|---|---|---|---|---|---|
| SWELL | Direction | | | | | | |
| | Size (ft) | 3-4 | 2-3 | 2 | 2 | 2-3 | 3 |
| WIND | Direction | | | | | | |
| | Force | F2-F3 | F2-F3 | F3 | F3 | F3 | F2 |
| WATER | Wetsuit | | | | | | |
| | Temp/°C | 29 | 30 | 29 | 29 | 29 | 29 |
| WEATHER | Rainfall/mm | 270 | 291 | 232 | 256 | 226 | 243 |
| | days/mth | 14 | 13 | 13 | 13 | 13 | 13 |
| | Min temp/°C | 24 | 24 | 24 | 23 | 23 | 24 |
| | Max temp/°C | 31 | 31 | 31 | 29 | 31 | 31 |

# Efate VANUATU

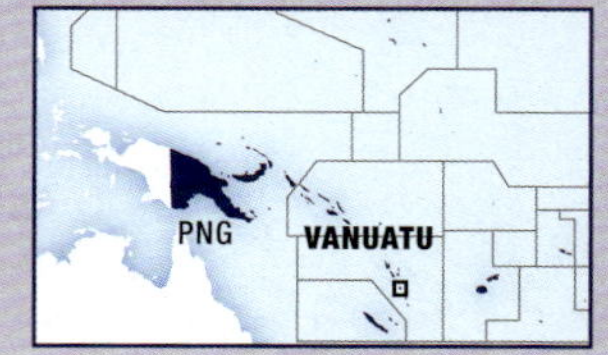


Situated 2,250km NE of Sydney, and 800km W of Fiji, Vanuatu would be an idyllic surf island if New Caledonia was not blocking any South Pacific swells. Vanuatu is the emerged part of an island arc, with a narrow rim delineated by a 2,000m isobath so when there is swell, it hits the coast with full strength. There are no lagoons or barrier reefs; there are only fringing reefs ranging from 100m to 2km wide. Sleepy capital city Port-Vila on Efate is set within a magnificent natural harbour inside Mélé Bay surrounded by half a dozen spots.

- **+ QUALITY CORAL REEFBREAKS**
- **+ YACHTING & SAILING STOP-OVER**
- **+ WARM AND EMPTY LINE-UPS**
- **+ GOOD TOURISM FACILITIES**

- **- S-SW SWELL SHADOW**
- **- LACK OF CONSISTENT SPOTS**
- **- SE SWELL/WIND EXPOSURE**
- **- EXPENSIVE FLIGHT AND TRIP**

JASON FEAST

Pango Point

To the west of Mélé is **Devil's Point**, a scary scene for radical lefts, offshore with the trades! On rare big swells, mediocre waves break inside Mélé Bay at **Black Sand Beach**. Many of the resorts are close to quality reefbreaks, which makes checking conditions easy. The tip of **Pango Point** (aka Pounders) is clad in coral, where lefts will speed down the line in SE swells at higher tides. Barrels from take-off then sectiony walls offer a few hits before shutting down over the aggressive polyps. **Breakas** can be described as a tube orgy when it is on, but the barrelling lefts need high tide and no trades. Sucky at the peak before shouldering off and there are some rights as well, especially if the swell has a bit of W in it. Take the free ferry to **Erakor Island**, a private resort island with many water activities, but few surfers to ride the short high tide lefts unfurling on the western reef. Lower swell exposure than Pango Pt or Breakas, but it does handle the trades better, as do the difficult, sectioning lefts a long walk out on Erakor Point. **Tapi Point** has probably the longest waves on Efate, albeit quite sectiony. There's also a right on the island, 700m from Eratap resort. **Teouma Bay**'s protected beachies break very softly, perfect for beginners, although its pseudonym Shark Bay reveals the main danger. Further away is **Soumabal Point**, a potential left reefbreak but again trade wind exposure is maximum, so it's likely to be disorganised. **Forari Bay** has a low consistency set-up, with some fast, hollow lefts in any E swell and any W wind. There's a right on the south side of the bay that will be cross/offshore in the trades and is definitely worth a regular check. The small cove at **Epao** (aka White Cows) holds a right reef that tends to stay smoother for longer in SE trades. 1-2km offshore from the Beachcomber, **Mangea Reefs**, soak up the worst the wind and waves can throw at them. Windy, shifty and sharky as hell. Boat out on a calm wind day. Check Tikilas Pass on Nguna where the right has some form.

Mangea Reefs
Epao
Forari Bay
Devil's Point
Black Sand Beach
Pango Point
Breakas
Erakor Island
Tapi Point
Teouma Bay
Soumabal Point

JASON FEAST

Breakas

New Caledonia blocks 100% of the SW swells and New Zealand makes it hard for straight S swells to make it right up to Vanuatu. SE groundswells from systems travelling east to South America or windswells from the trades, hit Vanuatu with some strength and consistency. Most exposed spots will be blown-out by 9am, so wake up at dawn. Surf is rarely big, 2-8ft being the normal range. Coral Sea cyclones produce occasional NW-W swells, with ideal NE-E wind conditions. From 1940 to 1985, 58 severe tropical storms and cyclones affected Vanuatu, 65% of which occurred in January and February. The trade winds are easterly in southern and central Vanuatu, and southerly in the far north where there is a clear equatorial climatic influence. Tidal range can reach 1.6m on spring tides, averaging out at 1-1.2m, but is enough to change the surf conditions on high tide only surf spots.

## TRAVEL INFORMATION

**Weather** – The best time for good weather is April/May to October when temps range from 18-28°C (64-82°F). January to March is hot (26-34°C/79-94°F), often wet and prone to cyclones, but being low season it's a good time of year to take advantage of travel deals. Water remains tropical year-round but in July-August, anticipate the windchill with a shorty.

**Lodging and Food** – Pango Paradise Cove Resort has 10 self contained units and 6 deluxe studios: $1087 for 5n/2p. Erakor Island Resort, waterfront bungalows (from $215/dble). Breakas Beach Resort $200/dble inc breakfast. Treetops Lodge bungalows $460/7 nights, inc breakfast. Kaiviti Hotel ($90/dble). Guest Houses like basic Tafea ($30/dble). Expect to pay $10 for a cheap meal.

**Nature and Culture** – It's heaven for diving, fishing and golf courses. Numerous kava 'nakamals' are found around Port Vila. Mele Cascades are only a 12km drive.

**Hazards and Hassles** – Shallow, razor-sharp reefs with no channels. Reef-cuts and snapped boards frequent. There is one hospital in Vila with limited resources. Efate is relatively malaria free. Tap water in urban areas is safe but not in rural areas.

**Handy Hints** – A gun is not needed. Don't forget reef boots, sunblock and alarm clocks. The Vanuatu are strongly linked with France, expect French ex-pats and Australian and Japanese tourists. Ni-Vans are the islanders. Locals surf here and have set up Pango Beach surf shop in the village.

| STATISTICS | | J F | M A | M J | J A | S O | N D |
|---|---|---|---|---|---|---|---|
| SWELL | Direction | | | | | | |
| | Size (ft) | 2-3 | 3 | 3-4 | 4-5 | 3-4 | 2 |
| WIND | Direction | | | | | | |
| | Force | F3 | F3 | F3-F4 | F3-F4 | F3 | F3 |
| WATER | Wetsuit | | | | | | |
| | Temp/°C | 28 | 28 | 26 | 25 | 26 | 27 |
| WEATHER | Rainfall/mm | 300 | 290 | 130 | 110 | 110 | 180 |
| | days/mth | 18 | 19 | 14 | 12 | 12 | 14 |
| | Min temp/°C | 23 | 23 | 21 | 19 | 20 | 22 |
| | Max temp/°C | 30 | 29 | 27 | 26 | 27 | 29 |

# South Province NEW CALEDONIA

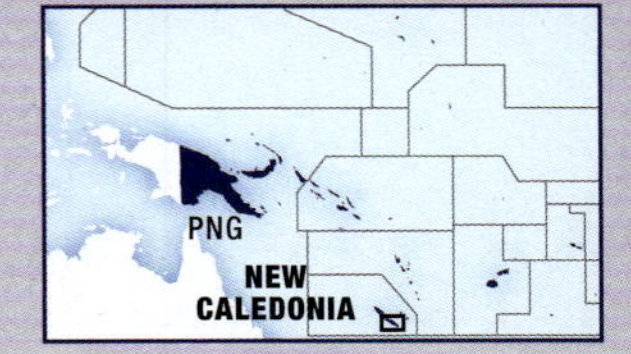




It's only recently that New Caledonia has begun to reveal its potential for outer reef barrels to the surfing world. Although the equal of anywhere else in the South Pacific, it is unlikely to become as popular as some of its neighbours because its waves break on reef passes between 5-20km offshore and are stretched along a 700km ribbon of barrier reef. This means that unless you can afford to be on an expensive charter yacht, or spend a couple of hours each day commuting, you aren't going to do a lot of surfing.

- + PERFECT REEF PASS WAVES
- + VARIETY OF BARRIER REEF SPOTS
- + EXOTIC YACHT TRIP
- + LOW CROWD FACTOR

- – BOAT ACCESS ONLY
- – EASILY BLOWN-OUT
- – VERY EXPENSIVE
- – INCONSISTENT

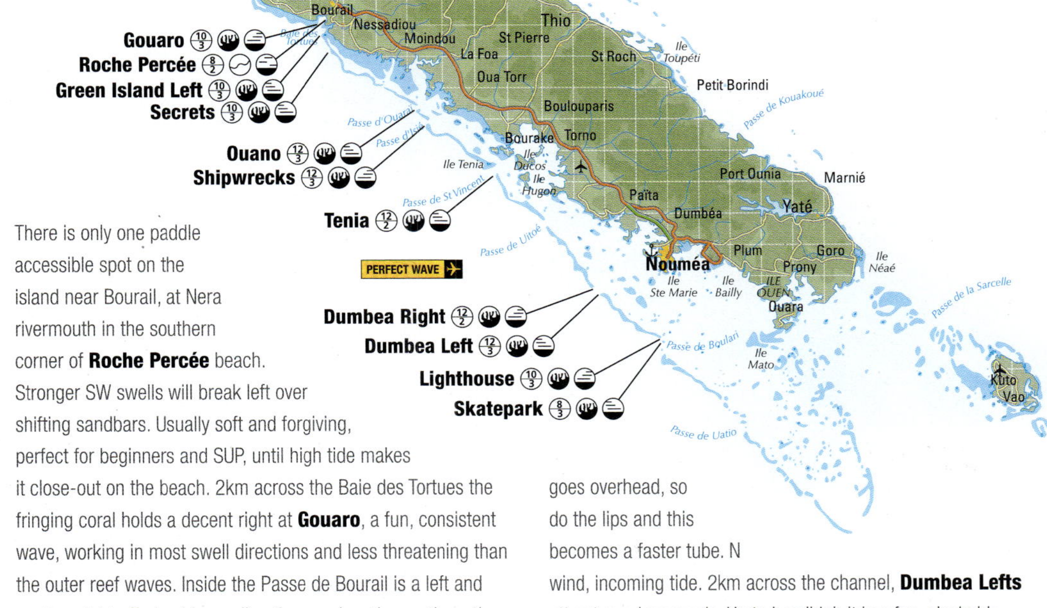


There is only one paddle accessible spot on the island near Bourail, at Nera rivermouth in the southern corner of **Roche Percée** beach. Stronger SW swells will break left over shifting sandbars. Usually soft and forgiving, perfect for beginners and SUP, until high tide makes it close-out on the beach. 2km across the Baie des Tortues the fringing coral holds a decent right at **Gouaro**, a fun, consistent wave, working in most swell directions and less threatening than the outer reef waves. Inside the Passe de Bourail is a left and another right offering big swell options and on the southern tip **Green Island Left** has three short sections that may wall or barrel and link up on good days for confident intermediates. The left at **Secrets** smacks the reef hard and tries to turn inside out on overhead days with fast, fluid, technical barrels. Since it is not a pass, getting caught inside is more likely. **Ouano** is one of New Caledonia's best lefthand pass waves with three sections of tubing, lip-smacking splendour. Handles any E wind, but morning glass is the real treat. Sometimes crowded with locals and visitors staying in La Foa, a 20min boat ride. Experienced surfers only. There are some much shorter lefts at **Shipwrecks** on smaller days and speedy rights across the Passe d'Isie. You can camp on **Tenia** Island and surf the left on the Passe de St Vincent, a half hour boat trip from Bourake. It has long carvable faces and crumbling lips, handles plenty of size and packs a punch. Ideal in SSW swell and ENE wind with an incoming tide – strong currents on dropping tides. 45mins from Nouméa **Dumbea Rights** are longish, predictable walls allowing turns galore in the 3-6ft range with some W in the swell. As the swell goes overhead, so do the lips and this becomes a faster tube. N wind, incoming tide. 2km across the channel, **Dumbea Lefts** attract regular crowds. Up to headhigh it has fun, slashable, walls and ramps with little pockets appearing along the 200m playground. Past 6-8ft throaty tubes scour the shallow inside coral. Multiple take-off zones and ENE is offshore. **Lighthouse** is another 100m edgy righthander that sucks hard from take-off with SW swell and NW-N winds. Gets super-shallow on the inside so caution and experience required. On smaller swells, the **Skatepark** reef is barely covered and from 6-8ft, this bowling wave can be thick and powerful with a reputation as a grower.

Roaring Forties SE-SW swells produce 2-10ft waves on the SW-facing coast from May to Sept. The shadow cast by New Zealand makes for shorter duration swells. During summer (Nov-Mar), consistency drops, but smaller 3-6ft SE swells will break on exposed passes. Coral Sea cyclones can bring NW swell, along with rain and destructive wind. Year-round the predominant wind is SE, 71% in Jan and 44% in Aug, cross or offshore for the lefts and ruinous for the rights. During winter the wind can blow anywhere from dead offshore NE round to blown out SW. Most reefs prefer mid incoming tide.

MIKE KEW

Ouano

## TRAVEL INFORMATION

**Weather** – The warm, sticky wet season lasts from December to April and the chances of torrential rain and cyclones are always present. The best surf months coincide with winter (Jun-Aug) when temperatures drop to 15-21ºC (59-70ºF) and can feel a little cold for a tropical destination. In deep winter, a light shorty for early or windy sessions is recommended, since water temps vary a lot from 22-26ºC (72-79ºF).

**Lodging and Food** – Nekweta in Bourail has package deals - full board accommodation + surf charter (up to 6 hours surfing) is $150/p/d. The luxury class charter boats are usually catamarans so somewhat cramped. Nights at sea can be noisy and rough. Food on board will have huge helpings of the freshest seafood available. The cost of living is 34% higher than Europe and imported food is 65% higher.

**Nature and Culture** – If you're not surfing then onboard activities are limited to snorkelling, fishing or scuba diving. On land there is trekking, horse riding and exploring many caves.

**Hazards and Hassles** – The only worries are reef cuts, sun stroke and marine life. There are a lot of sea snakes and sharks, with a 15yr old kitesurfer killed by a tiger shark in 2011 and a 19yr old surfer by a great white in 2009 at Bourail. The strong trades regularly hit 25 knots, which is why kitesurfing is so big.

**Handy Hints** – The French influence in New Caledonia is very strong and the standard of living is high. Surf boutiques in Noumea are pricey, so bring all your own equipment and booties for the reef.

ANDREW SHIELD

Gouaro

ANDREW SHIELD

Secrets

| STATISTICS | | J F | M A | M J | J A | S O | N D |
|---|---|---|---|---|---|---|---|
| SWELL | Direction | | | | | | |
| | Size (ft) | 2 | 3-4 | 4-5 | 5-6 | 4 | 1-2 |
| WIND | Direction | | | | | | |
| | Force | F4 | F4 | F3 | F3 | F3 | F4 |
| WATER | Wetsuit | | | | | | |
| | Temp/°C | 26 | 25 | 23 | 21 | 22 | 24 |
| WEATHER | Rainfall/mm | 110 | 135 | 95 | 83 | 47 | 60 |
| | days/mth | 10 | 11 | 11 | 9 | 6 | 6 |
| | Min temp/°C | 23 | 22 | 19 | 17 | 18 | 21 |
| | Max temp/°C | 29 | 27 | 24 | 23 | 25 | 28 |

# Mamanucas FIJI

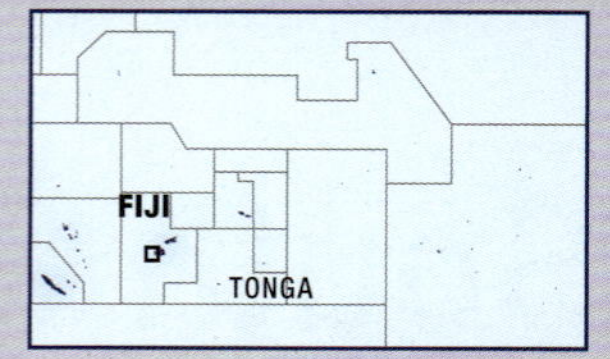


The 322 islands of Fiji form the epitome of the surf travel dream. A magical archipelago of white sand beaches and tropical vegetation ringed by shallow coral reefs, which get bombed by heavy, hollow lefthanders that set the standard for wave quality around the world. Most of the waves break on barrier reefs in the Mamanuca group of islands to the west of Fiji's main island, Viti Levu. Surf camps and boat access only to the waves around the Mamanucas make Fiji, or more to the point, Tavarua, an expensive, but essential surf experience. Yachties discovered Cloudbreak, probably in the '70s and kept it hush hush, until 1984, when Dave Clark began setting up the exclusive Tavarua resort and exclusive surfing rights to the offshore reef that has since been regarded as one of the planet's top lefthanders.

- + SUPER-CONSISTENT
- + VARIED WORLD-CLASS WAVES
- + CHOICE OF RESORTS
- + OPEN ACCESS TO CLOUDBREAK

- – DANGEROUS REEFS
- – STRONG CURRENTS
- – BOAT ACCESS TO MANY REEFS
- – EXPENSIVE RESORTS

Swimming Pools

STUART GIBSON

Malolo
MAMANUCA ISLANDS
Malolo Barrier Reef
Malolo Lailai Island
Nadi Bay
Nadi Waters
Nasoso
Denarau Island
Nadi
Voyualevu
Natawa
Nawaka
Swimming Pools
Wilkes Pass
Namotu Lefts
Restaurants
Tavarua Rights
Cloudbreak
Mini Cloudbreak
Namotu Island
Tavarua Island
WATERWAYS
ATOLL TRAVEL
PERFECT WAVE
NOMAD SURFERS
Nabila
Nalovo
Momi Bay
Momi
Uverite Point
VITI LEVU
2000
1000
500
Navutu
Lomowai
Kabisi
Mbatiri
Sanasana
Natadola
Malomalo
Voua
Cuvu
Sigatoka
Yadua
Olosara
Korotogo
Lulu's Bend
Sigatoka

To the N of Tavarua is **Wilkes Pass** named after a group of village warriors who escaped from the authorities through the reef pass here. It's a high tide right with long, fast, barreling waves finishing with a bowly inside section. Like most of Fiji's rights, it is sensitive to SE trade winds, so consistency suffers. Further north is the peak at Desperations, an exposed tip of the Malolo barrier reef where everyone ends up on those small swell days. N winds or glassy for both breaks. **Namotu Lefts** offer intermediates and longboarders a playful tapering wall on smaller swells from the S-SW. When it jumps well above headhigh, all bets are off as hefty barrels bend onto the reef, but it is still a notch down on Cloudbreak. Best with a bit of water covering the reef on the push and more NE wind than SE. Susceptible to very strong currents at low tide. On the other side of Namotu, **Swimming Pools** can be a tad faster, hollower and shallower than the lefts, but keeps the emphasis firmly on fun as it is always smaller than the surrounding breaks. **Restaurants** is the iconic wave that breaks off the resort island of Tavarua in full view of the diners and is the perfect back-up wave to big brother Cloudbreak. Always a bit smaller, but the utter predictability of the lip as it peels off for 2-300m means barrels and lip-smashing fun in equal measure. S to SW swell will wrap around the reef and S-SE winds will iron out the surface. It's still an experts only wave and gets way too risky at low as the corrugated coral contradicts the uniformity of the wave. Other waves on the island include Kiddieland, ideal rollers for beginners on soft-tops, SUPs and anything else, breaking regularly in close proximity to the Tavarua bar and on small swells, **Tavarua Rights** are ripable, fun-park walls, before rising to beautiful blue cylinders when the wind dies and glassy water envelops the southern tip of the island. All accessed by walking/paddling over reef or getting dropped outside by the resort boat. ✪**Cloudbreak** is the ultimate hotspot. When the swell is bigger, a couple of waves break at the entrance to Momi Bay, in front of the Seashell Cove resort. The rare and fickle right by the Lighthouse is usually blown out by the SE winds, but across the Navula Passage at **Mini Cloudbreak**, it's offshore and firing fast barrels, providing there is enough SW swell and high tide to cover the hungry reef. Always much smaller than Cloudbreak, but just as powerful, hollow and mean. **Natadola** is a beautiful resort

Namotu Lefts

JEREMY WILMOTTE

## TRAVEL INFORMATION

**Weather** – Fiji has a tropical climate that sees stable temps and ample rainfall, although compared to neighbouring island groups it is somewhat drier. The rainy season extends from Nov to April, peaking through Dec-March, when temperatures are at their warmest (32°C/90°F). Humidity levels can reach an uncomfortable 100%. Cyclones are an occasional occurrence. When the SE trades increase in strength in May the weather becomes much drier and cooler, but it rarely falls below 15°C (59°F), so being cold is never an issue. Year-round boardshorts and a rash vest, maybe a shorty for the coldest days in July-Aug.

**Lodging and Food** – Resorts are expensive! To stay at the Tavarua or Namotu surf camps during the peak season, book well in advance. Plantation Island resort is behind Wilkes and starts at $212/n/dbl for the cheapest hotel room. Fiji Surf run a 42ft trimaran boat as well a Bed N Surf service. Budget options, which don't include food and boat rides out to the reefs, may not always work out lots cheaper than surfer packages. There are backpacker and locally run establishments that offer everything from campsite (fr $10), to dorm (fr $12) to family rooms (fr $42). The Seashell@Momi from $65/n dorm room inc. all meals, or Surf Package (7n/dorm, 5x4hr surf boat + a'port trans = $395). Club Masa is just behind Sigatoka rivermouth and prices start at $50/d. The food is good, revolving around fish, taro, rice and fruit. Try some kava, the local brew.

**Nature and Culture** – Fiji is a tropical beach paradise. Diving, snorkelling, fishing and sailing are all excellent. Kiting has become very popular in the strong SE'ers, with or without waves on the lagoons. Hike the Tavoro Falls, Taveuni, or through the rainforest at Abaca. Check the sand dunes at Sigatoka, where they keep uncovering historical artefacts.

**Hazards and Hassles** – Ferries or fast catamarans service the Mamanucas, but you will need to hire local boats to take you to the surfing spots with prices varying depending on distance and destination (fr $50/p per surf). Check Unity for boat hire. Most surf camp accommodations include 1 surf transfer per day. Most surf spots are shallow so be careful of hitting the reef. Cover up from the sun, especially in the boats; take a surf hat and plenty of bottled water. Fijian people are very friendly, including those that surf.

**Handy Hints** – The Fiji Surf Shop is in Nadi stocking boards, rentals and accessories and is part of Fiji Surf Co that run a new surfboard factory, surf school, tours by road or trimaran and local comps for the growing number of Fijian surfers.

STUART GIBSON

CORY SCOTT

## Cloudbreak

LAT. -17.8875° LONG. 177.185°

Since the Fijian government 2010 "Surfing Decree", anyone can surf anywhere in Fiji waters, including this legendary reef pass. While the perfect pictures of Cloudbreak suggest flawless left barrels for one and all, this is a tricky wave with multiple sections and a malevolent side that keeps even the best surfers on their toes. The outside section at the top "Point" of the reef holds plenty of size and the vertiginous roll-ins lead into a flying wall section where speed carves are possible. Middles is where turns are less useful and the barrel starts to wind up, covering a lot of distance in a short time. Insides, or Shish-kabobs, is where the reef gets extremely shallow and the tubes get extremely... extreme! Less confident surfers thinking they can pick off a few on the inside are not going to find any easy rides here and the fingers of razor sharp reef are far less uniform than further out. The 3 sections rarely link up, but when they do, usually on a long period, SSW swell of epic proportions, it is one of the seven wonders of the surf world. Advanced to expert surfers should be able to deal with the heavy waves, currents and bump-inducing frisky trades, but there are other hazards. The live coral is slasher sharp and cuts have the tendency to flare up. The reef attracts some fauna that is also best avoided like sea snakes, stonefish and the odd well-fed shark, but the unavoidable bogieman is undoubtedly the sun. Once you have negotiated a seat in a boat (for a handsome sum), remember to take lots of water, sunscreen and a surf hat!

beach with a shorebreak that's good for bodysurfing and an inside reef peak for longboarding in big swells. 2kms outside of this at high tide, lefts leap out of deep water and hit the reef pass, bending and peaking along a disorganised line-up. Can be long walls and tubes when smallish, scary and sketchy when big, but the main problem is the howling SE wind. It's a 1km paddle over to the lesser right, which also needs NE winds. **Lulu's Bend** is another deep bay with high tide barrels breaking on both sides at the entrance. The north side peaks and hisses across the reef, before shutting down on virtually dry reef, while the south side left is prone to the same fate. Any N wind for the rights, glassy or NE-E for the lefts. The **Sigatoka** Sand Dunes National Park offers 5kms of beachbreaks in wonderful scenery without crowds. If there are N quadrant winds, A-frames will huff and puff along its length, but the real action is at the Sigatoka Rivermouth, where long, zippy lefts and shorter rights spin back into the river flow. Downsides are strong SE winds, strong rips and currents, murky water and sharks. Upsides are all abilities waves, friendly locals, low crowds and no coral heads lurking below!

Fiji is blessed by one of the best swell exposures in the world. For the Mamanuca group, the major source of swell is from the SW, generated by low pressures in the Tasman Sea, off Australia's east coast. Although New Zealand can block some size and warp the direction of these swells between due S 180º and SSW 205º, most low pressure systems will continue spinning east, providing Fiji with lesser SE-S swells. Swells range in size from 3-15ft, with occasional freak swells hitting 20ft+ at 18 seconds, during the favoured March-Nov South Pacific swell season. This is when wave height averages out at 5-6ft, with 10-12 second periods and consistently does so for 90% of the time. Despite year-round swell activity, the summer rainy season (Dec-Feb) has smaller, less consistent N-NE swells in the 2-6ft range. These are generated from remote NW Pacific lows which will hit the N shores of the archipelago (Yasawa, Vanua Levu). Through summer (Nov-March) the winds are generally lighter and from a SE-NE direction – NE is bang offshore in the Mamanuca's. Trade winds increase slightly in strength from May to Nov, averaging 16-32km/h and blowing mainly from the ESE to SE. Despite minor tidal ranges, most spots are very shallow and will be affected by low tide.

Restaurants

| STATISTICS | | J F | M A | M J | J A | S O | N D |
|---|---|---|---|---|---|---|---|
| SWELL | Direction | | | | | | |
| | Size (ft) | 4-5 | 5 | 6-7 | 7 | 6 | 5-6 |
| WIND | Direction | | | | | | |
| | Force | F4 | F3-F4 | F4 | F4 | F4 | F4 |
| WATER | Wetsuit | | | | | | |
| | Temp/°C | 28 | 27 | 26 | 25 | 25 | 26 |
| WEATHER | Rainfall/mm | 300 | 320 | 105 | 60 | 72 | 170 |
| | days/mth | 16 | 17 | 10 | 7 | 8 | 11 |
| | Min temp/°C | 23 | 23 | 21 | 20 | 21 | 22 |
| | Max temp/°C | 30 | 30 | 28 | 28 | 28 | 30 |

# Kadavu Passage FIJI

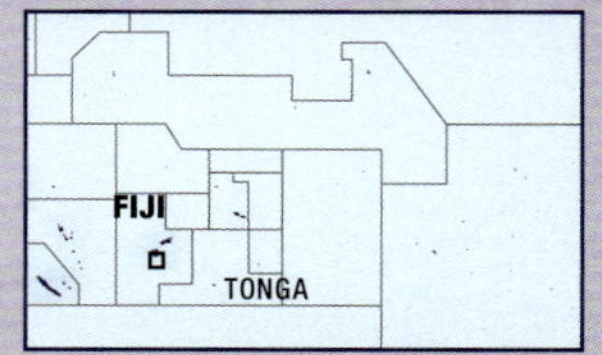


The southern coast of Fiji is dominated by a fringing reef, bringing the surf much closer to the white sand beaches of the resort studded Coral Coast. Powerful waves come surging in from deep water, hitting shallow reef ledges that unfortunately, are very exposed to the strong trade winds that buffet this coast. In order to find offshore conditions requires more long journeys in boats out to Frigates Pass or else an island-hopper flight to Kadavu Island where the contorted reef offers a selection of waves for all wind directions.

+ POWERFUL AND CONSISTENT
+ QUALITY TUBULAR LEFTS
+ WARM BULA SPIRIT
+ RESORT CROWD, FEW LOCALS

- BIG AND WINDY IN WINTER
- RARE SUMMER RIGHTHANDERS
- HEAVY RAIN
- OUTBOARD ACCESS ONLY

## TRAVEL INFORMATION

**Weather** – The cool dry months from May to October provide the best weather, but swells and winds are the wildest. In July and August, temps may drop to 18°C (64°F). Spells of cloudy, cool weather with occasional rains alternate with warm, sunny, humid days. The hot, wet season starts in November, but the stifling days are Jan-March. In winter, take a bit of thin neoprene for the windchill.

**Lodging and Food** – Matanivusi Eco Surf Resort at Vunanui fr. $2100/wk full board. Waidroka Bay starts from $170/dbl/n and surf boat cost $45p/p/ to local break or $70p/p Frigates. There are budget dorms from $15/n; doubles in 'bures' average $50. A meal plan, accommodation and transport to the surf will be at least $100/day. On Yanutha Island, Batiluva does all inclusive with great food and 1 daily trip to Frigates from $85/p/n. Naninya Island Resort (Nagigia) $165/n + $10 for each boat trip.

**Nature and Culture** – Beqa is Fiji diving spot #1 for pelagics and Kadavu Astrolabe Reef and Nagigia Island is world-class diving and fishing. Kava ceremonies with music and Meke dance and the fire walkers are a must.

**Hazards and Hassles** – Gutsy swells, gusty winds, sucky waves on razor-sharp reefs and rips. Crowds only occur at Frigates when several boats overpopulate the break. Waterproof bags and adequate clothing are a must.

**Handy Hints** – There are only the surf shops in Nadi. Many resorts have boards for rent and some like Nagigia give discounts to leave one behind. Surf lessons are available.

Frigates

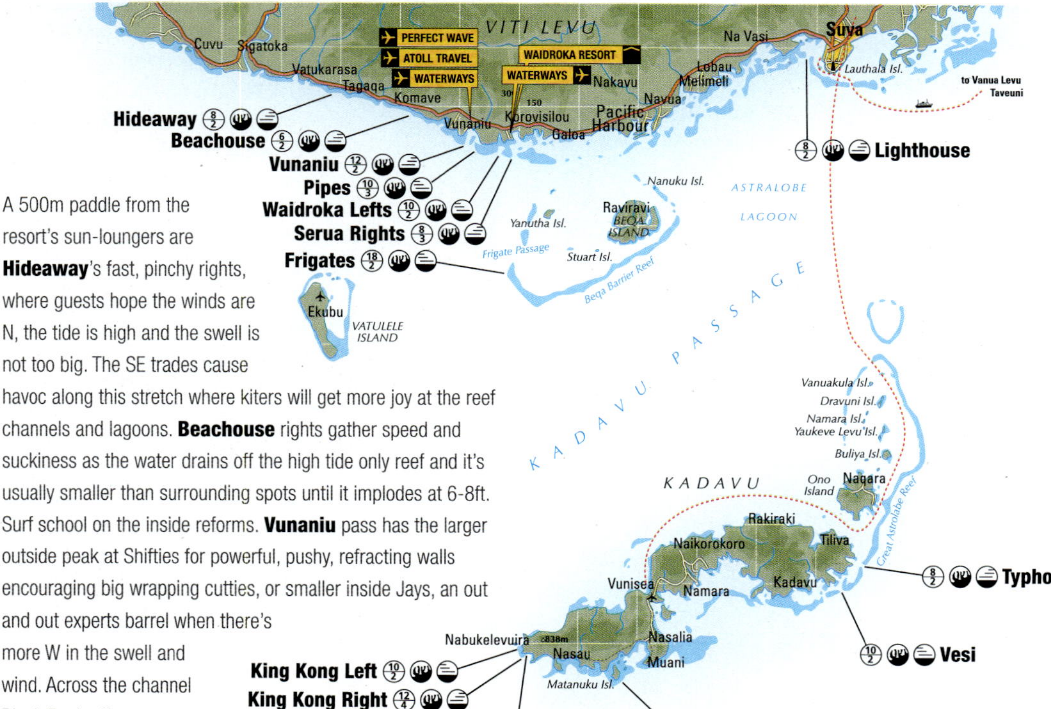


A 500m paddle from the resort's sun-loungers are **Hideaway**'s fast, pinchy rights, where guests hope the winds are N, the tide is high and the swell is not too big. The SE trades cause havoc along this stretch where kiters will get more joy at the reef channels and lagoons. **Beachouse** rights gather speed and suckiness as the water drains off the high tide only reef and it's usually smaller than surrounding spots until it implodes at 6-8ft. Surf school on the inside reforms. **Vunaniu** pass has the larger outside peak at Shifties for powerful, pushy, refracting walls encouraging big wrapping cutties, or smaller inside Jays, an out and out experts barrel when there's more W in the swell and wind. Across the channel Black Rock offers more high-octane ledgy rights.

Pipes

**Pipes** lives up to its name when a moderate SSE swell hits the bend of reef, sucks hard and throws lip for some pedal-to-the-metal tube rides. Improver-friendly **Waidroka Lefts** peak up in deeper water, where the steep-sloped take-offs lead to a hollow bowl before shouldering off. **Serua Rights** can be a long ride from the angled roll-in through the middle cutback shoulders to the sucky backdoor section as it hits the shallow inside reef. World-class **Frigates** boasts thick, bowly, fast, wrapping, hollow walls over a mid-ocean barrier reef for experienced surfers, staying at camps on Yanutha Island. Wind can chop up the face making the easy roll-in much harder and high tide will cover the dredgy inside section, adding to a long, long ride. There's a surprisingly decent right called **Lighthouse** at the entrance to Suva Harbour, a few minutes boat ride from the Suva yacht club. Fly to Vunisea on Kadavu Island then take a 45min boat ride to Nagigia Island. **King Kong Left** hits a notch in the otherwise straight fringing reef and wedges up a horseshoe peak that quickly opens up and barrels, before backing off then pitching again on the shallow inside. The fast, gnarly **King Kong Right** picks up a lot of swell, but it's usually blown out in the SE trades. **Daku** sees a split peak over a reef closer to the beach with fun rights and a few lefts in the morning before the wind gets up. If there is a N wind and a SE-S swell, pay for a long boat ride to **Uatotoka**, a superb right with long, makeable barrels. The left at **Vesi** needs rare NW winds and some wrapping SW swell. **Typhoon Alley** faces SE, so it only breaks occasionally, when the wind comes from the N to W quadrant.

This southern region receives all the same swells as outlined in the Mamanucas zone and in fact it has far better exposure to the residual SE swells. The SE trade winds mean most reliable Kadavu Passage spots are lefts as the occasional rights get fully blown out by the 15-25kph trades. Summer swell size drops from Dec-March, the main season for N-NE winds that favour the rights, but the E-SE breezes still blow for over 70% of the time. In winter, the surf can get pretty intimidating at exposed spots. Surprisingly for this latitude, spring tides reach 2.5m, affecting both reef and boat movements.

| STATISTICS | | J F | M A | M J | J A | S O | N D |
|---|---|---|---|---|---|---|---|
| SWELL | Direction | | | | | | |
| | Size (ft) | 3 | 5-6 | 6 | 7-8 | 7 | 2-3 |
| WIND | Direction | | | | | | |
| | Force | F4 | F3-F4 | F4 | F4 | F4 | F4 |
| WATER | Wetsuit | | | | | | |
| | Temp/°C | 28 | 27 | 26 | 25 | 25 | 25 |
| WEATHER | Rainfall/mm | 300 | 350 | 210 | 160 | 210 | 280 |
| | days/mth | 18 | 20 | 15 | 15 | 16 | 17 |
| | Min temp/°C | 23 | 23 | 22 | 20 | 21 | 22 |
| | Max temp/°C | 30 | 29 | 28 | 26 | 27 | 29 |

# Tongatapu TONGA

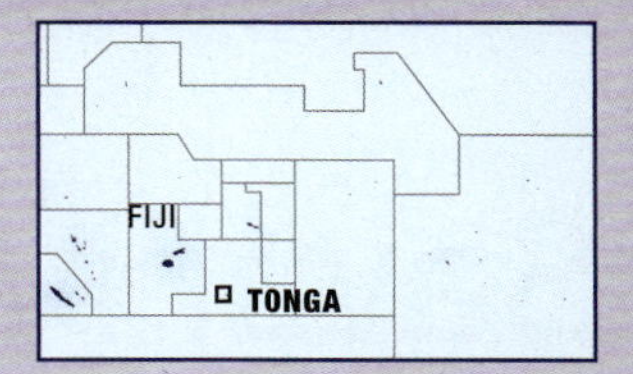


The Tonga archipelago includes 170 islands divided into 4 separate groups. Tongatapu is the main island, including the capital Nuku'alofa, which is made up of a raised coral platform. Constant wave action has cut a shelf into the cliff-bound south coast, unlike the north that's dotted with low-lying reefs and offshore islets. Most surf spots are all squeezed onto a remarkable reef bend on the W side of the island, where trade winds blow straight offshore and grinding lefts tour the coral fringe.

- **+ UNCROWDED SPOTS**
- **+ PERFECT REEFS**
- **+ GREAT CLIMATE**
- **+ LAID-BACK VIBE**

- **– LIVE CORAL REEF DANGERS**
- **– COOLER WINTER WATERS**
- **– LACKS VARIED ORIENTATION**
- **– EXPENSIVE LOCATION**

**The Pass** serves up a hollow left which is the most consistent small swell wave on the island, but it closes-out over 6ft. One of the few reefs that improvers will handle. Across the channel, **Pass Rights** (aka the Alley), break in a similar, stress free fashion during the summer season. It starts off a bit faster and hollower before hitting the deep channel where cutbacks are the order of the day. Both waves have generous depth and little current until it gets overhead. The other side of the peak can have an average left in winter S swells called Leftovers. The consistent lefts at **Motels** are fairly long with variable speed walls allowing big turns between the tuck sections before it ends on the reef fringe. Works on the smallest of swells and is user-friendly at small to medium sizes. Handles up to double overhead when it gets much heavier for advanced surfers. Straight in front of the main surf hang out Ha'atafu Beach Resort. **The Peak** is a small swell right that lines up a N swell into a high energy performance wall. Ends at a narrow crack in the reef so beware the end close-out section. **Kamikazes** is a tricky lefthander that often ends up being a straight-hander if the swell direction isn't bang on. Deep barrels on offer for those with the skill and possibly the skin to spare. Use rubber! **Corners** lefts work in both seasons, flipping between winter's short, sucky, intense barrels in due S swells and fun, ripable hotdog walls during summer NW-N pulses. Any W in the winter swell will make this the most dangerous left, while the summer version promotes big slashes and airs on the soft inside close-out. **Lighthouse** is a fast, dangerous, low tide righthander, split into two sections by The Surgeons Table. The short inside section demands higher tides to make the air drops into a rapid winding barrel ending in the safety of the channel. **The Bowl** doesn't break very often, but when it does it's an exceptional ride, holding almost any swell size and bending around the reef with a heavy bowl section. Take-off is next to the outside peak of Lighthouse. **Fishtraps**, another rifling left, is a case of the bigger the swell, the better and longer the wave. Variety of moods from tapered corners, through flying walls to nice hollow barrel sections. A rare all tides spot, but again low is really sketchy closer to the reef. A string of circular and barrier reefs extend to the NE where some fickle, but classic spots can be ridden in summer N swells. **E.T.'s** is a class act in summer NW-N swells and light NE-E winds, but is easily blown out and really inconsistent. Other spots with names like Loonies, Sharkie's and Razors are just as wind sensitive and require a long boat trip out to them.

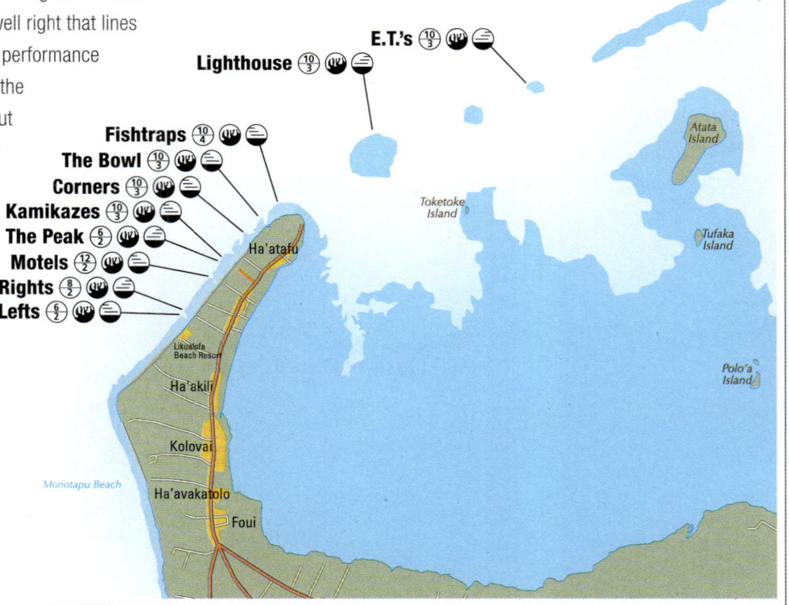

CRAIG PARRY

Corners

DAVID SPARKES

E.T.'s

Tonga is inconsistent because New Zealand blocks a big chunk of the SW swell window and only the strongest NW Pacific lows will register on the northern coast. Trade winds blow from the E-SE, year-round, but from Jan to April, some NW-NE quadrant winds arrive. The tidal range is minimal, but low tide is still too shallow for many spots.

## TRAVEL INFORMATION

**Weather** – Tonga's low latitude means subtropical conditions of less rain, but cooler temperatures. It lies within the cyclone belt and averages a major strike every 20 years, moderate cyclones every 3 years and small ones twice a year. The dry season is cooler, around the low 20°C's (68°F's) and occasionally a strong S wind bringing cold, wet spells. A springsuit is needed through the colder periods from June-Oct.

**Lodging and Food** – Excellent rooms available at the Ha'atafu Beach Resort (fr $70/n/p) including great breakfast and dinner. Otuhaka do rustic huts, backpacker style from $40/n. Great seafood everywhere.

**Nature and Culture** – Easy snorkelling, diving, excellent pelagic fishing and whale watching. Ha'atafu is a 15km Protected Beach Reserve. Lively clubs and bars in Nuku'alofa.

**Hazards and Hassles** – All of the reefs are live coral, so boots and a springy are a good idea. Locals are usually cool, but more than a couple of boats at E.T.'s will stress the line-up.

**Handy Hints** – Bring everything that you need with you. The Tonga Surfriders Association are based at Ha'atafu Beach Resort, but equipment is hard to find, so think about donating hardware. There are some inner reef reforms for kids or beginners. The "friendly islands" are the last Kingdom left in Polynesia. Respect local religious beliefs and try to adapt to the slow pace of life, especially on Sundays.

| STATISTICS | | J F | M A | M J | J A | S O | N D |
|---|---|---|---|---|---|---|---|
| SWELL | Direction | | | | | | |
| | Size (ft) | 4-5 | 5 | 6-7 | 7 | 6 | 5 |
| WIND | Direction | | | | | | |
| | Force | F4 | F4 | F4 | F4 | F4 | F4 |
| WATER | Wetsuit | | | | | | |
| | Temp/°C | 26 | 26 | 24 | 22 | 23 | 24 |
| WEATHER | Rainfall/mm | 210 | 287 | 102 | 107 | 112 | 120 |
| | days/mth | 11 | 13 | 11 | 8 | 9 | 9 |
| | Min temp/°C | 22 | 22 | 19 | 18 | 19 | 21 |
| | Max temp/°C | 29 | 29 | 26 | 26 | 26 | 28 |

# Savai'i and Upolu SAMOA

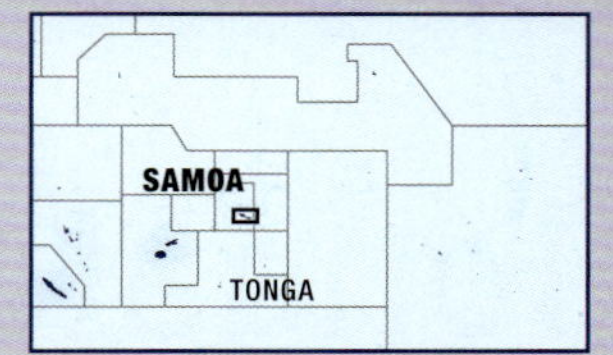


The Independent State of Samoa sits atop ancient volcanic cones rising up from the ocean bed and the two main islands of Upolu and Savai'i are amongst the largest in the South Pacific. Upolu is the more developed of the two islands with the majority of the resorts and decent surf spots for experienced surfers. The western island, Savai'i is much wilder with fewer known breaks and one-quarter of the coral reefs, but potential for discovery. Samoa is well situated to receive numerous swells from both the N and the S, creating very hollow, powerful waves, breaking over shallow barrier reefs around 500m offshore, but there are some big gaps that allow the surf to break on lava reefs, much closer to the shore.

**+ YEAR-ROUND CONSISTENT SWELL**
**+ POWERFUL BARRELS**
**+ WARM AND UNCROWDED**
**+ SAMOAN CULTURE**

**– MANY BLOWN OUT-DAYS**
**– REMOTE, DIFFICULT ACCESS**
**– SHARP, SHALLOW REEFS**
**– NO SURFING ON SUNDAYS**

## TRAVEL INFORMATION

**Weather** – The rainy season occurs during the summer (Nov-April) and the remainder of the year is dry with occasional showers. Samoa sits on the edge of the cyclone path, so they are a rare possibility, along with earthquake generated tsunamis (2009). Coastal temps are idyllic at around 27°C (80°F) year-round, water temps also never drop below 27°C (80°F), which is slightly above the South Pacific average. Even the trade winds are lighter than in many other South Pacific islands.

**Lodging and Food** – W Samoa is one of the cheapest countries in the South Pacific. If you're willing to rough it then there is accommodation fr $20 a night for a falé (thatched hut). To maximise water time, stay at one of the major surf camps on the south coast; Salani Surf Resort, Vaiula Beach, Maninoa, Coconuts, Samoana, Manoa Tours and Aganoa Beach on Savai'i. In Apia try the Samoan Outrigger Hotel. Green bananas, breadfruit, taro, fish, and lu'au are cooked on the stone fire (umu). Samoan sushi is called oka.

**Nature and Culture** – Most Samoans attend church and Sunday surfing near villages is frowned upon. Diving, snorkelling, deep-sea fishing, hiking, waterfalls (Papapapa Tai, Sauniatu, Sopoaga, Falefa), exploring caves, blowholes and lava tubes, To Sua Ocean Trench, Papase'ea sliding rock and all watersports. There's very little to do at night.

**Hazards and Hassles** – Many of the reefs are super-shallow and dangerous and hospital care is fairly rudimentary. Infections from reef cuts are a problem. Mosquitoes are plentiful, but there's no malaria. Drink only bottled water.

**Handy Hints** – Bring all surf gear including spare board(s), reef boots, rash vests and antiseptic for reef cuts. The wilds of Savai'i are best seen on an organised tour with Manoa Tours or Savai'i Surfaris. Boats to offshore spots, cost around $20/rtn/p from local tour operators (Manoa) or fishermen.

MANOA SURF TOURS

KEEGAN DOWNES
Anagoa

On Savai'i, **Salailua** has a deep channel and fun, intermediate-friendly walls breaking both ways. The lefts prefer more S in the swell and will handle the SE winds better. **Aganoa** is both a bowly righthander and screaming fast left situated right in front of the family run surf camp. The shorter rights can suck heavily, with barrels from take-off, before skirting the reef and bending through to an inside shut-down section where a coral head lurks. The swell direction sensitive lefts fly down the line with backdoor barrels aplenty, but no defined channel and sharp fingers of coral populate the straight reef. South coast options within an hour's drive include Middles peak, K-Land lefts, The Cross and Coconut Grove. Between the islands, **The Wharf** reef at Salelologa has clean rights on a moderate SE-S swell. Unfortunately it is dead onshore in any E wind. The north coast is also ringed with reef from **Fagamalo** to Sasina, then it's rocky lava until the coral returns at Asau. There are at least a dozen spots named from easy left walls to Sunset style, big swell rights, where the vagaries of swell direction will decide the venue and most are paddle accessible from land.

Upolu is way more populated with people and waves and the main spots all have a surf camp nearby. **Salamumu** is no exception, with swell direction dictating whether it's rights or lefts peaking up over the reef in front of Sa'Moana resort and a quality, quicksilver left peeling down a slight bend in the reef in front of the village. **Special K** is a mid to high tide, walled-up right that bends and bowls out at the end section. The rivermouth at Tafitoala village is where the fun lefts are called **Wackas** and although they bend a bit, are not quite protected enough from the SE trades. **Coconuts** is fully exposed on the tip of the fringing reef, cracking the coral with full-blooded lips that hiss and spit down the line, offering ample tube time and powerful pockets on the right side of the peak. The lefts can be doable when smaller and more SE in the swell. It's very sensitive to wind, tide and swell direction; glassy, high tide and SW swell are perfect. It's a hell of a long paddle from the resorts so hire a boat. Fresh water has gouged a deep inlet in the reef, providing easy boat and not so easy 10min paddle access to the lefts of **Siumu**. Another high tide reef with bowly lefts popping up, translating into good barrels and perfect lip lines on the best days, or shorter irregular ripable walls when the swell direction isn't ideal. Outside Siumu is another 300m up the reef offering more lefts, but a bit more wind exposure than nearby hotspot ✪**Boulders**. Salani Village has a long established surf resort thanks to the top drawer rides on either side of the channel. **Nu'usafee Island** is a real swell-magnet and makes the most of small swells, yet some think it is better when size starts to allow the three sections to pull off the reef a bit. Also named Devils Island and burning in coral hell is a real possibility on the exposed first section where speed and barrel riding skills are required in bulk and the higher the tide the better. The middle and end section rarely link, but the curve of reef makes it offshore in E winds and the barrels a bit more manageable. Boat access only with

SALANI SURF CAMP
Salani Right

### Boulders

**LAT. -14.0371° LONG. -171.77°**

**As the name Boulders suggests, this left breaks over a rocky mix of lava and the odd coral head, in pointbreak style, close to the headland. It is one of Samoa's classiest waves and handles as much size as the Pacific can throw at it, with triple overhead plus days a real possibility. A steep roll in leads to a flying wall that's thick and grunty, before turning totally tubular on the shallow end section. Major positive factors include rideable on lower tides and it's nicely tucked in out of the SE trade winds, which is also the ideal swell direction so only bigger pulses on the wrap will line-up properly. Negatives include crowds of advanced surfers on big swells as all the surf camps descend by boat and road; getting too close to the cliff at high tide or the inside coral heads at low tide; being under-gunned; the regular shark sightings in the vicinity.**

Tiavea Bay

ERIC HILLIARD/LUSH PALM

rentals available from Poutasi. Natural footers can motor east to Vaiula Beach where the fast righthand peelers of **Tafatafa** can be a long ride on SW swells or sectiony on a SE. Needs N winds so early or late for this rarely crowded spot. **Salani Right** will consistently barrel and fizz along the reef edge in any S swell and hopefully any N wind. More E in the swell will split the line-up with shorter, bowly hooks arriving from deep and shifting the take-off spot around, while SW will lengthen the ride and open up the face for turns. A little more flexible with lower tides and even onshore winds on certain days. Like most Samoan waves, plucky intermediates will handle the average days, but beyond overhead is for more experienced riders. **Salani Left** is a typical south coast left, requiring SE swell to wrap around and give a better chance of making this tube express that doesn't slow down until it hits the buffers 150m down the line. Onboard speed and taking the right track essential to reaping the long shade-time on offer. Compared to the right, it's less tide tolerant, handles less size, over a less user-friendly reef and is way less consistent. This means less people, albeit at a higher standard, striving to avoid the shallow inside shutdowns and dodging swinger sets on the paddle back out. On the S coast, the broken up reefs off **Aufaga Village** attract some smaller swell lefts and rights before the trades blow it out. Various good quality breaks can be found in **Tiavea Bay** a long, slow drive through the Uafato Conservation Area. The rivermouth is popular as a rest from the hazards of coral, peaking both ways with ramped-up walls and cover-up sections at mid tides. Further east is a powerful, fickle right peak and a distant right reef holds fun walls. At the western end there is also a fast sketchy left. The north-facing coast up to Apia is a mix of more extended fringes of coral and some steep, rocky volcanic coastline bringing the surf closer to the road. Fagaloa Bay is full of possibilities if you can get down to them and a boat becomes really handy. There are also a string of righthanders at Solosolo that are OK in E winds. Further east, **Luatuanuu** holds rocky rights beside Pudding Rock and abrupt peaks along the town reefs. Nearby, the suckier rights of Waterfalls break close to shore and unusually, is actually better on low tides. **Laulii** rights need a bigger swell to break so it can wrap around the reef and it handles plenty of E in the wind. Fun and ripable walls that are fine for average surfers, unlike the nearby monster barrels of the Dragons Breath.

Samoa is a swell-magnet, picking up swells from any direction, although SW-NW swells can be slightly filtered by neighbouring Tonga, Fiji, Tuvalu and the remote Gilbert Islands. Regular 3-12ft swells can arrive from the SE-SW year-round and the most prevalent direction is SSE with moderate 10-12sec periods. From Nov-March Samoa receives North Pacific NW-NE swells. While NE is more common, NW-N swells also occur and the period can be much longer than the S coast, helping with wave-height. Occasional cyclone swells can appear from any direction as the storm tracks are wildly unpredictable. The good news is that the E-SE trade winds are rarely too strong to surf, especially during the wet season when they are 15-25kph rather than 25-35kph in the middle of the year. The tidal range never exceeds 1.5m, but even small changes effect the shallow reefs and many of the south coast breaks are mid to high tide only.

| STATISTICS | | J F | M A | M J | J A | S O | N D |
|---|---|---|---|---|---|---|---|
| SWELL | Direction | | | | | | |
| | Size (ft) | 4-5 | 5 | 6-7 | 7 | 6 | 5 |
| WIND | Direction | | | | | | |
| | Force | F3 | F3 | F3-F4 | F4 | F3-F4 | F3-F4 |
| WATER | Wetsuit | | | | | | |
| | Temp/°C | 28 | 28 | 29 | 27 | 27 | 28 |
| WEATHER | Rainfall/mm | 397 | 300 | 152 | 100 | 162 | 315 |
| | days/mth | 20 | 16 | 10 | 9 | 12 | 9 |
| | Min temp/°C | 24 | 23 | 23 | 23 | 23 | 23 |
| | Max temp/°C | 30 | 30 | 29 | 29 | 29 | 30 |

# Tutuila AMERICAN SAMOA

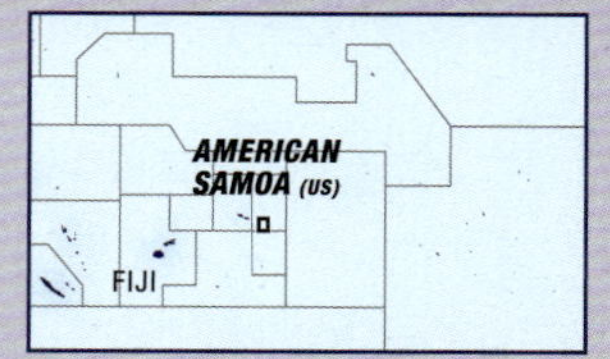


The only US land below the Equator, the territory of American Samoa consists of seven volcanic islands, with Tutuila the largest and most populated. Despite being surfed by Americans since the early '60s, the island's surfing population remains tiny and is mainly ex-pats. The waves are powerful reefbreaks with world-class potential, but the reality is that surf conditions are pretty fickle and surf spots dangerously shallow. Most breaks are located on the south coast, way too exposed to prevailing SE trades and the north coast of Tutuila is mostly sheer, black lava cliffs. Fortunately, the south coast has a relatively flat volcanic platform with fringing reefs and submerged coral banks, producing many surfable breaks.

- \+ RELIABLE SOUTH PACIFIC SWELLS
- \+ UNCROWDED POWERFUL REEFS
- \+ SOUTH COAST SPOT DENSITY
- \+ TROPICAL WARM WATERS

- \- NO NORTH COAST SPOTS
- \- SUPER-SHALLOW REEFS
- \- EXPOSED TO SE TRADES
- \- EXPENSIVE ACCESS

WILLIAM THOMAS

Pua Tree/Nu'uuli

The west end of Tutuila is the best surfing area with a superb coastal road skirting several quality surf spots. On occasional N swells, **Poloa** could be a blast, but be very careful with low tide close-outs. **Amanave Bay** is one of those archetypal South Pacific scenic bays, where waves have occasionally been surfed, with a left and right into the reef cut. **Nua** is the most likely venue to find classic lefts with the dominant combo of SW swells and SE winds. **Asili Point** may reveal its fun side with N winds, along with the most user-friendly break in the area, **Sliding Rock**. Rides are pretty long compared to the majority of short sucky ledges but favour high tides. Close by is Fagatele Bay Sanctuary Marine Reserve, a hotspot for divers and all nature lovers. Going eastward, the cliffs become sheer and Vaitogi stands as the only entry point to this area. From the airport, the good potential reefs start again and can easily be checked from the road. **Nu'uuli** mushes out after take-off and is usually onshore and empty. **Fatuuli Rock** offers long rights with a barrelling bowl on the inside. **Faganeanea**'s sectiony lefts get good with rare NW winds and a SE swell to run down the shelf. **Matuu** is another full-on barrel that breaks short and sharp, is onshore most of the time, but when it works it's a real contender. **Faga'alu** (aka Coral Heads) gets a small crowd as it is the closest wave to town, inside the harbour entrance. Not the best shape and rarely clean in the constant easterly onshores. Pago Pago Bay is exposed to the trades and swell shadowed by the Taema offshore bank. The best bet is **Lauli'ituai** with awesome lefts and rights under the right conditions, ideal for square barrel experts rather than the average surfer. Further east, the trade wind protected bowling lefts at **Liea Point** are also known as Gas Stations and **Amouli** entertains a long, high tide, lefthand pointbreak, plus some rights on the other side. Both are easy to check, unlike Aunu'u Island that requires a 15min ferry ride from Au'asi. The lefts on **Aunu'u** can be world-class with the last section dead offshore in the trades. On W-NW wind, check **Alao** or **Tula**; traditional American Samoan villages, which can be quite consistent and pleasant surf by Tutuilan standards.

Poloa Bay · Amanave Bay · Nua · Asili Point · Sliding Rock · Nu'uuli · Fatuuli Rock · Faganeanea · Matuu · Faga'alu · Lauli'ituai · Liea Pt · Aunu'u · Amouli · Alao · Tula

American Samoa has great year-round SE-SW swell exposure, varying from 3-15ft, but conditions are often too messy on the open south coast. Only huge NW swells make it down with any reasonable size, generally during Nov-Feb. Being right in the SE trade belt, Tutuila is plagued by strong prevailing 20-30km/h SE winds. The best conditions occur with the combination of clean S swells and rare N winds. Summer (Dec-March) is the season for clean conditions, but swell is not that plentiful and it frequently rains. Tidal range never goes over 1.5m, but is crucial over those shallow, low tide coral heads. Surfing bigger tides is preferable.

CHRISTOPHER LANTZ

Amanava Bay

## TRAVEL INFORMATION

**Weather** – The Tropical climate is usually divided into two seasons. During the hot and rainy season from December to April, temps go up to 30°C (86°F) and 3cm of rain may fall on a typical day. The Pioa Mountain overlooking Pago Pago is called Rainmaker Mountain! The rainy season is also the cyclone season. May to November is cooler and drier, with less humidity and pleasantly cool evenings.

**Lodging and Food** – In built-up Pago Pago the 3 star Sadie's by the Sea has rooms at $140/dble while in the more authentic Samoan area of Vaitogi, The Turtle and Shark Lodge has rooms fr $120/n. Local BBQ and stone baked breadfruit, pork, chicken and bananas are the local dish; expect $10 for a meal.

**Nature and Culture** – Climb lofty Mount Alava to view Pago Pago's natural harbour. Tutuila is covered in dense tropical rainforest, home to unique animals like the flying fox or the Pacific boa, much of it protected by National Parks. The 'turtle and shark' legend is performed in Vaitogi. Check Tisa's Barefoot Beach & Bar in Alega.

**Hazards and Hassles** – Be ready to airdrop into some shallow, square bowls: reef cuts are a given. There is a good hospital in town. Much of the coast around Pago Pago is quite developed. Religious beliefs dictate no surfing on Sunday apart from Sliding Rock.

**Handy Hints** – Bring at least 2 boards including a strong semi-gun. 90% of the population are native Samoans, they wear a lava lava (cloth wraparound) and dig Faía Samoa – the Samoan way. The int'l dateline passes west of Samoa; it's a day behind the rest of the world.

| STATISTICS | | J F | M A | M J | J A | S O | N D |
|---|---|---|---|---|---|---|---|
| SWELL | Direction | | | | | | |
| | Size (ft) | 4-5 | 5 | 6-7 | 7 | 5 | 4-5 |
| WIND | Direction | | | | | | |
| | Force | F3 | F3 | F3-F4 | F4 | F3-F4 | F3-F4 |
| WATER | Wetsuit | | | | | | |
| | Temp/°C | 28 | 28 | 29 | 27 | 28 | 28 |
| WEATHER | Rainfall/mm | 330 | 300 | 300 | 170 | 220 | 320 |
| | days/mth | 24 | 23 | 20 | 19 | 20 | 21 |
| | Min temp/°C | 24 | 24 | 24 | 23 | 24 | 24 |
| | Max temp/°C | 30 | 30 | 29 | 28 | 29 | 30 |

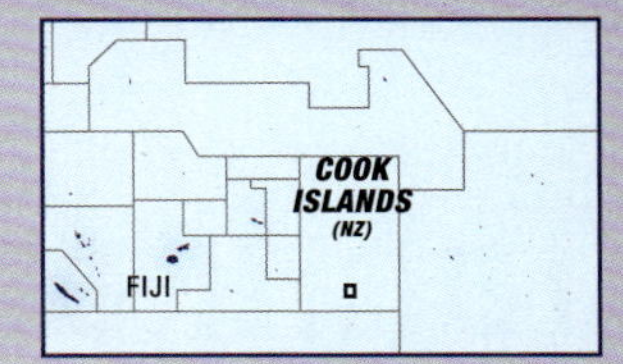




# Rarotonga COOK ISLANDS

Considering the 15 Cook Islands sit in between world-class locations like Fiji, Tonga, Samoa and Tahiti, you would be forgiven for thinking that they must have awesome waves somewhere. Unfortunately, the underwater topography and squeezed reef passes means the waves are fickle and rarely perfect. However, devoting a few weeks here should ensure some decent and definitely uncrowded waves.

**+ UNCROWDED REEF PASSES**
**+ N AND S SWELLS**
**+ EASY PADDLES FROM SHORE**
**+ OUTER ISLAND POTENTIAL**

**– LIMITED REEF PASS SET-UPS**
**– SHALLOW HIGH TIDE REEFS**
**– NO BEGINNER SPOTS**
**– EXPENSIVE LOCAL COSTS**

ANDREW SHIELD

Black Rock

Compared with other atolls, the lagoon surrounding Rarotonga is quite small. Most of the reef passes are too narrow, preventing waves from wrapping properly, and explains why there is only a handful of surf spots in the Cook Islands. The waves break over shallow reef, so it's usually safest to surf at high tide and a decent-size swell will also help the waves to break in deeper water. On the leeward side, the best spot is undoubtedly **Black Rock** (aka Socials/Golf Course) next to the airport. It's not a pass, more a curve in the reef that will bend prevailing swell into some slabby shacks on the rights. The lefts get really good too, barreling fast from a wedging take-off, but beware the coral heads and pitching lips. Plus points are it is really consistent because of its wide swell window, constant offshores, mid to high tide range and easy access. Minuses include short rides, close-outs, getting pitched, sharks and scrabbling over the reef on a dropping tide. This wave exudes true Polynesian power and although it is uncrowded, negotiating its imperfections requires skill and guts. Respect the local bodyboard crew. "The Boiler" of the Maitai Wreck (1916) sticks up off the **Avarua Harbour** reef and creates hollow lefts on major NW swells. Easier lefts peel down the harbour entrance on the inside, but NE winds are dead onshore. For righthanders, head to the reef off **Club Raro**, which regularly produces some good waves in smaller N swells. It's an ill-defined line-up and there's a good chance of taking a few on the head crossing the straight reef line. There's not much to recommend the east coast when the trades are shredding the waves to pieces, but on those rare, slack wind days, little scallops in the reef like **Norrie Park** (Matavera Point) can hold a decent right at high tide. Despite being on the windward side, one of the most surfed spots is **Avana**, breaking off the tip of Motutapu. The break is quite short and requires patience in selecting waves. The surf is neither that reliable nor challenging, even though it breaks over shallow reef, making it a bit too dangerous for beginners. On moderate SW swells and summer NE winds, the thick, ferocious rights off the **Avaavaroa Passage** provide pits for determined tube riders. Direction, size and period will be crucial to prevent the skinny channel closing-out and a dropping tide will see the currents race, so paddle in over the reef, well before mid tide approaches. **Rutaki Passage** favours the left side of another, thin 50m wide channel through the coral shelf. SE-S swell will help with the angle to the channel, but any wind lacking north will kill it. There's also a right on the other side when there's more W in the swell. Inconsistent, rarely crowded and not for intermediates. Just to the east, check anorexic Papua Passage on small, clean, organised swells.

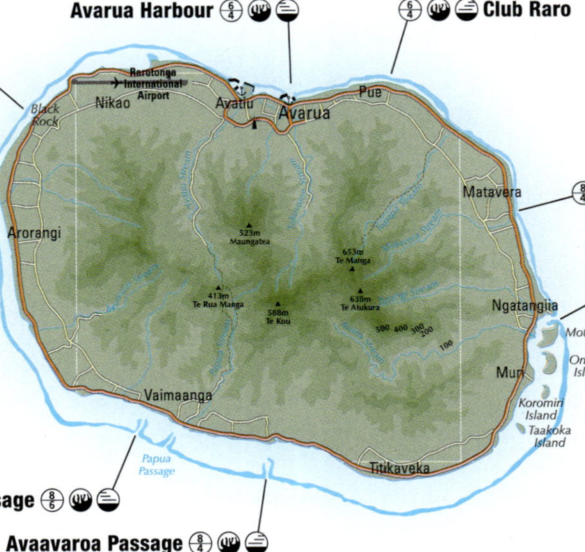


## TRAVEL INFORMATION

**Weather** – The surfing season, May-Sept, has the 'cooler' months, with average daily temps around 25°C (77°F), down to 19°C (66°F) at night. The summer rainy season, Dec-April, can be hot and humid 29°C (84°F) by day with bright sunny mornings and late afternoon downpours. Bring a shorty for windy winter days when water gets down around 22-23°C (72-74°F).

**Lodging and Food** – Prices are high for the South Pacific. Muri Beach Resort (from $165/n/dbl), Avana Waterfront apartments (fr $330/n sleeps 4). Avarua has the Paradise Inn from $85/n/single. Tiare Village is a cheap $21/n single, near the airport. Expect $15-20 for a meal.

**Nature and Culture** – Rarotonga is lush and peaceful. Go to Saturday morning's Punanga-nui Market. Fishing is world-class! Visit the other Cook islands who have joined the massive Pacific Oceanscape project along with 15 island nations to create the largest protected area network on the planet!

**Hazards and Hassles** – Watch the tides and currents in the narrow passes and surfing over shallow reef usually means reef cuts and urchins - booties essential. Most local riders are cool bodyboarders! There is no malaria but occasional outbreaks of dengue.

**Handy Hints** – No surf shops so bring all the gear you need. Adventure Cook Islands, near Rutaki has some limited hire equipment and advice. High tourist season is Dec to Feb.

JEREMY WILMOTTE

Rutaki Passage

South Pacific SE-SW swells ranging from 3-15ft arrive regularly between March and November and can also pop up in mid summer, when the focus has shifted to huge North Pacific NW swells. The prevailing trades oscillate between ENE in Jan to ESE in July, which is also the windiest month with speeds exceeding 20-40kmh. Tidal range never goes over 1m, but it really matters!

| STATISTICS | | J F | M A | M J | J A | S O | N D |
|---|---|---|---|---|---|---|---|
| SWELL | Direction | | | | | | |
| | Size (ft) | 4-5 | 5 | 6-7 | 7 | 5-6 | 4-5 |
| WIND | Direction | | | | | | |
| | Force | F4 | F4 | F4 | F4 | F4 | F4 |
| WATER | Wetsuit | | | | | | |
| | Temp/°C | 26 | 26 | 25 | 23 | 23 | 25 |
| WEATHER | Rainfall/mm | 238 | 226 | 170 | 109 | 114 | 187 |
| | days/mth | 15 | 14 | 12 | 10 | 9 | 11 |
| | Min temp/°C | 23 | 22 | 20 | 18 | 19 | 21 |
| | Max temp/°C | 29 | 28 | 26 | 25 | 26 | 27 |

# Tahiti and Moorea FRENCH POLYNESIA

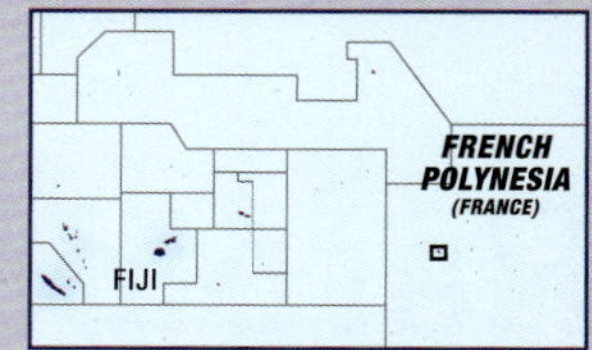


Tahiti sits at the centre of French Polynesia and now, thanks to the relatively recent discovery of Teahupoo, has become an undeniable focus for the surf world as the most challenging of playgrounds. There are dozens of islands in the Society Island chain that receive classic waves, but it's not all scary square barrels with some fun walls at various passes and even the odd beachbreak style wave to be found. On the whole, the quality of the spots is exceptional and the waves are varied, as swells arrive from both hemispheres, lighting up the coastlines of Moorea and Tahiti.

**+ POWERFUL BARRELLING WAVES**
**+ YEAR-ROUND CONSISTENCY**
**+ BEAUTIFUL LANDSCAPES**
**+ CHILLED-OUT ISLAND LIFESTYLE**

**– VERY EXPENSIVE**
**– DIFFICULT ACCESS**
**– LOCALISM AT SOME SPOTS**
**– SHARP CORAL REEFS**

## TRAVEL INFORMATION

**Weather** – During the wet season from Nov to April, there will be a heavy downpour every other day. El Niño years are very wet. Cyclones hit the country on occasions. In the dry season the high mountains effect the weather patterns and cause the S coast to see some rain. The temps are near perfect at 23°-30°C/74°-86°F year-round. The water hovers around 25-27°c (77°F-80°F).

**Lodging and Food** – At the bottom of the accommodation range are the dorm beds at Teamo (Papeete Youth Hostel), which charges at least $36/n. A mid-range favourite is Taharuu Surf Lodge in Papara (fr $85/n). In Teahupoo try Tauhanihani Village Lodge ($100/n), Vanira Lodge (fr$140/n), Te Pari Village or one of the other local "Faré" from $90/n. Moorea Surf Bed & Breakfast at Haapiti have private rooms with breakfast starting from $135. Board rental is $45 per day. There's plenty of motu style high end hotels and also Camping Nelson from $15/n. Eat from the roulottes (rolling food trucks) where locals eat simple island meals from $10, but more frequently you'll spend around $20-30 on a meal.

**Nature and Culture** – Head up into the beautiful mountains, visit some of the caves, go fishing, diving and snorkelling or just chill out amongst the lush landscape. Occasional dugout races are worth watching.

**Hazards and Hassles** – Respect the local's deep feeling of pride. The waves are super-heavy and the reefs are shallow and full of fire coral. Currents at the mouth of reef passes can be very strong. Teahupoo is one of the most dangerous waves in the world and should only be tackled by the most advanced of surfers. It has already seen one surf-related death. Sharks although common, pose no real threat. Don't eat poorly cooked fish, as there is a chance of catching ciguatera, a type of food poisoning. There are lots of mosquitoes, but no malaria.

**Handy Hints** – Equipment is very expensive in the Papeete and Maharepa surf shops. Bring at least two boards, including a longer pintail made especially for local conditions (heavy barrels!), reef boots, sun cream and possibly a helmet. Tahiti is a French speaking destination. New live HD webcams for numerous spots on tahiti-webcam.com.

LUIS BLANCO
Temae

LAURENT MASUREL
Vairao

When the N swells roll in, Moorea Island is worth the effort for its quality north coast reef passes. **Cooks Bay Pass** has what some call a fun left, despite the coral reef being close under fin. Too much E in the wind will mess it up although the shallower, nastier right across the channel will be cleaner. Take a dugout as currents and distance rule out paddling. **Hauru** is a narrow cut in the fringing reef near the Intercontinental on the north coast, which seems to favour lefthanders with a bit of W in the swell. Fast and shallow is the theme while the right is even worse and only for chargers with little regard for the boiling shut down sections. There is an easier left back at the entrance to Opunohu Bay. Currents get really strong and the nearby motu's are shark diving hotspots. At headhigh, **Haapiti** is an easy roll-in to a very long, slopey wall as it tours the curve of coral that is always deeper than the gin-clear water makes it seem. Even improvers can manage, but things hot up as the size increases to double overhead, when the drop steepens, the odd barrel section beckons and the river-like current heading out to sea cranks up. Extra inches of foam and shoulder muscle helps with the 20-40min paddle from town – better to hire canoes to get out there safely and quickly. Attracts plenty of surfers, but the vibe is often friendly and inclusive for all abilities. Wind can mess it up and kiters will descend in the afternoons. Moorea also gets plenty of decent waves through the S swell season, and if it's big enough, SE-SW lines will slip through the Chenal de Moorea then wrap around the eastern point near the airport. **Temae** hugs the coralline shelf, very close to shore, providing a righthand barrel spectacle on a par with Backdoor, but much longer. When it's on, which isn't often since it needs non-trade-winds, expect air drops into multiple caverns as it parallels the shoreline, getting shallower and uglier as it turns inside out. Temae locals covet this inconsistent right, so tread lightly and be sure of your abilities.

On Tahiti **Papenoo** can provide a fun, hollow range of peaks around the rivermouth, which helps shape some sand and rock bars, along with bringing pollution and a shark problem after rains. Holds the crowd that come in N swells and is usually cool, but there might be some vibe when the left is really firing. Cops the trades pretty bad so check it early. Out on an exposed, hammerhead reef, **Pointe Venus** follows the trend of Tahitian rights by being shallow and sketchy, requiring more than a little skill to negotiate the rapid tubes. Needs a small to moderate NE swell and S quadrant winds as it will get out of control in bigger swells. While the Bay de Matavai is famous for being

### ★ Teahupoo

LAT. -17.867243° LONG. -149.253582°

Often touted as the 'World's Heaviest Wave', Teahupoo has a fearsome reputation, encapsulated by the infamous Laird Hamilton tow-in shots that graced the cover of many surf mags in 2000. What sets Teahupoo aside is the sheer power and ferocity as a lip a few feet thick throws more out than up, creating a shape more rectangular than almond and making a mockery of most face measurements. More S in the swell will calm the beast slightly, but it is the straight on SW'ers that slam the reef and open up the caverns along the short 75-100m run for your life line-up. It's all about the drop really, which is hyper-critical here and those able to set an early rail into the gasping tubes will do better. Mistakes are swiftly and properly punished as the highly visible reef runs close to dry so quickly, pushing the unlucky ones into the lagoon and the coral is famed for infecting cuts. When it's smaller and from the W, there is even the odd right, a la Backdoor, but dont get caught paddling back out. Teahupoo consistently pulls in more swell than anywhere on Tahiti, but getting the ideal NE wind is less common, especially in the high season. Hazards like sharks, motorised traffic, the long paddle, crowds, localism and sunburn are nothing compared to the wave and the reef. There's a beachbreak at the rivermouth for the kids and it sometimes holds up a nice right wall for turns and airs, giving an opt out for most mortals that shouldn't really be attempting big Teahupoo.

Cook's landing spot, its long curve of volcanic sand is fairly poor for waves with lots of close-outs, but the bays towards **Arue** hold a few reefbreaks like Taharaa, surrounded by plush hotels and further on a very shallow left and right at La Fayette, where there is also some dumpy shorebreak, suited to bodyboards. Close to Papeete is **Taapuna**, the original Tahitian tube garden and popular destination wave for those who want a hollow, dredging and technically testing lefthander, a couple of notches below Teahupoo. Any W swell and any E wind will work, so it is consistent, crowded with good surfers and suited to experienced reefbreak surfers. Usual problems of being way out there, in waters strafed by current and a local crew who demand as much respect as the wave. Generally considered an easier alternative than Taapuna, **Sapinus** can still throw a decent tube especially on its inside section and offers some nice walled rides on the pass opposite the Tahiti Museum. Deep in the bay is a fun beach/shorebreak type set-up near the rivermouth when big W swells are running and there's something for everyone in a chilled out atmosphere. Just down the coast there's more waves in the bay and on the pass at Paea. Hollow, fast and shallow are often used to describe Tahitian waves and definitely apply to this distant fringe of reef at **Passe de Maraa**. Needs as much water as possible and some S in the swell to stop it shutting down horribly. The bonus is a lack of crowds and occasionally the right across the fast flowing channel will fire. Experts only. Beginners can head for the good beachbreak in **Papara**, which is a nice rest from the intensity of the surrounding reefs. Holds some curvy corners in larger swells and attracts some high performance riders looking to cut loose without getting cut. There's also some outside reef action for the chargers. On the Iti Peninsula, the Tapuehara Pass holds the flawless lefts of **Vairao**, yet another epic barrel spinning across the coral shallows 2km out. The S swell window and NE-E wind combo make it consistent, it packs some serious punch without huge crowds and like most waves in the world, is less intense than its neighbour, that freak of nature known as ★**Teahupoo**.

BEN THOUARD

Tahiti Iti

At a southern latitude of 17°, Tahiti is perfectly exposed to the super-consistent S/SW swells, which hammer the S coast year-round, but peak between April and Oct. Expect the surf to range from 4 to 15ft in season and 2-5ft in the off-season. Exposure to NW/N swells between Nov and March is less generous, arriving in the 3ft-8ft range. Dominant trade winds come from the E, tending towards SE during the May to Oct dry season (Maraamu), whilst the wet season (Toerau), sees the wind coming more from the NE. Mornings will usually be glassy and tidal range is very small.

| STATISTICS | | J F | M A | M J | J A | S O | N D |
|---|---|---|---|---|---|---|---|
| SWELL | Direction | | | | | | |
| | Size (ft) | 5 | 5-6 | 7 | 7-8 | 6-7 | 5-6 |
| WIND | Direction | | | | | | |
| | Force | F4 | F4 | F4 | F4 | F4 | F4 |
| WATER | Wetsuit | | | | | | |
| | Temp/°C | 27 | 27 | 26 | 25 | 26 | 27 |
| WEATHER | Rainfall/mm | 300 | 170 | 95 | 67 | 75 | 195 |
| | days/mth | 14 | 11 | 7 | 6 | 7 | 13 |
| | Min temp/°C | 23 | 23 | 21 | 20 | 21 | 23 |
| | Max temp/°C | 30 | 30 | 29 | 28 | 29 | 30 |

# Raiatea and Huahine FRENCH POLYNESIA

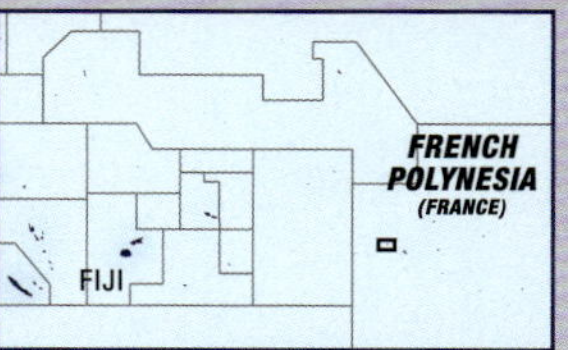


Raiatea is considered the traditional centre of French Polynesia's religion and culture, where many voyages of Pacific discovery started. The surf spots are more remote and quality is highly dependent on swell direction and wind exposure. Huahine is smaller, but boasts a number of quality reef passes including the matching pair of Faré Left and Faré Right, the region's most surfed waves. Because these islands are so remote, with a long history of resistance against the official government, a strong feeling of ownership of the spots, namely localism, has developed. The "Black Shorts" on Huahine and Raiatea will only let outsiders surf with them once they have proved themselves to be their friends and loyal to the surf.

**+ YEAR-ROUND SWELL**
**+ POWERFUL REEF PASSES**
**+ POSTCARD SCENERY**
**+ ALL TYPES OF ACCOMMODATION**

**- FIERCE LOCALISM**
**- REEF PASS DANGERS**
**- DIFFICULT ACCESS**
**- LONG PADDLE-OUTS**

JOLI

Faré Right

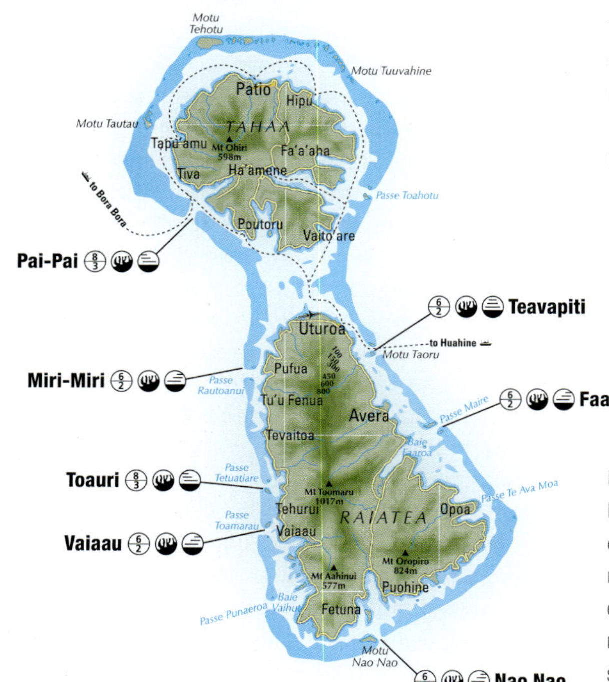


The coral reef surrounding Tahaa, the Vanilla Island, is crowned with 60 tiny, idyllic motus perched above the north shore. The **Pai-Pai** pass where major boats get in and out is too large for reliable surf but some days, it gets good with heavy rights or unpredictable lefts and is unlikely to have angry locals.

Located 220km NW of Tahiti, Raiatea is the largest and the administrative centre of the Leeward Islands. In the past named Havaii, it's the original land of the Maohi. **Miri-Miri**'s intense rights or **Toauri**'s classic lefts are the main names (again with some localism) working on smaller SW swells. **Vaiaau** is a rare right by Motu Toamarau, which peels unmercifully fast and works best with W in the swell. **Nao Nao** is very exposed on the south coast and the rights line up in SE swells. East Coast passes **Faaroa** and **Teavapiti** gather windswells, working erratically with hardly anyone to surf them. Huahiné is the best-known island since the Faré backpacker village sits within paddling distance of **Faré Rights**. A high quality wave with long, sectiony walls and plenty of short barrel opportunities. Paddle out from the jetty, just south of the hotel where kids learn on a tiny reform. **Faré Lefts** take about 20 mins to paddle to but are classic Polynesian surf: long powerful walls wrap into the *passe* but unfortunately are prone to localism. Out of the three classic spots here, **Fitii** probably has the best world-class potential with amazing rights providing open barrels and ideal launching pads for aerialists. A boat is advised to reach this localised break. Check the exposed southern pass of **Parea** on a flat windless day or on N wind, quality could be there with low crowd pressure. Another less surfed *passe* is **Motu Mahara** by the Sofitel Heiva where lefts offer fast walls in summer conditions. It's a year-round destination, favouring N winds for the epic rights. The northeasters blow from November-April, while swells are generated by massive lows in the North Pacific. The S swell season lasts the majority of the year, with the peak months being May-September, but it is not uncommon to have classic south swells before or after winter. Dominant winds are E-SE trades shifting NE and calming down in summer. Jan-March are the quietest and July-Sept the windiest. As for tides, it can only fluctuate by 0.6m max, but incoming or outgoing current will alter water heights.

SYLVAIN CAZENAVE

Faré Left

## TRAVEL INFORMATION

**Weather** – Cooled by the gentle breezes of the Pacific, the climate is sunny and pleasant – the year-round lowest temp is 21°C (70°F). Seasons are the reverse of those in the Northern Hemisphere. From November through May the climate is warmer and very humid, with daily temperatures of about 29°C (84°F) and from June through October, the climate is cooler and drier with daily temperatures of 27°C (80°F). Most of the rain falls during the warmer season. Water temps are just ideal around 27°C (80°F) and a bit of neoprene would only be useful to protect against coral cuts or gusty trades.

**Lodging and Food** – In Faré, Pension Chez Guynette starts at $20 for a dorm bed and Motel Vanille starts at $100 for a 2 person bungalow. In Uturoa, Hinano Hotel ($90 a/c room for 2) well located if you rent a boat. Expect $10 eating local food in 'Roulottes' or $20 in restaurants.

**Nature and Culture** – Faré comes to life on shipping day, Huahiné's people travel to town by le truck to sell their pigs, copra and melons and buy goods from the incoming supply ships. Tourist attractions include buying pearls, shark feeding, big game fishing or sailing cruises. In Raiatea, visit Taputapuatea, the largest marae (religious monument) in Polynesia or vanilla plantations. Brush up on your French.

**Hazards and Hassles** – Localism is the main issue, face it. Prepare for Polynesian power and take a first-aid kit for reef cuts. Passe rips can be intense, beware if paddling across the lagoon and wear sun-cream. When it rains for days, streams wash out a lot of trash and the channel gets brown with worrying debris. On Motus, mind the pigs!

**Handy Hints** – Although some beat-up boards are for rent in Faré, take two boards (with a step-up gun for 6ft+ days) and trying to trade one with a local could be a way to negotiate some surfing rights.

| STATISTICS | | J F | M A | M J | J A | S O | N D |
|---|---|---|---|---|---|---|---|
| SWELL | Direction | | | | | | |
| | Size (ft) | 4-5 | 5 | 6-7 | 7 | 5-6 | 4-5 |
| WIND | Direction | | | | | | |
| | Force | F3-F4 | F3 | F3-F4 | F4 | F4 | F3-F4 |
| WATER | Wetsuit | | | | | | |
| | Temp/°C | 28 | 28 | 27 | 26 | 26 | 27 |
| WEATHER | Rainfall/mm | 310 | 170 | 100 | 50 | 65 | 230 |
| | days/mth | 17 | 13 | 10 | 7 | 7 | 15 |
| | Min temp/°C | 22 | 22 | 21 | 20 | 21 | 22 |
| | Max temp/°C | 31 | 31 | 30 | 30 | 30 | 31 |

# Tuamotu FRENCH POLYNESIA

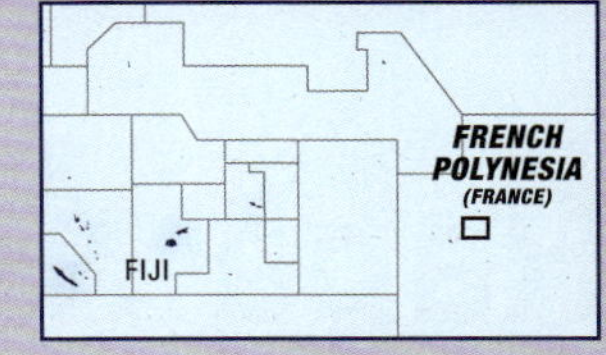


The vast majority of the world's 400 atolls are located in the Pacific and the Tuamotu, which cover a territory as vast as western Europe, is home to 77 of them. This dusting of islands is also called The Labyrinth, or the Archipelago of the Rough Sea and has remained essentially uncharted due to the difficulty of navigating the local waters.

+ YEAR-ROUND SWELLS
+ JUICY REEF PASSES
+ WORLD-CLASS FISHING/DIVING
+ LUXURY BOAT TRAVEL

- OCCASIONAL FLAT SPELLS
- NO SHELTER FROM TRADES
- LARGE DISTANCES BETWEEN BREAKS
- EXTREMELY EXPENSIVE SURF TRIP

To the east are the younger atolls, but it's the older atolls that are most likely to contain a reef pass, cut through the fringing reef to the inner lagoon. Out of 77 atolls, only 32 have at least one pass, only 10 have several, and most of these are found in the NW corner of the territory. Rangiroa is the world's second largest atoll, where the northern pass of **Avatoru** holds a long, hollow right that is regularly ridden by local surfers and bodyboarders, since it is accessible without a boat. Locals scamper barefoot across the sharp reef and it is a ripable wall when smaller, before turning nasty when overhead. It should be noted the rip in the pass averages at 5km/h and flows into the lagoon 35% of the time, while outgoing flow is 55%. This major current is a factor at all Tuamotu passes, including Tikehau, which is where most surf charters end up. **Tikehau Left** strafes the southern side of Tuheiava Pass, the only deepwater passage into the atoll. It can be both walled-up and hollow on the inside or just hollow from go to whoa, depending on the swell direction, which is usually best from the SW-W. **Tikehau Right** is usually slightly more forgiving than the left over the pass, although it has been known to go ballistic on rare large NW swells. It's hollower on the outside straighter reef line before hugging the channel into the inside which shoulders off at a slower pace. Again it's mid to high, preferably on the push and NE-E winds are offshore. The majority of N swells produce clean, mid-size rights while S swells generally result in punchier lefts. Some waves are hollower on the outside reef and then actually back off into a mushier bowl as they wrap into the deeper passes, giving less-experienced waveriders a chance, while the hardcore tube charger takes-off deeper, further up the reef.

N swells provide the best quality surf from Nov - April, getting to the Tuamotu 3-5 days later than Hawaii. Despite the large distances travelled and because they come out of deep water with nearly no shadowing en-route, they arrive with surprising ferocity and consistency, lasting about 2-3 days.

The S swell season runs the majority of the year, with the peak months being May-September, but it is not uncommon to have classic SE to SW swells during the N season. E-SE trades can be damn strong, Jan-March being the weakest and July-Sept the windiest. The Tuamotu Archipelago takes a lot more effort and money to get to, but rewards those surfers lucky enough to make it there, with an intense tropical experience in the Pacific wilderness. As for tides, it's not even 1ft max but incoming or outgoing currents can alter water heights.

Tuamotu

BEN THOUARD

Tuamotu

LAURENT MASUREL

## TRAVEL INFORMATION

**Weather** – Less difference between wet and dry seasons than Tahiti, because there are no mountains to gather clouds and mists. There are more short and heavy thunderstorms in the austral summer. It's warm year-round, but the period between May and October is the coolest (21°C/70°F min in August) and driest. There is more than 3000h of yearly sunshine. Statistically, there is only a serious cyclone every 25 years but there were 6 between Dec '82 and April '83. As there is no phreatic layer, the Tuamotu rely on rain for their water supply, so don't waste it. Water temps are ideal around 27°C (80°F) so neoprene would only be useful for coral cuts.

**Lodging and Food** – Long distances between waves are the main issue and so you must have a decent boat to explore. There is no dedicated surf charters but Haumana does cover surfing in full luxury and they have hosted many surfers including pros. Land-based accommodation is not ideal at all, but in Rangiroa/Tikehau there are one or two semi accessible waves possible by local boat hire. Expect lots of fish and French cuisine.

**Nature and Culture** – Early natives, the Paumotus, were aggressive towards visitors, indulging in tribal wars and cannibalism until it was annexed to French Polynesia in 1880. Tikehau atoll claims to have some of the best fishing in the world. Pearl farms (black pearls) and fish traps/farming provide the main economy.

**Hazards and Hassles** – Dogs chase small black tip sharks in 1ft of water: maos (sharks) are just about everywhere but attacks unlikely. Reef cuts, sunburn and rough seas are the main worries. Communication is possible via satellite phone but it will cost $5 a minute.

**Handy Hints** – Take a quiver incorporating pin tails or gunny shapes with spare leashes. Accomplished longboarders should survive, but this is not a beginner/improver zone. Bring reef booties, board shorts, rashies, helmet, ding repair, tropical wax and plenty of sun protection.

| STATISTICS | | J F | M A | M J | J A | S O | N D |
|---|---|---|---|---|---|---|---|
| SWELL | Direction | | | | | | |
| | Size (ft) | 4-5 | 5 | 6-7 | 7-8 | 5-6 | 4-5 |
| WIND | Direction | | | | | | |
| | Force | F4 | F4 | F4 | F4 | F4 | F4 |
| WATER | Wetsuit | | | | | | |
| | Temp/°C | 27 | 28 | 27 | 26 | 27 | 27 |
| WEATHER | Rainfall/mm | 200 | 130 | 95 | 70 | 110 | 170 |
| | days/mth | 17 | 14 | 12 | 11 | 14 | 18 |
| | Min temp/°C | 25 | 26 | 25 | 24 | 25 | 25 |
| | Max temp/°C | 23 | 23 | 22 | 21 | 22 | 23 |

# Rapa Nui

Known as Rapa Nui by its inhabitants, Easter Island is the most remote, inhabited place on earth. Its world-famous statues, the Moais, are 3-21m tall, carved out of the basalt rock and weigh up to 300 tonnes. Geologically, the coastline is young, formed by a single volcanic eruption and consists of rugged lava cliffs, making entry/exit points scarce. Most spots are heavy reefs dotted along the west and south coasts, plus two average quality beachbreaks with remarkable scenery on the north coast. Local surfers are friendly and open, showing typical Polynesian pride in their island and culture that demands as much respect as the waves.

**+ YEAR-ROUND SWELLS**
**+ POWERFUL LAVA REEFBREAKS**
**+ UNCROWDED SOUTH SHORE**
**+ GOOD WEATHER, CLEAR WATER**

**- BIG, WILD WAVES**
**- NO QUALITY BEACHBREAKS**
**- TRICKY EXIT/ENTRY POINTS**
**- EXPENSIVE AND REMOTE**

MAX MILLS
Hanga Nui

In Hanga Roa, both **Tahai** and **Toroko** reefbreaks are quite inconsistent. Toroko breaks more frequently with short rights and longer lefts in SW swells, but Tahai needs a massive NW swell to break. The next two breaks along this coast are quite consistent. Facing the fishermen's inlet, **Motu Hava**'s lefts and rights give decent rides before inside rocks spoil this fun, hot-dog reef. **Papas** will break even when it's onshore, providing lefts and rights ideal for the longboarder although in summer, at under 4ft, it might be rammed with local bodyboarders. Fickle **Mataveri** has the longest wave on the island with 800m rides possible, from the rocky outcrop that prevents it linking all the way through from the island. Needs a moderate swell with long period to work and the more W in it the better. Fast and tubular wave that is deceptive and always bigger than it looks. Plan your exit as getting out is very tricky! Local tow-in crew will be on it when big. Conditions on the south coast ("wild coast") can be deceptive, so have a good look before committing. Just beyond the oil terminal **Viri-Inga-O-Tuki** is a less critical wave, suitable for longboards or thicker guns. It can have more than a couple of peaks depending on swell size, with both lefts and rights that break on the full side, but still have plenty of push. **Tangaroa** made famous by Laird et al's second trip to the island in 2001, upped the ante as they towed-in on some insane heavy barrels over the reef. SE swells will make the entry/exit treacherous and bring down some deadly sections - avoid being caught inside the shallow, urchin-covered impact zone. The left looks makeable, but leads to a dangerous place. Popular with the local tow-in team and bodyboarders. Proper experts only wave. **Vaihu**'s impressive but deceptive lefts break over uneven reef and unless it is over 10ft, the ride will be short as it fades into deep water after take-off. The perfectly shaped, mini-pipe wave of **Huareva** provides a vert take-off on a short and intense lefthander. At 6ft, both **Koe Koe** and **Akahanga** will start to break and the pointbreak at Akahanga will continue to break up to 20ft, when it becomes the longest, big wave on the island. Heading east along this south coast, **Pakaia** is another short, intense, lava reef left, resembling a mutant Pipeline that will be perfect or non-existent depending on swell direction. It's an easy paddle out, like **Hanga Nui**, which has a small harbour to ease the usual entry/exit problems. The reef in the middle of a stunning bay has short lefts and longer rights that rarely close-out. On big NW swells, head to the north coast where both **Ovahe**'s pink-sand beach and **Anakena** will have waves, where the Moais overlook the scene and it's somewhere for beginners to get a wave occasionally.

Swells come from the SE-SW in winter (Apr-Sept) and W-NW in summer (October-March), so flat days are rare. The prevailing wind is E with a brief stint of NW in winter, but it's variable and often switches direction during the day. Tides are small and generally not an issue.

## TRAVEL INFORMATION

**Weather** – Air temps are never below 17°C (63°F) and never above 28°C (82°F). Winter is wet and summer is drier, with ever-present high humidity. Sub-tropical water temps from 19-24°C (66-75°F), plus the wind factor (20-50 km/h) makes a lycra/rubber vest handy in summer and a 2mm springy or steamer in winter.

**Lodging and Food** – There's a wide selection places in Hanga Roa. Lorana is ideally located: $200/night/dble full board. Camping Mihinoa is right next to the ocean ($18/n). Pea, facing Papa, or Te Moana in front of Motu Hava are great places to have lunch or dinner. Nightlife at Aloha Pub-Bar & Grill.

**Nature and Culture** – Enjoy open air, archaeological sites and the Sebastian Englert Museum, dive with orcas, trek or fish. The coastline is filled with natural caves containing many religious petroglyphs based on sea life.

**Hazards and Hassles** – Most of the lava reefs are flat with rare exposed rocks. South coast spots get very big but break in deep water. Take reef boots for the black sea urchins and a fast exit over the rocks. The hospital is modern but major surgery must be done in Chile.

**Handy Hints** – Take thicker longer boards. Big wave leashes are essential. No surf shops yet but boards can be fixed. Islanders show their hospitality with alcohol, mostly beers and Pisco.

PAUL KENNEDY
Mataveri

| STATISTICS | | J F | M A | M J | J A | S O | N D |
|---|---|---|---|---|---|---|---|
| SWELL | Direction | | | | | | |
| | Size (ft) | 3-4 | 4-5 | 6-7 | 7-8 | 6 | 3-4 |
| WIND | Direction | | | | | | |
| | Force | F3-F4 | F3-F4 | F4 | F4 | F4 | F3-F4 |
| WATER | Wetsuit | | | | | | |
| | Temp/°C | 24 | 23 | 21 | 20 | 20 | 22 |
| WEATHER | Rainfall/mm | 110 | 110 | 110 | 80 | 80 | 120 |
| | days/mth | 11 | 11 | 12 | 8 | 8 | 12 |
| | Min temp/°C | 21 | 19 | 16 | 13 | 15 | 17 |
| | Max temp/°C | 29 | 29 | 27 | 25 | 26 | 29 |

# Tabuaeran & Kiritimati LINE ISLANDS

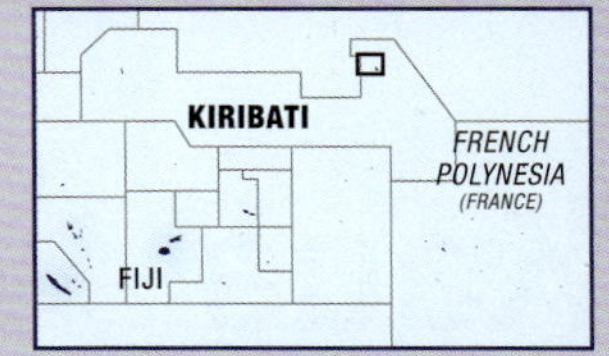


Kiribati (pronounced kee-ree-bass), comprises of 32 low-lying atolls, sprinkled across 3220km of the central Pacific. Most visitors arrive by cruise ship, stopping at Tarawa in the Gilbert's group and Kiritimati in the Line group mainly for diving, bone fishing and very occasionally for surfing. Formerly known as Christmas Island, Kiritimati is the biggest atoll in the world and comprises over 70% of the 850km/sq land area of the Republic of Kiribati. Tabuaeran (aka Fanning Island) means "heavenly footprint" as the island's shape suggests. Chuck Corbett left neighbouring Hawaii in 1979 in search of emptier line-ups and after 12 years around Tarawa, moved to Tabuaeran to surf English Harbor's freight train lefts.

**+ CLEAN N & S SWELLS**
**+ VARIOUS QUALITY SPOTS**
**+ LARGEST LAGOON IN WORLD**
**+ GREAT DIVING & FISHING**

**- DIFFICULT ACCESS TO SPOTS**
**- INCONSISTENT IN SUMMER**
**- INFREQUENT TRANSPORT LINKS**
**- REMOTENESS AND HIGH COSTS**

MICHAEL KEW
Bridges Point

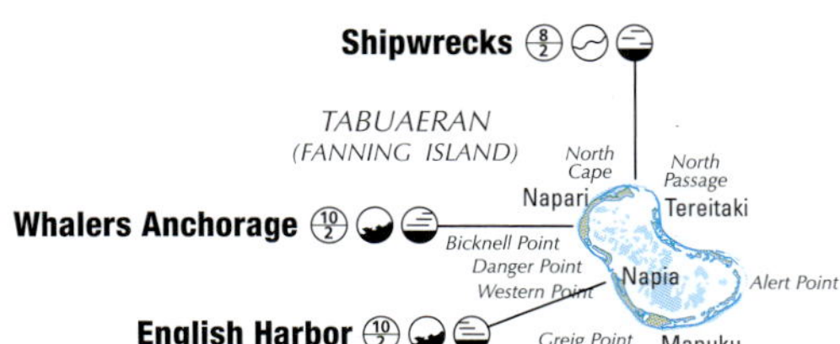


At the northern tip of Tabuaeran is **Shipwrecks**, a sandy bottom bay with lefts and rights breaking in winter N swells. **Whalers Anchorage** is very consistent and has small swell lefts and rights peeling into a channel. Along the southern edge of the main reef pass at **English Harbor** is a long, fast, top quality left that breaks consistently from April to September on SW to SE swells. Can be good rights across the channel on winter W-NW swells. Straight S swells for the left and due W for the right are very rare. The bottom is user-friendly coral rubble strewn on flat reef, as opposed to jagged live coral. Despite isolation, no local surfers, and poor inter-island flight service, Kiritimati has long been known to have good waves. There are breaks for all skill levels, from beginner to experts with gentle bathymetry, which means close-outs when big, but fun when small. Chuck reckons there are 18 spots in a 8km radius from London to Poland Point. **Bridges Point** is the obvious spot with a fun right, holding double overhead walls, sometimes referred to as a mix between Maalaea (fast) and Trestles (fun). NNW swells will make long and fast walls while W swells will bump up good bowls off the point which can shoulder and roll 150m to the lagoon, perfect for a longboard. Trades can mess it up as there is a 40km fetch blowing from the SE. Within paddling distance is **Cockrane's Reef**, a long, walled-up left that bends through almost 180° to join the rights, that are a good bet up to 4ft. On the northern end of Cook Islet is **Coral Head**, another good left up to 5ft, being well-sheltered from the trades. **Annie's** is a great left with 4 makeable sections, gets very hollow and is a guaranteed barrel for those with the balls. **Paris** is a stretch of 5 sheltered bays or cuts in the reefs, offering a swathe of fun spots which are trade wind protected, but close-out over 4-5ft. It only takes 30 min by boat from London, but by land, it's 2h30. Try **Poland Point**, which gets occasional rights off the exposed reef on the western corner, which can handle some N in the winds.

On Tabuaeran, surf is reliable year-round, getting overhead and much larger at times from November through March, which is when Kiritimati also gets good. The same winter swells that hit the north shore of Oahu arrive at a smaller size, but even longer periods. Winds are easterly trades that blow offshore year-round. Chuck Corbett shares his time between winters on Kiritimati and summers on Tabuaeran. Despite less than a metre tidal range, waves are often better at high tides and at English Harbor, there is strong side-shore rip to the wave on incoming tides.

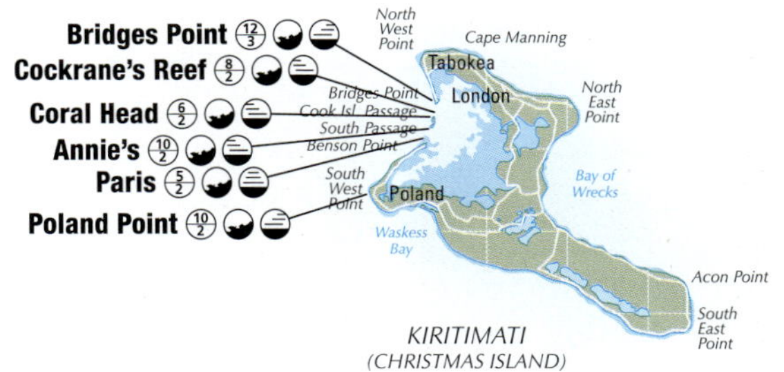

PETER HARDING
Paris

## TRAVEL INFORMATION

**Weather** – Temps vary little between days and nights throughout most of the year, ranging from 25-32°C (77-90°F) with an annual mean of 27°C (80°F). The Dec to April rainy season sees strong winds, occasional gales and even tornadoes, but it's safely between the hurricane and cyclone belts. Rainfall varies between 1020mm near the equator and 3050mm in the extreme north and south. It can be irregular and long periods of drought are not uncommon. Boardshorts only.

**Lodging and Food** – A handful of places in the $50-180 range. Captain Cook Hotel close to the airport have 24 rooms and bungalows. Mini Hotel is $30/60 single/dble. Meals are on a fixed cost of $40 a day. Both catholic and protestant parishes have basic rooms $30 a night. Christmas island surf offers all inclusive week long packages from $1200. Fanning island Surf has all in packages including local flights from $2350. Pegasus Lodges fly charters from Kiritimati to Tabuaeran for all inclusive surf and fishing tours (max 6 persons).

**Nature and Culture** – Internationally renowned for bone fishing and bird watchers are overwhelmed by thousands of migratory seabirds. Local dance is practised everywhere. Spectacular diving. Kiribati outrigger canoes, said to be the fastest in the Pacific are regularly raced in the lagoon. Second World War relics litter beaches in South Tarawa.

**Hazards and Hassles** – Besides reef dangers like cuts and sharks swimming around, pay attention to hepatitis A, B, and C. Stir in dengue fever, lice, ciguatera, staph and staph-spreading flies. Weekly Air Pacific flight from Nadi, Fiji or Hawaii: WKK supply ferry cruising 4-5 times per year,

**Handy Hints** – Chuck's Island Trader is for rent: Expect $2000/wk for 4pax. Trips would be 1 week for Kiritimati and 2 weeks for Tabuaeran. There is a divers association on Kiritimati. Strong Australian influence on Kiritimati means pay in AUD$. Kiribati bends the dateline to keep all its islands on the same side and is a full 24hrs ahead of Hawaii.

| STATISTICS | | J F | M A | M J | J A | S O | N D |
|---|---|---|---|---|---|---|---|
| SWELL | Direction | | | | | | |
| | Size (ft) | 4 | 2-3 | 2 | 3 | 3-4 | 4 |
| WIND | Direction | | | | | | |
| | Force | F3-F4 | F2-F3 | F3 | F3-F4 | F3-F4 | F3 |
| WATER | Wetsuit | | | | | | |
| | Temp/°C | 29 | 29 | 29 | 29 | 29 | 29 |
| WEATHER | Rainfall/mm | 149 | 324 | 326 | 110 | 164 | 134 |
| | days/mth | 10 | 18 | 19 | 8 | 12 | 11 |
| | Min temp/°C | 24 | 25 | 25 | 25 | 24 | 24 |
| | Max temp/°C | 30 | 30 | 30 | 30 | 30 | 30 |

# Kauai HAWAII

Known as the "The Garden Island", Kauai is an ancient and deeply eroded extinct volcano, rising 5000m above the sea floor. Kauai regulations state that no building may exceed the height of a coconut tree, preventing development from scarring the breathtaking scenery. There are more sandy beaches than many other islands and nearly 45% of its coastline is virtually deserted. Despite having over 300 surf spots, underwater topography is, allegedly, not as ideal as Oahu. The North Shore high volcanic cliffs hold few spots and the inaccessibility of the Na Pali coast makes it very dangerous to find and ride the few spots that face the brunt of the winter swells.

- + YEAR-ROUND SWELLS
- + HAWAIIAN POWER AND QUALITY
- + SUPER-SCENIC ISLAND
- + VARIETY OF COASTLINE

- – MOSTLY "EXPERTS ONLY" SURF
- – PROTECTIVE LOCALS
- – HIGH LOCAL PRICES
- – SHARKS

## TRAVEL INFORMATION

**Weather** – Kauai's seven micro-climates range from dry, desert, sunny areas, lush river valleys, balmy foothills and high mountain rain forests. Winter temps range 15°C (59°F) nights to 25°C (77°F) days, while summer is 20°C (68°F) and 30°C (86°F) respectively. The North Shore is 3-4°C (6-8°F) cooler than other parts. Trade winds bring rain to the eastern slopes, while the Waialeale summit is the wettest spot in the world, with a record of 11680mm (467"in) in the '60s! Boardies all year!

**Lodging and Food** – First timers may prefer package deals. The Marriott at Kalapaki starts at $480/dble and the prestigious Princeville Resort in Hanalei also costs as much as a surfboard per night. On the North Shore, try Hale Ho'o Maha in Kalihiwai: from $220/dble. Sheraton in Poipu ($315/dbl) or rent the condos. Expect $30 for a meal. Princeville is reportedly the most expensive supermarket in the USA.

**Nature and Culture** – While the nightlife can't rival Honolulu's, the natural beauty is unbeatable. Visit Waimea Canyon or Kokee State Park, kayak along the Wailua River, take a Na Pali Cruise or walk the Kalalau trail, fly in a helicopter above Niihau or Na Pali cliffs.

**Hazards and Hassles** – Any bad attitude in the surf will not be tolerated by the locals. Heavy, powerful sucky waves, regular big shark sightings and sharp reefs. Rains can be intense on the N-E sides, avoid river run-offs in the surf.

**Handy Hints** – Poipu hosts numerous surf schools like Kauai Surf School, or Margo Oberg's at the Nukumoi Surf Shop, at Brennecke's Beach. Check Hanalei Surf Company on the north shore. Cheap board rentals available. Shapers: Hamilton, Brewer, Wellman.

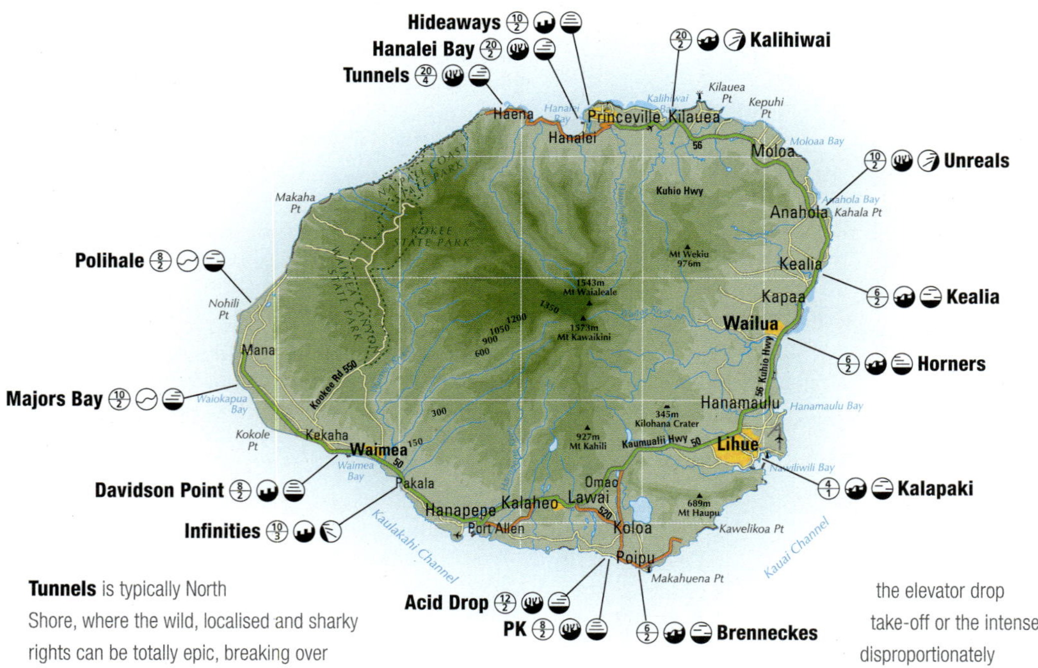


**Tunnels** is typically North Shore, where the wild, localised and sharky rights can be totally epic, breaking over sharp, live coral a long way from shore. **Hanalei Bay** is the focus of Kauai surfing, providing a range of waves in a small area. Below deluxe Princeville Resort is the righthand pointbreak that everyone wants to ride, crowding the sections of Impossible, Flat Rock and The Bowl on all sizes of board. Well-protected from the wind, it handles size but it's a very long paddle and of course, the locals are aggressive. Further round the bay there's average beachbreaks and some good reefs like Waikoko, Middles and Chicken Wing, or **Hideaways** further out in Princeville. The latter sits at the base of high cliffs and holds fun, scattered reefbreaks when small and not windy but has had a shark attack. Nestled beneath impressive cliffs is **Kalihiwai**, where even the best surfers can get thrashed by misjudging the elevator drop take-off or the intense, disproportionately massive barrels. Few people are permitted to partake. The Kilauea lighthouse marks entry to the rainy, onshore east coast, with low cliffs and extended valleys, aka the Coconut Coast. **Unreals** at Anahola is a right pointbreak working consistently on the regular E windswells and kona winds blow offshore. **Kealia**'s small, powerful (but predominantly onshore) waves can be a fun session and check **Horners** in Wailua, a traditional surfing locale for centuries. Wealthy beginners or longboarders might enjoy **Kalapaki**'s gentle reefbreak whilst staying at the Marriott right on the beach. Poipu is the best place to stay with lots of cheaper condos and close to several always offshore breaks. It's bodyboarding only at **Brenneckes**, but **PK**'s lefts, **Acid Drop**'s short barrelling rights and Center's treacherous righthand reefbreak are for experts only. The SW corner cloaks a few secrets plus the long perfect lefts of **Infinities** at Pakala. Will handle the bigger summer S swells while sharks, locals and sharp reef help regulate the crowd. Various quality reefs straddle the coast near Kekaha like **Davidson Point**. The Pacific Missile Range Base dominates the long and empty west coast beaches through Barking Sands up to **Majors Bay** and beyond to **Polihale**. Incredibly powerful beachbreaks with terrifying rips to match where one ride can equate to a long walk down the beach. On the horizon is Niihau, where only full-blooded Hawaiians are permitted to live a traditional existence with no electricity, no phones, no cars, no roads, no hotels...but there is surf!

Between October and March, 3-30ft W to N swells hit Kauai with periods around 15-20 seconds! From April to September, the South Shore gets long distance 2-8ft SW groundswell from the South Pacific. Year-round, 3-8ft constant NE windswell can be ridden on the windward side. Because the island is round, many swells refract around the coast. Stable NE-E trade winds vary from 27% (Dec) to 58% (Aug), with winter turning more SE. Occasionally kona S/SW winds provide perfect conditions for the North Shore. Tide ranges are slight but the coral reefs are particularly sharp.

Hanalei Bay

SYLVAIN CAZENAVE

| STATISTICS | | J F | M A | M J | J A | S O | N D |
|---|---|---|---|---|---|---|---|
| SWELL | Direction | | | | | | |
| | Size (ft) | 7-8 | 6-7 | 3-4 | 4 | 5-6 | 7-8 |
| WIND | Direction | | | | | | |
| | Force | F4 | F4 | F4 | F4 | F4 | F4 |
| WATER | Wetsuit | | | | | | |
| | Temp/°C | 24 | 24 | 25 | 26 | 27 | 25 |
| WEATHER | Rainfall/mm | 75 | 50 | 15 | 65 | 35 | 65 |
| | days/mth | 6 | 5 | 2 | 5 | 3 | 5 |
| | Min temp/°C | 16 | 17 | 18 | 20 | 20 | 17 |
| | Max temp/°C | 26 | 27 | 29 | 31 | 30 | 27 |

# Big Island HAWAII

Hawaii is known as the Big Island, since it's nearly double that of the others combined and, being a live volcano, continues to grow. Lava flowing from Kilauea is continually shaping a new landscape on its way to the sea where it can both create or destroy existing ones. Polynesian immigrants probably initiated surfing at Kealakekua Bay centuries ago, making the Big Island the birthplace of surfing and the aloha spirit. Crowds and localism do exist but remote spots requiring long hikes or 4WD access will be empty and conditions will be less competitive than most Hawaiian line-ups.

- + KONA SPOT DENSITY
- + REMOTE, UNCROWDED WAVES
- + VOLCANOES AND LAVA FLOWS
- + TROPICAL SNOW SPORTS

- – NW SWELL SHADOW
- – SUPER-RAINY EAST COAST
- – LOCALISED URBAN SPOTS
- – REMOTE SPOTS REQUIRE 4WD

ANDREW SHIELD

Kona Coast

## TRAVEL INFORMATION

**Weather** – Hawaii is full of microclimates, thanks to its high mountain peaks. During summer, the NE trades are more persistent and clear blue skies can last for weeks. In the winter, trades are frequently interrupted by fronts bringing SW-NW winds and intervals of widespread cloud and rain. 10cm of rain can fall in an hour and Hilo is the USA's wettest city, with 4500mm (180in) a year, while at Kawaihae, it's a mere 150mm (6in). Ascending the mountains, temperatures drop 1°C (3°F) every 150m and snow is likely above 10,660ft (3500m). Water is tropical-warm; bring a shorty for windy winter days.

**Lodging and Food** – Stay on Alii Drive for choice and mobility. Most of Kona's condos are well furnished with complete kitchens. The weekly rate is 6x daily rate and the monthly is 3x weekly rate. Check Hale Kona Kai and Kona Bali Kai close to Banyans. Expect $30 for a meal.

**Nature and Culture** – Climb to Observatory Hill, Mauna Kea's summit. Snowboard up there or slide the Kapoho crater. Register and hike the Pina Trail in Hawaii Volcanoes National Park when Kilauea is pumping red lava, see Kohala Coast petroglyphs and visit the Pacific Tsunami Museum in Hilo.

**Hazards and Hassles** – Don't enter the water with attitude – it will only bring trouble from the locals. Avoid Hilo and Kailua crowds. Beware while parking at remote spots; don't leave anything in the car. Reef cuts, rips and sunburn always a threat. Allow for long driving times.

**Handy Hints** – Pacific Vibrations in Kailua or order from Orchidland Surfboards in Hilo. Learners should try Hawaii Lifeguards Lessons in Keauhou or Ocean Ecotours in Honokohau.

The leeward Kohala Coast is fairly poor surf wise whereas the Kona Coast boasts the best conditions with offshore trades and a S to N swell window. **Kawaihae** Harbor is the island's official tidal measurement location and hosts several beginner-friendly reefs next to the breakwater. Plenty of rights in WNW swells, spied by a web cam. Most beaches are steep, narrow and strewn with grey to black sand like **Hapuna**, the island's largest. Ideal for bodysurfing or bodyboarding in the hollow dumpers plus a reef peak down the beach at this heavy, localised spot. **Anaehoomalu**, **Keawaiki** and **Kiholo** Bays lead onto the Kona Coast state park, allowing people to hike in to powerful, long, coral reefbreaks at **Mahailua** or Makalawena. **Pinetrees** is a quality wave-magnet, favouring lefts on any small to medium swell. **Banyans** is the locals favourite, shaping hollow rights in winter NW'ers and shorter lefts in summer souths. Kealakekua Bay is Hawaii's first surf beach, where competent surfers find a way out to **Ke'ei**'s fast breaking perfect lefts over shallow coral. On S swells, check spots around South Point like **Kahuku Ranch** where big, hairy peaks are offshore in NE trades and surf the long left pointbreak, sheltered from the trades, as is lonely **Kaalualu Point**. **Honuapo Bay** and **Punaluu** are easy access, messy, blown out, fairly mellow rides over rock and volcanic sand. On big S or SE swells, **Keauhou Point** holds long, walled-up lefts, or other peaks like Halape and Apua might work if it's big enough. **Pohoiki**'s three bays support some shallow lava reef rights and a left in bigger swells, but like **Kapoho Bay** further north, it's onshore in the trades. Hilo's strong wave-riding community remain cool at spots like **Richardsons**, where the mellow reefbreaks provide a good learning forum. At **Honolii Point** fast lefts and rights break into a rivermouth that is reliable in N-E swells and non trade winds. Check **Waipio Valley**'s black sand beachbreaks for quiet peaks but the hellish access road is 4WD material or a 1hr walk. **Kohala Lighthouse** is a good example of a secluded, localised hotspot. This classic left reefbreak is somewhat sheltered from NE trades despite its eastern location. Be very careful while parking there and keep a low profile.

Hawaii's winter swell supply is generally from the W-NW, but most NNW swells from 305° to 350° will suffer serious filtering on their way to Big Island shores. Only expect 3-12ft from October to March, NNE being the best directions for Hilo and Hamakua, or W swells for Kohala and Kona. NE-E trades bring a nearly constant supply of 1-5ft windswells, best surfed during winter SW kona winds. From April to September, South Pacific SW swells bring a regular supply of 2-8ft waves to the Kona, Kau and Puna areas. July to October is the hot period for East Pacific hurricanes pushing 3-8ft E-SE swells to Puna and Hilo, but there are also rare SW winter swells from SW Pacific cyclones. Because of the high mountains, it's offshore on both sides in the morning then Hamakua and Hilo get most of the onshore NE trades. 1m tidal range and tide times are different around the island.

| STATISTICS | | J F | M A | M J | J A | S O | N D |
|---|---|---|---|---|---|---|---|
| SWELL | Direction | | | | | | |
| | Size (ft) | 5-6 | 4 | 3-4 | 4 | 4-5 | 5-6 |
| WIND | Direction | | | | | | |
| | Force | F4 | F4 | F4 | F4 | F4 | F4 |
| WATER | Wetsuit | | | | | | |
| | Temp/°C | 24 | 23 | 25 | 26 | 27 | 25 |
| WEATHER | Rainfall/mm | 55 | 45 | 50 | 60 | 40 | 40 |
| | days/mth | 5 | 5 | 5 | 4 | 3 | 4 |
| | Min temp/°C | 18 | 18 | 20 | 21 | 20 | 19 |
| | Max temp/°C | 27 | 27 | 28 | 29 | 29 | 28 |

# Oahu HAWAII

Oahu is the third-largest Hawaiian island, yet it houses 70% of the state's population, attracted to the mix of spectacular, exotic scenery and the fantastic weather. Waikiki means "spouting waters", is the state's tourism mecca and the place where hundreds if not thousands of all kinds of waveriders are in the surf almost every day of the year, enjoying the fun, user-friendly conditions. Further afield there are some really good waves on the windward coast and a growing number of spots from Ewa Beach down south to the wild west coast where Makaha has already forged a famous reputation for everything from beginner curls to monstrous swells.

**+ CONSISTENT SWELLS**
**+ WORLD'S SURFING HERITAGE**
**+ BEGINNER-FRIENDLY WAIKIKI**
**+ PERFECT WEATHER**

**- MESSY WINDSWELLS**
**- INTENSE CROWDS & LOCALS**
**- SOME POLLUTION & SHARKS**
**- EXPENSIVE, LONG-HAUL**

## TRAVEL INFORMATION

**Weather** – Waikiki is situated on a drier narrow plain between the ocean and the Ko'olau mountain range that serves to block trade wind moisture. Warm, balmy weather year-round from 19-27°C (66-80°F) in winter to 21-30°C (70-86°F) in summer. From October to April, 3 or 4 kona storms (SW-W) bring hot, sticky air and thunderstorm activity, often with gusty winds and days of rain. Morning offshores descend from the interior mountains, before the perennial NE-E trade winds arrive, blowing hardest in summer. Boardshorts, year-round.

**Lodging and Food** – Boutique or historic hotels, condominiums, resorts and familiar chains; prices vary with the view. The Aloha Surf is a 3-star hotel: fr $145/nt dbl. Surfcondos fr $1500/wk for 4 pax. Every friday at camping. honolulu.gov you can reserve a campsite up to two weeks in advance (3d/$32, 5d/$52). No camping is allowed on either Wednesday or Thursday so 3-5 day max stay applies. Largest concentration of fancy restaurants and fast food in the state.

**Nature and Culture** – Being a prime honeymoon trip, Waikiki provides big-city amenities, shopping, culture and night-time entertainment. Honolulu was recently ranked first among America's largest cities for having the cleanest air and water, and the lowest crime rate. Visit the Bishop Museum for its archive of historical surf artefacts.

**Hazards and Hassles** – Sharp coral reefs and unpredictable shorebreaks have caused many serious neck and spinal injuries to all kinds of surfers. Strong currents frequently accompany big surf. Theft from cars is common at many of the bigger parking lots in and out of town. Localism also exists on the south shore - tread carefully.

**Handy Hints** – World famous Waikiki Beach Boys offer daily surf lessons & outrigger canoe rides. Low board hire rates from a huge number of surf shops and rental outfits; Standard NSP board ($45 for first 2 days then $10/day). Surftech Performance rental ($65/2 days then $10/day). SUP from $100/2 days then $20 a day. Delivery and pick up from anywhere on the island.

West Oahu

FABIEN HAEGELE

SEAN DAVEY

## THE WEST COAST

The Farrington Highway winds north to its denouement at Kaena Point, passing some pretty, rock-shrouded sands at Keaau Beach Park and Makua before skirting the SW-facing bay at **Yokohama**. While the scenery is relaxing, this wave is high octane, with fast, thumping lefts on a SW swell and just as angry rights on a NW. Only the swift need apply to try to get in quick enough and race it over the mosaic of coral heads, that are best covered at mid tide. There are four distinct breaks at **Makaha**: the Point, the Bowl, the Blowhole and the Inside Reef. Rideable at any size, these epic rights become a serious challenge over 10ft. Below that size there is something for everyone with inside rollers picked over by the groms, a nice left off the middle peak for the goofys, long wrapping walls for the charging longboarders and short sharp barrels for the shredders. Out on the point in a solid NW it's a committed, heart-stopping drop, then a full-bore race ahead of (or under) the axing lip towards the Bowl which may just turn into a cement-mixer close-out. With some luck it can link and reform all the way to shore, but watch out for backwash. Higher tides are preferred and getting caught inside over the reef can be a shallow, skin-threatening experience. Intermediates on small swells, experts with extra testosterone on the dig days. Visiting haoles (whites) need to be very respectful of the tight-knit Hawaiian families that live and play in Makaha. Featuring canoe, tandem, stand-up, bodysurfing and longboards over 10 feet, it brings together the entire community. Klausmeyers chunky lefts sit on the opposite side of the bay. The protected, fun reforms of **Rest Camp** in Pokai Bay are a laid-back option, unlike Sewers speedy rights in Waianae. **Maili Point** gets screaming fast lefts over shallow coral on bigger SW-W swell with trades. It breaks a long way offshore and shifts around, with regular clean-up sets. Entry and exit is a real rock dance, currents and sharks sweep the point, but the locals are usually on it. In Kahe Beach Park, **Tracks** long reef with a sandy inside produces lefts on S-SW swells, while good punchy rights break on NW-N swells. The main peak down near the power plant outputs electric rights and longer lefts, which are absorbed by a dominant pack of locals that have the place wired. There are some lesser peaks north towards Nanakuli and it's pretty much offshore here year-round. In Kalaeloa near the Campbell industrial park, **Barbers Point** sees lengthy lefts on headhigh S swells or broken up peaks on wrapping 3-5ft NW-N and W swells. Kauai blocks a bit of the NW, but there is usually some action here where the trades are offshore for the lefts further west or N winds are good around the lighthouse. The coral reef is strewn with rocky outcrops and entry and exit can be fraught depending on where along the curving coast the waves are best. Crowds and attitude are minimal while numbers of sharks spotted from the flights into the Kalaeloa airport are maximal! **White Plains Beach** could rival Waikiki as the best learning beach on the rock. It has lots of things going for it like fun, friendly, rolling peaks that are constantly reforming and running left or right across the flat dead coral shelf, which often has a nice dusting of sand over it. It's a super-wide playing field, soaking up swarms

SEE NORTH SHORE PAGE 287

7th Hole
Goat Island/ Mokuauia
PCC
Pounders
Crouching Lion
Pyramids
North Beach
Kailua Bay
Makapu'u
Sandy Beach
Yokohama
Makaha
Rest Camp
Maili Point
Tracks
Barbers Point
White Plains Beach
Ewa Beach Park

Pupukea
Waimea Bay
Waimea
Kahuku
Laie
Hauula
Punaluu
Puaena Point
Waialua Bay
Haleiwa
Waialua
Mokuleia
Kaena Point
Kaaawa
Wahiawa
Schofield Barracks
Waianae Mountain Range
Waikane
Kahaluu
Kane'ohe Bay
Kane'ohe Marine Corps Air Station
Moku Manu Island
Mokapu Point
Mokapu
Kailua
Kaneohe
Moku Lua Islands
Bellows Air Force Station
Makaha
Pokai Bay
Waianae
Maili
Maili Point
Nanakuli
Mililani
Pearl City
Waipahu
Pearl Harbour Naval Base
Kahe Point
Ko'olina
Barbers Point Naval Air Station
Ewa
Ewa Beach
Barbers Point
Honolulu International Airport
Mamala Bay
Honolulu
Kahala
Waikiki
Maunalua Bay
Hawai'i kai
Hanauma Bay
Ko'olau Mountain Range
Waimanalo Bay
Makapu'u Point

SEE SOUTH SHORE

### Ala Moana Bowls

LAT. 21.280296° LONG. -157.844067°

Long, shacking lefts peel down a shallow reef outside the Ala Wai Harbor. The wave was created by dredging a deepwater channel for boats to access the harbour and S swell will refract out of the channel and wedge up along the reef. Think big, round curves as it bowls over sections of reef, shoulders off, then gathers up another barrel section on the shallow inside. One of the best waves on Oahu, attracting many of the best surfers in Town, who don't often feel the need to share. Try the lesser rights or further down the reef at Rockpiles or Inbetweens in smaller swells. Paddle out from Magic Island when it's big or straight into the channel when small. Lower tides, not too much E in the swell and any wind with a sniff of N in it, although E is still OK. Can be consistent in summer, sometimes breaking every day for a month, but winter can be very patchy. This break ticks all the hazard boxes. Currents sweep the channel, as do large sharks and vessels, while the ugly sharp coral reef, urchins and maybe even the rusty remnants of the navigation pole all conspire to take their pound of flesh. Then there's the expensive parking, long paddle, locals, etc, etc!

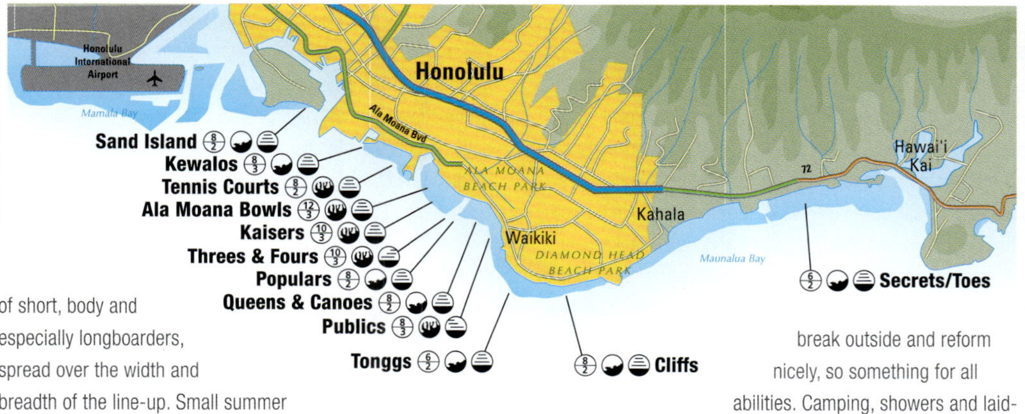


of short, body and especially longboarders, spread over the width and breadth of the line-up. Small summer swells and any N winds are ideal, although outside reefs will handle much bigger, but getting there is an ordeal as there are no defined channels and this place breaks with complete randomness. Massive parking lot fills up with families attracted to the excellent facilities including shops, shady picnic spots, BBQ pits, showers, etc. Always crowded in summer, but the vibe is friendly among the many servicemen and locals who regularly surf here. At Oneula Beach Park, Sandtracks will have rights on slack wind days. Around the rocky shoreline is Coves, where shortboarders can often find a punchier left at mid to high tide, plus some rights in the mixed-up line-up. Crowds aren't usually a problem but car security is. Further east are a bunch of localised spots like Lots, Shark Country and Haubush. **Ewa Beach Park** is a long SE-facing stretch with wind exposed sandbar and reefbreaks that only clean up on N winds. Size can be deceptive and there can be some long rides when it reforms and doubles-up through the inside. The military suburbs of Iroquois Point hold some appropriately named breaks like Marine Beach and Tank Traps near the entrance to Pearl Harbor.

## THE SOUTH SHORE – HONALULU

Screened by the hulking warehouses and shipyards on the industrialised **Sand Island**, this State Recreation Area and its brilliant white ribbon of sand holds a mish-mash of reefy peaks. Mainly surfed at the east end near the tower where waves can break outside and reform nicely, so something for all abilities. Camping, showers and laid-back uncrowded feel. **Kewalos** is super-consistent, dragging in swell toward the deep Kewalo Basin channel before unleashing a hollow, bad-tempered left that barrels, sections and shuts down with unpredictable regularity, shifting around the line-up and keeping the throng on their toes. The rights can also barrel, but quickly lead to shallow close-outs. Picks up all S and likes the angle from the E quadrant. Sharks are often spotted, lots of fishing boat traffic, some pollution and really nasty coral heads by the rip torn channel. Point Panic is across the channel, a mesmerizing, metronomic right tube that is reserved for the speedo and fin set, seen skillfully pirouetting and planing close to the rock seawall, as seen in the seminal bodysurf film *Come Hell or High Water.* **Tennis Courts** is a fun-filled, hot-dogging righthander that may start off a little slower for the longboard

ANDREW SHIELD

Queens

Queens to Tonggs

SEAN DAVEY

crew, but is soon racing and barreling over the inside double-up section. Likes S to W overhead swell, N winds and lower tides, while a SE swell will make the short, shouldering lefts a bit more interesting. Nearby various other named spots line the reef like Concession, Big Rights, Big Lefts and Little Haleiwa with Bomboras further out off the tip of Magic Island. Confident and patient surfers with a low profile may just have a chance of snagging a wave at the infamous ✪**Ala Moana Bowls**. From the Bowl more peaks comb the coral all the way down through Inbetweens and Rockpile to **Kaisers** where a superb right was created for tube-junkies not fazed by shallow coral, shipwrecks and a carpet of urchins when a channel was blown in the coral reef for boat access. The lefts are less intense but still worthy. **Threes and Fours** are a fair way from the beach, but this does little to dampen the crowd that rate Threes as one of the go to spots in a good S swell. Speed runs into some hollow sections end in a defined channel and then it's an easy paddle back out. Fours is more sectiony, with some cruisier lefts heading back towards Kaisers. **Populars** has slightly less crowded and less localised rights that run down the reef nicely in SE-S swells. There's a paddling channel to the right of the break and some shorter soft lefts. Further Inside **Queens** & **Canoes** are fabled, fun, Waikiki reefs packed with all kinds of surf crafts. Queen's rights offer ripable walls up to 6ft over forgiving reef, while Canoes can handle bigger, mushier waves for longboarders and learners. No danger from the reef but getting mowed down by anything from a soft top to an outrigger is real and present. Neither like big swell or wind and it is fair to say this could be the most crowded line-up on the planet most days. Named after a long gone public baths, **Publics** are the easy to spot left lines hugging the fringe of shallow reef on the east flank of Waikiki. Not for the unskilled, unlike further up the reef where the small swell spot Old Mans will have a mellow crowd on all craft. The lefts at **Tonggs** are improver-friendly with the odd hollow section as it doubles-up over the uneven coral. The right is faster before closing-out, while the left fades out in a deeper channel. All the breaks around Tonggs (Lighthouse, Graveyards, Suicide, Rice Bowl) handle NE trades much better than Cliffs. Paddle out from the tiny beach off of Kalakaua. Below the Diamond Head Rd lookouts, **Cliffs** is a scattering of 5-6 reefs and channels with consistently long walls that absorb the crowds of surfers and kites. Picks up S and E swell, so it's messy in trades, but it can be classic on N or glassy days and is often the biggest South shore spot. Near Kawaiku'i Beach Park, check the uncrowded offshore reefs of **Secrets** long rights & good shortboard lefts on high tide, plus **Toes** longboard peak when winds are calm or N.

## THE EAST COAST

**Sandy Beach** is a neck-breaking shorebreak for crazy, talented lids and fins on any E to S swell. Boards can head outside for the shallow left reef, which is usually blown to pieces by the trades. Arguably Oahu's best bodysurf/bodyboard spot, **Makapu'u Beach** has long trundling lefts ending in a huge shorebreak barrel that works best in winter with E swell and opposing winds. Really strong currents preside, keeping the lifeguards busy, who police the no surfboards policy at the Beach Park, but allow standups to take on the heavy barreling right over the lava shelf at Makapu'u Point, in front of Sea Life Park. It's also worth being curious about Rabbit Island in bigger NE swells. **Kailua Bay** is usually better suited for kitesurfing, but will hold a reef peak at the north end around Dunes Circle Dr. It's best on E swells and Kona W winds or try over at **North Beach** and **Pyramids** if it blows more from the S. Consistency is moderate at best and deteriorates as you head further north into the teeth of the trades where a scattering of breaks occasionally produce the goods at **Crouching Lion**, a right reef flanking Kahana Bay, or **Pounders** bodyboard wedges, that slam the sand in front of the cliffs at Laie Beach Park. Both **PCC** and **Goat Island** have exposed reefbreaks that are rarely clean, but most people come here to visit the biggest tourist destination on Oahu, namely the Polynesian Cultural Center. Final stop on the windward coast is the Kahuku Golf Course Beach where the **7th Hole** just may be worth the drive!

Between the prime South Shore months of April and October, South Pacific swells travel great distances with very long 14-22 sec wave periods, but small wave heights (1-4 ft). These groundswells are far from reliable and usually only last a couple of days, before the constant ENE trade wind swell returns to dominance. Wave height ranges from 4-12ft with short 5-8 sec periods. This will show up on the windward coast all the way round to Diamond Head, plus the Kaena Pt to Mokuleia stretch. North Pacific swells deliver the highest waves (8-20ft) with mid-to-long 10-18 second wave periods mostly from Oct - May. W-N direction will hit the leeward coast (although Kuaui does filter some swell) and spots like Makaha get famously big. This side of the island breaks year-round since it also picks up summer S swells. Waves from winter kona storms associated with fronts passing just north of Hawaii are very steep with moderate heights (10-15ft) and short to medium 8-10 sec periods. Kona storm waves have the greatest impact on south and west-facing coasts, but the associated winds mean it's prime time for the windward coasts. Waves from hurricanes and tropical storms (June-November) can reach extreme heights (10-35ft) and occur mostly on east, south and west-facing shores. The metronomic ENE trade winds rarely falter, gathering pace in summer and bending down the backside of Diamond Head, fanning Waikiki and the west coast with virtually permanent offshores. The micro tides make quite a difference to a select few South Shore breaks, but most spots are considered all tides, with high being a little mushier in most cases.

| STATISTICS | | J F | M A | M J | J A | S O | N D |
|---|---|---|---|---|---|---|---|
| SWELL | Direction | | | | | | |
| | Size (ft) | 5-6 | 4-5 | 2-3 | 4-5 | 5 | 5-6 |
| WIND | Direction | | | | | | |
| | Force | F4 | F4 | F4 | F4 | F4 | F4 |
| WATER | Wetsuit | | | | | | |
| | Temp/°C | 24 | 24 | 25 | 26 | 27 | 25 |
| WEATHER | Rainfall/mm | 104 | 86 | 43 | 43 | 65 | 108 |
| | days/mth | 10 | 9 | 8 | 8 | 9 | 11 |
| | Min temp/°C | 19 | 19 | 21 | 23 | 22 | 20 |
| | Max temp/°C | 25 | 27 | 29 | 29 | 30 | 28 |

Sandy Beach

LAURENT MASUREL

# Oahu North Shore HAWAII

There is no denying that the North Shore of Oahu is surfing's Mecca. Its undisputed attractions challenge every surfer on the planet, including all the pros, to find out if they have got what it takes. Conquering the fear of dropping into a bomb at Pipe, or paddling over the edge of a Waimea cliff represent the zenith of the surfing experience. There's no continental shelf or barrier reef to dampen the force of the powerful swells that come thundering out of the North Pacific and slam into the world's most famous surf zone. Reverentially dubbed 'The Seven Mile Miracle' this short, savage coastline between Haleiwa and Velzyland has it all from kiddies reforms to tow-in monsters. Most spots break on lava reef close to golden sand beaches with deep channels, which make paddling out easier but also create some strong rips in larger surf.

+ THE PROVING GROUND
+ SEVEN MILE MIRACLE
+ MYTHICAL SURF CULTURE
+ GREAT SPECTATOR ARENA

- DANGEROUS CONDITIONS
- AMAZING CROWD PRESSURES
- NOT SUITABLE FOR BEGINNERS
- EXPENSIVE

The town of **Haleiwa** provides a variety of facilities and amenities and is the commercial centre of the North Shore as well as being the breeding ground for many of the best Hawaiian talents, both past and present. Pulling up at the Ali'i Beach Park on a small day may be deceptive as broken peaks look easy, but when an overhead W-NW swell hits, a challenging, powerful right jumps the reef, outputting lightning fast walls and hollow hooks through to a shallow, inside shutdown section called the Toilet Bowl. Crazy crowds are guaranteed as is getting plenty of sets on the head trying to fight the ever-present rip. The rights of **Puaena Point** (Puni's) break into the Haleiwa boat channel, offering protection from unruly N swells and gusty NE trades. After slamming the exposed outside point, swells filter into a shelf that sucks hard and barrels before letting up and drifting into the deep channel. NW swell and mid tide is best for the dominant right while lefts appear when the swell is more W. The rip can be nasty and sharks patrol the harbour entrance. All the information you need is in the name. **Avalanche** is a proper bombproof bombora, rearing up from the depths to rumble left into a death or occasional glory end shack section. Best watched from the safety of Haleiwa unless packing jet propulsion or equipment and attitude to handle the power rips, random set shifts and limitless size range. **Laniakea** is a rare righthander that can be perfect when a N swell meets a light E wind at mid tide. When it finally fires, surfers descend, looking for their share of one of the North Shore's best rights, as it combines down-the-line speed with cylindrical beauty, especially on the inside wedge sections. Some lefts in W swells as the line-up breaks up, but going against the grain will involve some punishment over a reef prone to baring its teeth above water-level. Way offshore from Lani's, a predominant left peak entices the self assured to take on this scary, shifting monster called **Himalayas**. W-NW swells will wall lengthy lefts, while N will see rights off the peak, throwing up wildly fluctuating wave-heights and only experienced watermen will handle the rips and clean-ups. **Jocko's** is a sucky affair when a W-NW swell unfurls over coral heads and a gruesome, lava rock-strewn reef. Both the take-off peaks are steep and rapid, leading to mist exhaling tubes or wailing speed walls to another inside bowl section before the safety of the deep channel. Bonus right off outside suck leads to a rocky minefield. Handles plenty of size until the channel closes out to Chun's and the really strong out-going rip makes getting back to the beach an effort. One of the more improver-friendly spots on the North Shore, **Chun's** welcomes any swell onto three sections of righthand reef. The outside, middle and bowl all feature nice roll-ins, shredable walls and some inviting tubes in places. Best on small NW swells with any trade wind direction and even

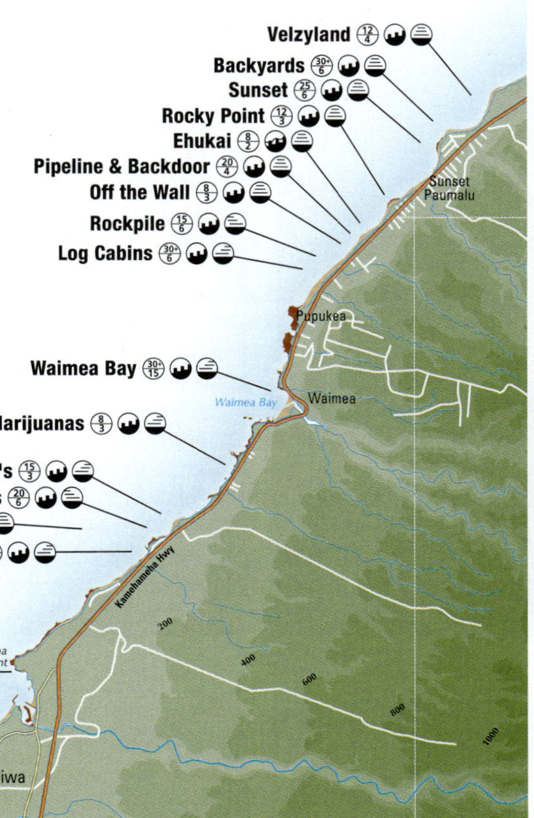


## TRAVEL INFORMATION

**Weather** – Between day and night, winter and summer, temps vary little from a near perfect 25°C (77°F). Sea surface water temps hover between 25-29°C (77-84°F), but winter kona fronts and a bit of upwelling will see lows of 24°C (75°F) at times. When NE-E trades blow, skies are usually clear.

**Lodging and Food** – The only North Shore hotel is the Turtle Bay Resort (from $199/n - 5th night free). Most people stay at Backpackers Vacation Inn and Plantation Village near Waimea (dorm bed from $27/n; private dbl rooms $62-$85/n; studio $120-$145/n; Cabins sleep 4-8p $160-$290; 10% off weekly rates.), B&B's in Haleiwa (fr $37/d) or rent a flat (from $600/w for 4 people). Winter is high season. Food is not cheap: $20 for a basic meal or buy it at Foodland.

**Nature and Culture** – Hike to Kaena Point or hit the Kahuku Sugarmill disco. Historic train tours through the Dole plantation outside of Haleiwa. The Hele Huli Adventure Center at Turtle Bay does surfing, stand up paddleboarding, golf, tennis, helicopter tours, horse riding, hiking, biking, fishing, glass bottom kayaking, whale watching and more. Check out the Polynesian Cultural Center, Oahu's biggest cultural attraction over on the windward side.

**Hazards and Hassles** – Drowning, collisions with the reef, heavy rips, flying boards and angry locals will all keep you on your toes! Surf the low-key spots and be patient and cautious in the line-up. Car rip-offs are common so leave nothing in it and leave it unlocked.

**Handy Hints** – Plenty of surf shops, both in Town (see South Shore) and Country (North Shore). Haleiwa has the biggest concentration; pick up a board designed for the local waves. Don't drop-in!

LAURENT MASUREL
Haleiwa

ANDREW SHIELD
Laniakea

LAURENT MASUREL

## ✪ Waimea

**LAT. 21.643213° LONG. -158.066465°**

**The benchmark, big-wave forum of Hawaii's North Shore. Deep water swells arrive suddenly, tripping on a lava shelf sitting a good 100m+ out from the northern headland. This creates a wave that lurches violently up, then out, resulting in the famous Waimea air drop take-off, followed by an endless plunge over boils, chops and gutters to the trough, then a race to the channel, chased by hundreds of tons of water. Strong trades, funneling down Waimea Valley are far from ideal, getting under the nose of your gun and holding you in a lip that's renowned for thick, high psi power, so light ESE wind is best, mid tide and a long period NW swell. On smaller days below 15ft, when The Bay proper isn't working, a sandbar and boulder section called Pinballs can reel off some juicy little pockets right along the lava rock point. Waimea's shorebreak is a gnarly mix of crashing lips and powerful pockets; once avoided, today it's packed with suicidal bodyboarders and even a few stand-up surfers. Getting in and out of the water requires timing through the shorebreak in the northern corner, while the overpowering current drags victims down to the jump rock. Crowds are thick, especially at the starting size around 15ft and sharing a set is common practice although flying boards and bodies heighten the risks. Specialist equipment, big wave experience and total commitment required.**

handles a bit of S wind. There's a sneaky left off the middle section, but the paddle back out is no fun. Absolutely always crowded since it's in full view of the Kam Highway, plus it's an easy, yet long paddle using the rip to the left. There are easier rolling waves to the north at Rightovers and Leftovers, plus some suckier action at Alligator Rock. Tricky, rock-hopping entry and exit keeps the crowds manageable. You would expect **Marijuanas** to be a mellow spot and compared to the smoking bombs further north it is, yet it can still spin off a speedy, walled right across a shallow-ish reef offering cover-ups and lip-bashing potential. Waist high to overhead NW swells and a bit of protection from the NE trades make it a tasty little number away from the crush. Halfway up the North Shore, the Kam Highway swings wide around a bay called ✪**Waimea** – the

Off-The -Wall

ANDREW SHIELD

spot that has set the standard for big wave surfing for over 50 years. **Log Cabins** is an underrated right that shifts around a lot over an ill-defined reef, relying on peaky N swells to prevent it from shutting down violently. It breaks over a treacherous lava bottom that has sharp, upthrusting fingers and sand fills the gaps in places. Way outside is Outer Log Cabins, a notorious tow-in reef that has held some of the biggest waves ever ridden. A good distance offshore lies a series of reefy protuberances that catch a NW swell and conduct it back towards Off-The-Wall in the shape of a meaty and often sketchy left. Heavily reliant on sand deposition, **Rockpiles** is notorious for lava fingers popping up when surfing it small, or when getting a beating paddling out. Therefore it's safer from mid and works in all N swell directions above headhigh and E-SE trades. There are some rights that head over towards Log Cabins, but the risk versus reward balance is all wrong. Crowds are lighter than Pipe, especially at size, but some say the consequences are heavier - be very sure of your ability. **Off-The-Wall** (a.k.a Kodak Reef) is the classic, high quality, super-crowded, right sprint that's been a favourite with photographers since the '70s. Separated from Pipe by a short channel, swells need to arrive with N in them to get the rights opening up over what is essentially a straight bit of reef. Shallow and unforgiving, but barrels guaranteed at mid-tide on an overhead NW swell. Smaller, less perfect lefts peel back towards Backdoor and may offer visitors more of a chance of actually catching a wave. ✪**Pipeline** & **Backdoor** form the most famous peak in the world. No other spot on earth quite matches the full Pipeline experience - the power, the barrels, the crowds, the glory, the humility......this is quintessential North Shore. Small day reef peaks at **Ehukai** offer some respite from the power of adrenaline-pumping surrounding waves, but not necessarily from the incessant crowds. Lefts and rights over the wildly uneven lava shelf can be hollow and epic when the sand has built up just right, giving less confident surfers a forum for turns, airs and barrels, when peaky headhigh N swells bounce around this Pupukea stretch that also includes the shallow spitting pits of Gas Chambers. All amenities at the Ehukai Beach Park area. The modest lava jut of **Rocky Point** is a swell magnet and a jam-packed theatre of progressive school surfing, logged by the ever-present surf photographers lining the beach. The rights reel off in N swells while the handful of speedy lefts prefer more W-NW. It's very consistent in all small to moderate swells and the curve of reef allows for some wind variation from NE-S depending on what section you are riding. Access path from the giant wood statue on Kamehameha Hwy. Past Kammieland, a fun near-shore peak opposite Kammies Market, the famous **Sunset Beach** starts its curve northwards. Incorporating Vals, Inside Bowl, West Peak, Middles and Sunset Point on the inside, this break has more personalities than reality TV. Under headhigh, NE windswell will still break at The Point, then overhead, W-NW swells start popping up over the fingers of reef at Middles, before double-overhead awakens Inside Bowl and maybe West Peak on a long period W-NW swell. Sunset's default mode is unpredictable as N swells will break up along the ragged hem of reef, while W will launch

JIMMY WILSON

## Pipeline

**LAT. 21.664939° LONG. -158.053075°**

**The most famous peak on the planet explodes onto an uneven, lava-slab reef a scant 80m offshore, forming the benchmark by which all other waves are measured. The left at Pipe is best awakened by swells with a generous helping of W in them, as too much N will cause a grisly shutdown over the dangerous, cave-pocked section of the reef. Outer reefs filter, bend and reform arriving swells, focusing energy and extra height on the peak, before abruptly releasing a lip that guillotines mercilessly along the first section until the explosion of spit heralds the shoulder and room for a turn or two. When the swell direction heads beyond NW, Backdoor swings open and welcomes the best tube-jockeys to an expansive room, but the door often slams shut across this tract of ultra-shallow, incongruous reef. Air drops are the only way in if you want the inside at Backdoor and ideal conditions include mid tide, ESE wind and headhigh to double-overhead faces (3-6ft Hawaiian). The lack of a paddling channel means it's often better to take the rip north and utilise the more defined access to the left, but expect serious beatings from the steroidal lips and whitewash. The legion of hazards is eclipsed by one defining factor - the crowd. This is the most sought after ride on the planet and normal rules don't apply. Avoid speculation, hesitation, lip-launches, trips over the falls and eye contact with the crew who will burn you into the pit of Pipeline purgatory.**

threatening slabs from wide, punishing the reckless in the turbulent inside. When the long, roller-coaster rights lead into the hollow Inside Bowl, board, leash and body snapping power is apparent, with many shutdowns and unmakeable sections before the wave fattens out into the channel. The real difficulty is trying to get a bomb set off the entrenched local crew on large boards who dominate, leaving mere mortals to dodge the bullets on the inside. 15ft Hawaiian for upper size limit when Outside Backyards sets start to wash through. Rips, phantom sets and the wide playing field help dismantle the pack. Shallow when small at The Point, but it is rare to bounce at size when depth increases and hold-downs are long rag-doll affairs in mid water at the West Bowl. Scattergun peaks stalk the exposed, wide reef flanking Sunset, providing a crowd-free option for those willing to take the inevitable beating **Backyards** is famous for. Extremely hard for paddle surfers to manage, it has become the domain of wind, kite and tow surfers when the swell jumps up. Outside Backyards will suck in more ocean swell than Waimea and 50ft + faces are on the cards. Shallow, urchin-covered reef adds to the heaviness. Almost a mile north of Sunset is **Velzyland**, perhaps the most localised and intensely crowded spot on the strip. Outer reefs like Phantoms filter the swell size before it reforms and lurches onto a sharp lava reef, spinning fast right bowls and shreddable walls before hitting a positively square inside barrel section. Less competitive, shorter lefts can be had, but there's no paddle channel to get back out. Mid tide, light SE and small to medium NW swell best. Experts or pros only and intermediates will be better off at Freddyland across the channel.

The winter season can extend as far as from Oct to May, but January holds the aces in the historical stats. Average swell height is 12ft, average period is 12secs and there are virtually no flat days! Peaks hit 27ft and 18secs respectively and the dominant E wind gusts to 20mph (32kmh) at least 1 day in 3. November, December and February figures are very similar, just a little less swell consistency and a bit more NE wind. From April to September, the North Shore is generally flat. NE wind is more sideshore, so if it gets strong, it will mess up the waves. S-W kona winds occur periodically in winter when a large frontal system associated with a deep low pressure appears to the W or NW of Hawaii. This can bring large swells, accompanied by wind and rain for a day or two before returning to trade winds from the opposite direction. While the max tidal range at Haleiwa never exceeds 2ft (0.6m), it is enough to cause real changes at many breaks.

GRANT ELLIS

Sunset and Backyards

| STATISTICS | | J F | M A | M J | J A | S O | N D |
|---|---|---|---|---|---|---|---|
| SWELL | Direction | | | | | | |
| | Size (ft) | 8-9 | 6-7 | 3-4 | 1-2 | 4-5 | 7-8 |
| WIND | Direction | | | | | | |
| | Force | F4 | F4 | F4 | F4 | F4 | F4 |
| WATER | Wetsuit | | | | | | |
| | Temp/°C | 24 | 24 | 25 | 26 | 27 | 25 |
| WEATHER | Rainfall/mm | 90 | 55 | 17 | 18 | 35 | 65 |
| | days/mth | 8 | 7 | 5 | 6 | 6 | 9 |
| | Min temp/°C | 19 | 19 | 21 | 23 | 22 | 20 |
| | Max temp/°C | 26 | 27 | 29 | 29 | 30 | 27 |

# Northwest Maui HAWAII

The legendary rights of Honolua and Maalaea are part of surfing's heritage and now Jaws, the biggest name of all can be added to Maui's list of insane waves. It's an island of contrasts, where lush green valleys give way to arid coastline, tropical fruits and flowers meet barren lava and cactus, beneath the towering peaks that dominate the landscape. The shroud of islands that include Molokai, Lanai and Kahoolawe block out some swell directions and there is an element of real luck and timing to score the big names, but there is a back-up cast of consistent, quality waves just waiting to keep the locals and visitors stoked.

+ WORLD-CLASS SPOTS
+ THINNER CROWDS THAN OAHU
+ WIND/KITESURFING HEAVEN
+ AMAZING VOLCANIC SCENERY

- SWELL SHADOWS
- STRONG TRADE WINDS
- SOME DIFFICULT ACCESS
- HIGH PRICES

JEREMIAH KLEIN

Honolua Bay

One of Hawaii's most famous summer spots is **Maalaea**, where a harbour breakwall has created a righthand wave that's considered to be the fastest in the world, but it needs a huge S-SW swell to break and is notoriously fickle. Use an F1 fast board to make the drop, bottom turn and pump into a racetrack so crowded that there will probably be someone dropping in with that chandelier section up ahead. Lahaina breaks all suffer from the split swell window so **Shark Pit**'s shallow, slabbing lefts like the S-SW swells more and the less hectic rights prefer the N swells. **Lahaina Breakwall** is an excellent, swell-sucking reef that squeezes snappy left walls and tubes from a S-SW pulse and high performance rights when winter N penetrates the narrow gap between Maui and Molokai. At **Lahaina Harbour** SW or N swells awaken either low tide rights into the busy boat channel or rapid lefthand, high tide walls. **Mala Wharf** is a popular longboard and intermediate spot on both S or N swells, as it spokes around a reef opposite the disused concrete pier and shoulders off into deeper water. Roping rights skirt the reef at **Rainbows** on winter pulses from the north, serving up some barrel action and grunty hooks, plus a shorter, bonus left barrel. Just south is Osterizers, another crisp A-frame that will always have some takers. **S-Turns** clutch of lava and coral reefs offer some nice peaks in less than perfect conditions and away from the heavy crowds of the surrounding well-known spots. **Little Makaha** can do a fair impression of its Oahu namesake, with sharp drops into bowly sections down a long point-style reef on the right N swell day when E-SE trades groom the mid tide sessions. A combination of length and ultra-round cylindrical sections set in the beautiful, cliff-lined amphitheatre of **Honolua Bay** make it the most coveted of Maui spots. The first section, Coconuts, breaks in front of the cliffs with the most size, accompanied by the most wind as the trades are funnelled down the valley. It then hits Outside, a classic barrel before propelling the lucky towards Cave, the hollowest and most crowded section, where it loses size leading into the inner Keiki Bowl. The Bay works on NNE, N, NNW and W swell, while NW swells are blocked by Molokai unless it is big enough to wrap. Honolua is definitely a wave for only the most experienced surfers. The intensity of the crowds matches the North Shore. The clue is in the name and **Windmills** is very exposed to all wind and swell at this due north-facing set of reefs. Long lefts and a couple of rights pound the rocky shoreline and really need calm winds or light S quadrant. Good check on small windswells, but still for advanced riders only, especially at size. A track runs down to a steep and deep bay at **Honokohau**, where a righthand boulder-strewn reef to the east and some lefts on the other side, will both break on any N swell. By no means perfect and maxes out when above double overhead, but a fun and changeable line-up without the thick crowds of other waves. Watch out for rocks and strong rips at size. **Waihee** is a broad amalgam of reefy peaks just off the golf course north of Kahului. Aspect means the trades mash the waves so early or kona winds required. Intermediate spot. The built-up area of Kahului has some basic boulder beach peaks at **Waiehu**, but just to the south, a brace of heavy localised reefs take plenty of N-NE swell, but need S-W winds. If the trades are blowing and the swell is maxing, there just might be a clean wave inside the Kahului Harbor, just a mile south. Water quality not great in this area. **Kanaha** is the start of the wind corridor, attracting kite and windsurfers to this north-facing stretch of coast near the airport. Usually messy wild peaks roll onto the cross-shore outside reefs for the wind crew, but kona winds can transform both Kanaha and the better reefs up at **Sprecklesville** into picture perfect left and right walls with tube opportunities. Cleans up a treat in S-W kona winds and gives intermediates a real run for their money. All

## TRAVEL INFORMATION

**Weather** – Between day and night, winter and summer, temps vary little from a near perfect 25°C (77°F). It's the same story in the water, which hovers around 24°C (75°F) year-round. The winter surf season has rainy periods, especially on S winds. When NE-E trades blow, skies are usually clear. The west shore is much drier than the easterly windward coast.

**Lodging and Food** – Accommodation prices are generally higher on Maui than Oahu. Good bases are Haiku or Paia near Hookipa in winter or Lahaina will have plenty of options in summer like Nani Kai Hale (fr $135 dbl). There are a couple of County Parks for camping near Hookipa. Avoid the low surf, tourist resorts on the SW coast around Kihei. Food is also pricey ($35+ per meal) so self catering is a good idea.

**Nature and Culture** – Haleakala Crater is the world's largest dormant volcano - see the sunrise from the summit. Flat-day activities include mountain biking, windsurfing, diving, and whale watching. For nightlife, head to Lahaina or Kaanapali.

**Hazards and Hassles** – To avoid trouble with the locals, don't surf the big name spots at the busiest times of the day. Don't leave valuables visible in your car.

**Handy Hints** – There are plenty of surf shops in Paia, including Da Kine, Hana Highway Surf and Honolua Surf Co, or Ole's in Lahaina, run by legendary shaper Bob Olsen. Honolua and others are real board snapping spots. Beginners should head to Nancy Emerson's surf school (fr $50/hr).

DAMIEN POULLENOT

Hookipa

tides, but higher will see less tubes and close-outs. **Baldwin Beach** is a real assortment of waves for all types of crafts and abilities ranging from mushy longboard peaks to crunching shoredump. Absorbs plenty of crowd and wind, continuing to break during moderate trades. Consistently breaks through the tide up to headhigh, giving the beginners a chance over the sand and patchy reef foundation. There's more easy options next door at Paia Bay. **Kuau** is a proper all out barreling left that will challenge most accomplished surfers and often win, thanks to its shallow, unpredictable nature. Easily blown-out and lashed by currents, the long paddle keeps the local crowd down a bit. The sort of break where keeping your feet up seems a good idea. **Hookipa** is home to some of the best wavesailing in the world, so expect strong cross-shore trade winds on most days after 11am. Hookipa is the centre of kite/windsurfing activity in Hawaii, but on windless mornings, this clutch of quality reefbreaks is always rammed. Furthest west is Lanes lefts, then there's shallow rights and lefts at the Point, just next to the main peak of Middles. The sailors are usually forced downwind on the rights, leaving plenty of long, roping lefts for packs of surfers to fight over. Hookipa is super-consistent, year-round, evidenced by the constantly jammed car parks of the Hookipa Beach Park off the Hana Hwy. Rips, rocks and windy-rigs falling from a great height are all part of the deal. The **Pavilions** section runs down the eastern point, crouched out of the wind and walling up beautifully into the defined channel, making the paddle back out easy. Ultra-performance walls that can barrel off on low, over a well-covered reef. Won't handle above double overhead, when Middles starts motoring, and its fun, ripable nature makes it super-popular with the locals, to the exclusion of all others, including the windsurfers. Finally, ✪**Peahi – Jaws** qualifies as the biggest hot spot on the planet!

Unfortunately, Maui is sheltered from many of the big SW, W, and NW swells by the smaller neighbouring islands of Molokai, Lanai and Kahoolawe, and the Big Island creates a very large shadow for the rare SE hurricane generated swells from Central America. Maui receives less swell and more wind than the North Shore on Oahu, but figures for swell consistency are 99% from Nov to Feb, averaging 8-10ft at 12secs. ENE-E trades are dominant and strongest from May to Aug, but winds can be much lighter in the mornings. The N coast needs ESE-S quadrant, but they only blow for 19% of the time in mid winter. Tidal range is small, but can have a drastic effect on shallow spots. Tide tables are widely available in surf shops.

### ✪ Peahi – Jaws

**LAT. 20.941597° LONG. -156.259343°**

The most notorious spot on Maui is a wave most surfers are extremely unlikely to ride. With the development of tow-in surfing in the early 90's, Jaws burst onto the scene, amazing the world with the sheer magnitude of the waves that were being ridden there by a select group of windsurfing and surfing hell-men. As big wave surfing has developed, Jaws has maintained the biggest and baddest tag, providing numerous winners for the XXL awards in almost every category. Takes any N swell, with more W favouring the long lefts, but it is the perfect, house-sized right tubes that most people associate with Jaws. Other waves have been discovered that challenge Jaws on height supremacy, but few can match its steroidal perfection. If you are thinking of tackling this wave, you will need far more knowledge of the spot than we can fit here and proper big wave experience so as not to be a liability in the increasingly zooed line-up. A few of the hazards include trade wind cross-chop and large speed-bump ribs that traverse the face, swatting surfers like bugs on a windshield. The impact zone is a washing machine all the way to the cliffs, regularly pulverizing boards, skis and bodies. Then there's launching at Maliko Gulch, where punching in and out of the closed-out bay is a game of Russian roulette. Take binoculars, a long lens and watch from the cliffs.

| STATISTICS | | J F | M A | M J | J A | S O | N D |
|---|---|---|---|---|---|---|---|
| SWELL | Direction | | | | | | |
| | Size (ft) | 7 | 5 | 3-4 | 2-3 | 4-5 | 6 |
| WIND | Direction | | | | | | |
| | Force | F4 | F4 | F4 | F4 | F4 | F4 |
| WATER | Wetsuit | | | | | | |
| | Temp/°C | 24 | 24 | 25 | 26 | 27 | 25 |
| WEATHER | Rainfall/mm | 90 | 55 | 17 | 18 | 35 | 65 |
| | days/mth | 8 | 7 | 5 | 6 | 6 | 9 |
| | Min temp/°C | 19 | 19 | 21 | 23 | 22 | 20 |
| | Max temp/°C | 26 | 27 | 29 | 29 | 30 | 27 |

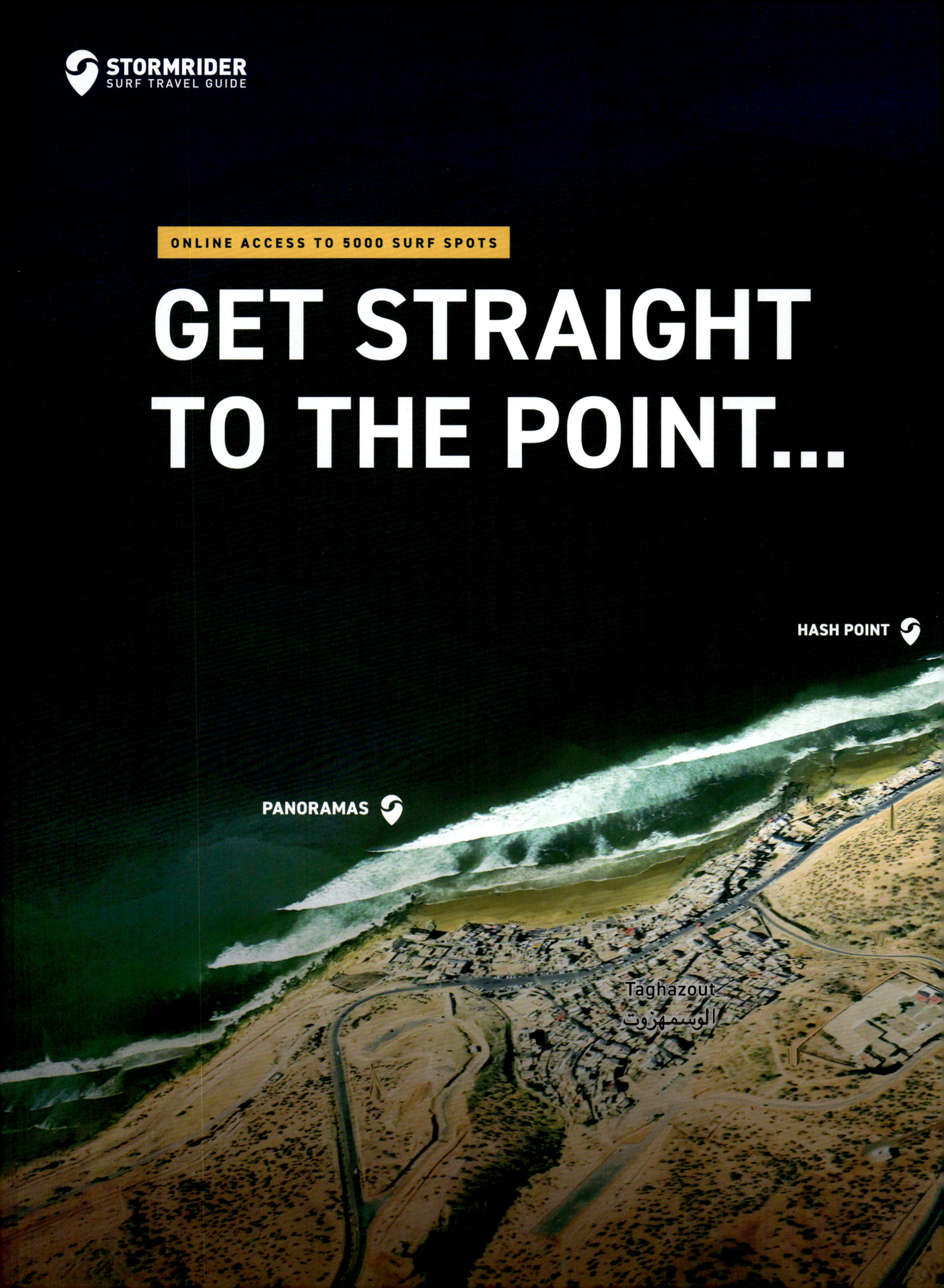
STORMRIDER
SURF TRAVEL GUIDE
ONLINE ACCESS TO 5000 SURF SPOTS
GET STRAIGHT
TO THE POINT...
HASH POINT
PANORAMAS
Taghazout

THE SOURCE
MYSTERIES
YOU ARE HERE
ANCHOR POINT
STORMRIDER
SURF TRAVEL GUIDE
Anchor Point, Taghazout
EXPLORE
RESOURCES
SHOP
DISCOVER YOUR PERFECT BREAK
CONTINENT
COUNTRY
TRAVEL DATE
WETSUIT
FILTER
→ STORMRIDERGUIDES.COM
EXPLORE

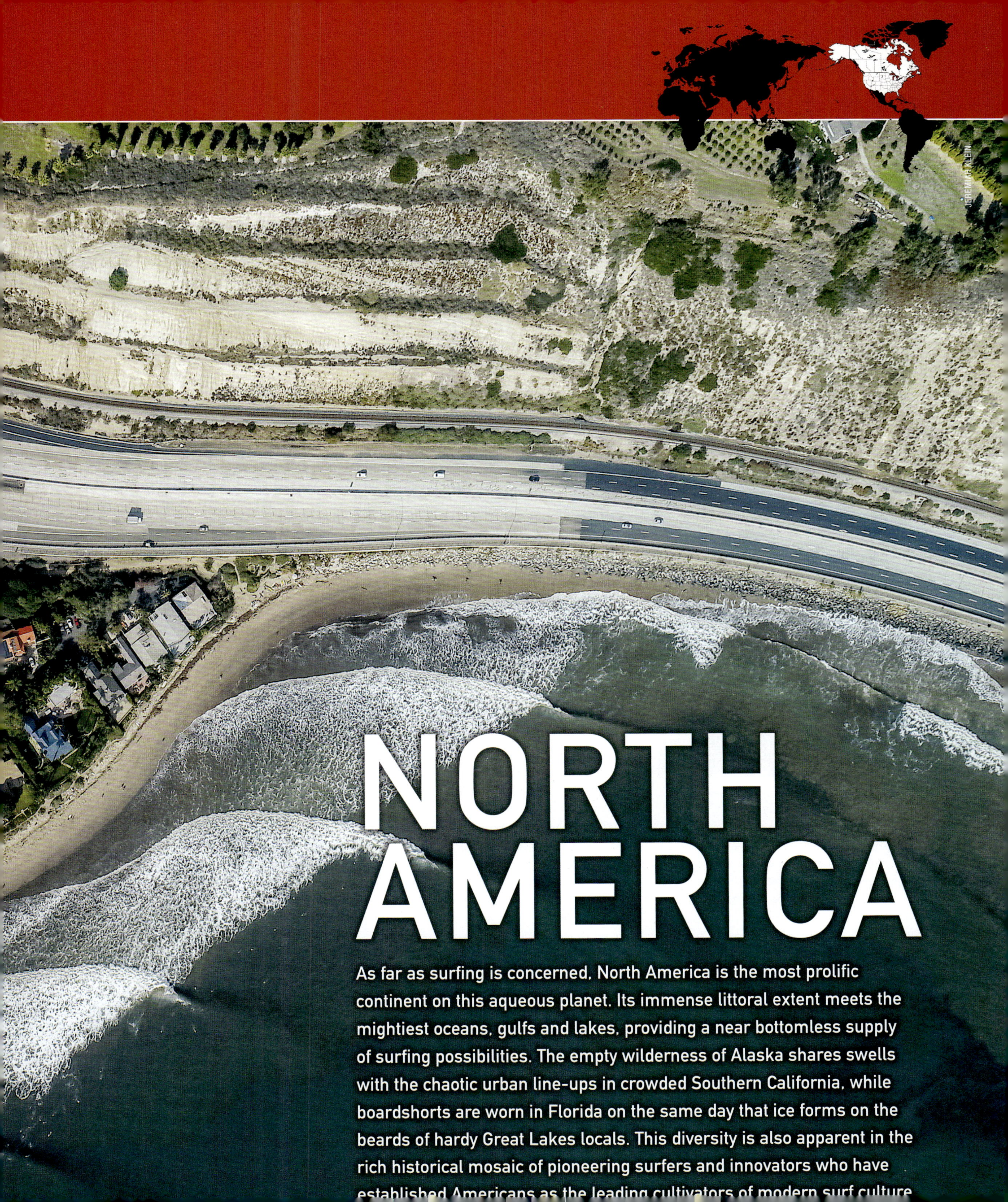

JEREMIAH KLEIN

# NORTH AMERICA

As far as surfing is concerned, North America is the most prolific continent on this aqueous planet. Its immense littoral extent meets the mightiest oceans, gulfs and lakes, providing a near bottomless supply of surfing possibilities. The empty wilderness of Alaska shares swells with the chaotic urban line-ups in crowded Southern California, while boardshorts are worn in Florida on the same day that ice forms on the beards of hardy Great Lakes locals. This diversity is also apparent in the rich historical mosaic of pioneering surfers and innovators who have established Americans as the leading cultivators of modern surf culture

# The Surf

MARK MCINNIS

British Columbia

MARK MCINNIS

Oregon

## THE PACIFIC NORTHWEST

**Alaska** is the USA's biggest state with its longest coastline (6,640mi/10,690km) yet it has barely been explored by the multitudes of US surfers living just down the coast in the Lower 48. Access is the key and flights or seasonal ferries provide the only viable means of transportation. This leaves thousands of watery miles to be mapped by surfers with a sturdy boat and complete faith in their ability to survive the cold, rain, fog, and fiercely unpredictable weather. Fortunately, the contorted coastline provides the shelter as bays, channels, estuaries, and fjord-like coves pock the islands and mainland, bending, refracting, and grooming unruly swells into more organised and manageable shapes. **The Aleutian Islands** get hit by serious swells, yet many expeditions have ended up getting no swell in the milder summer months. The north side is fully open to Bering Sea swells and spots on Adak have been surfed that work in NE swells. The Alaska Marine Highway ferry service runs from Seward to Unalaska twice a month in summer, briefly dropping in at tiny settlements along the Alaska Peninsula, throughout the 6 day return voyage. While it stops in the large fishing port of Dutch Harbor for 5-6 hours, it is not enough time to get wet despite there being some righthanders near the airport and a left spit in big N swells. Chartering a fishing vessel or quad bikes make it possible to search some of the Unalaska Bay coastline and great waves have been surfed to the east at road accessible Summer Bay, Morris Cove and Constantine Bays, but camping permits must be obtained from the Ounalashka land owners. One less worry for an expedition is the bare Aleutian landscape doesn't support any bears, unlike Kodiak Island that has perhaps the widest selection of readily accessible surf breaks in Alaska. Eastern Kenai Peninsula near Seward and the islands of Montague and Hinchinbrook do have surf potential and protect the Prince William Sound. Closer to Anchorage are some occasionally ridden waves in Homer, Nikiski and Anchor Point inside the Cook Inlet, which leads to the Turnagain Arm tidal bore in Girdwood. Located SE of Anchorage, huge 40ft (13m) tides flow into the Cook Inlet at a rate of 12 knots causing a wall of whitewater at Bird Point. 1-6ft waves can run for a couple of miles amongst the sand flats and channels, but sinking mud and viscous current makes this a dangerous thrill. The largest surfing community in Alaska (about 30 surfers) is now located in the remote town of Yakutat (pop. 600), home to good beachbreaks and a quality left on big swells. The **Southeast Alaska** coastline continues to provide an inexhaustible number of possible surf spots throughout the islands above the Canada border. Russian named islands like Chichagof, Kruzof and Baranof as well as the Prince of Wales and Outer Ketchikan areas present themselves as exploration areas. Sitka is the only population centre open to the Pacific and is the jumping off point for outer islands and has some road accessible surf to the south of town.

**British Columbia**'s western shores, from Queen Charlotte Islands in the north to Vancouver Island in the south, are closer to civilisation, but remain difficult to explore without concerted effort. The coastline north of Vancouver Island is akin to Alaska – under-explored and dotted with hundreds of islands and bays that will remain an area for boat exploration only. Part of the Queen Charlotte Islands is a world heritage site and access to many areas is by special permits only. The NW tip of **Vancouver Island** has inconsistent waves around Cape Scott at Lowrie and San Josef Bays, while Raft Cove is a hike-in bay with SW swell-pulling properties, but needs light or no winds. The tough access Nootka Trail boasts spectacular scenery and some surf breaks, at Bajo Beach where Calvin Creek waterfall cascades onto the sand, creating rivermouth peaks both sides and there are reefbreaks to the north. Surf huts are hidden in the woods nearby. Beano Creek also has river sculpted sandbars and is offshore in N winds.

Nested in the southern lee of Vancouver Island, **Washington** State appears strategically located to intercept the bountiful North Pacific storm pulses and transform them into great surf. The coastal angle evokes expectations of countless righthand point waves and huge, gnarly outer reef spots. Unfortunately, nothing could be further from the truth. While the Washington coast is indeed bombarded by an extravagance of winter swell, this rainy, bleak, shoreline offers just about the toughest and least rewarding wave grounds on the entire continent. Relentless storms bombard the Washington coast with huge swells, torrential rains, and wave-mangling S winds. There aren't too many places to hide, which is why many a Washington surfer seeks solace in the Strait of Juan de Fuca. Access is a problem to the few highly regarded surf spots, because entry is through tribal or private lands and past indiscretions have generally made surfers personae non gratae. The same applies at Washington's lost treasure, Point Grenville, a big headland that hooks out into the Pacific, interrupting the relentless NW winds and sheltering half a dozen tide dependant breaks under its southern flank. Located within the lands of Quinault Indian Nation, surfing is now banned thanks to bad behaviour in the past, trashing this beautiful corner of the coast. On the north side of the Grays Harbor inlet is Ocean Shores, a seaside town where the jetty creates a rare S wind block while leaving the way open to W and N swells plus some sandbars inside the entrance at Damon sandspit. Westport is the closest thing in the state to Surf City where the shelter of the long jetty can cut N winds in the corner or inside the estuary it's possible to enjoy smaller, cleaner swells, manicured by S winds. From Westport, it's mostly beachbreak south almost to the Columbia River. Not a lot of character – big beaches and nondescript sandbars open to the alternating surges of N and S winds, with only the occasional glassy or E wind day to set up some surfable peaks.

**Oregon** is a cold, wet, wild coast that is defined by a series of prominent headlands, rivermouths, vast coastal dunes, mighty spits and expansive beaches. The water's cold, there are lots of snappy white sharks, the wind and rain are intense and swells are often generated by storms so near to shore that it's hard to make it out through the short-period waves. Still, on a good day, surfing in Oregon can be as fun and rewarding as surfing anywhere in the world. Near the mouth of the Columbia River, Highway 101 connects the historic town of Astoria with the broad, sandy beaches of **North Oregon**. Highway 101 stays close to the coast leading into the surf hub of Lincoln City, with its surrounding beachbreaks and reefs, including big-wave comp spot Nelscott, then winds down through some lovely coastal geography past Boiler Bay, Otter Rock and the big beaches at Agate, which are both great learning spots. Then it's slim-pickings through the central coast from Waldport to Florence, where the jetties gentrify big swells between them or small summer pulses next to them in most directions and winds. Further south by the great dunes straddling Winchester Bay, the South Umpqua Jetty handles maximum beachbreak size, but not S winds. Coos Bay cradles a handful of popular breaks centred around Bastendorff Beach, benefiting from offshores when it blows S. From the NW exposed Bandon beaches out to the most westerly point at Cape Blanco is windblown until the south-facing hook of Port Orford. The southern corner of Oregon is a little more varied and esoteric, where both Gold Beach and Brookings offer attractive jetty protection and beachbreak peaks for all abilities when the wind cooperates.

## CALIFORNIA

**Northern California** is truly a land of feast or famine. The elements are harsh, the fickle reefs aren't perfect, the sandbars are temperamental and it's seemingly 20 feet and unrideable all winter. But classic days do exist and NorCal does occasionally serve up a heaping portion of coldwater perfection. **Del Norte County** starts with wide open miles of moody dune-backed beachbreak, accessed through the towns of Fort Dick and Smith River. The hub of the county's surfing is south-facing Crescent City, where popular South Beach is always a lot smaller and cleaner during the persistent N winds of spring. Otherwise it is mainly beachbreak that needs the small, clean windswells of summer to be manageable at spots like Wilson Creek, where the highway hits the sand. The second largest river in California empties at the Klamath Rivermouth, where the ever changing sandbars can be a barrel-fest, but the current and shark vibe are strong. Most of the **Humboldt County** coast is beachbreak, only surfable during small, clean swells, so during winter's big-time swells, surfers congregate at the jetties and points. South Humboldt has Shelter Cove, where a triad of boulder reefs keep the unfriendly locals happy in some seriously sharky waters. **Mendocino County** is not a stellar surfing destination and much of this coast is either inaccessible or unrideable. From Westport all the way south to Gualala, there are no world-class pointbreaks, reefs, or beachbreaks. On rare occasions during autumn or the smaller days of winter, surfers flock to North Mendocino spots like Virgin Creek and Chadbourne Gulch, but north of Westport, the forbidding cliffs of the Lost Coast remain unridden. Sheer cliffs and insanely rocky beaches are also the norm in South Mendocino, apart from a couple of fickle rivermouths. The main event is Point Arena where a thick, ledging righthander and a punchy left break on either side of the pier channels. The tranquil **Sonoma** coast has more quality wines than waves, since most of it is inaccessible or does not break at all due to deep water and sheer cliffs. The best spots (Secrets, Russian Rivermouth) are few and far between, so most surfers tend to congregate at all the same places. Salmon Creek is the county's best-known spot, where the beachbreaks are very consistent, but often junky. South-facing Doran Park is favoured by beginners thanks to its shallow, more graduated bottom and protection from the persistent NW winds. The fickle reefs are very tidally sensitive and many of the beachbreaks come up from deep water to throw treacherous shorepounds and don't break on small swell. **Marin** is the smallest of the NorCal counties and is also one of the sharkiest places on Earth. It is all beachbreak with rare exceptions and most of the county's shoreline is within the immense Point Reyes National Seashore. Point Reyes Beach is never flat, mostly messy and rippy, but a good option during the summer if the winds are calm. Bolinas is a hot area and does pull in the rare S swells, while nearby sheltered Stinson Beach catches more NW. Being first stop from the San Francisco Bay Area, Cronkhite Beach is by far the most crowded spot

**Central California** picks up the same swells and winds that buffet Northern Cal year-round, but here the coast angles a bit more to the SE, offering respite from the wind. Swell conditions can vary dramatically in a hurry – from too big to ride to small and piddly – while the weather will regularly switch from hot and sunny to cold and rainy with plenty of coastal fog sandwiched between. The City and County of **San Francisco** is a certified surfing metropolis, where you're only a few miles from a world-class beachbreak almost anywhere in the city. It's coupled with raw and rocky **San Mateo County**, home to huge-wave Mavericks. Surf-wise, **Santa Cruz** is just about the most diverse county in California and one of the most wave-rich areas on the entire West Coast. It's got the consistent, quirky reefs and beachbreaks of the north, user-friendly, ultra-clean and crowded points and reefs in '**Town**' and the powerful, uncrowded, often merciless beachbreaks of south county. There's always a wave somewhere, which translates into severely congested line-ups. In north county, Waddell, Scott Creek, Davenport, and Four Mile are all good options, offering anything from small, summer swell peaks to thick, sizeable reefbreaks and winter points. Just on the edge of town, crowds and quality increase at a handful of serious, hollow righthanders including Natural Bridges, Stockton Ave, Swift St and Mitchells Cove. South of town Manresa State Beach begins the beachbreak barrel-fest that crosses into **Monterey County** and one of the state's finest set-ups at Moss Landing, where a submarine canyon brings size and power to the expansive line-up. Winter storms are offshore at Lovers Point in Pacific Grove, while Asilomar and Spanish Bay are rarely flat, on the exclusive 17 Mile Drive toll road through the land of golf. Exclusive Carmel has a reliable, zippy beachbreak and sketchy surrounding reefs, before the world-famous, scenic route of Big Sur hugs the cliffs southwards. There are fickle, localised, semi-secret spots about, but the main access points have some good rides at Andrew Molera State Park, Sand Dollar Beach and Willow Creek. Kicked-back **San Luis Obispo County** is devoid of pointbreaks, though connoisseurs of fickle beachbreaks and quirky reefs will find something to ride. Very consistent in terms of swell and onshore wind, SLO has few sheltered spots and a lot of hit-and-miss reefs and beachbreaks, like the northern sand-slammers of San Carpoforo and Lighthouse. San Simeon's maddeningly volatile surf breaks, make Pico Creek the popular spot for fun sand and reef rights along with Santa Rosa Creek/Moonstone. Random, medium-quality reefs and spotty beachbreaks line the Highway 1 coast down through Cambria. Morro Bay occasionally converts an ordinary California

AL MACKINNON

Cortes Bank

RYAN CRAIG

Orange County

beachbreak into a magical mile or two of feathering A-frames and vomiting tubes. Hazard Canyon is a 24-karat spot and one of the most well-known breaks in California – a serious righthand reef with a legendary local posse. Neither Avila, Shell Beach, Pismo, or Oceano offer much in the way of perfection, but the Pismo Beach Pier is the hub of south-county surfing.

**Southern California** is the birthplace of modern surf culture and the surf industry. In SoCal, the water's relatively warm, the waves are generally small and forgiving and the weather's hard to beat. Just ignore that it's a vastly overpopulated concrete jungle, pulsing with rampant development, traffic jams and ever-thickening swarms of surfers. **Santa Barbara County** is cleaved in two, the north essentially a wind and swell exposed coast where powerful, gnarly beachbreaks offer isolated options at Santa Maria and cross-shore kiting spot Jalama, while round Pt Conception, south-facing Santa Barbara is all offshores and righthand points. **Ventura County** suffers less from the swell filtering capabilities of the Channel Islands, which hold some quality surf for the fishermen and boaters who don't mind taking a chance as shark bait. Santa Cruz, Santa Rosa, and San Miguel Islands have spots that take both winter N and summer S swells. A few spots sit on the border of Ventura and Santa Monica including crowded rights at County Line and Secos, which both get smoothed by the kelp on W or S swells. Zuma is a punchy sucky beachbreak at times, with a rocky right at Trancas and offshores funnelling down the canyons. With options from big-wave bays to the most gutless longboard reefs, **Los Angeles County** has all the bases covered and picks up a tad more swell than San Diego and Orange counties, especially around the Palos Verdes Peninsula. Most of LA is beachbreak; you can cruise for hours looking for a wave that holds up longer than five seconds, before the onshore wind hits at about 11am. A mixed bag, preferring SW pulses and zero wind, **Orange County** is more of a summer, small-wave beachbreak frontier. Due to island shadowing, N-NW swells miss large sections of coast as do WSW swells around Huntington. Water quality is horrendous after big rains and make sure you bring enough quarters for the parking meters. From the cobbles of Trestles in **North San Diego** down to the reefs and sands of **South San Diego** and on to the Mexican border, good surf is a common occurrence, especially in fall and winter. The huge population of SoCal surfers are blessed with plenty of options, plus there's a major resource right next door; it's called Baja.

## EAST COAST

**Canada**'s east coast surf scene is encapsulated on the peninsula of **Nova Scotia**. Further spots exist to the north in the frigid waters around cliff-bound **Newfoundland** Island and into the Labrador Sea, but few are ridden and local knowledge is required in these harsh frontiers of the surfing world.

New England boasts the American East Coast's best surfing areas with deep offshore waters, a wide swell window, pulling in the lion's share of non-hurricane swell from North Atlantic depressions, along with some hurricane swell, particularly in the SE. More importantly, New England provides a whole range of permanent surfing substrata, from Maine's cliffy, craggy coast of reefs, rivermouths and islands through New Hampshire's boulder-strewn points and slabs of submerged granite, right down to Rhode Island's cobblestone reefs and rocky protrusions. Any season other than summer is going to be your best bet, which means thick rubber, thick skin, and hopefully some thick waves. **Maine** gets the frontiersville tag if you're looking at surfing north of Portland. South of the capital, Ogunquit is the main focus, with its shifting rivermouth sandbars and both Short and Long Sands offer something for all abilities. Winter NE swells provide the most consistent source of sizeable waves since the Maine coast can find itself eclipsed from some hurricane swells by Cape Cod to the south. Winter water temperatures can plunge below freezing with the ocean "slushing" in places, while summer sees a fleeting period

JEREMIAH KLEIN

Los Angeles County

where a 3/2mm suffices. **New Hampshire** only has 17 miles of coastline, but it's probably the most action-packed stretch of surf on the whole East Coast. The Wall is a super consistent and powerful beachbreak, but it's the surrounding reefs that are the real challenge. The concentration of rock-bottomed breaks like Rye, Linkys and Foxhill makes it possible for experienced surfers to ride a range of wave types from walled-up right points to hollow left reefs, with or without some company. Summer can be a bummer for any sizeable swell, but winter will always throw up some heavy lines and there are sure to be a few classy days during the frequent offshore winds of spring and fall. North of Boston, **Massachusetts** appears to

ADAM CORNICK

Nova Scotia

NICK LAVECCHIA

York, Maine

be well set-up, with potential reefs and points everywhere, but they never seem to deliver the quality waves that this coastline suggests. There are a few fickle secret spots, tucked away, while places like Deveraux attract a dedicated crowd. South of Boston, the beachbreaks of Hull and the breaks around Scituate offer a haven for the city surfers. Cape Cod is a bit of a weird one; it's one big crescent of sand, producing shifting beachbreaks of variable quality. These hard-breaking, sand-bottom waves can reach epic size, plus it does tend to pick up any E swell and has the right aspect to pick up some hurricane swell too. Martha's Vineyard and Nantucket are the state's real gems, with wide swell windows and few surfers, but access and localism are apparent problems. **Rhode Island** has a lot of quality beach, reef and pointbreak surf in a relatively small area and the twisting coastline allows for a multitude of wind and swell options, making it the most consistent, year-round New England destination. Block Island is the icing on the cake, with a fickle, long left among its fruits, which are jealously guarded by aggressive locals. Connecticut lies to the west, blocked by Long Island to the south. It gets the occasional wave from rare due E swell, but the surf will be far better in Rhode Island.

The Mid-Atlantic surfing states are home to an abundance of good quality, hard-breaking beachbreaks, anchored by the endless man-made structures that litter the coast in the form of piers, jetties and breakwalls. The best time to find consistent waves along this Atlantic shoreline is right before, during, and just after the winter season. New York's **Long Island** juts due east out into the ocean, giving its south-facing beaches an excellent hurricane swell window and the ability to pick up some SW windswells, at the expense of regular wintertime NE swells. **New Jersey** boasts the most powerful, challenging beachbreaks on the East Coast. Long, straight barrier islands, punctuated by frequent inlets or jetties, are home to one of the largest East Coast surfing populations. The coasts of **Delaware** and **Maryland** are not the East Coast's most illustrious wave zone. A swell-stifling shelf extends out from Delaware Bay, so southern breaks like the Indian River Inlet and the Bethany beachbreaks are better. Ocean City, Maryland has a concentrated stretch of short jetties that shape some hollow, punchy waves each winter, particularly at the The Inlet and Pier. One way of escaping the bustle is to search by 4x4 the wild expanses of Assateague Island, where unstabilised, shifting, beachbreaks beckon. **Virginia** is notable because, apart from the extreme north and south of the state, there is little or no access to the plethora of offshore islands that dot the coastline. These islands undoubtedly hold some quality waves and a few privileged locals make forays into this wilderness by boat. Chincoteague National Wildlife Reserve offers miles of unspoiled beachbreak that usually has a big gutter between

## SWELL FORECASTING

### THE PACIFIC OCEAN

A constant procession of low pressure systems march across the northern Pacific from October to April. Their exact path is totally dictated by the meandering trajectory of the upper atmosphere jet stream, but they usually make landfall between British Columbia and Northern California. These lows are responsible for sending swells as far away as Peru, establishing the NW swell theme for California, plus any direction from W,SW round to SE up in Alaska and chaotic mixes of swell are common. Outside of these months, deep low pressure systems are rare, allowing large high pressure systems to establish themselves offshore. These highs generate the summer afternoon onshores and weak windswell from the W or NW, depending on how far south you are. This huge seasonal variation is most extreme during July and August, when the Southern Hemisphere storms are the most likely source of a salvation swell from the S or SW. Smaller storms and frontal activity can also send in SW lines from equatorial latitudes, or else the occasional 'chubasco' tropical storm appears off Central America as another unreliable source of summer S swells. Expect winter NW swells to usually be accompanied by S winds and summer S or SW swells to meet prevailing NW winds, dictating which side of the headland or jetty to head to. Considering Alaska's latitude, water temps should be colder, but as the Alaska Current splits off the Kuroshio extension, it moderates the whole Gulf of Alaska. The other arm forms the California Current, following the West Coast from BC to Baja, bringing cool water from the Kuroshio back to the equatorial gyres. Coastal upwelling is a feature that keeps the range of water temperatures down throughout the seasons. Depending on latitude and underwater topography, tidal ranges (heights) vary massively from one region to another. Much of the west coast is in the meso-tidal range, so spring tides oscillate between 7ft (2.3m) and 13ft (4.3m). Many tide sensitive spots will only work for about one third of the tide (low, mid or high). The Pacific Northwest experiences macro-tidal ranges of over 14ft (4.6m) on spring tides, resulting in extremely unstable surf conditions, where tide will be the main priority.

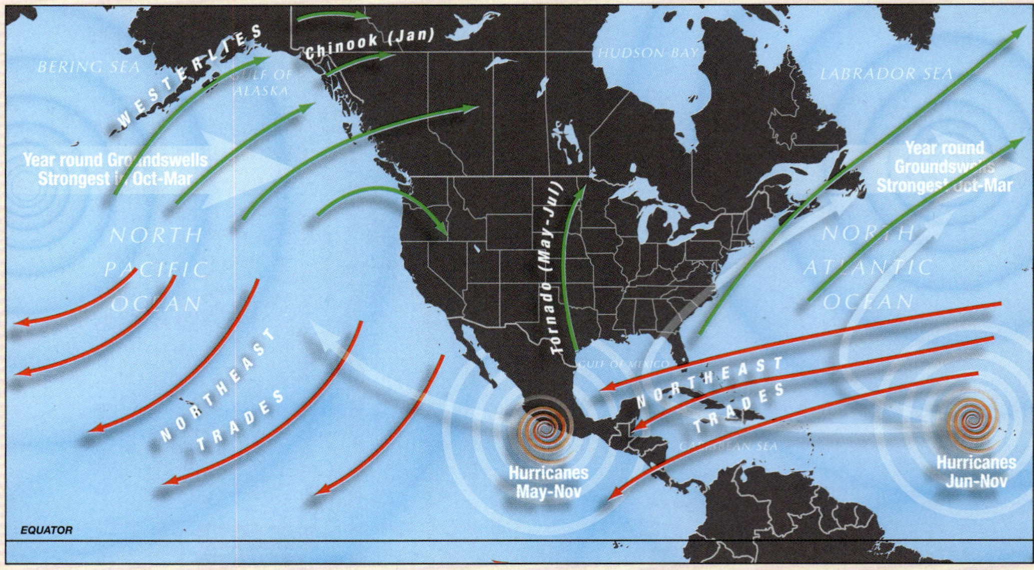


### NORTH ATLANTIC OCEAN

The jet stream also drags an incessant stream of winter storms across the northern latitudes of the Atlantic, but since these storms are travelling away from North America, the East Coast has to survive on the swells that propagate off the back of the low pressure systems. Many of these storms are spawned in Baffin Bay, between Newfoundland and Greenland and will pump NE swell down the East Coast, especially if they remain stationary, but they are usually quick to spin off toward Europe, taking the swell with them. Cold fronts sweeping across the continent hit the coast and wind up again providing another source of predominantly NE swell. In winter, these frontal systems can take a more southerly path, energised by the warmer waters of the Gulf of Mexico, and usually make oceanfall between Northern Florida and the Carolinas. Alternatively, cold air descending from the Canadian interior will arc down through the Mid Atlantic states, before swinging north again to join up with the established low pressure systems off Newfoundland. These fronts are dubbed Alberta (or Canadian) Clippers, and once again are most likely to send out NE pulses in their wake. Nova Scotia and New England score extra size from proximity to the weather systems, while the Outer Banks and Southern Florida protrude into the deep waters of the Gulf Stream current, which acts as a conveyor belt for the NE swell to head down the coast. Summer is a feast or famine scenario, with sizeable surf completely reliant on hurricane swells. These most powerful of tropical storms are the only low pressure cells that travel towards the East Coast, bringing large swells, but also the threat of widespread damage if they make landfall. Swell direction is dictated by the storm's track which can waver between due west into either the Caribbean Sea or the Gulf of Mexico or else following an arcing trajectory to the north, where cooler ocean temperatures signal it's demise. Hurricanes can appear anytime between June and November, with September and October providing the strongest possibility of scoring these swells, that usually have an element of S to them. 'Canes aside, summer can be diabolically flat, relying on weak E to SE windchop from the stationary Bermuda High, which dominates the western North Atlantic. Nova Scotia's Bay of Fundy can experience a depth difference of 50ft (16m) between low and high water, but most East Coast tides are low to moderate in the 4-5ft (1.2-1.6m) range.

### GULF OF MEXICO

Hemmed in by the Yucatan peninsula to the south and Cuba to the southeast, the Gulf Of Mexico must rely on weather systems to actually traverse some part of the expanse of water. From June to November it is hurricane season, but September and October are most likely to produce a storm that crosses into the Gulf from the Caribbean. This is also the time of year when the winter cold fronts will begin to sweep across the continent on the edge of Pacific low pressure systems. Strong winds from the SE will build up the swell for Alabama and the Florida Panhandle while Texas will see a more E to N airflow in the winter months. When the fronts pass through the winds will usually veer offshore, heralding the beginning of the end for most Gulf swells, which can disappear in a matter of hours. South-easterly windchop is the most likely source of summer waves, but flat spells can extend for months. Tidal fluctuations throughout the Gulf are small, but will still create strong currents at inlets and passes.

GRANT ELLIS

North Carolina

outside bars and the shorebreak. Virginia Beach, or "Va Beach" as the locals say, is another highly developed seaside resort that isn't associated with great surf, but it does have its share of days, both in town at the pier or 1st St Jetty and at the nearby spacious spots of Camp Pendleton.

Most East Coast surfers will make the pilgrimage to Cape Hatteras, North Carolina, at least once in their surfing lives. **The Outer Banks** pick up all available swell and provide a range of exposures to optimise different wind directions, making it the most consistent and highest quality East Coast surfing destination. **North Carolina** has a much longer coastline than the Outer Banks and the southern half of the state sweeps away to the SW, increasing the width of the continental shelf and weakening the energy of the waves. Atlantic Beach and Emerald Isle face due south and miss out on NE swells, but they light-up when there is a good S or a hurricane swell. Access restrictions to a lot of pier-surf areas mean hassles, particularly in summer, but winter brings some good conditions, since the prevailing angle of the coast is perfect for offshores during winter nor'easters. Wrightsville is one hotspot with punchy waves, where a dedicated crew of shredders competes with the crowds from the large campus at Wilmington. More

PATRICK EICHSTAEDT

Flagler, Florida

well-defined set-ups can be found near Carolina Beach before rounding Cape Fear to the sheltered, south-facing areas of Long Beach and Holden Beach. **South Carolina** is afflicted by the vast, gently sloping, shallow continental shelf, which reduces the power of the incoming waves. Nonetheless, Myrtle Beach is a seething cauldron of youth in the summertime, as college students descend en masse to party and hang out at the beach in the hot climate. This puts a stress on very limited wave resources, not to mention ordinances that restrict when and where you can surf along the built-up coastline. Even so, on its day, it can look good here, with clean, hollow waves and no shortage of dedicated year-round locals to capitalise on these infrequent conditions. The Charleston scene centres on Isle of Palms Pier and Folly Beach where The Washout provides the most consistent waves around. The continental shelf is at its maximum swell destroying width off **Georgia**, which is home to the friendliest crew of surfers on the East Coast. That good ol' Southern hospitality is strong in the surfing community, because they rarely have anything much to offer the traveler in the wave department. When there is enough swell to make it in over the shelf, a few spots around Tybee Island and St Simons Island will serve up average beachbreak surf, occasionally with a little power, but there is very little easy access to the lion's share of Georgia's coastline. Tales of long sandspits and peeling waves off some of the uninhabited islands aren't necessarily groundless, but the fickle nature of the area will deter all but the most intrepid explorers.

**Florida** encapsulates the East Coast surf scene unlike any other Atlantic State. The most southern point on mainland USA conjures up visions of warm weather, sub tropical water temperatures, and a perfect, year-round, beach-life environment. Despite the absence of regular groundswell and sizeable wave challenges, the average Florida surf can range from 1ft windchop to 20ft faces in a hurricane swell. Once again, it is the man made structures that provide the best line-ups, sprinkled along both coasts. **Northern Florida** from Jacksonville to Daytona includes plenty of well-defined waves courtesy of numerous piers and jetties. The long breakwaters of the St Johns River are real focal points for quality surf, attracting large surfing populations from inland cities like Gainesville and Orlando. Jacksonville Pier, St Augustine, Matanzas and Flagler Pier offer varying themes on the Florida beachbreak. Winters can be really good, but Northern Florida is way colder, requiring fullsuits, booties, and sometimes even gloves and hoods in the far north. The **Central Florida** zone is famed for the revered Sebastian Inlet wedges plus Cocoa Beach, since it's home to the greatest surfing professional, Kelly Slater. Florida is also the shark-attack capital of the world, but fatalities are rare. Smaller species like sand, spinner, lemon, and black-tip sharks join the more traditionally nasty mako, thresher, bull and occasional tiger sharks to chase the schools of bait fish and hang around the major inlets. Indian River County and St Lucie County remain under the radar and coquina reefs provide some stability and reliability to the surf at places like Stuart Rocks, while the inlet breakwater at Fort Pierce is a real swell magnet. **South Florida** may be a playground for the rich and famous, but where the Gulf Stream rubs against the continent in Palm Beach County, the surf can be overhead when barely 60 miles to the north it is 1ft slop.

## GULF OF MEXICO

The Gulf of Mexico is undoubtedly large, but a wide and gently sloping shelf strangles what limited fetch, short-lived swells that the landlocked Gulf can produce. Apart from the **Florida Panhandle** and southern Texas, there are very few powerful waves for the friendly, optimistic surfers of these southern states. Venice Beach is generally considered spot X on the southern Gulf Coast and subject to heavy crowds in heavy swells. The North and South Inlet Jetties are swell magnets, bending in serious waves at whichever one is opposed to the swell direction. The crowds are still apparent at Venice Pier, but recede at the beachbreaks that extend south past Englewood. Boca Grande and Naples Pier are literally, the last resorts on the Gulf Coast. Around Sarasota, Turtle Beach works on winter NW'ers, while Siesta Key needs summer S or W swells as it is protected from the N swells and winds. Holmes Beach or the three piers at Bradenton Beach are regularly crowded, plus nearby open beach can hold surprisingly punchy peaks. Anna Maria Key is a pier hotspot boasting outside and inside sandbars that will produce on any swell direction, size or tide. The offshore waters deepen off Tampa Bay and jetties are the focus for more hollow shorebreaks from St Pete to Reddington Shores, before beachbreaks along the Indian Shores to Indian Rocks curve, peak up and pitch close to shore. Sandwiched between the ultra-developed, surfer restricted stretch of Clearwater Beach and ultra-protective, elite residential beachbreaks of Belleaire lies an inlet jetty at Sand Key producing longer than average righthanders. From Clearwater to Cape St George surfing opportunities all but disappear as marshlands and very shallow offshore shoals take over. Florida's NW coast is called the Panhandle and directly offshore from Pensacola, the swell-sapping shelf is at its narrowest in the eastern Gulf. Strangely, there is enough fetch for E windswells to be produced, adding to the usual SE windchop, but SW to W swells have a lot of trouble getting over the shallow delta at the mouth of the Mississippi. Pensacola has miles of glaringly white, sandy beaches, where crumbly outside walls reform into a steeper inside shorebreak. A few precious waves exist at the barrier island extremities, or where piers and jetties provide solid foundations. Three of the best waves on the Panhandle are clustered around the long, inlet jetties at St Andrews State Park and Shell Island, which both have hard breaking peaks and wind protection, but the real gem is Amazons, a long, workable lefthander inside the inlet on the western side of the eastern jetty. Military bases, tidal currents, boat traffic, sharks and zealous, ticket issuing coast guards make access difficult. Panama City brings crowds, especially at the consistent Concrete Pier, while the Wooden Pier will provide a less-crowded, softer option. Henderson and Grayton Beach State Parks both offer respite from the shoreline development and a camping option beside miles of featureless peaks. Destin gives ample variation on straight, open beachies with inlet jetties forming wedging waves and helping shape consistent spots like NCO's and Jetty East. Fort Walton and Navarre piers help stack some sandbars then uninterrupted beachbreaks through the Avenues lead to Pensacola Beach, where the crowd is found close to the pier. **Alabama** sits between the worst and one of the best surfing areas of the Gulf, but generally displays a likeness to the former. Split by Mobile Bay into two areas of possibility, Alabama relies on hurricanes or SE windswell for any sort of wave action. Spots on the skinny, sandy strip of Dauphin Island tend to be weaker and less organised, but the surf breaks between Fort Morgan and the Florida state line provide the best chance of rideable waves around Orange Beach near the pier and jetty. **Mississippi** and **Lousiana** are so marginal for surf that the few local surfers are more likely to get wet in Texas or Florida. Pilot charts reveal a water depth of less than 35ft (11m) extending for miles offshore, courtesy of the silt-dumping Mississippi, choking the muddied waters for miles around the river's delta. Rumours of waves on offshore sandbanks out in the Mississippi delta can not be discounted and the East Bay peninsula may also hold surf as it protrudes out towards deeper water, but on the whole, these states are best avoided. **Texas** imitates the Atlantic coast barrier island theme, but there is a definite north-south split in wave size and consistency.

BOB HENSON

BSR Wave Park, Texas

# Alaska USA

Alaska's arc of wilderness seashore ranges from the far-western Aleutian Islands to Kodiak Island, then through the Gulf of Alaska to Yakutat and down to the islands and peninsulas around Sitka. A true surfing frontier containing untold surfing secrets in some of North America's most spectacular scenery, but this raw corner of the Pacific is not for the fainthearted.

+ VARIETY OF QUALITY SPOTS
+ EMPTY, WILDERNESS LINE-UPS
+ HUGE DISCOVERY POTENTIAL
+ GREAT SALMON/HALIBUT FISHING

- COLD, INCONSISTENT SURF
- LOADS OF RAIN AND WIND
- REMOTE, DIFFICULT ACCESS
- EXPENSIVE

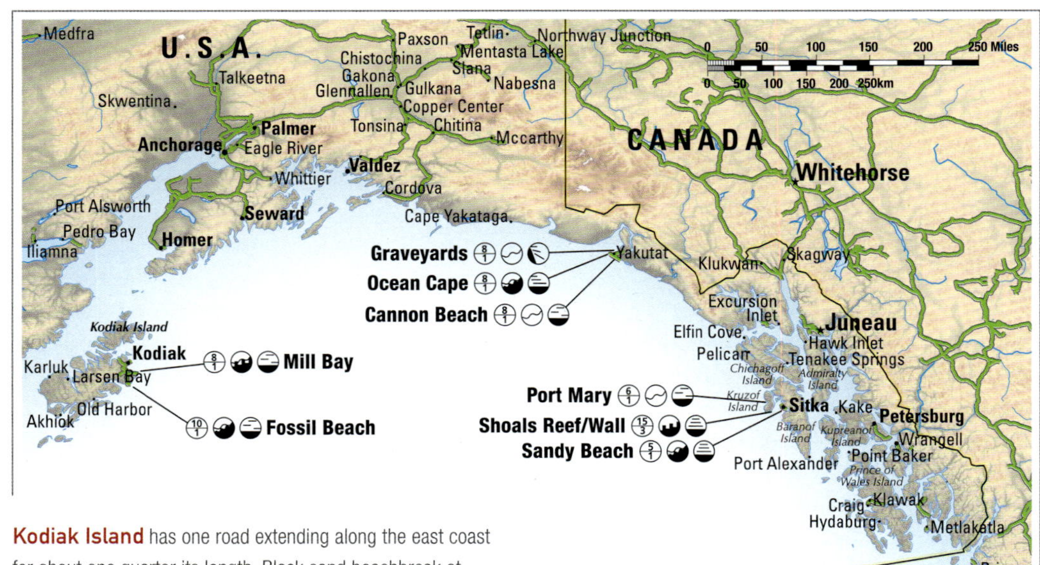


**Kodiak Island** has one road extending along the east coast for about one quarter its length. Black sand beachbreak at **Fossil Beach** is the most consistent swell-puller on the island as it is also open to the SW, but is often too big and blown out. Can be a bit sucky on the peak then usually backs off quickly and cruises for the longboard crew who frequent here. To the north is 3 Mile open beachbreak and some reefs below the cliffs before Pasagshak's indented bay and campground. The E-facing coast of Chiniak is mainly shoredump and cliffs, but some interesting fingers of reef and cobble points separate the straight beaches. Much of Kodiak City is in the swell shadow of Woody and Long Island, which definitely have some boat accessible spots on the north and east-facing coasts. **Mill Bay** provides sheltered waves in big NE-E swells and the Fort Abercrombie State Historic Park hides Boneyard, a testing reefbreak. **Yakutat** is the most well-known surf destination in SE Alaska and dubbed "The Far North Shore". Swells wrap around Point Carrew cleaning themselves up along shifting sandbars down to **Graveyards**, located inside the estuary itself. The original SW swell will be much smaller but cleaner as howling onshores become dead offshores. The sand is in constant flux, but the whole set-up favours lefts with barrels and power, plus a small swell right that's short and steep. **Ocean Cape** features some pockets of beachbreak held together with rocks and will receive the maximum SW swell, offering longer lefts as the coast bends away. **Cannon Beach** faces SW, is fully exposed to the swell and wind, so it's normally onshore and enormous. These spots are only worth a check in small summer swells. **Sitka** boasts one of the most accessible surf spots in SE Alaska provided the swell is up. To surf **Sandy Beach**, you need a moderate to big SW swell to hit the reef peak just north of the parking lot, but it is tidally sensitive, working best around mid incoming. Nice tapered forgiving walls and the best place to meet the local surfers to work out how to access the higher quality waves on Kruzof Island. **Shoals Reef/Wall** is about 30min boat ride from town. Primarily rights, this offshore brace of grizzled lava reef works best on S swells, although W will also break and it handles up to 15ft in any N wind at mid tide. Around the corner of the island west-facing spots include rights at Neva Bay, a peak at Red Tree Reef or the friendlier beachbreaks around the arc of sand at **Port Mary**.

A continuous procession of tight gradient tempests track the 50ºN line of latitude, assaulting the Gulf of Alaska with swell from a S-SW or sometimes W direction. Winter gales can persist for days with 60ft seas and hurricane force winds usually from the S-SE, before shifting more W for summer, when swell drops markedly. SE Alaska is better equipped for smaller, localised windswells than Kodiak Island, which needs NE-SE swells. Late spring and early fall are generally less changeable and more consistent seasons. Expect 14ft (4.3m) tidal range in Sitka and Kodiak, up to 16ft (4.9m) in Yakutat on spring tides with irregular semi-diurnal variations becoming more extreme further north.

BOB BARBOUR

Graveyards, Yakutat

## TRAVEL INFORMATION

**Weather** – The warmth brought by the Alaska Current supports a temperate rain-forest around Sitka but the weather is notoriously changeable. May and June are the driest months and summer temps hit 13°C (56°F) to 20°C (68°F) dropping to 5°C at night. There can be up to 20h of daylight in early summer but as low as 6h in January. Summer Yakutat and Sitka water temps mirror Northern California around 13°C (56°F), before bottoming out around 39°F (4°C). A 4/3mm fullsuit with 3mm boots at best, or a hooded 6/5/4mm with 5-7mm gloves and booties at worst. Kodiak is a bit colder!

**Lodging and Food** – Sitka has over 200 hotel rooms, plus campgrounds and RV facilities. The Yakutat accommodation is limited and expensive, with all mod cons lodges catering for fishermen and glacier sightseers. Expensive van rental. Kodiak City options or camp at Pasagshak. Local restaurants do halibut and other fine seafood - min $25 for a basic meal.

**Nature and Culture** – World-class salmon and halibut fishing (May–Sept), sea kayaking or hike up Mt Edgecumbe, SE Alaska's only volcano. Wildlife includes humpback whales, sea lions, sea otters, seabird rookeries, bald eagles and bears.

**Hazards and Hassles** – Camping in the wilderness requires special precautions to avoid trouble with bears! Rips can be fast and lava reef bottom is nasty on shallow parts of the Sitka reefs. King-sized mosquitoes in summer.

**Handy Hints** – Contact Scuba Do in Kodiak, Icy Waves in Yakutat, but unfortunately Cold Salt Surf Shop in Sitka has closed. Ideally, you need a boat, airplane, all terrain vehicle, camping equipment, fuel, gun, chainsaw and whiskey!

| STATISTICS | | J F | M A | M J | J A | S O | N D |
|---|---|---|---|---|---|---|---|
| SWELL | Direction | | | | | | |
| | Size (ft) | 6-7 | 5-6 | 4-5 | 3-4 | 6-7 | 7 |
| WIND | Direction | | | | | | |
| | Force | F5 | F5 | F4 | F3-F4 | F4-F5 | F5 |
| WATER | Wetsuit | | | | | | |
| | Temp/°C | 2 | 3 | 9 | 11 | 8 | 4 |
| WEATHER | Rainfall/mm | 18 | 13 | 15 | 54 | 61 | 26 |
| | days/mth | 6 | 5 | 5 | 12 | 13 | 7 |
| | Min temp/°C | -14 | -7 | 5 | 8 | 1 | -13 |
| | Max temp/°C | -5 | 4 | 15 | 18 | 10 | -4 |

# Vancouver Island CANADA

Canada has the world's longest coastline and with 52,455 islands, it should also host the largest number of surf spots. However, being located so far north between 45° to 80° latitude, frozen water is an issue, as well as a regular swell supply. Surfers exploring the southern corners of this vast country have found Vancouver Island to the west well-endowed with some quality reefs, points and beaches, but access is challenging without a boat or seaplane. Blessed with some reliable beachbreaks, Tofino is the closest thing to a surf town on the west coast, where stunning, old-growth, temperate rainforests provide the backdrop to some breathtaking beaches in this spectacular natural environment.

- + CONSISTENT SWELLS
- + BEACHES, REEFS & POINTS
- + WAVES FOR ALL ABILITIES
- + WILDLIFE

- – MESSY STORMY SWELLS
- – BEACHES OFTEN ONSHORE
- – RARE, LOCALISED POINTS
- – COLD AND SUPER RAINY

MARK MCINNIS

Vancouver Island

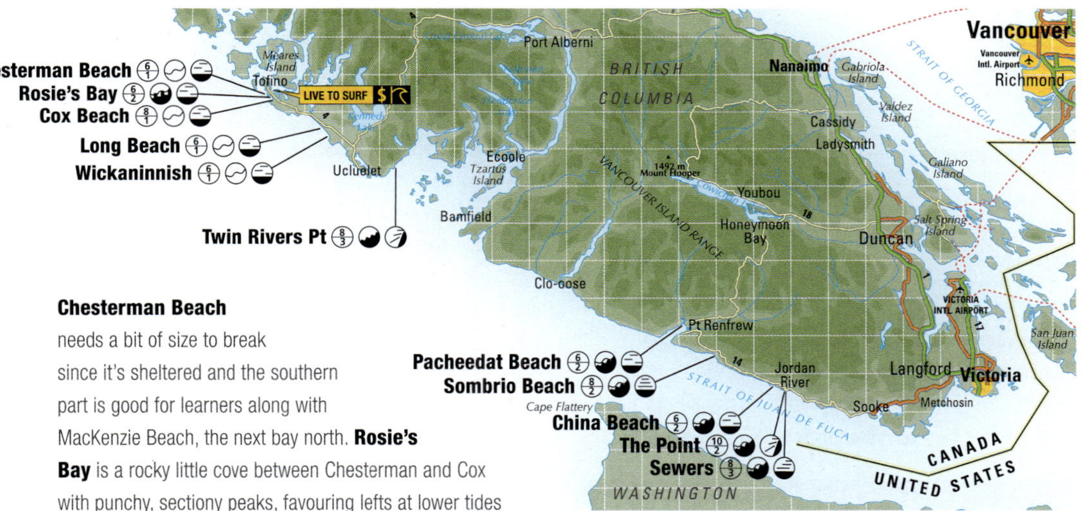


**Chesterman Beach** needs a bit of size to break since it's sheltered and the southern part is good for learners along with MacKenzie Beach, the next bay north. **Rosie's Bay** is a rocky little cove between Chesterman and Cox with punchy, sectiony peaks, favouring lefts at lower tides and is a haunt for local shortboarders. The main Tofino spot is **Cox Beach**, a crescent beach with tapering walls that line up best in the middle, while each end provides wind protection from the N and S respectively. **Long Beach** usually has mellow waves, providing an endless choice for the many surf schools that operate on this stretch. Closes-out when the waves get overhead and there can be some currents. **Wickaninnish** and its tourist Centre is protected from S winds, with more friendly beachbreak or try Florencia Bay for a bit more power. Ucluelet's Big Beach and Little Beach are unreliable, but **Twin Rivers** on a good W swell should see some fast tubing walls over sharp rocks. **Pacheedat Beach**, aka Gordon Rivermouth is a quality beachbreak, best on NE wind and a strong W swell. Most Juan da Fuca Strait spots are winter breaks and the misty, spooky at **Sombrio Beach** amongst the huge kelp beds includes 1st Peak, Chickens and 2nd peak, where the lefts are usually more walled up and faster. Further down the Strait is **China Beach**, a very average rocky beachbreak, next to Highway 14 where mellow peaks and easy rides make it a good place for beginner/improvers, but it wont break much in summer. Historically a logging camp, River Jordan has become a surfing town thanks to long wrapping rights known as **The Point**, Sewers, and Rock Piles, but it has also developed a reputation for intolerant, aggressive locals. Despite being somewhat inconsistent, these waves crank when it's on, which is mid-winter, big W-NW swell and a NE wind. The Point at the rivermouth can have very long rides (and some lefts back into the river), down-the-line speed walls and bowly barrel sections over the sand boulder mix. **Sewers** gets really hollow and fast, for experienced surfers only, since localism is a given. Further inside the Strait, there are other spots on huge swells, but remember that SE winds blow out most breaks.

Storms originating off Japan generate S-W swells that lash the coastline of British Columbia, from September through March. Summer, is reliant on localised windswells, as the distant Southern Hemisphere swells struggle to reach Vancouver Island, and Washington's Olympic Peninsula shadows the southern breaks. Winter swells vary between 3-15ft, lighting up the sheltered pointbreaks, while summer surf favours the Tofino beaches. NW wind is dominant in summer, while winter gets more W and SW. Spring tides are 3m max, affecting some rivermouth cobblestone breaks.

## TRAVEL INFORMATION

**Weather** – Vancouver Island weather is very wet and changeable, however, the winters are mild by Canadian standards and the summers are cool. Port Renfrew experiences about 12 days of snowfall over the year. The annual average rainfall can reach an impressive 6650mm (260in) in the mountains, dropping to a 10th of that in the rain-shadowed capital, Victoria. July is the driest month and November the wettest. A 4/3mm with booties in summer and a 5/4 mm hooded suit with 3/5mm gloves and boots in winter.

**Lodging and Food** – Many options for all budgets especially deluxe. Many B&Bs are located right on Tofino's beaches. Stay at Tofino Hostel (from $35/dorm bed). Cox Bay has the pricey private Pacific Sands Beach Resort. Camp near the surf at Greenpoint Campground with trail access to Long Beach. Try Sobo for delicious local seafood.

**Nature and Culture** – Tofino is a mecca for outdoor adventure like hiking the boardwalk trails in the ancient, dripping rainforest, biking on the beach at low tide, kayaking, sport fishing and whale watching. The West Coast Trail opens in summer for hiking, camping and exploring the surrounding wilderness, but surfing is not permitted.

**Hazards and Hassles** – River Jordan locals resent kooks showing up at their inconsistent pointbreak from the nearby cities of Victoria (pop: 300,000) and Vancouver (pop: 2M), and have been enforcing tough localism. Cold water, rain, wild surf and fast weather changes are the things to worry about. Beware of bears on the trails or beaches at remote spots.

**Handy Hints** – Surf gets big, so take a longer board with extra float for the full neoprene kit. Lots of surf schools in Tofino including local legends Bruhwiler, and Surf Sister female only surf camps. Many Tofino surf shops rent gear like Live to Surf, Storm Surf Shop and Long Beach Surf Shop who are also in Ucluelet. Read *The Cedar Surf* by Grant Shilling.

MICK GULLAN

Cox Beach

| STATISTICS | | J F | M A | M J | J A | S O | N D |
|---|---|---|---|---|---|---|---|
| SWELL | Direction | | | | | | |
| | Size (ft) | 7-8 | 6-7 | 4-5 | 3-4 | 6 | 7-8 |
| WIND | Direction | | | | | | |
| | Force | F5 | F4 | F4 | F3-F4 | F4 | F5 |
| WATER | Wetsuit | | | | | | |
| | Temp/°C | 7 | 9 | 11 | 15 | 14 | 10 |
| WEATHER | Rainfall/mm | 183 | 106 | 67 | 37 | 119 | 217 |
| | days/mth | 19 | 16 | 12 | 7 | 13 | 21 |
| | Min temp/°C | 0 | 3 | 9 | 12 | 8 | 3 |
| | Max temp/°C | 6 | 12 | 20 | 23 | 26 | 8 |

# Northern Oregon USA

North Oregon gets great surf when the conditions align, which unfortunately is rare. It's a windy place, but fortunately, the area has some protection either side of the major protruding points, capes and headlands. Some spots are crowded and well-known, while others are empty and rarely spoken of. Wetsuit technology has increased the surfing population, much of which drives over from Portland and the rest of the valley.

+ POWERFUL, BIG SWELLS
+ ACCESSIBILITY
+ BEAUTIFUL SCENERY
+ SPOT VARIETY

+ SWELLS OFTEN TOO BIG
+ STORMY CLIMATE
+ CROWDED
+ LOCALISM AND SHARKS

Fort Stevens State Park south to Seaside is a long, nondescript beachbreak, surfable only when small and clean. **Seaside Cove** is where the beach meets the rocks at the south end of the city. At high tide with SE wind, a right breaks into a rip that makes the paddle easy, so expect semi-hollow, sectiony walls with lots of longboarders on them. There are lefts, too, usually faster and more sectiony. **Seaside Point** consists of First and Second Point, which serve long, hollow, sling-shot lefts up to triple overhead-plus. First Point is the gem, while Second Point is shorter, heavier, and more exposed to wind. Gnarly locals revere both spots and maintain a reality of violent localism towards non-local surfers, even if you're low-key. Our advice: don't go there. **Indian Beach** can be worth checking; the mouth of Ecola Creek occasionally has a good bar sheltered from NW winds. The beach fronting pretty little **Cannon Beach** is basically all sandbars, only surfable when small and clean. Just south of Cape Falcon, hugely popular **Short Sands Beach** might as well be Portland-by-the-Sea due to its valley crowds after its wind protection, soft waves, and sandy bottom. The beautiful horseshoe cove is safe from all but W winds and entails a 20-minute walk through old-growth spruce forest. **Manzanita**

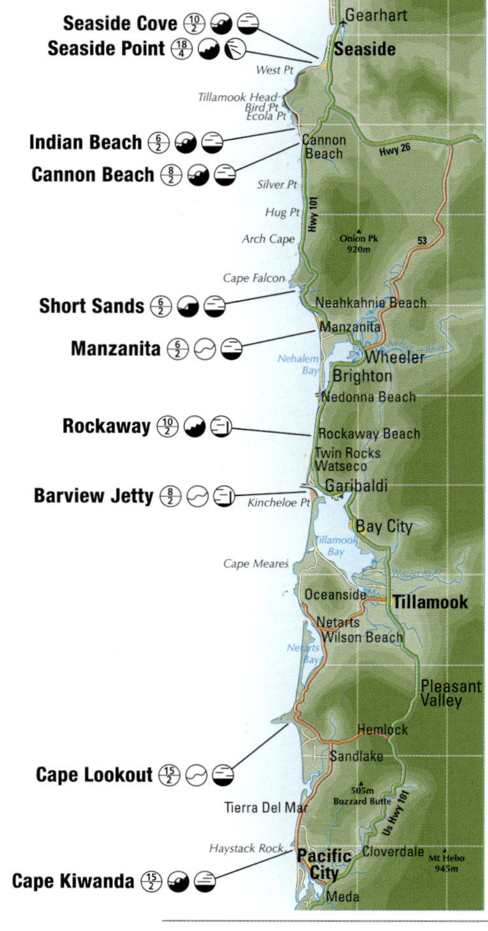

MICHAEL KEW

Cape Kiwanda

and **Rockaway Beach** are miles of typical, flat-bottomed beachbreak, backed by grassy dunes and wide open to wind and swell. The area is good during the summer with small, clean swells and east wind. **Barview Jetty** on the south entrance of Tillamook Bay offers organised jetty surf with fun, bowling waves. Before geological upheaval wrecked the reef (and the spot—R.I.P.), **Cape Lookout**, aka Boy Scout Camp, the longest cape on the West Coast, required W swells to get the best out of the once-quality righthand reef, sheltered from NW wind. Sometimes a good left breaks into the channel between the beachbreak and the point. Blows out on S wind. The north side has nice beachbreak too, which is naturally sheltered from winter S winds. Occasionally, good beachbreak rights unfurl at popular, heavily Instagrammed **Cape Kiwanda** (the Malibu of Oregon) and run south to Neskowin, all best when small and glassy.

The primary source of swell comes from the NW lows in the Gulf of Alaska during winter (Nov-Mar), ranging in size from 3-50ft. Summer is generally all local windswell; southern-hemisphere groundswells do not hit here. Check the Columbia River Bar Buoy 46029 on the Internet or weather radio for swell size, interval, and wind. Dominant winds are NW year-round, blowing cold and hard during spring (Mar-June) and bringing the fog during summer (June-Sept). Tides are a major factor at all spots; local tide tables are available at any surf shop or sporting goods store. Tread lightly.

MARK MCINNIS

Northern Oregon

## TRAVEL INFORMATION

**Weather** – Oregon is usually stormy from October to May; foggy in the summer; windy in the spring, and variable in the autumn. Autumn is the best (and sharkiest) time for this area when the summer fog leaves, the wind is lighter, and clean NW swells begin. Winter is far too big of a gamble for the visiting surfer – more often than not, it'll be raining with 35-knot SE winds, giant seas and few (if any) options for surfing. The water is always cold, requiring a 5/4mm hooded steamer, thick booties and gloves.

**Lodging and Food** - Camping is the ideal cheap option during the drier months. There is ample accommodation in all price ranges in Seaside, Cannon Beach, Tillamook and Pacific City. Drink good beer at Pelican Pub on the beach at Cape Kiwanda. Stuff your face at the Tillamook Cheese Factory.

**Nature and Culture** – North Oregon is rugged and beautiful, but most of the coast is not viewable directly from Highway 101. There are many places for hiking and general nature enjoyment. Not much nightlife to speak of unless you're a local.

**Hazards and Hassles** – Besides localism at the pointbreaks, the surf gets big and heavy. There are many bad currents. Hypothermia is a real possibility. White sharks are everywhere.

**Handy Hints** – Get a good printed map of the coast since cell phone reception is not widespread. Maintain a low profile and respect the locals. Don't go expecting good waves. Bring plenty of warm clothing and a big board. The friendly staffers at Cleanline Surf and Ocean Surf Adventures provide surfing lessons, gear rentals, and sales. They can also extend valuable advice regarding the best surf spots to suit your skill level. For "surf sisters," Northwest Women's Surf Camps offers private and group surf and stand-up (SUP) lessons, day camps, surf weekenders, and co-ed SUP excursions.

| STATISTICS | | J F | M A | M J | J A | S O | N D |
|---|---|---|---|---|---|---|---|
| SWELL | Direction | | | | | | |
| | Size (ft) | 6 | 4-5 | 4 | 4-5 | 5 | 6 |
| WIND | Direction | | | | | | |
| | Force | F4 | F4 | F5 | F4-F5 | F4 | F4 |
| WATER | Wetsuit | | | | | | |
| | Temp/°C | 12 | 13 | 13 | 14 | 14 | 13 |
| WEATHER | Rainfall/mm | 245 | 185 | 91 | 36 | 114 | 283 |
| | days/mth | 18 | 15 | 11 | 3 | 10 | 18 |
| | Min temp/°C | 6 | 8 | 11 | 12 | 11 | 7 |
| | Max temp/°C | 14 | 17 | 20 | 22 | 22 | 16 |

# Humboldt County CALIFORNIA, USA

North Humboldt is a beautiful and dramatic place, home to big trees and big waves. It is a rugged cold-water zone that appeals to a certain type of surfer, and while hardly a world-class surf trip the region can produce excellent winter waves. The spots are all beachbreaks, with a few rocky breaks near Trinidad. The surf is consistent and usually bad, but occasionally rewarding for those who time it right and like to charge.

- + BIG, CONSISTENT SWELLS
- + OFFSHORE DURING STORMS
- + BEAUTIFUL SCENERY
- + REDWOOD FORESTS

- – UNFRIENDLY LOCALS
- – SWELLS OFTEN TOO BIG
- – HARSH, STORMY CLIMATE
- – SHARKY

MICHAEL KEW

Patrick's Point

Heading south from Orick, **Freshwater Lagoon** is a commonly surfed spot in the Humboldt Lagoons State Park due to its paralleling Highway 101. Small, peaky swells are needed and the shifting sandbars make it a real lottery, particularly further south at Stone Lagoon and Dry Lagoon. Big Lagoon is usually the least surfable, featuring nasty shoredump. All the lagoon beaches are iffy, needing the optimum/rare conditions of clean, small swell, lower tide and E wind. All of these waves can suffer badly from strong currents. At the north end of Patrick's Point State Park, Agate Beach is a thick, righthand barrel that is fast and shallow. Hazards include crowds, scattered rocks, and gnarly shorebreak. The headland is **Patrick's Point** itself, a long, mushy, rocky, sectiony left that handles huge swells. Best at high tide in a southeast wind, on a clean west-northwest swell, 8-20ft+. College Cove is usually dumpy close-outs in a sheltered bay, so it's surfed on big swells and is protected from NW wind. **Trinidad State Beach** is a below-average, rocky beachbreak in scenic surroundings. **Camel Rock**, to the south, is a popular spot that at low tide can resemble a mushy right point, holding 3-8ft depending on the sand. Gets crowded. **Moonstone Beach** also attracts crowds to its wide, flat sands, and is sometimes fun during small, peaky swells and E wind. There have been four documented non-fatal shark attacks on surfers here. Clam Beach and **Mad River Beach** are funky, sharky breaks, rarely surfed. As with all the waves in this area, small, clean, peaky windswells with high tide and east winds are ideal. Along the north spit west of Eureka, Bunkers, Bay Street, and Power Lines are all shifty sandbars. **Bunkers** holds giant swells, resembling a cold Sunset Beach on its best days. The **North Jetty** of Humboldt Bay is the area's marquee spot. Fast, hollow rights and longer lefts can form off the jetty, with a river-like paddling channel along the rocks. Generally, lower tide is better, but North Jetty can break on any tide. The peak can handle triple-overhead plus – a SE wind and 3-12ft+ northwest swell is perfect. The jetty is the hub of surfing in North Humboldt, so it is crowded. Between the jetties, experts-only, black-diamond Humboldt Bay **Harbor Entrance** is known amongst mariners as the most dangerous in the state. For surfers, a heavy, sand-bottom peak breaks in the entrance. Access and exit is by jumping off and then clawing back onto the jetty. Serious lefts, and steep, dredging rights that barrel into the 45-foot-deep (15m) boat channel make this place strictly for the experienced. Handling 8-18'+, the Harbor Entrance also has strong currents. Low tide only.

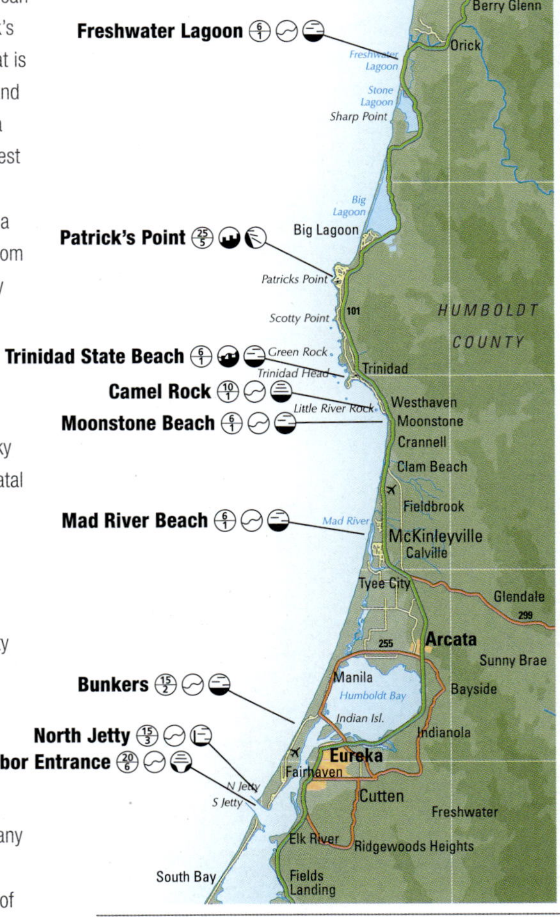


The source of waves for North Humboldt is the Gulf of Alaska in autumn/winter (Oct-Mar), with powerful storms brewing swell ranging in size from 3-50ft. Storms originating off Japan also produce long-range, organized W-NW groundswell. South swells do not hit here. Dominant winds are NW-N, often howling during spring (Mar-June) and bringing fog during summer (June-Sept). A few spots like the Harbor Entrance and Camel Rock can handle NW wind. SE winds can blow offshore at every other spot. All spots are fickle. Full cold-water rubber is required.

## TRAVEL INFORMATION

**Weather** – Winter is stormy, with consistent big swell. Spring has stiff, cold northwest wind, sunnier days, and colder water due to upwelling. Summer is usually foggy, with small to medium-sized and usually junky waves, plus the coldest water of the year. Autumn is the best chance to score good waves and weather simultaneously. A year-round 4/3 fullsuit as well as booties, gloves, and hood are required.

**Lodging and Food** – Eureka has lodging for every budget. McKinleyville and Arcata offer accommodation, but hotels are cheaper in Eureka. Trinidad and the Patrick's Point area have a few expensive B&Bs. There are campsites at Samoa Boat Ramp County Park, Clam Beach, Patrick's Point, Big Lagoon, Freshwater Lagoon, Gold Bluffs, and Prairie Creek. Good food is available in most of the towns.

**Nature and Culture** – Eureka is an unremarkable city, but heading north past Arcata, the renowned Redwood Coast scenery begins, featuring some of the world's biggest trees. Arcata is a liberal college town with plenty to do, whilst Trinidad is a quaint village. North of Trinidad is some of California's prettiest landscape. Arcata has the best nightlife in the region.

**Handy Hints** – A bigger board is necessary to surf Humboldt waves. This area is cold, sharky and powerful - all of these extremes should be planned for. Pleasant surprises await those who don't expect too much.

**Hazards and Hassles** – Large, unpredictable waves, heavy currents and the rocks at spots like Trinidad and Patrick's Point. Shark attacks are fairly common and the area is not known for friendly locals.

MICHAEL KEW

North Jetty

| STATISTICS | | J F | M A | M J | J A | S O | N D |
|---|---|---|---|---|---|---|---|
| SWELL | Direction | | | | | | |
| | Size (ft) | 12 | 10 | 7 | 6-7 | 8-9 | 12 |
| WIND | Direction | | | | | | |
| | Force | F5 | F4 | F3 | F3 | F3-F4 | F4-F5 |
| WATER | Wetsuit | | | | | | |
| | Temp/°C | 10 | 10 | 10 | 11 | 11 | 10 |
| WEATHER | Rainfall/mm | 267 | 153 | 50 | 14 | 76 | 256 |
| | days/mth | 20 | 15 | 8 | 5 | 15 | 20 |
| | Min temp/°C | 5 | 6 | 9 | 12 | 10 | 6 |
| | Max temp/°C | 12 | 13 | 15 | 16 | 16 | 13 |

# San Francisco and San Mateo USA

Despite being one of the world's most popular tourist destinations, San Francisco is often overlooked by travelling surfers tending to focus on the warmer waters and reliability of Southern California or the numerous pointbreaks of "Surf City USA," aka Santa Cruz. In recent years, city breaks like Ocean Beach have started to appear regularly in surf media, which is old news regarding Mavericks, California's premier big-wave reef. Every winter, paddle-in or tow-in acts of bravado remind us that one of the heaviest breaks on the planet lies less than 48km (30mi) away from San Francisco's rolling hills, cable cars, and famous bridge. Many surfers looking to escape city crowds will cross the Golden Gate Bridge and scout the isolated Marin County coast, but for such a large metropolis, there is still relative room to move in the wide-open space of Ocean Beach. Due to the proximity of the Farallon Islands, there are always the white sharks to think about, though fatalities have been few in the last 100 years.

- \+ NEVER FLAT
- \+ BIG-WAVE POTENTIAL
- \+ CITY ATTRACTIONS
- \+ ENTERTAINMENT & NIGHTLIFE

- – COLD WATER & BAD WINDS
- – URBAN CROWDS
- – SHARKY "RED TRIANGLE"
- – FICKLE

Fort Point

JEREMIAH KLEIN

On the south side of the Golden Gate Bridge, and breaking right below it, **Fort Point** is a funky but photogenic and fun left. It doesn't break often, but it will stay clean during large winter swells, low tide, and south winds. It suffers from strong currents, mushiness, rocks in the line-up, and occasional leftover crusty localism. **Deadmans** is the city's other lefthand reef/point. It's a bit more consistent, but apart from the sharks, the same hazards apply, although Deadmans is much hollower and dangerous, with somewhat difficult access. Needs low tide and bigger winter swell. **Kelly's Cove** distinguishes itself from other Ocean Beach peaks with a SW orientation that offers some protection from NW winds while helping to catch S swells. Easy access via the large, beachfront parking lots guarantees a high concentration of surfers. Often closed-out. Some of the peaks along **Ocean Beach** have their own name (Sloat, Fleishhacker, Taraval, VFWs, Noriega) but they all blend into a 5km (3mi) beachbreak that, on its very best days, rank among the best on the planet. It picks up all swells and a dropping tide increases the hollowness, but the random, shifting peaks remain makeable. Although it's easily and often trashed by wind, the strength of The Beach is its ability to hold any size without closing-out, by simply breaking further and further out. The biggest hurdle is paddling out through the seemingly endless, thundering lines of whitewater. **Sharp Park** in Pacifica is basically a continuation of Ocean Beach but on a smaller scale, with a few rocks and a pier to help hold the sand in place. Holds huge crowds when it's small and no crowds when it's huge. **Rockaway Beach** can produce clean peaks favoring rights on a NW swell during low tide. The reef/beachbreak set-up is protected during storms since SE winds blow offshore. This also applies to **Lindamar** (often just referred to as 'Pacifica'), a mushier, sheltered break very popular with longboarders and beginners. As a rule, Lindamar enjoys a higher tide than Rockaway. Fully exposed to large NW swells, **Pedro Point** is an interesting Mavericks alternative for goofyfooters. Starts breaking at double-overhead and does not stop. Has been surfed since the 1930s and always has a dedicated crew of local chargers on it. Clean, small W swells fire up the beachbreaks at **Montara State Beach**, but strong rips and the occasional shark can ruin a session. Considering paddling out at ✪**Mavericks** implies expertise in the field of big-wave riding. Only a legitimate charger with specific training

## TRAVEL INFORMATION

**Weather** – San Francisco has a temperate marine climate and enjoys mild weather year-round. Cool summers and mild winters seem to blend into one. Temperatures seldom rise above 21°C (70°F) or fall below 5°C (40°F). Morning and evening fogs roll in during the summer months. Unlike SoCal, days warm enough for boardies are few and far between. These patches of fog also make for fast temperature changes. Anytime is good to visit, although the warmer and drier months between August and October are considered the best. A 4/3 and 3/2 will cover most of the year, with booties needed for all but the warmest months.

**Lodging and Food** – Most lodging options are concentrated in downtown SF. To be closer to the surf try the Ocean View Motel next to Ocean Beach ($99/dble), Best Western Lighthouse Hotel in Rockaway ($140/dble) or San Benito House in Half Moon Bay ($110/dble). One budget option is Marin Headlands Youth Hostel near Fort Cronkhite ($31-37/p).

**Nature and Culture** – Tourist highlights include Fisherman's Wharf, Golden Gate Bridge, Chinatown, Alcatraz... It's simple to see a bit of everything following the well-indicated scenic drive. SF nightlife is great with many bars, restaurants, live music, sporting events—basically everything and anything.

**Hazards and Hassles** – Part of the Red Triangle, which accounts for 11% of great white shark attacks worldwide. Pollution risks are obvious around the city breaks. Stay out of the water on the day following heavy rain, when bacteria levels hit record highs. Localism gets serious at Fort Point and a couple of other spots. Unless you're qualified and experienced, don't even think about riding Mavericks.

**Handy Hints** – A full quiver should include big guns for out of control Ocean Beach and Mavericks (of course). Good news is that there are plenty of surf shops (Aqua, Wise, Mollusk) around Ocean Beach, and Mavs pioneer Jeff Clark shapes boards in HMB. Surfcamp Pacifica organises lessons.

RYAN CRAIG

Ocean Beach

RYAN CRAIG

### Mavericks LAT. 37.492362° LONG. -122.501421°

**World-famous, big-wave reef at Pillar Point for expert big-wave surfers only. Primarily a right, although the lefts have been ridden by a few brave men. Starts with an incredibly hollow, jacking take-off in front of a series of house-sized boulders known as "The Boneyard" and is followed by a long, huge wall ending in a deep channel. Starts to work at 12 feet, when the gnarled inside double-up known as Phlegm Balls will be breaking, before proper Mavs starts sucking in all size swells and never closes-out. One of the biggest, scariest waves in the world scoured by heavy currents and peppered with lethal rocks on the inside if you get dragged through the impact zone. This wave has already claimed the lives of big-wave surfers Mark Foo, Sion Milosky and a kayaker. There have been two reported shark attacks here, both non-fatal. Best access is via boat from Princeton Harbor. Otherwise, park south of Pillar Point and follow the footpath through the James Fitzgerald Marine Reserve past the harbor to a small beach protected by the north jetty. From here, paddle for 40mins around the boneyard to the line-up. Mavericks is part of the federally protected Monterey Bay National Marine Sanctuary, where regulations prohibit "motorized personal watercraft" although a new seasonal zone was established to allow tow-in surfing at Mavericks in December, January and February. The caveat is that the watercraft can only be used when the National Weather Service declares a high-surf warning, impacting water safety on moderate sized days.**

can expect to be able to ride one of the most challenging waves in the world. **Princeton Breakwater** is an easily accessible, wedgy, semi-hollow, rocky beachbreak sheltered from the huge outside surf and NW winds by a long jetty. Watch out for sharp inshore rocks. This is a popular spot with just about everybody in the county, so it gets very crowded. **Francis Beach** has a total exposure to all swell and winds, making it a good bet on clean, smaller days. Often maxed-out or blown-out, but sweet when it comes together. Located within Half Moon Bay city limits, but pay parking usually keeps the crowds down. **Martins Beach** is an exposed cove framed on the north side by Shark Tooth Rock, inside of which is a fun, mushy, west-facing righthand reef. Until recently, surfers, fishermen, and swimmers paid the previous owners a small fee to drive down the hill and park near homes at the water's edge, but public access is now threatened with a new landowner uphill claiming private property rights. There's a trio of exposed state beaches which all receive loads of swell, but are only surfable when small, peaky, and clean. **San Gregario** up to Tunitas Creek gets some punchy peaks on a medium-high tide with E wind, so it's usually best during the summer. **Pomponio** is a good S-swell beachbreak, similar to San Gregario. Always has some kind of surf, even on the smallest summer days. **Pescadero** has two spots: at the north end is a muscular beachbreak, offering virtually empty waves throughout the year. Best at higher tides with no wind, when it gets very peaky, hollow and always juicy. To the south is Pescadero Cove, a rock-strewn break with peaks aplenty. Best during a dropping mid tide with SE wind. Further beaches worth a check in small windswells are the little cove at **Bean Hollow** or the wider sands of **Gazos Creek**. Near the Santa Cruz county line is **Año Nuevo State Park**, a seal reserve with a wedging, shallow, low tide right that's always crowded when it's working, which is not that often, since it requires SW swell and N wind. Beware the abundant white sharks, which occasionally mistake surfers for seals—this is the centre of the Red Triangle, a triangular-shaped white shark habitat.

In winter, Aleutian lows are the primary source of NW swell. They push 3-35ft waves between October and March. Either side of summer sees frequent 2-6ft W groundswells from the W Pacific or near-shore windswell. Summer surf can originate from either SW groundswells or (rarely) tropical cyclones off Mexico between July and October. Waves can reach 10ft, but average 2-6ft. Dominant winds year-round are NW-N varying from 40% (Jan) to 70% (June); more S winds come in during the winter, and these can blow offshore at spots like Pedro Point and Lindamar. Only rare, dry E winds will be offshore around Ocean Beach. Tides are significant and getting hold of a tide table is easy. These tides push big currents; they are strong at Ocean Beach and get huge around Fort Point, posing a serious risk to water-users.

| STATISTICS | | J F | M A | M J | J A | S O | N D |
|---|---|---|---|---|---|---|---|
| SWELL | Direction | | | | | | |
| | Size (ft) | 6 | 4-5 | 4 | 4-5 | 5 | 6 |
| WIND | Direction | | | | | | |
| | Force | F4 | F4 | F5 | F4-F5 | F4 | F4 |
| WATER | Wetsuit | | | | | | |
| | Temp/°C | 12 | 13 | 13 | 14 | 14 | 13 |
| WEATHER | Rainfall/mm | 95 | 55 | 10 | 0 | 15 | 70 |
| | days/mth | 8 | 6 | 2 | 0 | 2 | 7 |
| | Min temp/°C | 6 | 8 | 11 | 12 | 11 | 7 |
| | Max temp/°C | 14 | 17 | 20 | 22 | 22 | 16 |

LAURENT MASUREL

Francis Beach

# Santa Cruz Town CALIFORNIA, USA

Two California beach towns are forever squabbling over the right to each call themselves "Surf City." Huntington Beach has miles of ho-hum beachbreak surf and plenty of people, but Santa Cruz has a huge variety of surf spots and perhaps the finest set-up of any zone on the West Coast. Hence, plenty of surfers. Situated just inside the northern point of the half circle of Monterey Bay, Santa Cruz enjoys all the benefits of a southern exposure, yet W, NW, and N swells wrap into the town and fire on several reefs, points, and beachbreaks. For surfers, the rocky green coastline around Santa Cruz is a cold-water paradise that more than deserves the title Surf City. Situated about 120km (75mi) south of San Francisco, Santa Cruz has a somewhat unique beach-town vibe but rampant gentrification and an increasing population. Millions live in the Bay Area cities to the north and east.

| | |
|---|---|
| + WIDE SWELL WINDOW | - COLD WATER |
| + SPOT VARIETY | - EXTREMELY CROWDED |
| + FREQUENTLY OFFSHORE | - NO SOUTH WIND SPOTS |
| + CONVENIENT AND EASY | - SHARKY |

## TRAVEL INFORMATION

**Weather** – The town area of Santa Cruz is a bit wetter than Southern California, but it's not fully exposed to the oceanic patterns of Northern California, like north of town is. Facing south and sheltered from N winds, Santa Cruz has a warmer micro-climate. Winters are mild and freezing temperatures are rare unless the bitter N winds blow. Spring is a weird time, often hazy (due to the difference between air and sea temperatures) with lots of wind but, like summer, it's sunny and dry. Autumn has nice weather and usually many swells. Because of the Monterey submarine canyon creating upwellings, the water remains cold year-round, always requiring a light steamer and occasionally a winter 4/3mm. O'Neill wetsuits were born in San Francisco in 1952 and moved to Santa Cruz in 1959.

**Lodging and Food** – There are dorm rooms (Carmelita Cottage) for around $30, but a motel room by the beach is $70-250 (Super 8, Dream Inn, Coastview Inn, Motel 6, Pacific Blue). There are dozens of options. Fast food is cheap ($10-15/meal), but restaurants are pretty expensive. Try the locally grown artichokes.

**Nature and Culture** – Visit the Lighthouse Surf Museum or the Shakespeare Santa Cruz Museum. Tour the university or hike in the redwoods. Take a stroll along the Wharf or the beach boardwalk. Santa Cruz has some cool nightlife, ranging from dive bars to proper nightclubs; check out the Catalyst, Moe's Alley, Motiv, Blue Lagoon, etc. The Swift/Ingalls Street Courtyard is a hip hangout with lots of shops and eateries.

**Hazards and Hassles** – Prepare to encounter lots of other water users. Some rock hazards and steep trails or stairs to beaches. To the south in Monterey Bay there is usually less crowd pressure and also north of town, but beware of white sharks and wind. If it rains much, rivermouth beaches can become polluted, but the sandbanks can be good (rare).

**Handy Hints** – There are plenty of surf shops like the O'Neill HQ on 41st Ave. Arrow, Haut, Freeline, Sawyer, etc. A new shortboard is around $700; you'll need a gun in the winter for tackling juicy rights. As a beginner, go to Richard Schmidt or Club Ed surf schools. Longboarding and SUP are popular.

Mitchell's Cove

JIMMY WILSON

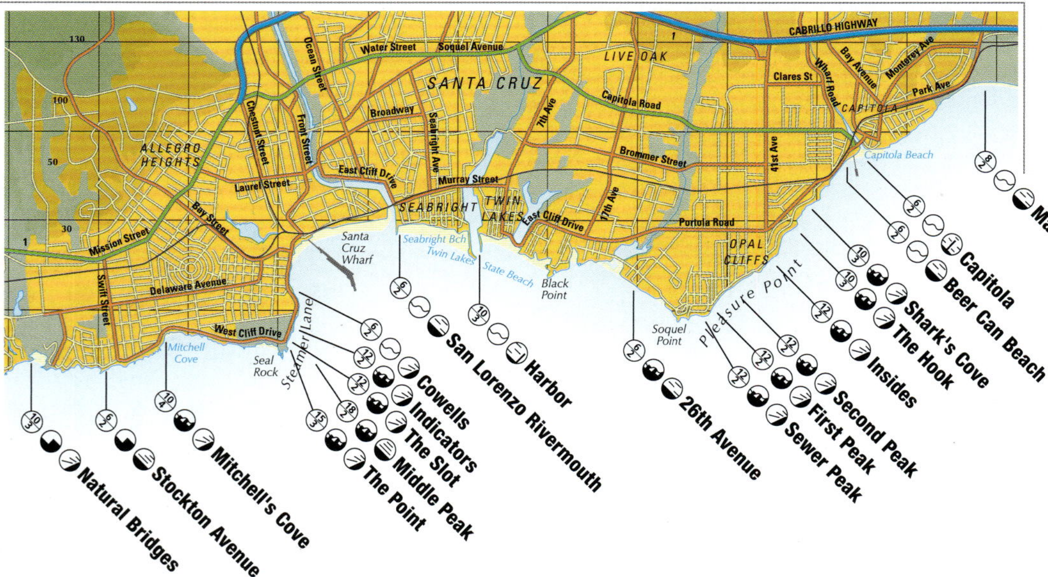

Harbor

RYAN CRAIG

The West Side of Santa Cruz town forms a series of points with a number of quality right reefs and a few pockets of beachbreak. The waves are usually punchy and can hold real size. Many spots have thick kelp beds that dampen the prevailing NW wind and smooth out the waves. **Natural Bridges** is a heavy righthand reef with a shallow bowl section over the inside rock ledge called "The Sidewalk." A dangerous high-intensity spot and not for beginners. Needs a low to medium tide with a clean NW swell and can handle up to a few feet overhead. **Stockton Avenue** hosts small, perfect righthand barrels made famous in the surf media as "Weasel Reef." The tiny take-off zone and aggressive locals make it nearly impossible for outsiders to get waves. Best during S-SW swells with low tides. Closes-Lane out as it exceeds headhigh size. One of the best spots in the county when the sections connect, **Mitchell's Cove** is a classic righthand pointbreak/sandbar set-up best during large, clean W to N swells and low incoming tides. Gets hollow, fast and crowded. ✪**Steamer Lane**, is a clutch of kelp covered reefs and pointbreaks that are mainly rights, which come thick & barrelling or long and slashable, plus a few short, steep, pitching lefts at this consistently crowded line-up. On a big W swell at mid tide rides can be had all the way around the point, into Cowells Beach and on towards the Municipal Pier – almost a mile! **Cowells** is a long, slow, mushy sand-bottomed point wave inside of Indicators, suitable for longboarding and beginners. Takes any bigger swell and works on all tides, frequently splitting into subsections that accommodate generous numbers of surfers. The best wave is usually closest to the cliff. The **San Lorenzo Rivermouth** is in the centre of town near the amusement park and, (depending on the rain and thus sandbar build-up) can turn on magic peaks. Beachbreaks east of the rivermouth can be classic. The **Harbor** also gets a sand build-up that creates a short, sucking barrel right off the south jetty, usually posted 'No Surfing,' but surfers will be surfers. **26th Avenue** represents the town's beachbreak action with a bit of rock reef thrown in for interest, culminating in the rocky reef peak at Little Windansea off the end of Rockview Street. Good spots during springtime SW-NW windswells and small summer S swells.

RYAN CRAIG

## Steamer Lane

LAT. 36.951415° LONG. -122.024013°

This collection of high-quality peaks breaks in any swell at any size, while being sheltered from the prevailing NW winds, making it a contender for most consistently crowded line-up in the country. There are four distinct spots. The farthest out is **The Point**, where hollow, thick rights rumble into life when it's on. Tight and hyper competitive take-off zone. Will accept any swell, but it's best on a S with medium-low tide to avoid backwash. **The Slot** also prefers lower tides on a W swell to bounce up some wedgy righthanders close to the cliff and is a good spot for tube rides or aerials, as it tends to close-out a bit. Straight out from the access stairs are several reefs, collectively called **Middle Peak**, then subdivided into First, Second, and Third reefs. Best during N-NW swells, each reef works at a different size, but each boast heavy elevator drops followed by a softer righthand shoulder. The lefts, however, are usually steeper and hollower, but they can leave you caught inside by the next set as Middle Peak shifts around alot, keeping the pack on the move. Further inside the headland is the heavily surfed, great hotdog wave **Indicators**. When swell and tide are perfect, it's a long, classic righthand point wave with a gaggle of speed sections and lips ripe for shortboard tricks. Best with a lined-up W-NW swell and medium-low tide.

The East Side scene is concentrated around the long righthanders of Pleasure Point, one of the most famous and popular spots in California due to its reliability, expanse, and frequent good shape, smoothed by the forests of kelp. Several take-off spots, the first being **Sewer Peak**, a top-to-bottom barrel over a rock shelf. The lefts can be decent, but the rights are generally cleaner and longer. Heavily surfed by excellent shortboarders. Best with S and W swells and low tide. Next comes **First Peak**, a quality righthander that's very predictable and very crowded, because it is surfable on a variety of swell angles and tides. Fun on a big day when it's makeable all the way through to Insides. Moving further down the point, there's **Second Peak**, less of a peak and more of a lined-up wall than First Peak. Not as stellar, but it does have its day. Popular with the grommet pack. Directly out in front of Jack O'Neill's house is **Insides** (aka, Middle Peak), a mushy reef peak occupied with longboarder cruisers and beginners. Some rocks on the inside; best with lower mid tides to minimise backwash, but choked with kelp on bigger low tides. **The Hook** is yet another excellent fast, hollow righthander. Best on lower tides and S swells up to a few feet overhead as NW swells lose a bit of size. The inside section can continue on and wrap into **Sharks Cove** which can also have a short left. Beside the wharf, **Beer Can Beach** is a decent beachbreak, best during small, clean, peaky swells with high tide. If there has been sufficient rainfall, **Capitola** can provide a decent rivermouth wave. The Jetty, next to the river, has a good sandbank with small punchy rights. Like all Santa Cruz breaks, there is always potential for a crowd. Perfect for improvers and longboarders. **Manresa** State Beach is a popular summertime beachbreak expanse; gets very crowded. Wicked littoral currents and shorepound. Closes-out easily. High tide and no wind best; peaky swells are the go.

NW swells come from lows off the Aleutian Islands (Oct-Mar), ranging in size from 3-20ft. Early and late summer will see frequent 2-8ft W swells originating far out in the western Pacific or as short distance windswells developing just offshore. Summer (July-Oct) surf can originate from either SW groundswells or hurricanes off Mexico. Waves can occasionally reach 10ft, but average 2-6ft. Check the harbour buoy or NOAA 46042 on the internet for the latest swell size. Dominant winds are NW-N year-round, varying from 40% of the time in Jan to 70% of the time in June; it blows the strongest in spring. Because Santa Cruz town faces south, prevailing winds are frequently offshore or cross-off. Town spots are generally better with lower tides.

TOM COZAD

Capitola

| STATISTICS | | J F | M A | M J | J A | S O | N D |
|---|---|---|---|---|---|---|---|
| SWELL | Direction | | | | | | |
| | Size (ft) | 6 | 4-5 | 4 | 4-5 | 5 | 6 |
| WIND | Direction | | | | | | |
| | Force | F4 | F4 | F5 | F4-F5 | F4 | F4 |
| WATER | Wetsuit | | | | | | |
| | Temp/°C | 13 | 13 | 14 | 15 | 15 | 14 |
| WEATHER | Rainfall/mm | 95 | 52 | 8 | 0 | 11 | 72 |
| | days/mth | 8 | 6 | 2 | 0 | 2 | 7 |
| | Min temp/°C | 5 | 7 | 10 | 12 | 11 | 7 |
| | Max temp/°C | 14 | 17 | 20 | 22 | 22 | 15 |

# Santa Barbara Co. CALIFORNIA, USA

Ah, Santa Barbara. The name alone evokes images of a swank Western Riviera of impressive homes, Euro tourists, soap operas, and celebrity sightings. Santa Barbara certainly has a ladle in the Southern California stew, and the south county rivals areas like Huntington Beach in terms of crowds and congestion—it's been said that while surfing here, you might as well be in L.A. The city of Santa Barbara is affluent and scenic, what with the wooded slopes of the Santa Ynez Mountains to the north and the Channel Islands to the south. Easily seen is the influence of Spanish settlers everywhere—especially so downtown, where brick, stucco, and adobe abut palm trees and tourist traps. Although Santa Barbara County's south coast faces due south (even southeast in some places), most swell from the S and SW is blocked by the Channel Islands. Point Conception further narrows the window of opportunity to N and NW swells that wrap around the cape. When this happens, what's lacking in quantity is made up in quality in a shapely series of right points. This set-up is the best in California on a medium to large W swell, but you can still burn a lot of gas chasing a wave—at least an uncrowded one. The Santa Barbara points have gotten overwhelmingly crowded in the past several years, partly because hundreds of surfers from the north and south (and an increasing number of foreign surf tourists) descend upon places like Rincon and El Capitan at every hint of winter west swell. Low-key spots that were rarely surfed 10 years ago are now heavily surfed.

| | |
|---|---|
| + RIGHT POINTBREAKS | – OFTEN SMALL OR FLAT |
| + OFTEN CLEAN | – EXTREMELY CROWDED |
| + NICE WEATHER | – POLLUTION |
| + SCENIC | – TRAFFIC |

El Capitan

JIMMY WILSON

## TRAVEL INFORMATION

**Weather** – Southern California is famous for its sunshine. It seldom rains. Spring-early summer dense fog and low clouds are common, often cleared by light afternoon onshores. The driest and sunniest time occurs when the easterly Santa Ana winds blow from the desert, usually in late summer and autumn. Winter is mild with a few rainy days, but bigger swells and favourable winds common. Water temp is cool, requiring a 3/2mm fullsuit most of the year, sometimes booties in the winter. El Niños bring warmer water, lots of swells (maybe too much), along with flooding rains and pollution. La Nina years are dismally flat.

**Lodging and Food** – Carpinteria has two Motel 6s at $60-$90. Goleta has several hotels but none at the beach. Santa Barbara (SB) has dozens of beachfront hotels from deluxe to budget, but even "budget" doesn't mean "cheap" in this very expensive city. Camping is available at Refugio, El Capitan, and Carpinteria state beaches ($30-$40, make reservations well in advance). Fast food is cheap ($10/meal), most restaurants are expensive. Great Mexican food is abundant.

**Nature and Culture** – Take a sailing lesson with Santa Barbara Sailing Center. Over on East Beach you can join a match of volleyball or go skateboard at the waterfront skate park. The mountains above the city are good for hiking and scenic vistas. Stroll along State Street for window-shopping and people-watching. Go wine tasting in the Santa Ynez Valley. Cruise around the new, hip Funk Zone.

**Hazards and Hassles** – Most pointbreaks visible from Highway 101 will be packed if breaking (even if tiny). Mind private properties. At low tide, the points expose rocks that hurt if hit (use a leash). There are white sharks here but sightings are rare. Beware of hyper-competitive wannabe pro surfers and a large number of kooks.

**Handy Hints** – Be mentally prepared to surf in a crowd. Don't bother bringing a gun. A new shortboard costs ±$750. Heaps of stores offer gear: Trim Shop, Rincon Designs, the Beach House, Surf Country, Channel Islands, etc. Have low expectations for the surf, even if there is a forecasted swell. This is the most fickle surf area in Southern California. The ocean here can look like a lake much of the year. The northern half of the county, however, is never flat—head north of Point Conception if you want some less-crowded (Jalama exempted) juice.

RYAN CRAIG

Below Point Conception are the private Bixby and Hollister ranches, a famous 14-mile stretch of coast containing several inconsistent albeit high-quality right points and reefs. Despite fronting private property, these spots get crowded, too. The Bixby spots are best during summer SW swells and NW wind; the Hollister spots are best generally during winter. Inaccessible to anyone lacking a HR real estate title, a good boat, or a drive-in connection. East of Hollister, south swells really do not hit anywhere because the Channel Islands do a fine job of blocking. Publicly accessible downcoast from Gaviota, **Tajiguas** offers various peaks along a small fetch of beach clearly visible from Highway 101, west of Refugio. Regularly surfed but not high-quality. Prefers medium tides and peaky windswells, best during the springtime. Park in the dirt on the ocean side of the road. **Refugio State Beach** is a small, mushy righthand sand cove wave favoured by beginners and longboarders. Needs big NW swells or the proper direction of W. Rideable at all tides but best with low. Can sometimes catch some summer SW swell. Waves can be long with a speedy section or two over the inside cove. Pleasant campground here. **Beavers/Hazards** is a small stretch of beach just east of Refugio where you can park along the road. Mediocre peaks, usually not very good, but it can get fun during windswells. Sometimes a fun right at the north end, sometimes a good left at the south end. Lower tides needed. Notoriously fickle and crowded, **El Capitan** State Beach is a perfect, hollow righthand point that rarely breaks properly. Needs a big W swell and low tide. Offshore with N wind. Can pick up SW swells. The beachbreak in front of the parking lot is best with windswells and higher tides. Camping near the beach and up the canyon. **Sands Beach** is popular with the UCSB college contingent, which makes sense since the spot picks up a lot of swell, best when peaky and smaller. Some rock hazards at the south end, which is also sometimes called Stu Peak (i.e. students). Often tar in the water. Gets hollow. Blows offshore in NE-SE wind. Just around the corner is **Devereux**, aka Coal

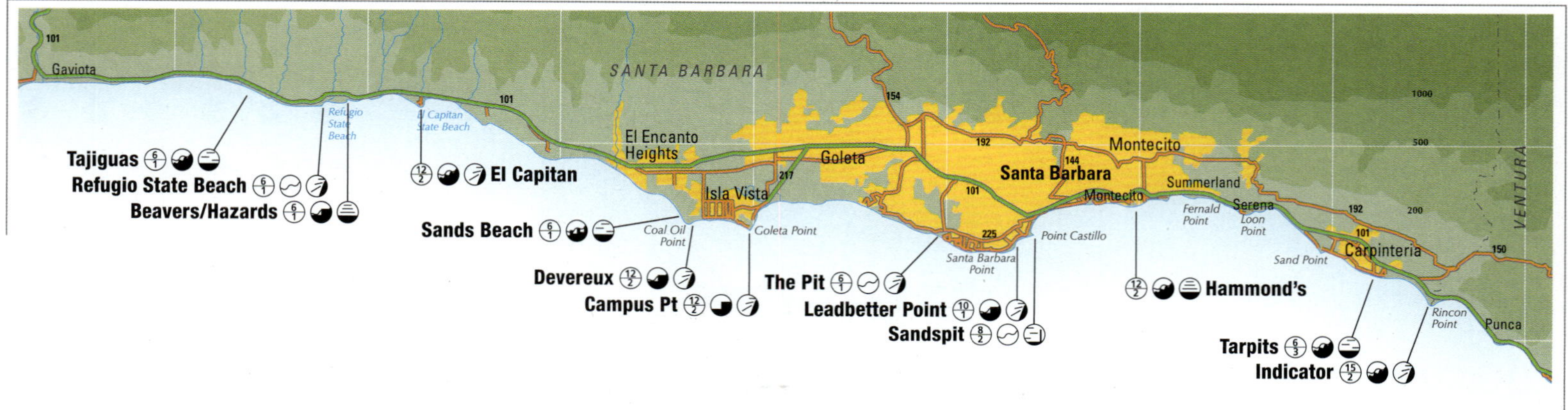

## Sandspit

**LAT. 34.404969° LONG. -119.687045°**

**A fairly rare righthand tube over an extremely shallow sand bottom, created by the Army Corps of Engineers when the breakwater was built to protect Santa Barbara Harbor. The wave is hard-hitting and dredging, beginning with a huge backwash coming out at an angle to the wave from the breakwater. Insanely competitive crowd and very dangerous – expert surfers with tuberiding experience only. Strong current requires constant paddling to stay in position. Rarely bigger than headhigh and needs big W or SE swells at low tide to work. Sheltered from NW wind and is often the cleanest spot on the sunny days between storms when big swells are in the water. Tom Curren got the all-time longest California tuberide here. The exposure and (hence) crowd factor has exploded in the last 5-10 years. Hundreds of surfers come to SB to give Sandspit a shot on big W swells. Doesn't break often. Park at the harbor and walk out along the breakwater; 90 minutes maximum free parking time allowed.**

Oil Point, a playful right that gets hollow on the rock ledge up top. Mushy otherwise, with lots of sections and room to move. Rides can be long. Often lots of kelp and tar. Gets a lot of swell, best with a WNW and lower tides and N wind. Park at the west end of Isla Vista and walk up. **Campus Point** is a fickle right point next to UCSB. Great spot when it breaks properly, which isn't very often. Big W swell and low tide needed. The other side of the point is a beachbreak left called Depressions, best with windswell or SE hurricane swells. **The Pit** (aka Arroyo Burro Beach) is a small beachbreak that gets fun and dumpy with windswells. Water is usually polluted after rains. Surf quality is normally poor, but it is still surfed regularly. Popular spot for groms, beachgoers, and dog-walkers. **Leadbetter Point** offers mushy, fairly long rights. Ideal spot for beginners, SUPs, and longboarders who come in numbers. Can get really fun with big W swells or windswells. More sectiony at low tide, too fat at high tide. **Sandspit** is an insanely crowded, famously draining/backwashy right barrel over a very shallow sand bottom. **Hammond's** is a classic righthand cobblestone reef/semi-pointbreak in ultra-rich Montecito. Similar to Lowers at Trestles. Fast and lined up; always crowded. Medium-high tides with clean W swells work best here. Accessible by walking up from the Miramar Beach access parking area. **Tarpits** (Carpinteria State Beach) is home to various reefy/sandbar peaks, best with medium tides and small, peaky swells. Rock boils at low tide, backwash at high tide. The beachbreak to the north can provide a lot of elbow room if Tarpits itself is crowded. Gets hollow; fun during the spring and summer; medium-low tide best. Campground here. Technically still in Santa Barbara County, **Indicator** is the outermost part of famous Rincon Point, best at high tide with a NW swell. Sometimes kelpy and very crowded, but usually not as bad as the crowds you'll find when you head toward the mouth of Rincon Creek, where you officially enter Ventura County and Rincon Cove, the best-quality wave in Southern California.

The primary source of swell comes from the NW lows out in the Aleutian Islands in winter (Oct-Mar). Waves can reach 12ft but average 3-8ft on W to NW swells; Point Conception blocks NNW-N swells. SW groundswells and hurricanes off Mexico are mostly blocked by the Channel Islands (San Miguel, Santa Cruz, Santa Rosa and Anacapa), especially in Santa Barbara County. Either side of summer, frequent 2-6ft W groundswell or windswell can occur. Calm days and offshores are more common in winter even though the E Santa Ana winds tend to blow in late summer. Dominant winds are W to NW, with NW at 28% (Dec) to 39% (Aug) – bringing choppy conditions from noon till dusk and sometimes earlier. Glassy days are more common here than elsewhere on the West Coast, with a noticeable difference between Santa Barbara and the frequently strong winds in the Point Conception area. Tides usually vary gently from 4ft-7ft (1.2-2.1m), but max range hits 8.5ft (2.6m).

JIMMY WILSON

Hammonds and Miramar Reefs

| STATISTICS | | J F | M A | M J | J A | S O | N D |
|---|---|---|---|---|---|---|---|
| SWELL | Direction | | | | | | |
| | Size (ft) | 4 | 3-4 | 1-2 | 1-2 | 4 | 4 |
| WIND | Direction | | | | | | |
| | Force | F3 | F4 | F4 | F4 | F4 | F3 |
| WATER | Wetsuit | | | | | | |
| | Temp/°C | 14 | 14 | 16 | 17 | 16 | 15 |
| WEATHER | Rainfall/mm | 85 | 49 | 3 | 0 | 11 | 52 |
| | days/mth | 4 | 3 | 1 | 0 | 1 | 3 |
| | Min temp/°C | 6 | 8 | 11 | 14 | 12 | 6 |
| | Max temp/°C | 18 | 19 | 21 | 24 | 23 | 20 |

# Ventura County CALIFORNIA, USA

Much more exposed than Santa Barbara, the scenic Ventura County coast is a haven for summertime S swells, wintertime NW swells, and just about everything in between. Consistent and high-quality surf is not uncommon, and there is a wealth of different surf spots to choose from on any given day, from pounding beachbreak barrels to slow beginner's waves. The Channel Islands do not have such a prominent swell-shadowing effect as they do for Santa Barbara, which can be waist high during a big winter swell while Ventura County is double-overhead. Onshore winds are usually stronger here than in Santa Barbara, and all Ventura spots blow out fairly easily. Strong offshore winds are a frequent occurrence, especially during the winter months in Oxnard, causing classic conditions. Rincon, one of the world's most famous pointbreaks, is in the extreme north end of the county, while to the south exist world-class beachbreaks like Silver Strands and the Santa Clara Rivermouth. South swells do better at the south county spots like County Line and Point Mugu, which is off-limits to anyone without a valid military identification card. W swells typically have the most power and are the most lined-up, but solid S swells tend to work wonders in south county. Most waves in the county can been seen from Highway 1 or Highway 101 and are easily accessible.

| | |
|---|---|
| + RINCON POINT | - WINDY |
| + POWERFUL BEACHBREAKS | - CROWDED |
| + NICE WEATHER | - POLLUTED |
| + FAIRLY CONSISTENT SURF | - TRAFFIC |

## TRAVEL INFORMATION

**Weather** – See Santa Barbara County

**Lodging and Food** – Ventura and Oxnard have many hotels and motels to suit any budget. Do a quick online search. Camping available at Hobson, Faria, Emma Wood, and McGrath ($30-$40, make reservations well in advance). Fast food is cheap ($8/meal). Mexican food is abundant. Enjoy some fresh beer at places like Surf Brewery, Topa Topa, and Poseidon.

**Nature and Culture** – Take a whale watching cruise or a day trip to the Channel Islands (islandpackers.com); go sport fishing or sailing; head up the 33 to lovely Lake Casitas; stroll out to the end of the pier or eat/drink/shop your way down Main Street in Ventura; ride a bike or skateboard along the boardwalks. Hike up to Two Trees or arrange for a tour of the Point Mugu naval base. Pretty much anything you can think of, you can do in this county (except snow sports).

**Hazards and Hassles** – All of the spots visible from Highway 101 will be crowded if they are good. At low tide, the points expose rocks that hurt if hit (use a leash). There are white sharks here but sightings are rare. Beware of hyper-competitive wannabe pro surfers and a large number of kooks at most spots. Rincon is the marquee destination in winter, and it's a scene. Traffic on the 101 can be bad at any time – Los Angeles is the next county south.

**Handy Hints** – Be mentally prepared to surf in a huge crowd at Rincon. A gun may be useful, especially at the Overhead. A new shortboard costs ±$750. Several stores offer gear: Ventura Surf Shop, Patagonia, Seaward, Beach Break, etc. Be low-key at spots like Silver Strand and Santa Clara Rivermouth. Wear a leash at the pointbreaks.

JEREMIAH KLEIN

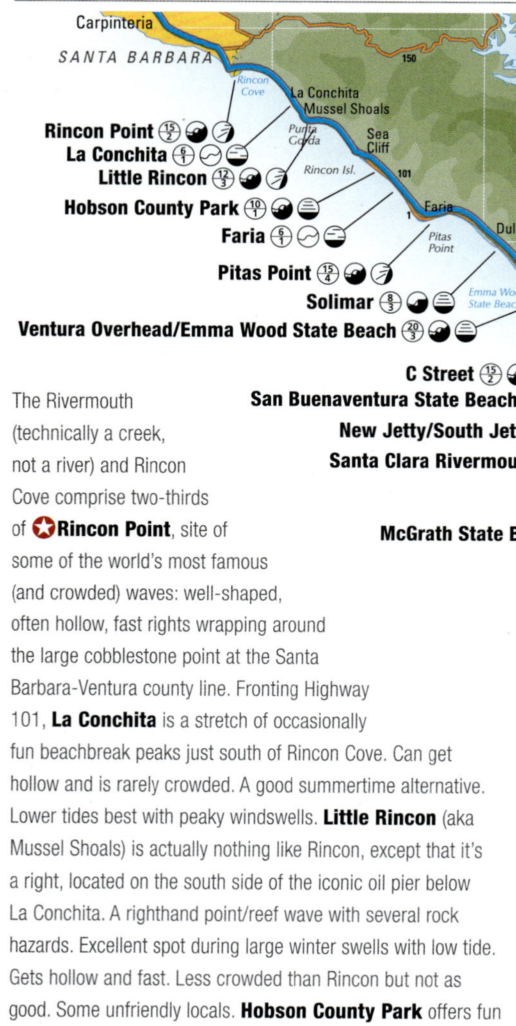


The Rivermouth (technically a creek, not a river) and Rincon Cove comprise two-thirds of **Rincon Point**, site of some of the world's most famous (and crowded) waves: well-shaped, often hollow, fast rights wrapping around the large cobblestone point at the Santa Barbara-Ventura county line. Fronting Highway 101, **La Conchita** is a stretch of occasionally fun beachbreak peaks just south of Rincon Cove. Can get hollow and is rarely crowded. A good summertime alternative. Lower tides best with peaky windswells. **Little Rincon** (aka Mussel Shoals) is actually nothing like Rincon, except that it's a right, located on the south side of the iconic oil pier below La Conchita. A righthand point/reef wave with several rock hazards. Excellent spot during large winter swells with low tide. Gets hollow and fast. Less crowded than Rincon but not as good. Some unfriendly locals. **Hobson County Park** offers fun cobblestone reef peaks; good with any swell and any tide. Long lefts can be had off the northern peak; long, mushy rights are the call at the south peak, which closes out on the inner sandbar. **Faria** is a long stretch of beachbreak; park along the old Pacific Coast Highway. Best with medium-high tides and small, peaky swells. A popular area with recreational vehicles as it's free to park here. **Pitas Point** (aka Faria County Park) is an extensive righthand cobblestone pointbreak. Lots of room for everyone but variable quality. Separate take-off areas and some long rides. Gets hollow and fast. Sheltered from the prevailing northwest wind. Can handle winter size and gets summer souths. A good alternative to Rincon but is getting more crowded each year. Campground up top. **Solimar** sometimes offers fun reef waves; mostly rights. Best with S swells and low tide. There is another wave on the inside, best with winter swells. Accessible by walking along pathways north and south of the community of Solimar. Park along the road. There is an outer reef here that is short, fast, and hollow, but very kelpy and a long paddle-out. **Emma Wood State Beach** is a very popular beachbreak/reef spot, punchy and hollow; mainly rights, but some good lefts on summer souths. Peaky swells are great. Gets a lot of swell and crowds, especially with kids. The outside reef is called Ventura Overhead, working only with big NW and W swells. Big-wave boards are recommended for the big drops and fat shoulders. Gets packed quickly amongst the kelp. **C Street** (aka California Street) is a very long righthand pointbreak fronting the Ventura County Fairgrounds. Very reliable spot that works on all tides

Little Rincon

RYAN CRAIG

TOM COZAD

**Rincon Point**

**LAT. 34.372395° LONG. -119.477495°**

Justifiably, Rincon Point is one of the world's most famous waves. A long, perfect righthand pointbreak; gets hollow and is usually very lined-up. Always very crowded. Try to wait your turn, or be aggressive. Watch out for flailing boards and bodies. Rides are possible from the very top of the point (above the river mouth) all the way to the highway, but the swell has to be big enough and of the proper direction (NW) not to section off. Rincon can be good at all tides, but low provides the most tube-time. The rivermouth generally likes a higher tide, while the cove likes medium-low. The rivermouth has some rock hazards at lower tides. Plainly visible from Highway 101. The inner cove is generally a mushier, softer wave popular with longboarders, but it too can be screaming fast. Avoid surfing Rincon after heavy rains (which are rare) since the septic tank sewage seeps into the ocean from the houses on the point. Accessible via two big free (for now) carparks off the Bates Road exit.

C-Street

JEREMIAH KLEIN

Oxnard Shores

with all swells up to double-overhead. Several take-off zones over a cobblestone and sand bottom. Rather mushy, but long and forgiving, so popular with longboarders. Paddling out can be difficult during big swells. Beware of water pollution after rains. **San Buenaventura State Beach** comprises a handful of jetties in the Pierpont Bay area, south of the Ventura Pier. Various beachbreak peaks; good with small, peaky swells. Fun during the summertime, but often windy. **New Jetty/ South Jetty** provides good, hollow beachbreak waves on the south side of the new jetty to the south of the Ventura Harbor mouth. Good with any swell up to a few feet overhead, making the locals territorial. **Santa Clara Rivermouth** can be a world-class sandbar, plus it gets good up and down the beach too. Severely polluted after heavy rainfall, which is when the shape can be flawless, dispatching A-frame peaks spinning off into long, fast walls in both directions. Holds up to several feet overhead. Gets crowded, but for good reason. One of California's best rivermouth breaks when everything comes together. **McGrath State Beach** is miles of beachbreak peaks that are uncrowded, but also suffer from pollution after rains. Needs smaller swells and higher tides. **Silver Strand** is a popular mile of powerful beachbreak flanked by two jetties. One of California's best beachbreaks. Site of nasty localism in years past; beware of potentially sour attitudes in and out of the water. Epic barrels during the wintertime. Seen in many surf magazines and videos. Always has some kind of surf. **Port Hueneme Beach Park** offers average beachbreak on both sides of the pier, with S swell lefts in summer. Can't handle any size, yet it's never flat. Higher tides and peaky swells work best. **Ormond Beach** is uncrowded beachbreak at the foot of Perkins Road, south of Port Hueneme. A good alternative to the crowds during peaky S swells.

The primary source of swell comes from the NW lows out in the Aleutian Islands in winter (Oct-Mar). Waves can reach 18ft, but average 3-8ft on W to NW swells; Point Conception shadows some N swells. SSW groundswells and SE hurricane swells from Baja are good at some of the southern spots. Either side of summer, frequent 2-6ft W groundswell or windswell can occur. Calm days and offshores are more common in winter even though the E Santa Ana winds tend to blow in late summer. Dominant winds are W-NW, NW – 28% (Dec) to 39% (Aug) – bringing choppy conditions from noon till dusk and sometimes earlier. Record tidal range is -1.6ft to 7.2ft (-0.5-2.2m).

| STATISTICS | | J F | M A | M J | J A | S O | N D |
|---|---|---|---|---|---|---|---|
| SWELL | Direction | | | | | | |
| | Size (ft) | 4 | 3-4 | 1-2 | 1-2 | 4 | 4 |
| WIND | Direction | | | | | | |
| | Force | F3 | F4 | F4 | F4 | F4 | F3 |
| WATER | Wetsuit | | | | | | |
| | Temp/°C | 14 | 14 | 16 | 17 | 16 | 15 |
| WEATHER | Rainfall/mm | 85 | 49 | 3 | 0 | 11 | 3 |
| | days/mth | 4 | 3 | 1 | 0 | 1 | 3 |
| | Min temp/°C | 6 | 8 | 11 | 14 | 12 | 6 |
| | Max temp/°C | 18 | 19 | 21 | 24 | 23 | 20 |

# Los Angeles County CALIFORNIA, USA

A sprawling metropolis with a population of approximately 10 million people, the city of Los Angeles is home to movie stars, extravagant homes, 12-lane freeways and nearly 96km (60mi) of Pacific Coast beaches. Among the surf spots of California's largest city, none can claim to be as famous as Malibu with its long righthanders breaking beside the coastal Highway 1. Tom Blake pioneered the break in 1926, then Miki Dora's stylish riding prowess and a movie based on a Malibu surfer girl, Gidget, exposed the wave to the world. LA County is mainly all beachbreak, but man-made structures like piers and jetties provide some good sandbars. Over-development of the LA basin has resulted in huge volumes of urban runoff from the coastal concrete jungle, causing regular beach closures from high bacteria counts and other toxic pollutants.

**+ CONSISTENT SWELL**
**+ LEGENDARY MALIBU**
**+ ENTERTAINMENT LA STYLE**
**+ SUNNY WEATHER**

**– MOSTLY BEACHBREAK**
**– URBAN POLLUTION**
**– EXPENSIVE**
**– HEAVY CROWDS/TRAFFIC**

## TRAVEL INFORMATION

**Weather** – Southern California is famous for its reliably sunny weather. It hardly ever rains especially from spring to fall, but there are many morning fogs, which dissipate by noon, unlike the constant LA smog. The sun shines, perpetuating light onshore sea breezes. The driest, sunniest time occurs with late summer Santa Ana conditions, when winds blow in from the desert. Nov to Feb brings mild winter weather with a few rainy days. Water temp is the warmest in California but still requires a 3/2 steamer most of the time. Water is warmer in Santa Monica Bay than San Diego because there is no upwelling. El Niño years have warmer water temps, lots of swells and flooding rains.

**Lodging and Food** – This is LA, so there is every kind of accommodation for every kind of budget. Also every kind of food. The Malibu Beach Inn is right on the beach south of the pier ($800/dble), Casa Malibu Inn is a bit cheaper, starting at $600. Malibu Creek State Park Campground is open year-round and affordable. Other options include the Hotel California in Santa Monica ($250) or Cadillac Hotel in Venice ($160). Comfort Inn Santa Monica is $144/night. The Santa Monica hostel is $50/night; the Venice Beach hostel is $135/night.

**Nature and Culture** – Cruising Highway 1 means checking the surf and the rich and famous's houses perched on the hillsides. Check Venice boardwalk for body-builders, posers, jugglers, and activists's. Of course LA offers endless entertainment possibilities. It is a true melting pot of the world. You can do anything you want.

**Hazards and Hassles** – Fires, floods, and earthquakes have taken their toll on the Los Angeles area. Crime is big in some areas. Gangs, drugs, etc. In the water crowds and pollution are the main issues. There are no secret spots around here, but the less accessible spots are definitely emptier. Many workers go for the dawn patrol; there may be fewer crowds during the day than early mornings.

**Handy Hints** – Only Redondo Beach Breakwater requires a gun, other breaks are best surfed on a regular shortboard or a longboard. Surf shops are numerous and a new shortboard costs around $800; try Mollusk in Venice and ZJ in Santa Monica. There are about 20 surf schools, including Malibu Makos and Aqua Surf.

JIMMY WILSON

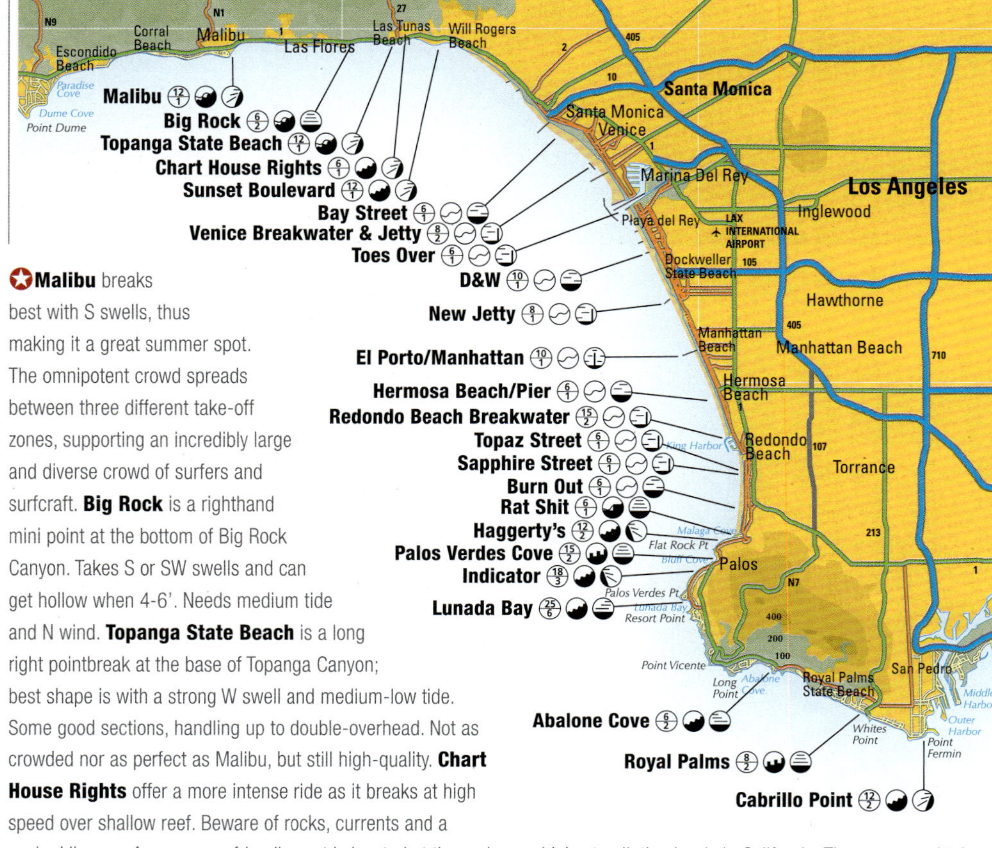


**Malibu** breaks best with S swells, thus making it a great summer spot. The omnipotent crowd spreads between three different take-off zones, supporting an incredibly large and diverse crowd of surfers and surfcraft. **Big Rock** is a righthand mini point at the bottom of Big Rock Canyon. Takes S or SW swells and can get hollow when 4-6'. Needs medium tide and N wind. **Topanga State Beach** is a long right pointbreak at the base of Topanga Canyon; best shape is with a strong W swell and medium-low tide. Some good sections, handling up to double-overhead. Not as crowded nor as perfect as Malibu, but still high-quality. **Chart House Rights** offer a more intense ride as it breaks at high speed over shallow reef. Beware of rocks, currents and a packed line-up. A more user-friendly spot is located at the end of **Sunset Boulevard**. On a large W swell, it offers mushy, sectiony walls and room for everyone. Likes low to mid tide. The crowded urban beaches of Santa Monica can occasionally offer good jetty surf to those not afraid to face some of the highest pollution levels in California. There are good tubes to be found on a solid S-SW swell and the Municipal Pier provides another surf option. For small beachbreak waves, the eternally popular **Bay Street** is best with peaky windswells and low tide. Needs to have holes in the sand bottom otherwise it is a close-out. Better known for outdoors gyms and basketball courts, **Venice Beach** holds some powerful winter peaks around the breakwater and jetty. With summer SW swells, Ballona Creek can have small, hollow rights at a spot called **Toes Over**, off the south jetty. The lefts south of there are better suited to longboarding and both spots suffer from high pollution levels. **D&W** can offer classic rights off the jetty, best with medium-low tides and 4-6' NW swell. El Segundo was supposed to receive a new break in the form of Pratte's artificial reef, but the project was a failure and the sandbags dumped there are only appreciated by the fish, while surfers keep hanging out at **New Jetty**. With W or SW swells, short, hollow waves break on a sandbar south of this jetty. The north side will pick-up winter's NW swells. **El Porto** is always bigger than surrounding beaches, can hold size and gets quite hollow. Downside is that it's always crowded and really wind sensitive. Several peaks up and down the beach can be good at all tides and up to a few feet overhead. Easy parking, but bring your quarters for the meters. Poor water quality. Good peaky waves at any tide can break on either side of **Manhattan Beach** Municipal Pier, attracting many surfers to the beach that Dale Velzy first rode in 1951. **Hermosa Beach/Pier** is another popular beachbreak, best with small, broken up swells, since it tends to close-out over 6ft. **Redondo Beach Breakwater** is a serious wedge of a lefthander, needing proper equipment and skills as it can hold triple-overhead winter swells. More beachbreaks extend

JEREMIAH KLEIN

Hermosa Beach

JIMMY WILSON

LA Secret

## Malibu

**LAT. 34.032090° LONG. -118.678089°**

**One of the world's most famous and most crowded righthand pointbreaks. Mainly a summertime spot best on S swells. Three separate take-off zones: Third Point: at medium tide, fast, hollow rides off the westernmost point. Big swells will connect up with Second Point: long, hollow, workable wall at medium tide, unmakeable at low. First Point: the most consistent and therefore the most surfed of the Malibu waves. Can show perfect shape, excellent for any type of surf craft. Works through the full tidal range, getting more hollow as the tide drops. The crowds are intense to say the least and with so many longboards about, sharing waves is common practice whether you like it or not. One of the worst beaches in the county for beach closures due to bacterial pollution after heavy rains. Malibu beachfront homes use outdated, ill-located septic tanks, which can leak directly into the Malibu Lagoon and line-up after heavy rain, leaving surfers with eye and ear infections, respiratory illnesses and rashes. After 35 years of debate the county is building a new treatment plant. There are full on-beach facilities, a small pay parking lot, and free parking along PCH.**

southwards to the Palos Verdes Peninsula. **Topaz Street** and neighbouring **Sapphire Street** provide jetty surf, while **Burn Out** is one of Torrance's best beachbreaks along Paseo de la Playa. **Rat Shit** is a rock/sand combo offering peaks up to about headhigh on W swells and lower tides; sheltered from S wind. **Haggerty's** offers thick wintertime lefts off a rocky headland, officially known as Malaga Cove. A few different take-off zones here, the main one being at the base of the church parking lot. Favours big W swells. **Palos Verdes Cove** (Bluff Cove) is one of California's first surf spots, boasting four different breaks. At the cove's north end is Ski Jump, a mushy righthand reef, slow and thick, breaking in front of Flat Rock Point. North Reef is just inside of Ski Jump, dishing up mainly fast rights and a few lefts. High tides work best here with smaller W swells. The cove's premier break is Middles; slow rights and lefts favored by longboarders. Needs winter swells. Then there's **Indicator**, a juicy, rocky, shallow left on the south end of the cove. **Lunada Bay** is a famous big-wave reef known for idiotic locals and its thick, world-class righthanders. One of the few bona fide Southern California big-wave spots. Needs big W-NW swells and any tide, lower the better. Perfect shape and very powerful; strong currents. Never closes-out. East wind is offshore. Rocky and unfriendly. **Abalone Cove** provides decent headhigh lefts off the rocky south end of the scenic cove during S swells. **Royal Palms** has two crowded spots. The rocky right point is called Palm Point, working with SW-W swells up to a foot or two overhead at low tide, when the waves line up better. The Jetty is a popular peak that prefers higher tides and small to medium SW swells. NW wind blows offshore at **Cabrillo Point**, where a rocky, often mushy righthander gets good on S and SW swells, but only breaks properly a few times per year.

The primary source of swell comes from the SW groundswells April to September or tropical cyclones off Mexico between July and October. Waves can reach 12ft but average 3-8ft as Santa Catalina Island can block some of the swell. Aleutian lows in winter (Oct-March), bring 2-8ft surf to the beaches, but it won't get in between Malibu and Santa Monica. Before and after summer, frequent 2-6ft W swells appear from distant West Pacific groundswell or near-shore windswell. Calm days and offshore days are more common in winter even though the magical E Santa Ana winds tend to blow in late summer. Dominant winds are W-NW. NW sea breeze usually chops things up from noon until dusk. Winds are rarely strong and glassy days are a SoCal feature. Tides vary from 4-7ft (1.2-2.1m).

| STATISTICS | | J F | M A | M J | J A | S O | N D |
|---|---|---|---|---|---|---|---|
| SWELL | Direction | | | | | | |
| | Size (ft) | 5 | 4 | 3-4 | 3 | 3 | 4 |
| WIND | Direction | | | | | | |
| | Force | F3 | F4 | F4 | F4 | F4 | F3 |
| WATER | Wetsuit | | | | | | |
| | Temp/°C | 14 | 14 | 16 | 19 | 19 | 16 |
| WEATHER | Rainfall/mm | 75 | 50 | 5 | 0 | 10 | 50 |
| | days/mth | 6 | 5 | 2 | 0 | 1 | 5 |
| | Min temp/°C | 8 | 9 | 13 | 16 | 13 | 9 |
| | Max temp/°C | 19 | 20 | 22 | 28 | 26 | 21 |

# Orange County CALIFORNIA, USA

Orange County surf is a mixed bag, stuffed full of a small-wave beachbreaks, catering to plenty of surfers living and working in the hub of the global surf industry. With warm temperatures and bikinied girls on the beach, Orange County can seem like the best place in the world at times, but it isn't. On the global scale, the generally weak, mediocre line-ups are often marred by the slightest onshore breeze and rarely last more than four seconds from take-off to close-out. Those big blue 'n sunny Salt Creek barrel photos in the magazines are actually glorified close-outs; same with Newport and Huntington. It can get good, especially when a fickle-as-hell S-SW pulse arrives with zero wind, outshining the neighbouring counties thanks to its SW-facing aspect. Wintertime W swells do get in quite handily, but due NW tends to approach the coast lacking intensity, while N swells are a miss. Jetties and piers play a major role from Seal Beach to Newport, which is all fairly consistent beachbreak. Surf size is never huge in Orange County unless you consider the Wedge, a freak of jetty engineering, yet there is generally something to ride every day, good or bad or somewhere between.

| + | – |
|---|---|
| + VARIETY OF SPOTS | – VERY CROWDED |
| + LOTS OF CLEAN WAVES | – TRAFFIC |
| + GREAT WEATHER | – POLLUTION |
| + ENTERTAINING AREA | – CONCRETE JUNGLE |

## TRAVEL INFORMATION

**Weather** – See Santa Monica Bay

**Lodging and Food** – This is the heart of coastal Southern California, so every kind of food and lodging is available, in all locations, for all budgets. A comfy double in a motel by the beach is $100-300 in Huntington Beach or Newport Beach. Laguna Beach hotels range $100-$160. Slightly cheaper places can be found in San Clemente. Youth Hostels cost $50 a night. Camp at Bolsa Chica or Newport Dunes Resort. Fast food and Mexican food is ubiquitous and cheap ($10/meal), restaurants can be pricey, especially those right on the beaches.

**Nature and Culture** – Great skate parks everywhere. Plenty of interesting surf and junk shops to browse. People-watching is fun. There's Disneyland, if that's your thing. Also check Knott's Berry Farm, Soak City and Wild River Water Park. Hollywood and LA's mean streets aren't far away.

**Hazards and Hassles** – The best way to avoid fierce crowds is to surf the less-accessible spots. Park close to gated communities and walk. Watch out for metered parking (tickets are forwarded by car rental agencies). There are a few stingrays and sea urchins, but not many sharks. Watch out for murky waters after heavy rain – sewage and stormwater run-off is a big problem.

**Handy Hints** – Don't bother with a big wave gun. Be ready to surf in crowds in subpar waves. A new retail shortboard costs ±$750, ($1000 for a longboard). Plenty of shops for gear – check Harbour, Katin, Jack's, HSS, Frog House, Hobie or Thalia.

PAT NOLAN

**7th Street to Dolphin Avenue** is a half-mile of sandbars exposed to wind and swell, including the Seal Beach Pier, which has average beachbreak peaks on both sides of the pier, with occasional epic shorebreak barrel wedges on the south side. At the end of 13th Street is a heavy, hollow sandbar peak when it breaks, which isn't very often. Shallow. Needs big winter swells with low tide. A great wave if you can catch it. Experienced surfers only. **Surfside/Sunset/Bolsa Chica** are eight miles of beachbreak peaks, best with low tides and peaky SW swells. One of the best waves is the right which bombs off of the **Surfside Jetty**, at the entrance to Anaheim Bay. Check it during a big W swell and low tide. Bolsa Chica fronts a 300-acre wetland preserve; easy to find your own peak. Needs smaller swells with medium tide and NE wind. **Huntington Cliffs** is more beachbreak, generally better than Bolsa Chica. Usually mushy and forgiving. Takes a low tide and SW-W swells. Windy. World-famous **Huntington Pier** is one of California's most iconic surf spots, site of much history over the years. Very reliable and consistent on both sides of the pier. Also very crowded. The north side often has excellent rights peeling into the pier, handling big winter size. The south side works best during SW swells, showcasing good lefts that wall right through the barnacle-encrusted pilings (this is the spot that made "shooting the pier" famous). Both sides can work at any tide, though medium is usually best. Blows out easily around the time surfing is "blackballed" in favour of swimmers and spongers during summer middays. Just south is **Huntington State Beach**, two miles of beachbreak, far less crowded than the pier area. The **Santa Ana River Jetties** produce consistent, hollow, polluted peaks between the two jetties at the river's mouth. Gets very good and crowded, needing low tide and smaller SW swells. **Newport Beach** is a long stretch of beachbreak interspersed with several small jetties. Popular sandbars lie at the ends of 36th, 54th and 56th streets. Hollow, peaky and crowded. Holds up to a few feet overhead. Best during summertime S swells, but can be good at any time of the year. Park anywhere you can find a spot, which can be easier said than done. **Blackies** sometimes offers crowded, epic, long, wintertime sandbar lefts north of Newport Pier, in front of Blackie's Bar. The rights do exist but pale in comparison. Better with lower tides. Some localism. **Newport Point** is a rare sandbar left renowned for producing world-class barrels during large S swells and Mexican hurricane pulses. Needs a low tide. Extremely crowded when it breaks. Located at 18th Street. ✪**The Wedge** is unlike any other wave in the country, and owes its existence to some serendipitous jetty placement that helps amplify the height and heft of this fearsome shorebreak. Nearby **Corona del Mar Jetty** produces quality, long sandbar rights during certain S swells, breaking off of the south jetty of Newport Bay. Gets epic and crowded. Needs low tide. **El Morro** is a smoking, shallow, sand-bottomed lefthander off Abalone Point during large S swells and a pushing tide; short, fast rides, hollow and draining. Fast and mostly closed-out. **Rockpile** (Heisler Park) is a hazardous, rocky righthander best during bigger SW swells. Needs high tide. Unfriendly local crew. **Laguna Beach** hosts a series of fickle reefbreaks, notably at the ends of Thalia, Oak and Brooks streets. Can get good during medium-sized winter swells, but very crowded when it does. Brooks Street

PAT NOLAN
Huntington Pier

## The Wedge

LAT. 33.593123° LONG. -117.881881°

Radical, world-famous freak wave dominated by bodysurfers, skimboarders, and bodyboarders, although surfers do enjoy some degree of success. Only big S or SW swells will work and N-NE winds are dead offshore. Waves refract off the west (northside) Newport Harbor jetty, amplifying the swell and creating a ridiculous wedging peak, primarily a left, which explodes over a treacherously shallow sand bottom. The swell period needs to be just right for the first wave to bounce off the jetty and then meet the next incoming swell at just the right moment to create the giant mutant peaks that can exceed 20ft faces. It's possible to catch the bounce before it meets the main wave, helping ride into the tube that rarely shows the manners to hold the exit door open. Broken bodies are routine, it's extremely crowded with extreme surfers and a real circus when it's working. Very dangerous spot, for experts only, with scant regard for their personal safety. Great spectator spot as it breaks so close to shore. Boards are banned for most of the day, keeping the bodybashers happy.

is a great left. Agate is a shifty, winter peak that can handle big NW swells at mid tide, when some rock hazards appear amongst the crowd. **Salt Creek** is a famous, long, sandy beach with three classic surfing areas over a sand and rock bottom. At the southern end of the beach is the **Point**, a south-swell left that gets epic, holding up to double-overhead. In front of the restrooms is **Middles**, a consistent peak and good with any swell. Very competitive crowd. To the north is **Gravels**, a shallow, grinding righthand barrel, often closed-out, but providing great tube views and action for surf photographers. Takes any swell. Very crowded, even by LA standards. **Doheny State Beach** is generally gutless righthand cobblestone reef waves, ideal for beginners and longboarders. Slow and mushy on any tide and swell. Crowded and polluted after rains. **Poche** has various average beachbreak peaks, popular during the summertime. Can get peaky and hollow. Needs a medium-high tide. Outer reef works during low tide. Take stairway from PCH beneath the trail tracks. **204** is an average beachbreak zone that can get quite good on peaky SW swells. Breaks fairly close to shore. Located at the 204-mile marker on the railroad tracks. **San Clemente Pier** offers crowded sandbar peaks on the pier's north side. Typical sand-bottomed peaks, sectiony and often hollow. No wind protection; any tide is fine. Fun during the summertime. High school scene. Located at the foot of Esplanade, **T Street** is the main spot in San Clemente and an early stomping ground for many professional surfers. There's a rock reef on the outside and beachbreak on the inside. Fun peaks best with S swells, when the lefts are usually better. Mushy with high tides, fairly hollow with low tides. **San Clemente State Park** can see hollow beachbreak peaks over a rock and sand bottom at the bottom of Avenida Calafia. Sectiony, mostly lefts, showing form during the summer. Campground here.

RYAN CRAIG

Rockpile

W-SW groundswells in the summer are a staple, although swell shadowing by Santa Catalina Island affects a few areas, especially during west-southwest swells around Huntington. In winter NW swells fluctuate between 2-12ft. In general Orange County's swell exposure is not as good as San Diego's but on any given day in spring or autumn there might be 2-6ft of W swell coming from groundswell in the western Pacific or nearshore windswell. Prevailing winds are W-NW, most common in December and least so in August. The 'Santa Ana' E winds blow in late summer, but offshore days are more common in winter. All year the winds are rarely strong and glassy days are one of California's finer features. Tidal range varies from -1.6 to 7.2ft (0.5-2.2m) at Newport Harbour Entrance.

JIMMY WILSON

Newport Beach

| STATISTICS | | J F | M A | M J | J A | S O | N D |
|---|---|---|---|---|---|---|---|
| SWELL | Direction | | | | | | |
| | Size (ft) | 4-5 | 4 | 2-3 | 4 | 5 | 4-5 |
| WIND | Direction | | | | | | |
| | Force | F3 | F4 | F4 | F4 | F4 | F3 |
| WATER | Wetsuit | | | | | | |
| | Temp/°C | 14 | 14 | 16 | 17 | 16 | 15 |
| WEATHER | Rainfall/mm | 72 | 37 | 3 | 0 | 7 | 45 |
| | days/mth | 4 | 3 | 1 | 0 | 1 | 3 |
| | Min temp/°C | 9 | 10 | 14 | 17 | 13 | 10 |
| | Max temp/°C | 18 | 19 | 22 | 25 | 24 | 21 |

# North San Diego Co. CALIFORNIA, USA

North San Diego County is a great place to be a surfer, as thousands (millions?) of us have discovered in the past 60+ years. That is, if you don't mind surfing with 60+ of your best friends at any given spot during any decent sort of conditions. North county has seen a sharp increase in the surfing population due to rampant housing development east of the Interstate 5 freeway and towns like Cardiff and Leucadia have become trendy relocation areas for East Coasters and Midwesterners. San Diego boasts a deep surfing history and a wealth of lore at spots like Windansea and San Onofre, while Trestles is one of the world's most famous waves. Much of the coast is laden with expensive homes, as basically all of San Diego's beach towns are quite rich to some degree. "Fair-weather surfer" is a good term to describe most surfers here as rain is rare and sunshine is the rule. Cloudy days keep a lot of people away from the beaches. There are so many surfers in San Diego that it is impossible to tell who is a local and who is not, but there is a solid longtime base of surfers claiming rights to certain spots like Swamis. San Diego surfers are typically a friendly breed, so travellers will have no problem fitting in to what's often called "America's Finest City".

**+ VARIETY OF SPOTS**
**+ LOTS OF CLEAN WAVES**
**+ GREAT WEATHER**
**+ FLAT DAY ENTERTAINMENT**

**– VERY CROWDED**
**– HEAVY TRAFFIC**
**– POLLUTION**
**– URBAN ATMOSPHERE**

**TRAVEL INFORMATION**

see San Diego – South

AARON CHECKWOOD

Oceanside Beach

AARON CHECKWOOD

Cardiff

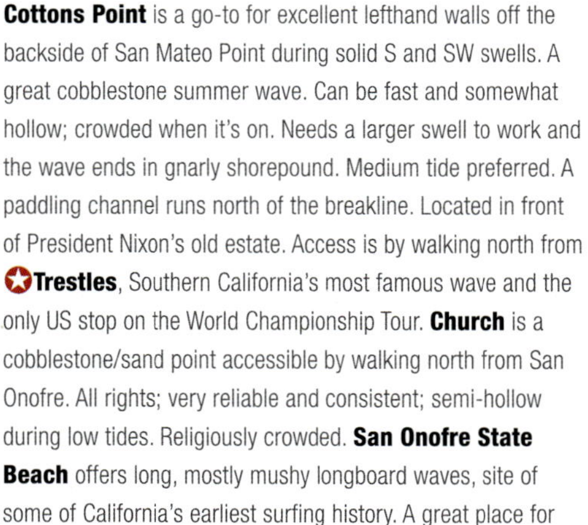

**Cottons Point** is a go-to for excellent lefthand walls off the backside of San Mateo Point during solid S and SW swells. A great cobblestone summer wave. Can be fast and somewhat hollow; crowded when it's on. Needs a larger swell to work and the wave ends in gnarly shorepound. Medium tide preferred. A paddling channel runs north of the breakline. Located in front of President Nixon's old estate. Access is by walking north from ✪**Trestles**, Southern California's most famous wave and the only US stop on the World Championship Tour. **Church** is a cobblestone/sand point accessible by walking north from San Onofre. All rights; very reliable and consistent; semi-hollow during low tides. Religiously crowded. **San Onofre State Beach** offers long, mostly mushy longboard waves, site of some of California's earliest surfing history. A great place for beginners and a family beach with mellow vibes. Old Man's is the premier reef peak at San Onofre, a summertime spot best with lower tides. The Point is just north, predominantly a righthander with occasionally good lefts. Campground here. **Trails** is about three miles of various beachbreak waves at the bottom of the bluffs west of I-5; somewhat secluded, but never empty. Trails 6 and 4 offer up the best bet for good surf. Needs peaky SW swells with lower tides; can't handle any size. **Oceanside Harbor** sometimes has good sandbar peaks at the north and south jetties. Crowded and consistent; better with higher tides and peaky SW swells up to a few feet overhead. Can get hollow. Usually bigger than spots to the south. **Oceanside Beach** is a decent beachbreak at the pier and to the north. Various access points along The Strand. Best with low tide and peaky S swells. Always busy. **Tamarack Avenue** is one of the better spots in Carlsbad, a sand/cobblestone break best during the summer. Handles up to a foot or two overhead. Down the beach is Warm Water Jetty, a decent right sandbar when it works. Camping nearby. At **Ponto**, what was once a quality reefbreak at the north end has been ruined with the installation of two small jetties in the middle of the beach. Now, the south end is the best spot, with hollow sandbar peaks galore. Directly in front of the jetties, at the lagoon mouth, is a hollow, shallow right-hand sandbar. Lots of currents, but a fun spot; popular with young shortboarders. **Grandview** is a crowded, consistent reef peak to the south of the stairs; less crowded but more walled to the north, which is also called Seascape, mostly beachbreak with some scattered reef. The reef lefts are best during summertime S swells with a medium tide; the rights get good with winter swells up to a foot or two overhead. Can line up nicely. At popular **Beacons**, the peak to the immediate south of the bluff trail is the main spot; a good, lined-up left and shorter, mushier right. Best with W swells up to a foot or two overhead. Needs a lower tide with small swells, higher tide with larger swells. Caters to longboarders and shortboarders. Crowded. Sandbars at the middle of the beach lead up to Bamboos, a fun righthand reef/sandbar in front of the bamboo patch in the bluff, under the houses. **Stone Steps** has variable beachbreak peaks at the bottom of the cement staircase off Neptune Avenue; usually uncrowded. Gets hollow and fast. Some reefy spots. Medium tides best with small, peaky swells from any direction. No beach here at high tide. **Moonlight Beach** is a highly developed sandy beach popular with tourists in the summer. Snack bar, volleyball courts, lifeguard tower, etc. The beachbreak out front gets good, best during the summertime with peaky, smaller swells and lower tides. Surfing restrictions here during the summer months. **D Street** is a good beachbreak just south of Moonlight. Hollow and powerful; usually has some kind of rideable surf when all else is flat. Best with medium tides and peaky SW swells. **Swamis** is a famous righthand reef/point

JEREMIAH KLEIN

JIMMY WILSON

Swamis

wave below the Self-Realization Fellowship Hermitage Grounds. Handles the most swell size out of any spot in the vicinity. The outer peak is a hollow, thick wall which can line up through the fast inside bowl over the inner shelf. Extremely crowded and competitive. Larger WNW swells work the best, with lower tides giving it hollowness. Holds up to triple-overhead. Often the best spot in Encinitas, always worth a look. **Pipes** is a scattering of reefs along the length of the San Elijo State Beach campground. Names include Traps, Turtles, Muffs and 8560s. Can't handle any size, but offers fun, punchy rides during smaller, peaky WSW swells on mid tide. **Cardiff Reef** has three high-quality reef waves, best with winter swells. The reef to the immediate north of the lagoon mouth is called **Tippers**, which is primarily a hollow, fast left and shorter, mushier right. Just south is **Suckouts**, a hairball righthand barrel over very shallow reef. Easy to get hurt here. Experts only. Then it's the more mellow **South Peak**, in front of the parking lot; quality rights peel into the channel. Some hollow sections; lines up during low tide. Crowded. You can almost always find something to surf here. **Seaside Reef** is a quality lefthand reef. A thick, hollow, leggy wall backing off in the middle before reforming on the inside. Competitive crowd. Needs good W swells with medium tide. High tide creates backwash. **Del Mar Rivermouth** is not a consistently epic rivermouth break by any standards, but it can get quite good, especially following heavy rainfall (somewhat of a rarity in SoCal) with a smaller W swell. Usually average beachbreak. **15th Street** is primarily a fun lefthand reef on SW swells, with adjacent beachbreak peaks. Needs a light E wind with any tide, although extreme highs tend to make the surf too fat and mushy. Low tide can generate tubes. The most popular spot in Del Mar. **South Del Mar** is a decent right reef that usually always has something to ride. Takes any small to medium-sized swell and any tide with no wind or morning offshores. Rather mushy but fun. Access is by walking north from **Torrey Pines State Beach**, a mile of accessible beachbreak backed by sheer sandstone bluffs. Best with small winter swells and high tide; E wind is offshore. Crowded with tourists during the weekends and summer months.

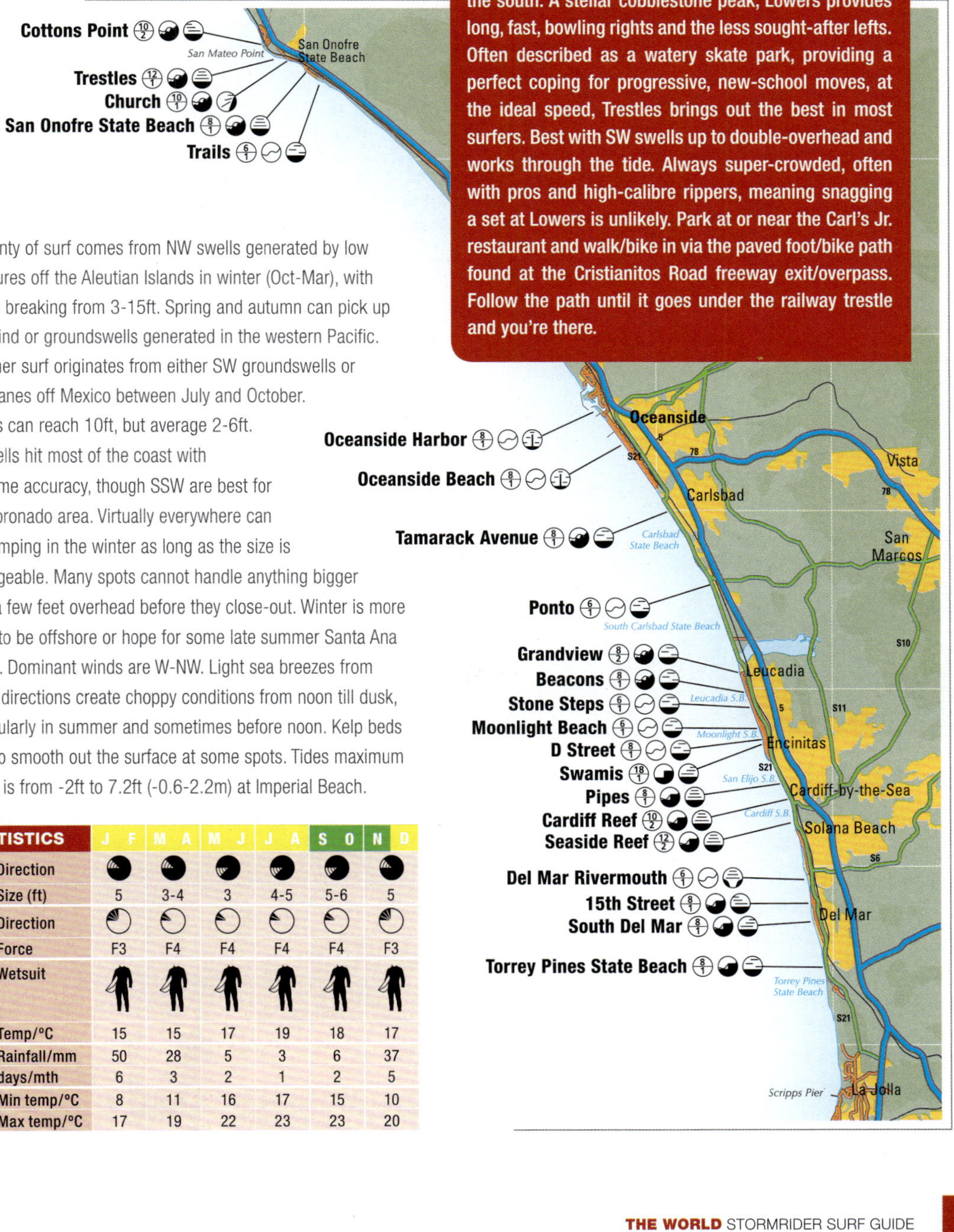

Plenty of surf comes from NW swells generated by low pressures off the Aleutian Islands in winter (Oct-Mar), with waves breaking from 3-15ft. Spring and autumn can pick up any wind or groundswells generated in the western Pacific. Summer surf originates from either SW groundswells or hurricanes off Mexico between July and October. Waves can reach 10ft, but average 2-6ft. W swells hit most of the coast with supreme accuracy, though SSW are best for the Coronado area. Virtually everywhere can be pumping in the winter as long as the size is manageable. Many spots cannot handle anything bigger than a few feet overhead before they close-out. Winter is more likely to be offshore or hope for some late summer Santa Ana winds. Dominant winds are W-NW. Light sea breezes from these directions create choppy conditions from noon till dusk, particularly in summer and sometimes before noon. Kelp beds help to smooth out the surface at some spots. Tides maximum range is from -2ft to 7.2ft (-0.6-2.2m) at Imperial Beach.

### Trestles

**LAT. 33.384399° LONG. -117.595007°**

One of the world's most famous waves, seen in countless magazines and videos, since it has been a pro-contest site for decades. Two breaks here: Uppers and Lowers. Uppers is a cobblestone mini-point featuring quality rights, often hollow and fast. The San Mateo Creek mouth can affect quality after rains, redistributing sand and cobbles, either creating unmakeable sections, or stitching together long rides. Lower tides best with W swells up to double-overhead and works on NW also. Generally less crowded than Lowers, which is just to the south. A stellar cobblestone peak, Lowers provides long, fast, bowling rights and the less sought-after lefts. Often described as a watery skate park, providing a perfect coping for progressive, new-school moves, at the ideal speed, Trestles brings out the best in most surfers. Best with SW swells up to double-overhead and works through the tide. Always super-crowded, often with pros and high-calibre rippers, meaning snagging a set at Lowers is unlikely. Park at or near the Carl's Jr. restaurant and walk/bike in via the paved foot/bike path found at the Cristianitos Road freeway exit/overpass. Follow the path until it goes under the railway trestle and you're there.

| STATISTICS | | J F | M A | M J | J A | S O | N D |
|---|---|---|---|---|---|---|---|
| SWELL | Direction | | | | | | |
| | Size (ft) | 5 | 3-4 | 3 | 4-5 | 5-6 | 5 |
| WIND | Direction | | | | | | |
| | Force | F3 | F4 | F4 | F4 | F4 | F3 |
| WATER | Wetsuit | | | | | | |
| | Temp/°C | 15 | 15 | 17 | 19 | 18 | 17 |
| WEATHER | Rainfall/mm | 50 | 28 | 5 | 3 | 6 | 37 |
| | days/mth | 6 | 3 | 2 | 1 | 2 | 5 |
| | Min temp/°C | 8 | 11 | 16 | 17 | 15 | 10 |
| | Max temp/°C | 17 | 19 | 22 | 23 | 23 | 20 |

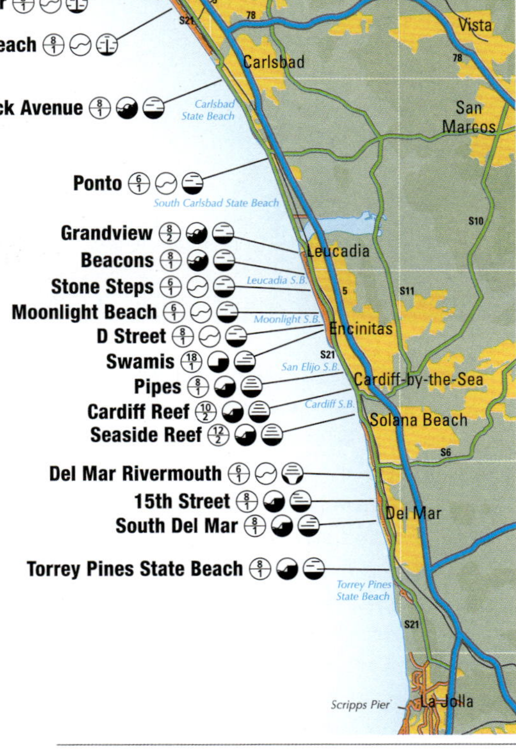

# South San Diego Co. CALIFORNIA, USA

Almost any kind of wave you seek can be found in South San Diego County, all the way to the Mexican border, especially during clean conditions of winter and autumn. As with the rest of California, there's a lot of beachbreak, but it is sprinkled with good reefs and semi-points. There are no true classic pointbreaks, unfortunately, but world-class sandbar waves are often found at Blacks and Imperial Beach. South San Diego's got it covered as far as quality reefbreaks go: Big Rock, Windansea, Sunset Cliffs, etc. The list goes on. Anything from the longboard sliders of PB Point to the behemoth left-handers of La Jolla Cove are at San Diego surfers' disposal. South county reef areas like La Jolla and Point Loma really shine during solid winter swells, but there exists a tinge of localism at select breaks. As a whole, South San Diego surf varies in aspects of power and consistency, but it's safe to say most spots are quite user-friendly and mild on a global scale. Lengthy flat spells are not unheard of and summer crowds can be stifling, but quality conditions occur several times a year.

**+ VARIETY OF SPOTS**
**+ LOTS OF CLEAN WAVES**
**+ GREAT WEATHER**
**+ FLAT DAY ACTIVITIES**

**- VERY CROWDED**
**- HEAVY TRAFFIC**
**- POLLUTION**
**- URBAN ATMOSPHERE**

✪**Blacks Beach** is the best beachbreak in the county, thanks to a swell sucking, submarine canyon. **Scripps Pier/La Jolla Shores** has good beachbreak on both sides of the pier, with the south side usually being better. Wide, sandy beach that becomes very crowded during the summer. Best with a medium tide; blows dead offshore with wintertime SE winds – a rarity with San Diego's predominantly SW-facing shoreline. **La Jolla Cove** is a long, big-wave left which works only during huge winter swells. Very thick and powerful, but not very hollow. Great drops. Gets crowded when it's on. Mid-low tide works best and S storm winds blow offshore here. Use caution and good timing when entering and exiting the water; very rocky and rough. Experts only. When La Jolla Cove is breaking, most everywhere else will be closed-out and there will be hundreds of spectators. Located off of Coast Boulevard, east of Girard Avenue. Strong W swells produce ledgy, high-quality peaks at **Horseshoe**, a shallow, jagged reef with little room for error. Heavy spot with edgy locals, so experts only. Medium tide with a solid swell works best. Not very consistent, but well-worth the wait. Walk north from Marine Street. **Little Point** is a fast summertime left, steep, and hollow. Crowded. High tide only and shortboards preferred. Breaks off the small point just north of Windansea. **Simmons** is a thick, barreling right-hander over shallow reef. Not a consistent spot but high-quality when it breaks. Broken boards and bodies are common. Low tide only with solid W swells working best. Also takes NW. Named after Bob Simmons, an early surfing innovator who drowned at Windansea in 1954. **Windansea Beach** is another famous reef with loads of surfing history. Powerful, thick peak with a long, tapering right and a shorter, hollower left. Best with SW swells and any tide. NE wind is offshore. Gets

AARON GOLDING PHOTOGRAPHY

La Jolla Cove

AARON GOLDING PHOTOGRAPHY

La Jolla Reef

## TRAVEL INFORMATION

**Weather** – San Diego is famous for its sunny, mild climate. It hardly ever rains, especially from spring to fall (autumn) when there are frequent morning fogs which disperse by noon. In summer the light onshores tend to crumble the waves, starting late in the morning. The driest, sunniest time occurs with 'Santa Ana' conditions when E winds blow from the desert. Winter is mild with occasional rainy days. Swells are bigger and the winds often favourable during these months.

**Lodging and Food** – Best to first search online. The cheapest coastal motel will cost around $140/night. There are several hostels, ranging from $30-$100/night. State Beach campgrounds are $30-$40 for a tent site. Good food is widely available, especially Mexican, but you can find absolutely everything in this highly developed metropolis. There are lots of bars and restaurants along Garnett Avenue in Pacific Beach. Also over 100 local microbreweries, many of them with excellent restaurants or food trucks. Ask for a "California burrito."

**Nature and Culture** – Check out the Del Mar Fairgrounds for all sorts of events year-round. Tour Legoland. Window-shop and people-watch in newly gentrified downtown Encinitas. Check out Torrey Pines State Reserve, site of the only natural continental habitat for the world's rarest pine, the Torrey. Visit Sea World, the SD Zoo, and the WaveHouse. Professional baseball (the Padres) is at Petco Park; also the Sockers (soccer) and the Gulls (ice hockey). Party on a rooftop in the Gaslamp District. Cruise downtown and Balboa Park. Check out the Midway aircraft carrier. Take the ferry to Coronado Island. Hike Potato Chip Rock. Get naked at Blacks. Go whale watching. Take a craft-beer tour. Golf at Torrey Pines.

**Hazards and Hassles** – The best way to avoid crowds is to surf the less accessible spots as local surfers tend to populate the most famous places. North County usually has less pressure and local people are generally extremely friendly. Stay low-key, respect lifeguards beach restrictions and local heavies. Don't stress if traffic is bad, because it always is. If it rains, watch out for polluted water. Wear sunscreen.

**Handy Hints** – Mentally prepare yourself for crowds and soft, average surf quality overall. A big wave gun will only be used rarely, usually at the Cove, Blacks and Swamis, which all get big and extremely powerful. There are plenty of shops to buy gear; try Surf Ride, Hansen's, Surfy Surfy, Encinitas Surfboards, Mitch's, Liquid Foundation, South Coast, PB Surf, or Bird's Surf Shed. SD offers easy access to the US border for Baja runs.

JEREMIAH KLEIN

## Blacks Beach

**LAT. 32.883254° LONG. -117.254590°**

**A famous, high-quality half-mile stretch of beachbreak, known for its consistency and power. Usually the biggest spot around. The La Jolla Submarine Canyon funnels swells directly into Blacks, which features three distinct spots. North Peak holds a brief but exciting righthand barrel. Middle Peak, is a two-way affair with the lefts usually being better. South Peak, can be a heavy, perfect left and all three handle huge swells from the W. Lower tide when small, but breaks right through at high. Long hold-downs and very painful if you get caught inside. Lots of severe rip currents and sneaker sets. Gets crowded for sure, but the long walk in via a very steep and rocky path down the crumbly cliffs prevents anyone grabbing a quick session. Wear grippy shoes and clothes, unless you're heading to the northern nudist area. Access at the south end of Blackgold Road, off of La Jolla Farms Road. Also known as Torrey Pines City Beach.**

very crowded; competitive atmosphere. Holds sizeable swells. Accessed from the end of Vista de la Playa and from Vista de la Playa at Fern Glen, and by stairways along Neptune Place, scuth of Fern Glen. **Big Rock** is a Pipeline-style barrel to the south of Windansea, also called Moids or Lobster Lounge. Very heavy, very shallow, very hollow. Holds up to several feet overhead; W swells work best. Dangerous rocks, so only rideable at mid or high tide. Tight take-off zone; lots of aggression. Expert tuberiders only. **South Bird Rock** is a fun, small summertime reefbreak best during outgoing tides and peaky SW swells. Backwash at high tide. Located at the end of Bird Rock Avenue. **Pacific Beach Point** offers popular, mellow peaks best with SW swells and higher tides. Good spot for longboarders and beginners. Gets crowded during summer. Park in the lot at the end of Tourmaline Street. **Pacific Beach/Mission Beach** is average beachbreak best with small, peaky SW swells and higher tides. Gets hollow, but often closed-out, so can be difficult to paddle back out. A paved promenade runs along the beach. The jetty at the south end of the beach can get good, with shorter rights ending in a channel and longer lefts. **South Jetty/Dog Beach** has decent sandbar peaks on any tide with peaky swell up to a foot or two overhead. Gets crowded like all the SD beaches. Punchy sections and some tubes. Consistent. Watch out for dog poop on the beach. Located at end of Voltaire Street. **Ocean Beach Jetty/Pier** is the longest pier on the West Coast and has fun beachbreak peaks on either side. Nice paddling channel for the rights on the north side. Occasionally gets hollow, attracting more people than usual. Located at the end of Niagara Avenue. Sunset Cliffs comprises several excellent reefbreaks in Point Loma, site of some unfriendly locals and stellar waves at the base of sheer cliffs. Steep, unsafe trails lead from the road down to the water. Best during the winter. Low tides work best with a W swell up to triple-overhead. Top spots include (from north to south): **Luscombs**, a thick peak with fast sections; **Rockslide**, more thick peaks; **North and South Garbage**, consistent rights and lefts; **Abs**, a long, lip-smacking left custom-built for performance; **New Break**, a hollow, zipper-fast right with protective locals – the jewel of Sunset Cliffs; **Chasm**, a tapering left across the channel from New Break. All spots are accessible by parking along Sunset Cliffs Boulevard or in the lot off Ladera Street. **Coronado City Beach** is a long fetch of powerful beachbreak, best with peaky summertime S-SW swells. Very hollow and unforgiving when it's firing. High tide works best. Blows offshore with a north wind. Unfriendly local crew. **Imperial Beach** is a consistent, powerful wintertime beachbreak, often back-breakingly hollow and never crowded. Long, reeling rights and lefts; difficult paddle-out when sizeable. Water is often polluted. Good sandbars can form around the pier, too. Located west of Ocean Lane, between Carnation and Encanto avenues.

Swell Forecasting and statistics see San Diego – North.

AARON CHECKWOOD

Imperial Beach

AARON CHECKWOOD

Sunset Cliffs

# Great Lakes USA/CANADA

Glaciers gouged out the 5 Great Lakes, creating the biggest lake system on the planet, containing 6 quadrillion gallons, or one fifth of the world's freshwater supplies. Their total shoreline, including islands and channels, extends for some 17,549km, more than the US West and East coasts combined! The sheer size of these lakes explain the presence of surprisingly large, surfable waves and despite poor consistency (10 days per month in season) and often inhospitable conditions, there are more freshwater surfers joining the line-ups each year.

+ UNIQUE FRESHWATER SURF
+ QUALITY SURF POSSIBLE
+ INLAND SURF CULTURE
+ GREAT LOCAL CAMARADERIE

- INCONSISTENT
- LONG DRIVES REQUIRED
- ICE AND THICK RUBBER
- SOME PRIVATE ACCESS BREAKS

Lake Superior is the largest surface, deepest and coldest of the Great Lakes, and unsurprisingly, has the biggest surfable waves. Its western end hosts the best spots, with optimal conditions being a strong, long duration, NE wind, followed by offshore NW. Bordering the town of Duluth, **Lester River** is a potentially excellent left point next to the rivermouth. **French River** is an easier spot with reef and shore breaks. Superior's best wave is **Stoney Point**, a steep, powerful, reef peak that gets big in NE blizzards. Long rides here and round the headland at Boulders. Other areas to check are the eastern end and southern fringe of Superior, plus the western base of the Keweenaw. With numerous cities and more than 70 potential spots, Lake Michigan is the most surfed lake. Sheboygan, Wisconsin, works in any N or rare SE windswells and **North Point** moulds hollow lefthanders with some power. **Elbow** is a soft, but long right, peeling off the bend in the breakwater. Racine breaks on all E wind/swell variations at the uncrowded breaks of **Wind Point**. The Chicago city beachbreaks (Osterman, Montrose, 57th Street and Rainbow) are best with spring N/NE winds and all the Illinois breaks from Chicago up to Zion will work on a NE wind. Indiana's short coast has some waves around Michigan City. Grand Haven is surf central in Michigan, and the **South Pier** handles the bigger SW to NW windchop. Lake Huron is the least explored and its dominant SW winds mean the best waves hit Ontario at Bayfield's south side **Harbor Jetty**, a noted bigger wave right. With a SW to NW wind, **Sauble Beach** can offer mellow to juicy waves, popular with kiters. In the southern confines of Georgian Bay, there are a few reefbreaks that break with size in the rarer NW gales. Lake Erie is the smallest of the lakes and the only one to completely freeze in winter. Consistent SW winds bring waves to the New York State coast beachbreaks from Buffalo down to Dunkirk at **Wright Park Beach**. A man-made jetty/reef holds tricky, rocky rights at **Palmwood Point**, Crystal Beach in large SW to W windswells. **Pleasant Beach** shows more shape and power for shortboarders. Lake Ontario is far deeper than Erie, so longer duration, cleaner windswells appear after the wind has died down. A summer E breeze can fuel some decent spots along the rocky, cobblestone shore at Grimsby, where **The Bridge** and beaches of Hamilton have been ridden for years. Toronto beachbreaks can pick up the SW windchop as it heads towards **Sandbanks**, which picks up all available swell along its 8km of beach, reef and pointbreaks. **Stony Point** receives the biggest Ontario lefts and rights over a dangerous rocky bottom.

Fetch is the key element, requiring several hours of wind blowing in excess of 37km/h over 80km of open water to produce surfable waves. The largest waves on the lakes easily surpass 10ft faces, and waves more than 20ft are occasionally recorded, usually in spring and fall. In summer, wind speeds are at their lowest, so surfable days are few and far between. In winter, inhospitable conditions (shelf ice, snow) make surfing pretty difficult. Spring sees variable and sometimes volatile weather. SW winds dominate summer, swinging N for winter.

INGRID LINDFORS
Grand Haven

SETH TYLER
Stoney Point

## TRAVEL INFORMATION

**Weather** – Winters are generally long and cold with night temps below 32°F (0°C). Prevailing winds from the west can produce very heavy snowfall along eastern lakeshores. During summer, storms pass to the north and warm, humid weather with occasional thunderstorms is followed by days of mild, dry weather. From November to April use a 6/5mm fullsuit with boots/gloves/hood, a 4/3 either side of summer, when a 3/2mm should do.

**Lodging and Food** – Basic motels ($90/dble) to luxury hotels. Lower rates out of summer. Try Fountain Park Motel (from $45/n) in Sheboygan. The cultural diversity means a huge variety of food in the Great Lakes region.

**Nature and Culture** – The lakes are exploited for their natural resources and mistreated for economic gain. Water quality across the lakes is variable. Sewage systems are designed to overflow into the lakes. Introduction of many non-native and invasive species like sea lampreys or zebra mussel are a real threat. Heaps of culture in major towns (Art Attack in Sheboygan, early May).

**Hazards and Hassles** – Cold shock and hypothermia are real dangers. Wave action can break up frozen sheets of shoreline ice sending big chunks into the line-up, creating heavy obstacles. Piers and jetties concentrate wave energy, but surfing close to them can be risky. Access to the coast can be a problem and surfing is currently banned at many beaches in Chicago.

**Handy Hints** – From boardshorts in summer to hooded 6 mil wetsuit for late fall and winter, along with thick gloves & booties. Rental and lessons available at the great Third Coast Surf Shop (New Buffalo, Michigan), Windward Sports in Chicago, Superior Surf System in Duluth, and TWC near Detroit. Use Vaseline on your face in winter.

| STATISTICS | | J F | M A | M J | J A | S O | N D |
|---|---|---|---|---|---|---|---|
| SWELL | Direction | – | – | – | – | – | – |
| | Size (ft) | – | – | – | – | – | – |
| WIND | Direction | | | | | | |
| | Force | F5-F6 | F5 | F4-F5 | F4 | F4-F5 | F5-F6 |
| WATER | Wetsuit | | | | | | |
| | Temp/°C | 2 | 2 | 4 | 13 | 17 | 7 |
| WEATHER | Rainfall/mm | 26 | 56 | 89 | 89 | 81 | 38 |
| | days/mth | 10 | 10 | 12 | 12 | 11 | 10 |
| | Min temp/°C | -17 | -4 | 6 | 12 | -4 | -10 |
| | Max temp/°C | -8 | 4 | 16 | 24 | 14 | -1 |

# Nova Scotia CANADA

Nova Scotia belongs to the Maritime Provinces of Canada, where it is impossible to be more than 56km away from the sea. Only a narrow isthmus connects Nova Scotia to mainland Canada and the Atlantic Ocean surrounds a coastline ranging from bays, inlets and cliffs to gravel or sand beaches. This rugged shoreline provides a wealth of pointbreaks, offshore reefs and plenty of beachbreaks, with a huge variety of wind and swell combinations.

+ GREAT HURRICANE SWELLS
+ BREAK QUALITY AND DIVERSITY
+ MINIMUM CROWDS
+ UNSPOILT COASTLINE

- ICY WATER TEMPS
- HARSH WEATHER
- INCONSISTENT SUMMER
- RISING LOCALISM

**Martinique** is Nova Scotia's longest sandy beach. A summer swell magnet, it is protected from SW winds and is more consistent and less crowded than nearby Lawrencetown. The popular Lawrencetown Beach is one mile in length and faces south, producing uninspiring beach peaks up to 5ft. **Lawrencetown Left Point** only breaks well 5-10 days/year, when winter or spring swells combine with W to NE winds. Really tubular and breaking close to the rocks, it has to be one of the heaviest spots around. Located at the centre of the beach, **The Reef** is a small swell peak ideal for longboards or beginners, and is a favourite hang-out for a few locals and old-timers. Surfed since the early 1960s, **Lawrencetown Right Point** can break on either small swells or anything up to 12ft. Good shape and length of ride coincides with a straight S swell, NW winds and mid tide. Cow Bay is another local's favourite, featuring numerous reefs including **Minutes**, named after timing rides that travel well over 500m. Very fast peelers, best on E-SE groundswells, it's slightly sheltered from W-NW winds and coveted by the locals. Around the corner is **Backyards**, a sheltered, higher tide, wedgy reef peak with a hollower left. **Osbourne** is a right pointbreak sheltered from all W winds and the long walk down the point can be worthwhile as it can offer very long rides around mid tide. The rocky beachbreak peak of **Moose** gets good on higher tides, S-SE swells and NW winds, creating hollow lefts in front of the giant moose statue. Closest wave to town so gets crowded. **Broad Cove** counts three pointbreaks with a cobble bottom. The main break is a long right, wrapping from the point into the bay. It works well on S swell with SW to NW winds. **Cherry Hill** is a long, white sand beach with a good left at one end, best checked on NE swell and NW winds. **Scott's Bay** is also known as Western Head Right and will have well-paced, whackable walls on S swell with any W in the winds. **Western Head** attracts long lefts to various sections of rock and cobblestone on NE wrapping swell. Breaks up into peaks a lot with NE offshore on the inside and NW out the end of the headland, where it gets big and unruly. **White Point** is one of the most popular beachbreaks around, sporting a surf school, rentals and sandbars that pick up any swell direction. **Summerville**'s long white sand beach offers good breaks at both ends, with the south end's rivermouth regularly producing the best sand bars.

Hurricane season offers the best potential for a combination of bearable water temps and quality surf, aided by North Atlantic storms bringing consistent NE swells, so Sept-Nov is best. These nor'easters send regular 12-15ft swells in winter, but usually come with storm force winds, heavy snowfall and water temps almost reaching freezing point. Spring is generally overlooked as water temps remain super-cold while the surf starts decreasing. Summer surf consists of small, locally-generated NE to SW windswells of 3-5ft. NW offshores are common in winter while sideshore SW winds prevail in summer. Tides in the Bay of Fundy, west of Nova Scotia are the highest in the world, reaching 52ft (16m), but are comparatively small in the east, with an 8ft (2.5m) range that affects most breaks.

Teahouse, Lawrencetown

ADAM CORNICK

## TRAVEL INFORMATION

**Weather** – Nova Scotia's mild oceanic winters, rarely see temps rise above freezing. Spring remains cool before summer highs average 15°C (59°F). Precipitation peaks in late fall and early winter when storms are more frequent and it snows regularly in winter. Spring fog is also a common occurrence. The Gulf Stream helps the water to reach 20°C (68°F) on the warmest late summer days, before it becomes the coldest ocean water in North America, rarely breaking the 4°C (39°F) barrier. Consistent sub zero air temperatures and tenacious NW polar winds means 6/5 suits, hoods, gloves and booties.

**Lodging and Food** – The Moonlight Beach Inn in Lawrencetown ($120/dble) or Eastern Passage B&B ($72/dble). In Port Joli, check the T.H. Raddall Park campground or the Emsik Beach House. White Point Beach Resort is $130/dble. Try the famous lobster.

**Nature and Culture** – Spot whales, seabirds and other marine creatures from the scenic, coastal routes. Halifax is a lively city with top restaurants and good nightlife. Check the Bay of Fundy's tidal bore.

**Hazards and Hassles** – Only the Lawrencetown-Cow Bay pointbreaks actually suffer from localism. Water quality is good at most spots due to the lack of coastal development. Booties are essential protection from rocks and cold.

**Handy Hints** – Longer, floatier boards help carry the necessary extra thick rubber. Several surf shops like Dacane Sports in Halifax, Rossignol in Port Joli and Happy Dude's in Seaforth. The first two offer lessons and rentals ($45/d board and suit). There are thousands of other spots to be found away from the main coastal towns.

Cow Bay

ADAM CORNICK

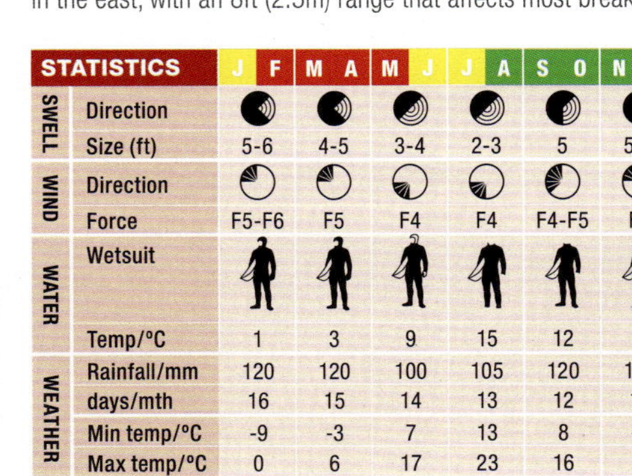

| STATISTICS | | J F | M A | M J | J A | S O | N D |
|---|---|---|---|---|---|---|---|
| SWELL | Direction | | | | | | |
| | Size (ft) | 5-6 | 4-5 | 3-4 | 2-3 | 5 | 5-6 |
| WIND | Direction | | | | | | |
| | Force | F5-F6 | F5 | F4 | F4 | F4-F5 | F5 |
| WATER | Wetsuit | | | | | | |
| | Temp/°C | 1 | 3 | 9 | 15 | 12 | 4 |
| WEATHER | Rainfall/mm | 120 | 120 | 100 | 105 | 120 | 140 |
| | days/mth | 16 | 15 | 14 | 13 | 12 | 15 |
| | Min temp/°C | -9 | -3 | 7 | 13 | 8 | -3 |
| | Max temp/°C | 0 | 6 | 17 | 23 | 16 | 5 |

# Rhode Island USA

Rhode Island may well be the smallest state in the USA, but over 640km of coastline and 100+ beaches have earned it the nickname "the Ocean State". Narragansett Bay splits the state in two parts with sand spits, barrier beaches, lagoons and salt ponds to the west, while low rounded hills and rocky headlands compose the landscape to the east. There's a good concentration of surf spots with cobblestone reefs helping to groom the lines of swell into nice defined peaks.

**+ CONSISTENT WINTER SWELLS**
**+ FALL HURRICANE SURF**
**+ SPOT DIVERSITY**
**+ SCENIC NEW ENGLAND**

**– COLD WATER**
**– WINDY**
**– SUMMER FLAT SPELLS**
**– SOME CROWDS**

## TRAVEL INFORMATION

**Weather** – Rhode Island is usually milder than the rest of New England and the warmest months of the year are April through October with highs averaging 21°C (70°F). Winter temperatures along the coast average –1°C (30°F) between December and March with snowfalls starting toward November's end. Hurricane damage occurs every 10 to 15 years. Water temps get down to 3°C (36°F), making the drysuit popular, yet springsuit/boardshort days are possible in July/August.

**Lodging and Food** – The Sea Gull Guest House (fr $76/n) is close to Narragansett Pier while The Lighthouse Inn of Galilee is located next to Pt Judith breaks ($120). Traditional local dishes are quahog clams, clam cakes, doughboys and johnnycakes.

**Nature and Culture** – Newport is an historic city from the early colonial era. Southern Rhode Island Green Trail offers parks, beaches, farmland, bird sanctuaries and wildlife refuges.

**Hazards and Hassles** – Crowds and lack of parking are an issue in summer around major spots like Ruggles. Sewage, seaweed, jellyfish, cold water and localism at certain breaks.

**Handy Hints** – Narragansett Pier has Warm Winds Surf Shop and Narragansett Surf & Skate Shop both do boards, rentals, lessons, repairs and equipment.

JOE MCGOVERN
Ruggles

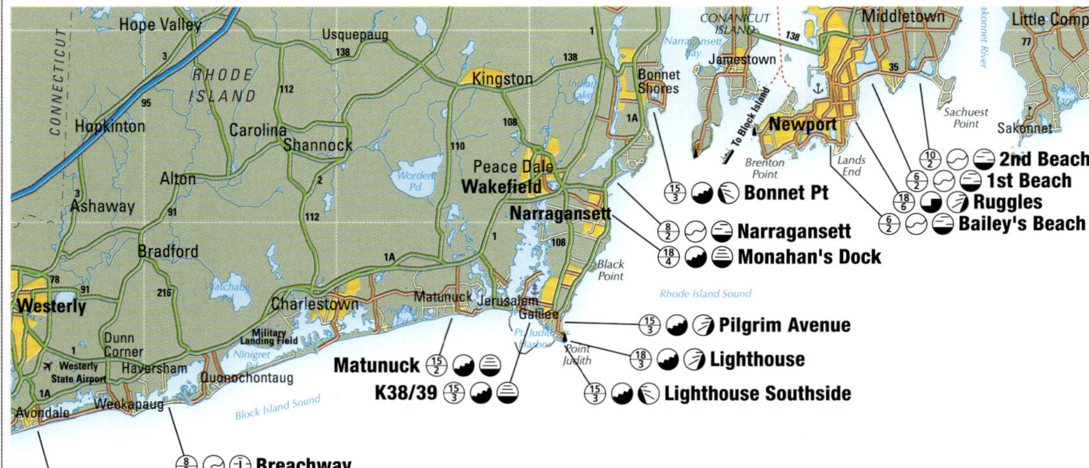


The large bay surrounding **Goosewing** Beach offers a mixture of beach, reef and pointbreaks, breaking on all tides and up to 10ft. There are many other spots around this peninsula but access is minimal. With a big parking lot, **1st Beach** (Eastons Beach) has small, soft-breaking waves up to headhigh for beginners and longboarders. **2nd Beach** (Sachuest Beach) has more appeal since it's usually bigger and better shaped with the extra treat of a protected left pointbreak cranking-up as the swell rises. With several righthand reefs lining a point, **Ruggles** reputation as the iconic east coast big wave entices a throng. It will only link-up on large S swells and NW winds with a low tide will make it truly classic. Turns massive SE hurricane swells into lines of cranking walls for riders with big wave expertise. Scoring a winter session at **Bailey's Beach** could mean hollow little peaks away from the mob, but the place seriously lacks consistency and parking spots. Inconsistent **Bonnet Point** lefthanders only break with a large S swell. Tube opportunities occur, but the walls are more adapted to linking turns. In contrast there are several consistent peaks along **Narragansett** Beach which makes the most of small summer swells in westerly winds and always attracts a glut of people. The crowded rights at **Monahan's Dock** are thick, top-to-bottom barrels for experts that can handle the critical, low tide take-off right in front of the dock. **Pilgrim Avenue** is a righthand point, which, although mushy, can handle size and strong SW winds. Two pointbreaks break either side of Point Judith. **Lighthouse** is the right with three sections combining into one long ride as the swell gets bigger. Breaking on a strong S swell steep, fast sections are followed by cutback shoulders and it can get up to triple overhead. At **Southside** lengthy lefthanders follow the same pattern. Inside the large Point Judith Harbor, **K38** and **K39** peaks offer the longest lefts on the East Coast with good S/SE swells. A long wall but never hollow enough to get barrelled, they're longboarders' favourites. **Matunuck** is the centre of Rhode Island surfing because there are three top quality peaks. Deep Hole is essentially a low tide left, breaking over the multi-coloured cobblestones that underpin all these peaks. The central peak is Trestles, showing some form similar to its Californian namesake, hollower on the rights and faster on the lefts. Furthest west, the bowly rights and longer, walled lefts of The Point, trundle towards the inside section known as The Bar, which is overlooked by a real bar, usually full of surfers and fishermen. All can handle some size and picking the right spot depends mainly on swell orientation. **Breachway** offers jetty surf at low tide, allowing for longer rides than the surrounding beachbreaks, but doesn't handle much size. **Masquamicut** State Beach is an average beachbreak, usually at its best with a combination of S swell, N wind and low tide. Offshore, Block Island presents some excellent surfing in hurricane and winter swells.

JOE MCGOVERN
Matunuck

Between August and October, SE-S hurricane swells can pump overhead waves for several days in a row. Slow moving, mid Atlantic lows send NE swells that have a long way to wrap around Cape Cod, reducing size, longevity and are often accompanied by high winds in winter. Summer is usually small with S-W winds dominating, while the offshore N winds occur more often in winter. The 1.6m tidal range will affect the pointbreaks on smaller swells.

| STATISTICS | | J F | M A | M J | J A | S O | N D |
|---|---|---|---|---|---|---|---|
| SWELL | Direction | | | | | | |
| | Size (ft) | 4 | 3-4 | 2-3 | 2 | 3-4 | 4 |
| WIND | Direction | | | | | | |
| | Force | F4-F5 | F4 | F4 | F3 | F3-F4 | F4-F5 |
| WATER | Wetsuit | | | | | | |
| | Temp/°C | 4 | 5 | 13 | 20 | 17 | 9 |
| WEATHER | Rainfall/mm | 90 | 110 | 80 | 75 | 85 | 110 |
| | days/mth | 11 | 12 | 11 | 9 | 9 | 12 |
| | Min temp/°C | -5 | 1 | 11 | 17 | 11 | 1 |
| | Max temp/°C | 3 | 10 | 20 | 26 | 20 | 8 |

# Long Island NEW YORK, USA

New York might not automatically conjure up images of epic surfing conditions, yet the Long Island peninsula has a south-facing coast with excellent swell exposure and some hard-breaking beachbreaks, jettybreaks and even some reefbreaks out at Montauk. From the cityscapes of Rockaway Beach to the spacious and audacious wealth of The Hamptons, New York offers surfers many options with a bucolic vibe close to the Big Apple.

+ MONTAUK REEFBREAKS
+ GOOD S SWELL WINDOW
+ LONG, EMPTY BEACHES
+ CLOSE TO NYC

– MISSES NE SWELLS
– DIFFICULT ACCESS & PARKING
– CROWDED
– CLOSE TO NYC

**North Bar** rights need an E or a big SE to wrap around the north side of Montauk Pt, with fast down-the-line sections that don't get hollow and rarely link up. The classic-looking righthand pointbreak at **Turtle Cove** can hold double-overhead powerful rights in a SE swell with W-NW winds. Very sectiony with multiple take-off points, short barrels occur along the boulder-strewn line-up. A strong, constant current helps disperse the crowds. **Ditch Plains** is absolutely always crowded as the steeper rights and mushy left with its workable wall and longer rides appeals to the longboard crew. Between here and the lighthouse, a long walk will reveal more rocky reef spots. A submerged reef of boulders at **Fortress** makes for some fun, walled-up, sections. Favours rights on a SE swell at all tides, but won't handle much size. **Atlantic Terrace** is sand with a sprinkling of boulders that breaks closer to shore with occasional good shape until high tide kills it completely. **Hitherhills** has a wide swell window, with SE on an incoming tide being the pick. Summer sand banks are best and it's easy access, all facilities in the State Park. Open shifting sandbars at **Indian Wells** can occasionally get good in winter S swells. Small SW swell is optimum for hollow rights when sand builds up on the east side of the **Georgia** jetties. **Flies** is the eastern jetty at Shinnecock Inlet that gets longer rights on a SW swell, while a SE swell can produce some hollow wedges. Exclusive suburbs make parking and access difficult in summer. **Cupsogue** Beach Park has an inlet jetty and peaks further up the beach if it's small. Pristine **Fire Island** has one access point, so a 4WD ($50 permit) is a must to explore the endless breaks that can get hollow and powerful. NW is offshore, and it will break on all tides and swell directions. Rarely crowded with lots of rips and currents. **Robert Moses** State Park has the easiest access and parking at 4 "fields", with more swell on the east side and smaller lined-up lefts further west. It always breaks close to the beach with hollow thumping sections and plenty of current. **Jones Beach** State Park has miles of unstabilized sandbars that are beginner and longboard friendly in summer, when the Gilgo area is generally the most consistent. Avoid high tide and crowds by walking. Due-south-facing **Lido Beach** needs a N wind and a SE swell to be at its best. Low to mid tide will have the hollowest waves and it gets plenty crowded. **Long Beach** faces a bit more SW, allowing it to handle the NE winds better. When the rest of Long Island is maxing out, Long Beach jetties will be smaller but can get hollow and perfect at lower tides. Being the closest surfing beach to NYC, the crowds at **Rockaway** Beach are more challenging than the inconsistent waves. Average beachbreaks that need a sizeable swell to make it in here with a big E bringing some decent lefts. Always crowded with surfers who are as aggressive as Yellow Cab drivers.

The best time to find consistent waves in New York is right before, during, and just after the winter season. The only hope during the warmer months is to luck into some summertime hurricane action from E around to SW. Regular wintertime NE swells can't get in to most spots. SW-NW winds dominate the surfing months, turning more onshore S in summer. NYC tidal range can hit 7.5ft (2.2m) but only 4.6ft (1.4m) at Montauk.

## TRAVEL INFORMATION

**Weather** – Summers see warm S winds and plenty of sunshine while winters are cold and snowy as the wind turns more N. Montauk is cooler and wetter than NYC averages. From November to April, use a 6/5 or a 5/4mm fullsuit with boots, gloves and hood. A 3/2mm fullsuit rest of the time or a springsuit for late July August.

**Lodging and Food** – Plenty of accommodation close to the city (AirBnB). In Montauk look up The Surf Lodge, Surf Club Montauk or camp at Hither Hills behind the surf or Fire Island. In Montauk, The Ditch Witch rules for munchies.

**Nature and Culture** – Long Island has a wild feel in places with numerous state and county parks. Fishing is big both sides of the island. Visit the Walt Whitman Birthplace and Interpretive Center in Huntington or Roosevelt's Summer White House.

**Hazards and Hassles** – Shark attacks number 10 in 180 years. Stinging lion's mane jellyfish are huge and regular summer visitors. Beach tags are enforced in summer by local councils and beach access or parking is near impossible in some towns. Long Island marine waters are polluted with PCBs, dioxin, cadmium and regular sewage spills from antiquated septic systems. Surfrider do lots of volunteer beach clean-ups.

**Handy Hints** – Many good surf shops including BungerSurf who have been on LI since 1961. Surf schools all along the coast from NYC to Montauk, many offering summer camps.

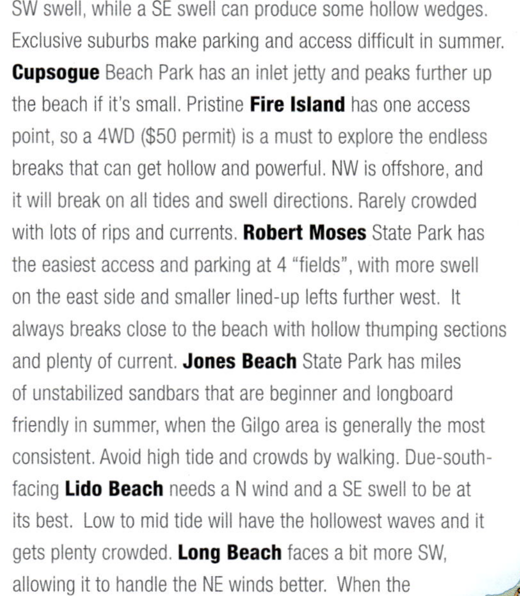

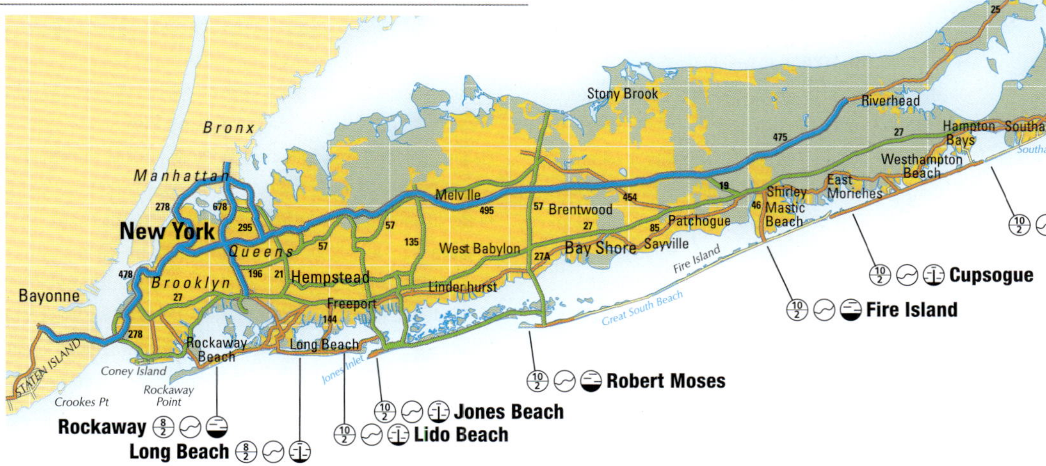

PAT NOLAN

Rockaway Beach

| STATISTICS | | J F | M A | M J | J A | S O | N D |
|---|---|---|---|---|---|---|---|
| SWELL | Direction | | | | | | |
| | Size (ft) | 4 | 3-4 | 2-3 | 2 | 3-4 | 4 |
| WIND | Direction | | | | | | |
| | Force | F4 | F3-F4 | F3 | F3-F4 | F3-F4 | F3-F4 |
| WATER | Wetsuit | | | | | | |
| | Temp/°C | 4 | 5 | 13 | 20 | 17 | 9 |
| WEATHER | Rainfall/mm | 97 | 86 | 81 | 107 | 86 | 84 |
| | days/mth | 11 | 11 | 10 | 11 | 9 | 9 |
| | Min temp/°C | -4 | 3 | 13 | 19 | 13 | 0 |
| | Max temp/°C | 3 | 10 | 22 | 27 | 23 | 8 |

# New Jersey USA

New Jersey is the most densely populated state of the USA, yet nobody spotted the surf potential until 1912 when Duke Kahanamoku introduced surfing to the East Coast at Atlantic City. The coastline of long, straight barrier islands bristles with a myriad of inlets and jetties, which help shape powerful, challenging beachbreaks for one of the largest Atlantic surfing populations. Constant erosion and beach replenishment programmes mean the surf breaks are in constant flux and it's one of the few states in the USA where you have to pay for the privilege of using the beach in the summer.

+ GOOD WINTER CONSISTENCY
+ WINTER MORNING OFFSHORES
+ SOME POWERFUL WAVES
+ PROXIMITY TO NYC

- BEACHBREAK ONLY
- RIPPY WHEN BIG
- BEACH TAGS IN SUMMER
- POLLUTION

## TRAVEL INFORMATION

**Weather** – Summers are humid and warm with an average temp of 75ºF (24ºC). Winters are cold with temps between 23-50ºF (-5-10ºC). Conditions in New Jersey change quickly: be prepared for 52ºF (11ºC) water in July and 75ºF (24ºC) air in January! From November to April, use a 5/4mm fullsuit with boots, gloves and hood. A 3/2mm fullsuit or a springsuit are fine during summer.

**Lodging and Food** – Large choice of accommodation (especially in Wildwood area), from basic motels ($50/dble) to luxury hotels. Prices usually double in summer. Huge portion, fast-food restaurants everywhere, but finding healthy food means searching and paying more.

**Nature and Culture** – Beach and gambling are the big attractions. Climb the 228-steps of Atlantic City's historic Absecon Lighthouse to check the sandbanks. Roller coasters all over the place. Whale watching from Cape May peninsula, also visit the Cape May Point State Park. NYC is close.

**Hazards and Hassles** – The numerous jetties and piers are not kind to boards or bodies! Sharks are around, but attacks occur very rarely. NJ beaches are famous for biting greenhead flies. Jellyfish swarms occasionally blow in. Beach tags enforced by local councils (from $5/10/25 day/week/seasonal).

**Handy Hints** – The Jersey shore is loaded with about 60 good surf shops. The perfect Jersey quiver would include a longboard for the small, busy summer waves, an all-round shortboard, plus a longer thruster for high performance in large surf. Many surf schools including Hammer surf school who offers advanced coaching along with regular lessons. Between these 15 spots are at least another 30 more.

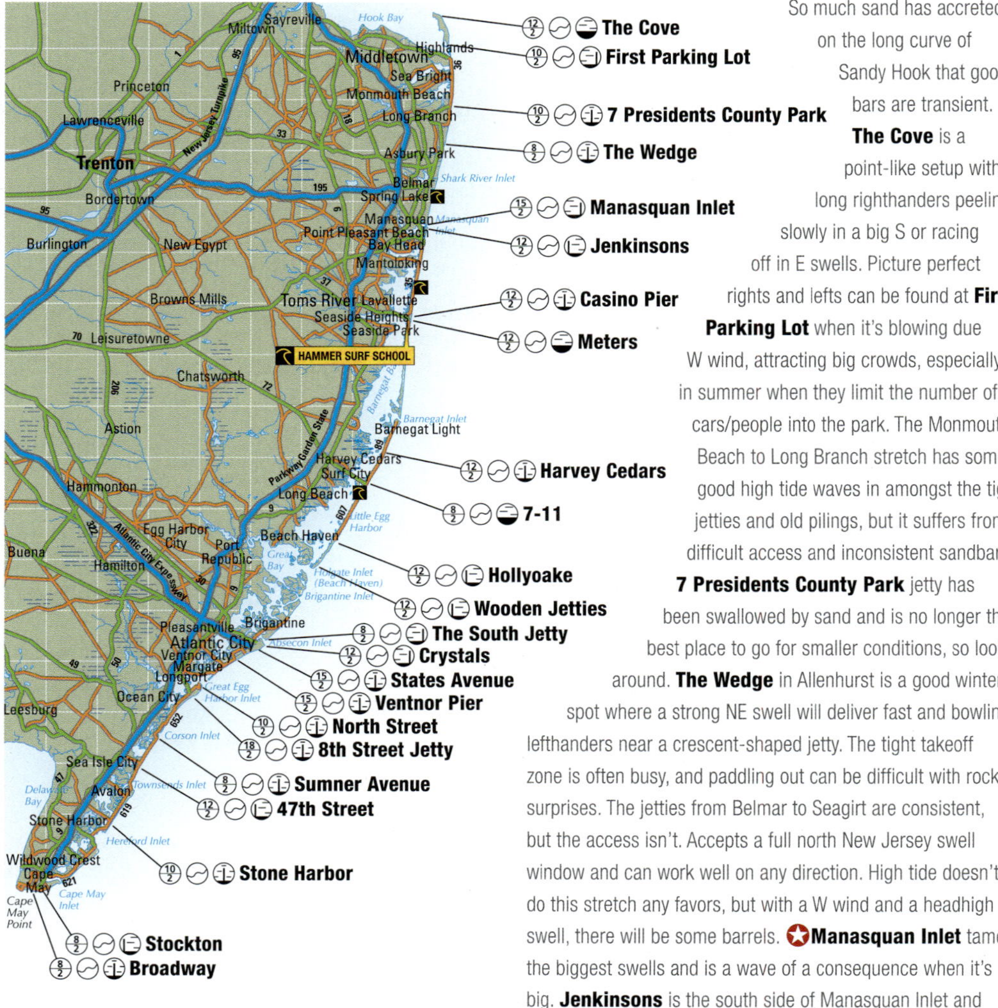


So much sand has accreted on the long curve of Sandy Hook that good bars are transient. **The Cove** is a point-like setup with long righthanders peeling slowly in a big S or racing off in E swells. Picture perfect rights and lefts can be found at **First Parking Lot** when it's blowing due W wind, attracting big crowds, especially in summer when they limit the number of cars/people into the park. The Monmouth Beach to Long Branch stretch has some good high tide waves in amongst the tight jetties and old pilings, but it suffers from difficult access and inconsistent sandbars. **7 Presidents County Park** jetty has been swallowed by sand and is no longer the best place to go for smaller conditions, so look around. **The Wedge** in Allenhurst is a good winter spot where a strong NE swell will deliver fast and bowling lefthanders near a crescent-shaped jetty. The tight takeoff zone is often busy, and paddling out can be difficult with rocky surprises. The jetties from Belmar to Seagirt are consistent, but the access isn't. Accepts a full north New Jersey swell window and can work well on any direction. High tide doesn't do this stretch any favors, but with a W wind and a headhigh swell, there will be some barrels. **Manasquan Inlet** tames the biggest swells and is a wave of a consequence when it's big. **Jenkinsons** is the south side of Manasquan Inlet and only works on a NE or E swell. Once again, the deep water offshore here focuses the swell, which throws up a powerful, low tide, left wedge that barrels for a short distance before the shoredump. Further south, Bay Head barrels hard around the short jetties, while Mantoloking to Lavallette is either impossible to park or impossible to get a wave off the hot young crew who shred these peaks in E-SE swells. **Casino Pier** in Seaside Heights got destroyed by Hurricane Sandy and the shortened rebuilt model is unlikely to be the quality wave of old, but good peaks in both directions will keep the huge crowds happy. **Meters** is a fun, snappy beachbreak with barrels and steep, workable walls just south of Casino Pier. Higher tides are now the preferred time to score some empty peaks in the wild Island Beach State Park. 4x4 permit or Herculean hike required. From Barnegat Lighthouse state Park through Loveladies, **Harvey Cedars**, and on to Northbeach, this stretch is home to a good percentage of Long Beach Island's heavy beachbreaks. A good NE or SE swell will come out of deep water and slam on the stretch of groynes at lower tides, creating sand-dredging, wide-open barrels, but prepare for a punishing paddle-out, particularly in winter. There are no great waves in Surf City, but the spot known as **7-11** works all-year-round, with all tides and swell directions and is perfect for beginners. **Hollyoake** in Beach Haven has a bay-like setup that produces long, punchy lefts on a NE swell with quite good NW wind protection. Situated in Holgate Wildlife Reserve on the southern tip of L.B.I., where a slight bend in the coast gives **Wooden Jetties** the capacity to hold the biggest NE swells. It will break on all tides, but low will be smaller and high will make it full, so mid is the pick. Lefts only, which seem to break below sea level with plenty of punch. The island of Brigantine has pretty standard straight beachbreaks until **The South Jetty** provides some wind protection and some stable sandbars for SE swells to unfurl on at mid to high tide. A fun summertime wave that usually gets chest-high peaks and a consistent crowd. Over Absecon

RYAN STRUCK/A-FRAME

## Manasquan Inlet

LAT. 40.1033° LONG. -74.0312°

A S/SE swell, a W wind, and the bigger the better for this famous jewel of Joisey. Deep water leading to the inlet, a beefy jetty and good sandbars conspire to provide long barreling righthanders and the odd left. Low to mid and closer to the beach if it's smaller, when the tall jetty will provide some protection in a southerly wind. Handles whatever the Atlantic can throw at it without shutting down. People have been known to paddle out the inlet in huge conditions. Generally regarded as the best wave in Jersey, this grinding board-snapper regularly gets as good as the photos. There are also good waves off the shorter jetties further up the beach. Always heavily crowded with plenty of attitude out in the water until it gets big enough to thin out the pretenders. Lots of currents and drift to contend with. Paddle-out rip by the jetty, where fishing lures become a hazard. Usual summer scramble for a parking meter and beach tags.

Long Beach Island

PAT NOLAN

Inlet, **Crystals** shallow beachbreak peak forms up close to the jetty in NE swells. Popular with bodyboarders looking for the steep, short lefts and occasional rights that break back towards the jetty. Depressed downbeat neighborhood and rip-offs are common. Atlantic City has non-stop casinos, the world's longest boardwalk and is home to several spots, like **States Avenue** (aka Gas Chambers), which accepts any swell, serving up long left walls off the wooden groin and the rights off the Steel pier have a high barrel potential. Neighbouring **Ventnor Pier** is also a magnet for all swell directions and fun peaks on both sides of the pier with some longer, peeling waves for all abilities. Both piers are often crowded, strafed by strong currents, and the nightmarish parking problems mean valet parking in some of the casinos is the best option. Try down at Margate Pier or the streets south for easier waves and access. Ocean City has consistent waves both sides of the **North Street** jetty, which is always bigger in size and larger in crowds. North Street is the closest to the inlet and receives plenty of sand, which builds up at the north end after a summer of S swells. Lower tides on the south side then the north side starts working after mid, which can have good rights. 5th Street gets a steep sucky left from a critical take-off point just in front of the end of the jetty, but **8th Street Jetty** is the famous contest site thanks to it's year-round consistency and ability to handle plenty of size, when paddling out gets very tricky. Very consistent, very crowded, beach tags needed and you can't surf the lefts south of the jetty between 10- 5pm in summer. The jetties to the south are disappearing under the sand at 12th Street and the old pier down at 58th is gone, but easier, ripable waves can be found along this stretch. A good beginner spot and longboard heaven is **Sumner Avenue** in Strathmere, which catches the smallest E-S swells and improves with the tide on this changeable beach. Sea Isle's 37th Street, **47th Street** and 52nd Street jetties have all been buried by beach nourishment programs but should have some lefthanders on a NE swell, and preferably from low to mid tide. In Avalon, 10th Street and 30th Street have built better banks thanks to the inlet jetty and fishing pier respectively. Facing a huge convent, **Stone Harbor** is another fun wave for everyone, from beginner to high intermediate. The Wildwood beach on Five Mile Island catches lots of sand in front of the resorts, working on all swells and tides, with fairly easy, mushy waves. The U.S. Coast Guard owns the island's prime surfing real estate down at the inlet jetty which is generally off limits to the public. Cape May is the country's oldest seaside resort, with good S swell exposure and excellent NW to NE wind protection, attracting crowds to the best spots. Bigger swells create lefthanders off the jetties like Queen Street or **Stockton**, but the sandbars are ever-changing with erosion and replenishment activity. **Broadway** is the spot everyone hits when it's huge and NE, fighting over the jetty lefts and a few bowly rights down the beach.

Typical fall to spring swells are S and NE windswells, usually bringing headhigh to double overhead surf for 2 to 4 days. In summer, Bermuda Highs can push in S windswell, but hurricanes in late summer and fall remain the best source for heavy S groundswell. Winds are lightest in summer with afternoon S sea breezes, then gusty offshores in fall and winter after storms. Expect a maximum tidal range of 5ft (1.5m) on springs.

| STATISTICS | | J F | M A | M J | J A | S O | N D |
|---|---|---|---|---|---|---|---|
| SWELL | Direction | | | | | | |
| | Size (ft) | 4 | 3-4 | 2-3 | 2 | 3-4 | 4 |
| WIND | Direction | | | | | | |
| | Force | F4-F5 | F4 | F4 | F3 | F3-F4 | F4-F5 |
| WATER | Wetsuit | | | | | | |
| | Temp/°C | 5 | 8 | 15 | 21 | 18 | 9 |
| WEATHER | Rainfall/mm | 84 | 92 | 77 | 102 | 73 | 86 |
| | days/mth | 11 | 11 | 9 | 10 | 8 | 11 |
| | Min temp/°C | -5 | 2 | 12 | 18 | 9 | 0 |
| | Max temp/°C | 5 | 13 | 24 | 29 | 22 | 10 |

# Outer Banks NORTH CAROLINA, USA

The Outer Banks are a bow-shaped string of narrow barrier islands, created by the merger of the cold Labrador Current from the north and the warm Gulf Stream from the south. These migrating islands with their transient sandbars pick up all types of East Coast swell and the dozens of piers provide some foundations, plus protection from wind and longshore drift. When it's happening, there are full-on beachbreak barrels to be had, which are not short of power.

- \+ WIDE SWELL WINDOW
- \+ POWERFUL BEACHBREAKS
- \+ UNCROWDED AREAS
- \+ WILD SCENIC AREA

- – WINDY CONDITIONS
- – BEACHBREAKS ONLY
- – COLD WINTERS
- – COSTLY ACCOMMODATION

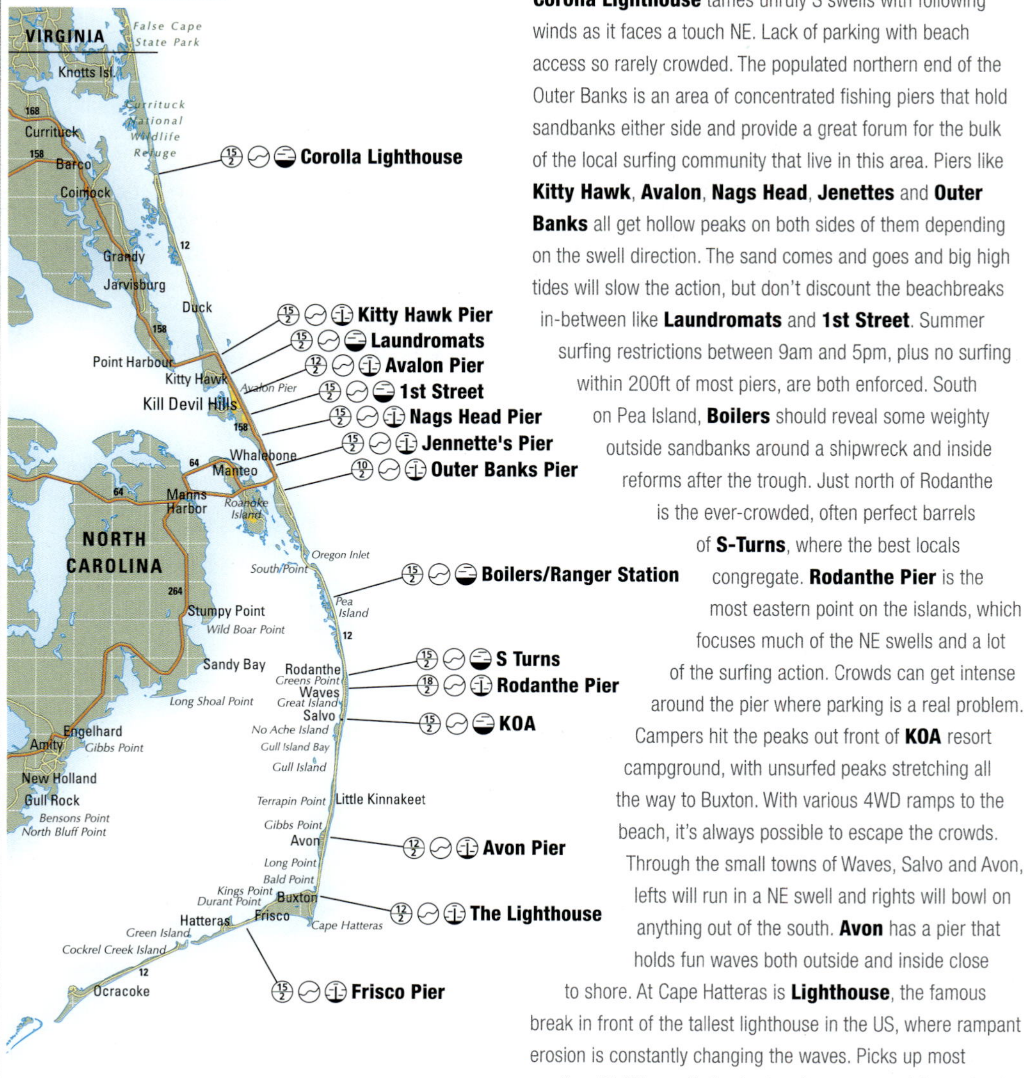


**Corolla Lighthouse** tames unruly S swells with following winds as it faces a touch NE. Lack of parking with beach access so rarely crowded. The populated northern end of the Outer Banks is an area of concentrated fishing piers that hold sandbanks either side and provide a great forum for the bulk of the local surfing community that live in this area. Piers like **Kitty Hawk**, **Avalon**, **Nags Head**, **Jenettes** and **Outer Banks** all get hollow peaks on both sides of them depending on the swell direction. The sand comes and goes and big high tides will slow the action, but don't discount the beachbreaks in-between like **Laundromats** and **1st Street**. Summer surfing restrictions between 9am and 5pm, plus no surfing within 200ft of most piers, are both enforced. South on Pea Island, **Boilers** should reveal some weighty outside sandbanks around a shipwreck and inside reforms after the trough. Just north of Rodanthe is the ever-crowded, often perfect barrels of **S-Turns**, where the best locals congregate. **Rodanthe Pier** is the most eastern point on the islands, which focuses much of the NE swells and a lot of the surfing action. Crowds can get intense around the pier where parking is a real problem. Campers hit the peaks out front of **KOA** resort campground, with unsurfed peaks stretching all the way to Buxton. With various 4WD ramps to the beach, it's always possible to escape the crowds. Through the small towns of Waves, Salvo and Avon, lefts will run in a NE swell and rights will bowl on anything out of the south. **Avon** has a pier that holds fun waves both outside and inside close to shore. At Cape Hatteras is **Lighthouse**, the famous break in front of the tallest lighthouse in the US, where rampant erosion is constantly changing the waves. Picks up most swells, with NE usually the best as it wraps round the ends of the battered jetties. Can get really dredgy but it all depends on where the sand is – barrels one week, mushy the next. Regular competition venue and the locals dominate the best waves. Big NE swells can wrap around the Cape for cleaner and smaller conditions on the south-east facing shoreline, but a S swell is needed to turn on **Frisco Pier**. It's inconsistent but capable of producing the goods when NE winds blow offshore. Take the ferry to reach Ocracoke Island and miles more deserted beachbreaks that are usually passed up by the hordes of wave-hungry surfers traversing the islands on Highway 12.

Winter NE swells arrive unhindered and offer the best consistency producing 2-12ft waves from September to May. Classic conditions come from late summer-early fall hurricanes producing perfect lines of 4-10ft swell. The Outer Banks are often swept by gusty winds but the islands' curve means it's possible to get sideshore, apart from a straight E wind. Dominant winter wind is NE plus some cold offshore westerlies and summer wind blows SW with NE sea breezes. Tidal range rarely exceeds 6ft (2m), but high tide in a small swell will fatten things out.

Rodanthe

DANIEL PULLEN

## TRAVEL INFORMATION

**Weather** – The conflicting temperatures of the Labrador Current and the Gulf Stream can bring very unstable weather. Winters are cold and stormy while summers are wet and warm. Mid-seasons can be anything in between - be prepared when hurricanes get close. Storms can wash right over the lowest parts of the islands, cutting road access when they breach the sand dune defences that are built up on the Atlantic side of Hwy 12. Weather changes are radical and statistics show some of the greatest contrasts seen in the atlas, especially water temps, which can get as low as 5°C (41°F). From boardshorts in the late summer, to 5/4/3, boots and hood in the winter, with everything in between.

**Lodging and Food** – Buxton is central but not right on the surf like Avon or Rodanthe. Motels/hotels from $80 upwards like Salvo Inn, Surf Motel, Cape Hatteras Motel. Campgrounds are cheap (Ocean Waves: $32-$52/n/4p). Expect to pay $20 for a fast food meal.

**Nature and Culture** – Great fishing potential! Climb the 248-step lighthouse to check the sandbanks. Visit the Wright Brothers Museum at Kitty Hawk – birthplace of modern aviation. Bars and nightclubs get lively in summer, but winter is ghostly quiet in the small towns, full of empty holiday accommodation.

**Hazards and Hassles** – Straying too close to a pier may see the grumpy, surfer-hating fisherman casting their biggest lead toward you. On town beaches you must wear a leash! Respect the swimming only zones. Mosquitoes, jellyfish and sea-lice in summer. 3 non-fatal shark attacks in a week in 2016. There are always strong rips.

**Handy Hints** – There are dozens of shops, including Whalebone, Secret Spot, Wave Riding Vehicles and Natural Art. Kiteboarding has literally taken off. Biggest towns are Nag's Head and Kill Devil Hills. Crowds from Virginia come down during summers and on weekends.

| STATISTICS | | J F | M A | M J | J A | S O | N D |
|---|---|---|---|---|---|---|---|
| SWELL | Direction | | | | | | |
| | Size (ft) | 5-6 | 4-5 | 3 | 2-3 | 4-5 | 5-6 |
| WIND | Direction | | | | | | |
| | Force | F4 | F4 | F4 | F4 | F4 | F4 |
| WATER | Wetsuit | | | | | | |
| | Temp/°C | 9 | 11 | 19 | 25 | 20 | 14 |
| WEATHER | Rainfall/mm | 122 | 99 | 101 | 142 | 134 | 119 |
| | days/mth | 10 | 9 | 10 | 12 | 8 | 8 |
| | Min temp/°C | 3 | 8 | 17 | 22 | 17 | 7 |
| | Max temp/°C | 11 | 17 | 25 | 29 | 24 | 15 |

# Central Florida USA

Florida's northern coast from Daytona to Jacksonville features a stretch of flat beaches with endless peaks between the occasional jetties and inlets. However, it is the centrally located 'Space Coast' that is the surf industry cradle and home to such famous locations as New Smyrna Beach, Cocoa Beach and Sebastian Inlet. Despite the generally poor sandbanks and small mushy conditions that occur most of the time, when a hurricane delivers powerful lines of swell, a few spots will turn on, with classic waves for the large local population, but the wait can be misery.

+ ENDLESS BEACHES
+ EASY WAVES
+ HURRICANE SWELLS
+ TOURISM HEAVEN

- SMALL WINDCHOP WAVES
- SUMMER FLAT SPELLS
- MAJOR SPOTS CROWDED
- HIGH SHARK BITE FACTOR

PATRICK EICHSTAEDT

New Smyrna Beach

**Daytona Beach** used to be the hot spot back in the '60s and is still popular with longboarders, learners and college break revellers. Better waves found at **Sunglow Pier** on all swells and tides. **Ponce Inlet** is popular when S-E swells of any size can peel right off the long jetty for long distances. **New Smyrna Beach** is super-consistent on N-E swells and the long stretch south of the inlet and jetty has good sandbars at high tides, spreading the heavy crowds. Beside the John. F. Kennedy Space Centre, **Playalinda** is a long beach that will pick up the best of a NE swell and pitch at low tide. Cape Canaveral is off limits, but when big winter NE swells roll in, the pier at **Cocoa Beach** can provide shelter from the accompanying winds, at a more manageable size, while nearby Jetty Park needs SE swell. There are plenty of sluggish, uninspiring peaks to choose from, that are usually longer and mushier at low tide and tend to become a shorebreak at high tide. **Patrick's Air Force Base**, picks up more of the NE swell with some consistent sandbars near the few parking opportunities. Between Patricks and Indialantic is **RCs**, one of the few big wave spots that breaks in NE swells with some power over coquina reef, a soft limestone containing crushed shells and coral. **Indialantic Boardwalk** has a steeper beach profile, which in turn provides a steeper, hollower wave. Jacking close-outs are interspersed with some makeable barrels, but the competition is heavy for these pits as well as the few meter parking spots. **Melbourne Beach** area is residential, so parking is even trickier and locals take advantage of it to improve their knowledge of these shifty but average sandbanks. Florida's most famous wave **Sebastian Inlet** sadly no longer bounces and wedges off the curving jetty after a beach replenishment program and major structural renovations altered the angle and currents, disappearing the iconic peaks almost overnight. Even Third Peak has suffered but can provide fast, hollow lefts when the swell shows some north in it.

Daytona Beach
Sunglow Pier
Ponce Inlet
New Smyrna Beach
Playalinda
Cocoa Beach
Patrick Air Force Base
RCs
Indialantic Boardwalk
Melbourne Beach
Spanish House
Chernobyl
Sebastian Inlet
Monster Hole

TOM DUGAN

Monster Hole

Further up the beach are **Chernobyles** and **Spanish House**, which need more swell to get the left tubes happening. All these peaks prefer low to mid tide incoming, but will break through to high, unless it's small in which case the backwash takes over. The intense crowds and weekend contests are awaiting the resurrection of the First Peak wedges. On a bigger swell, brilliant pointbreak style lefts and shorter rights can be ridden south of the inlet channel at rippy, localised and sharky **Monster Hole**.

Winter North Atlantic lows send NE swells, varying from 3-10ft, from October to March. Summer can see waves generated by the sea breeze, resulting in sloppy NE or SE wind chop. From August to October, an average of 10 hurricanes tracking from West Africa to the Caribbean may produce quality waves rarely exceeding 8ft. Winds are predominantly onshore with NE-E winds in winter and NW-SE in summer, but the offshores rarely coincide with decent swells. Expect of lot of 2-3ft wind chop conditions. Tidal range affect most spots at 9ft (3m).

## TRAVEL INFORMATION

**Weather** – Ideal climate for surfing apart from summers heavy rains, intense heat and lack of swells. September-October, the best surf months, are still rainy with short, pouring showers and thunderstorms which force surfers out of the water to avoid the constant lightning! Springsuit or a 2mm fullsuit from December to March whenever the water gets around 60°-64°F (16°-18°c).

**Lodging and Food** – Choose from ocean front hotels, spacious condos, beachside cottages, multi-bedroom bungalows to campground and RV sites. Heaps of raw bars, eclectic eateries and gourmet restaurants.

**Nature and Culture** – Orlando's Disneyland is notable for Typhoon Lagoon wavepool. The Orange Avenue nightclubs are lively. Check the Kennedy Space Centre in Cape Canaveral.

**Hazards and Hassles** – With 244 attacks (1 fatal) in last decade, Florida is the world's shark bite leader. Sebastian peaks get much crowd pressure but miles of average beaches spread the masses. Mosquitoes, sealice and sand sea-ums are a summer bummer. Respect lifeguard's beach restrictions, which often prevent surfing between 9am-5pm.

**Handy Hints** – Ron Jon's, the worlds' largest surf shop (or 9 acre tourist stop), is one of many in Cocoa Beach or Indialantic. Lots of fine shortboard shapers (Natural Art, Quiet Flight).

| STATISTICS | | J F | M A | M J | J A | S O | N D |
|---|---|---|---|---|---|---|---|
| SWELL | Direction | | | | | | |
| | Size (ft) | 3-4 | 3 | 1-2 | 1-2 | 3 | 3-4 |
| WIND | Direction | | | | | | |
| | Force | F4 | F4 | F3 | F3 | F4 | F4 |
| WATER | Wetsuit | | | | | | |
| | Temp/°C | 16 | 20 | 24 | 26 | 24 | 21 |
| WEATHER | Rainfall/mm | 50 | 80 | 175 | 175 | 225 | 57 |
| | days/mth | 5 | 6 | 10 | 13 | 14 | 6 |
| | Min temp/°C | 14 | 17 | 22 | 24 | 23 | 16 |
| | Max temp/°C | 25 | 28 | 31 | 32 | 30 | 26 |

# Southern Florida USA

Florida boasts the nation's longest coastline with some 1,350 miles, or over 8,000 if you count all the shorelines of its bays and islands! Southern Florida has a rich surfing heritage dating back to the 1930s and is home to some great winter waves, but summers of discontent are a given, thanks to the swell blocking shadow of the Bahamas. However, nearby Palm Beach County has a few breaks that handle the biggest NE swells, producing the best waves in the state.

- \+ GREAT N SWELL EXPOSURE
- \+ FLORIDA'S BIGGEST WAVES
- \+ WARMEST WATER IN USA
- \+ MIAMI NIGHT LIFE

- \- INCONSISTENT MUSHY WAVES
- \- CROWDED CITY LINE-UPS
- \- PARKING HASSLES
- \- FAIRLY EXPENSIVE

Hobe Sound · Coral Cove Park · Jupiter Inlet Sth Jetty · Juno Pier · Ocean Reef Park · Reef Road · Lake Worth Pier · Boynton Inlet · Delray Beach · South Beach Pavillion · Boca Raton Inlet · Deerfield Park Pier · Haulover · 21st Street · 5th Street · South Beach

**Hobe Sound** is the southernmost point of Florida's coast that is free of the Bahamas E swell shadow. On bigger N swells, at higher tides, lefts will link through to the beachbreak, reforming and standing up on the inside. **Coral Cove Park**'s flat tabletop reef cultivates good lefts on small northerly swells at low to mid tides. Fast and shallow. **Jupiter Inlet South Jetty** has a nice inside peak on all smaller swells and an outside right on bigger E swells. Lower tide on the push, and experienced surfers only will get waves off the locals. **Juno Pier** provides good sandbars without the trench between the outside low tide banks and the inside high tide shorebreak. Zippery, punchy lefts break off shoreline rock outcropping on small NE swells at **Ocean Reef Park**. Florida's undisputed best big-wave spot is **Reef Road**. This high-class lefthander can produce long, powerful, sucky rides when an overhead N to NE swell hits. Handles as big as Florida gets, best at low tide incoming, when it breaks over a coquina reef outside then a shallow sandbar inside. Always crowded with chargers. No parking within a mile of Reef Road – hike in from the south. Over the inlet, Pumphouse offers similar quality waves and access problems. **Lake Worth Pier** south side fires on a northerly swell and vice versa. Good sandbars give this break more punch, something the locals are also known for. Low tide in smaller swells, up to high in bigger swells. The southside shorebreak at **Boynton Inlet** shifts around six T-head jetties in NE swells, while SE windchop works on the north side at lower tides. An outside bar produces long, hollow lefts when a big NE swell combines with a low incoming tide. **Delray Beach** offers above average beachbreak that works best at the south end (Anchor Park). Will take both NE and SE swells from slop to sizeable, but tends to have better peaks on a NE'er at mid to high tides. **South Beach Pavilion** reef and sand-bottom wave needs a SE windchop to work as a NE'er will close-out. Hollow lefts and rights work up and down the beach, helping with crowding. Reefs appear up at Red Reef Park and beyond at Jap Rock that require overhead NE swells to show their quality lefts. Often a crew out when the SE wind blows. The south side of **Boca Raton Inlet** in the county park works on all tides in a NE swell. The peaks hold size and are much better than on the north side, which is very inconsistent. **Deerfield Park Pier** is best on a windchop SE with a low-incoming tide for above-average pier waves. NE swells don't line-up very well. The Fort Lauderdale stretch is pretty uninspiring - try Anglins Pier if desperate. Good sandbars can form around the **Haulover** jetties and pier. Lefts and rights along this stretch take N/NE swells and SE windchop and prefer lower tides. **21st Street** is a popular spot with more power for the long lefts peeling parallel to the beach on N-NE swells at low to mid tide. **5th Street** gets good banks and crowds from being close to the jetty. **South Beach** is Miami's best wave when a N-NE swell refracts off the jetty and wedges up into nice A-frames when the sand is there. Also takes a SE to S windswell, which wraps around and spins off lesser rights. Low incoming is best, when the ferocious crowd is at its worst.

NE swells arrive from October to March and hit Palm Beach County with more size and power thanks to its easterly position and the Gulf Stream acting as a swell corridor. ESE is the dominant wind year-round, kicking up weak and unreliable SE wind chop. Hurricanes are more likely later in the season. Tidal range never exceeds 5ft (1.5m).

## TRAVEL INFORMATION

**Weather** – Floridian weather and the warmest water in the US are attractive and rare cold winter mornings will see the ocean steaming. Rain backs off from Nov-Feb – the best surf months and a springsuit is needed for the 22-23°C (72-74°F) water.

**Lodging and Food** – Every type of accommodation option available under the sun. Miami and Palm Beach County are both full of good restaurants. Cuban, Haitian, Creole and many Caribbean fusion foods are local staples.

**Nature and Culture** – Take a trip down the Florida Keys for extraordinary natural beauty, or the bright lights of the big city in Miami.

**Hazards and Hassles** – The sharks can be seen from the beach during a baitfish run where the Gulf Stream touches the coast. Swarms of man-o-war in summer and tropical storms bring lightning. Access to the sand is nigh on impossible near some of the most expensive coastal real estate in the USA. Be prepared for some localism at the better spots.

**Handy Hints** – Surf shops scattered throughout the region with plenty of cheap equipment. Be prepared for expensive meter parking or a long walk.

| STATISTICS | | J F | M A | M J | J A | S O | N D |
|---|---|---|---|---|---|---|---|
| SWELL | Direction | | | | | | |
| | Size (ft) | 3-4 | 3 | 1-2 | 1-2 | 3 | 3-4 |
| WIND | Direction | | | | | | |
| | Force | F4 | F4 | F3 | F3 | F4 | F4 |
| WATER | Wetsuit | | | | | | |
| | Temp/°C | 22 | 24 | 28 | 30 | 28 | 23 |
| WEATHER | Rainfall/mm | 64 | 71 | 175 | 157 | 220 | 62 |
| | days/mth | 7 | 7 | 12 | 15 | 17 | 9 |
| | Min temp/°C | 16 | 19 | 22 | 24 | 23 | 18 |
| | Max temp/°C | 22 | 24 | 28 | 30 | 28 | 23 |

Reef Road

PATRICK EICHSTAEDT

# Texas USA

The Texas coastline accounts for a good proportion of the USA's beaches on the massive Gulf of Mexico, referred to by surfers as the Third Coast. The state may not be first choice when planning a USA surf trip, but its continuous string of barrier islands receive regular windswell and occasional hurricane swell from the Gulf. There are numerous passes, inlets, piers and jetties, providing the focus for waves along the endless, featureless strands. The intracoastal waterway creates access difficulties away from the bridges and ferries, but 4WDs are permitted on many of the public beaches.

+ WARM WATER
+ SOME UNCROWDED BREAKS
+ FRIENDLY LOCALS
+ NICE CLIMATE

- SMALL, SHORT-LIVED SWELLS
- RARE OFFSHORE WINDS
- HARD BARRIER ISLAND ACCESS
- SPRING BREAK CROWDS

GRANT ELLIS

Bob Hall Pier

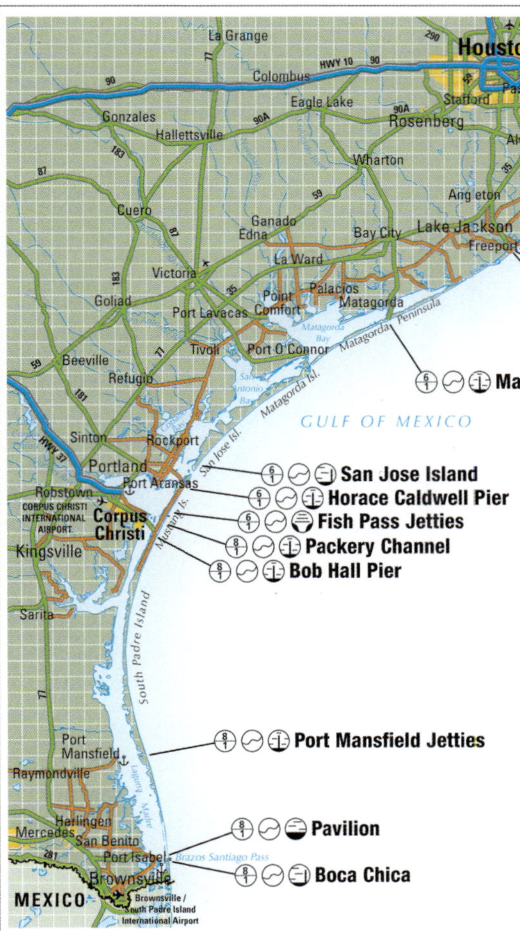


Meacom's mile-long pier was pulled down in 2009 and the Bolivar surf scene has drifted south to average peaks along **Crystal Beach**. Galveston Island has stable sandbars at **Flagship Pier** and the adjacent jetties, attracting longboard crowds unless the spot is overloaded by a really large swell. 37th Street and **61st Street** stand out as the best option for shortboarders since good sandbanks usually form north of the jetties. With the right conditions, peaks appear anywhere along the extensive seawall spreading the crowds. **Octagon** is a bit more consistent than Galveston, and the beachbreaks to the north, may yield a faster, hollower wave. On large S, even SW swells, **Surfside Jetty** is the place to be since it's possible to jump from the end of the jetty into longer cleaner lines as they wrap in. SW wind protection is a rare bonus. With a large E swell, action shifts to **Quintana**, an otherwise mushy break that finds power at size. The Colorado River inlet channel focuses all swell onto shallow sandbars at **Matagorda** forming hard-breaking beachies to the north of the pier or beside the jetties on both sides of the rivermouth. All get classic with a decent swell and any N wind. Getting to **San Jose Island** requires a quick boat or ferry ride, or long dangerous paddle. Soft triangular bars can be cleanish in S-SW wind and a strong SE swell. In Port Aransas, the **Horace Caldwell Pier** peaks up on either side, showing its best on a E-SE swell at mid tide. The silted up **Fish Pass Jetties** have both mushy and sucky waves with wind and current protection. The old broken J.P. Luby pier has been replaced by a long jetty at the **Packery Channel**, protecting good rolling peaks from S winds on all tides and swells.

## TRAVEL INFORMATION

**Weather** – Influenced by continental systems and the warm Gulf of Mexico Texas is constantly switching between periods of settled and unstable weather. South Padre Island enjoys a sub-tropical environment with mild dry winters, and warm breezy summers. Winters are usually mild averaging 18°C (65°F) and 28°C (82°F) in summer. Night temperatures are usually much cooler, but very rarely does the temperature drop to freezing. Hurricanes strike Texas once every 3 years on average. Water is warm enough to trunk it all summer long, but winter requires a 3/2 full suit.

**Lodging and Food** – A huge spring break hotel capacity ensures good deals the rest of the year. In SPI try La Quinta ($88/dble) or Tiki Condominiums ($100/dble). In Galveston, the Flagship on the pier gave its name to one of the best breaks, but got damaged and demolished. Eat at the Surf Club in Corpus Christi or the pier house next to Horace Caldwell Pier.

**Nature and Culture** – Beach is the big attraction here, plus a variety of amusement parks. Schlitterbahn Water Park has a standing wave you can bodyboard on, while Nland Surf Park has opened in Austin showcasing the Wavegarden technology.

**Hazards and Hassles** – 18 shark attacks have been recorded off Galveston and Padre Island. Be vigilant for soft sand, island breaches and immigration checks on long beach drives - travel in groups with tools, food, extra water. Hurricane surf is dangerous because of the strong currents it generates, especially around passes.

**Handy Hints** – Waves generally lack power, so big floaty boards tend to work the best. There are many fully stocked surf shops in Texas like Wind and Wave Water Sports in Corpus Christi or Beach Break in Galveston.

**Bob Hall Pier** is the most crowded, competitive surf spot in Corpus Christi, thanks to stable, shallow sandbars on both sides of the pier, that receive the full gamut of swells at all tides in all winds, producing punchier waves with steep drops and fast walls. **Port Mansfield Jetties** are isolated so crowds are minimal for some of the longest, lined-up waves in the state. More accessible are the Brazos Santiago Pass breaks located close to Port Isabel. **Pavilion** beachbreak gets classic, as powerful, hollow walls hold shape on the north side of the jetty. Best on E to SE swells, while the south side at **Boca Chica** prefers some N to get the lefts running down the beach. As with most Texan passes, in-between the two jetties there are a couple of quality waves that only break on the biggest swells when the beaches are closed out.

Weekly frontal activity brings several days of strong onshore NE-SE winds that can build surf up to the 4-6ft range, but the following W-N offshore winds diminishes the size quickly. Summer is usually flat and although the hurricane season stretches from Jun to Nov, Sept and Oct are more likely to produce storms that cross into the Gulf from the Caribbean. Tidal range is minimal but can affect the strength of the currents at inlets and passes.

| STATISTICS | | J F | M A | M J | J A | S O | N D |
|---|---|---|---|---|---|---|---|
| SWELL | Direction | | | | | | |
| | Size (ft) | 3 | 2-3 | 2 | 1-2 | 3 | 3-4 |
| WIND | Direction | | | | | | |
| | Force | F4 | F4 | F4 | F3-F4 | F4 | F4 |
| WATER | Wetsuit | | | | | | |
| | Temp/°C | 18 | 19 | 24 | 27 | 26 | 21 |
| WEATHER | Rainfall/mm | 40 | 40 | 80 | 60 | 110 | 40 |
| | days/mth | 8 | 5 | 7 | 6 | 7 | 7 |
| | Min temp/°C | 8 | 15 | 22 | 23 | 20 | 11 |
| | Max temp/°C | 10 | 25 | 31 | 33 | 30 | 22 |

Selina

JEREMY BRASSET

# CENTRAL AMERICA & THE CARIBBEAN

Central America has become a veritable surfing playground where the wave-rich deserts, jungles and tropical islands host some of the most fun and funky surf spots around. Perennial, long-period, Pacific swells break in bath-warm water, enticing the global surf community to not only taste the power of some of the world's best beachbreaks and points, but to buy into the region in a big way. Surf camps and schools manufacture new devotees, while local surfing populations grow steadily, yet crowds are the exception along much of this wild, undeveloped coast. Meanwhile, the Caribbean continues to pump in northern hemisphere winter, generally under the radar of much of the surf press, hiding behind a turquoise curtain of expensiveness, inconsistency and onshore winds. This somewhat misleading reputation leaves some top-class line-ups devoid of crowds and a chance to sample some tropical perfection in a beautiful and relatively safe environment.

Céron, Martinique

# The Surf

## MEXICO

Geographically considered more a part of North America, but surf-wise, **Mexico** is a different world from the Southern California hustle and bustle, starting off arid and rocky in **Baja**. Wooed by promises of long righthand points without the insane crowds of SoCal, a road trip down the dusty, potholed, washboard tracks of the Baja Peninsula has become a rite of passage. The Northern Baja region often resembles a hybrid of line-ups north of the border, sharing the same crowds, cool water and south-facing coves that wrap the winter NW swells onto cobble and reef. Between Punta Camalu and the beginning of the Central Baja zone at Punta Canoas lie a number of protected points like Cabo San Quintin, Puntas Baja and San Carlos, which all prefer winter W-NW swells and handle the prevalent, strong onshores. Beyond Rosarito and the desolate beachbreaks of Natividad begins what many regard as the true Baja since Mex1 veers over to the Gulf of California side and a labyrinth of 4x4 dirt tracks challenges the explorer to reach the coast. The rewards include the now well-known Punta Abreojos and the seven points of Scorpion Bay, both preferring SW swells, bringing warm water to these long peeling rights. There's hundreds of kilometres of rocky coast and endless beachbreak, but finding protection from the howling NW winds is the challenge. Los Cabos is a whole different world, swapping cactus and chilled-out camping for concrete and a party vibe amongst the throngs of US holiday makers. The Gulf of California breaks continue the natural footer's playground by wrapping in when a heavy S or local hurricane (chubasco) forms, but crowds and boardshorts make it a strangely alien Baja experience. **Sinaloa** state sits in a NW swell shadow behind Baja, but S swells arrive at a nice angle for lefthand points in San Miguel, Patole's and Marmol. The Mazatlan area holds hollow, spinning rights and lefts at multiple reefs including Valentinos, Los Patos, Chivos and A-frames behind La Isla de Piedra (Stone Island), where the ferry arrives from Cabo. Rivermouths are another dependable source of great waves at the shifting sandbars of Barron and Teacapan, located down the coast towards Nayarit and the crowds of San Blas and Puerto Vallarta. While summer rains can wash out the access roads to many of the small fishing villages on the northern coast of **Jalisco**, the beachbreaks (Penitas, Tomatlan, Tecuan, Arroyo Seco), rivermouths (Chamela, Barra de Navidad) and the odd pointbreak (Ranchito) are a good place for beginners and intermediates to get some quiet water time. The central mainland region faces directly into the the SW-S swells and also benefits from swell amplifying, deep-water bathymetry. Colima is home to ultra-powerful Pascuales, which is the state's best wave and like many of the waves in these three states, it's usually perfect in the morning NE offshores then blown-out junk in the afternoon, before a possible dusk glass-off. Michoacan is the place to go for challenging, fast peeling rivermouth waves like La Ticla and Nexpa, both awesome waves on their day. Grinding, sand-churning barrels can still be found at Petacalco, despite the coastal armouring and West Guerrero is chock-full of thumping beachbreak and a fair number of points and reef/sand combos. East of Acapulco's madness is almost exclusively sandy beach, punctuated by many estuaries, rivers and streams from the coastal lagoon systems. With the right swell (small to med) and some N or E in the wind, there's plenty of lightly surfed waves at places like Copala, La Bocana or the left point at Maldonado, which has S wind protection and more options in the immediate area. Oaxaca is home to Mexico's most famous wave, Puerto Escondido, where many believe the best beachbreak in the world hurls itself at the sands of Playa Zicatela. A huge scene revolves around these brutish, semi close-outs in West Oaxaca, but there are less-crowded options. One quiet beach in East Oaxaca has been put on the map when *The Search* competition was held there in 2006 and those that go the extra mile will discover this coastline is perfectly angled for righthand points. Bad coastal access is a theme repeated in **Chiapas**, which shares some geological features with Guatemala. Long, featureless beaches broken by entrances to salt-marsh lagoons and inland waterways. Scope Puerto Arista, Barras San Jose and San Simeon rivermouths, plus Puerto Madero offers some reliable form thanks to jetties, but water quality and security is suspect. The **Gulf of Mexico** needs onshore winds to drive the swell unless a cold front or hurricane has produced proper groundswell, so windchop is the norm. Jetties and rivermouths provide the sandbars and some wind protection on the long sandy stretches like Escolleras in Tampico. Veracruz is the best bet as the power-sapping shallow shelf is narrowest here. Worthy spots include the hollow left reefbreak at Marti, semi-consistent beachbreak at Destapador and the jetty breaks are down at Boca del Rio (Costalitos). There's a few more waves to the south like Camaronera and Barra de Sontecomopan but the continental shelf widens to the east and mushy, gutless waves are the norm all the way round the Yucatan Peninsula. Deep water returns on the east coast in the Caribbean Sea, where coral reefs fringe the islands and E-SE windswells have the longest fetch. Jan/Feb for cold fronts and hurricane season for swells from NW around to S, but it is just as likely to be flat. There's some shallow coral head rides off Punta Cancun and choppy onshore beach/rock/reef peaks right down the hotel strip (Chacmool, Palace Hotel, Club Med) including Playa Delphines, which has board hire. The offshore islands of Mujeres and Cozumel can hold surprisingly powerful beach/reef combos, but clean conditions and longevity are rare.

AL MACKINNON
Baja

RYAN CRAIG
East Oaxaca

## CENTRAL AMERICA

There are no real surprises along the exclusively sandy Pacific coast of Guatemala, where rivermouths and jetties are the focus for locals and a few visiting surfers, who are usually heading for the rocky geology to the south. The Caribbean coast is mostly unexplored and the straight, flat beaches of Izabal province gently shelve into the silted up bay and stretch down towards the Honduran border, offering negligible chances of scoring clean waves. There are however many small coral islands and cays offshore from **Belize** and more surfing options when the E to SE trades kick up a decent windswell. Check the left at East Cape on Half Moon Caye and Glovers Reef has a righthander on Long Caye. The far western coastline of **El Salvador** resembles Guatemala with straight unbroken beaches, except for the large rivermouth (la bocana) at Barra de Santiago. Acajutla faces due west and picks up smaller windswells, but the port and petroleum plant pollution is heavy. The Costa Balsamo provides the lion's share of the righthand pointbreaks stretching from as far west as Mizata back along the impossibly twisty, coastal mountain range road that allows glimpses of perfect regular foot set-ups like K59 and 61, before hitting the crowded line-ups of Zunzal and Punta Roca. Between La Libertad and the beginning of the Oriente Salvaje zone lies 120km of thumping beachbreak interrupted by many large rivermouths draining the muddy coastal estuarine wetlands. Check the playas at El Pimental, Costa del Sol and El Zapote. **Honduras** hogs the Caribbean coast and presents a massive 800km north-facing coast which definitely gets some swell. There are the coral fringed Islas de la Bahia out in the Gulf of Honduras which get battered in hurricane season with connections from the port town of Ceiba where small windswells might offer rideable waves on a not very regular basis. Towards the Nicaragua border, the infamous Mosquito Coast is the largest wilderness in Central America and access is only by boat to a swampy, sandy coastline that has very little to recommend it to surfers. Back on the Pacific coast, the scalloped Gulf of Fonseca is mostly Honduran, but the swell has to be large to make any impression on the mangrove lined bays and sheer islands and only a good boat will get you there. There is a lot more to **Nicaragua** than the increasingly popular, always offshore Rivas Province down south. While maybe not quite world-class, some of the Rivas set-ups provide the perfect balance between challenge and fun, making it an intermediate's paradise. Northern Nicaragua is lightly surfed due to difficult access (cliffs, rivers, swampy estuaries, no roads), shelving bathymetry and most notably, onshore winds in the afternoon. Jiquilillo is easy to get to, with expansive grey sand beachbreak plus some reef/point action down at El Manzano. Aserradores can have some booming beachbreak barrels in front of the isolated hotel and empty inaccessible beachies lead down to stabilised Playa Paso Caballos and the main port of Corinto. There are a couple of protected big swell spots, but without a good boat, access is minimal. Around Leon there are the resort beaches of Poneloya and Las Penitas, which have a bit more shape to their beachbreaks and don't pick up as much swell as down south, but when it does, it quickly gets heavy rips and closes-out. The Nicaragua zone extends from Puerto Sandino's firing lefts to the rare, sketchy left point at Sally Annes and has something for everyone along the way. The same NE breeze that grooms southwest Nicaragua all day is far from a blessing for the Caribbean coast, which is pretty much blown-out all day. Unlike Costa Rica and Panama, this coastline has a shallow continental shelf, knocking wave heights down and making it unlikely that any sheltered breaks in the lee of a headland will be big enough. Huge river estuaries and mangrove swamps silt up the famed Mosquito coast and the only real option for decent waves will be the coral reefs off the Corn Islands, but a kiteboard would make more sense. **Costa Rica**'s surf runs the full gamut of shapes, if not size, and each province boasts at least one draw card wave, often in the world-class category. Volcanic black sand, squeaky white sand and craggy reef can all be found in Guanacaste, including the well-documented wonder-walls like Potrero Grande, Roca Bruja and the peaks of Tamarindo, while off the map along the southern coast of the province lies plenty of less frequented beachbreak at Buena Vista, Samara, Carrillo and most notably Camaronal, where any sniff of S swell will hit the river-fed banks. Carillo has some sizeable, offshore reefs and local surf operators provide boat trips for the journeymen, while beginners

GRANT ELLIS

The Boom, Nicaragua

LAURENT MASUREL

Santa Rosa, Costa Rica

have an easy wave in the protected bay. The huge coastal province of Puntarenas begins on the Nicoya Peninsula, encapsulating the Golfo de Nicoya, where bigger S-SW swells push in and hit a number of breaks that are all offshore in NW winds, which can be handy in the wet season. Cabuya Island Reef is a low tide reef way out off the tip of the "Cemetery island" which is either a long reef platform walk or a boat ride. Los Reyes is nice righthand wall at the Lajas rivermouth and Playa Los Cedros gives goofies a short mellow fun run to slalom in idyllic scenery at high tide. Playa Grande is a solid 30min walk from Montezuma, but the rewards are proper hollow beachbreak peaks and a thick jungle backdrop in crowd-free pristine waters. The surf hub of Jaco/Playa Hermosa merges into Central Puntarenas Province, then down to the Panamanian border, encompassing the Golfo Dulce. More famous waves like Boca Baranca, Playa Hermosa, Playa Dominical and Pavones are encountered along the way, before switching over to the Caribbean coast and the surprisingly chunky reefbreaks of Limon. **Panama** has a torturously twisted coastline, pocked by islets and large estuaries, providing a wealth of surfing opportunities on both coasts. From the Costa Rican Pacific border at Punta Burica where lonely large lefts and rights expire on the extensive reef system which snakes into the west swell protected Gulf of Chiriqui. S swells start hitting around Puerto Armuelles where a few rights line-up down sandbanks built up by river flow. Repetitive grey sand beachbreak that is either junky, onshore, shorebreak close-outs or tapered shoulders depending on the prevailing conditions, leads eastwards to the growing resorts at Playa Barqueta. This is the beginning of Southwest Panama, the best surfing region that includes some remote offshore islands. Panama's biggest island, Coiba shadows the coast, absorbing the best of the swell at Manilla, a super-fun rivermouth left, plus there's a heaving bombora peak, a mellow righthand point on the east coast and miles of virgin beachbreak. Islas Jicarita, Jicaron and Montuosa are not well-endowed with good surfing reefs, but are an amazing wilderness adventure in this huge marine sanctuary. Past the west-facing coast of Veraguas Province and the south coast of Los Santos, SW swells have trouble getting into the east-facing coast before West Panamá Province, but there could be some good rights wrapping in on a big S. In the middle of the Gulf of Panama, the Pearl Islands are surrounded by jagged reef and pillars of volcanic rock, but the surfing options are limited and a boat is essential. Even more of a mission is the swell exposed southwest coast of Darien province, famed for drug running and kidnapping, where apart from Playa Mouerto and the rivermouth at Jaque, it's a jungle wilderness. The same theme continues over on the Caribbean coast, where there are vast tracts of inaccessible, un-navigable or simply unknown coastline. Bocas del Toro is now well-known, but the provinces of Ngöbe Buglé and Kuna Yala are indigenous regions that are only just beginning to allow tourists to visit. The Caribbean coast of Veraguas is deep in the Golfo de los Mosquitos and is the least exposed Carib shoreline, but neighbouring Colon province boasts numerous spots, starting with a fast, hollow right point at V-Land, facing Fort Sherman. Playa Maria Chiquita is the next easily accessible beachbreak, before heading northeast to the super regular reef peaks of Isla Grande, which break on all swells and work in the onshore trades. Further east will have opportunities at Nombre de Dios, Playa Palenque and the rivermouth at Cuango when N-NE swell arrives with size. The 365 San Blas Islands have numerous orientations of coral reefs making it possible to escape the prevalent NE-E onshores and the long fringing coral reef righthander of Kuna An is off Chichime Island with surfer-friendly accommodation.

## GREATER ANTILLES

Shaped like a shallow satellite dish, expectantly listening for the next broadcast of North Atlantic waves, the **Bahamas** occupy an enviable position facing the longest fetch to the NE. Great Abaco and Eleuthera regularly receive surfers from Florida and the US East Coast, plundering the offshore cays and reefs at Indica's, Garbanzo and Surfer's Beach, where a second generation of local riders are now ripping. Cays and reefs pimple the surface and many are either uninhabited or hard to reach unless you have access to an ocean going yacht, complete with good charts and a skilled captain, willing to explore the enormous potential of both the NE and SE Bahamas. In the past, charters have scoped the reef passes, points and beaches including Frenzies, NE Walkers, Drownies and Rushin Rights all up north, then Sandy Point on Cat Island, Cape Santa Maria on Long Island, Love Beach and Rigor Mortis on New Providence, Bonds Cay and Little Harbour Cay in the Berry Islands, Morgan's Bluff on Andros and Sumner Point's fringing reef has waves on Rum Cay. Tourists flòck to San Salvador for great snorkelling and diving, where there's plenty of potential waves on the east coast, plus a due N swell gets in down the NW side to Riding Rock. The list goes on with Conception Island, Crooked Island, Samana, Mayaguana and Inagua all on the yachties radar. The Turks and Caicos Islands share many Bahamian surf features. The straight barrier reef is a long way offshore, horribly exposed to the N winds, however the passes offer the possibility of bend and a safe boating/paddling channel. Northwest Point and Leeward Cut on Provo are offshore in E trades, while Mary's and Clark's Cut on North Caicos, plus the Lighthouse Reefs on Grand Turk get shralped. Learning to kiteboard on the calm, lagoon-like, near-shore waters makes far more sense, but equipment is hideously expensive to rent. The biggest island in the Caribbean should be a carnival of waves, but the Bahamas puts a damper on the party, filtering out all but the biggest winter swells from the NE coast of Cuba. The Atlantic swells have to squeeze through the gaps between the islands, then traverse the continental shelf, so the most reliable coast is around the eastern tip where the window is widest. Gulf of Mexico storm fronts can bring some half-decent waves to Havana and when a hurricane winds up in the Caribbean Sea, proper S groundswell pours through between Jamaica and Haiti, hitting the provinces of Granma, Santiago de Cuba and Guantanamo. The latter is particularly

RONAN GLADU

Shark Cove, Jamaica

rocky and bristling with reefs, but good shape can be found at rivermouth pointbreaks like Rio Duaba in Baracoa and occasionally near Cajobabo on the south coast. Santiago de Cuba has plenty of beaches from the rivermouth peaks in the Bacomao reserve to Playa Mar Verde in town and will work on SE-S swells from August to November. Its often, weak, onshore junk, driven by the E-SE winds until a proper swell hits, when the south coast can host the most powerful and sizeable surf in Cuba. Apart from the exposed western tip at Cabo San Antonio, the rest of southern Cuba is very unlikely to receive any reliable surf and is a much better diving and kiting destination among the cays and islands.

Jamaica is bigger than Puerto Rico, but has far fewer breaks, receiving far less swell. All the known spots on 'The Rasta Island' are clustered around the eastern tip on both the north and south coasts, picking up the corresponding winter NE and summer SE windswells. The north coast has waves all the way to Montego Bay, but the trade winds usually destroy the quality and without them, there's no waves anyway. A hurricane can bring SE and S groundswell to ignite bays and reefs that are usually flat year-round, especially along the southwest coast and the potential to ride junky wind-slop is always there, but generally speaking, stay east.

Little known Haiti is generally off most surfer's lists, yet it is home to some fun and even challenging waves on its coral fringed north and south coasts. While cruise ships stop at the deep-water anchorage off the sugar sands of Labadee Beach, passengers who have been riding the Flow-Rider onboard could be getting the real thing just around the corner at Haiti's best northern wave, Ginsu. Recent exploration has seen the country's inventory of surf spots skyrocket from 6 to at least 36, with the south coast containing the lion's share. The **Dominican Republic** has managed to duck the spotlight and remain relatively low-key until recently, as the Amber Coast north coast hotspots are now getting swamped by surfers from the US, Puerto Rico, Europe and a growing local contingent. It's hard to avoid the wind, which blows hard from the NE or E, resulting in towns like Cabarete becoming world-class kite and windsurfing centres. Eastward is the Samana Peninsula with friendly beachbreak at Nagua, Cayena, El Coson and La Bonita in touristy Las Terrenas. There's also a high concentration of hotels and resorts in Bavaro near Punta Cana and a few kilometres north is the reliably onshore, sandy peaks of El Macao, where straight N swells can produce short hollow waves plus there's some reef action at Caligula and more beachbreak at Uvero Alto. Close to the capital Santo Domingo and Las Americas airport is La Boya, the best right on the south coast, peeling over a rocky reef beside the polluted Boca Chica harbour. A bunch of locals have lobbied to protect La Boya (and nearby Banzai) from plans to expand the neighbouring Andres container terminal. There's more pollution at the reefbreak peaks of Guibia in downtown Santo Domingo and the reef at 3 Tabacos works in SE swells also. Half an hour southwest of the city is the huge port at Haina and some barreling beachies at Chinchorro and Nigua. Najayo el Ojo and Palenquito are outer reefs in San Cristobal, La Punta is misleadingly a rivermouth left, while rocky Patho is more like a pointbreak as is El Derrumbao, way off near Las Calderas. The SW province of Barahona, close to the Haitian border is where the mountain range meets the sea and a scenic coast road winds through thick jungle, and colourful, neat villages beside the turquoise waters of steep pebble beaches. There is not much choice between budget guest-houses and high-end hotels like Casa Bonita, overlooking Bahoruco, the best wave around. The cobblestone rivermouth peak gets pretty hollow, throwing up occasional tubes that head into the cold mountain river flow! Surfed by a handful of locals, who have a choice of a sandy lefthander La Cienaga, San Rafael shorebreaks, sucky rivermouth peaks at Paraiso, or lefts over the pebbles of Los Patos.

JS CALLAHAN/SURFEXPLORE

Haiti south coast

# SWELL FORECASTING

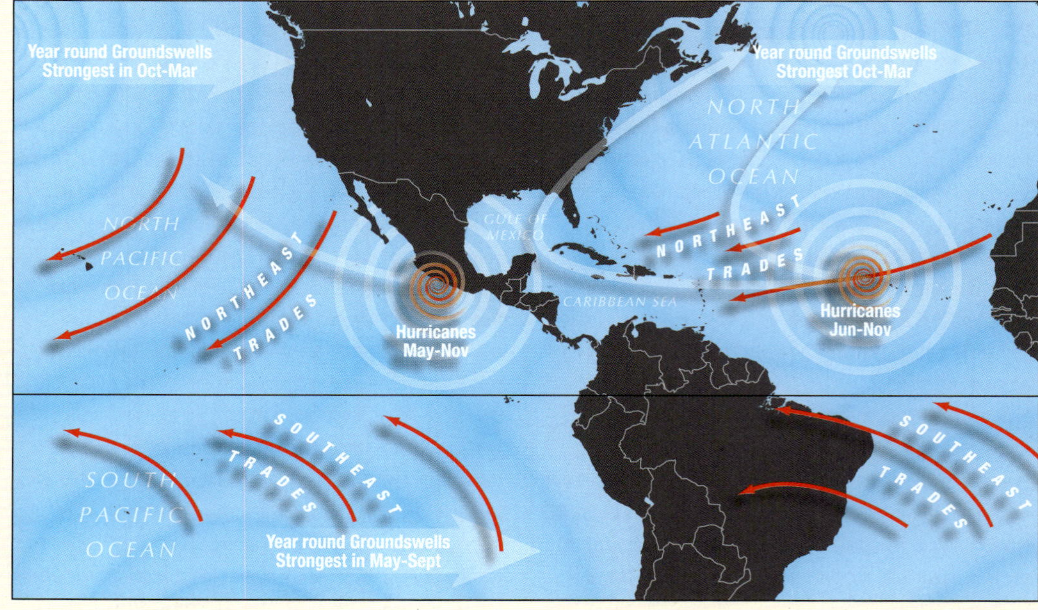


### THE PACIFIC OCEAN

Central America and the Caribbean form the link between North and South America, showing characteristics of both continents plus a character all of its own. The imbalance of swell distribution is apparent with the Pacific easily upstaging the Atlantic for size and consistency, but the Caribbean islands attract seasonal North Atlantic energy plus the Gulf Of Mexico is swept by windswell and occasional hurricanes. Most Pacific shores from Mexico to Panama rely on the dependable, year-round, long distance, SW swells from the South Pacific. Low pressure systems just to the east of New Zealand seem to produce the most epic waves, despite a journey of up to 12,000km. This is because the bulk of the swell is pushed off the weather system's leading edge as it travels east and the clockwise rotation aids a SW direction of origin. The southern regions of the Central American Pacific coast receive more of these southern swells but miss out on a lot of the North Pacific swells that Mexico enjoys. These NW swells rarely produce large waves, which will best strike the few WNW exposed regions like Baja, Nayarit, Jalisco or Guanacaste. The tropical storms that form off the Mexican mainland from May to November always take a northern trajectory, so S swell is produced for the northern regions of Mexico, Baja and California. Rarely will these hurricanes (locally known as chubascos or cordonazos) produce much for El Salvador, Costa Rica or Panama, and often just close-out on the Mexican beaches. Whenever Central America's Pacific shores go flat, which isn't very often, a short journey to the other side, opens up the possibilities offered by the Gulf of Mexico and the Caribbean Sea. The Gulf of Mexico produces windswell coming out of the north, but is less reliable than the sizeable and powerful waves that lash the Caribbean side of Costa Rica and Panama from December to April. Cold fronts and depressions north of Colombia are responsible for the unexpected winter waves, while rogue hurricanes can throw up swells through the June to November season. The wind set-up for Central America is nearly ideal with plenty of glassy or light wind conditions. In summer, after the early offshores, a light SW sea breeze will spring up, while winter is blessed by near constant northerly offshores, which can be a problem for the Caribbean coasts during the prime swell months.

### THE ATLANTIC OCEAN

Caribbean islands facing the North Atlantic accept swells travelling south from the high latitude band of low pressures that spin from Nova Scotia to Europe. These swells often bypass the North American East Coast, before reaching the exposed northern coasts of the Greater Antilles. Puerto Rico benefits from the maximum impact, with a swell-focusing 8km deep trench just offshore, helping to create reliable and occasionally huge waves from October to March. West of the Dominican Republic, the western Greater Antilles (Haiti, Cuba) are sheltered by the Bahamas, a string of islands and coral cays that hide some good waves. The Lesser Antilles also attracts a decent share of North Atlantic N/NE swells, but mainly rely on trade wind swell, hence the name tag of The Windward Islands. This area is also where the word hurricane originated from and the West Indies are always in the firing line of hurricane alley, so surfers pray for the swell without the devastation. If one of these storms crosses over the islands and into the Caribbean Sea, then the west coasts may come to life with perfect waves at breaks that are usually dead flat. Overall, the Caribbean is windy, dominated by an E/NE sea breeze which can produce cross/offshore conditions on NW-facing spots or consistent wind mush on windward coasts. This wind is almost always blowing, so it stands to reason that there are always going to be rideable waves on islands like Barbados.

The whole region is mainly fed by the North Equatorial Current on both the Pacific and Atlantic sides, meaning just one thing – boardshorts - unless you are in the central or northern Baja upwelling zone! Up to 4m changes in height of the semi-diurnal tides affects Panama and Costa Rica, while most of the region experiences less than 1.6m tidal range. Most of the Gulf of Mexico gets diurnal tides and the Caribbean Sea experiences semi-diurnal with different ranges.

**Puerto Rico** has so many surf spots it would be impossible to mention them all. For 40 years the surfing world has been well aware of the quality that resides on Northwest Puerto Rico and names like Gas Chambers and Tres Palmas have become synonymous with challenging, Hawaiian-style surf in the heart of the generally small surf Caribbean. Judiciously aided by the second deepest ocean trench, just offshore, PR sucks in the lion's share of winter ground and summer windswells to all its littoral extent. The north coast deserves its own map and is widely surfed by locals living in the capital, San Juan. There is no shortage of power and plenty of swell - it's just a matter of the wind, which blows some variation of E all year-long.

RYAN CRAIG

Puerto Rico Point

With break names like Los Tubos and Hollows, two spots near Arecibo, you know what you are going to get, along with a foot full of urchin spines. There are a bunch more reefs in this area, mostly all shallow, with treacherous rips and usually blown out by 11am. It's not all expert-only reefbreak and one of the main spots in San Juan is La Ocho, a reliable mix of waves for all abilities including a good righthander off a rock that is longboardable and a left wall called Fiji off the other side. The NE coast is ecologically protected and despite being in the teeth of the trade-winds, has many breaks like Chatarra in Loiza, a dead ringer for Pipeline on those rare W swell, S wind days with the same gladiatorial vibe in the thick crowd. Just down the reef is the more consistent and achievable A-frame, Aviones, but it's also super-crowded. In Loquillo, La Pared is no stress, bumpy beachbreak, while the long walk into La Selva is worth it for punchy, turn-fest walls beside an exposed slab reef. Even the east coast gets great headhigh days when the trades reverse to W-NW. The SE coast has Inches, a coral reef left beside a deep channel and long, loping walls with the odd hollow part on the inside. Can be long, fun and easy so it gets insanely crowded in summer, when a SE or S swell rumbles in. Also check out Patillas waves La Escuelita and Las Lajas. Dangers in PR are many and varied; the coral or lava reef is always ready for new flesh and the urchins are legion. Jellyfish and sea-lice add to the discomfort, but sharks are too well-fed to be a threat. Physical injury is far more likely if you get on the wrong side of the locals - choose your waves, sessions, parking and fights with the utmost care. Traffic can be hell.

L'Abbatoire, Guadeloupe

## LESSER ANTILLES

Strung out along a 1100km (685mi) oceanic front, the multitude of volcanic islands in the chain form an arcing Caribbean Sea barrier from the Atlantic swell train. Exotic, tropical, yet firmly Caribbean, each island group has its individual flavour in landscape, culture and also surf. The Windward and Leeward Islands offer a rich diversity of waves from perfect pointbreaks over fire-coral, barrier reef passes, tabletop reefs to flawless sand point barrels.

The Virgin Islands guard the northern border of the Leeward Islands and are first to receive the winter NW-NE swells, which are crucial to the recipe for Tortola's west coast diamond, Cane Garden Bay in the British Virgin Islands. Like Puerto Rico, a big N swell wrap and offshore NE-E is required and this can be replicated on the northwestern tips of islands like Jost Van Dyke and the far more accessible Saint Thomas in the **US Virgin Islands**. Hull Bay is the centre of the scene, holding a variety of fun, rolling waves over deeper water reefs, a long way from the beach and the tranquil waters of the yacht moorings, but expect austere wave heights as the 90° NE swell refraction saps plenty of size. There's fast, hollow, shallow waves at Caret Bay, where the locals are notoriously territorial. Over on St John, Trunk Bay holds guillotine lips over far out Johnson's Reef, plus there are a few SE swell options around Reef Bay and a couple of other rare south coast reefs.

St Martin and St Barthélémy are well-heeled yachting favourites, which can also be applied to **Barbuda** and Antigua, but each island maintains its own separate identity, along with some uncrowded perfection on the right swell/wind combo. That often means due N or even NW swells are required for some west coast action protected from the trades. That also means low consistency is the theme, especially on islands that are shielded by the outer chains, offshore islets and cays, like **St Croix**, **St Kitts and Nevis**, plus the steep, volcanic coasts of **St Eustace**, **Saba** and **Monserrat**. **Anguilla** is more exposed to swell and would seem to have the perfectly oriented NW coast, but the fringing reef way offshore is probably where the action is for those with a boat. Meads Bay has a hollow, backwashy, left reef down near the dolphinarium and the southeast coast has some left reef set-ups in Rendezvous Bay when it's big, or Savannah Bay when it's small.

**Guadeloupe** is the biggest land mass in this central zone and Grande Terre benefits from a deeper offshore valley pointing towards the Atlantic NE swell source. Basse Terre is not as fortunate and NE swells will generally struggle to reach the north and west coasts, but a big due N or those rare W hurricane swells will hit some prime spots. Offshore islets hide some action so check Ilet a Fajou, Caret and Kahouanne, which has a long right and left off the SE tip. The west coast beaches around Deshaies usually look like a lake, otherwise they can be thumping shorepound plus the odd reef corner in a swell. Down on the south coast there's some black sand beachbreak at Trois Rivieres and at Bananier, the most reliable beach. There's more waves up towards Roseaux, but east-facing beaches are rarely clean. The Iles des Saintes and Marie Galante offer some real possibilities for the marine mobile. A mere 25km south lies the relatively unspoiled island nation of **Dominica**, still cloaked in rainforest and the northernmost boundary of the Windward Islands. Cliffs make access tricky in places, but the 365 rivers cut valleys and build up black sand beaches, adding to the rocky reef inventory that dots the Atlantic coast. Check the mainly right reef of Calibishie up north, or the messy peaks of Pagua Bay beachie that has a few rivermouth paddling channels. Where the Rosalie river hits the coast can hold some shape providing the wind isn't too strong and there are many more potential waves down the east coast, but quality set-ups are few and far between. Scotts Head on the south coast can have waves in summer S swells and E wind is cross-off. The west coast is a very rare bird that gets a bit of swell in winter wrapping round to Portsmouth and a spot behind Ross University, or else it's destructive hurricane swells from the W.

Next island south is the French department of Martinique, where the waves are concentrated on the unusually protruding Caravelle Peninsula, allowing for offshores on a windblown east coast that is freckled with nearshore islets, cays and reefs. The French and the British battled over mountainous **St Lucia** 14 times, yet the island nation has remained low key as a surf destination. There are plenty of east-facing long sandy beaches that are joined by steep, plunging coastline that rarely provides the right bathymetry, but if the E wind stops blowing there are pocket beaches and rivermouths that may have good banks, like Can en Bas or Comerette in the north and Fond d'Or near Dennery. Down south, the kite-friendly sands around Vieux Fort are protected by offshore reefs and the Maria Islands, but it may be worth a look at the reefs to the west of the airport runway. The west coast is usually flat until hurricane swell provides some rights in unlikely bays like Marigot, or a straight N wakes up Windjammer and the far more consistent lefts of Rodney Bay, that handle SE winds. The Soufriere volcano erupted twice in the 20th Century, bringing widespread destruction to another French/British melange, **St Vincent and the Grenadines**. The main island of St Vincent poses the best chance of surf and the buffeted black sand beaches of the east coast are usually rideable but messy and uninviting. Possibly the best spot on St Vincent is a consistent left wall out on the shallow, rocky, coral encrusted reef pass entrance to the Blue Lagoon on the south coast. It's a long paddle from the marina and there are currents to deal with, so once again, those with access to a boat are ahead of the game. The Grenadines is all about sailing between protected anchorages and avoiding the windward side surf which undoubtedly exists; it's just hard to get to. Park Point on Bequia has a left and there are plenty more offshore reefs preventing the surf reaching some of the pristine, ivory sand beaches, a theme that continues on Mustique, Canouan, Mayreau, Palm and the larger, but terminally shadowed Union Island. A W or NW swell would have no such barrier and there must be some good set-ups for those rare days. Over the border into the **Grenada** governed islands of the Grenadines sees little difference in the geology and outer reefs are the only reliable swell catchers, as seen on the biggest island Carriacou and its

British Virgin Islands

Barbados

satellites, Petit St Vincent and Petit Martinique. The north coast of Caille Island has a proper, long, righthand reef setup that is cross-offshore in a SE wind, but it is next to the world's most expensive private island. The water deepens off Grenada and the barrier reefs become less prevalent, but the long and short east coast beaches still fail to produce any class waves in the face of the trades and getting around the island when a swell is running is hard work on the slow road system. Check the south coast at Prickly Bay for some fast lefts and rights or be lucky enough to score the island's best wave, Cherry Hill, tucked away on the protected west coast.

Out on the next oceanic ridge to the east lie the utterly reliable breaks of Barbados and the slightly less exposed shores of Trinidad and Tobago where classy breaks like Soup Bowls and Mount Irvine keep a large local surfing population well-fed.

# Northern Baja MEXICO

US surfers have been crossing the clandestine-proof border into the Baja (Lower) California desert peninsula for decades. Baja constitutes the major getaway for Californian waveriders, who jump in the 4x4 and drive the Mex1 Highway, looking for quality righthand pointbreaks, consistent beach and reefbreaks and cheaper, simpler living. Baja Norte has all the prerequisites to satisfy intermediate to expert surfers and the highway hugs the coast all the way down to Ensenada, making access to a varied range of breaks simple.

+ QUALITY RIGHT POINTBREAKS
+ CONSISTENT WINTER SWELLS
+ YEAR-ROUND DESTINATION
+ CHEAP TACOS, BEER & TEQUILA

- LACK OF LEFTHANDERS
- SURPRISINGLY COLD WATER
- USA STYLE CROWDS
- LOTS OF POTENTIAL DANGERS

On weaker S-NW swells, ex-party town **Rosarito** has highly consistent, year-round beachbreak for all levels around the pier, plus reefs and rivermouths, where pollution and the nuclear power plant are concerns. The right pointbreak at **Calafia** is mushy without a strong S swell and gets rocky at low tide. **K38** is a famous but very crowded right, peeling fast and hollow over an urchin farm. Best on a S swell, or a stronger W to NW pulse at low to mid. Working on similar swells but higher tides, **K38.5** is another fast, walled-up peak between rocky outcrops. Escape the thicker crowds by paddling to **K39**, an outside-breaking reef able to produce quality lefts and rights in any sizeable swell. Facing a guarded condo community, the semi-private reef off **Las Gaviotas** is more of a longboard wave for all levels. Sometimes sectiony and often crowded, it prefers a due S swell. **K55/Campo Lopez** is a very consistent setup similar to K38, where juicy barrels are common especially at the point on a NW swell. Decent beachbreak just N of the rocks. Guards try to restrict access to all these breaks for non-guests. The crowded Alisitos campsite at **K58/La Fonda** is where the best-shaped beachbreak in the area delivers very consistent barrelling lefts and rights, especially near the rivermouth. At size, paddling out can be punishing. **Salsipuedes**, the legendary right pointbreak has been privatised, so boating in is now the only way to enjoy the inconsistent, fast peeling rights at the point or the reef peak facing the ex-campground. **San Miguel** will get over-crowded when a W to NW swell fuels fast, powerful, tubing waves at low tide by the cobblestone rivermouth. Ensenada is the jumping-off point for Baja's most famous big-wave spot, **Killers**, 20km offshore on the Islas Todos Santos. An underwater canyon maximizes long period W-NW swell energy down the point, creating huge, powerful and shifty deepwater waves. South of Ensenada, dirt trails lead to wind-protected rights like **Santo Tomas**, a south-facing point plus some rocky beachbreak. **San Antonio del Mar** holds uncrowded and consistent beachbreaks. **Cabo Colonet** likes a solid S to W swell to kick-start the long but inconsistent rights hugging the cliff. Endangered by a project to build the third-largest port in the world. Construction would also threaten the fun but busy right pointbreak and reefs of **Quatro Casas**, best on a S swell and there's an excellent campsite on the bluffs that protect the break from NW wind. **Shipwrecks/Freighters** is best on a wrapping NW swell and holds some size. N wind protection is good, but the beached ship right in the line-up can shorten the long, mellow rights. There are some excellent reef options around to escape the crowds generated by the surf camp. A similar but more consistent and quieter pointbreak is found at **Punta Camalú**, with reef and beachbreak options up and down the cove.

Northern Baja is well-suited to the winter pattern of consistent W to NW swells and northerly winds. Long range S-SW pulses from summer storms, hit a select number of spots, but not all the pointbreaks. Spring is the worst time, as it is buffeted by the strongest winds. Tradewinds blow from the NW all year, with more N between November and February. The strong winds cause upwelling, which equals cold water. There's a big tide and a small tide with variations up to 2.8m.

Rosarito

DAMIAN DAVILA

Killers

AL MACKINNON

## TRAVEL INFORMATION

**Weather** – Sunny, mild and dry Mediterranean climate. Fresh ocean breezes and strong sun mean temperatures average from 16°-24°C (61-75°F) year-round. Winters are mild and windy with a little rain while a coastal fog occurs in early summer. Bring a 2/2mm steamer or springy in the summer, and a 4/3mm with booties in the winter.

**Lodging and Food** – Several hotels for all budgets in Rosarito and Ensenada fr $13/n. Club Marena rents holiday apartments at K38 and Las Gaviotas (fr $160/n). Baja Surf Adventures camp in Quatro Casas. Free-camping possible at places but campsites are safer and cheap. Great, spicy Mexican food

**Nature and Culture** – Good snorkelling and diving options; fishing is best during summer and fall. Whale watching at Ensenada from December through March. Strong winds offer great potential for kite/wind surf.

**Hazards and Hassles** – Things can get nasty near the border so get past Ensenada to avoid hassles. Drugs, theft, drunk drivers, police, gun-crime, pot-holes, car breakdowns, summer flash-floods, scorpions, snakes, etc. Do not run out of gas, water or food in remote areas. Travelling US surfers have been robbed at gunpoint even in proper campsites.

**Handy Hints** – Most surf shops are in Tijuana, San Miguel & Ensenada. Many spots can handle large swells so bring a gun (board!), wax, extra leash, ding and first-aid kit. English is widely spoken, US dollar accepted everywhere.

| STATISTICS | | J F | M A | M J | J A | S O | N D |
|---|---|---|---|---|---|---|---|
| SWELL | Direction | | | | | | |
| | Size (ft) | 4 | 3-4 | 2-3 | 3 | 4-5 | 5-6 |
| WIND | Direction | | | | | | |
| | Force | F3-F4 | F4 | F3-F4 | F3-F4 | F3-F4 | F3-F4 |
| WATER | Wetsuit | | | | | | |
| | Temp/°C | 15 | 15 | 18 | 20 | 19 | 16 |
| WEATHER | Rainfall/mm | 51 | 28 | 50 | 3 | 5 | 38 |
| | days/mth | 6 | 5 | 2 | 1 | 2 | 5 |
| | Min temp/°C | 8 | 11 | 14 | 17 | 15 | 10 |
| | Max temp/°C | 17 | 19 | 21 | 24 | 23 | 20 |

# Central Baja MEXICO

Baja California is a long, narrow peninsula extending south of San Diego, barely linked to the Mexican mainland by a thin strip of land. This arid, rocky finger has long been a playground for surfers from "Upper California" seeking righthand pointbreak perfection, without the urban crowds that dominate the USA line-ups. Central Baja is where the main highway heads inland, making the treasure trove of rights in the huge Bahia Sebastian Vizcaino and the beachbreak barrels of Isla Natividad harder to reach.

- + NUMEROUS RIGHT POINTS
- + NATIVIDAD TUBING WAVES
- + MILES OF UNCROWDED SURF
- + OFFSHORE TRADE WINDS

- – LACK OF LEFTS
- – UPWELLING
- – BAD ROADS, REMOTE NATIVIDAD
- – BASIC ACCOMMODATION

## TRAVEL INFORMATION

**Weather** – Central Baja weather is a cool and damp coastal desert climate, with periodic winter rains, and the summer is long and warm. If it gets really hot inland, the nights will get chilly on the coast (10°C/50°F). The hurricane season, stretching from June to October, may bring in some rain, but the cool ocean waters of the area limit storms northward trajectories.

**Lodging and Food** – Camping is the only type of accommodation available if you want to be close to the breaks. If you're willing to put in an hour's driving for more comfort, there's several places to stay in Guerrero Negro (El Morro) or try the hotels in Bahia Tortuga. Fresh lobster and cold Pacificos make a stylin' surf meal.

**Nature and Culture** – Besides fishing, main visitor attractions are the whale-watching tours to the nearby lagoons (Laguana Ojo de Liebre ) between January and April, or exploring nearby Sierras for Indian art. Nothing to do but surf on Natividad.

**Hazards and Hassles** – Roads are bad, gas stations are rare, you may get stuck in deep sand or lost for a while. Avoid night driving. Federales will pull you over for any reason and suggest you pay the fine directly to them – how convenient! Following them to the station could be even more costly in time and money.

**Handy Hints** – Take all your equipment including 4/3 wetsuits and boots in winter. English is widely spoken on the Baja peninsula. US dollars are accepted everywhere. Local fishermen know the ocean better than anyone, ask them for tips.

YEP

Punta Maria

Punta Eugenia and Cedros Island conspire to block S swells from much of Bahia Sebastian Vizcaino. **Punta Canoas** is one of the last spots able to pick up direct SW swells onto a series of points, where an outside reef and high cliffs offer good N wind protection. **Punta Blanca** is one of the series of seven major points known as the Seven Sisters. It's a fine right climb and drop pointbreak for able surfers, working best on a SW-W swell, offshore-ish in NW and is definitely among those requiring a 4WD. From **Punta Cono** south, only W to NW winter swells can be relied on. Cono bends these swells a full 180° and fans out endless carvable walls into the wind protected bay. **Punta Maria** is a class act; a long wrapping right, which can only be seen on major W swells that usually coincide with winter's offshore NE winds. **El Cardón** may be one of the smaller headlands in the area, but rides are actually really long and it is always bigger than Maria or Lobos. Rocky at the tip, sandy at the tail. Next door, **Punta Lobos** looks like an elongated version of El Cardón, complete with wind protection and an even sandier bottom. Sharks have been spotted among the guaranteed numbers of surfers in the line-up. Yet another good right pointbreak, **Punta Negra** enjoys offshore winds early and late in the day during the winter months. **Puerto San Andrés** receives strong offshores that attract a few windsurfers and surfers looking for real hollow waves. Whenever a really big W swell comes in, **Punta Santa Rosalillita** is an obvious choice with the point delivering truly classic, extra-long rides plus there's several other breaks around the bay, including waves beside the new harbour breakwalls. Punta Rosarito is so consistent, it has earned the nickname of **The Wall**, but winds, even if offshore, can get too strong to surf these powerful west-facing reefs.

Plenty of camping among the rock wall windbreaks. Cruise around El Tomatal fish camp in the area known as **Miller's Landing** to find the nice cobblestone right point and a neighbouring left/right reef. A big island like Isla Cedros seems attractive but it's really windy and breaks like **Playa Elefante** are only of medium quality. If you're gonna fly you should head to Isla Natividad. Located on the east side of the island, the dredging barrels of **Open Doors** are offshore every afternoon, but be prepared for powerful, board-snapping lefts and rights. Other breaks include Siren Bay's big wave option, Old Mans and Frijole. Back on the mainland, **Bahia Tortuga** is a seldom surfed area with numerous breaks, requiring S-W swell to penetrate the deep bay. From there air and water get warmer as you enter Baja California Sur and another bunch of excellent righthand points like Abreojos and Scorpion Bay.

Only spots above Punta Blanca or below Natividad can rely on the long-travelled, clean S-SW swells. The Seven Sisters only wake up when winter's W-NW swells hit from Oct to April. Winds blow NW-N. Upwelling keeps water temps lower than North Baja in winter. Tide range reaches 2.8m.

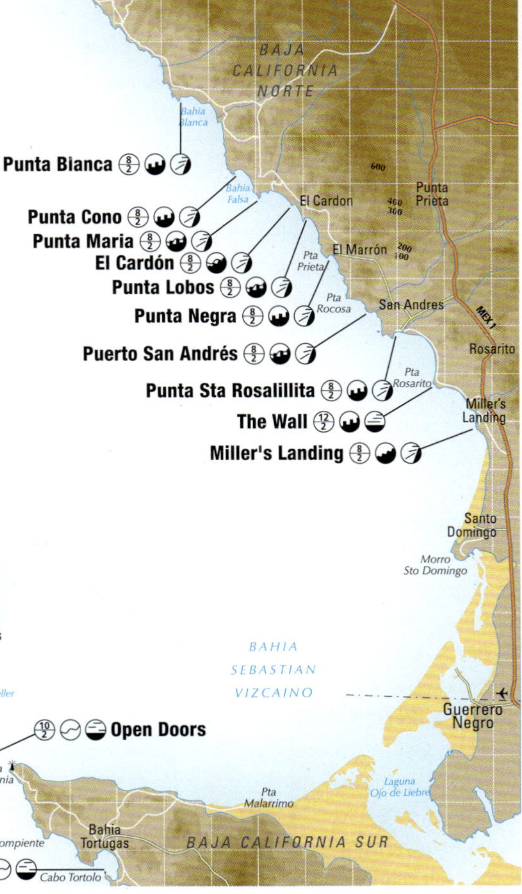

CHRIS CORONA

Open Doors

| STATISTICS | | J F | M A | M J | J A | S O | N D |
|---|---|---|---|---|---|---|---|
| SWELL | Direction | | | | | | |
| | Size (ft) | 4 | 3-4 | 2-3 | 3 | 3-4 | 4 |
| WIND | Direction | | | | | | |
| | Force | F4 | F4 | F4 | F3-F4 | F3-F4 | F4 |
| WATER | Wetsuit | | | | | | |
| | Temp/°C | 11 | 13 | 16 | 20 | 20 | 17 |
| WEATHER | Rainfall/mm | 35 | 15 | 5 | 15 | 75 | 30 |
| | days/mth | 4 | 3 | 1 | 2 | 4 | 4 |
| | Min temp/°C | 10 | 12 | 16 | 20 | 20 | 17 |
| | Max temp/°C | 21 | 24 | 27 | 30 | 28 | 24 |

# Los Cabos MEXICO

It's over 1200km in a straight line from the USA border to Cabo San Lucas at the southern tip of Baja California. Cabo is a distinctly civilised version of Baja and is one of Mexico's most developed ports, attracting US tourists to the burgeoning seaside resorts. Boardshort warm seas offer a 200° swell window from the SE around to the NNW, favouring S swells from either long distance lows or nearby hurricanes, but the W coast also receives a fair amount of NW swells.

- + WARM WATER AND WEATHER
- + RIGHT POINTS
- + GOOD SWELL/WIND PATTERNS
- + PLENTY OF SUNSHINE

- – LACK OF POWER
- – JELLYFISH AND DESERT BUGS
- – CABO CROWDS
- – SOME BAD ROADS

## TRAVEL INFORMATION

**Weather** – The desert climate is hot and dry for most of the year and summer gets steaming hot. Rain only comes from rare summer chubascos, provoking flash floods, lightning and gusty winds. Boardshorts at the tip, but west coast can get cold currents/upwelling so a thin springsuit or steamer for Jan-Feb.

**Lodging and Food** – Nov-Feb is the high season. The Los Cabos corridor is a set of hotels and resorts. Expect to pay at least $70/n for a good hotel. Cabo Surf Hotel overlooks the Costa Azul breaks ($285-625/n 4-8p). R.V parks and campsites are cheap (fr $10): San Pedrito, Pescadero, Cerritos, and Cabo Cielo. Free-camping possible outside the corridor. A good meal costs up to $20.

**Nature and Culture** – In Cabo San Lucas, The Squid Roe, Cabo Wabo and The Giggling Marlin go off at night. Whale watching or scuba diving in the Gulf is a flat day alternative.

**Hazards and Hassles** – Hurricanes, floods, jellyfish stings, scorpions, sea urchins and intense heat are all threats. Localism has got pretty bad around Monuments and Zippers. If you get pulled over by the Federales or military don't try to bribe them, just be cool.

**Handy Hints** – You can rent beginners boards on the beach at Costa Azul. Guns not needed and longboarders love Cabo. Los Cabos is the number one, long-weekend surf destination for Californians. The W coast is a laid-back place to hangout.

Shipwrecks

JIMMY WILSON

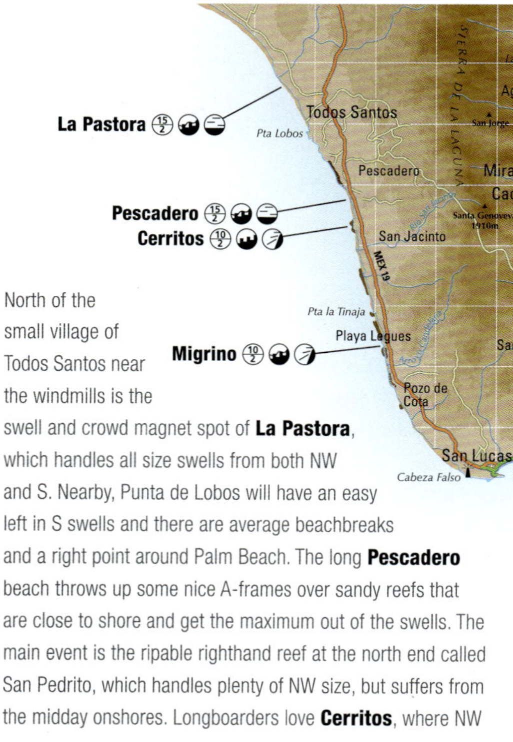


North of the small village of Todos Santos near the windmills is the swell and crowd magnet spot of **La Pastora**, which handles all size swells from both NW and S. Nearby, Punta de Lobos will have an easy left in S swells and there are average beachbreaks and a right point around Palm Beach. The long **Pescadero** beach throws up some nice A-frames over sandy reefs that are close to shore and get the maximum out of the swells. The main event is the ripable righthand reef at the north end called San Pedrito, which handles plenty of NW size, but suffers from the midday onshores. Longboarders love **Cerritos**, where NW swells wrap nice righthanders around the headland, or lefts break back into the wind-protected corner. Works at all tides with low making it steeper and faster. The beach peaks offer something for beginners when small. **Migrino** is a consistent right point that accepts winter swells and summer pulses along the numerous beach peaks. Only a short distance from town so gets pretty crowded when there's no waves in Cabo. On the east side of the Cabo San Lucas bay lies **Monuments**, a short, spinning left that works on any S-W swell and is offshore in N winds. Can get perfect, but it's a tight take-off zone and the rocks and urchins are lurking everywhere. Experience required especially at low tide. Just past Chileno is **El Tule**, a righthand reef that is quite consistent yet not too crowded, making the slopey walls ideal for improvers and intermediates. **Punta Palmilla** is a bay that is full of resorts and condos, hampering access. The outside point will break on only the biggest S swells, offering ledgy rights for skilled surfers only. The three waves of Costa Azul are the main surf focus in the region and all break over reef despite the sandy shoreline. **Acapulquito** is also know as Old Man's because it's a favourite of longboarders and is usually soft and mushy on the shoulder, giving longer, cruisey rides. **The Rock** is always crowded and offers a more challenging ride, especially as the tide drops out and the urchins get closer. Same applies to the rapid right called **Zippers**, but multiplied. It's almost impossible to get a wave off the dialled-in, un-sharing locals and below mid tide is a gamble. Best wave in Cabo. Hotels give way to desert, revealing numerous inconsistent right pointbreaks visible from the road like Punta Gorda. Plenty camp at **Shipwrecks** to ride the punchy right walls that rarely barrel, although the adjacent beachbreak left can. There are loads more reefs and points before **Nine Palms**, which is well sheltered from the wind and lines-up nicely in a big S. Fun, fast-crumbling walls as opposed to tubes, which can be found up the road at Punta Perfecta. **Los Frailes** is a large sandy bay with a left reef worth checking in a big SE swell. The **Punta Arenas** area is a long sand point that needs massive S or local storm swell from the N to offer anything other than flat water.

Acapulquito

PEDRO SALINAS

Summer (May-Oct) is consistent with long-distance, clean S-SW swell and deep tropical storms spinning off the Mexican coast providing raw SE swells for the breaks in the Sea of Cortez. In winter, major NW swells hit the west coast around Pescadero. Localised, storm generated windswells can hit both sides of the peninsula. Dominant NW winds blows onshore in the afternoons, while the S coast is mainly offshore. Winter sees more N in the wind and summer sees more W. Tide range maxes at 2.2m and is usually not a problem.

| STATISTICS | | J F | M A | M J | J A | S O | N D |
|---|---|---|---|---|---|---|---|
| SWELL | Direction | | | | | | |
| | Size (ft) | 3-4 | 2-3 | 3-4 | 4-5 | 4-5 | 3-4 |
| WIND | Direction | | | | | | |
| | Force | F3-F4 | F3-F4 | F3-F4 | F3 | F3 | F3 |
| WATER | Wetsuit | | | | | | |
| | Temp/°C | 23 | 23 | 25 | 28 | 28 | 26 |
| WEATHER | Rainfall/mm | 15 | 0 | 2 | 25 | 150 | 2 |
| | days/mth | 1 | 0 | 0 | 2 | 6 | 20 |
| | Min temp/°C | 12 | 13 | 17 | 22 | 21 | 15 |
| | Max temp/°C | 24 | 29 | 33 | 35 | 33 | 27 |

# Nayarit MEXICO

Mostly undeveloped, the scenic coastline of Nayarit has attracted hardcore surfers since the late '60s, hoping to score Matanchen Bay, known as being the longest right in the world. But things have changed with the fast rise of Puerto Vallarta, once a tiny fishing village in the neighbouring state of Jalisco, now attracting 4-5 million tourists each year.

+ SURFABLE YEAR-ROUND
+ TOP LONGBOARD/SUP SPOTS
+ SCHOOLS, CAMPS & BOATS
+ RESORTS OPTION

– LACK OF "MEXICAN JUICE"
– RESTRICTED ACCESS SPOTS
– SOME SHARKY LOCATIONS
– RAINY PEAK SURF SEASON

The remote offshore Isla Maria Cleofas has nice offshore peaks at **Hammerhead** accessed via surf charters leaving from Nuevo Vallarta. The banks of **Los Corchos** are powerless, but the peaks can get good shape from the river flow. San Blas has poor beachbreak at El Borrego, but paddle the rivermouth to **Stoner's Point**, a classic pointbreak that works in all swells and any N wind. More power and hollowness than other breaks, it's a consistent spot but hard to get to. **Las Islitas** is one of the longest waves in the world, with cover-up to cutback symmetry as the wall speeds up and slows down on the long journey down the point. It hardly ever breaks and only a huge S swell will do, along with a very long board. There are peaks right around Matanchen Bay for almost any wind direction and there is generally a good vibe in the water. The pointbreak lefts at **Aticama** are much more consistent in S-SW pulses and of excellent quality, but being so close to a fishery there's plenty of sharks drawn to the area. **Santa Cruz** needs a sizeable pure S or SW swell to get the left pointbreak peeling over the boulders beside the jungle cloaked cliff, otherwise check the sharky, polluted rivermouth if it's too small. Take a boat from Chacala to the rocky, urchin-infested lefts of La Caleta or **Lolas** especially in W swells. Gets crowded and a bit aggro, but the line-up has a few take-off spots. **San Pancho** is a fast lefthander off the point and sucky peak in front of the river that can hold some size and gets hollow around low tide. **Ostiones** is accessible by sea or land (long walk) and the lefts are worth checking on a big SW swell. The surf town of **Punta Sayulita** is ideally suited to beginners and longboarders. Rights off the point are slow and predictable for the surf school hordes, while the lefts at the rivermouth are steeper and faster. **Punta Mita** access is thoroughly guarded and requires a long paddle or a boat to these fast rights that need W in the swell. Well exposed to all swells, **The Cove** is a fast, sectiony right that lines up best in NW. Sensitive to wind and gets sucky at lower tides. The long workable rights of **El Faro** are the best in the bay when a W swell spokes around the point. Lower tides and N winds make for long rides through the multiple sections into the protection of the bay. Anclote beach has beginner beachies beside the rivermouth jetty and a righthand reefbreak to the west. **Costa Banderas** set-up favours rights and La Lancha, Punta Burros, Pools and Destiladeras are all worthy spots. Puerto Vallarta only works on big days when the beaches at el Tizate and the Holiday Inn in the hotel zone are pumping. Take a panga water taxi to **Quimixto**, a popular local beachbreak and rivermouth facing north.

Winter (Nov-Mar) is when W-NW swells wrap into Banderas Bay, losing some size but cleaning-up with the northerly offshores. Occasional W swells will provide the biggest conditions on most spots. March and April are usually windy, before summer pushes in long period S-SW swells in the 4-8ft range, the perfect direction for the northern lefthand breaks. Winter N winds progressively shift W-NW for summer. Semi-diurnal odd tidal range hovers around 1m (1.6m max).

Los Corchos
Stoner's Point
Las Islitas
Aticama
Sta Cruz
Hammerhead
Lolas
San Pancho
Ostiones
Punta Sayulita
Punta Mita
The Cove
El Faro
Islas Marietas
Costa Banderas
Quimixto
SURFHOLIDAYS
NOMAD SURFERS
PERFECT WAVE

## TRAVEL INFORMATION

**Weather** – Abundant rains and humidity in the summer, mixed with intense sunshine, regularly take temperatures beyond 30°C (86°F). The mountains generate cooler breezes at night, making the climate more bearable than further south. Winter sees daytime temperatures around 27°C (80°F), but nights get cooler, down to 15°C (59°F). Hurricanes usually stay out at sea, tracking W-NW towards Hawaii or Baja. Water temps range from 22-28°C (73-82°F) so a spring suit is advisable.

**Lodging and Food** – Resorts are plentiful in San Blas and PV. In Sayulita try Bungalows Las Gaviotas ($60) or Las Olas all women surfcamp ($2850/week). Viva Vallarta resort faces Punta del Burro, Punta de Mita's Meson de Mita is $60/dble. A $10 dinner lets you sample tasty specialties.

**Nature and Culture** – Sayulita is a laid-back city. San Blas is Nayarit's tourism centre and starting point for jungle river boating to La Tovara springs. Check out remote beaches, or snorkel/dive around Islas Marietas. Along the Malecón (downtown PV), a strip of restaurants, bars and clubs will provide all night entertainment.

**Hazards and Hassles** – Nayarit breaks are more adapted to intermediate level surfers. Locals don't always see the influx of surfers positively, but crowd levels are low on spots requiring a boat. San Blas surroundings are infested with jejenes (tiny sand gnats) that come out at night and provoke intense itching.

**Handy Hints** – Avoid Puerto Vallarta's polluted waters. Recommended quiver includes a longboard or fish. Equipment and rentals are available at Coral Reef Surf Shop in Bucerias or Acción Tropical Surf Shop in La Cruz de Huanacaxtle. Jalisco State (Puerto Vallarta) is 1h ahead of Nayarit (Sayulita).

NICK LAVECCHIA
Punta Sayulita

NICK LAVECCHIA
Punta Sayulita

| STATISTICS | | J F | M A | M J | J A | S O | N D |
|---|---|---|---|---|---|---|---|
| SWELL | Direction | | | | | | |
| | Size (ft) | 3 | 3-4 | 4 | 5 | 4-5 | 3-4 |
| WIND | Direction | | | | | | |
| | Force | F3-F4 | F3 | F3-F4 | F3 | F3 | F3 |
| WATER | Wetsuit | | | | | | |
| | Temp/°C | 23 | 23 | 25 | 28 | 28 | 26 |
| WEATHER | Rainfall/mm | 25 | 40 | 100 | 160 | 230 | 20 |
| | days/mth | 2 | 4 | 8 | 12 | 14 | 2 |
| | Min temp/°C | 16 | 18 | 23 | 24 | 24 | 19 |
| | Max temp/°C | 26 | 27 | 30 | 32 | 32 | 28 |

# Colima and Michoacan MEXICO

Mexico is a classic surf destination receiving ample swell into the numerous beaches, rocky headlands, rivermouths and reefs. Colima and Michoacan states have their fair share of waves, which include your typical, heavy Mexican beachbreaks like Pascuales along with the quality rivermouth destination wave at Rio Nexpa.

+ BIG SWELL CONSISTENCY
+ CALM WIND PATTERNS
+ UNCROWDED, BARRELLING WAVES
+ CHEAP AND EXOTIC

- SUMMER SWELL EXCESS
- WET SUMMER CLIMATE
- MUDDY ROAD ACCESS
- MOSQUITOES AND BANDIDOS

Most surfers arrive in **Manzanillo** where the big bay is great for learners around Playa Miramar on a small S or challenging for the local crew at Olas Altas in SW-W pulses. A super-protected right point works at La Boquita on huge days. **Cuyutlan** can be a huge close-out shorebreak, unless a small peaky S-W swell hits the straight black sandbanks, creating tube-time for the nimble. Up the beach, Tepalcates inlet groynes bend any swell, cut most winds and hold the sand nicely. At **El Paraiso**, a bend in the beach arranges nice triangular bars and some fast, hollow, yet more forgiving rides compared to its illustrious neighbour. **Pascuales** is a super-powerful peak, unloading top to bottom barrels up to double overhead and occasionally more. It's either perfect or a ferocious double-up close-out and is only for experts, before the midday onshores. **Boca de Apisa** is Colima's last option for a quality beachbreak; thick, fast and cracking in a medium S, which can produce long rivermouth lefts when the sand is settled. Peaks to the north and south also work well in the winter NW swells. Strong currents. Into Michoacan state, **San Juan de Alima** offers a relaxed vibe in and out of the water with plenty of good quality beachbreaks out in front of town, best ridden at high tide with light winds. To the southeast are 3 reefs with easy channels or Las Brisas fun peaks. **La Ticla** is visible from the Mex 200 and many stop to ride this epic wave. When it's small it's a good, fun beachbreak, but with a bit of S-SW swell, La Ticla becomes an awesome rivermouth left. The rights can be almost as good in W-NW and there is space to handle a crowd. Long history of banditry, theft, police corruption and general sketchiness, yet the surfers keep coming to ride this Mexican gem. On the road to Nexpa there are easier waves for all standards at numerous sparkling, crowd-free beaches like Ixtapilla, La Llorona, Colola, Maruata and El Zapote de Tizupa. **Huahua** rivermouth offers fast barrels over the sandy reef in both directions, depending on the season. Barra de Nexpa palapas (beach huts) face the long, tubing lefts of **Rio Nexpa**, a crowded rivermouth setup. Low to mid tide and due S swell can link all the sections making for hi speed rides over the boulders and sand. There can be much shorter, emptier rights off the peak, which break back into the rivermouth, especially if the swell is more W. The lefts can handle plenty of size and even NW wind, but get some strong currents and will dish out some poundings to the unwary. There are plenty of beachbreaks to the north at Playa Linda Vista and La Manzanilla for a break from the intensity of the waves and crowds here.

From Mar-Nov there are plenty of super-clean, lined-up S-SW groundswells, plus the bigger SE-SW June-Oct hurricane season. The beachbreaks are often too big for most surfers, reaching face heights of 25ft on the beaches, whilst the pointbreaks will be firing at 6-12ft. Due S swells fire up the left point/rivermouths, while W is good for the beachies and W-NW peels down the right rivermouth/reefs. Winter can see some clean 3-8ft swells and light W-N winds, plus many glassy days. Dominant N-NW winds shift to E-SE during the rainy period, which tend to be ok for the lefts. Tidal variation is slight (1.6m max) with a big and a small high tide.

LAURENT MASUREL

Pascuales

RICK COWLEY

Rio Nexpa

## TRAVEL INFORMATION

**Weather** – The Sierra Madre mountain range prevents cloud cover from reaching the coast. During the wet season (May-Sept) night-time thunderstorms can be torrential, as temps and humidity hit their peak. Winter is a far more pleasant time to visit, (±26°C/78°F), and the waves will be smaller. El Niño years are hotter and rainier than normal. A rash vest and boardshorts is all that is required.

**Lodging and Food** – San Juan has been developing more accommodation options (Maria Isabel $35-75 dble; Antonic $53-75/bungalow) than most of the small coastal towns, which offer dirt-cheap basic "palapas" (Pascuales or Nexpa from $15/d) or cheap camping (La Ticla or Maruata from $5/d). For more choice try Caleta de Campos or Playa Azul. Food is basic and very cheap at around $5/meal.

**Nature and Culture** – This area is very green with jungle all around and a lush, mountainous shoreline cut by large rivermouths. Wildlife is plentiful, but sharks are only a worry close to harbours and rivermouths. Colola is a famous turtle nesting site.

**Hazards and Hassles** – Thieves are a problem, especially at La Ticla campground and around Nexpa. Carry cash in small bundles and stash some. Travel in groups and never at night. Montezumas' Revenge is a particularly nasty stomach bug indigenous to Mexico.

**Handy Hints** – There is a surf shop in Tecoman. Bring spare boards, including guns in summer for the chargers. Come in the winter for good weather and clean, easy beaches and points.

| STATISTICS | | J F | M A | M J | J A | S O | N D |
|---|---|---|---|---|---|---|---|
| SWELL | Direction | | | | | | |
| | Size (ft) | 3 | 4-5 | 5-6 | 7-8 | 6-7 | 3-4 |
| WIND | Direction | | | | | | |
| | Force | F3 | F3 | F3 | F3-F4 | F3-F4 | F2-F3 |
| WATER | Wetsuit | | | | | | |
| | Temp/°C | 27 | 26 | 28 | 29 | 29 | 28 |
| WEATHER | Rainfall/mm | 4 | 1 | 158 | 254 | 254 | 18 |
| | days/mth | 1 | 0 | 8 | 13 | 12 | 2 |
| | Min temp/°C | 22 | 22 | 25 | 25 | 24 | 22 |
| | Max temp/°C | 31 | 32 | 33 | 33 | 32 | 32 |

# West Guerrero MEXICO

Guerrero catapulted Mexico onto the world tourism stage with the 1940's development of Acapulco, still the number one tourist destination in the country today. In the 1970's the federal government tried to repeat Acapulco's rapid growth, and promoted Ixtapa Zihuatanejo as the place to go. Surfing began in the extremely mountainous state in the 1960's, then '70s surf explorers Naughton and Peterson unveiled Petacalco, an insane, world-class right, in a land of mellow lefts.

+ LONG SURF SEASON
+ SALADITA LONGBOARD HEAVEN
+ SURF BREAKS GALORE
+ GOOD WEATHER

– NO STANDOUT THRUSTER WAVE
– EXPENSIVE RESORTS
– BANDIDOS AT WORK
– RAINY SEASON, HURRICANES

## TRAVEL INFORMATION

**Weather** – Guerrero enjoys 300 sunny days a year and in the winter months, between December and April the daytime temperature hovers around 31°C (88°F) with the nights going down 22°C (72°F). During this time there is little to no rainfall. The rainy season arrives during summer evenings or nights between late June and mid-October. Water temperature averages 26°C (79°F), so no neoprene required.

**Lodging and Food** – Winter is peak season with top prices. Itxapa is packed with luxury resorts; Zihuatanejo is more accessible with doubles around $40. Troncones area offers plenty of surf-facing accommodations. Try La Chuparosa de Saladita, Casa Delfin Sonriente or the Saladita SC (all fr $70). Enjoy shrimp and fish tacos or tiritas (fish & onions).

**Nature and Culture** – Explore the cave in Troncones. Fish and hike in the surrounding area. In Zihuatanejo check out the central market and walk over to the lighthouse (El Faro) from Las Gatas. Ixtapa is a modern resort with many nightclubs (Christine Club). Take a trip to the colonial town of Petatlán.

**Hazards and Hassles** – Guerrero has mostly mellow waves, but big days happen. Bandidos target campers and Highway 200 at night. Take hurricane warnings seriously, winds over 200km/h (120mph) are no laughing matter.

**Handy Hints** – Take a shortboard, step-up and a longboard. You can find gear at Catcha L'Ola Surf Shop in Ixtapa or Anfibios in Zihuatanejo. Lessons and rental boards at Jaguar Tours or The Inn at Manzanillo Bay.

Las Gatas

CHRIS CORONA

Manzanillo

WILLIAM MERTZ

The long port expansion at Lázaro Cárdenas turned **Petacalco** into an ugly close-out, but it has recently risen from the ashes and is now rideable on huge NW swells, or due S. Always powerful at any size, but the sandbar shape is crucial and close-outs are the rule. This polluted industrial city receives some thumping surf along a dozen jetties and **El Faro** is the most commonly surfed spot. No longer secret, **The Ranch** attracts experienced surfers staying in nearby resorts, who regularly drive or boat in to enjoy very consistent, long, sectiony, lip-bashing lefts, plus some rights and a rivermouth on the other side of the headland. Longboarders will prefer **La Saladita**, a soft-breaking lefthand pointbreak where rides over a minute long are not unusual. The left pointbreak at **Manzanillo** packs much more power, with steep drops and long, full speed sections, before shouldering off. Overhead days are safer as the wave breaks further away from the urchin-covered rocks. This is a surf rich area, with other points and a rivermouth as you head north. **Troncones** is a long stretch of beach marked with rock outcrops that encourage sandbar peaks, but it's the moody right reef at the south end that draws the crowds in a moderate SW swell. In Ixtapa, **Playa Linda** is usually mushy but the rivermouth can produce long left walls as the wave reels into a sandy lagoon. There's a ferry to Ixtapa Island, where a zipping right barrels over a flat rock ledge on the south coast. **Escolleras** at Playa del Palmar benefits from currents running along the marina, which sometimes shape a tubular right, but you won't be alone. **Las Gatas** takes a long walk, paddle, or a boat ride from the municipal pier. The inconsistent left there needs a good amount of S-W swell to break hollow and fast over a sharp reef, dominated by dialed-in locals. **Barra de Potosí** is really sheltered from S swells, but once or twice a year a left peels down the point in huge swells. There's also some average peaks in the rivermouth and a right pointbreak. **Loma Bonita** is a powerful stretch of beach and reef peaks, throwing out barrels in E winds and W swells at mid tides, plus there's the option of easier waves at La Barrita 2km south. Endless peaks line the coastal highway through Cayucal and further south to the **Mirador el Calvario**, which may be fun in small swells next to the northern headland. **Papanoa** is an average beachbreak with fast walls, but tends to close-out. **Playa Boca Chica** is a consistent beachbreak surfable year-round, and probably your last option before reaching Acapulco. Caca's Point is the only surfable spot within the Bay of Acapulco, otherwise there's more surf at Copa Cabana. At the northern end of **Revolcadero** beach is a big swell right and some beach peaks, rideable when the nearby beachbreaks of Punto Muerto and Playa Princess are closing-out. Playa Bonfil's consistent sucky beachbreak is directly in front of Acapulco Airport.

Guerrero works year-round with the biggest S swells arriving between April and October. Huge rideable surf is not a common occurrence – offshore hurricanes will produce two days of pounding surf up to 10ft, or messy, huge and rainy conditions if it gets too close but between November and March wave heights drop a notch – usually waist to headhigh. W-NW winds prevail all year, only July to September sees some regular SE winds. Expect offshore/calm wind in the morning before an afternoon seabreeze comes in. Tidal range hardly ever goes over 0.6m.

| STATISTICS | | J F | M A | M J | J A | S O | N D |
|---|---|---|---|---|---|---|---|
| SWELL | Direction | | | | | | |
| | Size (ft) | 3 | 4 | 5 | 6 | 5 | 4 |
| WIND | Direction | | | | | | |
| | Force | F3 | F3 | F3 | F3 | F3 | F3 |
| WATER | Wetsuit | | | | | | |
| | Temp/°C | 26 | 25 | 26 | 27 | 27 | 26 |
| WEATHER | Rainfall/mm | 5 | 0 | 160 | 250 | 270 | 25 |
| | days/mth | 0 | 0 | 6 | 11 | 11 | 1 |
| | Min temp/°C | 22 | 23 | 25 | 25 | 25 | 24 |
| | Max temp/°C | 31 | 31 | 32 | 33 | 32 | 32 |

# West Oaxaca MEXICO

Oaxaca is famous as the home of Puerto Escondido, one of the best beachbreaks in the world, where huge and spectacular barrels break with Hawaiian-style power on Playa Zicatela. The lack of any continental shelf and the offshore deep-water trench focuses the swell from both the Southern Hemisphere and frequent tropical storms that pass by this coast in summer time (April-Oct). These swells hit the sandbars in such a way that the waves jack-up in size, which can be emphasised by a backwash. Magazine photos of this place are misleading – the waves often close-out and the paddle-outs can be severe. Fortunately, Oaxaca (pronounced wah-hah-kah) is not only about huge death-defying barrels and there are a few user-friendly points, reefs and rivermouths for the average Joe.

+ WORLD'S "BEST" BEACHBREAK
+ CONSISTENT YEAR-ROUND
+ FAIRLY CHEAP
+ GOOD NIGHTLIFE

- LOTS OF CLOSE-OUTS
- CROWDS
- CRIME
- INSECTS

## TRAVEL INFORMATION

**Weather** – On average, daily temperatures are always high and the summer UV factor is often extreme. On average, the warmest month is April, hitting 32°C (90°F) but dropping to lows of 14°C (58°F) at night and it is also the month with the least humidity. The highest amount of precipitation falls in June, while August and September have more rainy days and the most humidity. Winter is more pleasant with dry weather (December is the driest month) and slightly less humidity, especially at night when it can drop below 10°C (50°F). The Pacific hurricane season runs from mid-May to November with storms peaking in early to mid September, producing torrential rains and heavy flooding, along with storm surges and waves up to 30ft+. Carlotta hit on June 15, 2012, and made landfall near Puerto Escondido, the first Pacific hurricane ever to make landfall that far east. Water temps are trunkable all-year-round, maintaining above 25°C (77°F), although some may don a thin vest for early winter mornings.

**Lodging and Food** – Puerto Escondido has everything from the cheapest, right up to top hotels. The beach road, Calle del Moro is a good place to be based giving you convenient access to the beaches and amenities. Hotels have been springing up all over the place – rooms from $40 upwards. Every type of food available, (great seafood at the port), from $4 a meal.

**Nature and Culture** – Visiting the archaeological site of Monte Alban or the picturesque city of San Cristobal de las Casas requires a real effort, but they are definitely worth the time and expense. The nightlife in Puerto Escondido goes off. A horse ride out to the Atotonilco hot wells is a good afternoon trip.

**Hazards and Hassles** – Muggings and petty theft are on the increase, sometimes accompanied by violence - don't carry valuables around with you. Bandidos are also a growing problem. Don't camp on beaches at night or drive down quiet roads. Some of the spots get crowded. When it's big, Puerto Escondido is a wave for advanced surfers. Insects, scorpions, stingrays, earthquakes, hurricanes, floods, heat and humidity are all part of the deal!

**Handy Hints** – Bring a couple of boards, plus a gun and be prepared to snap them - a helmet may be a good idea as well. Cheap boards can be bought at Central Surf or rented from the Cabañas Las Olas or Rockaway. Mexican surfers are hardcore and charge on the biggest of days - show them some respect. The Federales (police) are worth avoiding!

AL MACKINNON

LAURENT MASUREL

Chacahua

**Chacahua** throws up some access difficulties, as it is cut-off by a large system of estuarine lagoons, swamps and a national park. A local ferry crosses to the eastern side, where a fast, tubing right sometimes peels down a sandbar built up beside the rivermouth jetty. Works in both S and huge W-NW, plus there's plenty of surrounding beach peaks. It's not so consistent, with strong rips from the lagoon and aggressive locals. A reputation for big insects, theft and robbery has developed, but hotels haven't within this island-like community that offer basic accommodation with few amenities. The large lagoon system drains out to sea via the rivermouth at **Cerro Hermoso**. A jetty helps hold the sand that changes every time the boca breaks open. Lefts and rights will form in anything from the S, but it won't handle too much size. Nice quiet spot for all abilities to get some fun waves in the right conditions. Playa El Venada can have some short empty peaks and Playa Roca Blanca will often have a lazy right off the western headland rocks that is tucked out of the western breeze. **Carizalillo** is a small rocky bay that will have fun waves for all types of surfer on all types of craft. Needs a hefty swell to get the lumpy left walls and shallower, rock strewn rights going which prefer lower tides to avoid the bounce in a bay that is often flat and perfect snorkelling territory. Only medium consistency and sometimes crowded with local bodyboarders, longboarders and everything in between. Surf school operates here also. Around the rocky, hotel-studded headlands and past the lighthouse begins the peerless beachbreak of **Puerto Escondido** where spectacular, cavernous barrels unload close to shore right along the length of Playa Zicatela. Less assured surfers should take the long, hot walk (or catch the bus) down to the mellower, but busy lefts of **La Punta**, which offer the relief of a paddling channel and some long, fast, slashable walls. Fun shoulders outside can get hollow over the sandier

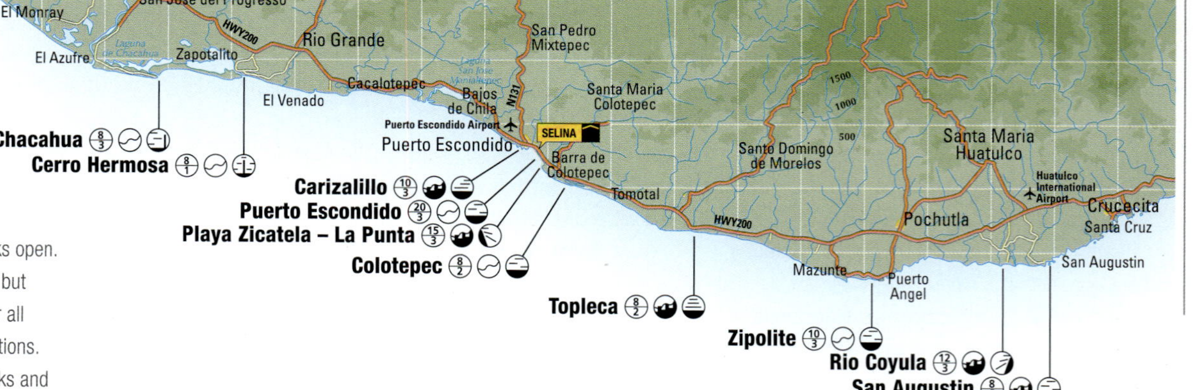


inside sections. Late afternoons should see the wind drop away and Puerto Escondido should clean up. Always crowded with the less adept visitors and locals. To the east of Puerto are the reliable rivermouth sculpted beachbreaks of **Colotepec**, which can still pack some punch and dredge some sand along the shifty, rippy and wind-exposed beach. **Topleca** is an isolated, peak over reef and sand that will be best in small swells. More beach and reef options in the area including Zapotengo. The renowned hippie community of **Zipolite** is a popular rest stop on the backpacker circuit and there can be some short, dumpy lefts and rights along the notoriously rippy beach, especially off the rock in the middle. The beach to the west has similar opportunities up towards San Augustinillo. Turn off the Mex 200 down a dirt track to **Rio Coyula** that will lead to a sandy pointbreak in front of Laguna Boca Vieja and a left and right at the eastern headland that all like a S-SE swell. It's a rarely surfed area with lots of good potential. Bandits operate on the small coastal roads in this area, robbing people at night.

## Puerto Escondido

**LAT. 15.843107° LONG. -97.053091°**

Swells hit the Puerto Escondido sandbars at Zicatela Beach in such a way that the waves jack-up in size, which is often emphasised by a backwash. Magazine photos of this place are misleading; guillotine lips make the paddle-outs punishing and there's always plenty of board-snapping close-outs, so wave choice is critical. Requires high skill level when it gets overhead, which is when the thick crowds start to thin out. Locals, pros and travellers fight for the 1 in 3 that hopefully won't shut down, but don't speculate in the lip. Committed surfers only need apply. Usually the rights break best on a due SW swell and will often be blown out by 11am when the ENE offshores stop. There's large numbers of skilled surfers in the water hoping for the bomb that stays open long enough to escape. Despite all this, it's still a year-round Mecca for big barrel hunters! Avoid eye contact with the local chargers - the line-up is a lottery so sit tight and one will come to you eventually. The rips are like tractor beams, holding you in the impact zone until you get blasted back to shore, where the lifeguards do their best to keep the death toll down. It's highly consistent and always crowded – dawn is best.

**San Augustin** needs a big S swell to work since it faces SE and an offshore island bounces the swell round the rocky bay. Nothing special but a beautiful spot. Bahias de Huatulco are well-protected tourist bays and offer little in the way of good waves, unless there is a really huge S swell, when Tangolunda may have a rideable shorebreak on this tourist hotel strip.

Oaxaca has consistent, year-round surf, but many consider summer (April-Oct) as the prime surf season. Quality swells are generated from lows off New Zealand, providing regular 3-10ft SW swells. Add the heavy action of the tropical storms or chubascos, generated off mainland Mexico, which churn up swells of 6-15ft between June-Oct. Many of these hurricane swells are just too unruly and close-outs are common. Double overhead days are far from rare and during the height of the swell you will often see waves getting to triple overhead. Some of the time the combination of wind and swell is far from ideal.

AL AMCKINNON

Zipolite

Between Nov and Feb, there will be lots of glassy or N wind days, but less of the strong swells. When the summer swells are pumping, there's more chance of onshore, due W winds, blowing from 39% of the time in April to 17% in July. Afternoon sea breezes are an almost daily occurrence, usually backing off after 5pm. The summer rainy season brings winds from all directions, but mainly a mild W-NW or a better E-SE. One big and one small tide a day can hit a maximum range of 1.5m, although it will usually be around half that figure, having a minimal effect on most spots.

LAURENT MASUREL

La Punta

| STATISTICS | | J F | M A | M J | J A | S O | N D |
|---|---|---|---|---|---|---|---|
| SWELL | Direction | | | | | | |
| | Size (ft) | 3 | 4-5 | 5-6 | 7-8 | 6-7 | 3-4 |
| WIND | Direction | | | | | | |
| | Force | F3 | F3 | F3 | F3 | F3 | F3 |
| WATER | Wetsuit | | | | | | |
| | Temp/°C | 27 | 27 | 28 | 28 | 28 | 27 |
| WEATHER | Rainfall/mm | 4 | 0 | 147 | 177 | 180 | 8 |
| | days/mth | 1 | 0 | 7 | 10 | 8 | 1 |
| | Min temp/°C | 22 | 23 | 25 | 25 | 24 | 22 |
| | Max temp/°C | 29 | 31 | 32 | 32 | 31 | 30 |

# East Oaxaca MEXICO

The third largest country in Latin America still has plenty of surf potential to be uncovered and those looking for warm water and offshore winds with no one else out, should seriously think about the eastern part of Oaxaca. Huatulco to Salina Cruz, is almost untouched by development and characterized by verdant jungle slopes meshing with spectacular white sand beaches. Dredging beachies, rifling points and secret jetties are visited by powerful southern hemisphere swells from April to October. Sketchy access to many spots keeps the crowds low.

- \+ CONSISTENT SUMMER SWELLS
- \+ CROWD-FREE OPTIONS
- \+ MANY CLASSIC BREAKS
- \+ NO MASS TOURISM

- – STRONG TRADE WINDS
- – SOME SKETCHY ACCESS
- – MAINLY RIGHTHANDERS
- – RAINY SURF SEASON

## TRAVEL INFORMATION

**Weather** – Oaxaca's "eternal spring" climate has a dry season from December to May, then a rainy season from June to November. Offshore hurricanes can have a strong impact on the amount of rainfall (1100mm/44in annual avg). Usually the rain lasts for just a few hours after which the sun comes out. The seasons deeply influence the vegetation, that switches from brown to lush green. Boardshorts only.

**Lodging and Food** – Punta Conejo resort has five day all inclusive packages from $900. Salina Cruz Surf Camp at Punta Chivo (with restaurant, bar & pool). Check Waterways for all incl. Salina Cruz stays or check local hotels and posadas in Salina Cruz ($30-80/dble). Wide variety of accommodations in Huatulco. Pepe's Cabana's ($15/nt) at Barra de la Cruz or luxury Villa las Tortugas at nearby Playa El Mojon (from $2000/wk). Diversity of regional cuisine, based on fish and shellfish.

**Nature and Culture** – Good diving options at Santa Cruz, also gentle rafting on Copalita and Zimatan rivers. Sea turtles nestling site at Morro Ayuta. See the ancient Zapotec ruins.

**Hazards and Hassles** – Waves aren't like Puerto Escondido, but big days happen. Banditos are known to work the Highway 200 at night. Don't get stuck on tracks during rainy season. Drive defensively as locals will pass on curves. Mosquitoes are a constant nuisance. Sharks are around.

**Handy Hints** – No surf shop in Salina Cruz, but Las Palmeras Surf Camp may have some basics. Ideally, a shortboard for hollow waves plus a longboard/fish for the classic points. Avoid travelling at night or alone. Bring a mosquito repellent. Beware of Federales.

**La Bocana** is a fun beachbreak, great for beginners staying in Huatulco and the highly sandbank dependant rivermouth is worth a check too. **Barra de la Cruz** was re-named La Jolla for the controversial Rip Curl Pro Search WCT event in 2006. A "once-in-a-decade swell" offered amazing conditions to the top 44 surfers, with deep barrel rides up to 12 seconds, being webcast all around the world.

The heavily localized, righthand pointbreak now gets crowded, despite its need for a big S or SE swell to even begin to show signs of life. Inconsistency aside, when it's on, it's worth the village access and beach charge to ride these long, epic rights in a beautiful setup. An out of service lighthouse marks **Morro Ayuta Point**, which is almost impossible to find without local knowledge or a surf guide. It's an excellent righthand sand pointbreak that is mainly surfed by a few locals. Barreling waves peel from the top of the headland, with very long rides when conditions are ideal (solid S swell, offshore NW winds). A long track in starts about 7kms east of Santiago Astata to the uncrowded, consistent waves of **San Diego**. There's a good right point at the mouth of the bahia and some peaks forming off the rocks to the east. Down a track beside quarries, **Concepción Bamba** is consistent and wind protected. A juicy, very hollow righthander peels off a small breakwall, offering short, intense rides if the tide is not too high (backwash). The longer breakwall delivers a heavy, thick barreling right. **Punta Chipehua** is a remote but quality right, peeling over rocks and sand when a solid S swell hits. Best from low to mid tide, they don't close-out when big, but have no tolerance to the regular 20-30 knot NE-E trade winds. **Punta Chivo** is a fun, tapered wall off the large sentinel rock and can have the odd hollow section. Great wave for longboarders or improvers and beginners can sit further inside. NE-E blows it out, but any W wind and S swell is fine. Working under similar conditions **Punta Conejo** is the premier pointbreak and is sometimes able to deliver rides up to 500m with a strong S swell. It's very inconsistent, but highly sought after and the crowd has increased, along with the number of Salina Cruz surf camps. The rocky tip of the sand engulfed **Salinas Cruz Jetty** holds some short, sucky rights and west of the big port, Playa Abierta can have thumping A-frames. East of Salina Cruz, **La Ventosa** is a highly consistent beachbreak, best with a small to medium summer S/SW swell and a low tide. There are miles of A-frame peaks to the east, but the offshore trade winds are sometimes too strong to surf here!

April to October is the surf season, when big southern hemisphere SW swells hit East Oaxaca and are usually a bit softer than around Puerto Escondido. Chubascos occasionally deliver 6-15ft waves and SE is a good direction. Strong "tehuano" trade winds whistle through the gap in the Sierra Madre range, between the warm Gulf and the colder Pacific. From October to April, these strong N-NE winds flatten the surf, but back off and become variable during the surf season. A rainy episode can turn off the fan, creating perfect glassy conditions. The semi-diurnal odd tides hit 2m, but won't stop you surfing.

AL MACKINNON
Barra de la Cruz

RYAN CRAIG
Punta Chivo

| STATISTICS | | J F | M A | M J | J A | S O | N D |
|---|---|---|---|---|---|---|---|
| SWELL | Direction | | | | | | |
| | Size (ft) | 3 | 4-5 | 5-6 | 7-8 | 6-7 | 3-4 |
| WIND | Direction | | | | | | |
| | Force | F4-F5 | F3-F4 | F3-F4 | F3-F4 | F4-F5 | F4-F5 |
| WATER | Wetsuit | | | | | | |
| | Temp/°C | 26 | 26 | 28 | 29 | 28 | 26 |
| WEATHER | Rainfall/mm | 4 | 1 | 165 | 197 | 181 | 14 |
| | days/mth | 1 | 1 | 8 | 10 | 7 | 1 |
| | Min temp/°C | 21 | 23 | 25 | 24 | 23 | 21 |
| | Max temp/°C | 30 | 32 | 33 | 32 | 31 | 30 |

# Guatemala

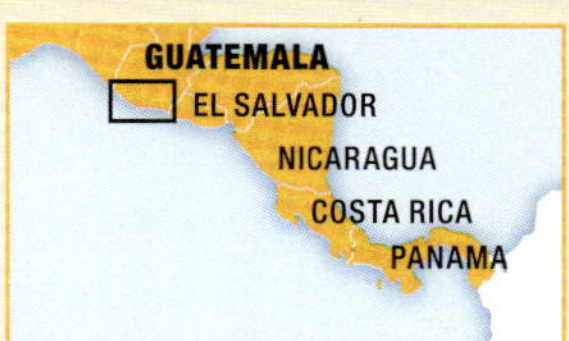




It may not be the best surf in Central America, but warm water and uncrowded beachbreaks will always find takers. With over thirty volcanoes and many peaks rising above 4,000m, it's surprising not a single rock can be spotted along the 250km coastline, making for a continuous stretch of mostly black-sand beachbreaks, only interrupted by the occasional rivermouth. Considered a transit zone between Mexico and El Salvador, the lack of coast roads means long drives between breaks, but few crowds to share the punchy beach, jetty and rivermouth peaks.

+ HARDLY EVER FLAT
+ DRY SEASON OFFSHORE WINDS
+ COMPLETELY UNCROWDED
+ CHEAP LODGING AND FOOD

- BEACHBREAKS ONLY
- NO COASTAL ROAD
- STRONG RIPS
- OCCASIONAL PETTY CRIME

PAIGE VUOTO

Iztapa

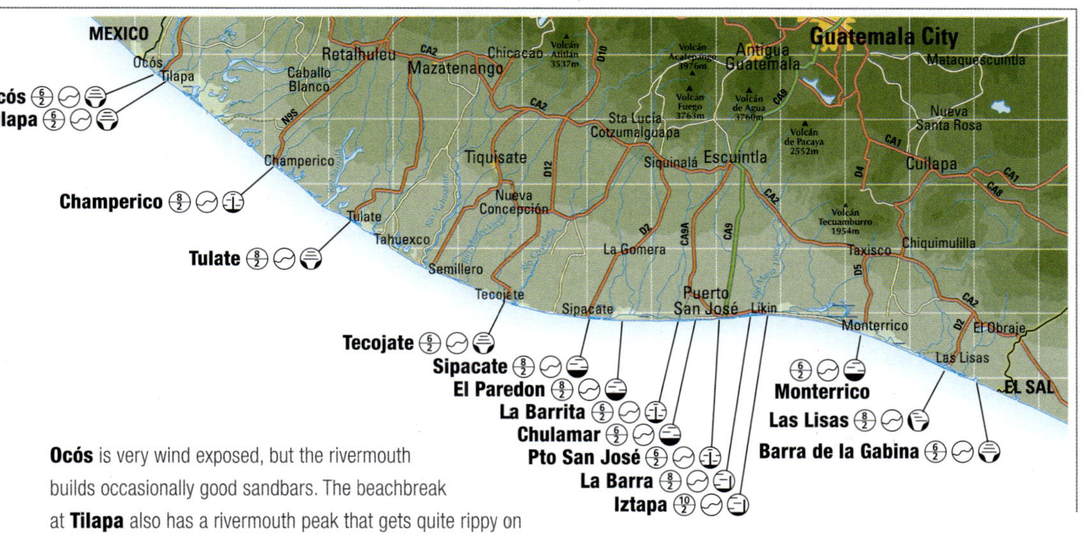


**Ocós** is very wind exposed, but the rivermouth builds occasionally good sandbars. The beachbreak at **Tilapa** also has a rivermouth peak that gets quite rippy on the dropping tide. The large pier at **Champerico** gives the sand and surfers a focus, breaking on a clean, small SW swell, with short barrels before it closes-out. Far more consistent are the rivermouth peaks of **Tulate** that handle bigger S-W swells and offers power with shape. The Rio Coyolate comes all the way from the central highlands, sometimes bringing enough sand to form a good sandbar in **Tecojate**. **Sipacate** is all about quality beachbreak peaks, and with miles of beach available, it's one of the best spots to catch some tube time when a peaky, head-high SW hits. Incoming tides and morning offshores complete the pretty picture. **El Paredon** is very consistent and popular with both local and foreign surfers, because the black sandbanks hold solid barrels on any S swell at higher tides. Rips get mad as the tide drops out and it's not for beginners above headhigh. Surf camps and schools here. Either side of the **La Barrita** jetties hold longer lefts and rights that come alive late spring and develop throughout summer. The adjacent Marina del Sur beachies get classic peaks with an incoming tide and the right swell angle. **Chulamar** beach isn't so steep and on a small swell there's well-organised waves. Rapidly accessed from Guatemala City, **Puerto San José** is Guatemala's most popular seaside resort, where average, all tide peaks break beside the derelict pier. Rips, some residential pollution and weekend warriors make this place less appealing. A coast road allowing easy surf checks starts at the upscale resorts of Balneario Likin, home of the challenging hollow rivermouth and jetty peaks at **La Barra**. The righthander is long and predictable, with hollow pockets interspersed by slashable shoulders. The left sucks hard and often closes-out onto the tip of the jetty. Rideable till slightly overhead, it needs low incoming tide or slack high to avoid the killer rip. Surf camp and adept crowd. The jetties in the fishing port of **Iztapa** build up the sand on the east side, offering longer, hollower waves on chunkier SW swells. Peaks also form between the jetties, offering a protected option in bigger swells. There's more peaks around, it just depends on whether the sand is in otherwise it'll be close-out city. Higher tides needed, rips guaranteed. The photogenic tourist town of **Monterrico** has a really steep beach angle that translates to rip-torn, shorepound close-outs best for bodyboarders. **Las Lisas**, via the inland freeway, avoids the usual shorebreak set-up and allows some bigger, longer waves to be ridden. The rivermouth left sandbar can line-up fun, whackable walls, but the rips can spoil it. Towards the border with El Salvador, several secluded beaches offer options to get wet, with rivermouths like **Barra de la Gabina** providing the best odds for creating some stable sandbars, despite swirling rips on the dropping tide.

Guatemala's rainy season between May and October, sees Southern Hemisphere swells arrive in the 3-12ft range, when winds will be offshore in the morning, then switch sideshore/onshore around 11am. Peaky, messed-up swells coming in at an angle are less likely to close-out, so many spots favour SW or occasional SE swells. Smaller South Pacific conditions are perfect for the beachbreaks during the off-season when E-NE offshores will be a regular occurrence. Tidal range can reach 2.5m, affecting the beachbreaks as much as the rivermouths, where the currents can be horrendous on the push and drop.

## TRAVEL INFORMATION

**Weather** – Guatemala is known for its mild highland temperatures, while the Pacific coast swelters in tropical temperatures, often hovering above 35°C (95°F). The seasonal difference is dramatic, with maximum rainfalls in July and September, often at night. The constant high humidity diminishes a little in the dry season from November to April. Water temperatures range between 27-29°C (80-84°F).

**Lodging and Food** – The tourism infrastructure isn't fully developed on the coast and low-standard hotels are the rule except in Chulamar, Iztapa and Monterrico. Check out surfinguatemala.com for accommodation options, surf school and rentals. El Parédon surf camp ($3.75/d tent; $8.50/d bunkbed; $27/d room) offers lessons and rentals. Complete meal = $12.

**Nature and Culture** – The Mayan ruins of Tikal are at the other end of the country. Turtle watching on many beaches during the full moon. Visit the Biotopo Monterrico-Hawaii nature reserve. Around Sipacate, bird watching, canoeing and fishing will fill a flat day.

**Hazards and Hassles** – No rocks to hit, but beware of the strong currents around rivermouths. Tourists are commonly targeted for robbery, bus and car-jackings. Travelling after sunset should be avoided. Malaria risk exists but dengue fever is the main concern in coastal areas.

**Handy Hints** – Take everything including favourite beachbreak board. Extra bars of warm water wax will befriend the locals. Early morning, low incoming tide, offshore wind and a 4-6ft SW swell should see ideal conditions everywhere.

| STATISTICS | | J F | M A | M J | J A | S O | N D |
|---|---|---|---|---|---|---|---|
| SWELL | Direction | | | | | | |
| | Size (ft) | 2 | 3-4 | 4-5 | 5 | 4-5 | 2 |
| WIND | Direction | | | | | | |
| | Force | F3 | F3 | F3 | F3 | F3-F4 | F3 |
| WATER | Wetsuit | | | | | | |
| | Temp/°C | 27 | 28 | 29 | 28 | 28 | 27 |
| WEATHER | Rainfall/mm | 5 | 50 | 280 | 310 | 350 | 35 |
| | days/mth | 1 | 3 | 14 | 15 | 15 | 3 |
| | Min temp/°C | 19 | 21 | 22 | 22 | 22 | 20 |
| | Max temp/°C | 31 | 32 | 31 | 31 | 30 | 31 |

# Costa del Balsamo EL SALVADOR

GUATEMALA
EL SALVADOR
NICARAGUA
COSTA RICA
PANAMA

El Salvador hides an insane array of long righthand pointbreaks making it a natural-footer's dream destination. Whilst its reputation has been built on the waves of Punta Roca in La Libertad, El Salvador has more than just one wave, and the whole country is literally bristling with awesome righthand pointbreaks. Considering its small size, El Salvador could easily claim the highest density of quality pointbreaks in Central America.

+ PERFECT RIGHT POINTS
+ MELLOW, WARM WAVES
+ GOOD WIND PATTERNS
+ CHEAP LIVING

- RARELY BIG
- FEW WINTER SWELLS
- RAINY SWELL SEASON
- THEFTS, DODGY SECURITY

RYAN CRAIG
Punta Roca

## TRAVEL INFORMATION

**Weather** – The dry season (Dec to April) is dusty and hot with extreme temperatures in March-April. Despite the heat, this is considered the best time to travel. The rest of the year receives heavy rainfall, which usually falls as afternoon and night time downpours and can make the roads impassable. However the cooler rainy nights make it easier to sleep. Apart from in Zunzal, the mosquitoes (zancudos) aren't that bad. The coast is much warmer than mountains and San Salvador.

**Lodging and Food** – La Libertad has a few decent hotels like Don Lito from $70p/n. Many tour operators include Epic Surfing Adventures (Zunzal, Mizata), K59 Surf Tours, Horizonte Surf Resort (El Zonte) and Tortuga Surf Lodge (Playa El Tunco). A meal will cost $10.

**Nature and Culture** – A city tour should include the San Salvador churches, and a visit to the national forest reserve WT Deininger or "Evil's Doorway". Volcano trips and Tazumal Maya ruins take a couple of days to visit. There's now a few small nightspots around El Tunco.

**Hazards and Hassles** – Boulders underlie many spots, which can get encrusted with sharp molluscs, plus there are plentiful urchins. Crowds occur at the main spots. Pollution, sea lice, thefts, hepatitis, malaria and typhoid are all potential problems, while decent medical attention is difficult to find.

**Handy Hints** – There are surf shops in San Salvador, La Libertad and Zunzal, but it's better to take your own gear and leave some. The points will require a fast board and a semi-gun for those big days. Take booties for the rocky points.

The west-facing **Los Cabanos** beachbreaks, just near the polluted port town of Acajutla, pick up W swells and may hide a few reefs as well. **Mizata** looks and acts like a long righthand point, but the short lefts can also be hollow and snappy off the peak. Works on any size swell at lower tides, to avoid the high tide backwash and it's super-consistent. **K61** looks good from a distance but is less lined-up, shiftier and a long paddle from the beach at K59. Gets a bit hollower and heavier when an overhead S swell arrives. **K59** can show good form at mid-tide on a S swell, warping across the inside, allowing experts a racetrack and intermediates a fun wall to shoulder on the wider sets. Handles some size with an easy paddle-out from the beach, avoiding the urchins. Pay for access or stay at the surf camp. **El Zonte** is another point/rivermouth peak where long, predictable rights amble down the boulders that start to show at lower tides. Mellower vibe than other Libertad breaks, catering for all abilities that stay at the multiple surf camps in the growing town. **Sunzal** seems to have waves every single day and makes the most of any S-W swell at lower tides. A big peak sucks up way outside (offering some lefts in due S swells) and then rumbles right for ages, shaping fun walls and cutback shoulders. Super-consistent and super-popular with intermediates and longboarders. If it's flat here, it's flat everywhere! The **Rio Grande Bocana** (rivermouth) sculpts the sand into long, hollow lefts and short, sharp rights but it needs a decent size swell and higher tides. Localism hotspot. Total respect required and the scattered rocks can be sharp. The small swell beachbreaks at **Playa Conchalio** can produce a fast barrelling wave, best in the dry season, when the chance of scoring the ultra-fickle San Blas righthand point in a W swell is higher. Famed **Punta Roca** is the top of the class, Central American, righthand pointbreak that pitches, walls up and races speedily over shallow, black boulders. Barrels and inviting open faces in medium-sized swells when length of ride can be leg burning. Handles double-overhead with ease when the drops and power increase exponentially. Hazards are many and varied including sharp shells on the rocks, bad pollution problems, hassling, localism and drop ins, armed robbery on the walk out the point, difficult entry and exit, crowds and powerful, butt-kicking waves. Right in town is the **La Paz** section, a less critical, fun point that's rocky, but popular with the locals and bodyboarders sheltering from the onshores. Another peak in town offers good lefts at **The Pier**, but it's usually full of kids who don't mind the close proximity of the sewage pipe!

BRUCE SUTHERLAND
K61

El Salvador faces south so it only receives S-SW swells and only a few places can pick up a due W. Big swells will produce 8-10ft conditions, which will remain rideable at most spots. The main swell season is March-October, but it could be considered a year-round destination as any small swell will produce surfable waves. The off-season is blessed by NE-E offshore winds, giving excellent water conditions. During the rainy season the winds will be offshore in the morning, then switch to sideshore around 10am and eventually onshore when the thunderstorms break out. Tidal range never goes over 2m, but it does affect most rocky pointbreaks.

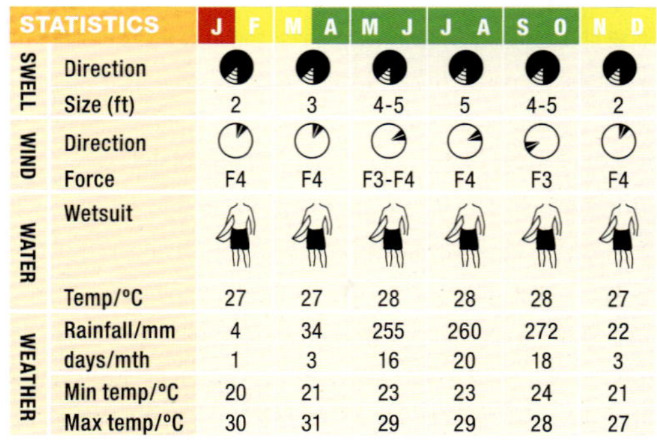

| STATISTICS | | J F | M A | M J | J A | S O | N D |
|---|---|---|---|---|---|---|---|
| SWELL | Direction | | | | | | |
| | Size (ft) | 2 | 3 | 4-5 | 5 | 4-5 | 2 |
| WIND | Direction | | | | | | |
| | Force | F4 | F4 | F3-F4 | F4 | F3 | F4 |
| WATER | Wetsuit | | | | | | |
| | Temp/°C | 27 | 27 | 28 | 28 | 28 | 27 |
| WEATHER | Rainfall/mm | 4 | 34 | 255 | 260 | 272 | 22 |
| | days/mth | 1 | 3 | 16 | 20 | 18 | 3 |
| | Min temp/°C | 20 | 21 | 23 | 23 | 24 | 21 |
| | Max temp/°C | 30 | 31 | 29 | 29 | 28 | 27 |

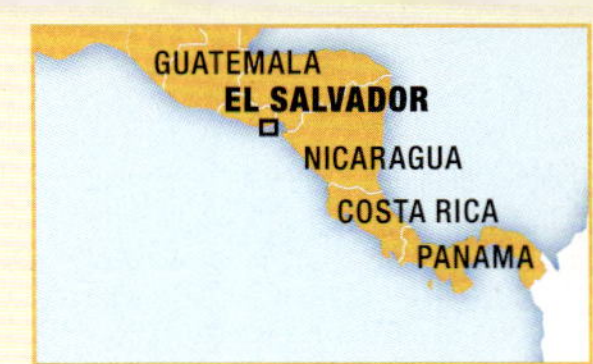


# Oriente Salvaje EL SALVADOR

**El Salvador has gone through a tumultuous time with civil war followed by economic devastation and violent social unrest. Things have improved dramatically and surfers have discovered there's more to this country than the famous La Libertad rights. In fact, the Oriente Salvaje (Savage East) now attracts more and more travellers to some epic right points where surf camps and a range of accommodation is available in a quiet bucolic setting.**

+ WORLD-CLASS RIGHT POINTS
+ UNSPOILED BEACHES
+ WARM WATER, FRIENDLY WINDS
+ CHEAP LIVING

- SOUTH SWELLS ONLY
- RAIN THROUGH SWELL SEASON
- GETS CROWDED IN SEASON
- QUIET NIGHTLIFE

Easily accessed by road, the seaside resort of **El Espino** sits on a 12km long beachbreak surrounded by mangroves, a rivermouth and the impressive Chaparrastique volcano in the background. It is mainly a beginner spot, but the sand banks can line-up and offer tubes to the more experienced surfers. **Punta Mango** is the main attraction, an epic right pointbreak peeling over barnacle encrusted boulders. With a solid S-SW swell and an incoming tide, hollow racetrack walls deal out juicy barrels to the inevitable crowd of boaters, especially at its ideal size, from headhigh to double overhead. It's possible to drive during the dry season, but the bad roads and thefts make the 30 minute boat ride from El Cuco or Flores advisable. **La Ventana** named after the hole in the cliff is a super-fun and very consistent beachbreak ideal for the smaller days. East of the headland has short peaks, while the west end of Ventana Beach has a righthander that can connect and get long rides in moderate swells. Best by boat and usually empty. Not for the faint-hearted, **Toro de Oro** is best accessed by boat due to the nasty, volcanic rock shoreline. Better with a bit of W in the swell to stop it sectioning off and swatting the unwary into a rock-strewn dead-end, it can look very appealing from the side, but only the best will negotiate the fast, long rides. Further inside in the next bay, **La Vaca** acts as a pressure valve for Las Flores, which gets a bit slow at high tide. The occasionally hollow rights are faster but shorter, and favour swells in the 2-6ft range. Intermediate to experienced surfers will focus on **Las Flores**, a Salvadorian dream set-up and one of the premier surfing locations in Central America. Compatible with the largest swells and always better at low tide, the waves first wrap around a rocky point full of palm trees, jack up over the take-off rocks, then reel off down a sandbar offering more speed and barrelling sections. Lengthy rides up to 300m are common, but the increasing crowds make it hard to get priority. Mellower shoulders at high tide but still fun. Beware of panga traffic through the line-up. El Cuco, a tiny village abandoned during the civil war is now home to several surf camps and consistent beachbreak that is often slow and mushy, but great for beginners and especially good on high tide with a 4ft swell. Characterized by its floundering ranchos on the beach, the village of **Las Tunas** has lots of rocky beachbreaks as well as a ever-changing rivermouth with potential quality sand banks. Also check the nearby Playa Torola and its similar setup. The majestic Gulf of Fonseca, bordered by Nicaragua and Honduras, offers a beautiful setting but inconsistent surf. The easternmost right pointbreak known as **Lucky Man's** needs a big S swell to wrap around and generate long, fun performance walls over a rock/sand bottom. There are other fickle beach and reef breaks to discover between Playitas and El Tamarindo, best by boat since it is a very wild area.

The narrow swell window favours S-SW swells, SW being the best direction. A true W swell will rarely get in to Eastern El Salvador unless it is huge. Highest consistency occurs during the wet invierno season from May-Oct, with some 8-12ft days. Winds are usually offshore in the mornings then shift to light to moderate SW onshores at mid-day, yet the points remain well wind-protected. Nov-Apr is the dry verano season, offering consistent surf in the 3-5ft range, when sunny offshore conditions prevail, often for days. The lack of strong local offshores prevents upwelling and the tidal range never goes over 1.8m, which only slightly affects most rocky pointbreaks.

CHRISTOPHER LANTZ

Punta Flores

## TRAVEL INFORMATION

**Weather** – See Costa Balsamo. Water temps vary between 26-28°C or hotter (79-82°F) so boardshorts only.

**Lodging and Food** – Several levels of accommodation in El Cuco from basic to luxury. Waterways do packages at Miraflores (fr $200) and the newly-built hotel overlooking Punta Mango (fr $457). Try corn and rice flour pupusas, as well as the local pilsner beer. No nightlife.

**Nature and Culture** – Conchagua volcano is the highest point around La Union Bay where there's good fishing. Visit the Laguna de Olomega. Parrots nest in the rocks at Punta Mango. Heaps of butterflies, often in the line-up. 7 active volcanoes including nearby Chaparrastique that erupted in 2015.

**Hazards and Hassles** – Theft is a major issue - make use of hotel safes. Hepatitis A/B, tetanus, diphtheria, cholera, typhoid and dengue fever constitute significant threats. Avoid public transportation and hanging out alone, making yourself a target for armed robbers. No real shark threat, but earthquakes are a possibility.

**Handy Hints** – Limited surf supplies, take ding repair & extra fins. Reef booties at low tide and strong sun protection required. Water quality much better during dry season. Avoid Semana Santa (week before Easter). Best to bring US$ and speak Spanish. Women should not venture out alone, especially at night.

JIMMY WILSON

Punta Mango

| STATISTICS | | J F | M A | M J | J A | S O | N D |
|---|---|---|---|---|---|---|---|
| SWELL | Direction | | | | | | |
| | Size (ft) | 2-3 | 4-5 | 6 | 6-7 | 5-6 | 3-4 |
| WIND | Direction | | | | | | |
| | Force | F4 | F4 | F3-F4 | F4 | F3-F4 | F3-F4 |
| WATER | Wetsuit | | | | | | |
| | Temp/°C | 26 | 27 | 28 | 28 | 28 | 27 |
| WEATHER | Rainfall/mm | 7 | 28 | 226 | 306 | 227 | 26 |
| | days/mth | 1 | 3 | 16 | 20 | 18 | 3 |
| | Min temp/°C | 20 | 22 | 23 | 22 | 21 | 20 |
| | Max temp/°C | 30 | 31 | 30 | 30 | 29 | 29 |

# Nicaragua

GUATEMALA
EL SALVADOR
NICARAGUA
COSTA RICA
PANAMA

The bulk of Nicaragua's coastline makes up the Mosquito Coast on the Caribbean side, where an extensive, shallow shelf drains what meagre swells are available. Most of Nicaragua's better-known surf spots are concentrated in the developed southwest corner where a narrow stretch of coastline separates Lake Nicaragua (the largest lake in Central America) from the Pacific. This huge body of water creates the perfect atmospheric conditions for offshore winds to blow most of the year, grooming a wealth of excellent beachbreaks and left points.

+ LONG SWELL SEASON
+ DOMINANT OFFSHORE WINDS
+ WAVES FOR ALL ABILITIES
+ QUICKLY DEVELOPING COUNTRY

- HARD ACCESS TO SURF SPOTS
- NO STANDOUT RIGHTHANDERS
- NATURAL DISASTERS THREAT
- LACKS TOURIST INFRASTRUCTURE

**Puerto Sandino** is touted as one of Nicaragua's best waves and could also be the longest with rides up to 400m possible, when the reef anchored rivermouth sands pile up in the perfect triangle. Take-offs can be fast and vert straight into the first of multiple barrel sections, broken up by lip-smacking walls. Likes a higher, pushing tide when the outside peaks soften and the NE winds are dead offshore. Most local surf camps access via boat, otherwise it's a long, current swept paddle. **Punta Miramar** holds consistently good lefts, with fast inside runners and tubes on the inside sections of reef at higher tides. When the swell cranks, so does the outside section, offering mean, heavy, hollow rides for those with the skills to handle the low tide bombs. **Pipes** is the rocky beachbreak barrels to the north in small to medium swells. Flatter slab-like reef at **Shacks** requires sand, swell and tide to be right for some fun inviting barrels and walls for blasting. The lefts are always better and it needs moderate swells to work. **El Transito** vacuums up all available swell onto constantly moving sandbars, shaped by refraction off the reef protrusions at either end. Fun waves for all until it gets overhead and quickly closes-out. **Playa Ausuchillas** consistently handles swells of most sizes and is a go to for small peaky days when there will be some nice peelers for all abilities. Gets demanding at size, with big challenging barrels. Likes low tide. The left reef at **Hemorrhoids** prefers more water over the rocks and can have some rapid-fire walls and barrels for the guaranteed crowd that come from the Gran Pacifica resort and beyond. **Chiggas** is popular because it handles any size and is an easier deepwater roll-in to barrel and turn sections, just north of Playa San Diego, an exposed stretch of black sand beachbreak for all abilities on small days. The private, all-inclusive beach resort of **Montelimar** fronts an average beachbreak with a sluggish left sometimes forming off the southern point. Best ridden on a small peaky swell and pushing tide, when the odd inside tube section can spice up a session. **Masachapa's** rights will only go off on a rare combination of big W swell and low tide on a windless day since NE is sideshore. Also check out the nearby pier on the protected beach. **Pochomil** is a popular vacation spot only 1h drive from Managua. It picks up plenty of S swell and there are 3 rivermouths to help sculpt sandbars. Check for a slow, rolling A-frame down Pochomil Viejo. **Casares** needs a good swell to get through the offshore reefs and focus in on the rocky shoreline where several peaks will work, usually at higher tides. Fickle and hard to read. Boat in to remote **Playgrounds**, where sweet, inviting lefts and shorter rights scurry across the barnacle encrusted cobbles, offering fun skatepark walls in moderate swells from the S-SW. Predictable, ripable and good

Hemorroids

NICOLAS FOJTU

Playa Santana

CALLUM MORSE

## TRAVEL INFORMATION

**Weather** – The Pacific lowlands of Nicaragua are always extremely hot, but the air feels fresher during the rainy season (May to Nov). Torrential downpours and flooding can be expected around October. The dry season (Dec to April) brings winds that send clouds of brown dust across the plains, especially in the last months (mid-April to mid-May). The early dry season is generally considered as the most pleasant time to visit, but is not the optimum swell season. The constant, strong, offshore winds create upwelling and make the water temperatures drop quickly. Some neoprene may be necessary despite the average water temp staying between 26-30°C (79-86°F).

**Lodging and Food** – Recent years has seen a huge increase in the number of surf camps along the whole southern coastline from San Juan del Sur to Popoyo offering everything form budget to high end options. In the Popoyo area, Las Plumerias Lodge has all-inclusive packages from $750 p/w. Waterways has packages from $1399 p/w. Surf Tours Nicaragua around Puerto Sandino further north has packages starting from $1050/wk. Try "Gallo Pinto" the local rice & beans combo.

**Nature and Culture** – Around San Juan del Sur go to the refuge at La Flor beach, where thousands of turtles lay their eggs between July and January. Walk to the lighthouse or the "antennas" for stunning views of neighbouring Costa Rica. Take the trip to 'Isla de Ometepe' on Lake Nicaragua, which is inhabited by freshwater sharks.

**Hazards and Hassles** – After over 40 years of dictatorship and 11 years of Sandinista rebel's power, Nicaragua shifted to a democracy in 1990. The country has also had its share of natural disasters with hurricane Mitch and the 1972 earthquake that destroyed a large part of Managua. Like all Central American countries, use caution and avoid traveling at night.

**Handy Hints** – Surf shops in SJDS include Nica Surf, Good Times, Chica Brava and repairers like Mosco. Popoyo has NSR and Bordport. Lots of surf schools and rentals. Expect all rooms to be sold out for Semana Santa.

RYAN CRAIG

**Popoyo**

LAT. 11.458120° LONG. -86.111567°

The peak at Popoyo displays alluring symmetry over the flatfish reef and sand slab at the southern end of Playa Guasacate. Peels off predictably at a nice pace for vertical whacks and the odd crumbly cover-up. Better at low incoming tide, the peak will hold up to double overhead with longer barrel sections before closing-out and a considerable crowd as well. The Outer Reef, found 400m offshore, is only really an option for the very bravest and skilled big wave riders. The lefts look deceptively perfect from distance but close inspection reveals shallow rocks, boils and riverine currents sculpting heaving, bloodthirsty barrels with a do or die end section. Easily handles 20ft faces at this higher tide spot and it gets scarier by the minute on the drop, which doesn't deter the local hellmen that have it wired. Popoyo is one of the most consistent and crowded waves in the country and site of the 2015 ISA World Surfing Games.

RYAN CRAIG

Colorado

for intermediates, but avoid touching the sharp bottom. **Lance's Left** pointbreak offers easy rollers and shoulders in most swell directions and sizes. Best accessed by boat on a dropping tide for fun rides for most abilities unless big. **El Astillero** gets great beachbreaks, particularly up by the rivermouth where the rights get hollow and pack plenty of punch. **Popoyo** has become a surf town with multiple surf camps and accommodation close to the super-consistent A-frame peak that has been attracting surfers for decades. Other reefs like La Piedrita and Stoneys left help spread the crowd. There's also easy waves at Beginners Bay and along Playa Guasacate. **Playa Santana** has heavy beachbreaks barrels that are highly sought after and always crowded on higher tides. It's in a gated community with direct access to **Playa Rosada**, a straight-shooting, short, speedy left over a carpet of craggy, urchin sprinkled reef. **Panga Drops** bombora style horseshoe-shaped reef picks up everything going and offers whizzing walls, inside barrels and fading shoulders that shift all over the large playing field. Super-fun for mere mortals on both short and longboards. The rivermouth sandbars at **Playa Colorado** are quite possibly the hollowest, fastest barrels in the country when a SW or even better a W swell arrives. Quite sensitive to tide and wind, arrive by boat and avoid the copious stingrays in the shallows.

Playa Gigante has a few fickle breaks (Amarillo, Hongo) and is the closest launch spot for the classic, draw-card left of **Manzanillo** when the specific SSW swell wraps in. A wedgy, cliff bounce take-off, leads into a series of walled, occasionally hollow sections, before racing into the beachbreak on the inside. A longish ride from tip to tail and definitely best around mid tide on moderate swells below 225°. Only accessible by panga or the 5 star resort. Often crowded because it appeals to the average surfer, but the long paddle back out and various sections can spread the bodies. Beware of rocks and urchins. The beachbreak of **Playa Maderas** is probably the best around San Juan. Very consistent, sometimes hollow, it gets challenging in overhead swells. Often crowded with all types of surfer and surfcraft. San Juan del Sur has become a cruise port and seaside resort, popular with Nicaraguan teenagers as much as gringo surfers. The surf isn't very good within the city's horseshoe-shaped bay, so some locals go south to surf second-rate beachbreaks at the picturesque cove of **El Remanso**. Better sessions should be found at the next beach, **Playa Tamarind**, where quick barrel opportunities occur on clean small swells, although on most days, the right pointbreak will prove too sectiony. **El Yanke** is a good beachbreak with well-defined peaks, but even better are the high tide peaks found two beaches north at Playa Hermosa, where all abilities will find something to their liking without the crowd. Just south **El Coco** isn't as good, but the main road hits the coast for easy access. Beyond the turtle nesting sites along the beach of Playa la Flor, the long, hollow left point just south is known as Sally Ann's and should only be attempted on huge swells, because when it's under double overhead, rocks litter this break.

The major swell season stretches from March to Oct, concurrent with the rainy season, when continuous 3-10ft swells, with occasional 15ft bursts arrive from the S-SW. The middle of the dry season (Dec to April) sees fewer swells, but is rarely flat and the offshore winds are at their strongest, often reaching gale-force. These northern winds, called papagayos, are produced by an intensification of the northeast tradewinds in the Caribbean, and can be experienced all the way from Guatemala to Costa Rica. Without opposition, they shriek over Nicaragua's large lakes, producing a continuous jet of offshore wind from November through to September. Only Sept seems to suffer from regular SW-W onshore winds. The tidal range reaches 2.5m, becoming a crucial element at many of the rocky spots.

| STATISTICS | | J F | M A | M J | J A | S O | N D |
|---|---|---|---|---|---|---|---|
| SWELL | Direction | | | | | | |
| | Size (ft) | 2-3 | 3-4 | 5 | 5-6 | 4-5 | 2-3 |
| WIND | Direction | | | | | | |
| | Force | F4 | F4 | F3-F4 | F4 | F3-F4 | F3 |
| WATER | Wetsuit | | | | | | |
| | Temp/°C | 26 | 27 | 28 | 28 | 27 | 26 |
| WEATHER | Rainfall/mm | 10 | 5 | 200 | 170 | 300 | 50 |
| | days/mth | 1 | 1 | 14 | 19 | 20 | 6 |
| | Min temp/°C | 21 | 23 | 24 | 23 | 22 | 21 |
| | Max temp/°C | 33 | 35 | 34 | 31 | 31 | 31 |

# Guanacaste COSTA RICA

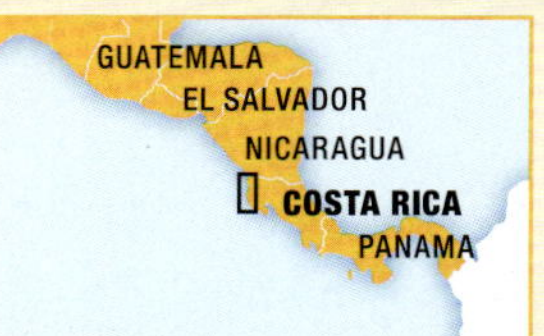


Volcanic black sand, squeaky white sand and craggy reef can all be found in the northern province of Guanacaste, where long distance Pacific swells arrive from the near 180° swell window with reliable consistency, firing up the well-documented wonder-walls like Potrero Grande, Roca Bruja and the busy peaks of Tamarindo. Quality reefs at Avellanas and Playa Negra provide the challenge and laid-back beachbreaks around Nosara cater for the steady influx of new surfers. Tamarindo has become the epicentre of Costa Rican surfing, particularly during the dry season when clean, offshore conditions, sunshine and easy access make it a veritable tropical paradise for experienced surfers and beginners alike.

- + CONSISTENT YEAR-ROUND
- + FUN-SIZED WAVES
- + WAVES FOR ALL ABILITIES
- + RICH IN WILDLIFE

- – CROWDED
- – OPPRESSIVELY HOT WEATHER
- – MILLIONS OF INSECTS
- – TOURIST PRICE INFLATION

NICK LAVECCHIA

Tamarindo

Located on the Pacific coast near the Nicaraguan border is the famous, perfect, right rivermouth pointbreak of **Potrero Grande**, aka Ollie's Point and featured on Endless Summer II. It was named because an airstrip nearby was used by US Colonel Oliver North to land weapons for the Nicaraguan Contras. While US Colonel Oliver North is long gone, the name Ollie's Point has stuck to this way above average righthand pointbreak. While an expensive, long boat trip from Playas del Coco is the only way in, it doesn't deter the crowds who flock here in a big S or medium W swell to sample the plenty-long, ruler-edged walls perfect for thwacking and the cover-ups that section off at low tide. Ideal for dialling in some moves thanks to its predictability and forgiving nature, Potrero Grande is one of the funnest rides in CR. Access through the national park is only possible in the dry season and hazards include getting bogged, small crocs, small sharks and very large mosquitoes! This is the wave featured on "Endless Summer II". It's not possible to stay on land in the national park, but there is a charter boat that can spend the night offshore and get you into the line-up first thing before other boats have been able to make the 35km, up to 3hr journey from Playa Cocos. The 6km long **Playa Naranjo** is another world-class wave. The north-facing bays of Potrero and Brasilito are fairly poor beachbreak with some smaller straight-handers for beginners, but the left off **Flamingo Point** is more consistent with sloping walls over a gnarly reef and occasional good form without a frothing crowd. Needs lower tides and a bigger SW swell to be a destination, while the left at Brasilito in front of the golf course will be better in W-NW. Tamarindo's wide, rivermouth-dissected bay has become Costa Rica's blueprint surf town with its handful of user-friendly waves and a laid-back vibe. At the northern end is **Playa Grande**, which is an excellent beachbreak and famous turtle breeding ground, 30mins walk or 20 mins drive from Tamarindo. It picks up the maximum S-SW swell available and unpackages it along a choice of quality triangular bars at mid tide. Goldilocks factor means low is too closey, while high gets a bit backwashy. With a decent swell several good spots break in **Tamarindo** itself, including Estero's consistent, fast rivermouth peaks, as well as smaller, beginner-friendly, straight-hander beachbreaks and several reefbreaks like Pico Pequeño, Diria and Henry's. They're all well situated for SW-NW swells, but crowds are a constant theme from clueless beginners to ripping locals. South of town, **Langosta** rivermouth holds some lefts and rights over scattered rocks that tend to appear at lower tides. The beachbreak to the south of the river can hold some thumping barrels on occasion without huge numbers. **Avellanas** is blessed with six named breaks along the 2km strand starting with Little Hawaii way up at the northern point that holds bigger SW swells and smaller crowds. El Estero is the rivermouth break which is always bigger and peaks up at a big rock. El Palo and the Right are classic beachbreak style sandbars anchored by reef, attracting a crowd to the skate-park walls and pits that draw in both SW and NW swells. The Left is right in front of the parking lot and zooms over some unfriendly lava, getting sketchy as the tide drops. Finally, there's an outside bommie peak for fearless experts. Outstanding, crystal-blue rights form off the north end reef of **Playa Negra** attracting plenty to the mid tide barrels and easy accommodation. Will break through the tide with enticing walls, hooks and ramps before the lower tide brings the draining tubes, which require speed and positioning to make. There are some lefts to the north and more reefy peaks to the south. The coast leading to Nosara is full of potential surf, easily

## TRAVEL INFORMATION

**Weather** – Guanacaste is the driest part of Costa Rica with lots of sunshine and hot temperatures, often accompanied by oppressive 100% humidity. A fan or A/C is a must for sleeping. The dry season runs from December to April, but the rest of the year is not excessively rainy anyway, unlike the Caribbean side. Expect evening rain pretty much every day and clear mornings. San José, at 1100m escapes the worst of the heat. The water is warm year-round; a rash vest will protect you from the sun and maybe a shorty for the occasional strong NE wind raising the wind chill factor in the dry season.

**Lodging and Food** – Costs have risen fast over the years, stay in one of the many Tamarindo hotels ($90+/dble) or in cheaper cabinas ($35/dble). Avellanes, Junquilla and Nosara are good places to stay. A typical restaurant bill is $12-15.

**Nature and Culture** – National parks (e.g. Santa Rosa) swarm with monkeys, toucans, crocodiles and snakes. Lots of the beaches are prime turtle nesting sites. On the odd flat day the volcanoes (Arvenal) are spectacular.

**Hazards and Hassles** – Playa Grande saw a fatal shark attack in 2011, plus 3 crocodile attacks in 4 years at the rivermouth. Although it's almost malaria-free, there are tons of zancudos (insects). Stingrays, sea-lice and the occasional jellyfish swarm will sting you in the line-up. Non-violent rip-offs (cameras, cash etc.) occur, especially from vehicles or on the beach.

**Handy Hints** – Reading the Tico Times can reveal some bargains for rental cars and hotels. There are a multitude of surf shops in Tamarindo or Nosara and many surf camps and hotels rent boards. Surf schools and lessons are easy to find. Costa Ricans are well educated and often speak good English.

JEREMIAH KLEIN

accessible in the dry season with a 4WD. **Playa Marbella** holds some picture perfect spinning peaks over scattered rocks and black sands south of Playa Frijola. Lefts at the south end off the point work at high and are always smaller, while the north end beachbreaks like low and draw in the SW swell. Breaks with power and purpose and works in both the wet and dry season. Often crowded with rippers looking to get shacked. **Playa Ostional** offers, fun, lip-smacking walls without a big crowd, making it perfect for intermediates and longboarders. Prefers NW swell to get the longer rights going that break off one of the rock outcrops that divide this long beach. Better at higher tides and won't handle bigger swells. A thin ribbon of rock separates Ostional from **Playa Nosara**, a long crescent of black sand that entertains the multitudes of surf schools and beginners that have been drawn to this area. From knee to headhigh these peaks are quite manageable and not too powerful, while still holding good shape. Playa Pelada is a clutch of small bays with a bit of S wind and swell protection. Slow, shouldering left at the south end may appeal to improvers, but it's the righthander off the middle reef that needs NW swell and a pushing tide, which pulls in the crowds for some fun rip and race walls when it eventually gets good. Ride the current out close to the rocks. Postage stamp take-off area means the locals can get twitchy. Nosara has grown into a major coastal town with an array of lodging and surf camp options, who have set up to take advantage of **Playa Guiones** consistent and user-friendly waves. Multiple peaks pop-up along its length and can peel for deceptively long distances. It's not the most powerful set-up and below headhigh, currents are usually mild. Holds shape as it gets bigger, but becomes a chore to get out the back beyond the regular close-outs, especially at low tide. Loads of room to move for all abilities, but advanced surfers will want to head north or south to find more powerful, hollow waves. Lots of stingrays about so shuffle your feet when walking out at low tide.

Playa Negra

LAURENT MASUREL

**Playa Naranjo**

LAT. 10.791988° LONG. -85.678387°

Facing a huge rock called Roca Bruja meaning Witches Rock, which was deposited in the sea by an angry volcano 50k's away, ultra-fast, zippy walls streak down the sand, offering ample crystalline tubes and good length of ride. Needs higher tides to prevent the close-outs and some S in the swell. Most surfers coagulate just south of the rivermouth, where the sandbars pile up, but there are always more peaks to the south. North of the rivermouth is usually smaller. The only effective way to reach these spots is by boat from Playa del Coco (where there is an inconsistent left) or by 4x4 in the dry season, but like most national parks, there's no accommodation so camping is the only possibility. Crowds have grown massively in recent years. Hazards include saltwater crocodiles around the rivermouths.

The major swell season is April to Oct, when swells hit from a variety of angles. S-SW swells coming off the Roaring Forties produce numerous 3-10ft swells - lows located off New Zealand give the best direction. Tropical storms off Mexico produce NW swells. Dec to April sees NW arctic swells, which, when combined with frequent offshores and no rain, makes this the best season for clean 3-4ft waves almost every day. Winds are not usually a factor, however there is a wet but gentle SW-W monsoon period from May to December. Typically, mornings are offshore, afternoons onshore. Winter sees a dry period with a lot of light winds from-any direction, but predominately from the NNE-E. Tides can reach 4m, drastically changing the waves.

| STATISTICS | | J F | M A | M J | J A | S O | N D |
|---|---|---|---|---|---|---|---|
| SWELL | Direction | | | | | | |
| | Size (ft) | 2 | 3 | 4-5 | 5 | 4-5 | 2 |
| WIND | Direction | | | | | | |
| | Force | F3 | F2 | F3 | F3 | F3 | F3 |
| WATER | Wetsuit | | | | | | |
| | Temp/°C | 26 | 27 | 28 | 27 | 27 | 26 |
| WEATHER | Rainfall/mm | 4 | 18 | 205 | 202 | 270 | 70 |
| | days/mth | 1 | 2 | 16 | 18 | 20 | 7 |
| | Min temp/°C | 23 | 23 | 22 | 23 | 23 | 22 |
| | Max temp/°C | 35 | 35 | 33 | 32 | 32 | 31 |

# Golfo de Nicoya COSTA RICA

GUATEMALA
EL SALVADOR
NICARAGUA
COSTA RICA
PANAMA

US surfers looking for exotic waves close to home, usually choose Costa Rica, since it's possible to be surfing a perfect, peeling pointbreak, or a thunderous beachbreak barrel within a couple of hours drive of San Jose airport. With waves all-year-round, Puntarenas surf towns have sprung up at Jaco and further afield on the Nicoya peninsula around Santa Teresa/Mal Pais. Despite shocking access roads requiring 4WD in the wet season, this wild area has become a surf-school heaven, trading on idyllic tropical scenery, incredible national park wildlife and mellow beachbreaks.

+ GREAT LEFTS AND RIGHTS
+ CONSISTENT, POWERFUL BEACHES
+ BOTH SOUTH AND NORTH SWELLS
+ EXOTIC, WARM AND FRIENDLY

– BEST SWELLS IN RAINY SEASON
– BEACHES CLOSE-OUT EASILY
– CROWDED BREAKS, BUSY RESORTS
– BAD ROADS AND PETTY CRIME

LAURENT MASUREL

Playa Hermosa

**Playa Coyote** stretches up to equally long Playa San Miguel, so finding an empty peak is simple, especially around the two rivermouths at higher tides on small swells. There's an average left off the rocks on the point that holds size and rights when it's a NW swell. Further north, there's plenty of less frequented beachbreak at Buena Vista, Samara, Carrillo and most notably Camaronal. Deserted beachbreak **Playa Caletas** leads down to a large rivermouth and more of the same at Playa Ario. Small swells, mid tide or check the high tide right reef on the northern headland. Offshore reefs catch W-NW swell at **Manzanillo**, shaping some lefts and rights that are fickle but fun for good surfers. The beach is a perfect nursery for kids and newbies. **Playa Hermosa** is a cruisey beachbreak creating the perfect slow rollers for the stream of surf school softoppers, plus a reefy righthander off the northern point. **Playa Santa Teresa** is hollow and consistent, especially at lower tides. Lava rock ledges protrude out and catch the sand at a number of named spots like Suck Rock, La Lora Amarilla and Casa Cecilia. **Playa Carmen** starts the Mal Pais section and is better suited to improvers and intermediates with fatter, slower, longer rights and shorter steeper lefts, including a high tide reef at the north end. Bigger SW swell awakens the **Punta Barigona** lefts and the easier inside Mar Azul walls at high tide. Hard to predict whether it will be cutbacks or cover-ups, mals or pintails. **Sunset Reef** is a full bore, high speed, left tunnel over ugly lava reef at the end of the Mal Pais coast road. Spots inside the Nicoya gulf include Cabuya Island Reef, Los Reyes, Playa Los Cedros and Playa Grande in Montezuma. On a major S-SW swell, **Boca Barranca** is an exceedingly long left wall that trickles and peels through up to 750m of fun-filled sections for all craft and abilities in the polluted rivermouth. **Puerto Caldera** has a faster, ripable left rivermouth bar in front of the bridge on big swells and higher tides. El Hoyo throws up quality wedges and ramps off the west jetty and there's an all tides left point at Punta Corrallillos. All are polluted and localised. **Titives**' beachbreaks easily close-out except for the rights into the rivermouth and the Mini Valor lefts off the point in strong S swell. Sharky and crocy! The reliable racey lefts and bending rights at **Playa Escondida** are boat access only, but their quality means crowds. **Jacó** is Costa Rica's main surf town with plenty of hotels, surf shops, bars and discos where the beachbreak has consistent higher tide peaks and easy learner waves. **Roca Loca** is a great right on a good SW-W swell, breaking in front of or beside a big rock cluster. Powerful, tricky ride with lots of rocks to avoid at low. The long, black sand, zooed-out beachbreak at **Playa Hermosa** exudes serious power and punishes plenty on double overhead days when close-outs rule. Rips are legendarily strong, sand is stupidly hot. The walk down to **Boca Tusubres** reveals less-crowded peaks on lower tides and bigger, punchier waves. South-facing **Esterillos Oeste**, consists of a long sandy stretch with some lava reefs outside and a slow righthander called La Sirena.

Swell Forecasting – see Guanacaste and Puntarenas.

## TRAVEL INFORMATION

**Weather** – see Guanacaste and Puntarenas

**Lodging and Food** – Plenty of choices to stay in Jaco, but favour Playa Hermosa for its proximity to quality surf: prices keep going up so ask for winter or long stay discounts! Mal Pais is surf camp central with all sorts of different packages. A typical food bill would be $12-15.

**Nature and Culture** – Lots of outdoor activities like horseriding, kayaking or river rafting. In Jaco/Hermosa area try the Waterfalls and Canopy Tour in the jungle forest, or fly tandem paragliding! Nightlife in Jaco is heavy; check Disco La Central or Papagayo. In Mal Pais, it's quieter with plenty of wildlife. Don't miss Cabo Blanco National Park.

**Hazards and Hassles** – Black sand at noon can burn feet. Take booties for sharp lava reefs at low tide (3m range). Dense crowds of experienced expats, hot ticos and surf schools. People have drowned in Playa Hermosa's heavy waves, competent swimming ability is necessary when double overhead. Bugs, caterpillars and mosquitoes can be pretty bad in the wet season. Sea-lice!

**Handy Hints** – Because of heavy airlines tax, it may be cheaper to rent or buy boards in Jaco/Hermosa. A quality shortboard costs $450, longboards are $650. Rentals from $15/d. Lots of ding repairers. Plenty of surf shops in Jaco like Chucks WOW, Jass, Walter or Carton and Santa Teresa has Denga, Kina, Nalu, 360 or Lost in Santa. Travel off-season (Sept-Oct) and save up to 25%.

JS CALLAHAN SURFEXPLORE

Boca Barranca

# Central Puntarenas COSTA RICA

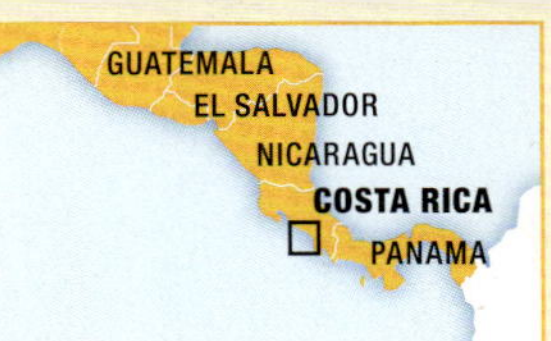


Costa Rican surf tours first began in 1985 and some areas have become a crowded victim of their own success. Central Puntarenas province has largely remained off the surfers beaten tracks and the area that extends south of Dominical to the Corcovado National Park on the Osa Peninsula still offers a lot to explore in lush tropical scenery. The wet season from May to November, is synonymous with consistent S-SW swells hitting a variety of quality rock and sand set-ups.

+ HIGH SUMMER CONSISTENCY
+ LOW CROWDS
+ OSA NATIONAL PARK RAINFOREST
+ GREAT EXPLORATION POTENTIAL

– NO WORLD-CLASS WAVES
– HEAVY SUMMER RAINS
– CROCS AT RIVERMOUTHS
– TRICKY ACCESS TO DRAKES

BLUETRAILZ.COM

Drake's Bay

Boca Damas · Quepos Jetty · Quepos Bombie · Playitas · Playa El Rey · Playa Matapalo · Playa Dominical · Dominicalito · Punta Dominical · Playa Hermosa · Punta Uvita · Playa Ballena · Rio Sierpe Rivermouth · Drake's Bay · Rio Claro Rivermouth

PERFECT WAVE · SURFHOLIDAYS · SELINA

Punta Judas · Parrita · Damas · Paquita · Quepos · Playa Isla Damas · Punta Quepos · Playa Espadilla · Manuel Antonio Nat. Park · Playa Savegre · Savegre · Matapalo · Hastillo · San Juan · San Isidro · Palmares · Dominical · Playa Dominical · San Pablo · Uvita · Punta Uvita · Trinidad · Coronado · Bahia de Coronado · Cortes · Drake · Punta Agujas · Isla del Caño · Rincon · San Pedrillo · Punta Llorona · Corcovado National Park · Sirena

The rivermouth of **Boca Damas** delivers long, fast, sectiony and sometimes hollow lefts plus shorter broken-up rights. Usually bigger than nearby breaks and best with incoming tide. The strong currents, crucial tide factor and local crocs should convince most to get a boat ride from Damas or Quepos. Marina construction should have destroyed **Quepos Jetty** but the new harbour wall and river estuary have built an even better version of the wave. Mushy and slow at waist to chest (longboards), but anything bigger will peel extremely fast, with inside barrel sections and ripable walls. Needs solid SW to W swell and lower tides. Also weak beachbreak best on big S swell as is the rare tow-in option off the point at **Quepos Bombie**. The tourist magnet Manuel Antonio National Park has fun, semi-consistent waves for all standards along Playa Espadilla, but the northwest corner at **Playitas** holds the best waves from mid to high tide and there is also an outer reef righthander with a solid swell and a high tide. **Playa El Rey** is an isolated long stretch of ebony beach that hides good quality peaks, especially near Rio Naranjo rivermouth. Closes-out when big, but is always bigger than the nearby breaks. Camping possible, but bring all supplies. Another similar spot with endless peaks and no crowds is found at **Playa Matapalo**. Dominical is a laid-back surf city, with a highly consistent, strong barrelling beachbreak at **Playa Dominical**. It can hold serious size without closing-out, gets bigger near Rio Baru rivermouth, prefers some W in the swell and pushing tides. The protected bay of **Dominicalito** is popular with beginners/improvers since it is a smaller, softer beachbreak, but watch out for some hidden rocks at low. Another great wave for intermediates when small is the left at **Punta Dominical**, but when it's fuelled by a serious swell, it holds up to triple overhead with long, hollow rides. Go at higher tides and don't get caught inside! The incredibly scenic **Playa Hermosa** usually breaks half the size of Dominical, but the northern end in a S swell will have some fast hollow sections for speedsters. **Punta Uvita** is the gateway to the stunning Marino Ballena marine park. The whale-tail-shaped point creates good shelter for the soft beachbreaks when the area is maxed-out and onshore NW is blowing. **Playa Ballena** is one of the best beginners waves in the area thanks to gently rolling, long rides. Also check the uncrowded beaches of Piñuela, Ventanas, Tortuga rivermouth or get a boat in Ojochal (or walk) to Terraba rivermouth, a perfect peeling left. Fly, drive or catch a boat to Drake's Bay, near the boat only **Rio Sierpe Rivermouth**, a spot that can get excellent on incoming tide with long, powerful lefts and rights. **Drake's Bay** is a remote spot hidden in the rainforest with expensive accommodation and many breaks to explore including an offshore reef. The **Rio Claro Rivermouth** is a wilderness left on the most exposed fringe of the Corcovado National Park, so getting there without a boat is a mission.

May to November S-SW swells range from 3-12ft. Dec to April WNW swells hardly reach this stretch of coast, except for a few west-facing breaks around Drake's Bay. There is a gentle SW-W monsoon-like period from May to December (wet season), with light and variable winds. Typically, mornings are offshore before a sea breeze picks up. The significant 3m tides seriously influence all breaks.

## TRAVEL INFORMATION

**Weather** – The dry season between late December and April is referred to as "summer", despite being in the northern hemisphere. The green or wet season lasts from May to November, but still offers an average of about 5hrs of daily sunshine. September and October are the rainiest months including sudden tropical thunderstorms, lightning and heavy rains. Temps vary little between seasons, ranging from 29-32°C (84-90°F) during the day and 20-23°C (68-74°F) during the night. Water is boardshort warm 26-30°C (79-86°F).

**Lodging and Food** – Quepos & Manuel Antonio have dozens of hotels. Large choice in Playa Matapalo and Dominical from cheap camping to all inclusive surf camps. Drake Bay area is more expensive. A typical food bill would be $12-15.

**Nature and Culture** – Abundant wildlife. Manuel Antonio, Marino Ballena and Corcovado National Parks deserve a visit. Canopy Safari in Manuel Antonio ($85). SUP and kayak tour the waterways. Great night life in Quepos, quieter in Dominical.

**Hazards and Hassles** – CR is the safest nation in Central America. The surf and theft are the main dangers, along with the crocodiles, bugs, spiders, scorpions. Dangerous roads at night, many potholes. A 4x4 is a plus during rainy season.

**Handy Hints** – English is widely spoken. Plenty of surf shops in Quepos and Dominical. Renting a board is easy, cheap (from $10/day) and often a good solution. Booties can be useful to walk on reef. It always pays to get up early. Take mosquito repellent and hiking boots.

GUILLUAME LARRE

Punta Dominical

| STATISTICS | | J F | M A | M J | J A | S O | N D |
|---|---|---|---|---|---|---|---|
| SWELL | Direction | | | | | | |
| | Size (ft) | 2 | 3 | 4-5 | 5 | 4-5 | 2 |
| WIND | Direction | | | | | | |
| | Force | F2-F3 | F2-F3 | F3 | F3 | F3 | F3 |
| WATER | Wetsuit | | | | | | |
| | Temp/°C | 28 | 28 | 28 | 28 | 28 | 27 |
| WEATHER | Rainfall/mm | 4 | 19 | 203 | 201 | 270 | 72 |
| | days/mth | 1 | 2 | 16 | 18 | 20 | 7 |
| | Min temp/°C | 23 | 23 | 22 | 23 | 23 | 22 |
| | Max temp/°C | 35 | 35 | 33 | 32 | 32 | 31 |

# Golfo Dulce COSTA RICA

GUATEMALA
EL SALVADOR
NICARAGUA
COSTA RICA
PANAMA

The southern extremity of Costa Rica cradles Pavones, the most awe-inspiring wave in the country and one of the longest lefts in the world. Perfect, ruler-edged, freight-train fast envelopes spinning down a benign cobble and sand point deep in the jungle. The Golfo Dulce provides a watery divide between Pavones lefts and Matapalo's rights over on the Osa Peninsula, whilst the surrounding lush curtain of rainforest hides many other spots.

+ PAVONES ULTRA-LONG POINT
+ QUALITY MATAPALO RIGHTS
+ CALM WINDS
+ EXOTIC RAINFOREST WILDLIFE

- CROWDED & INCONSISTENT
- INTENSE RAINY SEASON
- LACK OF ROADS
- TROPICAL DISEASES/INSECTS

If it's flat around Matapalo, try **Playa Carate**, just before the Corcovado National Park, which picks up any S or W swell onto exposed sandbanks near the murky rivermouth that attracts both types of toothed locals. A string of quality, low tide, right point/reefbreaks skirt the rocks of **Cabo Matapalo**. The most consistent spot is the outside point (aka Hog Hole), which produces very steep, fast walls. This is a challenging break, getting wild and heavy when it's big with a nasty mix of ledges, boulders and cobblestone on the inside. **Backwash** is the middle cove and usually a bit smaller than the outer point, but hollow fast sections make this a crowded wave at low-mid tide. If the S swell gets to a decent size, **Pan Dulce** becomes a Rincon-style right point, meaning really long, mellow cutback shoulders and zippy walls perfect for longboarding, often breaking as two separate sections on a rocky bottom deep inside the Golfo. The tiny inside beachbreak is ideal for newbies. **Playa Zancudo** is a beautiful beach sheltered far inside the Golfo Dulce near a large rivermouth. It can have a decent wave when swell size and direction are right, but is generally small and soft for beginners especially at high tide. Low tide is suckier and shorter, offering dumpy waves up to a little overhead. Playa Pilon at the far southern end of Zancudo faces a few left points at Rancho del Mar and Punta Salea that provide a quiet alternative if the SW swell is pumping. The crowds at **Pavones** come for insanely long lefts, sectioning down a sandy, cobblestone point, close to shore. It's incredibly inconsistent, as only big S-SW swells will penetrate the Golfo Dulce. Modern swell forecasting means plenty of surfers will be on hand when it does work including the locals and expat crew who are notorious for sewing up the best set waves and making it past the hollower low tide rivermouth section all the way down to the cantina where the breakneck speed lets up a bit. This La Esquina del Mar section breaks better at high tide unless it is big, offering rides of up to a kilometre for those quick enough to beat the longer sections. Main problem is the crowd and jelly-legs, which get little respite on the long hot walk back up the point. If the crowd gets too much there are more ruler-edged lefts spinning off around the next headland into the El Higo section. At the end of the road is **Punta Banco** where beachbreak peaks are flanked by multiple reefbreaks that draw in plenty of swell. Fun for all abilities when small, but handles some size amongst the various reefs that include the ridiculously rocky La Pina and loping lefts at La Nicaragua. **Eclipse** has lefts and rights at both the rocky point and the beachbreak beside the rivermouth. It's well-placed to pick up even NW swell, but prefers peaky smallish SW at lower tides. Punta Burica is super-exposed and produces large peaks breaking on many different offshore reefs in a largely unexplored area that requires a sturdy panga.

NW swells or hurricane swells off Mexico wont get into Pavones, which needs due S or a bit SW. The maximum tidal range can reach 3.65m, which has a great effect on where you will surf. Some breaks are non-existent at low, then overhead at high and most beachies work better on the push. See also – Guanacaste and Central Puntarenas.

MARK MCINNIS

Pavones

UNA OLA

Pavones

## TRAVEL INFORMATION

**Weather** – see Central Puntarenas - This area has a wet tropical climate with high temperatures and humidity year-round, with more rainfall and thunderstorms than the rest of the Pacific coast. May to Dec rainy season sees intense downpours, especially in the afternoons. The short dry season occurs when the wind turns to the N between Jan and April. The water remains very warm year-round; take boardshorts and a long sleeve rash vest for the strong sun.

**Lodging and Food** – Pavones has multiple B&Bs, lodges and holiday rentals from $15/n upwards. Una Ola all inclusive 7 day package fr $1033. Punta Banco basic rooms cost $20/n. Matapalo has many private properties with upmarket jungle bungalows (Bosque del Cabo, Bahia Esmeralda: min $150+) while waveless Puerto Jimenez is much cheaper. Pavones legendary cantina La Esquina del Mar burnt down in 2011.

**Nature and Culture** – National parks (e.g. Corcovado) are home to monkeys, scarlet macaws, crocodiles and snakes. Wildlife and flora in the rainforests is stunning! Only Golfito and Puerto Jimenez offer some night action.

**Hazards and Hassles** – Mind the rocks, especially at low tide Matapalo spots. Crowds at Pavones and Matapalo get thick and the locals/expats get angry at times. Malaria tablets are necessary. Sea lice, jellyfish and swarms of daytime feeding mosquitoes, have caused a few cases of Dengue fever.

**Handy Hints** – The local name for men is ticos, for women it's ticas. Local people are really friendly and most people speak English. Pura vida (pure life) means hello. Cases of muggings and thefts from cars and hotels are growing.

| STATISTICS | | J F | M A | M J | J A | S O | N D |
|---|---|---|---|---|---|---|---|
| SWELL | Direction | | | | | | |
| | Size (ft) | 2 | 3 | 4-5 | 5 | 4-5 | 2 |
| WIND | Direction | | | | | | |
| | Force | F3 | F2 | F3 | F3 | F3 | F3 |
| WATER | Wetsuit | | | | | | |
| | Temp/°C | 26 | 27 | 28 | 27 | 27 | 26 |
| WEATHER | Rainfall/mm | 4 | 18 | 205 | 202 | 270 | 70 |
| | days/mth | 1 | 2 | 16 | 18 | 20 | 7 |
| | Min temp/°C | 23 | 23 | 22 | 23 | 23 | 22 |
| | Max temp/°C | 35 | 35 | 33 | 32 | 32 | 31 |

# Limón COSTA RICA

GUATEMALA
EL SALVADOR
NICARAGUA
COSTA RICA
PANAMA

Costa Rica's Caribbean coastline receives fairly big and wild waves from short-lived, seasonal storms, mainly centred off Colombia. These powerful, short-fetch Caribbean swells break in the 2-12ft range on some excellent reefs, concentrated around Puerto Limón and Puerto Viejo. The Caribbean coastline is short (212km) and the majority is within the barely accessible Tortuguero National Park, a long sandy line backed by huge waterways with countless beachbreaks, potential rivermouths, and brimming with sea-life.

+ CONSISTENT, SEASONAL SWELL
+ POWERFUL REEFBREAKS
+ INSIGNIFICANT TIDAL RANGE
+ LAID-BACK CARIBBEAN STYLE

– FLAT BETWEEN SEASONS
– LACK OF GOOD BEACHBREAKS
– EXTREMELY WET
– PETTY CRIME

RYAN CRAIG

Limón

A boat from Puerto Moin is best for accessing the lonely, empty and average northern beachbreaks of Parismina, **Tortuguero Beach** or Barra Colorado. The regular rivermouths bring brown murky water and big crocs to the already sharky line-up. In Portete, the industrialised keyhole harbour is flanked by the rare rights of **Cocaine Point**, which need plenty of N in the swell to start peeling off down the 100m sharp coral reef. Always crowded **Playa Bonita** is the main beach in the area and features a chunky mid-tide left reef at the north end which gets slamming hollow in a strong NE swell. The high tide beachbreak closes-out at headhigh and the low tide Los Tumbos rights are short and sucky over a rocky minefield favoured by bodyboarders. The serious right ledges of **Roca Alta** get shallow and tricky at low tides. **Isla Uvita**, where Columbus landed in 1502, is a long lefthander that picks up everything and shunts along a shallow ledge, offering challenging, bowly lefts for assured tube-hunters only. Air drops to get in and lines-up best on NE swells at mid tide. If there aren't any boats for hire in Limón, the paddle from the mainland takes about 20mins; jellyfish rather than sharks are the major cause for concern. En route to Cahuita there is 35km of average but consistent beachbreaks like **Westfalia**, where sandbanks are deserted, but close-out easily. Check the **Barco Quebrado** at the Rio del Banano rivermouth where better shaped banks are often seen. In Cahuita, the main beachbreak, **Playa Negra**, occasionally gets good with easy rollers for beginners in small swells at high tides, but it can get overhead and hollow on a NE pulse. There's a fun low tide, longboarding left off the point in Playa Blanca, which speeds up with size. Full of power and menace, the notorious **Salsa Brava** holds any size Carib swell in cylindrical uniformity. Air drop first peak into the pit and race for the shoulder, possibly linking up with the shiftier second peak where mere mortals are allowed to take their turn in the competitive line-up that some call the 'Caribbean Pipeline'. A short, intense left can appear and low tide will be sketchier over the salivating coral reef. Needs the mid-winter NE to SE swells or a July hurricane to really get going and early morning slack winds to reach its fine potential. Beware of the reef, urchins, locals, expats and some pollution. The beachbreaks of **Playa Cocles** are mellow and fun, perfect for beginners, while a short left breaks beside an island at the north end, offering mid tide slashable walls, until the swell gets overhead. At the south end, **Little Shoal** is a coral shelf mix of mainly rights, plus a few lefts that are less intense than nearby reefs. **Punta Uva** is a bit more challenging as the scattered peaks can get hollow and sucky along the sandy reefs and shorebreak. Outside, the point can line-up playful right walls. **Manzanillo** beachbreaks pick up small swells and are wind exposed, plus there are right reef options off the headlands which requires a bit of trek through the beautiful jungle of the national refuge area.

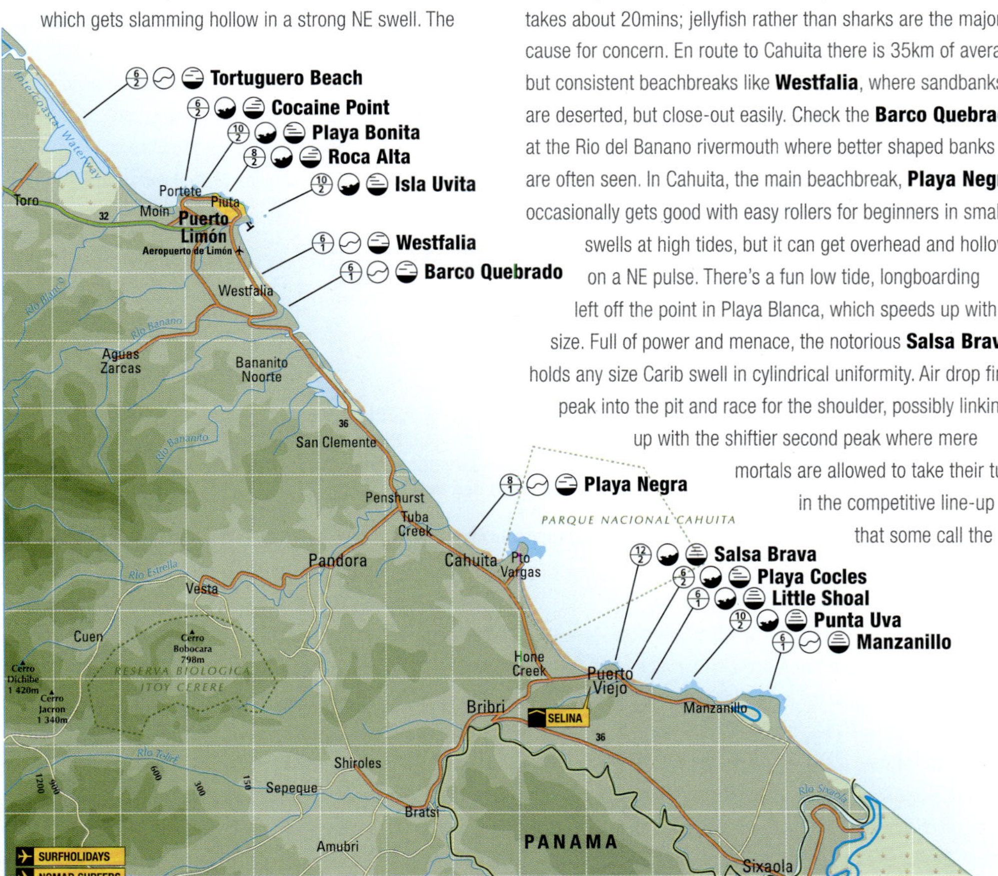


The main winter season from Dec to March sees many storms churning off Cartagena in Columbia, aiming ENE swells and stormy weather directly at Costa Rica. There is also a June-August season, July being the safer bet. The Talamanca coastal range helps to calm down local squalls and induces offshore winds in the morning. Tidal phases are only 1m, but that's enough to make the heavy coral reef platforms even more dangerous at spots like Isla Uvita and Salsa Brava.

## TRAVEL INFORMATION

**Weather** – The Talamanca coastal region is extremely wet and the rainiest months (Dec/Jan, July/Aug) correspond with swell. Rain can come in heavy downpours, often at night, followed by clearing skies. Temps are similar throughout the year. Typically the lows will be above 21°C (70°F) and the highs below 30°C (86°F). Expect high humidity and cooling breezes. Water temps from 26.5°C (80°F) in Jan to 30.3°C-87°F) in June – boardies.

**Lodging and Food** – For nice hotels, avoid Limón (except Park Hotel). Playa Cocles, Finca Chica (fr$45). Hotel Puerto Viejo is central and cheap ($18/basic room). Rocking J's party hostel hammocks (fr $7). Carib style meals cooked in coconut milk, curry, and ginger!

**Nature and Culture** – Cahuita National Park wildlife includes howler monkeys, sloths, iguanas, parrots, hummingbirds and toucans. Flat day diving and snorkelling can be good. Serious nightlife influenced by Rastafarian culture. Tasty Waves across from Cocles Beach and in PV (Johnny's). Have a look at Bri-Bri handicrafts.

**Hazards and Hassles** – Be prepared to face intense downpours. These waves have power and intensity and can be dangerous especially at Salsa Brava, the most crowded spot. Jellyfish appear in the murky water at certain times of year. Things to avoid: Rasta wannabees selling drugs, street crime, bugs and mosquitoes!

**Handy Hints** – Take a semi-gun for Salsa/Limon spots. There are surf shops in San José (Mango, Planeta Surf y Skate) and gear to rent in Puerto Viejo. Bring wet weather clothing!

| STATISTICS | | J F | M A | M J | J A | S O | N D |
|---|---|---|---|---|---|---|---|
| SWELL | Direction | | | | | | |
| | Size (ft) | 3-4 | 3 | 1-2 | 3 | 1 | 3 |
| WIND | Direction | | | | | | |
| | Force | F4 | F4 | F4 | F4 | F3 | F4 |
| WATER | Wetsuit | | | | | | |
| | Temp/°C | 26 | 26 | 27 | 27 | 27 | 27 |
| WEATHER | Rainfall/mm | 260 | 240 | 280 | 350 | 180 | 390 |
| | days/mth | 18 | 14 | 16 | 21 | 14 | 21 |
| | Min temp/°C | 20 | 21 | 22 | 22 | 22 | 21 |
| | Max temp/°C | 30 | 30 | 31 | 30 | 30 | 30 |

# Southwest Panama

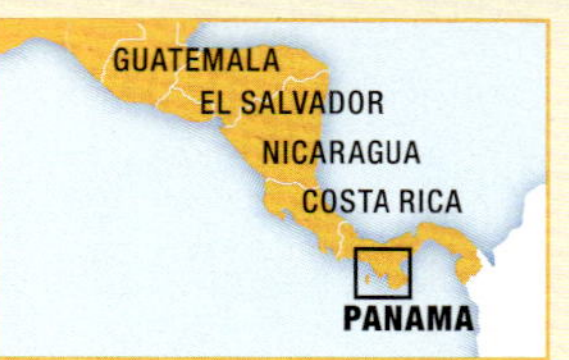


Southwest Panama feels like an uncrowded version of neighbouring Costa Rica with the added bonus of offshore islands to explore. The Southwest Panama zone includes the Provinces of Chiriqui, Veraguas and Los Santos, which can draw in swell from due S to WNW onto a smorgasbord of points, reefs and impressively beautiful beaches. Surf towns have sprung up at the hotspots like Santa Catalina, which is Panama's most sought-after righthander and was the venue for the ISA World Surfing Games.

+ WORLD-CLASS REEFBREAKS
+ CALM WIND CONDITIONS
+ UNCROWDED SPOTS
+ WILD EXOTIC AREA

– CROWDED SANTA CATALINA
– INTENSE RAINY SEASON
– LACK OF ROADS
– TROPICAL DISEASES

From the regional capital David, many locals hit the straight beachbreaks of La Barquetta or **Las Lajas**, which offer variable quality beginner/improver waves over the flat sands at higher tides, but might hide more challenging rides towards the rivermouths at either end. The island of Silva de Afuera is the focus, a 30min boat ride offshore. **P-Land** wraps around the southwestern tip, peaking on a tabletop reef that creates fast, tubing lefts and pinching shoulders in equal measure. Usually bigger than other spots, it's best at higher tides and the tight take-off zone doesn't handle a crowd. Further down the reef is the much easier ride at Leftovers. A 10min paddle to the east is **Nestles**, an explosive, but short peak, where experts will get tube time after the sucky drop on the favoured rights before emerging onto the fat shoulder. The lefts head straight for some rocks. Morro Negrito surf camp is close to two rocky lefthanders for competent surfers or better. **Emily's** is right in front of the accommodation and peels over some sharp reef and barnacle encrusted rocks at variable speed flicking between whackable walls and a few tight tubes. 20 mins walk south is **The Point** that needs a sizeable swell to build some fast, pitching lefts at lower tides. For length of ride, the rivermouth south of the camp is unbeatable, sculpting a **Sandbar** that offers 200-400m rides down both sides of the triangle depending on swell direction. Soft forgiving shoulders and faster, crumbling sections offer something for all levels and it is fairly consistent, despite being shadowed by Coiba Island, where more waves await the intrepid. **Punta Roca** sucks hard over a ledgy reef making the drops beyond vertical and the tube nice and round. Short, shallow and shoulders off quickly after the initial rush. **Santa Catalina** has the reputation as one of the best waves in Central America, thanks to unrivalled reliability and year-round offshores. At the far end of beginner-friendly Playa Estero is **Punta Brava**, a challenging, low tide left and suicidal right in a small rocky bay that offers no paddling channel and is littered with nasty rocks. Always bigger than anywhere else, it's far safer surfing from a boat and avoiding getting caught inside. Offshore, the island of Sebaco offers radical rights, fun lefts and empty beachbreak in a wilderness setting. Playa Reina near **Mariato** has various rocky peaks, ideal for intermediates up. A string of good beachbreaks to the south include Playas Torio, Mata Oscura and Plaza, plus some lined-up lefts near Punta Duarte and the rivermouths. **Corto Circuito** is a heaving tube over an outside slab off the point, which quickly reverts to a long slashable wall through to the inside. Powerful, awesome wave that's best with due S swell at lower tide. **Horcones** beach arcs through 3kms of black-sand-pounding-beachbreak that includes a rivermouth and a pointbreak at the western end called Dos Rocas. Mid to low tide dropping on any S swell. The road runs by the scattered reef peaks of **Dinosaurios** that pick up plenty of swell and shape up well at higher tides. **411** (Cuatro-once) is the most surfed pointbreak in the Cambutal area, with high tide righthanders hugging the rock shelf and keeping intermediates

SURFERS PARADISE SURF CAMP
P-Land

## TRAVEL INFORMATION

**Weather** – Expect a wet tropical climate with high temperatures and humidity year-round, even more so on the Caribbean side of the highlands. The seasons are determined by rainfall rather than temperature changes. There is a prolonged rainy season between May and Dec with intense downpours, especially in the afternoons. The short dry season occurs when the wind turns to the N between Dec and April. Water can drop to 24ºC (75ºF) in Feb, but hits 30ºC (86ºF) by June so boardies and rashie.

**Lodging and Food** – There's a range of accommodation options lining the cliffs above Santa Catalina, ranging from camping at Oasis, Estero Beach (15min walk to SC) from $5. Cabanas Rolo are one of the cheaper options in town with local legend Rolo, who also has a boat. In the Quebrada de Piedra area, Surfers Paradise Surf Camp has 7 day deals starting from $560. In Venao try BeachBreak Surf Camp ($595/7/d), or Surf Camp Guanico to the west ($350/7/n). Food is basic with plenty of fish available.

**Nature and Culture** – Despite rampant clearing of the jungle for livestock and crops, the monkeys, birds, crocodiles and snakes are still around. The closest city is David or Panama. A trip out to Coiba to see the National Park centre and hopefully surf the south coast is unforgettable.

**Hazards and Hassles** – Due to large tidal ranges, hitting the shallow reef is a real possibility. The surf at Santa Catalina gets real busy and the locals have it wired. Yellow fever injection and malaria tablets are necessary. The heat can get very intense from May-Sept.

**Handy Hints** – Booties may come in handy for the long walk rock hop out to La Punta or Punta Brava. Try some of the other obvious reefs near Santa Catalina, or rent a boat and explore the great waves in both directions (Sebaco, Punta Rocas). FluidAdventurespanama.com offer surf/nature trips around SC and out to Coiba. Panama uses the US dollar.

RICHARD BRADY

Las Lajas
P-Land
Nestles
Emily's
The Point
Sandbar
Punta Roca
La Punta
Punta Brava
Mariato
Playa El Toro
Playa Lagarto
Playa los Destiladeros
Ciruelo
Playa Venao
Playa Raya/Madrono
Guánico Point
Playa Cambutal
411
Dinosaurios
Corto Circuito
Horcones

RICHARD BRADY
Mariato

Playa Venao

happy with groomed climb and drop walls, plus some hollow pockets for the rippers. **Playa Cambutal** has all tides, all abilities beachbreak in front of the hotel with the same name. Fun and cruisey, beginners can get some shelter at the western end as outside reefs filter the swell. Just out of town is Punta Negra, a reliable reef peak visible from the road. **Guanico Point** needs low tide and some size to wrap into the protected southern corner of Guanico Beach. The other end is super-consistent, but not the most powerful or perfect sandbars, so it's usually empty. Takes a long hike over the fields to reach **Playa Raya**, a rivermouth that grooms the sand on both sides for long, strong, lefts and rights into the empty beach. Low incoming better as rips will be running on the drop. Named after all the manta and stingrays found here. Sharky rivermouth as well. Confident surfers only. **Playa Madrono** benefits from a stream outfall creating fast peeling, top-to-bottom tubes at low tides in any S swell and any light N wind. It's a half hour walk in and not always working, but the good days will attract those in the know. Popular crescent bay beachbreak at **Playa Venao** (Venado) usually has some kind of wave to ride for the range of surfers that come here. Avoid extremes of tide and size. The encircling hills offer some wind protection making it a regular contest site. The fishing harbour at **Ciruelo** is flanked by a weighty lefthander that only appears in long period SW swells on slack wind days. Thick and bowly with some challenging tubes, which keeps the crowds minimal. At **Playa los Destiladeros** the shingle beachbreak and scruffy lefts off the point are barely worth the effort, but the righthand point has some decent waves on a moderate SW swell at low to mid tide. **Playa Lagarto** almost faces due E, so isn't the most consistent spot, but a moderate headhigh SE-S swell will throw up some nice tubular corners, particularly at the rocky point. Light W winds and mid tides to avoid the close-outs. Just outside Pedasi, **Playa El Toro** is even more protected than Lagarto and really needs a good S pulse to hit the rocky fingers of reef off this beach. Short lefts and longer rights on the wrap will form at mid to low. Only the locals are likely to see it at its best and the rocks are a problem getting in and out.

**Santa Catalina**

**LAT. 7.623544° LONG. -81.257672°**

Long, racy Panamanian reefbreak that is ultra-consistent thanks to the swell-pulling power of a deep offshore trench and consistent all day offshores. At high tide, the defined peak offers a big drop both ways, although the left is short-lived and fats out fairly quickly. Meanwhile, those lucky enough to snag a set off the talented crew will wind down the long reef, hitting a few critical corners where the dash is best done behind the curtain. Ruler-edged walls bring out the best in intermediates, who can pick up waves further down the line. Low tide is very sketchy and makes getting in/out arduous. Ultra reliable during southern-hemi swell season and handles the surf camp crowds.

The major swell season is April to Oct, relying on the usual Roaring Forties swell generator that produces numerous 3-12ft swells from the S-SW. The NW hurricane swells off Mexico will struggle to get into the Gulf of Chiriqui but may awaken some dormant waves on west-facing coasts. Dry season in Santa Catalina experiences a regular breeze off the mountains and even NW will be OK for the rights. Light winds and evening glass-offs are common – stay alert. There is a gentle SW-W monsoon period from May to December (when it's wet). S-SW predominance occurs for 44% of the time in May to 68% of the time in Oct. Typically, mornings are offshore and afternoons see a light onshore seabreeze. The dry winter period has a lot of low wind days with winds from any direction with a NW-NE dominance. Tides can reach a huge 5m, so get a tide chart.

| STATISTICS | | J F | M A | M J | J A | S O | N D |
|---|---|---|---|---|---|---|---|
| SWELL | Direction | | | | | | |
| | Size (ft) | 2-3 | 3-4 | 5 | 5-6 | 5 | 2-3 |
| WIND | Direction | | | | | | |
| | Force | F3 | F2 | F3 | F3 | F3 | F3 |
| WATER | Wetsuit | | | | | | |
| | Temp/°C | 26 | 27 | 28 | 28 | 27 | 27 |
| WEATHER | Rainfall/mm | 110 | 67 | 315 | 387 | 365 | 510 |
| | days/mth | 7 | 7 | 15 | 17 | 16 | 15 |
| | Min temp/°C | 24 | 25 | 24 | 24 | 24 | 24 |
| | Max temp/°C | 29 | 30 | 31 | 31 | 31 | 29 |

# Panamá Oeste Province PANAMA

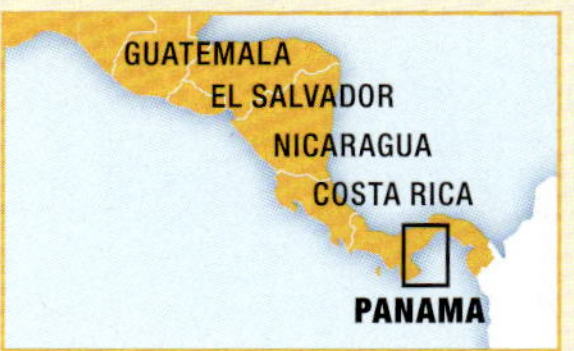


Panama deserves its nickname of "The crossroads of the World". This narrow strip of land not only makes the link between Central and South America, but also joins the mighty Pacific and Atlantic oceans via the Panama Canal. The cosmopolitan metropolis of Panama City hugs the eastern bank of the Pacific entrance to the Canal, deep in the sheltered Golfo de Panama, where only the strongest south swells can penetrate. However, an hour's drive west on the Pan-American Highway leads to another string of sandy beaches with better surf and much cleaner waters.

+ HIGH WAVE DENSITY
+ EASY, FUN WAVES
+ SIMPLE ACCESS/TRAVEL
+ PANAMA CITY ENTERTAINMENT

– NARROW SWELL WINDOW
– FLAT IN OFFSHORE SEASON
– FICKLE QUALITY SPOTS
– POLLUTED, CROWDED CITY SPOTS

**Rio Mar** is a long walk to reach the extensive rock ledge where a fun right breaks down the point at low tide. If the tide is too high, give the adjacent beachbreaks a try. Bigger swells light up **Punta Palmar**'s fast, powerful, outside righthanders at high tide, but it still works on smaller swells, breaking fatter and slower inside the headland. There's also the popular Frente Palmar beachbreak close-outs for contests and beginners. **Hawaiisito** (Little Hawaii) favours fun, easy lefts over the boulders, but will not handle swell above head high. **San Carlos Point**, (aka Jeffreys) can supply long, fast sections down the rock and sand point at lower tides. **Costa Esmeralda** has an inconsistent high tide peak that is slopey and mushy when small, but livens up with a solid S swell. The changeable rocks and sand of **Punta Teta** are shaped by the river outflow, allowing some fast low to mid tide lefts to break into the Frente Teta area, where more A-frame peaks will appear at high. Locals favourite and is often crowded at weekends. As the name **Rinconsito** (Little Rincon) suggests, this is a long, workable, hot-dog wall with time and space for all sorts of turns, but it requires sizeable swell and is very inconsistent. **Rocky Point** needs just the right size swell to be breaking without closing-out. It's predominantly rights but there are a few lefts too which are constantly shifting in front of the rivermouth. The impressive righthand pointbreak of **Playa Serena** peels hard and hollow from the take-off in front of the twin condo towers, before turning into a long and easy wall ideal for longboarding. Best at low tide, it's dependent on sand distribution, so it's quite fickle and therefore crowded. **Playa Malibú** rivermouth break always picks up more swell than other spots in the area and is surfable at all tides. Count on fast tubular waves when the Chame River and tidal action combine to shape the black sand. Between Punta Chame and Panama City, the swell is blocked by Punta Chame itself and a few offshore islands, while Bahia Chorrera is simply too shallow for the surf to reach the coast. The next spots lie within the city itself and will break on very large swells, but be aware that water quality is appalling. Right in the middle of the Casco Viejo (Old Quarter), **Las Bóvedas** is a rock-bottomed reef peak with good lefts ending on a large rock. Such a location insures maximum crowds and minimum safety (pollution and thievery). Right in front of the Corredor Norte expressway, **Boca La Caja** is a fickle right breaking next to a large protruding rock. Always crowded with unsharing locals and there's general insecurity in this neighbourhood. **Panamá la Vieja** is a rare case of "mudbreak" since most of the sand previously there was used for construction. Highway pilings block the swell and even on the biggest days with the biggest tide, it's a mushy, messy wave rolling in from a long way out. **Mojon Beach** offers a choice of three peaks, with Las Piedras and Nuevo Ride breaking around high tide, while La Lama is a low tide break. These are OK breaks if confined to the city, but none are really worth facing the crowd and pollution.

See Southwest Panama. A SSW angle (around 210°) is the optimum swell direction to penetrate the gulf, where it will be about half the size of Santa Catalina, but it is usually clean. During the winter Dec-May dry period, offshore N winds are the rule; but regular swells aren't. The wet or "green season" is typically morning offshores before a sea breeze picks up and onshore SW winds dominate between Sept and Nov. Tides can reach a huge 5.5m!

PATRICK CASTAGNET

Playa Malibú

## TRAVEL INFORMATION

**Weather** – see Southwest Panama

**Lodging and Food** – Accommodation is affordable but not dirt cheap as in other Central Am countries. The Rio Mar Surf Camp has rooms from $25/p/n, dorms $15/n. More hotels are available in Coronado and Gorgona. $15 gets you a great meal, try patacones (plantains).

**Nature and Culture** – A tour of Panama City should include the ruins of the 16th Century original city, Casco Viejo – the colonial city, and the modern skyscraper city. See ships passing through the Panama Canal at the Miraflores locks. Taboga is an attractive island with nature and wildlife. Panama City nightlife has something for everybody.

**Hazards and Hassles** – All city spots suffer from pollution. Compared to other countries in Central America, Panama feels richer and safer, but some areas of the capital are best avoided at night. The risk of malaria is low in this part of the country. It's safe to drink the water.

**Handy Hints** – Boa Surfboards are made locally. Rio Mar Surf Camp rents boards ($10/day) and can arrange lessons ($20/h). National currency, the Balboa is equivalent to the American dollar, use whichever.

| STATISTICS | | J F | M A | M J | J A | S O | N D |
|---|---|---|---|---|---|---|---|
| SWELL | Direction | | | | | | |
| | Size (ft) | 1-2 | 2-3 | 3-4 | 4 | 3-4 | 1-2 |
| WIND | Direction | | | | | | |
| | Force | F3-F4 | F3-F4 | F3 | F3 | F3 | F3-F4 |
| WATER | Wetsuit | | | | | | |
| | Temp/°C | 26 | 26 | 27 | 27 | 27 | 26 |
| WEATHER | Rainfall/mm | 30 | 45 | 200 | 190 | 225 | 190 |
| | days/mth | 3 | 3 | 12 | 11 | 13 | 11 |
| | Min temp/°C | 22 | 23 | 23 | 23 | 23 | 23 |
| | Max temp/°C | 32 | 32 | 31 | 31 | 30 | 30 |

GUATEMALA
EL SALVADOR
NICARAGUA
COSTA RICA
PANAMA



# Bocas del Toro PANAMA

Columbus left his name to the main island of this archipelago consisting of nine major islands, 59 smaller islands and a myriad of mangrove cays. Located off Panama's northwest coast, modern travellers will find that much of the medieval natural environment that greeted the explorers remains intact. The wooden city of Bocas del Toro exudes a decidedly Caribbean style and flavour. There are some remarkable surf spots in this zone, but the two windows of surf throughout the year are slender.

- \+ CONSISTENT SEASONAL SWELL
- \+ QUALITY, ALL TIDE REEFS
- \+ CHEAP AND SAFE AREA
- \+ LESS CROWDS THAN COSTA RICA

- – FLAT BETWEEN SEASONS
- – LACK OF RIGHTS
- – WET AND WINDY AFTERNOONS
- – TIME-CONSUMING TRIPS TO SPOTS

RYAN CRAIG

Silverbacks

Furthest north from Bocas del Toro, is the consistent stretch of beach known as **Bluff**. Hollow & powerful waves break super-close to the shore, plenty of which close-out. Pick the right ones for a quick barrel at this spot that is ideally suited to bodyboards. **Dumpers** gets its name from the garbage dump across the road, an unsightly blemish in such beautiful surroundings. The wave is short and super-hollow, only suited to experienced surfers wearing booties as it ends on a stupidly sharp ledge of dry reef. On big days, Inside Dumpers breaks a bit longer, with more walls and not so square tubes. A 10-15min drive from town is the quality reefbreak of **Paunch**. The lefts start with a tubular section, before wrapping into a more workable wall and a bonus inside cover-up. A fun, ripable, rampy wave when small, it gets real sucky with a bigger swell. There is also the option of a few rights off the peak, but they are a shadow of the lefts. It can get crowded and even the surf schools are seen around here, despite the sharp reef. The water-taxi option is best used to navigate around the slim island of **Careñeros** to check the surf at its northern tip. This urchin-dusted left reefbreak peels down the east coast of the island, for a ride that can top 200m in a N-NE swell. It's an all-rounder with nice lip-line and cutback shoulders, but it holds size and can have some long tubing sections too. On Bastimientos island, **Silverbacks** coral encrusted, righthand reefbreak starts thumping its chest in the winter months. Surrounding exposed beaches need to be overhead to awaken this muscular, angry wave that sucks up volumes of water and hurls it at the shallow ledge, turning into large kegs that are as intense as they are short. Only experienced, air-drop specialists will gain much from this wave as the under-gunned and under-skilled are punished by the shifting peak and scarily long hold-downs. **First Beach**, (aka Wizard Beach) is a basic beachbreak with patches of reef that picks up more swell than any other spot. Can get suckier and dumpier on a bigger, longer period swell and there is often a left at the north end, with stronger rips through the channels between the scattered reefs. Same story around the corner at Red Frog Beach, but less quality and crowd. There is more messy wind-exposed beach and reef on Bastimentos out to Punta Vieja and the Zapatillas Keys, two islands located on a coral platform. The rest of the archipelago is open to exploration if you can find a boat driver willing to venture across the strong currents flowing between the open sea and the lagoon of Chiriqui. Cayo de Agua's NE shore could be a better bet with a series of points (Nispero and Tiburon) surrounded by coral. The Valiente Peninsula principally attracts biologists and geologists, but Isla Escudo de Veraguas has some fun lefts and a slabby right. The area has great swell exposure and points are plentiful.

The Caribbean Sea produces strong windswells with 5-10sec period, creating consistent 2-12ft surf during the two distinct seasons. Dec to March sees many storms churning off Cartagena in Columbia. There is also a June-August season. The main ENE direction aims perfectly at this corner of Panama and it's far enough away from the storms to let the swell clean-up and avoid constant onshore winds. Hurricane swells are rare. Tides only fluctuate about 1m so spots will be breaking all day, but favour mornings for windless sessions.

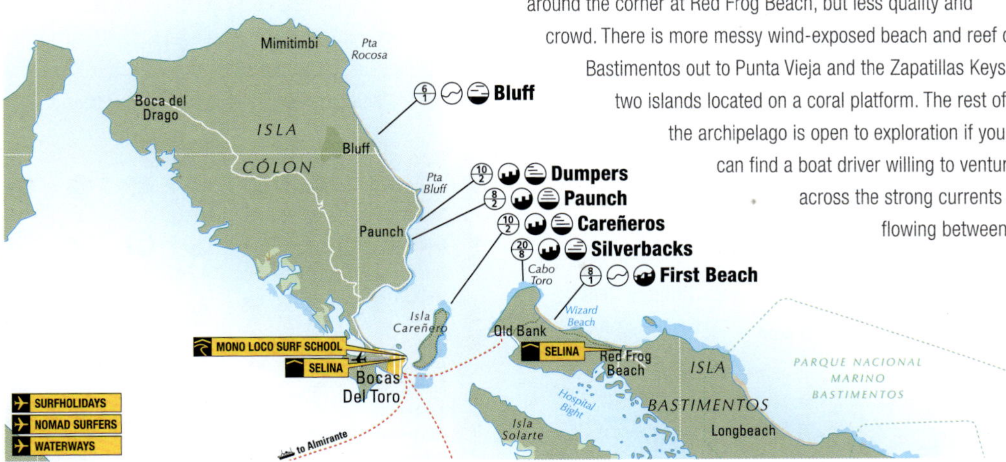


## TRAVEL INFORMATION

**Weather** – Temps are similar throughout the year and would get real hot if it wasn't for the cooling sea breeze. The rainiest months (Dec/Jan, July/Aug) correspond to the swell season. Water temps are very stable in the 27-30°C (80-86°F) range, boardies time, any time.

**Lodging and Food** – Large range of basic hostels in Bocas starting from $10. Waterways has all inclusive packages at Red Frog Bungalows from $155 per night. Selina offer various options - dorm $16/n, private room $79/n. Lots of good food at great prices. Check Hungry Monkey. Drink local beer (Balboa).

**Nature & Culture** – Trek through the rainforest, or enjoy the coral reefs and clear waters while diving or snorkelling. Best nightlife spots are the Barco Hundido (a.k.a. the Wreck Deck) and Iguana.

**Hazards & Hassles** – Getting in and out at Paunch or Dumpers may require reef boots. Take mosquito repellent, but there's no/low risk of malaria in Bocas. Sessions may turn into missions as getting to and from some spots is time consuming. Boards over 7ft a hassle on internal flights.

**Handy Hints** – Bring your own equipment including a step-up for Silverbacks. Some surf camps have limited equipment for sale or rental (Tajada de Sandia). Mono Loco offer road and boat tours as well as surf lessons.

NICK LAVECCHIA

Paunch

| STATISTICS | | J F | M A | M J | J A | S O | N D |
|---|---|---|---|---|---|---|---|
| SWELL | Direction | | | | | | |
| | Size (ft) | 3-4 | 3 | 1-2 | 3 | 1 | 3 |
| WIND | Direction | | | | | | |
| | Force | F4 | F4 | F4 | F4 | F3 | F4 |
| WATER | Wetsuit | | | | | | |
| | Temp/°C | 26 | 26 | 27 | 27 | 27 | 27 |
| WEATHER | Rainfall/mm | 200 | 170 | 215 | 250 | 120 | 300 |
| | days/mth | 18 | 14 | 16 | 21 | 14 | 21 |
| | Min temp/°C | 20 | 21 | 22 | 22 | 22 | 21 |
| | Max temp/°C | 30 | 30 | 31 | 30 | 30 | 30 |

# Abaco and Eleuthera BAHAMAS

These 700 low-lying islands, along with over 2,400 islets called cays, are surface projections of two oceanic banks composed of coral with a limestone base. Extending from 80km east of Florida to 80km northeast of Cuba and crossing the Tropic of Cancer, technically speaking, the archipelago is not a part of the Caribbean. All the eastern "out islands" have good surfing potential but only Abaco and Eleuthera receive travelling surfers on a regular basis.

+ GOOD, VARIED REEFBREAKS
+ LOW CROWD PRESSURE
+ INCREDIBLY CLEAR WATER
+ CLOSE TO FLORIDA

- FLAT SUMMERS
- UNRELIABLE HURRICANE SWELLS
- UNPREDICTABLE WINDS
- CLOSE TO FLORIDA

ALEX WILLIAMS

Garbanzo

**Willawahs** is on the main beach of Guana Cay, where a sandy, flat reef shapes small swell peaks for all abilities. Elbow Cay seems to hold all the popular spots. Hopetown's "Down Along" road runs along the water, leading to **Four Rocks**, a rare beachbreak in a sea of coral reefs. **Indicas** may well be the best barrel in the Bahamas, forming stand-up tubes over a shallow, live coral reef. It's a great left up to 6ft, before turning into the area's proving grounds, holding up to double overhead. **Rush Reef** is a quality wave on a larger swell as the peaks break way offshore, in deep water. The rights are longer, plus there are nearby options on the inside at Hamburger and the fun Pools peaks in front of the Abaco Inn. Mid to high tide essential and the lefts are usually the go in NE swells. **Garbanzo** is easy and forgiving when small, as consistent, long lefts and some rights break along the deeper reef, with enticing walls and ramps. Gets serious at size, which it handles and is the locals go to spot, so expect company. There are more breaks on the way to **Tilloo Cut** that receives consistent surf on the remote, southern tip of the cay, which is boat access only. Long and thin, Eleuthera is under 2km wide for 160km (100mi) of shoreline with pink and white beaches, sheltered coves and dramatic cliffs. The deep water, bowling A-frame on the west side of **Egg Island** takes a good N swell to work, but is usually clean since the trades will blow offshore there. Ride a boat from Spanish Wells to check it out. Harbour Island lefts run down the reef nicely in E swells and across the deep channel, **Whale Point Cut** will have a righthand point setup in big N swell and slack or S winds. Both need dropping tides. **Holiday Beach** is Eleuthera's most radical wave. Steep and hollow, the left is usually the wave of choice. Overhead NE swells and mid-tide are optimal conditions. Gregory Town's **Surfer's Beach** draws long lefts from any swell and some steep rights appear once in a while. It's a fast wave with an intense inside section breaking over a sand bottom. Hatchet Bay cuts a long, fat, workable left known as **Ledges** on the northern side and The Dump works best on low to mid tide and an E to SE swell off the southern point. Rainbow Bay area catches lots of swell but will be only heavy beachbreak unless it's big enough for **Hidden Beach**'s point to reveal itself. On an E to SE wind, inside **James Point** will be offshore and the place to be for clean, hollow and very shallow rights in a N swell. The main headland to the east is an exposed deep-water reef that handles big rights wrapping into the bay. Big sea-life, mega urchins and impossible reef access mean it's a super-long paddle. **North Palmetto Point** holds powerful peaks a long way off the beach at Diamond Cay. **Rock Sound** can occasionally fire on NE-E swells, with perfect lefts angling down sharp reef near the airport.

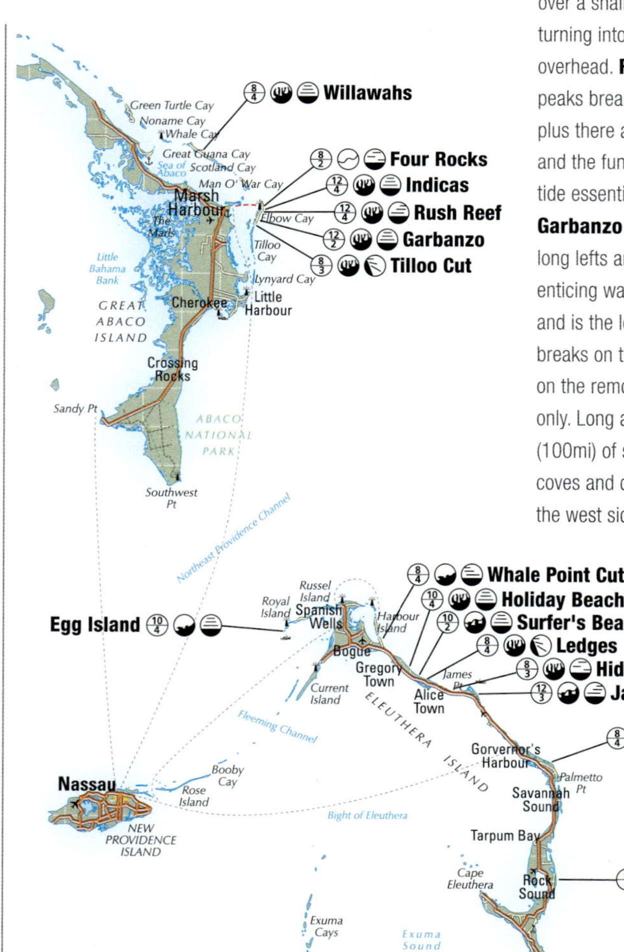


Between October and April, North Atlantic lows and fronts deliver numerous NE swells from 3-10ft. Summer is flat most of the time before August to October brings the possibility of small but clean hurricane swells between days of SE windchop. Moderate onshore easterlies blow more from the NE (Oct-April) then SE (May-Sept). Offshores arrive as soon as a cold front leaves the US East Coast, but winds remain unpredictable. Tidal range (1.5m) affects the shallower spots and mid tides are best.

## TRAVEL INFORMATION

**Weather** – The winter temperatures are commonly 5°C (9°F) warmer than Florida and the summer highs are generally lower, moderated by the surrounding waters. Rainfall is low during the winter surf season but heavy squalls or thundershowers occur during the hurricane months of June through October. Water temps stay well above 21°C (70°F) year-round, but a neoprene vest/shortie will protect against winter windchill.

**Lodging and Food** – Expensive destination, winter is peak tourism season. On Elbow Cay, the Abaco Inn is the place to be ($125/dbl). Bahamas Out-Island Adventures offers guided camping surfaris on Eleuthera. Other lodging options include The Cove Eleuthera in Gregory Town ($245/dbl). Surfers Haven Guesthouse from $40/n/dbl camping.

**Nature and Culture** – Fishing, snorkelling and diving are great, live coral, tropical fish and dolphins are abundant. The Abacos are known as the 'Sailing Capital of the World'. In Hopetown, take photos from the lighthouse.

**Hazards and Hassles** – Crowd levels are lower than 30 years ago. Live coral heads and urchins lurk, so take reef boots. Many shark attacks on spearfishers, snorkelers and divers - only 1 on a surfer at Elbow Cay in 2010. The burning sun is much more of a threat; use plenty of sunscreen.

**Handy Hints** – Take a regular shortboard plus a longer one for those steep waves on Eleuthera. Rebecca's beach shop in Gregory Town rents boards. There are many more islands with good surf in the Bahamas.

| STATISTICS | | J F | M A | M J | J A | S O | N D |
|---|---|---|---|---|---|---|---|
| SWELL | Direction | | | | | | |
| | Size (ft) | 4-5 | 4 | 2-3 | 1-2 | 3 | 4 |
| WIND | Direction | | | | | | |
| | Force | F4-F5 | F4 | F3-F4 | F3 | F4 | F4 |
| WATER | Wetsuit | | | | | | |
| | Temp/°C | 22 | 23 | 25 | 27 | 26 | 24 |
| WEATHER | Rainfall/mm | 40 | 60 | 130 | 130 | 170 | 50 |
| | days/mth | 5 | 5 | 11 | 13 | 14 | 7 |
| | Min temp/°C | 18 | 20 | 22 | 24 | 23 | 20 |
| | Max temp/°C | 24 | 26 | 29 | 31 | 30 | 26 |

# Cuba

Beyond the postcard clichés of Mojitos, salsa dancing and cigars, Cuba hides some decent waves in warm, tropical and largely empty water. The Bahamas filters the bulk of Atlantic wave activity on the NE coast, but the Gulf of Mexico sends stormy swell to the NW corner of the island, around Havana and hurricanes can produce massive waves for the S coast of Cuba. The island lacks consistency, but when the waves arrive they hit all manner of beaches, bays and rocky headlands.

+ UNCROWDED OUTSIDE HAVANA
+ EXPLORATION POSSIBILITIES
+ PERFECT WINTER CLIMATE
+ CULTURAL INTEREST

- SHORT, INCONSISTENT SEASON
- ONSHORE WINDS
- DIFFICULT TRAVEL LOGISTICS
- EXPENSIVE LODGINGS AND FOOD

**La Setenta** (aka Calle 70, Playa 70) is the pick of the Havana spots, just in front of the distinctive Russian Embassy in the Miramar district. A shallow table of flat, dead but painfully sharp coral produces messy peaks that often close-out. In fact, were it not for the slab of concrete sticking out into the ocean here that provides a marginally easier entry and exit point, this spot hardly differs from any other part of the reef that lines the Havana coastline. Rides are short and usually mushy in the onshores. It can get very busy and, unfortunately, surf etiquette doesn't appear to have caught on in a big way in Cuba. Much quieter than La Setenta are the long sandy beaches of the **Playas del Este**. Generally gathering less swell, they are worth checking out when La Setenta is too big or stormy. There are a number of individual beaches here, but the overriding feature is strong currents. Due to the nature of the sandbar waves, their exact form varies from day to day. Heading east from Havana to Varadero, **Sun Beach** is the number one tourist spot in Cuba. There is an average beachbreak with exposure to the NW, but beware, lifeguards sometimes shut the beach when the surf is up. In Ciego de Avila province, a 27km long causeway links the mainland to **Cayo Coco**, a good option for package tour surfers staying at some of the largest resort hotels in the country. There's a mixture of sandy beach, rocks and coral reef but shallow waters and the Bahamas shadow make Cayo Coco very inconsistent. Between here and the tourist town of Holguin there are definitely other waves. Just to the west of the pretty port of **Gibara** is a fast and hollow left breaking on a shallow rock shelf. The wave is short and intense, with a tube section, but it does need a good swell to get going. More waves shadow the road all the way back to Playa Caletones, where a fringe of reef holds possibilities in NE swells. Further E, Guardalavaca beach is usually tiny junk, but the offshore reef has rights out off the northern headland. Even further east, the best wave in Cuba, **Boca de Yumuri**, is found near Baracoa. A classic cobblestone right point, it reels into a stunning bay for up to several hundred metres. Breaks from 3-8ft and gathers any sign of a NE swell through a gap between the Bahamas and the Turks and Caicos. It also handles any tide, and is offshore in an E wind. The south coast of Cuba has plenty of potential, but it only really breaks on rare hurricane swells, or SE windchop. Explore Cajobabo rivermouths, Playa Juragua lefts and Playa Aguadores or Playa Mar Verde beachbreak peaks on each side of Santiago de Cuba. The ledgy and unpredictable righthand reefbreak called **Windmills** is found inside the Guantanamo Bay military base, so only the armed forces get to surf it.

Cuba is a winter-only surf destination as only the bigger NE Atlantic groundswell will manage to seep in through gaps in the Bahamas. These swells suffer from a reduction in size and power but 6-8ft waves are not unheard of. The dominant wind is from the NE so early mornings or sheltered bays are the way to go. Havana receives weekly winter swells from the NW, which are generated by intense storms in the Gulf of Mexico, bringing onshore winds, rain and poor quality surf. Rare hurricane swells can strike from the north or the south and produce big waves. These are highly unpredictable but September and October are the most likely periods. Tidal variation is small, not exceeding 0.6m.

JUAN FERNANDEZ

La Setenta

## TRAVEL INFORMATION

**Weather** – During the short winter occasional cold air masses come from the north, but they are short duration. The average temperatures throughout the year oscillate between 20 and 35°C (68-95°F). The Eastern region enjoys warmer, drier weather. Aug to Oct main hurricane season occurs during the rainy season (May-Oct), before the dry season (Nov- April). North coast water temps can drop to 23°C (74°F). A light vest or shorty in the winter will meet all needs.

**Lodging and Food** – Casa particulars are Cuba's take on AirBnB - rented rooms in private homes fr $15-30/n. Hotel Copacabana, Panorama and Neptune are close to La Setenta (fr $115/n). Most tourists get package deals in the huge Costa Verde resorts. Try ropa vieja (old clothes) stew.

**Nature and Culture** – Old Havana is fully deserving of UNESCO World Heritage Status. The town of Baracoa and the countryside surrounding it are a perfect place to relax under a palm tree and soak up the atmosphere. Kiting and diving throughout Cuba is superb.

**Hazards and Hassles** – Escape the tourist resort bubble. Shallow reefs like Setenta can be ridiculously sharp. Travel times are ridiculously long.

**Handy Hints** – Take all surfing equipment and spares for the locals. No surf equipment is available anywhere in the country, along with many imported goods most people take for granted.

| STATISTICS | | J/F | M/A | M/J | J/A | S/O | N/D |
|---|---|---|---|---|---|---|---|
| SWELL | Direction | | | | | | |
| | Size (ft) | 2-3 | 2 | 1-2 | 1 | 1-2 | 2-3 |
| WIND | Direction | | | | | | |
| | Force | F4 | F4 | F3-F4 | F4 | F4 | F4 |
| WATER | Wetsuit | | | | | | |
| | Temp/°C | 25 | 26 | 28 | 29 | 29 | 27 |
| WEATHER | Rainfall/mm | 58 | 52 | 142 | 130 | 161 | 68 |
| | days/mth | 5 | 4 | 9 | 10 | 11 | 6 |
| | Min temp/°C | 18 | 20 | 22 | 24 | 23 | 20 |
| | Max temp/°C | 26 | 28 | 31 | 32 | 31 | 27 |

# Jamaica

**Famous for Bob Marley, reggae music and Rastafarian culture, Jamaica is the third largest island in the Caribbean, but it is relatively obscure in terms of Caribbean surf destinations. Despite its size, only the eastern tip receives a decent amount of windswell worth exploring, with options for both north and south coasts. The north coast boasts some bigger NE swells, white-sand beaches and quality rivermouths favouring rights, but it is often onshore. The south shores enjoy better consistency and some good lefts, often brushed by NE offshores, along crowd-free grey sand beaches.**

+ DECENT WINTER CONSISTENCY
+ WARM WATER, FRIENDLY WAVES
+ LOW CROWD FACTOR
+ RASTAFARI CULTURE AND MUSIC

- FREQUENT ONSHORE CONDITIONS
- SOMETIMES SMALL & GUTLESS
- POOR ROADS ON EASTERN SIDE
- DIFFICULT ACCESS, PRIVATE COAST

Plump Point **Lighthouse** is one of the south coast's most consistent spots, where a long and soft left pointbreak peels lazily down the point, but it's the shorter barrelling rights that the regular crowds covet. **The Groynes** were installed to stop erosion taking out the road around the large harbour and have built up nice sandbars for all abilities. Usually longer lefts in SE swells. The Zoo reef that held short, perfect, barrelling lefts and rights was blown away by hurricane Ivan in 1994. The rivermouth is working its magic and some lesser lefts have reappeared. Facing the Wilmot family's Jamnesia guest-house is **Copa**, possibly the best rights on the south coast when strong SE swells hit. **Makka's** is the main option for fun ripable lefts, providing very long rides when it connects on any SE swell. Often a contest site, Makka's can accommodate large hurricane swells and crowds. SE swells and any N wind will be ideal for the long left point at **Roselle** that draws in the absolute maximum swell on the south coast. Exposed **Prospect Point** bends in bigger SE swells onto a rocky reef where lefts explode with cylindrical regularity. Fast and technical, so lesser surfers will do better at Prospect Middle Reef where lefts pitch then wall through to a sandy inside. Third Reef needs macking swell to get the long peaks peeling. All best at low tide. Holland Bay also hides some waves, but access can be a problem. **Hector's River** is a typical example where fun lefts & rights over sandy reef are visible from the scenic look-out, but walking down the cliffs is not an easy task. **The Ranch** overlooks 4 reefbreaks; the northern left is reliable in smaller NE swells while over the channel is a sectiony right that barrels in E-SE swells. Another left spins off the peak and an outside right rumbles to life in big pulses. **Long Bay** picks up all the NE windswell creating a decent left off a coral bulkhead in winter. Summer SE rights appear, but lack quality. **Boston Bay** is Jamaica's first recognised surf spot, offering white sand beach, crystal clear water and its notorious spicy jerk chicken or pork, which always draws a small crowd of locals, expats and tourists. Lefts wedge off the outside rock or there's a fat right on the other side of the tight, wind protected bay. Less consistent than Long Bay and perfect for beginners in the usual chest-high soft breakers. **Peeny Wally's** is the best right point around, breaking on most conditions, making it a regular contest site. Performance walls perfect for gouging manoeuvres, it's easier to walk back after a long one. Not far is the Shark's Cove private property; ask the Jamnesia guys to take you there. The whole north coast up to Montego Bay has waves but quality is a problem with constant onshore NE trades often wrecking the surf. Try **Runaways** for a small wave on bigger NE windswells and hopefully offshore SE winds.

Jamaica is largely cut-off from the North Atlantic NE swells by Cuba and Haiti/Dominican Republic although some filters around both ends of Hispaniola. Hurricanes could provide a good S-SE swell or else slam into the island and wreak havoc! Winter (Dec-March) is the best time to expect NE-SE windswells, typically 2-6ft at 5-7 second period. Summer (June-Sept) also produces S-SE swells with plenty of small, playful waves on the south coast. Expect scattered 1-2 week flat spells and 3ft is the biggest semi-diurnal tide.

Lighthouse

BILLY MYSTIC

Makka's

BILLY MYSTIC

## TRAVEL INFORMATION

**Weather** – Jamaica's year-round air temps are 25-30°C (77-86°F). Warm trade winds bring intense but brief rainfall throughout the year, with peaks in May and October. Refreshing onshore breezes blow during the day and cooling offshores at night. Jamaica lies at the edge of Hurricane Alley and sometimes scores direct hits. Boardshorts only.

**Lodging and Food** – Expect $50 for a room and $10 a meal. Jamnesia Camp in Bull Bay offers camping from $15 and simple rooms from $35/n or $45/dble. Try Boston Style Chicken and Ital (rasta veggie cooking).

**Nature and Culture** – Kingston is close for bars & nightlife. Lots of natural sights like Reach Falls, the Bath Fountain hot mineral spring and the Blue Mountains (best coffee in the world?). The Rasta Brethren's mission at Zion Hill is to educate others to the true words of Haile Selassie. Bob Marley Museum.

**Hazards and Hassles** – Kingston has some really rough neighbourhoods like Trenchtown. Police often harass Rastas for weed possession, don't smoke anywhere with anyone. Mind the sea urchins, fire coral, jellyfish, sea lice and sunburn. Crowd pressure is minimal; local surf operators will take clients to semi-secret gems.

**Handy Hints** – Jamnesia Surf Club, at Bull Bay was established by the Wilmots to help the development of surfing through surf events with a surf school, board repair & rental facilities and Patrick Mitchell making Quashi boards. No surfshop.

| STATISTICS | | J F | M A | M J | J A | S O | N D |
|---|---|---|---|---|---|---|---|
| SWELL | Direction | | | | | | |
| | Size (ft) | 3-4 | 2 | 0-1 | 2-3 | 2 | 2 |
| WIND | Direction | | | | | | |
| | Force | F4 | F4 | F4 | F4 | F3-F4 | F4 |
| WATER | Wetsuit | | | | | | |
| | Temp/°C | 27 | 27 | 28 | 29 | 29 | 28 |
| WEATHER | Rainfall/mm | 19 | 33 | 97 | 85 | 143 | 60 |
| | days/mth | 3 | 3 | 4 | 6 | 8 | 5 |
| | Min temp/°C | 19 | 20 | 22 | 23 | 23 | 21 |
| | Max temp/°C | 30 | 31 | 32 | 33 | 32 | 31 |

# Haiti

Haiti is the western end of the second largest Caribbean island, Hispaniola and gets surf and on both its north and south coasts. It takes real determination to check Haiti's empty surf since multiple natural and political disasters have ravaged the poorest nation in the western hemisphere. Along Haiti's north coast shallow reefs greet the winter NE swells and there is plenty to explore for the curious trailblazers who fancy some empty Caribbean juice.

+ N AND S COAST SEASON
+ MORNING OFFSHORES
+ TOTALLY EMPTY SPOTS
+ TROPICAL PARADISE

- SMALL, SHALLOW, INCONSISTENT
- WRECKED INFRASTRUCTURE
- CHAOTIC PORT-AU-PRINCE
- TRANSPORT HASSLES

JS CALLAHAN SURFEXPLORE

Les Anglais

**Caracol** has lefts and rights over coral on both sides of the reef pass, but access is via a taxi boat and it is inconsistent. The main north coast attraction for cruise ship tourists is Labadee Beach and for surfers it's nearby **Ginsu**. Really consistent and open to all NE energy, the take-off can throw out some nice short and intense tubes, then it curves and bowls through to "chopping board rock" on the inside. Difficult road access and the reef is so shallow and urchin-covered that it's best to paddle out from the next cove west from the break at lower tides. **Limbe** hosts a shallow fast left, with steep performance sections and an end bowl. **Chouchou** sleeps in a steep bay until a big NE swell breaks clear into the channel for a short critical barrel section, then a wrapping face. **Le Borgne** is a right reefbreak/rivermouth, close to Pointe Boeuf, that can peel down the line for a long way and give some E wind protection. There are tapering rights and also short playful lefts in oily, diesel blue water. **Cap Rouge** overlooks a spectacular wedging right reef, with long curving walls followed by a lively and shallow end section over a flat coral reef. Works in both NE wind and groundswells. Although fickle and needing a solid NE swell, **St Louis du Nord**'s long sand bottom point can deliver perfect longboard rights on low tides. There are way more spots to discover both sides of Turtle Island's massive NE swell shadow. Way out west on the Tiburon peninsula are numerous potential SE swell rights and left slabs on the **Tiburon Reefs** just south of the town via the decent coastal road. Empty **Les Anglais**' outstanding, sprawling, left point/rivermouth, breaks way up the top on small swells, before 7 seconds plus period conjures the longest wave in Haiti, peeling stylishly through three sections past the town. Consistent tight-to-shore wedging lefts and rights meet in an eye-stinging silty shoredump at **Chevalier**. Inconsistent **Torbek** becomes an excellent, long rivermouth right peeling easily over boulders and sand in longer period SSE swells. **Baie Du Mesle** is a high quality, super-shallow, long left reef with hollow sections and walling faces. **Aquin** has sandy Rainbow Beach for beginners and the offshore islands hold two excellent left reefs plus a speedy short righthander with a critical takeoff and a bowling section on Grande Caye. **L'Hemitage Beach** receives all available SE swell and handles afternoon onshores to deliver long, powerful, performance lefts, with a pounding shorebreak. Offshore bathymetry makes **Brasiliene** a swell magnet with reeling rivermouth lefthanders snapping over large cobblestones. The main Jacmel wave **Pistons** shapes good lefts over the sand topped reef in the morning offshores. **Cayes Jacmel** tames chaotic windswell into good peaky take-offs, fast walls and open faces for cutbacks. There's an emerging local surf scene at the friendly Kabik beachies, or try Ti Mouillage's shallow, slabby lefts. Photgenic **Cotterelle Point** entices walkers to playful, performance walls over shallow boils of urchin reef estate. Consistent **Cotterelle Beach** is rideable in sub 5 second period junk, with wedgy peaks into shorebreak close-outs. Finally, **Marigot** can deliver fast, tight-to-shore lefts over boulders, with hollow sections.

Winter (Nov-March) is when NE trade winds and Atlantic lows produce almost constant swells. True NW-N groundswells are shadowed by the Bahamas and the Turks & Caicos islands. Typically, the surf will be 2-5ft with possible 6-8ft days. The south coast really scores some decent E-SE windswell between July and September. Expect 2-4ft surf, unless a hurricane swell hits from Sept-Oct jacking up 10-12ft waves. Irregular semi-diurnal tides hit 1.1m (north) and 0.8m (south).

## TRAVEL INFORMATION

**Weather** – Temps range from 15-25°C (59-77°F) during winter and from 25-35°C (77-95°F) through summer. NE trade winds bring heavy rainfall to the northern plains and the hurricane exposed southern peninsula between April and Nov. Warm water year-round – take booties for shallow reefs.

**Lodging and Food** – Only the main tourist beaches have good places to stay like Cormier Plage near Cap Haitien, Kayanol Village in Labadee or Hotel Florita And Hotel Cyvadier in Jacmel. Expect to pay $60, but there are local rooms for $10. Local meals can be anything from dirt cheap ($1-2) to $25 for international standard cuisines. Great coffee and Rhum Barbancourt is a fine cognac.

**Nature and Culture** – Mountainous and wild. Don't miss the Bassin Blue waterfalls near Jacmel. Visit Citadelle Laférière from Cap Haitien. Artisan's Market, located near the beach has rich art and crafts. Play soccer or dominos with locals.

**Hazards and Hassles** – Many travel warnings because of natural disasters and political protests. More local kids are riding broken boards and a few expats may appear. Beware of the staghorn coral, urchins and really shallow spots. Local transport can be tough over bad roads.

**Handy Hints** – Longboards and learning some Haitian creole (closest to French) are both useful. Rent local fishing boats to get to the islands and inaccessible spots. Get up early for morning mountain offshores. Earthquakes and hurricanes have left Haiti battered - donate some equipment to the local groms.

| STATISTICS | | J F | M A | M J | J A | S O | N D |
|---|---|---|---|---|---|---|---|
| SWELL | Direction | | | | | | |
| | Size (ft) | 3 | 2 | 0-1 | 2-3 | 1-2 | 3 |
| WIND | Direction | | | | | | |
| | Force | F4 | F4 | F4 | F4 | F4 | F4 |
| WATER | Wetsuit | | | | | | |
| | Temp/°C | 26 | 26 | 28 | 28 | 29 | 28 |
| WEATHER | Rainfall/mm | 43 | 123 | 161 | 108 | 168 | 60 |
| | days/mth | 4 | 9 | 10 | 9 | 12 | 6 |
| | Min temp/°C | 22 | 23 | 24 | 24 | 24 | 23 |
| | Max temp/°C | 31 | 31 | 32 | 33 | 32 | 31 |

# Amber Coast DOMINICAN REPUBLIC

The Dominican Republic is the second largest and most populous country in the Caribbean, occupying the eastern two thirds of the island of Hispaniola. Both the Atlantic Ocean and the Caribbean Sea produce rideable surf on an ideally indented coastline, centred around the hotels and resorts on the Amber Coast, between Puerto Plata and the kiteboarding mecca of Cabarete.

+ GREAT SURF/WIND/KITE COMBO
+ GOOD REEFBREAKS
+ ALL-INCLUSIVE RESORTS
+ CHEAP FOR THE CARIBBEAN

- SHORT SWELL SEASON
- UNFAVOURABLE TRADE WINDS
- AFTERNOON SEABREEZES
- URCHIN-INFESTED REEFS

FLORIAN LANG

La Derecha

Next to the colonial fort in Puerto Plata, a channel splits the reefs of **La Puntilla**, offering intense rights and lefts on a head high northerly swell. The city's other option, **Coffee Break** is a reef peak worth checking when it's too small for La Puntilla. On the biggest northern swells when Encuentro spots start closing-out, peaks will appear in **Sosua Bay**, groomed by the offshore trades, creating a short, clean, sucky ride that's best going left. Also check La Boca to the southwest. **El Canal** is a good but fickle left reef with a shorter right that needs a headhigh swell to work. Encuentro is the Dominican Republic's surf hotspot with a concentrated variety of waves. **Destroyers** is a very shallow, urchin covered reef, holding fast, round lefts in NW-NE swells and the neighbouring left of Mini Tavarua is even faster and hollower - pros only! **La Izqierda** is a lower tide left with plenty of push and barrel sections, especially in NW swells, but all these lefts are very exposed to the wind. **La Derecha** is the most consistent wave in Encuentro with long, walling rights for shredders on the outside reef plus the occasional left in all swells, especially NE. **Bobo's** rights and lefts are a bit faster, less-crowded and there's easier rollers in deeper water over the sandier inside for the many surf schools. The treacherous peak at **Coco Pipe** is for experts only who can handle the heavy drop, barrel, get out quick sequence that the better rights demand. The whole Encuentro stretch usually gets blown-out by 10am in summer trades, yet winter can have plenty of glassy days. **Kite Beach** hosts an outer reef A-frame that's a long paddle and handles the biggest N-NE swells. The rights are best and it's never crowded until the kiteboarders appear around midday. Beyond Punta Goleta is **Bozo Beach** a thumping, fast, experts only shorebreak that pits and spits, keeping bodyboarders and shut-down tube hunters happy. In east Cabarete just opposite the **Police Station**, there's more sandy reefbreak that seems to line-up better in an E swell. Both **La Bomba** (opposite an old gas station) and **Mananero** are curvaceous beachbreaks leading down to the La Boca rivermouth kite spot and providing there is little wind, short barrels are plentiful amongst the shifting peaks. East of Rio San Juan, rights peel down a reef in front of the main entrance to the **Playa Grande**. Around the corner and a long paddle against the sweeping current, **La Preciosa** peak is known to get picture perfect, especially going left. Needs more size than Encuentro, but gets real good in a due N without the same crowd factor. Tucked into the next bay east, the wreck of **El Barco** helps another A-frame reef sculpt some speedy rights and it will handle a bit of E-SE wind. Even better protected is the experts only pointbreak **La Muela** that doesn't start breaking until it's overhead, but will hold shape as big as it gets, rumbling down the point with power and purpose.

FLORIAN LANG

La Preciosa

Between November and March, 2-15ft N swells arrive from lows located off Florida. Early winter is usually good despite regular rain which diminishes before the trade winds pick-up from mid-January. Prevailing winds are either side of E all year-round, getting super strong in winter, so surf early before the trades kick in. Hurricanes and SE windswells awaken the south coast, mainly through the summer months. Tidal range remains under 0.6m.

## TRAVEL INFORMATION

**Weather** – The so-called "cool" season (Nov to March) is pleasantly warm with low humidity and a few days rain each month. The temperature hovers around 29°C (84°F) during the day and 20°C (68°F) at night. Summer temperatures range between 28C-35°C (60-95°F). The highlands are considerably cooler. June to September is the hurricane season, with one blowing through every 8-16yrs. Boardies only.

**Lodging and Food** – Lots of resorts between Sosua and Cabarete. Hooked Cabarete have apartments from $25/n behind the beach at Encuentro. DR Surf Tours (book via Waterways) offer surf packages and explore the whole coast. Dominican dishes come with brown beans (habichuelas) and rice. Presidente is the local beer and the local Brugal rum is cheap and cheerful.

**Nature and Culture** – Cabarete is busy with bars, restaurants and nightclubs. Check Lake Dudu's tarzan swing and 10m zipline jump. Visit the beautiful island of Cayo Lavandado, in the Bay of Samana or travel through the highest mountain chain in the Caribbean. World-class kitesurfing in Cabarete.

**Hazards and Hassles** – SUP is not allowed at the Encuentro breaks west of Coco Pipe. Urchins cover many reefs, so bring booties (surf schools supply them). Most areas are quite safe, although Sosua's nightlife can lean towards the seedy.

**Handy Hints** – You can pick up surf essentials in Cabarete, but there's only a small selection of surfboards. At Encuentro you can find several surf schools with board rentals and lessons. Various hotels/camps organise daily transfers from Cabarete to Encuentro (Hotel Villa Taina). The peso is the national currency, but many businesses prefer US$.

| STATISTICS | | J F | M A | M J | J A | S O | N D |
|---|---|---|---|---|---|---|---|
| SWELL | Direction | | | | | | |
| | Size (ft) | 3-4 | 3 | 1-2 | 1 | 3 | 3-4 |
| WIND | Direction | | | | | | |
| | Force | F4 | F4 | F4 | F4 | F4 | F4 |
| WATER | Wetsuit | | | | | | |
| | Temp/°C | 25 | 26 | 27 | 28 | 28 | 27 |
| WEATHER | Rainfall/mm | 170 | 140 | 90 | 75 | 110 | 280 |
| | days/mth | 11 | 10 | 8 | 7 | 9 | 14 |
| | Min temp/°C | 21 | 22 | 24 | 25 | 24 | 22 |
| | Max temp/°C | 27 | 27 | 29 | 30 | 30 | 28 |

# Northwest Puerto Rico

**Puerto Rico is to Florida what Hawaii is to California. It gets big, it's exotic, and it has fierce locals. Located in what is regarded as the best corner of the Caribbean for surf, Puerto Rico's premier surf spots are found on the northwest coast of the island. A deep-water trench offshore means NW-NE swells hit the north shore with little loss in size and power, breaking on slab reefs of coral and lava.**

+ CONSISTENTLY OFFSHORE
+ QUALITY POINTBREAKS
+ WARM, POWERFUL WAVES
+ EASY ACCESS

- WINDY
- HEAVY CROWDS AND LOCALS
- CAR CRIME
- POLLUTION PROBLEMS

The north coast town of Isabela has some mellower protected beachbreak with a rolling right off the point, but the next bay is **Middles**, where seriously heavy right tubes and lesser lefts unload on the lava and coral reef. **Dunes** has many quality, wind-exposed reefs that are usually crowd-free. **Playa Montones** is a consistent, hollow wave - always worth a look and gets a bit of wind protection from the point. **Jobo's** is a consistent long right breaking onto a sand-covered reef plus a left and more peaks down the beach. Works best on small swells and gets a hassley crowd. **Shack's** is considered a kite/windsurfing spot because of the consistent cross-shore conditions, but on windless days it is a well-shaped reefbreak. **Table Top** is another heaving right barrel, starting next to an exposed platform of rock and running into a shallow coral reef scattered with dangerous rocks on the inside. **Surfers Beach** is a consistent, accessible reef peak on the Ramey Air Force Base and ranges from fun shoulders to punchy barrels, with longer sections on the crowded right. In big wrapping NE swells, **Wilderness** entices some of the tallest, wildest rights, onto a wide, crowd-spreading expanse of WNW-facing reef. The lefts are more bowly when it's small. Sharp nasty reef, strong rips and local vibe. Aguadilla spots are only worth checking on big NW-NE swells when **Gas Chambers** dishes out square, warp-speed barrels a dozen times a year. Crazed experts only have to deal with the drop, backwash, crowds and salivating locals, but the rewards are crack-high. **Crash Boat** is just on the south side of the jetty where wedgy rights line-up over the sandy reef bottom. Decent swell with a bit of W in it is needed. Lots of aggressive local bodyboarders. Downtown Aguadilla features fickle slash and burn rights at Bridges, when the W swell awakens it deep in the wind-protected bay. **Table Rock** is a righthand barrel that fizzes over an urchin-covered reef and is another experts-only spot. More consistent reef and sand peaks break at **BC's** in Aguada town. **Sandy Beach** lines-up a good left off the rocks plus there's some beachbreak in the area (Pools) that may suit beginner/improvers. Rincon is the surfing epicentre and **Domes** is the first point to bend long rights onto its lava rock bottom. It's offshore in the trades, picks up the most swell and is often the only show in town, so crowds fight over the sectiony walls and odd left that bounces around in the small bay. Next point down is **Indicators**, a nasty stretch of shallow, testing reef where rocks, urchins and punishing paddle-outs keeps crowds down. **Maria's** draws the hordes on all types of watercraft to a stretch of kinder reef that grooms the N swells into down-the-line walls perfect for high performance surfing. NW swell and lower tides will produce hollower waves. **Tres Palmas** is Puerto Rico's big wave testing ground and can hold waves up to 20ft when a really big winter NW swell hits. Tough drops into the trade-wind offshores lead to wailing walls, coveted by the local chargers, but beware of wide sneaker sets. Tucked into a bay is **Little Malibu**, which has small, fast, tubey rights over a shallow, fire coral reef that's half the size of Rincon breaks.

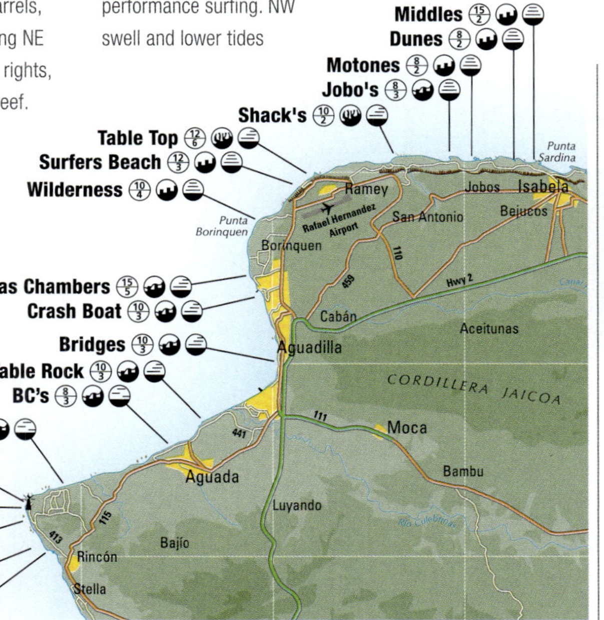


US East Coast cold fronts send NW-NE 2-15ft swells down to the most consistent NW tip of the island. The swells wrap onto the W coast giving clean, offshore conditions. NE, E and SE windswells, plus occasional hurricanes in the Caribbean will produce waves in other parts of the island. The wind blows predominantly from the E, veering NE in the winter and SE in the summer. Tidal ranges are minimal (0.72m), but affect many of the shallow reefs.

JIMMY WILSON

Table Top

STEVE FITZPATRICK

Gas Chambers

## TRAVEL INFORMATION

**Weather** – Winter highs of around 24°C (75°F) and night-time lows that never drop under 15°C (58°F) at the coast, where there is no distinct wet and dry season. High rainfall in the mountains and in Sept-Oct, when strong hurricanes occasionally hit the island. Mainly boardshorts or a shorty for early, windy, late winter sessions.

**Lodging and Food** – The surf and tourist season are concurrent, meaning higher prices, but PR is lower on the Caribbean scale. Quality accommodation options include La Cima in Isabella, ($60/d), Cielo Mar in Aguadilla, ($55/d), or Surf & Board Surfari in Rincón, ($45/sgle/d). A good meal can be had for $15.

**Nature and Culture** – Great windsurfing and diving. San Juan is the second oldest city in the Americas - check the historic old town and El Morro. There's good hiking in the El Yunque rainforest national park. The nightlife is very lively.

**Hazards and Hassles** – Shallow reefs, urchins and some very crowded spots. Localism, car theft, high crime rate (lots of guns) and sewage are all serious concerns. Hurricane Maria flattened the island in 2017, causing 66 deaths.

**Handy Hints** – Quality surf shops include Ramey Surf Zone, West Coast and Mar Azul in Rincon. Wear sunblock in the water and mosquito repellent in the evenings.

| STATISTICS | | J F | M A | M J | J A | S O | N D |
|---|---|---|---|---|---|---|---|
| SWELL | Direction | | | | | | |
| | Size (ft) | 4-5 | 3-4 | 2 | 1-2 | 4 | 4-5 |
| WIND | Direction | | | | | | |
| | Force | F4 | F4 | F4 | F4 | F4 | F4 |
| WATER | Wetsuit | | | | | | |
| | Temp/°C | 25 | 26 | 27 | 28 | 28 | 26 |
| WEATHER | Rainfall/mm | 65 | 75 | 132 | 137 | 150 | 127 |
| | days/mth | 13 | 10 | 13 | 16 | 15 | 16 |
| | Min temp/°C | 21 | 22 | 23 | 24 | 24 | 22 |
| | Max temp/°C | 28 | 28 | 31 | 31 | 31 | 30 |

# British Virgin Islands

Tortola is the largest of the British Virgin Islands and the capital, thanks to an important deep-water harbour in Road Town. The north shore of the island is dotted with a series of bays and beaches offering a good diversity of surfing locations, including one the Caribbean's sparkling gems, namely Cane Garden Bay.

+ WORLD-CLASS CANE GARDEN BAY
+ CONSISTENT BEACHBREAKS
+ SAFE TROPICAL DESTINATION
+ EXPLORATION POTENTIAL

- SHORT SWELL SEASON
- LACK OF CONSISTENT REEFS
- BOAT ACCESS ONLY BREAKS
- EXPENSIVE

ALEX DICK-READ

Cane Garden Bay

**Capoon's Bay**, aka Little Apple Bay, holds a perfectly symmetrical A-frame reef where a user-friendly wave handles everything from 2ft to big swells. There's another, softer right on the E side of main peak, generally used by SUPers and often known as Gay Rights. Around the corner, Long Bay, has more beachbreak peaks. World-class **Cane Garden Bay** faces west, so the right pointbreak will only break 20-30 times a year, but when it's on, fast walls peel down the shoreline for several hundred metres. Throaty barrels at the tip of the point hit the numerous shallow coral heads, then race down the line to a fast, hollow end section. Try to time a big NW-NE swell (Anegada saps due E) with NE-E wind. SE messes up Cane, but is dead offshore around the point at fickle Brewers Bay, which has a much shallower, more dangerous/unpredictable left pointbreak. **Josiah's Bay** is the most consistent beachbreak and is slightly off the beaten track. The quality of the wave depends on the shape of the sandbanks, but there's always something to ride. It's ideally suited for longboarding and learning - hence the local surf school. "JBay" holds lots of surfers but above 1.5m it becomes less defined with arduous paddle-outs. There are more waves on Tortola, including powerful beachies in remote, roadless locations. Finding them would require boating along the coast or making friends in the small, local surfing community. There are a couple of spots on nearby Virgin Gorda – **Yacht Harbour**'s reef at Spanish Town is worth checking on a large NW swell. It's a tubular A-frame with long rights and a quick, hollow left. Anegada is completely different from all the other BVIs in that its highest point is only 10m above sea level. The whole island looks just like a giant beach but it's actually a raised reef. It's wild coast is popular with divers and fishermen.

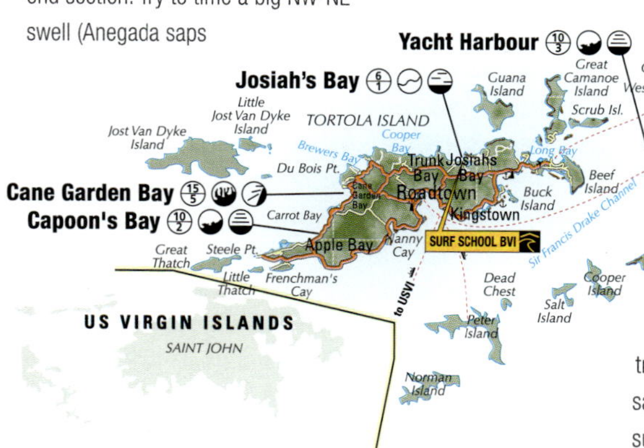

ALEX DICK-READ

Capoon's Bay

## TRAVEL INFORMATION

**Weather** – Constant trade breezes temper humid summer temperatures around 30°C (86°F); winter is slightly cooler. Average water temperatures remain around 26°C (79°F) year-round. Total rainfall is quite low (<5d/month). BVI is in the hurricane zone; watch out between June and November. Post Christmas is the ideal time to visit.

**Lodging and Food** – The BVI is not a cheap destination: food is pricey and accommodation is in short supply. Most visitors sleep on their chartered yachts and on land the only budget options since Hurricane Irma are AirBnB-type rentals. Starting at around $110/dble in season, Sebastian's is a middle price hotel and is right on the beach in Little Apple Bay. The Tamarind Club is a similar price, in Josiah's Bay.

**Nature and Culture** – Cruise the islands on a yacht or using local ferries, depending on your budget. Top diving spots include the sunken RMS Rhone, off Salt Island, and Horseshoe Reef (Anegada). Good snorkelling in Smugglers Cove and Brewer's Bay. Check out the Baths on Virgin Gorda, a network of giant granite boulders and take a paddle around the mangroves on Beef Island or hike in the hills with GroundSea Adventures.

**Hazards and Hassles** – Minor threats include sunburn, fire coral, urchins and jellyfish. Sharks abound but risks are low. Locals are friendly, but need to be respected. Hurricane Irma decimated the whole BVI so, as of publication time, many of the old established places and activities of note might or might not return as the islands recover.

**Handy Hints** – Take usual shortboard and step-up or longboard. Breeze Paddleboards is a small surf shop in Road Town and Surf School BVI in Josiah's Bay have a ton of boards and other gear to rent or buy. In West End, SUP rental company Island Surf&Sail also has some boards and veteran Huntington Beach/Cocoa Beach shaper and BVI resident, Bob Carson was still shaping up until Hurricane Irma struck. For lessons, head to Josiah's Bay where Surf School BVI's Steve Howes and Icah Wilmot are the hugely popular teachers/coaches.

**West End** is actually a great kite/windsurf spot, but if the wind drops or goes southeast, a long righthand pointbreak will reveal itself. It can either be a mellow, cruisey wave or turn heavy with huge rips and some big barrels bowl sections. Another option on the island is **Loblolly Bay**, which is usually onshore since it is exposed to east winds, but it picks up maximum swell. This spot is very remote and it's a long paddle from the beach to the peak. On a windless day, there's a long, relaxed left and a much more intense and hollow right. Sharky.

Peak surf season is between November and March, when winter lows leave the US East Coast, sending 2-15ft surf to the exposed shores. E windswell and the occasional hurricane swells will sometimes provide summertime surf on SE exposed shores for desperate locals, but long flat spells are way too common to plan a surf trip at this time of the year. The wind blows E year-round, with more NE winds between November and March, and more SE for the rest of the year. The tidal range hovers between 30-60cm max.

| STATISTICS | | J F | M A | M J | J A | S O | N D |
|---|---|---|---|---|---|---|---|
| SWELL | Direction | | | | | | |
| | Size (ft) | 4 | 3 | 1-2 | 2 | 3-4 | 4 |
| WIND | Direction | | | | | | |
| | Force | F4 | F4 | F4 | F4 | F4 | F4 |
| WATER | Wetsuit | | | | | | |
| | Temp/°C | 25 | 25 | 26 | 27 | 28 | 26 |
| WEATHER | Rainfall/mm | 40 | 60 | 85 | 85 | 110 | 100 |
| | days/mth | 4 | 3 | 4 | 5 | 5 | 6 |
| | Min temp/°C | 22 | 23 | 25 | 25 | 24 | 23 |
| | Max temp/°C | 28 | 29 | 30 | 31 | 30 | 29 |

# St Martin and St Barthélemy

**Together with Anguilla, St Martin and St Barthélemy sit right on the northeastern corner of the Caribbean islands. St Martin is the smallest island in the world to be shared by two sovereign governments, with French Saint Martin taking-up about two-thirds of the landmass to the north and Dutch Sint Maarten to the south. Good exposure to northern swells and a mixture of sand, rock and coral breaks make these islands a quality Caribbean surf trip, if you can afford it.**

+ GOOD REEFS AND POINTS
+ MANY SWELL/WIND COMBOS
+ SMALL-SIZED ISLANDS
+ UNCROWDED, FRIENDLY

- SHORT SWELL SEASON
- WIND SENSITIVE BREAKS
- FICKLE BEST BREAKS
- VERY EXPENSIVE

Just north of Marigot, the small mellow waves of **Friar's Bay** make it an ideal longboard spot. It breaks on a large flat shallow reef and will be best on N-NW swells. At the northern tip of the island, **Wilderness** is a classy right pointbreak that goes off with an overhead N swell and any S in the wind. Park at the rubbish dump, where there may be wind-blown peaks and walk the 1.5km path around the mountainous jungle backdrop. The popular Orient Beach is protected from the swell by a coral ridge, but jetskis can take you to surrounding breaks on the islands (Pinel, Tintemarre) outside the bay. **Le Galion** is paddle accessible, but the easy peaks will usually be blown-out by the trade winds. Across the bay, **The Bowl** is a premium right reefbreak with a sizeable E hurricane swell. Getting in and out is quite tricky and booties are required. **Guana Bay** is a mediocre beginners beachbreak where wind-blown straighthanders hit the sugary sands. **Mullet Bay** packs more punch, with hollow shoredump making it an ideal bodyboard wave on a big NW-N swell or rare SW-W hurricane swell. Another serious righthand reefbreak is **Cupecoy**; if it's big and coming from the NW, the wave will pitch a couple of barrelling sections before ending right on a cliff.

The exclusive French island of St Barthélémy has many coves and bays mostly protected by coral reefs. **Anse des Lézards** is a small swell, consistent reefbreak with very accessible lefts and the odd right on a N/NE swell. A mellow and occasionally very long left can be found at **Anse des Cayes**. There is also a hollow right with a sketchy, super-shallow coral reef ending. The decent rights and lefts in **St-Jean** suffer from both wind exposure and some badly placed coral heads. The cross/onshores attract wind/kitesurfers, who shred underneath the small planes that land at the adjacent airstrip. Lorient is St Barths' surfing hub, where members of the Reefer's Surf Club meet before or after a session at **The Ledge**, a shallow A-frame reef on larger N swells. Hot locals will also tackle the offshore rights of **Picket Fence**. It only breaks on the largest northerly swells and the very shallow end section over live coral reef, ensures few takers. The same conditions will produce awesome powerful rights on **Pointe Milou**, which is well-protected from the winds and a great spectating arena. The island of **La Tortue** hosts a great spot where the trades blow offshore, shaping nice walls which speed up as the wave peels over the reef. Inconsistent and a gruelling paddle against strong currents from the western tip of Grand Cul-de-Sac bay. **Toiny** faces SE, so summer/autumn hurricane swells or on big wrap-around swells from the NE. Produces fast barrels going both ways, a short gnarly right and a long, glorious walling left that are both hollow and shallow, so incoming tides best. There are further fickle reef peaks to the west at each end of Grand Fond and Washing Machine.

Late November until early April sees 2-10ft surf on the NE exposed shores with occasional 12ft faces at L'Orient. Otherwise, choppy windswell is all there is to ride on east-facing shores, but the reefs make the most of it. Occasional hurricane swells will provide summertime surf on the SE exposed shores. The wind is predominantly E year-round with more N winds between Nov and March. Surf early or right after a storm for glassy conditions. Minimal 0.3m tidal range.

Wilderness
SAINT-MARTIN (FRANCE)
Friar's Bay
Le Galion
The Bowl
Guana Bay
Cupecoy
Mullet Bay
SINT-MAARTEN (NETHERLANDS)

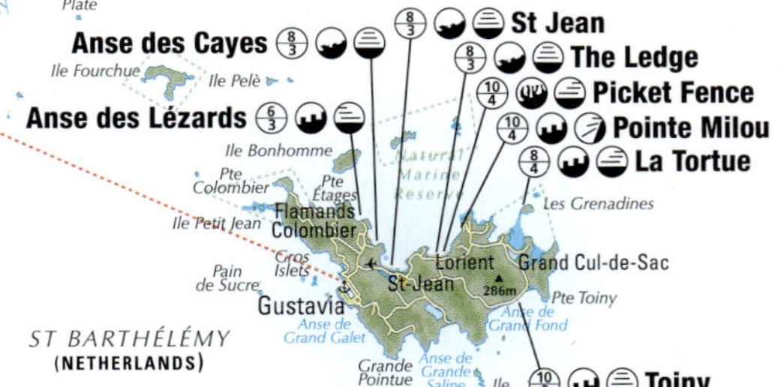


## TRAVEL INFORMATION

**Weather** – The tropical, dry climate keeps the temperature constant at 28°C (82°F) in winter and 30°C (86°F) in summer. Moist, Atlantic trade winds bring regular orographic rainfall to the lush eastern coast, leaving the western sides drier. Hurricane season, (July-Nov) brings extra precipitation and occasional damage to vegetation and buildings. Water temperature will range from 26°-30°C (79°-86°F).

**Lodging and Food** – St Martin is about big resorts and hotels while half the beds in St Barths are in privately owned villas and apartments. Moderate to very expensive – no budget options. In St Barths, the surf season is tourist season with top rates. Try La Plantation in St Martin (Orient Bay, fr$120), Maho Beach hotel in St Maarten ($240-$600) or Les Mouettes in St Barths (fr$155).

**Nature and Culture** – Naturalists will enjoy Eden Park and the Butter Fly Farm, naturists Orient Beach. There's great diving and fishing in St. Barths, but the accent is on civilised living like shopping and eating.

**Hazards and Hassles** – Some reefs are shallow and the coral is sharp – take booties. Respect the growing local populations and the strong sunshine.

**Handy Hints** – Rentals and lessons on St Martin at Le Galion (SXM), Orient Bay or check Soul Seeker Surf Shop. On St Barths there's Hookipa Surf Shop in Saint Jean and Totem Surf, in Gustavia. Each island has their own currency but US$ are accepted everywhere.

PIERRE CARREAU

Toiny

PIERRE CARREAU

The Ledge

| STATISTICS | | J F | M A | M J | J A | S O | N D |
|---|---|---|---|---|---|---|---|
| SWELL | Direction | | | | | | |
| | Size (ft) | 4 | 3 | 1-2 | 2 | 3-4 | 4 |
| WIND | Direction | | | | | | |
| | Force | F4 | F4 | F4 | F4 | F4 | F4 |
| WATER | Wetsuit | | | | | | |
| | Temp/°C | 25 | 25 | 26 | 28 | 28 | 26 |
| WEATHER | Rainfall/mm | 50 | 50 | 75 | 90 | 110 | 95 |
| | days/mth | 12 | 9 | 11 | 12 | 14 | 13 |
| | Min temp/°C | 23 | 24 | 25 | 25 | 25 | 24 |
| | Max temp/°C | 28 | 29 | 30 | 30 | 31 | 29 |

# Antigua

PUERTO RICO
ANTIGUA
TRINIDAD & TOBAGO

Antigua and Barbuda are located on the Leeward side of the Eastern Caribbean, ideally positioned in the NE corner of the island range. Mostly low-lying, the rocky coastlines of Antigua has numerous bays and inlets, some of which have been turned into harbours. The water offshore is shallow, reducing the impact of the swell and cutting the number of surfable spots down to around ten.

+ WINTER GROUNDSWELLS
+ UNCROWDED CONDITIONS
+ SAILORS PARADISE
+ DELUXE TOURISM SERVICES

– VERY INCONSISTENT
– SHALLOW CORAL REEFS
– LACK OF LAND ACCESS SPOTS
– UBER EXPENSIVE

Antigua has a greater density of spots. Just south of the beach resorts at Dickenson Bay and Runaway Bay is **Sand Haven** (also called Lashings). With a NW-NE swell running, a semi-consistent left and right reefbreak breaks near to the St. James Club. The beaches most convenient to St. John's are Fort James, a popular public beach, and Deep Bay but neither hold much shape or size. **Fort Barrington** is a left pointbreak that gets impressively long and ripable on the handful of good days a year. Visible in the distance is **Galley Bay**, the most consistent north side spot, where the outside lefts are stupidly shallow, breaking fast and hollow over staghorn coral. The series of four crescent beaches at **Hawksbill** have pretty disorganised surf and several reefs are exclusive to the hotels and therefore private. Offshore, Sandy Island can get all-time conditions but requires the fickle combination of good N swell and no wind, not to mention a boat to access the spot. Lefts wrap down the east side and the rights can be offshore in SE winds. On the south coast is **Fisher's Hill**, where rare lefts spin over shallow reef and it will be sideshore in NE winds. Land access is almost impossible, so take a boat and also check the outer reef of **Rendez-Vous Bay**. It's a a popular beach with messy shoredump for boogie boarding or bodysurfing when SE trades blow and there are some more shoreline reefs to the east. The best wave on the south coast is **Turtle Bay** near Proctor's Point, a scenic set up with a quality, long left reefbreak on S-SE swell. Gets hollow, racy sections over ridiculously shallow reef, attracting the local crew from English Harbour. **Half Moon Bay**'s reef off the northern headland is fairly consistent pulling in any E swell. A sucky take-off leads to some faster walls with a bit of speed and power and it can wrap into the bay and clean up a bit. Needs a bit of size to clear the reef and handles overhead swells.

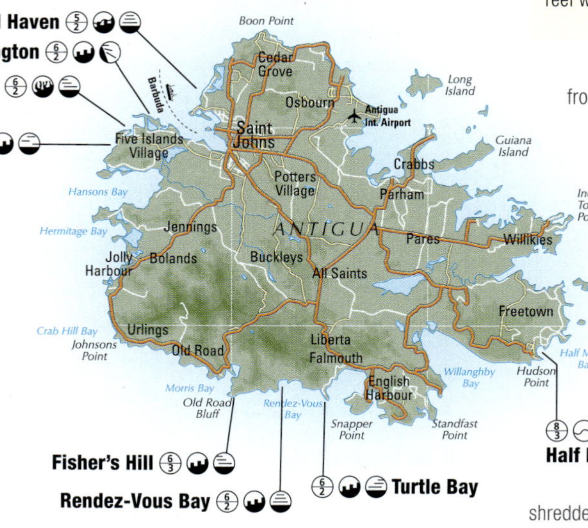


JIMMY WILSON

Galley Bay

Neighbouring Barbuda sits 40km north of Antigua and has a coastline of long pink and white sand beaches protected by barrier reefs. Unfortunately, the island took a direct hit from Hurricane Irma and 90% of the buildings were damaged along with all the island's infrastructure. The population was evacuated and the island remains eerily deserted with only a third of the 1800 population returning to rebuild. Surfwise, apart from some very rare waves on the west coast, Barbuda is not the best Caribbean surf destination for consistent waves. Spanish Point on the southeast tip of the island, is a barrier reef with sectioning lefts and some scruffy rights that need calm wind to break. A line of barrier reefs parallels the eastern shore, but they are usually shredded by onshores, unless it's a rare W or windless day.

A large underwater plateau between the two islands has a shadowing effect on most of the north Antigua spots and the swells lose a lot of energy and size. Bad winter storms and cold fronts will produce 3-6ft groundswell, but most surf is made up of 2-4ft windswell. Most of the consistent spots are onshore, breaking small on razor-sharp coral. The winds are NE almost all year, but during summer, SE trades blow. Good windswells are quite rare, the surf quality is often a choice between onshore mush over sand with a bit of size, and smaller side-shore walls over sketchy reef bottoms. Hurricane season (summer) can have epic days, lighting up dormant breaks. Tide changes are almost nil with 0.3m range max.

JIMMY WILSON

Fort Barrington

## TRAVEL INFORMATION

**Weather** – Antigua is drier than most other Caribbean Islands. Average daily temperature drops a few degrees in winter (Dec-Mar) from the usual high of around 30°C (86°F). Rainy season (mid Sept-Nov) is when daily showers can be expected. Hurricane season runs from June to Sept; keep an eye on the forecast during this period. Boardshorts only.

**Lodging and Food** – Mainly luxury self-contained hotels or all-inclusive resorts like Galley Bay start at $575/n. Beach hotels under $100 will be hard to find. $50 rooms at the Capuccino Lounge in St-Johns. Barbuda had high-end tourism but Hurricane Irma, the most powerful Atlantic storm ever, destroyed most buildings and infrastructure in Sept 2017.

**Nature and Culture** – English and Falmouth Harbours become lively from Dec to April, culminating in the Antigua Sailing Week, a world-class regatta since 1967. Calypso and Soca music are big. Barbuda is home to an abundance of birdlife and great snorkelling and scuba diving.

**Hazards and Hassles** – Reefs are shallow and dangerous with staghorn coral. Be careful when it's small. Many remote breaks can only be accessed by boat. Barbuda will take a long time to be rebuilt and cater for tourists again.

**Handy Hints** – Turtle Surf Shop sells accessories, boards and SUP board rentals are available. Kiteboarding is big on the enclosed waters of Nonsuch Bay. Take a strong board for small reef waves or fast beachbreaks.

| STATISTICS | | J F | M A | M J | J A | S O | N D |
|---|---|---|---|---|---|---|---|
| SWELL | Direction | | | | | | |
| | Size (ft) | 3-4 | 3 | 2 | 2-3 | 3-4 | 4 |
| WIND | Direction | | | | | | |
| | Force | F4 | F4 | F4 | F4 | F3-F4 | F4 |
| WATER | Wetsuit | | | | | | |
| | Temp/°C | 25 | 26 | 28 | 30 | 28 | 26 |
| WEATHER | Rainfall/mm | 64 | 64 | 101 | 126 | 150 | 125 |
| | days/mth | 9 | 8 | 9 | 12 | 12 | 13 |
| | Min temp/°C | 23 | 24 | 25 | 26 | 25 | 24 |
| | Max temp/°C | 28 | 29 | 30 | 31 | 30 | 29 |

# Grande Terre, Guadeloupe

**Guadeloupe consists of two main islands joined in the middle, which viewed from above, reveal a butterfly shape. It is a 'département' of France, with strong French-influenced culture, plus its own unique Creole style. It's one of the east Caribbean's most consistent surf destinations, receiving regular trade wind swell coupled with North Atlantic groundswell, producing small to moderate waves on all three coasts.**

+ SMALL, EASY WAVES
+ CONSISTENT SURF
+ ALTERNATIVE WATER SPORTS
+ LAID-BACK ATMOSPHERE

– SLOPPY ONSHORE WAVES
– SCHOOL CROWDS
– TOURIST DEVELOPMENT
– PRICEY

PIERRE DE CHAMPS

Anse Salabouelle

Grande Terre has the majority of the surf spots while Basse Terre only gets surf from S and W hurricane swells. There are also the exposed islands of Marie Galante and La Désirade offshore, which have good potential for explorers. On Grande Terre, **Le Moule** is the main surfers hangout. Facing NE, it has the best exposure to swell and is the most consistent wave around. Normally this reef works as a waist to headhigh onshore left with a juicy take-off and ripable vertical walls directly in front of the car park. Short, ultra-fast rights are possible off the peak and there's more waves on the adjacent Damencourt reefs. Not for beginners or improvers and there's a local pecking order. Difficult entry off the jetty when bigger and watch out for rocks and urchins. The expert only outside reef at **La Station** has critical take-offs into fast barrel sections on moderate N to E swells. Draws in plenty of swell and can have some scary sections. **Caille Dehors** bends a bit more on the inside allowing for more turns, but is challenging and shifty as the wave height moves into double figures. Off the beach at **Alizé** can be some easier, fun waves for all abilities. **Anse Salabouelle** (a la Bouelle) is a quality stretch of reef where snappy, hollow lefts share a channel with walled-up rolling rights that pick up all E swells. Hope for S winds and there will be barrels. Pulls a crowd with vibe when it is on, which is often. A keyhole leads to **Anse à la Gourde**'s structured rights off a protruding rock, that are fun when small, challenging when big. **Pointe des Chateaux** has messy onshore lefts that are suited to improvers. Summer SE swells will light up **La Chaise**, a fast left with a bit of E wind protection. **Port St-François** is generally an easy reef peak, but still shallow and urchin covered. Crowded **La Caravelle** in St Anne, has two consistent, shallow lefts (longer La Digue and short hollow La Table), plus a pushy right called Calif. The left at **Petit-Havre** is quality, attracting plenty of surfers from the capital, looking for short barrels, long slashable shoulders and some NE/E wind protection. There's wind and swell protection for beginners and kids at Hotel Novotel, while experts can search for some juice on Gosier Island. **Port-Louis** boasts the best wave on the island – a peak with long mellow rights and a shorter left, but needs a moderate N-NE groundswell. **Anse Bertrand** has a choice of walled-up, easy peaks. The area conceals some excellent reefs like Plombier, Anse Laborde or Pointe d'Antigues, all of which break rarely, get crowded and are for experts only.

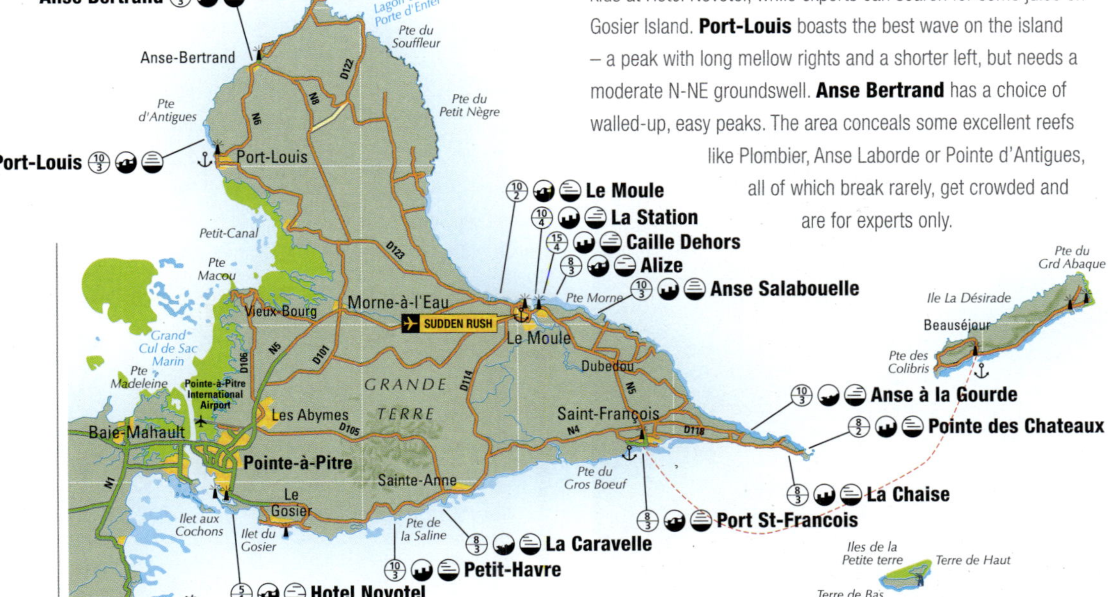


## TRAVEL INFORMATION

**Weather** – Like most tropical islands, the climate varies according to exposure to the trades. Grande Terre is the windward side of Guadeloupe, but being mainly flat it doesn't attract many rain squalls from out at sea. Most of the rain falls over higher Basse Terre. The wettest season starts in June and sometimes lasts until December, with heaviest rains possible during the hurricane season of June-October. Temperatures remain around 26°C (79°F) all year with little variation.

**Lodging and Food** – If you can't stay in Le Moule, try St. François. Freddo Surf Camp from $340/wk. Most of the hotels are on the south shore, costing anything from $32-245/n. Renting a flat can be much cheaper (Airbnb from $40/n). Creole cuisine is very tasty - try ti-punch, the local drink of rum, lime and cane syrup. A meal will cost around $20.

**Nature and Culture** – Apart from visiting spice markets or sailing, Basse Terre offers enjoyable trekking around La Soufrière volcano. Diving is best at Îlets Pigeon, on the Carib side. There are mangrove swamps between the two islands.

**Hazards and Hassles** – Many of the spots break on limestone or coral, often in shallow water, so watch out for reef cuts. Some spots have many urchins. Avoid hurricane season because Guadeloupe is right in their paths and the surf is usually small at this time of year.

**Handy Hints** – Gear is expensive but available at Gwada Surf Shop (Le Moule) and Surf Rider, (Saint-François). Two surf schools in Le Moule. Most surfers are local Guadeloupe and French expats or tourists. There are lots of bodyboarders. French is the official language though most locals speak Creole.

DAMIEN POULLENOT

Port-Louis

The main swell season is from late October to March, with 2-10ft N-NE groundswells mixed with consistent 2-5ft E wind swells. Onshore trade wind swell occurs year-round, but it will usually be small. Dominant E trades vary from 44% of the time in November to 70% in July. It tends to have a slightly more frequent NE pattern than SE, except during May-June and Sept-Oct. This is unfortunate as SE winds produce more offshores on Grande Terre. The hurricane season (June-Oct) offers a better chance to surf spots exposed to the Caribbean Sea, but at this time of year there is no regular groundswell. Maximum tidal variation is 0.5m.

| STATISTICS | | J F | M A | M J | J A | S O | N D |
|---|---|---|---|---|---|---|---|
| SWELL | Direction | | | | | | |
| | Size (ft) | 4 | 3 | 1-2 | 2 | 3-4 | 4 |
| WIND | Direction | | | | | | |
| | Force | F4 | F4 | F4 | F4 | F4 | F4 |
| WATER | Wetsuit | | | | | | |
| | Temp/°C | 25 | 25 | 27 | 28 | 28 | 26 |
| WEATHER | Rainfall/mm | 75 | 95 | 152 | 197 | 245 | 175 |
| | days/mth | 13 | 11 | 14 | 17 | 18 | 17 |
| | Min temp/°C | 19 | 20 | 22 | 23 | 22 | 20 |
| | Max temp/°C | 28 | 29 | 30 | 31 | 31 | 30 |

# Martinique FRANCE

PUERTO RICO
MARTINIQUE
TRINIDAD & TOBAGO

Martinique lies in the heart of the Lesser Antilles, or Windward Islands and is dominated by the peaks of the Carbet and the Mont Pelée dormant volcanoes. The southern shores are highly regarded by tourists seeking picture perfect beaches, leaving surfers to focus on the northern and eastern coastline, ideally exposed to winter's North Atlantic swell. Volcanic and coral reefs pepper the island plus the southern beaches provide a summer swell bodyboard option.

- \+ GOOD RIGHT REEF SET-UPS
- \+ CONSISTENT TARTANE SPOTS
- \+ LOW TIDAL INFLUENCE
- \+ SAFE TOURIST HAVEN

- – SEASONAL NORTH SWELL
- – ONSHORE TRADE WINDS
- – SHARP SHALLOW REEFS
- – SOME CROWDED SPOTS

## TRAVEL INFORMATION

**Weather** – Jan to June are the cooler and drier months (carême), and the wet season runs from July to Dec (hivernage). The southern area of the island tends to be drier. Daytime temperatures can reach 30°C (86°F) and there's only about a 5°C (9°F) difference between summer and winter temperatures. Two regular, alternating wind directions from NE and ESE.

**Lodging and Food** – Accommodation options range from large hotels to family-run "Relais Créoles," or "Gîtes de France", usually studios in private homes. Around Tartane, try Résidence Océane (fr $90/n), L'hôtel La Caravelle ($90/dble) or Bliss from $325/wk. Sample Martinique's culinary magic, a marriage of French and Creole cuisines.

**Nature and Culture** – Hiking, diving and mountain biking are great. A wealth of sightseeing: white sand beaches, tropical rainforest, floral gardens and the majestic Mount Pelee. Sample product at rum distilleries before dancing to Biguine and Zouk.

**Hazards and Hassles** – Spots around Tartane can get crowded, but it's easy to move to less popular spots. Stay clear of the poisonous manchineel trees that border some beaches; they are sometimes marked with red paint. Martinique has the best medical care in the Eastern Caribbean.

**Handy Hints** – Surfing equipment at Itacaré Surfshop. Reef boots are advisable. Bliss surf school located on Plage des Surfeurs, offers surf lessons (group $36/1.5h) and board rentals ($30/d; $120/w).

DAMIEN POULLENOT
Pelle à Tarte

**Tomate** has long predictable right walls for honing turns and it's always offshore over the intermediate-friendly rock and sand reef/point. Needs a sizeable N swell, just like **Céron**, which is a bit shorter, but packs more punch as it ends in a shorebreak on a beautiful black sand beach. Both are good waves, but mere shadows of neighbouring **Anse Couleuvre**, possibly the best wave on the island. These long, tubular rights start with an easy take-off, but the walls are fast and powerful, before the wave ends over coral and urchins. Skills are required to ride this inconsistent, wind-protected beauty. Not a place to hassle for waves, despite Couleuvre meaning snake! Grand-Rivière hosts two quality breaks. **Bagasse**'s powerful, barrelling rights and lefts will attract tube seekers while **Charlot** reefbreaks will cater to those looking for longer rides. Charlot's reefbreaks are powerful, sucky affairs and some longer rights are possible, but only experienced surfers should make the long paddle from the harbour against the sweep. The rights of **Basse-Pointe** break directly into the port and getting in is tricky. Consistently has long workable walls in NE swells, but rarely gets the SW offshores to be clean. **Le Lorrain** is perfect for beginner/improver surfers as it's a mellow beachbreak with no hazards away from any crowds. **Charpencaye** is Anse Charpentier's right reefbreak. The take-off is straight into a tube section, followed by a fast, peeling wall that ends on an urchin-covered reef ledge. Tricky in and out requires a bit of reef dancing and that the strong currents have led to a complete ban on swimming at the beachbreak on the other side of the wild bay. The best concentration of consistent spots is found on the Caravelle peninsula that juts into the Atlantic near La Trinité. Anse l'Etang Bay has a number of spots including easy rights at WF (camping), the fast-peeling Entre-deux lefts in the middle, plus **Cocoa**, a technically challenging fast and powerful, big swell left. Anse Bonneville hosts the **Plage des Surfeurs**, the most consistent (although often messy) and best known spot on the island. After paddling around a large coral patch, mellow rights and lefts can be surfed, with some longer rides possible on the rights. A surf school takes advantage of the smaller inside wave. Out on the point, Roukoukou is a sucky, barreling left and right that handles swell, but not wind. **Pelle à Tarte** is a short walk or a 15min paddle from there. This wave is much more shallow and powerful with a hollow but makeable right and a death defying left that only a few bodyboarders dare tackle. On the south shore of the island, the reefbreaks give way to a string of beachbreaks that tend to close-out quickly and therefore only attract bodyboarders looking for launch ramps. The road to **Anse Trabaud** crosses private property and the owner charges $2.50 for the privilege. The wave is a shorebreak on the left side of the beach. There's also a reef outside, but it's an exhausting paddle and rarely worth it. Around Le Diamant a few regulars take on violent shorebreaks such as **Diams** or Banzaï. **Anse Cafard** is just more of the same stuff and should only appeal to bodyboarders.

The main swell season is from November to March, with 3-10ft N-NE North Atlantic groundswells. Constant 2-5ft E windswells occur year-round, so surfing small sloppy waves is always an option around the Caravelle peninsula. The highly unpredictable hurricane season can bring some of the largest swell of the year between July and September. Dominant E trade winds vary from 44% (Nov) to 70% (Jul), blowing more NE than SE. Max 0.8m tides.

DAMIEN POULLENOT
Basse-Pointe

| STATISTICS | | J F | M A | M J | J A | S O | N D |
|---|---|---|---|---|---|---|---|
| SWELL | Direction | | | | | | |
| | Size (ft) | 4 | 3 | 1-2 | 2 | 3-4 | 4 |
| WIND | Direction | | | | | | |
| | Force | F4 | F4 | F4 | F4 | F4 | F4 |
| WATER | Wetsuit | | | | | | |
| | Temp/°C | 25 | 25 | 26 | 28 | 28 | 26 |
| WEATHER | Rainfall/mm | 95 | 80 | 160 | 240 | 240 | 170 |
| | days/mth | 15 | 12 | 17 | 22 | 19 | 18 |
| | Min temp/°C | 21 | 22 | 23 | 24 | 24 | 23 |
| | Max temp/°C | 27 | 28 | 29 | 29 | 30 | 29 |

# Trinidad and Tobago

Located only 7km from the South American continent, Trinidad's convoluted north coast presents beachbreaks, reefbreaks and a huge amount of unexplored coastline stretching east from Port-Of-Spain. Two thirds of Tobago is volcanic and mountainous, cloaked in tropical rainforest, while the flatter, drier southwest coast is where all the surf spots are located, including Mount Irvine, generally considered one of the best waves in the Caribbean.

+ MAGIC MOUNT IRVINE
+ SPOT DENSITY ON TOBAGO
+ CHEAP, EXCELLENT FOOD
+ CRAZIEST CARNIVAL

- INCONSISTENT LARGER SWELLS
- STRONG LOCALISM
- LONG DRIVES TO TRINIDAD SURF
- THIEVERY/POLICE ROADBLOCKS

BABY MARMOOTTE

Mount Irvine

The crescent bay of **Las Cuevas** holds hollow, fast beachbreak peaks in N to E swells, is always better at mid to high tide and bigger at the western end. Further west is Tyrico Bay with gentle peelers for beginners. **Blanchisseuse** is a nice sandy beach with some rocks on its eastern side and the best peaks usually at the western end, but there can be some very strong rips requiring strength and endurance. The trade wind and swell-protected bay and rivermouth of **Grande Rivière** is the place to head in huge swells when the rest of the north coast is maxed-out. Nice clean peaks over rocks at the eastern side, but it is often crowded, small and the adjacent beachbreak is bigger. Another good bigger swell reefbreak can be found back at Matelot. **Sans Souci** sandbars develop on either side of the bay depending on the currents and when the left is working, it is usually the best. Takes N round to E swells at 2-15ft and is excellent during hurricane season when it gets huge, clean and hollow. To the right of the main jetty in front of the fishing depot, **Toco** is a super-hollow right that breaks only in a N swell. It's very inconsistent and the locals are all over it when it does break – surf elsewhere. **Salybia** is the only real barrier reefbreak on the island a short distance from the Toco lighthouse. It's a bit of a paddle to the outer reef where hollow, sectioning lefts and rights break best at low to mid tide on N–NE swells in the winter months. Down the beach from **Balandra** fishing depot is an exposed, powerful, ultra-consistent, all tides beachbreak. Nearby Saline Bay has an inner reef and an outer island break with N wind protection. On Tobago, **Mount Irvine** is a fast, racy wall with pits to park in and lips to float as it peels down the colourful live coral platform. N-NE swells from Nov-April are the key, it's usually offshore all-day and will be better at mid to high tides. There's also a left further down the reef on the biggest swells. Crowds get thick when it's on, parking is scarce, the paddle is long and the locals expect to dominate the peak. Dead flat in summer. Walk about a mile up the beach from Store Bay to access **Sunset Left**, a reef that's a short paddle off the private Pigeon Point area. It gets nice and hollow, and works well with a 3-6ft N–NE swell. It is a good alternative when Mount Irvine is packed and breaks in similar conditions. Half way along the beach towards Sunset Left is **Sunset Rights**, a very shallow, hollow righthander, especially at low tide. It rarely gets above headhigh and only works when Mount Irvine and Sunset Left are breaking huge. Very inconsistent, but very good. Predictably located right at the end of the runway, **Airports** is a hollow, punchy righthander. It works during wintertime, from 4-6ft and is best at low tide. Big swell spot that's not as rare as Sunset Right, but not as consistent as Mount Irvine. **Crazy's** is the only break on the east coast of the island, located north of Scarborough, in Goldsborough Bay. Very poor quality, desperation wave working in junky E windswells only. Never reaches headhigh, consistently bad.



Dec to April, NE trades drive windswell in the 4-8ft range and longer period (12-15sec), 4 to 6ft N-NE groundswells. June to Oct relies on smaller NE-SE trade wind swells or large (12-30ft), long period (15sec) hurricane swells, creating the best surfing conditions of the year. Winds are generally due E, ranging from 25-45km/h, often lighter and more variable in the wet season. The tidal range is 0.3-1.2m and a rising tide can increase the size of the surf at some spots.

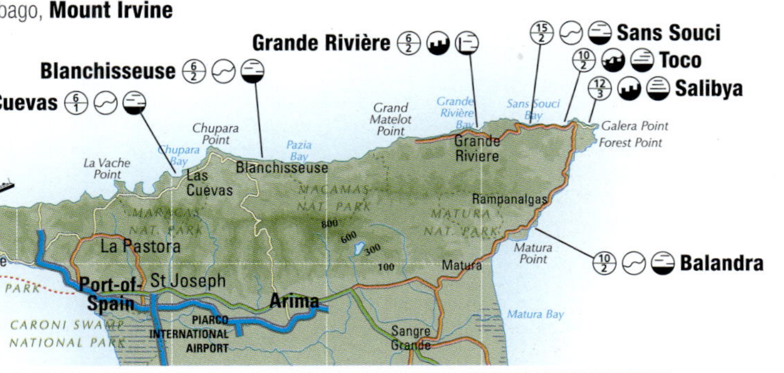


## TRAVEL INFORMATION

**Weather** – The climate of both islands is warm and humid, with the dry season running from Nov to April, and the wet season from May until October. Hurricanes generally track to the north of Trinidad, generating significant swell without the carnage. Dry season winds can see 37km/h averages for weeks on end.

**Lodging and Food** – Guest houses in Grande Rivière (Mt. Plaisir) or Toco (Patrice Bravo). Staying in Trinidad hotels entails very long drives. Most hotels in Tobago are scattered around Mt Irvine and Pigeon Point. Tasty inexpensive curry, rotis or shark 'n' bakes.

**Nature and Culture** – Bird or turtle watching, diving (Speyside), snorkelling and mountain biking tours. Birth place of Soca music and the famous February Trinidad Carnival.

**Hazards and Hassles** – Expect violence for a lack of respect towards the locals at breaks like Mount Irvine. Car-jacking banditos and theft is a possibility. Be watchful for poisonous snakes and giant centipedes.

**Handy Hints** – Take mosquito repellent, long-sleeve rash vest and a light-weight springsuit for dawn patrols. Alan Davis shapes and repairs boards in Cascade, Trinidad. Rent boards from the locals like Cool Runnings at Mount Irvine beach.

SIMON MCCOMB

Sunset Right

| STATISTICS | | J F | M A | M J | J A | S O | N D |
|---|---|---|---|---|---|---|---|
| SWELL | Direction | | | | | | |
| | Size (ft) | 3-4 | 2-3 | 1 | 1-2 | 3 | 3-4 |
| WIND | Direction | | | | | | |
| | Force | F4 | F4 | F4 | F3-F4 | F3-F4 | F3-F4 |
| WATER | Wetsuit | | | | | | |
| | Temp/°C | 26 | 26 | 27 | 28 | 28 | 27 |
| WEATHER | Rainfall/mm | 55 | 50 | 147 | 232 | 181 | 154 |
| | days/mth | 12 | 9 | 15 | 22 | 18 | 17 |
| | Min temp/°C | 20 | 20 | 22 | 22 | 22 | 21 |
| | Max temp/°C | 31 | 32 | 32 | 31 | 32 | 32 |

# Barbados

Barbados belongs to the Windward Islands, sitting east of the main Caribbean chain in solitary isolation. Famous for its holiday resorts, clear blue water and white sand beaches, it also has the eastern Caribbean's most consistent surf. Strong, constant trade winds whip up year-round swell on the windward coast, while in winter, regular N-NE groundswells will bring challenging waves to the iconic east coast break Soup Bowls as well as lighting up the north and west coasts. The south coast also has a cluster of breaks working on multi-directional swells, as they sweep around the tear-drop shaped island. Barbados offers some heavy waves and fun waves in equal measure, catering for all abilities on this friendly, laid-back rock.

+ CONSISTENT SWELLS
+ FUN, PUNCHY WAVES
+ VARIETY OF SPOTS
+ PERFECT CLIMATE

– CONSTANT TRADE WINDS
– RARITY OF BIG SWELLS
– CROWDED
– RELATIVELY EXPENSIVE

## TRAVEL INFORMATION

**Weather** – Known as "Little England", Barbados is blessed with a near perfect climate. The island receives 3000hrs of sunshine a year and 1500mm (60in) of rain, and the constant trade winds help to keep the humidity and heat at bearable levels. The wettest season is from July-November when tropical fronts pass over the region. The wind is lightest at this time of year. February-May is the driest and windiest period. Hurricanes tend to pass further to the north. In the water, boardshorts and a rash vest suffice for most of the year, although early morning sessions in the winter may call for a shorty.

**Lodging and Food** – Peak tourist season is Dec to March, when prices shoot up. Pay around $50/dble in a local guest-house. On the south coast try Zed's Surfer's Point Guesthouse at $100-180/n per studio. Near Soup Bowl, stay at Sea-U Guesthouse (fr $95) or Atlantis do a surf package fr $320/dbl. Surfholidays have multiple options across the island. Great spicy food with plenty of fish. A meal usually costs around $15 including beer or rum.

**Nature and Culture** – Stopping at small rum shops and village stores is the best way to meet the warm, friendly local people. There is good diving and snorkelling on the west coast and wind/kite surfing on the SE tip of the island. Organised tourist excursions include the Jolly Roger pirate ship or Sam Lord's coral castle. Try Harbour Lights or The Boatyard for a good night out. In some night spots a $15 cover charge includes free drinks.

**Hazards and Hassles** – The onshore winds on the E coast are the biggest nightmare and there can be intense rips north of Bathsheba. Take precautions against the strong sun, mosquitoes and reef cuts. The popular surf spots get busy, but usually the atmosphere is cool as long as you're respectful. Drugs are frowned upon by the general community despite extensive use. Police will not hesitate to lock up tourists. Crack problems contradict the generally safe, easy-going reputation of the island, leading to robberies and occasionally violence.

**Handy Hints** – It's very easy to rent gear at Zed's (Inch Marlowe) or Dead or Dread Surf Shop in Bridgetown. Many surf schools and tours available like surfbarbados.com. Barbados line-ups are full of U.K. and East Coast American surfers. Take a semi-gun for the bigger days in winter. Immigration will be particularly slow unless you have the name of a guest house or hotel where you are intending to stay.

TOM CAREY

Parlours

JIMMY WILSON

**Sandbank** (aka Cattlewash), is usually messy beachbreak, strafed by rips and currents, so it's better suited to experienced surfers who will get the best from the dumpy close-outs and onshore slop. Bathsheba, halfway up the east coast, is home to **Soup Bowls**, the island's most famous break. Clever observers may spot the peak just south at High Rock, offering an empty alternative with chambered rights and walled lefts heading down to Parlours. It's only a 300m paddle down to **Parlours**, an expanse of peaking right and left runners that seem to improve as the swell builds. Less power and intensity than Soup Bowls and almost as reliable, just without the hassling for set waves. The scatter gun line-up keeps crowds low and paddling high, especially at double-overhead. **Tent Bay**, a powerful left, walls up and spins down the reef on a straight N swell. Never crowded because somewhere else is usually better. Breaks outside the deep water anchorage in front of the rebuilt Atlantis Hotel. Beneath the lighthouse at **Ragged Point**, a powerful, mid to high tide shorey hits the rocky shoreline when the swell is E-SE. Any N in the swell will mean plenty of close-outs, but the cliffy headlands help with the wind and it consistently picks up all available energy. Dangerous cliff path access and lots of rocks around. **Long Beach** is a dumpy, erratic beachbreak facing SE that is a favourite with bodyboarders as it sometimes holds banging barrels close to shore. Early mornings on a clean, small to moderate SE swell will look good from the cliffs. Access is free and easy from the Foul Bay parking, while exclusive Crane Bay to the north requires payment and is usually smaller. **Surfers Point** can be a fun left set-up with cruisey shoulders bending into the bay and providing a bit of protection from the nor'easters. There are some rights too, with the emphasis on fun, easy rides, breaking over a dead coral platform that is fairly benign. **Silver Sands** holds peaks over a beach/reef combo that sucks in SE swell and produces some hollow rights. It's short and dumpy and often crowded. NE wind is cross-shore so the wind and kite crew will be around, along with some protective locals. At the bottom tip of the island, **South Point** offers long lefts over a live coral reef in front of the lighthouse. Breaks up into sections that may link up when big enough, the theme is long, fast left walls with cover-ups or shorter, bowly rights that catch the wind a bit more. Prefers mid to high tide, when it gets a bad backwash. Lots of urchins and local surfers who have the place wired. **Freights** probably has the best lefts on the south coast, but it rarely lines-up, since a big S swell is required. Long, fast and hollow when on, there are three defined sections starting at the cliffs on the point, where feathered walls flow into the central reef barrels and if you are lucky, more bowls through the inside. Has many moods when small with plenty of shorter rights and lazy, longboard shoulders that make this a useful beginner spot. Access down the cliffs is sketchy and if it is working properly everyone will be on it. Close to Bridgetown is **Brandons**, a sandy reef peak that only works on big hurricane or SE windswells and is offshore in NE trades. Mainly groomed, speedy lefts with the odd tuck section, or fleeting, rounder rights. It gets crowded in winter and is dominated by town locals who love the place. Sloppy and beginner-friendly in summer.

Duppies
Maycocks
Tropicana
Sandy Lane
Batts Rock
Brandons
Freights
South Point
Silver Sands
Surfers Point
Long Beach
Ragged Point
Sandbank
Soup Bowls
Parlours
Tent Bay

### Soup Bowls

**LAT. 13.215318° LONG. -59.521318°**

Famous east coast right, full of power and intensity. Vertical drops, thick bowls and big shut down sections that even work in the regular onshore trade winds. Kelly Slater puts Soup Bowls in his "top three waves in the world" thanks to its "really good curve that allows all sorts of manoeuvres and airs". Winter N swells bring the heavy "Bowls", while a SE direction may provide the fun "Soup" part of the name, while still holding excellent shape. No matter what direction, this is a wave of consequence as it shifts up the size scale. Some days you do need to be Slater to get a set off the dialled-in local crew, but there's rarely a flat day and average midweek crowds will often be mellow. Another unavoidable constant is the army of urchins on the inside along with the omnipresent NE-E trade winds.

The west coast only breaks on the biggest N swells so it's the least consistent part of the island, but the E trade winds will provide the cleanest conditions. The most consistent spot is **Batts Rock**, a perfect A-frame peak that is well-known among Bridgetown locals and like most west coast spots, five guys is a crowd. Powerful, hollow fast lefts are common. **Sandy Lane**, mid-way down the island, is a short, perfect left, but it's either fantastic, or totally flat. Backwash airs are all the rage over this sharp, shallow reef. Lowest consistency around, meaning the locals will be out in force when it finally breaks. Speedy left barrels over urchin-covered, fire coral reef makes **Tropicana** a treacherous left for experts only, who usually choose high tide for their tube time. There are more challenging reefs up towards Speightstown like Fort and Sandridge. The long, tapering shoulders of **Maycocks** are a fun alternative to Duppies and will always be smaller and more manageable on a wrapping N swell. Low to mid tide is preferred and the trades are always offshore. Handles the biggest swells on an outside section that keeps the chargers happy. Set in beautiful scenery, but difficult to find without directions. On the NW tip of the island is **Duppies**, a consistent, powerful right that suffers from strong currents. Probably the best wave on the island after Soup Bowls, it is not for the faint-hearted. It breaks some distance offshore, is reputed to be sharky (no attacks in 100 years!) and the name refers to malevolent spirits and ghosts, so the vibe is heavy. Cliffs mean getting caught in the north to south current is a scary proposition.

The best season for groundswells is from late Oct to March, when 2-12ft N-NE swells wrap around the northern tip of the island to produce clean 1-10ft waves on the west coast and bigger onshore waves on the east coast. The other main swell source is the E wind, which consistently kicks up 2-5ft swells. Sometimes they get big enough to wrap onto the S coast where they clean up dramatically. This wind occurs year-round so you're likely to find a rideable wave most days. Barbados rarely gets hit by major hurricanes (avg every 72yrs), but their swell often reaches the east coast and when they're big, can light up the west and south coast as well. From June to October, it's mainly flat on the south coast. The prevailing wind comes from between the NE-SE for 50-70% of the time. NE is more common than SE, except in the summer months. Throughout the year the mornings will often be glassy with residual wind swell offering superb conditions. Despite small tidal variations (1m max), most of the best surf occurs at low tide, especially on the south coast.

ROGER SHARP

South Point

JS CALLAHAN/SURFEXPLORE

Tropicana

| STATISTICS | | J F | M A | M J | J A | S O | N D |
|---|---|---|---|---|---|---|---|
| SWELL | Direction | | | | | | |
| | Size (ft) | 4-5 | 3-4 | 2-3 | 2-3 | 4 | 4-5 |
| WIND | Direction | | | | | | |
| | Force | F4 | F4 | F4 | F4 | F3-F4 | F4 |
| WATER | Wetsuit | | | | | | |
| | Temp/°C | 25 | 26 | 27 | 28 | 27 | 26 |
| WEATHER | Rainfall/mm | 47 | 34 | 85 | 147 | 174 | 150 |
| | days/mth | 10 | 8 | 12 | 17 | 15 | 15 |
| | Min temp/°C | 21 | 21 | 23 | 23 | 23 | 22 |
| | Max temp/°C | 28 | 30 | 31 | 31 | 31 | 29 |

# SOUTH AMERICA

Some of the finest Pacific surf real estate on the planet can be found snaking down the western shoulder of South America, sandwiched between the lofty spine of the Andes and the limitless blue fetch of the South Pacific. Curving to face the onslaught of SW Antarctic swell, this arid, long coastline has been shaped by a generous, goofy-footed god, who created an abundance of over-long, leg-shattering left pointbreaks. The chilly Humboldt Current acts as a swell super-highway, bringing year-round waves, topped up by North Pacific vagabond pulses.

More cold water, stormy waves stalk the southern Atlantic side of the continent, before giving way to warmer tropical waters and a carnival of beachbreaks, ready to party when either a local windswell or a well-travelled groundswell arrives from either hemisphere. The cherry on top is the seasonal offering for Caribbean coastlines, adding extra flavour to South America's already tasty feast of waves.

Chicama, La Libertad, Peru

# The Surf

Ecuador

## THE CARIBBEAN SEA

Opening the South American chapter with the island zone of **Isla Margarita and Sucre** brings the final leap from the Caribbean islands to the continental landmass. **Venezuela** suffers from a due north aspect with filtered swell and is not the most promising of South American destinations. Recent political and civil upheaval doesn't help, but if you are looking for waves between Sucre and the **Caracas** zone, then avoid the mainland coast and stay offshore looking at outside reefs on the Archipielago de Los Roques. The windward beaches on Bonaire, Curacao and especially Aruba have some established spots and a local crew to ride them in any E windswells. Hurricane swell transforms these islands, but it is usually only the wind crew who are having fun. The remote arid coast of **Colombia** on the Guajira Peninsula is smattered with shipwrecks which is usually a good sign for swell, but more an indicator of the strong winds that buffet this coast down to the **Caribbean Colombia** zone where the Andes meet the sea.

## THE PACIFIC OCEAN

The thick jungle north of the **Pacific Colombia** zone is a notoriously lawless region which will have some waves towards the Panama border, but it'll be better and safer further south. Muddy rivermouths slice through the steamy jungle all the way down to Ecuador, leaving plenty of exploration opportunities for those with a seaworthy lancha and strong anti-malarials.

Over the border into **Ecuador** starts off with unpromising, NW-facing hard-packed beaches and silted bocanas (rivermouths), but quickly improves from the city of Esmereldas into the **Northern Ecuador** zone. Playas and puntas offer something for everyone, although the wait for a decent swell can be long. The Panama Current keeps the water warm and the balmy beach parties going through the holiday seasons, especially in **Southern Ecuador** surf towns like Montañita and Playas. 900km due west, the **Galapagos Islands** sit in splendid isolation, offering unique wildlife and waves on the two main surfing islands of **San Cristóbal and Santa Cruz** while keeping other islands off limits from tourism including surfing.

Northern **Peru** is well-known for its speed barrels around Mancora, courtesy of North Pacific, mid-winter swells when the rest of Peru is in the grip of summer swell patterns. There are however, more waves to the north in the **Tumbes** region, a warm sub-tropical zone cloaked in equatorial rainforest and mangroves, contained within a number of sanctuaries and national parks. Anomalous with the rest of the Peruvian coastal landscape, the waves are also weird, with wide, open beachbreaks receiving NW-N swells from December to March. Major fishing towns on the mangrove estuaries like Puerto Pizarro are no good, but further south there are some swell magnet spots like south of the piers in La Cruz and Zorritos, or the bigger rivermouths like Bocapan. There is still a propensity for lefts, wrapping around sandy curves rather than headlands and the most crowded spot will be Punta Mero, where rocks help hold the shape. The road parallels the beach at Cancas, allowing an easy surf check of the occasionally perfect reefs and semi-point bends in the coast north of the pier. Exclusive houses and hotels line the beach at Punta Sal where a left runs down the headland, but it is inconsistent and a good locale for alternative ocean sports. Mancora is the best place to stay and explore Tumbes, or head south to the famous spots like Cabo Blanco in the **Northern Piura** surf zone. **Southern Piura** begins the arid, isolated trend that recurs all the way down the west coast of the continent through Chile and offers crowd-free left points like Nonura for those willing to take on the harsh transport and living conditions the Sechura Desert creates. Bayovar is a real outpost, sandwiched between the warm northern barrels and the long, cold left points that begin in **Lambayeque** region and keep going through **La Libertad** where the world's first nationally protected surf break resides at Chicama. Some rate Pacasmayo as even longer in the makeable, single ride category and there are a handful more, ridiculously long points to choose from as you head south into the cliffs and islands of **Ancash**. This region is often by-passed by the hordes heading north to shang-ri-left and can be a quiet retreat for those looking for a few rights. **Lima** is the bustling, growing capital that could be the continent's ideal surf city, blessed with a range of waves from rolly beachbreaks to terrifying tow-ins and just about everything in-between. This includes the urban beaches of the **Costa Verde**, which have been surfed since 1939 and **Punta Hermosa**, a concentrated wave-park just south of the city. Empty and clean it isn't, so the crowd and pollution averse need to blow off San Bartolo and Miraflores to explore the points of **Southern Lima and Ica**, including Cerro Azul and San Gallen, a rare righthander of top quality. The **Arequipa** region has some spots worth checking around Chira, Camana and Quilca, where the heavy beachbreak wedges at the south end of San Malloy work nicely before the wind gets up. The **Moquegua** and **Tacna** regions are covered in the **Southern Peru** zone which extends down to the Chilean border, offering a more size, less people equation.

Since the advent of the barrel-rich *Rip Curl Search* pro surfing contest at **Arica** in 2007, more people are aware that **Chile** has some quality waves. El Gringo and El Buey burst onto the scene, from a tight urban surf zone in an industrialised northern city that already has a healthy surfing population. Wander south out of town into the **Tarapaca** region and a blank 180km canvas of gnarled, eroded cliffs dip their toes in the cool current, broken by the occasional alluvial plain of dark desert sand deposited by a canyon carving river. Checking these rivermouths may uncover some thumping beachbreaks at Caleta Camarones, Caleta Chica and near the rocky bays of

Peru

Pisagua. There are some good short slabs and rocky pocket beaches that fire on just the right conditions, but to find them would take luck and lots of time, better spent elsewhere. There is barely a break in the bristling desert cliffs before hitting the short coastal flats of **Iquique**, where thunderous tubes unload over the unforgiving reefs that scoop up the SW swell and amplify it. These lurching, spitting waves have dictated that Chile has a far greater proportion of bodyboarders to take on the challenging spots that would otherwise go virtually unridden. Long, lonely beaches stretch out beside the ocean hugging Ruta 1 down to Barrancon, a slab peak with good rights about 34kms north of Tocopilla, where shorepound hits the city beaches in the shadow of the industrial port and power station. Along this coast there are other waves that are on clear display from the road, but surfers tend to stick to the known spots, which start again over the border towards **Antofagasta**. This zone starts setting the scene for wild, rugged coastline and continues the power theme from Arica and Iquique. There is a bit more variety to the set-ups with close to shore reef slabs being complimented by some rocky points and beachbreaks. Beyond the gasping chambers of Nuluhaga, plunging cliffs return and the fabulous

Ruta 1 struggles with the mountainous terrain, so heading inland to the 5 and by-passing the next 50kms is a good idea. From Caleta el Cobre south to the beginning of the **Atacama** region, there are going to be some rocky opportunities when the swell steps up, but you have got to want it bad to overcome the steep access and isolation problems. Northern Atacama flattens out a bit as the Andes split away from the Chilean Coastal Range and coastal access improves markedly with long, grey-white sands holding below average beachbreaks at playas Blanca, Chanaral, Flamenco and the protected bays just west of Copiapo.

**Atacama and Coquimbo** (aka Norte Chico region) has plenty to offer, although most just hit the growing surf/holiday town of Totoralillo, thanks to the concentration of waves and facilities. Strong winds and waves buffet the exposed southern flank of **Coquimbo**, sea fog is common and the roads through the Fray Jorge national park are slow and rough, but there are some waves at the ends of the coastal access tracks. Talcaruca, El Sauce and the rivermouth of the Rio Limari are worth checking in small to medium swells as anything big overpowers the coast here. Size is not a problem for the reef peak at El Teniente where the long, high tide rights are usually empty.

## SWELL FORECASTING

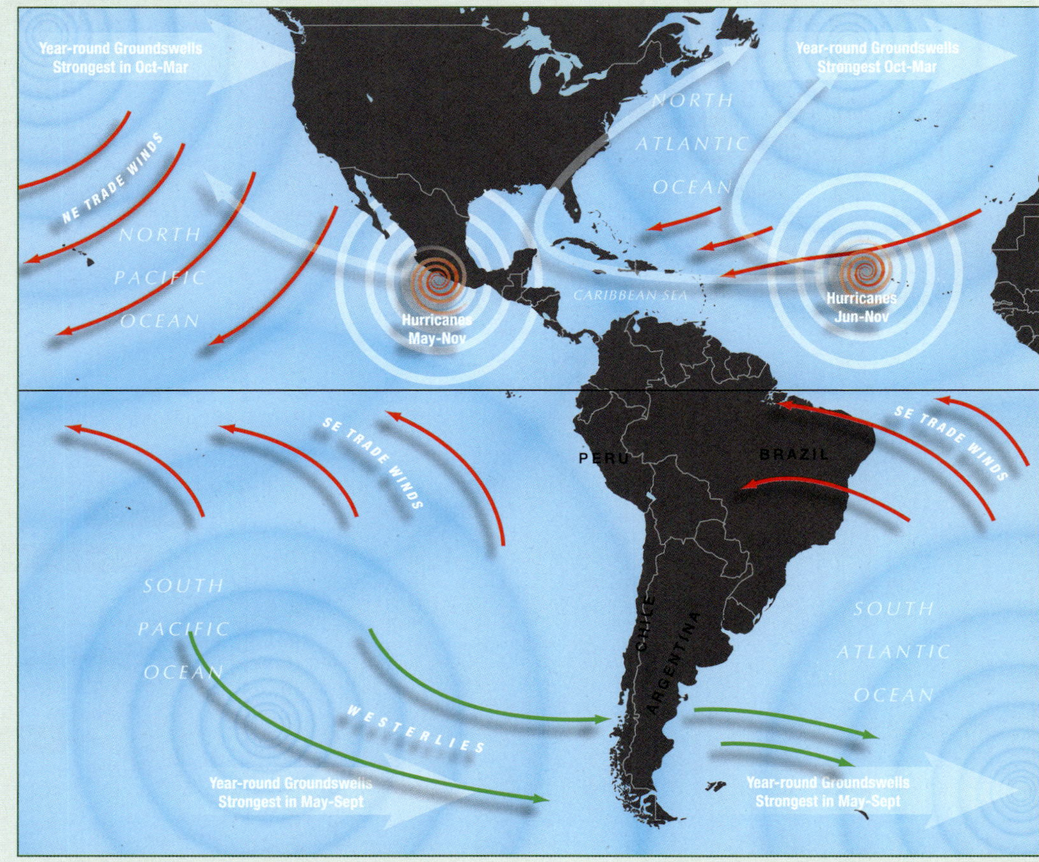


### THE PACIFIC OCEAN

Following the trend set by the rest of the Americas, South America is also a clear case of split personality in terms of swell exposure. The Pacific coast from Ecuador to Peru and on to Chile is perfectly poised to soak up the best of the SW swells from the South Pacific surf factory. Low pressures trundle along a path from New Zealand to Cape Horn nearly all-year-round, marching out of the southwest onto the rocky shoreline of Pacific South America. These swells are helpfully guided by the Humboldt (or Peru) Current, which tends to drag more SW swells up the coast of Chile and into Peru. Some spots in Chile and Peru can be ridden every day, which is a rare privilege on Planet Surf's inconsistent shorelines. While Chile and most of Peru rely on generous SW swells, Northern Peru and Ecuador protrude enough to pick up the end of the wave train from the North Pacific Aleutian lows. These long-distance, long period, winter NW swells have to march for up to 10 days from their point of origin and consequently lose much in the way of height and lulls between sets are long. Waves are seasonally erratic and water temps are balmy unless surfing the Galapagos Islands, where the end of the Humboldt Current deposits the coldest water found at equatorial latitudes. Central to Southern Peru, along with all of Chile, can get pounded by big waves through the southern hemisphere winter (April-Oct) and these swells don't necessarily stop in summer, rather they just decrease in frequency.

Thousands of kilometres of desert fringe the coast where the constant S to SW winds blow, bringing tailor-made offshores to the seemingly endless array of lefthand pointbreaks that nestle inside the protection of southern headlands. Winds veer more westerly in Chile, while in Northern Peru and Ecuador, the S wind is lighter and mornings can be windless glass.

The extensive Atacama Desert (the driest on earth) is sandwiched between the lofty peaks of the Andes to the east and the predictable massive upwelling that occurs off Southern Peru and Northern Chile. Compounded by the Humboldt Current, chilly year-round water temps bring thick fog, yet a complete absence of rain in places. When the El Niño current crosses the Pacific, a warm layer of water can disturb the balance, causing chaos via heavy rain and mudslides in areas that usually receive no rain at all. Semi-diurnal tidal ranges are 1-2m for most of the Pacific coast, although Colombia can hit 5m in the north.

### THE ATLANTIC OCEAN

Like most east-facing coasts, South America suffers from a lack of decent groundswells. South Atlantic lows quickly travel eastward to Africa, putting too much W in the swell, leaving the bulk of the coast reliant on SE-S pulses, coming off the back of the clockwise spinning pressure systems. This is compounded by the fact that the South Atlantic is the only ocean within tropical latitudes that virtually never receives any tropical storm action (only one recorded storm, Catarina in 2004). The third detracting factor is the extensive continental shelf that robs the waves of height and power. South America's east coast rarely gets epic big swells, but its saving grace is the consistent and favourable NE, E and SE windswell that hits year-round. Most of the surf in Argentina and Uruguay relies on these windswells outside of winter when wave heights can really suffer. Brazil accounts for the bulk of the eastern seaboard and not surprisingly gets the lion's share of consistently small onshore surf conditions. The southern surf regions provide the best chance of size from the southern hemisphere winter lows, which will send in SE swells and occasionally SW swells from cold fronts, or make do with the windswell whipped up by the constant E sea breezes. Further north, the tropical region of Brazil gets SE trades in winter, producing windswell mush, but very little to surf in summer. Atlantic South America is almost devoid of islands, but winter North Atlantic swells have Fernando do Noronha in their sights and can also reach NE-facing states of Brazil like Ceara, but wave heights will be austere.

Currents are courtesy of the large gyre that feeds cooler water from the Benguela Current off Africa into the warmer Brazilian Current before sinking south to complete the circuit. The North Brazilian Current offshoot warms the waters of the NE before merging with the Caribbean Current. The cold Malvinas Current chills the coastal waters of Patagonia where one of the few areas of coastal upwelling on an east-facing coast lowers the water temperature even further. This area also experiences diurnal tides and a massive tidal range up to 9.5m, as does the NE equatorial coast of Brazil especially around the mouth of the Amazon where it hits 4m+.

RICARDO BRAVO

Southern Chile

Massive wind turbines dot the coast southwards – never a good sign for surfers, but subtle changes see more scalloped bays and fun sandy beaches for beginners and longboarders as you enter the **Valparaiso** region. Check near the ports of Los Vilos, the crowded beaches of Los Molles, peaks at Pichicuy, lefts at Salinas de Pullally or Papudo and the wide-open beachbreaks at Cachagua. This heralds the beginning of the **Valparaíso and O'Higgins** regions, including the most famous surf town in Chile, Pichilemu. The large coastal cities of Valparaiso and San Antonio are the closest to the land-locked capital, Santiago and get very busy during holidays, but are blessed with plenty of strong beaches and reefs. South of San Antonio, there is a shift in the topography that begins to favour left points and rivermouths in the southern corners of the bays and none are better than the ultimate South American pointbreak, Punta de Lobos. Small and fun or large and life threatening are both on offer here and the boom to bust seasonal variation is being conquered as Pichilemu establishes itself as Chile's surf city. Our zone finishes at Lobos, but the waves don't and a hatful of southern corner rivermouths connected to sensitive strands of hard-pack grey sand with rocky fringes extend for over 100kms,

SURFOTOS.CL

Southern Chile

beckoning the inquisitive to the rolling green countryside. Constitución is the next big coastal town at the mouth of the river in region VII **Maule** and apparently marks the southern limit of the old Inca Empire. There is a real concentration of waves around the town beaches, which can have some decent lefts on windless days, but the smoke from the cellulose factory and industrial backdrop is quite a deterrent. Maule also hides some big waves, like the outer reef of Santos del Mar and there are even some righthand points, thanks to the surf-friendly geology. The NW orientation of the ensuing coast southwards allows plenty of scope for protected lefts in the lee of the headlands (check around Loanco) before the beginning of the **Bío Bío** region (VIII) at Pullay. Rivermouth sculpted pointbreaks are the main attraction and while some tried to keep them secret, recent environmental and natural disasters have firmly put the fickle lefthander Buchupureo on the map. is one of the largest coastal conurbations in Chile. Beyond the city of Concepción, one of the largest coastal conurbations in Chile, starts the big adventure. Anyone willing to take on regions IX **Araucanía**, XIV **Los Ríos** (they created a new region in 2007 and stuck it between 9 and 10!) and X **Los Lagos**, will need to have a lot of time on their hands as the remnants of the Pan American Highway, Ruta 5, stays a good 60-100kms inland and coastal arteries diminish rapidly. Rivers are the key to access and roads often follow them as they carve through the green carpet of hills. Unfortunately, **Araucania** features far too much straight beachbreak that is both wind and swell-blown, plus there are relatively few southern headlands that provide either rivermouth or pointbreak opportunities. Try around Queule for either swell protection or exposed beachies at Playas Ronca and Cheuque, just north of the easily accessed town of Mehuin, where a quality left rivermouth squares up in the corner of the beach. As the Los Rios name suggests, this is the place to find your own rivermouth left before the ever-strengthening wind turns the sea into a frothy cappuccino. Curinanco area is rife with possibilities, provided swell is small and winds are low, plus it is fairly close to the main city of Valdivia. Steep hills and rocky coves run down the coast to Playa Chaihuin, where the NW angle and rivermouth can help tame and sculpt the raw swell. Next road-serviced rivermouth is Hueicolla and finally Barra del Rio Bueno that has a lot of river-scoured bars. The spaghetti roads and forestry trails that lead into Los Lagos are best attacked with 4x4 since roads regularly flood and getting cut off is common. Little is known about the surf down here so follow the few roads to Llico Bajo, Huahuar or Playas Pinuno and Mar Bravo, in the hope you are not greeted by a freezing, blown-out mess. A car ferry plies the treacherous Chacao Channel, while the proposed bridge to link Chiloé Island with the mainland remains unbuilt, but this truly is the end of the road for the PanAm. This incredibly beautiful, wild and desolate landscape is mainly settled on the east coast, huddling away from the gales that sweep in from the Pacific. Around the main town of Ancud, there are some proper north-facing protected options inside the channel and also out on the craggy Peninsula de Lacuy. The rocky west coast is comprised of the Chiloé National Park, with road access into Cucao. Here, the long, wind-battered, west-facing beach is not a good surf option with strong currents and whitewash as far as you can see, unless it is a tiny summer swell. It's probably a safe bet to assume that somewhere along this indented, craggy coast there are some good set-ups, but nothing better than the waves found further north in Biobio. Armed with the knowledge that quality recedes as you head deeper south, only the super-adventurous will attempt to explore region XI **Aisén** and only the clinically insane will be drawn to region XII **Magallanes** and **Antártica Chilena**, where the clue to conditions is in its name. If standing in the teeth of the Roaring Forties, hurling constant rain, sleet or snow in your face as you don your 6/5mm to enter glacial-fed water patrolled by orcas doesn't faze you, then start planning your serious south Chile expedition and marvel at the fact that you are surfing at the bottom of the world!

## THE ATLANTIC OCEAN

Continental east coasts have always suffered from a dearth of swell compared to their western counterparts as the global weather systems circulate in their established corridors from west to east. Coastal angle sometimes helps, but unfortunately in southern **Argentina** it is relatively steep, requiring more SE than due S swells to penetrate the large east-facing bays. The freakishly powerful winds in Patagonia can not be overstated, creating havoc with the surf, driving a vehicle and controlling a surfboard, in or out of the water. South America's most extreme tides, extensive cliffs, steep beach angles, no roads and difficult access compounded by by the fact most of the coastal real estate is privately owned as part of huge, Gaucho owned ranches. This is the real frontier, so plan well and hope you don't have a mishap, although everyone looks out for each other in Patagonia. Furthest south, Isla de los Estados has been surfed and on Tierra del Fuego, the Rio Grande beachbreaks near the rivermouth is the main surfing spot on this weather-lashed island.

Out on the British territory of the **Falkland Islands**, the local surfers usually ride small, short, fast peelers at Surf Bay or the slightly better exposed military area Bertha Beach beside a signposted minefield. You'll be sharing with a menagerie of creatures including dolphins, sea lions and penguins at these east-facing beaches, where the offshores can often be too strong and shralp the waves to bits.

Back on the mainland, it's the main towns/cities that are always founded on a large rivermouth or port where most travellers will scope for waves. The unremarkable urban beach of Rada Tilly is often ridden and Playa Union, Chubut a cool little town with a nice little surf scene. The road hugs the coast around the north of Golfo San Mattias, overlooking miles of brown sand beachbreak, below cliffs heading into El Condor where the kiters hang. Bahia Blanca is shallow, but Monte Hermoso picks up plenty of S and dumps it hard on the shorebreak. From here the coast curves northeastwards, opening up to more swell and the possibility of quieter beachbreaks around Claromeco and some proper lefts spoking off the jetty at Necochea. Across the river, Quequen will fire around the shipwreck and its iconic propeller. **Mar del Plata** has always been the centre of both the Argentinian surf scene and summer beach parties. There are waves closer to Buenos Aires (Santa Clara del Mar, Pinamar, San Clemente del Tuyú), but they are adversely affected as the coast bends away from the swell and you get closer to the widest rivermouth in the world.

PEDRO SALINAS

Uruguay

Across the Rio del Plata the capital of **Uruguay**, Montevideo rarely has any rideable size in the turbid brown waters of Playa Honda, so the Uruguayan surfers head east to the far more reliable breaks of party towns like Punta del Este, La Paloma and Santa Teresa.

The transition into **Brazil** is seamless, as long, lonely, windy sands like Praia do Hermenegildo, partition the lagoons into **Rio Grande do Sul State**. Rivermouth jetties are fine relief from straight beachbreaks, but none exist up through the big coastal conurbations of Balneario Gaivota, Balneario Rincao, Arroio do Silva and Praia de Jaguaruna, before hitting the rocky headland at Farol de Santa Marta where the quality suddenly jumps and heralds the beginning of probably Brazil's best surfing state of **Santa Catarina**. The southern section of coast is stacked with dozens of great waves and serves as a pressure valve from the crowds at highlight praias like Cardozo, Ipoã, the jetties and beachies of Laguna or either side of the knobbly headland at Itapirubá. The tap doesn't just

Matinhos, Paraná

switch off north of Florianopolis, although it is less open to S swells and works better on E or SE. Try Itapema Central or Marambaia at Balneário Camboriú if you love high-rise and an audience, or scout out the quieter beaches like Quatro Ilhas, Brava and Atalaia. Barra Velha beaches like NE to E swells at Praia do Sol, Costão or the long skinny peninsula leading up to the rivermouth jetty at Foz do Itapocu then the exposed straight sands at Barra do Sul. The peninsula at São Francisco do Sul welcomes a variety of swells and winds and both Praia Grande or Prainha are really reliable for solid peaks and solid crowds. The three bays interrupting Itapoa's straight beaches hold a longer ripable right off Third Rock and fuller peaks flow north to Barra do Saí and **Paraná State**. The two main surf towns are Guaratuba and Matinhos which support a large local population at any of the 17 breaks in the area. Highlights include the peak at the north end of another Praia Brava or Direitas in front of Morro do Cristo with long rights off the rocks, but neither are empty or friendly. Working in all swells, Pico de Matinhos is a proper throaty righthand barrel coveted by many for its great length and intensity of ride. The Baia de Paranagua dominates the coast and there are a few waves on the Ilha do Mel in the mouth of the estuary. The rest of Paraná is one featureless straight beach with virtually no road access and the same can be said of southern **São Paulo State** until Peruíbe where the urban sprawl meets the sand again. No less than 12 breaks are strung along this coast up to Praia Grande and the beginning of the **Littoral Paulista** zone, with Mongaguá Pier offering something different from straight beachbreak. There is an incredible richness of surf between the Sao Paulo zone and the beaches of Rio, overshadowed by the same coastal mountain range thats makes this a beautiful coastline to surf. Massaguaçu, Maranduba and Lagoinha all have fun quality waves on their day, but the undisputed surf town on this coast is Ubatuba. Long term location for professional contests at all levels, the rights off the rivermouth at Itamambuca are good training for the best Brazilian surfers and there are multiple peaks up the beach in various swell directions. Back in town there is something for all abilities at Praia Grande and it's a destination for both foreign and local surfers. The coast gets steep and forested in Parati which is in **Rio de Janeiro State** and the waves can be excellent at little rocky points like Cepilho or sheltered coves like Laranjeras, Sono or Martim de Sá. Ilha Grande blocks the swell to the mainland, (although Mambucaba has a rivermouth peak in big swells) catching it at two big beaches called Aventureiro and Lopes Mendes. Then the 42km long arm of the Restinga de Marambaia is restricted access army land leading into the city of **Rio de Janeiro** and its famously overcrowded beaches. North of Buzios, the SE-facing coast of Rio state will always have surfers in the water at the main coastal cities of Rio das Ostras and Macaé, before the Jurubatiba Sandbank National Park shorepound stretches for 44kms northwards.

There's not much action until the border with the next state **Espirito Santo**, a mix of long, lonely, natural beaches and built-up, crowded urban sands. The north of Espirito Santo curves away from the swell, with less surf but waves to be found for holidaymakers at popular summer beaches like Guriri, or among the strange parabolic armouring of Praia da Barra, Conceição. Entering Bahia state, the 200km wide Abrolhos Bank continental shelf extension saps swells of power so this is a stretch of coast worth avoiding until the beginning of the **South Bahia** zone. The northern **Bahia State** coastline turns to face the SE swells from Salvador and multiple beaches make the most of any far off pulses. Scout from the south-facing spots near the entrance to the huge Baia de Todos Santos up to Aleluia and on to Praia da Onda at Itacimirin. A platform of dead coral parallels the long beaches and while there may be a few occasional spots, the onshores are fairly consistent and the surf is often junky all the way to the border with Sergipe. The main surf spot in **Sergipe State** is Atalaia, where the large rivermouth barely improves the slow, fat mushy nature of the surf throughout the region. Neighbouring **Alagoas State** sees a vast improvement in the surf at Praia do Francês, which picks up anything from the E-SE-S and offers something for everyone at three defined peaks. Advanced surfers will prefer the faster, hollow rides at Coqueirais, or in front of the ancient Leprosarium. Fortunato is calmer and slower, so very good for beginners. The barrier reef starts again, running up to the long L-shaped pier at Maceió, which has peaks on both sides and up to the busy port. Off Pajucara beach a defined left reefbreak peels, but it's a mission to paddle the 2km then climb over the low tide rocks to get out there. Praia de Cruz das Almas can have some hollow dumpers on the good days, weak mush on the bad. North to Praia Sereias there are some high tide only peaks at Praia do Riacho Doce and lower tide hollower options at New Orleans, both involving some rock avoidance. Broken reefs and skerries screen the beaches north with a few gaps at Praia do Morro and Tamandaré just before the beginning of the **Pernambuco** zone. Also part of **Pernambuco State** is probably Brazil's best waves on the far-off island of **Fernando de Noronha**. North of Recife the rivermouths and estuaries feel sharky with low quality waves and into **Paraíba State**, the capital João Pessoa has regularly ridden, but not very exciting beachbreaks at Bessa, plus a north-facing jetty break at Intermares, Cabadelo.

The barrier reef stops at Baía da Traição and long, dead straight sands lead into **Rio Grande de Norte**, a state with much better surf potential. A cluster of breaks around the Baía Formosa headland can show quality form in winter with long righthand peelers at the Porto, shorter but bangin' rights at the Ponta and peaks for all at Mar Aberto. Next major cluster of surf is between Pipa and Tibau do Sul, with rock and sand breaks at the local competition beach Amor, beneath beautiful ochre cliffs. Beginners, longboarders, SUP'ers, kiters and just about everyone else will have fun at Madeiro, a long rock and sand right with S wind protection. Cacimbinha has extensive, uncrowded N swell peaks leading up to the sweet righthanders

Baia Formosa, Rio Grande do Norte

of Abacateiro and especially Lajão, where long rights tour the headland with hollow and ripable sections in equal measure. Tabatinga has waves both off the headland reefs and on the long Buzios beach below huge desert dunes that extend up the coast into surfing hotspot Natal. Multiple quality spots like Escadaria and Manary are strung out along popular Ponta Negra, where pros and foundlings share the many peaks that thrive on E swell and S winds. Low tide tubes and small fun peaks at Praia Artistas are slightly less crowded than neighbouring Miami in the shadow of the bridge expressway. The NE shoulder of the country would appear to be a rich hunting ground, but the continental shelf expands, supporting more coral reefs and power-sapping protrusions. It's not devoid of surf but lacks quality and the constant trade winds suit the kiteboarders who frequent Zumbi beach. Small weak and windblown waves continue into the huge coastal sand dune system which extends for 150km towards **Ceara State** and the next regularly surfed zone of **West Ceara**. Winter northern hemisphere swells are required for this coastline so don't come here in the middle of the calendar year. Jericoacoara, aka Jeri, 300kms west of Fortaleza is an established stop for the travelling surfing community and neighbouring Malhada beach has good rights in a NE swell. Search around the lighthouse on the point of Praia de Pedra do Sal near the town of Parnaíba in **Piaui State**, as you might get some long righthanders on the lee side from the wind.

The final extension of the Brazilian coast runs into the Amazon basin, where the coast becomes a bewildering jumble of creeks, estuaries, mangrove swamps and small islands, interspersed with some of the most remote beaches in Brazil! The main reason to come to this zone is to try one of the many river bore waves that are a feature of the Amazon. Known as the pororoca in the local dialect, these powerful, destructive tidal phenomenons appear on several rivers, including the Pindaré/Mearim, Guama/Capim, Marajo Island, Moju, Guajara, Macapa Canal do Norte, Cassipore and the Rio Araguari. Travelling at 15-25 km/h, the tidal bore comes approximately every 12h50min so there's only one chance to ride per day and there's a shift of 40mins every day. Usually, there are rideable waves up to 3 days before and after full or new moon phases and these spring tides have a range of 6-7m max. Unlike other bores, the wetter the season, the better because droughts mean more mud & sand banks will be exposed in the estuary and dissipate the bore energy. River contours and depth are constantly changing and sets of waves can have 2 to 3 rideable waves, but the first one is usually the best option. Sometimes the second wave can have more power, break further away from the bank or be cleaner if there's some windchop. Most sections break either right or left with plenty of space for several surfers to ride at a time. Ocean waves in this northern zone usually range from 2-5ft on a coast plagued by countless shallow sandbanks. Best season for **Maranhão State** is winter (Dec-April) when NE groundswells are running, while Para gets more waves in summer (July-Nov) with constant E-SE trade winds. Extreme tidal ranges mean surf is mostly high tide. Maranhão's extensive coastal dunes terminate at Travosa, a collection of fishing huts on an endlessly long and wind exposed beach. French influenced Sao Luis, the capital of Maranhão is not the best wave zone, but the safest bet is Araçagi, where the peaks break with more power and shape. Sao Marcos has little to recommend it - the water is murky, unnaturally hot, heaps of tankers pass by to enter the rivermouth and there has been 3 shark attacks on surfers in the '90s. Ponta da Areia is deeper in the rivermouth and has occasional classic days with E wind protection. Across the wide river, beaches like Itatinga are more famous for shell collecting than surf, as the sands migrate massively in the estuary. Because it can be offshore in N winds, it's flat most of the time, but lefts can line up on the shifty banks with a strong NE swell. Arari (the capital of watermelon!) is a 3h drive away and offers the cleanest bore conditions thanks to better weather and a narrower river. The Rio Mearim breaks in as many as 12 sections in a 1h30min journey from the rivermouth mudbank known as Cement Mix to the Arari village. The wave can range in size from a 8ft wall of whitewater to a tiny but superclean 1 to 2ft right. Over a period of 5 days, surfing can be had early morning from between 5-8am to 7-10am. **Pará State** is for surf desperadoes, with small mushy windchop on remote, boat or walk in beaches like Camaraçu that occasionally lines-up some long rights off a drifting sandbank. Across the wide bay, Praia de Ajuruteua is long and shapeless except at the creek and river mouths or make the low tide walk into NE-facing Chavascal, a stretch of mushy beachbreak best on N/NE swells up to 6ft. Check the ivory strands at Marieta, a half hour boat ride from Salinas in summer NE swells. Offshore sandbars can block the swells but NE should slide down the long righthander-friendly beach. Atalaia is the centre of the Salinas scene with long stretches of mushy beachbreak best on N/NE swells pushed in by a rising tide. Bigger and more consistent than most Pará waves, the sand dunes provide more sandbars in the surf and it attracts big beach crowds during holidays. Around the headland, Praia do Farol Velho might have some smaller righthand runners. Take a 40min boat ride out to the beautiful, slow-paced island of Maiandeua where waves hit both the NE exposed Praia de Princesa and Vila do Algodoal, which is good with NW swell and SE winds. Praia do Crispim is another popular, road accessible holiday beach with chaotic banks and mushy rides. The much larger nearby town of Maruda may have waves in straight NE swells. Rio Capim passes near Belem, in the State of Para and Sao Domingo do Capim provides easy access from land for those who can't afford the expense of hiring a boat. Locals wait for the bore on the mud flats and ride all sorts of surfcraft including pirogues (canoes/small boats). This 600km (370mi) tributary of Rio Guama, has lots of rideable bore sections for those armed with a boat and local knowledge. The Rio Araguari was the biggest and longest bore wave in the Amazon, on the largest river of **Amapá State**, its source being high in the western Tumucumaque mountain range about 350km away. Unfortunately, because of river dams upstream and extensive buffalo breeding creating tributaries that lower the water levels, the Araguari river bore has been downgraded from 5 star to 1star. A recent discovery of a new bore wave in the Bailique Islands means that hiring a boat out of Macapa and surfing the mouth of the Amazon is still possible with the right guide. There are no "normal" ocean waves in the region and the river affects wave quality all the way into **French Guiana**.

MARCELO MARAGNI

Rio Capim, Pará

The capital Cayenne is regularly surfed along the suburban Rémire-Montjoly beaches and the coast-hugging Route des Plages overlooks some low quality NE-facing beachbreak. Inside the Mahury rivermouth is an occasional longer, brown-water left and just offshore another left pointbreak on Ilet la Mère. Mid to high tides are always better to bring the swell over the coastal shoals. Further large rivers drain into the Atlantic, but a lack of swell and sandbars make kiteboarding far more popular at Kourou. The best surf in the country can be found on Les Iles du Salut, with reefs off both Royal and Devil's island. **Suriname**'s 386km coastline is one of the worst for surfing on the continent, with straight gently shelving, sediment loaded beaches bookended by large equatorial rivers. Moderate to strong ENE winds bring choppy seas over short period waves and up to 3m tides keep the waves guessing where to crumble. The capital Paramaribo is too deep inside the mouth of the large chocolate-brown Suriname river. Matapica is probably the best chance of a wave, sandwiched between extensive national parks that protect the many species of turtle nesting along these shores. **Guyana** is an adaption of an Amerindian word for "The land of many waters" and it suffers from all the same problems as Suriname. Brown, sometimes polluted waters flow from the Demerara and Essequibo rivers, silting up the coast for miles around. There are some jetties and groynes around Jonestown that protrude into high tide waters, but generally speaking, avoid all The Guianas if you are looking for anything more than chest-high choco-slop.

# Isla Margarita & Sucre VENEZUELA

Just 40km (25mi) off mainland Venezuela, Margarita Island emerges out of the warm Caribbean Sea, showcasing beautiful beaches, majestic mountains and verdant valleys. This rich natural backdrop overlooks a hedonistic, beach-going, tax-free shopping, party-orientated crowd. While the social life is hardcore, the surfing is not, but provides a small wave, warm water option for those looking for good times under the sun.

+ ISLAND AND MAINLAND SURF
+ BEAUTIFUL WHITE SAND BEACHES
+ TOURIST HEAVEN, GOOD NIGHTLIFE
+ PERFECT WEATHER

- ALWAYS SMALL
- WINDY, CHOPPY CONDITIONS
- UNSTABLE POLITICAL SITUATION
- NOT SO CHEAP

THIERRY GIBAUD

Puerto Cruz

The fishermen's huts of **Punta Arena** extend along a pretty beach that can produce hollow waves provided the surf is big enough to get there; locals swear it only happens a couple of times a year. The curving beach from **La Pared** through to El Tunal will be clean in SE winds, but just needs enough swell to be more than a close-out shoredump. The monumental Playa Restinga joins the two islands but is mainly a kitesurfing venue. The N-facing white sand beach of **Playa Caribe** is usually just more small shorebreak, but the eastern end past the island gets more swell and better shape. **Puerto Cruz** has good shelter from virtually any E or S wind. This right pointbreak reels over a rocky bottom and the long rides it offers are worth the long wait, since it rarely breaks. The northeast coast of Margarita is perfectly orientated to receive any available swell and has become the surf hub of the island. Among Margarita's 27 beaches, covering 53km of its 160km shoreline, **Playa el Agua** is one of the longest and widest, and definitely the busiest. Venezuelans like to come here to exhibit their tanned bodies while drinking cocktails on the water's edge. While the peaks are usually crumbly and easily blown-out, early mornings can be glassy and fun, with the odd hollow section, attracting crowds of all abilities surfers. Taking its name from the red snapper fish, **Parguito** is the island's primo surf spot. Gets some hollow short rides at times and there can be a few nice A-frames along its length when the rips break up the close-outs. Regularly onshore but still enough push for some ramps, attracting plenty of locals. Less swimmers to avoid than at El Agua. Its extra consistency makes it the pick for surf contests and national championships are regularly organised here. Closer to town is **Guacuco**, which picks up plenty of swell at this wide open, 5km long beach. Often messy with lines of whitewash making it the ideal beach for the local surf school. Some fun easy waves without the crowd of better surfers who will be up the coast. A good way to get away from Margarita's crowded scene is to cruise the mainland. Stretching for 70km under Margarita, the Peninsula de Araya is sheltered from the swell by the Isla Coche, itself sitting in water too deep for waves to break. However el Morro de **Chacopata** is fully exposed, and the reefbreak represents the closest reliable spot for Cumana's surfing community. On the way to Carupano, check out **La Esmeralda** and **Punta de Guiria** which should pick-up more swell than most of the coast. **Playa Copey**'s righthand pointbreak and other peaks, 7km before Carúpano, have been the site of national surfing championships. There are good waves in **Carúpano** itself, but be prepared to surf in troubled water around the rivermouth. Further east, there are more breaks on the way to Rio Caribe, which could serve as a base for expeditions to the Peninsula de Paria. A 4WD is advised to access most of these beaches. The uncrowded rights and left reefs of **Chaguarama** are only 10 minutes away from Rio Caribe and an extra 20mn will take you to **Pui Puy**, a consistent, uncrowded, long stretch of beachbreaks where several peaks can be found. Further investigation of the Peninsula de Paria should bring some rewards.

## TRAVEL INFORMATION

**Weather** – Weather changes little between seasons; the dry season stretches between Dec and April, matching the surf season when it seldom rains and the temperatures remain just under 30°C (86°F). The island is out of the hurricane belt. Rains occur mostly at night, in strong and heavy showers. Sun radiation is extremely strong; don't forget sunscreen and boardshorts.

**Lodging and Food** – Hotels around Playa El Agua ranging from $20-135/n. Try the local posadas in Playa Copey (fr $29 dble). A meal is around $20; try the local Catalana fish and arepanas (stuffed pancakes).

**Nature and Culture** – Windsurfers will head to famous El Yaque. Take a boat tour on the Lagoon of the Restinga national park or hike to the Castle of Santa Rosa. Go to Porlamar for tax-free shopping or raging nightlife (Senor Frog's...)

**Hazards and Hassles** – 2003 a surfer lost his leg at El Yaque. Locals are keen surfers and usually friendly. The political and economic crisis in 2017 brought riots and food shortages.

**Handy Hints** – Take a fish or a longboard for the numerous small, mushy days. A few shops carry surf equipment (Nathacha's Surf Shop). Escuela De Surf Guacuco Roots does lessons and rentals at Playa Guacuco.

| STATISTICS | | J F | M A | M J | J A | S O | N D |
|---|---|---|---|---|---|---|---|
| SWELL | Direction | | | | | | |
| | Size (ft) | 3 | 2-3 | 1 | 1 | 1-2 | 2-3 |
| WIND | Direction | | | | | | |
| | Force | F4 | F4 | F4 | F3-F4 | F3 | F3-F4 |
| WATER | Wetsuit | | | | | | |
| | Temp/°C | 26 | 26 | 27 | 28 | 28 | 27 |
| WEATHER | Rainfall/mm | 10 | 10 | 75 | 120 | 70 | 40 |
| | days/mth | 6 | 2 | 5 | 7 | 5 | 9 |
| | Min temp/°C | 24 | 25 | 25 | 26 | 26 | 25 |
| | Max temp/°C | 28 | 29 | 30 | 30 | 31 | 29 |

Premium wave season is Dec to April, when North Atlantic groundswells wrap around the West Indies island chain and hit the NE-facing coasts. The biggest ones will wrap around the island to produce cleaner surf on the other side. Expect year-round, kneehigh E windswell, chased by summertime E trade winds and stronger N-NE winds between Dec and March. Mornings can have calm conditions. The tide range is minimal at 0.45m.

# Caracas VENEZUELA

Underexposed as a surf destination, Venezuela is more quantity than quality, with the majority of waves being punchy onshore shorebreaks or fun pointbreaks ruffled by sideshore winds. This quiet corner of the Caribbean offers surfers year-round, warm water, small waves to practice getting speed and making big moves. Catastrophic mudslides in 1999 buried whole towns and the coast has remained a bit of a wreck. More recently political and socio-economic upheaval has resulted in travel warnings being issued, but there are some good waves to be found for the more adventurous.

- + CONSTANT NE WINDSWELLS
- + LOTS OF RIGHT POINTBREAKS
- + EPIC HURRICANE SWELLS
- + RELATIVELY UNCROWDED

- – SMALL, SHORT PERIOD SWELLS
- – ONSHORES AND TURBID WATER
- – SOCIAL AND POLITICAL INSTABILITY
- – CAR THIEVES & MUDSLIDE RISK

NASSER

Cuyagua

There are a high number of little boulder and rock right points, like **Los Caracas**, a popular beach about 2hrs drive east from Caracas, where the waves can be excellent near the El Rio rivermouth. **Anare** may not be an epic beachbreak, but it's consistent and there can be some rights spinning off the harbour wall into the rivermouth. Safe and friendly with a good hotel, plus a board shaper called Prisma. **Punta Care** is a quality right pointbreak, which gets really good with a solid swell, offering steep walls for up to 200m rides. Gets crowded. **Fido Point** offers short punchy rights off a broken jetty where the locals may be a little less welcoming. The whole beach is guarded on Sundays like **Playa Pantaleta**, a consistent beachbreak, which is best in weather fronts and can handle large swells. Pelua reef lefts work on rare occasions, but on a big swell, **Otro Pais**, (aka Camuri Grande Club or Paraiso) is the place to be. It's a fast, powerful, right pointbreak, where barrels are possible, but strong rips and restricted access require lots of paddling. In front of the private **Puerto Azul** club is another righthander that peels off the jetty protecting the mouth of the Rio Naiguatá. Long rides over the sandbar when it's on form. **Carmen D'Uria**'s great rights are clearly visible from the coastal highway, but hardly anyone surfs there because it's dangerous to park near the favellas (slums). **Los Cocos** is the most popular, consistent break with super-fun lefts near the Los Coquitos jetty and peaks down the beach, but expect crowds with attitude and pollution. **Tanaguarena** (aka La Playita or Boca del Rio) sports rocky rights peeling down beside the jetty that are shallow, dangerous and really powerful but unfortunately, all too rare. Another **Playita**, just north of the airport is also a fickle right pointbreak, with good jetty options just to the west. **Mamo** rights can be very long, breaking next to the Officer's Club that has restricted access, so park outside and paddle wide. Nice walls with various sections and shouldering off on the inside. The pretty colonial village of Choroni shelters legitimate reefbreak rights at **El Malecon**, and a decent shorebreak at Playa Grande. One of Venezuela's best beachbreaks is **Cuyagua**, where the hollow waves near the rivermouth hold some size. It can be short rides and closes-out a lot, but there's E wind protection from the headland and room to move up or down the beach. Good accommodation and weekend party scene. Check **El Playon** and the wedgy lefts and rights at La Punta, the beach furthest west past the rock jetty. Dumpy close-outs attract the bodyboard crew between the rock jetties. The beautiful archipelago of Los Roques is famous for excellent kitesurfing, world-class diving, plus there is at least one consistent small-wave surf spot.

## TRAVEL INFORMATION

**Weather** – Caracas lies in a series of valleys surrounded by majestic tree-clad mountains. Annual average temps oscillate between 25-27°C (77-81°F) and vary little year-round. The dry season runs from Dec to April and the rainy season from May to Nov. Heavy showers are common but usually last an hour at most, leaving high daily sunshine hours. Boardies only.

**Lodging and Food** – Many high-rise hotels (Ole Caribe) in Naiguata or La Guaira, (fr $55-90/day). In Playa Anare, Villa Anare is $50/dble. In Cuyagua, posadas are $30/dble (Doña Meche, Cuyagua Mar). Meals cost around $5 in small places.

**Nature and Culture** – Crazy beach party scene with music and cars on the beach. Breathtaking mountain scenery plunges into the ocean. Caracas is close and you can take the Cable Car back to the coast. Ambiance in Cuyagua is unreal, while Carnival is perfect for heavy party animals.

**Hazards and Hassles** – After the 1999 mudslides, many coastal districts were destroyed; thievery and muggings have been on the rise since. Don't park or walk around Naiguata, La Guaira or Maiquetia at night. Stay out in the quiet areas from Punta Care to Los Caracas. Roads can be really bad. Beware of boulders.

**Handy Hints** – Fish and shortboards are ideal. There are lots of good shapers like Bachaco, Prisma and Kannibal charging $350 for a good shortboard, but they're not easy to find and there are no large surf shops. Check the peaceful Los Roques archipelago. Carnival time (February), Christmas and Easter week can be very busy with flights & pensions booked up.

Caribbean ENE trade winds are boosted when they hit the steep, mountainous coast, bringing a constant supply of 2-6ft short-period windswell from Nov to March. Summer winds turn more E and wave size decreases to 1-4ft, unless a hurricane swell tracks into the Caribbean Sea, producing epic 8-10ft conditions with low winds. Winds and waves are usually calmer in the morning, then build during the day. Sometimes, mountain canyons can create localised offshore winds. There is one big tide and one small tide twice a day reaching 0.5m range.

| STATISTICS | | J F | M A | M J | J A | S O | N D |
|---|---|---|---|---|---|---|---|
| SWELL | Direction | | | | | | |
| | Size (ft) | 3-4 | 3 | 2-3 | 2 | 3 | 3-4 |
| WIND | Direction | | | | | | |
| | Force | F4 | F4 | F4 | F4 | F4 | F4 |
| WATER | Wetsuit | | | | | | |
| | Temp/°C | 26 | 26 | 27 | 28 | 29 | 29 |
| WEATHER | Rainfall/mm | 27 | 19 | 41 | 55 | 52 | 55 |
| | days/mth | 4 | 3 | 8 | 12 | 10 | 10 |
| | Min temp/°C | 21 | 21 | 23 | 23 | 24 | 22 |
| | Max temp/°C | 30 | 30 | 32 | 32 | 33 | 32 |

# Caribbean Colombia

Colombia is a beautiful, sensuous country of music and dance, unexplored jungles and sophisticated towns and cities. In terms of security, the situation has improved over the last decade and tourism has begun to increase. Colombia's Pacific coastline works best from April to October, while the more developed and easier-going Caribbean coastline is the focus for consistently fun beachbreaks, reefbreaks and a few rivermouths from November to March.

**+ VERY CONSISTENT**
**+ UNCROWDED**
**+ DRY SURF SEASON**
**+ MOUNTAIN SCENERY**

**- POOR QUALITY, MESSY WAVES**
**- FREQUENT ONSHORES**
**- SOME DIFFICULT ACCESS**
**- STREET CRIME & DRUG TRADE**

STEPHANE ROBIN

Los Naranjos

The vanilla yellow city of Cartagena de Indias has a sheltered spot in in front of the **Hilton**, where short jetties catch big swells with W in them and deeper in the bay Castillogrande beach only breaks rarely as it faces S. The longest jetty on Cartagena's beachfront holds surprisingly punchy lefts in front of the **Las Velas** hotel and is more consistent than the jetties stretching north. These waves break on localised windswell and are usually weak, messy and a muddy brown colour. Things improve marginally along the strip of coastline between here and Barranquilla, which has better exposure and Caribbean Colombia's only known reefbreaks. **Pradomar** is well-known for its soft rights off the jetty and lefts further down the beach, but the more consistent option is the slow, fat rights of **El Bolsillo** the next jetty north. It picks up all the NE swell, but maxes out in overhead conditions and the rips get really strong. **Punta Roca** is probably the best wave on the Caribbean coast, a heavy, ledgy A-frame reef that can get hollow. It's easily blown-out and will be busy with Barranquilla's friendly surf community, breaking best at higher tides and holding up to 6ft. A good respite from the hustle of the cities is the Parque Nacional Tayrona – the jungle-cloaked bays and inlets house numerous perfect beaches. **Arrecifes** is a highly consistent wave and unlike the Barranquilla and Cartagena areas is not battered by constant wind. The right breaking off the huge granite boulders at the eastern end of the beach is the best wave, though it does close-out a lot and beginners will struggle with the paddle and power. With accommodation or hammock camping possible right on the beach, this is a truly idyllic spot to hang out for a few days and the waves are rarely crowded since better, easier access options are found nearby. It's an hour-long walk through the jungle to reach the beach and visitors must pay a fee to enter the park. A small stream emerges at **Los Naranjos** and creates a reliable low tide sandbar in front of the dramatic rock pillars. It gets hollow and is generally a cleaner wave than Arrecifes, holding up to 6ft and only small numbers in the line-up. There are some lefts over rock heading west, plus more playas to scope at Castilletes and Cañaveral. **Casa Grande** is a suckier, powerful peak that will either tube or close-out depending on the state of the bank. If the mouth of the Rio Mendihuaca is open, look for some longer lefts. Further east still, **Buritaca** has two right pointbreaks and hollow waves in the rivermouth breaking in a beautiful, natural setting. **Viento Fresco** also has a quality righthand point, consistently breaking on all swells. Opposite Club **Las Gaviotas** is another long right rivermouth that deposits sand along a sectiony line-up. There are further right points in the Finca de los Rivera area, with numerous exploration possibilities.

Locally produced windswells with very short wave periods result in messy and confused surf. On the plus side, it's consistent, with rarely a flat day between December and March. The Barranquilla to Cartagena stretch is always windy during this period, but winds are often lighter in the morning. Hurricane swells are rare for this part of the Caribbean. Most swells are in the 3-4ft range, often building through the day before dropping off again as the wind dies overnight. Tidal variation rarely exceeds 0.3m.

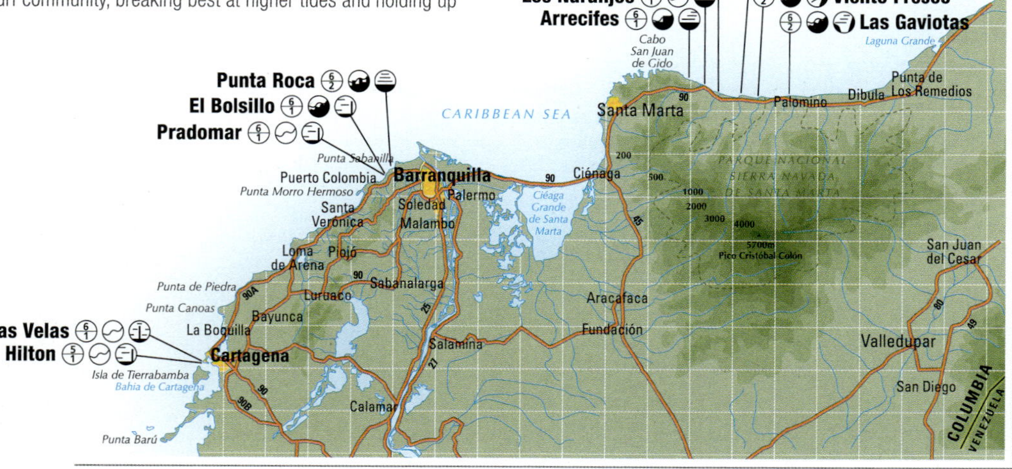


## TRAVEL INFORMATION

**Weather** – Year-round hot weather, with averages between 25-30°C (77-86°F). Dec to April is the driest and the evenings are freshened by a light breeze, making the heat more tolerable. May to August temperatures can reach 45°C (113°F), with regular light showers adding to the humidity. Sept to Nov are the least appealing, with daily torrential downpours, flooding certain areas. Boardshorts and a rash vest year-round.

**Lodging and Food** – Every town has at least one basic hotel and all the coastal tourist cities have dozens of options suiting all price ranges. Colombia is cheap, with clean double rooms available for as little as $10. Many seafood and meat dishes like cazuela de mariscos, ceviche de camarones or carne asada and fried chicken, all usually served with plantains.

**Nature and Culture** – Cartagena is a World Heritage Site renowned for its beauty and extraordinary street life. The Parque Nacional Tayrona has good jungle trekking and the remains of a lost city called Pueblito. The twin peaks of the Sierra Nevada de Santa Marta are the world's highest coastal mountains at 5775m. Ciudad Perdida is a Colombian highlight.

**Hazards and Hassles** – After decades of guerrilla insurgency, paramilitary death squads, massively powerful drug cartels, kidnapping and a daunting petty crime rate, Colombia is finally becoming more secure. Stick to tourist areas, listen to local advice and avoid displays of wealth (jewellery, watches, phones etc).

**Handy Hints** – Limited surf spares are available from Etniko in Barranquilla. Kayakitesurfing school do surfing and SUP lessons and rentals (fr$20/h). Colombia can be very dangerous in places, but don't be paranoid; most people leave with nothing but good memories.

| | STATISTICS | J F | M A | M J | J A | S O | N D |
|---|---|---|---|---|---|---|---|
| SWELL | Direction | | | | | | |
| | Size (ft) | 3 | 3 | 2 | 2-3 | 1-2 | 2-3 |
| WIND | Direction | | | | | | |
| | Force | F5 | F4-F5 | F4-F5 | F4-F5 | F4 | F4 |
| WATER | Wetsuit | | | | | | |
| | Temp/°C | 26 | 26 | 27 | 27 | 28 | 27 |
| WEATHER | Rainfall/mm | 2 | 13 | 110 | 117 | 185 | 82 |
| | days/mth | 0 | 2 | 11 | 12 | 15 | 7 |
| | Min temp/°C | 23 | 24 | 25 | 25 | 25 | 24 |
| | Max temp/°C | 30 | 31 | 31 | 31 | 31 | 30 |

# Pacific Colombia

The Pacific shores of Colombia have remained an obscure, difficult to access surf destination since much of Choco Province has no roads and it is one of the wettest shores in the world. Getting there entails flying in on a small plane to the Nuqui area, which receives long-distance swell from all over the Pacific. There are average breaks close to town, but to get to the better waves in the region requires a powerboat. To make it economical, a group of four is ideal to hire a boat and explore.

**+ N & S GROUNDSWELLS**
**+ GOOD LEFTS & RIGHTS**
**+ AMAZING JUNGLE WATERWAYS**
**+ CHEAP, EXOTIC COLOMBIA**

**- BOAT ACCESS ONLY**
**- RARELY BIGGER THAN 6FT**
**- EXTREMELY WET**
**- AIR ACCESS - NO LONGBOARDS**

The town of **El Valle** has a couple of powerful, all tides beachbreaks with something for everyone between El Almejal and the peaks beside the large rivermouth of La Bocana. Beware the scattered rocks in the line-ups especially at the north end of El Almejal. There's a local surf camp and some rental boards available. There's a beautiful vista of offshore islands from **Jurubidá**, which requires a solid swell with W in it, to form a decent righthand, sand-bottom point at the rivermouth. Fun to surf, this low tide wave is best in morning offshores before the wind switches to light NW. The **Tribugá** rivermouth has both rights and lefts, but the longer lefts are better. At high tide it breaks close to shore and has good shape. Hazards at this spot include strong rips and occasional sharks. **Nuquí** itself has a fickle rivermouth left, which is a long, mellow ride when it works, although it needs a big SW swell. Most of the time the adjoining beachbreak is fairly poor. **El Cantil**, where most surfers stay, has a beachbreak that works in NW or big SW swell. The waves here are average, with shifting peaks best in early morning glassy conditions. Within easy reach are the lefts at **Terco**, which again requires Dec-Mar NW swell or a big W/SW to get going. The peak is anchored by rock and can have some faster, hollower sections. The **Termales** rivermouth sandbanks dictate whether the lefts or rights will be better on either NW or big SW swells. So named thanks to the thermal hot pools just behind the beach. More accommodation options have opened in this area. If the swell is big and from the SW, check **El Mystic**, a sectiony left reef, way out off the end of the bay, but it's very rare hence the name. Most surfers bypass all of these breaks and take the 45 minute powerboat trip to **Pico de Loro**, which is regarded as the best wave in Nuqui. It's a great lefthander with walls, shoulders and barrel sections that get better in SW swells. Mid-tide is the optimum time to hit it with any E wind, but watch out for the big rocks and it gets a crowd on occasion. Under similar conditions, **Pela Pela** is another left with barrel sections and a sharp, shallow inside over rocks. Just 5km north of Cabo Corientes, **Juan Tornillo** is a good west-facing beach that picks up all W swell and handles a bit of size. Round the cape is **Secret Right**, a big, open barrel on SW or big NW swells. This wave works best at low tide and can run for 100 metres or more. There are other spots in the area and further south large estuarine rivermouths interrupt the straight grey beachbreak in a jungle wilderness.

Low pressures spinning near New Zealand rather than Chile, will deliver SW swell and surf in the 3-6ft range with possible 8ft days, along with a light onshore seabreeze and heavier rainfall. In winter (Dec-Feb), clean, long-distance NW swells and winds arrive with slightly less rain, but consistency might be at stake. Surf in this season is typically 2-4ft and very clean. Transition months are November and May, neither of which are ideal. Tidal variation can be as much as 5m, so take charts or a tide program.

## TRAVEL INFORMATION

**Weather** – The slopes of the Andes face the Pacific Ocean across a 100km coastal plain. The average rainfall in Nuqui is 5250mm (207in)! Rainfall has more variation throughout the hours of the day than the months of the year. In some places, rain falls on more than 300 days per year. The good news is that the coastal and offshore rain begins after midnight, then propagates westward over the ocean during the morning and sometimes afternoon hours. The sun does come out every day for a few hours; just don't expect to see much of the moon. The water is always boardshorts warm.

**Lodging and Food** – Basic accommodation and new eco-lodges around Nuqui are available. Hotel Nuquimar (fr $55/n). 6 nights & 3 boat trips in El Cantil Ecolodge is around $790, with full board, transfers and netted beds in double rooms. High Season can be more expensive. Food is good but not always varied, and a small store sells basic stuff.

**Nature and Culture** – Great outdoor activities like fishing (Jan-June best), humpback whale watching (June-Oct), diving (big fish, some coral) and the honeymoon trip to the Del Amor Cascades (Love Waterfalls). Nature is everywhere and the wild forest houses native people and endemic species.

**Hazards and Hassles** – Nuqui to Cabo Corriente has become much safer now, particularly as it has grown as an eco-tourism zone. It is worth avoiding big rivermouths around Cali, where boats with illicit cargo might transit. Bull sharks frequent rivermouths but no attacks recorded. Rips can be a concern but the main hazard is rain and the threat posed by chloroquine resistant malaria below 800m. There is one hospital for minor emergencies.

**Handy Hints** – Regarding safety, always ask in Medellin before departure. Beginners can take surfing lessons with the El Cantil Ecolodge, who also rent boards ($27/d), SUP's ($33/d) and boats ($438/d/4p). The region plays host to amazing jungle life and whale watching, so take binoculars.

MEMO GOMEZ

Pico de Loro

MEMO GOMEZ

Pela Pela

| STATISTICS | | J F | M A | M J | J A | S O | N D |
|---|---|---|---|---|---|---|---|
| SWELL | Direction | | | | | | |
| | Size (ft) | 4 | 3 | 2-3 | 4 | 2 | 2-3 |
| WIND | Direction | | | | | | |
| | Force | F4 | F3-F4 | F3 | F3-F4 | F3-F4 | F3-F4 |
| WATER | Wetsuit | | | | | | |
| | Temp/°C | 26 | 26 | 28 | 28 | 28 | 27 |
| WEATHER | Rainfall/mm | 590 | 597 | 649 | 623 | 609 | 532 |
| | days/mth | 23 | 24 | 25 | 26 | 26 | 27 |
| | Min temp/°C | 24 | 24 | 23 | 23 | 23 | 23 |
| | Max temp/°C | 32 | 32 | 32 | 32 | 32 | 31 |

# Northern Ecuador

**Ecuador is a warm-water fix after enduring the cold Humboldt Current that pervades the South American Pacific Coast. The Montañita area in the south is popular but the perfect left point set-up in Mompiche has attracted the more adventurous to the lush tropical rainforest of Esmeraldas Province, aided and abetted by a pick'n'mix of reefs, rivermouths and beachbreaks in a variety of swells.**

+ N & S SWELL EXPOSURE
+ EXPLORATION POTENTIAL
+ LESS CROWDS THAN S ECUADOR
+ BEAUTIFUL NATURAL AREA

- SHORT N SWELL SEASON
- FLAT SPELLS
- HARD TO REACH MOMPICHE
- RAINY SURF SEASON

**Atacames** is a massive tourist resort with lively beach bars, while the beachbreak ranks highly on the fun scale with barrels at low tide and long rides at high tide. It needs a NW or strong W swell to function. Samé is an elite resort where the beachbreaks are short and often close-out, but **Casa Blanca** may hold up if the swell is from the SW. Solitude-seekers may feel better in the fishing village of **Tonchigue**, but the local left pointbreak is usually quite sectiony. **Punta Galera** is like a slow copy of Suspiro and Mompiche. It's usually worth checking in the mornings when a NW or strong W swell shows up. The tedious access keeps the crowd levels down. **Estero del Plátano** has a good high tide reef peak that works on any W swell and regularly barrels in the morning offshores. One of Ecuador's best waves, **Mompiche** is all about long tubular rides in perfect scenery. This left pointbreak starts with a steep barrelling first section over a sharp rock ledge, before winding into the bay where it is well protected from the S dry season winds. NW and W swells work best, but it has been surfed on strong SW swells. Gets packed with locals when it's on, so be respectful. A few clicks south, **Punta Suspiro** is an underrated wave needing the same conditions and is used as a crowd escape from Mompiche. It's another left pointbreak with shorter, but classy rides. **Portete** is a powerful righthander just on the other side of Suspiro, that breaks with any swell direction but gets blown-out easily. There's a rivermouth and beachbreak peaks to the south. Dangerous at low tide and now overshadowed by a massive resort. There's no surf right in **Cojimies**, the first stop in Manabí Province, but with the help of a boat, hardcore explorers will reach the outer sandbanks (a couple of km offshore) where a bunch of beachbreaks can prove worth the effort.

On the way down to **Perdernales** are more beachbreaks that sometimes get epic. NW or W swells, morning offshores and a 4WD to access the beach are vital. Predominantly a major hub for the shrimp industry, Pedernales also has a stretch of fun beachbreaks, which occasionally get heavy and square. Over the Equator, the long rides of **Punta Ballena** would be a longboard paradise if it wasn't so fickle. Sometimes the lines do connect for long rides, other times it gets crumbly, un-makeable sections. It needs NW, W swells and wind can be an issue. **Cabo Pasado** is a way offshore reefbreak only accessible by boat from Canoa. With NW to W swells it can provide perfect, crystal water barrels, provided the wind is down. 16kms of beach stretch south of **Canoa**; the beachbreaks are top quality, with long walls or tubes depending on what the tide is doing. Conversely they can be junky and mushy and perfect for beginners. Again, NW and W swells are best and individual spot names include The Bridge, The Lab and Briceño. There's some jetty surf on the exposed side of Bahía de Caráquez and the fickle pointbreak lefts of **Punta Bellaca** will fire occasionally. When on (with good SW-W swells), a bunch of locals will be there to enjoy powerful waves around the low tide. If the swell comes from the NW it's best to go down to **La Mesita**, a remote left pointbreak offering long rides away from any crowd.

PAUL KENNEDY

Mompiche

Ecuador is exposed to 2-10ft NW swells that slowly decay over the 8-10 days they take to reach the Equator, arriving during the wet surf season when glassy N-NE or light onshore conditions prevail. SW swells in the austral winter are more consistent but unfavourable exposure and trade winds mess up the surf and bring colder temps. S-SW winds dominate up to 90% of the time. Puerto de Bahia Caraquez tides reach 3.2m, mainly affecting the reef and pointbreaks.

## TRAVEL INFORMATION

**Weather** – Esmeraldas is the wettest coastal province and Guayas the driest. The surf season matches the rainy season, between Jan and March. Days typically awaken to bright sunshine before tropical showers start pouring in the afternoon and continue at night. Temperatures are stable year-round from 23-27°C (74-80°F). Boardies up north or springsuit down south.

**Lodging and Food** – Budget hotels from $9 a night. Same, Atacames and Esmeraldas have high-end resorts. Mompiche beach's Casablanca resort fr $75/d; Try Sancocho Esmeraldeño' (fish soup) and 'mariscos encocada', seafood in a coconut sauce.

**Nature and Culture** – Check out the Manglares Mataje/ Cayapas Ecological Reserve. Wild partying in Atacames' beach bars and discos. Sua and Muisne island have a quieter, relaxed atmosphere.

**Hazards and Hassles** – Dysentery, hepatitis A and cholera are the main concerns: drink purified water and avoid ceviches (raw fish dishes). Mosquitoes love the rainy season - mild risk of malaria in Esmeraldas. Esmeraldas city and Atacames beach are unsafe after dark. Drugs are cheap, jail terms are long.

**Handy Hints** – The surf shops are further south. Bring regular boards and lycra sun protection. Crowds are rarely a problem. Ecuador is a very cheap visit.

| STATISTICS | | J F | M A | M J | J A | S O | N D |
|---|---|---|---|---|---|---|---|
| SWELL | Direction | | | | | | |
| | Size (ft) | 4 | 3 | 2-3 | 4 | 2-3 | 2-3 |
| WIND | Direction | | | | | | |
| | Force | F3 | F2-F3 | F3 | F3-F4 | F4 | F3-F4 |
| WATER | Wetsuit | | | | | | |
| | Temp/°C | 26 | 26 | 25 | 24 | 23 | 23 |
| WEATHER | Rainfall/mm | 144 | 122 | 90 | 15 | 14 | 26 |
| | days/mth | 23 | 24 | 23 | 7 | 8 | 1 |
| | Min temp/°C | 23 | 24 | 23 | 23 | 23 | 23 |
| | Max temp/°C | 27 | 28 | 27 | 27 | 27 | 27 |

# Southern Ecuador

Ecuador receives plenty of small, long distance, Pacific swells that roll in with moderate power, breaking onto forgiving reefs and sandy beaches. While some spots only light up with a big swell, there is usually something to surf for most of the year as southern Ecuador benefits from both N and S swells. North of Salinas is generally better exposed to N swells, while southern spots only break on S-SW swells.

+ TWO SURF SEASONS
+ WARM WATER
+ CALM WINDS
+ VERY CHEAP

– LACK OF HEAVY WAVES
– SOME CROWDS
– RAINY WINTER SEASON
– PETTY THEFTS IN THE CITIES

KEVIN MONCAYO

Montañita

Ecuador's surf city is Manta, full of bodyboarders who bust out some big moves on the hollow waves of **Murcielago** beachbreak. There's a wedge off the harbour wall that the locals covet – not the best beginner break. **San Mateo** was the longest wave in the country until a massive port was built, cutting the wave in half. It's still possible to get 400m walls rumbling down the line-up, offering up plenty of vertical lips for smashing and the odd barrel. Wont break until the beaches are overhead with a NW swell, so the few times a season it fires, it's crowded. **Puerto Cayo** picks up all swells, but excels on a moderate NW, handling overhead days. The peaks can get sucky at low tide and it is best in the morning glass conditions. Just south of busy Puerto Lopez is the isolated beach at **Punta Mala**, where some quality lefthanders spin down the line under the shadow of a majestic sea stack. **Rio Chico** welcomes long, consistent, uncrowded lefts to wrap around a rock shelf and bend into the private beach, inviting high energy turns on the steep walls. Better at lower tides with slack winds and W in the swell, pay to park and surf at the hotel. Further south are decent beachbreaks through Las Tunas and Ayambe. **Montañita** is Ecuador's most popular surf break and is identified by a phallic-shaped rock. It catches most swells, but NW will connect the inside and outside sections, easily holding double overhead on the sets and breaks with power and consistency. Hollower at lower tide or big open carvable faces as it pushes in, Montañita ticks many boxes for experienced surfers. Beginners and improvers should try the adjacent beachbreak where many of the surf schools operate. Montañita has become a bustling, noisy, party town with myriad bars, restaurants and places to stay. The local pecking order at the point is enforced so be patient and pick off the inbetweeners. **Punta Chulluype** takes a NW swell down both sides of a craggy reef, bending rip bowl lefts and open walls on the right. Large rocks in the line-up make low tide sketchy, especially if it is small. Named after the long dissolved shipwreck that used to grace this reef, **El Barco**'s lefts and higher tide rights entertain a lot of the Salinas surf community when a N or big SW swell manages to wrap around the promontory. Gets shallow but remains ripable fun for all sorts of surfcraft. N swells are bisected by the rocky island at **Playero de Miramar** and the peaks improve as the tide pushes. Another wall of fun for blasting turns, airs or cruising into deeper water on the lefts. La Bahia or **Shit Bay** is well exposed to the N with a great left by the rocks that awakens with moderate NW or big SW swells and S-SW winds. The tip of the Salinas peninsula catches both N and S swells at the wild exposed tourist viewpoint of **Chocolatera**. This windy, rippy, rocky spot can have a righthander bending around the point and some sketchy lefts, but it's normally blown-out and rarely worth the effort. Competition beach **FAE** has a very consistent workable left wall off the point plus some strong hollow beachbreak peaks. Best with small to moderate SW swell as it gets hectic when too big. Down the long Mar Bravo beach to Punta Carneros has good sandbars and is popular with Salinas locals and bodyboarders. **Puerto Engabao** has a consistent right pointbreak with punchy, performance orientated walls in average-sized SW-W swells. Tiny take-off zone close to the rocks means crowds are an issue. The powerful, long rights of **El Pelado** need a decent S-W swell and dropping tides to produce the barrels in front of the rock on the point. Walls through to another hollow section inside and 300m rides are possible. Almost always blown-out by the S winds, along with the string of seven pearler right points leading into Playas (El Faro, El Hambre, Las Paso, El Posada, Shark Bay, Olas Verdes, Chabella). Get up very early to beat the wind.

When the long distance, North Pacific NW swells finally arrive, only the spots north of Salinas will benefit. The southern half of the zone thrives on year-round 5-6ft SW swells, which average around 13secs period, even in the austral summer. The real problem is the wind that is even more consistent than the swell and blows from the SSW-WSW the whole year, albeit at windspeed lower than F3. Tidal range is lower than in the north at 2.7m for La Libertad.

## TRAVEL INFORMATION

**Weather** – See Northern Ecuador zone

**Lodging and Food** – Waterways offer a full 5 day tour package fr $945 with a base in Montañita. There is also plenty of cheap accommodation from camping and hostels (Tiki Limbo). Casa Coco house overlooks the point ($165/n/6p) as does Baja Montañita ($67/dble). All levels of accommodation options in Manta, Salinas or Playas. Basic food costs start from $7 a meal.

**Nature and Culture** – A visit to the high Sierras and the fabulous Andes mountains is a must. Quito is a great place to hangout, whilst Otavalo, Banos and Vilcabamba are all unique.

**Hazards and Hassles** – Mosquitoes are abundant everywhere in the rainy season, but no malaria down south. Rental cars are targeted by theives.

**Handy Hints** – Sumbawa surf shop is in Montañita. Faro is the cheapest place on earth to buy balsa wood boards and you can learn to surf on one at Camp Balsa Surf School. Crowds are only a problem near the cities and Montañita.

| STATISTICS | | J F | M A | M J | J A | S O | N D |
|---|---|---|---|---|---|---|---|
| SWELL | Direction | | | | | | |
| | Size (ft) | 4 | 3 | 3-4 | 4 | 3-4 | 3-4 |
| WIND | Direction | | | | | | |
| | Force | F3 | F3 | F3 | F3 | F3 | F3 |
| WATER | Wetsuit | | | | | | |
| | Temp/°C | 24 | 24 | 22 | 21 | 22 | 23 |
| WEATHER | Rainfall/mm | 244 | 196 | 18 | 18 | 2 | 7 |
| | days/mth | 16 | 15 | 3 | 1 | 1 | 2 |
| | Min temp/°C | 21 | 22 | 20 | 18 | 19 | 20 |
| | Max temp/°C | 31 | 32 | 31 | 29 | 31 | 31 |

# Santa Cruz, San Cristóbal GALAPAGOS

It was through observing the unique and diverse wildlife of the Galapagos Islands that led Charles Darwin to expand upon his theory of evolution. These 17 isolated, oceanic oases have been declared a national park and even today, only five of the islands are inhabited. The coastal fringe of this active volcanic archipelago is made up of lava reefs and boulders, because the water is too cold for coral formation. Some islands don't have that many good spots thanks to steep and broken up lava outcrops, while other islands like San Cristóbal have a concentration of top quality waves in a small area. Waves jack up suddenly out of deep water and have plenty of power, drawing the odd comparison with Hawaii. Further exploration may reveal more breaks, but many islands are off limits and permits are required to leave the main tourist areas. The predominant S-SE trade winds mean that the most consistent spots are to be found on the north-facing shores during the Northern Hemisphere winter, but there are also options to ride swells that have made the long journey from the Southern Ocean throughout the year. Most of the reefs are sharp and difficult to gauge depth through the ultra-clear, coldest equatorial water on earth. The Humboldt Current brings nutrient rich water and plenty of swell from Antarctica, attracting the prolific marine wildlife, along with experienced, wilderness seeking surfers.

**+ POWERFUL REEFBREAKS**
**+ WAVES YEAR-ROUND**
**+ UNCROWDED**
**+ WILDLIFE MECCA**

**- INCONSISTENT**
**- COOL WATER**
**- FEW SPOTS**
**- TOUGH ACCESS**

## TRAVEL INFORMATION

**Weather** – Despite its equatorial position, the Galapagos enjoys a relatively dry climate. The dry season, also called "Garua", causes low clouds, fog and drizzle on the hillsides from May to Dec but virtually no substantial rain. This is supposedly the cold season with constant SE to S winds. March and April are both the hottest and wettest months of the short wet season from Jan to May, when a springsuit should suffice, while around Aug/Sept, a light steamer is needed. El Niño years are much warmer in the sea and wetter on land.

**Lodging and Food** – Unless you stay on a boat, you have plenty of choice for Baquerizo Moreno basic hotels (Orca, Miconia, Casa Blanca, etc from $40/n), or the higher end Golden Bay Hotel (Wavehunters package including boat transfers fr $1990/wk/dbl), or the Hotel Pimampiro, used by Waterways for all inclusive guided tours ($1850/5d/dbl). Cheaper hostels and home stays in Puerto Ayora from $20/n/dorm. Galapagos Vision catamaran from $850/p/3n. Food is generally fish & rice. Veggies and beers are expensive.

**Nature and Culture** – The Galapagos is a World Heritage Site due to the amazing wildlife, which shows little fear of people. From midnight to 6am all electricity is switched off - don't expect any nightlife.

**Hazards and Hassles** – In the case of an emergency, adequate hospitals are far away. Most lava reefs are shallow and the rocks have sharp edges. Three shark attacks on surfers (Isabella and Santa Cruz islands) between 2007-2014 all non-fatal. Male sea lions are swimming around and have been know to nip at surfers. The true local surfers are few and friendly.

**Handy Hints** – Bring everything you may need with you. A couple of boards (a semi-gun may be needed), leashes, fullsuit and springsuit, booties, hats, sunscreen, insect repellent, flashlight and a conservationist attitude, especially when it comes to the scarce water supplies. The National Park entry fee is $100, payable in cash at the airport. To get to most spots, you'll have to walk or take a taxi ($2-5). Be careful of the sun, it's strong and shade is rare; people have died getting lost! Take strong footwear, hat and lots of water.

JUAN FERNANDEZ

PAUL KENNEDY

El Cañon

JUAN FERNANDEZ

Loberia

Baltra Island is the main airport and tourist arrival point, where most cruises start from. It's a military base and outside the National Park, so no problem for accessing the surf. The main break is 20mins sail north on tiny **Seymour Norte**, where a top quality, 100m long, right pointbreak will peel over rocky reef and boulders in NW-N swells. There can be shorter, hollow peaks dotting the west coast and it is a fairly consistent bet for your first surf off the plane. Baltra also has a chunky left wall inside **Aeolian Cove** that handles plenty of size and rumbles over the reef that is a mere stone's throw from the airport terminal. **Las Salinas** is just a bit further down the west coast of Baltra and is a classic cruiser's righthander, with long rolling walls around headhigh. Unusually for these islands, most of the reef is covered by sand, making this a lower risk wave for improvers and longboarders.

On Santa Cruz island, 1.5hr sail west of the largest population centre at Puerto Ayora, will anchor you by the solid lefthander at **Palmas Grandes**. This coast relies on S-SW swells and Palmas seems to receive and handle more size than other islands, with big drops into a longish, squared-off wall. There are three more left line-ups within sight and plenty more exploration potential to the north. **Cerro Gallina** or "Chicken Hill" overlooks a rolling left that rumbles and crumbles down a long boulder point into a bay that offers a bit of E-SE afternoon wind protection. It's a fun, hassle-free ride, with deeper water, but enough power to keep all abilities happy. Very consistent in any S swell and only accessible from a surf tour boat. A rare arc of sandy beachbreaks can be had at **Bahia Tortuga**, a 3km walk from Puerto Ayora. Wont take too much swell and is often onshore, but some fun corners can be found and it's the ideal learners spot. Take food and water and pack your trash at this once pristine spot. Back in town there's a sketchy, rocky right at Playa de la Estacion in front of the Darwin Research Station.

On San Cristóbal, Puerto Baquerizo Moreno, has the greatest concentration of decent surf spots in the Galapagos. It's also the administrative capital of the islands and holds the bulk of the islands accommodation. **Manglecito** is 15kms NE of Puerto Baquerizo by boat, where the point fires off fast lefts that are shallow and heavy at the peak before walling out into the bay. Long, fast and a real blast on an overhead NW pulse. Experienced surfers when bigger, plus there's a consistent A-frame reef nearby. ✪**Carola** is by far the most awesome, most consistent

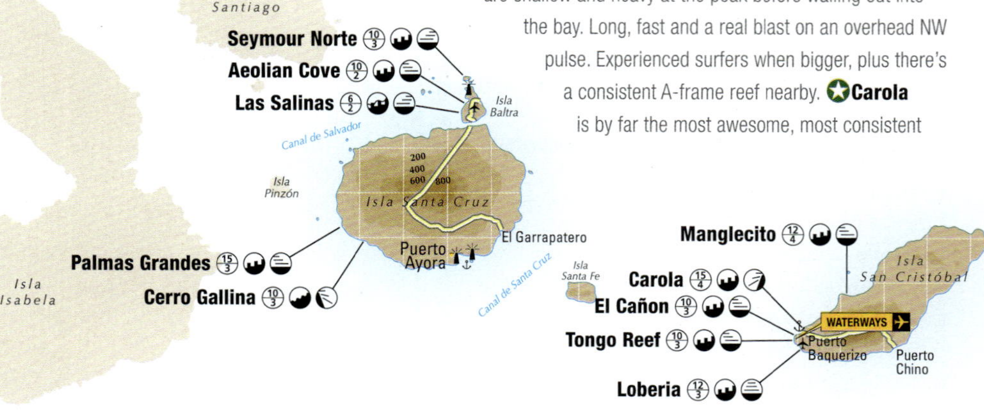

## Carola

LAT. -0.889159° LONG. -89.614200°

**Carola is the rapid righthander in front of the lighthouse, a short boat ride or 2km walk from the port. Mainly working on NW-N swells, plus a SW can also sneak in. It's a long, tubular wave, rideable from 4-15ft+, with a fast, heavy drop, made more difficult by the SE trades blowing into the barrel. Mid tides usually help with makability and expect to get get caught inside, where the duck-diving is fierce. The boulder strewn lava rock reef and semi-crowded conditions make this an experienced surfers spot, especially at size.**

and most crowded wave on the island. To surf **El Cañon**, you have to enter the military zone and leave your passport (or surf permit/i.d. from the San Cristobal Surf Club) at security! This left breaks in front of the cannon, close to the bouldered shore, when small N pulses come in, but holds waves up to 8-10ft on wrapping SW swells. High and tight tuck-in moments between the open walls that shoulder into the busy bay. A kilometre offshore, the Outer Reefs have some great lefts and rights depending on the swell angle, for those with access to a boat. **Tongo Reef** is a 30min walk round the coast from Cañon, or a short boat ride if the military refuse entry. It's a multi-sectioned left that starts steep and keeps going with fast down-the-line walls that may get hollower at the last section or shoulder off into the bay. When it connects up in S swells it is pure stoke for fast driving goofies and breaks through the tides. On the southwest-facing coast, **Loberia** is another Galapagos gem that can hold epic barrels on its day. From the A-frame peak, it's thick and fast, pitching over a shallow, spiky lava reef and will rifle off both ways, depending on what flavour of S groundswell is hitting. It's not always barreling with plenty of smaller, high performance days and the left point opposite the right can be a fun, ripable wall. NW swell does wrap in, but won't line it up like a good SW. Scores a 6 for consistency and 5 for crowds. Aggressive male sea lions will bite surfers that get too close to the females and pups, especially during mating season. Loberia also has a few nasty rocks sticking up out of the line-up. It's a 10min cab ride from town. There are many more possibilities around San Cristobal like La Perdida, Puerto Grande, Crateres and Punta Pitt in the north, but access is always the issue and getting permits from the National Parks plus a surf guide (San Cristobal Surf Club or tour operator) is essential to travel to out of the way breaks. Isla Isabela has the longest sandy beach in the Galapagos at Puerto Vilamil, where fun peaks arrive in any S swells, but it catches the wind quite badly.

The good news about being located right on the equator is that the islands receive the cleanest swells from both N and S, but the bad news is that these swells are generated more than 5,000km away and can suffer from heavy decay. Nevertheless, during the peak season from Dec-Mar, NW swells throw up steady waves in the 2-8ft range, with occasional forays into the 12-15ft range and winds have more E angle at much lower speeds. During April to Dec, early season SW swells dominate, before swinging more S, showing super-high groundswell consistency, long periods and greater wave height. At the same time, the trade winds pick up pace and clock around to the SE or due S, bringing cross-onshore winds to mess up exposed spots, so the early season months (Apr-May) are the best bet for good conditions at southern spots. Deep in the Austral winter, water temps can drop as low as 18-20°C (64-68°F) due to upwelling, la niña and the Humboldt Current. Be aware of the tides varying from 1-2.5m, which can make for a difficult time at certain spots, especially on small to medium-sized days when rocks can suddenly pop out of the water.

Tongo Reef

PAUL KENNEDY

| STATISTICS | | J F | M A | M J | J A | S O | N D |
|---|---|---|---|---|---|---|---|
| SWELL | Direction | | | | | | |
| | Size (ft) | 4 | 3-4 | 4 | 4-5 | 4 | 3-4 |
| WIND | Direction | | | | | | |
| | Force | F3 | F3 | F3 | F3 | F3 | F3 |
| WATER | Wetsuit | | | | | | |
| | Temp/°C | 23 | 24 | 22 | 21 | 20 | 21 |
| WEATHER | Rainfall/mm | 57 | 60 | 9 | 4 | 7 | 6 |
| | days/mth | 7 | 4 | 2 | 3 | 6 | 8 |
| | Min temp/°C | 23 | 23 | 21 | 19 | 18 | 20 |
| | Max temp/°C | 30 | 30 | 28 | 25 | 25 | 27 |

# North Piura PERU

The northwest corner of Peru enjoys waters warmed up by the southern extremity of the Panama Current and the coastline favours swells coming out of the N Pacific. It's not as consistent as the rest of Peru and is only worth visiting in the middle of the Southern Hemisphere summer, concentrating the crowds at Christmas. While heavy reefs like Cabo Blanco attract the experts, there is much for improvers and intermediates to get their teeth into like El Nuro, Cabo Blanquillo and Lobitos in a mixture of swell sizes and directions.

+ SUMMER NW SWELLS
+ GREAT LEFTS WITH GOOD WINDS
+ WARM WATER, PLENTY OF SUN
+ CLOSE TO S SWELL EXPOSURE

- SHORT SWELL SEASON
- FAIRLY INCONSISTENT
- HOT SPOT LOCAL CROWDS
- SOME SHARP ROCKS

Cabo Blanco

JAVIER FERNANDEZ

**Mancora** has a rolling lefthand pointbreak with nice walls, a few tube sections and inside shoulders where cutbacks prevail. Prefers incoming tides, is consistent and busy. **Punta Ballenas** picks up more SW-W swell, is much faster and hollower than the main point, but it's a messy, sectiony wave and will close-out over the sharp rocks at low tide. The shallow rock ledge at **Los Organos** needs W-N swell to create short, sharp left barrels and even shorter rights. More tide, glassy conditions and bags of experience, otherwise try fun Organitos. **El Nuro**'s sand-covered reef picks up N swell for uncrowded, high-performance waves with crumbling lips and forgiving cutback walls. On a big N swell, world-class **Cabo Blanco**'s fast tubes attract Peru's best surfers. The take-offs are usually late, straight into a spacious cavern, then race off past the elbow of the reef and down towards the pier 100m away. Frustratingly fickle, it explodes dangerously close to exposed, board-chewing rocks, there's a constant rip to fight and it's the most crowded, aggressive line-up in the country. Suitably named **Panic Point** is another challenging left that regularly works when S-SW swells wrap into a minefield of sharp, barnacle encrusted rocks, throwing up punchy, rapid tube sections that require high skill to survive. Dominated by a small local crew at mid to high tide. Check uncrowded **Cabo Blanquillo**, a left reef that needs some sand and no wind to get classic. **Punta Restin** is exposed and isolated, bending in S swells to a disorderly line-up that sections off and closes-out, plus the water will be 2-3°C (5-7°F) colder than in Mancora. **Piscinas** breaks beside a seawater pool built into the rocks, where a nice, easy left offers fun walls and a bit of steeper stuff in the shallower shorebreak. **Lobitos** is another perfectly shaped Peruvian point where long mechanical peelers will wall and run with lots of lip climbing and floating to link it up. Works in winter S and summer NW swells with higher tides making the inside steeper section less susceptible to close-outs. Rates highly for both crowds and consistency; expect vibes and drop-ins or go down to the easier, emptier El Muelle peaks. **El Hueco** is a heavy, heaving barrel hitting the reef off the tip of the point at Lobitos. You need a solid swell from the S-SW, negative tides and air-drop to casual tube-stance skills and it may link into the faster Frontera section. **Baterias** offers smaller S swell options at low tide with barrel sections and thick walls in strong currents. Inconsistent, windy **Punta Arenas** is a quality but sectiony left at low tide with a moderate swell. South of Talara where the water temps drop sharply, **El Golf** pitches hollow, punchy, fast righthanders, often when all the points are sleeping. Thorough workout with swirling currents. **Negritos** town beach can hold some nice triangular sandbars at La Brea with some fun corners amongst the close-out barrels. Head towards the southern headland at Balconies or maybe up at the huge concrete pier at Puerto Negritos for wind protection.

Máncora
Punta Ballenas
Los Organos
El Nuro
Cabo Blanco
Panic Point
Cabo Blanquillo
Punta Restin
Piscinas
Lobitos
El Hueco
Baterias
Punta Arenas
El Golf
Negritos
Pta Sal
TUMBES
Máncora
SURFHOLIDAYS
Vichayito
Los Organos
WATERWAYS
SUDDEN RUSH
Nuro
Cabo Blanco
El Alto
Restin
Panamericana Norte
Pta Piedras
PIURA
Lobitos
NOMAD SURFERS
Pta Capullana
Bahia de Talara
Cap. FAP Victor Montes Arias International Airport
Talara
Pta Arena
Negritos
Pta Parinas

Only the heart of the NW swell season (Nov-Feb) will see reliable 2-8ft conditions. Being long distance swells, the waves will be perfectly lined-up with long lulls between sets. There is lots of due W swell throughout summer, or it's only a short drive to the SW-facing coastline beyond Bayovar and the consistent S swells. S winds are straight offshore for most of the left points, while a light SW afternoon sea breeze can affect the more exposed spots. Light winds in the prime swell season. 2m tidal ranges; waves are better at low tide.

Lobitos

STU GIBSON

## TRAVEL INFORMATION

**Weather** – Peru's semi-arid climate is ideal for travelling - it hardly ever rains, daily variations are minimal, temps are never too hot or too cold (except, maybe in deepest winter). Most of the year is hot and sticky with plenty of sunshine. Wind patterns are light. Boardshorts or springsuit for most spots, but around Lobitos/Talara a light fullsuit is the go.

**Lodging and Food** – Many surfers stay at "Crillon", a cheap, rough pension in Mancora. Point Mancora Beach Hostel from $20/n. Mancora Beach Bungalows ($165/dbl/n). Mancora Bay hotel (fr $50/dbl). Talara has the best range of accommodation for all budgets. Cheap seafood – ceviche & rice costs about $6.

**Nature and Culture** – Much of coastal Peru is desert. It's a long trip inland to the Inca ruins of Cajamarca. Renowned big-game fishing for giant swordfish. During El Niño years all the fish vanish.

**Hazards and Hassles** – Be vigilant for pickpockets in popular tourist areas. Eat only well-cooked or boiled food.

**Handy Hints** – Surf shops in Mancora and Lobitos. This area could be combined with a trip to Ecuador. Basic Spanish is essential if you're travelling here without a guide.

| STATISTICS | | J F | M A | M J | J A | S O | N D |
|---|---|---|---|---|---|---|---|
| SWELL | Direction | | | | | | |
| | Size (ft) | 4 | 3 | 1-2 | 1 | 1-2 | 3-4 |
| WIND | Direction | | | | | | |
| | Force | F3 | F2-F3 | F3 | F3 | F3-F4 | F3-F4 |
| WATER | Wetsuit | | | | | | |
| | Temp/°C | 24 | 25 | 23 | 22 | 21 | 22 |
| WEATHER | Rainfall/mm | 3 | 45 | 0 | 0 | 0 | 1 |
| | days/mth | 0 | 4 | 0 | 0 | 0 | 0 |
| | Min temp/°C | 23 | 23 | 21 | 20 | 20 | 21 |
| | Max temp/°C | 30 | 31 | 30 | 28 | 29 | 29 |

# South Piura PERU

Heading towards remote Bayovar seems unnecessary when the ultra-long rides of Chicama are just a few hours south and the deep tubes of Cabo Blanco a few hours north. Conditions are extremely harsh in this vast desert region of sand dunes and granite cliffs, which remains fairly untouched by tourism, so you better be well prepared for camping and desert survival in your 4x4. The rewards are the long, lonely left caverns at Nonura and Punta Tur, plus a handful of other spots scattered across a wide, empty landscape. Not for those looking to move on from surf school success, this is a hardcore destination suited to rippers with rippling muscles to keep abreast of the serious currents.

+ WORLD-CLASS LEFTS
+ COMPLETELY UNCROWDED
+ ALWAYS OFFSHORE
+ PRISTINE NATURAL AREA

– 4WD ACCESS ONLY
– HEAVY LINE-UPS AND RIPS
– ZERO FACILITIES
– "EL NINO" RISK

Punta Tur

GONZALO BARANDARIAN

The 20km long beach of **Colán** has mushy, small waves hitting the gently shelving sand and rolling in with little decent shape. Good for complete beginners. **Punta Negra** is a small S-SW swell option, hopefully producing some fast lefts across the straight sandbars, instead of shut-downs. It's a mission to find the right dirt roads to this empty, cliff-lined beach. **Yacila** is protected from the strong winds by a large rock, attracting local bodyboarders to the mediocre, beachbreak close-outs in summertime NW swells. Handles onshore W wind quite well. On the north side of **La Islilla** fishing village, a righthand pointbreak can get really hollow when a summer N swell meets any wind from the east. Natural footers will want to try this one, but it doesn't break too often. Beachbreak further north will be more consistent. Forget the Bay Of Sechura, unless you are looking for small, close-out mushburgers. **Punta Aguja** marks the spot where the Equatorial Counter Current loses the battle against the Humboldt, meaning the water gets radically colder south of this rocky point. The beaches leading down to Nonura can hold a fun, easy peak or two when the point is too small. Bayovar's world-class spot, **Nonura** is only accessible by 4WD and camping is the only accommodation option. A long, tough paddle out against strong currents, leads to the classic tubular pointbreak lefts. Nonura will take any moderate swell from the SW to the NW and maxes-out around 10-12ft. Everyone who gets it on agrees with two things; it's a hell of a wave and a hell of a current. **Punta Faro** also holds lefts at breakneck speed with break-arm currents, but smaller, straighter swells from W-NW can be more manageable. Ecolodge accommodation on the beach. **Punta Tur** is another great lefthander that breaks further away from the shore than Nonura, resulting in really long, fast peeling waves split into different sections. When everything aligns like 10ft of SW swell, ESE winds and low incoming tide, T-Land can resemble its Indonesian namesake. Suffers from really strong currents, is inconsistent, gets blown-out and is only suited to fast, confident surfers. Basic desert camping in a pristine environment – leave it that way. A dirt track parallels the **Reventazón** beach for endless kilometres, surveying unappealing, usually out of control, onshore beachbreak that's only worth a look on the smallest, windless days. There's more exposed empty below average beachbreak in **Cabo Verde**, at the Piura/Lambayeque border, opposite Lobos de Tierra island.

April-October is the best season for regular 3-12ft S-SW swells coming from lows down in the southern latitudes, with a minimum of 2-3ft swell produced by the southerly winds accompanying the cold Humboldt Current. Between November and February, NW swells will come down from the North Pacific 5-6 days after pounding the Hawaiian shores. The constant temp difference between dry land and relatively cold water, drives prevailing S winds 40-55% of the time and SE 30-45%, which is offshore on NW exposed bays like Nonura. Usually, SE morning winds turn to the S after noon. The tidal range doesn't exceed 1.5m, but that's enough to affect the pointbreaks.

## TRAVEL INFORMATION

**Weather** – Desert and semi-desert climate caused by the cold waters of the Humboldt Current flowing northwards. Rain is scarce, even during the rainy season running from January through March, but when the El Niño phenomenon arises, the water temps rise, and the skies open, causing flooding with widespread damage to roads, bridges and towns. Nights are colder with mild mornings in the Andean region. The differences in water temps are radical from the north to the south of the zone, ranging from boardies/springy to a light steamer.

**Lodging and Food** – The Punta Luna Ecolodge is $100/n and you must bring all food and water supplies from Piura before heading there in your own 4x4. No guided tours currently available. Hotel Náutico de Paita ($20/dbl) or rent a bungalow in Playa Colán Lodge ($75 triple). Gustatory delights include baby goat and rice, and seco de chevalo (pork, rice and plantains).

**Nature and Culture** – There's great diving in places like Colán, Punta Bapo and Isla Lobos de Tierra. Yacila and Colán are beautiful beaches in Paita. Witness archaeological remains of the Vicús Culture, masters of ceramics and goldsmithing, in Catacaos. The Virrilá estuary is a bird (watching) paradise.

**Hazards and Hassles** – Crowds or localism definitely won't be a problem, but being absolutely alone is much less enjoyable when out of fresh water or food, lost, or stuck in the sand. Driving skills on unpaved or sand roads is recommended. Wild animals may steal food.

**Handy Hints** – Be environmentally aware – recent complaints about surfers leaving litter and not using adequate latrines could jeopardise the issuing of permits, which are required for some of the distant and virgin beaches. Before driving on sand, deflate tyres to avoid getting stuck. Try to go with someone that already has good knowledge of the area.

| STATISTICS | | J F | M A | M J | J A | S O | N D |
|---|---|---|---|---|---|---|---|
| SWELL | Direction | | | | | | |
| | Size (ft) | 4 | 3 | 4 | 4-5 | 4 | 3-4 |
| WIND | Direction | | | | | | |
| | Force | F3 | F3 | F3-F4 | F3-F4 | F3 | F3 |
| WATER | Wetsuit | | | | | | |
| | Temp/°C | 22 | 22 | 19 | 18 | 17 | 19 |
| WEATHER | Rainfall/mm | 10 | 10 | 0 | 0 | 0 | 0 |
| | days/mth | 0 | 0 | 0 | 0 | 0 | 0 |
| | Min temp/°C | 23 | 22 | 19 | 17 | 17 | 19 |
| | Max temp/°C | 32 | 31 | 28 | 26 | 28 | 30 |

# La Libertad PERU

The region of La Libertad is home to Chicama, generally considered the world's longest left. It breaks mainly on sand, is consistently offshore, is relatively gentle and doesn't suffer too badly from crowds. Amazingly, there are more leg-burning, endless walls like Pacasmayo, which probably lines-up a bit better than Chicama and is possibly a bit longer in the makeable single ride category. Add in Punta Huanchaco, another 800m of sectiony lefts in the home of the Totora reed Caballito riders and this La Libertad zone looks like the place to go for the quintessential South American lefthander experience.

**+ PERFECT UNCROWDED LEFTS**
**+ EXCELLENT WIND PATTERNS**
**+ CLOSE TO THE ANDES**
**+ HISTORICAL SITES**

**- STRONG CURRENTS**
**- WINDY AFTERNOONS**
**- FOGGY**
**- DIFFICULT, TEDIOUS ACCESS**

## TRAVEL INFORMATION

**Weather** – Peru's ideal travelling temperatures and lack of rainfall are overshadowed by a near permanent sea mist (garúa), which leaves a grey, depressing blanket over the bleak countryside. Dec-March is about the only time that you can expect clear skies. Avoid El Niño years when it will rain all day, every day, bridges and roads will be washed away and the water will turn a muddy brown. In the water you will require a 3/2 steamer from May-Nov and a springsuit for the rest of the time.

**Lodging and Food** – Chicama town is Puerto Malabrigo, as signposted and there are now every type of surfer accommodation from budget to luxurious. The boutique Chicama Surf Hotel and Spa has luxury rooms starting from \$100/n/p or \$130/n/dbl that includes breakfast, sauna, gym, jacuzzi, wifi, etc. Their big draw card is the zodiac tow-back service; \$30/d/p for two sessions. Huanchaco also has multiple accommodations for all budgets. Seafood is excellent value at around \$8 a meal or some guest houses let you use the kitchen to self cater.

**Nature and Culture** – The Huanchaco Festival with the "Caballitos de Tortora" and some surf contests take place in May. Close by are the remains of Chan-Chan, an old Moche Indian site. For hiking and climbing Huaraz is home to the Cordillera Blanca, a mountain range with several 6000m peaks.

**Hazards and Hassles** – There aren't many hazards to be aware of. Petty thefts, especially on crowded buses are very common. Eat only boiled and cooked food.

**Handy Hints** – Rental boards are available from many of the camps/hotels (SurfHouse, Chicama Surf Hotel) from \$11/day. Take booties for hopping over rocks, a light fullsuit and an everyday board. A longboard would be ideal for some of the long slow waves. Basic Spanish essential for independent travellers.

WILSON FLORES

Puemape
CARLOS SANCHEZ

Pimentel
CARLOS SANCHEZ

In the region of Lambayeque, **Pimentel**'s long, dishevelled pier points directly into the SW swells, catching sand and heaping it up into long bars, promoting rolling peaks and plenty of fun corners. Prefers summer NW swells to hit the winter build-up, when good lefts set up on the south side. **Puerto Eten** also has a long, busted-up pier, with rights in summer swells back towards the pier and some more interesting peaks anchored to the rocks just south of the pier. The best wave is the left point found below the lighthouse (Punta La Farola) in the next bay, when SW swells wrap onto the rocks and wall up nicely for a few hundred metres. **Pacasmayo** catches loads of swell, peels forever and is often referred to as Chicama's big brother, as it will always hold much larger waves. It is also claimed to be a longer ride on the rare occasions that a 12ft S-SW swell transports surfers on a 2.5km marathon from the tip of the point till it smashes into the pier in town.

Rides have been timed at 4mins and it doesn't section off or have gaps in the wave like Chicama. Pacasmayo starts off with a hollower, squirting section, then mellows into a wall of varying steepness with little pockets and crumbling lip-lines, perpetually motoring northwards with symmetrical precision. A perfect day would see low tide incoming, double-overhead SSW swell, light ENE wind and hope it is a weekday for lower crowds. The current reaches epic proportions when it's big. Most walk back up, but getting through the rocks, wreck, urchins and stingrays can be tricky. Local surf businesses have bought zodiacs to the line-up, greatly increasing the wave count of the wealthy and annoying the paddlers with fumes, wake and bad etiquette. Kite-surfing has grown massively as the afternoon cross-shore provides the power to launch and saves the arms from the paddling. Very high consistency for some kind of rideable wave and these days it is often crowded with large groups of foreign and South American travellers. **Puemape** is a bit more reefbreak than typical point. The exposed shelf sitting in front of a rocky tongue of land, is very open to S-W swells and is usually a bit bigger than Pacas on small days. The drop is sharp with plenty of rocks in the periphery of your vision and it starts off fast and steep with some cover-up potential, before bending into the sandy bay and going fatter, but maintaining plenty of push

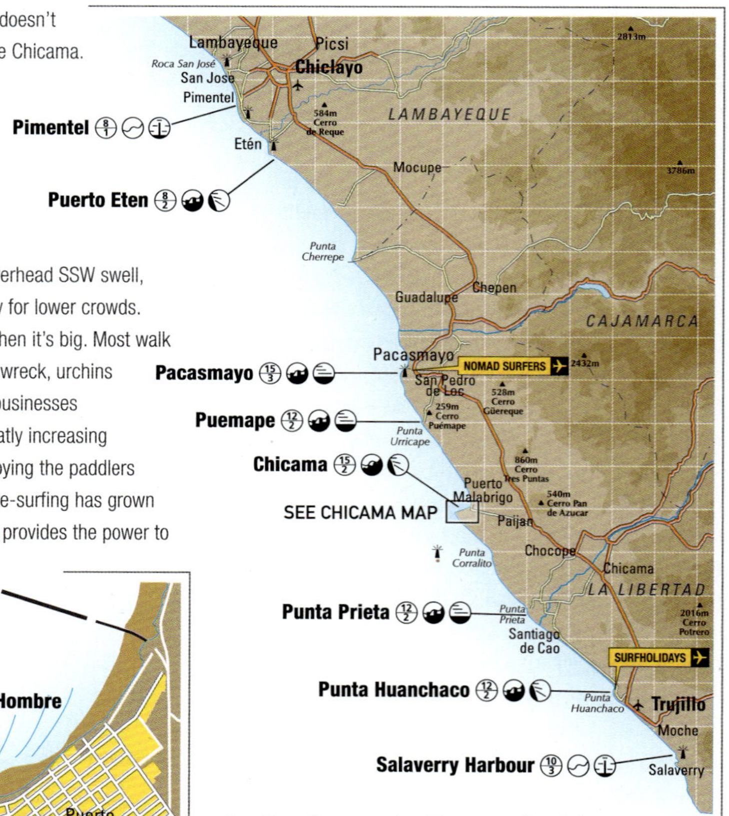

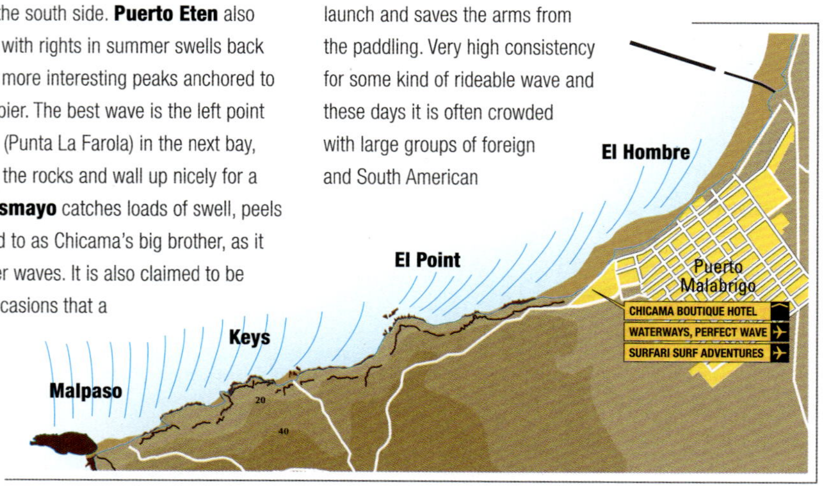

## ✪ Chicama

LAT. -7.704944° LONG. -79.452749°

Chicama is invariably offered as the longest wave in the world, measuring 4km, although no one has actually ridden it for that distance. Most people drift down through the four defined breaks and walk back up the point. Furthest out is El Cape aka Malpaso, which starts fast and sucky before becoming the familiar, slightly tapered, lip-feathering walls that demand a repetitive approach of drive, lip bash, float and pump until a temporary shoulder gives respite for a roundhouse or two. It's a neat but unmakeable kilometre to the racy walls of Keys, where barrels with wind protection need a moderate to strong swell and higher tides to transport you up to three-quarters of the way towards the main point. The big protrusion of El Point is a 20+min walk from town and the exposed rocks make a good marker in this faceless line-up. It starts off fast with some hollower, close-out sections, but quickly settles into an ideal tempo that peels like it was designed in a laboratory. Foam-climb re-entries will help negotiate the longest makeable stretch of Chicama that spins for 1.1kms, before reaching the last El Hombre section, where you are most likely to get barrelled as the swell hits a clump of rocks and sandbanks, then speeds up on its 800m sprint to the pier. Lower tides and E-SE winds favour the two end sections, but sometimes the wind is so strong it will blow the waves to shreds.

along the tapered slopey shoulders. Summer swells can disturb the sand so winter souths are the go. Blows out really easily so it's early or nothing, since NE winds are fairly rare all day. Urchins and more of those arm-burning rips flowing north. Few waves on the planet have the level of fame that ✪**Chicama** enjoys, yet it remains fairly low key as a "must surf" destination. Many factors help dissuade pilgrims like the wave height rarely reaching double overhead with a 12ft swell barely producing overhead conditions at El Point. The north-sweeping current is so strong, you spend more time walking back up the point than surfing. The Point could happily handle a crowd of 100 surfers, because most of the time at least half will be either out of the water or out of position. Surfers paying a hefty price for zodiac assist will bank more set waves, while the strong-paddling locals pick off the peaches. Drop-ins are common by those speculating that the guy on the inside wont make it. The whole Chicama show is consistent if you don't mind surfing small, broken-up, soft-shouldered sections and the days of real quality S-SW heaving swell are much rarer, when the crowds descend hoping for a slice of the legend. Discoveries of ancient civilisations have been unearthed at **Punta Prieta** (aka El Brujo), where exposed, wind-affected reefbreak just might line-up some nice shorter left sections on small S swells and glassy or E winds. There's some beach peaks to the north, but it's only worth the detour for the archeology. **Punta Huanchaco** is the home of the totora reed Caballito riders, who may be the world's first surfers. Fishermen have been riding the lefts back to shore at this spot for the last 2000 years. For today's surfer it offers easy and super-consistent waves, as it is very exposed to all swells. There are no cliffs on the headland, making it more of a reefbreak style set-up and more open to being blown-out. From the tip to past the long pier is a good 800m, but it hardly ever links up, preferring to peak and wall in a disorganised fashion, with some nice punchy hooks and corners linking the flatter trundling walls. All the various sections have names like La Posa and Sunset, plus there are some waves on the north side of the pier including a rare but welcome righthander. Huanchaco is party central compared to the other surf towns and attracts a lot of tourists from Trujillo and beyond, checking out the UNESCO protected mud city of Chan Chan. The line-up is sometimes crowded, but the typically strong Peruvian left point current spreads the punters. Surf shops, schools and rentals available. Between the jetties at **Salaverry Harbour**, an A-frame peak breaks that holds big waves and has a handy channel on either side of it. Beachbreak extends up to another jetty at Delicious Beach, but good shape is hard to find. There's exposed beaches and headlands to the south leading down to the heavily sheltered and somewhat hoaxy lefts of Puerto Mori. Nice beginner beach when small, but gets heavy once it is overhead.

Regular 4-12ft S-SW swells come from lows circulating the southern ocean between New Zealand and Cape Horn, propagating mainly SW pulses off their leading edges. The average size of 5-6ft for autumn, winter and spring means flat days are really rare on the most exposed points. Swell consistency exceeds 95% from March to August and only drops to the high 80s during summer. The other noteworthy fact is the average period never drops below 13 seconds, with 18-20 second days a regular occurrence, especially in April, May and June when the biggest swells are expected. Dominant winds are due S, with more SE early and maybe a touch of SW in the afternoon. This means offshore in many of the NW-facing bays, where most of the lefthand points are located. Tidal ranges are small with a maximum range of 1.7m.

CHICAMASURF.COM

Pacasmayo

| STATISTICS | | J F | M A | M J | J A | S O | N D |
|---|---|---|---|---|---|---|---|
| SWELL | Direction | | | | | | |
| | Size (ft) | 2-3 | 3 | 4 | 4-5 | 4 | 2-3 |
| WIND | Direction | | | | | | |
| | Force | F3 | F3 | F3 | F3 | F3 | F3 |
| WATER | Wetsuit | | | | | | |
| | Temp/°C | 21 | 21 | 18 | 17 | 17 | 18 |
| WEATHER | Rainfall/mm | 3 | 4 | 0 | 0 | 0 | 1 |
| | days/mth | 0 | 0 | 0 | 0 | 0 | 0 |
| | Min temp/°C | 21 | 20 | 18 | 16 | 16 | 17 |
| | Max temp/°C | 29 | 29 | 25 | 22 | 23 | 25 |

# Ancash PERU

Ancash is a Quechua word meaning blue and this region is where the first Peruvian civilisation, known as Chavín, originated and flourished in 600BC. It is a land of contrasts, with vast sand deserts hemmed in by the 6,768m white summit of the Andes mountains lying only 100km from the coast. Despite being blessed by highly consistent swells and a bunch of quality spots, travelling surfers usually by-pass this area, but as crowd levels increase everywhere, this rich, empty surf region is definitely one worth checking out.

+ NO CROWDS
+ GREAT SWELL EXPOSURE
+ CLOSE TO LIMA
+ ANDEAN LANDSCAPES

- LACK OF BEACHBREAKS
- MOSTLY LEFTHANDERS
- FOGGY DAYS
- PETTY THEFT

**Playa Grande** is home to good righthand beachbreaks and an excellent lefthand reefbreak that fires with S-SW swells. Extremely shallow even at high tide, the hungry reef delivers a very fast and tubular but short wave that never closes-out or gets busy. The vert take-off is followed by a slabby, square barrel that is one of the most dangerous waves in Peru! Experts only. **Bermejo** hosts an uncrowded, perfect, lefthand pointbreak where the trade winds blow offshore. The first section is fast and hollow in places, peeling over a stony bottom and best at low tide with a S swell. The second sandy section is a fun, easy wall, ideal for improvers. If a small to moderate SW swell hits, then the fickle righthand reef known as **El Pico** can deliver some excellent, powerful righthand tubes from mid to high tide. Big swells shut down this stretch. A labyrinth of dirt tracks makes it hard to find **Centinela**, one of the country's best left pointbreaks, with up to 4 consistent sections. Best with a W swell and definitely better at low tide, the outside sections (4-10ft) are for experienced riders only, as they are very rocky with frequent rips. The sandy inside sections (2-7ft) wall up very nicely too and suit all standards. On S swells only the powerful first section breaks, but the more the swell turns to the W and even NW the sandy inside section walls up and very long rides are on offer. Watch out for cliff bounce, barely submerged rocks, rips at size and weekend crowds. A shorter, smaller and much less consistent lefthander hugs the hilly headland at **Carquin**. The 1st section can be tubular on a solid S swell, unfortunately the rides are shorter than the ones of Centinela and an ugly industrial area lies in the background. The rare summer N swells won't suit many breaks in the area except the inconsistent, high tide lefthander at **Paraiso**. Nearby spots include El Rebote, La Antena, and Punta Salinas which has a similarly jutting southern headland that blocks all but the biggest S swells. **Pasamayo** is a very powerful, well-shaped reef peak, throwing out plenty of tubes and long ripable walls. It's very consistent and often too big, so a small to medium swell on windless early mornings is best. Take a boat rather than the insanely steep sand dune below the Pan-American truck lane. Ancón has a N swell option at Playa **Conchitas**, where a semi consistent righthander breaks over flat rocks and sand. It is a popular, crowded town beach in summer with nearby facilities, but it suffers from poor water quality.

SEE COSTA VERDE MAP

GONZALO BARANDARIAN

Playa Grande

Central Peru is consistently exposed to 4-15ft S-SW swells that can occur anytime from March through November, while the NW swell season (November to March) will turn on a few spots, but is definitely not the best time to surf here. Prevailing winds are from the SE-S and blow all through the year, offering a lot of sideshore conditions for much of the SW angled coast and offshores for a few points. Usually, SE morning winds turn more S after noon, so wake up early, especially in winter when windspeed increases. Tidal ranges are up to 1.8m with most spots breaking better at low tide.

## TRAVEL INFORMATION

**Weather** – Ancash has a spring-like climate all-year-round. Foggy and sunny days intermingle around the humid sand dunes throughout the year. Summers have warm temps around 30°C (86°F), winters are very humid around 18°C (64°F), while spring and autumn are bang in the middle 24°C (75°F). The only rainfall is a light sea mist drizzle locally known as garua. Many use a 4/3mm fullsuit with boots between June and November and a 3/2mm fullsuit the rest of the year thanks to the wind-driven upwelling

**Lodging and Food** – The Centinela surf camp has folded. Cheap accommodation in Barranca (Hotel Chavin or hostels from $20/dble). In Huacho, 25mins drive from the point is Hotel Centenario (fr $50/n). Try the ceviche del pato, picante de cuy, jaca-casqui, pecan-caldo and humitas de chochoca.

**Nature and Culture** – Visit the highest summit of Peru, Huascarán in the glacier-filled National Park. Lots of ancient archaeological sites of Chavin de Huantar & Caral cultures, plus Paramonga pyramids. Check the Rataquenua view-point and Ancash Regional Museum in Huaraz.

**Hazards and Hassles** – Hidden rocks, currents, sea urchins and the shallow reef at Playa Grande constitute the main dangers while surfing. Avoid driving at night, heavy traffic and thefts in Lima, don't get lost near Paraiso.

**Handy Hints** – No surf shops in Ancash region, boards & gear must be rented or bought in Lima (Klimax, Wayo Whilar, Boz, Sofia Mulanovich surf shop). Bring a 6'6" to 7'4" thick board for heavy waves. Booties and helmet are a plus (few hospitals). Due to petty theft even from taxis, leave a copy of your passport or ID card with your hotel in Lima. Free camping possible but not recommended.

| STATISTICS | | J F | M A | M J | J A | S O | N D |
|---|---|---|---|---|---|---|---|
| SWELL | Direction | | | | | | |
| | Size (ft) | 4 | 3 | 4 | 4-5 | 4 | 3-4 |
| WIND | Direction | | | | | | |
| | Force | F3 | F3 | F3-F4 | F3-F4 | F3-F4 | F3 |
| WATER | Wetsuit | | | | | | |
| | Temp/°C | 21 | 20 | 18 | 17 | 16 | 18 |
| WEATHER | Rainfall/mm | 0.5 | 0 | 0.7 | 2 | 2 | 0.3 |
| | days/mth | 1 | 0 | 1 | 2 | 1 | 1 |
| | Min temp/°C | 13 | 15 | 12 | 12 | 12 | 12 |
| | Max temp/°C | 26 | 26 | 23 | 20 | 21 | 24 |

PEDRO SLAINAS

Bermejo

# Costa Verde PERU

Lima is the bustling, growing capital that could be the continent's ideal surf city, blessed with a range of waves from rolly beachbreaks to terrifying tow-ins and just about everything in-between. The urban beaches of the Costa Verde at Miraflores are perfect for beginners and longboarders as it usually breaks softly outside and reforms multiple times. Those looking for more of a challenge will find it at La Herradura, the iconic South American left pointbreak.

**+ HIGHLY CONSISTENT SWELL**
**+ GREAT SPOT DENSITY**
**+ EASY ACCESS AND CHEAP**
**+ LIMA ENTERTAINMENT**

**- NOT PERU'S BEST SURF**
**- COLD WATER**
**- COASTAL WINTER FOG**
**- CITY CROWDS AND POLLUTION**

## TRAVEL INFORMATION

**Weather** - See Punta Hermosa and Ancash

**Lodging and Food** – City prices, but a wide range of options. In Miraflores try the Imperial Inn ($40/n) or the trendier Hostal Lucerna ($47/n). Both are a short cab ride to the Costa Verde beaches. Backpackers should head to 151 ($11/n) or Mochilero's in Barranco ($8/n).

**Nature and Culture** – Witness the Inca's wealth and culture in the city museums. Pachacamac ruins are among the largest pre-Columbian settlement on the Peruvian coast. Budget for a short hop to the Andes.

**Hazards and Hassles** – Crowds are common especially at La Herradura. Rolling boulders in the shorebreak may result in sprained ankles. Razorblade maestros (pickpockets) operate on buses and all main tourist areas. Eat only cooked & boiled food.

**Handy Hints** – Many city surf shops (Klimax, Sofia Mulanovich, Quicksilver, O'neill). Good, competitively priced, locally made boards by Wayo Whilar and wetsuits by Boz. Take a 3/2 steamer and booties for urchins & rocks.

PEDRO SALINAS

**Barranquito to Triangulo**

CARLOS SANCHEZ

**La Herradura**

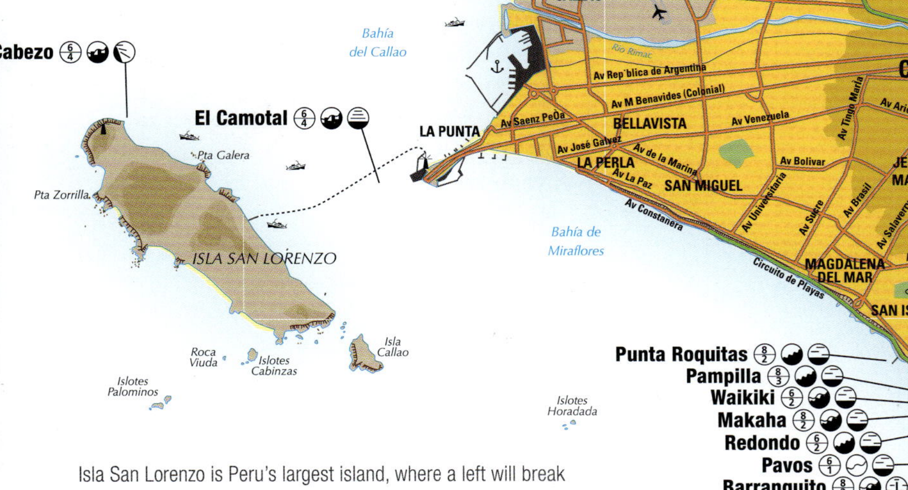


Isla San Lorenzo is Peru's largest island, where a left will break at **El Cabezo** below the lighthouse on the largest NW/SW swells, but only locals with boats will ever surf it. **El Camotal** is another 'secret island' and it's possible, although not recommended, to paddle from la Punta. The wave breaks both ways and gets occasionally hollow, but wind exposure usually makes the wave face choppy. The Costa Verde is a string of beaches located at the foot of the cliffs that plunge down from the Miraflores district of Lima. Unchallenging, consistent lefts and rights break at **Punta Roquitas**, where stones/boulders roll around in the shorebreak. Better at lower tides, it usually has a bit more push than the other jetties, attracting crowds of the better surfers and bodyboarders. **La Pampilla**'s shifty peaks develop into a better right in larger swells. Rolling faces and easy shoulders make this a longboarders favourite and contest site. There's more waves at the adjacent beaches of Tres Picos. **Waikiki**'s soft breaking rights and lefts prove enjoyable on a longboard as it breaks outside and reforms when bigger, or else mushy peaks inside the jetties on SW swells. The original Waikiki Surf Club is definitely worth a visit to check out their old logs. **Makaha** is on the north side of the huge jetty, but like the neighbouring beaches, power is lacking and rolling, slopey walls are the norm. It can also be a long tiring paddle searching for the outside sets and closes-out when it gets overhead. On the southern side of the jetty is **Redondo**, where a fairly reliable left breaks with all the same hallmarks; soft, slow and forgiving for the crowds of beginners. Barranco district's beaches face NW, requiring NW swell or larger S to SW swells to wrap in. **Pavos** beachbreak is only suitable for bodyboarders with shoredump launchpads and deep water to the outside bar. **Barranquito** is an organised jetty left, plus rights also break on the other side of the jetty and back towards the left. It's usually smaller but shows a bit better shape than the breaks to the north, when the boulders and sand are just right. Another Hawaiian-named break, **Laniakea** is a decent righthander that's popular with dawn patrol surfers from Lima as S wind will ruffle it. Sombrillas or **Ala Moana** lefts get fast walls and the odd hollow section when strong southerly swells hit the area. It has an easy paddling channel and winds are offshore most of the time. There are more boulder beaches in the Agua Dulce area and **Triangulo** attracts a crowd when all the other beaches are closed-out. It's very protected from both swell and wind, creating mellow, rolling peaks that don't break well very often. **La Herradura** is the best pointbreak in Lima, isolated in a relatively deserted, horseshoe bay in the Chorrillos district. This powerful left breaks along a high cliff for rides up to 500m split into 3 sections. The steep, hollow take-off becomes a long workable wall before spinning through a tubular inside section. Requires a solid swell to start breaking and gets better as the size increases, holding up to 12ft faces on the best days. Winds are usually not a problem since the dominant S wind blows offshore and low tide is better. Such a quality wave in the middle of such a big city draws plenty of crowds to this experts only break and it is the only show in town when a big swell hits. Prepare to be burnt repeatedly as the locals show little appetite for waiting. The rip gets stronger on the inside sections and thefts are a problem if walking around the point to take photos, etc. Some paddle from the surf club, others make the long walk. South of Lima, **Villa** is a small swell beach where hollow, punchy peaks need slack wind conditions, but it can get heavy closeouts and strong longshore currents.

Swell Forecasting – See Punta Hermosa and Ancash

# Punta Hermosa PERU

Less than an hour south of central Lima, the low cliffs and pocket bays of the well-heeled beach suburbs of Punta Hermosa and San Bartolo attract beach-goers throughout the year. Surfers the world over will have heard of Pico Alto, a perfectly named big wave peak capable of holding XXL size, but there is plenty more for the average surfer to get excited about. A concentration of super-consistent reefs stud the coast, plus there are a handful of beachbreaks that work great in small summer swells. With such dependable swells creating a variety of waves for all abilities, Punta Hermosa is one of those rare places that keeps most surfers happy, most of the time.

**+ CONSISTENT SWELLS**
**+ GREAT DENSITY OF SPOTS**
**+ BIG WAVE POTENTIAL**
**+ CHEAP AND EASY LIVING**

**- LACK OF PERFECT CONDITIONS**
**- COLD WATER, COASTAL FOG**
**- BARREN COASTLINE**
**- WEEKEND CROWDS**

CARLOS SANCHEZ
Caballeros

**Pulpos** is a wide-open, exposed beachbreak that picks up all available S and N swell, providing it is not too big to transform the banks into one big straight-hander. Can be steep and fast with barrels that favour rights and those happy to hit lips as it closes-out, namely bodyboarders. The cove at **El Silencio** has a rocky reef inside the northern headland where a variable right will break in moderate S or better still W-NW swells. Inconsistent and often disorganised, the rights can be sucky over the sharp boulders before fattening out on the shoulder then shutting down on the sandier inside. There are some lefts at the southern end and also around the headland back towards Pulpos at La Timba. Caballeros and Señoritas are so named, because in the past, men and women were segregated into their own beaches. **Caballeros** is probably the best and most reliable righthander in the Punta Hermosa region, drawing in S to W swells onto a jutting headland reef. It starts off with a sucky spurt, then walls and shoulders as it bends onto the shallower parts of the reef and some hollow sections on the inside. Good power and just the right speed make it a favourite with intermediate and experienced regular-footers. **Señoritas** breaks left with power and purpose across 3 sections of rocky reef attached to the southern headland of the Señoritas/Caballeros bay. Purposeful walls with slabby lips and the odd tube moment, march across the line-up in most swells and there is a bit of S wind protection. Both waves work best at mid incoming, require a long paddle against fast currents, urchins are everywhere and the rocks are home to colonies of razor sharp picos de loro barnacles. They're super-consistent, crowded and for good surfers only. **Pico Alto** provides some of the biggest rideable waves in South America. The rights at the north end of **Playa Norte** can have some shape over the mix of boulders and sand, but are usually short slammers for the bodyboard crew. Around the headland is El Paso, a powerful, punishing righthander over boulders in a strong S-SW swell. The main resort beach of Punta Hermosa is flanked by **La Isla** and in the middle of the bay, a reliable peak forms on waist-high days and keeps breaking right up to double-overhead. It starts as a rambling righthand wall, thick at the base with crumbling lip-line and open faces perfect for carves and gouges. As it heads to the inside section, steeper hooks and cover-ups are possible before it fills and reforms into the shorebreak section called La Puntilla. The left is usually super-soft, so only cutbacks will do. **Punta Rocas** is by far the most consistent and crowded spot in the area. It's a peak off a blunt headland and the line-up favours rights, which work from tiny to triple overhead without closing-out. Muscular walls bump and grind down the bouldery reef, with a receding lip-line that invites blasting off the top and snapping back towards the power, of which there is plenty. Can have some hollow moments, especially at higher tides as it breaks closer on the rocks, while the lefts are more tubey in smaller SW swells. Most paddle-out from the southside, where the shorebreak is often ridden by bodyboarders. Any E in the wind will be fine. **Santa Rosa** is furthest north in a string of longer lefthanders and occasional short rights that run down this San Bartolo headland when the swell picks up from the W. At size it is an angry stretch of water, standing up hard from take-off and offering a further tube section before shutting down mercilessly on the boulder strewn beach.The paddle-out is tricky and the currents get motoring on big days. NW will open up the rights and fast, juicy walls are then available for a short distance. Mid tide is safest at this challenging spot that requires experience. **El Huayaco** peaks up directly in front of the dry creek mouth, doing a 200m left point impression, plus a bonus short right. From a predictably vertical drop-in, tapered ripable walls fan down the boulders with a mix of crumbly lips to launch from and some sucky chandelier pipes at the shallower spots. Works on smaller swells than Santa and Pena Rosa and is a bit less intimidating. Better with W in the swell and incoming tides. Furthest out on Punta Negra is **Peña Rosa**, the third of the boulder reef, left points with accompanying short rights back into the rocks. Like the others, S swell isn't ideal here so a bit of W goes a long way to stop the

## TRAVEL INFORMATION

**Weather** – Peru's semi-arid climate is ideal for travelling - it hardly ever rains, daily variations are minimal, temps are never too hot or too cold (except, maybe in the deepest winter), but this doesn't mean unbroken sunshine every day. The big difference between land and sea temps brings a near constant mist, called garúa, which occurs regularly from April-Nov. The Andes usually has superb visibility. El Niño years never stop raining. A 3/2 is needed from May-Dec and a springsuit or 2/2 for summer.

**Lodging and Food** – There are places to stay nearly everywhere, with several cheap lodging possibilities in Punta Hemosa or San Bartolo from as little as $15/n. Food is cheap; fast food (Bembos), the local seafood (ceviche) and beer (Pilsen Callao) should be sampled.

**Nature and Culture** – Cool place to hang out, with plenty of nightlife and some interesting wildlife. Take some time out from the surf and take a flight over the mysterious Nazca lines, or visit the stunning Macchu Picchu site high in the Andes.

**Hazards and Hassles** – On the down side, there are muscular crowds and rips, spiky urchins and picos de loros, lurking rocks and thieves, plus some real board-breaking potential at some spots. Lima has a high crime rate - take care.

**Handy Hints** – Costa Verde has the bulk of the surf shops. Take booties and a light fullsuit (or buy a Boz to blend in). Try to combine this trip with a visit to the Chicama/Mancora area.

CARLOS SANCHEZ

**Pico Alto**

**LAT. -12.337744° LONG. -76.837768°**

**South America's big-wave spot is an offshore bombora peak that breaks with Hawaiian power and proportions, 1.5km out to sea off the point at Playa Norte. It's mainly the rights that the tow crews and gun-toting paddle-ins are after and like most monster breaks, it's all about the drop, but Pico Alto also has an exceptional length of ride with a long, thunderous wall on offer to those who manage to negotiate the exploding peak. It's a 30-min paddle just to get in position, and is only rideable when the wave face is very clean and smooth. The left has far less wall, but is just as intense on the drop as the right, then fades into deeper water. Needs a good 8ft of swell to feel the reef and will hold as big as you like. Needless to say this is for big wave nuts only. It may look do-able from the headland but it is a different story out there. Specialist equipment and experience riding some of the biggest waves in the world are essential. One for the voyeurs, otherwise paddle out from Playa Norte, dodging the close-outs when it is really pumping.**

lefts shouldering off too much. Can have some sucky, barrelly moments on the right day. Less of a crowd as it is a bit of walk past Huayaco and people are too lazy to go the extra distance for what is probably a lesser wave. **Peñascal** appears off the southern tip of the wave-lashed San Bartolo headland, doing a scaled-down impression of a big-wave bombora. It arrives from deep and rears up quickly, giving those on longer boards the time to stroke into some serious drops and race along a series of wide walls and grunty lips. Mainly a long right, but there are some lefts depending on the swell direction, although the paddle back out is likely to result in a few on the head. The right can throw up a mean barrel when it is nicely lined-up in a S-SW swell, but it is more of a pedal to the metal wall. Great fun when smaller on the inside El Bajo section, before getting serious from double-overhead up on the point proper. High tide kills it a bit, but it will handle some onshore wind and works well in a S swell N wind combo, unlike the other lefts around the corner. The picos de loro cover the boulders and will even rip booties to shreds, so better to take the longer paddle from the beach. It is fairly high-consistency and crowds are well-spread by the shifting nature of the peak. Not for novices, who can try the mellower peaks in the bay near the jetties at the popular **Playa Norte** beachbreak in San Bartolo. Relatively friendly rolling peaks out the back with some rampy rights heading back towards the central jetty. The reliable left off the southern jetty is a ripable open face that handles some size and the whole stretch has something for all abilities and surfcraft so gets very busy on weekends.

CARLOS SANCHEZ

Punta Rocas

PEDRO SALINAS

San Bartolo

Lima receives super-consistent 4-15ft S-SW swells off the Roaring Forties lows, plus a minimum of 2-3ft of windswell produced by the constant S winds that accompany the cold Humboldt Current. It is rare to find it totally flat, with the worst month for swell consistency being January when it drops down to 95% and for 6 months of the year average swell height hovers around 6-8ft! Punta Hermosa stats show marginally more size and consistency than Costa Verde. The dominant wind is S, which is offshore at the NW-facing spots and southern corners. Usually, SE morning winds turn to S or SW after noon and can mess up the west-facing beachbreaks and reefs that need SE or glass. Tides have little effect on most spots if it is big enough.

| STATISTICS | | J F | M A | M J | J A | S O | N D |
|---|---|---|---|---|---|---|---|
| SWELL | Direction | | | | | | |
| | Size (ft) | 3-4 | 4 | 5 | 6 | 5 | 3-4 |
| WIND | Direction | | | | | | |
| | Force | F3 | F3 | F3 | F3-F4 | F3-F4 | F3 |
| WATER | Wetsuit | | | | | | |
| | Temp/°C | 20 | 19 | 18 | 16 | 16 | 18 |
| WEATHER | Rainfall/mm | 1 | 0 | 5 | 8 | 5 | 2 |
| | days/mth | 0 | 0 | 1 | 2 | 0 | 0 |
| | Min temp/°C | 19 | 18 | 15 | 14 | 14 | 16 |
| | Max temp/°C | 26 | 25 | 21 | 18 | 20 | 23 |

# South Lima and Ica PERU

**Few bother to make it all the way down to the points of Southern Lima and Ica regions for some isolated, desert waves. Certainly Cerro Azul and San Gallen should be on any Peruvian itinerary and there are many little fishing villages where the waves can get really good when the sand is all lined up. From Puerto Caballas in Ica to Playa Molendo in Arequipa lies 450kms of real desert frontier where onshores buffet the exposed sandy stretches and there's potential to explore this savage and daunting coast by 4x4.**

- **+ CONSISTENT S SWELL**
- **+ SAN GALLEN RIGHTHANDER**
- **+ ASIA SUMMER PARTIES**
- **+ NEVER RAINS**

- **– DISTANCE BETWEEN BREAKS**
- **– MORE ONSHORES**
- **– DESERT TERRAIN**
- **– OFTEN TOO BIG**

Novelty shorebreak inside deeply protected **Naplo** harbour, bends bigger or N swells into dumpy closeouts and short steep lefts and rights for the bodyboarders. Rippy, bouncy, rocky and dirty. When a nice W-NW swell hits **Playa Chilca** at the right angle, perfect A-Frames shack up on the sandbars, creating fast, makeable tubes. It can take a good 12ft swell and seems to jack up the wave height in all conditions, but if it comes from the S, the current is unbearable. **Puerto Viejo** proffers one of the longest rides in Lima region when a good S swell wraps around the headland, where it is well protected from all S winds. The linear walls will excite both short and longboarders with little hollow pockets and a lip-line coping perfect for flick, float or fly. When small, head up the beach to Puerto Nuevo and snag some short but sick sandbank shacks. **Asia** sits on a gargantuan stretch of resort playas with varying quality beachbreak peaks. Can be hollow and zippy one day, sloppy and slow the next. Usually best around Playa Cocos behind the islands where the sandbars are more varied. **Cerro Azul** nestles nicely between a tall headland and a long fishing pier, allowing a triangular bar to build up and sculpt a performance ride for a good 2-300m. Starts off steep in front of Eagle Rock then slopes off into the shoulder and cruises through the sections towards the pier. S wind is dead offshore, it's rideable from waisthigh to overhead and loved by longboards and learners. There's a proper sucky, tubular right on the north side of the pier. Walk back round after a wave to avoid the current, stingrays and to spread the crowd. Predominantly a left boulder reef, **Pepinos** gives rise to some fast left slides with barrel potential and nice inside shoulders for cutbacks and snaps. Doesn't like any wind or too much swell and the line-up can shift around with swell direction. Touted as one of the best rights in Peru, **San Gallen** is in a protected National Park area, brimming with wildlife. Moderate due S swells slip up the island's east coast, hitting the boulders from deep water and breaking through a series of sections that alternate between throaty, thick-lipped tubes to ramped up shoulders and hooks. Early morning glass will be classic, but can be ridden through the day if sea breeze is W enough and the second Banana section is more protected. Power is the theme, so advanced surfers only. Gets unbelievably crowded with boatloads of frothy surfers making the expensive boat trip from the tiny port of Chaco. Middle of nowhere ghost town, **Puerto Caballas** sees steep and flat walls mix it up through the sections, but the two scalloped bays don't really link up unless it is large. Windy region good for kiters.

This zone combines the characteristics of Lima and Southern Peru, in some of the most inhospitable desert environment in the country. Big, unruly swells often shut down the beaches beside the Pan Am Hwy and leave few options in the miles of unsurfed coast between Lima and Arequipa. Autumn to spring expect 3-15ft of S-SW swell and don't hold your breath for anything from the NW as the coast veers away from it. Also, the regular SE-S winds are more onshore here than anywhere else in Peru, so early glass is the best hope for many spots. San Gallen needs N quadrant winds for the best sections. 1.3m tides are the norm in spring.

GOOGLE EARTH

San Gallen

PEDRO SALINAS

Cerro Azul

## TRAVEL INFORMATION

**Weather** – Low rainfall, mild temperatures and less garua fog, especially from Dec-April. Water temps range from 21°C (70°F) in the north in summer to 15°C (59°F) down south in winter. That means springsuit to 4/3, depending on where and when.

**Lodging and Food** – Asia has exploded with expensive holiday homes, resorts and hotels. Summers are packed and prices are higher. Cerro Azul has more options for budget travellers. Pisco is considered the home of pisco sour.

**Nature and Culture** – The Paracas National Reservation, (aka the Peruvian Galapagos) includes the Islas Ballestas, which are off limits to people, but boat tours can get close to see the many birds, sea lions, turtles, dolphins, and whales. A standing wave pool was installed at Boulevard de Asia, 97.5 km south of Lima. The cemeteries in Arequipa are worth a visit

**Hazards and Hassles** – There's plenty of sea-life but shark attacks are unheard of. The sharp rocks, picos de loros and currents are more of a problem. There may be some hassling at crowded breaks like Cerro Azul and San Gallen.

**Handy Hints** – Lima has the bulk of the surf shops so get all your gear before heading south. Take booties and a range of rubber for protection. Summer is party time around the resorts of Asia. Hiring a boat out to the Islas Ballestas is difficult and expensive as most are for sightseeing tourists (fr$15).

| STATISTICS | | J F | M A | M J | J A | S O | N D |
|---|---|---|---|---|---|---|---|
| SWELL | Direction | | | | | | |
| | Size (ft) | 3-4 | 4 | 5-6 | 6-7 | 5-6 | 4 |
| WIND | Direction | | | | | | |
| | Force | F3 | F3 | F3 | F3-F4 | F3-F4 | F3 |
| WATER | Wetsuit | | | | | | |
| | Temp/°C | 20 | 19 | 17 | 16 | 15 | 18 |
| WEATHER | Rainfall/mm | 0.5 | 0.4 | 3 | 6 | 5 | 1 |
| | days/mth | 1 | 1 | 1 | 2 | 3 | 1 |
| | Min temp/°C | 18 | 16 | 13 | 11 | 12 | 15 |
| | Max temp/°C | 27 | 25 | 21 | 19 | 20 | 24 |

# Southern Peru

Those seeking consistency and big waves should seriously consider heading south to Arequipa, Moquegua and Tacna, the country's southernmost regions, where all that is needed is a spirit of adventure, a good wetsuit and ideally a 4WD. Ilo is the place for left reefs; some large like El Olon and some hollow like Piedras Negras, but both are affected by pollution from the massive copper smelter nearby. This zone is more suited to advanced riders, although there are fun beachbreaks when the swell calms down.

| | |
|---|---|
| + GOOD CONSISTENCY | – COLDER WATER |
| + VARIETY OF BREAKS | – REMOTE AREA, FEW SERVICES |
| + NO CROWDS | – 4X4 REQUIRED |
| + VERY FRIENDLY PEOPLE | – POLLUTION ISSUES |

GONZALO BARANDARIAN

El Colegio

The popular resort of **Mollendo** has some highly consistent, but often mushy beachbreaks that easily close-out above headhigh. Banks vary greatly with the swell direction and W is often best. A short drive to Caleta Mejía will reveal strong, sometimes hollow shorebreaks at **Tiro Alto**, but it must be a small to medium summer swell, since it's easily overpowered by stronger swells. Overlooked by a huge statue of Christ, **Punta de Bombón** offers a similar setup to Tiro Alto, except that the Rio Tambo rivermouth can create better sandbanks. Offers beginners some easy walk out turn and catch whitewash rides, while experienced surfers will find some A-frames out the back before the afternoon breeze sets in. Can get some strong longshore drift - mark your position. An oasis of sand amongst a rocky, cliffy shoreline that extends for miles, SW-facing **Playa Platanales** can either spit out quality, sizeable barrels or mushy beginners waves in small swells and onshore winds. In front of the Hacienda Pocoma, inconsistent **El Olon** is the second biggest wave in Peru after Pico Alto. The long lefts get tubular at the right stage of tide, hold up to 20ft of S or SW swell, and should be left to experienced big-wave surfers only. There is a shorter right and it's always way bigger than it looks from the road and cliffs. Heavy to get out through the boulders of the shorebreak and even worse to get in. Proper equipment and a big desire to launch off the ledge and into some cavernous bombs. Crowds? You wish! **Piedras Negras** is another high quality, lefthand reefbreak with powerful, barreling, take-off section from mid to high tide and is only surfed by a friendly local crew, many of whom are bodyboarders. Flawless sparkling tubes breathe down the reef in most small to moderate swells with some S in them. Only 2km from large copper smelter and refinery, belching out large amounts of air and water pollution. The reef peak **El Colegio** faces the school's stadium and is user-friendly in offshore conditions. There are smaller, more protected waves south towards the rivermouth. Beyond the harbour is the hefty big wave slab called Big Sister where some crushing A-frames will appear in big swell, no wind scenarios. **Pozo de Lizas** is Ilo's patrolled summer beach attracting crowds of tourists and any small S swells onto good banks for learners. Gets blown-out easily. Check **Caleta Sama** in moderate to large S-SW swells, where a semi-consistent pointbreak generates short, steep, powerful lefthanders. About 20kms further south along the Inca Trail is a superbly hollow right reef at **Punta Colorado** that is a favourite of bodyboarders from Tacna. Close to Tacna, **Boca del Rio** is a small recreation town, offering some nightlife and a collection of beaches with well-formed peaks. There is a large choice of waves, from beach to reefbreaks, but don't expect more than mostly short rides. From here starts a long, linear stretch of wind and current swept beach that extends to Arica, Chile.

The biggest winter storms send oversized waves and huge close-outs, with breaking waves varying between 3-15ft and bigger at El Olon. There is still a fair amount of S-SW in the summer, complimented by the occasional summer NW swells. SE-S winds dominate, blowing for 65% of the year, with more SE, except between Oct-Nov. Glassy conditions occur for 10-12% of the year as mornings are typically windless, then around noon a gentle S sea-breeze creates a little chop on the wave face. The spots around Ilo benefit from better S wind protection. Tidal range never exceeds 2m (6ft), but is important at the shallow reefs.

## TRAVEL INFORMATION

**Weather** – During summer, skies are clear, then winter sees occasional fog and persistent drizzles that peak in August and September. Annual rainfall averages 40mm (1.6in), officially making this area a desert. Although average water temps shouldn't require more than a 3/2mm, from May to December, many use a 4/3mm fullsuit with boots and a 3/2mm fullsuit the other months.

**Lodging and Food** – Ilo has different levels of hotels, facilities, and is strategically situated near all the surrounding waves. Cheap hotels are Arequipa, Porteno, El Eden, Romicor, San Martin, Paraiso. For more comfort try Gran Hotel ($80/dble). Hospedaje El Tigre en Boca del Rio. Incredible seafood, excellent wines and piscos produced near Tacna.

**Nature and Culture** – On a flat day visit the Algarrobal museum (archeology & agriculture) near Ilo or the Naval Museum in town. Sandboarding in Boca del Rio. Miculla is an extensive petroglyph site east of Tacna, estimated to be 1,500 years old.

**Hazards and Hassles** – No sharks cruise the area. Massive winter waves, rocks and strong currents constitute the main risks, along with earthquakes, tsunamis and volcanic eruptions.

**Handy Hints** – Peruvian boards are good and inexpensive (surf shops in Arequipa and Lima). Bring ding repair and extra leash. Camping not recommended (winter is cold). Basic Spanish essential.

| STATISTICS | | J F | M A | M J | J A | S O | N D |
|---|---|---|---|---|---|---|---|
| SWELL | Direction | | | | | | |
| | Size (ft) | 3-4 | 4 | 5-6 | 6-7 | 5-6 | 4 |
| WIND | Direction | | | | | | |
| | Force | F2-F3 | F2-F3 | F2-F3 | F2-F3 | F2-F3 | F2-F3 |
| WATER | Wetsuit | | | | | | |
| | Temp/°C | 21 | 19 | 17 | 15 | 16 | 19 |
| WEATHER | Rainfall/mm | 0.5 | 0.4 | 2 | 5 | 6 | 0.5 |
| | days/mth | 1 | 1 | 1 | 2 | 3 | 1 |
| | Min temp/°C | 18 | 15 | 11 | 9 | 11 | 14 |
| | Max temp/°C | 28 | 26 | 22 | 20 | 21 | 25 |

# Arica CHILE

The extreme north of Chile showcases a string of gnarly reefbreaks, breaking close to the shore, on the wave-rich Alacran Peninsula. These shallow, hard-breaking line-ups like El Gringo have achieved international notoriety since the pro circus arrived in 2007, when even the world's best struggled to tame the tubes, so this is definitely not a zone for beginners. It is super-consistent for swell and light winds in this city of eternal spring in the world's driest desert, the Atacama.

- \+ ULTRA-CONSISTENT SWELL
- \+ POWERFUL REEFBREAKS
- \+ BIG WAVE RIDING OPTIONS
- \+ DRY, WARM CLIMATE

- \- SHALLOW REEFS AND URCHINS
- \- BOARD-BREAKING CONDITIONS
- \- INCREASING CROWDS
- \- FAR FROM INTERNATIONAL HUBS

RICARDO BRAVO

Alacran Peninsula

RICARDO BRAVO

El Gringo

**Las Machas**' long stretch of beach is super-consistent and peaks abound. The waves are usually better around high tide and the sandbanks shift a lot with the rips. Check the Rio Lluta mouth and Playa Chinchorro to the south. El Tubo was a right breaking next to the pier, but both disappeared in 2012. **Playa Chinchorro** is more of a beginner-friendly break where the surf schools operate and it will work better on NW swells at higher tide. **La Puntilla** is a rare left breaking at the mouth of the San Jose river. Due to its tucked-in location, only the largest swells will produce rideable waves and it is often sectiony and crowded because everywhere else may be maxed-out. Seldom ridden rights break south of **El Puerto** and the construction of the port transformed Alacrán island into a peninsula. Few will see or score **El Brazo**'s sand-covered reef that breaks at the northern tip of the island off the elbow jetty and requires a large wrapping swell and S-SW winds to produce a large tubular A-frame. **La Isla** is one of the most highly regarded breaks around, especially on summer northerly swell days where the lefthander forms a hollow wall with tubing sections. It breaks really close to the rocks and needs a medium-size swell to be at its best. Treacherous **Tojo Viejo** is an intense left breaking on the western tip of the peninsula. It's only ridden when over 6ft of S swell and good days are rare. Nicknamed the Chilean Pipeline, **El Gringo** is another tubular A-frame crashing close to the shore with serious power. The left is the real deal with fast, compression tubes and a more predictable rate of speed and openness, once the lurching air-drop has been negotiated. The right holds a bigger SW swell and throws wide before triangulating the wall into deeper water that provides a far safer paddling channel than the left. Tide is dependant on size, as it is usually the small swells that lure victims onto the barely watered rocky platform. Ultra-shallow sharp reef studded with urchins and some barnacles, swept by currents and occasionally patrolled by aggressive sea-lions and the areas best surfers. **El Buey** is an offshore big wave arena, where the left will focus S-SSW swells into booming barrels, while the right will wall up anything with more W in it and offer roller coaster walls. The spot can hold 20ft (6m), but is quite wind sensitive. **Arenillas Negras** is a wider exposed beachbreak, but still scattered with rocks and rarely lines up much more than some short mid tide slides and calmer inside whitewash for the beginners. Just to the south however, is a mental bodyboarding, righthand slab called El Rancio where super-thick, below sea-level tubes explode in SW-W swells up to 12ft and any E wind. Pollution flows from the commercial sector round here, including the rancid waste from the fish processing factory.

Large S-SW swells arrive in winter so it's advantageous to be located in the north to avoid the constant storms. Some of the spots will break even better with the very occasional summer NW swells between November and March. SE-S wind dominance remains around 65% year-round, with more SE, except between Oct-Nov. Mornings are typically windless, then light offshores pick up till noon when gentle S sea breezes create a little chop on the wave face. Tidal range never exceeds 1.4m, but is relevant for the shallow Alacran reefs.

## TRAVEL INFORMATION

**Weather** – Nicknamed The city of eternal spring, Arica is mild with lows only going to 13°C/56°F in winter. It never rains in the Atacama and less than 1mm of precipitation per year makes it the driest spot on Earth. The coastal fog, known as camanchaca doesn't stick around as long as the Peruvian garua. Water temps can vary by +/- 3°C from the averages.

**Lodging and Food** – There are many budget hotels in town and $25 will get you a nice double. Hotel Lynch ($47/dble) or Hotel San Marcos ($32/dble). $12 gets an excellent seafood meal, which can be accompanied by Chilean wine or Pisco Sour.

**Nature and Culture** – Arica is the gateway to the Altiplano, check out geoglyphs (pictures drawn on the hillsides) and pukaras (Indian fortresses). El Morro Hill is a national historic monument, offering great panoramic views. The San Marcos de Arica church was designed by Gustav Eiffel. People meet around El Alacrán at night time.

**Hazards and Hassles** – Wave dangers are obvious - big peaks, powerful lips, shallow, sharp reefs and urchins. Crowds are mostly bodyboards and foreigners and 10 guys are enough to fill the take-off zone.

**Handy Hints** – Arica has several surf shops (Huntington, Solari, Gringo, Tomate) and schools. Bring a quiver, with big wave guns. Booties essential. Most men work in mines in the desert so the city often feels like it is only inhabited by women.

| STATISTICS | | J F | M A | M J | J A | S O | N D |
|---|---|---|---|---|---|---|---|
| SWELL | Direction | | | | | | |
| | Size (ft) | 4 | 4-5 | 5-6 | 6-7 | 5-6 | 4-5 |
| WIND | Direction | | | | | | |
| | Force | F2 | F2-F3 | F2-F3 | F3 | F3 | F2-F3 |
| WATER | Wetsuit | | | | | | |
| | Temp/°C | 21 | 19 | 17 | 15 | 15 | 18 |
| WEATHER | Rainfall/mm | 0 | 0 | 0 | 0 | 0 | 0 |
| | days/mth | 0 | 0 | 0 | 0 | 0 | 0 |
| | Min temp/°C | 18 | 17 | 14 | 13 | 14 | 16 |
| | Max temp/°C | 27 | 25 | 21 | 19 | 21 | 24 |

# Iquique CHILE

**Iquique holds a very concentrated stretch of challenging reefbreaks breaking close to the shore, with cylindrical barrels slamming down hard onto shallow reefs full of urchins. It's often big and gnarly and many of the spots are more suitable for bodyboarders or the most skilled of surfers. Fortunately, there are channels, which enable safe paddle outs to most line-ups. Wave height can be deceptive from the main coastal road where crowds gather to watch the big swells which happen often in Chile!**

**+ VERY CONSISTENT, ALL YEAR**
**+ BIG, POWERFUL WAVES**
**+ CHILLED AND UNCROWDED**
**+ PERFECT CLIMATE**

**– SHALLOW URCHIN-COVERED REEFS**
**– NO MELLOW WAVES**
**– TIDALLY SENSITIVE**
**– REMOTE CITY**

Almost all the waves in Iquique suck hard off the rocky slabs of reef and lurch forward in a hurry from take-off. Dry sucks, boils and urchins are all part of the equation, so skill and caution needed in equal measure. **Punta Dos** is no exception where barrels explode on a gnarled reef. It is mainly a righthand point-style set-up, but there are lefts depending on the swell angle. An uncompromising wave mainly ridden by bodyboarders along with the crazy lefts just north at La Cosa. **Intendencia** is a challenging and very heavy left that has to be perfect in order to be makeable. Massive power is concentrated on the peak and it gets square and slabby when there is less than a full tide covering the reef. This makes the take-off beyond vert and often unmakeable for all but the best stand-ups and bodyboarders, who have this place dialled in. Often breaks, but good days are rare. **Las Urracas** starts off looking all the world a nice peak, but only the left has a future as it walls and barrels down the surprisingly shallow reef to a narrow channel. The right becomes El Colegio a bit further down and many use the easier paddle-out via Urracas to get there. Like all the Iquique breaks, getting caught straightening out can be sketchy on the urchin-studded rocks. Iquique's banner spot is **Colegio**, a thick, muscle-bound right that pumps up nicely as the swell increases and will handle up to the triple-overhead mark fairly effortlessly. Following the local trend for vertical drops into a draining barrel section, the difference here is it can keep spinning down the line for a good 100m. Picture perfect in the sparkling morning glass, it is still a challenging prospect and lesser surfers should beware. Handles most tides through the size range and prefers the push, with high giving more room for error on the peak. Needs at least headhigh conditions to start breaking and just gets better from there. Crowds of rippers and bodyboarders will be on hand when it is firing, which is fairly often and travellers need to show respect to both the locals and the wave. Watch out for clean-up sets that close out the channel by keeping an eye on the outside indicator bomboras. **Punta Una** sucks hard off the reef with the end section going almost dry, especially at high tide. The left on the other side of the peak is called Mauro and is shorter, but just as intense. Another booger wave with room for only the best air-drop to tube stand-ups. Works well in smaller swells hence the crowding problems. The main city beach **Playa Cavancha** is usually just a big, rip-torn closeout, but in winter and on windswells with a bit of W or N in them there will be a few corners for beginners and cruisers. The small swell beachbreaks of Playa Brava and Huayquique are usually too big to surf and blown-out. Pioneered by Chilean charger Ramon Navarro and Gabriel Villaran (Peru), the jaw-dropping bombora of **La Bestia** has tubes on a grand scale. Tow-ins and paddle-ins now regularly take place on the handful of days it breaks each winter. Definitely a spectator sport, preferably from 20 floors up in one of the apartment blocks or hotels that loom on the Punta Cavancha.

Constant S-SW swells between 3-15ft come pouring off the Roaring Forties year-round, although winter obviously sees more of the bigger swells that hit double figures. The predominant wind is from the S with more SSW blowing into the wind sensitive rights. Glassy mornings are common, especially in summer when wind speeds back off and long period 20 second swells can arrive in the 6-8ft range. Mid to high tide is the go for most spots with a small 1.4m range.

RICARDO BRAVO
Las Urracas and Colegio

## TRAVEL INFORMATION

**Weather** – The Atacama Desert is one of the driest places in the world with rain falling only once every 15 years on average. Big canyons behind Iquique help collect moisture from sea humidity, making it surprisingly green. Little variation in temperatures from 24°C (75°F). The water is warmer than most of the country, especially in the summertime when a light 3/2 steamer or springsuit will do.

**Lodging and Food** – Cheap residentals/hostels will give you a bed for $25 or hotels like the Prat from $70. Seafood is cheap and widely available, the local brew is Pisco Sour.

**Nature and Culture** – The spectacular Lauca National Park is an 8hr-bus ride from Iquique. Other worthwhile sites include the Atacama Giant, Pintados and the ghost town of Humberstone.

**Hazards and Hassles** – Your main danger is from the shallow, urchin-covered reefs and thick, heavy waves. Most locals are bodyboarders, but even ten people in a tight take-off zone can make for a crowded line-up.

**Handy Hints** – Opposite Colegio is Vertical surf shop with a range of stock. Bring big-wave guns, boots and a helmet. Many Chilean men work in mines out in the desert and so Iquique seems to be populated almost entirely by women.

ADRIAN ARAYA
Intendencia

| STATISTICS | | J F | M A | M J | J A | S O | N D |
|---|---|---|---|---|---|---|---|
| SWELL | Direction | | | | | | |
| | Size (ft) | 4 | 4-5 | 5-6 | 6-7 | 5-6 | 4 |
| WIND | Direction | | | | | | |
| | Force | F2 | F2-F3 | F2-F3 | F3 | F3 | F2-F3 |
| WATER | Wetsuit | | | | | | |
| | Temp/°C | 19 | 19 | 18 | 16 | 17 | 18 |
| WEATHER | Rainfall/mm | 0.5 | 0 | 0 | 0 | 0 | 0 |
| | days/mth | 0 | 0 | 0 | 0 | 0 | 0 |
| | Min temp/°C | 18 | 17 | 14 | 13 | 13 | 16 |
| | Max temp/°C | 27 | 25 | 21 | 19 | 21 | 24 |

# Antofagasta CHILE

Much like Chile itself, the city of Antofagasta is long and narrow, sandwiched between the Pacific and the Andes, on the Tropic of Capricorn. With 20km of sandy beaches scattered among rocky coves, this unattractive port city is off the beaten path for surfers, who tend to congregate at the northern cities of Arica and Iquique. There is more variety to the surf here, with beachbreaks among crazy rock formations, some longer left points as well as the obligatory Chilean death slab known as Nuluhaga, south of town. Not beginner territory, but intermediates will be able to manage the points.

+ GREAT LEFT POINTS
+ CONSISTENT SWELL
+ SPOT DIVERSITY
+ NEVER RAINS

- FEW RIGHTS
- COOL WATER
- DESERT AREA
- LACK OF TOURIST INTEREST

ADRAIN ARAYA

Pozo Verde

ADRAIN ARAYA

Nuluhaga

The small bay of **Pozo Verde** has both left and right points that get perfect around 6ft. Long drive, but gets a little crowd on small summer swells. The popular coastal resort of **Hornitos** has good, shorter rides for learners, with low wind and tide. Head toward the southern cliffs for more protection or around to Playa Itata for more size. On the southern part of Mejillones' hammer-shaped headland, **Choralillo** is a fun, left point and a good playground for practicing manoeuvres. There might be some wave sailors and kiters who also like the rolling walls. **Isla Santa Maria** hosts three distinct breaks. One is a giant, deep-water A-frame, while the other two reefbreaks are left points best surfed around headhigh. Boat access only so crowds are never a problem. The rights at **Peñarol** can be quite long, but swell needs to be more W to avoid being too sectiony. Lefts are more common, but it needs over 10ft of open swell as it is tucked into the massive bay behind Isla Santa Maria. In the Bahia Moreno, **Cordeles** is a very consistent, less-rocky beachbreak with further pocket beaches extending all the way north to La Rinconada. The eroded sandstone arch of **La Portada** soars 50m above a rocky point-style reef that offers zippy lefthanders across 3 sections. The natural environment is impressive, but unfortunately the point is extremely wind sensitive. **Budeo** is an excellent right reefbreak, powerful and tubular. It's regularly crowded with bodyboarders looking for small but clean tubes. Urchins love it here too. The W-NW orientation of the coast between Antofagasta and Cabo Jara makes for some good lefthand set-ups. **Piedra del Lobo** is a classic left holding up to 10ft with rides 100m long. Heavy wipe-outs are not uncommon but rocks are no threat at this spot. Use the two purple poles to line-up on. The hollow and powerful right called **Andrómeda** holds well-overhead waves and is never too crowded. **La Puntilla**'s left reefbreak is Antofagasta's most central and famous wave, with lots of sections to accommodate the regular city crowds. **Ram5** is a very powerful left breaking very close to the rocks, making entry and exit quite difficult. Often crowded with experienced surfers despite only medium consistency. Regularly picked as a national contest site, **Cúpula** is regarded as the best wave in the zone. It breaks best at 6-12ft and locals compare it to Tavarua. Exaggeration or not, the wave is indeed a long left with several tubular sections, breaking over magma rock reef. The occasional shorter right can be ridden as well. Friendly locals may give tips on how to handle the rocks sticking out in front of the wave and the urchins and seashells covering the seafloor. In the discotheque sector, **Huáscar** is yet another left point, but this one breaks better in the summertime, when the largest northern swells roll in, so it's inconsistent. Las Garumas camping just to the north. **Nuluhaga** stands as the most impressive wave around showing some Teahupoo characteristics. Wedges up into a thick-lipped peak but it's the left that is ridden. Heavy drops are followed by stratospheric tubes with little water over the reef. It only breaks when the outside swell is moderate to heavy, and it has to be glassy or light E-SE. Absolute chargers only and the local bodyboarders dominate.

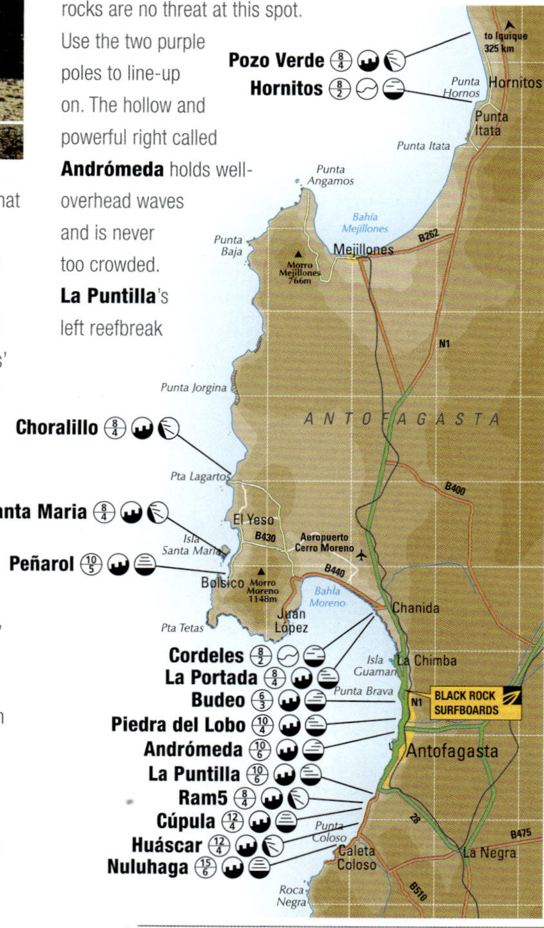


Rosy average annual statistics; 7-8ft SSW swell at 12-13 second period with 98% swell consistency! Summer shifts the lighter wind to SSW and SW. Winter will kink back towards due S and increase in speed. Early/late glass-offs happen 5% of the time, year-round. Many all tides spots, despite 1.45m change in height. Just off the coastline here, the Peru-Chile Trench plunges to depths of 8064m.

## TRAVEL INFORMATION

**Weather** – Coastal desert climate with cool sea breezes tempering summers at 24°C (75°F) and around 17°C (63°F) in winter. Not a drop of rain and the clearest skies in the world with clouds appearing only 20 days per year. The large peninsula deflects the cold Humboldt Current, making water temps a little higher. A 3/2 steamer year-round.

**Lodging and Food** – Budget rooms under $20 are widely available. Beach facing Hotel Tatio and Hotel Antofagasta (fr$80/n). Hotel Capitania in Mejillones fr $32. Excellent seafood is available around the Terminal Pesquero.

**Nature and Culture** – A non-touristy modern city with European architecture (replica of Big Ben), good restaurants and entertainment spots. The Ruta 1 coastal highway to Iquique is an epic 400km journey. "Mano Del Desierto" (Hand of the Desert) is a large sculpture 50km south of Antofagasta.

**Hazards and Hassles** – With surfing and bodyboarding becoming increasingly popular among young Chileans, crowds are developing and vibes are not always positive. Sharp reefs and urchins, so bring reef boots.

**Handy Hints** – Bring a good all-round board or Black Rock surfboards in Antofagasta has shortbaords starting at $500. Padang Padang surf shop is well equiped and has a surf school.

| STATISTICS | | J F | M A | M J | J A | S O | N D |
|---|---|---|---|---|---|---|---|
| SWELL | Direction | | | | | | |
| | Size (ft) | 4 | 4-5 | 5-6 | 7 | 5-6 | 4 |
| WIND | Direction | | | | | | |
| | Force | F2-F3 | F3 | F3 | F3 | F2-F3 | F2-F3 |
| WATER | Wetsuit | | | | | | |
| | Temp/°C | 19 | 19 | 16 | 14 | 15 | 18 |
| WEATHER | Rainfall/mm | 0 | 0 | 1 | 2 | 1 | 0 |
| | days/mth | 0 | 0 | 0 | 0 | 0 | 0 |
| | Min temp/°C | 16 | 14 | 12 | 10 | 12 | 14 |
| | Max temp/°C | 24 | 21 | 19 | 16 | 18 | 21 |

# Atacama and Coquimbo CHILE

Distances are so vast, Chile has a numerical naming system and this 'Norte Chico' zone straddles the regions of Atacama (Region 3) and Coquimbo (Region 4). Totoralillo has sprung up as a popular summer resort and crowds flock to the beach hotels overlooking a hammerhead peninsula that bends lefts and rights down both sides with impressive regularity. Coupled with fancy La Serena, this area holds something for everyone from fast barrels to rolling points and a multitude of beachbreaks.

+ VERY CONSISTENT SWELLS
+ QUALITY LEFT & RIGHT POINTS
+ ALL ABILITIES CATERED FOR
+ CULTURAL LA SERENA

- HEAVY WAVES
- YEAR-ROUND COLD WATER
- EXPOSED TO WINDS
- ROCKS AND BOULDERS

**La Vedette** faces NW, bending solid S-SW swells into standout barrelling lefts along a rocky point. Beware of rocks on the inside and check the long beach north if the swell is too small. Most contests happen at the consistent, learner-friendly, summer beaches of **Tres Playitas**, where a few corners will be sprinkled about amongst the scattered rocks and rip gullies. From Huasco, cross the phenomenal desert full of purple flowers to remote, exposed **Playa Brava**, which offers a wild shorebreak, providing the SW swell is small and the S winds aren't blowing. The long, slow roads into Pinguino de Humboldt National Reserve, lead to **Agua Dulce**, a large, southwest-facing beach that works with the smallest swells over shallow sandbars. Breathtaking scenery and more pocket beaches nearby like Playa Palocillo. It's a 6km boat ride from the fun beachies at Punta Choros to get to **Isla Damas**, which gets some nice surf, including a sweet right reef, facing the SW swell and some pristine water beachbreaks at Playa Las Tijeras. Feels like the Galapagos with so much wildlife around including sea-lions and penguins. **Punta Teatinos** is a semi-right pointbreak capping a long beachbreak lined with good resorts, a golf course and a lagoon. Consistent and empty, but the paddling can be heavy when the A-frames hit overhead. La Serena's a popular beach resort, straddles the long Avenida del Mar, which joins 12 beaches, but it's **El Faro** that is the most consistent of these below average beachbreaks with lots of close-outs. The surf village of Totoralillo has a small circular peninsula of rocks and sand, holding 3 pointbreaks plus a sandbar in the shorebreak. The left is called **Pipe**, since it produces the most radical wave, a lightning fast barrel that's far from easy to thread, making it a popular bodyboard spot. On the south side of the peninsula, the long righthand point of **El Muro** is broken into three sections, with bigger, faster walls outside at Cabañas, through the shallow El Muro mid section and into the easier inside of Rocas, that will handle N winds. One thing they all have in common is some shallow rocks. In summer, the beach gets a bit crowded and dirty, with hotels right on the point. Beginners will do better down the beach at **Derecharcha** for fun summer rights. Uncrowded because it often closes-out. **Las Tacas** is a NW-facing beachbreak that stays clean in S winds, but mostly closes-out in front of the Med-style 5-star hotel circling the sands. **Playa Blanca** is sheltered from S-W swells by Punta Lengua de Vaca, but it's close-out city and really only suited to beginners staying in the beachfront condos.

Winter wave face heights sometimes reach 20ft with 12-14 second period, but late summer is the best time for clean surf in the 6-8ft range. There are rideable waves almost every day of the year, but deep winter can feel chilly, so mid-seasons are best for swell, winds and weather. Summer is fine especially on the WSW-facing beachbreaks with potential for very long distance (20sec +) NW swells. In the northern half of Chile, atmospheric circulation is largely controlled by the South Pacific High, resulting in winds blowing parallel to the coast north of 31°S. Further south, the winds take a more onshore westerly direction. Tides are semi-diurnal and can reach 1.77m on extreme phases.

WILLY URIBE

Pipe

## TRAVEL INFORMATION

**Weather** – Coquimbo enjoys a transitional climate between the arid northern desert of the Atacama and the pleasant Mediterranean climate of the central coast. In summer (Dec-Feb), daytime temps range between 11-25°C (52-77°F) whereas during winter (Jun-Aug), it drops by 4°C to average at 7-22°C (45-72°F) with lows reaching -5°C at night. There is a lack of precipitation with annual average rainfall under 100mm (4in). Use a 4/3mm fullsuit with optional boots from May to December and a 3/2mm between January and April.

**Lodging and Food** – Try Hostal Nomade in Barrio Inglés at Coquimbo fr $13-$32/dble. Luxury Jardim del Mar in La Serena is $95-160/dble. In Totoralillo, Polynesian style Tiki Tano has 9 cabins (fr $95/cabin). Expect $5 for a basic meal; lots of cheap seafood. Plenty of people free-camp Tres Playitas.

**Nature and Culture** – La Serena has beautiful stone architecture, 29 churches, shady avenues and pretty plazas. Check the astronomical observatories of La Silla, European Southern Observatory and El Tololo. Visit Elqui Valley or the villages of Pisco Elqui and Vicuña.

**Hazards and Hassles** – Water gets cold and mornings can be gloomy; pack booties and maybe a hood too. Don't get caught inside, some boulders and rocks are nasty plus there's urchins. Most spots are uncrowded, more seals than surfers.

**Handy Hints** – There are surf shops in La Serena (Lurop, Good Vibes), but better bring everything, including a gun and a second wetsuit so you can always put on a dry one. Total Surf School do lessons, accommodation and have a shop in Totoralillo.

| STATISTICS | | J F | M A | M J | J A | S O | N D |
|---|---|---|---|---|---|---|---|
| SWELL | Direction | | | | | | |
| | Size (ft) | 4 | 4-5 | 5 | 6-7 | 5-6 | 3-4 |
| WIND | Direction | | | | | | |
| | Force | F3 | F3 | F3-F4 | F4 | F3-F4 | F3-F4 |
| WATER | Wetsuit | | | | | | |
| | Temp/°C | 18 | 17 | 15 | 13 | 14 | 16 |
| WEATHER | Rainfall/mm | 0 | 1 | 21 | 22 | 6 | 0 |
| | days/mth | 0 | 0 | 2 | 5 | 1 | 0 |
| | Min temp/°C | 14 | 11 | 7 | 7 | 9 | 11 |
| | Max temp/°C | 25 | 25 | 18 | 16 | 19 | 23 |

# Valparaiso and O'Higgins CHILE

Pichilemu is probably the most famous surf town in Chile, situated in the south of this zone, which combines Region V and VI.

+ SUPER-CONSISTENT
+ LOTS OF LONG LEFT POINTS
+ BIG WAVE OPTIONS
+ LAID-BACK PEOPLE

– COLD WATER YEAR-ROUND
– RAINY WINTERS AND WINDY
– HARD ACCESS TO SOME SPOTS
– LACK OF NIGHT ENTERTAINMENT

Both Valparaiso & O'Higgins encircle the Región Metropolitana de Santiago, so there are plenty of weekend warriors making the 120km trip to the beaches from the capital. Long lefthand points begin to appear in the southern corners of the bays along with some strong beachbreaks along the Vina del Mar stretch. Pichilemu is where the awesomely long and handsome lefts of Puertecillo, La Puntilla and Punta de Lobos await in a cold water, goofy-footers paradise.

RICARDO BRAVO

Viña del Mar

**Maitencillo** rivermouth is usually where the best mid tide A-frames can be found along this 2km stretch of coarse, golden sand on small swells. Produces some real quality in the morning glass conditions at the northern end known as Abanico. If it's big from the S then La Punta in **El Claron** has a left pointbreak, peeling over sand-covered rocks at lower tides. Needs to be big to wrap in and is well-protected from S to SW winds. **Papagayo** is an uneven reef in the bay at Quintero where a long left setup shunts and sometimes barrels over the shallower sections at lower tides. Will handle a good slice of swell and the channel is deep enough to not close-out, but it doesn't like the SW wind. The wave wraps around to an inside reef almost behind the island, shedding size and offering a friendly option for improvers and groms. Across the channel is a mutant bodyboard slab right and on the southern headland, Puntilla has wind protected lefts. Surfing started in Chile in the early '70s around **Ritoque**, which has powerful and super-consistent beachbreaks that are clean on N winds. The north end has a defined left next to the paddling channel that flanks the headland and makes getting out the back a breeze. The walled rights off the peak lead into the rips and close-outs that characterise the centre and south end, where wave height usually increases. **La Boca** has become a popular spot for beginners and surf schools, since it's well-sheltered from all S winds and sometimes the sand aligns for some good rides. Closes-out in W swells and prefers lower tides. Head north up the beach towards Punta del Piedra if it is too small. Con Con's NW-facing beaches at Amarillo, Negra and Las Bahamas offer some more beginner-friendly set-ups and occasional barrels on big days. Real pollution problems, bad rips, crowds of bodyboarders and beginners. The **Reñaca** beachbreaks get packed in summer and the action is concentrated near the pile of boulders up the north end that help hold the sandbanks and form some short sharp wedges that barrel quickly before shutting down. The pocket beach at **Las Salinas** needs a 6-10ft S-SW swell to start breaking and isn't a very long ride with tapered walls and short bowls over the bigger boulders at higher tides. There's plenty of straighthander shoredump down to Viña del Mar. **Algarrobo** has a range of rock and sand breaks. El Mejoral is a powerful left reefbreak that needs to be approaching headhigh and mid tide to start clearing the rocks properly, then when the swell gets seriously big, a new section called Detroit breaks further out and links into the main line-up. There are hollow rights around the point at La Chilena which prefers W-NW swells. **El Quisco** is a rocky beach with a few options including La Derecha in the middle of the beach, a shorey for the boogers to the south and a rare right at the north end that needs NW swell. **La Castilla** is the best left around with powerful and pushy walls that can be long and speedy, without really barreling. The small cove at **Las Cruces** can have a good left, which starts at the southern headland and zips across the bay, but it's often just a mushy closeout. Head north towards El Tabo when it's small. **La Boquilla** rivermouth can align wide-ranging lefts in a SW swell and SE winds, but it gets rippy and messy. Navidad and **Matanzas** both need the sand to join the rocky dots and create anything decent. Often disorganised with unmakeable sections, Matanzas has some outside and inside low tide lefts that keep the small crowds and the wind/kitesurfers happy. **Puertecillo** is one of Chile's most sought after left pointbreaks and renowned for epic, long, sand-dredging barrels. It's nestled in the lee of the stubby headland with good S wind protection, but needs a decent dose of swell to get going. Always much smaller than the waves in Pichilemu, ideal conditions include at least a 10ft SW swell, SE or no wind, outgoing tide from mid and hopefully a mellow, mid-week crowd. When the sand is parked, waves of up to

## TRAVEL INFORMATION

**Weather** – Looking at the vegetation reveals a mixed climate of mild Mediterranean and wet Oceanic. Due to the relatively low latitude, winter is a period to avoid because of cold temperatures, frequent showers and changeable weather. It is possible at this time to snowboard in the mountains, 4hr away. Sunshine levels vary from 2-3hr in winter to 8-9hr in the summer. Summers are dry and quite warm, but the coast is sometimes shrouded in mist. The Humboldt Current cools the water year-round and it rarely exceeds 17°C (62°F), so 4/3 or 3/2 in summer.

**Lodging and Food** – Lots of hostels and B&B's from ($15/d). Hotels in Pichilemu from $27 or Punta Lobos Surf Lodge is $95/dbl. Hostal Punta de Lobos has Cabins from $40 p/n or Dorm rooms fr $10 p/n. There is lots of cheap seafood at cafeterias - Curanto is a must. Pisco is the drink of choice. Expect to pay $15 a meal.

**Nature and Culture** – Pichilemu and other coastal resorts get crowded with city tourists during the summer. Pichilemu has some nightlife, while Valparaiso and Cartagena are lively. Don't miss the Andes and the volcanoes.

**Hazards and Hassles** – Strong rips make getting to the line-up difficult when it's big. Otherwise the locals are cool, crowd pressure is low, rocks are well-covered with seaweed and the numerous seals are curious, but harmless.

**Handy Hints** – There are surf shops in Santiago (Surfers Paradise, Stoked), Vina del Mar (Waimea, Tablas) and Pichilemu (World Jungle) with reasonable stocks of boards and suits.

SURFOTOS.CL

### Punta de Lobos

LAT. -34.423878° LONG. -72.049645°

Proclaimed "The best left pointbreak in Chile" by local big-wave maestro Ramon Navarro and few could argue when witnessing a monster SW swell detonating way outside the iconic rocks that guard the entrance to the bay. Lobos is not just for XXL days either, with a ripable, sand-bottomed section known as Diamante on the inside for the groms and the pilots. Further up the point, the El Mirador section has summer peelers rotating past the shoreline rock clusters, or muscle-bound walls linking from the rocks all the way to the beach sections in a lined-up SW-W swell. Too much S swell will ramp up the current, while W will shut down the outside barrels so SW @ 235° should be perfect. Prefers lower tides, but will break right through. The paddle-out from the island rocks (Los Morros) has achieved legendary status for sketchiness – dashing across the slippery shelf from a hiding place in the rocks when there is a lull has caught many out. Experts only when it gets above double-overhead. Summer beach party scene, surf shop on point and skate ramp on the beach for flat days, which are pretty rare so don't expect to get it to yourself.

700m are possible. It's pretty inconsistent with summer crowds topping 100, drop-ins are a given and the constant rip current is a drain. The private land has been impacted by decades of camping and construction of a large housing development has begun. **Topocalma** is an exposed major headland that draws in swell onto a scruffy array of fringing rocks. There will be more lefts off the north side of the "Pan de Azúcar" rocks leading into the beachbreaks, which can get scoured by the river when it opens. Nothing epic but an escape from the Puertocillo crowds. Laid-back Pichilemu has grown massively and is now a popular summer resort for Chileans from Santiago. The kilometre-long line-up of **La Puntilla** has treated many to the longest rides in the country, provided the sand is cooperating and linking it all up. This is a rare occurrence and most will find loping, sloping walls, barging down the point for triple figure sections inviting down the line scribes and hacks back to the power source in equal measure. The paddle-out is exhausting against the drift and many elect to walk after a long one. Gets unruly at size, but will still hold up through the deep channel in the bay. Crowds are spread amongst the sections, with lots of locals, but generally a mellow scene since it is so consistent. When the swell is small **Infiernillo** picks up the most, but is often too fast for most average surfers. It's a full-on barreling left, open to all swells, but with no wind protection, so it's only worth checking on small to moderate size, glassy days. Proper pedal-to-the-metal grinders sweep over the rocky protrusions that build up the bridging sand, but predictability is hard to come by. Low tide will be faster, while high can improve make-ability,

SURFOTOS.CL

El Mirador, Lobos

but the paddle-out is always fraught and getting pinned on the inside is guaranteed despite its pointbreak status. Strong, experienced intermediates upwards and it will have a fair pack on it when it's firing. **Punta de Lobos** is one of the most consistent spots in the southern hemisphere, let alone Chile.

S to SW and even due W swells appear from Antarctica lows, with sizes varying from 2-18ft year-round. The dominant wind comes from the S varying from 32% of the time in June to 55% of the time from Oct through to Feb. The winter period of May-July also gets a lot of NW-NE winds (30-40%), which is unheard of further north. The remainder of the year sees a light S or SW pattern. This means that the north-facing coves will often be offshore, favouring lefts. The tidal range of 1.8m is significant and mid to high tides are the go at most spots.

MARK MCINNIS

Infiernillo

| STATISTICS | | J F | M A | M J | J A | S O | N D |
|---|---|---|---|---|---|---|---|
| SWELL | Direction | | | | | | |
| | Size (ft) | 4-5 | 5 | 6 | 7-8 | 6 | 4 |
| WIND | Direction | | | | | | |
| | Force | F4 | F4 | F4 | F4 | F4 | F4 |
| WATER | Wetsuit | | | | | | |
| | Temp/°C | 17 | 16 | 14 | 13 | 13 | 15 |
| WEATHER | Rainfall/mm | 18 | 62 | 230 | 210 | 82 | 37 |
| | days/mth | 2 | 7 | 16 | 15 | 10 | 7 |
| | Min temp/°C | 12 | 9 | 7 | 5 | 7 | 11 |
| | Max temp/°C | 27 | 25 | 18 | 17 | 21 | 26 |

# Bío Bío CHILE

The word frontier is often used to describe this verdant southern region, but considering there is another 2500kms of coastline stretching down to the tip of the continent, it's probably more like the gateway to the real frontier further south. Left pointbreaks are clustered in the north, while heavily sand-dependant, left rivermouths dominate the central and southern parts of the zone. There are some mushy, beginner-friendly waves, plus a healthy number of open beachbreaks that just love a small, peaky, summer pulse.

**+ WORLD-CLASS LEFTS**
**+ BEAUTIFUL REGION**
**+ VERY CONSISTENT SWELLS**
**+ CHEAP, FRIENDLY**

**- REALLY COLD WATER**
**- SANDBANK DEPENDENT**
**- SOME POLLUTION PROBLEMS**
**- NOT EASY TO REACH**

SCOTT WALLS

Bío Bío

PAUL KENNEDY

Bío Bío

En route for **Curanipe** is Santos del Mar, a tow-in outer reef where 30ft lefts have been ridden, but the lefthand rivermouth at the coastal resort is much friendlier and often used as a contest site. The first section breaks further up off the rocks, becoming hollower down by the black sand rivermouth. It's offshore with S-SW winds and fires at low tide. **Tregualemu** holds lefts in swells up to 15ft, peeling over rock and sand with fast walls in front of a rivermouth. It's a private track to the beach, so ask for permission or walk down beach, 1km from the north. Easier access **Pullay** is a sandy left point that throws up some whackable berms and lazy shoulders, which are fun for improvers, but it's not quite tucked in enough out of the wind. Coveted **Buchupureo** is the standout break with the rivermouth grooming the sand into really long lefts, breaking in 2-3 sections and it's protected from S winds. Barrel time can reach a handful of seconds and comparisons with Mundaka means it gets crowded at times. Some vibe is bound to be encountered and consistency is as variable as the flow of sand from the rivermouth. **Rinconada** is a similar set-up, but it doesn't get very hollow with rumbling long walls and great cutback shoulders attracting crowds of learners in summer. In small swells, try **Playa Monte del Zorro** for dumpy beachbreak and a protected left in the southern corner. **Praia Mela** is yet another rivermouth set-up that depends on the sand for speed of ride and has adjacent scruffy beachbreak. A huge pulp mill was built on the nearby Rio Itata. Industrial

## TRAVEL INFORMATION

**Weather** – Talcahuano has a temperate Mediterranean climate and the winter months, from May to September, are cool and rainy with temps ranging from 3-17°C (37-63°F). The summer months, from December through February, are mild 6-24°C (43-75°F) with the least rain. Use a 4/3 mm fullsuit with boots and 5/4mm with gloves and hood in winter gales. The water rarely tops 15°C (59°F).

**Lodging and Food** – Expect $20-30 for a cheap room and $5-10 for a basic meal. Lots of cheap seafood. Cabañas Mirador Alto Las Brisas or Hostal Refugio del Mar in Curanipe, well used by surfers. Contact Curanipetur for bookings.

**Nature and Culture** – Biobio river has world-class white water rafting. Impressive rock formations like Iglesia de Piedra are near Buchupureo. Temuco City south is the gateway to the lakes and volcanoes like Pucon. Near Cobquecura is La Loberia, where 3000 seals live on 4 big rocks. In Concepcion Naval base, take a tour on the Peruvian battleship Huascar.

**Hazards and Hassles** – Cold waters and windchill can cut down water time, so avoid winter. Lefts break mostly on sand, but some large rocks stick out. Pollution at some of the rivers is becoming an issue. A soupy fog can cling to the coast for days. Some localism likely.

**Handy Hints** – Take a gun along for 8-10ft days. There's no surf shop in Concepcion (Aloha has closed). Learn some Spanish. Educated people, gorgeous mountains, snow resorts, quality wines: Chile is very addictive, stay as long as you can.

Concepción is the second largest city in Chile, sitting alongside the Bio Bio river, which enters the sea at **Desembocadura**. Scattered rocks lurk in the beachbreak that picks up plenty of swell for the local bodyboarders. Often closes-out, but can show some real form when the sand has been allowed to settle. Water quality is variable. **Playa Sector El Piure** is one of 6 SW-facing beachbreaks, best in summer peaky swells, set in a wildly beautiful landscape. On small swells, **Cueva del Toro** may have some shape or walk north through the tunnel to get to Playa Millaneco. The main spot for experts and bodyboarders is **El Faro**, where explosive lefts hit the reef off the cape, plus there are 2 jetties and a protected rivermouth sandbank for all abilities. The long rivermouth lefts below **Punta Quidico** can be leg-achingly long, tubular and comparable with Buchupureo up north. The river flow can mess up the banks, but there's usually some sort of left breaking somewhere in the lee of the tall headland. **Tirua** is a messier set-up, with strong currents from the large river. Winter wave heights can reach 20' with 12 to 18 second period, but the winds have a lot more W and even N direction that blows out the southern corners. Summer beachbreaks may pick up super-long distance NW or local windswells, but the points/rivermouths need wrapping S-SW. The first swells of autumn should hit perfectly sculpted, rivermouth sandbanks and spring flow rates can also build up the bars. Tides are semi-diurnal and can reach 1.87m on extreme phases, affecting most of the rivermouths.

| STATISTICS | | J F | M A | M J | J A | S O | N D |
|---|---|---|---|---|---|---|---|
| SWELL | Direction | | | | | | |
| | Size (ft) | 5 | 5-6 | 6-7 | 7 | 6-7 | 4-5 |
| WIND | Direction | | | | | | |
| | Force | F4 | F3-F4 | F3 | F3-F4 | F3-F4 | F3-F4 |
| WATER | Wetsuit | | | | | | |
| | Temp/°C | 14 | 14 | 13 | 11 | 12 | 14 |
| WEATHER | Rainfall/mm | 19 | 57 | 216 | 202 | 75 | 31 |
| | days/mth | 1 | 5 | 12 | 14 | 5 | 3 |
| | Min temp/°C | 8 | 6 | 5 | 3 | 4 | 6 |
| | Max temp/°C | 24 | 22 | 15 | 13 | 17 | 22 |

# Mar del Plata ARGENTINA

Argentina counts around 300km of surfable beaches, most of them located in Buenos Aires Province. The eastern Pampas, consists mainly of grassy plains, while the western regions climb into the vertiginous Andes. Mar del Plata stands as the main summer getaway for "Porteños" escaping their Buenos Aires lives, where the city beaches are bisected by dozens of piers and jetties creating many surf spots in a variety of swell and wind directions.

+ SPOT CONCENTRATION
+ BREAK DIVERSITY
+ WIND AND SWELL OPTIONS
+ RANGE OF ACCOMMODATION

- CROWDED URBAN SPOTS
- SUMMER SURFING BANS
- FREEZING WINTERS
- BUILT-UP AND POLLUTED

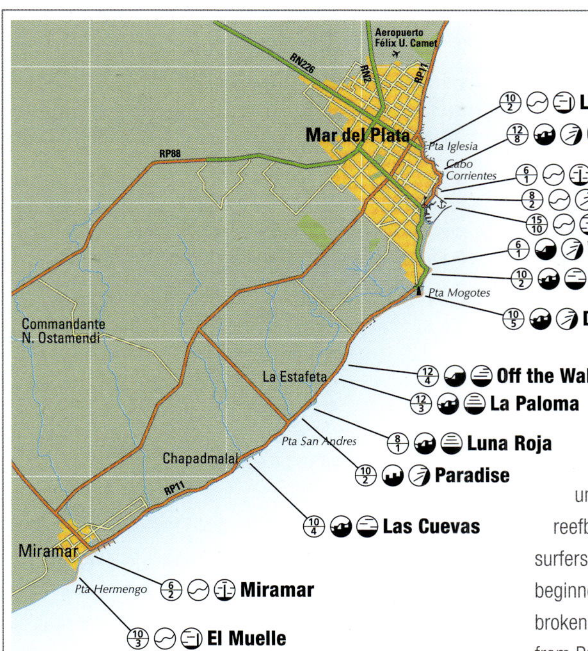


The solid concrete pier of **El Muelle** accommodates larger S swells without closing-out so much. Longer rights can form off the end and faster walls will peel into the rocky beach. There are more powerful peaks among the rocks to the south of the pier at El Pomol. **Miramar** has been inundated with stubby jetties, resulting in plenty of beachbreak options. Honores near the rivermouth gets good banks and a crowd. Chapadmalal is home to **Las Cuevas**, which includes a decent left reef, a shallow right and good beachbreak peaks in between. **Paradise**'s pointbreak rights can be long and will hollow out with SE swells and NW winds. **Luna Roja** breaks over a rock bottom in front of some large cliffs, with fun peaks when it's small and heavier lefts as the swell picks up. Negotiate the dangerous cliff path down to **La Paloma**, a testing, advanced wave over a rocky minefield, with barrels and power aplenty on a SE groundswell and dropping tide. Fickle **Off the Wall** is a treacherous right breaking over a rock shelf with super-fast barrel sections for experts. High tide makes entry and exit virtually impossible and it's often blown-out. **Diva** is a queen of the coast when it reels perfectly in front of the lighthouse. Low consistency since it needs NE-E overhead swells so not usually a winter spot. **Mariano** (aka Honu Beach) picks up the most swell in the region, unleashing short powerful peaks plus some barreling reefbreak lefts that should only be tackled by experienced surfers and bodyboarders. **Waikiki** is the best place for beginners or longboarders looking for small, fun, mushy broken-up rights, shouldering off the point. The beachbreaks from Punta Mogotes out to the rarely surfed big swell peak at **Escollera Sur** are usually not worth riding. At the south end of Playa Grande **Yacht** is protected from winter's S winds, which makes it possible to ride this long, classic right when most of the other spots are blown-out. At the north end, crowded **Biologia** breaks left off the tip of the jetty in any E swells. Rights break back towards the rocks and there can be a right off the end into the next bay, depending on swell direction. Can get really hollow on lower tides, which attracts crowds of locals that will be quick to drop-in. **Cabo Corrientes** pointbreak was once the best wave in Argentina, but building a jetty in the middle of the wave pretty much killed it except on the biggest E swells of the year. Inside that jetty, the beginner-friendly sands of Playa Varese are nicely protected from S wind and swells. Further round the city's polluted bay, multiple jetties and T-head groynes create varying quality waves for all surfers. Try La Popular, La Perla, Sunrider or **La Pepita** which turns SE swells into nice rights with an inside wedge. Unfortunately, such days will attract great crowds, and bad vibes are not uncommon.

JAVIER AMEZAGA

Yacht

## TRAVEL INFORMATION

**Weather** – The coastal central area is relatively humid with great variations in temperatures. The winter is dry and cold with temperatures remaining between 5-13°C (41-56°F) in July/August. Rainfall brings shallow summer flooding to the flat Pampas areas. Between June and Sept, the water drops to 9°C (48°F), requiring a 5/4/3 fullsuit, booties, gloves and hood. 3/2 fullsuits are good between seasons before Jan-March hovers between 18-22°C (64-72°F) allowing springsuits.

**Lodging and Food** – Surf hostels (Flor de Lis, Del Mar), surf hotels (Alma Viva, La Maquinita), surf houses (Sternschein, Rufus), plus Cabanas Maripesca and Fincas del Oceano, right on the sea. Argentina's beef is the best in the world.

**Nature and Culture** – MDP in summer is as packed as a city can be and everything revolves around hanging-out at the beach, bar-hopping around Plaza Mitre and dancing all night. Visit the Museo del Mar, which displays over 30,000 shells.

**Hazards and Hassles** – Most of the crowds happen in the summer when the city is assaulted by Porteños and free surf schools give everyone a chance to hit the waves. Local surfers remain friendly towards foreigners.

**Handy Hints** – Take a regular shortboard. Many surf shops in MDP (Birdband, Carricart, Natural, Sunset) or Crow in Miramar. Some of the country's best spots are actually located in Necochea, 80km (50mi) south of Miramar.

PEDRO SALINAS

Las Cuevas

Roaring Forties depressions send 3-12ft SE-S swell before tracking east towards Africa. Summer is dominated by constant NE winds that will send smaller, inconsistent windswells between Nov and Feb, but paddle out early or late to avoid these onshores. NW winds dominate mid-year, before SE increases in Sept/Oct. The indented shape of the coast and the numerous jetties help shelter from strong winds, but as a rule the best sessions occur when the winds go back to blowing offshore after the howling SE'er that sent the swell. Tides hit 1.8m, heavily affecting certain breaks.

| STATISTICS | | J F | M A | M J | J A | S O | N D |
|---|---|---|---|---|---|---|---|
| SWELL | Direction | | | | | | |
| | Size (ft) | 2-3 | 3 | 4 | 4-5 | 4 | 2-3 |
| WIND | Direction | | | | | | |
| | Force | F4 | F3-F4 | F4 | F4 | F4 | F4 |
| WATER | Wetsuit | | | | | | |
| | Temp/°C | 20 | 18 | 13 | 10 | 11 | 16 |
| WEATHER | Rainfall/mm | 70 | 70 | 60 | 50 | 55 | 65 |
| | days/mth | 7 | 8 | 7 | 7 | 8 | 8 |
| | Min temp/°C | 15 | 12 | 6 | 5 | 7 | 12 |
| | Max temp/°C | 25 | 22 | 15 | 13 | 17 | 22 |

# Uruguay

Uruguay is a fairly unknown surfing destination, despite being neighbours with Brazil. There are more than 80 breaks scattered along just 200km of Atlantic coast, with everything from pointbreaks to beachbreaks, not to mention the rivermouths and even outer reefs with big waves. Some of the best spots are not easy to get to and so are seldom crowded, even yielding mellow waves in the middle of the summer.

**+ UNCROWDED SPOTS**
**+ SEMI-CONSISTENT POINTS**
**+ CHEAP AND SAFE**
**+ RELAXED LINE-UPS**

**- LACK OF POWERFUL SPOTS**
**- SMALL, AVERAGE IN SUMMER**
**- BROWNISH, MUDDY WATER**
**- COLD WINTER TEMPS**

La Paloma

NICOLAS OLIVERA

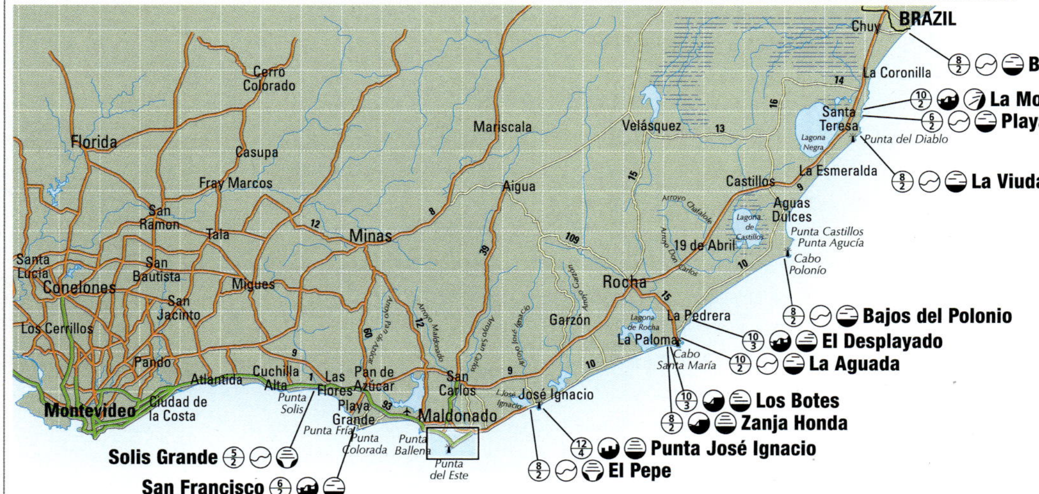


Montevideo gets some brown-water waves inside the wide mouth of the Rio de la Plata and big stormy swells can produce occasional waves at numerous spots like Arroyo Pando, St Lucia del Este, Cuchilla Alta and the long, ever-shifting rivermouth peaks at **Solis Grande**. They all need strong, long-period SE-SW swells and get city crowds. **San Francisco** includes a right pointbreak, an E wind-protected beachbreak at El Pewe and some rocky peaks out on Punta Colorado called Faroleta. In built-up Punta del Este, **La Virgen** is a challenging left reef/point set-up with rumbling walls and barrels on the drop. Holds some size and the tricky access through a jumble of urchin dusted rocks, currents and vertical drops make this an experts only wave. **El Emir** attracts crowds to a diminishing beach that can hold powerful, sometimes hollow peaks, particularly in an E swell. **Los Dedos** has no real punch in the line-up, but a huge sculpture of giant fingers half-buried in the sand. **La Olla** is a fun left wall in E swells allowing most abilities time for turns and and a longer cruise to the beach. **La Barra**'s rivermouth helps shape good sandbars off the rocky coast. Long lefts or shorter steeper rights provide a wide playground for many surfers of all abilities. Mid tide, any N wind and a ESE swell should be

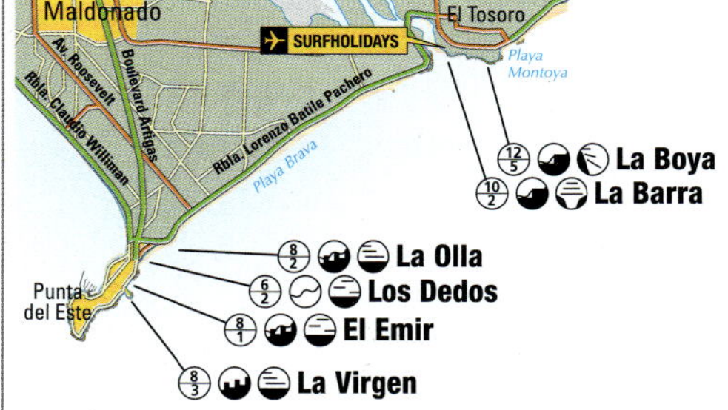


primo. Out on the point, **La Boya** hosts fast, hollow lefts over flat rocks and a crowd is guaranteed. The other side of the point, hollow rights peel into Playa Montoya and a rolling left breaks at the far end of Bikini Beach. **El Pepe** is a rivermouth that can sculpt good banks and is sometimes called La Boca de la Laguna. Consistent summer left and right at **Jose Ignacio** handles SW wind if swell is big enough to clear the nasty rocks. In La Paloma **Zanja Honda** is the best spot with longer lefts and hollower rights over rock and sand, just west of **La Botes**, a spinning left point with 150m rides. Popular **La Aguada** picks up plenty of swell and outputs spinning peaks for all abilities. **El Desplayado** has some top quality rights that wall up off a small reef at the southern end of the beach and reel off in SE swells. Hollow and powerful. **Bajos del Polonio** has thumping sandbars, can pick up all swell directions and is sheltered by Cabo Polonio. Other beaches to explore on the north side include Calavera, Valizas and Aquas Dulces. Santa Teresa and Punta Del Diablo form the other main surf hub in Uruguay, sporting 15 major spots within a 25km drive. **La Viuda** faces SE and picks up plenty of swell onto shifting sandbanks that often form up hollow peaks in the northern corner. **Playa del Barco** is a quality curve of open beachbreak with the northern access through Chero Chato and Las Achiras. There is plenty of potential for quality rights along this undeveloped coastline that has few hotels, but lots of campsites. **La Moza** is the best righthand point around, attracting weekend crowds to ride long walls with cover-up sections off the rocks at the southern end of a long beach. **Barra del Chuy**, is the most consistent wave in the country blessed with shorebreak power, but plagued by onshore winds.

In winter, lows form between the Falklands and Argentina, then veer on a NNE path towards Africa. SE swells are quite regular, reaching 12ft+ but averaging 4-10ft. Summers are really small, often going flat as the swell drops below 3ft. Autumn is the best season. Onshore winds are frequent after mid-morning and the best winds are S-SW for rights and NW-NE for lefts. July, August and September water temps can drop to 10ºC (50ºF) but may be 13ºC (56ºF) in a mild year. 4/3 with boots, a 3/2, a springsuit and maybe boardshorts in the hottest summers at 24ºC (75ºF). Max tidal range is 0.8m in Montevideo.

## TRAVEL INFORMATION

**Weather** – Cold fronts in winter bring overcast, drizzly spells and sometimes a violent SW Pampero wind blowing in from Argentina. Summer thunderstorms are frequent when high humidity and fog are common. Spring is usually damp, cool, and windy, summers are warm, autumns are mild and winters are chilly and uncomfortably damp.

**Lodging and Food** – Punta del Este, hostels/hotels from $20-500/n. Many hostels in La Paloma fr $13/n or Santa Teresa Nat Park camping. Lively nightlife. Lots of BBQ's serving sausages, blood sausages, stout beer or first-class red wines. Pay around $15 for a full meal.

**Nature and Culture** – Punta del Este's Gorlero Avenue has restaurants, bars, shops, cinemas and the Feria Artesanal. Isla de Lobos, 8km offshore, is one of the world's largest sea-lion colonies. Whales may be seen October-November.

**Hazards and Hassles** – Aside from rocks & some jellyfish in summer, things are pretty safe. Wind changes are fast and without warning so surf when you see good waves.

**Handy Hints** – Cheap and decent quality equipment is available to buy or rent from surf shops in the main beach towns. Use a thicker, longer board for the mellow waves and reduced buoyancy in the rivermouth.

| STATISTICS | | J F | M A | M J | J A | S O | N D |
|---|---|---|---|---|---|---|---|
| SWELL | Direction | | | | | | |
| | Size (ft) | 2-3 | 3 | 4 | 4-5 | 4 | 2-3 |
| WIND | Direction | | | | | | |
| | Force | F4 | F4 | F4 | F4 | F4 | F4 |
| WATER | Wetsuit | | | | | | |
| | Temp/°C | 22 | 21 | 15 | 12 | 14 | 19 |
| WEATHER | Rainfall/mm | 80 | 82 | 86 | 92 | 89 | 76 |
| | days/mth | 8 | 9 | 10 | 10 | 11 | 15 |
| | Min temp/°C | 18 | 16 | 11 | 9 | 11 | 15 |
| | Max temp/°C | 25 | 23 | 17 | 15 | 17 | 22 |

# Rio Grande do Sol BRAZIL

The "Great River of the South" is the southernmost State of Brazil, bordered to the north by Santa Catarina, to the west by Argentina, to the south by Uruguay and to the east by the Atlantic Ocean. Gaúcho cattle herders and ranchers have settled the pampa regions and the state is highly regarded for its hospitality and excellent quality of life. The coast is one straight sandy beach stretching 500km, broken only by 3 rivermouths, where the construction of jetties is the only other help for creating sandbanks, yet there are a few good surprises and consistent winter swells.

- **+ BIG WAVE OPTION IN TORRES**
- **+ NOT POLLUTED**
- **+ BEACH & PARTY VIBE**
- **+ FRIENDLY GAÚCHO HOSPITALITY**

- **– AVERAGE QUALITY BEACHBREAKS**
- **– NOT TOO CONSISTENT**
- **– ALMOST NO WIND PROTECTION**
- **– REGULAR STRONG RIPS**

Just south of the huge jetties protecting the mouth of the Rio Grande, Cassino Beach (not on map) needs small, clean swells without onshore winds to have anything worth riding. **Cidreira** is a less-developed resort town with waves often breaking beyond the pier in a jumble of whitewater, but the locals are on the best peaks either side of the pier channels. Porto Alegre surfers can pack the busy peaks of **Tramandaí** on both sides of the pier and there will be some barrels on a W wind day. Another option can be the fickle peelers at the Barra de Imbe rivermouth.

The t-shaped pier in busy **Atlântida** helps to hold the sand banks for bigger, longer rides, mostly rights in a S swell. Trendy, urbanised **Capão da Canoa** has 18km of open beachbreak, but hope for a windless day to catch some hollow peaks in clean water thanks to proper sewage water treatment. Quieter breaks are found along the wide open beach of **Itapeva** that will be better in the mornings on smaller peaky swells. With pristine beaches and famous basalt rock formations, Torres is the state's prettiest and varied surf town. If it blows from the N/NE, **Guarita** will have protected peaks, peeling over a rocky bottom just outside of the tiny bay. **Praia da Cal** is a very consistent break located just below the tall cliffs south of the lighthouse hill that offer decent S wind shelter. A S swell will deliver faster, longer righthanders, but it gets real busy. **Prainha** is another punchy beachbreak with often hollow peaks thanks to rock-anchored sandbars. It's consistent, crowded and a place to hang-out admiring the view. **Ilha dos Lobos** is a rocky offshore islet, home to sea lions and the "Brazilian Teahupoo", but surfing the thick, barrelling lefthander has been banned for wildlife conservation. Various peaks can be found along the 2km **Praia Grande** beach, but locals usually prefer its southern end for the rock & sand bottom. Can be a good spot when stormy in winter. Mostly lefts forming outside the point & then reforming on the inside, losing power along the way. **Praia dos Molhes** starts from the S jetty, offering a decent left wall and protection from the N wind. When the sandbanks are well-shaped and an E swell hits, this popular contest site becomes very busy. **Barra do Mampituba** is the north jetty that lines up good righthanders, best in a S swell. The canal between the jetties has smaller, hollower waves, but watch out for the dangerous boat traffic and nets.

BASILIO RUY

Guarita

## TRAVEL INFORMATION

**Weather** – The dominance of the warm and moist maritime air creates humid summers with temps between 25-35°C (77-95°F). Winter reveals mild average temps, but it's changeable and sudden windy, rainy weather can drop to 2-15°C (35-59°F). Autumns tend to be as changeable as winters but warmer. Rainfall is regular throughout the year but spring is slightly drier. Use a 3/2 steamer from June to December, with optional 4/3 and boots in colder winter spots like Chui. A springsuit is sufficient for the rest of the year.

**Lodging and Food** – Large choice of accommodation from pousadas to luxury hotels. In Torres, try Hotel Samambaia, A Furninha ($50/n) or Guarita Park Hotel ($65/n). The barbecue, locally known as churrasco is one of the most important elements of everyday life.

**Nature and Culture** – Ecotourism is well developed. Lots of historical tours to Jesuit Missions. Torres is home of the Guarita Park biosphere reserve and a hot air balloon festival.

**Hazards and Hassles** – Never leave valuables (phones, cameras, watches, rings) unattended or in cars. Brazilian thieves are experts and know every trick! Local water is usually not safe to drink; go for mineral water, beer or guarana. When driving, go with the flow. Localism is not a problem if you respect the rules. Watch out for the dangerous fishing nets.

**Handy Hints** – Plenty of surf shops where quality equipment is pretty cheap. Bring any board that works in small to medium beachbreaks. Wake up early for offshore conditions. Try sandboarding in Itapeva or Cidreira.

BOOZE TENTACLE

Atlântida Pier

Autumn to winter cold fronts moving in a NE direction constitute the main source of swell. Due S swells have a longer fetch, offer a better period and also tend to be cleaner than the E swells that are generated closer to the shore. April and May usually see better-shaped waves over summer sculpted sandbars, while June, July and August are usually the biggest. From Nov-April, summer flat spells can be interrupted by locally generated windswell or an occasional weak cold front. Expect heavy currents running parallel to the coast when a strong swell is around. Winds are usually calm to light offshore on early mornings, then they pick up at mid-morning to 10-15 knots SE (onshore). When a storm passes, the SE winds get stronger (15-25 knots). The small mean tidal range (0.7m max) has little influence on the surf.

| STATISTICS | | J F | M A | M J | J A | S O | N D |
|---|---|---|---|---|---|---|---|
| SWELL | Direction | | | | | | |
| | Size (ft) | 2 | 2-3 | 3-4 | 4 | 3-4 | 2 |
| WIND | Direction | | | | | | |
| | Force | F4 | F4 | F4 | F4 | F4 | F4 |
| WATER | Wetsuit | | | | | | |
| | Temp/°C | 24 | 23 | 19 | 16 | 18 | 21 |
| WEATHER | Rainfall/mm | 128 | 119 | 94 | 120 | 130 | 104 |
| | days/mth | 8 | 8 | 9 | 10 | 10 | 7 |
| | Min temp/°C | 20 | 17 | 13 | 9 | 12 | 18 |
| | Max temp/°C | 26 | 25 | 20 | 19 | 19 | 24 |

# Santa Catarina BRAZIL

The south of Brazil offers the best surf in the country, with bigger swells and more coastal variations than the north. The best option is Santa Catarina Island, facing ESE and is commonly referred to as Florianopolis (or Floripa), the state capital and port on the island's west side. It is a great destination, with a concentration of 20 breaks covering a 225° swell window, providing waves for all abilities, plus further south are the quality spots around Guarda de Embau, Garopaba and Imbituba.

**+ GREAT CONSISTENCY**
**+ WIDE RANGE OF SPOTS**
**+ TROPICAL SCENERY**
**+ SAFE, DEVELOPED AREA**

**- COOL WATER**
**- RELATIVELY CROWDED**
**- FISHING SEASON BEACHES CLOSURES**
**- WET CLIMATE**

Santinho
Moçambique
Galheta
Mole
Joaquina
Campeche
Morro das Pedras
Matadeiro
Lagoinha do Leste
Naufragados
Praia da Pinheira
Guarda do Embau
Gamboa
Silveira
Ferrugem
Praia Rosa
Praia da Vila

Imbituba holds the biggest waves in Brazil at **Praia da Vila**, where chunky rights unfurl on an outside reef in E to S swells. It's more of a steep, grunty, rolling wall than a barrel, but requires skill to negotiate at double-overhead plus. On smaller swells there are hollow lefts and various peaks along the rest of the beach. Mid tides, any N winds and any swell over chest-high will attract thick competitive crowds. **Praia Rosa** has good exposure, particularly at the N end where the crowds will jockey for A-Frames with NE wind protection in most swells. **Ferrugem** is a multi-directional swell magnet, where the super-consistent beachies pack some punch. Lefts at N end in NE swell, rights off rocks at S end and a number of rip bowls in-between. In Garopaba, **Silveira**'s grunty, right pointbreak lays down testing sections over urchin-infested rocks. Both the south end and north end beachies can turn on grinding barrels and the whole stretch is often better at higher tide. The south end of **Gamboa** has some handy gullies making the paddle easier holding up some lefts and rights for the smaller crowd of intermediates and longboarders. The **Guarda do Embau** lefthand rivermouth forms steep peaks off the point that run down the changeable bars, with a mix of wall and tube sections. Scimitar shaped **Praia da Pinheira** is fairly average beachbreak, biggest in the middle of the protected bay. Hike or boat into **Naufragados** a hollow wave with a tendency to close-out. S swells with N winds ideal to get the right off the rocks working or a left back into the rivermouth. **Lagoinha do Leste** is a mission to reach, but perfectly angled to pick up SE swell, producing sharp drops and some fast rides, especially when the lagoon opens and creates some channels. The lefts at **Matadeiro** rivermouth can be epic but are extremely fickle and inconsistent. The sandbars shift and there may be more rights going back towards the river or short, sharp, close-outs stretching down the beach. Reliable righthanders break at the S end of **Morro das Pedras** in SE groundswell. **Campeche**'s long, hollow right needs a major S swell to wrap around the sand point and spin off fast, leaving many behind. **Joaquina** beach is the most consistent and usually the best beachbreak in Santa Catarina. Any swell direction and size, any tide and any W wind. It's always powerful, often hollow and never empty. Encircled by steep hills, **Praia Mole** offers S wind protection and average beachbreaks that improve to the north. The **Galheta** nudist beach is a bit of a hike, but it gets hollow waves with fewer surfers. **Moçambique** is the longest beach, where smaller swells on light wind days will have an endless selection of peaks, that get sucky on lower tides. Cruisers will find the Barra da Lagoa south end less boisterous while rippers should head N for faster, walled-up waves at Ponta das Aranhas. **Santinho** regularly welcomes decent peaks to this undeveloped beach, particularly at the north end, which picks up more swell and is offshore in NW-N winds.

This part of Brazil receives the most swell in the country and the 2-10ft SE-S swells are reasonably powerful and frequent, especially from April to Oct. Unusually, spring is better than autumn with more E in the swells coming off deep lows to the SE. Wind speeds are high, blowing primarily from the N-SE in the summer and flipping between S-SW to N-NE in the winter. SW winds mean stormy weather, while 'lestadas' (easterlies) are the usual sea breezes, which blow with force after lunch. Less than 1m tidal variation has little affect on spots.

Praia da Vila

FLAVIO VIDIGAL

## TRAVEL INFORMATION

**Weather** – The climate is wet/subtropical with as much rain in the winter as in the summer. Deep winter brings cold, stormy weather, while the summer has afternoon thunderstorms. Imbituba water temps are 15°C (60°F) in July and top out at 27°C (81°F), so 3/2, springsuits and boardies are all needed.

**Lodging and Food** – Summer is tourist high season when cheap accommodation is hard to find. Florianopolis has something for every budget plus surf camps (Floripa, Brazil Surfing Adventure, Luex) and also in I mbituba (Camp Surf, Camping Padang).

**Nature and Culture** – "Floripa" is an extreme sport wonderland with sandboarding, windsurfing, kitesurfing, wakeboarding, paragliding, hang-gliding, mountain biking, horse riding, rock climbing etc, plus plenty of apres-surf nightlife – biggest party of the year is Oktoberfest in Blumenau.

**Hazards and Hassles** – Although crowds are much thinner than in São Paulo, you're in Brazil and all Brazilians love to surf. During the fishing season from May-June some beaches ban surfing. Mussels and urchins at a few spots, notably Silveira.

**Handy Hints** – Boards are cheap - check surf shops in Floripa (Lombok, Reefifi, Tikehau), Garopaba (Sulnativo) and Imbutuba (Atma, New Life). Plenty of surf schools (Praia de Imbituba, Casa do Surf, Evandro Santos).

| STATISTICS | | J F | M A | M J | J A | S O | N D |
|---|---|---|---|---|---|---|---|
| SWELL | Direction | | | | | | |
| | Size (ft) | 2 | 2-3 | 3-4 | 4 | 3-4 | 2 |
| WIND | Direction | | | | | | |
| | Force | F4 | F4 | F4 | F4 | F4 | F4 |
| WATER | Wetsuit | | | | | | |
| | Temp/°C | 25 | 24 | 21 | 18 | 19 | 23 |
| WEATHER | Rainfall/mm | 227 | 117 | 65 | 42 | 102 | 167 |
| | days/mth | 14 | 11 | 8 | 5 | 10 | 14 |
| | Min temp/°C | 23 | 22 | 19 | 18 | 19 | 21 |
| | Max temp/°C | 30 | 28 | 28 | 26 | 26 | 29 |

# São Paulo BRAZIL

São Paulo is one of the world's largest cities and so it's no surprise to discover that the sub-tropical shores of the Littoral Paulista (city beaches), are teeming with hot surfers. This zone of mainly sandy beachbreaks has numerous quality setups, but regular pumping swells are never guaranteed so patience is required for the good days. A way of avoiding the worst of the crowds is to take a long hike or a boat to some of the harder access spots that can be found along the more rugged stretches of coastline.

- \+ CONSISTENT CLEAN SURF
- \+ EASILY ACCESSIBLE
- \+ GOOD QUALITY FACILITIES
- \+ URBAN ENTERTAINMENT

- \- HEAVY CROWD PRESSURE
- \- LACK OF BIG WAVES
- \- POLLUTION
- \- BUILT UP, HEAVY TRAFFIC

Pitangueras

TONY FLEURY

## TRAVEL INFORMATION

**Weather** – Although the Tropic of Capricorn runs through São Paulo, the Serra do Mar mountain range makes this area wetter and cooler than you would expect. São Paulo is at an altitude of about 800m, and can get cold and grey while the coast is warm and sunny. During the winter (May-Sept) surf period, temps average 23°C (74°F), rarely falling under 18°C (64°F). Summers are hot and humid. The bad air pollution can make it very uncomfortable. Springsuits are generally sufficient, although, on some cooler winter mornings, 18°C (64°F) water will need a steamer.

**Lodging and Food** – There is the full range of accommodation possibilities in Guaruja. Surf season is the off-season for tourists, although July is still busy. Finding a room (fr $30/n) in a 'pousada' or 'chales' in Maresias/Trindade is easy. Basic foodstuffs are cheap. When eating out, stick to the 'prato do dia' (dish of the day) or the pay by weight system in order to keep costs down.

**Nature and Culture** – Maresias is a packed beach, where people go to be seen. Scenic Ilhabela is a nice place to escape the crowds. Parati to the north, is an enjoyable colonial town.

**Hazards and Hassles** – The worst problems are the crowds in the water, localism and bad pollution. Crime is not as high as in Rio, but be careful in the outskirts of São Paulo.

**Handy Hints** – Boards are cheap and easily available from surf shops along the coast (Crizca, Raizes, Skull). Plenty of surf schools in Sao Sebastiao, Ilhabela and beyond in Ubatuba.

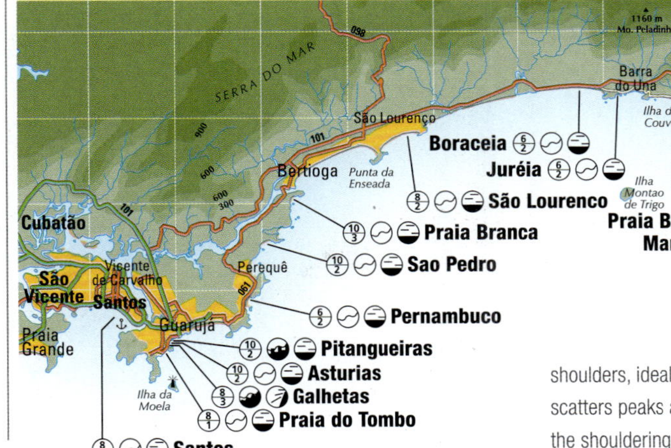


The crowded **Santos** beaches need SE-S swells which are bigger at Praia do Itaraé while Embaré will be more offshore in E winds. **Praia do Tombo** has some good lefts off the jumbled rocks of the high-rise covered headland. When an E swell hits, **Galhetas** can get big, hollow and powerful down at the southern point of **Playa Asturias**, which holds standard, fun, easy beachbreak for all abilities and surfcraft. **Pitangueiras** is a very consistent spot, making the most of any swell direction, but it's ultra-crowded and a fight for every wave. There are four main peaks; Canal & Monduba are usually fuller, while it's hollower at Ilha and Canto do Maluf, which is the NE corner of the beach on the other side of the island. Beginners should go to Enseada, but not packed **Pernambuco**, which gets consistent, hollow peaks with rights rolling into the northern corner. Handles a bit of S wind, but needs E in the swell to break. Exclusive resorts restrict road access to the northern beaches like **Sao Pedro**, where lefts spin off the rocks in solid swells. If the wind is S try Pinheiro and Iporanga, otherwise **Praia Branca** is reliable and powerful, with hollow peaks at either end. **São Lourenco** has small rivermouth formed sandbars along its length, creating deeper channels and easier sloping walls and shoulders, ideal for improvers and longboarders. **Boraceia** scatters peaks and the crowd along its length, inviting turns on the shouldering walls. Quiet **Juréia** is a short bay with waves off either headland, particularly the left in E swells. **Camburi** can produce some excellent lefts on a major S swell and rights at the other end in an E. Sucky and slabby over a rock sand mix. **Praia Brava**'s dumpy, short close-outs will occasionally line-up something better in a wilderness setting. Picturesque **Maresias** is one of Brazil's best beachbreaks when a SE-S groundswell, groomed by NE winds produces hollow, fast, top-to-bottom tubing lefts and rights. Challenging Canto do Moreira wedges heavily off the western headland and the eastern end will be smaller, but no less-crowded with the finest surfers in the region, including local Gabriel Medina. **Pauba** is the suckiest shorebreak on the coast with heavy bowls, air drops and slamming lips for lids and loonies. On beautiful Ilhabela, **Bonete** needs S or even SW swell to start triangulating off the headland and throwing some high and wide tubes for the few that make the 3hr+ trek there. **Castelhanos** has hollow surf on any E swell and is 4x4 road accessible. Further east around Ubatuba are another dozen multiple-aspect beaches with a range of waves for all abilities and surfcraft.

The Littoral Paulista is well-exposed to frequent winter S-SE swells coming up from Antarctica. From April-Oct you can expect plenty of 3-8ft days. Unusual, late winter E swells produced by lows tracking way off the coast or by the strong E winds sometimes caused by high pressures, will send short-lived ENE groundswells onto Brazil's beaches. Swells rarely get very big and when they do there are few spots that can hold much size. The dominant summer E wind veers more N or S to SW through winter when a cold front approaches the coast. It is usually offshore in the mornings, but by 10am the E sea breeze picks up. Tidal ranges are small (1.7m max) and don't really effect most spots.

| STATISTICS | | J F | M A | M J | J A | S O | N D |
|---|---|---|---|---|---|---|---|
| SWELL | Direction | | | | | | |
| | Size (ft) | 1-2 | 2 | 3 | 3-4 | 3 | 1-2 |
| WIND | Direction | | | | | | |
| | Force | F3 | F3-F4 | F3 | F3 | F3 | F3 |
| WATER | Wetsuit | | | | | | |
| | Temp/°C | 26 | 26 | 23 | 21 | 21 | 24 |
| WEATHER | Rainfall/mm | 227 | 117 | 65 | 42 | 102 | 167 |
| | days/mth | 14 | 11 | 8 | 5 | 10 | 14 |
| | Min temp/°C | 23 | 22 | 19 | 18 | 19 | 21 |
| | Max temp/°C | 30 | 28 | 28 | 26 | 26 | 29 |

Praia do Tombo

TONY FLEURY

# Rio de Janeiro BRAZIL

Rio's physical features are dominated by the Sierra do Mar mountain range, which is cloaked by the Mata Atlantica forest. Mountains plunge into the sea, forests meet the beaches and granite cliff faces rise abruptly from the extended lowlands. The Wonderful City is one of the most densely populated places on earth, with almost 7 million "Cariocas" indulging in dancing, drinking, beach-going and sunbathing. The waves can get hollow and powerful enough to run World Tour contests at the best beaches, where the crowds can be intense.

**+ BRAZIL'S BEST BEACHBREAKS**
**+ CONSISTENT YEAR-ROUND**
**+ DRIER WINTER TIME**
**+ RIO ACCESS AND SERVICES**

**– LACK OF POINTS AND REEFS**
**– RARE EPIC CONDITIONS**
**– ULTRA-CROWDED MAIN SPOTS**
**– HIGH STREET CRIME RATE**

## TRAVEL INFORMATION

**Weather** – Rio is tropical, warm and humid, with local variations due to differences in altitude, vegetation and proximity to the ocean. Hot summer days (Dec-March) are followed by heavy and rapid evening rains. Most surfers tend to come in winter; Oct water temps can be as cold as 20°C or as hot as 26°C (70-76°F)! Springy or boardshorts rule this coast. Upwelling makes Saquarema and Cabo Frio cold!

**Lodging and Food** – Copacabana is where most int'l hotels are located. Try Pousada Barra Sol in Tijuca (fr$36). In Saquarema, Itauna Inn Casal fr $45 with ideal surf views. Plenty of pousadas in Buzios. Expect tasty Prato do dia to cost ±$5.

**Nature and Culture** – The beach in Rio is the main place to go for action, sport, parties, shows...Futvolei is big! Don't miss Pão de Azucar (400m) or Corcovado Cristo Redentor (710m) for sunset views of the city from a cable car. Pillion flights with a pilot hang/para-gliding off the 510m Pedra Bonita can be arranged. Excellent hiking and climbing.

**Hazards and Hassles** – Expect thick, aggressive crowds and localism at any urban spot. Hike down long beaches for hassle-free line-ups. Pollution is a massive issue. Drug abuse, street violence and muggings/car jackings are rife. Avoid strolling along beaches at night, or in favelas like Rocinha.

**Handy Hints** – Local boards are cheap (fr$2-300 shortboard) and good quality. Shapers: Lelot, André Cebola, Akio, Udo Bastos. Shops: Rocky Center, Rico, Local, Geriba Surf. Surf schools: Escola de Surf Rico (Ipanema, Barra), Saquarema Surf School, Sunset (Buzios). Rio has a surf bus that goes to all the beaches. Avoid Carnival time!

JS CALLAHAN SURFEXPLORE

HENRIQUE PINGUIM

Ipanema

Rio's westernmost surf is located on the southern coast of Ilha Grande. Restinga de Marambaia represents 40kms of mostly off-limits beachbreaks because of military restrictions. The unreliable rivermouth left at **Barra de Guaratiba** can be Rio's best wave when the cylindrical walls spin down the triangulated sandbar. Fast, throaty barrels, but the crowds, localism, sharks and pollution detract heavily. Cradled in a beautiful and protected natural setting, **Grumari** is really consistent and open to all swells, lining up nicely in SW swells and any N wind. Fun for all when small, then it takes some skill to just get out on overhead days. If there's no surf at **Prainha**, then give up for the day. Swells from the E will get lefts wrapping round the point, while the rights at the other end will handle anything around to the SW. Powerful and pretty peaks fill the middle stretch and can be hollow. Unusually for this coastline, **Praia Macumba** is usually a fat rolling wall, ideal for longboarders and learners since the take-off is slopey and easy. Handles plenty of size but has enough deep channels to get out at the main peak on the eastern point. Can be a bit steeper down the west end and at the sucky bodyboard spot Secrets. Such an easy wave is gonna attract a lot of older, wiser surfers and those not so wise - be careful on the paddle-outs. **Barra da Tijuca** stretches for 14km so there are many local names for different sandbars, often named after the lifeguard post numbers. Furthest west is Recreio which always has a decent sandbar and a crowd to match. The undeveloped foreshore of Reserva in the middle up to Barramares can hold some serious tubes in S swells. Pepe's near the rivermouth shapes some rapid lefts, but pollution is a big worry. When it's small, Barra da Tijuca is fairly gentle and user-friendly for all abilities. The main peaks will be crowded, but you can walk up or down to another peak. Once overhead, the waves get fast, often closing-out with guillotine lips and few regular channels. Rips,

HENRIQUE PINGUIM

Copacabana

### Arpoador

LAT. -22.989554° LONG. -43.192694°

Arpoador is Brazil's surfing birthplace and usually entertains the best surf of the Zona Sul (South Side), easily recognised by its giant granite rock lookout. On medium to big E-SE swell, lefts can reach 10ft, wrapping around the point and catching on the sandbar that builds up next to it. Longish walls with hollow slots and plenty of punch for a full repertoire of manoeuvres, before doing the run back up the beach and jumping off the point. Will show its best in SE swell, lower tides and NE wind, but unfortunately this doesn't occur too often and when it does, thick crowds of Rio rippers will be all over it. Has hosted top-level surf contests, but its inconsistency makes it a lottery. Since the city installed lighting, night time sessions are entirely doable and far less popular with the locals. Wandering down Ipanema beach won't escape the crowds, but the people-watching is special.

jellyfish and severe sewage pollution add to the risks. **São Conrado** is a heaving shorey barrel-fest on better SE swells, attracting large numbers of bodyboarders from the large local favela, Rocinha. Both the lefts off the rocky eastern end and the middle peak will lurch from air drop to spitting barrel with lots of wedge and close-out ramps. Not the place to get cocky or leave anything in the car. The pollution is sickening after rains. **Leblon** outputs beefy rights up to 12ft in S swells that are sheltered from W winds at the pointbreak and there are sucky, dumpy beach peaks as well, running right through famous Ipanema down to ✪**Arpoador**, Rio's favourite pro contest site. This stretch is totally zooed from dawn till dusk and the locals will not be very accommodating. It's the same vibe around the headland in the short, sucky sliders of **Diabo**. **Copacabana** may be the world's most famous beach, attracting the beautiful, bronzed local Cariocas and tourists to an endless party along Avenida Atlantica. During a strong SE swell and W-NW wind, big tubes pop up and slam the shorebreak at lower tides, making the bodyboarders happy and the lifeguards nervous. The SW corner offers more south wind and swell protection around Posto 6, up to more exposed Posto 5 and then Leme at the north end occasionally gets fast hollow, suck-out lefts. When it's small and onshore, beginners will be OK, otherwise it's for intermediates/experts when huge and barreling. This is the ultimate beach crowd and the line-up will never be empty. Take the 14km Niteroi bridge to cross the Bahia de Guanabara (which has a few waves in storm swells) and reach **Itacoatiara**. This is one of the heavier, hollower beachbreaks in Brazil, sucking in S swells and exploding them on shallow, challenging bars. West end Pampo can have good rights on SW, Meio lurches hard in the middle while Costão will turn out E-SE lefts. Any N wind and a pushing tide is usually the go. It's not always perfect, but when it picks up, only experienced, fleet-footed surfers should take on the air-drops. A long, rigidly straight beach leads past the extensive lagoon system to **Ponta Negra**, where powerful beachbreak can arrive with E-SE swell, but it is usually closing-out or messy and blown-out. **Jaconé** prefers a SW swell angle to help with the close-outs that sometimes spin off some cylindrical corners. Many Cariocas consider Saquarema to have the most consistent, quality waves in Brazil. To the west of the lagoon channel, **Praia da Vila** piles up sand off the point with a peak and a left that can get hollow and hard-breaking on a moderate swell with E in it. Nice intermediate-friendly walls when smaller. **Itauna** is often referred to as the Maracanã of surf as it holds major contests in some of the most consistent and competitive waves in the land. 10-12ft and clean is not that rare an occurrence when the outside lefts roll through on E-SE swells. Powerful tubular rights grind through on a S-SW, but won't handle so much size. Like most beaches, it is accessible to most abilities when small, but requires skills once overhead conditions arrive, along with the best, dialled-in locals. Massambada Restinga is another endless beach with myriads of potential peaks, best on E-S mid-size swells and N winds. Check as many access points as possible, like **Seca** about halfway down and Praia Grande, which shapes all size S swell into some superb lefts. **Praia Brava** also holds long, perfect lefts in Arraial do Cabo, when NE winds clean an E-S swell. There are also peaks along the narrow beach that disappears at high tide. Cabo Frio gets consistent surf by a 1616 built fort, thus it's called Praia **Forte**. It's pretty urban so expect competitive crowds, when the SE swell gets in. There are empty waves all the way down the long arc of beach through Foguete and Pontal where there is also a left reef off the island. **Geriba** is ritzy Buzios' most consistent beachbreak, best on

BASILIO RUY

Itauna

NW-NE wind and E to S swell, but it gets super-crowded on weekends. Nice peaks, sometimes hollow and plenty of walls to work with. Heading south to Tucuns or even Dunas de Pero will result in a mellower wave and line-up. The outside reefbreaks of **Laje Rasa** are slopey cutback shoulders perfect for cruising and SUP. Be ready for a 30min paddle or get a boat out there.

The Littoral Carioca receives the same swells as Littoral Paulista (prev page), but big swells are rare, which is convenient because few spots can hold size. Dominant wind comes from the E varying from 16% (June) to 32% (Oct); NE-SE is the usual direction plus the winter S-SW winds when cold fronts move towards the coast. Offshores only occur on calm mornings before 10am, or on SW-facing spots with NE winds. Tidal range is usually low (1.5m max) and doesn't matter most of the time.

| STATISTICS | | J F | M A | M J | J A | S O | N D |
|---|---|---|---|---|---|---|---|
| SWELL | Direction | | | | | | |
| | Size (ft) | 2 | 2-3 | 3-4 | 4 | 3-4 | 2 |
| WIND | Direction | | | | | | |
| | Force | F3-F4 | F3-F4 | F3-F4 | F3-F4 | F4 | F3-F4 |
| WATER | Wetsuit | | | | | | |
| | Temp/°C | 25 | 25 | 23 | 22 | 22 | 23 |
| WEATHER | Rainfall/mm | 110 | 120 | 85 | 55 | 90 | 130 |
| | days/mth | 11 | 12 | 9 | 7 | 10 | 13 |
| | Min temp/°C | 23 | 22 | 20 | 19 | 20 | 22 |
| | Max temp/°C | 30 | 29 | 26 | 26 | 26 | 28 |

# Espirito Santo BRAZIL

Brazilian surfers have traditionally overlooked the waves in the Holy Spirit State, but that is to ignore its ideal positioning for picking up both winter groundswells from the southern ocean and summer windswells from the reliable onshore trades. The capital Vitória along with Vila Velha and Guarapari are located in the south, where the diversity of waves includes top quality spots breaking over coral reefs, rock slabs and sandy rivermouths.

**+ SURPRISING VARIETY OF SPOTS**
**+ LESS CROWDS THAN SOUTH ZONES**
**+ YEAR-ROUND SWELL ACTION**
**+ WARM WATER AND AIR TEMPS**

**- CROWDED MAIN SPOTS**
**- SUMMER JUNKY WINDSWELLS**
**- CONSTANT ONSHORES**
**- SOME LOCALISM**

## TRAVEL INFORMATION

**Weather** – Vitoria and its satellite city Vila Velha expirence a tropical climate with rainfall concentrated in the summer months of Nov/Dec and March/April. Average air temperature is 26 °C (79°F) and rainfall is 2302 mm. Water temps can drop below 23°C (74°F) for July-Sept so a springsuit is needed.

**Lodging and Food** – South of the capital, there's good hotel infrastructure, inns, restaurants and many vacation homes for rent. Brazil Evolution Surf Camp and Regência Surf in the north do packages. Moqueca Capixaba is a local seafood delicacy.

**Nature and Culture** – ES is all about the beach from long and empty natural strands to the short, crowded and built-up urban scene of Vila Velha, which parties hard in summer. Brazilian navy personnel may be scoring the offshore islands of Trindade and Martin Vaz. Visit the inland national parks of Pedra Azul and Caparaó.

**Hazards and Hassles** – No shark attacks recorded in ES. Expect some bad attitude at the reefbreaks and don't leave valuables in cars or on the beach.

**Handy Hints** – Surfing is growing fast and the state government has invested heavily in coastal city infrastructure and safety. Lots of surf shops in Vila Velha, Jacaraipe and Serra. Capixaba is nickname for ES people.

DUDU MELAO
Regência

Regência
Xangão
Jacaraipe
Praia de Carapebus
D2
Itaparica
Barra do Jucu
Ponta da Belina
Praia Ponta da Fruta
Setiba Pina
Praia do Morro

The town beach of Guarapari bristles with high-rise apartments on the curving sands of **Praia do Morro**, attracting tourists and plenty of surfers to a consistent beachbreak in winter S or summer E-SE windchop. The northern end is usually bigger up towards the marlin statue on the little reef. Teeming with summer holidaymakers and surfers when it is good. **Setiba Pina** is the opposite vibe in a nature reserve with crystal clean water and some punchy A-frames up towards the central rocks. Likes an E swell to get the lefts spitting and has a low crowd factor mid-week. From Praia D'ulé up to **Praia Ponta da Fruta**, average banks can form in SE swells, with crumbling walls and pitching peaks often seen on the same day. Further south will be more challenging and sometimes gets a crowd when word gets out that Ulé is firing. **Ponta da Belina** is one of the state's best waves, offering long, strong, righthand walls stretching over some fingers of reef. Thick fast walls and feathering coping make it a high performance wave with sections more for bashing than ducking, but quality will depend on the sand formation. Handles any size swell from E-S and there can be a short left off the peak in more easterly swells. Guaranteed a crowd of slick locals who know the set-up. The headland at **Barra do Jucu** shields a few waves, the most popular being the peak at Barrão which often has a longer-running left that's super-fun and ultra-reliable in any S swell and NE winds are fine. The bodyboarders love the thick shoredump off the rocks of Praia de Concha and there are further peaks down by the cemetery. Absolutely always crowded with some of the best surfers because if it isn't breaking here, then find another activity for the day. A wall of concrete apartment blocks line the beach at **Itaparica** where sometimes hollow corners stalk the straight banks, especially behind the island. SE-S swells are usually better and there will still be some crumbly peaks and ramps in a SE wind. Similar deal at adjacent Praia de Itapoã which picks up E swells better. Numerous rocky islets sit offshore including **D2**, a barely submerged slab reef where the bodyboard crew go to get some serious shacks. Draws loads of water off the reef and reshapes it into a thick, squarish righthander. There are similarly brutish lefts nearby at Coral do Céu. It's a 1.35km paddle so hiring a boat is a good idea. The rocky point at **Praia de Carapebus** holds a ripable right wall that works better on E swells and dropping tides. Out the tip of the point at Praia Mole are more good reef-anchored peaks that the locals covet. Very consistent at Mole, but always smaller at Carapebus. The extensive sands of **Jacaraipe** pick up all swell undulations along the Serra coastline with easy rollers for beginners and occasional hollow days. Water quality is suspect down near the rivermouth jetty so try up towards Laranjeiras and Solemar. In Barra do Sahy, an offshore reef catches E-SE swells at **Xangão**, a localised righthander with a sucky take-off and a long wall. The long beach at **Regência** is one of the best waves in the state, serving stately lefts with roomy barrels in E-S swells and being perfectly happy with a NE sea breeze. The rivermouth can line up on big days when the beach is closed-out. Powerful waves without a clear paddling channel and rips make this spot unsuitable for beginners. Check the nearby rivermouth for a super-long but rare lefthander at Boca do Rio. Dirty river water and the potential for a few sharks. Regienca is part of a protected sea turtle nesting site.

Swell Forecasting - see **South Bahia**

| STATISTICS | | J F | M A | M J | J A | S O | N D |
|---|---|---|---|---|---|---|---|
| SWELL | Direction | | | | | | |
| | Size (ft) | 2 | 2 | 3 | 3 | 2-3 | 2 |
| WIND | Direction | | | | | | |
| | Force | F4 | F4 | F4 | F4 | F4 | F4 |
| WATER | Wetsuit | | | | | | |
| | Temp/°C | 26 | 27 | 25 | 24 | 24 | 25 |
| WEATHER | Rainfall/mm | 55 | 51 | 88 | 38 | 78 | 260 |
| | days/mth | 17 | 20 | 18 | 16 | 22 | 25 |
| | Min temp/°C | 22 | 21 | 19 | 17 | 20 | 22 |
| | Max temp/°C | 33 | 30 | 25 | 29 | 29 | 32 |

# South Bahia BRAZIL

Brazil is famed for Carnival and Salvador de Bahia undoubtedly hosts the most intense one. Surfers in the mid '70s searching the coast south of Salvador found the Bahia State capital Itacaré had an abundance of juicy, warm-water beachbreaks, reefbreaks and an amazingly long rivermouth right.

- \+ CONSISTENT WINDSWELLS
- \+ EASY BEGINNER'S WAVES
- \+ BOCA DA BARRA LONG RIDES
- \+ LESS-CROWDED HIKING SPOTS

- \- RARELY EPIC
- \- CROWDED MAIN BREAKS
- \- RAINY AUTUMN/WINTER
- \- DISTANT AIRPORTS

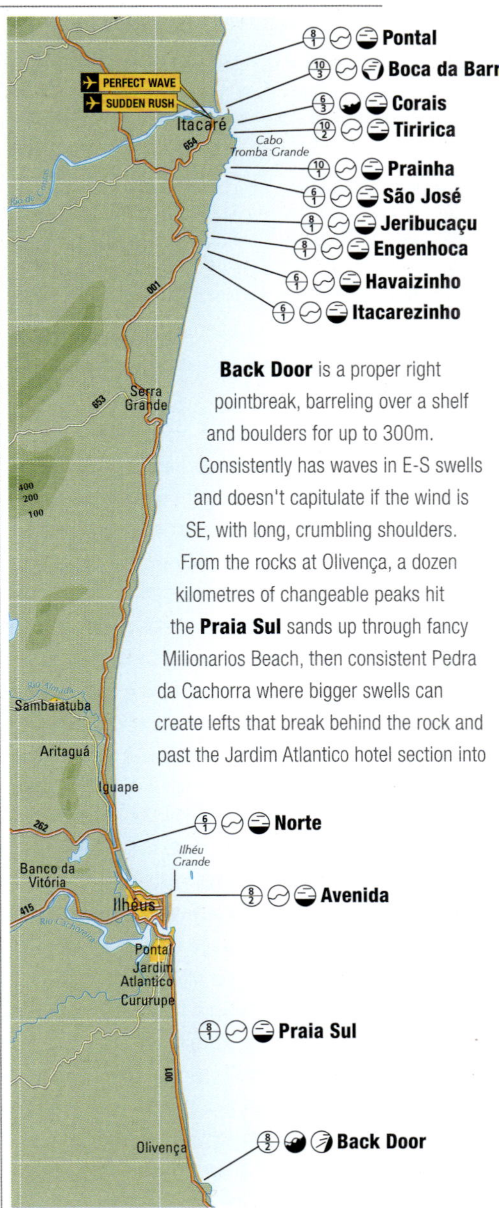


**Back Door** is a proper right pointbreak, barreling over a shelf and boulders for up to 300m. Consistently has waves in E-S swells and doesn't capitulate if the wind is SE, with long, crumbling shoulders. From the rocks at Olivença, a dozen kilometres of changeable peaks hit the **Praia Sul** sands up through fancy Milionarios Beach, then consistent Pedra da Cachorra where bigger swells can create lefts that break behind the rock and past the Jardim Atlantico hotel section into the rockier northern corner at Ilhéus proper. The best peaks get crowded, but there are endless options for those bothered to walk from the access points. **Avenida** Soares Lopes parallels the beach through town and picks up all swells onto average banks with the odd hollow day. The north end will be bigger and quieter on SE swells. Ilheus' most consistent beach is **Norte** stretching for 50km of low tide barrels. Consistent variable grade beachies in any E swell and any W flavour wind. In front of the Eden One pousada is a good spot, but this beach soaks up and spreads any crowd. **Itacarezinho** is a long beach with trenches inside and some coral reefs outside, which creates currents aplenty. The waves can be long rollers, making this a favourite summertime longboard and beginners wave. **Havaizinho** has a set of three inconsistent beaches, which produce some decent lefts on low tide with E swell, amongst the many scattered rocks. It's a 15min walk to **Engenhoca**'s beautiful horseshoe-shaped beach, holding mainly lefts in a NE swell with a paddling channel whatever the swell size. Perfect for beginners and longboarders as the waves are usually fat, particularly above mid tide. The beautiful **Jeribucaçu** rivermouth holds small, crumbly, junky walls or bigger lined-up triangles for those willing to make the steep 20-30min walk! **São José** is a smaller beach, with room for a peak and maybe a right off the rocks at the south end. It's a very long 50min walk in through the rainforest from Ribeira Beach, but it's only 40min to busier **Prainha**. The waves can be steep and punchy, especially the lefts off the rocks at the north end in a NE swell and it likes due S also. **Tiririca** is the main spot in Itacaré, thanks to regular barreling waves unloading on banks at the north, central and southern end of this short beach. Neighbouring beaches Resende, Costa and Ribeira just don't compare in the quality or consistency stakes. Hardcore shortboarders should walk round to **Corais** for tubular and fast peaks over a dead coral reef in moderate E swells at low tide. **Boca da Barra** is a super-long, righthander at the Contas rivermouth. With a SE-S swell and a low incoming tide, streaking across long walls for 600m is possible. There are fat lefts off the peak into the river flow, which is the conveyor belt out to the distant line-up. Only experienced surfers and strong paddlers should take it on and dropping tides can have horrendous rips. Boat access only leaves **Pontal** a quiet, exposed beach that will set-up some nice sucky peaks in a SE-S swell at lower incoming tides.

Winter is rarely flat because of a constant windswell pushed by the E-SE trade winds. Most beachbreaks hover in the 2-6ft range, while the 6-8ft swells necessary for the rivermouth rights are pretty rare. Because most beaches are well-sheltered by headlands, S-SE winds must be really strong to ruin the surf. In winter, storms bring wind, then rain, then glass-off. There can be several cycles during the day, so stay alert. Spring is usually the best time with decent swell activity and calm winds. Tidal range can reach 2.4m, causing low tide beachbreaks to tend to close-out.

Jeribucacu

EASYDROP.COM

## TRAVEL INFORMATION

**Weather** – Bahia coastal weather is hot and humid, without a real dry season and high annual rainfall creating the coastal rainforest (Mata Atlantica). Despite regular rainfall, sunshine is plentiful varying from 12 days a month in July-August to 29 days in Dec-Jan. Oct-Nov are the calmest months and the best period for uncrowded sessions. Water temps vary between 24-30°C (75-86°F), take a shorty or vest for the coldest spells.

**Lodging and Food** – Itacaré has three lodging areas: Tiririca, Caminho da Praia (Beachway) or in town. Easydrop is the main operator for beginners who stay in Pousada Belfort or Pousada Ilha Verde. Try Lawrence's Surf House, Hawaii Aqui or Sao José Eco resort. Meat with beans, rice and salad is ±$5.

**Nature and Culture** – The Contas River is great for SUP & rafting. Canoeing, ecobike, rappel or trekking are easy to do with specialised guides. Capoeira is big! During New Year and Carnival, people dance and party hard.

**Hazards and Hassles** – No malaria, but some dengue fever cases. Keep valuables hidden and don't walk at night in cities like Ilhéus or Bahia. Crowds occur at Tiririca and Corails and the high summer season is super-busy so avoid it.

**Handy Hints** – A longboard would be great for Boca da Barra and a gun unnecessary. Buy a quality shortboard for $300 and longboard for $450 or rent cheaply.

Corais

EASYDROP.COM

| STATISTICS | | J F | M A | M J | J A | S O | N D |
|---|---|---|---|---|---|---|---|
| SWELL | Direction | | | | | | |
| | Size (ft) | 1-2 | 2-3 | 3-4 | 4 | 3 | 1-2 |
| WIND | Direction | | | | | | |
| | Force | F3 | F3 | F3-F4 | F4 | F3-F4 | F3-F4 |
| WATER | Wetsuit | | | | | | |
| | Temp/°C | 28 | 28 | 27 | 25 | 25 | 26 |
| WEATHER | Rainfall/mm | 160 | 270 | 190 | 150 | 110 | 170 |
| | days/mth | 9 | 14 | 11 | 10 | 6 | 9 |
| | Min temp/°C | 22 | 21 | 19 | 19 | 21 | 21 |
| | Max temp/°C | 30 | 29 | 28 | 26 | 28 | 29 |

# Pernambuco BRAZIL

Nordeste is the Brazil of clichés… colourful, vibrant and always exciting. The 70km coastal strip that makes up the seaboard of Pernambuco State is a low lying, fertile plain with a great mix of beaches and reefs. Most of the reefs lie within 200m of the shore and offer powerful waves on offshore days, whilst the beaches are better surfed on the more common onshore days. However there has been a ban on surfing in Recife since shark attacks on surfers sky-rocketed through the '90s.

- + EASY, UNCROWDED BEACHES
- + RARELY FLAT
- + PARADISE BEACHES
- + GREAT ATMOSPHERE

- – SMALL ONSHORE SURF
- – SHARK ATTACK HOTSPOT
- – RECIFE SURF BAN
- – PETTY CRIME IN RECIFE

## TRAVEL INFORMATION

**Weather** – Pernambuco's rainy season lasts from May to Aug, when afternoons see heavy thunderstorms. Winter temps hardly ever drop below 20°C (68°F), but the onshore E-SE trade winds prevent the air from getting too hot. Water never drops below 25°C (77°F) so boardshorts and a rash vest year-round.

**Lodging and Food** – Porto da Galinhas: Pousadas - Pedras or Farol do Porto. Maracaipe: Pousadas Maracaipe, dos Coqueiros and Brisas are close to the beach. Meals from $10; try eating peixadas and macaxeira. The local drink is caipiriñha.

**Nature and Culture** – The coastline is a beautiful blend of low sand dunes and palm trees. The waters are murky in the winter. Good diving off Santo Aleixo Island. Olinda is the former capital of Brazil.

**Hazards and Hassles** – No shark attacks north of Boca de Suape for a while now, mainly because of the surfing ban. Big beaches like Maracaipe only get crowded at weekends, but if one of the good reefs turns on it will be busy whatever time. In Recife and Boa Viagem stay alert for pickpockets and muggers.

**Handy Hints** – Porto da Galinhas: Surf schools - Escola de Surf Marroquim & Atahalley. Surf shops - Katu, Republica de Surf, MySurf.

LAURENT MASUREL

Maracaipe

LAURENT MASUREL

Recife

To the north of Barra da Sirinhaem you will find outside reefs such as the hard to get to mysto left **Impolsivel**, off Ilha Santo Aleixo. **Ponta de Serrambi** is a quality spot thanks to shallow reefs providing hollow, spitting barrels, but only on the rare days when the wind is offshore or glassy. There is a left that wraps around the pocked, pointy reef into a channel and a right that holds some good size. Pushing tide is safer. Localism has increased here in recent years due to an increase in the amount of surfers coming down from Recife since the surfing ban, plus it is surrounded by luxury apartments. The most consistent beach in this zone is **Maracaipe**, which hosted the 2000 World Surfing Games. Although the middle of the beach is usually the best, there are dozens of other sandbanks to choose from. Quality is variable as the wave tends to roll through from fatter outside banks, reforming several times on its journey to the hollower, close-out shorebreak that keeps the bodyboarders happy. High tide tends to be better and it's always busy, especially on weekends. It's a 10min paddle from **Galinhas** harbour to a shallow, outside reef that can have a punchy righthander on glassy mornings plus there's an occasional left. Some hollow beachbreaks can be found in town at Borete, which are usually fairly empty. South of the 2.5km long jetty at Porto de Suape, **Cupe** has a consistent, long stretch of peaks with enough shape and power to attract a regular local crew. Can be hollow on the right tide and offer a mix of walls and barrels. The city of Recife has banned surfing along a 60km stretch of coast since 1998, due to a large surge in shark attacks from 1992-2013 which include 63 attacks with 25 fatalities. The construction of a huge harbour in Boca de Suape, along with irresponsible coastal development and some serious over-fishing are blamed for the spate of attacks on surfers and swimmers. Although the **Gaibu** Peninsula is located inside the prohibited zone, the authorities have allowed the locals access to the surf and there have been no attacks so far. The beach at Enseadas has a line of reef that can make for some thick-lipped peeling pipes among the close-outs and everyday onshore junk. Gets ultra-jammed on weekends as it's the only show in town, unless you are flaunting the ban at the other city spots like Pedra Preta, the reliable SE-facing beachbreaks of Paiva, the quality, hollow reefs of Quebra Mar, Abreus and Acaiaca up in the resort area of Boa Viagem, or Praia del Chifre and Olinda, one of the most picturesque colonial towns in the country. All these beaches have witnessed multiple shark attacks, so best to obey the warning signs posted everywhere that say: *Bathers in this area are at greater than average risk of shark attack.* Locals still surf and don't believe the situation is as dangerous as the government suggest and believe the ban should be lifted.

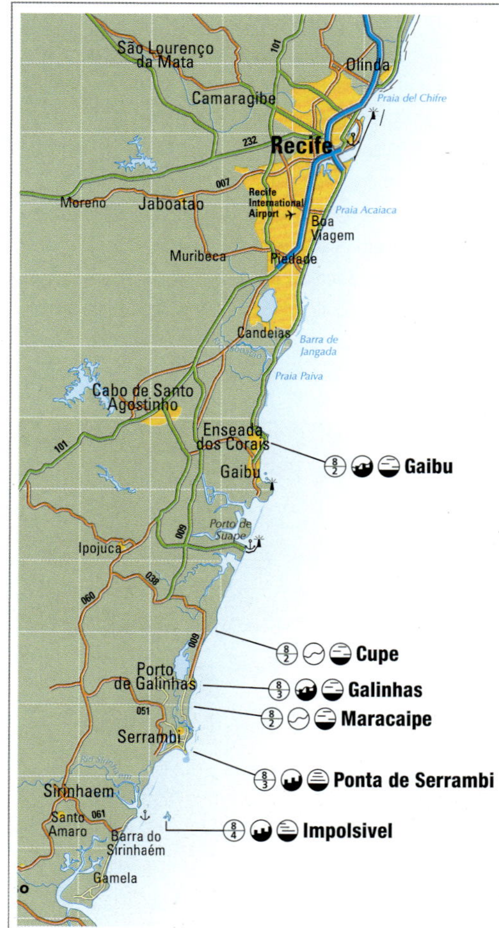


During the winter rainy season it's rarely flat due to a constant windswell created by the E-SE trade winds. Most waves are in the 2-5ft range and have a lack of shape and power on the beaches, but remain rideable with onshore wind. The reefs will only produce quality, clean surf when the wind is in the W quadrant (never!) or very light (<4% of the time). Groundswells are rare and come from lows to the S, most frequently from May to Oct. These swells can reach 8ft, but suffer diminishing size from travelling such a long distance. The E-SE wind is constant, blowing more E in Jan before veering more SE through the middle of the year. With a tidal variation of up to 2.6m, shallow reefbreaks can be unsurfable at low tide or too full at high.

| STATISTICS | | J F | M A | M J | J A | S O | N D |
|---|---|---|---|---|---|---|---|
| SWELL | Direction | | | | | | |
| | Size (ft) | 0-1 | 1-2 | 2-3 | 2-3 | 2 | 1 |
| WIND | Direction | | | | | | |
| | Force | F4 | F4 | F4 | F4 | F4 | F4 |
| WATER | Wetsuit | | | | | | |
| | Temp/°C | 28 | 29 | 27 | 26 | 26 | 27 |
| WEATHER | Rainfall/mm | 70 | 190 | 270 | 203 | 45 | 26 |
| | days/mth | 11 | 15 | 22 | 20 | 10 | 6 |
| | Min temp/°C | 25 | 24 | 23 | 22 | 23 | 24 |
| | Max temp/°C | 30 | 29 | 28 | 27 | 28 | 29 |

# West Ceara BRAZIL

A significant supply of North Atlantic winter swells provides a separate surf season on this north-facing coast of Brazil.

+ TWO SOURCES OF SWELL
+ QUALITY HOLLOW WAVES
+ PUNCHY BEACHIES & RIGHT POINTS
+ EASY ACCESS & CLOSE FACILITIES

– BLOWN-OUT IN SUMMER
– LACK OF SIZE
– HEAT, CROWDS & POLLUTION
– BIG TIDAL VARIATION

The uniform, meandering beaches of the Ceara coast are rarely interrupted by the odd narrow rivermouth and backed by scrubby sand dunes and coconut palms. The surf scene is centred around Natal, Fortaleza and Paracuru, a proper surf town with four main righthand pointbreaks that fire from November to February.

If not blown-out, **Praia do Futuro** with 5kms of exposed beachbreaks has fewer crowds and cleaner water than Fortaleza, and average peaks with plenty of shoulder for turns when NE-E windswells blow in. **Titanzinho** is Fortaleza's most consistent reefbreak. There are rights running down the reef in E-SE and wedgy lefts breaking back towards the pocket beach and the long jetty. Both spots suffer from aggro localism. Along the bustling **Volta da Jurema** there are many beachbreaks like Praia do Nautico, Jacqueline, Apito, Iracema, Meireles and Diarios, all favouring lower tides. Fun waves for all abilities and it's rare to see it empty. Jump from the old steel pier to ride **Ponte Metalica**'s quality reefbreak peaks. A slab of limestone reef holds the sand and the sometimes sucky peaks are best with N swell and low tides. Between the marina and a long jetty, **Leste Oeste**'s urban beachbreak can be weak and junky or steep and dumpy, depending on its mood. **Barra do Ceara**'s polluted peaks break right beside the rivermouth and rarely have the quality to outweigh the risk. **Icarai** is Ceara's most consistent beachbreak, picking up any size swell from both the N or the E, occasionally distributing some short sucky barrels before the inevitable close-out. It's a regular WQS contest site and attracts intense crowds. There is a major working port in **Pecém**, where the surf is notoriously inconsistent, even in a decent swell, leaving the outside lefts to the windsurfers. **Tabinha** is a real swell magnet beachbreak, best on mid-tide and spreads out the crowds of Paracuru surfers who go there when it's on. The right off the rocks known as Pesqueira can get good on bigger NE-E swells and a pushing tide, resulting in long ripable walls. **Outside**'s coral reef lefts near Petrobras Pier are shallow and shape up best with a N swell. Needs S winds as E will be cross-shore, inviting the kiters to move up here from Quebramar. Potentially the longest right point on a northerly swell, **Boca Do Poço** walls up along the sand-covered reef on a pushing tide. Right in town, **Ronco do Mar**'s hard-breaking rights are dangerous when low tide exposes the rocky reef, but it's consistent from mid tide up. Always crowded on the small take-off zone as this is the best break in the area and hosts high-level pro contests. Suited to longboarders, **Curral**, works on any tide and has long, fun walls near the fish trap pilings. Last option for a right point is **Pedra do Meio**, only a few kms west, identified by big boulder rocks next to the take-off and it's somewhat sheltered position from E winds. Praia do **Havaizinho** is an alternative to the crowded points and can fire on mid to high tides, offering nice peaks in the rocky corner. Long stretch of empty beachbreak leading up to Barra do Rio Curu.

The North Atlantic winter groundswells arrive from October to March, but decay due to the distance travelled means it's safer to focus on the Nov-Feb heart of the season. North-facing breaks are better exposed and size varies from 2-8ft, producing 4-6ft quality lines on the right pointbreaks, with pulses usually lasting 2-3 days. Then, the E-SE trades start kicking in and produce mushy 2-5ft windswell with predominantly onshore conditions, favouring the steep NE-facing beachbreaks. July-August has the strongest wind, often preferred by the kite/windsurfing community. Avoid transitional months like March-April or September. Funnily enough, the wind tends to back off around noon and be stronger morning and evenings. Tidal range increases heading west, reaching up to 3.2m in Paracuru.

## TRAVEL INFORMATION

**Weather** – Ceara has a warm and relatively wet climate with the main rainfall in March-April. Some years, rainfall is low causing drought and desertification in most semi-arid areas. The Mata Atlantica (forest) of Ceara is shattered into relatively small 'islands' deep inland. During the surf season, the sun is fierce so a rashie is essential for protection.

**Lodging and Food** – Surf and high tourist season coincide. In Fortaleza, lots of hotels along Futuro Beach (Gran Marero, Crocobeach fr$72) or Carmel Cumbuco Resort. In Icaraí, Pousada Baiano, or Planalto Hotel (fr$15). In Paracuru, try Pousada Villa Verde or Club Tropical hotel. Expect $7 for a meal.

**Nature and Culture** – Paracuru 'Cidade alegre' is a pleasant resort for wealthy Cearense & Brazilians. Carnival gets pretty big there, including Corridas de Buggy and sand surfing. Hit Jericoacoara if kite/windsurfing and Quixad for hang-gliding.

**Hazards and Hassles** – Ceara is on the Equator so bring high SPF sunblock. Street crime is much lower than other major urban parts of Brazil. Crowds and pollution can be appalling around Fortaleza, which apparently has the wildest Monday nights in the world.

**Handy Hints** – Boards in Brazil are super-cheap, but light: FeC, Super Série, World Boards (shortboard for $250-300). In Fortaleza, try the Surf Beat, Flora or Pranchas Xboards shops. Bodyboarding is big and longboarding's popularity is increasing. Surf schools include Chandler Surf and Futuro.

Volta da Jurema

FRANCIS CHAGOS

| STATISTICS | | J F | M A | M J | J A | S O | N D |
|---|---|---|---|---|---|---|---|
| SWELL | Direction | | | | | | |
| | Size (ft) | 3-4 | 2-3 | 2 | 2-3 | 1-2 | 2-3 |
| WIND | Direction | | | | | | |
| | Force | F3-F4 | F3-F4 | F4 | F4-F5 | F4 | F4 |
| WATER | Wetsuit | | | | | | |
| | Temp/°C | 27 | 27 | 27 | 26 | 26 | 26 |
| WEATHER | Rainfall/mm | 160 | 330 | 160 | 30 | 10 | 25 |
| | days/mth | 7 | 12 | 5 | 1 | 1 | 1 |
| | Min temp/°C | 25 | 23 | 23 | 22 | 24 | 25 |
| | Max temp/°C | 31 | 30 | 30 | 30 | 31 | 31 |

# Fernando do Noronha BRAZIL

Surprisingly, Fernando de Noronha's main source of swell is not from the S like most of Brazil, but from the North Atlantic lows that provide Europe with its surf. These swells have to march thousands of miles south, helped along by favourable winds and ocean currents. The island has had a colourful recent history, having been used as a battlefield, jail, air base and weather station, but has now become a tourist heaven for divers and surfers. It is never under 2ft during Dec-Feb, and swells last for 5-6 days. Like Hawaii, the island is the summit of a huge underwater volcano, rising 4.3km from the ocean floor. The surrounding deep water and lack of continental shelf allows the swells to hit with unimpeded speed and power, jacking up wave heights in the process. The SE-facing side of the island is too steep and mountainous for any surf, whereas the NW oriented coastline has perfect topography and offshore winds. The steeply sloping beaches make for some fast barrels, which sometimes tend toward the straighthander category, but are perfectly suited to bodyboarders and tube junkies.

- **+ POWERFUL TUBES**
- **+ REEF AND BEACHBREAKS**
- **+ CONSISTENTLY OFFSHORE**
- **+ UNTOUCHED, WILD ENVIRONMENT**

- **– SHORT SURF SEASON**
- **– DIFFICULT ACCESS**
- **– ISOLATED ISLAND LOCATION**
- **– VERY EXPENSIVE LIVING COSTS**

LAURENT MASUREL

Cachorro

## TRAVEL INFORMATION

**Weather** – Being located just south of the Equator, Fernando do Noronha enjoys a hot and humid climate split between a dry and wet season. SE trades bring the heaviest rain, (nearly every day), from Feb to July and even into Aug. Temps are very stable, with the air and water being around 26°-27°C, (80-82°F). In the dry season from August to Jan everything turns from verdant green to very brown and burnt. For the best surf and weather come earlier in the season (Nov).

**Lodging and Food** – There are over 70 pousadas (guesthouses) and most have full-board prices from $80/n/dbl to $590/n/dbl for Pousada Triboju. Try Dolphin Hotel, Colina or Aleffawi pousadas at Boldró or Topázio and Alto Mar at Meio. Food and drink wise you have a choice of either expensive imported items, (like beer), and cheap repetitive seafood served in the launchonetes.

**Nature and Culture** – An appreciation of nature and hiking will greatly enhance your enjoyment of the island. Aquatic life is very rich with fish, shark, dolphins, (swimming with them is not allowed, nor is spear fishing) and turtles as well as birds and big lizards. There is no nightlife on the island or urban entertainment (except during the competition), if there's no surf then occupy yourself by hiking, snorkelling, fishing or diving.

**Hazards and Hassles** – There are plenty of sharks, stingrays and moray eels around but they don't pose much threat (a diver lost his hand to a small tiger shark in 2015). In the wet season there are lots of mosquitoes and bugs. Be careful of sunburn and reef cuts.

**Handy Hints** – 1hr flights from Recife or Natal. The island is a national park with a Nature Tax that favours shorter visits ($15/d, $88/7d, $235/14d). In addition, there is a Ecological Tax or entrance ticket to the park that costs 65R$ ($20) for Brazilians and 130R$ ($40) for foreigners and is valid for ten days. There are few real locals, but Brazilians from the mainland stay here for weeks on end. Bring absolutely everything you need with you. Boards are available to rent, but like most goods on the island, it's expensive (100R$/$31/d). There's an Escola de Surf in Meio.

HENRIQUE PINGUIM

LAURENT MASUREL

Praia do Meio

When a moderate to big NW swell slams into the northern-most point of Noronha, the classic righthander at **Baia da Rata** offers powerful righthand walls for experts with a boat. Paddling the 2kms or island hopping is not the best idea as there are many sharks swimming the channels. If the swell is big enough and the tide low enough, then you may get to surf fickle **Abras**, the best left reef on the island. It starts off as an open barrel before turning into a carvable wall that in turn becomes a fast hollow, close-out section on the gnarled reef shelf. Low tide only adds to the inconsistency and SW winds are even rarer, but S-SE will blow into the barrel. Nasty rocks pop up everywhere, making entry and exit a real pain. On the other side of Isla **São José** from Abras, a groomed righthander sometimes breaks into the bay that is usually full of moored up boats awaiting passengers for island and dive tours. Needs W in the swell and lower tides as the island gets cut off by high water. Intermediates should handle the punchy walls. Just down from the harbour at **Boboca**, a hollow, chunky left will rip across the reef in NW swell and is perfectly offshore in the SE winds. Rights will also appear along the uneven reef line with sand filling in the holes. Boboca handles some size and most tides, attracting the locals to the mid tide sessions on the good days. Requires experience when it gets big. **Cachorro** is a pocket beach located below the famous vista from the Fort Remedios. Scattered rocks at each end will either hold some swift, sucky rights off the headland or longer left walls skirting around the mini-point from Praia Meio. Gets really dumpy as it closes out on the sparse sand in the middle of the beach. Good place to escape the crowds and ride some slightly easier waves, despite it being the closest beach to Vila dos Remedios where most of the accommodation is centred. **Praia do Meio** holds various decent peaks that usually work best on mid tides. More good waves are to be found at Praia do Italcabe, in **Conceição**, which is a fast beachbreak and is the centre of the island's beach bar scene. Closes-out quite a bit at the extremes of tide, but can have a right off the eastern corner or some lefts beneath the towering monolith of the Pico do Morro. Mellow crowds, particularly in the mornings and beginners will have plenty of safe, sandy whitewash to catch. **Boldró** is a hazardous reef with some very good lefts and rights that barrel when it's small, but it gets a little crazy when the swell is over 6ft. Lower tides are needed to pull the waves off the rock shelf and what flavour of N swell direction will decide which side fires. Fast and wedgy at the peak, coupled with sharp rocks and some protective locals make this an experienced surfers spot. The northeastern end of the main Cacimba beach surf spot is called **Bode** and it catches some nice peaks in smaller broken-up swells at mid tides. If the swell arrives from the NE then a righthand tunnel will grind off the slab of reef for a longer, pedal to the metal ride. Worth checking to avoid the pack at ✪**Cacimba do Padre**. Not an easy place for beginners unless it is small.

Low pressures sitting off the North American east coast generate plenty of 2-12ft NW-N swells between Nov and March. As these systems move towards the Azores, the swell arrives from a more NE direction, helped by the prevailing NE trades and Canaries Current, but slightly hindered by the Cape Verde islands shadow. Fernando de Noronha is also exposed to tropical depressions as they head from Africa to the Americas and will send an off-season swell if they develop into hurricanes quickly enough. South swells hit between April-Oct, but due to onshore winds and steeply rising beaches, they don't produce good quality waves, however, it will always be 1-2ft at this time. Wind patterns are extremely stable, SE is the predominant direction varying from 41% in April to 70% in Sept, when it's not blowing SE it will almost certainly be due E. In fact for 94% of the time it blows from one of these two directions.

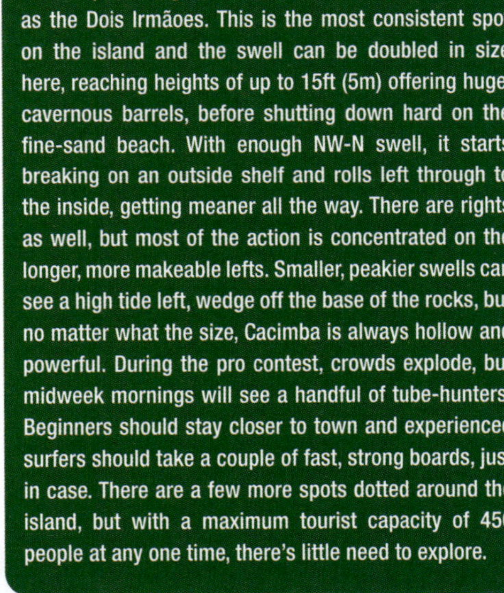

**Cacimba do Padre**

**LAT. -3.848619° LONG. -32.438816°**

Looking down from the mirantes (viewpoints), Cacimba do Padre appears as a picturesque tropical beach with perfect clean waves in crystal clear water, against the backdrop of the gnarled volcanic rock brothers known as the Dois Irmãoes. This is the most consistent spot on the island and the swell can be doubled in size here, reaching heights of up to 15ft (5m) offering huge, cavernous barrels, before shutting down hard on the fine-sand beach. With enough NW-N swell, it starts breaking on an outside shelf and rolls left through to the inside, getting meaner all the way. There are rights as well, but most of the action is concentrated on the longer, more makeable lefts. Smaller, peakier swells can see a high tide left, wedge off the base of the rocks, but no matter what the size, Cacimba is always hollow and powerful. During the pro contest, crowds explode, but midweek mornings will see a handful of tube-hunters. Beginners should stay closer to town and experienced surfers should take a couple of fast, strong boards, just in case. There are a few more spots dotted around the island, but with a maximum tourist capacity of 450 people at any one time, there's little need to explore.

This means perfect offshore conditions on the NW-facing surf coastline. There are some slight variations at the beginning of the wet season, (Feb-April), when there may be NE and S winds. The semi-diurnal tidal range maximum is 2.36m and affects the waves a lot, with low tide required for some reefs, while the beachbreaks are usually happiest at mid.

DAMIEN POULLENOT

Bode

| STATISTICS | | J F | M A | M J | J A | S O | N D |
|---|---|---|---|---|---|---|---|
| SWELL | Direction | | | | | | |
| | Size (ft) | 4-5 | 3-4 | 1 | 1 | 1-2 | 4 |
| WIND | Direction | | | | | | |
| | Force | F4 | F3 | F4 | F4 | F4 | F4 |
| WATER | Wetsuit | | | | | | |
| | Temp/°C | 27 | 28 | 27 | 26 | 26 | 27 |
| WEATHER | Rainfall/mm | 70 | 190 | 270 | 203 | 45 | 26 |
| | days/mth | 11 | 15 | 22 | 20 | 10 | 6 |
| | Min temp/°C | 25 | 24 | 23 | 22 | 23 | 24 |
| | Max temp/°C | 30 | 29 | 28 | 27 | 28 | 29 |

# Europe

atlantic surf lodge
EAT/SLEEP/SURF
ACCOMMODATION FOR SURFERS AND FRIENDS
surf and yoga lessons available
vieux boucau • france / +33 6 08 92 18 29 / uli@atlantic-surflodge.com / www.atlantic-surflodge.com

Boardingmania
Surf School & Camp
tripadvisor
Seignosse - South West France

4, Place De La Vigie, 40510, Seignosse, France
Email info@boardingmania.com
or visit www.boardingmania.com

Sushi Hossegor
www.cjsushis.fr

LAGOONDY
SURF CAMP ★ BIARRITZ ★ BIDART ★ FRANCE
ECOLE DE SURF - LOCATION
LAGOONDY
BIARRITZ • BIDART • FRANCE
SURF SCHOOL ★ SURF TRIP ★ SURF RENTAL
★ +33(0)6 09 74 25 19 ★
www.lagoondy.com
lagoondy.surfcamp@wanadoo.fr

LIFE S A BEACH... SINCE 2004!
SURF CAMPS, LESSONS, RENTALS, YOGA
UNCROWDED SURF & BEACHFRONT LOCATIONS
IN PORTO & ESMORIZ, PORTUGAL
SURF CAMP
SURFIVOR
www.surfivorcamp.com

PORTUGAL
SURF RENTALS
WHY FLY WITH THEM,
WHEN YOU CAN RENT THEM!?
www.portugalsurfrentals.com

surf
SURF
CHAMPION
SURF GUIDE
SINCE 1985
TOURS
with...
www.championsurfguide.com

# Europe

## Euro Surfari?

Get the super-detailed, 400 page Europe Guide or regional eBooks at www.stormriderguides.com

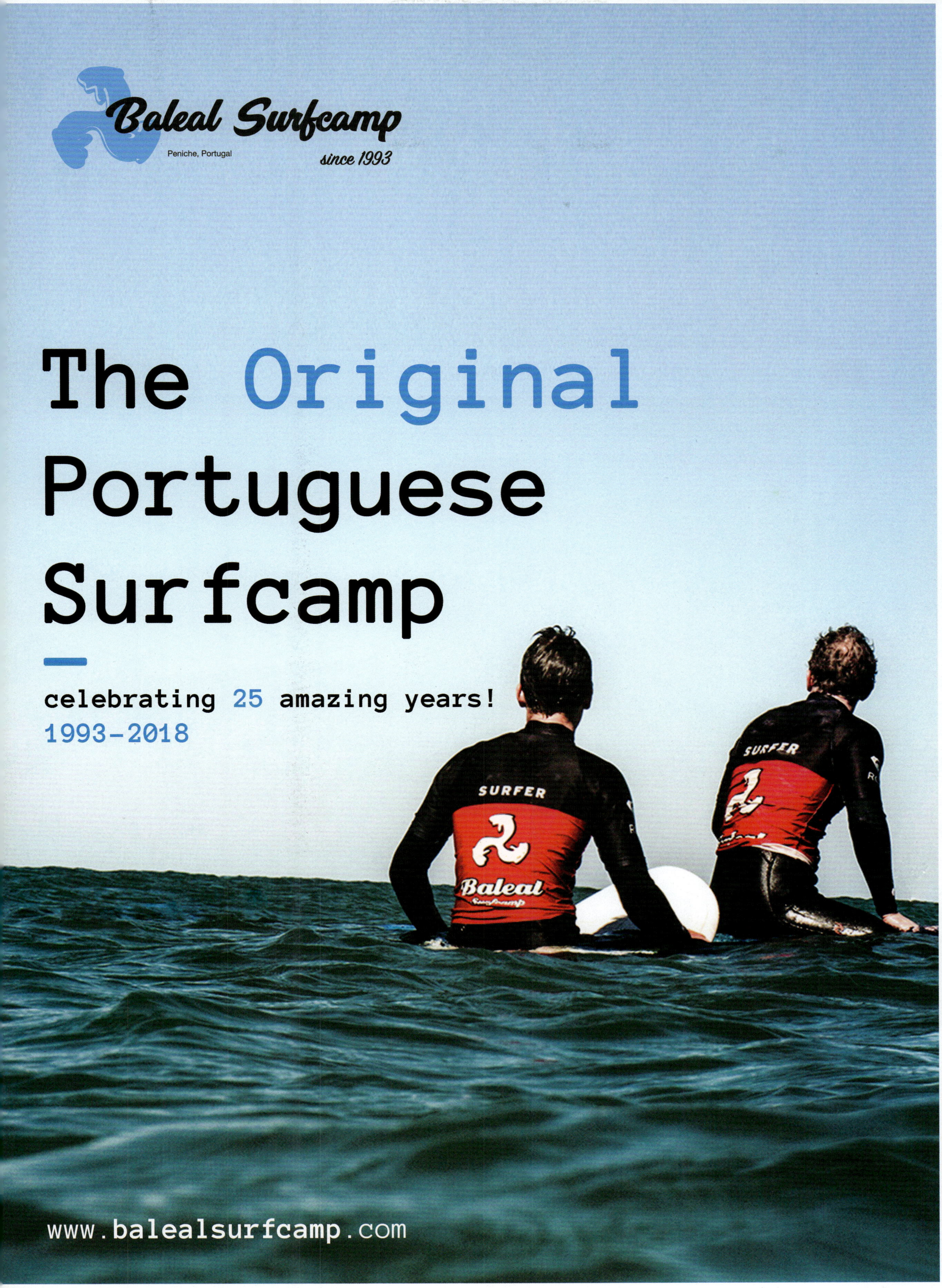

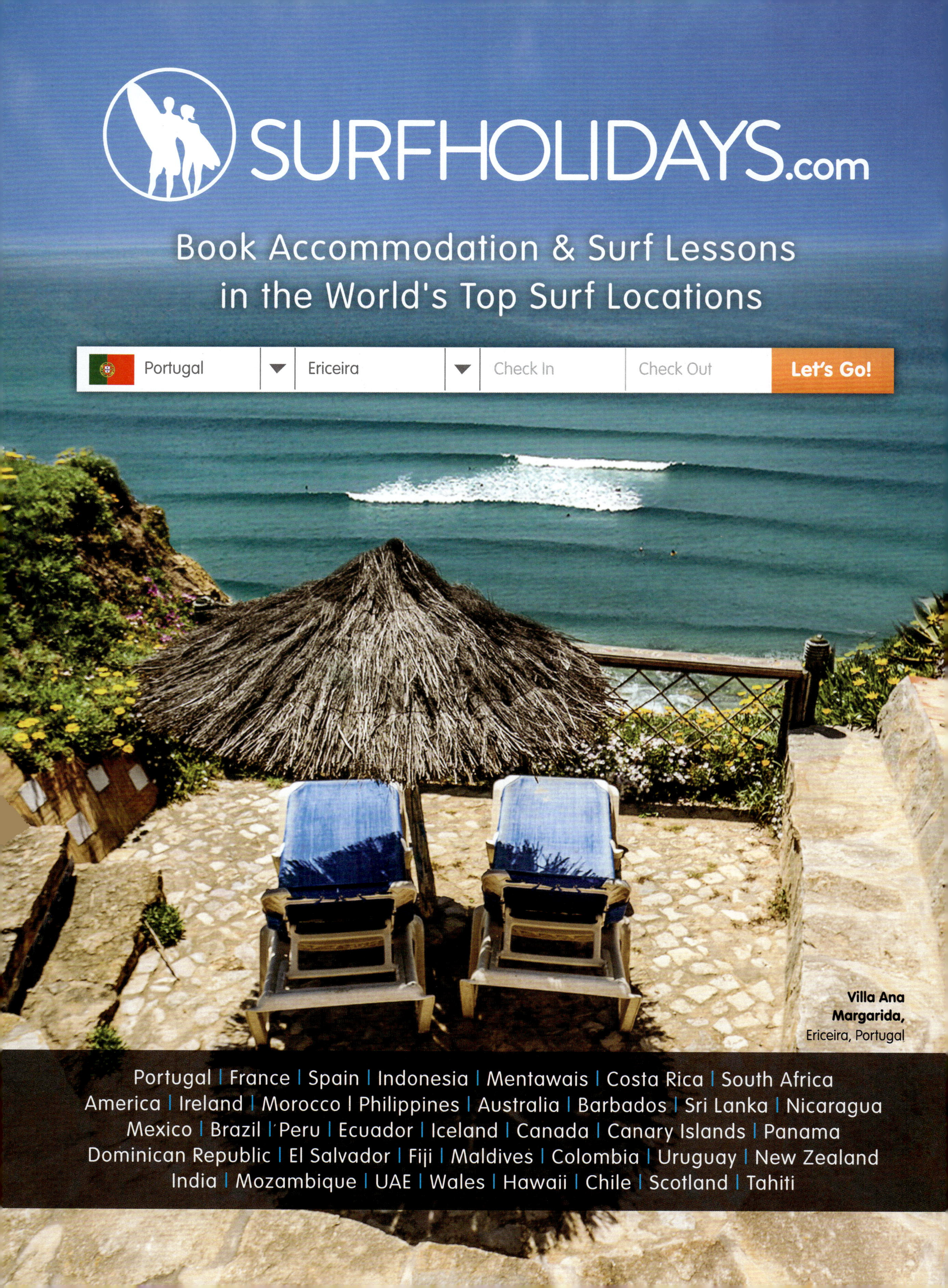
SURFHOLIDAYS.com
Book Accommodation & Surf Lessons
in the World's Top Surf Locations
Portugal
Ericeira
Check In
Check Out
Let's Go!
Villa Ana Margarida, Ericeira, Portugal
Portugal | France | Spain | Indonesia | Mentawais | Costa Rica | South Africa
America | Ireland | Morocco | Philippines | Australia | Barbados | Sri Lanka | Nicaragua
Mexico | Brazil | Peru | Ecuador | Iceland | Canada | Canary Islands | Panama
Dominican Republic | El Salvador | Fiji | Maldives | Colombia | Uruguay | New Zealand
India | Mozambique | UAE | Wales | Hawaii | Chile | Scotland | Tahiti

# Europe / Africa

# Africa / Indian Ocean

We make surf travel easy for you...
...and we guarantee the best price.
the perfect wave
surf experience
www.perfectwavetravel.com

# Indian Ocean

NOMAD SURFERS
Book Your Next Surf Trip
ONLY ONE CLICK AWAY AT NOMADSURFERS.COM
NOMAD TROPICAL
RESORT
WEST SUMBAWA
WEST SUMBAWA SURF RESORT
SURF CAMPS TO IMPROVE YOUR SKILLS
SURF CAMPS FOR CHILDREN
PERFECT FOR YOUR PARTNER OR FAMILY

# Pacific / Americas

Est. 1984

LIVE TO SURF

# Americas

Punta Conejo Resort was created with the vision of providing a unique and tranquil year round ocean front resort experience in Salina Cruz, Mexico. It is the only ocean front resort of its kind in the region that offers "all inclusive" accommodations, including a full menu & bar, Wi-Fi, A/C and pool. The authentic feel of the property is enhanced by embracing local artisans, culture, and the surrounding natural environment.
PUNTA CONEJO
RESORT
MEXICO
Steps away from one of the most ripable right points in all of Mexico allowing you to strike when conditions are best, assuring you get pristine, uncrowded point surf. This region is literally stacked with quality beach breaks and some of the best sand-bottom points in the world, offering fun surf for every level of surfer. The water is always warm and the cerveza is always cold.
puntaconejoresort.com
tel: 979-639-7873
puntaconejoresort@gmail.com
Ryan Chaci Craig
Bryce Lowe White

LTL
LIVETHELIFE.TV
SURF RENTALS
& REAL ESTATE
www.livethelife.tv
nicaragua / costa rica / france / portugal / spain / bali
morocco / south-africa / réunion / mauritius / maldives
mentawai / australia / new zealand / fiji / hawaii / california

swell consulting
Wanna make your Surf Lodge grow?
www.swell-consulting.com

# Americas

CHICAMA
BOUTIQUE HOTEL & SPA

Chicama Boutique Hotel offers surfers from around the globe the opportunity to surf the longest left point break on Earth. Our 20 room property has been carefully designed to provide the best comfort for surfers. Tow-Back Service, Saunas, Gym, ocean view hot-taps and an exquisite restaurant available for you year round.

ticket to ride
EXPAND YOUR HORIZONS
SURF TOURS, HOUSES AND COURSES IN SOME OF THE
WORLD'S MOST ADVENTUROUS SURFING DESTINATIONS.
TICKETTORIDEGROUP.COM
Life's Good
EST 2005

## S



## T



## U



## V



## W



## X



## Y



## Z

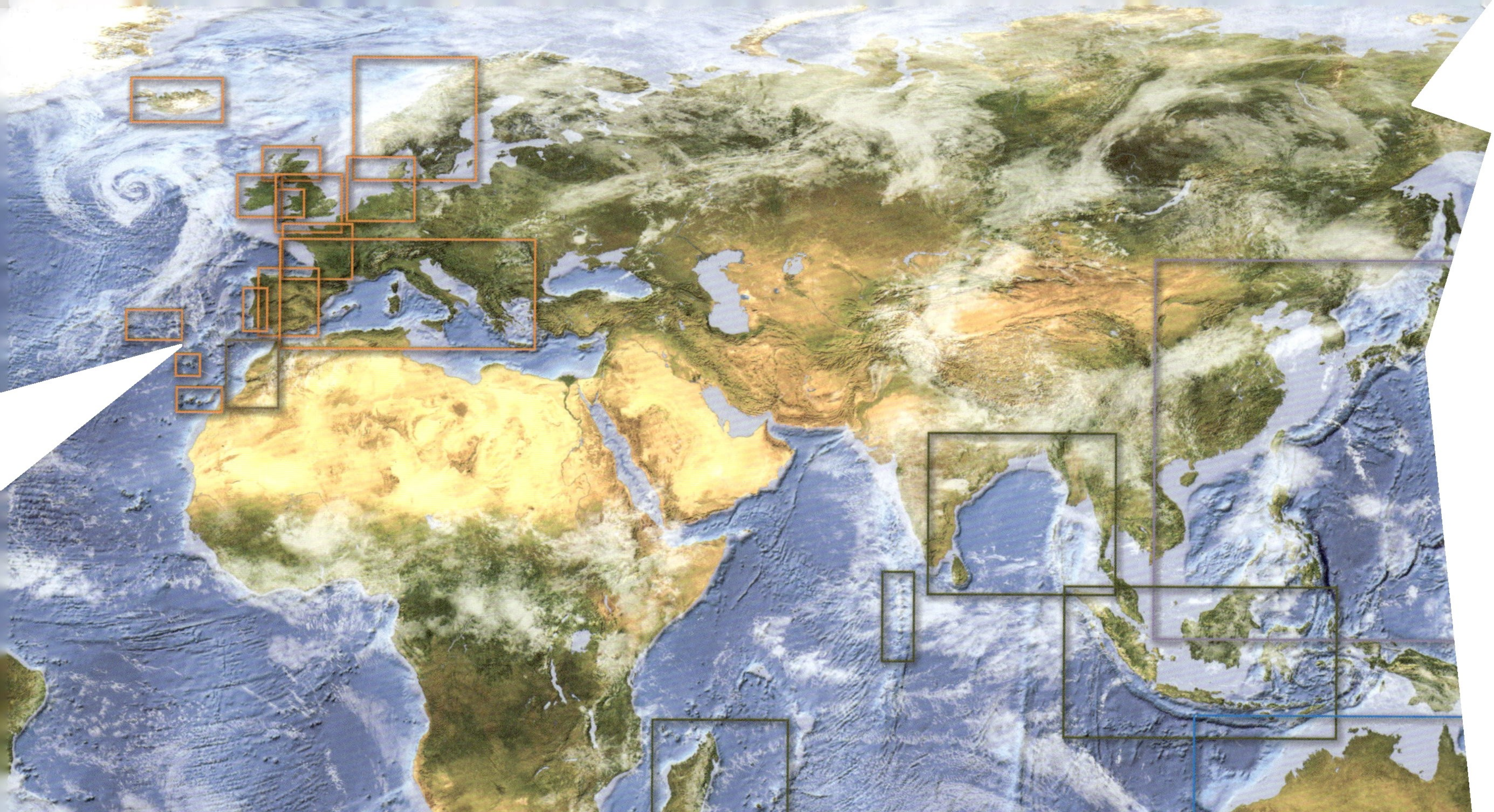

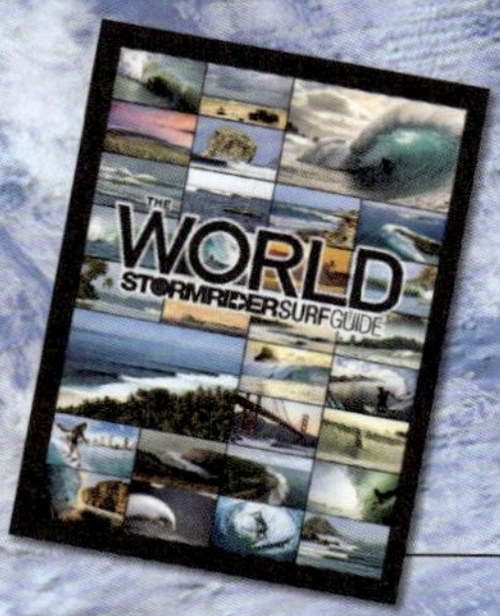

# BIBLIOGRAPHY

## TRAVEL PRODUCTS

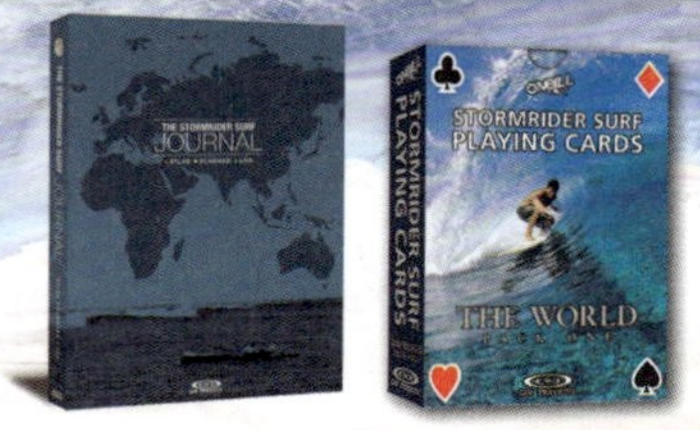

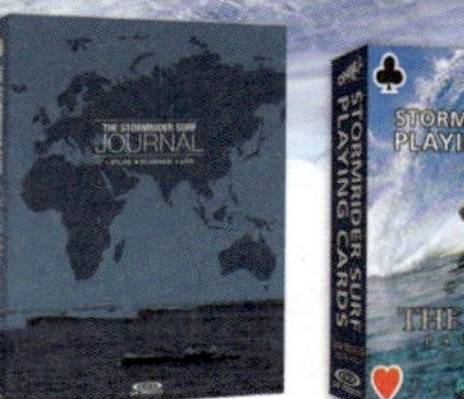

## STORMRIDER EBOOKS

Covers with folded corners are available as Stormrider eBooks.

Download on iBooks

amazonkindle

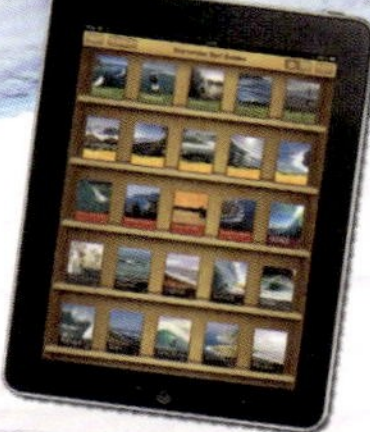

## AFRICA

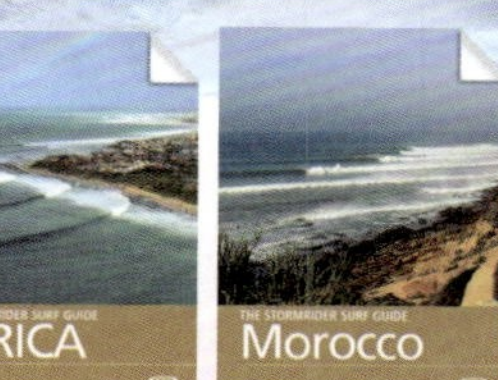

## AUSTRALIA

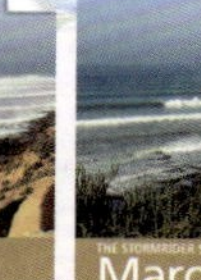

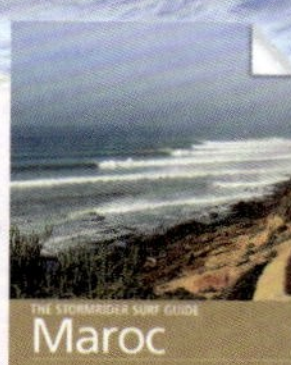

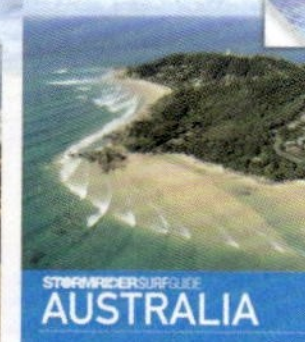

## EUROPE

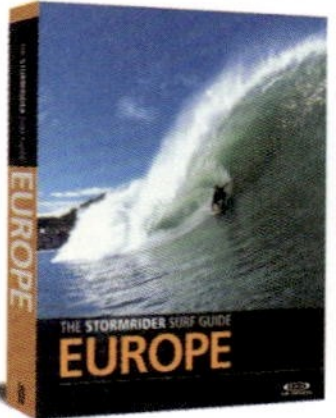

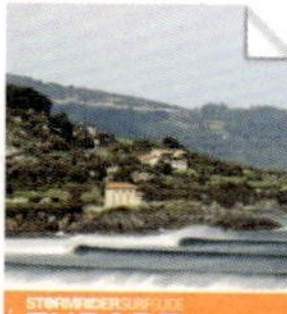

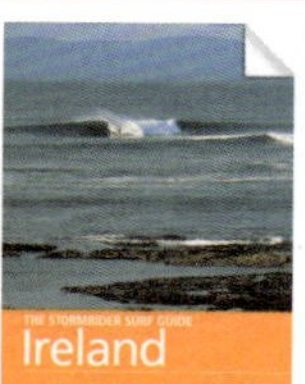

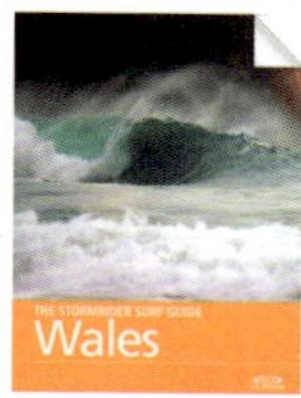

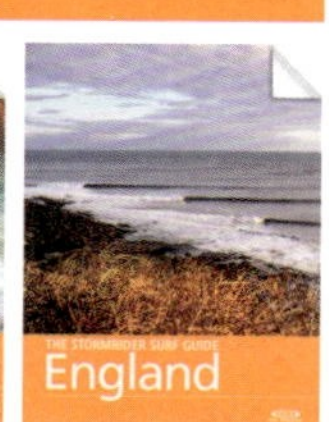

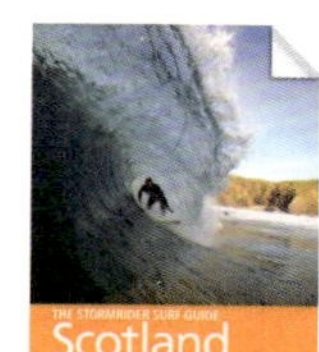

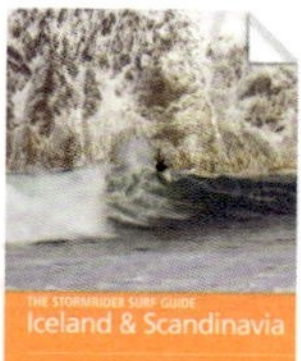

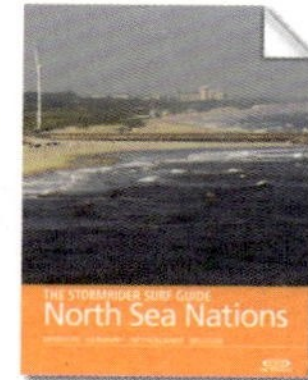

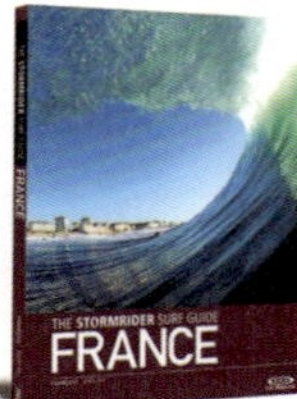

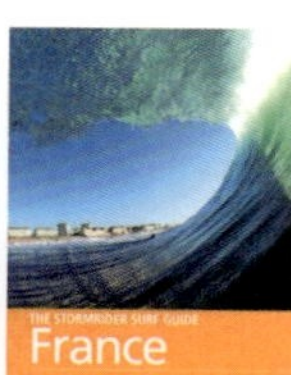

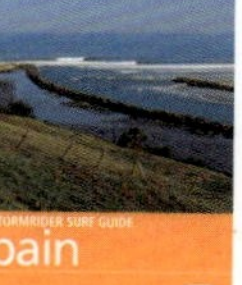

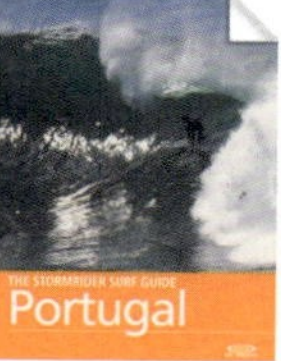

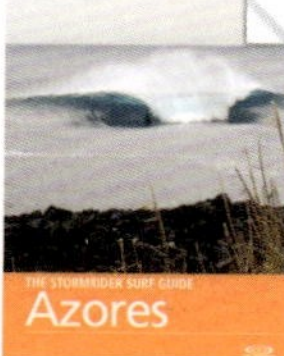

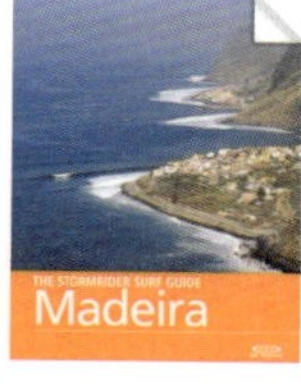

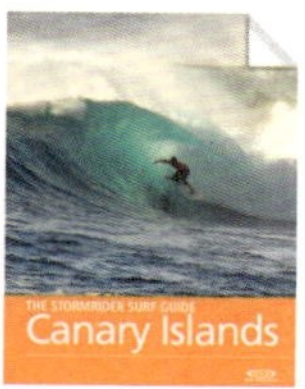

## INDIAN OCEAN

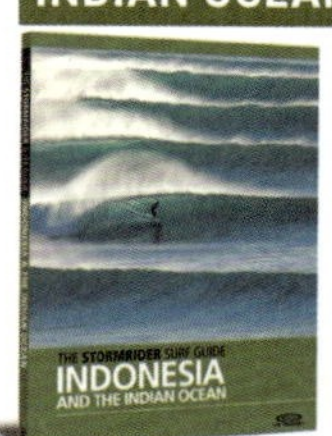

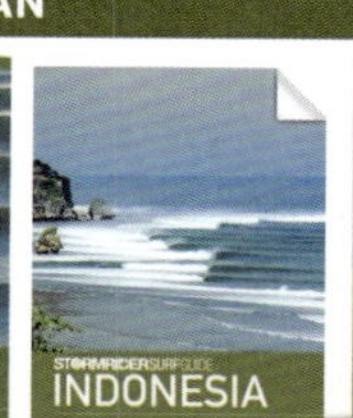

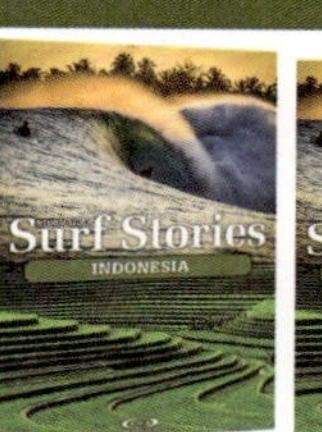

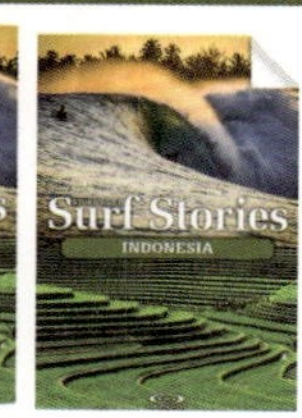

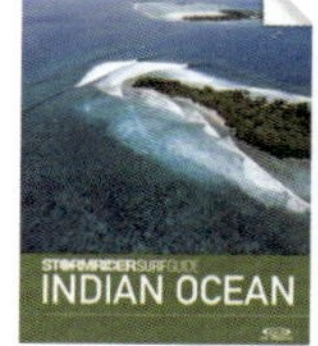

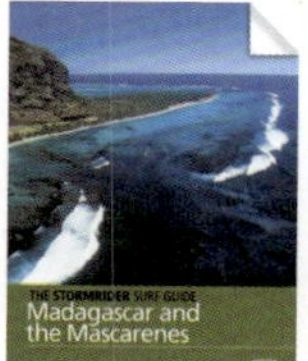

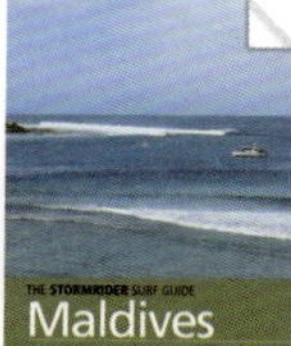

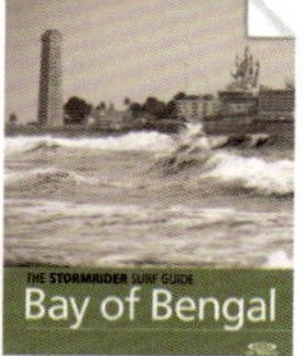

## PACIFIC OCEAN

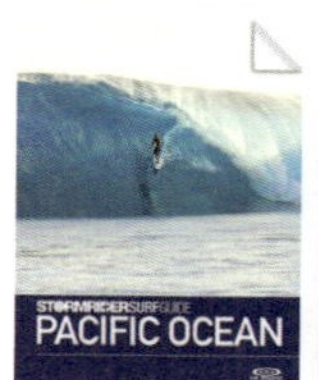

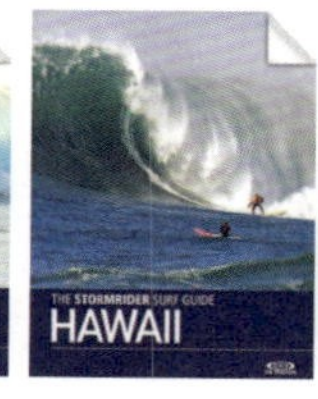

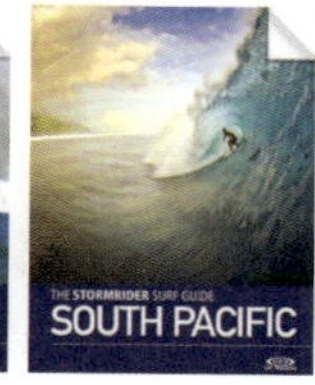

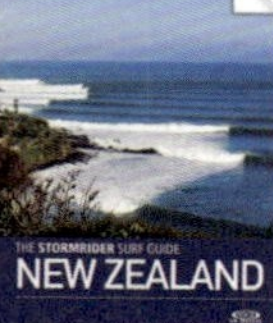